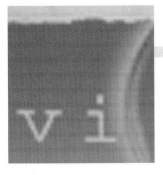

REVISED EDITION

EXCELLENCE IN BUSINESS

COURTLAND L. BOVÉE

Professor of Business Administration
C. Allen Paul Distinguished Chair
Grossmont College

JOHN V. THILL

Chief Executive Officer
Communication Specialists of America

MICHAEL H. MESCON

Founder and Chairman, The Mescon Group
Atlanta, Georgia

Regents Professor of Management, Ramsey Chair of Private Enterprise
Andrew Young School of Policy Studies, Georgia State University

PEARSON

Prentice
Hall

Upper Saddle River, NJ 07458

Library of Congress Cataloging-in-Publication Data

Excellence in business / Courtland L. Bovée, John V. Thill, Michael H.
Mescon.—Rev. ed.
   p. cm.
  Rev. ed of: Business today / Michael H. Mescon, Courtland L. Bovée, and John V.
Thill.
  Includes bibliographical references and index.
  ISBN 0-13-141438-0
   1. Business. 2. Management—United States. I. Thill, John V. II. Mescon,
  Michael H. Business today. III. Title
HF1008.M372 2005
658—dc21   2003051733

Acquisitions Editor: Jennifer Simon
Editor-in-Chief: Jeff Shelstad
Assistant Editor: Ashley Keim
Editorial Assistant: Melissa Yu
Media Project Manager: Jessica Sabloff
Marketing Manager: Anke Braun
Marketing Assistant: Patrick Danzuso
Senior Managing Editor (Production): Judy Leale
Production Editor: Virginia Somma/Mary Ellen Morrell
Production Assistant: Joe DeProspero
Permissions Supervisor: Suzanne Grappi
Associate Director, Manufacturing: Vincent Scelta
Production Manager/Manufacturing Buyer: Arnold Vila
Design Manager: Maria Lange
Art Director: Blair Brown
Interior Design: Laura Gardner
Cover Design: Blair Brown
Cover Illustration/Photo: Xavier Bonghi/Getty Images, Inc.
Illustrator (Interior): EletraGraphics, Inc.
Manager, Print Production: Christy Mahon
Composition/Full-Service Project Management: Carlisle Communications, Ltd.
Printer/Binder: RR Donnelley/Willard

Credits and acknowledgments borrowed from other sources and reproduced, with
permission, in this textbook appear on pages R-18–R-26. Photo credits appear on
pages R-26–R-27.

Pearson Prentice Hall™ is a trademark of Pearson Education, Inc.
Pearson® is a registered trademark of Pearson plc
Prentice Hall® is a registered trademark of Pearson Education, Inc.

Pearson Education LTD.   Pearson Education Australia PTY, Limited
Pearson Education Singapore, Pte. Ltd   Pearson Education North Asia Ltd
Pearson Education Canada, Ltd   Pearson Educación de Mexico, S.A. de C.V.
Pearson Education–Japan   Pearson Education Malaysia, Pte. Ltd

10 9 8 7 6 5 4 3 2 1
ISBN 0-13-141438-0

BRIEF CONTENTS

CONTENTS

Part 5   Developing Marketing Strategies to Satisfy Customers   298

Setting a New Standard in Introduction to Business Textbooks

In our goal of setting a new standard in introduction to business texts, we dedicated ourselves to four important objectives: (1) to provide the most current and up-to-date introduction to business textbooks in the market, (2) to provide a clear and complete description of the concepts underlying business, (3) to illustrate with real-life examples and cases the remarkable dynamism and liveliness of business organizations and of the people who operate them, and (4) to incorporate the valuable recommendations of instructors who use this book daily.

The Leader in Currency

Instructors of business have contributed their viewpoints on the latest trends in business. In addition, we have conducted an exhaustive study of the literature of business, including thousands of the very latest reports, monographs, books, and articles. As a quick glance of the extensive references and acknowledgments sections near the end of this book will show, *Excellence in Business* is the most carefully researched and currently documented introductory business textbook on the market. Topics include the challenges of cyberterrorism in the global business environment (pp. 77–78); ◆ investors and the landmark settlement by ten of Wall Street's biggest investment firms (pp. 469, 471); ◆ how the trustees of Hershey's opted to turn down a $12.5 billion buyout after protests from workers, retirees, and officials of the township where Hershey is located (p. 257); ◆ turmoil in the airline industry (p. 31); ◆ wasteful technology spending (p. 105); ◆ corporate ownership and governance (p. 148); ◆ shareholder's rights and shareholder's power (pp. 148–149) ◆ radio frequency identification (RFID) (p. 229); ◆ the latest on the DaimlerChrysler merger (p. 155) ◆ new discussion of Six Sigma (pp. 233–234); ◆ new ways to train employees on computers (p. 283); ◆ United Airlines and the drawback of employee ownership stock plans (ESOP) (pp. 295–296); ◆ questionable marketing tactics on campus (p. 317); ◆ the latest about e-money and digital wallets (p. 447); ◆ computer viruses and the threat to the economy (p. 106).

In-Depth Coverage

Our practice in this text is to provide the most in-depth coverage of material suitable for an introductory business course, compared with any book on the market. This book not only tells what is happening in the world of business, it explains why (or perhaps why not). Furthermore, our company examples expose students to more than a company name or a person. We make sure that we include a fair amount of detail about each company or person we mention. In addition, we explain difficult concepts by using a variety of interesting examples and metaphors to which students can relate.

In short, we believe that no other textbook in the field will be as successful in drawing students into the subject matter, presenting both sides of the story—the advantages and disadvantages—and preparing students to obtain and pursue satisfying business careers.

More Real-World Focus and Real Company Examples

Excellence in Business offers the most contemporary look at business of any book in the field. Dozens of companies are featured in our chapter vignettes, cases, exercises, special feature boxes, and videos. And we spotlight hundreds of small and large companies throughout each chapter, looking closely at the issues their managers and employees struggle with on a daily basis. Each company example has been carefully selected to draw students into the real world of business and to offer students the opportunity to learn from other people's successes and failures. Examples include the following:

> American Express's virtual environment ◆ the world's largest private employer: Wal-Mart ◆ Patagonia helps save the environment ◆ technology delivers new business opportunities for UPS ◆ GeniusBabies.com builds a smart business ◆ restructuring Kinko's partnerships to duplicate success ◆ producing perfect Krispy Kreme doughnuts ◆ "The Soul of Dell," a computer maker's program for success ◆ creating company loyalty at SAS Institute ◆ blending a successful workforce at Jamba Juice ◆ Botox: marketing a facelift in a bottle ◆ how Costco makes living more affordable ◆ Charles Schwab uses a new model to operate in a tough investment environment ◆ JetBlue airline's use of innovative strategies

Integrated Approach to E-Business

Through its integrated approach, this book reinforces the importance of e-business to students.

1. *Chapter coverage.* Internet technology and its impact on the way companies do business are explored in detail in Chapter 4.
2. *"Keeping Pace with Technology and Electronic Commerce"* boxes. Special feature boxes
   - highlight the differences that exist between conducting business in the e-world versus
   - conducting business in a traditional business environment.
3. *Featured e-businesses.* Chapter vignettes, case studies, boxes, and in-text examples feature popular e-businesses such as Cisco, Dell, E*Trade, eBay, Amazon, and more.
4. *Video cases with exercises.* Selected video cases give students a first-hand look at critical e-commerce issues that companies are facing. Companies include Sketchers, BMW motorcycles, and Body Glove among others.
5. *Internet exercises.* Students become acquainted with the wealth of information on the Web by completing the text's "Best of the Web" and "Explore on Your Own" exercises.

Learning Tools That Help Develop Skills and Enhance Comprehension

Excellence in Business uses a variety of helpful learning tools to reinforce and apply chapter material as well as stimulate higher-level thinking skills. These include the following:

- **Learning Objectives.** Chapter-opening learning objectives establish benchmarks for measuring success. Each numbered objective is clearly stated to signal important concepts students are expected to master. The numbered objectives reappear in the text margins close to the related material. The end-of-chapter "Summary of Learning Objectives" reinforces basic concepts by capsulizing chapter highlights for students.

- **Questions for Review.** Five end-of-chapter questions reinforce learning and help students review the chapter material.

- **Questions for Analysis.** Five end-of-chapter questions help students analyze chapter material. One of these questions is ethics-based and marked with a special callout.

- **Questions for Application.** Four end-of-chapter questions give students the opportunity to apply principles presented in the chapter material. Two of these questions are integrated and give students the opportunity to apply principles learned in earlier chapters. Marked with a special callout, these integrated questions encourage students to think about the "big picture."

- **Four-Way Approach to Vocabulary Development.** The text's four-way method of vocabulary reinforcement helps students learn basic business vocabulary with ease. First, each term is printed in boldface within the text. Second, a definition appears in the margin adjacent to the term. Third, an alphabetical list of key terms appears at the end of each chapter, with convenient cross-references to the pages where the terms are defined. Fourth, all marginal definitions are assembled in an alphabetical glossary at the end of the book.

- **Lively, Conversational Writing Style.** Read a few pages of this textbook and then read a few pages of another introduction to business textbook. We think you will immediately notice how the lucid writing style in *Excellence in Business* makes the material pleasing to read and easy to comprehend. We have carefully monitored the text's content and reading level to ensure that it's neither too simple nor too difficult.

Acknowledgments

A key reason for the continued success of *Excellence in Business* is an extensive market research effort. The advice of hundreds of instructors around the country aided us in our attempt to create a textbook suited to the unique needs of the introductory business market. Our sincere thanks are extended to the individuals who responded to our surveys as well as to the individuals who provided us with their insights through detailed market reviews.

Survey Reviewers of Prior Editions

Lee Adami, Northern Wyoming College; **Robert Alliston**, Davenport College of Business; **Lorraine Anderson**, Marshall University; **Doug Ashby**, Lewis and Clark Community College; **Fay Avery**, Northern Virginia Community College; **Sandra Bailey**, Indiana Vocational Technical College; **James Baskfield**, Northern Hennepin Community College; **Gregory Baxter**, Southeastern Oklahoma State University; **Charles Beavin**, Miami-Dade Community College; **Larry Beck**, Cohin County Community College; **Joseph Berger**, Monroe Community College; **James Boeger**, Rock Valley College; **Riccardo Boehm**, Hostos Community College; **Mary Jo Boehms**, Jackson State Community College; **Glennis Boyd**, Cisco Junior College; **Jeffrey Bruehl**, Bryan College; **Carl Buckel**, College of the Canyons; **Howard Budner**, Borough of Manhattan Community College; **John Bunnell**, Broome Community College; **Van Bushnell**, Southern Utah University; **William Carman**, Bucks County Community College; **Paul Caruso**, Richard Bland College; **Eloise Chester**, Suffolk County Community College; **Carmin Cimino**, Mitchell College; **Ellen Clemens**, Bloomsburg University of Pennsylvania; **James Cleveland**, Sage Junior College of Albany; **Debra Clingerman**, California University of Pennsylvania; **Herbert Coolidge**, Southern College of Seventh-Day Adventists; **Gary Cutler**, Dyersburg State Community College; **Giles Dail**, Edgecombe Community College; **Joe Damato**, Cuyamaca College; **James Day**, Shawnee State University; **Patrick Ellsberg**, Lower Columbia College; **Alfred Fabian**, Indiana Vocational College; **Jennifer Friestad**, Anoka-Ramsey Community College; **Joan Gailey**, Kent State University, East; **Joyce Goetz**, Austin Community College; **Barbara Goza**, Southern Florida Community College; **Phyllis Graff**, Kauai Community College; **Hugh Graham**, Loras College; **Vance Gray**, Bishop State Community College; **Gary Greene**, Manatee Community College; **Marciano Guerrero**, LaGuardia Community College; **Delia Haak**, John Brown University; **Maurice Hamington**, Mount St. Mary's College; **E. C. Hamm**, Tidewater Community College; **Carnella Hardin**, Glendale Community College; **Marie Hardink**, Anne Arundel Community College; **Diana Hayden**, Northeastern University; **Elizabeth Haynes**, Haywood Community College; **Sheila Devoe Heidman**, Cochise College; **Diana Henke**, University of Wisconsin at Sheboygan; **Norman Humble**, Kirkwood Community College; **Liz Jackson**, Keystone Junior College; **Michael Johnson**, Chippewa Valley Technical College; **Carol Jones**, Cuyahoga Community College; **Lonora Keas**, Del Mar College; **Sylvia Keyes**, Northeastern University; **Sharon Kolstad**, Fort Peck Community College; **Ken LaFave**, Mt. San Jacinto Community College; **Richard Larsen**, University of Maine at Machias; **Philip Lee**, Campbellsville College; **Richard Lenoir**, George Washington University; **Martha Leva**, Pennsylvania State University; **Kathy Lorencz**, Oakland Community College; **James Loricchio**, Ulster County Community College; **Tricia McConville**, Northeastern University; **Cheryl Macon**, Butler County Community College; **Ann Maddox**, Angelo State University; **Marie Madison**, Harry S. Truman College; **Barry Marshall**, Northeastern University; **George Michaehides**, Franklin Pierce College; **Norman Muller**, Greenfield Community College; **Lucia Murphy**, Ursinus College; **Alita Myers**, Copiah-Lincoln Community College; **Eric Nielsen**, College of Charleston; **Patricia Parker**, Maryville University of St. Louis; **Clyde Patterson**, Shawnee State University; **Corey Pfaffe**, Marantha Baptist Bible College; **Noel Powell**, West Georgia College; **Allen Rager**, Southwestern Community College; **Roy Roddy**, Yakima Valley Community College; **Ehsan Salek**, Virginia Wesleyan College; **Bernard Saperstein**, Passaic County Community College; **Kurk Schindler**, Wilbur Wright College; **Mark Schultz**, Rocky Mountain College; **Arnold Scolnick**, Borough of Manhattan Community College; **David Shepard**, Virginia Western Community College; **Stephanie Smith**, Lander University; **Susan Smith**, Finger Lakes Community College; **George Stook**, Anne Arundel Community College; **David Stringer**, DeAnza College; **Ben Tanksley**, Sul Ross State University; **John Taylor**, University of Alaska, Fairbanks; **Chris Tomas**, Northeast Iowa Community College; **Palmina Uzzolino**, Montclair State University; **Martha Valentine**, Regis University; **Juanita Vertrees**, Sinclair Community College; **IngoVon Ruckteschel**, Long Island University; **Chuck Wall**, Bakersfield College; **Jay Weiner**, Adams State College; **Lewis Welshofer**, Miami University of Ohio; **Charles White**, Edison Community College; **Richard Williams**, Laramie County Community College; **Clay Willis**, Oklahoma Baptist University; **Ira Wilsker**, Lamar University; **Ron Young**, Kalamazoo Valley Community College; **Sandra Young**, Jones County Junior College; **Harold Zarr**, Des Moines Area Community College; **Nancy Zeliff**, Northwest Missouri State University; and **Gene Zeller**, Jordan College.

Market Reviewers of Prior Editions

Harvey Bronstein, Oakland Community College; **Debra Clingerman**, California University of Pennsylvania; **Bill Dempkey**, Bakersfield College; **John Heinsius**, Modesto Junior College; **Alan Hollander**, Suffolk Community College; **Bob Matthews**, Oakton Community College; **Jerry Myers**, Stark Technical College; **Dianne Osborne**, Broward Community College; **Mary Rousseau**, Delta College; **Martin St. John**, Westmoreland Community College; **Patricia Setlik**, William Rainey Harper College; **Richard Shapiro**, Cuyahoga Community College; **Shafi Ullah**, Broward Community College; **Randy Barker**, Virginia Commonwealth University; **James D. Bell**, Southwest State University; **Joe Brum**, Fayetteville Technical Community College; **Steven Cassidy**, Howard University; **Jan Feldbauer**, Austin Community College; **Lorraine Hartley**, Franklin University; **Donald Johnson**, College for Financial Planning; **Jeffery Klivans**, University of Maine-Augusta; **Paul Londrigan**, Mott Community College; **Ted Valvoda**, Lakeland Community College; **William Warfeld**, Indiana State University; **Lewis Scholossinger**, Community College of Aurora; **Ronald Cereola**, James Madison University; **Mohammed Ahmed**, Webster University; **Dennis Foster**, Northern Arizona University; **Marshall Wick**, Gallaudet University; **Anthony Cafarelli**, Ursuline University; **Sandra Johnson**, Shasta College; **Robert Fouquette**, New Hampshire College; **Judy Domalewski**, Community College of Aurora; **Gerald Crawford**, University of North Alabama; **Gary Walk**, Lima Technical College; **Pamela Shindler**, Wittenburg University; **John Mozingo**, University of Wisconsin, Oshkosh; **C. Russell Edwards**, Valencia Community College; and **David Sollars**, Auburn University, Montgomery.

Market Reviewers for *Excellence in Business*

Steven Huntley, Florida Community College; **Sara Huter**, Webster University; **Sally Wells**, Columbia College; **Roosevelt Martin**, Chicago State University; **George Crawford**, Clayton College and State University; **William Grimes**, Washtenaw Community College; **David DeCook**, Arapahoe Community College; **Ronald Akie**, Mount Ida College; **Barbara Van Syckle**, Jackson Community College; **Jeri Rubin**, University of Alaska; **Michael Scrivens**, Monroe Community College; **Marne David Schmitz**, Front Range Community College; **Janet Seggern**, Lehigh Carbon Community College; **Michael Shapiro**, Dowling College; **Cynthia Nicola**, Carlow College; **Robert Myers**, Palm

Beach Atlantic College; **Don Richie**, Oregon Institute of Technology; **Richard Stewart**, Western Nevada Community College; **David Chandler**, Indiana University; **Lorena Edwards**, Belmont University; **Jaidev Singh**, University of Washington; **Rick Baldwin**, Prairie View A&M University; **Pat Tadlock**, Horry-Georgetown Technical College; **PK Shukla**, Chapman University.

Personal Acknowledgments

We are grateful to Jackie Estrada for her remarkable talents and special skills; to Gail Olson for her astute attention to details and exceptional abilities; and to Joe Glidden for his research efforts and database supervision.

The authors wish to acknowledge the contributions of Dr. David Rachman, including his work on the outline for the First Edition of *Business Today*. Dr. Rachman was a named author for editions one through eight of *Business Today*.

A very special acknowledgment goes to Barbara Schatzman, whose superb communication skills, distinguished background, and wealth of business experience assured this project of clarity and completeness.

The supplements package for *Excellence in Business* has benefited from the able contributions of numerous individuals. We would like to express our thanks to them for creating the finest set of instructional supplements in the field. The supplement authors include Barbara Gorski, University of St. Thomas and Jimidene Murphy, Clarendon College, who worked on the instructor's manual; Barbara Van Syckle, Jackson Community College, who developed the test bank; Myles Hassell, University of New Orleans, who created the PowerPoint package; Brandi Guidry-Hollier, University of Louisiana at Lafayette, who updated the study guide; Trisha Clark, University of Phoenix, who created the online courses; Andy Saucedo, University of New Mexico at Las Cruces, who developed the online chapter quizzing; David Tooch, University of New Hampshire who authored *Building a Business Plan*; James S. O'Rourke, IV, University of Notre Dame who authored *Beginning Your Career Search*; and Marian Burk Wood, who authored both *Business Ethics in Uncertain Times* and *Building Your Personal Stock Portfolio*.

We also wish to extend our warmest appreciation to the devoted professionals at Prentice Hall. They include Jerome Grant, president; Jeff Shelstad, vice president and editor in chief; Jennifer Simon, editor; Anke Braun, marketing manager; and Ashley Keim, assistant editor, all of Prentice Hall Business Publishing, and the outstanding Prentice Hall sales representatives. Finally, we thank Judy Leale, managing editor of production; Blair Brown, designer; and Virginia Somma and Mary Ellen Morrell, production editors for their dedication. And we are grateful to Lynn Steines, project manager at Carlisle Communications and Melinda Alexander, photo researcher, for their superb work.

Courtland L. Bovée
John V. Thill
Michael H. Mescon

DESIGNED FOR STUDENT LEARNING

Learning Objectives

Chapter-opening learning objectives establish benchmarks for measuring success.

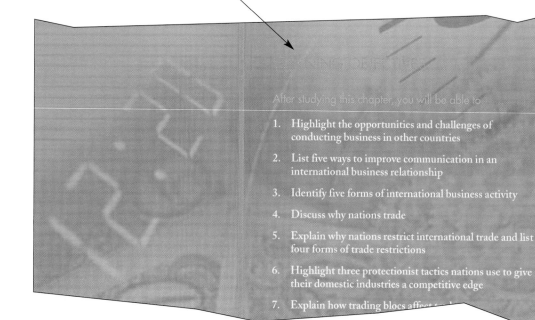

LEARNING OBJECTIVES

After studying this chapter, you will be able to

1. Highlight the opportunities and challenges of conducting business in other countries

2. List five ways to improve communication in an international business relationship

3. Identify five forms of international business activity

4. Discuss why nations trade

5. Explain why nations restrict international trade and list four forms of trade restrictions

6. Highlight three protectionist tactics nations use to give their domestic industries a competitive edge

7. Explain how trading blocs affect t...

Lance Armstrong, winner of five consecutive Tour de France races (1999–2003) boldly displays his Trek affiliation.

INSIDE BUSINESS TODAY

Trek Bikes: Trekking Around the Globe

It's a world away from the bright lights of Paris. But the little town of Waterloo, Wisconsin, captured the world's attention during the recent Tour de France. When Lance Armstrong zoomed across the finish line in 1999, 2000, 2001, 2002, and 2003 at Paris's Champs-Elysées, the American cycler raced to victory on a bike made by Trek Bicycle Corporation of Waterloo.

Not far from Trek's headquarters in downtown Waterloo sits a nondescript building. It's within these wall that the next generation of Trek bikes are born, created by Trek's Advanced Concept Group, known as ACG. For Lance Armstrong and the U.S. Postal Services team, that means making bikes that are lighter, stron... ...d faster than anyone thought possible.

As more exporting opportunities opened up, Keehn experimented with other foreign distribution methods. For instance, to minimize cultural and language barriers, she relied on the expertise and knowledge of local distributors instead of approaching retailers directly. In other countries, she advised Trek to create wholly-owned subsidiaries for handling sales, inventory, warranties, customer service, and direct distribution to retail outlets. Such subsidiary offices allowed Trek to maintain higher profits and more control over its products.

Still, Keehn hit some bumps in the road as she ventured into the global marketplace. For example, customs delays cre... ...urance and financial problems; some ship- ...clearances in Mexico.

Inside Business Today

Each chapter begins with a vignette, "Inside Business Today," that attracts student interest by vividly portraying the business challenges faced by a real businessperson. Each vignette ends with thought-provoking questions that draw students into the chapter.

THE OPTIMAL SUPPORT FOR YOUR COURSE

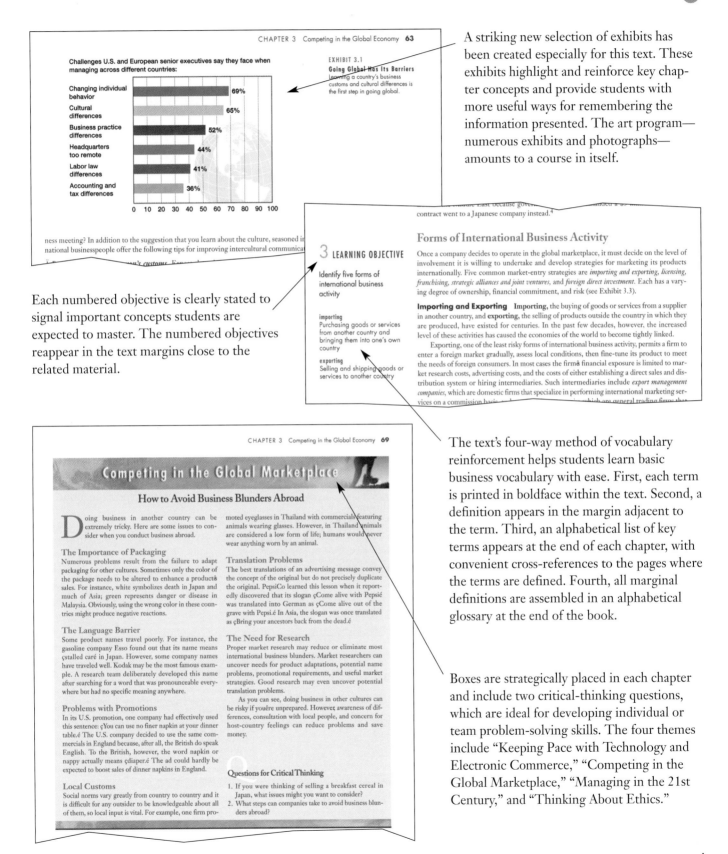

A striking new selection of exhibits has been created especially for this text. These exhibits highlight and reinforce key chapter concepts and provide students with more useful ways for remembering the information presented. The art program—numerous exhibits and photographs—amounts to a course in itself.

Each numbered objective is clearly stated to signal important concepts students are expected to master. The numbered objectives reappear in the text margins close to the related material.

The text's four-way method of vocabulary reinforcement helps students learn basic business vocabulary with ease. First, each term is printed in boldface within the text. Second, a definition appears in the margin adjacent to the term. Third, an alphabetical list of key terms appears at the end of each chapter, with convenient cross-references to the pages where the terms are defined. Fourth, all marginal definitions are assembled in an alphabetical glossary at the end of the book.

Boxes are strategically placed in each chapter and include two critical-thinking questions, which are ideal for developing individual or team problem-solving skills. The four themes include "Keeping Pace with Technology and Electronic Commerce," "Competing in the Global Marketplace," "Managing in the 21st Century," and "Thinking About Ethics."

CHECK YOUR UNDERSTANDING, EXPAND IT AND EXPLORE . . .

The end-of-chapter "Summary of Learning Objectives" reinforces basic concepts by capsulizing chapter highlights for students.

begins to see itself as ...

Summary of Learning Objectives

1. **Highlight the opportunities and challenges of conducting business in other countries.**
   Conducting business in other countries can provide opportunities such as increased sales, operational efficiencies, exposure to new technologies, and consumer choices. At the same time, it poses challenges, such as the need to learn unique laws, customs, and ethical standards. Furthermore, it exposes companies to the risks of political and economic instabilities, volatile currencies, international trade relationships, and the threat of global terrorism.

2. **List five ways to improve communication in an international business relationship.**
   To improve international communication, learn as much as you can about the culture and customs of the people you are working with; keep an open mind and avoid stereotyping; anticipate misunderstandings and guard against them by clari-

   fying your intent; adapt your style to match the style of others; and learn how to show respect in other cultures.

3. **Identify five forms of international business activity.**
   Importing and exporting, licensing, franchising, strategic alliances and joint ventures, and foreign direct investment are five of the most common forms of international business activity. Each provides a company with varying degrees of control and entails different levels of risk and financial commitment.

4. **Discuss why nations trade.**
   Nations trade to obtain raw materials and goods that are unavailable to them or too costly to produce. International trade benefits nations by increasing a country's total output, offering lower prices and greater variety to its consumers, subjecting domestic oligopolies and monopolies to competition, and allowing companies to expand their markets and achieve production and distribution efficiencies.

Five end-of-chapter questions reinforce learning and help students review the chapter material.

TEST YOUR KNOWLEDGE

Questions for Review

1. How can a company use a licensing agreement to enter world markets?
2. Why would a local businessperson need to learn about the global business environment?
3. What is the balance of trade, and how is it related to the balance of payments?
4. What is dumping, and how does the United States respond to this practice?
5. What is a floating exchange rate?

Questions for Analysis

6. Why would a company choose to work through intermediaries when selling products in a foreign country?
7. How do companies benefit from forming international joint ventures and strategic alliances?
8. What types of situations might cause the U.S. government to implement protectionist measures?
9. How do tariffs and quotas protect a country's own industries?
10. *Ethical Considerations:* Should the U.S. government more closely regulate the practice of giving trips and other incentives to foreign managers to win their business? Is this bribery?

Five end-of-chapter questions help students analyze chapter material. One of these questions is ethics-based and marked with a special callout.

Four end-of-chapter questions give students the opportunity to apply principles presented in the chapter material. Two of these questions are integrated and give students the opportunity to apply principles learned in earlier chapters. Marked with a special callout, these integrated questions encourage students to think about the "big picture."

80 PART 1 Conducting Business in the Global Economy

Questions for Application

11. Suppose you own a small company that manufactures baseball equipment. You are aware that Russia is a large market, and you are considering exporting your products there. What steps should you take? Who might be able to give you assistance?
12. Because your Brazilian restaurant caters to Western businesspeople and tourists, much of the food you buy is imported from the United States. Lately, the value of the real (Brazil's currency) has been falling relative to the dollar. This change makes your food imports much more costly, and it negatively affects your profitability. You have three options: which one will you choose? (a) Raise menu prices across the board. (b) Accept only U.S. dollars from customers. (c) Try to purchase more of your food items locally. Please explain your selection.

13. *Integrated:* Review the theory of supply and demand discussed in Chapter 1. Using this theory, explain how a country's currency is valued and why governments sometimes adjust the values of their currency.
14. *Integrated:* You just received notice that a large shipment of manufacturing supplies you have been waiting for has been held up in customs for 2 weeks. A local business associate tells you that you are expected to give customs agents some "incentive money" to see that everything clears easily. How will you handle this situation? Evaluate the ethical merits of your decision by answering the questions outlined in Exhibit 2.3 on page 00.

END-OF-CHAPTER MATERIAL

Five categories of exercises include "Handling Difficult Situations on the Job," "Building Your Team Skills," "Discovering Career Opportunities," "Developing Your Research Skills," and "Exploring the Best of the Web."

PRACTICE YOUR KNOWLEDGE

Handling Diffcult Situations on the Job: English Only Defending a Tough Policy

When Frances Torres read the memo announcing that employees should speak only English on the job, she was outraged. Torres, a lens inspector for Signet Amoralite, a lens-manufacturing firm in southern California, is fluent in both English and Spanish but feels that the English-only rules constitute discrimination. Now Torres and a group of her co-workers have brought their complaints to you, a manager in human resources.

More than half of Signet Amoraliteŝ 900 employees are Asian, Filipino, or Hispanic. The company policy states that çspeaking in another language that associates cannot fully understand can lead to misunderstandings, is impolite, and can even be unsafe.é While the policy carries no punishment, it is considered by some critics to violate federal discrimination laws.[50]

Your task: You know that you must defend the companyŝ English-only policy to Torres and the others; youêve been told by upper management that it will not be eliminated or altered. To help clarify your thinking and see things from the employeesê perspective, imagine that you have been hired by a company in another country that uses a language different from your own. How would you feel if you were required to learn and use that language exclusively, even if some of your co-workers were able to speak and understand your native tongue? To defend Signet Amoraliteŝ policy, what can you do or say or write that will help Torres and her co-workers accept it? Also, what do you think will be the best way to present this information?

Building Your Team Skills

In todayŝ interdependent global economy, fluctuations in a countryŝ currency can have a profound effect on the flow of products across borders. The U.S. steel industry, for example, has been feeling intense competition from an influx of Korean, Brazilian, and Russian steel imports. After the currencies of those countries plummeted in value, the price of steel products exported to the United States dropped as well, making U.S. steel much more expensive by comparison.

Fueled by low prices, steel flooded into the United States, hurting sales of U.S. steel. Over the course of several months, the volume of steel imports nearly doubled. Stung, U.S. steelmakers slashed production and laid off more than 10,000 U.S. workers. U.S. trade officials charge that the cheap imported steel is being dumped, and they are considering protectionist measures such as imposing quotas on steel imports.[51]

With your team, brainstorm a list of at least four additional ways the United States might handle this situation. Once you have your list, consider the probable effect of each option on these stakeholders:

Ä U.S. businesses that buy steel
Ä U.S. steel manufacturers
Ä U.S. businesses that export to Korea, Brazil, or Russia
Ä Employees of U.S. steel manufacturers

On the basis of your analysis and discussion, which option will your team recommend? Select a spokesperson to explain your selection and your teamŝ reasoning to the other teams. Compare your recommendation with those of your classmates.

This classic device assists students in evaluating situations, using good judgment, learning to make decisions, and developing critical thinking skills.

A CASE FOR CRITICAL THINKING

Doing Everybody's Wash—Whirlpool's Global Lesson

Everybody is talking about going global these days, but most people donât understand what that means. David Whitwam, chairman and CEO of Whirlpool, does. When he first began eyeing the global marketplace, this Michigan-based appliance maker was concentrating only on the U.S. market, producing and marketing washers, refrigerators, and other household appliances under the Whirlpool, KitchenAid, Roper, and Kenmore brand names.

The Right Way to Go Global

Determined to convert Whirlpool from a U.S. company to a major global player, Whitwam purchased N. V. Philipsŝ floundering European appliance business in 1989. The CEOŝ first challenge was to integrate and coordinate the many European operations with the U.S. operation. Some companies accomplish this task by imposing the parentŝ systems on the acquired companies, but Whitwam started down a more ambitious path. He created cross-cultural teams with members from the European and North American operations, and together they designed a program to ensure quality and productivity throughout Whirlpoolŝ worldwide operation. In the eyes of other corporate leaders, Whirlpool was doing everything right. The company was even featured in a 1994 *Harvard Business Review* article titled çThe Right Way to Go Global.é

Spinning Out of Control

Whitwam soon discovered, however, that developing global strategies was easier than executing them. Whirlpool had not counted on the difficulty in marketing appliancesÑa largely homogeneous process in the United StatesÑto the fragmented cultures of Europe, Asia, and Latin America. For instance, clothes washers sold in northern European countries such as Denmark must spin-dry clothes much better than washers in southern Italy, where consumers often line-dry clothes in warmer weather. And consumers in India and southern China prefer small refrigerators because they must fit in tight kitchens.

Despite these challenges, Whitwam was convinced that he could remake Whirlpool into a truly global company. But Whirlpoolŝ timing couldnât have been worse. Just as the company was planting its feet in international markets, economic turmoil hit Asia and Europe. Wildly fluctuating foreign exchange rates wreaked havoc in Asia, where Whirlpool had participated in several joint ventures. Fortunately, less than 5 percent of Whirlpoolŝ sales came from Asia, so the company was not seriously hurt. Still, ongoing global economic woes contributed to Whirlpoolŝ multimillion dollar losses overseas.

Rearranging the Global Load

The global economic crisis forced Whitwam to fine-tune his expansion plans. Whirlpool dropped one joint venture in China (costing the company $350 million) and rearranged others as intense competition and weak economic conditions drove appliance prices down and sapped profits. çThe thing we misjudged was how rapidly Chinese manufacturers could improve their quality,é notes Whitwam.

In Brazil, where Whirlpool had long been profitable, a currency crisis coupled with inflation worries slowed appliance sales to a trickle. Still, Whitwam remained committed to the market. Anticipating future growth opportunities in this emerging market, Whirlpool invested hundreds of millions of dollars to modernize operations, cut costs, and solidify its position as the countryŝ market leader in refrigerators, room air conditioners, and washers.

David Whitwamŝ global strategy, however, was not widely copied by rivals. As Whirlpool continued to expand in Europe, Latin America, and Asia, the companyŝ major competitor, Maytag, was selling its European and Australian businesses to refocus on the lucrative North American market. Nevertheless, Whitwam was willing to ride out the storm, even as global economic troubles dragged on.

Whitwam expedited Whirlpoolŝ entry into foreign markets by using licensing arrangements and by forming strategic alliances with others. Whirlpool also developed standardized products,

CHAPTER 4 Fundamentals of Information Management, the Internet, and E-Commerce 113

Conducting Business in the Global Economy

PART I

Mastering Global and Geographical Skills—Why Finland Leads in Wireless Technology

Despite its small size and relative isolation in the Arctic Circle, Finland is a nation of what marketing jargonists like to call "early adopters," the people most willing to try out new technologies and to make them their own. In the 1970s Finns were the first people in Europe using fax machines. In the early 1980s Finnish universities were wired to their counterparts in California using early forms of the Internet. By the late 1990s, Finland had the world's highest level of Internet and mobile phone use as a percentage of population. While a national predilection for gadgetry plays a part in Finland's emergence as a hub of information technology, more concrete factors are at work.

Part of the reason for Finland's advancement is its geography. When telecommunications developed in the 1970s, Finns were more inclined to pursue wireless options because the costs of running cable to isolated pockets of a vast and frozen nation were daunting. Thus, wireless technology became a priority for the government and the private business sector. Today the wireless mentality is so ingrained in Finland that many new homeowners don't bother ordering fixed-line service.

Finland's mobile communications flagship supports a network of research centers, feeding start-ups that now plan to provide content and services for an expected wireless Internet boom. It is largely because of Nokia that at least 60 percent of Finns have mobile phones. Among young professionals the figure is closer to 100 percent.[35]

Your task: Learn more about Finland's geography and infrastructure and other factors that have influenced its technological advancements. Internet resources such as the CIA World Factbook (www.odci.gov/cia/publications/factbook), the U.S. State Department (www.state.gov), and Virtual Finland (http://virtual. finland.fi) can help you get started. Use these resources and others you may find on the Internet or at the library to answer the following questions:

1. Briefly describe Finland's terrain and climate. How might they have played a role in the country's lead in wireless telecommunications?
2. How does the size of Finland's economy compare to other nations in the world? What industries are strongest in Finland? What products does Finland manufacture? Export?
3. How has Finland's investments in research and technological development paid off?
4. How has information technology penetrated Finnish society?

This part-ending geographic exercise describes a real-world business situation and asks students to answer questions and complete activities.

VIDEO CASE

Giving Global Law and Order a Helping Hand: Printrak

Learning Objectives

The purpose of this video is to help you:

1. Understand how and why a company adapts to the needs of foreign customers.
2. Identify the levels of international involvement that are available to companies.
3. Discuss the differences that can affect a companyŝ international operations.

Synopsis

Scotland Yard and the Canadian Mounties are only two of the many organizations around the world that use security technology from Printrak www.printrakinternational.com, a Motorola company. Starting with a computerized fingerprint management system, Printrak has added a number of security and criminal information products as it expanded from its California headquarters to serve customers around the globe. General manager Darren Reilly and his management team study each countryŝ legal, political, economic, and cultural differences, as well as analyzing local demand and customer needs. Rather than invest in local plants and equipment, Printrak works through local sales agents to ensure that its products are presented in a culturally savvy way for each market. Despite country by country differences in business customs and ethics, the decisions and actions of Printrakŝ employees are guided by Motorolaŝ code of conduct.

Discussion Questions

1. ***For analysis:*** What are some of the barriers that affect Printrakŝ ability to do business in foreign markets?
2. ***For analysis:*** From Printrakŝ perspective, what are the advantages and disadvantages of hiring and training local sales agents to work with customers in each foreign market?
3. ***For application:*** In addition to establishing users committees, what else should Printrak do to track changing customer needs in other countries?
4. ***For application:*** How would you suggest that Printrak build on its relations with çbeachhead customersé to expand in particular regions?
5. ***For debate:*** Printrak employees and managers must comply with Motorolaŝ global ethics policy. Should local sales agents be allowed to take any actions they deem necessary to make sales in local markets, regardless of Motorolaŝ policy? Support your chosen position.

Online Exploration

Browse Printrakŝ home page at www.printrakinternational. com, see where the company has customers, and read some of the news releases about international operations. Also look at the resource links that Printrak has posted for customers and site visitors. Why would Printrak publicize its customer list in this way? Why would it include a glossary of security-related terms and acronyms on the website? Finally, do you think the company should translate some or all of its website to accommodate foreign customers? Explain your response.

Professionally produced videos take students behind the scenes at some of the world's most fascinating organizations. Each case includes a synopsis, five discussion questions, and an online exploration exercise.

JUST FOR STUDENTS

- Text website with open access to a variety of features including quizzes, section summaries, learning activities, hot links for websites mentioned throughout the text, and student PowerPoints.

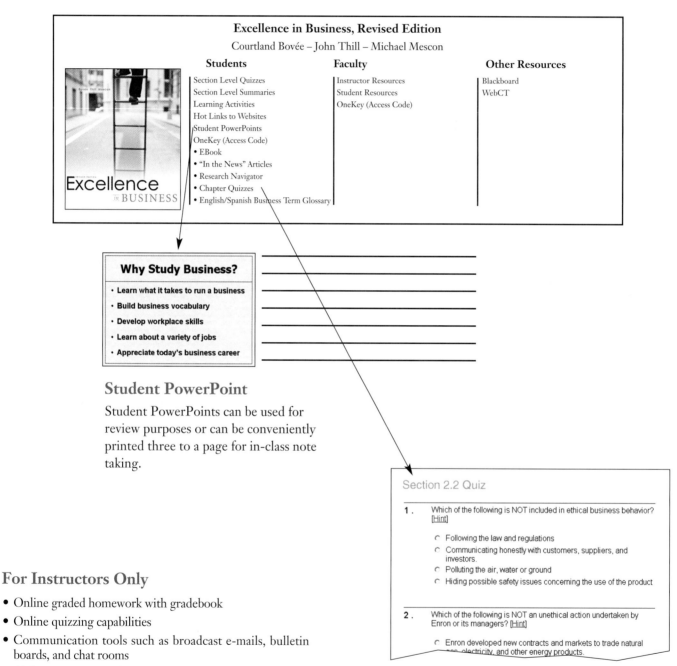

Excellence in Business, Revised Edition

Courtland Bovée – John Thill – Michael Mescon

Students	Faculty	Other Resources
Section Level Quizzes	Instructor Resources	Blackboard
Section Level Summaries	Student Resources	WebCT
Learning Activities	OneKey (Access Code)	
Hot Links to Websites		
Student PowerPoints		
OneKey (Access Code)		
• EBook		
• "In the News" Articles		
• Research Navigator		
• Chapter Quizzes		
• English/Spanish Business Term Glossary		

Why Study Business?

- Learn what it takes to run a business
- Build business vocabulary
- Develop workplace skills
- Learn about a variety of jobs
- Appreciate today's business career

Student PowerPoint

Student PowerPoints can be used for review purposes or can be conveniently printed three to a page for in-class note taking.

Section 2.2 Quiz

1. Which of the following is NOT included in ethical business behavior? [Hint]

- Following the law and regulations
- Communicating honestly with customers, suppliers, and investors.
- Polluting the air, water or ground
- Hiding possible safety issues concerning the use of the product

2. Which of the following is NOT an unethical action undertaken by Enron or its managers? [Hint]

- Enron developed new contracts and markets to trade natural gas, electricity, and other energy products.

For Instructors Only

- Online graded homework with gradebook
- Online quizzing capabilities
- Communication tools such as broadcast e-mails, bulletin boards, and chat rooms
- Ability to customize the online textbook for your students

Section Level Quizzes

Section level quizzes are composed of a multiple-choice pretest and post-test for each major section of the chapter.

ONLINE LEARNING TOOLS

With the access code packaged with each new copy of the book, students have access to the exciting new website, OneKey. In addition to the features listed, students can use the E-book, and English/Spanish Business Terms Glossary, "In the News" articles, Research Navigator, and Chapter Quizzes.

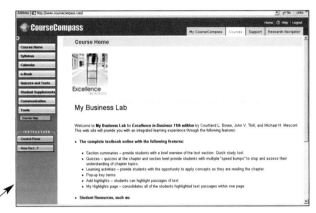

- Free access to "Research Navigator." This is the easiest way for students to start a research assignment or research paper. Complete with extensive help on the research process and three exclusive databases of credible and reliable source material including the EBSCO Academic Journal and Abstract Database, *New York Times* Search by Subject Archive, and "Best of the Web" Link Library.

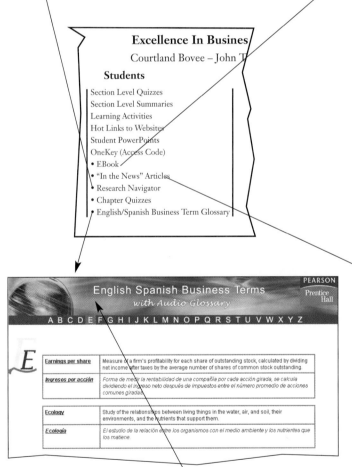

Excellence In Busines

Courtland Bovee – John T

Students

Section Level Quizzes
Section Level Summaries
Learning Activities
Hot Links to Websites
Student PowerPoints
OneKey (Access Code)
- EBook
- "In the News" Articles
- Research Navigator
- Chapter Quizzes
- English/Spanish Business Term Glossary

- The **complete textbook** online with the following integrated features:

  ■ Section summaries—provide students with a brief overview of the text's sections.

  ■ Quizzes—give students the opportunity to access their understanding of chapter topics at the end of every section and cumulative chapter.

  ■ Learning activities—allow students to apply concepts as they are reading the chapter.

  ■ Pop-up key terms

  ■ Customizable learning experience

    • Add highlights—students can highlight passages of text.

    • My Highlights page—consolidates all of the students' highlighted text passages within one page.

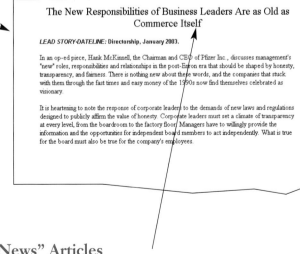

English/Spanish Glossary

In the English/Spanish glossary, key business terms are presented in English and Spanish with definitions and a short audio clip stressing the correct punctuation.

"In the News" Articles

"In the News" Articles: Updated once a semester, the "In the News" articles feature current news about companies featured in this text, on this text's videos, or in the *Excellence in Action* photo essay book.

ADDITIONAL SUPPLEMENTS FOR YOUR STUDENTS

- Mastering Business Essentials CD
- Study Guide
- Student discounts for *New York Times*, *Wall Street Journal*, and *Financial Times* subscriptions

Building Your Personal Stock Portfolio
by Marian Burk Wood, M.B.A.—
ISBN 0131176242

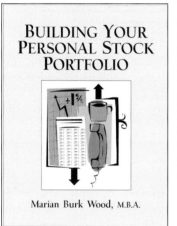

Week by week, through a series of cumulative lessons, students learn the basics of investing, from understanding risk to researching and trading stocks. Worksheets guide students through the process of analyzing information, making decisions, and monitoring their stock portfolio. Teaching Notes appear on this text's website.

Building Your Personal Career Portfolio: A Step by Step Guide for Building Your Career Portfolio, Third Edition, by James S. O'Rourke, IV, University of Notre Dame—
ISBN 0131008021

Students build their individualized career portfolio through the process of self-assessment, matching career opportunities, initiating the job search, using the latest Internet-based search vehicles, preparing all job-search related documents, and building interview skills. Upon completion of this workbook, students will have a career portfolio they can use and build on as their career progresses.

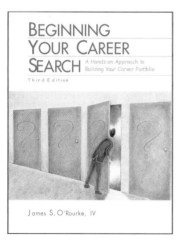

Building a Business Plan featuring Business PlanPro Software
by David Tooch, University of New Hampshire—
ISBN 0131047094

Step-by-step lessons with actual case studies prepare students to write a business plan. Upon completion of all the cumulative lessons, each student will have created a polished and professional business plan, whether he or she chooses to do so by hand or with Palo Alto's Business PlanPro Software. Teaching Notes appear on this text's website.

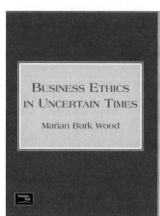

Building a Business Plan is available stand-alone for students who wish to complete their business plan by hand, without the use of the Business PlanPro Software. To order the stand-alone supplement, use ISBN 0131008005.

Business Ethics in Uncertain Times
by Marian Burk Wood, M.B.A.—
ISBN 0131414224

Covering management's accountability, corporate governance, accounting practices, stakeholder relations, and ethical decisions and behavior. This supplement provides students with a thorough foundation of business ethics. Dedicated sections analyze ethics at Enron, Arthur Andersen, and WorldCom. Teaching Notes appear on this text's website.

Real results. In real time.

Put student results at your fingertips.

Assess your students' progress with the **Prentice Hall Personal Response System** (PRS)—a wireless polling system that enables you to pose questions, record results, and display those results instantly in your classroom.

The PRS enables each student to respond privately to questions posed, giving you immediate feedback that will provide valuable insight into student learning. Over 200 universities and colleges are already using the Personal Response System. Join the movement to interactive classrooms and real-time feedback.

How does it work?

- Each student gets a cell-phone-sized transmitter which they bring to class. You have a receiver (portable or mounted) connected to your computer. The number of receivers in the classroom depends on class size.
- You ask multiple-choice, numerical-answer, or matching questions during class, and students answer using their transmitters.
- The receiver, connected to your computer, tabulates the answers and displays them graphically in class.
- You can record the results for grading, or simply use them as a discussion point.

How much does it cost?

Students need only purchase the transmitter once for just *$15 net** with a Prentice Hall text. Once purchased there is no additional cost, and students can use the transmitter in any relevant class.

Plus, for every 40 transmitters ordered by your bookstore, Prentice Hall will give adopting institutions one free receiver—a $250 value—and the software needed to run the system.

IMAGINE THE POSSIBILITIES.

Increased Interactivity

Immediate Insight

Higher Attendance

100% Participation

Just-In-Time Teaching Potential

In-class Surveys & Polls

Interested?

For more information on using the Prentice Hall PRS in your courses, just contact your Prentice Hall representative. You can find the name of your local representative via our website at **www.prenhall.com**.

*Prices effective September 2003 and subject to change without notice.

JUST FOR FACULTY

Teach with an Unparalleled Supplements Package

- **Presentation Manager CD**
- **OneKey Website**
- **18 video segments tied directly to in-chapter video cases**
- **16 additional video segments that reenforce business concepts**
- **Instructor's Manual**
- **Color Overhead Transparencies**
- Adopters can receive a 15-week discounted subscription to the *New York Times*, *Wall Street Journal*, and *Financial Times*

FINANCIAL TIMES
World business newspaper.

- **Electronic test generator powered by Test Gen EQ**
- **Test Item File**—In addition to page references and difficulty levels, each test question is based on the levels of Bloom's Taxonomy, and correlation tables begin each chapter to assist in the creation of tests.
- For those instructors who prefer not to use the computerized Test Item File, Prentice Hall provides a special call-in service.

---

4 Fundamentals of Information Management, the
Internet, and E-Commerce

Learning Objectives
1. Discuss the responsibilities of the chief informati...
2. Differentiate between operations information s...
   tion systems
3. Discuss the role of hardware, software, and net...
4. Discuss how businesses are using the Internet
5. Name three broad categories of e-commerce a...
   involves
6. Explain how to conduct an effective database s...
7. Identify and discuss five challenges businesses ...

Summary of Learning Objectives
1. **Discuss the responsibilities of the chief info...**
   The chief information officer (CIA) is responsi...
   the company's information systems. This task i...
   needs, deciding on what data to track, and deve...
   process, retrieve, and distribute the data. Addit...
   installing computer hardware and software and...
   the collection and distribution of information.

2. **Differentiate between operations informati...**
   support systems.
   Operation information systems include transac...
   control systems, and office automation systems...
   operations and provide the information lower-...
   need to operate and control company processes...
   port systems provide managers with informatio...
   decisions. Categories of management support s...
   mation systems, which provide data for routine...
   port systems, which help managers solve nonro...
   mation systems, which are designed to facilitat...
   and expert systems, which use artificial intellig...

Discuss the role of hardware, software, and ne...

CHAPTER 15
PROMOTIONAL STRATEGIES

MULTIPLE CHOICE QUESTIONS

What is Promotion?

1. Of the four marketing mix components, _____ is the one most often associated with marketing.
   a) Place
   b) Price
   c) Product
   d) Promotion (page, Level 1, Easy)

2. Promotin may take the form of _____.
   a) Face-to-face communication
   b) Indirect communication
   c) Direct communication
   d) All of the above (page, Level 1, Easy)

Setting Promotional Goals

3. Which of the following is the persuasive communication that motiva...
   goods, services, or ideas that an organization is selling?
   a) Marketing strategy
   b) Product strategy
   c) Promotion (page, Level 4, Difficult)
   d) Strategic planning

4. Promotional activities have all but which of the following goals?
   a) To appeal (page, Level 2, Moderate)
   b) To inform
   c) To persuade
   d) To remind

5. Sarita's confection store makes scrumptious chocolate fudge with ch...
   Because the chocolate market is saturated, which promotional strateg...
   get people to try her fudge?
   a) Appealing
   b) Informing
   c) Persuading (page, Level 3, Moderate)
   d) Reminding

6. Andrew has come out with a new laundry detergent that revolutioniz...
   become when washed. Which promotional strategy should he use?
   a) Informing (page, Level 3, Moderate)
   b) Persuading
   c) Reminding

CORRELATION TABLE FOR CHAPTER 15

Question Type	Level 1 Easy Knowledge	Level 2 Moderate Comprehension	Level 3 Moderate Application	Level H Difficult Analysis Synthesis Evaluation
Multiple Choice	2, 3, 10, 12, 13, 18, 19, 23, 34, 36, 37, 40, 41, 45, 46, 47, 48, 53, 55, 57, 60	1, 4, 5, 6, 9, 11, 20, 21, 24, 25, 26, 28, 29, 31, 33, 38, 43, 50, 59	7, 14, 15, 16, 17, 22, 27, 30, 32, 35, 39, 44, 54, 56, 58, 61	8, 42, 49, 51, 52
True/False	64, 65, 67, 71, 77, 78, 79, 80, 84, 90, 91	62, 63, 66, 69, 72, 75, 76, 83, 88	81, 82, 85, 89	68, 70, 73, 74, 86, 87
Fill In the Blank	94, 95, 96, 97, 99, 101, 102, 105	93	92, 98, 103, 106	100, 104
Essay	----------------	108	109, 110	07, 111

Total Number of Test Questions: 135
(67 Multiple Choice; 40 True/False; 23 Fill In the Blank; 5 Essay)

- The authors of this text are on call to answer any questions or address any concerns adopters might have while using their text or supplements. Just send an e-mail to **bovee@leadingtexts.com,** and the authors will respond as quickly as possible.

PRESENTATION MANAGER ON CD-ROM

This Instructor's Resource CD-ROM is an interactive library of presentation and classroom resources. By navigating through this CD, adopters can collect the materials including images from the text most relevant to their interests, edit to create powerful class lectures, copy them to their own computer's hard drive, and/or upload them to an online course management system. This CD writes custom "index" pages, which assist the user in navigating through and viewing the various assets they have collected. This CD runs on both the Windows and Mac platforms and employs interactive techniques that will be familiar to those who use Internet-based search engines.

Select a chapter from the table of contents, and you can see a list of resources, such as Instructor's Manual, Test Bank, Exhibits, and PowerPoints. The resources are further broken down into subcategories, so you can find what you need. Or, you can simply search by keyword. All of the resources have been associated with the appropriate text keywords.

After you've found the files you'd like to present or post to a website, select them with one click, put them into your export list (like a shopping cart), and export them to your hard drive or disk. The Presentation Manager will organize them for you into folders according to file type, and even provide a simple webpage for easy viewing.

On the Presentation Manager CD, you will also find the following faculty supplements:

- **PowerPoints**—Two PowerPoint packages are available with this text. The first is the standard set of instructor's PowerPoints. The second is an enhanced, interactive version of the first with video clips and weblinks in each chapter. Both versions contain teaching notes.
- **Online Courses** in WebCT, Blackboard, and CourseCompass
- **Electronic test generator powered by Test Gen EQ**
- **Instructor's Manual**
- **Test Item File**
- **All of the art files from the text**

CUSTOM VIDEOS

Chapter-ending custom videos help students see how real-life businesses and the people who run them apply fundamental business principles on a daily basis. Companies include the following:

• **U.S. Department of Commerce**, 2004, running time 10:26. Learn how the U.S. economic system works, through an interview with Bobby Hines, an international trade specialist whose job is to help companies used to the U.S. economic system expand into world markets and, as a result, different economic systems. This video looks at the U.S. economic system, how that system is affected by supply and demand, and the resources the United States has for assisting businesses.

• **American Red Cross**, 2004, running time 10:31. The American Red Cross was founded to aid the victims of war. Since that time, the role of the Red Cross has been increased to aid victims of natural disasters, as well as victims of manmade disasters such as nuclear attacks and the terrorist attacks of September 11. With more than 1,000 local chapters, how does this organization maintain its high moral ideals? Get the answer to this question in this video.

• **Printrak International**, 2004, running time 11:42. Fingerprint tracking originated in the United States and companies like Printrak International have helped move this innovative technology into the countries that need it most. Discover how Printrak leveraged capital to expand into foreign markets, how it negotiated trade barriers, and accounted for differences in the demands and expectations of various foreign markets.

• **Boeing Satellite Systems**, 2003, running time 12:11. Many of us would love to have a television in our computer at work. At Boeing Satellite systems, IPTV is just one of the ways its more than 8,000 employees are kept in communication with other offices around the world. In a technologically-driven market, Boeing Satellite explains how information systems have changed its business and how Boeing uses information systems to save money in daily processes.

• **Durango Pro-Focus Flight Training Center**, 2004, running time 12:47. Find out how, step-by-step, a retired Air Force colonel started a business providing military-style training for commercial airline pilots.

• **Amy's Ice Creams**, 2002, running time 13:36. Americans consume nearly 1.6 billion gallons of ice cream a year! Learn how a small Texas ice-cream store chain got its start

in this big business and how it came to be successful through planning and differentiating its product.

• *Creative Age Publications*, 2004, running time 9:49. Learn from the president and CEO of Creative Age what goes into managing a publishing company that produces seven different magazines ranging in topics from nail care to kidney dialysis. Students will hear what long- and short-term goals have been set for the company, what management skills are looked for in prospective managers, and how corporate culture can stimulate creativity and teamwork.

• **Nantucket Nectars**, 2002, running time 14:46. In 1989, the Juice Guys started their business with a blender and sold their blended peach nectar drinks off their boats to people visiting Nantucket. See how this company has changed dramatically since it first started, how it keeps lines of communication open within its headquarters, and how it uses technology to keep its remote office in touch.

• **Body Glove**, 2004, running time 13:52. This well-known maker of wetsuits has expanded to other products ranging from cell phone covers to resort hotels. How did it get there? Interviews with Scott Daley (vice president of marketing) and Russ Lesser (president) explain how the company came up with its product ideas, where it found the materi-

als used in many of its products, and how services (like diving cruises) fit into the whole picture.

• **Kingston Technology**, 2004, running time 13:30. The owners of the company don't have corner offices. When a new employee starts, the owners stop by to introduce themselves; and everyone at the company receives 10 percent cash back on company profits. Sound like a great company to work for? Developing a feeling of family, loyalty, and trust has been the key in creating Kingston Technology's happy family of more than 1,500 employees who are all committed to the success of the company.

- **Park Place Entertainment**, 2004, running time 13:19. What do Caesar's Palace, Bally's, the Las Vegas Hilton, and Paris Hotel & Casino have in common? Each of these hotels is owned and operated by Park Place Entertainment, the world's largest gaming company. With more than 52,000 employees, learn how the Park Place Entertainment human resources department recruits and develops its management team, and evaluates each worker's performance.

- **Sketchers USA**, 2004, running time 12:19. Sketchers designs cool shoes for cool people. Sketchers makes sure its shoes are seen in cool places, cool magazines, and on cool television shows. But how did it get there? The success of Sketchers is a culmination of its employees, the branding of its product, address-

ing the needs of consumers through in-house market research, communicating one-on-one with consumers, and differentiating its product from others.

- **MCCI**, 2004, running time11:25. For a company that makes parts on a customized client-by-client basis, how can it strategize most effectively, how can it maintain the zero failure rate necessary in its business, and what are the risks of selling such unique goods. Mike Kujawa, CEO, answers these questions in MCCI's segment.

- **Clos du Bois Winery**, 2004, running time 11:12. Riding a

tidal wave of U.S. consumer interest in California wines, Clos du Bois Winery sells its wines from coast to coast. The company now produces and ships more than one million cases of wine

every year, although less than 20 percent is sold in California. In order to keep its distribution organized, Clos du Bois ships its wines from a central warehouse to more than 300 wholesalers' warehouses around the United States.

- **BMW Motorcycles**, 2004, running time 12:52. How does BMW Motorcycles create a memorable brand image?

What is the goal of BMW's message to consumers? How is the web used when marketing BMW motorcycles? Laurence Kuykendall, director of marketing, provides answers to these and many more questions in this segment.

- **McDonald's**, 2002, running time 12:27. With billions served in nearly every country in the world, McDonald's explains how accounting information flows through such a

large organization, what regional differences it had to manage in unifying financial information, and what tracking methods it uses to collect and process financial reports and projections.

- **Coast Business Credit**, 2004, running time 9:51. Find out why it's often difficult for start-up businesses to find venture capital, what Coast Business Credit looks for in a loan prospect, and what type of companies one should avoid when making financial loans.

- **Understanding Investments: Motley Fool**, 2002, running time 16:53. The chances of winning the lottery are probably about a million to one, and unless you come up with the next great idea—the pet rock has already been taken—becoming a millionaire overnight may not be in your future. Chances are you will have a better chance of getting rich if you learn to select investments that are appropriate for your long-term financial goals. Motley Fool educates us about securities and investment strategies in this risky business.

ADDITIONAL CUSTOM VIDEOS

A second set of custom videos is available with this text. These videos further enforce the concepts and principles in the life of a business and the people that work there. Guides to accompany these videos are available on the text's website. Videos include all of the following:

- **Education and Earnings**, 2004, running time 10:33. College students sacrifice earnings while attending school in return for greater earnings potential in the future. Interviews with an economist, a recruiter, and a social worker who has seen her earnings go up as her level of education increased provide great context for discussion on how much these costs should weigh on the decision-making process.

- **Conducting Business Ethically and Responsibly: Patagonia**, 2002, running time 7:33. Yvon Chouinard founded Patagonia over 20 years ago, making climbing gear by hand for his friends. In addition to its commitment to customers, "serious users who rely on the product in extreme conditions," the firm is also responsible to its employees, providing a family-friendly workplace, and for the environment, donating millions of dollars to grassroots environmentalist groups in the United States and abroad.

- **Nidek—Responding to the Challenges of Globalization**, 2003, running time 9:34. When David Yeh, direc-tor of sales at Nidek, USA, was recently faced with an unusually high turnover rate in his sales force, he knew that things needed to change—and fast! By taking into consideration the discrepancies between Japanese-style management practices and American culture, he was able to resolve the problem, while also giving employees more job satisfaction.

- **Emotion—Beyond Pictures and Video Clips to Virtual Images**, 2003, running time 5:11. Who would have thought that Nike, The Discovery Channel, and the motion picture industry had something in common? All three companies—along with a host of others—are using the  media asset management services of EMotion, a software company based in northern Virginia. By striving for ease of use, a pay-per-use system, and a completely digital database, EMotion is one of the first companies to think globally across industries.

- **Sytel—A CEO Who Makes Things Happen**, 2003, running time 3:58. Not many companies have a CEO like Jeanette Lee White, who can tell customers confidently "When you hire Sytel, you get the entire company, including the CEO." Sytel's history of meeting customer demands with a blend of creativity, accuracy, and speed have earned it accolades in both the government and the private sector. Learn how Jeanette Lee Whitel's cutting-edge approach to  leadership has helped her company to make the *Inc.* 500 list several times, and why she has won a national entrepreneur award from *Working Woman* magazine.

- **Quova: Leading with Integrity and Compassion**, 2003, running time 7:08. In the crowded field of information technology, leadership can make all the difference. By adopting a "hands-under" leadership style, Quova Inc.'s President and CEO Marie Alexander has created a corporate culture that strives to help people not only achieve the company's goals, but to achieve their personal goals as well. As a female CEO, Alexander has never considered being a woman as an obstacle in her professional life. See her leadership style in action in this video.

- **Organizational Change at Student Advantage**, 2002, running time 8:44. Change is one of the challenges every manager, as well as every college student, can count on facing. In the business world, acquisition can be a company's most successful growth strategy, but it can also mean a strong potential for corporate cultures to collide. Students will learn how to avoid these conflicts and other conflicts associated with corporate change.

- **Beyond Components**, 2004, running time 5:05. Lou Dinkel's company, Beyond Components, not only strives to be a socially responsible company—it is actually able to accomplish it. Not many other CEOs can say that their company donates 10 percent of corporate profits to charity, or that they encourage their employees to earn college degrees! Lou Dinkel sets his company apart from others in the industry by "doing all the little things better."

- **Labor Relations**, 2002, running time 10:28. Watch as HR professional Daryl Hulme deals with the sensitive situation of putting a young woman just starting out in her career at ease at hotjobs.com. Sara Lancaster has just accepted a position in HotJobs' computer programming department as a full-time programmer. At her last job, she was in the union and is concerned that HotJobs doesn't offer one. Without a union, Lancaster feels she lacks job security. Students will see what other human resources' professionals think about this situation and the steps they would take to calm Sara's fears.

- **Recruitment and Placement,** 2002, running time 13:57. Bertelsman, one of the world's top music distributors, counts Santana, the Dave Matthews Band, and TLC among its long list of recording artists. Go behind the scenes with Paul Fiolek, vice president of human resources at Bertelsman BMG, where he faces the possibility that the wrong person has been hired for a job.

- **Starbucks**, 2004, running time 14:00. Starbucks' strategy is based on four pillars: (1) providing the best coffee, (2) offering the finest products associated with coffee, (3) creating an environment that is inviting, and (4) being socially responsible. The phenomenal growth of this Seattle-based company can be found through the implementation of these pillars by its employees. The result is a company that is passionate about creating a coffeehouse experience.

- **Snapple**, 2004, running time 11:00. Snapple is an example of a brand that started as an American success story, lost its way, then rediscovered itself over a period of 20 years. This video chronicles Snapple's successes and failures over this time.

- **A Walk Down a Store Aisle**, 2004, running time 8:00. Federated Direct, which owns Bloomingdale's and Macy's, was losing market share due to intense competition from discount stores, online retailers, and specialty shops until Dawn Robertson, president and chief merchandising officer, stepped in. See what Dawn and her group implemented to keep customers happy and keep them coming back.

- **Exile on 7eventh: Thriving in the Wake of the "Tech Wrek,"** 2003, running time 5:10. In a time when many dot-coms have folded, Exile on 7eventh is alive and well. With clients like Earthlink, Microsoft, and eBay, Exile on 7eventh is striving to find cost-effective online advertising solutions when the climate of the advertising industry is plagued by a lack of confidence. Learn how the company's ability to marry creativity to accountability has led to its success.

- **The Federal Reserve System**, 2004, running time 9:50. What three words appear across the top of the front of a one-dollar bill? The answer is Federal Reserve Note. But what does this mean and what does the Federal Reserve do? Wayne Ayers, a former Federal Reserve economist, and Deb Bloomberg, an economic education specialist at the Federal Reserve Bank of Boston, provide an overview of the Federal Reserve System and its impact on the economy.

- **Business Ethics**, 2004, running time 12:17. Over the past few years it seems we are hearing more and more about companies acting unethically. This section discusses the incentives for firms to engage in fraud and the role regulators play. Reference is made to Enron, Tyco, and Worldcom. The Securities and Exchange Commission (SEC), its goals, and its obligation to protect small investors are also discussed.

CHAPTER

Fundamentals of Business and Economics

LEARNING OBJECTIVES

After studying this chapter, you will be able to

1. Define what a business is and identify four key social and economic roles that businesses serve

2. Differentiate between goods-producing and service businesses and list five factors contributing to the increase in the number of service businesses

3. Differentiate between a free-market system and a planned system

4. Identify the factors that affect demand and those that affect supply

5. Compare supply and demand curves and explain how they interact to affect price

6. Discuss the four major economic roles of the U.S. government

7. Explain how a free-market system monitors its economic performance

8. Identify five challenges that businesses are facing in the global economy

Wal-Mart's success is based on the simple idea of making the customer Number 1, offering low prices, and squeezing costs.

INSIDE BUSINESS TODAY

Bagging Success at Wal-Mart

In its forty-some year reign, Wal-Mart has amassed a jaw-dropping trophy rack of titles, including "World's Largest Private Employer in the United States," "World's Largest Corporation," and "100 Best Companies to Work For." But perhaps its biggest claim to fame occurred in 2001, when it passed General Motors and Exxon to become the first service company to rise to the number-one position on *Fortune* magazine's list of the 500 biggest U.S. companies. That's an amazing feat considering that Wal-Mart didn't even exist in 1955, when *Fortune* first published its list. So how did a peddler of inexpensive shirts and fishing rods become the mightiest corporation in America?

Sam Walton always knew that he wanted to be in the retailing business. He started his career by running a Ben Franklin franchise, and in 1962 he founded Wal-Mart. Walton went on to build his empire by buying stuff at the lowest cost possible and passing the savings on to consumers through super low prices. Walton also controlled expenses better than the competition. Wal-Mart uses sophisticated information technology and fully automated distribution centers to squeeze costs out of its operation and maximize selling efficiencies.

Walton's focus on the bottom line now permeates all levels of Wal-Mart's operation. Its aesthetics in architecture and advertising are decidedly no-frills; its corporate offices are stark; its executives pay for their own coffee and even share hotel rooms on business trips; and to curtail frivolous energy consumption, lights, heat, and air conditioning at all U.S. Wal-Marts are controlled from the company headquarters in Bentonville, Arkansas.

But Wal-Mart's low prices and cost savings are not the only driving force behind its success. Walton pushed sales growth relentlessly by preaching the first commandment of today's service economy: The customer rules. Wal-Mart strives to exceed customers' expectations by providing the kind of service that keeps customers satisfied. Moreover, Sam Walton, who died in 1992, believed in sharing profits with employees and treating them as partners—valuing their opinions, communicating with them, and listening to them. He demonstrated his concern for employees in small but effective ways: time-and-a-half pay for work on Sundays and an "open door" policy that let workers bring concerns to managers at any level—to name a couple.

Today, Wal-Mart accounts for a staggering 60 percent of all U.S. retail sales. It is the nation's biggest seller of DVDs, groceries, toys, diamonds, and sporting goods—to name a few. The company manifests itself in four main forms in the United States: Some 1,600-plus traditional Wal-Mart retail stores, which carry everything from panties to Pennzoil and average about 90,000 square feet; some 500 Sam's Clubs, warehouse stores where "members" pay an annual fee to receive greater discounts on dry goods and groceries; some 1,140 Supercenters, combination retail and full-sized grocery stores clocking in at 190,000 square feet and similar in scope to a European hypermarket; and over 30 neighborhood markets similar in scope to small grocery stores. Wal-Mart also operates some 1,200 stores overseas. And it is the number one U.S. supermarket: With over $56 billion in grocery sales, the company is so feared by competitors that the mere announcement of its imminent arrival in a market is enough to send some grocery chains packing.

Overall, Wal-Mart attributes its remarkable success to its willingness to swim upstream. If everybody else is going in one direction, Wal-Mart moves the opposite way. For instance, Sam Walton ignored critics who said that towns with a population of less than 50,000 could not support a discount store for long. Then he set out to prove that the critics were wrong, opening store after store in small towns and putting mom-and-pop retailers out of business. Today the corporation employs over 1.3 million people worldwide and plans to hire over 1 million more in the near future. Its annual revenue exceeds $218 billion—making Wal-Mart bigger than the economy of Switzerland.[1]

Why Study Business?

1 **LEARNING OBJECTIVE**

Define what a business is and identify four key social and economic roles that businesses serve

business
Activity and enterprise that provides goods and services that a society needs

profit
Money left over after expenses and taxes have been deducted from revenue generated by selling goods and services

Business is everywhere. Whether you're shopping at a Wal-Mart, flying in an airplane, watching a movie, buying a CD over the Internet, enjoying your favorite coffee drink, or withdrawing money from an ATM, you're involved in someone else's business. In fact, you engage in business just about every day of your life. But like many college students, for most of your life you've been observing and enjoying the efforts of others. Now that you're taking an introduction to business course, however, your perspective is about to change.

In this course you'll learn what it takes to run a business. As you progress through the course, you'll begin to look at things from the eyes of an employee or a manager instead of a consumer. You'll develop a fundamental business vocabulary that will help you keep up with the latest news and make more-informed decisions. By participating in classroom discussions and completing the chapter exercises, you'll gain some valuable critical-thinking, problem-solving, team-building, and communication skills that you can use on the job and throughout your life.

Should you decide to pursue a career in business, this course will introduce you to a variety of jobs in fields such as accounting, economics, human resources, management, finance, marketing, and so on. You'll see how people who work in these business functions contribute to the success of a company as a whole. You'll gain insight into the types of skills and knowledge these jobs require. And most important, you'll discover that a career in business today is fascinating, challenging, and often quite rewarding.

With some 500 new stores opening each year, Walgreens provides consumers with pharmaceutical and health-care needs, society with over 130,000 jobs, investors with quarterly dividends, and charities with over $1 million in annual donations.

What Is a Business?

A **business** is profit-seeking activity that provides goods and services that satisfy consumers' needs. Wal-Mart, for example, sells a variety of goods and services to consumers in hopes of earning a **profit**—what remains after all expenses have been deducted from business revenue. The goal of earning a profit from engaging in business is commonly referred to as a *profit motive*. Profits are the lifeblood of a free-market economy. Without a chance to earn a profit, businesses have no incentive for innovation. They won't spend money on research and development, and they won't invest in producing and marketing new products.[2]

In addition to earning a profit, businesses provide a society with necessities such as housing, clothing, food, transportation, communication, health care, and much more; they provide people with jobs and a means to prosper; they pay taxes that are used to build highways, fund education, and provide grants for scientific research; and they reinvest their profits in the economy, thereby creating a higher standard of living and quality of life for society as a whole. Wal-Mart, for example, contributes hundreds of millions to support local communities and nonprofit organizations. The company is one of the leading financial supporters of education in the United States, and its recycling programs collect millions of pounds of plastic annually.[3]

Not every organization exists to earn a profit, however. **Nonprofit organizations** such as museums, public schools and universities, symphonies, libraries, government agencies, and charities exist to provide society with a social or educational service. Nonprofit organizations receive revenues from a number of sources, including donations, government grants, memberships, fundraising activities, and sales of promotional products such as Girl Scout cookies. The American Red Cross, for example, is a nonprofit organization that provides relief to victims of disasters and helps people prevent, prepare for, and respond to emergencies. The organization took in over $1 billion in monetary and in-kind donations in 2002 and spent most of that money on its programs and supporting services.[4]

Although nonprofit organizations such as the Red Cross do not have a profit motive, they must operate efficiently and effectively to achieve their goals. And they face many of the same business opportunities and challenges experienced by profit-seeking businesses. For instance, both profit-seeking and nonprofit organizations need resources to produce goods and services. Wal-Mart, for example, needs buildings, electricity, cashiers, and knowledgeable managers. American Airlines needs planes, fuel, trained pilots, cash, and airports. And the American Red Cross needs volunteers, computers, and money.

Economists call these resources **factors of production**, which they categorize into five general types:

- *Natural resources*—commodities that are useful inputs in their natural state, such as land, forests, minerals, and water
- *Human resources*—anyone (from company presidents to grocery clerks) who works to produce goods and services
- *Capital*—resources (such as money, computers, machines, tools, and buildings) that a business needs in order to produce goods and services and get them to consumers
- *Entrepreneurs*—people who are innovative and willing to take risks to create and operate new businesses (see Exhibit 1.1)
- *Knowledge*—the combined talents and skills of the workforce

Profit-seeking enterprises maximize a company's profit by using these five factors of production in the most efficient way possible.

Goods-Producing Businesses Versus Service Businesses

Most businesses can be classified into two broad categories (or industry sectors): goods-producing businesses and service businesses. **Goods-producing businesses** produce tangible goods by engaging in activities such as manufacturing, construction, mining, and agriculture. Boeing, the world's largest manufacturer of commercial jetliners, military aircraft, and satellites, is a goods-producing business. The company's Everett, Washington, factory is the largest building, by volume, in the world. Spanning 98 acres under one roof, the facility is big enough to handle construction of 20 widebody jets at once.[5] Of course, most manufacturing operations do not require a facility as big as Boeing's. Nonetheless, it's difficult to start a goods-producing business without substantial investments in buildings, machinery, and equipment. For this reason, most goods-producing businesses are **capital-intensive businesses**; that is, they generally require large amounts of money or equipment to get started and to operate.

---

nonprofit organizations
Firms whose primary objective is something other than returning a profit to their owners

factors of production
Basic inputs that a society uses to produce goods and services, including natural resources, labor, capital, entrepreneurship, and knowledge

natural resources
Land, forests, minerals, water, and other tangible assets usable in their natural state

human resources
All the people who work for an organization

capital
The physical, human-made elements used to produce goods and services, such as factories and computers; can also refer to the funds that finance the operations of a business

entrepreneurs
People who accept the risk of failure in the private enterprise system

knowledge
Expertise gained through experience or association

2 LEARNING OBJECTIVE

Differentiate between goods-producing and service businesses and list five factors contributing to the increase in the number of service businesses

goods-producing businesses
Businesses that produce tangible products

capital-intensive businesses
Businesses that require large investments in capital assets

EXHIBIT 1.1 Rags to Riches

Few start-up companies are resource-rich. Still, they become successful because an entrepreneur substitutes ingenuity for capital resources.

THE COMPANY	ITS START
Clorox	In May 1913, five men pooled $100 each and started Clorox. The group had no experience in bleach-making chemistry but suspected that the brine found in salt ponds in San Francisco Bay could be converted into bleach.
The Limited	In 1963, 26-year-old Leslie Wexner left his family's retail store after having an argument with his father. He opened one small store in a strip mall in Columbus, Ohio. Today the company operates more than 5,000 stores in the United States.
Gateway 2000	Using $10,000 he borrowed from his grandmother, Ted Waitt started the company in his father's South Dakota barn in 1985. Because a typical computer-industry campaign would have been too costly, Waitt invented its now-famous faux-cowhide boxes. Today Gateway's revenues exceed $5 billion.
Coca-Cola	Pharmacist John Pemberton invented a soft drink in his backyard in 1886. Asa Chandler bought the company for $2,300 in 1891. Today it is worth over $170 billion.
E & J Gallo Winery	Ernest and Julio Gallo invested $6,000 but had no wine-making experience when they rented their first warehouse in California. They learned wine making by studying pamphlets at the local library.
Marriott	Willard Marriott and his fiancée-partner started a nine-seat A & W soda fountain with $3,000 in 1927. They demonstrated a knack for hospitality and clever marketing from the beginning.
Nike	In the early 1960s, Philip Knight and his college track coach sold imported Japanese sneakers from the trunk of a station wagon. Start-up costs totaled $1,000.
United Parcel Service	In 1907, two Seattle teenagers pooled their cash, came up with $100, and began a message and parcel delivery service for local merchants.
Wrigley's Gum	In 1891 young William Wrigley Jr. started selling baking soda in Chicago. To entice new customers, he threw in two packages of chewing gum with every sale. Guess what the customers were most excited about?
Amazon.com	In 1994 Jeff Bezos came across a report projecting annual web growth at 2,300 percent. So Bezos left his Wall Street job, headed to Seattle in an aging Chevy Blazer, and drafted his business plan en route. His e-business, Amazon.com, initially focused on selling books over the Internet, but Bezos later expanded his product offerings to include toys, consumer electronics, software, home improvement products, and more. Today Amazon.com is exploding in size. The company now generates over $2.7 billion in annual sales.

service businesses
Businesses that provide intangible products or perform useful labor on behalf of another

labor-intensive businesses
Businesses in which labor costs are more significant than capital costs

electronic commerce (e-commerce)
The general term for the buying and selling of goods and services on the Internet

barriers to entry
Factors that make it difficult to launch a business in a particular industry

Service businesses, by contrast, produce intangible products (ones that cannot be held in your hand) and include those whose principal product is finance, insurance, transportation, utilities, wholesale and retail trade, banking, entertainment, health care, repairs, or information. Wal-Mart, Nordstrom, Jiffy Lube, and eBay are examples of service businesses. Most service businesses are **labor-intensive businesses**. That is, they rely more on human resources than on buildings, machinery, and equipment to prosper. A consulting firm is an example of a labor-intensive service business because its existence is heavily dependent on the knowledge and skills of its consultants. A group of consultants can go into business simply by purchasing some computers and some telephones.

Keep in mind that some companies produce both goods and services. IBM, for example, is primarily a manufacturer of computers and other business machines, but at least one-third of the company's sales come from computer-related services such as systems design, consulting, and product support.[6] Similarly, Boeing provides flight training, fleet and logistics support, and a number of aviation services to support sales of its commercial aircraft. As more and more manufacturers such as Boeing and IBM focus on servicing and supporting their products, it becomes increasingly difficult to classify a company as either a goods-producing or a service business. Still, such broad classifications are useful for reporting and analytical purposes.

Growth of the Service Sector

Services have always played an important role in the U.S. economy. For more than 60 years, they accounted for half of all U.S. employment. In the mid-1980s services became the engine of growth for the U.S. economy (see Exhibit 1.2).[7] Today the U.S. services sector provides 80 percent of the nation's jobs.[8] Wal-Mart's ascendancy to the title of largest U.S. company underscores the increasing importance of service businesses to the U.S. economy.

The growth in the service sector is attributable to five key factors:

- *Consumers have more disposable income.* The 76 million baby boomers in the United States (people born between 1946 and 1964) are in their peak earning years. These consumers find themselves with more disposable income and look for services to help them invest, travel, relax, and stay fit.

- *Services target changing demographic patterns and lifestyle trends.* The United States has more elderly people, more single people living alone, more two-career households, and more single parents than ever before. These trends create opportunities for service companies that can help people with all the tasks they no longer have time for, including home maintenance, food service, and child care.

- *Services are needed to support complex goods and new technology.* Computers, home entertainment centers, recreational vehicles, security systems, and automated production equipment are examples of products that require specialized installation, repair, user training, or extensive support services. As new technology is incorporated into more and more products, companies will need to provide more of these types of product-support services to remain competitive.

- *Companies are increasingly seeking professional advice.* To compete in the global economy, many firms turn to consultants and professional advisors for help as they seek ways to cut costs, refine their business processes, expand overseas, and engage in **electronic commerce (e-commerce)**—buying and selling over the Internet.

- *Barriers to entry are low for service businesses.* Capital-intensive manufacturing businesses generally have high **barriers to entry**, which means that conditions exist that make entry into these businesses extremely difficult. Such conditions include significant capital requirements, high learning curves, tightly controlled markets, strict licensing procedures, the need for highly skilled employees, or the

Manufacturers of resistance-training machines have characteristics of both goods-producing and service-producing businesses. In addition to producing high-quality equipment, they must provide product training, technical support, warranties, and on-site repair and maintenance; some manufacturers even offer seminars on resistance training and how to maintain a healthy lifestyle.

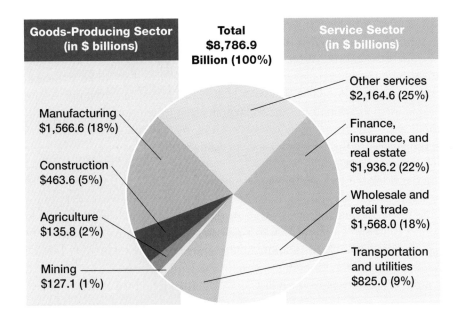

EXHIBIT 1.2
Sectors of the U.S. Economy
The service sector accounts for 74 percent of U.S. economic output, and the goods-producing sector accounts for the remaining 26 percent.

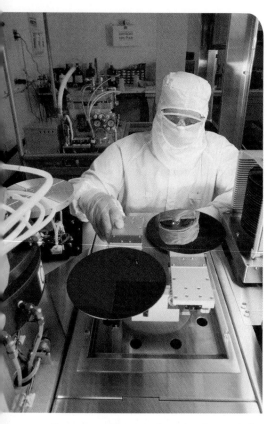

Computer-chip manufacturing is a capital-intensive business. A new state-of-the art factory costs about $2 billion to build and that's only the start. Add to that the costs of manufacturing equipment, supplies, equipment repairs, utilities, and skilled workers, and you can see why the barriers of entry into this industry are extraordinarily high.

economics
The study of how society uses scarce resources to produce and distribute goods and services

microeconomics
The study of small economic units, such as individual consumers, businesses, and industries

macroeconomics
The study of a country's overall economic issues, such as competition, the allocation of scarce resources, and government policies

economic system
Means by which a society distributes its resources to satisfy its people's needs

use of specialized equipment or skills. By contrast, the barriers to entry for most service companies are low.

Whether you're running a service or a goods-producing business, world economic situations affect all businesses that compete in the global economy. Thus, running a successful business today requires a firm understanding of basic economic principles, of the major economic systems in the world, and of how businesses compete in the global and electronic economy.

What Is Economics?

Economics is the study of how a society uses its scarce resources to produce and distribute goods and services. The study of economic behavior among consumers, businesses, and industries who collectively determine the quantity of goods and services demanded and supplied at different prices is commonly referred to as **microeconomics**. By contrast, the study of a country's larger economic issues, such as how firms compete, the effect of government policies, and how an economy maintains and allocates its scarce resources, is commonly referred to as **macroeconomics**. The role that individuals and government play in allocating a society's resources depends on the society's **economic system**, the basic set of rules for allocating a society's resources to satisfy its citizens' needs.

Types of Economic Systems

All societies must deal with the same basic questions: How should limited economic resources be used to satisfy society's needs? What goods and services should be produced? Who should produce them? How should these goods and services be divided among the population? In countries with *free-market systems*, these decisions are made by individuals (or households) when they decide how to spend or invest their income and by businesses when they decide what kinds of goods and services to produce; in countries with *planned systems*, these decisions are made by governments.

Free-Market System In a **free-market system**, individuals are free to decide what products to produce, how to produce them, whom to sell them to, and at what price to sell them. Thus, they have the chance to succeed—or to fail—by their own efforts. **Capitalism** is the term most often used to describe the free-market system—one in which individuals own and operate the majority of businesses and where competition, supply, and demand determine which goods and services are produced. Capitalism owes its philosophical origins to eighteenth-century philosophers such as Adam Smith. According to Smith, in the ideal capitalist economy (pure capitalism), the *market* (an arrangement between buyer and seller to trade goods and services) serves as a self-correcting mechanism—an "invisible hand" to ensure the production of the goods that society wants in the quantities that society wants, without regulation of any kind.[9]

Because the market is its own regulator, Smith was opposed to government intervention. He held that if anyone's prices or wages strayed from acceptable levels that were set for everyone, the force of competition would drive them back. In modern practice, however, the government sometimes intervenes in free-market systems to influence prices and wages or to change the way resources are allocated. This practice of limited intervention is called *mixed capitalism*, which is the economic system of the United States. Other countries with variations of this economic system include Canada, Germany, and Japan. Under mixed capitalism, the pursuit of private gain is regarded as a worthwhile goal that ultimately benefits society as a whole. This is not the case in a planned system.

Planned System In a **planned system**, governments control all or part of the allocation of resources and limit the freedom of choice in order to accomplish government goals. Because social equality is a major goal of planned systems, private enterprise and the pursuit of private gain are generally regarded as wasteful and exploitive.

The planned system that allows individuals the least degree of economic freedom is **communism**, which still exists in countries such as North Korea and Cuba. (Note that even though communism and socialism are discussed here as economic systems, they can be political and social systems as well.) The degree to which communism is actually practiced varies. In its purest form, almost all resources are under government control. Private ownership is restricted to personal and household items. Resource allocation is handled through rigid centralized planning by a handful of government officials who decide what goods to produce, how to produce them, and to whom they should be distributed.[10] Although pure communism still has its supporters, the future of communism is dismal. As economists Lester Thurow and Robert Heilbroner put it, "It's a great deal easier to design and assemble the skeleton of a mighty economy than to run it."[11]

Socialism lies somewhere between capitalism and communism in the degree of economic freedom that it permits. Like communism, socialism involves a relatively high degree of government planning and some government ownership of land and capital resources (such as buildings and equipment). However, government involvement is limited to industries considered vital to the common welfare, such as transportation, utilities, medicine, steel, and communications. In these industries, the government owns or controls all the facilities and determines what will be produced and how the output will be distributed. Private ownership is permitted in industries that are not considered vital, and in these areas both businesses and individuals are allowed to benefit from their own efforts. Taxes are high in socialist states because the government must cover the costs of medical care, education, subsidized housing, and other social services.

The Trend Toward Privatization

Although varying degrees of socialism and communism are practiced around the world today, several socialist and communist economies are moving toward free-market systems. Anxious to unload unprofitable businesses for badly needed cash and to experiment with free-market capitalism, countries such as Great Britain, Mexico, Argentina, Israel, France, Sweden, and China are **privatizing** some of their government-owned enterprises by selling them to privately held firms. Great Britain, for example, has sold the national phone company, the national steel company, the national sugar company, Heathrow Airport, water suppliers, and the company that makes Rover automobiles. France is reducing its controlling stake in Air France, the country's national airline, to under 20 percent. And China plans to convert more than 60 percent of its state-owned industries in the near future.[12]

Microeconomics: The Forces of Demand and Supply

At the heart of every business transaction is an exchange between a buyer and a seller. The buyer wants or needs a particular service or good and is willing to pay the seller in order to obtain it. The seller is willing to participate in the transaction because of the anticipated financial gains from selling the service or good. In a free-market system, the marketplace

3 LEARNING OBJECTIVE

Differentiate between a free-market system and a planned system

free-market system
Economic system in which decisions about what to produce and in what quantities are decided by the market's buyers and sellers

capitalism
Economic system based on economic freedom and competition

planned system
Economic system in which the government controls most of the factors of production and regulates their allocation

communism
Economic system in which all productive resources are owned and operated by the government, to the elimination of private property

socialism
Economic system characterized by public ownership and operation of key industries combined with private ownership and operation of less-vital industries

privatizing
The conversion of public ownership to private ownership

4 LEARNING OBJECTIVE

Identify the factors that affect demand and those that affect supply

demand
Buyers' willingness and ability to purchase products

supply
Specific quantity of a product that the seller is able and willing to provide

(composed of individuals, firms, and industries) and the forces of demand and supply determine the quantity of goods and services produced and the prices at which they are sold. **Demand** is the quantity of a good or service that consumers will buy at a given time at various prices. **Supply** is the quantity of a good or service that producers will provide on a particular date. Both work together to impose a kind of order on the free-market system.

On the surface, the theory of supply and demand seems little more than common sense. Consumers should buy more when the price is low and buy less when the price is high. Producers would offer more when the price is high and offer less when the price is low. In other words, the quantity supplied and the quantity demanded continuously interact, and the balance between them at any given moment should be reflected by the current price on the open market. However, balancing supply with demand by adjusting price isn't quite that simple.

Understanding Demand

Consider the airline industry. When the economy is robust, consumers are willing to spend more on discretionary travel. When the economy falters, they cut back on such discretionary spending. Airlines can respond to changes in consumer demand by reducing ticket prices or by offering promotions. But factors other than price influence consumer demand, including

- consumer income
- consumer preferences (such as increased safety or reduced travel time for the airline industry)
- the price of substitute products (such as rail or automobile travel or videoconferencing for the airline industry)
- the price of complementary goods (such as hotel accommodations or restaurant dining for the airline industry)
- advertising and promotional expenditures
- consumer expectations about future prices

Still, price generally is considered the most important variable. In most cases as the price of a good or service goes up, people buy less. In other words, as the price rises, the quantity demanded declines. Alternatively, at lower prices, consumers generally are willing to purchase more goods and services.

5 LEARNING OBJECTIVE

Compare supply and demand curves and explain how they interact to affect price

demand curve
Graph of the quantities of product that buyers will purchase at various prices

A **demand curve** is a graph showing the relationship between the amount of product that buyers will purchase at various prices. (Demand curves are not necessarily curved; they may be straight lines.) To draw the graph, we assume that all variables except price remain constant. Demand curves typically slope downward, which means that lower prices generally attract larger purchases. For instance, when airlines reduce their ticket prices, the demand for airline travel generally rises. Exhibit 1.3 shows a possible demand curve for the monthly number of economy tickets (seats) for an airline's Chicago to Denver route at different prices.

It is important to understand that there is a difference between changes in the quantity demanded at various prices and changes in *overall* demand. A change in quantity demanded, such as the change that occurs at different airline ticket prices for a market, is simply movement along the demand curve. A change in overall demand resulting from changes in a number of variables besides price produces an entirely new demand curve. Exhibit 1.4 highlights the expected movement of the new demand curve as key variables change.

Looking back at our airline example, if consumer concerns for travel safety increase or the consumer income decreases, we would expect our original demand curve for airline tickets to drop at every price. As Exhibit 1.5 shows, such an overall drop in demand would result

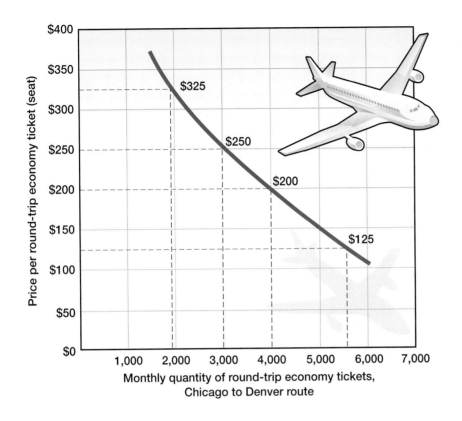

EXHIBIT 1.3
Demand Curve for Monthly Airline Tickets (Economy Seats): Chicago to Denver Route
This demand curve shows that the higher the ticket price, the smaller the quantity demanded, all else being equal.

in a new demand curve for airline ticket sales for the same Chicago to Denver route. The new demand curve shifts to the left of the original demand curve depicted in Exhibit 1.3. If conditions change and overall demand increases beyond the original demand depicted in Exhibit 1.3, the new demand curve would shift to the right of the original demand curve.

Understanding Supply

Demand alone is not enough to explain how a company operating in a free-market system sets its prices or production levels. In general, a firm's willingness to produce and sell a good or service increases as the price it can charge and its profit potential per item increase. In other words, as the price goes up, the quantity supplied generally goes up. The depiction of the relationship between prices and quantities that sellers will offer for sale, regardless of demand, is called a **supply curve**. Movement along the supply curve typically slopes

supply curve
Graph of the quantities that sellers will offer for sale, regardless of demand, at various prices

EXHIBIT 1.4   How Changes in Variables Shift the Demand Curve
The demand curve is affected by changes in these variables.

	EXPECTED SHIFTS IN DEMAND CURVE	
VARIABLE	**SHIFTS TO THE RIGHT WHEN:**	**SHIFTS TO THE LEFT WHEN:**
Consumers' incomes	increase	decrease
Consumer preferences	are more favorable toward product	are less favorable toward product
Prices of substitute products	increase	decrease
Prices of complementary goods	decrease	increase
Advertising or promotional expenditures	increase	decrease
Consumer expectations become more	optimistic	pessimistic
Number of buyers	increases	decreases

EXHIBIT 1.5

Shift in Demand Curve for Monthly Airline Tickets (Economy Seats): Chicago to Denver Route

Heightened concerns about travel safety and a weakened economy are two factors that have decreased overall demand for airline economy tickets (seats) at all prices.

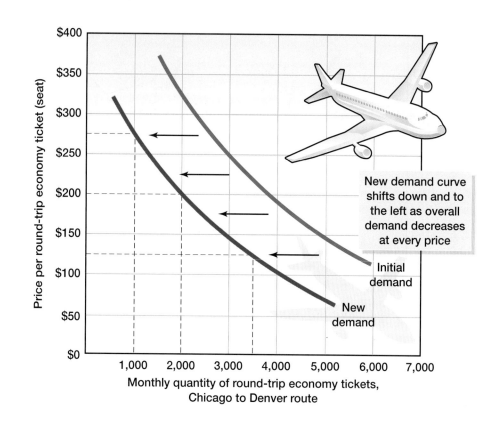

upward. So as prices rise, the quantity sellers are willing to supply also rises. Similarly, as prices decline, the quantity sellers are willing to supply declines.

Exhibit 1.6 shows a possible supply curve for the monthly number of economy tickets (seats) supplied on an airline's Chicago to Denver route at different prices. The graph shows that increasing prices for economy tickets on that route should increase the number of tick-

EXHIBIT 1.6

Supply Curve for Monthly Airline Tickets (Economy Seats): Chicago to Denver Route

This supply curve shows that the higher the price, the larger the quantity of economy tickets (seats) airlines are willing to supply, all else being equal.

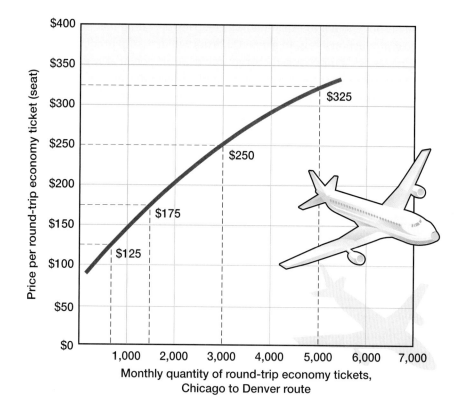

EXHIBIT 1.7   How Changes in Variables Shift the Supply Curve
The supply curve is affected by changes in these variables.

	EXPECTED SHIFTS IN SUPPLY CURVE	
VARIABLE	*SHIFTS TO THE RIGHT WHEN:*	*SHIFTS TO THE LEFT WHEN:*
Costs of inputs	decrease	increase
Number of competitors	decreases	increases
New technology	decreases production costs	increases production costs
Suppliers expect that future sales prices	will decline	will increase

ets (seats) an airline is willing to provide for that route, because the airlines are motivated by the possibility of earning growing profits.

As with demand, several factors affect a seller's willingness and ability to provide goods and services at various prices. These variables include the cost of inputs (for example, pilot wages, fuel, and planes for the airlines), the number of competitors in the marketplace, and advancements in technology that allow companies to operate more efficiently. A change in any of these variables can shift the entire supply curve, either increasing or decreasing the amount available at every price, as Exhibit 1.7 suggests.

For example, if the cost of fuel rises, airlines may respond by cutting back the number of economy seats assigned to its routes, shifting the supply curve to the left (see Exhibit 1.8). But if new technologies allow the airline to save fuel or reduce the costs of training pilots, airlines may increase the number of economy seats assigned to its routes. Such increase in supply would shift the supply curve to the right.

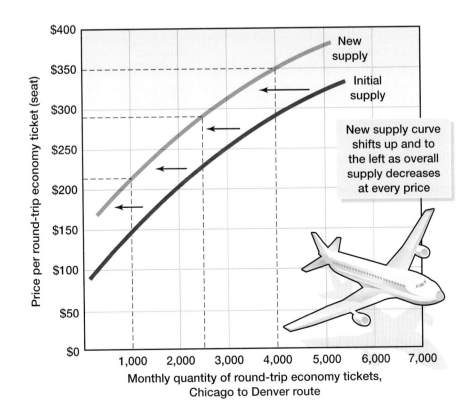

New supply

Initial supply

New supply curve shifts up and to the left as overall supply decreases at every price

Price per round-trip economy ticket (seat)

Monthly quantity of round-trip economy tickets, Chicago to Denver route

EXHIBIT 1.8

Shift in Supply Curve for Monthly Airline Tickets (Economy Seats): Chicago to Denver Route
Airlines have responded to heightened concerns about travel safety and a weakened economy by reducing the supply of airline tickets (seats) at all prices. This new supply curve shifts up and to the left, signaling that the quantity supplied decreases at every price.

EXHIBIT 1.9

The Relationship Between Supply and Demand
In a free-market system, prices aren't set by the government, nor do producers alone have the final say. Instead, prices reflect the interaction of supply and demand. The equilibrium price (E) is established when the amount of a product that producers are willing to sell at a given price equals the amount that consumers are willing to buy at that price.

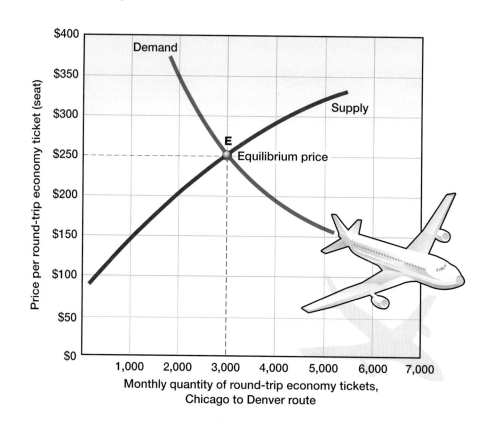

equilibrium price
Point at which quantity supplied equals quantity demanded

Understanding How Demand and Supply Interact

In the real world, variables that affect demand and supply do not change independently. Instead, they change simultaneously and continually. Exhibit 1.9 shows the interaction of both supply and demand curves for monthly airline economy tickets (seats) on a single graph. The two curves intersect at the point market **E**, or $250. This price is known as the **equilibrium price**. At that price the airline is willing to sell 3,000 round-trip economy tickets and consumers are willing to buy 3,000 economy tickets for its Chicago to Denver route. In other words, the quantity supplied and the quantity demanded are in balance.

As variables affecting supply and demand change, so will the equilibrium price. For example, increased concerns about passenger safety or longer lines at airport security checkpoints could encourage travelers to make alternative economic choices such as automobile travel or videoconferencing, and thus reduce the demand for air travel at every price. Suppliers might respond to such a reduction in demand by either reducing the number of flights offered or reducing ticket prices in order to restore the equilibrium level. As this chapter's case study shows (see pages 31–32), several airlines are experimenting with a number of options to find a new equilibrium point because of an expected long-term decline in overall demand.

Macroeconomics: Issues for the Entire Economy

In the previous section we discussed a variety of individual factors that affect the forces of supply and demand simultaneously. In this section we will expand on that discussion by showing how a number of larger economic forces also influence market behavior and ultimately affect supply and demand. These issues include how firms and industries compete in an economic system and the role government plays in fostering competition, regulating industries, protecting stakeholders, and contributing to economic stability.

competition
Rivalry among businesses for the same customer

Competition in a Free-Market System

In a free-market system, customers are free to buy whatever and wherever they please. Therefore, companies must compete with rivals for potential customers. Wal-Mart, for example, competes with Target, Toys "R" Us, Sears, and a number of discount retailers that sell the same goods and services. **Competition** is the situation in which two or more suppliers of a product are rivals in the pursuit of the same customers.

In theory, the ideal type of competition is **pure competition**, which is characterized by three conditions: a marketplace of multiple buyers and sellers; a product or service with nearly identical features such as wheat or cotton; and low barriers to entry (that is, the ability to easily enter and exit the marketplace). When these three conditions exist, no single firm or group of firms in an industry becomes large enough to influence prices and thereby distort the workings of the free-market system. By contrast, in a **monopoly** there is only one producer of a product in a given market, and thus the producer is able to determine the price. A situation in which an industry (such as commercial aircraft manufacturing) is dominated by only a few producers (in this case, Boeing and Airbus Industries) is called an **oligopoly**.

Although oligopolies have few players, they can be extremely competitive—especially if the players become involved in a bidding war. Such was the case when Iberia Airlines was looking to purchase 12 new planes to modernize its long-haul fleet. In 2003 the airline solicited bids from rivals Boeing and Airbus, but first Iberia executives made it clear that the airline was looking for discounts exceeding 40 percent. Whichever company could meet or exceed Iberia's target price would win the race. After a months-long dogfight between the two aviation titans, the contract was awarded to Airbus. Heightened competition between the two rival jet makers helped Iberia nail down a deeply discounted price and valuable concessions.[13]

Between pure competition and monopoly lie varying degrees of competitive power. Most of the competition in advanced free-market economic systems is **monopolistic competition**, in which a large number of sellers (none of which dominates the market) offer products that can be distinguished from competing products in at least some small way. Toothpaste, cosmetics, soft drinks, Internet search engines, and restaurants are examples of products that can vary in the features each offers.

When markets become filled with competitors and products start to look alike, companies use price, speed, quality, service, or innovation to gain a **competitive advantage**—something that sets one company apart from its rivals and makes its products more appealing to consumers. For example, Wal-Mart upstages competitors by selling goods at low prices. Jiffy Lube competes on speed: Mechanics change a car's oil and oil filter in 15 minutes or less while customers wait. Starbucks competes on quality by delivering a premium product that has changed the definition of "a good cup of coffee." And Macys.com competes on customer service. Not only are Macy's customers allowed to return their online purchases to any physical Macy's store, but those who live near a Macy's retail outlet can call its customer service department to have a store employee pick up unwanted Internet purchases at their home. The service is free—the customer just has to be home when the Macy's employee arrives.

Product innovation is another way that companies compete in the free-market economy. For nearly a century, 3M's management has promoted innovation by giving employees the freedom to take risks and try new ideas. Beginning with the invention of sandpaper in 1904, 3M has produced such staples as masking tape, cellophane tape, magnetic tape, videotape, and Post-it Notes. Sometimes product innovation can revolutionize an entire industry, just as Razor aluminum scooters, Rollerblades, AbFlex, Atomic hour-glass skis, and Burton & Sims snowboards did by creating new market opportunities for the sporting goods industry.[14]

pure competition
Situation in which so many buyers and sellers exist that no single buyer or seller can individually influence market prices

monopoly
Market in which there are no direct competitors, so that one company dominates

oligopoly
Market dominated by a few producers

monopolistic competition
Situation in which many sellers differentiate their products from those of competitors in at least some small way

competitive advantage
Ability to perform in one or more ways that competitors cannot match

It doesn't take long before innovative products such as scooters catch on. But just rolling out a "me-too" product in today's competitive marketplace will not guarantee success. Today's products must be exciting and create perceived consumer value to catch the savvy buyer's eye.

Government's Role in a Free-Market System

6 **LEARNING OBJECTIVE**

Discuss the four major economic roles of the U.S. government

Although the free-market system generally works well, it's far from perfect. If left unchecked, the economic forces that make capitalism succeed may also create severe problems for some groups or individuals. To correct these types of problems, the government serves four major economic roles: it enacts laws and creates regulations to foster competition; it regulates and deregulates certain industries; it protects stakeholders' rights; and it intervenes to contribute to economic stability.

Fostering Competition   Because competition generally benefits the U.S. economy, the federal government and state and local governments create thousands of new laws and regulations every year to preserve competition and ensure that no single enterprise becomes too powerful. For instance, if a company has a monopoly, it can harm consumers by raising prices, cutting output, or stifling innovation. Furthermore, because most monopolies have total control over certain products and prices and the market share for those products, it's extremely difficult for competitors to enter markets where monopolies exist. For these reasons, over the past century or so, a number of laws and regulations have been established to help prevent individual companies or groups of companies from gaining control of markets in ways that restrain competition or harm consumers.

Antitrust Legislation   Antitrust laws limit what businesses can and cannot do, in order to ensure that all competitors have an equal chance of producing a product, reaching the market, and making a profit. Some of the earliest government moves in this arena produced such landmark pieces of legislation as the Sherman Antitrust Act, the Clayton Antitrust Act, and the Federal Trade Commission Act, which generally sought to rein in the power of a few huge companies that had financial and management control of a significant number of other companies in the same industry. Usually referred to as *trusts* (hence the label *antitrust legislation*), these huge companies controlled enough of the supply and distribution in their respective industries to muscle smaller competitors out of the way.

One of the highest-profile antitrust cases of the 1990s involved the software giant Microsoft. Microsoft makes the operating-system software used by 90 percent of personal computers in addition to producing a wide array of application software that runs on those operating systems. In the late 1990s the U.S. Justice Department accused Microsoft of using its vast clout to give itself an unfair advantage in the application-software business by bundling its popular Internet Explorer web browser with its Windows operating system. Competitors such as Netscape alleged that Microsoft was willing to use every tool at its disposal to damage competition by forcing or persuading companies to install Internet Explorer as a condition of licensing the Windows operating system.

After a much-publicized two-year trial, on June 7, 2000, U.S. District Judge Thomas Jackson ordered that the company be split up after ruling that Microsoft was indeed a monopoly and that it had repeatedly and willfully abused its monopoly power to thwart competition and stymie innovation. But in July 2001 the U.S. Court of Appeals reversed Judge Jackson's order to split Microsoft into smaller companies and sent the case back to district court to develop remedies to prevent Microsoft from using its Windows operating system monopoly in an anticompetitive manner.[15] One such remedy issued by Judge Kollar-Kotel required Microsoft to disclose the communications protocol in its Windows PC software so competitors' software can work more smoothly with Windows.[16]

Mergers and Acquisitions   To preserve competition, the government may also stipulate requirements companies must meet to gain approval for a proposed merger or acquisition. Before the government would approve the AOL and Time Warner merger, it insisted that the companies make their powerful cable and Internet networks available to competitors. Without such requirements, regulators were concerned that Time Warner, by virtue of its enormous size, would have too much power and influence over access to the Internet.

If the government thinks a proposed merger or acquisition might restrain competition, it may deny approval altogether. United Airlines and U.S. Airways terminated their merger plans when the U.S. government said it would block the deal. The government asserted the combination would reduce competition, raise airfares, and harm consumers on nationwide airline routes.[17] Similarly, bookstore chain Barnes & Noble scrapped its planned $600 million acquisition of Ingram Book Group, the largest book wholesaler in the United States, when regulators alleged that the merger would stifle competition by giving Barnes & Noble an advantage over smaller booksellers.[18]

Regulating and Deregulating Industries Sometimes the government imposes regulations on specific industries to ensure fair competition, ethical business practices, safe working conditions, or general public safety. The establishment of the Transportation Security Administration and the federalization of U.S. airport security following the September 11, 2001, terrorist attacks is an example of one such case in which the U.S. government has assumed control of a private industry for the safety of its citizens.

In a *regulated industry*, close government control is substituted for free competition, and competition is either limited or eliminated. In extreme cases, regulators may even decide who can enter an industry, what customers they must serve, and how much they can charge. For years, the telecommunications, airline, banking, and electric utility industries fell under strict government control. However, the trend over the past few decades has been to open

Competing in the Global Marketplace

Is Big Government Back in Style?

For the past two decades, America's mantra, both at home and overseas, has been "Government is not the solution to our problems. Government is the problem." But the unexpected bursting of the technology bubble, the unnerving terrorism of September 11, the shocking revelations of corporate corruption, and declines in equities and personal wealth have changed that mantra. Public demand has brought back government in its traditional role—as guardian of the country's safety.

The early 21st century has witnessed an expansion in government's size, reach, and authority. Following the September 11, 2001, terrorist attacks, America has seen a large increase in national defense spending to develop a department of homeland security, to rout al Qaeda from Afghanistan, to tighten airport security, and to increase its defenses against global terrorism. America has also seen an increase in legislative oversight and government intervention in business and the economy following a surge in reported corporate wrongdoings.

But government's expanded reach does not mean that its citizens and policymakers have lost their faith in the importance of free markets. They just realize that in these troubled times, the relationship between government and society must change. A recent ABC News poll showed that 68 percent of respondents trust the U.S. government to do what's right "when it comes to handling national security and the war on terrorism." The danger, of course, is that the government could go too far. By regulating too heavily it could increase friction in the markets. By bloating its defense and security spending, it could shift too much capital away from productive enterprise. By enticing high-tech companies to depend on fat defense contracts, it could reduce corporate efficiency and competitiveness. There is even a danger that the budget deficit could grow to such an extent that interest rates are hiked, hurting consumers and businesses alike. The economic stakes of big government are high. Thus, the challenge ahead is to get the calibration right.

Questions for Critical Thinking

1. How does the U.S. government play an important role in the global economy?
2. How is the role of the U.S. government changing?

up competition in regulated industries by removing or relaxing existing regulations. Hopes are that such *deregulation* will allow new industry competitors to enter the market, create more choices for consumers, and keep prices in check. But the debate is ongoing about whether deregulation achieves these goals.

Take the telecommunications industry, for example. The 1996 Telecommunication Act promised to bring vibrant competition to an industry that had previously been dominated by the Baby Bell companies (which were created from the government's break up of AT&T in 1982). The Act required that the Baby Bells share their vast network of phone lines with competition. By 1999 nearly 400 new carriers were poised for a telecom revolution. But the Baby Bells have consistently made life difficult for the little guys by imposing onerous conditions on new competitors and by merging with each other to form four huge Papa Bell organizations. Still, a recent FCC report found that non-Bell carriers served about 16.4 million U.S. phone lines and control about 8.5 percent of the market, with as high as 20 percent in New York. However, experts estimate that of the 200 still-remaining new carriers, only 50 will survive.[19]

Protecting Stakeholders In addition to fostering competition, another important role the government plays is to protect the stakeholders of a business. Businesses have many **stakeholders**—groups that are affected by (or that affect) a business's operations, including colleagues, employees, supervisors, shareholders, customers, suppliers, governments, and society at large. In the process of serving one or more of these stakeholders, a business may sometimes neglect the interests of other stakeholders. For example, managers who are too narrowly focused on generating wealth for shareholders might not spend the funds necessary to create a safe work environment for employees or to reduce waste. Similarly, a public company that withholds information about its true financial performance may hamper the ability of investors to make solid decisions and may even harm the wealth of stakeholders, as we will see in our discussion of Enron in Chapter 2.

To protect consumers, employees, shareholders, and the environment from the potentially harmful actions of business, the government has established several regulatory agencies (see Exhibit 1.10). Many of these agencies have the power to pass and enforce rules and regulations within their specific area of authority. Such regulations are intended to encourage businesses to behave ethically and in a socially responsible way. Chapter 2 takes a closer look at society's concerns for ethical and socially responsible behavior, specific government agencies that regulate such behavior, and the efforts by businesses to become better corporate citizens.

Contributing to Economic Stability A nation's economy never stays exactly the same size. Instead, it grows and contracts in response to the combined effects of such factors as technological breakthroughs, changes in investment patterns, shifts in consumer attitudes, world events, and basic economic forces. *Economic expansion* occurs when the economy is growing and people are spending more money. Consumer purchases stimulate businesses to produce more goods and services, which in turn stimulates employment. *Economic contraction* occurs when such spending declines. Businesses cut back on production, employees are laid off, and the economy as a whole slows down.

If the period of downward swing is severe, the nation may enter into a **recession**, traditionally defined as two consecutive quarters of decline in real gross domestic product. The United States has experienced only 10 recessions since World War II.[20] When a downward swing or recession is over, the economy enters a period of *recovery:* Companies buy more, factories produce more, employment is high, and workers spend their earnings.

These recurrent up-and-down swings are known as the **business cycle**. Although such swings are natural and to some degree predictable, they cause hardship. In an attempt to avoid such hardship and to foster economic stability, the government can levy new taxes or

stakeholders
Individuals or groups to whom a business has a responsibility

recession
Period during which national income, employment, and production all fall

business cycle
Fluctuations in the rate of growth that an economy experiences over a period of several years

EXHIBIT 1.10 Major Government Agencies and What They Do
Government agencies protect stakeholders by developing and promoting standards, regulating and overseeing industries, and enforcing laws and regulations.

GOVERNMENT AGENCY OR COMMISSION	MAJOR AREAS OF RESPONSIBILITY
Consumer Product Safety Commission (CPSC)	Regulates and protects public from unreasonable risks of injury from consumer products
Environmental Protection Agency (EPA)	Develops and enforces standards to protect the environment
Equal Employment Opportunity Commission (EEOC)	Protects and resolves discriminatory employment practices
Federal Aviation Administration (FAA)	Sets rules for the commercial airline industry
Federal Communications Commission (FCC)	Oversees communication by telephone, telegraph, radio, and television
Federal Energy Regulatory Commission (FERC)	Regulates rates and sales of electric power and natural gas
Federal Highway Administration (FHA)	Regulates vehicle safety requirements
Federal Trade Commission (FTC)	Enforces laws and guidelines regarding unfair business practices and acts to stop false and deceptive advertising and labeling
Food and Drug Administration (FDA)	Enforces laws and regulations to prevent distribution of harmful foods, drugs, medical devices, and cosmetics
Interstate Commerce Commission (ICC)	Regulates and oversees carriers engaged in transportation between states: railroads, bus lines, trucking companies, oil pipelines, and waterways
Occupational Safety and Health Administration (OSHA)	Promotes worker safety and health
Securities and Exchange Commission (SEC)	Protects investors and maintains the integrity of the securities markets

adjust the current tax rates, raise or lower interest rates, and regulate the total amount of money circulating in our economy. These government actions have two facets: monetary policy and fiscal policy.

Monetary Policy Monetary policy involves increasing or decreasing a nation's money supply to regulate the economy. In the United States, monetary policy is controlled primarily by the Federal Reserve Board (the Fed), a group of appointed government officials who oversee the country's central banking system. The Fed influences the money supply to make certain that enough money and credit are available to fuel a healthy economy. However, it must act carefully, because altering the money supply affects interest rates, inflation, and the economy. When the money supply is increased, more money is available for loans, so banks can charge lower interest rates to borrowers. On the other hand, an increased money supply can lead to more consumer spending and can result in the demand for goods exceeding supply. When demand exceeds supply, sellers may raise their prices, leading to inflation. In turn, inflation can slow economic growth—a situation the Fed wants to avoid. And, because so many companies now buy and sell across national borders, the Fed's changes may affect the interlinked economies of many countries, not just the United States.[21] That's why the Fed moves cautiously and keeps a close eye on the size of the money supply.

As Chapter 17 discusses in detail, the Fed uses four basic tools to influence the money supply: changing the reserve requirement, changing the discount rate, conducting open-market operations, and establishing selective credit controls. For instance, if the Fed increases the interest rate on money it lends to banks, the banks pass this increase on to borrowers. This action prompts businesses and consumers to borrow less and spend less, thus slowing the economy. Similarly, if the Fed decreases the interest rate on money it

monetary policy
Government policy and actions taken by the Federal Reserve Board to regulate the nation's money supply

Mortgage rates at 30-year lows sparked a wave of new-home construction at the beginning of the 21st century, in spite of an overall economic recession.

fiscal policy
Use of government revenue collection and spending to influence the business cycle

lends to banks, banks pass this decrease on to its borrowers. This action prompts businesses and consumers to borrow more and spend more, thus stimulating the economy. In 2001 the Fed lowered interest rates 11 times to prod the economy into recovery.[22]

Money injected into the economy has a *multiplier effect* as it makes its way through the system. For example, if a company borrows money to build a large office complex, thousands of construction workers will be gainfully employed and earn wages. If some of these workers decide to spend their extra income to buy new cars, car dealers will have more income. The car dealers, in turn, might spend their income on new clothes, and the salesclerks (who earn commissions) might buy compact disks, and so on. This *circular flow* of money through the economic system links all elements of the U.S. economy by exchanging goods and services for money, which is then used to buy more goods and services, and so on.

Fiscal Policy **Fiscal policy** involves changes in the government's revenues and expenditures to stimulate or dampen the economy. Government spending is indeed an important factor in U.S. economic stability. For one thing, the U.S. federal and state governments are responsible for supplying and maintaining such *public goods and services* as the highways, military, public water works, fire and police protection, and so on. The U.S. government gets money to provide such public goods by collecting a variety of taxes such as those listed in Exhibit 1.11.

Each year the president of the United States proposes a federal budget, a blueprint for how the U.S. government will raise and spend money during the coming year. The proposed budget is then presented to Congress for approval. When the U.S. government spends more money than it takes in, it creates annual budget deficits. The accumulated amount of annual budget deficits (the U.S. national debt) fluctuates, and now amounts to over $6 trillion.[23] Interest payments on the national debt alone can cost U.S. taxpayers over $300 billion a year—or $10,000 per second. To pare down the national debt, Congress passed a 1997 law to balance the budget by 2002—which it did.[24] But the balanced budget was short lived, as federal spending soon increased to fund a war on terrorism and to give the U.S. economy a lift as it emerged from a recession.[25]

EXHIBIT 1.11

Types of Taxes
From road repair to regulation, running a government is an expensive affair. To fund government operations and projects, national governments, states, counties, and cities levy and collect a variety of revenue-raising taxes.

TYPE OF TAX	LEVIED ON
Income taxes	Income earned by individuals and businesses. Income taxes are the government's largest single source of revenue.
Real property taxes	Assessed value of the land and structures owned by businesses and individuals.
Sales taxes	Retail purchases made by customers. Sales taxes are collected by retail businesses at the time of the sale and then forwarded to the government.
Excise taxes	Selected items such as gasoline, tobacco, and liquor. Often referred to as "sin" taxes, excise taxes are implemented to help control potentially harmful practices.
Payroll taxes	Earnings of individuals to help fund Social Security, Medicare, and unemployment compensation. Corporations match employee contributions.

How a Free-Market System Monitors Its Economic Performance

Each day we are deluged with complex statistical data that depict the current status and past performance of the economy. Sorting, understanding, and interpreting these data are difficult tasks even for professional economists. **Economic indicators** include statistics such as interest rates, unemployment rates, and housing data that are used to monitor and measure economic performance. Statistics that point to what may happen to the economy in the future are called *leading indicators;* statistics that signal a swing in the economy after the movement has begun are called *lagging indicators.*

Watching Economic Indicators

Economists monitor the performance of the economy by watching a variety of indicators. Unemployment statistics, for example, signal future changes in consumer spending. When unemployment rises, people have less money to spend, and the economy suffers. Housing starts, another leading indicator, show where several industries are headed. Housing is very sensitive to interest rate changes. If mortgage rates are high, fewer people can afford to buy new homes. As a result, housing starts to drop and builders stop hiring. Some may even lay off workers. Meanwhile, orders fall for plumbing fixtures, carpets, and appliances, so manufacturers decrease production and workers' hours. These cutbacks ripple through the economy and lead to slower income and job growth, and weaker consumer spending.[26] Another leading indicator is durable-goods orders, or orders for goods that typically last more than three years (which can mean everything from desk chairs to airplanes). A rise in durable-goods orders is a positive indicator that business spending is turning around. Besides unemployment data, housing starts, and durable-goods orders, economists closely monitor a nation's price changes and output.

Measuring Price Changes

Price changes, especially price increases, are another important economic indicator. In a period of rising prices, the purchasing power of a dollar erodes, which means that you can purchase fewer things with today's dollar than you could in a prior period. Over time, price increases tend to lead to wage increases, which in turn add pressures for higher prices, setting in motion a vicious cycle.

Inflation and Deflation   **Inflation** is a steady rise in the prices of goods and services throughout the economy. When the inflation rate begins to decline, economists use the term *disinflation.* **Deflation**, on the other hand, is the sustained fall in the general price level for goods and services. It is the opposite of inflation; that is, purchasing power increases because a dollar held today will buy more tomorrow. In a deflationary period, investors postpone major purchases in anticipation of lower prices in the future. Keep in mind that although prices in the overall economy tend to increase year after year, not all industries and product categories necessarily follow this trend. In the electronics industry, for instance, prices tend to drop as technology advances and production becomes more efficient. When DVD players first hit the market, they were priced at about $1,000. Today you can purchase one for under $100.

Price Indexes   The **consumer price index (CPI)** measures the changes in prices of a representative basket of about 400 goods and services purchased by a typical consumer, such

7 LEARNING OBJECTIVE

Explain how a free-market system monitors its economic performance

economic indicators
Statistics that measure variables in the economy

inflation
Economic condition in which prices rise steadily throughout the economy

deflation
Economic condition in which prices fall steadily throughout the economy

consumer price index (CPI)
Monthly statistic that measures changes in the prices of about 400 goods and services that consumers buy

as clothing, food, housing, and utilities over time. A numerical weight is assigned to each item in the representative basket to adjust for each item's relative importance in the marketplace. The CPI has always been a hot topic because it is used by the government to index Social Security payments, and it is widely used by businesses in private contracts to calculate cost-of-living increases. But, like most economic indicators, the CPI is far from perfect. For one thing, the representative basket of goods may not accurately represent the prices and consumption patterns of the area in which you live. For another, the mix in this basket may not include new innovations or capture the shift of consumer purchases to products with falling prices. To adjust for these deficiencies, in 2002 the Labor Department began publishing a "superlative" or "chained" CPI.[27]

producer price index (PPI)
Monthly statistic that measures changes in the prices at the producer or wholesaler level

The **producer price index (PPI)** is another economic indicator used to track price changes. In contrast to the CPI, the PPI measures prices at the producer or wholesaler level. Three major categories of goods tracked in the PPI are finished goods sold to retailers, intermediate goods such as product components that require further processing, and crude goods or raw materials.

Measuring a Nation's Output

gross domestic product (GDP)
Dollar value of all the final goods and services produced by businesses located within a nation's borders; excludes receipts from overseas operations of domestic companies

The broadest measure of an economy's health is the **gross domestic product (GDP)**. The GDP measures a country's output—its production, distribution, and use of goods and services—by computing the sum of all goods and services produced for *final* use in a market during a specified period (usually a year). The goods may be produced by either domestic or foreign companies as long as these companies are located within a nation's boundaries. Sales from a Honda assembly plant in California, for instance, would be included in the GDP.

gross national product (GNP)
Dollar value of all the final goods and services produced by domestic businesses; includes receipts from overseas operations and excludes receipts from foreign-owned businesses within a nation's borders

A less-popular measure of a country's output is the **gross national product (GNP)**. This measure excludes the value of production from foreign-owned businesses within a nation's boundaries (such as Honda U.S.), but it includes receipts from the overseas operations of domestic companies—such as sales from Wal-Mart's stores in Germany. Put another way, the GNP considers *who* is responsible for the production; the GDP considers *where* the production occurs. Although far from perfect, the GDP enables a nation to evaluate its economic policies and to compare its current performance with prior periods or with the performance of other nations.

Exhibit 1.12 summarizes the common indicators used to measure a nation's economic performance. By any objective measure, the U.S. economy was in a period of economic con-

EXHIBIT 1.12 **Ten Common Indicators of a Nation's Economic Performance**
Economists use a number of economic measures to evaluate a nation's economy. Here are 10 of the most significant measures.

ECONOMIC MEASURE	DESCRIPTION
Prime interest rate	Lowest interest rate that banks charge preferred borrowers on short-term loans
Unemployment rate	Percentage of a nation's workforce unemployed at any time
Housing starts	Number of building permits issued by private housing units
Durable-goods orders	New orders for goods that last more than three years
Labor productivity rate	Rate of increase or decrease in the average level of output per worker
Balance of trade	Total value of a country's exports minus the total value of its imports, over a specific period of time
Inflation rate	Percentage increase in prices of goods or services over a period of time
Producer price index	Monthly index that measures changes in wholesale prices
Consumer price index	Monthly index that measures changes in consumer prices of a fixed basket of goods and services
Gross domestic product	Dollar value of all final goods and services produced by businesses located within a nation's borders

traction as it ushered in the new millennium. But a look into the country's economic history shows that U.S. growth has been a series of ups and downs.

History of U.S. Economic Growth

The first economic base in the United States was the small family farm. People grew enough food for their families and used any surplus to trade for necessary goods provided by independent craftspeople and merchants. Business operated on a small scale, and much of the population was self-employed. With fertile, flat terrain and adequate rainfall, farmers soon prospered, and their prosperity spread to the townspeople who served them. Nonetheless, the success or failure of crops influenced every aspect of the U.S. economy.

In the early 19th century, people began making greater use of rivers, harbors, and rich mineral deposits. Excellent natural resources helped businesspeople accumulate the capital they needed to increase production—fueling the transition of the United States from a farm-based economy to an industrial economy.

Age of Industrialization: 1900–1944

During the 19th century, new technology gave birth to the factory and the industrial revolution. Millions of new workers came to the United States from abroad to work in factories where each person performed one simple task over and over. Separating the manufacturing process into distinct tasks and producing large quantities of similar products allowed businesses to achieve cost and operating efficiencies known as **economies of scale**.

economies of scale
Savings from manufacturing, marketing, or buying in large quantities

As demand for manufactured goods increased, businesses focused on producing more and more goods. By the early 1920s, large, powerful operations populated the landscape and put smaller competitors, workers, and consumers at a disadvantage. By popular mandate, the government passed laws and regulations to prevent the abuse of power by big business. At the same time, workers began to organize into labor unions to balance the power of their employers. Meanwhile, U.S. businesses enjoyed such an enormously diverse market within the country's borders that they didn't need to trade overseas. But prosperity soon ended. In 1929 the U.S. stock market crashed, ushering in a period of economic collapse known as the Great Depression. Millions of people lost their jobs. By 1941, 1 in 10 workers remained unemployed, the birth rate was stagnant, and the hand of the U.S. government strengthened as people lost confidence in the power of business to pull the country out of hard times. That same year the United States entered World War II.

The Postwar Golden Era: 1945–1969

The postwar reconstruction, which started in 1945, revived the economy and renewed the trend toward large-scale enterprises. The G.I. Bill of Rights opened advanced education to the working classes. The middle class grew and prospered. By 1950 the birth rate had jumped, and the baby boom was on. Accustomed to playing a major role in the war effort, the government continued to exert a large measure of control over business and the economy. President Eisenhower's highway system fueled expansion and the growth of the suburbs. Sales of new homes and U.S.-manufactured automobiles skyrocketed. And nearly half of the world's output bore the proud label "Made in the U.S.A."

Stimulated by a boom in world demand and an expansive political climate, the United States prospered throughout the 1960s. Expanding world trade provided limitless markets for U.S. goods. But once Europe and Japan had recovered from the war, they began challenging U.S. industries—Italy with shoes, Switzerland with watches, and Japan with cameras.

By the end of the 1960s, Japanese transistor radios dominated the world market, and manufacturing accounted for less than 30 percent of the U.S. GDP. Still, the more advanced technological industries and their products—televisions, copying machines, and aircraft—remained U.S. preserves.

The Turbulent Years: 1970–1979

In the early 1970s, inflation depressed demand and U.S. economic growth began to slump. In 1973 the price of a barrel of oil skyrocketed from $3 to $11, forcing companies to invest in ways to save energy instead of investing in new manufacturing equipment. Meanwhile, with virtually no investment money floating around, and no money for new business start-ups, the U.S. economy wasn't particularly competitive. Companies had no incentive to lower their costs and consumers had fewer product choices, which helped sustain higher prices.

The U.S. economy had barely recovered from the 1973 oil shock when it got hit again in 1979 (oil jumped from $13 to $23 per barrel), resulting in galloping inflation and sky-high interest rates. Exports from Asia began to pour into the United States—some bearing U.S. labels—and the United States entered an era of diminishing growth.[28] Meanwhile, a takeover binge was changing the structure of corporate America. Giant organizations called *conglomerates* emerged as companies acquired strings of unrelated businesses to grow and diversify their enterprises. At the same time, deregulation in several large markets, including transportation and financial services, made it possible for newcomers such as People Express (airline) to enter the marketplace. Even though some of these companies failed, their presence forced significant restructuring in the industries they entered.

Rise of Global Competition: 1980–1989

During the 1980s, global competition slowly crept up on the United States. Since the 1950s, Japanese firms had been refining their manufacturing processes to become more efficient, and by 1980 they had a 30-year head start on the United States. (Ironically, the United States had supplied its foreign competitors with the resources and know-how to stake a claim in the world marketplace.) Sony moved into the fast lane and introduced new product innovations such as the Walkman and the VCR, while pricing them affordably. By the mid-1980s, it became almost impossible to buy a consumer electronic device that was made in the United States.

To regain a competitive edge, many U.S. companies restructured their operations. Some corporations merged with others to produce economies of scale; others splintered into smaller fragments to focus on a single industry or a narrower customer base. The tough times of the 1970s planted the seeds for the entrepreneurship of the early 1980s. Little companies such as Staples, Dell, and Home Depot started popping up with founders who said, "We went to work for the safe, big company and it wasn't safe at all."[29] Meanwhile, new technological developments such as the microprocessor and genetic engineering tools were embraced not by leading companies of the day but by new entrants (such as Microsoft, Cisco, and Oracle) who swiftly attacked the status quo.[30]

Highway to the New Economy and Beyond: 1990 to the Present

In the early 1990s U.S. businesses got hit again. The U.S. economy went into a full-blown recession, and many companies that had loaded up on debt in the 1980s to expand their operations or to acquire other companies went bankrupt. During this period of upheaval, unemployment soared, as hundreds of thousands of jobs were eliminated. General Motors alone laid off 130,000 workers—enough to fill two football stadiums. Had the United States continued in the direction it was headed at the beginning of the 1990s, it might well have experienced the disaster that many economists feared. But it didn't.

Manufacturing improvements helped move the United States from a position of near-terminal decline to renewed world dominance.[31] Managers at IBM and AT&T breathed new life into these two U.S. manufacturing classics. Meanwhile, Motorola struck back at Japan's dominance in the electronics field with its pagers and cell phones, Hewlett-Packard took over the high-volume market in low-cost computer printers, and once-sleepy Kodak challenged the Japanese with digital and disposable cameras.[32] As more and more U.S. companies reengineered their operations to improve productivity and to focus on product quality, U.S. industries experienced remarkable turnarounds. But it was investments in new technology and the promise of e-commerce that ultimately pushed the U.S. economy into a remarkable period of prosperity.

Managing in the 21st Century

What's New About the New Economy?

The phrase *new economy* is more than a decade old. In the beginning, some people used the term to describe a period of unprecedented U.S. economic prosperity. Others used it to describe a period during which start-up dot-coms were supposed to topple industry giants. Still others used it to describe a period marked by new rules of business.

One new rule, so they thought, was that profitability didn't matter. Many Internet start-ups tried to convince people that if you sold enough product at a loss, eventually you'd earn a profit. They played a game of "don't look there, look here" by conjuring up a host of new ways to gauge a company's performance. They even convinced investors that market share, growth, number of people who see a webpage, and length of each site visit had a greater value than profitability. But these new measures soon turned out to be largely irrelevant. When dot-coms began to implode at the beginning of the 21st century, and when the Nasdaq dropped below 2500, many concluded that the new economy was just a phase whose time had passed.

Make no mistake. The new economy is not—and never was—just about dot-coms and exuberant stock markets. It never did belong to just one industry or one part of the country. The new economy is about three things:

- *The expansion of individual opportunity.* Never before in the history of business has the individual mattered more—as a talented performer, as a leader in an organization, as a consumer in the marketplace, and as an investor.

- *Innovation.* The era of stable, predictable, competition is over. The only way to stay in business today is to be fully, constantly, and instantly alive to new ideas, new practices, and new opportunities. In the new economy, intangible assets such as knowledge are more valuable than physical ones.

- *The transformative power of information technology and communications.* In the new economy, networked digital technologies will unleash new possibilities—in the ways we work and in the ways companies operate—but only if they are used wisely.

These three forces apply equally to companies of all sizes, of all ages, in all industries. And they continue to reinvent, reenergize, and redirect everything about business today.

So, whether the performance of the U.S. economy is stalled, in a slump, or producing at full steam, the new economy is indeed very much alive today. It's faster, more volatile, and less predictable; it knows no geographical boundaries; it's very dependent on the use of information technology; and it has been released from its kidnapping by the get-big-fast, get-rich-quick crowd.

Questions for Critical Thinking

1. How has the definition of the term *new economy* evolved?
2. How do the three forces of the new economy compare and contrast to the five factors of production?

Characterized by faster growth, lower inflation, technology-driven expansion, and thrift, this new era (referred as the *new economy*) ushered in a period in which customers began using the Internet to deal directly with sellers and manufacturers and to become more informed buyers, as Chapter 12 points out. Meanwhile, a flood of money into new companies put pressure on older ones to raise productivity and innovate rapidly. For a good part of the 1990s the new economy became synonymous with rapid growth, improved living standards for millions, plentiful jobs, and glorious—or so it seemed—investment opportunities.

But by the turn of the century, the tech sector that had led the economy upward led it right back down. Those who thought the new economy meant good times forever were mugged by reality. An abrupt economic slowdown ushered in a brief recession, the tenth recession since World War II. The Big Bust vaporized corporate profits, scorched investment portfolios, laid waste to technology sectors, and humbled scores of dot-com visionaries. The stock markets that had reached record highs gagged, then plunged. The economic downturn forced companies to renew their focuses on such quaint concepts as serving customers and producing profits. And it spurred aggressive cost cutting that fueled a wave of corporate layoffs. Bad news was met head on with the September 11 terrorists attacks and a series of corporate scandals that pummeled the stock market, shook Americans' faith in the nation's institutions, and tarred the images of highly admired organizations and executives. Terrorism, a war with Iraq, and an outbreak of severe acute respiratory syndrome (SARS) in predominately Far Eastern countries heightened concerns for the safety of U.S. citizens traveling abroad. The drive to thwart global terrorism, improve the ethical practices of businesspeople, and drive economic growth are just a few of the challenges facing business today.

Challenges of a Global Economy

8 **LEARNING OBJECTIVE**

Identify five challenges that businesses are facing in the global economy

Whether economic indicators suggest that the economy is in a period of contraction or expansion, businesses must be prepared to meet the many challenges of a global economy. These include:

- ***Producing quality products and services that satisfy customers' changing needs.*** Today's customer is well informed and has many product choices. For many businesses, such as Wal-Mart, competing in the global economy means competing on the basis of *speed* (getting products to market sooner), *quality* (doing a better job of meeting customer expectations), and *customer satisfaction* (making sure buyers are happy with every aspect of the purchase, from the shopping experience until they're through using the product).

- ***Starting and managing a small business in today's competitive environment.*** Starting a new business or successfully managing a small company in today's global economy requires creativity and a willingness to exploit new opportunities. Small companies often lack the resources to buffer themselves from competition. Furthermore, once a new product or process is brought to the market, competitors need only a short time to be up and running with something similar. Thus, the biggest challenge for small businesses today is to make a product or provide a service that is hard to imitate.

- ***Thinking globally and committing to a culturally diverse workforce.*** Traditionally, a business was considered to have an economic advantage if it was located in a country with a plentiful supply of natural resources, human resources, capital, and entrepreneurs. But in the global economy knowledge is the key. Today, companies can obtain capital from one part of the world, purchase supplies from another, and locate production facilities in still another. They can relocate their operations to wherever they find a steady supply of affordable workers. **Globalization**—the increasing tendency of the world to act as one market instead of a series of national ones—opens new markets for a company's goods and services, increases competition, and changes the composition of the workforce into one that is more diverse in race, gender, age, physical and mental abilities, lifestyle, culture, education, ideas, and background. By 2010 minorities will account for 50 percent of the U.S. population, and immigrants will account for half of all new U.S. workers.[33] Thus, to be competitive in the global economy, companies must commit to a culturally diverse workforce, think globally, and adopt global standards of excellence.

globalization
Tendency of the world's economies to act as a single interdependent market

- *Behaving in an ethically and socially responsible manner.* As businesses become more complex through global expansion and technological change, they must deal with an increasing number of ethical and social issues. These include the marketing of unhealthful products, the increasing pollution of the environment, and the use of questionable accounting practices to compute financial results. In the future, businesses can expect continued pressure from environmental groups, consumers, employees, and government regulators to act ethically and responsibly.

- *Keeping pace with technology and electronic commerce.* Everywhere we look, technology is reshaping the world. The Internet and innovations in computerization, miniaturization, and telecommunication are tearing down the walls of geography, allowing businesses to reach markets anywhere in the world. Such technologies are spawning new businesses, transforming existing ones, saving companies money, and changing the way customers, suppliers, and companies interact. Technology is also changing the way people shop for books, cars, vacations, advice—even the way they wash clothes. The Internet is also forcing companies of all sizes and types to face new competition, explore new business opportunities, and adopt new ways of conducting business. In short, the Internet has touched every business and industry and is changing all facets of business life.

As these challenges suggest, doing business in the 21st century means working in a world of increasing uncertainty, where change is the norm, not the exception. In the coming chapters, we explore specific challenges that businesses are facing in the global economy, and we provide real-world examples of how companies are tackling and meeting these challenges.

Summary of Learning Objectives

1. **Define what a business is and identify four key social and economic roles that businesses serve.**
A business is a profit-seeking activity that provides goods and services to satisfy consumers' needs. The driving force behind most businesses is the chance to earn a profit; however, nonprofit organizations exist to provide society with a social or educational service. Businesses serve four key functions: They provide society with necessities; they provide people with jobs and a means to prosper; they pay taxes that are used by the government to provide services for its citizens; and they reinvest their profits in the economy, thereby increasing a nation's wealth.

2. **Differentiate between goods-producing and service businesses and list five factors that are contributing to the increase in the number of service businesses.**
Goods-producing businesses produce tangible goods and tend to be capital intensive; whereas service businesses produce intangible goods and tend to be labor intensive. The number of service businesses is increasing because (1) consumers have more disposable income to spend on taking care of themselves; (2) many services target consumers' needs brought about by changing demographic patterns and lifestyle trends; (3) consumers need assistance with using and integrating new technology into their business operations and lifestyles; (4) companies

are turning to consultants and other service professionals for advice to remain competitive; and (5) in general, barriers to entry are lower for service companies than they are for goods-producing businesses.

3. **Differentiate between a free-market system and a planned system.**
   In a free-market system, individuals have a high degree of freedom to decide what is produced, by whom, and for whom. Moreover, the pursuit of private gain is regarded as a worthwhile goal. In a planned system, governments limit the individual's freedom of choice in order to accomplish government goals, control the allocation of resources, and restrict private ownership to personal and household items. The pursuit of private gain is nonexistent under a planned system.

4. **Identify the factors that affect demand and those that affect supply.**
   The factors that influence demand include the price of the product or service, consumer income, consumer preference, the prices of substitute products, the prices of complementary goods, advertising and promotional expenditures, and consumer expectations about the future. The factors that influence supply are the costs of inputs, the number of competitors in the marketplace, and advancements in technology.

5. **Compare supply and demand curves and explain how they interact to affect price.**
   A demand curve is a graph showing the relationship between the amount of product that buyers will purchase at various prices. Because lower prices typically lead to larger purchases, demand curves usually slope downward as they move to the right. A change in overall demand shifts the demand curve further to the right if overall demand increases, or to the left if overall demand declines. A supply curve is a graph showing the relationship between various prices and quantities that sellers will offer for sale, regardless of demand. Because sellers are willing to supply more goods as prices rise, demand curves usually slope upward as they move to the right. Increases in overall supply shift the supply curve to the right; whereas decreases in overall supply shift the supply curve to the left.

When the interests of buyers and sellers are in balance, an equilibrium price is established. This is the point at which the demand curve and supply curve intersect and represents the price at which buyers are willing to buy the same quantity as sellers are willing to sell.

6. **Discuss the four major economic roles of the U.S. government.**
   The U.S. government fosters competition by enacting laws and regulations, by enforcing antitrust legislation, and by approving mergers and acquisitions, with the power to block those that might restrain competition. It regulates certain industries where competition would be wasteful or excessive. It protects stakeholders from potentially harmful actions of businesses. And it contributes to economic stability by regulating the money supply to encourage growth or control inflation, by raising taxes, and by spending for the public good.

7. **Explain how a free-market system monitors its economic performance.**
   Economists evaluate economic performance by monitoring a variety of economic indicators, such as unemployment statistics, housing starts, durable-goods orders, and inflation. They compute the consumer price index (CPI) and producer price index (PPI) to keep an eye on price changes—especially inflation. In addition, economists measure the productivity of a nation by computing the country's gross domestic product (GDP)—the sum of all goods and services produced by both domestic and foreign companies as long as they are located within a nation's boundaries.

8. **Identify five challenges that businesses are facing in the global economy.**
   The five challenges identified in the chapter are (1) producing quality products and services that satisfy customers' changing needs, (2) starting and managing a small business in today's competitive environment, (3) thinking globally and committing to a culturally diverse workforce, (4) behaving in an ethically and socially responsible manner, and (5) keeping pace with technology and electronic commerce.

KEY TERMS

barriers to entry **(7)**	consumer price index (CPI) **(21)**	entrepreneurs **(5)**
business **(4)**	deflation **(21)**	equilibrium price **(14)**
business cycle **(18)**	demand **(10)**	factors of production **(5)**
capital **(5)**	demand curve **(10)**	fiscal policy **(20)**
capital-intensive businesses **(5)**	economic indicators **(21)**	free-market system **(8)**
capitalism **(8)**	economic system **(8)**	globalization **(27)**
communism **(9)**	economics **(8)**	goods-producing businesses **(5)**
competition **(15)**	economies of scale **(23)**	gross domestic product (GDP) **(22)**
competitive advantage **(15)**	electronic commerce (e-commerce) **(7)**	gross national product (GNP) **(22)**

human resources **(5)**	monopoly **(15)**	pure competition **(15)**
inflation **(21)**	natural resources **(5)**	recession **(18)**
knowledge **(5)**	nonprofit organizations **(5)**	service businesses **(6)**
labor-intensive businesses **(6)**	oligopoly **(15)**	socialism **(9)**
macroeconomics **(8)**	planned system **(9)**	stakeholders **(18)**
microeconomics **(8)**	privatizing **(9)**	supply **(10)**
monetary policy **(19)**	producer price index (PPI) **(22)**	supply curve **(11)**
monopolistic competition **(15)**	profit **(4)**	

TEST YOUR KNOWLEDGE

Questions for Review

1. Why do businesspeople study economics?
2. What are the five factors of production, and why are knowledge workers the key economic resource in today's economy?
3. How is capitalism different from communism and socialism in the way it achieves key economic goals?
4. Why is government spending an important factor in economic stability?
5. Why might the government block a merger or acquisition?

Questions for Analysis

6. Why is it often easier to start a service business than a goods-producing business?
7. Why is competition an important element of the free-market system?
8. Besides price, what factors might influence consumers' demand for new automobiles? What factors, besides price, might influence manufacturers' supply of new automobiles?
9. How do countries know whether their economic system is working?
10. *Ethical Considerations:* Because knowledge workers are in such high demand, you decide to enroll in an evening MBA program. Your company has agreed to reimburse you for 80 percent of your tuition. You haven't revealed, however, that once you earn your degree, you plan to apply for a management position at a different company. Is it ethical for you to accept your company's tuition reimbursement, given your intentions?

Questions for Application

11. Company sales are skyrocketing, and projections show that your computer consulting business will outgrow its current location by next year. What factors should you consider when selecting a new site for your business?
12. How would a decrease in Social Security benefits to the elderly affect the economy?
13. Graph a supply and demand chart for America Online's monthly subscription pricing structure. Make up any data you need, but show the company's equilibrium price to be $23.95.
14. Think about the many ways that technology has changed your life as a consumer. Record your thoughts on a sheet of paper. On that same sheet of paper, make a second list of how you envision technology will change your life in the near future. Compare your thoughts to those of your classmates.

PRACTICE YOUR KNOWLEDGE

Handling Difficult Situations on the Job: Beating the Chains

You're a manager at the Blue Marble, an independent children's bookstore in Fort Thomas, Kentucky. Owner Tina Moore competes successfully with the big chains by supplying personalized service along with her products, thus earning customer loyalty. When your hand-picked staff sells a book, they draw on their extensive knowledge of children's literature to help customers choose.

But when it comes to the ever-popular *Harry Potter* series (now also a movie series about the famous boy wizard), Moore enters a global competition. Author J.K. Rowling's British and U.S. publishers coordinate a simultaneous release for every new book in the series (called a "strict on sale date"). Many stores stay open until midnight the night before so they can sell the hotly anticipated books the instant their agreements allow.

When *Harry Potter and the Order of the Phoenix* came out, many of Moore's regular customers drove miles to reach the Barnes & Noble superstore, which threw a midnight pajama party, giving away "Harry Potter spectacles," ladling out "butter beer" (ginger ale), and showcasing a live owl for the fans who showed up in droves. By the time you opened at 9 a.m., your customers were already at home, sipping hot chocolate and reading the 734-page book they'd bought from your competitors.[34]

Your task: "*Harry Potter VI*" will be released soon. Moore wants you to brainstorm ideas for drawing customers to the Blue Marble instead of losing them to the chains. What competitive advantages do you hold? How can you maximize and apply them to this situation? Since the product is identical, can you differentiate yourselves? How? Can you extend the excitement (and sales) beyond the release date? List your ideas, with points indicating benefits for each of them. Then finalize a plan for the next *Harry Potter* strict on sale date.

Building Your Team Skills

Economic indicators help businesses and governments determine where the economy is headed. You may have noticed news headlines such as the following, each of which offers clues to the direction of the U.S. economy:

1. Housing Starts Lowest in Months
2. Fed Lowers Discount Rate and Interest Rates Tumble
3. Retail Sales Up 4 Percent over Last Month
4. Business Debt Down from Last Year
5. Businesses Are Buying More Electronic Equipment
6. Industry Jobs Go Unfilled as Area Unemployment Rate Sinks to 3 Percent
7. Telephone Company Reports 30-Day Backlog in Installing Business Systems

Discuss each of those headlines with the other students on your team. Is each item good news or bad news for the economy? Why? What does each news item mean for large and small businesses? Report your team's findings to the class as a whole. Did all the teams come to the same conclusions about each headline? Why or why not? With your team, discuss how these different perspectives might influence the way you interpret economic news in the future.

EXPAND YOUR KNOWLEDGE

Discovering Career Opportunities

Thinking about a career in economics? Find out what economists do by reviewing the *Occupational Outlook Handbook* in your library or online at www.bls.gov/oco/home.htm. This is an authoritative resource for information about all kinds of occupations. Under Search By Occupation, enter "economists."

1. Briefly describe what economists do and their typical working conditions.
2. What is the job outlook for economists? What is the average salary for starting economists?
3. What training and qualifications are required for a career as an economist? Are the qualifications different for jobs in the private sector as opposed to those in the government?

Developing Your Research Skills

Gaining a competitive advantage in today's marketplace is critical to a company's success. Look through recent copies of business journals and newspapers (online or in print) to find an article about a company whose practices have set that company apart from its competitors. Use your favorite online search engine to find more information about that company online.

1. What products or services does the company manufacture or sell?
2. How does the company set its goods or services apart from its competitors? Does the company compete on price, quality, service, or innovation?
3. Does the company have a website, and if so, how does the company use it? What kinds of information does the company include on its website?

Exploring the Best of the Web

URLs for all Internet exercises are provided at the website for this book, www.prenhall.com/bovee. *When you log on to the text website, select Chapter 1, then select "Student Resources," click on the name of the featured website, and review the website to complete these exercises.*

Explore these chapter-related websites, review their content, and answer the following questions for each website you visit:

1. What is the purpose of this website?
2. What kinds of information does this website contain? Please be specific.
3. How is the information provided at this website useful for businesspeople? Consumers?
4. How did you expand your knowledge of business fundamentals and economics by reviewing the material at this website? What new things did you learn about these topics?

Find the Right Stuff

Getting information on a specific company can be a challenge, especially if you don't know where to begin. One of the best starting points is Hoover's Online. This website provides an incredible gateway to over 10,000 companies and the latest information on each (such as brief profiles, financial data, history, and current events). Log on and use the toolbox to browse company data. Type in the full name of a company and check it out. Be sure to explore the special Hoover Features. You might want to read about some of the emerging companies. www.hoovers.com

Step Inside the Economic Statistics Briefing Room

Want to know where the economy is headed? Visit the White House Economic Statistics Briefing Room to get the latest economic indicators compiled by a number of U.S. agencies. Click on Federal Statistics by category to enter the room, and check out the stats and graphs for new housing starts; manufacturers' shipments, inventories, and orders; unemployment; average hourly earnings; and more. Are monthly housing starts, unemployment, and annual median household income increasing or decreasing? Make your own projections as to which direction the economy is heading. www.whitehouse.gov/fsbr.esbr.html

Discover What's in the CPI

The CPI is an important tool that allows analysts to track the change in prices over time. But the CPI doesn't always match a given individual's inflation experience. Find out why by visiting the official CPI website maintained by the U.S. Bureau of Labor Statistics. Be sure to check out how the CPI measures homeowners' costs, how the CPI is used, what goods and services it covers, and whose buying habits it reflects. Then click on the Most Requested Series, find your region, and trace the CPI for your area by entering some information in the boxes. http://stats.bls.gov

Learning Interactively

Companion Website

Visit the Companion Website at www.prenhall.com/bovee. For Chapter 1, take advantage of the interactive "Study Guide" to test your changing knowledge. Get instant feedback on whether you need additional studying. Read the "Current Events" articles to get the latest on chapter topics, and complete the exercises as specified by your instructor. Expand your learning with a visit to the "Research Area." There you will find a wealth of information you can use to complete your course assignments.

A CASE FOR CRITICAL THINKING

Turmoil in the Airline Industry

Even before the September 11 terrorist attacks, the major airlines were flying into stiff head winds. Slim to nonexistent profits, bankruptcies and buckets of red ink, poor service, late arrivals, overexpansion, frequent air-traffic-control breakdowns, some of the worst labor–management relations in business, high fuel costs, a full-blown economic downturn, and the collapse of business travel had cast this industry into one of the worst periods in aviation history.

Road Warriors Get Smart

For years, the major airlines had succeeded in getting business travelers (road warriors) to pay premium fares by pampering them with special business-class seats and other perks. Business travel was their lifeblood. Sales of unrestricted fares and last-minute tickets generated about two to three times as much as economy fares and contributed about 70 percent of a major airline's revenue. But with corporate profits hitting the skids in late 2000, companies put the brakes on travel spending.

The corporate exodus hit the major airlines hard. Resourceful business travelers used substitute products such as videoconferencing or other transportation modes—even if it meant putting up with inconveniences—to reduce travel expenses. Some turned to the Internet to find cheaper airfares. Others moved their business downstream to discount airlines such as Southwest and Jet Blue. Major airlines tried to raise round-trip leisure tickets to make up for their lost business revenues, but fierce competition from discounters prevented them from doing so.

Air Travel Is "Wal-Marted"

Just as Wal-Mart did in retailing, the discounters of the air such as Southwest and Jet Blue are squeezing the major airlines from all ends. Low-cost carriers now account for nearly 20 percent of the U.S. domestic air capacity, up from 6 percent in the early 1990s. They can afford to sell travel tickets for less because they have many cost advantages over full-service rivals. To begin with, they have younger fleets, which require less maintenance, and younger labor forces that aren't tied to complicated, inefficient labor contracts. Moreover, low-fare carriers typically fly one airplane model, thus minimizing maintenance, operating, and training costs. By contrast, big carriers typically fly six or seven types of aircraft. And unlike the big guys, the discount airlines don't operate expensive hub-and-spoke systems.

Caught Between a Hub and a Hard Place

Using a hub-and-spoke route system, major airlines scoop up traffic from smaller cities (the spokes) and funnel it through a few gathering points (the hubs). This practice allows airlines to serve small markets and offer passengers more destinations and more frequent flights. But it also presents a logistical nightmare. It forces major airlines to schedule lots of flights to arrive and depart within narrow windows of time in order to minimize passenger layover times. This means that ground crews, such as gate attendants and baggage handlers, often sit idle between waves of connecting flights. By contrast, point-to-point carriers, such as Southwest and Jet Blue, schedule flights as if passengers are moving to their final destination. Instead of having planes and crews sit around and wait for passengers, point-to-point carriers maintain fast-paced schedules, which means minimal downtime for aircraft and fewer personnel on the ground.

In the past, hub-and-spoke airlines were able to charge high fares for refundable and last-minute tickets to cover the additional costs of running a costly system. But with competition from point-to-point carriers heating up, a stalled economy, and the defection of many business travelers to discount airlines, this is no longer possible. Thus, the higher costs of operating a hub-and-spoke system have turned a competitive advantage into a competitive disadvantage.

Turbulent Skies for the Big Carriers

Today, one in four tickets sold is on a discount airline. As pressure from low-fare carriers mounts, major airlines are reevaluating every aspect of their operations. The major carriers are undergoing radical change just to stay in business. They are experimenting with changes in costs, capacity, pricing, and product features in ways they haven't seriously contemplated since the industry was deregulated in 1978. They are stripping billions of dollars from their operations by revamping their hub system, cutting jobs, eliminating flights, ending food service, and removing first-class seats, and by simplifying their fleets to cut training and maintenance costs. Some are replacing agents with self-service kiosks. Others are wrangling concessions from unions for huge pay cuts to

reduce labor costs—a major differentiating factor when you consider that in 2002 a United Airlines captain earned $9,000 to $11,000 more a month than a Jet Blue captain. Still others, such as U.S. Airways and United Airlines have filed for Chapter 11 bankruptcy protection to reorganize their outstanding debt and lower their operating costs.

In spite of these efforts, questions loom as to whether all the major airlines can survive. Even with huge cost cuts, all airlines remain susceptible to possible terrorist attacks, economic turns, or employee unrest. As experts claim that this is just the beginning of an industry-wide shakedown. After all, no airline can fly forever losing billions of dollars.

Critical Thinking Questions

1. What supply and demand factors have changed the equilibrium point for airline ticket sales?

2. How has information technology affected the airline industry?

3. How are complementary products affected by problems in the airline industry?

4. Take a closer look at the airline industry by logging on to hoovers.com, selecting Companies and Industries, Industries, Industry Snapshots, and Airlines. Who are the major industry competitors? Why do U.S. airlines form alliances with overseas partners?

VIDEO CASE

Helping Businesses Do Business: U.S. Department of Commerce

Learning Objectives

The purpose of this video is to help you:

1. Understand world economic systems and their effect on competition.

2. Identify the factors of production.

3. Discuss how supply and demand affect a product's price.

Synopsis

The U.S. Department of Commerce seeks to support U.S. economic stability and help U.S.-based companies do business in other countries. In contrast to the planned economy of the People's Republic of China, the United States is a market economy, where firms are free to set their own missions and buy from and sell to any other business or individual. In the United States, companies must comply with governmental regulations that set standards such as

minimum safety requirements. When doing business in other countries, they must consider tariffs and other restrictions that govern imports to those markets. In addition, supply and demand affect a company's ability to set prices and generate profits.

Discussion Questions

1. *For analysis:* If a U.S. company must pay more for factors of production such as human resources, what is the likely effect on its competitiveness in world markets?

2. *For analysis:* Is the equilibrium price for a company's product likely to be the same in every country? Explain your answer.

3. *For application:* To which factors of production might a small U.S. company have the easiest access? How would this affect the company's competitive position?

4. *For application:* Is a company likely to see more competitors enter a market when supply exceeds demand or when demand exceeds supply?

5. *For debate:* Should the U.S. Department of Commerce, funded by citizens' tax payments, be providing advice and guidance to U.S. companies that want to profit by doing business in other countries? Support your chosen position.

Online Exploration

Visit the U.S. Department of Commerce (DOC) website at www.commerce.gov, and follow some of the links from the home page to see some of this government agency's resources for businesses. Also follow the link to read about the DOC's history. What assistance can a U.S. business expect from this agency? How have the agency's offerings evolved over the years as the needs and demands of business have changed?

CHAPTER 2

Ethical and Social Responsibilities of Business

LEARNING OBJECTIVES

After studying this chapter, you will be able to

1. Discuss what it means to practice good business ethics and highlight three factors that influence ethical behavior

2. Identify three steps that businesses are taking to encourage ethical behavior and explain the advantages and disadvantages of whistle-blowing

3. List four questions you might ask yourself when trying to make an ethical decision

4. Explain the difference between an ethical dilemma and an ethical lapse

5. Discuss the relationship between corporate social responsibility and profits

6. Discuss how businesses can become more socially responsible

7. Outline activities the government and businesses are undertaking to improve the environment

Environmentally friendly products such as those sold by Patagonia give consumers a chance to make a difference while satisfying their needs.

INSIDE BUSINESS TODAY

Beyond the Pursuit of Profits: Patagonia Gears Up to Save the Environment

Some business executives believe they have to concentrate on the bottom line before they can turn their attention to worthy causes. But Yvon Chouinard, founder and owner of Patagonia, a leading designer and distributor of outdoor gear, sees things differently. A passionate environmentalist, Chouinard believes everyone—from consumers to corporations—should do his or her part to save the earth's resources. In fact, Chouinard refuses to sacrifice the environment for the sake of his company's profitability. Instead, Chouinard strives for the best of both worlds—profits and environmental responsibility—by making both a key part of his business strategy.

Patagonia works hard to develop production techniques that reduce the environmental impact of the company's operations. Employees also reap the benefits of the company's environmental values. For instance, employees receive full pay for two-month internships at environmental nonprofit organizations. Moreover, Patagonia gives environmental groups about $1 million each year—more money than the company allocates for advertising—through a self-imposed "earth tax" on annual profits.

Nevertheless, blending profitability with social responsibility isn't always easy. Back in the 1990s, adhering to rigid environmental standards in the production of its high-priced goods created enormous operating expenses for the company. Faced with sagging sales and a severe cash crunch, Patagonia was forced to scale back its operations and lay off one-fifth of its workforce.

Consultants advised Chouinard to sell the company and create a charitable foundation for environmental causes instead of donating a million or so from company profits each year. But

he hadn't established Patagonia for the sole purpose of giving money away to environmental groups. He wanted to "use the company as a tool for social change" and was convinced that Patagonia could serve as an example for others.

So Chouinard launched an extensive effort to improve Patagonia's bottom line while retaining the company's focus on saving the earth's resources. First, he took his case to the public, educating consumers on environmental issues. Lengthy catalog essays by Chouinard explained the company's philosophies about saving the earth's resources and Patagonia's rationale for developing environmentally sensitive techniques in the production of merchandise. Then he refined Patagonia's public image of a "green" business, creating an internal assessment group to evaluate the company's environmental performance. He also constructed a new distribution center with recycled materials and an energy-saving heating system.

Next Chouinard focused on his suppliers. He challenged them to improve their performance and helped them develop techniques for meeting the company's environmental standards. Working with outside contractors, Patagonia developed Synchilla fleece (a fabric made from recycled plastic soda bottles), which now accounts for the recycling of some 8 million plastic bottles each year. Patagonia also worked with farmers to produce 100 percent organic cotton—grown without artificial pesticides or fertilizers. To offset the higher production costs for the cotton, the company split the increased costs with consumers, hoping that they would find value in an environmentally sensitive product. They did. Once the catalogs reached consumers, Patagonia immediately sold out of its new line of all-organic cotton sweaters.

Today, Patagonia is a proven leader and pioneer of "green" profits. Named one of *Fortune* magazine's "100 Best Companies to Work For," Patagonia has proven that companies can achieve success while supporting their environmental values.[1]

Ethics in the Workplace

Yvon Chouinard works hard to make sure that Patagonia does the right thing. But as Chouinard knows, a business can't take action or make decisions; only the individuals within a business can do that. From the CEO to the newest entry-level clerk, every individual in an organization makes choices and decisions that have moral implications. These choices and decisions affect the company and its stakeholders. Moreover, they ultimately determine whether the company is recognized as a responsible corporate citizen.

This chapter explains what it means to conduct business in an ethically and socially responsible manner and discusses the importance of doing so. Many people use the terms *social responsibility* and *ethics* interchangeably, but the two are not the same. **Social responsibility** is the idea that business has certain obligations to society beyond the pursuit of profits. **Ethics**, by contrast, is defined as the principles and standards of moral behavior that are accepted by society as right versus wrong. To make the "right choice" individuals must think through the consequences of their actions. *Business ethics* is the application of moral standards to business situations.

We begin our discussion of ethics by explaining what it means to behave ethically. Next we highlight factors that influence ethical behavior and provide examples of what some companies are doing to improve their ethical behavior. In the second part of the chapter we discuss what it means to be a socially responsible business and explore business's efforts to become more socially responsible.

social responsibility
The concern of businesses for the welfare of society as a whole

ethics
The rules or standards governing the conduct of a person or group

What Is Ethical Behavior?

LEARNING OBJECTIVE

Discuss what it means to practice good business ethics and highlight three factors that influence ethical behavior

As Yvon Chouinard knows, wanting to be an ethical corporate citizen isn't enough; people in business must actively practice ethical behavior. In business, besides obeying all laws and regulations, practicing good ethics means competing fairly and honestly, communicating truthfully, and not causing harm to others.

Competing Fairly and Honestly Businesses are expected to compete fairly and honestly and not knowingly deceive, intimidate, or misrepresent customers, competitors, clients, or employees. While most companies operate within the boundaries of the law, some do knowingly break laws or take questionable steps in their zeal to maximize profits and gain a competitive advantage. For example, to get ahead of the competition, some companies have engaged in corporate spying, stolen patents, hired employees from competitors to gain trade secrets, and eavesdropped electronically. Although businesses need to gather as much strategic information as they can, ethical companies steer clear of such practices.

In some cases, the line between legal and ethical behavior is blurred. For instance, breaking into an office to gather sensitive information or crucial documents from the trash is illegal, but once the refuse makes its way to a dumpster on public property, it's fair game. Still, rifling through a competitor's trash bins—a practice commonly referred to as *dumpster diving*—is unethical. Companies that practice good ethical behavior frown on dumpster diving and even take corrective steps to make sure their employees compete fairly and honestly in the workplace. Procter & Gamble (P&G) did so when the company admitted that several of its employees had hired corporate detectives to retrieve documents related to Unilever's hair care operations from a dumpster outside Unilever's Chicago offices. While P&G denied doing anything illegal, the company voluntarily told Unilever that it had obtained information "in a way that was clearly outside our company's policies in the area of business information gathering." Executives at P&G voluntarily returned the documents to Unilever, agreed to pay their rival $10 million, and promised not to use any of the information it had obtained.[2]

Communicating Truthfully   Companies that practice good ethical behavior refrain from issuing false or misleading communications. Publishers Clearing House learned this ethical lesson the hard way. The company paid $34 million to settle lawsuits by 26 states claiming that it had deceived consumers by mailing "you are winner" notices that looked like checks for large amounts. The company was also charged with accompanying such notices with deceptive communications that led consumers to believe they could increase their chances of winning a grand prize by purchasing magazine subscriptions. As part of the settlement agreement, Publishers Clearing House promised it would stop mailing simulated checks and stop sending consumers misleading information. It also promised that future mailings would disclose the odds of winning and inform the public that buying subscriptions would not increase their chances of winning.[3]

Not Causing Harm to Others   According to a recent *Business Week*/Harris poll, some 79 percent of Americans believe corporate executives put their own personal interests ahead of the interests of workers and shareholders.[4] Placing one's personal welfare above the welfare of the organization can cause harm to others. For instance, every year tens of thousands of people are the victims of investment scams. Lured by promises of high returns, investors sink more than a billion dollars annually into nonexistent oil wells, gold mines, and other fraudulent operations touted by complete strangers over the telephone and the Internet.

In fact, the Internet's ability to reach millions of people, combined with its protective cloak of anonymity, makes it a breeding ground for all sorts of unethical behavior. Cyberspace abounds with stories about auction rip-offs, top company executives who steal one another's intellectual property, offerings of shares in start-up companies that don't exist, and e-commerce sites that fail to deliver what they promise. And it's not just gullible consumers who are being duped. Businesses of all sizes are becoming targets. Hot Internet business scams include hijacking webpages and diverting traffic to sites that can charge higher ad fees based on the new audience, making fraudulent Internet access offers, and webpage design outfits preying on small companies.

Businesspeople can also harm others by getting involved in a **conflict of interest**. A conflict of interest exists when an individual chooses a course of action that advances his or her personal interests over those of his or her employer or when choosing a course of action will benefit one person's interests at the expense of another. For example, a lawyer would experience a conflict of interest if he represented both the plaintiff and defendant in a lawsuit. Similarly, independent auditors have a conflict of interest if their firm also serves as the client's consultants, as Chapter 16 discusses in detail (see "Where Were the Auditors?" on page 410).

conflict of interest
Situation in which a business decision may be influenced by the potential for personal gain

Another way that unethical business executives take advantage of the investor is by using the company's earnings or resources for personal gain. For instance, they may cheat on expense accounts or pad invoices and then split the overcharge with the supplier. Other tactics include using "creative accounting" (also known as "cooking the books") to make a company look good, selling company secrets to competitors, or using confidential, nonpublic information gained from one's position in a company to benefit from the purchase and sale of stocks. Such **insider trading** is illegal and is closely checked by the Securities and Exchange Commission (SEC).

insider trading
Use of material nonpublic information to further one's own fortune or those of one's family and friends

The new millennium has ushered in a wave of fraud, investment scams, and ethical lapses unprecedented in scope. Worse yet, such corruption has cost thousands of employees their jobs, clipped investors' stock portfolios by billions, and destroyed the faith of many in Corporate America and its underlying securities markets. Here are some examples:

Martha Stewart sold her ImClone shares on December 27, 2001, raising suspicions that she might have had inside information about a Food and Drug Administration decision on December 28 that subsequently caused the shares to plummet.

- *Adelphia.* For 50 years, John Rigas, the founder of the sixth largest U.S. cable company, lived the American Dream. But his oversized ambitions led him into an American Nightmare when he and his two sons—Timothy and Michael—were accused of committing one of the largest frauds ever perpetrated on investors and creditors. The Justice Department and the U.S. Postal Service allege that they used the company jet for personal vacations, lived rent-free in Adelphia-owned apartments, used company assets to secure some $3.1 billion in loans for family-run partnerships, stole hundreds of millions of dollars from the company, and inflated Adelphia's cable TV subscriber numbers to make investors think the company was still growing at a healthy pace. Adelphia declared bankruptcy in June 2002.[5]

- *ImClone.* Samuel Waksal (founder and former CEO of biotechnology company, ImClone) pleaded guilty to 6 of 13 charges of insider trading, fraud, and conspiracy brought by the U.S. Attorney's office. Waskal had tried to dump $4.9 million of ImClone stock one day before the Food and Drug Administration rejected the company's application to market a much-anticipated new cancer drug named Erbitux. Waksal was also charged with tipping off family members about the FDA rejection before the news became public. The news decimated the stock's market value. In a related transaction, Martha Stewart, Waksal's close friend, was allegedly informed by her Merrill Lynch stockbroker that members of the Waksal family were dumping their shares. Stewart, who profited by selling her 4,000 ImClone shares one day before the FDA announcement, claimed to have a previous agreement with her broker to sell the stock if the price fell below $60 a share. But lawmakers questioned Stewart's account of her trade and turned the matter over to the Justice Department and the SEC for further investigation. Facing ever-increasing scrutiny over the trade, Stewart resigned from her board position on the New York Stock Exchange in late 2002.[6]

- *WorldCom.* This long-distance telecom giant shocked investors when it revealed in 2002 that it had engaged in one of the biggest frauds in corporate history. The company admitted to overstating cash flow by $3.9 billion by reporting ordinary expenses as capital expenditures. The accounting fraud allowed WorldCom to post a 2001 profit of $1.4 billion instead of reporting a loss for that year (see Chapter 16 for an explanation of such accounting trickery). Several WorldCom executives were charged with falsifying the company's books. Some have pleaded guilty and may cooperate with federal prosecutors who are trying to pin charges on others. Prosecutors claim that the company had a culture of misbehavior. In July 2002, WorldCom filed for Chapter 11 bankruptcy protection—the largest bankruptcy filing ever. The resulting plunge in WorldCom shares cost investors some $175 billion—nearly three times what was lost in the Enron implosion.[7]

- *Tyco.* In 2002, former Tyco CEO L. Dennis Kozlowski and former Tyco CFO Mark H. Swartz were charged with having stolen more than $170 million from the company and with defrauding investors by illegally reaping $430 million from company stock sales. Tyco is a sprawling conglomerate with annual revenue of about $36 billion. Kozlowski and Swartz allegedly authorized the forgiveness of tens of millions of dollars of loans to dozens of Tyco executives to keep them loyal. And they granted themselves and others excessive compensation and bonuses without board approval. In addition, Kozlowski allegedly siphoned company money for lavish personal expenditures, including a $16.8 million apartment in New York City, $14 million in real estate renovations and furnishings, a $72,000 yacht, and a $6,000 shower curtain—to name a few.[8]

- *Enron.* The most highly publicized corporate financial scandal of the new millennium involved energy-trading giant Enron and its auditors, Arthur Andersen. Company executives have been charged with grossly inflating company profits by hiding debt and engaging in numerous accounting shenanigans. The debacle shred public confidence and trust in Corporate America, setting off a chain of governmental proposals to reform big business. For a discussion of the events leading up to the Enron and Andersen implosions and the fallout from the Enron-Andersen scandal, see this chapter's Case for Critical Thinking, "Enron: A Case Study in Unethical Behavior" (pages 58–59), A Case for Critical Thinking: "Consulting Pushes Arthur Andersen Out of Balance" (pages 428–429), and "Where Were the Auditors?" (page 410).

Factors Influencing Ethical Behavior

Although a number of factors influence the ethical behavior of businesspeople, four in particular appear to have the most impact: cultural differences, knowledge, organizational behavior, and legislation.

Cultural Differences   Globalization exposes businesspeople to a variety of cultures and business practices. What does it mean for a business to do the right thing in Thailand? In Africa? In Norway? What may be considered unethical in the United States may be an accepted practice in another culture. Consider bribes, for example. In the United States bribing officials is illegal, but to get something done in Mexico, it's common to pay officials *una mordida* ("a small bite"). In China, businesses pay *huilu*, and in Russia, *vzyatka*. Although the Foreign Corrupt Practices Act makes it illegal for U.S. businesses operating abroad to pay bribes, U.S. companies are allowed to make small payments under certain conditions.

To crack down on illegal payoffs, the industrialized nations have now signed a treaty that makes bribes to foreign officials a criminal offense. Still, bribery won't end just because a treaty has been signed or because it is illegal.

Knowledge   In most cases, a well-informed person is in a position to make better decisions and avoid ethical problems. Making decisions without all the facts or a clear understanding of the consequences could harm employees, customers, the company, and other stakeholders. As an employee or manager, you are held accountable for your decisions and actions. So be sure to ask questions and gather enough information before making a decision or choosing a course of action. For instance, if a business superior tells you to shred a file drawer full of documents, you might want to ask why and inquire whether doing so would be in violation of the law.

Organizational Behavior   The foundation of an ethical business climate is ethical awareness. Organizations that strongly enforce company codes of conduct and provide ethics training help employees recognize and reason through ethical problems. Similarly, companies with strong ethical practices set a good example for employees. On the other hand, companies that commit unethical acts in the course of doing business open the door for employees to follow suit.

To avoid such situations, many companies proactively develop programs designed to improve their ethical conduct. Boeing, for example, requires all employees to undergo at least one hour of ethical training a year; the company's senior managers must undergo five hours. Lockheed Martin has created a newspaper called *Ethics Daily* that runs articles showcasing ethical problems employees have faced and how they resolved them.[9]

In addition, more than 80 percent of large companies have adopted a written **code of ethics**, which defines the values and principles that should be used to guide decisions

2 **LEARNING OBJECTIVE**

Identify three steps that businesses are taking to encourage ethical behavior and explain the advantages and disadvantages of whistle-blowing

code of ethics
Written statement setting forth the principles that guide an organization's decisions

EXHIBIT 2.1 IEEE Code of Ethics
The Institute of Electrical and Electronics Engineers promotes the public policy interests of its U.S. members. The organization's code of ethics serves as a model for members to adopt.

THE INSTITUTE OF ELECTRICAL AND ELECTRONICS ENGINEERS, INC.
CODE OF ETHICS

We, the members of the IEEE, in recognition of the importance of our technologies affecting the quality of life throughout the world, and in accepting a personal obligation to our profession, its members and the communities we serve, do hereby commit ourselves to the highest ethical and professional conduct and agree:

1. to accept responsibility in making engineering decisions consistent with the safety, health and welfare of the public, and to disclose promptly factors that might endanger the public or the environment;

2. to avoid real or perceived conflicts of interest whenever possible, and to disclose them to affected parties when they do exist;

3. to be honest and realistic in stating claims or estimates based on available data;

4. to reject bribery in all its forms;

5. to improve the understanding of technology, its appropriate application, and potential consequences;

6. to maintain and improve our technical competence and to undertake technological tasks for others only if qualified by training or experience, or after full disclosure of pertinent limitations;

7. to seek, accept, and offer honest criticism of technical work, to acknowledge and correct errors, and to credit properly the contributions of others;

8. to treat fairly all persons regardless of such factors as race, gender, disability, age, or national origin;

9. to avoid injuring others, their property, reputation, or employment by false or malicious action;

10. to assist colleagues and co-workers in their professional development and to support them in following this code of ethics.

(see Exhibit 2.1 for an example). By itself, however, a code of ethics can't accomplish much. "You can have grand motives, but if your employees don't see them, they aren't going to mean anything," says one ethics manager.[10] To be effective, a code must be supported by employee communications efforts, a formal training program, employee commitment to follow it, and a system through which employees can get help with ethically difficult situations.[11]

Codes of ethics are so important that according to the Federal Sentencing Guidelines (1991), a company found to be violating federal law might not be prosecuted if it has the proper ethics policies and procedures. As one ethics expert explains, "If you have an active ethics program in place ahead of time, then bad things shouldn't happen; but if they do happen, it won't hurt you as badly."[12] Perhaps inspired by these guidelines, some companies have created an official job position—the ethics officer—to guard morality. Originally hired to oversee corporate conduct—from pilfering company pens to endangering the environment to selling company secrets—many ethics officers today function as corporate coaches for ethical decision making. Of course, ethical behavior starts at the top. The CEO and other senior managers must set the tone for people throughout the company. At Aveda, a cosmetics company, the corporate mission is to bring about positive effects through responsible business methods. "We do this, quite frankly, out of self-preservation," says founder and chairman Horst Rechebecher.[13]

Another way companies support ethical behavior is by establishing a system for reporting unethical or illegal actions at work, such as an ethics hot line. Companies that value ethics will try to correct reported problems. If a serious problem persists, or in cases in which management may be involved in the infraction, an employee may choose to blow the whistle. *Whistle-blowing* is an employee's disclosure to the media or government authorities of illegal, unethical, or harmful practices by the company. But whistle-blowing can bring with it high costs: Public accusation of wrongdoing hurts the business's reputation, requires

Thinking About Ethics

Actions Speak Louder Than Codes

Once you write a code of ethics and establish an ethics hot line, what more does your business need? A lot more, according to experts. When Walker Information surveyed 2,000 U.S. employees, it found that many people still didn't trust their employers' ethics. Nearly 30 percent of respondents said that employers sometimes ignored ethics and even deliberately broke the law. Fewer than half trusted employers: Only 46 percent believed leaders take responsibility for their actions; just 45 percent believed leaders act with fairness; and only 40 percent believed employers keep promises.

Some companies developed detailed codes of behavior and established ethics hot lines only to pay them lip service. Perhaps that's why 81 percent of top managers believe they use ethics in day-to-day decision making, whereas 43 percent of employees believe managers routinely overlook ethics. When leaders make decisions that clearly show profits winning out over ethics, employees become skeptical and mistrustful, attitudes that lead to unethical behavior.

To avoid the lip service trap, support your ethics programs with a dose of reality:

- *Inspire concretely.* Tell employees how they will personally benefit from participating in ethics initiatives. People respond better to personal benefits than to company benefits.
- *Acknowledge reality.* Admit errors. Discuss what went right and what went wrong. Solicit employee opinion:

What do you think? What's your view? And act on those opinions.

- *Incorporate reality into your solutions.* Use practical strategies that can be accomplished in the time available. Obtain real feedback by asking employees to name three realities the company isn't facing, three reasons the company won't meet its goals, and three competitive weaknesses the company exhibits in the marketplace.
- *Be honest.* Tell employees what you know as well as what you don't know. Talk openly about real results, not about what you'd like them to be. Accept criticism—and listen to it.

Make personal benefits, company errors, and tactical solutions more concrete by being straightforward and specific. By acknowledging the realities in every situation, you turn your words into action and build trust with your employees.

Questions for Critical Thinking

1. How does building trust encourage employees to be more ethical?
2. Some companies ask job candidates to take pre-employment tests such as drug tests or lie detector tests. Does such testing build trust with potential employees? Explain.

attention from managers who must investigate the accusations, and damages employee morale. Moreover, whistle-blowers risk being fired or demoted, and they often suffer career setbacks, financial strain, and emotional stress. The fear of such negative repercussions may allow unethical or illegal practices to go unreported. Still, all things considered, many employees do the right thing, as Exhibit 2.2 suggests.

Legislation   Recent government legislation designed to punish corporate wrongdoings is another factor influencing ethical behavior. A 2002 corporate accountability bill signed by President George W. Bush established new standards for prosecuting wrongdoers, gave corporate whistle-blowers broad new protections, and created an independent regulatory board with investigative and enforcement powers to oversee the accounting industry and punish corporate auditors. It also required corporate executives to certify their companies' financial statements and set new penalties for securities fraud and document shredding.[14]

EXHIBIT 2.2
Doing the Right Thing
According to a survey of 1,002 randomly selected adults, when it comes to ethics in the workplace, most employees try to do the right thing.

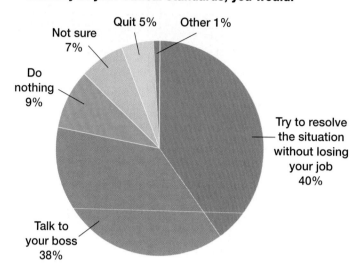

If you found out your employer was doing something contrary to your ethical standards, you would:

- Quit 5%
- Other 1%
- Not sure 7%
- Do nothing 9%
- Try to resolve the situation without losing your job 40%
- Talk to your boss 38%

3 LEARNING OBJECTIVE

List four questions you might ask yourself when trying to make an ethical decision

How Do You Make Ethical Decisions?

Determining what's right in any given situation can be difficult. One approach is to measure each act against certain absolute standards. In the United States, these standards are often grounded in teachings, such as "Do not lie" and "Do not steal." Another place to look for ethical guidance is the law. If saying, writing, or doing something is clearly illegal, you have no decision to make; you obey the law.

Even though legal considerations will resolve some ethical questions, you'll often have to rely on your own judgment and principles. When trying to decide the most ethical course of action, you might apply the Golden Rule: Do unto others as you would have them do unto you. Or you might examine your motives: If your intent is honest, the decision is ethical; however, if your intent is to mislead or manipulate, your decision is unethical.

You might consider asking yourself a series of questions:

1. Is the decision legal? (Does it break any laws?)
2. Is it balanced? (Is it fair to all concerned?)
3. Can you live with it? (Does it make you feel good about yourself?)
4. Is it feasible? (Will it actually work in the real world?)

4 LEARNING OBJECTIVE

Explain the difference between an ethical dilemma and an ethical lapse

ethical dilemma
Situation in which both sides of an issue can be supported with valid arguments

ethical lapse
Situation in which an individual makes a decision that is morally wrong, illegal, or unethical

When you need to determine the ethics of any situation, these questions will get you started. You may also want to consider the needs of stakeholders, and you may want to investigate one or more philosophical approaches such as those mentioned in Exhibit 2.3. These approaches are not mutually exclusive. On the contrary, most businesspeople combine them to reach decisions that will satisfy as many stakeholders as possible without violating anyone's rights or treating anyone unjustly.

Most ethical situations can be classified into two general types: ethical dilemmas and ethical lapses. An **ethical dilemma** is a situation in which one must choose between two conflicting but arguably valid sides. All ethical dilemmas have a common theme: the conflict between the rights of two or more important groups of people. The second type of situation is an **ethical lapse**, in which an individual makes a decision that is clearly wrong, such as divulging trade secrets to a competitor. Be careful not to confuse ethical dilemmas with ethical lapses. A company faces an ethical dilemma when it must decide whether to continue operating a production facility that is suspected, but not proven, to be unsafe. A company

EXHIBIT 2.3   Itemized List for Making Ethical Decisions
Companies with the greatest success in establishing an ethical structure are those that balance their approach to making decisions.

IS THE DECISION ETHICAL?	DOES IT RESPECT STAKEHOLDERS?	DOES IT FOLLOW A PHILOSOPHICAL APPROACH?
Is It Legal? ☐ Does it violate civil law? ☐ Does it violate company policy? **Is It Balanced?** ☐ Is it fair to all concerned, in both the short and the long term? **Can You Live with It?** ☐ Does it make you feel good about yourself? ☐ Would you feel good reading about it in a newspaper? **Is It Feasible?** ☐ Does it work in the real world? ☐ Will it improve your competitive position? ☐ Is it affordable? ☐ Can it be accomplished in the time available?	**Will Outsiders Approve?** ☐ Does it benefit customers, suppliers, investors, public officials, media representatives, and community members? **Will Supervisors Approve?** ☐ Did you provide management with information that is honest and accurate? **Will Employers Approve?** ☐ Will it affect employers in a positive way? ☐ Does it handle personal information about employees discreetly? ☐ Did you give proper credit for work performed by others?	**Is It a Utilitarian Decision?** ☐ Does it produce the greatest good for the greatest number of people? **Does It Uphold Individual, Legal, and Human Rights?** ☐ Does it protect people's own interests? ☐ Does it respect the privacy of others and their right to express their opinion? ☐ Does it allow people to act in a way that conforms to their religious or moral beliefs? **Does It Uphold the Principles of Justice?** ☐ Does it treat people fairly and impartially? ☐ Does it apply rules consistently? ☐ Does it ensure that people who harm others are held responsible and make restitution?

makes an ethical lapse when it continues to operate the facility even after the site has been proven unsafe. Other examples of ethical lapses would include inflating prices for certain customers, hiring employees from competitors to gain trade secrets, selling technological secrets to unfriendly foreign governments, switching someone's long-distance service without his or her consent (a practice known as *slamming*), slipping unauthorized charges into phone bills (a practice known as *cramming*), and using insider information to profit on the sale of company securities.

Social Responsibility in Business

In addition to practicing ethics in the workplace, companies such as Patagonia strive to encourage social responsibility in their policies and among their employees. Social responsibility is a concept with decades-old roots. In the 19th and early 20th centuries, the prevailing view among U.S. industrialists was that business had only one responsibility: to make a profit. "The public be damned," said railroad tycoon William Vanderbilt, "I'm working for the shareholders."[15] *Caveat emptor* was the rule of the day—"Let the buyer beware." If you bought a product, you paid the price and took the consequences. No consumer groups or government agencies would help you if the product was defective or caused harm.

In the mid-20th century, Milton Friedman's view of a company's responsibility toward society was representative and remained influential for many years: "There is only one social responsibility of business," said Friedman. "To use its resources and engage in activities designed to increase its profits so long as it stays within the rules of the game, which is to say, engages in open and free competition without deception or fraud." Friedman argued that only real people, not corporations, could have responsibilities and that corporate executives were obligated to make decisions to maximize the shareholders' returns. Moreover, maximizing shareholders' returns would enable them to contribute to the charities and causes of their choice.[16] As he saw it, the only social responsibility of business was to provide jobs and pay taxes.

Social Responsibility and Profits

5 **LEARNING OBJECTIVE**

Discuss the relationship between corporate social responsibility and profits

Of course, the ideal relationship between business and society is a matter of debate. Historically, investors have been primarily interested in a company's financial performance. But many investors and managers now support a broader view of social responsibility. They argue that a company has an obligation to society beyond the pursuit of profits and that becoming more socially responsible can actually improve a company's profits. This line of thinking is best captured by a *New York Times* headline: "Do Good? Do Business? No, Do Both!" "You can't put one in front of the other. You can't be successful if you can't do both," says Seth Goldman, co-founder of Honest Tea, a company that manufactures barely sweetened ice tea and totally biodegradable tea bags. In other words, companies must be profitable businesses to advance their social mission, and their socially responsible activities should enhance the business.

Companies that support this line of thinking link the pursuit of socially responsible goals with their overall strategic planning. Such socially responsible companies are just as dedicated to building a viable, profitable business as they are to hewing to a mission—and they think strategically to make both happen. Increasingly, companies and employees are caring about their communities and want to be a part of the greater cause. They want to be good corporate citizens and satisfy shareholders' needs for a return on their investment. Still, finding the right balance can be challenging.

Exactly how much should businesses contribute to social concerns? This is a difficult question for most companies because they have limited resources. They must allocate their resources to a number of goals, such as upgrading facilities and equipment, developing new products, marketing existing products, and rewarding employee efforts, in addition to contributing to social causes. This juggling act is a challenge that every business faces. For example, if a company consistently ignores its stakeholders, its business will suffer and eventually fold. If the company disregards society's needs (such as environmental concerns), voters will clamor for laws to limit the offensive business activities, consumers who feel their needs and values are being ignored will spend their money on a competitor's products, unhappy investors will put their money elsewhere, and employees whose needs are not met will become unproductive or will quit and find other jobs. As Exhibit 2.4 shows, stakeholders' needs sometimes conflict. In such cases, which stakeholders should be served first—society, consumers, investors, or employees?

When word spread that Ben & Jerry's founders were interested in selling the company, protesters gathered to voice their concerns. Many worried that buyers would not carry forward the social responsibility programs at the core of Ben & Jerry's existence.

Ben & Jerry's: Balancing Social Responsibility and Profits

Ben & Jerry's founders Ben Cohen and Jerry Greenfield have long struggled to balance the company's social initiative with shareholder demands for better profits. Since its inception in

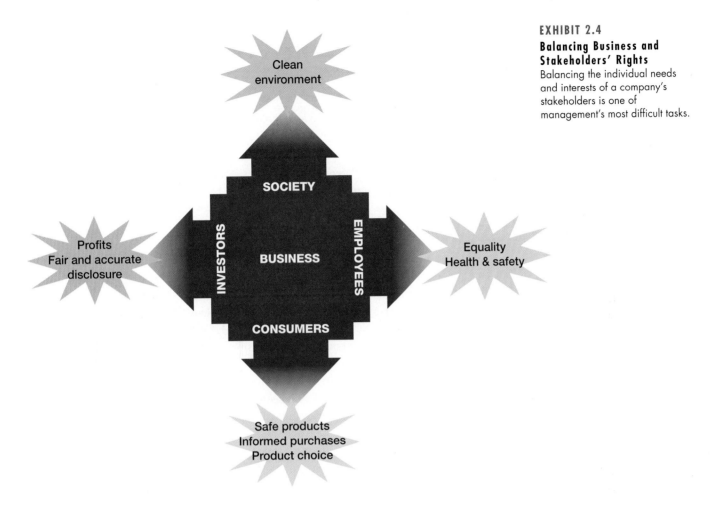

EXHIBIT 2.4
Balancing Business and Stakeholders' Rights
Balancing the individual needs and interests of a company's stakeholders is one of management's most difficult tasks.

1978, Ben & Jerry's Homemade Ice Cream has donated 7.5 percent of pretax profits to various causes (including saving the family farm, promoting world peace, saving the world's rain forests, and keeping French nuclear testing out of the South Pacific). Unfortunately, the company fell on hard times in the 1990s, nearly confirming the view that socially responsible companies would ultimately go out of business. But Perry D. Odak became CEO in 1997 and proved the skeptics wrong.[17]

When Odak took over, sales were down, and so was company morale. Employees didn't want to abandon Ben & Jerry's social mission in a search for profits. Many of them regretted the cancellation of efforts such as the Peace Pop program and its "One Percent for Peace." But as colorful as some of those programs were, they had also been inefficient. However, things changed under Odak. By focusing on the balance sheet, he managed not only to tighten Ben & Jerry's business practices and improve its bottom line but also to enhance its ability to contribute to worthy causes.[18]

In 1999 Ben & Jerry's was sold to Unilever, a $45 billion global giant that owns Breyer's and Good Humor ice cream brands, for $325 million in cash. Critics were concerned that the new owner would not preserve the company's commitment to social causes. But Unilever assured them that Ben & Jerry's social mission would be encouraged and well funded. Unilever agreed to donate an initial $5 million and 7.5 percent of Ben & Jerry's annual profits to the Ben & Jerry's Foundation. Moreover, it promised not to reduce jobs or alter the way the ice cream is made. In spite of strong resistance from Vermont residents and loyal customers, some saw the sale as an opportunity to project social consciousness onto a large multinational corporation.[19]

Business's Efforts to Increase Social Responsibility

6 **LEARNING OBJECTIVE**

Discuss how businesses can become more socially responsible

social audit
Assessment of a company's performance in the area of social responsibility

philanthropic
Descriptive term for altruistic actions such as donating money, time, goods, or services to charitable, humanitarian, or educational institutions

As Ben & Jerry's and Patagonia show, socially responsible businesses can indeed make a difference in the world. *Industry Week*'s 100 Best Managed Companies all actively engage in socially responsible activities. Some work to curb child abuse or domestic violence. Others provide generous benefits packages for employees. Still others have strong recycling programs to keep the environment clean. Those that give back to society are finding that their efforts can lead to a more favorable public image and stronger employee morale. Thus, more and more organizations are attempting to be socially responsible citizens by conducting a *social audit*, by engaging in *cause-related marketing*, or by being *philanthropic*.

A **social audit** is a systematic evaluation and reporting of the company's social performance. The report typically includes objective information about how the company's activities affect its various stakeholders. Companies can also engage in *cause-related marketing*, in which a portion of product sales help support worthy causes. For example, Johnson & Johnson gives the World Wildlife Fund a cut from sales of a special line of children's toiletries. Similarly, Peaceworks encourages joint business ventures among people of different backgrounds who live in volatile regions of the world. One of the company's product lines is *spraté*, uniquely flavored spreads produced in Israel by a Jewish-owned company that buys all its ingredients from Israeli Arabs and Palestinians. When consumers buy a jar of spraté, they not only get a tasty spread but also support the peace process in the Middle East.[20]

Some companies choose to be socially responsible corporate citizens by being **philanthropic**; that is, they donate money, time, goods, or services to charitable, humanitarian, or educational institutions. Newman's Own gives away its profits. The company, which annually sells $100 million of popcorn, lemonade, ice cream, and salad dressing, has donated $115 million for hunger relief, for medical research, and to fund camps for seriously ill children.[21] Similarly, corporations such as Microsoft, General Electric, Dell, and Wal-Mart donate billions of dollars in cash and products to charity each year. In short, businesspeople are doing whatever they can—donating computers, taking kids on field trips, supporting basketball teams, building houses for people, or helping people find jobs.

Chairman William Ford helps in the clean-up effort of the Rouge, where the Ford Motor Company will build a new environment-friendly assembly plant.

Responsibility Toward Society and the Environment

Environmental issues exemplify the difficulty that businesses encounter when they try to reconcile conflicting interests: Society needs as little pollution as possible from businesses, but producing quality products to satisfy customers' needs can cause pollution to some degree. Business executives such as Patagonia's Yvon Chouinard try to strike a balance by making environmental management a formal part of their business strategy—along with quality, profits, safety, and other daily business operations.[22] Still, merging industrialism with environmentalism is not an easy task, says William Clay Ford Jr., chairman of Ford Motor Company, who persuaded his board to spend $2 billion to tear down the old assembly plant in Dearborn, Michigan, and transform the Rouge, an environmental wasteland covered with contaminated soil, into an environment-friendly manufacturing plant.[23]

The Pervasiveness of Pollution   For decades, environmentalists have warned businesses and the general public about the dangers of **pollution** (contamination of the natural environment by the discharge of harmful substances). Our air, water, and land can easily be tainted by industrial discharges, aircraft and motor vehicle emissions, and a number of chemicals that spill out into the environment as industrial waste products. Moreover, the pollution in any one element can easily taint the others. For instance, when emissions from coal-burning factories and electric utility plants react with air, they can cause acid rain, which damages lakes and forests.

pollution
Damage to or destruction of the natural environment caused by the discharge of harmful substances

The Government Effort to Reduce Pollution   Widespread concern for the environment has been growing since the 1960s, with the popularization of **ecology**, or the study of the balance of nature. In 1963 federal, state, and local governments began enacting laws and regulations to reduce pollution (see Exhibit 2.5). In December 1970 the federal government established the Environmental Protection Agency (EPA) to regulate air and water pollution by manufacturers and utilities, supervise the control of automobile pollution, license pesticides, control toxic substances, and safeguard the purity of drinking water.

Many individual states have also passed their own tough environmental laws. For example, California now requires that 10 percent of all new vehicles sold in the state be pollution-free. In response, both large and small car manufacturers are working to produce cars that use alternative fuel technology such as hybrid electric vehicles and hydrogen fuel cells.

Progress has also been made in reducing water pollution. Both government and private business have made major expenditures to treat and reuse wastewater, as well as to upgrade sewage systems. Unfortunately, the war on toxic waste has not been quite as successful. Government attempts to force businesses to clean up toxic-waste dumps have yielded many

 **LEARNING OBJECTIVE**

Outline activities the government and businesses are undertaking to improve the environment

ecology
Study of the relationships between living things in the water, air, and soil, their environments, and the nutrients that support them

EXHIBIT 2.5   Major Federal Environmental Legislation
Since the early 1960s, major federal legislation aimed at the environment has focused on providing cleaner air and water and reducing toxic waste.

LEGISLATION	PROVISION
National Environmental Policy Act (1999)	Establishes a structure for coordinating all federal environmental programs
Clean Air Act and amendments (1963, 1965, 1970, 1977, 1990)	Assists states and localities in formulating control programs; sets federal standards for auto-exhaust emissions; sets maximum permissible pollution levels; authorizes nationwide air-pollution standards and limitations to pollutant discharge; requires scrubbers in new coal-fired power plants; directs EPA to prevent deterioration of air quality in clean areas; sets schedule and standards for cutting smog, acid rain, hazardous factory fumes, and ozone-depleting chemicals
Solid Waste Disposal Act and amendments (1965, 1984)	Authorizes research and assistance to state and local control programs; regulates treatment, storage, transportation, and disposal of hazardous waste
Resource Recovery Act (1970)	Subsidizes pilot recycling plants; authorizes nationwide control programs
Federal Water Pollution Control Act and amendments (1972)	Authorizes grants to states for water-pollution control; gives federal government limited authority to correct pollution problems; authorizes EPA to set and enforce water-quality standards
Safe Drinking Water Act (1974, 1996)	Sets standards for drinking-water quality; requires municipal water systems to report on contaminant levels; establishes funding to upgrade water systems
Noise Control Act (1972)	Requires EPA to set standards for major sources of noise and to advise Federal Aviation Administration on standards for airplane noise
Toxic Substances Control Act (1976)	Requires chemicals testing; authorizes EPA to restrict the use of harmful substances
Oil Pollution Act (1990)	Sets up liability trust fund; extends operations for preventing and containing oil pollution

lawsuits and much expense but disappointing results. At some sites, the groundwater may never be restored to drinking-water purity.

The Business Effort to Reduce Pollution   While some companies must be pressured by the federal government or private citizens to stop polluting the environment, others do a good job regulating themselves. 3M's decision to discontinue making Scotchguard fabric protector is a noteworthy example of company self-regulation. 3M was under no government mandate to stop manufacturing products with perfluorooctane sulfonate (PFOs). Moreover, no evidence existed that PFOs harmed humans. But when traces of the chemical showed up in humans, 3M decided to pull the plug on the product and not wait until scientific evidence might someday link PFOs to a disease. This decision cost 3M $500 million in annual sales because the company did not have a substitute product to fill Scotchguard's void.[24]

Like 3M, many companies are addressing environmental concerns by taking actions such as the following[25]:

- Considering environmental issues a part of everyday business and operating decisions
- Accepting environmental staff members as full-fledged partners in improving the company's competitiveness
- Measuring environmental performance
- Tying compensation to environmental performance
- Determining the long-term environmental costs *before* such costs occur
- Considering environmental impact in the product-development process
- Challenging suppliers to improve environmental performance
- Conducting environmental training and awareness programs

In addition to these actions, companies are reducing the amount of solid waste they send to landfills by implementing companywide recycling programs. Companies and individuals alike generate enormous amounts of solid waste—more than 200 million tons in the United States each year, much of which is electronic waste (computer monitors, circuit boards, and so on).[26] Companies are also cleaning up land pollution created years ago by careless—but legal—disposal of substances (now known to be unhealthy) in landfills.

Hundreds of thousands of tons of waste have also been eliminated through conservation and more efficient production. Some companies are using high-temperature incineration to destroy hazardous wastes or are giving their wastes to other companies that can use them in their manufacturing processes. Some even neutralize wastes biologically or have redesigned their manufacturing processes so that they don't produce the wastes in the first place.

Businesses that recognize the link between environmental performance and financial well-being are discovering that spending now to prevent pollution can end up saving more money down the road (by reducing cleanup costs, litigation expense, and production costs). From building eco-industrial parks to improving production efficiency, these activities are a part of the *green marketing* movement, in which companies distinguish themselves by using less packaging materials, recycling more waste, and developing new products that are easier on the environment.

One such innovative product on the horizon is the fuel-cell car. Every U.S. automaker has developed a prototype

Electronics recycling centers like this one near the Lianjiang River in China are releasing toxic pollutants, environmental groups say.

version of an electric car powered by hydrogen. Full-scale production models are expected to come out within the next 10 years as costs go down. Hydrogen-powered cars are quieter than gas-powered vehicles and are virtually pollutant-free.[27]

Responsibility Toward Consumers

The 1960s activism that awakened business to its environmental responsibilities also gave rise to **consumerism**, a movement that put pressure on businesses to consider consumer needs and interests. Consumerism prompted many businesses to create consumer-affairs departments to handle customer complaints. It also prompted state and local agencies to set up bureaus to offer consumer information and assistance. At the federal level, President John F. Kennedy announced a "bill of rights" for consumers, laying the foundation for a wave of consumer-oriented legislation (see Exhibit 2.6). These rights include the right to safe products, the right to be informed, the right to choose, and the right to be heard.

consumerism
Movement that pressures businesses to consider consumer needs and interests

The Right to Safe Products   The U.S. government imposes many safety standards that are enforced by the Consumer Product Safety Commission (CPSC), as well as by other federal and state agencies. Theoretically, companies that don't comply with these rules are forced to take corrective action. Moreover, the threat of product-liability suits and declining sales motivates many companies to meet safety standards. After all, a poor safety record can damage a company's reputation. But with or without government action, many consumer advocates complain that some unsafe products still slip through the cracks.

EXHIBIT 2.6   Major Federal Consumer Legislation
Major federal legislation aimed at consumer protection has focused on food and drugs, false advertising, product safety, and credit protection.

LEGISLATION	PROVISION
Food, Drug, and Cosmetic Act (1938)	Puts cosmetics, foods, drugs, and therapeutic products under Food and Drug Administration's jurisdiction; outlaws false and misleading labeling
Cigarette Labeling Act (1965)	Mandates warnings on cigarette packages and in ads
Fair Packaging and Labeling Act (1966, 1972)	Requires honest, informative package labeling; labels must show origin of product, quantity of contents, uses or applications
Truth-in-Lending Act (Consumer Protection Credit Act) (1968)	Requires creditors to disclose finance charge and annual percentage rate; limits cardholder liability for unauthorized use
Fair Credit Reporting Act (1970)	Requires credit-reporting agencies to set process for assuring accuracy; requires creditors who deny credit to tell consumers the source of information
Consumer Product Safety Act (1972)	Creates Consumer Product Safety Commission
Magnuson-Moss Warranty Act (1975)	Requires complete written warranties in ordinary language; requires warranties to be available before purchase
Alcohol Labeling Legislation (1988)	Requires warning labels on alcohol products, saying that alcohol impairs abilities and that women shouldn't drink when pregnant
Nutrition Education and Labeling Act (1990)	Requires specific, uniform product labels detailing nutritional information on every food regulated by the FDA
American Automobile Labeling Act (1992)	Requires carmakers to identify where cars are assembled and where their individual components are manufactured
Deceptive Mail Prevention and Enforcement Act (1999)	Establishes standards for sweepstakes mailings, skill contests, and facsimile checks to protect U.S. consumers against companies that use such tactics to deceive and exploit consumers

By the time Bridgestone/Firestone finally admitted that it had made "bad tires," the company had been aware of peeling tire tread problems for at least three years. Most of the recalled tires were sold with Ford Explorer vehicles.

Take medical devices, for example. Millions of Americans sport some kind of implanted medical device, be it a pacemaker, heart valve, artificial knee or hip, breast implant, or about 240 other types of products. Now some patients are discovering the hard way that faulty surgical devices, which were implanted into their body, have been recalled. Patients complain that they are not being notified of such recalls. "It can be easier to find out that your car has been recalled than your pacemaker or your artificial hip," notes one patient. Under current law only 12 of the most high-risk types of implant devices are required to be tracked by manufacturers. Even for those, when a recall is issued, no one is required to directly notify patients. European countries track patients who receive implant devices, but similar U.S. efforts have been stymied by concerns about liability, patient privacy, and the high cost of doing so. Then there is the issue of whom to notify—the doctor or the patient. In addition, many recalls are quite complex and don't affect every patient given a particular device. In short, the likelihood of a national databank of implant recipients is remote unless manufacturers are required by law to participate.[28]

Even when a defective product is acknowledged by manufacturers, the recall process can be a nightmare. Consider Firestone tires, for example. Critics claim that Ford and Firestone didn't act fast enough once they suspected problems with Firestone Wilderness AT and ATX tires (see "Failure to Yield . . . or Asleep at the Wheel?"). Not only did Ford and Firestone handle the recall of 6.5 million tires poorly, but they waited much too long before they removed the defective tires from the marketplace.[29]

The Right to Be Informed Consumers have a right to know what is in a product and how to use it. They also have a right to know the sales price of goods or services and the details of any purchase contracts. Without such information, they have no practical means for making rational product choices. The 1966 Fair Packaging and Labeling Act requires producers to provide information such as the size of a product, its ingredients, nutritional content, and its expiration date (if it is perishable) on product labels. The Nutrition Labeling and Education Act of 1990 strengthened the 1966 act by further requiring producers to include information such as the percentage of the recommended daily intake of certain vitamins and minerals, the total number of calories, and the caloric breakdown of a standard serving size. It further defined terms such as *low fat*, *light*, and *healthy* to prevent manipulation of such claims by manufacturers.

The Food and Drug Administration, the Federal Trade Commission, and the Agriculture Department are the federal agencies responsible for regulating product labels to make sure no false claims are made. These agencies are concerned not only with safety but also with accurate information. For instance, if a product is sufficiently dangerous, a warning label is required by law, as in the case of cigarettes. However, warning labels can be a mixed blessing for consumers. To some extent, the presence of a warning protects the manufacturer from product-liability suits, but the label may not deter people from using the product or from using it incorrectly. The billions of dollars a year still spent on cigarettes in the United States illustrates this point.

The Right to Choose Which Products to Buy Especially in the United States, the number of products available to consumers is truly amazing. But how far should the right to choose extend? Are we entitled to choose products that are potentially harmful, such as cigarettes, liquor, or guns? To what extent are we entitled to learn about these products? Consumer groups and businesses are concerned about these questions, but no clear answers have emerged. Moreover, some consumer groups say that government does not do enough. For example, when a product has been proven to be dangerous, does the fact that it is legal

Thinking About Ethics

Firestone and Ford: Failure to Yield . . . or Asleep at the Wheel?

For nearly a decade, lawsuits claimed that treads on tires manufactured by Bridgestone/Firestone were peeling off without warning, causing Ford Explorers to flip over. Mounting consumer complaints and damaging media reports led to a federal investigation in 2000, putting pressure on Firestone to recall 6.5 million defective tires. But the public soon learned that trouble had started long before the massive tire recall.

As early as 1998, Ford Motor Company received reports of Firestone tire tread separations on Ford Explorers in countries with hot climates, such as Saudi Arabia and Venezuela. Ford took the complaints to Firestone because it didn't have enough information to investigate the problem itself. (Tires are the only significant part of the car guaranteed by the supplier, not the automaker.) Firestone reassured Ford that the tire problems resulted from a combination of variables: hot climate, fast drivers, and improper tire care by consumers. Meanwhile, Ford was getting an early warning about tire safety problems from its own warranty data. Still, Firestone refused to recall the tires.

Convinced that its tire supplier was not owning up to problems, Ford stepped in and unilaterally replaced Firestone tires on nearly 50,000 vehicles in 16 foreign countries. The problem is, neither Ford nor Firestone bothered to inform U.S. authorities about the overseas tire recall. Soon similar failures began to occur in the United States at unusually high rates, and Ford initiated its own investigation in early 2000. About that same time, the federal government entered the scene.

Meanwhile, the recall and surrounding recriminations set off a bitter fight between the two companies over responsibilities for the crashes. Convinced that tread separations were related to inadequate tire pressures, Firestone claimed Ford had ignored the tire maker's warnings to boost the recommended tire pressure for Explorers. But Ford pinned the blame on Firestone, claiming the company stalled in analyzing and sharing its warranty-claims data. Firestone executives, in turn, argued that Explorers had been involved in 16,000 rollover accidents within the past decade—but fewer than 10 percent had involved tread separation of Firestone tires. The dispute ended the 96-year relationship that began when Harvey Firestone sold tires to Henry Ford for the Model T.

Even though over 174 deaths and 700 injuries have been linked to Explorers equipped with Firestone tires, both companies claim that they didn't realize the extent of the lethal tire problems until just before the recall. But one U.S. congressman claimed both companies had been asleep at the wheel. "What does it take to put a company . . . on notice that perhaps they've got a defective product out there?" the congressman challenged. "You've got a lawsuit, you've got people killed . . . Doesn't that tell you that something is probably wrong with your product?"

Questions for Critical Thinking

1. Why did Bridgestone/Firestone wait so long to recall the defective tires?
2. What lesson(s) can other companies learn from the Ford/Firestone debacle?

---

justify its sale? Should the government take measures to make the product illegal, or should consumers be allowed to decide for themselves what they buy?

Consider cigarettes, for example. Scientists determined long ago that the tar and nicotine in tobacco are both harmful and addictive. In 1965 the Federal Cigarette Labeling and Advertising Act was passed, requiring all cigarette packs to carry the now-famous Surgeon General's warnings. Over the years, tobacco companies have spent billions of dollars to defend themselves in lawsuits brought by smokers suffering from cancer and respiratory diseases. As recently as 1996, the Liggett Group (a major U.S. tobacco company) admitted publicly that cigarettes cause cancer, are addictive, and have been promoted to encourage

Recent media blitzes by antismoking organizations have appeared in magazines, on billboards, and in television commercials. The hope is that ads such as this one will elevate consumer awareness about the health problems related to cigarette smoking.

smoking among minors. And in 1997 the tobacco industry agreed to pay $368.5 billion over 25 years and an additional $15 billion per year after that to settle lawsuits brought by smoking victims and 40 state governments. Even so, consumers can still purchase cigarettes in the marketplace. RJR Nabisco chairman Steve Goldstone reminds us that "behind all the allegations . . . is the simple truth that we sell a legal product."[30]

The Right To Be Heard Many companies have established toll-free numbers for consumer information and feedback, and print these numbers on product packages. In addition, more and more companies are establishing websites to provide product information and a vehicle for customer feedback. Companies use such feedback to improve their products and services and to make informed decisions about offering new ones.

Responsibility Toward Investors

Historically, investors have been primarily interested in a company's financial performance. Clearly, a business can fail its investors by depriving them of their fair share of the profits. But a business can also fail its shareholders by being too concerned about profits. That's why a growing number of investors are concerned about the ethics and social responsibility of the companies in which they invest.

  The job of looking out for a company's investors falls to its board of directors. Lately, more investors are turning up the heat on the individuals who sit on those boards (as we discuss in Chapter 6). Concerned investors are targeting board members who fail to attend meetings, who sit on the boards of too many companies, who are underinvested (own very little stock in the companies they direct), and who sit on boards of companies with which their own firms do business. Aggrieved investors are also filing lawsuits not just against the management of companies that admit to "accounting irregularities" but against their boards of directors and their audit committees.

  As Chapter 16 points out, the audit committee signs off on all financial statements and is supposed to protect shareholders, acting as a check on management's corporate reporting methods and asking tough questions about accounting practices. Looking out for investors is no easy task, but investors are finding that holding individual directors more accountable improves overall performance. Of course, any action that cheats the investors out of their rightful profits is unethical.

Responsibility Toward Employees

Patagonia's Yvon Chouinard has always emphasized employee relationships that are ethical and supportive. For some companies, the past 30 years have brought dramatic changes in the attitudes and composition of the workforce. These changes have forced businesses to modify their recruiting, training, and promotion practices, as well as their overall corporate values and behaviors. (Consult Chapter 10 for an in-depth discussion of the staffing and demographic challenges employers are facing in today's workplace.)

The Push for Equality in Employment The United States has always stood for economic freedom and the individual's right to pursue opportunity. Unfortunately, until the past few decades many people were targets of economic **discrimination**, relegated to low-

discrimination
In a social and economic sense, denial of opportunities to individuals on the basis of some characteristic that has no bearing on their ability to perform in a job

paying, menial jobs and prevented from taking advantage of many opportunities solely on the basis of their race, gender, disability, or religion.

The Civil Rights Act of 1964 established the Equal Employment Opportunity Commission (EEOC)—the regulatory agency that battles job discrimination. The EEOC is responsible for monitoring the hiring practices of companies and for investigating complaints of job-related discrimination. It has the power to file legal charges against companies that discriminate and to force them to compensate individuals or groups who have been victimized by unfair practices. The Civil Rights Act of 1991 extended the original act by allowing workers to sue companies for discrimination and by granting women powerful legal tools against job bias.

Affirmative Action   In the 1960s, **affirmative action** programs were developed to encourage organizations to recruit and promote members of minority groups. Proponents of the programs believe that minorities deserve and require preferential treatment to boost opportunities and to make up for years of discrimination. Opponents of affirmative action believe that creating special opportunities for women and minorities creates a double standard that infringes on the rights of other workers and forces companies to hire, promote, and retain people who are not necessarily the best choice from a business standpoint. Moreover, studies show that affirmative action has not been entirely successful, because efforts to hire more minorities do not necessarily change negative attitudes about differences among individuals. Regardless, any company that does business with the federal government must have an affirmative action program.

In addition to affirmative action programs, about 75 percent of U.S. companies have established **diversity initiatives**. These initiatives include increasing minority employment and promotion, contracting with more minority vendors, adding more minorities to boards of directors, and targeting a more diverse customer base. Many companies also offer employees diversity training to promote understanding of the unique cultures, customs, and talents of all employees.

People with Disabilities   In 1990 people with a wide range of physical and mental difficulties got a boost from the passage of the federal Americans with Disabilities Act (ADA), which guarantees equal opportunities for an estimated 50 million to 75 million people who have or have had a condition that might handicap them. As defined by the 1990 law, *disability* is a broad term that protects not only those with obvious physical handicaps but also those with less-visible conditions, such as cancer, heart disease, diabetes, epilepsy, AIDS, drug addiction, alcoholism, and emotional illness. In most situations, employers cannot legally require job applicants to pass a physical examination as a condition of employment. The law also forbids firing people who have serious drinking or drug problems unless their chemical dependency prevents them from performing their essential job functions.

Occupational Safety and Health   Each day about 15 workers lose their lives on the job, while another 15,500 are injured in the private workplace.[31] During the activist 1960s, mounting concern about workplace hazards resulted in passage of the Occupational Safety and Health Act of 1970, which set mandatory standards for safety and health and which established the Occupational Safety and Health Administration (OSHA) to enforce them.

Today, OSHA's ergonomic safety regulations protect millions of workers from repetitive stress injuries such as carpal tunnel syndrome (from repetitive keyboarding) and back injuries (from repetitive lifting). The rules grant workers up to 90 days of employer-paid sick leave for people injured on the job as a result of repetitive actions. Studies show that about 1.8 million U.S. workers each year suffer musculoskeletal injuries at work from performing repetitive actions and that about one-third of the cases are serious enough to require time off.[32]

Concerns for employee safety have also been raised by the international expansion of businesses. Many U.S. companies subcontract production to companies in foreign countries,

affirmative action
Activities undertaken by businesses to recruit and promote women and minorities, based on an analysis of the workforce and the available labor pool

diversity initiatives
Company policies designed to enhance opportunities for minorities and to promote understanding of diverse cultures, customs, and talents

Protestors parade in a Santa Monica, California, shopping district. The group claimed that some of the shops in the area carry merchandise manufactured in sweatshops.

making it more difficult to maintain proper standards of safety and compensation for workers. For example, when a local labor advocacy group inspected a Nike factory in Vietnam, members discovered violations of minimum wage and overtime laws, as well as physical abuse of workers. Nike has been criticized in recent years for similar conditions in its other Southeast Asian and Chinese factories. Many other companies, including the Gap, Guess, and the Body Shop, have come under similar criticism. In 1997 a presidential task force composed of apparel industry representatives, labor unions, and human rights groups drafted a code of conduct to uphold the rights of foreign workers of U.S. manufacturing companies. Among the provisions of the code are minimum wage requirements and limits on the number of hours employees work in a week.[33]

Ethics and Social Responsibility Around the World

As complicated as ethics and social responsibility can be for U.S. businesses, these issues grow even more complex when cultural influences are applied in the global business environment. Corporate executives may face simple questions regarding the appropriate amount of money to spend on a business gift or the legitimacy of payment to "expedite" business. Or they may encounter out-and-out bribery, environmental abuse, and unscrupulous business practices. In Chapter 3 we discuss global business and highlight how a country's ethical codes of conduct, laws, and cultural differences are indeed put to the test as more and more companies transact business around the globe.

Summary of Learning Objectives

1. **Discuss what it means to practice good business ethics and highlight three factors that influence ethical behavior.**

   Businesspeople who practice good business ethics obey all laws and regulations, compete fairly and honestly, communicate truthfully, and do not cause harm to others by putting themselves ahead of others or by placing themselves in a conflict of interest situation. Of the many factors that influence ethical behavior, the four most common are cultural differences, knowledge of the facts and consequences involving a decision or action, the ethical practices and commitment to ethical behavior at one's place of work, and legislation.

2. **Identify three steps that businesses are taking to encourage ethical behavior and explain the advantages and disadvantages of whistle-blowing.**

   Businesses are adopting codes of ethics, appointing ethics officers, and establishing ethics hot lines. In spite of these efforts, if illegal, unethical, or harmful practices persist, an employee may need to blow the whistle, or disclose such problems to outsiders. Doing so may force the company to stop the problematic practices. But bringing these issues into the public eye has consequences. It can hurt the company's reputation, take managers' time, damage employee morale, and affect the informant's job with the company.

3. **List four questions you might ask yourself when trying to make an ethical decision.**

   When making ethical decisions ask yourself: (1) Is the decision legal? (Does it break any law?) (2) Is it balanced? (Is it fair to all concerned?) (3) Can you live with it? (Does it make you feel good about yourself?) (4) Is it feasible? (Will it work in the real world?).

4. **Explain the difference between an ethical dilemma and an ethical lapse.**

   An ethical dilemma is an issue with two conflicting but arguably valid sides, whereas an ethical lapse occurs when an individual makes a decision that is illegal, immoral, or unethical.

5. **Discuss the relationship between corporate social responsibility and profits.**

   For years, many companies believed that the only role of a company was to make money and that social problems were the concern of the state. It was believed that socially responsible companies could not be profitable. But supporters of social responsibility now argue that a company has an obligation to society beyond the pursuit of profits and that companies can be both socially responsible and profitable. In fact, being a socially responsible company can help improve profits, and being profitable can help companies stick to their social mission.

6. **Discuss how businesses can become more socially responsible.**

   Companies can conduct social audits to assess whether their performance is socially responsible; they can engage in cause-related marketing by using a portion of product sales to help support worthy causes; and they can become philanthropic by donating their money, time, goods, or services to charitable, humanitarian, or educational institutions. Companies can also protect and improve the environment by taking a variety of

actions to reduce pollution. They can become good citizens by considering consumers' needs and respecting their four basic rights: the right to safe products, the right to be informed—which includes the right to know a product's contents, use, price, and dangers; the right to choose which products to buy; and the right to be heard, such as the right to voice a complaint or concern. They can look out for a company's investors and protect the value of their interests. And they can foster good employee relationships by treating employees fairly and equally, and by providing a safe working environment.

7. **Outline activities the government and businesses are undertaking to improve the environment.**

   In 1970 the government set up the Environmental Protection Agency to regulate the disposal of hazardous wastes and to clean up polluted areas. Many individual states have also passed their own tough clean air laws. Companies are taking these steps to improve the environment: (1) considering the laws a part of everyday business and operating decisions, (2) making environmental staff members full-fledged partners in improving competitiveness, (3) measuring environmental performance, (4) tying compensation to environmental performance, (5) determining environmental costs *before* they occur, (6) considering the environmental impact of the product-development process, (7) helping suppliers improve their environmental performance, and (8) conducting training and awareness programs.

KEY TERMS

affirmative action **(53)**

code of ethics **(39)**

conflict of interest **(37)**

consumerism **(49)**

discrimination **(52)**

diversity initiatives **(53)**

ecology **(47)**

ethical dilemma **(42)**

ethical lapse **(42)**

ethics **(36)**

insider trading **(37)**

philanthropic **(46)**

pollution **(47)**

social audit **(46)**

social responsibility **(36)**

TEST YOUR KNOWLEDGE

Questions for Review

1. Who shapes a company's ethics?
2. What is a conflict of interest situation?
3. How do companies support ethical behavior?
4. How are businesses responding to the environmental issues facing society?
5. What can a company do to assure customers that its products are safe?

Questions for Analysis

6. Why can't legal considerations resolve every ethical question?
7. How do individuals employ philosophical principles in making ethical business decisions?
8. Why does a company need more than a code of ethics to be ethical?
9. Why is it important for a company to balance its social responsibility efforts with its need to generate profits?

10. *Ethical Considerations:* How do unethical acts committed by company executives affect all businesses?

Questions for Application

11. You sell musical gifts on the web and in quarterly catalogs. Your two-person partnership has quickly grown into a 27-person company, and you spend all your time on quality matters. You're losing control of important environmental choices about materials suppliers, product packaging, and even the paper used in your catalogs. What steps can you take to be sure your employees continue making choices that protect the environment?

12. At quitting time, you see your new colleague filling a briefcase with expensive software programs that aren't supposed to leave the premises. What do you do? Explain your answer.

13. *Integrated:* In Chapter 1 we identified knowledge workers as an important economic resource of the 21st century. If an employee leaves a company to work for a competitor, what types of knowledge would be ethical for the employee to share with the new employer, and what types of knowledge would be unethical to share?

14. *Integrated:* Is it ethical for state and city governments to entice businesses to relocate their operations to that state or city by offering them special tax breaks that are not extended to other businesses operating in that area?

PRACTICE YOUR KNOWLEDGE

Handling Difficult Situations on the Job: Children at Risk

This morning Perrigo Company discovered that a batch of its cherry-flavored children's painkiller contains more than the label-indicated amount of acetaminophen. Marketing department reports indicate that 6,500 four-ounce bottles of the "children's nonaspirin elixir" (a Tylenol look-alike) are already in the hands of consumers; 1,288 bottles remain on store shelves. The problem is that the acetaminophen contained in the painkilling liquid is up to 29 percent more than labels state, enough to cause an overdose in young children, which can cause liver failure and even death. So far, thankfully, no injuries have been reported. Only lot number 1AD0228 contains the excess dosage.

Your job responsibility in the Customer Support and Service Department is to the retailers who sell Perrigo's 900 over-the-counter pharmaceuticals and nutritional products as "store brands." These are the "better buys" found beside brand-name products such as Tylenol, Motrin, Aleve, Centrum, or Ex-Lax, featuring such store names as Kroger or Hy-Vee. They're priced a bit lower and they offer "comparable quality and effectiveness." Retailers yield higher profits from them, while consumers save money by buying them.[34]

Your task: Perrigo has publicly announced its recall of the product. Consumers can return bottles from the faulty batch to stores, and stores can return them to Perrigo for full refunds. Your job is to notify stores in writing, as legally mandated. What information should you include in your letter? What information should you omit, if any? How can you use your letter to preserve Perrigo's fine reputation?

Building Your Team Skills

Choosing to blow the whistle on your employees or co-workers can create all kinds of legal, ethical, and career complications. Here are five common workplace scenarios that might cause you to search your soul about whether or not to go public with potentially damaging charges. Read them carefully and discuss them with your teammates. Then decide what your team would do in each situation.[35]

1. You believe your company is overcharging or otherwise defrauding a customer or client.

2. With all of the headlines generated by sexual harassment cases lately, you'd think employees wouldn't dare break the law. But it's happening right under your company's nose.

3. You discover that your company, or one of its divisions, products, or processes, presents a physical danger to workers or to the public.

4. An employee is padding overtime statements, taking home some of the company's inventory, or stealing equipment.

5. You smell alcohol on a co-worker's breath and notice that individual's work hasn't been up to standard lately.

EXPAND YOUR KNOWLEDGE

Discovering Career Opportunities

Businesses, government agencies, and not-for-profit organizations offer numerous career opportunities related to ethics and social responsibility. How can you learn more about these careers?

1. Search the Occupational Outlook Handbook (print or online edition at http://stats.bls.gov/oco) to identify jobs related to ethics and social responsibility. One example is Health and Safety Specialist, a job concerned with a company's responsibility toward its employees. What are the duties and qualifica-

tions of the jobs you have identified? Are the salaries and future outlooks attractive for all of these jobs?

2. Select one job for further consideration. What other sources of employment information might provide more details about this job? Which of these sources are available in your school or public library? What additional sources can you consult for more information about the daily activities of this job and for ideas about locating potential employers?

3. What skills, educational background, and work experience do you think employers are seeking in applicants for the specific job you are researching? What key words do you think employers would search for when scanning electronic résumés submitted for this position?

Developing Your Research Skills

Articles on corporate ethics and social responsibility regularly appear in business journals and newspapers. Look in recent issues (print or online editions) to find one or more articles discussing one of the following ethics or social responsibility challenges faced by a business:

- Environmental issues, such as pollution, acid rain, and hazardous-waste disposal
- Employee or consumer safety measures
- Consumer information or education
- Employment discrimination or diversity initiatives
- Investment ethics
- Industrial spying and theft of trade secrets
- Fraud, bribery, and overcharging
- Company codes of ethics

1. What was the nature of the ethical challenge or social responsibility issue presented in the article? Does the article report any wrongdoing by a company or agency official? Was the action illegal, unethical, or questionable? What course of action would you recommend the company or agency take to correct or improve matters now?

2. What stakeholder group(s) are affected? What lasting effects will be felt by (a) the company and (b) these stakeholder group(s)?

3. Writing a letter to the editor is one way consumers can speak their mind. Review some of the Letters to the Editor in newspapers or journals. Why are letters to the editor an important feature for that publication?

Exploring the Best of the Web

URLs for all Internet exercises are provided at the website for this book, www.prenhall.com/bovee. *When you log on to the text website, select Chapter 2, then select "Student Resources." Click on the name of the featured website, and review the website to complete these exercises.*

Explore these chapter-related websites, review their content, and answer the following questions for each website you visit:

1. What is the purpose of this website?

2. What kinds of information does this website contain? Please be specific.

3. How is the information provided at this website useful for businesspeople? Consumers?

4. How did you expand your knowledge of ethics and social responsibility in business by reviewing the material at this website? What new things did you learn about this topic?

Build a Better Business

One way to distinguish your business as an ethical organization is to join the Better Business Bureau (BBB). Members of this private, not-for-profit business group agree to maintain specific standards for operating ethically and addressing customer complaints. The BBB website is packed with information about the organization, member businesses, and programs that benefit businesses and consumers alike. You can find reports on companies, register complaints, get help with consumer problems, and access publications on all kinds of consumer issues, such as avoiding business scams and investigating charitable organizations. www.bbb.org

Surf Safely

Although the majority of telemarketing and online businesses are legitimate, unethical businesses bilk consumers out of billions of dollars every year. Fortunately, the National Fraud Information Center (NFIC) can help consumers fight back. The center was established by the National Consumers League (NCL) to safeguard consumers against telemarketing and Internet fraud. Resources on the center's website include reports about current online and telephone scams, tips for online safety, advice on how to file a fraud report, statistics about telemarketing fraud, and special advice for seniors, who are targeted by con artists. Even if you consider yourself a savvy consumer, the site contains a lot of valuable information to help you avoid being ripped off. www.fraud.org

Protect the Environment

For 30 years, the United States Environmental Protection Agency (EPA) has been working for a cleaner, healthier environment for American people. Visit the agency's website to get the latest information on today's environmental issues. Become familiar with the major environmental laws and proposed regulations and learn how to report violations. Expand your knowledge about air pollution, ecosystems, environmental management, and hazardous waste. Visit the EPA newsroom to get regional news. Read the current articles and follow the links to hot lines, publications, and more. This site is a must for all businesses. www.epa.gov

Learning Interactively

Companion Website

Visit the Companion Website at www.prenhall.com/bovee. For Chapter 2, take advantage of the interactive "Study Guide" to test your changing knowledge. Get instant feedback on whether you need additional studying. Read the "Current Events" articles to get the latest on chapter topics, and complete the exercises as specified by your instructor. Expand your learning with a visit to the "Research Area." There you will find a wealth of information you can use to complete your course assignments.

A CASE FOR CRITICAL THINKING

Enron: A Case Study in Unethical Behavior

Formed in 1985, Enron began as a transmitter of natural gas through pipelines. The company later evolved into the leading market maker in electricity and natural gas by buying power from generators and selling it to customers. The company also traded in coal, fiber optics, bandwidth, plastic, and other energy-related goods. From 1998 to 2000 Enron's annual revenue rose from $31 billion to more than $100 billion, making it the seventh-largest company on the Fortune 500 list.

In 1999 Enron was cited by *Fortune* magazine as one of the "100 best companies to work for in America." Enron's past chairman Kenneth Lay boasted to the press that "our corporate culture and our world-class employees make Enron a great place to work." He added, "We are proud to receive recognition as a top workplace; it's a reflection of our commitment to our employees and their key role in our company's success." Less than two years later, the company's empire unraveled, exposing one of the biggest business scandals in U.S. history.

Who's Accountable?

It could take years to untangle the Enron mess as Congress, investigators, and regulatory agencies try to piece together clues that could explain how a company that reported revenues exceeding $100 billion and profits of $979 million became worthless overnight. Several Enron executives have been indicted on charges of fraud, conspiracy, and other illegal behavior but have yet to be proven guilty (at the time this book was printed). Nonetheless, several acts of unethical behavior have been uncovered during congressional hearings and reviews of company documents: Enron's accountants used wildly creative accounting practices to grossly overestimate company profits and hide losses through a web of partnerships; financial analysts, who also served as Enron's investment bankers, continued to urge investors to buy Enron stock even as the company headed toward bankruptcy; and several top Enron executives allegedly used insider information and withheld information from the public as they cashed out more than $1 billion of company stock when it was at its peak.

Although these acts contributed to Enron's failure and subsequent bankruptcy filing in December 2001, the company's fate was sealed by the negligence of its managers and auditors, who were either unaware of the company's lurking financial problems or chose to look the other way—even as warning lights began to flash. Enron's managers kept its company's employees and stakeholders in the dark. And they continued to paint a rosy picture of the company's financial health even as the giant energy conglomerate was sliding toward financial ruin. "The continued excellent prospects in Enron's market position make us very confident in our strong earnings outlook," Kenneth Lay told Wall Street executives, after he was allegedly advised of questionable accounting practices by Enron's vice president Sherron Watkins.

Watkins had sent a seven-page letter to Lay informing him, among other things, that Enron executives "consistently and constantly" questioned the company's accounting methods to senior officials. "I am incredibly nervous that we will implode in a wave of accounting scandals," wrote Watkins. Upon receiving the letter, Lay asked Watkins not to blow the whistle while he tried to deal with the situation. But Lay did nothing, and Watkins, believing that he would investigate as promised, did not inform outside authorities.

One Cozy Bunch

Unethical behavior by Enron's auditors, Arthur Andersen Company, also contributed to the company's demise. Andersen, which had recently settled allegations of fraud stemming from its audits of Waste Management and Sunbeam (for which a $110 million settlement was paid), entered into a conflict of interest situation by acting as both Enron's independent auditors and management advisors. The accounting firm was paid fees of $1 million a week and maintained unusually close ties with Enron executives, compromising the firm's independence. (See Chapter 16 for a discussion of the conflict posed when a firm serves as both auditors and consultants to a client.)

Long before Enron's collapse, Arthur Andersen accountants knew of the company's growing losses. But they continued to bend to the wishes of Enron executives who didn't want to recognize the losses or make them public. Once the losses were disclosed, Andersen managers began a massive shredding campaign of Enron documents—which they claimed was standard company procedure. On June 15, 2002, a federal jury convicted Arthur Andersen on a single felony count of obstruction of justice for interfering with a federal investigation of its failed client, Enron. Although the accounting firm was originally indicted for shredding Enron-related documents, the firm was convicted because an Andersen lawyer ordered critical deletions to an internal memo for the purpose of impeding an official proceeding. The conviction will forever stain the legacy of this once-revered American institution. In August 2002 the 89-year-old, 85,000-employee firm ceased auditing public companies—the core of its worldwide business. What's left of Andersen now faces a raft of Enron-related lawsuits.

The Ripple Effect

In short, Enron serves as an example of how negligent conduct by a company's managers and advisors and the failure to communicate truthfully to stakeholders can severely harm a company's employees, investors, customers, and other innocent stakeholders. Enron's 21,000 employees lost their jobs and saw their retirement savings wiped out. And tens of thousands of shareholders—including some of the nation's biggest institutional investors—lost billions of dollars when Enron's stock value plummeted from $80 to pennies a share.

Critical Thinking Questions

1. What unethical acts did Enron's managers and auditors commit?
2. How did such acts affect the company's stakeholders?
3. What factors may have influenced Enron's unethical behavior?

4. Log on to C-Span online (www.c-span.org/enron) to get the latest news on the Enron investigation. Read Sherron Watkins' letter to Kenneth Lay. Why did Watkins write this letter? What new events have been uncovered in the Enron investigation?

VIDEO CASE

Doing the Right Thing: American Red Cross

Learning Objectives

The purpose of this video is to help you:

1. Identify some of the social responsibility and ethics challenges faced by a nonprofit organization.
2. Discuss the purpose of an organizational code of ethics.
3. Understand the potential conflicts that can emerge between an organization and its stakeholders.

Synopsis

Founded in 1881 by Clara Barton, the American Red Cross is a nonprofit organization dedicated to helping victims of war, natural disasters, and other catastrophes. The organization's 1,000 chapters are governed by volunteer boards of directors who oversee local activities and enforce ethical standards in line with the Red Cross's code of ethics and community norms. Over the years, the Red Cross has been guided in its use of donations by honoring donor intent. This helped the organization deal with a major ethical challenge after the terrorist attacks of September 11. The Red Cross received more than $1 billion in donations and initially diverted some money to ancillary operations such as creating a strategic blood reserve. After donors objected, however, the organization reversed its decision and—honoring donor intent—used the contributions to directly benefit people who were affected by the tragedy.

Discussion Questions

1. *For analysis:* What are the social responsibility implications of the American Red Cross's decision to avoid accepting donations of goods for many local relief efforts?

2. *For analysis:* What kinds of ethical conflicts might arise because the American Red Cross relies so heavily on volunteers?
3. *For application:* What can the American Red Cross do to ensure that local chapters are properly applying the nonprofit's code of ethics?
4. *For application:* How might a nonprofit such as the American Red Cross gain a better understanding of its stakeholders' needs and preferences?
5. *For debate:* Should the American Red Cross have reversed its initial decision to divert some of the money donated for September 11 relief efforts to pressing but ancillary operations? Support your chosen position.

Online Exploration

Visit the American Red Cross site (www.redcross.org) and scan the headlines to read about the organization's response to recent disasters. Also look at the educational information available through links to news stories, feature articles, and other material. Next, carefully examine the variety of links addressing the needs and involvement of various stakeholder groups. What kinds of stakeholders does the American Red Cross expect to visit its website? Why are these stakeholders important to the organization? Do you think the organization should post its code of ethics prominently on this site? Explain your answer.

Competing in the Global Economy

Lance Armstrong, winner of five consecutive Tour de France races (1999–2003) boldly displays his Trek affiliation.

INSIDE BUSINESS TODAY

Trek Bikes: Trekking Around the Globe

It's a world away from the bright lights of Paris. But the little town of Waterloo, Wisconsin, captured the world's attention during the recent Tour de France. When Lance Armstrong zoomed across the finish line in 1999, 2000, 2001, 2002, and 2003 at Paris's Champs-Elysées, the American cycler raced to victory on a bike made by Trek Bicycle Corporation of Waterloo.

Not far from Trek's headquarters in downtown Waterloo sits a nondescript building. It's within these wall that the next generation of Trek bikes are born, created by Trek's Advanced Concept Group, known as ACG. For Lance Armstrong and the U.S. Postal Services team, that means making bikes that are lighter, stronger, and faster than anyone thought possible.

At first glance, Waterloo seems like an unlikely place for the headquarters of an international business. Dairy farms dominate the rural landscape. Green Bay Packers' fans support their favorite team—and promote the state's most famous commodity—by wearing foam cheese wedges on their heads. And here, Trek opened for business in 1976 with five workers assembling bicycle frames by hand in an old wooden barn.

During the company's first few years, Trek sold its bicycles exclusively in the United States. But all that changed in 1985 when Joyce Keehn, now Trek's worldwide sales director, received several inquiries about exporting Treks to Canada. A novice in international trade, Keehn consulted the state's export agency and sought advice from local exporters at state-sponsored trade seminars. After considering Trek's close proximity to Canada, Keehn decided that selling directly to Canadian bicycle shops was the company's best option for international expansion.

As more exporting opportunities opened up, Keehn experimented with other foreign distribution methods. For instance, to minimize cultural and language barriers, she relied on the expertise and knowledge of local distributors instead of approaching retailers directly. In other countries, she advised Trek to create wholly-owned subsidiaries for handling sales, inventory, warranties, customer service, and direct distribution to retail outlets. Such subsidiary offices allowed Trek to maintain higher profits and more control over its products.

Still, Keehn hit some bumps in the road as she ventured into the global marketplace. For example, customs delays created frequent insurance and financial problems; some shipments even disappeared during customs clearances in Mexico. On one occasion, Trek halted distribution of its catalog after discovering that a featured cartoon character was offensive to Germans. And customizing bikes for the European markets increased Trek's production costs.

Cyberspace presented even more challenges for Keehn. Trek's international dealers must charge higher prices than those charged by U.S. sellers to cover costs such as shipping and tariffs. Moreover, international prices must take into consideration fluctuating foreign exchange rates. To avoid this confusion and to protect its international sellers, Trek does not sell bicycles or reveal prices on its website. Instead, Trek refers customers to authorized dealers in their area.

Today, whether you're in cyberspace, Cincinnati, or Cyprus, you won't have to travel far to find a Trek. Keehn has established a network of 65 distributors on six continents and seven wholly-owned subsidiaries in Europe and Japan.

From its humble beginnings in Waterloo, Trek is now the world's largest maker of racing bikes, mountain bikes, and other types of specialty bikes. The company sells more than a half million bikes in more than 70 countries every year. In 10 years, annual revenues have grown from $18 million to over $400 million, of which 40 percent now come from international business.[1]

The Global Business Environment

1 LEARNING OBJECTIVE

Highlight the opportunities and challenges of conducting business in other countries

Like Trek, more and more enterprises are experiencing the excitement of conducting business in the global marketplace. Even firms that once thought they were too tiny to expand into a neighboring city have discovered that they can tap the sales potential of overseas markets with the help of fax machines, overnight delivery services, e-mail, e-commerce, and the Internet. Even if you're working for a small local firm, chances are your company will use foreign-made materials or equipment, hire employees of different nationalities, or sell over the Internet.

In fact, more and more companies are realizing that selling goods and services in foreign markets can generate increased sales, produce operational efficiencies, expose companies to new technologies, and provide greater consumer choices. But venturing abroad also exposes companies to many new challenges, as Trek's Joyce Keehn discovered. For instance, each country has unique ways of doing business, which must be learned: Laws, customs, consumer preferences, ethical standards, labor skills, and political and economic stability—all of these factors can affect a firm's international prospects. Furthermore, volatile currencies, international trade relationships, and the threat of terrorism can make global expansion a risky proposition.

Still, in most cases the opportunities of the global marketplace greatly outweigh the risks. Consider UPS. When this company began its rapid global expansion program in the 1980s, it had to attain air rights into each country, unravel a patchwork of customs laws, learn how to deal with varying work ethics and employment policies, and so on. But the company's efforts paid off. Today UPS delivers over 13 million documents and packages daily in more than 200 countries. Over 13 percent of the company's revenue now comes from international package deliveries.[2]

Cultural Differences in the Global Business Environment

Cultural differences present a number of challenges in the global marketplace. Consider the Internet, for example. In many Asian countries, shopping is a revered family outing. Thus, getting Asian consumers to shop online is a task. Moreover, most commercial transactions in Asia still require cash and written receipts, making e-business a more complex process. And, e-business is seen as too American in some Islamic and former communist countries.

When doing business in the global environment, companies must recognize and respect differences such as social values, language, ideas of status, decision-making habits, attitudes toward time, use of space, body language, manners, and ethical standards. Otherwise these differences can lead to misunderstandings in international business relationships, particularly if differences in business practices also exist (see Exhibit 3.1). Furthermore, companies that sell their products overseas must often adapt the products to meet the unique needs of international customers, as Trek discovered.

The best way to prepare yourself for doing business with people from another culture is to study that culture in advance. Learn everything you can about the culture's history, religion, politics, and customs—especially its business customs. Who makes decisions? How are negotiations usually conducted? Is gift giving expected? What is the proper attire for a busi-

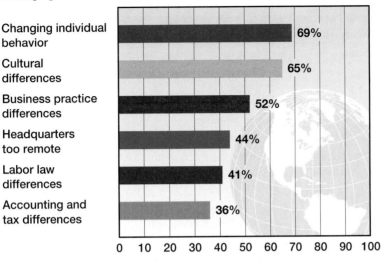

Challenges U.S. and European senior executives say they face when managing across different countries:

Changing individual behavior	69%
Cultural differences	65%
Business practice differences	52%
Headquarters too remote	44%
Labor law differences	41%
Accounting and tax differences	36%

0 10 20 30 40 50 60 70 80 90 100

EXHIBIT 3.1
Going Global Has Its Barriers
Learning a country's business customs and cultural differences is the first step in going global.

ness meeting? In addition to the suggestion that you learn about the culture, seasoned international businesspeople offer the following tips for improving intercultural communication:

- *Be alert to the other person's customs.* Expect the other person to have values, beliefs, expectations, and mannerisms different from yours. For instance, don't be surprised when businesspeople in Pakistan excuse themselves in the middle of a meeting to conduct prayers. Moslems pray five times a day.

- *Deal with the individual.* Don't stereotype the other person or react with preconceived ideas. Regard the person as an individual first, not as a representative of another culture.

- *Clarify your intent and meaning.* The other person's body language may not mean what you think, and the person may read unintentional meanings into your message. Clarify your true intent by repetition and examples. Ask questions and listen carefully. The Japanese are generally appreciative when foreigners ask what is proper behavior, because it shows respect for the Japanese way of doing things.[3]

- *Adapt your style to the other person's.* If the other person appears to be direct and straightforward, follow suit. If not, adjust your behavior to match. In many African countries, for example, people are suspicious of others who seem to be in a hurry. Therefore, you should allow plenty of time to get to know the people you are dealing with.

- *Show respect.* Learn how respect is communicated in various cultures—through gestures, eye contact, and so on. For example, in Spain let a handshake last five to seven strokes; pulling away too soon may be interpreted as a rejection. In France, however, the preferred handshake is a single stroke.

These are just a few tips for doing business in the global marketplace. Exhibit 3.2 can guide you in your efforts to learn more about a country's culture before doing business abroad.

Legal Differences in the Global Business Environment

All U.S. companies that conduct business in other countries must be familiar with U.S. law, international law, and the laws of the specific countries where they plan to trade or do business. For example, many governments burden e-commerce with a maze of rules, regulations, and tax laws. To protect neighborhood stores, German regulations prohibit most price discounting on consumer goods. Similarly, in some foreign countries, online auctions run into legal tangles because laws require the physical display of goods to be sold at the

2 LEARNING OBJECTIVE

List five ways to improve communication in an international business relationship

EXHIBIT 3.2 Checklist for Doing Business Abroad
Use this checklist as a starting point when investigating a foreign culture.

UNDERSTAND SOCIAL CUSTOMS

✓ How do people react to strangers? Are they friendly? Hostile? Reserved?

✓ How do people greet each other? Should you bow? Nod? Shake hands?

✓ How are names used for introductions?

✓ What are the attitudes toward touching people?

✓ How do you express appreciation for an invitation to lunch or dinner or to someone's home? Should you bring a gift? Send flowers? Write a thank-you note?

✓ How, when, or where are people expected to sit in social or business situations?

✓ Are any phrases, facial expressions, or hand gestures considered rude?

✓ How close do people stand when talking?

✓ How do you attract the attention of a waiter? Do you tip the waiter?

✓ When is it rude to refuse an invitation? How do you refuse politely?

✓ What are the acceptable patterns of eye contact?

✓ What gestures indicate agreement? Disagreement? Respect?

✓ What topics may or may not be discussed in a social setting? In a business setting?

✓ How is time perceived?

✓ What are the generally accepted working hours?

✓ How do people view scheduled appointments?

LEARN ABOUT CLOTHING AND FOOD PREFERENCES

✓ What occasions require special clothing? What colors are associated with mourning? Love? Joy?

✓ Are some types of clothing considered taboo for one sex or the other?

✓ What are the attitudes toward human body odors? Are deodorants or perfumes used?

✓ How many times a day do people eat?

✓ How are hands or utensils used when eating?

✓ What types of places, food, and drink are appropriate for business entertainment?

✓ Where is the seat of honor at a table?

ASSESS POLITICAL PATTERNS

✓ How stable is the political situation? Does it affect businesses in and out of the country?

✓ How is political power manifested? Military power? Economic strength?

✓ What are the traditional government institutions?

LEARN ABOUT ECONOMIC AND BUSINESS INSTITUTIONS

✓ Is the society homogeneous?

✓ What minority groups are represented?

✓ What languages are spoken?

✓ Do immigration patterns influence workforce composition?

✓ What are the primary resources and principal products?

✓ What vocational/technological training is offered?

✓ What are the attitudes toward education?

✓ Are businesses generally large? Family controlled? Government controlled?

✓ Is it appropriate to do business by telephone? By fax? By e-mail?

✓ Do managers make business decisions unilaterally, or do they involve employees?

✓ How are status and seniority shown in an organization? In a business meeting?

✓ Must people socialize before conducting business?

APPRAISE THE NATURE OF ETHICS, VALUES, AND LAWS

✓ Is money or a gift expected in exchange for arranging business transactions?

✓ What ethical or legal issues might affect business transactions?

✓ Do people value competitiveness or cooperation?

✓ What are the attitudes toward work? Toward money?

✓ Is politeness more important than factual honesty?

✓ What qualities are admired in a business associate?

auction. And legislative mazes turn the simple act of registering a web address into a long and complex process.

In addition to understanding and obeying foreign laws, all companies doing international business must also comply with the 1978 Foreign Corrupt Practices Act. This U.S. law outlaws actions such as bribing government officials in other nations to approve deals. It does, however, allow certain payments, including small payments to officials for expediting

Competing in the Global Marketplace

When Will China Get Real?

Welcome to the People's Republic of China, where copies of well-known foreign products are as available as tea and rice at meals. China produces more fakes than any other nation—everything from autos to aircraft parts, beer to razor blades, soap to shampoo, TVs to toilets. Nearly half of the world's 14 billion batteries are produced in China. But most of them are fake versions of Panasonic, Gillette, and other big brands. By some estimates, foreign companies lose at least $1.5 billion a year in China to piracy.

Counterfeiting has infiltrated nearly every sector of China's economy. Most counterfeiters work at small to midsized factories, but many stay at home, doing things like filling Head & Shoulders bottles with concoctions from large vats in their living rooms. Overall, the amount of China's manufacturing base that is dependent on fakes and other illegal knockoffs is estimated to be 10 percent to 30 percent. Copyright piracy has thrived during the past decade, thanks to the influx of foreign technology and lax enforcement of existing copyright laws. In fact, counterfeiting is so ingrained in China's culture that many Chinese view it as harmless.

Worse still, the fakes are exported everywhere—to Europe, Russia, the Middle East. Unilever says that fake Dove soap is making its way from China into Europe. Bose, a maker of high-end audio systems, is finding Chinese fakes in overseas markets. The pirates have indeed moved to a whole new level of sophistication. Ten years ago, China's knockoffs were below Western standards. Now many fake Duracells look so genuine that Gillette has to send them to a forensics lab to analyze them. Fake watches even contain full-sized Swiss movements and real gems. It's scary to think about what could wind up on the world's shelves.

So what are pirated brand owners to do? Some multinationals are shutting or shrinking some product lines in China because these products are overrun by counterfeits. But China's market is so vast and promising, few companies are willing to pull out entirely. So most foreign companies are trying to boost government enforcement. U.S. sunglasses maker Oakley has gotten Chinese authorities to close counterfeiters' factories. And Yamaha Motor Company recently won a landmark judgment against a Chinese company accused of manufacturing copied versions of its motorcycles, although it was awarded only a fraction of the $3.6 million in damages it sought. Meanwhile, China has launched campaigns against counterfeit products and claims to be making remarkable progress. Authorities have revoked some 35,000 business licenses and closed some 32,000 violating businesses, showing signs that Beijing is getting serious in its battle against corporate piracy.

Still, it will be a tough task for China to get real soon. The country's legal system is riddled with loopholes. And a real crackdown on counterfeiting could create serious social turmoil and costs to the central government, because fake making is the livelihood of so many citizens. "Entire villages live off counterfeiting. If you suddenly throw these people out of work, you'll have riots," says one spokesperson for a leading private anti-counterfeiting agency. So while China's lawmakers grapple with a solution, endless raids, fines, and revoked licenses are all China has to offer—for now.

Questions for Critical Thinking

1. Why doesn't China use its manufacturing skills to make its own products?
2. Honda recently set up a joint venture to make and sell motorcycles with a Chinese company that used to produce Honda knockoffs. Why would Honda do this?

routine government actions. Critics of this U.S. law complain that payoffs are a routine part of world trade, so forbidding U.S. companies to follow suit cripples their ability to compete. Others counter that U.S. exports haven't been affected by this law and that companies can conduct business abroad without violating antibribery rules. Regardless of whether they agree or disagree with the law, some companies have had to forgo opportunities as a result of it. For example, a U.S. power-generation company walked away from a $320 million contract in the Middle East because government officials demanded a $3 million bribe. The contract went to a Japanese company instead.[4]

Forms of International Business Activity

3 LEARNING OBJECTIVE

Identify five forms of international business activity

importing
Purchasing goods or services from another country and bringing them into one's own country

exporting
Selling and shipping goods or services to another country

Once a company decides to operate in the global marketplace, it must decide on the level of involvement it is willing to undertake and develop strategies for marketing its products internationally. Five common market-entry strategies are *importing and exporting, licensing, franchising, strategic alliances and joint ventures,* and *foreign direct investment.* Each has a varying degree of financial commitment, risk, control, and profit potential (see Exhibit 3.3).

Importing and Exporting   **Importing,** the buying of goods or services from a supplier in another country, and **exporting,** the selling of products outside the country in which they are produced, have existed for centuries. In the past few decades, however, the increased level of these activities has caused the economies of the world to become tightly linked.

Exporting, one of the least risky forms of international business activity, permits a firm to enter a foreign market gradually, assess local conditions, then fine-tune its product to meet the needs of foreign consumers. In most cases the firm's financial exposure is limited to market research costs, advertising costs, and the costs of either establishing a direct sales and distribution system or hiring intermediaries. Such intermediaries include *export management companies,* which are domestic firms that specialize in performing international marketing services on a commission basis, and *export trading companies,* which are general trading firms that will buy your products for resale overseas as well as perform a variety of importing, exporting, and manufacturing functions. Still another alternative is to use foreign distributors.

Working through a foreign distributor with connections in the target country is often helpful to both large and small companies because such intermediaries can provide you with the connections, expertise, and market knowledge you will need to conduct business in a foreign country.[5] In addition, many countries now have foreign trade offices to help importers and exporters interested in doing business within their borders. Other helpful resources include professional agents, local businesspeople, and the International Trade Administration of the U.S. Department of Commerce. This trade organization offers a variety of services, including political and credit-risk analysis, advice on entering foreign markets, and financing tips.

EXHIBIT 3.3
Market-Entry Strategies
The degree of financial commitment, risk, control, and profit potential varies with each foreign market-entry strategy.

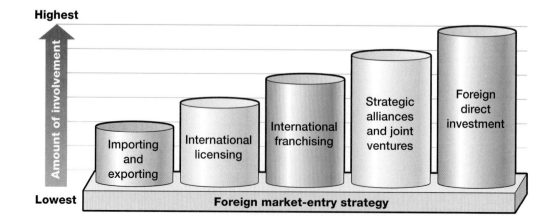

International Licensing   **Licensing** is another popular approach to international business. License agreements entitle one company to use some or all of another firm's intellectual property (patents, trademarks, brand names, copyrights, or trade secrets) in return for a royalty payment. Underwear manufacturer Jockey licenses the rights to use the Jockey name to certain foreign manufacturers of women's active wear, sleepwear, and slippers. Jockey licenses its products in more than 120 countries but is careful that all such arrangements add value to the Jockey name.[6]

Many firms choose licensing as an approach to international markets because it involves little out-of-pocket cost. A firm has already incurred the costs of developing the intellectual property to be licensed. Pharmaceutical firms, for instance, routinely use licensing to enter foreign markets. Once a pharmaceutical firm has developed and patented a new drug, it is often more efficient to grant existing local firms the right to manufacture and distribute the patented drug in return for royalty payments. Israel's Teva Pharmaceutical Industries, for example, has a license to manufacture and market Merck's pharmaceutical products in Israel. This arrangement saves Merck the expense of establishing its own Israeli salesforce.[7] Of course, licensing agreements are not restricted to international business. A company can also license its products or technology to other companies in its domestic market.

International Franchising   Some companies choose to expand into foreign markets by *franchising* their operation. International franchising is among the fastest-growing forms of international business activity today. Under this arrangement, a franchisor enters into an agreement whereby the franchisee obtains the rights to duplicate a specific product or service—perhaps a restaurant, photocopy shop, or video rental store—and the franchisor obtains a royalty fee in exchange. Holiday Inn Worldwide has used this approach to reach customers in over 65 countries. So have KFC, McDonald's, and scores of others. Smaller companies have also found that franchising is a good way for them to enter the global marketplace.[8] By franchising its operations, a firm can minimize the costs and risks of global expansion and bypass certain trade restrictions. (The advantages and disadvantages of franchising in general will be discussed in detail in Chapter 5.)

International Strategic Alliances and Joint Ventures
A **strategic alliance** is a long-term partnership between two or more companies to jointly develop, produce, or sell products in the global marketplace. To reach their individual but complementary goals, the companies typically share ideas, expertise, resources, technologies, investment costs, risks, management, and profits.

Strategic alliances are a popular way to expand one's business globally. The benefits of this form of international expansion include ease of market entry, shared risk, shared knowledge and expertise, and synergy. In other words, companies that form a strategic alliance with a foreign partner can often compete more effectively than if they entered the foreign market alone. Consider the strategic alliance established by American Airlines, British Airways, Cathay Pacific Airways, Quantas, and others. Named *oneworld*, this partnership makes global travel easier for consumers. Benefits include integrated frequent flyer programs, common airport lounges, and more efficient ticketing among member carriers so that a change of airlines is transparent when booking international flights.[9]

licensing
Agreement to produce and market another company's product in exchange for a royalty or fee

strategic alliance
Long-term relationship in which two or more companies share ideas, resources, and technologies in order to establish competitive advantages

In the past few years, China's major cities have sprouted American franchises and restaurants, including McDonald's, Pizza Hut, and Starbucks.

joint venture
Cooperative partnership in which organizations share investment costs, risks, management, and profits in the development, production, or selling of products

A **joint venture** is a special type of strategic alliance in which two or more firms join together to create a new business entity that is legally separate and distinct from its parents. When Starbucks ventures overseas, it uses three business strategies: joint ventures, licenses, and company-owned operations. Currently, the chain operates 1,200 international outlets from Beijing to Bristol and is expanding overseas at a rapid pace. Partnering with locals makes it easier to start and operate a coffee shop on foreign turf, but it also reduces the company's share of the profits by some 20 to 50 percent.[10]

In some countries, foreign companies are prohibited from owning facilities outright or from investing in local business. Thus, establishing a joint venture with a local partner may be the only way to do business in that country. In other cases, foreigners may be required to move some of their production facilities to the country to earn the right to sell their products there. For instance, the Chinese government would not allow Boeing to sell airplanes in China until the company agreed to move half of the tail-section production for its 737s to Xian.[11]

Foreign Direct Investment Exporting, licensing, franchising, and strategic alliances allow a firm to enter the global marketplace without investing in foreign factories or facilities. However, many firms prefer to enter international markets through ownership and control of assets in foreign countries.

The most comprehensive form of international business is a wholly-owned operation run in another country, without the financial participation of a local partner. Many U.S. firms conduct business this way, as do companies based in other countries. These operations vary in form, size, and purpose. Some are started from scratch; others are acquired from local owners. Some are small sales offices; others are full-scale manufacturing facilities. Some are set up to exploit the availability of raw materials; others take advantage of low wage rates; still others minimize transportation costs by choosing locations that give them direct access to markets in other countries. In almost all cases, at least part of the workforce is drawn from the local population.

multinational corporations (MNCs)
Companies with operations in more than one country

foreign direct investment (FDI)
Investment of money by foreign companies in domestic business enterprises

Companies with a physical presence in numerous countries are called **multinational corporations (MNCs)**. Since 1969, the number of multinational corporations in the world's 14 richest countries has more than tripled, from 7,000 to 24,000.[12] Some multinational corporations increase their involvement in foreign countries by establishing **foreign direct investment (FDI)**. That is, they either establish production and marketing facilities in the countries where they operate or purchase existing foreign firms, as Wal-Mart did in the late 1990s, when it acquired large retail stores in Germany and Great Britain and later converted them into Wal-Mart supercenters. Such foreign direct investment constitutes the highest level of international involvement. Moreover, it carries much greater economic and political risk and is more complex than any other form of entry in the global marketplace.[13]

The U.S. Commerce Department reports that foreign direct investment in the United States remains high, following three years (1998–2000) of unprecedented levels of spending to acquire or establish U.S. businesses.[14] In addition to the United States, areas such as the Chinese Economic Area (China, Hong Kong, and Taiwan), South Korea, Singapore, Thailand, Malaysia, Indonesia, Vietnam, India, South Africa, Turkey, and Brazil are attractive spots for foreign investment. Labeled *big emerging markets*, these countries make up 70 percent of the world's land, 85 percent of the world's population, and 99 percent of the anticipated growth in the world's labor force.[15] As such, they have been identified by the U.S. International Trade Administration as having the greatest potential for large increase in U.S. exports over the next two decades.

China is becoming too big a PC market for anyone to ignore. Dell, which recently opened its fourth PC factory in the world on China's southeastern coast, can now deliver PCs to Chinese customers as fast as it does to North American ones.

Competing in the Global Marketplace

How to Avoid Business Blunders Abroad

Doing business in another country can be extremely tricky. Here are some issues to consider when you conduct business abroad.

The Importance of Packaging

Numerous problems result from the failure to adapt packaging for other cultures. Sometimes only the color of the package needs to be altered to enhance a product's sales. For instance, white symbolizes death in Japan and much of Asia; green represents danger or disease in Malaysia. Obviously, using the wrong color in these countries might produce negative reactions.

The Language Barrier

Some product names travel poorly. For instance, the gasoline company Esso found out that its name means "stalled car" in Japan. However, some company names have traveled well. Kodak may be the most famous example. A research team deliberately developed this name after searching for a word that was pronounceable everywhere but had no specific meaning anywhere.

Problems with Promotions

In its U.S. promotion, one company had effectively used this sentence: "You can use no finer napkin at your dinner table." The U.S. company decided to use the same commercials in England because, after all, the British do speak English. To the British, however, the word napkin or nappy actually means "diaper." The ad could hardly be expected to boost sales of dinner napkins in England.

Local Customs

Social norms vary greatly from country to country and it is difficult for any outsider to be knowledgeable about all of them, so local input is vital. For example, one firm pro-

moted eyeglasses in Thailand with commercials featuring animals wearing glasses. However, in Thailand animals are considered a low form of life; humans would never wear anything worn by an animal.

Translation Problems

The best translations of an advertising message convey the concept of the original but do not precisely duplicate the original. PepsiCo learned this lesson when it reportedly discovered that its slogan "Come alive with Pepsi" was translated into German as "Come alive out of the grave with Pepsi." In Asia, the slogan was once translated as "Bring your ancestors back from the dead."

The Need for Research

Proper market research may reduce or eliminate most international business blunders. Market researchers can uncover needs for product adaptations, potential name problems, promotional requirements, and useful market strategies. Good research may even uncover potential translation problems.

As you can see, doing business in other cultures can be risky if you're unprepared. However, awareness of differences, consultation with local people, and concern for host-country feelings can reduce problems and save money.

Questions for Critical Thinking

1. If you were thinking of selling a breakfast cereal in Japan, what issues might you want to consider?
2. What steps can companies take to avoid business blunders abroad?

Fundamentals of International Trade

The success of U.S. businesses such as Trek, Wal-Mart, UPS, and others that operate in the global marketplace depends, in part, on the international economic relationships the United States maintains with other countries. Basically, the U.S. objective is to devise policies that balance the interests of U.S. companies, U.S. workers, and U.S. consumers. Other countries are trying to do the same thing. As you might expect, the many players in world trade sometimes have conflicting goals.

Why Nations Trade

4 **LEARNING OBJECTIVE**

Discuss why nations trade

No single country has the resources to produce everything its citizens want or need. Businesses and countries specialize in the production of certain goods and engage in international trade to obtain raw materials and goods that are unavailable to them or too costly for them to produce. International trade has many benefits: It increases a country's total output, it offers lower prices and greater variety to consumers, it subjects domestic oligopolies and monopolies to competition, it creates jobs, and it allows companies to expand their markets and achieve cost, production, and distribution efficiencies.[16]

How does a country know what to produce and what to trade for? In some cases, the answer is easy. A nation may have an **absolute advantage**, which means it can produce a particular item more efficiently than *all* other nations, or it is virtually the only country producing that product. Absolute advantages rarely last, however, unless they are based on the availability of natural resources. Saudi Arabia, for example, has an absolute advantage in crude oil production because of its huge, developed reserves. Thus, it makes sense for Saudi Arabia to specialize in providing the world with oil and to trade for other items it needs.

absolute advantage
A nation's ability to produce a particular product with fewer resources per unit of output than any other nation

In most cases, a country can produce many of the same items that other countries can produce. The **comparative advantage theory** explains how a country chooses which items to produce and which items to trade for. The theory states that a country should produce and sell to other countries those items it produces more efficiently or at a lower cost, and it should trade for those it can't produce as economically. To see how the theory works, consider the United States and Brazil. Each can produce both steel and coffee, but the United States is more efficient at producing steel than coffee, while Brazil is more efficient at producing coffee than steel. According to the comparative advantage theory, the two countries will be better off if each specializes in the industry in which it is more efficient and if the two trade with each other, with the United States selling steel to Brazil and Brazil selling coffee to the United States.[17] The basic argument behind the comparative advantage theory is that such specialization and exchange will increase a country's total output and allow both trading partners to enjoy a higher standard of living.

comparative advantage theory
Theory that states that a country should produce and sell to other countries those items it produces most efficiently

How International Trade Is Measured

balance of trade
Total value of the products a nation exports minus the total value of the products it imports, over some period of time

trade surplus
Favorable trade balance created when a country exports more than it imports

trade deficit
Unfavorable trade balance created when a country imports more than it exports

balance of payments
Sum of all payments one nation receives from other nations minus the sum of all payments it makes to other nations, over some specified period of time

In Chapter 1 we discussed how economists monitor certain key economic indicators to evaluate how well their country's economic system is performing. Two key measurements of a nation's level of international trade are the *balance of trade* and the *balance of payments*. The total value of a country's exports minus the total value of its imports, over some period of time, determines its **balance of trade**. In years when the value of goods and services exported by the United States exceeds the value of goods and services it imports, the U.S. balance of trade is said to be positive: People in other countries buy more goods and services from the United States than the United States buys from them, creating a **trade surplus**. Conversely, when the people of the United States buy more from foreign countries than the foreign countries buy from the United States, the U.S. balance of trade is said to be negative. That is, imports exceed exports, creating a **trade deficit**. As Exhibit 3.4 shows, in 2001 the U.S. trade deficit amounted to $350 billion.[18]

The **balance of payments** is the broadest indicator of international trade. It is the total flow of money into the country minus the total flow of money out of the country over some period of time. The balance of payments includes the balance of trade plus the net dollars received and spent on foreign investment, military expenditures, tourism, foreign aid, and

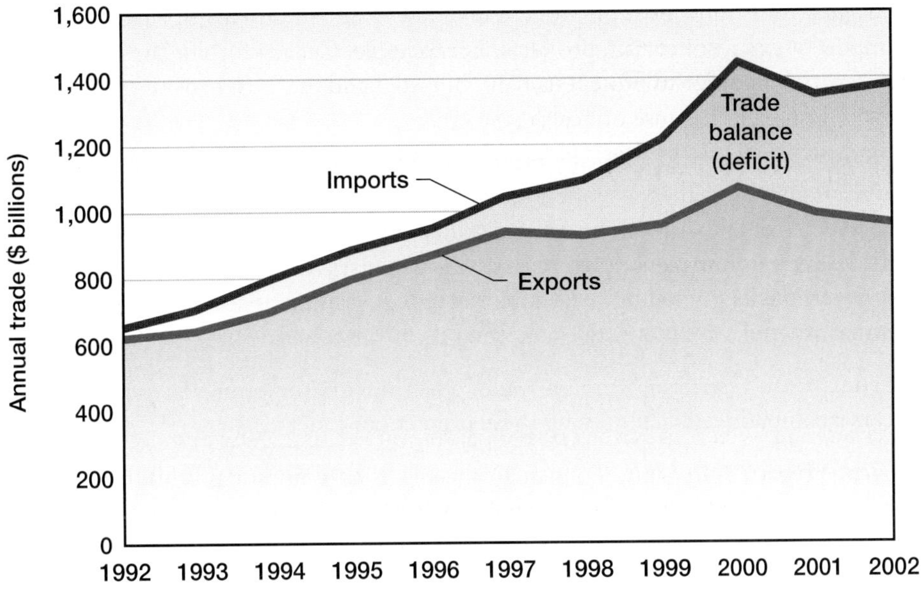

EXHIBIT 3.4

U.S. Trade Deficit

Because the United States imports more than it exports, the country creates a deficit trade balance.

other international transactions. For example, when a U.S. company such as Whirlpool buys all or part of a company based in another country, that investment is counted in the balance of payments but not in the balance of trade. Similarly, when a foreign company such as Daimler-Benz buys a U.S. company such as Chrysler or purchases U.S. stocks, bonds, or real estate, those transactions are part of the balance of payments. The U.S. government, like all governments, desires a favorable balance of payments. That means more money is coming into the country than is flowing out.

Trade Restrictions

5 LEARNING OBJECTIVE

Explain why nations restrict international trade and list four forms of trade restrictions

Even though international trade has many economic advantages, sometimes countries practice **protectionism**; that is, they restrict international trade for one reason or another. Sometimes they restrict trade to shield specific industries from foreign competition and the possible loss of jobs in these industries. Sometimes they try to protect certain industries that are key to their national defense and the health and safety of their citizens. And sometimes they engage in protectionist measures to give new or weak industries an opportunity to grow and strengthen.[19]

protectionism
Government policies aimed at shielding a country's industries from foreign competition

Are trade restrictions a good idea or a bad idea? Study after study has shown that in the long run, they hurt a country because they remove competition, stifle innovation, and allow domestic producers to charge more for their goods. The most commonly used forms of trade restrictions include:

tariffs
Taxes levied on imports

- ***Tariffs.*** **Tariffs** are taxes, surcharges, or duties levied against imported goods. Sometimes tariffs are levied to generate revenue for the government, but more often they are imposed to restrict trade or to punish other countries for disobeying international trade laws. In 2002, the United States began imposing tariffs of up to 30 percent on certain imported steel products. The action was taken to protect the steel industry from a surge of imports.[20]

quotas
Fixed limits on the quantity of imports a nation will allow for a specific product

- ***Quotas.*** **Quotas** limit the amount of a particular good that countries can import during a year. The United States puts ceilings on foreign sugar, peanuts, and dairy products. Limits may be set in quantities, such as pounds of sugar, or in values, such as total dollars' worth of peanuts. In some cases, a product faces stiff tariffs once it reaches its quota. After foreign tobacco products hit their quotas, for example, additional shipments face 350 percent tariffs.[21]

embargo
Total ban on trade with a particular nation (a sanction) or of a particular product

- *Embargoes.* In its most extreme form, a quota becomes an **embargo**, a complete ban on the import or export of certain products. For example, Canada forbids the importation of oleomargarine in order to protect its dairy industry, and the U.S. bans the importation of toys with lead paint because of health concerns.

- *Sanctions.* Sanctions are politically motivated embargoes that revoke a country's normal trade relations status; they are often used as forceful alternatives short of war. Sanctions can include arms embargoes, foreign-assistance reductions and cutoffs, trade limitations, tariff increases, import-quota decreases, visa denials, air-link cancellations, and more. Most governments (including the United States) use sanctions sparingly, because studies show that sanctions are ineffective at getting countries to change.[22]

6 LEARNING OBJECTIVE

Highlight three protectionist tactics nations use to give their domestic industries a competitive edge

In addition to restricting foreign trade, governments sometimes give their domestic producers a competitive edge by using these protectionist tactics:

- *Restrictive import standards.* Countries can assist their domestic producers by establishing restrictive import standards, such as requiring special licenses for doing certain kinds of business and then making it difficult for foreign companies to obtain such a license. For example, Chiquita claims that an eight-year European Union restriction on banana imports from Latin America cost the company $1.5 billion.[23] Other countries restrict imports by requiring goods to pass special tests.

- *Subsidies.* Rather than restrict imports, some countries subsidize domestic producers so that their prices can compete favorably in the global marketplace. Airbus, originally an alliance of state companies from Germany, France, England, and Spain, was subsidized for years to help the company compete against rival Boeing. Now that Airbus is a strong competitor, the complex alliance has been sold to a joint venture composed of two private companies—the French–German–Spanish European Aeronautic Defense and Space Company and Britain's BAE Systems PLC.[24]

dumping
Charging less than the actual cost or less than the home-country price for goods sold in other countries

- *Dumping.* The practice of selling large quantities of a product at a price lower than the cost of production or below what the company would charge in its home market is called **dumping**. This tactic is often used to try to win foreign customers or to reduce product surpluses. Most industrialized countries have antidumping regulations. Section 301 of the U.S. Trade Act of 1988, for instance, obligates the U.S. president to retaliate against foreign producers that dump products on the U.S. market. So when reports showed that Japan was dumping coated steel, which is used primarily in metal containers, cans, bakeware, and home builders' hardware, on the U.S. market, the United States imposed a 95 percent antidumping penalty on the coated steel to prevent Japan from materially injuring the U.S. steel industry.[25]

Agreements and Organizations Promoting International Trade

To prevent trade disputes from escalating into full-blown trade wars, and to ensure that international business is conducted in a fair and orderly fashion, countries worldwide have created trade agreements and organizations. Philosophically, most of these agreements and organizations support the basic principles of **free trade**. The assumption is that each nation will ultimately benefit by freely exchanging the goods and services it produces most efficiently for the goods and services it produces less efficiently. The major trade agreements and organizations include the GATT, the WTO, the APEC, the IMF, and the World Bank.

free trade
International trade unencumbered by restrictive measures

The General Agreement on Tariffs and Trade The General Agreement on Tariffs and Trade (GATT) is a worldwide pact that was first established in the aftermath of World War II. The pact's guiding principle—most favored nation (MFN)—is one of nondiscrimination: Any trade advantage a GATT member gives to one country must be given to all GATT members, and no GATT nation can be singled out for punishment. In 1995 GATT established the World Trade Organization (WTO), which has replaced GATT as the world forum for trade negotiations.

The World Trade Organization The World Trade Organization (WTO) is a permanent forum for negotiating, implementing, and monitoring international trade procedures and for mediating trade disputes among its 144 member countries. The organization's goals include facilitating free trade, lowering the costs of doing business, enhancing the international investment environment, simplifying customs, and promoting technical and economic cooperation. Experts believe that the WTO should ultimately prove to be more effective than the GATT because the WTO has a formal legal structure for settling disputes.

Admission to the organization is through an application process and requires approval by two-thirds of the members. All WTO members enjoy "favored" access to foreign markets in exchange for adhering to a long list of fair-trading rules and laws governing patents, copyrights, and trademarks. After 15 years of negotiations, China was finally admitted to the WTO in November 2001. As a condition of its membership, China made extraordinary concessions. Over a five-year period, China must eliminate many tariffs and quotas on a wide range of products and open its market of 1.4 billion people to foreign goods. One group that spoke out strongly against China's admission to the WTO was U.S. textile workers, who feared that the lifting of U.S. quotas on foreign textiles by 2005 will increase imports of foreign textiles and severely affect the U.S. textile industry.[26]

China's Trade Minister Shi Guangsheng claps as China joins the World Trade Organization. Among the many advantages of trading with China are its enormous population and good infrastructure.

The Asia Pacific Economic Cooperation Council The Asia Pacific Economic Cooperation Council (APEC) is an organization of 18 countries that are making efforts to liberalize trade in the Pacific Rim (the land areas that surround the Pacific Ocean). Among the member nations are the United States, Japan, China, Mexico, Australia, South Korea, and Canada. In 1994 the members agreed to eliminate all tariffs and trade barriers among industrialized countries of the Pacific Rim by 2010 and among developing countries by 2020.[27]

The International Monetary Fund The International Monetary Fund (IMF) was founded in 1945 and is now affiliated with the United Nations. Its primary function is to provide short-term loans to countries that are unable to meet their budgetary expenses. As such, the IMF is often looked upon as a lender of last resort. For example, the IMF has provided well over a combined total of $150 billion in loans to South Korea, Indonesia, Brazil, Thailand, and other countries to help rescue them from a global financial crisis at the end of the twentieth century.[28]

The World Bank Officially known as the International Bank for Reconstruction and Development, the World Bank was founded to finance reconstruction after World War II. It now provides low-interest loans to developing nations for the improvement of transportation, telecommunications, health, and education. Currently the World Bank is focused on bringing the Internet to the less-developed regions of the world, such as Africa. World Bank officials and telecommunication executives hope that Internet connections will attract more companies to the region and lead to more rapid economic development.[29] Both the IMF and the World Bank are funded by deposits from its 182 member nations. The bulk of the funds come from the United States, western Europe, and Japan.

Trading Blocs

trading blocs
Organizations of nations that remove barriers to trade among their members and that establish uniform barriers to trade with nonmember nations

7 LEARNING OBJECTIVE

Explain how trading blocs affect trade

Trading blocs are another type of organization that promotes international trade. Generally comprising neighboring countries, trading blocs promote free trade among regional members. Although specific rules vary from group to group, their primary objective is to ensure the economic growth and benefit of their members. As such, trading blocs generally promote trade inside the region while creating uniform barriers against goods and services entering the region from nonmember countries. Trading blocs are becoming a significant force in the global marketplace.

Trading blocs can be advantageous or disadvantageous in promoting world trade, depending on one's perspective. Some economists are apprehensive about the growing importance of regional trading blocs. They fear that the world is splitting into three camps, revolving around the Americas, Europe, and Asia. Any nation that does not fall into one of these economic regions could suffer, they say, because members of the trading blocs could place severe restrictions on trade with nonmember countries. The critics fear that overall world trade could decline as members become more protective of their own regions. As a result, consumers could find themselves with fewer choices, and many producers could lose sales in lucrative foreign markets.

Others claim that trading blocs could improve world trade. The growth of commerce and the availability of customers and suppliers within a trading bloc could be a boon to smaller or younger nations that are trying to build strong economies. The lack of trade barriers within the bloc could help member industries compete with producers in more-developed nations, and, in some cases, member countries could reach a wider market than before.[30] Furthermore, close ties to more stable economies could help shield emerging nations from fluctuations in the global economy and could promote a greater sharing of knowledge and technology; both outcomes could aid future economic development.

The four most powerful trading blocs today are the Association of Southeast Asian Nations (ASEAN), South America's Mercosur, the North American Free Trade Agreement (NAFTA), and the European Union (EU), with the latter two being the largest and most powerful (see Exhibit 3.5). Because many trading nations see Latin America as an area for large-scale economic growth in the future, they are eager to establish ties with Mercosur, which links Argentina, Brazil, Paraguay, and Uruguay and encompasses a population of

EXHIBIT 3.5

Members of Major Trade Blocs
As the economies of the world become increasingly linked, many countries have formed powerful regional trade blocs that trade freely with one another and limit foreign competition.

European Union (EU)*	North American Free Trade Agreement (NAFTA)	Association of Southeast Asian Nations (ASEAN)	Mercosur
Austria	Canada	Brunei	Argentina
Belgium	Mexico	Indonesia	Brazil
Finland	United States	Malaysia	Paraguay
France		Philippines	Uruguay
Germany		Singapore	
Ireland		Thailand	
Italy			
Luxembourg			
Netherlands			
Portugal			
Spain			
Denmark			
Great Britain			
Greece			
Sweden			

*Boxed countries are members of the Economic and Monetary Union (EMU).

210 million people who produce more than $1 trillion in goods and services.[31] Like other trading blocks, Mercosur's objectives include the free movement of goods and services across the borders of its members. Furthermore, the group seeks an economic integration that it hopes will make the four countries more competitive in the global marketplace.[32] Some U.S. officials hope that Mercosur will eventually join NAFTA to form a Free Trade Area of the Americas (FTAA).[33]

NAFTA   In 1994 the United States, Canada, and Mexico formed a powerful trading bloc, the North American Free Trade Agreement (NAFTA). The agreement paves the way for the free flow of goods, services, and capital within the bloc by eliminating all tariffs and quotas on trades among the three nations. So far the score card for NAFTA seems positive. It has been a huge success in promoting trade between the United States and its Mexican and Canadian neighbors. Canada and Mexico now send more than 85 percent of their exports to the United States and get a similar percentage of their imports from the United States. That mighty stream can total $2 billion a day.[34] Fears that NAFTA would move U.S. jobs across the border have proven unfounded. Moreover, the impact of NAFTA on U.S. jobs has been relatively small.[35] Ultimately, NAFTA's supporters would like to see the agreement expanded to include all of Central and South America—making it the largest free-trade zone on the planet.[36]

The European Union   One of the largest trading blocs is the European Union (EU), which combines 15 countries and more than 370 million people. Talks are under way to admit more countries, including the Czech Republic, Estonia, Hungary, Slovenia, and Poland.[37] EU nations are working to eliminate hundreds of local regulations, variations in product standards, and protectionist measures that limit trade between member countries. Eliminating barriers enables the nations of the EU to function as a single market, with trade flowing between member countries as it does among states in the United States.

European Union's Impact on the Rules of Global Trade   Increasingly, the rules governing the food we eat, the software we use, and the cars we drive are set in Brussels, the unofficial capital of the European Union. The European Union, which regulates more frequently and more rigorously than the United States—especially when it comes to consumer protection—has a significant impact on global product standards. Twenty years ago if manufacturers designed something to U.S. standards, they could pretty much sell it all over the world. Now items must conform to EU standards.

When it comes to consumer or environmental protections, EU regulators believe it's better to be safe than sorry. That approach evolved partly from a series of food scares in Europe over the past 10 to 14 years, such as mad-cow disease. It also reflects the fact that Europeans are more inclined than Americans to expect government to protect them. Because of stricter EU rules, McDonald's has stopped serving soft-plastic toys with its Happy Meals and United Technologies has redesigned its Carrier air conditioners to comply with European recycling rules, which are tougher than U.S. standards.[38]

U.S. farmers also tend to cater to European tastes—especially when it comes to genetically modified food. The U.S. Food and Drug Administration has approved the use of most genetically modified crops in human food, but the EU has placed strict limits on which genetically modified seeds can be planted and how they can be used in Europe. Thus, many U.S. food processors won't buy genetically modified corn or soybeans so they can sell their products internationally.[39]

The Euro   In 1999, 11 of the 15 EU countries formed the economic and monetary union (EMU) and turned over control of their individual monetary policies to the newly created European Central Bank. With a combined population of about 376 million people, these 11 countries account for about 20 percent of the world's gross domestic product (GDP), making them the world's second largest economy.[40] The four countries that did not join the

The euro eases price comparisons for products sold by the 12 European member countries.

EMU are Greece (which did not meet the strict qualification requirements), Britain, Denmark, and Sweden, which chose not to participate initially. One of the driving forces behind the decision to join the EMU was the anticipated advantages these 11 countries would enjoy by creating a unified currency called the **euro**.

Officially launched in 1999 (with notes and coins available in 2002), the euro got off to a rocky start. But European leaders believe it will build a bond among Europe's cities and improve trade. Moreover, the euro could wipe out some $65 billion annually in currency exchange costs among participants and cut the middleman out of trillions of dollars' worth of foreign exchange transactions. U.S. businesses and travelers alone could save as much as 50 percent of the costs they now pay to convert dollars into multiple European currencies. And, with prices in these 11 nations now visible in one currency, consumers can compare prices on similar items whether they are sold in Lisbon or Vienna.

Foreign Exchange Rates and Currency Valuations

euro
A planned unified currency used by European nations that meet certain strict requirements

When companies buy and sell goods and services in the global marketplace, they complete the transaction by exchanging currencies. For instance, if a Japanese company borrows money from a U.S. bank to build a manufacturing plant in Japan, it must repay the loan in U.S. dollars. Or if a South Korean car manufacturer imports engine parts from Japan, it must pay for them in yen (Japan's currency). To do so, companies exchange their currency at any international bank that handles *foreign exchange*, the conversion of one currency into an equivalent amount of another currency. The number of yen or pounds that must be exchanged for every dollar or won is known as the **exchange rate** between currencies.

exchange rate
Rate at which the money of one country is traded for the money of another

Most international currencies operate under a *floating exchange rate system;* thus, a currency's value or price fluctuates in response to the forces of global supply and demand (as we discussed in Chapter 1). The supply and demand of a country's currency are determined in part by what is happening in the country's own economy. Moreover, because supply and demand for a currency are always changing, the rate at which it is exchanged for other currencies may change a little each day. Japanese currency might be trading at 137.6 yen to the dollar on one day and 136.8 on the next.

Even though most governments let the value of their currency respond to the forces of supply and demand, sometimes a government will intervene and adjust the exchange rate of its country's currency. Why would a government do this? One reason is to keep the price of a nation's goods and services more affordable in the global marketplace and to protect the nation's economy against trade imbalances. Another is to boost or slow down the country's economy.

Devaluation, or the drop in the value of a nation's currency relative to the value of other currencies, can at times boost a country's economy because it makes the country's products and services more affordable in foreign markets while it increases the price of imports. Because fewer units of foreign currency are required to purchase the devalued currency, such situations tend to raise a country's exports and lower its imports. Conversely, a strong currency boosts imports and dampens exports.

Some countries fix, or peg, the value of their currencies to the value of more stable currencies, such as the dollar or the yen, instead of letting it float freely. Hong Kong, for example, pegs its currency to the U.S. dollar. If a currency is pegged, its value fluctuates proportionately with the value of the foreign currency to which it is linked. So if the U.S. dollar declines, so will the Japanese yen and other currencies that are pegged to it. This system works well as long as the proportionate relationship between the two currencies remains valid. But if one partner suffers economic hardship, demand for its currency will decline significantly and the exchange rate at which the two are pegged will become unrealistic. Such was the case with Thailand's currency (the baht), Indonesia's currency (the rupiah), and Argentina's currency (the peso). When these countries unpegged their currencies from the U.S. dollar to let them gradually seek their true value, the currencies went into a freefall.

Terrorism's Effect on the Global Business Environment

Argentines gathered in front of a Buenos Aires currency exchange, as the government lifted restrictions against citizens' trading pesos at a free-floating rate against the dollar.

In the global marketplace, the problems of one country can greatly affect world economics. The September 11 terrorist attacks on the World Trade Center in New York City and the Pentagon in Washington, D.C., were targeted at the American people and the free-market system, but economically the attacks knew no borders. When American's stop buying—even if for only a short period of time—the world feels the impact.

To get a perspective of how important U.S trade is to the world economies, consider the following: Each day U.S. Customs processes about 38,000 trucks and railcars, 16,000 containers on 600 ships, and 2,600 aircraft, most of which are filled with foreign goods brought into the United States.[41] Foreign trade, which accounted for 20 percent of U.S. economic activity a decade ago, now accounts for almost 30 percent. U.S. exports alone have been responsible for a third of the 20 million jobs created since 1986.[42] And while the 2,500 largest U.S. companies sold about 12 percent of their goods and services outside the United States in 1980, that figure has tripled the past two decades.[43]

Of course, no one knows for certain what impact terrorism will have on the attitudes of U.S. businesspeople toward globalization. Some high-profile firms such as Merrill Lynch, Morgan Stanley, Charles Schwab, Home Depot, Ford Motor Company, and Gateway Computers have pulled back or canceled their global expansion plans, but no broad evidence exists to indicate that many others will follow suit.[44] In fact, a recent survey by the United Nations shows that 70 percent of respondents expect investment and employment in their foreign operations to rise in the near term.[45]

KFC, for example, is one firm that doesn't plan on hitting the brakes. KFC has around 5,000 U.S. restaurants and 6,000 abroad. It has 158 franchises in Indonesia, which has the world's largest Muslim population. It has a restaurant in the holy city of Mecca, Saudi Arabia. In all, KFC has restaurants in more than 80 countries, including Japan, Australia, Egypt, Mexico, Malaysia, and Swaziland. In China, where

8 **LEARNING OBJECTIVE**

Discuss terrorism's impact on globalization

In spite of terrorism, Burger King is expanding its operations overseas, even though it faces many obstacles. Here Lebanese students in Beirut hold a sit-in to protest U.S. foreign policy.

Terrorism isn't the only issue affecting global trade. Here, in Hong Kong, a waitress and patrons wear masks to protect themselves from catching SARS (severe acute respiratory syndrome). The 2003 outbreak of the disease, particularly in the Asia-Pacific region, caused the worst economic crisis in southeast Asia since a wave of bank failures and currency devaluations in 1997. Nervous customers stayed away from stores and restaurants, travelers canceled trips, and industries that offer services to people such as retail stores, restaurants, hotels, airlines, or cinemas were hit particularly hard. Also hurt were global suppliers to these industries.

KFC has more than 500 restaurants, it is opening about 10 new stores a month. And it's not about to slow down. KFC plans to open more than 1,000 stores a year overseas for the foreseeable future. As the company's CEO David Novak sees it, KFC's long-standing presence in so many countries makes it an accepted part of the landscape, and therefore less likely to be a major target of terrorism. "We're going to have some radical situations, but not to the extent we think it's going to alter our business plan."[46] "We're still on a fast track overseas, in fact it's one of the keys to our company's growth," adds the VP of marketing.[47]

One of the more likely outcomes of the September 11 terrorist attacks is that world trade will face new obstacles. The war on terrorism has changed the rules of international travel, with tighter security, longer delays at borders, cargo restrictions, and higher transport costs. Every container entering the United States at the Mexican border must now be opened and inspected. As a result, cargo-laden trucks now take up to seven hours to cross, compared with one or two hours before the attacks. Similarly, where a cargo jet could make five stops a day before the attacks, now it makes four.[48] Such delays force companies to inventory more spare parts and increase their manufacturing and operating costs (as Chapter 9 points out).

In spite of these obstacles, most businesses have too much riding on globalization to give up on it now. For multinationals such as Whirlpool, globalization is the key to their future. And some even believe that rather than deterring globalization, the terrorist attacks could accelerate it.[49] The more countries cooperate against terrorism, the more the world begins to see itself as one place.

Summary of Learning Objectives

1. **Highlight the opportunities and challenges of conducting business in other countries.**
   Conducting business in other countries can provide opportunities such as increased sales, operational efficiencies, exposure to new technologies, and consumer choices. At the same time, it poses challenges, such as the need to learn unique laws, customs, and ethical standards. Furthermore, it exposes companies to the risks of political and economic instabilities, volatile currencies, international trade relationships, and the threat of global terrorism.

2. **List five ways to improve communication in an international business relationship.**
   To improve international communication, learn as much as you can about the culture and customs of the people you are working with; keep an open mind and avoid stereotyping; anticipate misunderstandings and guard against them by clari-

   fying your intent; adapt your style to match the style of others; and learn how to show respect in other cultures.

3. **Identify five forms of international business activity.**
   Importing and exporting, licensing, franchising, strategic alliances and joint ventures, and foreign direct investment are five of the most common forms of international business activity. Each provides a company with varying degrees of control and entails different levels of risk and financial commitment.

4. **Discuss why nations trade.**
   Nations trade to obtain raw materials and goods that are unavailable to them or too costly to produce. International trade benefits nations by increasing a country's total output, offering lower prices and greater variety to its consumers, subjecting domestic oligopolies and monopolies to competition, and allowing companies to expand their markets and achieve production and distribution efficiencies.

5. **Explain why nations restrict international trade and list four forms of trade restrictions.**

   Nations restrict international trade to boost local economies, to shield domestic industries from head-to-head competition with overseas rivals, to save specific jobs, to give weak or new industries a chance to grow strong, and to protect a nation's security. The four most commonly used forms of trade restrictions are tariffs (taxes, surcharges, or duties levied against imported goods), quotas (limitations on the amount of a particular good that can be imported), embargoes (the banning of imports and exports of certain goods), and sanctions (politically motivated embargoes).

6. **Highlight three protectionist tactics nations use to give their domestic industries a competitive edge.**

   From time to time countries give their domestic producers a competitive edge by imposing restrictive import standards such as requiring special licenses or unusually high product standards, by subsidizing certain domestic producers so they can compete more favorably in the global marketplace, and by dumping or selling large quantities of a product at a lower price than it costs to produce the good or at a lower price than the good is sold for in its home market.

7. **Explain how trading blocs affect trade.**

   Trading blocs are regional groupings of countries within which trade barriers have been removed. These alliances ease trade among bloc members and strengthen barriers for nonmembers. Critics of trading blocs fear that as members become more protective of their regions, those not in the bloc could suffer. Proponents see them as a way to help smaller or younger nations compete with producers in more developed nations. The four most powerful trading blocs today are the Association of Southeast Asian Nations (ASEAN), the Mercosur, the North American Free Trade Agreement (NAFTA), and the European Union (EU).

8. **Discuss terrorism's impact on globalization.**

   Terrorism could prompt companies to withdraw from the global marketplace and focus more on doing business within their national borders. But the likelihood of moving in that direction is remote. Most multinational organizations have too much at stake to move backward; they see globalization as the key to their future. Global terrorism, however, does pose new challenges to world trade. Tighter security, border crossing delays, cargo restrictions, and higher transportation costs are having an impact on the free flow of goods in the global marketplace. These obstacles are forcing some companies to rethink their inventory and manufacturing strategies.

KEY TERMS

absolute advantage **(70)**

balance of payments **(70)**

balance of trade **(70)**

comparative advantage theory **(70)**

dumping **(72)**

embargo **(72)**

euro **(76)**

exchange rate **(76)**

exporting **(66)**

foreign direct investment (FDI) **(68)**

free trade **(72)**

importing **(66)**

joint venture **(68)**

licensing **(67)**

multinational corporations (MNCs) **(68)**

protectionism **(71)**

quotas **(71)**

strategic alliance **(67)**

tariffs **(71)**

trade deficit **(70)**

trade surplus **(70)**

trading blocs **(74)**

TEST YOUR KNOWLEDGE

Questions for Review

1. How can a company use a licensing agreement to enter world markets?

2. Why would a local businessperson need to learn about the global business environment?

3. What is the balance of trade, and how is it related to the balance of payments?

4. What is dumping, and how does the United States respond to this practice?

5. What is a floating exchange rate?

Questions for Analysis

6. Why would a company choose to work through intermediaries when selling products in a foreign country?

7. How do companies benefit from forming international joint ventures and strategic alliances?

8. What types of situations might cause the U.S. government to implement protectionist measures?

9. How do tariffs and quotas protect a country's own industries?

10. *Ethical Considerations:* Should the U.S. government more closely regulate the practice of giving trips and other incentives to foreign managers to win their business? Is this bribery?

Questions for Application

11. Suppose you own a small company that manufactures baseball equipment. You are aware that Russia is a large market, and you are considering exporting your products there. What steps should you take? Who might be able to give you assistance?

12. Because your Brazilian restaurant caters to Western business-people and tourists, much of the food you buy is imported from the United States. Lately, the value of the real (Brazil's currency) has been falling relative to the dollar. This change makes your food imports much more costly, and it negatively affects your profitability. You have three options: which one will you choose? (a) Raise menu prices across the board. (b) Accept only U.S. dollars from customers. (c) Try to purchase more of your food items locally. Please explain your selection.

13. *Integrated:* Review the theory of supply and demand discussed in Chapter 1. Using this theory, explain how a country's currency is valued and why governments sometimes adjust the values of their currency.

14. *Integrated:* You just received notice that a large shipment of manufacturing supplies you have been waiting for has been held up in customs for two weeks. A local business associate tells you that you are expected to give customs agents some "incentive money" to see that everything clears easily. How will you handle this situation? Evaluate the ethical merits of your decision by answering the questions outlined in Exhibit 2.3 on page 43.

PRACTICE YOUR KNOWLEDGE

Handling Difficult Situations on the Job: English Only—Defending a Tough Policy

When Frances Torres read the memo announcing that employees should speak only English on the job, she was outraged. Torres, a lens inspector for Signet Amoralite, a lens-manufacturing firm in southern California, is fluent in both English and Spanish but feels that the English-only rules constitute discrimination. Now Torres and a group of her co-workers have brought their complaints to you, a manager in human resources.

More than half of Signet Amoralite's 900 employees are Asian, Filipino, or Hispanic. The company policy states that "speaking in another language that associates cannot fully understand can lead to misunderstandings, is impolite, and can even be unsafe." While the policy carries no punishment, it is considered by some critics to violate federal discrimination laws.[50]

Your task: You know that you must defend the company's English-only policy to Torres and the others; you've been told by upper management that it will not be eliminated or altered. To help clarify your thinking and see things from the employees' perspective, imagine that you have been hired by a company in another country that uses a language different from your own. How would you feel if you were required to learn and use that language exclusively, even if some of your co-workers were able to speak and understand your native tongue? To defend Signet Amoralite's policy, what can you do or say or write that will help Torres and her co-workers accept it? Also, what do you think will be the best way to present this information?

Building Your Team Skills

In today's interdependent global economy, fluctuations in a country's currency can have a profound effect on the flow of products across borders. The U.S. steel industry, for example, has been feeling intense competition from an influx of Korean, Brazilian, and Russian steel imports. After the currencies of those countries plummeted in value, the price of steel products exported to the United States dropped as well, making U.S. steel much more expensive by comparison.

Fueled by low prices, steel flooded into the United States, hurting sales of U.S. steel. Over the course of several months, the volume of steel imports nearly doubled. Stung, U.S. steelmakers slashed production and laid off more than 10,000 U.S. workers. U.S. trade officials charge that the cheap imported steel is being dumped, and they are considering protectionist measures such as imposing quotas on steel imports.[51]

With your team, brainstorm a list of at least four additional ways the United States might handle this situation. Once you have your list, consider the probable effect of each option on these stakeholders:

- U.S. businesses that buy steel
- U.S. steel manufacturers
- U.S. businesses that export to Korea, Brazil, or Russia
- Employees of U.S. steel manufacturers

On the basis of your analysis and discussion, which option will your team recommend? Select a spokesperson to explain your selection and your team's reasoning to the other teams. Compare your recommendation with those of your classmates.

EXPAND YOUR KNOWLEDGE

Discovering Career Opportunities

If global business interests you, consider working for a U.S. government agency that supports or regulates international trade. For example, here are the duties performed by an international trade specialist at the International Trade Administration of the U.S. Department of Commerce: "The incumbent will assist senior specialists in coordination and support of government trade programs and events; perform research and analysis of trade data and information on specific topics or issues within a larger project or assignment; and disseminate trade information and materials on government products/services to U.S. businesses and associations. Incumbent will attend meetings and engage in other activities for developmental purposes. As a condition of employment, applicants must be available for reassignment and relocation within the United States."[52]

On the basis of this description, what education and skills (personal and professional) would you need to succeed as an international trade specialist? Why? How does this job description fit your qualifications and interests?

1. Given their duties, where would you expect international trade specialists to be situated or transferred? Would you be willing to move to another city or state for this type of position?

2. What sources would you contact to locate trade-related jobs with government agencies such as the International Trade Administration?

Developing Your Research Skills

Companies involved in international trade have to watch the foreign exchange rates of the countries in which they do business. Use your research skills to locate and analyze information about the value of the Japanese yen relative to the U.S. dollar. As you complete this exercise, make a note of the sources and search strategies you used.

1. How many Japanese yen does one U.S. dollar buy right now? Find yesterday's foreign exchange rate for the yen in the *Wall Street Journal* or on the Internet. (*Note:* One Internet source for foreign exchange rates is www.x-rates.com.)

2. Investigate the foreign exchange rate for the yen against the dollar over the past month. Is the dollar growing stronger (buying more yen) or growing weaker (buying fewer yen)?

3. If you were a U.S. exporter selling to Japan, how would a stronger dollar be likely to affect demand for your products? How would a weaker dollar be likely to affect demand?

Exploring the Best of the Web

URLs for all Internet exercises are provided at the website for this book, www.prenhall.com/bovee. *When you log on to the text website, select Chapter 3, select "Student Resources," then click on the name of the featured website to complete these exercises.*

Explore these chapter-related websites, review their content, and answer the following questions for each website you visit:

1. What is the purpose of this website?

2. What kinds of information does this website contain? Please be specific.

3. How is the information provided at this website useful for businesspeople? Consumers?

4. How did you expand your knowledge of conducting business in the global environment by reviewing the material at this website? What new things did you learn about this topic?

Navigating Global Business Differences

In today's global marketplace, knowing as much as possible about your international customers' business practices and customs could give you a strategic advantage. To help you successfully conduct business around the globe, navigate the resources at USA Trade.gov. Begin with the Trade Information Center and follow the links to Country Information and Export Programs Guide. Prepared by U.S. embassy staff, these guides contain helpful information on foreign marketing practices, trade regulations, investment climate, and business travel for a number of countries. And if your international plans include a business trip, begin your journey here. You'll be glad you did. www.usatrade.gov

Going Global

Have you ever thought about getting into the world of exporting? Where would you go for information and help? Many small and large companies have gotten valuable export assistance from online material such as the *Basic Guide to Exporting*. This joint publication by the U.S. Department of Commerce and Unz & Company has a wealth of information about export procedures; foreign markets, industries, companies, and products; export financing; unfair trade practices; trade statistics; and more. www.unzco.com/basicguide/index.html

Banking on the World Bank

The World Bank plays an important role in today's fast-changing, closely meshed global economy. Do you know what this organization of five closely associated institutions does? Do you know who runs the bank, where the bank gets its money, and where the money goes? Learn how this organization's programs and financial assistance help poorer nations as well as affluent ones. Log on to the World Bank website and find out why global development is everyone's challenge. www.worldbank.org

Learning Interactively

Companion Website

Visit the companion website at www.prenhall.com/bovee. For Chapter 3, take advantage of the interactive "Study Guide" to test your chapter knowledge. Get instant feedback on whether you need additional studying. Read the "Current Events" articles to get the latest on chapter topics, and complete the exercises as specified by your instructor. Expand your learning with a visit to the "Research Area." There you will find a wealth of information you can use to complete your course assignments.

A CASE FOR CRITICAL THINKING

Doing Everybody's Wash—Whirlpool's Global Lesson

Everybody is talking about going global these days, but most people don't understand what that means. David Whitwam, chairman and CEO of Whirlpool, does. When he first began eyeing the global marketplace, this Michigan-based appliance maker was concentrating only on the U.S. market, producing and marketing washers, refrigerators, and other household appliances under the Whirlpool, KitchenAid, Roper, and Kenmore brand names.

The Right Way to Go Global

Determined to convert Whirlpool from a U.S. company to a major global player, Whitwam purchased N. V. Philips's floundering European appliance business in 1989. The CEO's first challenge was to integrate and coordinate the many European operations with the U.S. operation. Some companies accomplish this task by imposing the parent's systems on the acquired companies, but Whitwam started down a more ambitious path. He created cross-cultural teams with members from the European and North American operations, and together they designed a program to ensure quality and productivity throughout Whirlpool's worldwide operation. In the eyes of other corporate leaders, Whirlpool was doing everything right. The company was even featured in a 1994 *Harvard Business Review* article titled "The Right Way to Go Global."

Spinning Out of Control

Whitwam soon discovered, however, that developing global strategies was easier than executing them. Whirlpool had not counted on the difficulty in marketing appliances—a largely homogeneous process in the United States—to the fragmented cultures of Europe, Asia, and Latin America. For instance, clothes washers sold in northern European countries such as Denmark must spin-dry clothes much better than washers in southern Italy, where consumers often line-dry clothes in warmer weather. And consumers in India and southern China prefer small refrigerators because they must fit in tight kitchens.

Despite these challenges, Whitwam was convinced that he could remake Whirlpool into a truly global company. But Whirlpool's timing couldn't have been worse. Just as the company was planting its feet in international markets, economic turmoil hit Asia and Europe. Wildly fluctuating foreign exchange rates wreaked havoc in Asia, where Whirlpool had participated in several joint ventures. Fortunately, less than 5 percent of Whirlpool's sales came from Asia, so the company was not seriously hurt. Still, ongoing global economic woes contributed to Whirlpool's multimillion dollar losses overseas.

Rearranging the Global Load

The global economic crisis forced Whitwam to fine-tune his expansion plans. Whirlpool dropped one joint venture in China (costing the company $350 million) and rearranged others as intense competition and weak economic conditions drove appliance prices down and sapped profits. "The thing we misjudged was how rapidly Chinese manufacturers could improve their quality," notes Whitwam.

In Brazil, where Whirlpool had long been profitable, a currency crisis coupled with inflation worries slowed appliance sales to a trickle. Still, Whitwam remained committed to the market. Anticipating future growth opportunities in this emerging market, Whirlpool invested hundreds of millions of dollars to modernize operations, cut costs, and solidify its position as the country's market leader in refrigerators, room air conditioners, and washers.

David Whitwam's global strategy, however, was not widely copied by rivals. As Whirlpool continued to expand in Europe, Latin America, and Asia, the company's major competitor, Maytag, was selling its European and Australian businesses to refocus on the lucrative North American market. Nevertheless, Whitwam was willing to ride out the storm, even as global economic troubles dragged on.

Whitwam expedited Whirlpool's entry into foreign markets by using licensing arrangements and by forming strategic alliances with others. Whirlpool also developed standardized products, which it could modify to meet specific market needs. For instance, feature-rich German appliances were combined with efficient, low-cost Italian technologies to produce a "world washer." Then Whirlpool modified the machines for local preferences. Front-loading washing machines were scaled down for European homes, as were refrigerators for India. Despite their widely different exteriors and sizes, the appliances had plenty of common "innards."

Ultimate Reward

In less than a decade, Whitwam transformed Whirlpool from essentially a U.S. company into the world's leading manufacturer of major home appliances. With 11 major brands sold in 170 countries, international sales now account for about 45 percent of the company's $10 billion annual revenue. Moreover, the outlook for growth in the global appliance industry looks promising. Still Whitwam understands that doing business in the global marketplace is fraught with risk; conditions can change at the drop of a baht, ruble, or dollar.

Critical Thinking Questions

1. What did Whirlpool find to be the advantages and disadvantages of doing business around the world?
2. How did global expansion affect Whirlpool's products?
3. Should Whirlpool be concerned about a currency devaluation in a country where it sells few appliances?
4. Find out how Whirlpool is faring with its global strategy. Go to Chapter 3 of this book's website at www.prenhall.com/ bovee, and click on the Whirlpool hotlink to read more about Whirlpool's financial performance, international operations, and plans for expansion. How are Whirlpool's sales doing outside the United States? Where is the company strongest? Where is it struggling? What changes, if any, is the company making to its global strategy?

VIDEO CASE

Giving Global Law and Order a Helping Hand: Printrak

Learning Objectives

The purpose of this video is to help you:

1. Understand how and why a company adapts to the needs of foreign customers.
2. Identify the levels of international involvement that are available to companies.
3. Discuss the differences that can affect a company's international operations.

Synopsis

Scotland Yard and the Canadian Mounties are only two of the many organizations around the world that use security technology from Printrak www.printrakinternational.com, a Motorola company. Starting with a computerized fingerprint management system, Printrak has added a number of security and criminal information products as it expanded from its California headquarters to serve customers around the globe. General manager Darren Reilly and his management team study each country's legal, political, economic, and cultural differences, as well as analyzing local demand and customer needs. Rather than invest in local plants and equipment, Printrak works through local sales agents to ensure that its products are presented in a culturally savvy way for each market. Despite country by country differences in business customs and ethics, the decisions and actions of Printrak's employees are guided by Motorola's code of conduct.

Discussion Questions

1. *For analysis:* What are some of the barriers that affect Printrak's ability to do business in foreign markets?
2. *For analysis:* From Printrak's perspective, what are the advantages and disadvantages of hiring and training local sales agents to work with customers in each foreign market?
3. *For application:* In addition to establishing users committees, what else should Printrak do to track changing customer needs in other countries?
4. *For application:* How would you suggest that Printrak build on its relations with "beachhead customers" to expand in particular regions?
5. *For debate:* Printrak employees and managers must comply with Motorola's global ethics policy. Should local sales agents be allowed to take any actions they deem necessary to make sales in local markets, regardless of Motorola's policy? Support your chosen position.

Online Exploration

Browse Printrak's home page at www.printrakinternational.com, see where the company has customers, and read some of the news releases about international operations. Also look at the resource links that Printrak has posted for customers and site visitors. Why would Printrak publicize its customer list in this way? Why would it include a glossary of security-related terms and acronyms on the website? Finally, do you think the company should translate some or all of its website to accommodate foreign customers? Explain your response.

CHAPTER 4

Fundamentals of Information Management, the Internet, and E-Commerce

LEARNING OBJECTIVES

After studying this chapter, you will be able to

1. Discuss the responsibilities of the chief information officer

2. Differentiate between operations information systems and management support systems

3. Discuss the role of hardware, software, and networks in information systems

4. Discuss how businesses are using the Internet

5. Name three broad categories of e-commerce and explain what each category involves

6. Explain how to conduct an effective database search

7. Identify and discuss five challenges businesses are facing in the Information Age

UPS is widely recognized for its brown trucks that move more than 13 million packages a day. The company is guided by one of the most sophisticated information systems on the planet.

INSIDE BUSINESS TODAY

Technology Delivers New Business Opportunities for UPS

On the outside, United Parcel Service (UPS) may look like a delivery company that moves packages from point A to point B. But on the inside, UPS is really an information technology company. That may seem like an odd way to describe a company with nearly 150,000 vehicles and several hundred planes, but information technology is one of UPS's most important strategic assets. UPS uses technology to improve its own business and to help other companies with everything from supply chain management to product repair.

Technology has always played a key role at UPS, even back in 1907, when leading-edge technology meant a telegraph machine and a sturdy bicycle. Nineteen-year-old founder Jim Casey and his crew started out delivering handwritten messages and telegrams around Seattle. As another new technology—the telephone—caught on and took business away from the telegraph, Casey shifted the company from messages to packages, offering home delivery services for local retail stores. Sure enough, the automobile caught on next and people started taking their purchases home themselves, so Casey shifted again, this time to the general package-delivery model that is still the core of the company's business.

For a long time, UPS saw investments in new technology as little more than a way to make sure the birthday sweater from Grandma arrived on time. Then, in the early 1990s, it caught on to the real power of information, and UPS began using technology to explore the millions of transactions it made every day to look for ways to make its truck routes more efficient, optimize truck sizes, and improve delivery time. Company drivers ditched their clipboards and paper in favor of wireless handheld

computers, known as the Delivery Information Acquisition Device (DIAD). These mobile devices capture electronic signatures and delivery details and feed this information into the company's data centers in New Jersey and Georgia, which house some 15 mainframes and 140 terabytes of company and customer data. Initially, this system allowed UPS managers to pinpoint the whereabouts of a package and to deliver that information to customers over the telephone. But this was just the first step in a bigger plan.

In 1995 UPS began offering package tracking on its website. "We were so efficient at getting packages through on time and on schedule, we could never really understand why people wanted tracking or other information about packages," says UPS vice chairman Mike Eskey. But once UPS started turning that information over to customers, it learned that access to data was more than a convenience; it was a phenomenon. Today the UPS website gets more than 80 million visits a day.

Finally grasping how important information had become to its own operations, UPS realized it could gain a competitive edge by giving other corporations access to similar kinds of information about their own companies. The company formed a subsidiary, UPS Logistics, to sell logistics and information management and warehousing expertise to other companies. Today Ford Motor Company lets UPS Logistics manage the transportation and distribution of 4.5 million vehicles a year—from 21 manufacturing sites, through five railroad yards, to 55 destination railroads, to 6,000 dealers in North America. Ford now saves $125 million a year through faster deliveries while increasing dealer and customer satisfaction. Samsung and Nike are among the other well-known companies who've turned to UPS for warehousing and distribution expertise. And UPS offers to help when products go in reverse, too, managing returns and even product repairs for the likes of Toshiba and Lexmark.

As UPS approaches its one hundredth birthday with 370,000 employees and some $30 billion in revenue, technology is driving the company in a new direction. Those humble brown trucks rumbling through your neighborhood don't look much fancier than Jim Casey's original bicycle, but they're now guided by one of the most sophisticated information systems on the planet.[1]

How Businesses Manage Information

As UPS demonstrates, all businesses rely on the fast distribution of information for just about everything they do. Organizations need quality information to make good decisions and to help managers and employees accomplish their goals. They need information to increase organizational efficiencies, stay ahead of competitors, find new customers, keep existing customers, develop new products, and so on. Fortunately, we live in the Information Age, where information is easily accessible and readily available. But having too much information can be overwhelming and at times counterproductive. As the amount of information continues to increase, employees must learn how to discriminate between useful and useless information and between what is truly important and what is routine.

According to Bill Gates, "The most meaningful way to differentiate your company from your competition is to do an outstanding job with information."[2] But what exactly does this job involve? To begin with, information is most useful to those people who can act on it. A computer technician, for example, doesn't need to know the costs of office supplies, and the advertising manager doesn't need to know the repair schedules for the company's fleet of delivery equipment. Therefore, doing a good job with information means making sure that the *right information* reaches the *right people* at the *right time*, and in the *right form*.[3] Moreover, for information to be useful, it must be accurate, timely, complete, relevant, and concise. The closer information comes to meeting these five criteria, the more it will facilitate the company's decision-making process.

Technology, of course, plays a key role in managing a company's information. Computers, computer networks, and telecommunication devices enable organizations to track, store, retrieve, process, and share information that can be leveraged to achieve competitive advantages. But in addition to using technology to gather and manage information, companies must develop strategies and systems for analyzing and presenting information, so managers and employees can use it in their daily decision making.

This chapter explains the basics of information systems, technology, the Internet, and e-commerce. It discusses how companies use information systems and Internet technology to run their operations, generate revenues, cut costs, enhance communication, and find information. And it highlights the challenges businesses are facing as they increasingly rely on technology to achieve new goals. We begin the chapter by discussing some technology basics.

How Companies Use Information Systems

data
Recorded facts and statistics; data need to be converted to information before they can help people solve business problems

Each day companies collect, generate, and store vast quantities of **data** (recorded facts and statistics) that are relevant to a particular decision or problem. For example, the accounting department may have price and sales data for hundreds of products, the marketing department may have customer data, the purchasing department may have inventory data, and so on (see Exhibit 4.1). However, data do not become information until they are used to solve a problem, answer a question, or make a decision.

EXHIBIT 4.1 Information Flow in a Typical Manufacturing Company
Many kinds of manipulations and transfers of information support daily operations and decision making in a manufacturing company.

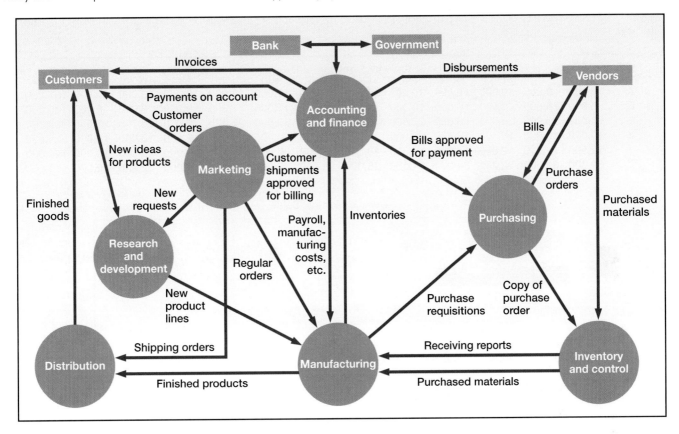

Data are stored in **databases**, the equivalent of a centralized electronic filing cabinet that stores collections of data that can be used by people throughout an organization. When a manager wants to know the average monthly sales of say products X, Y, and Z, he or she must cross-reference the data. Through a process known as **data warehousing**, data are moved from separate databases into a well-organized central database, where they are sorted, summarized, and stored. Managers from the various functional areas can then make complex *queries*, or ask questions of the central database to review and analyze the data, solve problems, answer questions, or make decisions (see Exhibit 4.2). Such multidepartmental queries are not possible when data are stored in separate databases throughout the organization.

When a query is made, the computer software sifts through huge amounts of data, identifying what is valuable to the specific query and what is not. This process, known as **data mining**, is the task of using sophisticated technology to identify useful trends. Effective data mining helps turn mountains of data into useful information.

Most large organizations employ a top-level manager, called a **chief information officer (CIO)**, to develop and oversee a company's data collection, storage, and information systems. The CIO's responsibilities include finding out who in the organization needs what types of information, how these individuals will use this information, how often they will need it, and how they will share it with others. Once the company's information needs have been assessed, the CIO determines the types of data to track and develops systems to collect, track, store, process, retrieve, and distribute the data. In addition, the CIO oversees the purchase and installation of computer hardware and software and other technologies to facilitate the collection and distribution of information. In smaller companies, these tasks may be handled by the company accounting manager, controller, or data processing manager.

databases
Centralized, organized collections of data

data warehousing
Building an organized central database out of files and databases gathered from various functional areas, such as marketing, operations, and accounting

data mining
Sifting through huge amounts of data to identify what is valuable to a specific question or problem

 **LEARNING OBJECTIVE**

Discuss the responsibilities of the chief information officer

chief information officer (CIO)
Top corporate executive with responsibility for managing information and information systems

EXHIBIT 4.2   Data Versus Information
The table at the top represents sales data for a small company's six products. In this form, the data are just statistics that answer no particular question and solve no particular problem. Therefore, they are not considered information. When a manager queries the database to identify the average monthly sales for each product, he or she is asking for specific information. The sales data are used to generate the graph that illustrates the requested information.

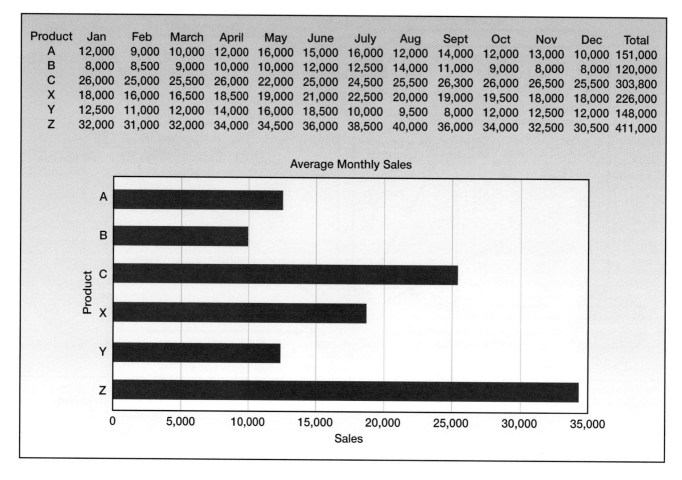

Product	Jan	Feb	March	April	May	June	July	Aug	Sept	Oct	Nov	Dec	Total
A	12,000	9,000	10,000	12,000	16,000	15,000	16,000	12,000	14,000	12,000	13,000	10,000	151,000
B	8,000	8,500	9,000	10,000	10,000	12,000	12,500	14,000	11,000	9,000	8,000	8,000	120,000
C	26,000	25,000	25,500	26,000	22,000	25,000	24,500	25,500	26,300	26,000	26,500	25,500	303,800
X	18,000	16,000	16,500	18,500	19,000	21,000	22,500	20,000	19,000	19,500	18,000	18,000	226,000
Y	12,500	11,000	12,000	14,000	16,000	18,500	10,000	9,500	8,000	12,000	12,500	12,000	148,000
Z	32,000	31,000	32,000	34,000	34,500	36,000	38,500	40,000	36,000	34,000	32,500	30,500	411,000

2 LEARNING OBJECTIVE

Differentiate between operations information systems and management support systems

transaction processing system (TPS)
Computerized information system that processes the daily flow of customer, supplier, and employee transactions, including inventory, sales, and payroll records

process control systems
Computer system that uses special sensing devices to monitor conditions in a physical process and makes necessary adjustments to the process

The types of information systems used by a company generally fall into two major categories: operations information systems and management support systems. As Exhibit 4.3 illustrates, each category typically corresponds to business operations at specific levels of the organization.

Operations Information Systems   Operations information systems include transaction processing systems, process and production control systems, and office automation systems. These systems typically support daily operations and decision making for lower-level managers and supervisors.

Transaction Processing Systems   Much of the daily flow of data into and out of the typical business organization is handled by a **transaction processing system (TPS)**, which captures and organizes raw data and converts these data into information. Common transaction processing systems take care of customer orders, billing, employee payroll, inventory changes, and other essential transactions. For example, UPS uses a TPS to accept charges and to bill customers. Another example is the TPS system used by airlines to assign you a seat on your flight.

Process and Production Control Systems   Operations information systems are also used to make routine decisions that control operational processes. **Process control systems** monitor conditions such as temperature or pressure change in physical processes.

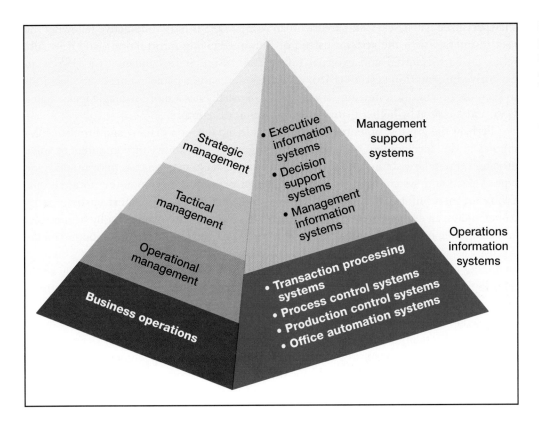

EXHIBIT 4.3
Information Systems and Organizational Levels
Managers and employees at the various levels of an organization rely on different types of information systems to help them accomplish their goals.

These systems use special sensing devices that take measurements, enabling a computer to make any necessary adjustments to the process.

Production control systems are used to manage the production of goods and services by controlling production lines, robots, and other machinery and equipment. In Chapter 9 we will discuss how computer-aided manufacturing can increase efficiency and improve quality by automating production processes. In some cases, manufacturing software is linked with design software to automate the entire design-and-production cycle. For instance, an engineer designing a new component for a car engine can electronically transfer the design to the production department, which will then control a milling machine that automatically carves the part from a block of steel.

Office Automation Systems   **Office automation systems (OAS)** include any type of operations information system that helps you execute typical office tasks. Whether the job is producing a report or calculating next year's budget, an OAS allows you to complete the task more efficiently by converting the process into an electronic format. Office automation systems range from a single personal computer with word-processing software to networks of computers that allow people to send electronic mail and share work among computers.

Management Support Systems   Management support systems are designed to help managers make decisions. A variety of such systems are available that allow users to analyze data, identify business trends, and make forecasts. A **management information system (MIS)** provides managers with information and support for making routine decisions. An MIS takes data from a database and summarizes or restates the data into useful information such as monthly sales figures, daily inventory levels, product manufacturing schedules, employee earnings, and so on. This information is generally organized in a report or graphical format, making it easier for managers to read and interpret.

Whereas a management information system provides structured, routine information for managerial decision making, a **decision support system (DSS)** assists managers in solving highly unstructured and nonroutine problems through the use of decision models

production control systems
Computer systems that manage production by controlling production lines, robots, and other machinery and equipment

office automation systems (OAS)
Computer systems that assist with the tasks that people in a typical business office face regularly, such as drawing graphs or processing documents

management information system (MIS)
Computer system that supplies information to assist in managerial decision making

decision support system (DSS)
Information system that uses decision models, specialized databases, and artificial intelligence to assist managers in solving highly unstructured and nonroutine problems

executive information system (EIS)
Similar to decision support system but customized to strategic needs of executives

artificial intelligence
Ability of computers to reason, to learn, and to simulate human sensory perceptions

expert system
Computer system that simulates the thought processes of a human expert who is adept at solving particular problems

speech-recognition system
Computer system that recognizes human speech, enabling users to enter data and give commands vocally

and specialized databases. Compared with an MIS, a DSS is more interactive (allowing the user to interact with the system instead of simply receiving information), and it usually relies on both internal and external information. Similar in concept to a DSS is an **executive information system (EIS)**, which helps executives make the necessary decisions to keep the organization moving forward. An EIS usually has a more strategic focus than a DSS, and it is used by higher management to plan for the future.

Perhaps the greatest potential for computers to aid decision making and problem solving lies in the development of **artificial intelligence**—the ability of computers to solve problems through reasoning and learning and to simulate human sensory perceptions. One type of computer system that can simulate human reasoning by responding to questions, asking for more information, and making recommendations is the **expert system**. As its name implies, an expert system essentially takes the place of a human expert by helping less knowledgeable individuals make critical decisions. For instance, the troubleshooting methods used by an experienced auto mechanic could be programmed into an expert system. A beginning mechanic could describe a sick engine's symptoms to the system, which would then apply the expert mechanic's facts and rules to suggest which troubleshooting methods might reveal the cause of the problem.

Several software companies have taken expert systems a step further by giving them the ability to suggest innovative solutions for problem solving. Drawing on their preprogrammed knowledge of inventive principles, physics, chemistry, and geometry, such systems often come up with solutions to problems that lead to new product inventions. One example of such an innovation is a flash for pocket cameras that eliminates "red eye."

A second advance in artificial intelligence to make its way into business is the **speech-recognition system**. Using computer software, a generic vocabulary database, and a microphone, speech-recognition systems enable the user to interact with the computer verbally. Artificial intelligence techniques enable the computer to learn the user's speech patterns and update its vocabulary database continually. In this way, the system evolves, becoming more intelligent, versatile, and easy to use. Businesses are increasingly using speech-recognition systems to replace touch-tone activated menu systems. For example, UPS uses a speech-recognition system to respond to customers' telephone inquiries on the whereabouts of their packages. Similarly, airlines use speech-recognition systems to respond to telephone inquiries regarding the status of flight departures and arrivals.

The Role of Hardware, Software, and Networks in Information Management

Now that you have an idea of how businesses manage information, it's time to take a closer look at the role hardware, software, and networks play in the information management process.

Hardware and Software Hardware represents the tangible equipment used in a computer system, such as disk drives, keyboards, modems, printers, scanners, fax machines, pagers, and personal digital assistants (PDAs). All-in-one devices address your multiple communication needs by combining the separate functions of a printer, fax, scanner, and phone into one machine.

Software encompasses the programmed instructions, or applications, that direct the activity of the hardware. Software applications in today's business world are almost limitless. Companies use them to set goals, hire employees, order supplies, manage inventory, sell products, store data, communicate with employees, and perform countless other tasks. The term *application* refers both to

Personal digital assistants (PDAs) have become an indispensable technological tool for most businesspeople. Some PDAs have small keyboards for inputting data; others require special pens. Most share data with desktops so users can keep their desktop data and PDA data in sync.

an actual task, such as preparing reports and memos, and to the *software* that is used to complete the task.

Systems software is perhaps the most important software category because it includes **operating systems**, which control such fundamental actions as storing data on disk drives and displaying text or graphics on monitors. Commonly used operating systems include MS-DOS, Windows (which increases the usability of MS-DOS by incorporating a graphical user interface), UNIX, IBM's OS/2, and Apple's Macintosh System. When you first turn on a computer, the operating system begins to direct the actions that enable the various computer hardware devices and software applications to interact in ways that are useful to you. A word-processing program, for instance, can't read the hard disk or write text to the display by itself; it relies on the operating system to direct the computer's hardware and to manage the flow of data into, around, and out of the system.

Application software encompasses programs that perform specific user functions, such as word processing, database management, desktop publishing, and so on. The array of software packages is vast, as suggested by Exhibit 4.4. Many of these individual programs are available in *suites*—bundled together as integrated software programs such as Microsoft Office or Claris Works, making it easier to incorporate the work from one program into another.

Networks   A **network** is a collection of hardware, software, and communications media that are linked so they can share data and expensive hardware. This linking of computers and communication devices allows businesspeople to easily stay in touch with their offices, their computers, their associates, and their families while they travel the world. It is also much easier for workers in remote locations to share work, ideas, and resources. What makes all of this possible are complex networks of linked computers and communication devices.

Networks are classified by the size of their geographic area. In a **wide area network (WAN)**, computers at different geographic locations, such as the branches of a nationwide bank, are linked through one of several transmission media. In contrast, a **local area network (LAN)**, as its name implies, meets data communications needs within a small area, such as an office or a university campus. Any computer can be part of a network, provided it has the right hardware, software, and transmission media.

Transmission Media   One of the most common ways to communicate over a network is by using standard telephone lines and a **modem** (modulator–demodulator), which can be either a stand-alone unit or a circuit board that is plugged into the computer. The transmitting computer's modem converts digital computer signals to analog signals so that they can be transmitted over telephone lines. The receiving computer's modem converts the signals from analog back to digital. Although slow by comparison with other technologies, conventional dial-up modems are used by roughly 88 percent of all Americans to access the Internet.[4] The other 12 percent use cable lines and cable modems, digital subscriber lines (DSL), or other high-speed technologies, such as fiber optic cable, that have an increased data transmission capacity and speed, also known as **bandwidth**.

Wireless Communication   Wireless communication offers an alternative to standard telephone, coaxial, and fiber optic lines. Just as humans can now communicate without wires via cellular telephones, pagers, and other wireless communication devices, so computers can send and receive data without being "hardwired" to a network. This feat is accomplished by transmitting data as microwave signals or radio signals to the receiving computer via stations located on mountains, towers, or tall buildings or by satellites orbiting the earth. Wireless transceivers are small devices attached to the computer that transmit and receive data. Wi-Fi (short for Wireless Fidelity) works best when the wireless device used to transmit and receive data (such as a laptop) is no more than 1,500 feet from a cable Internet or

3 LEARNING OBJECTIVE

Discuss the role of hardware, software, and networks in information systems

hardware
Physical components of a computer system, including integrated circuits, keyboards, and disk drives

software
Programmed instructions that drive the activity of computer hardware

operating systems
Class of software that controls the computer's hardware components

application software
Programs that perform specific functions for users, such as word processing or spreadsheet analysis

network
Collection of computers, communications software, and transmission media (such as telephone lines) that allows computers to communicate

wide area network (WAN)
Computer network that encompasses a large geographic area

local area network (LAN)
Computer network that encompasses a small area, such as an office or a university campus

modem
Hardware device that allows a computer to communicate over a regular telephone line

bandwidth
Maximum capacity of a data transmission medium

EXHIBIT 4.4   Software Application Programs
Software applications have been developed to satisfy almost every business need. Here's a quick review of their features.

Software Application Programs

Word processing: Word-processing programs enable users to type, store, edit, format, and print documents for almost any purpose. Text and graphics can be added, deleted, and moved without retyping the entire document. Special word-processing features include spelling checkers, grammar checkers, automatic text entry, mail merge (a feature that allows you to insert names into a generic form letter, giving the appearance that the letter is personalized), and automatic page numbering. Repetitive keystrokes or tasks can be recorded in a macro, a customized program you create to handle the typing or task automatically.

Desktop publishing (DTP): Desktop publishing software goes a step beyond typical word processors by allowing designers to lay out printer-ready pages that incorporate artwork, photos, and a large variety of typographic elements. Together with scanners and other specialized input devices, publishing programs let businesspeople create sophisticated documents on their computers in a fraction of the time it once took. Flyers, brochures, user manuals, annual reports, and newsletters are just a few of the documents that can be produced in camera-ready formats that go directly to the print shop.

Spreadsheets: A spreadsheet is a program designed to let users organize and manipulate data in a row–column matrix. The intersection of each row-and-column pair is called a cell, and every cell can contain a number, a mathematical formula, or text used as a label. Among the spreadsheet's biggest strengths is the ability to quickly update masses of calculations when conditions change—it will automatically update a record if one of the records to which it is linked is changed. Businesspeople use spreadsheets to solve a wide variety of problems, ranging from statistical analysis to simulation models used in decision-support systems.

Databases: Database management software allows users to create, store, maintain, rearrange, and retrieve contents of databases. Almost anywhere you find a sizable amount of data in electronic format, you'll find a database management program at work. Such programs help users produce useful information by allowing them to look at data from various perspectives.

Graphics and presentation: Graphic programs allow users to create and modify charts, graphs, tables, and diagrams. Together with specialized output devices such as plotters and color printers, business-graphics software can produce overhead transparencies, 35-mm slides, posters, and signs. The graphic images created with these software packages can be imported in publishing and word-processing programs for incorporation into documents and presentations. Popular presentation software programs such as PowerPoint allow users to create electronic slides with clip art, video clips, sound clips, and animation.

Personal information managers (PIMs): Also known as contact managers, these database programs let users track communication with their business contacts, organize e-mail, maintain a work calendar and appointment schedules, store contact information, and much more.

Integrated programs: Also known as suites, these programs offer multiple applications in one package that allows you to easily share information among the individual applications. Common software suites such as Microsoft Office and Lotus SmartSuite include word-processing, database management, spreadsheet, graphics, presentation, and communication applications.

other high-speed connection. The mobility offered by this configuration is ideal for many applications.

At Wal-Mart Stores, for example, customers no longer pace the aisles while an employee checks whether an item missing from the shelf is available. With a few keystrokes on a wireless hand-held computer, employees can find out on the spot whether merchandise is in the stockroom or at a nearby store. Similarly, hand-held wireless computers do double duty as roving employees ring up items in a shopper's cart and print out a claim check that can be processed by the cashier.[5] Moreover, as this chapter's opening vignette shows, wireless technology and the Internet are changing the way UPS works.

Still, not everyone is happy about Wi-Fi's potential. Cellular carriers have spent billions of dollars over the past few years upgrading their wireless networks to accommodate higher data speeds so that consumers can send e-mail, browse the web, and make use of other applications from their phones and other hand-held devices. But Wi-Fi, which allows laptop users with Wi-Fi connections to piggyback on a nearby high-speed Internet connection, is far faster than cellular carriers' latest-generation offerings.[6]

How Businesses Are Using the Internet

The world's largest computer network is the **Internet**. Started in 1969 by the U.S. Department of Defense, the Internet is a voluntary, cooperative undertaking; no one individual, organization, or government owns it. The Internet is accessible to individuals, companies, colleges, government agencies, and other institutions in countries all over the world. It links thousands of smaller computer networks and millions of individual computer users in homes, businesses, government offices, and schools worldwide. Exhibit 4.5 highlights some key Internet terms you should know. You can learn more about Internet fundamentals by visiting the whatis website at http://whatis.techtarget.com.

The Internet is revolutionizing all facets of business life. In the space of just a few years, it has penetrated virtually every aspect of business and the economy. Look at JetBlue, for example. Born smack in the middle of the Internet age, JetBlue has abandoned the long-time practice of forcing pilots to tote several heavy flight manuals onboard their aircraft. Instead, JetBlue uses the web to transmit the manual updates and technical notices to pilots wherever they are in the United States. Pilots are able to receive basic information about their upcoming flights or other critical data, such as how to maneuver specific equipment or operate parts of the plane in emergency situations. In the future, the company hopes to link aircraft-parts manufacturers and fuel suppliers to JetBlue's internal systems to make business transactions such as buying jet fuel easier and more efficient.[7]

As the JetBlue example shows, the Internet is becoming a lifeline for many companies, who use it to generate new revenues, cut costs, enhance communication, and find information. It has changed the way customers, suppliers, and companies interact, creating huge opportunities as well as unforeseen competitive threats. And it has changed the way companies work internally—collapsing boundaries and redefining relationships among various functions, departments, and divisions.

Generating New Revenue

As Chapter 14 discusses in detail, companies are using their websites and e-mail to reach new markets and customers, promote their products and services, find new business partners, and provide customers with product information, product support, and customer service. UPS

An employee at the Electronic Boutique in Schaumburg, Ill., scans a shopper's selections, charges his card, and prints a receipt using a portable check-out station.

4 LEARNING OBJECTIVE

Discuss how businesses are using the Internet

Internet
A worldwide collection of interconnected networks that enables users to share information electronically and provides digital access to a wide variety of services

EXHIBIT 4.5 Key Internet Terms You Should Know
Many people confuse these key terms when discussing Internet applications.

Bookmark	A browser feature that places selected URLs in a file for quick access, allowing you to automatically return to the website by clicking on the site's name
Browser	Software, such as Netscape Navigator or Microsoft's Internet Explorer, that enables a computer to search for, display, and download the multimedia information that appears on the World Wide Web
Digital subscriber line (DSL)	High-speed phone line that carries both voice and data
Domain name	The portion of an Internet address that identifies the host and indicates the type of organization it is. The abbreviation following the period is the top-level domain (TLD). The original seven TLDs identified businesses (com), educational institutions (edu), government agencies (gov), international sources (int), the military (mil), network resources (net), and nonprofit organizations (org). To keep up with demand, additional TLDs (such as pro, biz, info, coop, museum, and name) are being introduced.
Download	Transmitting a file from one computer system to another, on the Internet, bringing data from the Internet into your computer
File transfer protocol (FTP)	A software protocol that lets you copy or move files from a remote computer—called an FTP site—to your computer over the Internet; it is the Internet facility for downloading and uploading files
Homepage	The primary website for an organization or individual; the first hypertext document displayed on a website
Hyperlink	A highlighted word or image on a webpage or document that automatically allows people to move to another webpage or document when clicked on with a mouse
Hypertext markup language (HTML)	The software language used to create, present, and link pages on the World Wide Web
Hypertext transfer protocol (HTTP)	A communications protocol that allows people to navigate among documents or pages linked by hypertext and to download pages from the World Wide Web
Internet service provider (ISP)	A company that provides access to the Internet, usually for a monthly fee, via telephone lines or cable; ISPs can be local companies or specialists such as America Online
Telnet	A way to access someone else's computer (the host computer) and to use it as if it were right at your desk
Uniform resource locator (URL)	Web address that gives the exact location of an Internet resource
Upload	To send a file from your computer to a server or host system
Webpages	Related files containing multimedia data that are made available on a website
Website	A related collection of files on the World Wide Web
World Wide Web (WWW or web)	A hypertext-based system for finding and accessing Internet resources such as text, graphics, sound, and other multimedia resources

customers, for instance, use the company's website to arrange for package pickups and to track a package's whereabouts. Dell customers use the Internet to obtain product information, place an order for a new computer system, and obtain product and technical support. Lands' End customers use the Internet to get helpful product information and wardrobe ideas. They can even chat with a live company representative online. And Starbucks's customers log on to the Starbucks's Express website to preorder their beverage and pastry selections. Then they pick up their orders at a local Starbucks outlet without waiting in line.[8] As you can imagine, the uses for the Internet in business are endless.

Consider Eli Lilly and Company. Facing a major loss of revenue when its patent for Prozac expired in 2001, Eli Lilly launched InnoCentive LLC, a website designed to attract a virtual community of scientists. It takes 12 to 15 years and a sizable budget (about $800 million) to bring a major drug to market. InnoCentive cuts the cost and time involved in drug discovery by using outside scientists to help Eli Lilly and other chemistry-driven companies unravel problems. Here's how it works: Drug companies, called "seekers," go to the website and put up a "Wanted" poster that describes the problem they are trying to nail. Bounty-hunter scientists, called "solvers," sign a confidentiality agreement and then go to

Keeping Pace with Technology and Electronic Commerce

Create a Winning Website

These days anyone can learn to design and construct webpages. All you need is the right web-authoring software and a reasonably good computer to create pages with text, photos, and animated graphics. But if you want to create a winning website, here are a few suggestions to consider:

- *Present a professional corporate image.* Be sure to provide a corporate profile that tells people a little bit about your company. Include news releases or articles about your business so that customers can see how well known or dynamic you are in the industry. Make sure your material is accurate, interesting, and related to your products. Identify the key benefits of your product (include product details on a second page). Check out other websites for inspiration—especially your competitors' sites—and decide what you like or dislike about their appearance. Think of ways to distinguish your site.

- *Don't forget the basics.* Always give visitors a person to call and a place to send for information. Be sure to list your postal and e-mail addresses and phone and fax numbers. And remember, because the Internet is international, list the nation where your company or its dealers are located.

- *Make your website easy to use.* Web surfers have a short attention span, so keep large graphics (which take forever to load) to a minimum. If you must include any large, embedded graphics or photos, provide an option for users to select a text-only interface, or provide small images of photos (called thumbnails) for users to click on if they want to view larger, more detailed versions.

Always provide hyperlinks at the bottom of each page to allow users to move backward and forward through a multipage site.

- *Anticipate your customers' needs.* Plan ahead. By including answers to frequently asked questions, chances are you'll cover about 90 percent of your customers' concerns. Remember, users tend to provide both frank and useful input, but only if you ask them for it. So be sure to include an active customer feedback mechanism such as e-mail, open feedback forms, or structured survey forms. Don't require users to register before they can see your site. You may drive them away.

- *Promote your website.* Be sure to list with numerous search engines—giant indexes that allow web users to find information by entering key words. Most of these listings are free. Maximize the number of times your site will be listed by jamming in as many words as you can that best describe your site. Take out an ad in the newspaper and list your company in the Internet yellow pages. Finally, don't just sit back and expect your website to perform magic. Use it to find out as much as possible about your customers. Ask yourself: How can I benefit from all this customer information?

Questions for Critical Thinking

1. Why do web surfers have a short attention span?
2. List some of the ways companies can benefit from having a website on the Internet.

---

one of the site's secure "project rooms," which contains data and product specifications related to the problems. Solvers perform the work in the hopes of obtaining a large reward (as much as $100,000) for their solutions. To date, some 7,000 scientists have created 2,400 project rooms that are organized around 33 problems.[9]

In addition to using company websites for the functions we just highlighted, companies are using Internet technology to engage in e-commerce. They are generating new revenue streams by creating new online markets for existing products, creating new products specifically designed for online markets, and expanding existing or new products into international markets. In Chapter 1 we defined electronic commerce (e-commerce) as the buying and selling of goods and services over an electronic network. The type of e-commerce conducted is generally categorized by the parties involved in the transaction.

5 LEARNING OBJECTIVE

Name three broad categories of e-commerce and explain what each category involves

business-to-consumer e-commerce
Electronic commerce that involves transactions between businesses and the end user or consumer

mobile commerce (m-commerce)
Transaction of electronic commerce using wireless devices and wireless Internet access instead of PC-based technology

Business-to-Consumer E-Commerce   Referred to as *B2C, e-tailing,* or *electronic retailing,* **business-to-consumer e-commerce** involves interactions and transactions between a company and consumers, with a strong focus on selling goods and services and marketing to consumers. Typical business-to-consumer transactions include such functions as sales, marketing (promotions, advertising, coupons, catalogs), order processing and tracking, credit authorization, customer service, and electronic payments.

In the mid-1990s, experts advised physical retail stores to keep their e-commerce initiatives separate. The thinking was that creating separate e-businesses would allow the web entity to speed up decision making, be more flexible, be more entrepreneurial, act independently, and thus compete more effectively with *pure-play e-businesses* (those that exist only on the Internet, such as Amazon.com). Some retailers embraced this approach, but others worried that creating separate e-businesses would cannibalize their physical-store sales and upset their entire distributions systems.

As Chapter 14 points out, experts now agree that integrating a retailer's physical store operation with its web operation is the most effective approach to e-commerce. Consider Barnes & Noble. To compete with Amazon.com, Barnes & Noble established a completely separate division—Barnesandnoble.com—and later spun the division off as a stand-alone company. But barnesandnoble.com lacked a sense of urgency about the web and let Amazon.com capture the lion's share of online book selling. Moreover, Barnes & Noble customers became confused and angry when they tried to return books purchased from barnesandnoble.com to the physical Barnes & Noble bookstores, only to be turned away. It didn't take long for Barnes & Noble to realize that its decision to separate its online and physical stores was flawed. So in 2000 Barnes & Noble integrated the two operations, making it possible for web customers to return purchases at a company's physical store. The practice of integrating a store's web and physical stores so that they appear as one operation is known as *clicks-and-bricks* or *clicks-and-mortar.*

Mobile commerce, commonly referred to as *m-commerce,* is the conduct of e-commerce by using wireless Internet access and wireless handheld devices, such as cell phones, palm pilots, and pagers to transact business. Wireless Internet connections hold immense potential for businesses. In Europe and Asia people are using their mobile phones to send text messages, to exchange e-mail, to read the morning news, to surf websites, and to purchase movie tickets or items from vending machines. But it may be some time before that kind of m-commerce takes off in the United States. The biggest reason for the U.S. lag in m-commerce is the lack of a uniform standard for digital communications. Europe, Japan, and other countries have mandated one standard technology for mobile communication, called Global System for Mobile Communications, or GSM. By contrast, the United States has adopted several wireless standards that make data retrieval more expensive, complicated, and unreliable.

In spite of this obstacle, U.S. wireless carriers are betting that recent developments in third-generation technology (known as 3G) and future developments in fourth-generation technology (known as 4G) will entice Americans to use their cell phones, hand-held computers, and other mobile devices to shop and conduct business. Both 3G and 4G promise the greater bandwidth and speed that are now possible only with wired broadband connections.

For businesses, m-commerce promises to help companies streamline their operations and increase efficiency by allowing workers to conduct business away from the office. It will enable businesses to develop new forms of m-services, m-entertainment, and m-advertising. For consumers, m-commerce offers the tantalizing prospect of shopping for books, baseball tickets, and other items on portable gadgets while commuting on the subway or standing in line at the post office. But before that can happen, companies must develop new portable devices with bigger screens and new applications that will entice users to go mobile. They must also make improvements in voice-recognition technology that will eliminate the need to type on miniature keypads.[10]

Business-to-Business E-Commerce Known as *B2B*, **business-to-business e-commerce** uses the Internet to conduct transactions between businesses. This form of e-commerce typically involves a company and its suppliers, distributors, manufacturers, and retailers who participate in large online trading hubs or electronic marketplaces to purchase supplies and transact business. Generally, the types of goods sold in business-to-business transactions include office materials, manufacturing supplies, equipment, and other goods a company needs for operations.

B2B exchanges can be run by an independent third party or by existing competitors who join forces to form a new venture. They can be as basic as a manufacturer putting up a bare-bones website to let distributors securely order products, or they can be as complex as a public marketplace where buyers, sellers, distributors, and shippers share all kinds of information about inventory, prices, markets, purchase orders, invoices, payments, credit, approvals, and so on.

The two most common types of B2B exchanges are *buyer exchanges* and *supplier exchanges*. *Buyer exchanges* are marketplaces formed by large groups of buyers (even competitors) who purchase similar items. By joining forces and aggregating demand for a product, they can achieve economies of scale that are not possible individually. *Supplier exchanges* are formed by suppliers who band together to create marketplaces to sell their goods online. The groups typically sell complementary products, offering buyers one-stop shopping for most of their needs. Covisint, for example, is a B2B exchange founded by DaimlerChrysler, Ford, and General Motors that allows auto industry participants to purchase products ranging from office supplies to vehicle parts in one convenient location.

Although B2B electronic marketplaces sound intriguing on paper, they have been slow to evolve, for a number of reasons. In order for the exchanges to succeed, competitors who join forces must be willing to share business processes—even ones that give them a competitive advantage. They must be willing to dump the network of suppliers they've built up over the years and make all their purchases through a new, unproven exchange. Moreover, they must restructure their software packages, accounting systems, data management systems, and manufacturing schedules so they can communicate with the operating systems of other exchange members. Despite these roadblocks, some industry experts anticipate that the business-to-business segment of e-commerce will grow significantly in the near future.[11]

Consumer-to-Consumer E-Commerce **Consumer-to-consumer e-commerce** involves consumers selling products directly to each other using the Internet as the intermediary. This form of e-commerce can be as simple as a website that functions as a swap exchange for used textbooks or it may be as complex as an auction site such as eBay. As an online middleman, eBay has brought together millions of buyers and sellers around the world and sold more than $21 billion of goods without ever taking possession of them. Sellers list their products with eBay and buyers bid on listed sellers' products. Once a bid is accepted, the seller ships the product directly to the buyer. To grow company sales to a goal of $30 billion to $40 billion, eBay is now targeting giant retailers to use the auction site as a dumping ground for their excess inventory.[12]

Cutting Costs

In addition to generating revenues, Internet technology helps companies cut costs. Companies are using the Internet to search for the best prices for parts and materials from domestic

business-to-business e-commerce Electronic commerce that involves transactions between companies and their suppliers, manufacturers, or other companies

consumer-to-consumer e-commerce Electronic commerce that involves transactions between consumers

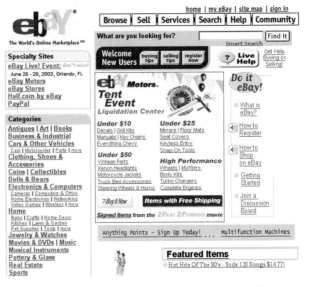

Founded in September 1995, eBay is the leading online marketplace for the sale of goods and services by a diverse community of individuals and businesses.

Job Recruiting Moves to the Net

In the late 1990s, e-cruiting (recruiting over the Internet) was just catching on. Today it's an integral part of the recruiting strategy for companies of all sizes. Companies have discovered that the Internet is a fast, convenient, and inexpensive way to find prospective job candidates. And job candidates are finding that the Internet is a convenient way to gather company information, search for job vacancies, and post résumés for large-volume distribution using career websites such as Monster.com, HotJobs.com, and CareerBuilder.com (also known as job boards).

Companies are using the Internet to search for résumés of promising candidates, take online applications, accept electronic résumés, conduct interviews, and administer tests. In comparison to traditional recruiting methods, the benefits of Internet recruiting are many:

• *Speed.* The Internet allows job seekers to search for jobs quickly, from any place and at any time, and to communicate via e-mail with potential employers. Companies can also save time in the hiring process by using the Internet to become a 24-hour, seven-days-a-week recruiter and to give applicants quick responses to their queries. Determined nocturnal headhunters can snap up hot résumés posted on the Internet before dawn and contact candidates immediately by e-mail. Some companies report receiving responses and résumés only minutes after posting a job opening.

• *Reach.* The Internet allows employers to contact a broader selection of applicants more quickly, target specific types of applicants more easily, and reach highly skilled applicants more efficiently. Some com-

pany websites bring in thousands of résumés in one week, a volume that would be far too cumbersome to manage through traditional means.

• *Cost savings.* Electronic ads typically cost much less than traditional print ads, career fairs, and open houses. Moreover, processing electronic application forms is more efficient than processing paper forms. Intelligent automated search agents can filter or prescreen potential applicants and find résumés that match job descriptions and specific employer criteria.

Still, e-cruiting is not without drawbacks. The biggest complaint voiced by companies is that the Internet produces more job applicants than ever before. The number of résumés one company received went from 6,000 to 24,000 annually after going online. The increased volume of résumés makes it more difficult to cull promising candidates from unqualified ones. Companies get résumés from such far away places as Albania and Timbuktu. "People will send their résumé because its very simple to cut and paste. But, they're no way qualified for the position," notes one HR director. Another drawback is that not everyone has Internet access or uses the Internet to search for jobs.

Questions for Critical Thinking

1. How are job seekers and employers using the Internet in the recruiting process?
2. What are the benefits and drawbacks of Internet recruiting?

and international suppliers. They are using electronic marketplaces and auction sites to manage inventories more effectively. They are saving costs by allowing employees to telecommute and work from remote locations. They are using the Internet to cost-effectively recruit and train employees. They are reducing costly travel expenses by substituting Internet-based videoconferences for in-person meetings. And they are using the Internet to reduce the costs of publishing, processing, distributing, and storing paper-based information by converting information into an electronic format and placing it on company websites, intranets, and extranets.

Consider Boeing. Before the Internet, this Chicago-based aerospace giant would ship a mountain of technical manuals, parts lists, and other maintenance documents to its 600 air-

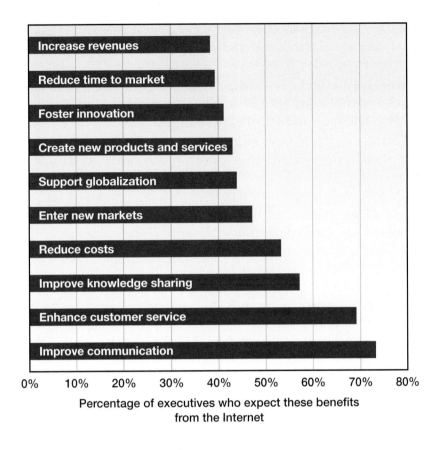

Increase revenues

Reduce time to market

Foster innovation

Create new products and services

Support globalization

Enter new markets

Reduce costs

Improve knowledge sharing

Enhance customer service

Improve communication

0% 10% 20% 30% 40% 50% 60% 70% 80%

**Percentage of executives who expect these benefits
from the Internet**

EXHIBIT 4.6
Greatest Internet Benefits
Over 525 executives who responded to a survey by Booz-Allen & Hamilton and the Economist Intelligent Unit listed these business benefits as the key contributions of the Internet.

line customers—enough papers to make a stack 130,000 feet tall—at an annual cost of millions of dollars. Now Boeing places all this information on the Internet so customers can review the data, obtain product updates, and discuss maintenance issues in chat areas.[13]

Enhancing Communication

According to a recent survey by Booz-Allen & Hamilton and the Economist Intelligent Unit, communication is the most important benefit of the Internet (see Exhibit 4.6). Companies are using the Internet to conduct meetings and collaborate with local, national, and international business partners; communicate with customers and employees; share text, photos, slides, videos, best practices, and other data within the organization; and inform investors, industry analysts, government regulators, customers, and other stakeholders about business developments.

Great Harvest Bread Company is a good example of how companies use the Internet to enhance communication. The company's 140 franchisees collaborate, swap ideas, compare notes, and help one another succeed by using a company website called Breadboard and by communicating via e-mail, the most popular form of Internet communication.[14]

In addition to e-mail, the Internet offers businesses a variety of choices for online communication, including:

- *Discussion mailing lists.* **Discussion mailing lists**, also known as a *listservs*, are discussion groups to which you subscribe by sending a message to the list's e-mail address. From then on, copies of all messages posted by any other subscriber are sent to you via e-mail. It's like subscribing to an electronic newsletter to which everyone can contribute.

- *Newsgroups.* **Usenet newsgroups** consist of posted messages on a particular subject and the responses to them. Newsgroups differ from discussion mailing lists in two key ways. First, messages are posted at the newsgroup site, which you must access by using a news

discussion mailing lists
E-mail lists that allow people to discuss a common interest by posting messages, which are received by everyone in the group

Usenet newsgroups
One or more discussion groups on the Internet where people with similar interests can post articles and reply to messages

instant messaging (IM)
Technology that allows people to carry on real-time, one-on-one, and small-group text conversations. Unlike e-mail, instant messages are not automatically recorded or saved.

chat
A form of interactive communication that enables computer users in separate locations to have real-time conversations. Usually takes place at websites called chat rooms.

Telnet
A way to access someone else's computer (the host computer), and to use it as if it were right on your desk.

Internet telephony
Using the Internet to converse vocally

file transfer protocol (FTP)
A software protocol that lets you copy or move files from a remote computer—called an FTP site—to your computer over the Internet; it is the Internet facility for downloading and uploading files

intranet
A private network, set up within a corporation or organization, that operates over the Internet and may be used to link geographically remote sites

reader program. Second, messages posted to a newsgroup can be viewed by anyone. You can think of a newsgroup as a *place* you visit to read posted messages, whereas a discussion mailing list *delivers* posted messages to you.

- *Instant messaging and chat.* Many companies encourage the use of **instant messaging (IM)** and **chat** to collaborate. Both allow online conversations in which any number of computer users can type in messages to each other and receive responses in real time.

- *Telnet.* **Telnet** is a class of Internet application program that allows you to communicate with other computers on a remote network even if your computer is not a permanent part of that network. For instance, you would use Telnet to access your county library's electronic card catalog from your home computer.

- *Internet telephony.* Internet users can converse vocally over the Internet using **Internet telephony**. Converting traditional voice calls to digital signals and sending them over the Internet is much less expensive than calling over standard phone lines. It can also be more efficient, allowing an organization to accommodate more users on a single line at once.

- *File transfers.* **File transfer protocol (FTP)** is an Internet service that enables you to download files (transfer data from a server to your computer) and to upload files (transfer data from your computer to another system). FTP also allows you to attach formatted documents to your e-mail messages and download formatted files. Sometimes users compress or *zip* large files—such as graphics files—to make them easier and faster to transfer. If you receive a zipped file, you must use special software (usually provided with your web browser) to decompress it before you can read it. The Internet also makes *peer-to-peer file sharing* possible. Using the Internet and software, people can exchange files directly (from user to user) without going through a central server.

In addition to these communication choices, companies can use intranets and extranets—two types of websites specifically designed for internal and external communication.

Intranets   Companies that want to set up special employee-only websites can use an **intranet**, a private internal corporate network. Intranets use the same technologies as the Internet and the World Wide Web, but the information provided and the access allowed are restricted to members of the organization (regardless of their actual location). Whereas employees can use a password to log onto the corporate intranet and then move to public areas of the Internet, unauthorized people cruising the Internet can't get into the internal site.

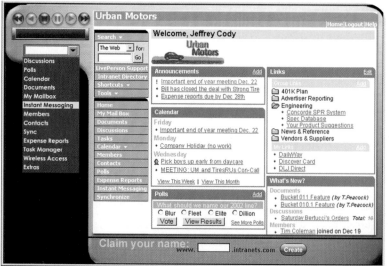

Intranets have become an increasingly popular vehicle for Internet communications in organizations. Ford Motor Company, for example, uses its intranet to enable engineers and designers worldwide to collaborate in real time on the design of new car models. Every model has its own internal website to track design, production, quality control, and delivery processes. And IBM employees can log onto the company intranet to conveniently check their health care benefits.[15] Other companies are using intranets to publish company forms, reports, phone directories, company newsletters, and other information, such as[16]

- *Policy manuals.* The most current version is always available to all employees without having to reprint manuals when policies change.

Jeff Cody logs into his company intranet to get the latest company announcements, event calendar, reports, directories, and more.

- *Employee benefits information.* Employees can find out about benefits, reallocate the funds in their retirement and benefit plans, fill out electronic W-4 forms, view an electronic pay stub, and sign up for training programs.

- *Presentation materials used by marketing and sales departments.* Sales representatives can download marketing materials at customer sites all over the world. In addition, changes made by marketing representatives at company headquarters are immediately available to field salespeople.

- *Company records and information.* Company directories, customer information, employee skills inventories, project status reports, company calendars and events, and many other records can be stored on an intranet so they're accessible from anywhere in the world, using an Internet connection and a password.

Putting this material on an intranet allows employees at any location to find information quickly and easily.

Extranets   Once a company has an intranet in place, the cost of adding external capabilities is minimal, but the benefits can be substantial. An **extranet** is an external intranet that allows people to communicate and exchange data within a secured network. Unlike intranets, which limit access to employees, extranets allow qualified people from the outside—such as suppliers and customers—to enter the network using a password. Extranets can enhance communication with clients, suppliers, and colleagues, and they can save companies time and money.

Most business-to-business e-commerce uses extranet technology as the backbone for the trading hubs and exchanges. Extranet technology also offers a cheaper alternative to **electronic data interchange (EDI)**, a private network system that facilitates the exchange of critical business documents (such as invoices and purchase orders) and information about payments, products, services, and logistics over a special telephone or leased data line. Setting up an EDI link can run $100,000, and monthly maintenance can cost $1,000.[17]

extranet
Similar to an intranet, but extending the network to select people outside the organization

electronic data interchange (EDI)
Information systems that transmit documents such as invoices and purchase orders between computers, thereby lowering ordering costs and paperwork

Finding Information

The Internet is rich in business information. You can find current news, discussions of business issues, industry trends, and company information such as financial performance, products, goals, and employment. In fact, the web is so vast and changes so constantly that it's easy for users to get sidetracked. If you've ever been lost in cyberspace, take heart—it happens to everybody. Chances are good that you'll find information on the Internet about almost any research topic. However, finding that information can be frustrating if you don't know how to conduct an effective search.

One important thing to keep in mind is that anyone (including you) can post anything on a website. No one filters it. No one checks it for accuracy. And no one can be sure of who is producing the information or why they are placing it on the Internet. For that reason, it's best to refrain from seriously surfing the web for business information until you've had a chance to learn a bit about your topic from journals, books, and other sources that are carefully edited for the accuracy of their content. That way you'll be able to detect skewed or erroneous information, and you can be more selective about the websites and documents you choose to use as a resource.

If you are looking for specific company data, your best source may be the company's own website (assuming it maintains one). Websites generally include detailed information about the company's products, services, history, mission, strategy, financial performance, and employment needs. Furthermore, many sites provide links to related company information, such as public records and financial statements, news releases, and more.

Keep in mind that a lot of the information that you may want simply isn't on the web. If you're researching small organizations, for instance, you may find nothing or just an address

6 LEARNING OBJECTIVE

Explain how to conduct an effective database search

search engines
Internet tools for finding websites on the topics of your choice

and phone number. Furthermore, even if the information you're seeking does exist on the web, you may not be able to locate it. Even the best **search engines**—Internet tools that identify and query web content—manage to index only about a third of the pages on the web.[18] Then again, when a search engine turns up what you're looking for, it will probably also turn up a mountain of stuff you won't need. You can produce more targeted search results by following these search strategies and tips to conduct an effective database search:

- *Select appropriate databases.* You'll want a good business database. However, journals on your topic may be in a database that also includes journals on psychology, computers, or medicine.

- *Use multiple search engines.* Don't limit yourself to a single search engine, especially if you are looking for less popular topics. Try your search on several engines by using *metacrawlers*, special engines that search several search engines at once.

- *Translate concepts into key words and phrases.* For instance, if you want to determine the "effect of TQM on company profits," you should select the key words *TQM*, *total quality management*, *profits*, *sales*, *companies*, and *corporations*. Remember, use synonyms or word equivalents whenever possible, and use quotation marks around phrases to look for the entire phrase instead of separate words.

- *Use a short phrase or single term rather than a long phrase.* Search engines look for the words exactly as you key them in. If the words occur, but not in the same order, you may miss relevant hits.

- *Do not use stopwords.* Stopwords are words the computer disregards and will not search for. Database documentation will identify any stopwords in addition to the common ones: *a, an, the, of, by, with, for,* and *to*.

- *Do not use words contained in the name of the database.* Using words such as *business* or *finance* in a business database will work, but they appear so often that searching for them slows the processing time and adds no precision to your results.

- *Use variations of your terms.* Use abbreviations (*CEO, CPA*), synonyms (*man, male*), related terms (*child, adolescent, youth*), different spellings (*dialog, dialogue*), singular and plural forms (*man, men*), nouns and adjectives (*manager, management, managerial*), and open and compound forms (*online, on line, on-line*).

- *Specify a logical relationship between the key words.* Must the document contain both *companies* and *corporations*, or is either fine? Must it contain both *profits* and *companies*, or should it contain *TQM* or *total quality management* and *profits* or *sales*?

Boolean operators
The term *boolean* refers to a system of logical thought developed by the English mathematician George Boole; it uses the operators AND, OR, and NOT

- *Use Boolean operators.* Narrow or broaden your search by including AND, OR, and NOT. As Exhibit 4.7 shows, such **Boolean operators** can help you create complex, precise search strategies. For example, you could create a search strategy such as "(marketing or advertising) AND (organizations or associations) AND NOT consultants." This means that qualifying documents or websites must have either the word *marketing* or *advertising* and must have either the word *organizations* or *associations*, but they can't have the word *consultants*. Many search engines automatically include Boolean operators in their strategies even though you can't see them on the screen. Either insert your own (which should override automatic operators) or review the instructions for your search engine.

- *Use proximity operators.* To specify how close one of your key words should be to another, use a proximity operator such as NEAR. For example, the search phrase "marketing NEAR/2 organizations" means that *marketing* must be within two words of *organizations*.

- *Use wildcards.* Wildcard characters help you find plurals and alternative spellings of your key words. For example, by using a question mark in the word *organi?ations*, you'll

EXHIBIT 4.7   Improving Your Search Results
Using these Boolean operators, proximity operators, and wildcards will vastly improve the effectiveness of your electronic searches.

SEARCH OPERATOR	EFFECT	STRATEGY	RESULTS
AND	Narrows the results. Searches for records containing both of the words it separates. Words separated by AND may be anywhere in the document—and far away from each other.	Rock AND roll	Music
OR	Broadens the results. This is a scattergun search that will turn up lots of matches and is not particularly precise. Searches for records containing either of the words it separates.	Rock OR roll	Igneous rocks; gemstones; crescent rolls; music
NOT, AND NOT	Limits the results. Searches for records containing the first word(s) but not the second one. Depending on the database, AND is not always included in combination with NOT.	Snow skiing NOT water skiing; Snow skiing AND NOT water skiing	Snow skiing; cross-country skiing
WITHIN OR NEAR	Proximity operators. Searches for words that all appear in a specified word range.	Snow WITHIN/2 skiing	Terms in which *skiing* is within 2 words of *snow*
ADJ	Adjacency operator. Searches for records in which the second word immediately follows the first word (two words are next to each other).	Ski ADJ patrol	Ski patrol
?	Wildcard operator for single character; matches any one character.	Ski?	Skit; skid; skin; skip
*	Wildcard operator for string of characters.	Ski*	Ski; skiing; skies; skill; skirt; skit; skinny; skimpy
""	Exact match. Searches for string of words placed within quotation marks.	"2002 budget deficit"	2002 budget deficit

find documents with both *organisations* (British spelling) and *organizations*. Similarly, by using an asterisk at the end of the stem *chair**, you'll find *chairman, chairperson, chairs,* and *chairlift.*

- ***Evaluate the precision and quality of your search results to refine your search if necessary.*** If you end up with more than 60 to 100 links to sort through, refine your search. If your first page of results doesn't have something of interest, you've entered the wrong words or too few words. Also, pay attention to whether you are searching in the title, subject, or document field of the database. Each will return different results.

Challenges Businesses Are Facing in the Information Age

Electronic commerce and new technologies may be a dream for companies and consumers, but they also present a number of challenges to today's businesses. Among them are employee privacy, employee productivity, wasteful technology spending, data security, and sabotage and cyberterrorism.

Employee Privacy

Employee privacy in today's workplace is a hot issue. Worried by productivity losses in a failing economy, the leaking of trade secrets, and lawsuits for discrimination, more and

7 LEARNING OBJECTIVE

Identify and discuss five challenges businesses are facing in the Information Age

more employers are monitoring the online behavior of employees. New technologies enable supervisors to eavesdrop on employees' telephone conversations and call up a data processors' computer output and input on a supervisor's terminal. Hidden cameras and microphones observe workers without their knowledge. Computers record employees' telephone calls, along with the calls' duration and destination.[19]

According to an American Management Association survey, 74 percent of major U.S. companies keep tabs on workers by recording phone calls or voice mail and by checking employees' computer files and e-mail.[20] Companies claim that such surveillance helps crack down on abuse: Just months after Xerox began monitoring web usage, it fired 40 employees for viewing inappropriate websites—primarily pornographic sites.[21] The fact is that employers have the legal right to monitor everything from an employee's web access to the content of their company e-mail or voice mail messages. In addition, both e-mail and voice mail can be used as evidence in court cases.

Employee Productivity

Maintaining a high level of employee productivity is another challenge companies are facing. E-mail, voice mail, conference calls, and faxes interrupt employees while they work. Chat or real-time conversation windows can pop up on computer screens and demand immediate conversation. Technology has created an expectation for instant answers, making it virtually impossible for employees to tune out these interruptions.

Moreover, the percentage of employees who use company resources for personal business is alarming (see Exhibit 4.8). Sending personal e-mail and faxes, surfing the Net, and shopping online are common employee abuses. In fact, 50 percent of U.S. web purchases occurred in the workplace, compared with 37 percent from home, and 4 percent from schools, reports ComScore Networks of Reston, Virginia, which monitors more than 1.5 million Internet users.[22]

Electronic traffic jams are another productivity problem that companies face. The Internet was originally designed to be like a single-lane highway with unlimited access points and no traffic control. These features make accessibility, which is the Internet's strength, into a weakness for users who need to move large amounts of data more quickly. When traffic gets heavy, the Internet slows down. To get around this problem, several universities have created an ultra-high-speed Internet2, with connections 400 times faster than standard high-speed lines. But this service is available to only a limited number of users.[23]

EXHIBIT 4.8

On Company Time
Everyone's doing it: photocopying tax returns on the office copier, faxing a loan application, or slipping personal mail into an overnight delivery envelope. According to a recent Ziff Davis survey, the Net is still the top company resource most people use for personal business.

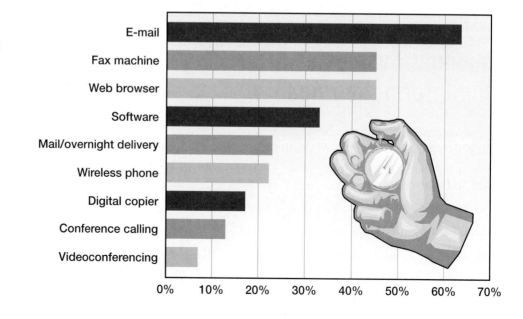

Wasteful Technology Spending

Morgan Stanley estimates that in a recent two-year period U.S. companies threw away $130 billion on unneeded software and other technology. Worldwide, companies waste as much as 20 percent of the $2.7 trillion they spend annually on new technology, estimates Gartner research firm. They do so because they stampede into wrong technology, overbuy and purchase more features and functions than they need, and fail to implement new technology properly. They also underestimate the time needed to make new technology work. They think they can install new systems fast and immediately reap the results touted by salespeople. But many find out the hard way that the deployment of complex systems can take years.

Consider candymaker Hershey Foods, for example. The company finished installing three new software packages in the summer of 1999, just as retailers placed orders for Halloween. But the software, part of a $112 million system, proved incompatible with earlier programs. The results were disastrous. Chocolate Kisses and other treats piled up in warehouses because of missed or delayed deliveries. Meanwhile, Hershey lost about $120 million in sales.[24]

Data Security

Before computers, companies typically conducted business mainly on paper, locking up sensitive documents and using security precautions when transporting important files. Furthermore, only a limited number of people had access to vital company data. But the move from paper-based systems to electronic data management poses a real threat to corporate data security.

Experts report that technically skilled thieves and rank-and-file employees are stealing millions if not billions of dollars a year from businesses in the United States and abroad. But the exact amount of losses suffered by organizations as a result of computer crime is difficult to quantify. Businesses are reluctant to report and publicly discuss electronic theft for fear of attracting other cyberattacks or undermining the confidence of their customers, suppliers, and investors. Nonetheless, according to a 2002 survey of 500 computer security practitioners conducted by the FBI and Computer Security Institute, 80 percent of survey respondents acknowledged financial losses to computer breaches, with an average loss ranging from $2 million to $6 million per incident.[25]

Two common forms of computer infiltration crime are *hacking*, or breaking into a computer network such as an intranet to steal, delete, or change data; and, *cracking*, or entering a computer network for nondestructive reasons, such as to play a prank or show off. Thieves are hacking computers to divert cash from company bank accounts, pilfer valuable information—like business-development strategies, new product specifications, or contract bidding plans—and sell the data to competitors. Hacking on the Internet is expected to grow exponentially in frequency and complexity. Some attribute the increase to a tightening economy, the increasing amount of riches flowing through cyberspace, and the relative ease of such crimes. "If people found out how astoundingly large this problem is, they'd be shocked," says one technology consultant.[26]

Experts estimate that 70 percent of computer systems intrusions are orchestrated by company employees who steal company passwords and other forms of identification. Other violators include laid-off workers, contractors, and consultants who destroy, alter, or expose critical data.[27] One of the best known cases of insider computer crime involved two accountants at Cisco Systems, who broke into the company's computer system and issued themselves nearly $8 million in company stock. The two were sentenced to 34 months in prison.[28]

To guard against such unauthorized computer access by outsiders, most companies install security software called a **firewall**, a special type of gateway that controls access to

firewall
Computer hardware and software that protects part or all of a private computer network attached to the Internet by preventing public Internet users from accessing it

the company's local network. The firewall allows access only to users who present the proper password and system identification. In addition to firewalls, companies protect their data by (1) determining which employees should receive passwords to vital networks; (2) providing ongoing security enforcement and education; (3) conducting background checks on all new employees; (4) adopting a security policy that requires employees to use passwords, turn computers off when not in use, encrypt sensitive e-mail, and apply stronger security measures to safeguard trade secrets; and (5) developing a plan for data recovery if disaster strikes.[29]

Taking these measures will, of course, deter potential offenders, but doing so will not guarantee the security of information or completely protect data from sabotage or cyberterrorism.

viruses
Form of computer sabotage embedded in software or passed from one computer to the next that changes or deletes computer files or programs

worms
Form of computer sabotage sent by e-mail that reproduces—taking up network space and snarling connections

cyberterrorism
Orchestrated attacks on a company's information systems for political or economic purposes

Sabotage and Cyberterrorism

Today, criminals are using technology to disrupt website and computer operations and cause other problems for companies, governments, and individuals. Among the most common forms of sabotage are viruses and worms:

- **Viruses** are programs that can change or delete files or programs. Embedded in legitimate software (without the manufacturer's knowledge) or in files passed from one computer to another, vicious viruses can quickly do tremendous damage.
- **Worms** are programs specifically designed to replicate over and over again. Spread by e-mail, they send more worms to everyone in the recipient's e-mail address book—taking up precious network space and snarling connections.

Nearly every workplace has had one or more computers infected with a virus. In a recent study, 85 percent of the firms surveyed said they had been victims of viruses. And virus damage can be costly. Cleaning up the wreckage and protecting against additional viruses has forced companies to spend billions annually on virus protection programs and other safeguards.[30]

Cost is not the only concern. As worms and viruses spread, they can disrupt other interconnected government and company systems and slow Internet traffic. Even a relatively simple sabotage technique such as repeatedly trying to access an Internet address can tie up a site or crash its equipment, as eBay, E*Trade, Amazon.com, and other web-based businesses have learned.[31]

Cyberterrorism—orchestrated attacks on a company's information systems for political or economic purposes—is a form of cybercrime that is being taken even more seriously since the terrorist attacks in New York City and Washington, D.C., in September 2001. Computer security experts say that the country's computer networks and the Internet are vulnerable to coordinated attacks that could interrupt power supplies to millions of homes, disrupt air traffic control systems, shut down water supplies, cut off emergency 911 services, and cripple corporate America, causing billions of dollars in business losses.[32]

To better police data security threats from domestic and international sources, the U.S. Justice Department has set up the National Infrastructure Protection Center (NIPC) at the FBI. The FBI has also begun using a software program called Carnivore to screen e-mail messages for clues to potentially

Fatou Kinteh inputs an order on a touch screen computer at a Silver Diner in Rockville, Md. The 13-restaurant chain was knocked offline for about four days when the Code Red computer worm infected their system.

crippling electronic and physical terrorist attacks. Although privacy advocates fear that Carnivore and other security measures are too intrusive and could lead to false accusations, government officials—and many citizens—are willing to trade off some privacy for a higher degree of security against all types of terrorism.[33]

Summary of Learning Objectives

1. **Discuss the responsibilities of the chief information officer.**

   The chief information officer (CIO) is responsible for designing and developing the company's information systems. This task involves assessing the company's needs, deciding on what data to track, and developing systems to track, store, process, retrieve, and distribute the data. In addition, the CIO is responsible for installing computer hardware and software and other technologies to assist with the collection and distribution of information.

2. **Differentiate between operations information systems and management support systems.**

   Operation information systems include transaction processing systems, process control systems, and office automation systems. These systems support daily operations and provide the information lower-level managers and supervisors need to operate and control company processes. By contrast, management support systems provide managers with information they need to make strategic decisions. Categories of management support systems include management information systems, which provide data for routine decision making; decision support systems, which help managers solve nonroutine problems; executive information systems, which are designed to facilitate higher-level strategic planning; and expert systems, which use artificial intelligence to simulate human reasoning.

3. **Discuss the role of hardware, software, and networks in information systems.**

   Effective information systems require hardware (tangible equipment such as keyboards, printers, computers, and fax machines) and software (the applications that direct the activity of the hardware). Companies share electronic data and expensive hardware by using networks to link their computers. Wide area networks connect computers in distant geographical locations, whereas local area networks connect computers in nearby areas such as local offices or college campuses. Networks rely on telephone lines, cable lines, or wireless devices to transmit data. The capacity and speed at which data are transmitted is governed by a system's bandwidth.

4. **Discuss how businesses are using the Internet.**

   Business are using the Internet in four key ways: To generate new revenue streams by conducting electronic commerce, finding new business partners, providing customer and product support, and promoting their goods and services online; to cut costs by purchasing supplies and inventory online, recruiting and training employees via company websites and intranets, and conducting business away from the office; to communicate with customers, employees, and other stakeholders by using a variety of Internet-based communication tools such as e-mail, newsgroups, instant messaging and chat, videoconferencing, and data file transmission; and to obtain information by conducting online research and subscribing to online media.

5. **Name three broad categories of e-commerce and explain what each category involves.**

   Business-to-consumer e-commerce (B2C) involves interactions between a company and consumers, such as sales and marketing functions. Business-to-business e-commerce (B2B) involves interactions between businesses, such as establishing online trading hubs or exchanges where businesses can purchase inventory and supplies and exchange information. Consumer-to-consumer e-commerce involves the interaction between consumers such as the buying and selling of personal items via auction sites or personal websites.

6. **Explain how to conduct an effective database search.**

   To search databases effectively, you should select databases that store the specific information you need, use multiple search engines (if searching the Internet), translate concepts into key words and phrases, use short phrases rather than long ones, avoid stopwords and words contained in the name of the database, vary your search terms, specify a logical relationship between the keywords, use Boolean operators, use proximity operators, use wildcards, and evaluate your search results, refining your strategy if necessary.

7. **Identify and discuss five challenges that businesses are facing in the Information Age.**

   Technology and information enhance productivity in many ways, but they can also create new workplace challenges. These include drawing the line between protecting the organization and invading an employee's privacy, maintaining a high level of employee productivity, curbing wasteful spending on unnecessary technology, maintaining data security, and protecting against computer sabotage and cyberterrorism.

KEY TERMS

application software **(91)**

artificial intelligence **(90)**

bandwidth **(91)**

Boolean operators **(102)**

business-to-business e-commerce **(97)**

business-to-consumer e-commerce **(96)**

chat **(100)**

chief information officer (CIO) **(87)**

consumer-to-consumer e-commerce **(97)**

cyberterrorism **(106)**

data **(86)**

data mining **(87)**

data warehousing **(87)**

databases **(87)**

decision support system (DSS) **(89)**

discussion mailing lists **(99)**

electronic data interchange (EDI) **(101)**

executive information system (EIS) **(90)**

expert system **(90)**

extranet **(101)**

file transfer protocol (FTP) **(100)**

firewall **(105)**

hardware **(90)**

instant messaging (IM) **(100)**

Internet **(93)**

Internet telephony **(100)**

intranet **(100)**

local area network (LAN) **(91)**

management information system (MIS) **(89)**

mobile commerce (m-commerce) **(96)**

modem **(91)**

network **(91)**

office automation systems (OAS) **(89)**

operating systems **(91)**

process control systems **(88)**

production control systems **(89)**

search engines **(102)**

software **(90)**

speech-recognition system **(90)**

Telnet **(100)**

transaction processing system (TPS) **(88)**

Usenet newsgroups **(99)**

viruses **(106)**

wide area network (WAN) **(91)**

worms **(106)**

TEST YOUR KNOWLEDGE

Questions for Review

1. What are the purposes of data warehousing and data mining?

2. Would employee records be considered data or information? Explain your answer.

3. How are companies using the Internet to generate revenues?

4. What kinds of information are companies placing on intranets?

5. Why has business-to-business electronic commerce been slow to evolve?

Questions for Analysis

6. Why do companies need information and information management systems?

7. What concerns might you have when citing information from a website?

8. How are companies today using speech-recognition systems? Why are such systems important for m-commerce?

9. Why is new technology considered both a benefit and a curse?

10. *Ethical Considerations:* You finally saved enough money to buy a CD-RW drive so you can burn your own CDs and save lots of money. You log onto the Internet but before you can download your favorite tunes you must first agree to all those WARNING messages. Of course, you're in too much of a hurry to actually read them, so you simply check "agree" and begin downloading songs. What do you think is the purpose of these warning messages? Is it ethical for you to agree to them without understanding what you are agreeing to? What happens if you disagree?

Questions for Application

11. Select a well-known e-commerce website, review its content, and answer these questions:

    a. What kinds of product and company information does the website provide?

    b. What information does the website ask customers to provide about themselves?

    c. What are some of the features the website includes to facilitate the ordering of products? (For example, can you check the status of your order? Does the site advise you if the product is out of stock?)

    d. How does the website provide customers with assistance if they have a question or need help?

12. How has the Internet changed the way you interact with businesses?

13. *Integrated:* Most small businesses can't afford to hire a chief information officer. If you owned a small business, how would you go about setting up effective information systems? (*Hint:* think about using both internal and external resources.)

14. *Integrated:* How might an increased interest in m-commerce (from a consumer perspective) stimulate the economy?

PRACTICE YOUR KNOWLEDGE

Handling Difficult Situations on the Job: Controlling Techno-Tantrums

This is the third time in a month your company, Metro Power, has had to escort an employee from the building after a violent episode. Frankly, everyone is a little frightened by this development, and as a department manager, you have the unhappy task of trying to quell the storm. All of these episodes began with some failure of company technology to perform as expected.

One man punched out his computer screen after the system failed. Another threw his keyboard across the room when he couldn't get access to the company's intranet. A woman started kicking her stalled printer and screaming obscenities before terrified co-workers stopped her. You're afraid these incidents may be just the beginning.

Your business depends on technology at all levels. Common as they are, technology failures are sometimes seen as disastrous and unacceptable by tired, stressed, and overworked employees. Tempers flare and physical violence too often follows. You're just grateful that, so far, none of that anger or frustration has been taken out on co-workers.[34]

Your task: You need to decide how to reduce the rising tide of temper tantrums over technology failure. How can you help your workers deal with this fairly routine frustration? Equipment failures are inevitable; what can you suggest to help frazzled employees respond more calmly? What steps might they take before (prevention), during (response), and after (repair) techno glitches? You need to be prepared if another employee explodes in a violent outburst against company equipment. How will you handle that worker? Can you think of ways to defuse such a situation?

Building Your Team Skills

A computer virus shut down the computer system of your major competitor last month, and you heard from a friend that they are still experiencing serious problems. So you decide to learn from their experience. As manager of the data processing department you have assembled your team of data processors to brainstorm a list of precautions and steps your department should take to protect the company's data against computer viruses. Using teams of students, generate this list of recommendations and then group the recommendations into logical categories. Compare your team's recommendations with those generated by the other teams in your class.

EXPAND YOUR KNOWLEDGE

Discovering Career Opportunities

You love technology but cringe at the thought of sitting in front of the computer all day, writing miles of code for new programs or designing complicated networks. But before you prejudge what you may or may not have to do at work if you pursue a career in information management, why not consult an expert. Log onto Prentice Hall's Student Success SuperSite at www.prenhall.com/success/MajorExp and select the Information Technology major. What courses do you need to take for this major? What can you do with a degree in Information Technology? How might you use these courses to prepare you for a general business career?

Developing Your Research Skills

Scan recent business journals and newspapers (print or online edition) for an article showing how computers or other new technology helped a company gain a competitive advantage or improve its profitability.

1. What new technology did the company acquire and how did they use it to gain a competitive advantage or improve profitability?

2. Did the article mention any problems the company had implementing its new technology? What were they? Do you think the problems could have been avoided? How?

3. Did the technology require employees to learn new skills? If so, what were they?

Exploring the Best of the Web

URLs for all Internet exercises are provided at the website for this book, www.prenhall.com/bovee. *When you log on to this text's website, select Chapter 4. Then select "Student Resources," click on the name of the featured website, and review the website to complete these exercises.*

Explore these chapter-related websites, review their content, and answer the following questions for each website you visit:

1. What is the purpose of this website?

2. What kinds of information does this website contain? Please be specific.

3. How is the information provided at this website useful for businesspeople? Consumers?

4. How did you expand your knowledge of information management, the Internet, and e-commerce by reviewing the material at this website? What new things did you learn about these topics?

Stay Informed with CIO

Chief information officers make smart business decisions by staying current in the field of information technology. Resources such as CIO Online, a leading resource for information managers, provides expert advice and links to many industry-related resources. Log onto the journal and research critical information topics, listen to industry experts, receive career advice, get the latest Internet survey information, visit the reading room, join a discussion forum, and more. Don't worry if you missed an issue or two—access to the archives is as easy as a click of the mouse. www.cio.com

Ride the Technology Wave

Computer technology advances at a dizzying pace. Today's industry standards in hardware and software can become dinosaurs almost overnight. This situation can be especially problematic for businesses that spend thousands, or even millions, of dollars on computer systems intended to improve productivity. Fortunately, a number of excellent resources are available on the Internet to help both businesspeople and home computer users stay on top of the advancing waves of technology. *PC Magazine Online* is one such resource. This website offers news on future technologies, reviews of current hot products, and hints for effective information and technology management, as well as hundreds of free software downloads. Take some time to explore this resource. In business today, any extra information you can get about technology trends may become a competitive advantage. www.zdnet.com/pcmag

Learn the Rules of the Road

The road to creating a successful online store can be a difficult and confusing one if you are unaware of the concepts and principles behind e-commerce. Learn how e-commerce works and how to get started in the exciting world of e-commerce by visiting the eCommerce Guidebook. Discover how to get an Internet merchant bank account. Search for available domain names. Get the latest Internet and e-commerce statistics. And stay on top of the latest e-commerce news by clicking on one of the featured e-magazines, by visiting an industry association, or by following the online resource links provided at this website. www.online-commerce.com

Learning Interactively

Companion Website

Visit the Companion Website at www.prenhall.com/bovee. For Chapter 4, take advantage of the interactive "Study Guide" to test your chapter knowledge. Get instant feedback on whether you need additional studying. Read the "Current Events" articles to get the latest on chapter topics, and complete the exercises as specified by your instructor. Expand your learning with a visit to the "Research Area." There you will find a wealth of information you can use to complete your course assignments.

A CASE FOR CRITICAL THINKING

Nokia Dials Up Wireless Innovations

Hold up one of Nokia's clever new mobile phones with a built-in camera, and it's hard to picture the Finnish company's humble beginnings as a maker of everything from toilet paper to tires. Founded in 1865 as a forest products company, Nokia saw more than 125 years of profitable operations skid to a halt in the early 1990s when a global recession and the Soviet Union's collapse stalled demand for the company's rubber, paper, and chemical products. Nokia was making mobile phones by that time, but it couldn't match competitors' mass-production techniques. When Jorma Ollila took over as CEO in 1992, Nokia was floundering.

Strong Connections

In a bold move to survive, Ollila ditched the conglomerate's other interests to focus on wireless telecom. His hands-off management style inspired innovation and creativity, and employees worked in teams to turn the company around. Nokia beefed up its research and development efforts and designed the 2100 series with stylish, contemporary features. The company had predicted sales of 400,000 units when it launched the 2100 series in late 1993. Actual sales were 20 million.

Operating profits soared to $1 billion in 1995, but Ollila was determined to stay ahead of the competition. Nokia began introducing models that appealed to specific market segments, from user-friendly phones that required only one hand to operate to models with switchable covers and selectable ringing tones. A series of market winners pushed Nokia past Motorola as the world's top mobile maker by the end of the 1990s, with nearly 30 percent of the global market and more than one-third of the U.S. market.

Nokia's Secret Code

From the beginning of Nokia's dramatic turnaround, the company realized that teamwork, focus, and innovation were key to success. At annual meetings known as the Nokia Way, employees now help determine Nokia's priorities. Nokia executives then translate these priorities into a strategic plan and make sure they stay on track by monitoring annual revenue growth. If growth of a product line falls below 25 percent, employees shift their focus to other products with more potential.

Another element of Nokia's success is the company's ability to innovate with an eye on the future. More than a third of its employees work in research and development, fostering new technologies, creating new products, and even envisioning new business models. Not unlike clothing designers and car manufacturers, Nokia realizes that a constant stream of new designs with breakthrough capabilities is critical to maintaining consumer interest.

Smart strategy and fast, creative implementation continue to pay off. Nokia entered the new millennium as the world's top mobile phone maker, with sales above $30 billion and profits of more than $3 billion.

Dialing in to New Challenges

Ollila knows that sustaining this phenomenal growth requires constant attention and reinvention. As he puts it, "This isn't a business where you do one big strategic thing right and you're set for the next five years." Nokia must keep evolving and innovating to stay on top, and everything from the organizational structure to technology investment is fair game. The company continues to sharpen its focus on mobile communications, having sold off more than a dozen peripheral business units between 1996 and 2001.

Maintaining profitability is among the biggest challenges. Nokia used to hold a strong lead in unique phone technologies, but as often happens in electronics, many of these once-unique features and functions are now available off the shelf in inexpensive integrated circuits. Several companies even sell "phone kits" that are ready to assemble, making it much easier for Nokia's competitors to build phones. Such advances help lower prices for consumers but blunt Nokia's advantages and put tremendous pressure on profit margins.

Meanwhile, many mobile phone markets are reaching saturation, and convincing existing customers to move up to new phones is a tough sell. A key step in this effort will be persuading millions of people to surf the web on their phones or use built-in digital cameras, music players, and other new phone capabilities. Elsewhere, the vast Chinese market beckons, but the question of which phone standard China will settle on—and therefore which phone companies will be best positioned to sell there—has yet to be answered.

If anyone has demonstrated the ability to make it happen, though, it's Jorma Ollila, and he is convinced Nokia is ready to lead the industry with the next generation of wireless phones. But only time will tell whether this company can repeat its stunning performance.

Critical Thinking Questions

1. Why did Nokia shift its focus to wireless communications?
2. How does Nokia stay ahead of its competitors?
3. What new challenges does Nokia face today?
4. Visit Nokia's website and answer these questions: Has Nokia managed to continue growth and maintain profits? How does Nokia encourage consumers to try new features and functions such as digital photography? How does Nokia explore new technologies and business possibilities that aren't in its immediate corporate focus? How does the Nokia Research Center help the rest of the company?

VIDEO CASE

Space Age Information Systems: Boeing Satellite Systems

Learning Objectives

The purpose of this video is to help you:

1. Recognize why a business must manage information.
2. Consider the role of information systems within an organization.
3. Recognize how information systems and communication technology contribute to a company's efficiency and performance.

Synopsis

The world's leading manufacturer of commercial communications satellites, Boeing Satellite Systems is a wholly owned subsidiary of Boeing and serves customers in 14 countries. Each of the company's more than 8,000 employees is equipped with a personal computer or laptop, which can also serve as a television to receive broadcasts about company activities. The company's information system collects data from all departments, analyzes the information, and then disseminates the results to help management make decisions that will boost performance, productivity, and competitiveness. The chief information officer also oversees security precautions and disaster recovery plans to safeguard the company's valuable data.

Discussion Questions

1. *For analysis:* What role do information systems play in the Boeing Satellite Systems division?
2. *For analysis:* What are some of the ways in which information technology can improve productivity and performance at Boeing Satellite Systems?
3. *For application:* What potential problems might Boeing Satellite Systems have encountered when introducing computer kiosks into factory operations?

4. *For application:* In addition to showing Boeing-made satellites being launched, what else should the company broadcast to employees' computers? Why?

5. *For debate:* Should Boeing Satellite Systems use software to prevent potential abuses by monitoring how its employees use their personal computers and laptops? Support your chosen position.

Online Exploration

Visit the Boeing Satellite Systems website at www.boeing.com/ satellite and follow links or search the site to learn more about its state-of-the-art integration and test facility. Also browse the site to see what the company says about its use of information systems and communication technology. Why would the company discuss technology in detail on a public website? What specific benefits of information systems does Boeing Satellite Systems highlight? Why are these benefits important to customers who buy satellites?

PART 1

Mastering Global and Geographical Skills—Why Finland Leads in Wireless Technology

Despite its small size and relative isolation in the Arctic Circle, Finland is a nation of what marketing jargonists like to call "early adopters," the people most willing to try out new technologies and to make them their own. In the 1970s Finns were the first people in Europe using fax machines. In the early 1980s Finnish universities were wired to their counterparts in California using early forms of the Internet. By the late 1990s, Finland had the world's highest level of Internet and mobile phone use as a percentage of population. While a national predilection for gadgetry plays a part in Finland's emergence as a hub of information technology, more concrete factors are at work.

Part of the reason for Finland's advancement is its geography. When telecommunications developed in the 1970s, Finns were more inclined to pursue wireless options because the costs of running cable to isolated pockets of a vast and frozen nation were daunting. Thus, wireless technology became a priority for the government and the private business sector. Today the wireless mentality is so ingrained in Finland that many new homeowners don't bother ordering fixed-line service.

Finland's mobile communications flagship supports a network of research centers, feeding start-ups that now plan to provide content and services for an expected wireless Internet boom. It is largely because of Nokia that at least 60 percent of Finns have mobile phones. Among young professionals the figure is closer to 100 percent.[35]

Your task: Learn more about Finland's geography and infrastructure and other factors that have influenced its technological advancements. Internet resources such as the CIA World Factbook (www.odci.gov/cia/publications/factbook), the U.S. State Department (www.state.gov), and Virtual Finland (http://virtual.finland.fi) can help you get started. Use these resources and others you may find on the Internet or at the library to answer the following questions:

1. Briefly describe Finland's terrain and climate. How might they have played a role in the country's lead in wireless telecommunications?

2. How does the size of Finland's economy compare to other nations in the world? What industries are strongest in Finland? What products does Finland manufacture? Export?

3. How has Finland's investments in research and technological development paid off?

4. How has information technology penetrated Finnish society?

CHAPTER

5

Small Business, Entrepreneurship, and Franchises

LEARNING OUTCOMES

After studying this chapter, you will be able to

1. Highlight the major contributions small businesses make to the U.S. economy

2. Cite the key characteristics common to most entrepreneurs and list the reasons that they start their own small businesses

3. Discuss three factors contributing to the increase in the number of small businesses, and name three small-business ownership options

4. Highlight the advantages and disadvantages of franchising

5. Explain the two essential functions of a business plan and the importance of preparing a business plan

6. Identify four sources of small-business assistance

7. Discuss the principal sources of small-business private financing

Michelle Donahue-Arpas founded her home-based business GeniusBabies.com to sell gift baskets to parents of newborn babies.

INSIDE BUSINESS TODAY

GeniusBabies.com Builds a Smart Business

Like many entrepreneurs, Michelle Donahue-Arpas's idea for a new business grew out of career experience and personal passions. In her case, working with emotionally disturbed children sparked an interest in music and toys that stimulate mental development in newborns and infants. Throw in a strong desire to stay at home with her first child, and GeniusBabies.com was born.

Donahue-Arpas's first step was to identify an existing product that she figured needed improvement: the gift baskets that families and friends often send to new parents. Donahue-Arpas thought these products offered little real value in relation to their high price tags, and she saw an opportunity to meet the same gift-giving need but with beneficial learning products instead of baby lotion and talcum powder. The gift baskets her company now creates contain a selection of puzzles and other toys that stimulate a baby's cognitive and physical development. Moreover, the baskets fulfill the founder's interest in quality learning products for infants.

Donahue-Arpas established her company as an Internet-only retailer, meeting her need to run the business from home. But unlike so many dot-com businesses that piled up investor cash then went looking for sales under the pressure to generate insane growth, Donahue-Arpas emphasized sensible, sustainable growth from the start. In fact, she started with less than $5,000 and coaxed the business along for $300 or so a month in the beginning. She managed her finances carefully and stayed focused on her target market—parents of newborns—both to avoid speculative investments in unproven markets and to concentrate her limited advertising budget for maximum impact.

Her career as a social worker gave plenty of insight into children, parents, and the products she was offering at GeniusBabies.com, but Donahue-Arpas knew she lacked experience in both business management and the technology needed for a successful Internet operation. So she turned to more experienced business owners for help. She teamed up with fellow "mompreneurs" with similar business goals to share advice, ideas, and even marketing support through a cooperative website called MyBabyShops.com. This advice and lots of trial-and-error learning have expanded Donahue-Arpas's business and technical skills and improved the operation along the way. For example, she redesigned her website to make it easier to find through Internet search engines and discontinued international sales when she realized the company couldn't satisfy overseas customers to the standard she wanted. Dropping international sales also meant she and her family could scale back their hours a bit, approaching something like a normal life at times.

Without the huge marketing budgets that many dot-coms have (or had) GeniusBabies.com emphasizes positive word of mouth, cooperative online marketing with similar companies, and a personal touch that keeps customers happy. Donahue-Arpas knows that simple moves such as personal notes and thank-you messages with orders can pay back big time in customer satisfaction and positive referrals. She says that consumers are so used to impersonal treatment from large corporations that they're pleasantly shocked when her small company communicates in such an intimate way.

Success naturally leads to growth, but Donahue-Arpas has kept it a mom-friendly, family affair. The staff now includes two full-time moms, two-part moms, and the newest addition to the GeniusBabies.com family: her husband George. Her mother and grandmother even pitch in, along with a small army of temporary help during the holiday season.

Managing with limited resources, learning on the fly, digging deep for inspiration—these are all classic elements of the entrepreneurial experience. And so is hard work. Donahue-Arpas routinely works nights and weekends to keep customers satisfied and to manage the many facets of a growing business. Like most entrepreneurs, she has to put more into her work than the average job, but she wouldn't have it any other way. From staying at home to being her own boss to doing work she truly believes in, Michelle Donahue-Arpas has made her personal dream of entrepreneurship come true.[1]

Understanding the World of Small Business

Many small businesses start out like GeniusBabies.com: with an entrepreneur, an idea, and a drive to succeed. In fact, the United States was originally founded by people involved in small businesses—the family farmer, the shopkeeper, the craftsperson. Successive waves of immigrants carried on the tradition, launching restaurants and laundries, providing repair and delivery services, and opening newsstands and bakeries. This trend continued for decades, until improvements in transportation and communication enabled large producers to manufacture goods at low costs and pass the savings on to consumers. Many smaller businesses could not compete with larger retailers on price, so scores of them closed their doors, and big business emerged as the primary economic force. The trend toward bigness continued for several decades, then it reversed.

The 1990s was a golden decade for entrepreneurship in the United States. Entrepreneurs launched small companies in droves to fill new consumer needs. Many took advantage of Internet technologies to gain a competitive edge. Some succeeded; others failed. But the resurgence of small businesses helped turn the U.S. economy into the growth engine for the world.

Today, over 5.8 million small companies exist in the United States.[2] But defining what constitutes a small business is surprisingly tricky, because *small* is a relative term. For example, a manufacturing firm with 500 employees might be considered small if it competes against much larger companies, but a retail establishment with 500 employees might be classified as big when compared with its competitors.

One reliable source of information for small businesses is the Small Business Administration (SBA). This government agency serves as a resource and advocate for small firms, providing them with financial assistance, training, and a variety of helpful programs that are discussed later in this chapter. The SBA defines a **small business** as a firm that is (a) independently owned and operated, (b) is not dominant in its field, (c) is relatively small in terms of annual sales, and (d) has fewer than 500 employees. The SBA reports that 80 percent of all U.S. companies have annual sales of less than $1 million and that about 60 percent of the nation's employers have fewer than five workers.[3]

Economic Roles of Small Businesses

Small businesses are the cornerstone of the U.S. economy. They bring new ideas, processes, and vigor to the marketplace. They generate about 51 percent of private sector output.[4] And they fill a niche market that generally is not served by large businesses. Here are just some of the important roles small businesses play in the economy:

- *They provide jobs.* Small businesses create about 67 to 75 percent of new jobs. Moreover, some 22 million small businesses employ more than 51 percent of the private nonfarm U.S. workforce and generate more than half of the private U.S. gross domestic product.[5]

---

1 LEARNING OBJECTIVE

Highlight the major contributions small businesses make to the U.S. economy

---

small business
Company that is independently owned and operated, is not dominant in its field, and meets certain criteria for the number of employees and annual sales revenue

- *They introduce new products.* The National Science Foundation estimates that small businesses produce 55 percent of U.S. product innovations, a high percentage given the fact that small companies spend considerably less on research and development than large companies do.[6]

- *They supply the needs of large corporations.* Small businesses provide new workers (those entering the labor force for the first time) with basic job training. In addition, many small businesses are distributors, servicing agents, and suppliers who service the needs of larger corporations. Consider Parallax. This 150-employee firm inspects nuclear power plants, implements safety procedures, and cleans up hazardous and nuclear waste at power plants and weapons complexes across the nation. A large percent of Parallax's business comes from servicing the needs of large corporations such as Westinghouse and Lockheed Martin. Not bad for a company launched out of the founder's home with $10,000 in personal savings.[7]

- *They provide specialized goods and services.* Michelle Donahue-Arpas launched GeniusBabies.com to sell a specialized good—gift baskets for parents of newborns. As another example, when Mike Woods tried to teach his son how to read, he couldn't find any toys on the market that helped teach phonics. So he left his job as a partner in a big law firm and started LeapFrog. The company's initial product was the Phonics Disk, a $50 toy that teaches children shapes, sounds, and pronunciation of letters and words. Since 1995, LeapFrog, now a division of Knowledge Universe, has created more than 50 interactive learning products and 40 interactive books.[8]

In addition to these economic roles, small businesses spend about $2.2 trillion annually, just a bit less than the $2.6 trillion spent by big companies.[9]

Characteristics of Small Businesses

Small businesses are of two distinct types: lifestyle businesses and high-growth ventures. The self-employed consultant working part-time from a home office, the corner florist, and the neighborhood pizza parlor fall into the category of *lifestyle businesses*—firms built around the personal and financial needs of an individual or a family. Lifestyle businesses, such as GeniusBabies.com, are modest operations with little growth potential (although some have attractive income potential for the solo businessperson).

In contrast to lifestyle businesses, some firms are small simply because they are new. Many companies—such as FedEx, Microsoft, and UPS—start out as small entrepreneurial firms but quickly outgrow their small-business status. These *high-growth ventures* are usually run by a team rather than by one individual, and they expand rapidly by obtaining a sizable supply of investment capital and by introducing new products or services to a large market. But expanding from a small firm into a large enterprise is no easy task; there's a world of difference between the two.

Compared to large businesses, small businesses generally have fewer products or services, they usually focus on a narrow group of customers, and they remain in close contact with their markets. Small businesses also tend to be more open-minded and willing to try new things than big businesses. Case studies show that small businesses can make decisions faster because the owners are more accessible and they give employees more opportunity for individual expression.

Nonetheless, most small businesses tend to have limited resources, so owners and employees must perform a variety of job functions in order to get the work done. Being a jack-of-all-trades is not for everyone, however (see Exhibit 5.1). When Bob Hammer and Sue Crowe purchased Blue Jacket Ship Crafters, a mail-order model-ship-kit manufacturer, they quickly learned that running a small company was not like running Motorola, where the two had been senior managers for the better part of their careers. It took a lot more

EXHIBIT 5.1

How Small-Business Owners Spend Their Time
The men and women who start their own companies are jacks-of-all-trades, but they devote the lion's share of their time to selling and producing the product.

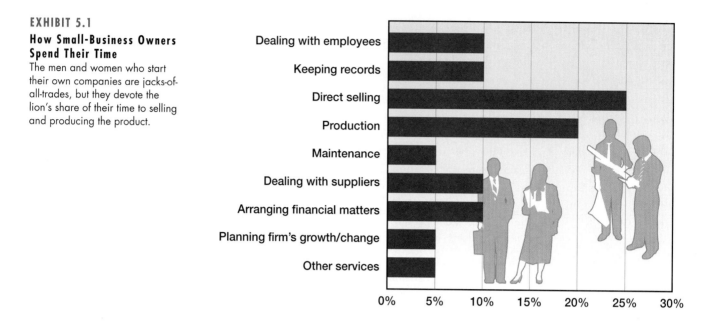

work and time than they had imagined. Even Crowe admits, "You will put in more money than you thought you would, you will take out a lot less, and you will work harder than you did when you were making a six-figure salary at your large corporation."[10] Many executives who leave the corporate world to start a small business have trouble adjusting to the daily grind of entrepreneurship. They miss the support services, conveniences, and fringe benefits they enjoyed in large corporations.

2 LEARNING OBJECTIVE

Cite the key characteristics common to most entrepreneurs and list the reasons that they start their own small businesses

Characteristics of Entrepreneurs

Not everyone has the wherewithal to start a new business. In Chapter 1, we defined an entrepreneur as a person who creates a new business in the face of risk and uncertainty for the purpose of achieving profit, growth, and other opportunities. So what does it take to be an entrepreneur? To begin with, entrepreneurs usually start with nothing more than an idea and then organize the resources necessary to transform that idea into a sustainable business.

Consider the Srivastava sisters. Alka and Mona Srivastava gave up their plans to pursue advanced studies in economics and law to start Florentyna Intima, a lingerie firm. They wanted to create a product that was of higher quality than the average department store lingerie item yet not too expensive. Although they had no experience in manufacturing lingerie, they used their knowledge of economics and business to study the industry. They traveled around Asia to find a designer and manufacturer and eventually chose one based in Bangkok. Then they created prototypes and attended trade shows to display their items to owners of lingerie boutiques. Today their bras, underwear, and camisoles are sold in more than 200 U.S. specialty shops and through catalogs.[11]

Jim Throneburg's idea for a new business involved innovative socks. In the late 1970s, Throneburg noticed that Americans were purchasing multiple pairs of sneakers. "If the shoe changed for the function, I figured I needed to design a sock that complemented the shoe," recalls Throneburg. Since then, he has transformed his family's North

Sisters and partners Alka, left, and Mona Srivastava started Florentyna Intima, a lingerie firm. "We had to learn everything as we went along," Mona says.

Carolina hosiery company, Thorlo Inc., from a commodity business into one of the most innovative sock manufacturers in the world. So far the company has created more than 25 varieties of sport-specific socks.[12]

Throneburg's and the Srivastava sisters' experiences illustrate that innovation can happen anywhere, in any industry, and at any time. Innovation is rarely the product of pure inspiration. Rather, innovation happens when people see things differently. Gary Hamel, chairman of innovation consulting firm Strategos, says that innovators typically view the world through four lenses. They look for deeply held conventions and challenge them; they look for change in the world and understand the revolutionary potential of the change; they empathize with customers and anticipate their needs; and they view their organizations less like businesses and more like skill sets, constantly asking, "How can I creatively recombine what I know to make new things?"[13]

Besides the ability to see things differently, commonly known as vision, entrepreneurs tend to have these qualities in common:

- They are highly disciplined.
- They like to control their destiny.
- They listen to their intuitive sense.
- They relate well to others.
- They are eager to learn whatever skills are necessary to reach their goal.
- They learn from their mistakes.
- They stay abreast of market changes.
- They are willing to exploit new opportunities.
- They seldom follow trends (rather, they spot and interpret trends).
- They are driven by ambition.
- They think positively.
- They prefer the excitement and potential rewards of risk taking over security.

Entrepreneurs who start their own businesses do so for a number of reasons, as Exhibit 5.2 shows. Most, like Michelle Donahue-Arpas, start with relatively small sums of money and operate their business informally from their homes, at least for a while. They have diverse backgrounds in terms of education and business experience. Some come from companies unlike the ones they start; others use their prior knowledge and skills—such as editing, telemarketing, public relations, or selling—to start their own businesses. Still others have less experience but have an innovative idea or a better way of doing something. They find an overlooked corner of the market, exploit a demographic trend unnoticed by others,

EXHIBIT 5.2   Why Entrepreneurs Went into Business
Entrepreneurs seldom cite "making more money" as a primary reason for starting a business.

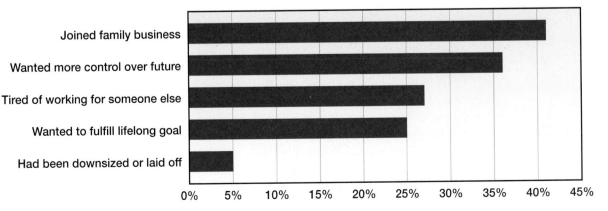

or meet an unsatisfied consumer need through better service or a higher-quality product. Moreover, they often plan and develop their product quickly, while the rest of the business world ponders whether a market for the product exists.

Consider Kate Spade, for example. Spade quit her job as accessories editor for *Mademoiselle* and launched her own handbag company out of her home in 1991. Priced at $100 to $400, Spade's nylon bags weren't cheap, and she had a tough time getting them into trade shows because she didn't "do leather." But Spade's instincts were better than the style-makers'. On an impulse the night before her first trade show, Spade ripped the labels "kate spade new york" from the inside of her bags and stitched them on the outside, sewing until her fingers got puffy. Good move. Barneys ordered 18 of her bags, and *Vogue* decided to feature them on its glossy accessories page. It wasn't long before Julia Roberts and Gwyneth Paltrow (who saw the bags in fashion magazines) had them on their shoulders. Nevertheless, the company didn't become profitable until 1996, when Saks and Neiman Marcus each ordered 3,000 bags for all their stores. Then in 1999 Neiman Marcus purchased a majority stake in the company. Since its inception, Kate Spade's business has flourished. She now sells shoes, accessories, and much more than purses.[14]

Of course, not all entrepreneurs start a new business. Some work within an established enterprise with the mission of developing new products and business opportunities. Called *intrapreneurs*, these individuals may head up small groups in larger organizations.

Factors Contributing to the Increase in the Number of Small Businesses

Several factors are contributing to the growth in the number of a small businesses. One factor is that small-business ownership allows founders to gain control over their own destiny. Although owners face many economic risks, such as uncertainty of income and the risk of losing their entire invested capital, they do not have to worry about being fired or laid off. Moreover, they have the chance to make a difference in the world and an opportunity to combine their concerns for social issues with the desire to earn a good living.

Small-business owners also have a chance to reap unlimited profits by doing work that they enjoy. A common sentiment among small-business owners is that their work really isn't work. Although they work long hours, small-business owners generally love what they do.

In addition to the many benefits of small-business ownership, three other factors are contributing to the increase in the number of small businesses today: technological advances, an increase in the number of minorities and women starting businesses, and corporate downsizing.

Technology and the Internet Personal computers, laptops, fax machines, copiers, printers, answering machines, e-mail, and the Internet have made it easier and more affordable for people to start and operate small businesses. ShippingSupply.com is a good example of how technology is driving the increase in the number of small businesses. Karen Young, a collector of knickknacks, founded this small business when she was looking for affordable packing and shipping materials for her mail-order items. On a whim Young decided to market bubble wrap, plastic foam, and shipping tubes she purchased direct from manufacturers to eBay sellers. Like many businesses, ShippingSupply.com uses the Internet to communicate with customers and suppliers all over the world—any time of the day—and to access the types of resources and information that were previously available only to larger firms. Today ShippingSupply.com has eight full-time employees, occupies 7,000 square feet of warehouse space, and has over 35,000 customers in its database.[15]

Technology and the Internet also make it easier for people like Donahue-Arpas to run their businesses from home. In the past, home-based businesses tended to revolve around crafts or hobbies. But now accountants, writers, lawyers, and consultants can use technolo-

Six Strategies for Working Effectively from Home

If you're seriously considering working from home, you're not alone. Millions of Americans are currently doing so and the number increases daily. Many people start a home office by turning a hobby or interest into a business. Others use existing skills from their salaried job. Whatever the reason, follow these six strategies to increase your chances for home business success.

1. ***Start slowly.*** Moonlight by keeping your full-time job and developing your business as a sideline until it takes off; work a part-time job to provide a base income while you're building your business; or take a major client from your previous job to help launch your fledgling venture.

2. ***Don't sell yourself short.*** When pricing your services, remember perception is important. If potential customers perceive your price as being too high, you'll end up without a sale. If they perceive it as being too low, they'll worry that it may be inferior in quality.

3. ***Select the best at-home office location.*** If you can't designate a separate room, choose a location where you will be disturbed the least. Set aside a space large enough to include these basic work areas: space for a desk and chair and for your equipment; a space where you can collect your thoughts or hold meetings; storage space for books, files, and reference materials; and a large work space for activities such as assembling materials and doing mailings or shipping.

4. ***Don't allow disruptions.*** Separate work time from the time needed to handle household responsibilities, family obligations, and conversations with friends. If disruptions continue, try relocating your office to a different area of the home or changing your office hours.

5. ***Don't overdo it.*** Home offices make it easy to become a workaholic and neglect your personal life. If you find yourself with less and less free time, set up a firm work schedule, protect your free time by making sure clients know your work hours, and establish minibreaks throughout the work day for your personal enjoyment.

6. ***Stay in touch with the outside world.*** Network, attend professional seminars, join community organizations, read business journals, and schedule regular breakfast or luncheon meetings. Building and maintaining professional relationships are a great way to stay current in your field and to gain new clients.

Questions for Critical Thinking

1. Why is the location and physical set-up of a home office important?
2. How can you maintain a professional image when working from home?

gies to set up shop at home—or on the web. In fact, according to the Small Business Administration, about 53 percent of all small businesses are home based.[16]

Increase in the Number of Minorities and Women Starting Small Businesses

An increase in the number of minority and women entrepreneurs like Donahue-Arpas is also fueling small business growth. Data from the U.S. Small Business Administration show that between 1987 and 1997, the number of minority-owned firms grew 168 percent—more than triple the 47 percent growth rate of U.S. businesses overall. Minority-owned firms now make up 18.6 percent of all small businesses.[17]

Consider Mashti Shirvani. He has been making ice cream since he was a child. By the ninth grade, he was running the family ice cream shop in Iran. He came to the United States in 1978 to study electronics. To support himself, Shirvani worked as a chef in various restaurants and eventually opened his own restaurant. But ice cream was his first love. So in 1980, he bought an existing establishment and named it Mashti Malone. Initially the store sold almost all its ice cream to some 300 Persian and Armenian restaurants, whose customers

Customers can order exotic ice cream flavors from the Mashti Malone website and have their purchases shipped anywhere in the United States.

love flavors like Rosewater because the taste reminds them of home. But in the late 1990s, after an intense marketing campaign and a publicity stint on the Food Channel, Mashti Malone grew in popularity. Until that time "we didn't take the retail part of our business very seriously," said Shirvani's brother and partner. Today, Mashti Malone is a fixture in a Los Angeles neighborhood, satisfying locals who flock to the store on weekends. Over 60 percent of the store's retail customers are non-Persian. The company also sells its unusually flavored ice creams via its website.[18]

The number of women starting small businesses has also increased sharply over the past three decades—from 5 percent of all small businesses to over 39 percent. These businesses now employ more than 18.5 million people and ring up more than $3.1 trillion in annual sales.[19] As Exhibit 5.3 shows, women start small businesses for a number of reasons. Some choose to run their own companies so they can enjoy a more flexible work arrangement; others start their own business because of barriers to corporate advancement, known as the *glass ceiling*. Josie Natori, is a perfect example of such a scenario. By her late 20s, Natori was earning six figures as the first female vice president of investment banking at Merrill Lynch. But Natori knew that her chances of further advancement were slim in the male-dominated financial world. So she started her own lingerie line. Today Natori is the owner of a multi-million-dollar fashion empire that sells elegant lingerie and evening wear.[20]

Corporate Downsizing Contrary to popular wisdom, business start-ups soar when the economy sours. In fact, several well-known companies were started during recessions. Tech titans William Hewlett and David Packard joined forces in Silicon Valley in 1938 during the Great Depression. Bill Gates started Microsoft during the 1975 recession. And the founders of Sun Microsystems, Compaq Computer, Adobe Systems, Silicon Graphics, and

EXHIBIT 5.3

Women Starting Businesses
More than half of all women business owners started their own businesses because they had an entrepreneurial idea or wished to advance their careers.

What women with companies less than a decade old say is the main reason they started a business:

Reason	Percentage
Entrepreneurial idea	35%
Glass ceiling	22%
Bored in job	14%
Downsized	10%
Fell into it	10%
Family event	5%
Born entrepreneur	3%
Reenter workforce	1%

Lotus Development all started their companies in 1982—in the midst of a recession and high unemployment.[21]

During hard times, many companies downsize or lay off talented employees, who then have little to lose by pursuing self-employment. Armed with years of experience, a working knowledge of their industries, and a network of connections, these former employees set out to establish companies of their own. Consider Nancy Rodriguez, an ex-employee of Swift & Co., a meat-processing company. When Swift downsized its research and development (R&D) staff in the mid-1980s, Rodriguez left to start her own venture, Food Marketing Support Services. Her staff of 20 food-science experts now assist big-food companies like Swift in bringing new-product concepts to market. The food companies come up with the idea, but hire Food Marketing to fully develop the concept, create prototypes, and so on. Using outsiders such as Food Marketing's staff of experts saves the food companies time and money in the crucial trial-and-error stage of developing the new concept. It also allows them to maintain smaller R&D staffs.[22]

Starting a Small Business

Could you or should you join the thousands of entrepreneurs who start some 800,000 new businesses every year?[23] No matter how fast you learn and how much investigating you do, you're likely to find that the challenges of running a business are far greater than you anticipated. If you decide to take the risk, you can get into business for yourself in three ways: Start from scratch, buy an existing business, or obtain a franchise.

Small-Business Ownership Options

Roughly two-thirds of business owners launch **start-up companies**; that is, they start from scratch rather than buy an existing operation or inherit the family business. Starting a business from scratch has many advantages and disadvantages, as Exhibit 5.4 points out. Of the three options for going into business for yourself, starting a new business is the most common route, and in many cases, the most difficult.

Another way to go into business for yourself is to buy an existing business. This approach tends to reduce the risks—provided, of course, you check out the company carefully. When

start-up companies
New ventures

EXHIBIT 5.4   Weighing the Advantages and Disadvantages of Starting a New Business
Owning a business has many advantages, but you must also consider the potential drawbacks.

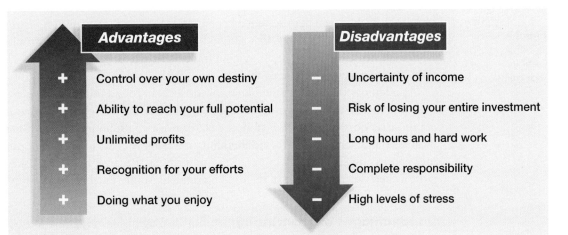

Advantages	Disadvantages
+ Control over your own destiny	− Uncertainty of income
+ Ability to reach your full potential	− Risk of losing your entire investment
+ Unlimited profits	− Long hours and hard work
+ Recognition for your efforts	− Complete responsibility
+ Doing what you enjoy	− High levels of stress

Panera, which means "time for bread" in Latin, is starting to do for bread what Starbucks did for coffee. The St. Louis–based chain has over 250 locations, with franchise commitments for 500 more.

you buy a business, you generally purchase an established customer and supplier base, functioning business systems, a proven product or service, and a known location. You don't have to go through the painful period of building a reputation, establishing a clientele, finding suppliers, and hiring and training employees. In addition, financing an existing business is often much easier than financing a new one; lenders are reassured by the company's history and existing assets and customer base. With these major details already settled, you can concentrate on making improvements.

Still, buying an existing business is not without disadvantages. For one thing, the business may be overpriced. For another, inventories and equipment may be obsolete. Furthermore, the location may no longer be satisfactory, the previous owner may have created ill will, your personality may clash with those of existing managers and employees, and outstanding bills owed by customers may be difficult to collect.

The Franchise Alternative

An alternative to buying an existing business is to buy a **franchise** in somebody else's business. This approach enables the buyer to use a larger company's trade name and sell its products or services in a specific territory. In exchange for this right, the **franchisee** (the small-business owner who contracts to sell the goods or services) pays the **franchisor** (the supplier) an initial fee (which can range from $1,000 to $10 million) and monthly royalties (which can range from 1 percent to 12 percent of sales).[24]

Types of Franchises   Franchises are of three basic types. A *product franchise* gives you the right to sell trademarked goods, which are purchased from the franchisor and resold. Car dealers and gasoline stations fall into this category. A *manufacturing franchise*, such as a soft-drink bottling plant, gives you the right to produce and distribute the manufacturer's products, using supplies purchased from the franchisor. A *business-format franchise* gives you the right to open a business using a franchisor's name and format for doing business. Fast-food chains such as Papa John's, KFC, Taco Bell, and Pizza Hut typify this form of franchising.

Advantages of Franchising   Franchises are a factor of rising importance in the U.S. economy. The International Franchise Association estimates that franchising accounts for about 40 percent of all U.S. retail sales.[25]

Why is franchising so popular? For one thing, when you invest in a franchise, you know you are getting a viable business, one that has "worked" many times before. If the franchise is well established, you get the added benefit of instant name recognition, national advertising programs, standardized quality of goods and services, and a proven formula for success. As one franchise owner put it, "Buying a franchise is like buying a cookbook: The recipe is there, but you have to do the cooking yourself."[26]

In addition to a ready-made blueprint for success, for an initial investment (from a few thousand dollars to upward of a million, depending on the franchise), franchisees generally get these services: site-location studies, market research, training, a support network, technical assistance, and assistance with building or leasing your structure, decorating the building, purchasing supplies, and operating the business. Because few franchisees are able to write a check for the amount of the total investment, some franchisors also provide financial assistance.

Disadvantages of Franchising   Although franchising offers many advantages, it is not the ideal vehicle for everyone. First, owning a franchise is no guarantee of wealth. Even

4 LEARNING OBJECTIVE

Highlight the advantages and disadvantages of franchising

franchise
Business arrangement in which a small business obtains rights to sell the goods or services of the supplier (franchisor)

franchisee
Small-business owner who contracts for the right to sell goods or services of the supplier (franchisor) in exchange for some payment

franchisor
Supplier that grants a franchise to an individual or group (franchisee) in exchange for payments

though it may be a relatively easy way to get into business, not all franchises are hugely profitable. In fact, some franchisees barely survive. Furthermore, when a chain loses its cutting edge in the marketplace, being stuck with a franchise can be painful. Franchisees are usually bound by contracts to sell only authorized goods, often supplied by the franchisor itself at whatever price the franchisor wants to charge. By contrast, if independent retailers run into trouble with their product lines, they can change suppliers or perhaps switch rapidly to a whole new line of business.

Another disadvantage of franchising is the monthly payment, or royalty, that must be turned over to the franchisor. Royalties are not necessarily bad as long as the franchisee gets ongoing assistance in return. An additional drawback of owning a franchise is loss of independence. Franchisors can prescribe virtually every aspect of the business, down to the products and supplies purchased, the details of employee uniforms, and the color of the walls. To protect their public image, franchisors require franchisees to maintain certain standards and to operate their outlets according to the terms spelled out in the franchisor's operations manual. If a franchise fails to meet the minimum standards established for the operation, the franchisor may terminate its license.

Prospective Subway franchisees must attend company training classes and pass a final exam before they can own a Subway sandwich shop.

Of course, some franchisors give franchisees a voice in how advertising funds are used and a voice in the franchising system by establishing franchise advisory boards. Successful franchisors recognize that franchisees are closest to the customer and can be hotbeds for innovation. Few, however, grant their franchisees the degree of autonomy that Great Harvest does. To promote innovation, Great Harvest Bread franchisees are free to run their bakeries as they see fit—on just one condition: They must share what they learn along the way with other franchise owners.[27]

How to Evaluate a Franchise   How do you protect yourself from a poor franchise investment? The best way is to study the opportunity carefully before you commit. Since 1978 the Federal Trade Commission has required franchisors to disclose information about their operations to prospective franchisees. By studying this information, you can determine the financial condition of the franchisor and ascertain whether the company has been involved in lawsuits with franchisees. Before signing a franchise agreement, it's also wise to consult an attorney. Exhibit 5.5 suggests some points to consider as you study the package of information on the franchise.

Nevertheless, some people find out too late that franchising isn't the best choice for them. They make a mistake common among prospective franchisees—buying without really understanding the day-to-day business. Often, prospects simply don't get beyond the allure of the successful name or concept—or the mistaken notion that a franchise brings instant success. "People go into a sub shop at the noon hour and see the cash register opening and closing," says one franchise expert. "What they don't see is having to get there at 4:00 A.M. to bake the bread." Buying a franchise is much like buying any other business: It requires analyzing the market, finding capital, choosing a site, hiring employees, and buying equipment. The process also includes an element not found in other businesses—evaluating the franchisor.

One of the best ways to evaluate a prospective franchisor is by talking to other franchisees. At a minimum, you should find out what other franchisees think of the opportunity. If they had it to do over again, would they still invest? You might even want to spend a few months working for someone who already owns a franchise you're interested in.

Market saturation is another important issue to consider when evaluating a franchise opportunity. Many growth-seeking franchisors have exhausted most of the prime locations

EXHIBIT 5.5   Ten Questions to Ask Before Signing a Franchise Agreement
A franchise agreement is a legally binding contract that defines the relationship between the franchisee and the franchisor. Because the agreement is drawn up by the franchisor, the terms and conditions generally favor the franchisor. Before signing the franchise agreement, be sure to consult an attorney.

1. What does the initial franchise fee cover? Does it include a starting inventory of supplies and products?
2. How are the periodic royalties calculated and when are they paid?
3. Are all trademarks and names legally protected?
4. Who provides and pays for advertising and promotional items?
5. Who selects the location of the business?
6. Is the franchise assigned an exclusive territory?
7. If the territory is not exclusive, does the franchisee have the right of first refusal on additional franchises established in nearby locations?
8. Is the franchisee required to purchase equipment and supplies from the franchisor or other suppliers?
9. Under what conditions can the franchisor and/or the franchisee terminate the franchise agreement?
10. Can the franchise be assigned to heirs?

and are now setting up new franchises in close proximity to existing ones. Owners of General Nutrition Companies (GNC) franchises learned this lesson the hard way. The franchisees were besieged by cold-eyed competition—not from other vitamin merchants, but from the parent company itself—when GNC began opening company stores not far from their existing franchises. The franchisees took GNC to court, claiming that company stores benefited from purchasing inventory at wholesale prices and thus could undercut the selling prices of vitamins at franchised stores. After a lengthy court battle, GNC reached a settlement agreement with the franchisees.[28]

Preparing a Business Plan

5 LEARNING OBJECTIVE

Explain the two essential functions of a business plan and the importance of preparing a business plan

Whether you're purchasing a franchise, buying an independent business, or starting a new venture of your own as Donahue-Arpas did, all three options require a lot of work (see Exhibit 5.6), not the least of which is planning. Although many successful entrepreneurs claim to have done little formal planning, even the most intuitive of them have *some* idea of what they're trying to accomplish and how they hope to do it. Jeff Bezos, founder of Amazon.com, planned the world's first online bookstore in the backseat of his car as his wife drove them from New York to Seattle. As Bezos and other entrepreneurs know, planning is essential for success. No amount of hard work can turn a bad idea into a profitable one: The health-food store in a meat-and-potatoes neighborhood and the child-care center in a retirement community are probably doomed from the beginning.

Planning forces you to think ahead. Before you rush in to supply a product, you need to be sure that a market exists. You must also try to foresee some of the problems that might arise and figure out how you will cope with them. For instance, what will you do if one of your suppliers suddenly goes out of business? Can you locate another supplier quickly? What if the neighborhood starts to change—even for the better? An influx of wealthier neighbors may cause such a steep increase in rent that your business must move. Also, tough competition may move into the neighborhood along with the fatter pocketbooks. Do you have an alternative location staked out? What if styles suddenly change? Can you switch quickly from, say, hand-painted crafts to some other kind of artwork?

One of the first steps you should take toward starting a new business is to develop a **business plan,** a written document that summarizes an entrepreneur's proposed business venture, communicates the company's goals, highlights how management intends to achieve

business plan
A written document that provides an orderly statement of a company's goals and how it intends to achieve those goals

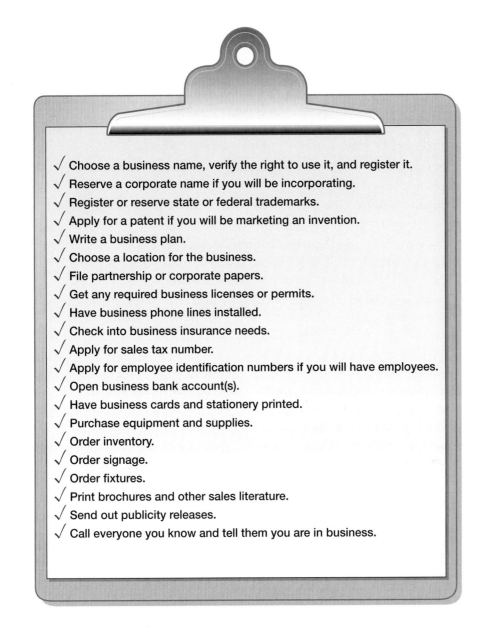

- ✓ Choose a business name, verify the right to use it, and register it.
- ✓ Reserve a corporate name if you will be incorporating.
- ✓ Register or reserve state or federal trademarks.
- ✓ Apply for a patent if you will be marketing an invention.
- ✓ Write a business plan.
- ✓ Choose a location for the business.
- ✓ File partnership or corporate papers.
- ✓ Get any required business licenses or permits.
- ✓ Have business phone lines installed.
- ✓ Check into business insurance needs.
- ✓ Apply for sales tax number.
- ✓ Apply for employee identification numbers if you will have employees.
- ✓ Open business bank account(s).
- ✓ Have business cards and stationery printed.
- ✓ Purchase equipment and supplies.
- ✓ Order inventory.
- ✓ Order signage.
- ✓ Order fixtures.
- ✓ Print brochures and other sales literature.
- ✓ Send out publicity releases.
- ✓ Call everyone you know and tell them you are in business.

those goals, explains its marketing opportunities and strategy, and shows how consumers will benefit from the company's products or services.

Preparing a business plan serves two important functions: First, it guides the company operations and outlines a strategy for turning an idea into reality. Writing a plan requires you to gain an in-depth understanding of the industry in which you plan to compete, and it subjects your ideas to the test of reality. It forces you to make important decisions about personnel, marketing, facilities, suppliers, and distributors and to develop programs that will help you succeed. Second, a business plan serves as a vehicle to attract lenders and investors. In fact, if you don't have a business plan, many investors won't even grant you an interview. A solid business plan is written proof to potential investors that an entrepreneur has performed the necessary research and has studied the business opportunity adequately. It demonstrates that the entrepreneur has considered both the positive and the negative aspects of the new venture. It may even deliver the hard truth—that the concept just won't work. Discovering this fact on paper can save considerable time and money.

As you can imagine, writing a business plan requires a great deal of thought. There are no shortcuts. If you are starting out on a small scale and using your own money, your business plan may be relatively informal. But at a minimum, you should describe the basic concept of the business and outline its specific goals, objectives, and resource requirements. A formal plan, suitable for use with banks or investors, should cover these points:

- *Summary.* In one or two pages, summarize your business concept. Describe your product or service and its market potential. Highlight some things about your company and its owners that will distinguish your firm from competition. Summarize your financial projections and the amount of money investors can expect to make on their investment. Be sure to indicate how much money you will need and for what purpose.

- *Mission and objectives.* Explain the purpose of your business and what you hope to accomplish.

- *Company and industry.* Give full background information on the origins and structure of your venture and the characteristics of its industry.

- *Products or services.* Give a complete but concise description of your product or service, focusing on its unique attributes. Explain how customers will benefit from using your product or service instead of those of your competitors.

- *Market and competition.* Provide data that will persuade the investor that you understand your target market and can achieve your sales goals. Be sure to identify the strengths and weaknesses of your competitors in addition to the features and benefits of your product or service.

- *Management.* Summarize the background and qualifications of the principals, directors, and key management personnel in your company. Include résumés in the appendix.

- *Marketing strategy.* Provide projections of sales and market share, and outline a strategy for identifying and contacting customers, setting prices, providing customer services, advertising, and so forth. Whenever possible, include evidence of customer acceptance, such as advance product orders.

- *Design and development plans.* If your product requires design or development, describe the nature and extent of what needs to be done, including costs and possible problems.

- *Operations plan.* Provide information on the facilities, equipment, and labor needed.

- *Overall schedule.* Forecast development of the company in terms of completion dates for major aspects of the business plan.

- *Critical risks and problems.* Identify all negative factors and discuss them honestly.

- *Financial forecasts and requirements.* Include a detailed budget of start-up and operating costs, as well as projections for income, expenses, and cash flow for the first three years of business. Identify the company's financing needs and potential sources.

- *Exit strategy.* Explain how investors will be able to cash out or sell their investment, such as through a public stock offering, sale of the company, or a buyback of the investors' interest. When covering these points, keep in mind that your audience wants short, concise information—not lengthy volumes—and realistic projections for growth.

For additional information on writing business plans, see the Appendix "Your Business Plan," and complete the Business PlanPro exercises at the end of each text part.

Understanding Why New Businesses Fail

Even if you write a winning business plan, you have no guarantee of success. In fact, you may have heard some depressing statistics about the number of new businesses that fail. Some reports say your chances of succeeding are only one in three; others claim that the odds are even worse, stating that 85 percent of all new business ventures fail within 10 years. Actual statistics show otherwise, however. Among all companies that close their doors, only

EXHIBIT 5.7   Why New Businesses Fail
Experts have identified these 10 reasons as the most likely causes of new business failure.

1. Management incompetence
2. Lack of industry experience
3. Inadequate financing
4. Poor business planning
5. Unclear or unrealistic goals
6. Failure to attract and keep target customers
7. Uncontrolled growth
8. Inappropriate location
9. Poor inventory and financial controls
10. Inability to make the entrepreneurial transition

about one in seven actually fails—that is, goes out of business leaving behind unpaid debts.[29] Moreover, the true failure rate is much lower if you remove the operations that Dun & Bradstreet (D&B) business analysts say aren't "genuine businesses." For instance, a freelancer who writes one article for a magazine and then stops writing would be counted as a failed business under the traditional measurement (which is based on tax returns).

Most new businesses fail for a number of reasons, as Exhibit 5.7 suggests. Lack of management skills, experience, and proper financing are among the top 10 reasons for failure. So is uncontrolled growth. Growth forces changes throughout the organization that affect every aspect of the business operation. In general, growing companies need to install more sophisticated systems and processes. They must staff positions that never existed and learn how to delegate responsibilities and control. They must hire experienced managers. And they must stay focused. When growth is too rapid, it can force so much change that things spin out of control. And nothing can kill a successful business faster than chaos.[30]

Doug and Jill Smith learned this lesson the hard way. With a 50 percent increase in sales in one year alone, their company, Buckeye Beans & Herbs, was spinning out of control. They needed more people to take the orders, fill them, package the product, and so on. It took the couple a while to realize they weren't running a little mom-and-pop operation anymore. "We just couldn't do it all, and we didn't have the people in place yet," note the Smiths, who eventually got things back on the right track.[31]

If turning away potential business sounds like a bad idea, consider the experience of Chase Bobko, a Seattle software company. Founded in 1987, Chase Bobko steadily built a successful business on programs that allowed clients to manage huge volumes of information on the Internet. The website management business took off in late 1998, and overnight Chase Bobko became the category leader. It signed up new clients at a furious pace, bringing in both Motorola and Boeing in a single week. Revenues ballooned from $2.2 million in 1999 to $5.6 million in 2000. Unfortunately, those new clients were more demanding than the company had anticipated. Chase Bobko hired strategists to help new clients solve their problems, but it couldn't hire and train them fast enough. In hindsight, the company should have turned down some new business, admits the founders. "Our people tried to be attentive, but they were overwhelmed."[32]

Besides growing too rapidly, another mistake entrepreneurs make is to stray too far from the original product or market. Take Lifeline Systems, a provider of personal-response systems for the elderly. Fewer than 10 years after it was founded, the company went public and was distributing its monitoring devices in more than 700 hospitals across the United States. Fearing that its focus was too small, the company diversified by introducing a new version of its monitoring device that could be used by children and college students in emergencies. It sold these devices to drug, electronics, and department stores at roughly half the price of the original model. But the mass-market strategy found few buyers. Worse, it alienated the company's hospital customers, whose demand for the original product was already falling as a result of slashed hospital budgets. Lifeline began reporting losses. When a new CEO was hired to turn things around, one of the first things he did was undo the company's diversification efforts and restore the company's original focus.[33]

Managing in the 21st Century

Why Did the Dot-Coms Fall to Earth?

In the late 1990s, just about any dot-com company that wanted to hawk wares over the Net found plenty of eager investors. The web was underdeveloped territory. Young entrepreneurs with a good idea and a business plan could make a couple of phone calls to venture capitalists (VCs) and raise millions.

But amidst the popping of champagne corks, troubles soon began to brew. Entrepreneurs learned the hard way that successfully launching a public company was much different from successfully running one. Cyberspace got crowded. New dot-coms went unnoticed. Desperate to get consumers' attention and business, e-tailers spent lavishly on advertising. Some pumped out discount offers and free-shipping promises—hemorrhaging cash and piling up losses. Investors watched in shock as dot-com stock prices fell through the floor and companies vanished.

Why did the dot-comes run out of steam? Experts now cite these reasons:

- *Poor management.* Many dot-coms were founded by people with cool ideas but no business sense. Some entrepreneurs were in such a rush to go public, they forgot one small detail: they needed a sound business plan. They were more attracted by the potential to get rich than by the need to create a company "built to last."

- *Unrealistic goals.* Many dot-com start-ups were dedicated to achieving the impossible—launching companies in weeks and attracting millions of customers in months. But the evolution of consumers was far slower than most people predicted. People were not ready to buy mortgages and new cars in volume over the Internet. The hoped-for volume simply did not exist.

- *Going public too soon.* Venture capitalists, eager to back the next Amazon or eBay, tossed huge sums of money at companies that had barely a prayer of prospering. In many cases the VCs took the dot-coms public too soon—long before the company or its management could prove consistent performance to the public.

- *Extravagant spending.* Companies spent recklessly to lure customers with special promotions and silly marketing campaigns—no matter the cost. For instance, drkoop.com, an online health site, burned through three-quarters of the $84 million it raised in an IPO in less than 1 year. Some dot-coms even began to act like conventional retailers—building costly warehouses and adding staff—to compete. Online grocer Webvan, for example, built distribution centers that could handle up to 8,000 orders a day—many times more than a traditional warehouse—arguing that it would give the upstart a big cost advantage over its bricks-and-mortar competitors. But it never gained the sales volume to take full advantage of the efficiencies. After tearing through $830 million in start-up and IPO funds, Webvan closed up shop.

Today's entrepreneurs have more reasonable expectations about the time and effort required to build a business. They realize that they must prove their ability to manage costs and show a clear sign of profitability before venture capitalists will even consider them. Moreover, without stock market euphoria and a source for easy capital, many entrepreneurs must rely on the cash generated from their business to finance growth.

Questions for Critical Thinking

1. Why did many dot-com businesses fail at the beginning of the 21st century?
2. Why is it more difficult for entrepreneurs to start a dot-com business in today's environment?

Even when signs of failure begin to surface, some entrepreneurs don't pull the plug fast enough. Jeff Schwarz worked three years without drawing a salary and used up $100,000 of his personal savings before closing his photography business, Remarkable Moments.[34]

Keep in mind that failure isn't always the end of the world. Many presidents of big, successful companies, including Fred Smith of FedEx, can spin long tales about how failure got them where they are today or how failure was a valuable learning experience. Moreover, many sources of small-business assistance exist to help you plan your new business and overcome these obstacles.

Helping New Businesses Get Started

6 LEARNING OBJECTIVE

Identify four sources of small-business assistance

Many local business professionals are willing to serve as mentors and can help you avoid the pitfalls of business. As a small-business owner, you may turn to small-business resources such as the Service Corps of Retired Executives (SCORE), incubators, the Internet, and the Small Business Administration. These resources can help you evaluate your business idea, develop a business plan, locate start-up funding sources, and show you how to package your business image professionally.

SCORE

Some of the best advice available to small businesses costs little or nothing. It's delivered by SCORE's 12,000 volunteers. The men and women of this SBA resource partner are working and retired executives and active small-business owners who offer advice and one-on-one counseling sessions on topics such as developing a business plan, securing financing, and managing business growth. To date, more than 4.5 million clients have been helped by SCORE counselors.[35]

Michael Bornstein, president of Skate America, relied on the advice of SCORE counselors to help him build a website so he could sell his skateboarding equipment and accessories online. "My SCORE counselors were a tremendous help in setting up the website. They advised me on systems requirements, advertising opportunities, and some key people to utilize when setting up Skate America," says Bornstein. Today Skate America's profits continue to outpace projections, and the company's prospects are as exciting as some of the tricks performed by its daredevil customers.[36]

Whether you use a SCORE counselor or find a private mentor, having someone to bounce your ideas off or to help you create a five-year financial forecast can increase the chances of your business's survival, as Lynelle and John Lawrence discovered. Owners of the Mudhouse Café in Charlottesville, Virginia, the Lawrences used a SCORE representative to help them prepare a detailed business plan and obtain financing. "There's no way we would be here without SCORE," confesses the couple.[37]

After a friend referred John and Lynelle Lawrence to SCORE, counselor Joe Geller (right) helped the couple through each stage of preparation for their Mudhouse Café in Charlottesville, Virginia.

Incubators

Incubators are centers that provide "newborn" businesses with just about everything a company needs to get started—office space, expert advice, legal and accounting services,

incubators
Facilities that house small businesses during their early growth phase

clerical services, marketing support, contacts, and more.[38] Some incubators are open to businesses of all types; others specialize in a specific industry or product. Regardless, the goal is to convert "tenant" firms into "graduates," so most incubators set limits—from 18 months to 5 years—on how long a company can stay in the nest.[39]

Studies show that firms that start out in incubators typically increase sales by more than 400 percent from the time they enter until the time they leave.[40] Furthermore, 8 of 10 businesses nurtured in incubators succeed. Incubators, of course, are not a new idea. Thousands of them hatch successful businesses each year. For instance, a Milwaukee, Wisconsin, business incubator gave Yolanda Cross the chance to move her catering-related business from her home into a more professional setting, where it has flourished.[41]

The Internet

The Internet is another source of small-business assistance. Sonja Edmond, owner of Heavenly Bounty Giftbaskets, a hand-crafted gift-basket business, had to look no farther than her computer screen when she needed help. Although she enjoyed making gift baskets as a hobby, she wasn't sure whether a viable market existed to support a home-based business. So she posted a price-setting question on CompuServe's Working from Home and Handcrafts forum. Within 24 hours, her e-mail box was flooded with answers from forum members, who "convinced me I could do this," she says. Edmond struck a resource gold mine: Not only did she find the encouragement she needed to plunge into entrepreneurship, she also got valuable business leads and advice on licensing her product.[42]

Small Business Administration

The Small Business Administration provides a number of support services for small-business owners. A look at the organization's website (www.sba.gov) highlights the type of informational services the SBA provides. These include an answer desk to help callers with questions about starting and running a small business; online business courses that cover topics such as starting a small business, business planning, and growing your business; online publications that cover such topics as working for a family business, financing businesses, pricing products and services, finding and paying employees, and much more.

The Small Business Association is also a good source for financial assistance. Guaranteed loans provided by the SBA launched FedEx, Intel, and Apple Computer. To get an SBA-backed loan, you apply to a regular bank, which actually provides the money; the SBA guarantees to repay up to 80 percent of the loan if you fail to do so. The average SBA-backed loan is about $100,000; the upper limit is $1 million with a 75 percent guarantee.[43] Microloans range from $100 to $25,000, with the average loan of $10,000 paid back over four years.[44] From the businessperson's standpoint, SBA-backed loans are especially attractive because most have longer repayment terms than conventional bank loans—nine years as opposed to two or three. A longer repayment term translates into lower monthly payments.

In addition to operating its loan guarantee program, the SBA provides a limited number of direct loans and special services to minorities, women, and veterans.[45] The SBA 8(a) program, for example, helps disadvantaged companies

With plenty of perseverance and a $19,000 microloan from the SBA, Karla Brown was able to start her business, Ashmont Flowers Plus.

obtain contracts with the U.S. government. Optimum Management Systems (OMS) is one successful 8(a) company. Founded in 1998, the information technology consulting company did about $40,000 in revenue. Thanks to assistance from the 8(a) program, the company initially concentrated on government contracts before breaking into other markets. Today OMS employs about 65 people and projects $5 million to $6 million in annual revenues.[46]

The SBA's Small Business Investment Companies (SBICs) and Minority Enterprise Small Business Investment Companies (MESBICs) also provide financing to minority-owned businesses. These organizations are similar in operation to venture-capital firms, but they tend to make smaller investments and are willing to consider businesses that private financiers may not want to consider.[47]

Financing a New Business

7 LEARNING OBJECTIVE

Discuss the principal sources of small-business private financing

If you're starting a new business or purchasing an existing operation, chances are you may not qualify for an SBA-backed loan or you'll need more money than the SBA can provide. Companies need money to pay employees, purchase inventory, and acquire assets such as land, production facilities, and equipment before they can generate revenue.

Private Financing Sources

Like GeniusBabies.com, most new businesses turn to private financing sources, such as family, friends, and loans from banks, finance companies, or other commercial lenders to finance their needs. As the start-up grows, owners can raise additional funds by selling shares of stock to the public.

One good source of private financing is big business. Companies such as Coca-Cola and Procter & Gamble fund young companies in exchange for stock or exclusive rights to future products. By working with start-ups, larger companies hope to hasten product development and infuse their own operations with more of the entrepreneurial spirit.[48]

Bank loans are another source of private financing, but obtaining such financing can be difficult for most start-ups. "They pretty much laughed me out of the bank and wouldn't give me a loan," recalls Kirt Perron, founder of Jamba Juice. So instead Perron sold a real estate investment and borrowed the rest of the money he needed to start his business from family and friends. Today Perron is a minority owner of the privately held company, which sells smoothies, juices, bread, and hot soups in over 350 stores across the United States.[49]

Most banks consider start-ups such as Jamba Juice or GeniusBabies.com risky so they shy away from lending money to them. Moreover, the risk inherent in some start-ups justifies higher interest rates than banks are allowed to charge by law. Thus, most banks will finance a start-up only if they can obtain payment guarantees from other financially sound parties or to the extent that the business has marketable collateral, such as buildings and equipment, to back the loan.[50] (In Chapter 17, we'll discuss the advantages, the disadvantages, and the risk of financing with borrowed money, or debt versus financing with equity by selling shares of stock in your firm to the public.) If corporate or bank loans are not an option, you may be able to turn to other sources of private financing assistance such as venture capitalists, angel investors, or credit cards.

venture capitalists
Investment specialists who provide money to finance new businesses or turnarounds in exchange for a portion of the ownership, with the objective of making a considerable profit on the investment; also called VCs

Venture Capitalists **Venture capitalists** are investment specialists who raise pools of capital from large private and institutional sources (such as pension funds) to fund ventures that have a high, rapid growth potential and a need for large amounts of capital. Venture capitalists, or VCs as they're called in entrepreneurial circles, do not simply lend money to a small business as a bank would. Instead they provide money and management expertise in return for a sizable ownership interest in the business. Once the business becomes profitable, venture capitalists reap the reward by selling their interest to other long-term investors for a sizable profit.

Burned by the dot-com fallout at the end of the millennium, many VCs have become more selective about whom they lend money to. Of the 600,000 or so businesses that started up in 2000, only some 5,000 received venture capitalist funding.[51] In addition to being more selective, venture capitalists are also becoming more aggressive in their oversight and management of firms they've already funded. For instance, they are shutting down firms that show little promise and pumping extra cash into those they think can survive. VCs are also scrutinizing the business plans of capital seekers more skeptically. Applicants must now show real revenue, real customers, and a clear path to profits.[52] Still, most venture capitalist firms will only finance firms that need $10 million or more.[53] Thus, if you're looking for only $1 or $2 million of financing, you might want to find an angel instead.

Angel Investors   Comfortable with risks that scare off many banks, *angel investors* put their own money into start-ups with the goal of eventually selling their interest for a large profit. These wealthy individuals are willing to loan smaller amounts of money than are VCs and to stay involved with the company for a longer period of time.

Start-ups that seek out angels typically have spent their first $50,000 to $100,000 and are now looking for the next $250,000 to grow their business.[54] In addition to providing financing, angels can be a great source of business expertise and credibility. High-profile angels include such experts as Bill Gates (chairman of Microsoft), Marc Andresseen (founder of Netscape), and others.[55]

Credit Cards   According to a recent study by the Federal Reserve, approximately one-third of small businesses use credit cards to finance their new business ventures.[56] Many people turn to credit cards because credit card companies don't care how borrowers spend the money just as long as they pay the bill. Others use credit cards because they are the only source of funding available to them. But high penalties and hidden fees can make credit cards a risky way to finance a business, as Jorge de la Riva discovered. He used personal credit cards to start up his industrial wholesale business—an experience he calls "playing with the tiger." As de la Riva put it, "You can make it work only if you have a definite plan to pay back the debt."[57] Unfortunately, many do not.

Going Public

Public financing is achieved by selling shares of a company's stock. Whenever a corporation offers its shares of ownership, or **stock**, to the public for the first time, the company is said to be *going public*. The initial shares offered for sale are the company's **initial public offering (IPO)**. Going public is an effective method of raising needed capital, but it can be an expensive and time-consuming process filled with regulatory nightmares. Public companies must file a variety of statements with the Securities and Exchange Commission, pay costly fees, and prepare audited financial statements, as Chapter 17 points out. Moreover, public versus private ownership has a number of advantages and disadvantages, as Chapter 6 will discuss next.

stock
Shares of ownership in a corporation

initial public offering (IPO)
Corporation's first offering of stock to the public

Summary of Learning Objectives

1. **Highlight the major contributions small businesses make to the U.S. economy.**

   Small businesses bring new ideas, processes, and vigor to the marketplace. They generate about 51 percent of private sector output. They provide about 67 to 75 percent of all new jobs and employ over half of the private nonfarm U.S. workforce. Small businesses introduce new goods and services, provide specialized products, and supply the needs of large corporations. In addition, they spend almost as much as big businesses in the economy each year.

2. **Cite the key characteristics common to most entrepreneurs and list the reasons that they start their own small businesses.**

   Entrepreneurs are highly disciplined, intuitive, innovative, ambitious individuals who are eager to learn and like to set trends. They prefer excitement and are willing to take risks to reap the rewards. Some of the reasons that they start their own small businesses are that they have an innovative idea or see an opportunity that others don't see, they want more control over their future, they are tired of working for someone else, they want to fulfill a lifelong goal, and they have been laid off.

3. **Discuss three factors contributing to the increase in the number of small businesses, and name three small-business ownership options.**

   One factor is the advancement of technology and the Internet, which makes it easier to start a small business, compete with larger firms, or work from home. A second factor is the increase in the number of minority and women entrepreneurs. Finally, corporate downsizing has made self-employment or small-business ownership an attractive and viable option. When starting a small business, you have three options: you can start a new company from scratch, you can buy a going concern, or you can invest in a franchise. Each option has its advantages and disadvantages when it comes to cost, control, certainty, support, and independence.

4. **Highlight the advantages and disadvantages of franchising.**

   A franchise has the advantages of having wide name recognition and being a blueprint for a viable business. It offers franchisees mass advertising, financial help, training, a support network, and assistance with such start-up tasks as site and property selection, market research, and operations. But owning a franchise also has disadvantages. These include monthly royalty payments to the franchisor, constraints on the franchisee's independence to operate the business as he or she sees fit, the risk of being stuck with a losing enterprise, and the risk of market saturation.

5. **Explain the two essential functions of a business plan and the importance of preparing a business plan.**

   Two essential functions of a business plan are to guide the company operation by outlining a strategy for turning an idea into reality and to serve as a vehicle to attract lenders and investors. Preparing a business plan is important because it helps owners understand their industry, their market, and their competition. It helps them foresee challenges, critical risks, and opportunities so they are better prepared for the future. It helps them plan for the hiring of management and employees, as well as the selection of facilities and suppliers. It forces them to plan and develop company goals and objectives and develop a marketing and distribution strategy to reach these goals and objectives. And it forces them to prepare financial forecasts, identify sources for financial assistance, and determine whether the venture will work from an operational and financial viewpoint.

6. **Identify four sources of small-business assistance.**

   One source for small-business assistance is SCORE—an organization staffed by retired executives and active small-business owners who provide counseling and mentoring for free. Incubators are another source. They provide facilities, business resources, and all types of start-up support. The Internet is also an excellent resource for product and market research, business leads, advice, and contacts. Finally, the Small Business Administration provides small-business advice via help desks, online business courses, and electronic publications. It is also a good source for financial assistance and SBA-backed loans.

7. **Discuss the principal sources of small-business private financing.**

   The Small Business Administration, although not an actual source, can assist entrepreneurs by guaranteeing small bank loans up to 80 percent of the amount borrowed. Bank and corporate loans are another principal source of private financing. So are family and friends. Other alternatives include venture capitalists, angel investors, and credit cards.

KEY TERMS

business plan **(126)**

franchise **(124)**

franchisee **(124)**

franchisor **(124)**

incubators **(131)**

initial public offering (IPO) **(134)**

small business **(116)**

start-up companies **(123)**

stock **(134)**

venture capitalists **(133)**

TEST YOUR KNOWLEDGE

Questions for Review

1. What are the advantages of buying a business rather than starting one from scratch?

2. What factors should you consider when evaluating a franchise?

3. What are the key components of a business plan?

4. What are the key reasons for most small-business failures?

5. What is a business incubator?

Questions for Analysis

6. Why is writing a business plan an important step in starting a new business?

7. Why is it important to establish a time limit for a new business to generate a profit?

8. What things should you consider when evaluating a franchise agreement?

9. Why would a company seek financing from an angel investor instead of using a venture capitalist or going public?

10. ***Ethical Considerations:*** You're thinking about starting your own hot dog and burger stand. You've got the perfect site in mind, and you've analyzed the industry and all the important statistics. It looks as if all systems are go. Uncle Pete is even going to back you on this one. You really understand the fast-food market. In fact, you've become a regular at a competitor's operation (down the road) for over a month. The owner thinks you're his best customer. He even wants to name a sandwich creation after you. But you're not there because you love Frannie's fancy fries. No, you're actually spying. You're learning everything you can about the competition so you can outsmart them. Is this behavior ethical? Explain your answer.

Questions for Application

11. Briefly describe an incident in your life pertaining to a particular failure. What was it and what did you learn from this experience?

12. Pick a small business whose general operation you understand (example: dry cleaner, local restaurant, college book store). If you were starting a similar business operation, what critical risks and problems might you identify in your business plan?

13. ***Integrated:*** Entrepreneurs are one of the five factors of production as discussed in Chapter 1. Review that material plus Exhibit 1.1 (Rags to Riches; see page 6), and explain why entrepreneurs are an important factor for economic success.

14. ***Integrated:*** Pick a local small business or franchise that you visit frequently and discuss whether that business competes on price, speed, innovation, convenience, quality, or any combination of those factors. Be sure to provide some examples.

PRACTICE YOUR KNOWLEDGE

Handling Difficult Situations on the Job: Getting the Inside Scoop on a Franchise

You know that franchises can be a smart first move for aspiring business owners. But you've also read that they demand long hours, steep investments, and rigid rule following. Still, you're seriously investigating buying into an existing franchise system. You've narrowed down the choices, and this week you're investigating the Subway franchise, hoping for a location near your hometown of Bartlesville, Oklahoma. With 14,700 stores worldwide, Subway seems like a good investment, but you need to be certain.

When you called Subway's headquarters and asked for references, you were told about Tharita Jones, who operates a Subway store in Tulsa, about 30 miles from Bartlesville. "She's been with us for about five years now," said the woman as she gave you Jones's name and number. Jones generously agreed to meet with you for a brief time next week, despite her daily avalanche of work (watching over employees, doing paperwork, ordering supplies, talking to customers, checking restrooms, fixing problems . . .). You want to make the meeting as efficient as possible, for your sake and hers.[58]

Your task: Considering all you've learned in this chapter about franchise advantages and disadvantages, and small businesses in general, what questions will be most pertinent for your meeting with Jones? Jot them down as you think of them so you'll be prepared. Remember, you won't want to waste Jones's time with questions you can get answered from other sources, so focus on eliciting her unique insights as a franchisee.

Building Your Team Skills

The 10 questions shown in Exhibit 5.5 cover major legal issues you should explore before plunking down money for a franchise. In addition, however, there are many more questions you should ask in the process of deciding whether to buy a particular franchise.

With your team, think about how to investigate the possibility of buying a pizza franchise. First, brainstorm with your team to draw up a list of sources (such as printed sources, Internet sources, and any other suitable sources) where you can locate basic background information about the franchisor. Also list at least two sources you might consult for detailed information about buying and operating your franchise. Next, generate a list of at least 10 questions any interested buyer should ask about this potential business opportunity.

Choose a spokesperson to present your team's ideas to the class. After all the teams have reported, hold a class discussion to analyze the lists of questions generated by all the teams. Which questions were on most teams' lists? Why do you think those questions are so important? Can your class think of any additional questions that were not on any teams' lists but seem important?

EXPAND YOUR KNOWLEDGE

Discovering Career Opportunities

Would you like to own and operate your own business? Whether you plan to start a new business from scratch or buy an existing business or a franchise, you will need certain qualities to be successful. Start your journey to entrepreneurship by reviewing this chapter's section on entrepreneurs. Now delve deeper into the career opportunities of owning and running a small business.

1. Which of the entrepreneurial characteristics mentioned in the chapter describe you? Which of those characteristics can you develop more fully in advance of running your own business?

2. Using library sources or an Internet search engine, find a self-test on entrepreneurial qualities or use the entrepreneurial test at the website www.onlinewbc.gov/docs/starting/test.html. Analyze the test's questions. Which of the characteristics discussed in this chapter are mentioned or suggested by the questions included in the test?

3. Answer all the questions in the entrepreneurial self-test you have selected. Which questions seem the most critical for entrepreneurial success? How did you score on this self-test and on the questions you think are most critical? Before you go into business for yourself, which characteristics will you need to work on?

Developing Your Research Skills

Scan issues of print or online editions of business journals or newspapers for articles describing problems or successes faced by small businesses in the United States. Clip or copy three or more articles that interest you and then answer the following questions.

1. What problem or opportunity does each article present? Is it an issue faced by many businesses, or is it specific to one industry or region?

2. What could a potential small-business owner learn about the risks and rewards of business ownership from reading these articles?

3. How might these articles affect someone who is thinking about starting a small business?

Exploring the Best of the Web

URLs for all Internet exercises are provided at the website for this book, www.prenhall.com/bovee. *When you log on to the text website, select Chapter 5, then select "Student Resources," click on the name of the featured website, and review the website to complete these exercises.*

Explore these chapter-related websites, review their content, and answer the following questions for each website you visit:

1. What is the purpose of this website?

2. What kinds of information does this website contain? Please be specific.

3. How is the information provided at this website useful for businesspeople? Consumers?

4. How did you expand your knowledge of small business, entrepreneurship, and franchising by reviewing the material at this website? What new things did you learn about this topic?

Guide Your Way to Small-Business Success

Inc.com has an outstanding selection of articles and advice on buying, owning, and running a small business that you won't want to miss. If you're considering a franchise, the tools and tips at this site will help you find your ideal business. Concerned about financing? Check out the articles on raising start-up capital, finding an angel, or attracting venture capital. You can also find information on how to create or spruce up a website, set up your first office, develop entrepreneurial savvy, and overcome burnout. Running a small business is no easy feat, so get a head start by reading the Inc.com guides online. www.inc.com/guides

Start a Small Business

Thinking about starting your own business? The U.S. Small Business Administration (SBA) website puts you in touch with a wealth of resources to assist you in your start-up. Perhaps you would like some professional business counseling, financial assistance, or advice on developing a business plan. Starting a new business or buying an existing one can be an overwhelming process. But you can increase your chances of success by taking your first steps with the SBA's Startup Kit. So log on to find out if entrepreneurship is for you. Then do your research and discover some of the secrets of success. www.sba.gov

Learn the ABCs of IPOs

Taking a company public is not for the faint of heart. But like a Broadway opening, a successful debut can launch a relatively unknown company into stardom—or allow it to quietly disappear from the public eye. Even today's largest corporations were at some point small start-ups looking for public financing. Which company is the next Coca-Cola, Home Depot, or Microsoft? How do IPOs work? How does a young company play the IPO game? You can

find the answer to these questions and more by checking out the Beginner's Guide to IPOs at Hoover's IPO Central. www.hoovers.com/ipo

Learning Interactively

Companion Website

Visit the Companion Website at www.prenhall.com/bovee. For Chapter 5, take advantage of the interactive "Study Guide" to test your chapter knowledge. Get instant feedback on whether you need additional studying. Read the "Current Events" articles to get the latest on chapter topics, and complete the exercises as specified by your instructor. Expand your learning with a visit to the "Research Area." There you will find a wealth of information you can use to complete your course assignments.

A CASE FOR CRITICAL THINKING

Why Is Papa John's Rolling in Dough?

As a high school student working at a local pizza pub, John Schnatter liked everything about the pizza business. "I liked making the dough; I liked kneading the dough; I liked putting the sauce on; I liked putting the toppings on; I liked running the oven," recalls Schnatter. "From the get-go, I fell in love with the business." Working his way through college by making pizzas, Schnatter was obsessed with perfect pizza topping placement and bubble-free melted cheese. But he knew that something was missing from national pizza chains: a superior-quality pizza delivered to the customer's door. And his dream was to one day open a pizza restaurant that would fill that void.

Humble Beginnings

Schnatter got his chance shortly after graduating from Ball State University with a business degree. His father's tavern was $64,000 in debt and failing. So Schnatter sold his car, purchased some used restaurant equipment, knocked out a broom closet in the back of his father's tavern, and began selling pizzas to the tavern's customers. Soon the pizza became the tavern's main attraction and helped turn his father's business around.

With a recipe for success, Schnatter opened the first Papa John's restaurant in 1985 in Louisville, Kentucky. Then he set about growing his business. After all, he was no novice. He knew the grass-roots of the pizza business, had an intuitive grasp on what customers wanted, and knew how to make pizzas taste a little bit better than the competition's.

Expanding the Pie Chart

John Schnatter used franchising to grow the business. Today about 75 percent of Papa John's are franchised; the rest are company-owned. But Papa John's doesn't just move into an area and open up 200 stores. It expands one store at a time. Before a single pizza hits

the ovens, franchisees spend six months to a year assessing an area's potential. Once a store is up and running, the company puts enormous effort into forecasting product demand. Franchisees project demand one to two weeks in advance. They factor in anything from forthcoming promotions to community events to the next big high school football game. If a major sports event is on TV, store owners are ready for the surge in deliveries.

Papa John's made its European debut in 1999 by acquiring Perfect Pizza Holdings, a 205-unit delivery and carryout pizza chain in the United Kingdom. The acquisition gave Papa John's instant access to proven sites that would have been difficult to obtain. Besides the real estate, Perfect Pizza had a good management team that Schnatter could fold into his organization.

The Perfect Crust

If one strength rises above the others in Schnatter's path to success, it's his ability to recruit and retain the right people. "There's nothing special about John Schnatter except the people around me," Schnatter says. "They make me look better" and they make Papa John's what it is—committed to its heritage of making a superior-quality, traditional pizza.

Quality control is another important part of Schnatter's secret recipe for success. To ensure a high-quality product, Papa John's keeps things simple. About 95 percent of the restaurants are take-out only. They offer just two types of pizza, thin crust or regular—no salads, no sandwiches, and no buffalo wings. Owners are trained to remake any pies that rate less then eight on the company's 10-point scale. If the cheese shows a single air bubble or the crust is not golden brown, out the offender goes. To make sure everything is in order, Schnatter visits four to five stores a week. His attention to detail has helped the company earn awards. Papa John's was twice voted number one in customer satisfaction among all fast-food restaurants in the American Consumer Satisfaction Index.

Piping-Hot Performance

Now the third-largest pizza chain, Papa John's has more than 2,700 stores in 47 states and nine international markets. Annual sales have mushroomed to about $1.7 billion. But like many companies today, Papa John's faces challenges. Although Americans consume pizza at the rate of 350 slices a second, restaurant pizza sales are as flat as a thin-crust pie. Papa John's opens new restaurants and closes unprofitable outlets all the time to keep profitability in line. But it's becoming increasingly difficult to expand the company's share of the pie in a highly competitive and stagnant industry. Which means that to succeed, Papa John's must grab market share from giants such as Pizza Hut, Little Caesar's, and delivery king Domino's. And that's becoming increasingly difficult.

Critical Thinking Questions

1. What steps did John Schnattner take to turn Papa John's into a successful pizza chain?

2. If you were drafting Papa John's initial business plan, what would you need to know about competition?

3. Why does Papa John's rely on franchising to grow its concept?

4. Go to Chapter 5 of this text's website at www.prenhall.com/bovee. Click on the Papa John's link to read about Papa John's franchise system. What kind of assistance does Papa John's provide new franchisees? What are Papa John's minimum requirements for new franchisees? How much does it cost to open a Papa John's restaurant?

VIDEO CASE

Flying High in Small Business: Durango Pro-Focus Flight Training Center

Learning Objectives

The purpose of this video is to help you:

1. Identify the characteristics of an entrepreneur.
2. Consider the reasons why a small business succeeds or fails.
3. Understand the financing needs of a small business.

Synopsis

Durango Pro-Focus Flight Training Center aims to be a high-flying small business. Working with Midland College and Mesa Airlines, the company provides classroom, simulator, and in-flight training for airline pilots. The entrepreneurial founder and his top managers have a passion for their business—working 80 hours per week or more at the outset—but also keep a critical eye on the market to be sure they are satisfying a real need. To start, management funded the purchase of a flight simulator and other equipment as well as the construction of an administrative wing for office space, in anticipation of attracting future investors. Now Durango wants to expand by setting up training centers in other areas with good flying weather, a nearby airport, and a college partner.

Discussion Questions

1. *For analysis:* What specific factors are contributing to Durango's success?

2. *For analysis:* Why are passion and skill important characteristics for Durango's founders?

3. *For application:* What specific factors might cause Durango to fail—and what can management do to avoid failure?

4. *For application:* What might Durango do to assess the need for its services in other areas of the United States?

5. *For debate:* Do you agree with Durango's decision to expand by setting up its own training centers rather than franchising the operation? Support your chosen position.

Online Exploration

Visit the Pro-Focus website at www.pro-focuspilots.com to see how Durango is working with Midland College and Mesa Airlines to train pilots. Then follow the link to read more about Durango, its history, and its top managers. How does the company use this site to convey an image of quality and competence for its training services? How does it communicate the benefits for students who use its training services?

CHAPTER 6

Forms of Business Ownership and Business Combinations

LEARNING OBJECTIVES

After studying this chapter, you will be able to

1. List five advantages and four disadvantages of sole proprietorships

2. List five advantages and two disadvantages of partnerships

3. Cite four advantages and three disadvantages of corporations

4. Delineate the three groups that govern a corporation and describe the role of each

5. Explain the differences between common and preferred stock from a shareholder's perspective

6. Highlight the advantages and disadvantages of public stock ownership

7. Identify the key advantages and disadvantages of business combinations

Kinko's, once known simply as the leading chain of printing and copy shops, has recast itself for the work-obsessed digital age.

INSIDE BUSINESS TODAY

Restructuring Kinko's Partnerships to Duplicate Success

Paul Orfalea knew he would run a big company someday. He just never envisioned Kinko's as that dream. At 22, Orfalea borrowed enough money to open a copying service near the University of California, Santa Barbara. The store was so small that he had to wheel the single copier onto the sidewalk to make room for customers. Nevertheless, it met the needs of local college students.

By 1995 (some 25 years later), Kinko's—named after Orfalea's reddish, curly hair—had grown into a chain of 815 stores operating in five countries. But Kinko's wasn't managed as a single entity. Instead, the business consisted of 130 separate partnerships, each operating groups of stores. Even though Orfalea retained a majority interest in each partnership, the partners were free to operate their stores as they saw fit. As a result, not all Kinko's were the same. And that was a problem. Some reinvested their earnings in high-tech equipment while others cashed in their profits. This meant that traveling customers would find color copiers and high-speed Internet access at spruced-up outlets in one city and dilapidated storefronts with little more than black-and-white copy machines in another.

Orfalea knew that to succeed in a high-tech marketplace, all Kinko's stores would have to look alike and offer comparable services. Moreover, with more and more people working at home, in cars, in airports, or in other remote locations, the stores would have to invest in expensive equipment such as digital printers, high-speed copiers, fast Internet connections, and even videoconferencing equipment to service the growing needs of these virtual workers. Such services, of course, would require lots of money and the help of experts. So in 1997 Orfalea selected private investors Clayton, Dublier & Rice (CD&R) to help turn things around.

Plunking down $219 million in exchange for a 30 percent share of Kinko's, CD&R rolled the 130 individual partnerships into a single privately held corporation and gave each partner shares of stock in the newly formed organization. It took the original partners some time to adjust to the new corporate structure—after all, they were accustomed to being their own bosses. But eventually they came around. Besides, they realized that having a private equity stake in Kinko's could be worth a sizable fortune if the company went public some day.

With Kinko's now a corporate entity, everyone was working in the same direction. The store managers expanded their services to include onsite rental of computer time, document binding and finishing, custom printing, passport photos, mailing services (including overnight delivery drop-off), videoconferencing facilities, and more. In addition, the company launched KinkonetSM, a proprietary document distribution and print network that allows customers to transmit information from one Kinko's site to another. Now customers can go into any of the 1,100 Kinko's stores in such far-flung places as Australia, Japan, South Korea, or the United Kingdom and find the same equipment, supplies, and services, making it possible for small-business owners and travelers to rely on Kinko's as their office away from home.

Restructuring the partnerships has helped turn Kinko's into the world's leading provider of document solutions and business services. But it has also launched a behind-the-scenes feud. Orfalea and the former partners are demanding that CD&R either take Kinko's public or buy their remaining shares. CD&R has rejected both requests. The former partners claim that CD&R is dragging its feet because it will lose $5 million in annual management fees it collects under the present arrangement. "Nonsense," says CD&R's president. "We would love this company to go public. But going public is difficult to do. It's like Gallo wine: You don't go public before its time."[1]

Forms of Business Ownership

As Paul Orfalea knows, one of the most fundamental decisions you must make when starting a business is selecting a form of business ownership. This decision can be complex and can have far-reaching consequences for your business. Picking the right ownership structure involves knowing your long-term goals and how you plan to achieve them. Your choice also depends on your desire for ownership and your tolerance for risk. Furthermore, as your business grows, chances are you may change the original form you selected, as Orfalea did.

The three most common forms of business ownership are sole proprietorship, partnership, and corporation. Each form has its own characteristic internal structure, legal status, size, and fields to which it is best suited. Each has key advantages and disadvantages for the owners. Exhibit 6.1 contrasts the characteristics of the three forms of business ownership.

Sole Proprietorships

sole proprietorship
Business owned by a single individual

A **sole proprietorship** is a business owned by one person (although it may have many employees); it is the easiest and least expensive form of business to start. Many farms, retail establishments, and small service businesses are sole proprietorships, as are many home-based businesses (such as caterers, consultants, and computer programmers).

1 LEARNING OBJECTIVE

List five advantages and four disadvantages of sole proprietorships

Advantages of Sole Proprietorships   A sole proprietorship has many advantages. One is ease of establishment. All you have to do to launch a sole proprietorship is obtain necessary licenses, start a checking account for the business, and open your doors. Another advantage is the satisfaction of working for yourself. As a sole proprietor, you can make your own decisions, such as which hours to work, whom to hire, what prices to charge, whether to expand, and whether to shut down. Best of all, you can keep all the after-tax profits, and profits are taxed at individual income tax rates, not at the higher corporate rates.

As a sole proprietor, you also have the advantage of privacy; you do not have to reveal your performance or plans to anyone. Although you may need to provide financial information to a banker if you need a loan, and you must provide certain financial information when you file tax returns, you do not have to prepare any reports for outsiders as you would if the company were a public corporation.

unlimited liability
Legal condition under which any damages or debts attributable to the business can also be attached to the owner because the two have no separate legal existence

Disadvantages of Sole Proprietorships   One major drawback of a sole proprietorship is the proprietor's **unlimited liability**. From a legal standpoint, the owner and the business are one and the same. Any legal damages or debts incurred by the business are the owner's responsibility. As a sole proprietor, you might have to sell personal assets, such as your home, to satisfy a business debt. And if someone sues you over a business matter, you might lose everything you own if you do not have the proper types and amount of business insurance.

In some cases, the sole proprietor's independence can also be a drawback, because the business depends on the talents and managerial skills of one person. If problems crop up, the sole proprietor may not recognize them or may be too proud to seek help, especially given the high cost of hiring experienced managers and professional consultants. Other disadvantages include the difficulty of a single-person operation obtaining large sums of capi-

EXHIBIT 6.1 **Characteristics of the Forms of Business Ownership**
The "best" form of ownership depends on the objectives of the people involved in the business.

STRUCTURE	OWNERSHIP RULES AND CONTROL	TAX CONSIDERATIONS	LIABILITY EXPOSURE	BASE OF ESTABLISHMENT AND TERMINATION
Sole proprietorship	One owner has complete control.	Profits and losses flow directly to the owner and are taxed at individual rates.	Owner has unlimited personal liability for business debts.	Easy to set up but leaves owner's personal finances at risk. Owner must generally sell the business to get his or her investment out.
General partnership	Two or more owners; each partner is entitled to equal control unless agreement specifies otherwise.	Profits and losses flow directly to the partners and are taxed at individual rates. Partners share income and losses equally unless the partnership agreement specifies otherwise.	Personal assets of any operating partner are at risk from business creditors.	Easy to set up. Partnership agreement recommended but not required. Partners must generally sell their share in the business to recoup their investment.
Limited partnership	Two or more owners; the general partner controls the business; limited partners don't participate in the management.	Same as for general partnership.	Limited partners are liable only for the amount of their investment.	Same as for general partnership.
Corporation	Unlimited number of shareholders; no limits on stock classes or voting arrangements. Ownership and management of the business are separate. Shareholders in public corporations are not involved in daily management decisions; in private or closely held corporations, owners are more likely to participate in managing the business.	Profits and losses are taxed at corporate rates. Profits are taxed again at individual rates when they are distributed to the investors as dividends.	Investor's liability is limited to the amount of his or her investment.	Expense and complexity of incorporation vary from state to state; can be costly from a tax perspective. In a public corporation, shareholders may trade their shares on the open market; in a private corporation shareholders must find a buyer for their shares to recoup their investment.

tal and the limited life of a sole proprietorship. Although some sole proprietors pass their business on to their heirs as part of their estate, the owner's death may mean the demise of the business. And even if the business does transfer to an heir, the founder's unique skills may have been crucial to the successful operation of the business.

Partnerships

If starting a business on your own seems a little intimidating, you might decide to share the risks and rewards of going into business with a partner. In that case, you would form a **partnership**—a legal association of two or more people as co-owners of a business for profit. You and your partners would share the profits and losses of the business and perhaps the management responsibilities. Your partnership might remain a small, two-person operation or it might have multiple partners, like Kinko's did. Of the three forms of business ownership, partnerships are the least common (see Exhibit 6.2).

Partnerships are of two basic types. In a **general partnership**, all partners are considered equal by law, and all are liable for the business's debts. For instance, when accounting

partnership
Unincorporated business owned and operated by two or more persons under a voluntary legal association

general partnership
Partnership in which all partners have the right to participate as co-owners and are individually liable for the business's debts

EXHIBIT 6.2
Popular Forms of Business Ownership
The most popular form of business ownership is sole proprietorship, followed by corporations, then partnerships.

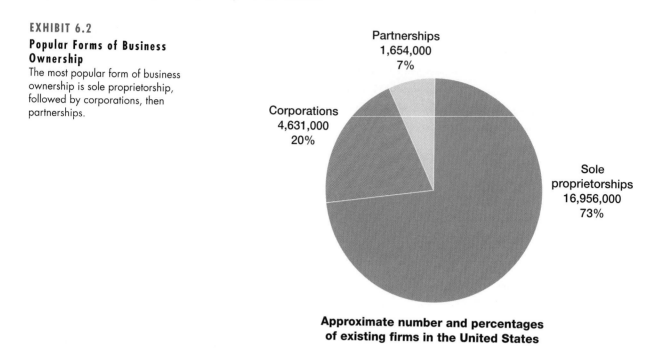

Partnerships
1,654,000
7%

Corporations
4,631,000
20%

Sole proprietorships
16,956,000
73%

Approximate number and percentages of existing firms in the United States

limited partnership
Partnership composed of one or more general partners and one or more partners whose liability is usually limited to the amount of their capital investment

firm Laventhol and Horwath plunged into bankruptcy, the partners had to dig into their own pockets to satisfy creditors.[2] To guard against personal liability exposure, some organizations choose to form a **limited partnership**. Under this type of partnership one or more persons act as *general partners*, who run the business, while the remaining partners are passive investors (that is, they are not involved in managing the business). These partners are called *limited partners* because their liability (the amount of money they can lose) is limited to the amount of their capital contribution. Many states now recognize *limited liability partnerships* (LLPs) in which all partners in the business are limited partners and have only limited liability for the debts and obligations of the partnership. The limited liability partnership was invented to protect members of partnerships from being wiped out by claims against their firms. Most states restrict LLPs to certain types of professionals such as attorneys, physicians, dentists, and accountants.[3]

Advantages of Partnerships Proprietorships and partnerships have some of the same advantages. Like proprietorships, partnerships are easy to form. Partnerships also provide the same tax advantages as proprietorships, because profits are taxed at individual income-tax rates rather than at corporate rates.

However, in a couple of respects, partnerships are superior to sole proprietorships, largely because there's strength in numbers. When you have several people putting up their money, you can start a more ambitious enterprise. In addition, the diversity of skills that good partners bring to an organization leads to innovation in products, services, and processes, which improves the chances of success.[4] The partnership form of ownership also broadens the pool of capital available to the business. Not only do the partners' personal assets support a larger borrowing capacity, but the ability to obtain financing increases because general partners are legally responsible for paying off the debts of the group.

Arthur Andersen partners and limited partners must rely on the provisions spelled out in the firm's partnership agreement to determine their rights and liabilities once they no longer are a member of the firm. Some ex-partners are concerned about their personal liability as Enron creditors, shareholders, and employees seek to recover the billions of dollars they have lost as a result of poor audit practices.

Finally, forming a partnership increases the chances that the organization will endure, because new partners can be drawn into the business to replace those who die or retire. For example, even though the original partners of the accounting firm KPMG Peat Marwick (founded in 1897) died many years ago, the company continues.

Disadvantages of Partnerships   Except in limited liability partnerships, at least one member of every partnership must be a general partner. All general partners have unlimited liability. Thus, if one of the firm's partners makes a serious business or professional mistake and is sued by a disgruntled client, all general partners are financially accountable. At the same time, general partners are responsible for any debts incurred by the partnership.

Another disadvantage of partnerships is the potential for interpersonal problems. Difficulties often arise because each partner wants to be responsible for managing the organization. Electing a managing partner to lead the organization may diminish the conflicts, but disagreements are still likely to arise. Moreover, the partnership may have to face the question of what to do with unproductive partners. And if a partner wants to leave the firm, conflicts can arise over claims on the firm's profits and on capital the partner invested. Provisions for handling the departure and addition of partners are usually covered in the partnership agreement.

Partnership Agreement   A *partnership agreement* is a written document that states all the terms of operating the partnership by spelling out the partners' rights and responsibilities. Although the law does not require a written partnership agreement, it is wise to work with a lawyer to develop one. One of the most important features of such an agreement is to address sources of conflict that could result in battles between partners. The agreement spells out such details as the division of profits, decision-making authority, expected contributions, and dispute resolution. Moreover, a key element of this document is the buy/sell agreement, which defines the steps a partner must take to sell his or her partnership interest or what will happen if one of the partners dies.

Corporations

A **corporation** is a legal entity with the power to own property and conduct business. Its unlimited life span, combined with its ability to raise capital, gives it the potential for significant growth. The modern corporation evolved in the 19th century, when large sums of capital were needed to build railroads, steel mills, and manufacturing plants. Such endeavors required so much money that no single individual or group of partners could hope to raise it all. The solution was to sell shares in the business to numerous investors, who would get a cut of the profits in exchange for their money. These investors got a chance to vote on certain issues that might affect the value of their investment, but they were not involved in managing day-to-day operations. The investors were protected from the risks associated with such large undertakings by having their liability limited to the amount of their investment.

It was a good solution, and the corporation quickly became a vital force in the nation's economy. As rules and regulations developed to define what corporations could and could not do, corporations acquired the legal attributes of people. Like you, a corporation can receive, own, and transfer property; make contracts; sue; and be sued. Unlike the case with sole proprietorships and partnerships, a corporation's legal status and obligations exist independently of its owners.

Advantages of Corporations   No other form of business ownership can match the success of the corporation in bringing together money, resources, and talent; in accumulating assets; and in creating wealth. As it grows, a corporation gains from a diverse labor pool, greater financing options, and expanded research-and-development capabilities. The corporation has certain inherent qualities that make it the best vehicle for reaching those objectives. One such quality is limited liability. Although a corporate entity can assume

2 LEARNING OBJECTIVE

List five advantages and two disadvantages of partnerships

corporation
Legally chartered enterprise having most of the legal rights of a person, including the right to conduct business, to own and sell property, to borrow money, and to sue or be sued; owners of the corporation enjoy limited liability

3 LEARNING OBJECTIVE

Cite four advantages and three disadvantages of corporations

tremendous liabilities, it is the corporation that is liable and not the private shareholders. Take Johannes Schwartlander, who ran his San Francisco marble and granite business as a sole proprietorship for seven years. When the company began to grow, Schwartlander decided to incorporate to protect himself. "When we had so many employees and started installing marble panels ten stories up, I realized that if five years later something fell down, I would be responsible," he says.[5] Incorporation also protects him from personal liability should his business go bankrupt.

In addition to limited liability, corporations that sell stock to the general public have the advantage of *liquidity*, which means that investors can easily convert their stock into cash by selling it on the open market. This option makes buying stock in a corporation attractive to many investors. In contrast, liquidating the assets of a sole proprietorship or a partnership can be difficult. Moreover, shareholders of public corporations can easily transfer their ownership by selling their shares to someone else. Thus, corporations tend to be in a better position than proprietorships and partnerships to make long-term plans, with their unlimited life span and funding available through the sale of stock. As they grow, corporations can benefit from the diverse talents and experience of a large pool of employees and managers. Moreover, large corporations are often able to finance projects internally.

Of course, a company need not be large to incorporate. Most corporations, like most businesses, are relatively small, and most small corporations are privately held. The big ones, however, are *really* big (see Exhibit 6.3). The 500 largest corporations in the United

EXHIBIT 6.3

Top 25 U.S. Corporations
These are the top 25 U.S. corporations ranked by 2001 sales as reported by *Fortune* magazine.

RANK COMPANY	REVENUES ($ MILLIONS)
1 Wal-Mart Stores	219,812
2 Exxon Mobil	191,581
3 General Motors	177,260
4 Ford Motor	162,412
5 Enron	138,718
6 General Electric	125,913
7 Citigroup	112,022
8 Chevron Texaco	99,699
9 International Business Machines	85,866
10 Philip Morris	72,944
11 Verizon Communications	67,190
12 American International Group	62,402
13 American Electric Power	61,257
14 Duke Energy	59,503
15 AT&T	59,142
16 Boeing	58,198
17 El Paso	57,475
18 Home Depot	53,553
19 Bank of America	52,641
20 Fannie Mae	50,803
21 J.P. Morgan Chase	50,429
22 Kroger	50,098
23 Cardinal Health	47,948
24 Merck	47,716
25 State Farm Insurance	46,705

States, as listed by *Fortune* magazine, have combined sales of over $7.4 trillion.[6] Wal-Mart, the largest U.S. company, employs more than 1.2 million people, which is greater than the population of Detroit, Michigan.[7]

Disadvantages of Corporations Corporations are not without some disadvantages. The paperwork and costs associated with incorporation can be burdensome, particularly if you plan to sell stock. The complexity varies from state to state, but regardless of where you live, it is wise to consult an attorney and an accountant before incorporating. In addition, corporations are taxed twice. They must pay federal and state corporate income tax on the company's profits, and individual shareholders must pay income taxes on their share of the company's profits received as dividends.

Another drawback for publicly owned corporations is that they are required by the government to publish information about their finances and operations. Disclosing financial information increases the company's vulnerability to competitors and to those who might want to take control of the company against the wishes of the existing management. It also increases the pressure on corporate managers to achieve short-term growth and earnings targets in order to satisfy shareholders and to attract potential investors. Some cite such earnings pressure as the driving force behind the aggressive accounting practices recently adopted by some corporations, as Chapter 16 discusses.

Special Types of Corporations Certain types of corporations enjoy special privileges if they adhere to strict guidelines and rules. One special type of corporation is known as the **S corporation** (or subchapter S corporation). An S corporation distinction is made only for federal income tax purposes; otherwise, in terms of legal characteristics, it is no different from any other corporation. Basically, the owners receive the tax advantages of a partnership while they raise money through the sale of stock. In addition, income and tax deductions from the business flow directly to the owners, who are taxed at individual income-tax rates, just as they are in a partnership. Corporations seeking S status must meet certain criteria: (1) They must have no more than 75 investors, none of whom may be non-resident aliens; (2) they must be a domestic (U.S.) corporation; and (3) they can issue only one class of common stock, which means that all stock must share the same dividend and liquidation rights (but may carry different voting rights).[8]

Limited liability companies (LLCs) are another special type of corporation. These flexible business entities combine the tax advantages of a partnership with the personal liability protection of a corporation. Furthermore, LLCs are not restricted in the number of shareholders they can have, and members' participation in management is not restricted as it is in limited partnerships. Members of an LLC normally adopt an operating agreement (similar to a partnership agreement) to govern the entity's operation and management. These agreements generally are flexible and permit owners to structure the allocation of income and losses any way they desire, as long as certain tax rules are followed. In addition, the agreements can be designed to meet the special needs of owners, such as special voting rights, management controls, and buyout options. The only limit to what can be done is the owners' imagination.[9]

Some corporations are not independent entities; that is, they are owned by a single entity. **Subsidiary corporations**, for instance, are partially or wholly owned by another corporation known as a **parent company**, which supervises the operations of the subsidiary. A **holding company** is a special

S corporation
Corporations with no more than 75 shareholders that may be taxed as a partnership; also known as a subchapter S corporation

limited liability companies (LLCs)
Organizations that combine the benefits of S corporations and limited partnerships without the drawbacks of either

subsidiary corporations
Corporations whose stock is owned entirely or almost entirely by another corporation

parent company
Company that owns most, if not all, of another company's stock and that takes an active part in managing that other company

holding company
Company that owns most, if not all, of another company's stock but that does not actively participate in the management of that other company

Binney & Smith, the manufacturer of Crayola crayons and Silly Putty, is a subsidiary corporation wholly owned by its parent company, Hallmark Cards.

type of parent company that owns other companies for investment reasons and usually exercises little operating control over those subsidiaries.

Corporations can also be classified according to where they do business. An *alien corporation* operates in the United States but is incorporated in another country. A *foreign corporation*, sometimes called an *out-of-state corporation*, is incorporated in one state (frequently the state of Delaware, where incorporation laws are lenient) but does business in several other states where it is registered. And a *domestic corporation* does business only in the state where it is chartered (incorporated).

LEARNING OBJECTIVE

Delineate the three groups that govern a corporation and describe the role of each

shareholders
Owners of a corporation

proxy
Document authorizing another person to vote on behalf of a shareholder in a corporation

chief executive officer (CEO)
Person appointed by a corporation's board of directors to carry out the board's policies and supervise the activities of the corporation

5 LEARNING OBJECTIVE

Explain the differences between common and preferred stock from a shareholder's perspective

common stock
Shares whose owners have voting rights and have the last claim on distributed profits and assets

dividends
Distributions of corporate assets to shareholders in the form of cash or other assets

Corporate Ownership and Governance

The corporation is owned by its **shareholders**, who are issued shares of common or preferred stock in return for their investments. Shareholders of a corporation can be individuals, other companies, nonprofit organizations, pension funds, and mutual funds. In theory, common shareholders are the ultimate governing body of the corporation. But shareholders are rarely involved in managing a corporation, particularly if the corporation is publicly traded. Instead, the common shareholders elect a board of directors to represent them, and the directors, in turn, select the corporation's top officers, who actually run the company (see Exhibit 6.4). Those who cannot attend the annual meeting in person vote by **proxy**, signing and returning a slip of paper that authorizes management to vote on their behalf. Most individual shareholders in large corporations—where the shareholders may number in the millions—vote for directors recommended by management.

The center of power in a corporation often lies with the **chief executive officer, or CEO.** Together with the chief financial officer (CFO) and the chief operating officer (COO), the CEO is responsible for establishing company policies, managing corporate direction, and making the big decisions that will affect the company's growth and competitive position, as Chapter 7 discusses in detail. Keep in mind that the chief executive officer may also be the chairman of the board, the president of the corporation, or both. Moreover, because corporate ownership and management are separate, the owners may get rid of the managers (in theory, at least) if the owners vote to do so.

Shareholders' Rights

Most stock issued by corporations is **common stock**. As we just discussed, owners of common stock have voting rights and get one vote for each share of stock they own. They can elect the company's board of directors in addition to voting on major policies that will affect ownership—such as mergers, acquisitions, and takeovers. Besides conferring voting privileges, common stock frequently pays **dividends**, payments to shareholders from the company's profits. Dividends can be paid in cash or stock (called *stock dividends*). They are declared by the board of directors but their payment is not mandatory. For example, some companies, especially young or rapidly growing ones, pay no dividends. Instead, they reinvest their profits in new product research and development, equipment, buildings, and other assets so they can grow and earn future profits.

EXHIBIT 6.4 Corporate Governance
In theory, the shareholders of a corporation own the business, but in practice they elect others to run it.

In addition to dividends, common shareholders can earn a return on their investment. If shareholders sell their stock for more than they paid for it, they stand to pocket a handsome gain. But because the value or price of a company's common stock is subject to many economic variables besides the company's own performance, common-stock investments are risky and shareholders may not get any profit at all.

In contrast to common stock, **preferred stock** does not usually carry voting rights. It does, however, give preferred shareholders the right of first claim on the corporation's assets (in the form of dividends) after all the company's debts have been paid. This right is especially important if the company ever goes out of business. Moreover, preferred shareholders get their dividends before common shareholders do. The amount of preferred dividend is usually set (or fixed) at the time the preferred stock is issued and can provide investors with a source of steady income. Like common stock, however, dividends on preferred stock may be omitted in times of financial hardship. Still, most preferred stock is *cumulative preferred stock*, which means that any unpaid dividends must be paid before dividends are paid to common shareholders.

Avis has never paid cash dividends to shareholders. The company believes that shareholders are best served by reinvesting profits back into the company to foster long-term growth.

preferred stock
Shares that give their owners first claim on a company's dividends and assets after paying all debts

Shareholders' Power

The shareholders' degree of power is governed, in part, by whether the company is privately or publicly held. The stock of a **private corporation** such as Kinko's is held by only a few individuals or companies and is *not publicly traded.* By withholding their stock from public sale, the owners retain complete control over their operations and ownership. Such famous companies as Hallmark and Hyatt Hotels have opted to remain private corporations (also referred to as *closed corporations* or *closely held companies*). These companies finance their operating costs and growth from either company earnings or other sources, such as bank loans.

By contrast, the stock of a **public corporation** is held by and available for sale to the general public; thus the company is said to be *publicly traded.* This means that shares of a public corporation may be bequeathed or sold to someone else. As a result, the company's ownership may change drastically over time while the company and its management remain intact (as long as the company is economically sound).

Typically, the more shareholders a company has, the less tangible the influence each shareholder has on the corporation. However, some shareholders have more influence than others. In recent years, *institutional investors,* such as pension funds, insurance companies, mutual funds, and college endowment funds, have accumulated an increasing number of shares of stock in U.S. corporations. As a result, these large institutional investors are playing a more powerful role in governing the corporations in which they own substantial shares, especially with regard to the election of a company's board of directors.[10] Furthermore, at companies such as Avis and United Airlines, employees are major shareholders and so have a significant voice in how the company is run.

private corporation
Company owned by private individuals or companies

public corporation
Corporation that actively sells stock on the open market

Hyatt's owners, the Pritzker family, have opted to retain control of their enterprise because they appreciate the long-term value of doing so. That status also has a profound effect on the way Hyatt runs its 190 hotels and resorts worldwide. Public companies, which have an eye trained on the stock price, tend to overlook the long-term effects of a decision in favor of short-term gains. But Hyatt's general managers are free from concern about quarterly earning reports and stock prices. This gives them a certain entrepreneurial attitude that other hotel managers might not enjoy.

Advantages and Disadvantages of Public Stock Ownership

Highlight the advantages and disadvantages of public stock ownership

In Chapter 5 we discussed the concept of going public in the context of financing the enterprise. Bear in mind that in addition to providing a ready supply of capital, public ownership has other advantages and disadvantages. Among the advantages are increased liquidity, enhanced visibility, and the establishment of an independent market value for the company. Moreover, having a publicly traded stock gives companies flexibility to use such stock to acquire other firms. This was one of the primary reasons UPS decided to sell 10 percent of its stock to the public in 1999, after nearly a century of remaining a privately held organization.[11] Nevertheless, selling stock to the public has distinct disadvantages: (1) the cost of going public is high (ranging from $50,000 to $500,000), (2) the filing requirements with the SEC (Securities and Exchange Commission) are burdensome, (3) ownership control is lost, (4) management must be ready to handle the administrative and legal demands of heightened public exposure, and (5) the value of the company's stock becomes subject to external forces beyond the company's control.

Consider Ralph Lauren, for example. For three decades Ralph Lauren ran his own show, parlaying a $50,000 loan and a knack for neckties into a multibillion-dollar fashion empire. Then, in 1997 Lauren went public. But after putting 29.5 million shares (11 percent of the voting control) in public hands and pocketing a half a billion dollars, Lauren suddenly found himself answering the prying questions of institutional investors, fund managers, and analysts who all wanted to know: Are you really as good as you say you are?

"It's been a rocky romance with Wall Street ever since," notes Lauren. "The stock goes up and we ask, 'What did we do?' It goes down and we ask the same thing. Every quarter your report card comes out. There's no privacy, there's no comfort." Nonetheless, after a rocky start, the designer soon caught on to being in the public eye. "You start to realize, now you have to play another game, you are marketing to another market—Wall Street," notes Lauren.[12]

board of directors
Group of people, elected by the shareholders, who have the ultimate authority in guiding the affairs of a corporation

Responsibilities of the Corporation's Board of Directors

Representing the shareholders, the **board of directors** is responsible for declaring dividends, guiding corporate affairs, reviewing long-term strategic plans, selecting corporate officers, and overseeing financial performance. Depending on the size of the company, the board might have anywhere from 3 to 35 directors, although 15 to 25 is the typical range for traditional corporations. The board has the power to vote on major management decisions, such as building a new factory, hiring a new president, or buying a new subsidiary. The board's actual involvement in running a corporation varies from one company to another. Some boards are strong and independent and serve as a check on the company's management. Others act as a "rubber stamp," simply approving management's recommendations.

Such was the case at Enron. When the Enron auditors told board members that Enron was following high-risk accounting, none of the directors drilled deep enough to learn the details or object to the procedures described by the auditors. Nor did they request a second opinion. They failed to ask probing questions. And they even approved $750 million in cash bonuses to Enron executives in a year when the Houston-based company reported net income of $975 million. Enron directors failed miserably. They failed to provide sufficient oversight and restraint. As a result, they contributed to the company's collapse because they watched passively as the firm engaged in financial shenanigans that put the firm at grave risk.[13]

Ralph Lauren spent his life creating a luxury brand. Before going public, Lauren had to answer to no one.

The Debate over Director Independence and Compensation During most of the 1990s, corporate governance seemed to hardly matter. The buoyant stock market rewarded both the good and the bad boards. But when the stock-market bubble burst, that changed. Enron, and the corporate disasters that followed, forced many companies to get serious about governance. The scandals exposed just how vulnerable even the largest companies were to fraud and manipulation. They are shedding new light on the importance of director independence, compensation, duties, and integrity.

One topic under heated debate is director independence. At most large corporations, boards are composed exclusively of directors from outside the company, with only the CEO and a senior executive or two from inside the organization. This arrangement helps ensure that the board provides diligent and independent oversight.[14] Proponents of director independence claim that a board with too many insiders can give management too much power over a group whose function is to protect shareholders' rights and investments. Still, director independence has its drawbacks. Outside directors are at a serious information disadvantage. Thus, they must rely largely on the CEO's portrayal of the firm's condition and prospects. Moreover, many outside directors are selected for their accomplishments and stature and are often exceedingly busy. Most are top executives at other companies and typically work 50 to 70 hours per week, travel extensively, and incur a lot of stress in their jobs. Many also serve on the boards of several large companies. In fact, a 2002 study revealed that boards of the nation's leading companies had a startling amount of overlap. In 11 of the 15 largest companies, at least two board members sat together on another board.[15]

Director compensation is another hot topic. To compensate directors for their time and contributions, most large companies pay their directors a sizable fee and issue them stock options—the right to purchase a set number of shares of stock at a specific price (see Chapter 11). Some think compensation in the form of company stock aligns the directors' interests with those of other stockholders and is the most effective way to get outside directors to vigorously represent the shareholder. Evidence shows that companies in which directors own large amounts of stock and take an active role in guiding the company usually outperform those with more passive boards. Nonetheless, critics of this practice claim that directors with excessive stockholdings could compromise their independent decision making by placing too much focus on a company's short-term stock performance.

Board Reform on the Horizon Across Corporate America, a governance revolution is under way. Directors whose main contribution to boardroom debate had been golf scores and gossip are returning to the classroom to learn how to read a balance sheet. Board committees that routinely awarded massive pay packages to poorly performing CEOs are having second thoughts. Recent legislation by Congress now requires boards to appoint a greater number of independent directors to the board and to include at least one financial expert on board audit committees.[16]

Boards are going even further with reform. They are instituting sweeping changes in their composition, structure, and practices on an unprecedented scale. They are grappling with tough questions: How much is enough when it comes to paying the chief executive? What's the best way to account for stock options? What kinds of ties should be banned between directors and the companies they oversee? How many boards can directors serve on without being stretched too thin? How should the audit committee be staffed and run? And how much additional consulting, if any, is acceptable for the outside accounting firm? The recent scandals have made it all too clear that the decisions boards make on these issues can have profound consequences for their companies.[17] "There has been a massive failure in corporate governance," says the retired chairman and CEO of Medtronic, the world's leading medical technology company. "Too many directors

It's getting tough to fill a boardroom. These days, outside directors are thinking twice before accepting a seat on a company's board.

don't take their responsibilities seriously, and the firms that have gotten in trouble are indications of that failure.[18]

For the boards that are reforming, the changes are likely to be profound. The remade boards will include fewer company executives and other insiders and more independent directors. The new board will become more involved in long-term strategic planning and in evaluating management performance. And the job itself will become more difficult, requiring more time and more technical knowledge. "Boards of directors will be rolling up their sleeves and becoming more closely involved with management decision making," says one governance expert.[19]

But all this means much more work and potential personal liability for directors. "It makes you think: Why would you ever want to be a director?" says one independent director. Which is why some directors are heading for the exits. And that puts companies in a major bind: To satisfy regulations and shareholder demand, companies need outside experts on their boards. But finding such qualified candidates and keeping them on board is a formidable challenge.[20]

Business Combinations

7 LEARNING OBJECTIVE

Identify the key advantages and disadvantages of business combinations

Companies have been combining in various configurations since the early days of business. Joining two companies is a complex process because it involves every aspect of both companies. For instance, executives have to agree on how the combination will be financed and how the power will be transferred and shared. Marketing departments need to figure out how to blend advertising campaigns and salesforces. Data processing and information systems, which seldom mesh, must be joined together seamlessly. And companies must deal with layoffs, transfers, and changes in job titles and work assignments.

Mergers, Consolidations, and Acquisitions

merger
Combination of two companies in which one company purchases the other and assumes control of its property and liabilities

consolidation
Combination of two or more companies in which the old companies cease to exist and a new enterprise is created

acquisition
Form of business combination in which one company buys another company's voting stock

leveraged buyout (LBO)
Situation in which individuals or groups of investors purchase a company primarily with debt secured by the company's assets

Two of the most popular forms of business combinations are mergers and consolidations. The difference between a merger and a consolidation is fairly technical, having to do with how the financial and legal transaction is structured. Basically, in a **merger** one company buys another company, or parts of another company, and emerges as the controlling corporation. The controlling company assumes all the debts and contractual obligations of the company it acquires, which then ceases to exist. A **consolidation** is similar to a merger except that an entirely new firm is created by two or more companies that pool their interests. In a consolidation, both firms terminate their previous legal existence and become part of the new firm.

A third way that a company can acquire another firm is by purchasing that firm's voting stock. This transaction is generally referred to as an **acquisition** and is completed when the shareholders of the acquired firm tender their stock for either cash or shares of stock in the acquiring company. A **leveraged buyout (LBO)** occurs when one or more individuals purchase a company's publicly traded stock by using borrowed funds. The debt is expected to be repaid with funds generated by the company's operations and, often, by the sale of some of its assets. For an LBO to be successful, a company must have a reasonably priced stock and easy access to borrowed funds. Unfortunately, in many cases, the acquiring company must make huge interest and principal payments on the debt, and those payouts then deplete the amount of cash that the company has for operations and growth.

Keep in mind that the purpose and outcome of mergers, consolidations, and acquisitions are basically the same, which is why you will often hear these terms used interchangeably.

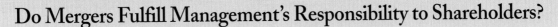

Thinking About Ethics

Do Mergers Fulfill Management's Responsibility to Shareholders?

For over a century, mergers and acquisitions have continually changed the face of business in the United States. Corporations claim that mergers make them more competitive and thus increase shareholder value. But do shareholders really benefit from mergers? Strong evidence suggests that often they do not.

Recent studies show that over 80 percent of mergers failed to produce any benefits for shareholders—supposedly the key beneficiaries. And the most recent mergers actually destroyed shareholder wealth. Bank One's merger with First Chicago and NationsBank's merger with BankAmerica, for example, promised hefty shareholder returns by cross-selling an extensive arsenal of products and achieving economies of scale by eliminating duplicate operations. Both failed to deliver. In fact, as is usually the case with mergers, the only winners appear to have been the shareholders of the acquired firm who sold their company stock for more than it was really worth.

Why do such a high percentage of mergers and acquisitions fail? Although no one answer applies to every situation, experts cite these common mistakes:

- Companies often rush into deals in search of synergies but then fail to develop them. Once the merger is done, management simply assumes that the computer programmers, sales managers, and engineers will cut costs and boost revenues according to plan.
- Companies pay excessively high premiums for the companies they acquire. According to one expert, anytime an acquiring company pays a premium of 25 percent or more over the trading price of the acquired company's stock, the acquiring company is exposing itself and its shareholders to substantial risk.

- Bigger does not always equate with better. As one expert put it, if you combine two lumbering companies, you get one that runs worse, not better.
- Companies are unable to reconcile differences in corporate cultures. A successful merger requires more than respecting each partner's differences. Procedures must be established to settle disputes and to integrate workforces and product lines strategically.

Without question, some mergers and acquisitions are beneficial to companies and shareholders in both the short term and the long term. Synergies can be realized. However, managers need to approach mergers and acquisitions with caution by answering these questions: Will the regulatory environment change? How will competitors respond? Do the expected gains justify the up-front costs? Will the cultures of the two companies blend well? Without seeking honest answers to these questions, management may find it difficult to fulfill its obligation to the company's shareholders.

Questions for Critical Thinking

1. If you were on the board of directors at a company and the CEO announced plans to merge with a competitor, what types of questions would you want answered before you gave your approval?
2. If a CEO has the opportunity to merge with or acquire another company and is reasonably certain that the transaction will benefit shareholders, is the CEO obligated to pursue the deal? Why or why not?

Advantages of Mergers, Consolidations, and Acquisitions   Business combinations provide several financial and operational advantages. Combined entities hope to eliminate expenditures for redundant resources; increase their buying power as a result of their larger size; increase revenue by cross-selling products to each other's customers; increase market share by combining product lines to provide more comprehensive offerings; eliminate manufacturing overcapacity; and gain access to new expertise, systems, and teams of employees who already know how to work together. Often these advantages are grouped under umbrella terms such as *economies of scale*, *efficiencies*, or *synergies*, which generally mean that the benefits of working together will be greater than if each company continued to operate independently.

Disadvantages of Mergers, Consolidations, and Acquisitions Despite the promise of economies of scale, studies of merged companies show that most of these deals fail to actually achieve the promised efficiencies.[21] Part of the problem with mergers is that companies often borrow immense amounts of money to acquire a firm, and the loan payments on this corporate debt gobble up cash needed to run the business. This debt becomes even more of an issue if a company pays a premium to acquire an entity. Another problem is that many managers do not understand what they are purchasing. Often, they envision grand synergies that prove unworkable, as this chapter's AOL and Time Warner case study shows. Not only do they overestimate cost savings but they underestimate the difficulty involved in combining the operations of the two entities. They fail to keep key employees on board, they fail to keep existing customers happy, and they fail to recognize that integrating acquisitions well is both an art and a science.[22]

Another key obstacle that companies face when combining forces is that they tend to underestimate the difficulties of merging two cultures. In Chapter 7 we discuss organizational culture in detail. A company's culture is the way people in the organization do things. Culture includes not only management style and practices but also the way people dress, how they communicate, or whether they punch a time clock. *Culture clash* occurs when two joining companies have different beliefs about what is really important, how to make decisions, how to supervise, how to communicate, and so on (see "DaimlerChrysler: Merger of Equals or Global Fender Bender?"). Experts note that in too many deals the acquiring company imposes its values and management systems on the acquired company without any regard to what worked well there.

Current Trends in Mergers, Consolidations, and Acquisitions The years from 1992 through 2000 saw the completion of 71,811 corporate mergers, consolidations, and acquisitions at a combined value of $6.66 trillion—many with significant implications in the marketplace.[23] Consider, for instance, the $160 billion merger of America Online (the world's biggest Internet provider) and Time Warner (the world's biggest media company). This megadeal, announced only 10 days into the new millennium, linked AOL's 20 million subscribers and e-commerce capabilities with Time Warner's extensive collection of world-class media, entertainment, news brands, and broadband delivery systems to produce the world's first fully integrated media and communications company.[24] Similarly, the 1998 acquisition of Travelers by Citicorp (valued at $83 billion) spliced together a global bank, an insurance company, a brokerage firm, a credit card operation, and some 100 million customers in 100 countries.[25] And the $81 billion marriage of Exxon and Mobil in 1999 created the world's largest oil company, while the $36 billion combination of Daimler-Benz and Chrysler in 1998 was the biggest acquisition of any U.S. company by a foreign buyer. From telecommunications to banking to oil to automobiles, mass consolidation among industry competitors is one strategy for competing in the global marketplace. As one economist put it, "If you don't play the game as a global company, you're going to wind up a niche player."[26]

Still, after a decade of unprecedented megamergers, some of the largest U.S. companies are now shedding their unprofitable acquisitions and focusing on generating internal growth from their core businesses. Factors contributing to this trend reversal include an economic slowdown, increased political uncertainty, global market saturation, and pressure from shareholders to generate profits and keep things simple. Moreover, Wall Street is becoming increasingly suspicious of companies with too many unrelated business operations or products.[27]

hostile takeovers
Situations in which an outside party buys enough stock in a corporation to take control against the wishes of the board of directors and corporate officers

Defenses Against Merger, Consolidation, and Acquisition Although 95 percent of all business combinations result from friendly deals, some 5 percent are **hostile takeovers,** in which one party fights to gain control of a company against the wishes of the existing management.[28] Of course, not all hostile takeovers are bad. In November 1999

Competing in the Global Marketplace

DaimlerChrysler: Merger of Equals or Global Fender Bender?

The champagne was on ice when Chrysler and Daimler-Benz announced a stunning $36 billion merger in May 1998. Headquartered in Germany, DaimlerChrysler would be the world's third-largest automaker. On paper, the companies were a perfect fit—one was strong where the other was weak. Daimler's engineering was legendary, and it was strong in technology. Chrysler excelled at new product design and development. Complementary products and geographical mix would allow them to challenge rivals around the world. Moreover, anticipated synergies would save the combined operation $3 billion annually.

Charged with excitement and curious about each other's cars and culture, the two companies began the integration process. But fundamental differences in management, operational, and decision-making styles made the transition difficult. For example, a German decision would work its way through the bureaucracy for final approval at the top. Then it was set in stone. By contrast, the Americans valued consensus building and shared decision making. Moreover, they allowed midlevel employees to proceed on their own initiative, sometimes without waiting for executive-level approval.

Turf battles also bogged down the combination process. Mercedes executives closely guarded their parts and designs for fear of eroding the Mercedes mystique. Managers from both sides spent more time defending their way of doing things than promoting the integration of systems. Issues that should have been resolved by managers were bumped up to the company's board of directors. Differences in salary levels and management perks fueled an undercurrent of tension. The Americans earned two, three, and in some cases four times as much as their German counterparts. But the expenses of U.S. workers were tightly controlled compared with those of the German system. Daimler-Benz employees thought nothing of flying to Paris or New York for a half-day meeting, then capping the visit with a fancy dinner and a night in an expensive hotel. The Americans blanched at the extravagance.

Friction led to the departure of talented Chrysler midlevel managers and several top Chrysler executives—including Chrysler's president Thomas Stallkamp, who had played an instrumental role in orchestrating the merger. Soon the management board was scaled down from 17 members to 13 (eight Germans and five Americans), and the reality became clear: Daimler executives were indeed running the show. DaimlerChrysler wasn't a merger of equals. Instead, Daimler-Benz had acquired Chrysler, and an American icon had lost its independence.

Questions for Critical Thinking

1. What prevented DaimlerChrysler from achieving the promised synergies?
2. Which of these stakeholders benefited the most from the merger: the original Chrysler shareholders or the new DaimlerChrysler shareholders? Explain your answer.

---

pharmaceutical giants Warner-Lambert and American Home Products (AHP) announced a $54.5 billion merger. The two were caught off guard when that same day rival Pfizer launched an unfriendly takeover bid for Warner-Lambert and eventually sweetened its bid as an inducement to wrap things up quickly. In February 2000, Pfizer succeeded in its hostile bid to buy Warner-Lambert for $90 billion. Warner-Lambert conceded that Pfizer's hostile bid was better for shareholders than its planned merger with AHP had been.[29]

As mentioned earlier, every corporation that sells stock to the general public is potentially vulnerable to takeover by any individual or company that buys enough shares to gain a controlling interest. Basically, a hostile takeover can be launched in one of two ways: by tender offer or by proxy fight. In a *tender offer*, the raider offers to buy a certain number of shares of stock in the corporation at a specific price. The price offered is generally more

Hewlett-Packard's CEO Carly Fiorina claimed victory in the proxy fight over its merger with Compaq Computer Corp. Now Fiorina's mettle will be tested in almost every dimension. She has to merge two struggling companies with divergent corporate cultures, restore the confidence of investors, and win over the many employees who opposed the deal.

than the current stock price so that shareholders are motivated to sell. The raider hopes to get enough shares to take control of the corporation and replace the existing board of directors and management. In a *proxy fight*, the raider launches a public relations battle for shareholder votes, hoping to enlist enough votes to oust the board and management.

Proxy fights sound easy enough, but they are tough to win. The insiders have certain advantages: They can get in touch with shareholders, and they can use money from the corporate treasury in their campaign. Walter Hewlett, son of Hewlett-Packard's (HP's) co-founder, faced this uphill battle when he launched a five-month proxy fight against HP's proposed $19.4 billion acquisition of Compaq. Hewlett, whose family foundation and trusts owned 5.7 percent of HP's shares, hoped to kill the largest technology merger in history, arguing that it was too expensive and too risky. Following a narrow victory margin for HP in 2002, dissident Hewlett refused to concede. He sued HP, alleging that the company had engaged in "improper means" to secure votes that resulted in a "slim but sufficient" majority vote. But after a short trial, the Delaware Chancery Court judge dismissed the lawsuit stating that Hewlett "failed to prove" claims that HP had withheld information from shareholders and had perpetrated a vote-buying scheme.[30] Hewlett, who did not wish to further a controversy that might adversely affect the value of the company, accepted the decision and agreed to move forward.

Corporate boards and executives have devised a number of schemes to defend themselves against unwanted takeovers:

- *The poison pill.* This plan, triggered by a takeover attempt, makes the company less valuable in some way to the potential raider; the idea is to discourage the takeover from actually happening. A good example is a special sale of newly issued stock to current stockholders at prices below the market value of the company's existing stock. Such action increases the number of shares the raider has to buy, making the takeover more expensive. Many shareholders believe that poison pills are bad for a company, because they can entrench weak management and discourage takeover attempts that would improve company value.[31]

- *The golden parachute.* This method is designed to benefit a company's top executives by guaranteeing them generous compensation packages if they ever leave or are forced out after a takeover. These packages often total millions of dollars for each executive and therefore make the takeover much more expensive for the acquiring company. Thus, a golden parachute has an effect similar to that of a poison pill.

- *The shark repellent.* This tactic is more direct; it is simply a requirement that stockholders representing a large majority of shares approve of any takeover attempt. Of course, such a plan is viable only if the management team has the support of the majority of shareholders.

- *The white knight.* This tactic uses a friendly buyer to take over the company before a raider can. White knights usually agree to leave the current management team in place and to let the company continue to operate in an independent fashion. Starwood Lodging Trust, a large hotel investment firm, used this tactic to block the hostile takeover attempt of ITT by Hilton Hotels.[32]

Sometimes a group of investors is able to take a publicly traded company off the open market by purchasing all of the company's stock. This tactic is known as "taking the company private." Descendants of Levi Strauss, for example, borrowed $3 billion to buy back all the shares of Levi's stock so that the family could maintain control of the company.[33]

Although companies such as Levi Strauss may go private to thwart unwanted takeovers, this is a radical action. First, stockholders must be willing to sell, and second, buyers must have enough cash on hand to repurchase all the company's stock. Moreover, going private eliminates the firm's ability to raise future capital by selling authorized shares to the public, so it's not a move that many corporations make.

Strategic Alliances and Joint Ventures

In Chapter 3 we discussed strategic alliances and joint ventures from the perspective of international expansion. We defined a strategic alliance as a long-term partnership between companies to jointly develop, produce, or sell products, and we defined a joint venture as a special type of strategic alliance in which two or more firms jointly create a new business entity that is legally separate and distinct from its parents. In this chapter we look at these forms of business combinations as an alternative to a merger, consolidation, or acquisition.

Many strategic alliances are driven by the realization that no single company can offer customers everything they need. RadioShack's strategic alliances with Verizon Wireless and Sprint PCS is one good example of how companies benefit from entering into such arrangements. "Our strategic alliances and innovative store-within-a-store concepts with Sprint PCS and Verizon Wireless helped make RadioShack the single largest retailer of wireless phones," says RadioShack's CEO, Leonard Roberts. Meanwhile, Sprint PCS and Verizon Wireless benefit from the strategic alliance by building on RadioShack's household name and existing customer base. Customers can view and purchase wireless phones and sign up for national, regional, and local services offered by these partners at any of the 4000-plus RadioShack locations.[34]

Starbucks's strategic alliance with Barnes & Noble bookstore is another example of the benefits derived from these special types of partnerships. Originally, Starbucks opened company-owned and operated stores inside Barnes & Noble bookstores in markets where Starbucks already had a retail presence. Both companies benefited from the arrangement—Starbucks drew customers into the bookstore and Barnes & Noble generated sales for Starbucks. But when Barnes & Noble began to build stores in areas where Starbucks was not already present or had no immediate plans to expand, the companies collaborated to develop Barnes & Noble Cafes. The 400 or so cafes are now run by Barnes & Noble, which licenses the Starbucks brand and serves its coffee. Starbucks prefers forming such alliances and licensing its brand to others for a fee in lieu of franchising its stores so that it can retain more control over the Starbucks brand.[35]

As these examples show, strategic alliances can accomplish many of the same goals as a merger, consolidation, or acquisition without requiring a painstaking process of integration.[36] They can help a company gain credibility in a new field, expand its market presence, gain access to technology, diversify offerings, and share best practices without forcing the partners to become fast friends for life. If the arrangement does not work out or its usefulness expires, the partners can simply go their separate ways.

Companies can also form joint ventures to accomplish the same benefits enjoyed by strategic alliances. Joint ventures are similar to partnerships except that they are formed for a specific, limited purpose. America Online, Philips Electronics, and Direct TV formed a joint venture to develop and offer an interactive service that lets customers access the Internet via their TV sets. Like strategic alliances, joint ventures have many advantages. They allow companies to use each other's complementary strengths that might otherwise take too long to develop on their own, and they allow companies to share what may be the substantial cost and risk of starting a new operation.[37]

Summary of Learning Objectives

1. **List five advantages and four disadvantages of sole proprietorships.**
   Sole proprietorships have five advantages: (1) They are easy to establish, (2) they provide the owner with control and independence, (3) the owner reaps all the profits, (4) profits are taxed at individual rates, and (5) the company's plans and financial performance remain private. The four main disadvantages of a sole proprietorship are (1) the company's financial resources are usually limited, (2) management talent may be thin, (3) the owner is liable for the debts and damages incurred by the business, and (4) the business may cease when the owner dies.

2. **List five advantages and two disadvantages of partnerships.**
   In addition to being easy to establish and having profits taxed at individual rates, partnerships offer a greater ability to obtain financing, longevity, and a broader base of skills. The two main disadvantages of partnerships are unlimited liability for general partners and the potential for personality and authority conflicts.

3. **Cite four advantages and three disadvantages of corporations.**
   Because corporations are a separate legal entity, they have the power to raise large sums of capital, they offer the shareholders protection from liability, they provide liquidity for investors, and they have an unlimited life span. In exchange for these advantages, businesses pay large fees to incorporate, and they are taxed twice on company profits—corporations pay tax on profits and individuals pay tax on dividends (distributed corporate profits). Finally, if publicly owned, corporations must adhere to strict government reporting requirements.

4. **Delineate the three groups that govern a corporation and describe the role of each.**
   Shareholders are the basis of the corporate structure. They elect the board of directors, who in turn elect the officers of the corporation. The corporate officers carry out the policies and decisions of the board. In practice, the shareholders and board members have often followed the lead of the chief executive officer. However, some board members are more active

than others. The hands-on role that directors play in a corporation will likely increase as a result of the Enron debacle and the collapse of several high-profile corporations. Reform efforts are underway to restructure board compensation, composition, and responsibilities.

5. **Explain the differences between common and preferred stock from a shareholder's perspective.**
   Common shareholders can vote and can share in the company's profits through discretionary dividends and adjustments in the market value of their stock. In other words, they can profit from their investment if the value of the stock rises above the price they paid for it, or they can lose money if the value of the stock falls below the price they paid for it. In contrast, preferred shareholders cannot vote, but they can get a fixed return (dividend) on their investment and a priority claim on assets after creditors.

6. **Highlight the advantages and disadvantages of public stock ownership.**
   Public stock ownership offers a company increased liquidity, enhanced visibility, financial flexibility, and an independently established market value for the stock. The disadvantages of public stock ownership are high costs, burdensome filing requirements, loss of ownership control, heightened public exposure, and loss of direct control over the market value of the company's stock.

7. **Identify the key advantages and disadvantages of business combinations.**
   By combining their operations, companies hope to eliminate redundant costs, increase their buying power, increase their revenue, improve their market share, eliminate manufacturing overcapacity and gain access to new expertise and personnel. But these advantages come with a price. Companies must borrow immense amounts of money to acquire a firm. Moreover, managers tend to overestimate cost savings, underestimate the difficulty of the transaction, and fail to keep employees and customers happy. Furthermore, many combined companies experience culture clash—the difficulty of joining two companies with different beliefs, values, and practices.

KEY TERMS

acquisition **(152)**
board of directors **(150)**
chief executive officer (CEO) **(148)**
common stock **(148)**
consolidation **(152)**

corporation **(145)**
dividends **(148)**
general partnership **(143)**
holding company **(147)**
hostile takeovers **(154)**

leveraged buyout (LBO) **(152)**
limited liability companies (LLCs) **(147)**
limited partnership **(144)**
merger **(152)**
parent company **(147)**

TEST YOUR KNOWLEDGE

Questions for Review

1. What are the three basic forms of business ownership?
2. What is the difference between a general and a limited partnership?
3. What is a closely held corporation, and why do some companies choose this form of ownership?
4. What are the responsibilities of a company's board of directors?
5. What are the benefits of strategic alliances and joint ventures?

Questions for Analysis

6. Why is it advisable for partners to enter into a formal partnership agreement?
7. To what extent do shareholders control the activities of a corporation?
8. How might a company benefit from having a diverse board of directors that includes representatives of several industries, countries, and cultures?
9. Why do so many mergers fail?
10. *Ethical Considerations:* Your father sits on the board of directors of a large, well-admired, public company. Yesterday, while looking for an envelope in his home office, you stumbled on a confidential memorandum. Unable to resist the temptation to read the memo, you discovered that your father's company is talking with another publicly traded company about the possibility of a merger, with Dad's company being the survivor. Dollar signs flashed in your mind. Should the merger occur, the value of the other company's stock is likely to soar. You're tempted to log on to your E*Trade account in the morning and place an order for 1,000 shares of that company's stock. Better still, maybe you'll give a hot tip to your best friend in exchange for the four Dave Matthews Band tickets your friend has been flashing in your face all week. Would either of those actions be unethical? Explain your answer.

Questions for Application

11. Suppose you and some friends want to start a business to take tourists on wilderness backpacking expeditions. None of you has much extra money, so your plan is to start small. However, if you are successful, you would like to expand into other types of outdoor tours and perhaps even open up branches in other locations. What form of ownership should your new enterprise take, and why?
12. Selling antiques on the Internet has become more successful than you imagined. Overnight your website has grown into a full-fledged business—now generating some $200,000 in annual revenue. It's time to think about the future. Several competing online antique dealers have approached you with a proposal to merge their website with yours to create the premier online antique store. The money sounds good, but you have some concerns about joining forces. What might they be? What other growth options should you consider before joining forces with another business?
13. *Integrated:* In Chapter 3 we discussed international strategic alliances and joint ventures. Why might a U.S. company want to enter into those types of arrangements instead of merging with a foreign concern?
14. *Integrated:* Look back at Chapter 5. How might each of the following small-business scenarios affect your selection of a form of business ownership.

    a. You have decided to purchase a franchise operation instead of starting a business from scratch.
    b. You can't tap into your personal financial resources or rely on friends or family for financial assistance.
    c. You are a hard worker, visionary, a risk taker, highly disciplined, and very bright. But you lack managerial experience.

PRACTICE YOUR KNOWLEDGE

Handling Difficult Situations on the Job: Determining Accountability in a Crisis

Like other board members, you agreed to management's recommendation that the Westlake Therapy and Rehabilitation Center invest in an Endless Pool. This new invention by a Philadelphia manufacturer produces an adjustable current flow, so that physical therapy patients can swim "endlessly" against it. Westlake could offer patients year-round water therapy, in an indoor pool small enough to fit a standard living room.

Management chose the optional six-foot depth, which required (1) a special platform and (2) installation in a room with a high ceiling. Westlake's old gymnasium would become the new Water Therapy Pavilion. Total cost: $20,080, plus $8,000 budgeted for installation. According to the manufacturer, the Endless Pool could be assembled by "two reasonably handy people with no prior installation experience following detailed procedural videos." Playing it safe, management hired professionals—Abe's Pool Installation—to build the platform and install the pool. Owner Abe Hanson was given the instructional videos, the manufacturer's hotline number, and was told that Endless Pool would provide free, preinstallation engineering consultations.

Weeks later, Westlake's chief administrator flipped the switch at the dedication ceremony and the new pool's hydraulic motor started moving 5,000 gallons of water a minute through a grill at the front of the pool. But instead of entering the turning vane arrays, the wave surged out the back, onto the platform and gathered board members, staff, patients, and reporters. Final damage: a collapsed platform, a ruined floor, an incorrectly installed pool, and numerous dry-cleaning bills. Fortunately, no injuries. Estimated cost with floor repair: $10,000. Local newscasters aired the footage on the evening news; they're coming back tomorrow for an interview. Abe is not returning management's calls.[38]

Your task: You must help to decide how to handle this much-publicized fiasco. What actions should the board take, and what should it leave to management's discretion? Consider the impact on company image, profitability, liability, and daily operations. Whom will you hold accountable? How?

Building Your Team Skills

Directors often have to ask tough questions and make difficult decisions, as you will see in this exercise. Imagine that the president of your college or university has just announced plans to retire. Your team, playing the role of the school's board of directors, must decide how to choose a new president to fill this vacancy next semester.

First, generate a list of the qualities and qualifications you think the school should seek in a new president. What background and experience would prepare someone for this key position? What personal characteristics should the new president have? What questions would you ask to find out how each candidate measures up against the list of credentials you have prepared?

Now list all the stakeholders that your team, as directors, must consider before deciding on a replacement for the retiring president. Of these stakeholders, whose opinions do you think are most important? Whose are least important? Who will be directly and indirectly affected by the choice of a new president? Of these stakeholders, which should be represented as participants in the decision-making process?

Select a spokesperson to deliver a brief presentation to the class summarizing your team's ideas and the reasoning behind your suggestions. After all the teams have completed their presentations, discuss the differences and similarities among credentials proposed by all the teams for evaluating candidates for the presidency. Then compare the teams' conclusions about stakeholders. Do all teams agree on the stakeholders who should participate in the decision-making process? Lead a classroom discussion on a board's responsibility to its stakeholders.

EXPAND YOUR KNOWLEDGE

Discovering Career Opportunities

Are you best suited to working as a sole proprietor, as a partner in a business, or in a different role within a corporation? For this exercise, select three businesses with which you are familiar: one run by a single person, such as a dentist's practice or a local landscaping firm; one run by two or three partners, such as a small accounting firm; and one that operates as a corporation, such as Target.

1. Write down what you think you would like about being the sole proprietor, one of the partners, and the corporate manager or an employee in the businesses you have selected. For example, would you like having full responsibility for the sole proprietorship? Would you like being able to consult with other partners in the partnership before making decisions? Would you like having limited responsibility when you work for other people in the corporation?

2. Now write down what you might dislike about each form of business. For example, would you dislike the risk of bearing all legal responsibility in a sole proprietorship? Would you dislike having to talk with your partners before spending the partnership's money? Would you dislike having to write reports for top managers and shareholders of the corporation?

3. Weigh the pluses and minuses you have identified in this exercise. In comparison, which form of business most appeals to you?

Developing Your Research Skills

Review recent issues of business newspapers or periodicals (print or online editions) to find an article or series of articles illustrating one of the following business developments: merger, acquisition, consolidation, hostile takeover, or leveraged buyout.

1. Explain in your own words what steps or events led to this development.

2. What results do you expect this development to have on (a) the company itself, (b) consumers, (c) the industry the company is part of? Write down and date your answers.

3. Follow your story in the business news over the next month (or longer, as your instructor requests). What problems, opportunities, or other results are reported? Were these developments anticipated at the time of the initial story, or did they seem to catch industry analysts by surprise? How well did your answers to question two predict the results?

Exploring the Best of the Web

URLs for all Internet exercises are provided at the website for this book, www.prenhall.com/bovee. When you log on to this text's website, select Chapter 6, then select "Student Resources," click on the name of the featured website, and review the website to complete these exercises.

Explore these chapter-related websites, review their content, and answer the following questions for each website you visit:

1. What is the purpose of this website?
2. What kinds of information does this website contain? Please be specific.
3. How is the information provided at this website useful for businesspeople? Consumers?
4. How did you expand your knowledge of forms of business ownerships and business combinations by reviewing the material at this website? What new things did you learn about these topics?

Choose a Form of Ownership

Which legal form of ownership is best suited for a new business? Answering this question can be a challenge—especially if you're not familiar with the attributes of sole proprietorships, partnerships, and corporations. That's where Nolo Self-Help Centers can help. Because there's no right or wrong choice for everyone, your job is to understand how each legal structure works and then pick the one that best meets your needs. Start your research by browsing the small business law center at Nolo. Be sure to check out the FAQs and Legal Encyclopedia. www.nolo.com

Follow the Fortunes of the Fortune 500

Quick! Name the largest corporation in the United States, as measured by annual revenues. Give up? Just check *Fortune* magazine's yearly ranking of the 500 largest U.S. companies. For years, General Motors has topped the list with its $170 billion-plus in annual revenues, but now Wal-Mart has taken over with over $200 billion in annual revenues. The Fortune 500 not only ranks corporations by size but also offers brief company descriptions along with industry statistics and additional measures of corporate performance. You can search the list by ranking, by industry, by company name, or by CEO. And to help you identify the largest international corporations, there's a special Global 500 list as well. www.fortune.com

Build a Great Board

Want a great board of directors? This inc.com guide contains the best resources for entrepreneurs who are ready to recruit outside directors for their boards. Find out how to recruit board members and how to persuade top-notch people to come on board. Once you've selected your members, learn how to maximize your board's impact and resolve conflicts among board members. Check out one expert's five practical tips for good nuts-and-bolts boardsmanship. www.inc.com/guides/growth/20672.html

Learning Interactively

Companion Website

Visit the Companion Website at www.prenhall.com/bovee. For Chapter 6, take advantage of the interactive "Study Guide" to test your chapter knowledge. Get instant feedback on whether you need additional studying. Read the "Current Events" articles to get the latest on chapter topics, and complete the exercises as specified by your instructor. Expand your learning with a visit to the "Research Area." There you will find a wealth of information you can use to complete your course assignments.

A CASE FOR CRITICAL THINKING

AOL and Time Warner: Fragile Promises

Industry experts laughed in his face. The Silicon Valley elite sneered at his audacity. Back in 1995, Steve Case's predictions about the future of his fledgling company, America Online (AOL), seemed outrageous to everyone—except Steve Case. Nonetheless, Case doggedly pursued his dream, turning AOL into one of the darlings of Wall Street. "We could be bigger than AT&T," Case predicted. "The future is online." It was a vision that Case refused to abandon, in spite of the odds against him.

Near the end of the 20th century, AOL was a profitable Internet giant, serving over 22 million customers around the globe and delivering more mail than the U.S. Postal Service. Its high-flying stock price gave it the financial clout to grow its customer base by acquiring such companies as Netscape Communications, rival CompuServe, and ICQ with its instant messaging software. But CEO Case knew AOL needed access to compelling content and the high-speed cable TV lines that could zap information and entertainment into homes at lightning speed.

Deal of the Century

Determined to transform itself into a global communications company, AOL orchestrated the deal of the century. When AOL approached Time Warner about the merger possibility, Time Warner was reeling from its own costly, repeated, and failed efforts to move the company into the digital era. Hitching a ride into the future with AOL was an attractive option. For AOL, capturing Time Warner seemed to herald the dawning of the digital century. Melding AOL's Internet empire with the diverse and revenue-rich Time Warner colossus (which included Time Warner Cable, HBO, CNN, TBS, Warner Bros. Pictures, Warner Music Group, and such magazines as *Time*, *People*, and *Sports Illustrated*) would produce the first fully integrated media and communications company.

Visions of a Blockbuster

In January 2000 the two announced their intended $160 million merger. AOL Time Warner (AOLTW) promised grand synergies and slam-dunk revenues from its unrivaled combination of print and television content with cable and online distribution. Together, the companies could pipe a dazzling array of movies, music, magazines, and more to their combined 100 million customers. And the merged companies could reap economies of scale by promoting and selling each other's products and by eliminating duplicate operating costs.

Jeers from the Balcony

Not everyone was excited about the prospects of the merger. Critics feared that merging AOL, a "new economy" Internet company based in Virginia, with Time Warner, an "old economy" media company headquartered in New York City, could create communication and cultural problems. At worst, they feared, the merger would shackle AOL's flexibility, speed, and entrepreneurial drive and sink its rapidly rising stock price. And Time Warner's shareholders, who were getting paid in AOL stock, worried that the share price was highly inflated.

Regulators and members of Congress were concerned that AOLTW would be too big and too powerful—that it might be able to single-handedly dominate and control the coming era of broadband access to the Internet. They wanted to ensure that the cable TV system, just like the federal highways, would be open to everyone.

Merger Mayhem

The wrangling with regulators, shareholders, and other stakeholders lasted a full year, but the government finally approved the largest merger in U.S. history on January 11, 2001. Shortly thereafter the company ran into an economic firestorm. A dot-com shakeout along with a declining economy spurred the worst advertising recession in a decade. The resulting slump in ad sales hammered AOLTW's magazine, television, and online businesses. As the economy continued to sour, so did AOL's subscriber growth and the company's performance. AOLTW reported a 2002 net loss of $98.7 billion—the biggest annual corporate loss in history. The

total value of its stock plunged by some 70 percent (from a high of $335 billion), vaporizing shareholder wealth, rendering employee stock options nearly worthless, damaging employee morale, and confirming doubters' fears that Time Warner made a huge mistake by merging with AOL.

Can AOLTW Be Saved?

Meanwhile, cultural clashes between the two companies led to severe infighting. In late 2002 the suit-and-tie Time Warner team wrested control from the Polo-shirt-and-khakis AOL crowd. Most of the senior executives associated with the merger have left the company—including Case—who resigned in 2003, stating that he did not want his presence to continue to be a distraction.

Amidst the flurry, speculation about the company's future grew rampant. Attempts to line up AOL subscribers to AOL's own broadband package (via third-party access) have, for the most part, failed. Critics of the merger even suggested that the company spin off the online and cable businesses. In September 2003 Time Warner dropped "AOL" from the company name. In hindsight, analysts called the merger the worst deal in history. Even Steve Case admitted that the company was "too aggressive" in its promises: "We had higher expectations for the economy and advertising than what turned out to happen." Indeed, only time will tell if the world's largest media merger can be rescued.

Critical Thinking Questions

1. Why did the media refer to the merger as the deal of the century?
2. Why was Time Warner eager to merge with AOL?
3. What challenges did AOL and Time Warner face as a merged company?
4. Visit the Time Warner website: www.aoltimewarner.com. Review the site to get the latest news about the fate of the merger. How is the company doing financially? How much turnover has occurred among high-level executives? If any parts of the business have been sold off, what has the acquiring company said about future prospects?

VIDEO CASE

Doing Business Privately: Amy's Ice Cream

Learning Objectives

The purpose of this video is to help you:

1. Distinguish among the types of corporations.
2. Consider the advantages and disadvantages of incorporation.
3. Understand the role that shareholders play in a privately held corporation.

Synopsis

Amy's Ice Creams, based in Austin, Texas, is a privately held corporation formed in 1984 by Amy Miller and owned by Miller and a small group of family members and friends. At the outset, one of the most important decisions Miller faced was choosing an appropriate legal ownership structure for the new business. Fueled by the founder's dedication to creating happy ice cream memories for customers, Amy's has continued to evolve and grow. The company now operates nine stores and rings up close to $3.5 million in annual sales. Applying for a job is an adventure in creativity, and Miller welcomes employees' suggestions for new flavors and new promotions to keep sales growing.

Discussion Questions

1. *For analysis:* How does Amy's Ice Cream differ from a publicly held corporation?

2. *For analysis:* What are some of the particular advantages of corporate ownership for a firm like Amy's Ice Cream?

3. *For application:* How well do you think Amy's is working to ensure its continued survival and success? Looking ahead to future growth, what marketing, financial, or other suggestions would you suggest?

4. *For application:* What are some of the issues that Amy Miller may have to confront because her 22 investors are family members and friends?

5. *For debate:* Should Amy's Ice Cream become a publicly held corporation? Support your chosen position.

Online Exploration

Find out what is required to incorporate a business in your state. You might begin by searching the CCH Business Owner's Toolkit site at www.toolkit.cch.com. If you were going to start a small business, would you choose to incorporate or choose a different form of legal organization? List the pros and cons that incorporation presents for the type of business you would consider.

Conducting Business in the Global Economy

PART 2

Mastering Global and Geographical Skills: Communicating with International Suppliers

With 95 percent of the world's population living outside the United States, more and more U.S. businesses today are purchasing and selling their products globally. Chances are, even if you own a small business in a strip mall, you're purchasing merchandise or supplies from somewhere else in the world. Take a moment to think about just how international your own daily life is becoming. Look at your clothes, your car, the food you eat, the movies you see, the materials that built and decorated your home. How many of these items came, in whole or in part, from another country? As a new business owner, you will be communicating with many international businesses and customers. In preparation, visit several local small stores and learn how they do business in the global marketplace.

1. Look at 10 products sold in the store and note where they are made. How many of the products can you easily identify as coming from outside the United States?

2. Arrange to meet with the stores' owners or managers. Find out how they order these international products. Do they submit their orders by mail? telephone? fax machine? Internet? Find out whether these local stores sell any of their products overseas. How do their international customers purchase products from them? Do they have a website? Do they send out international mailings or catalogs?

3. Although it's easier today, doing business around the globe increases your need to understand world geography. Consider time differences, for example. Your U.S. business hours certainly won't coincide with the store hours of your suppliers in Europe or Asia. How will you adjust for these differences? The Internet, of course, is one way. But what if you really need to talk to the store manager? When should you place the call? Visit your local library or use resources such as the *World Almanac* to learn more about international time.

   a. How many time zones are there in the United States (including possessions)?

   b. If it's noon in New York City, what time is it in Cape Town, South Africa? Copenhagen, Denmark? Sydney, Australia? Tokyo, Japan? Athens, Greece? Honolulu, Hawaii? Moscow, Russia?

4. As a new business owner, you will be communicating with people who speak many different languages. Visit the Travlang Foreign Language for Traders webpage (www.travlang.com/languages). How do you say "inventory" in Italian? Portuguese? German? French?

CHAPTER

7

Functions and Skills of Management

LEARNING OBJECTIVES

After studying this chapter, you will be able to

1. Define the four basic management functions

2. Outline the tasks involved in the strategic planning process

3. Explain the purpose of a mission statement

4. Discuss the benefits of conducting a SWOT analysis

5. List the benefits of setting long-term goals and objectives

6. Cite three leadership styles and explain why no one style is best

7. Identify and explain important types of managerial skills

8. Summarize the six steps involved in the decision-making process

Michael Dell keeps Dell Computer ahead of its competitors by constantly pushing for change.

INSIDE BUSINESS TODAY

Adding Soul to the Winning Ways of Dell Computer

It's a true story that sounds like a Texas-sized tall tale. In 1984, 19-year-old Michael Dell started selling personal computers from his dorm room at the University of Texas at Austin. He started with a simple idea: purchase computer components from suppliers, assemble the components, cut out the intermediaries and sell PCs directly to customers. A mere eight years later, Dell Computer Corporation joined the ranks of the Fortune 500—*Fortune* magazine's annual roster of the world's largest companies. By 2001 the company led all PC manufacturers in global market share and posted annual revenues of over $32 billion.

Along the way, Michael Dell earned many honors for his leadership. One secret to his success: always pushing the company to be self-critical in its quest for ever-greater efficiency in everything it does. He also has an uncanny ability to visualize and then capitalize on changes in the business world before they occur.

However, no one's foresight is perfect, and the company struggled to sustain its amazing growth during an economic downturn that stretched from 2000 into 2003. Every computer company got hit hard, and Dell was no exception.

When growth slows, managers face tough decisions: How could the company boost revenues? Where could it cut expenses? How could it hang on to talented people? True to Michael Dell's aggressive spirit, the company pursued solutions in all three areas. One of the most difficult choices was to cut expenses by laying off nearly 6,000 people. The most daring move was to boost revenues by launching several new product lines. Dell already offered more than just PCs, but these other items were products made by Cisco, Palm, Hewlett-Packard (HP), and others that Dell simply resold. So in 2002 Dell began applying its own name to printers, routers, and other items previously manufactured by others. The move grew revenues, but also caused former partners to sever their ties with Dell. Finally, the most farsighted initiative was the search for a larger purpose that would help Dell inspire and retain its remaining employees.

This search for a larger purpose was a sign of a maturing senior management team. In the aftermath of a large layoff, a typical company would respond by encouraging its people to work harder, do more, and still produce good results. In other words, do the same old things but faster. However, Dell applied its find-a-better-way mentality and started searching for answers to a bigger question: Beyond pure financial performance, what does it mean to be a great company? The program, called "The Soul of Dell," examined the company's culture and looked for ways to make Dell into more than just the world's most efficient and competitive computer maker.

Leading the way was president and chief operating officer Kevin Rollins, a former management consultant who had advised Michael Dell during the company's vigorous growth days. Rollins searched for models of success, starting with other companies that were recognized as being great places to work. All had a strong culture, a well-defined leadership model, and an overarching purpose that went beyond financial rewards. He also studied the ideas and habits of Thomas Jefferson, Theodore Roosevelt, and other great leaders.

165

The results of this search are captured in five core elements that expanded the company's vision: (1) create loyal customers by providing a superior experience at great value and by outperforming the competition; (2) base continued success on teamwork and the opportunity for each team member to learn and grow; (3) be direct in all ways—business model, ethics, communication, relationships, and more; (4) participate responsibly in the global marketplace; and (5) maintain a passion for winning.

In the hypercompetitive PC market, success is never guaranteed, but Dell is surviving the extended slowdown better than every other U.S. competitor. And with an expanded vision now firmly in place, the company is ready to thrive when favorable business conditions return.[1]

The Four Basic Functions of Management

1 LEARNING OBJECTIVE

Define the four basic management functions

management
Process of coordinating resources to meet organizational goals

Michael Dell knows that when managers possess the right combination of vision, skill, experience, and determination, they can lead an organization to success. Dell also knows that not everyone is equipped to be an effective manager. So he focuses on finding the right managers to help him turn his vision into reality. In this chapter we explore the four basic functions that **management** entails: planning, organizing, leading, and controlling resources (land, labor, capital, and information) to efficiently reach a company's goals (see Exhibit 7.1). And we highlight the skills required of effective managers.

In the course of performing the four management functions, managers play a number of roles that fall into three main categories:

- *Interpersonal roles.* Managers perform ceremonial obligations; provide leadership to employees; build a network of relationships with bosses, peers, and employees; and act as liaison to groups and individuals both inside and outside the company (such as suppliers, competitors, government agencies, consumers, special-interest groups, and interrelated work groups).

- *Informational roles.* Managers spend a fair amount of time gathering information from and delivering information to employees, customers, suppliers, and other stakeholders.

- *Decisional roles.* Managers use the information they gather to encourage innovation, to resolve unexpected problems that threaten organizational goals (such as reacting to an economic crisis), to decide how organizational resources will be used to meet planned objectives, and to run the business. They also negotiate with many individuals and groups, including suppliers, employees, and unions.

Being able to move among these roles while performing the four basic management functions is just one of the many skills that managers must have. But these functions are not discrete; they overlap and influence one another. Let's examine them in detail.

EXHIBIT 7.1   The Four Basic Functions of Management
Some managers, especially those in smaller organizations, perform all four managerial functions. Although these functions tend to occur in a somewhat progressive order, sometimes they occur simultaneously, and often the process is ongoing.

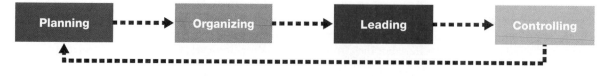

The Planning Function

Planning is the primary management function, the one on which all others depend. Managers engage in **planning** to develop strategies for success, establish goals and objectives for the organization, and translate their strategies and goals into action plans. To develop long-term strategies and goals, managers must be well informed on a number of key issues and topics that could influence their decisions. A closer look at the strategic planning process will give you a clearer idea of the types of information managers need to help them plan for the company's future.

Understanding the Strategic Planning Process

Strategic plans outline the firm's long-range (two to five years) organizational goals and set a course of action the firm will pursue to reach its goals. These long-term goals encompass eight major areas of concern: market standing, innovation, human resources, financial resources, physical resources, productivity, social responsibility, and financial performance. A good strategic plan answers: Where are we going? What is the environment? How do we get there?

To answer these questions and to establish effective long-term goals, managers require extensive amounts of information. For instance, managers must study budgets, production schedules, industry and economic data, customer preferences, internal and external data, competition, and so on. Managers use this information to set a firm's long-term course of direction during a process called strategic planning. Consisting of seven interrelated critical tasks, the strategic planning process is an ongoing event, as Exhibit 7.2 suggests.

Develop a Clear Vision   Most organizations are formed in order to realize a **vision**— a realistic, credible, and attainable view of the future that grows out of and improves on the present. Henry Ford envisioned making affordable transportation available to every person.

planning
Establishing objectives and goals for an organization and determining the best ways to accomplish them

strategic plans
Plans that establish the actions and the resource allocation required to accomplish strategic goals; usually defined for periods of two to five years and developed by top managers

2 LEARNING OBJECTIVE

Outline the tasks involved in the strategic planning process

vision
A viable view of the future that is rooted in but improves on the present

EXHIBIT 7.2
Seven Tasks of the Strategic Planning Process
In today's rapidly changing economy, strategic planning is an ongoing process comprising these seven tasks.

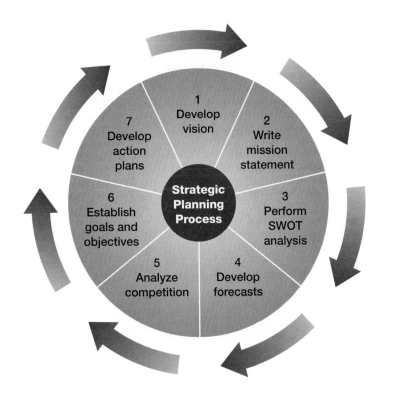

When Wendelin Wiedeking took over as CEO of Porsche in 1992, the company was racing toward record losses of $150 million. Few people believed that Wiedeking could get Porsche back on track. But Wiedeking had a clear vision for the company—one that adopted lean and efficient Japanese production systems at Porsche. Thanks to Wiedeking's vision and leadership, Porsche is back in the fast lane. By the turn of the century, it was racking up some of the highest profit margins of any manufacturer in the automobile industry.

Fred Smith (founder of FedEx) envisioned making FedEx an information company (besides being a transportation company). Bill Gates (chairman of Microsoft) envisioned empowering people through great software, anytime, anyplace, and on any device. And as early as 1994, Michael Dell envisioned the Internet as an efficient way to sell directly to customers. That same year an informal team launched Dell.com and loaded the website with technical support and product information. Today Dell operates one of the highest-volume e-commerce websites in the world.[2] Without such visionaries as Ford, Smith, Gates, and Dell, who knows how the world would be different? Thus, developing a clear vision is a critical task in the strategic planning process. But having a vision alone is no guarantee of success; it must also be communicated to others, executed, and modified as conditions change.

Translate the Vision into a Meaningful Mission Statement   To transform vision into reality, managers must define specific organizational goals, objectives, and philosophies. A starting point is to write a company **mission statement**, a brief document that defines why the organization exists, what it seeks to accomplish, and the principles that the company will adhere to as it tries to reach its goals.

3 LEARNING OBJECTIVE

Explain the purpose of a mission statement

mission statement
A statement of the organization's purpose, basic goals, and philosophies

Put differently, a mission statement communicates what the company is, what it does, and where it's headed. Typical components of a mission statement include the company's product or service; primary market; fundamental concern for survival, growth, and profitability; managerial philosophy; and commitment to quality and social responsibility.

From day one, Dell's mission has been the same: Build better computers and sell them at lower prices. And it is this simple mission that keeps Dell's management focused on doing what it does best (see Exhibit 7.3). Furthermore, it drives management to continually ask, "What is the most efficient way to do things?"[3]

Another important function of a mission statement is to bring clarity of focus to members of the organization. A mission statement helps employees understand how their role is tied to the organization's greater purpose. Thus, it should inspire and guide employees and managers in such a way that they can understand the firm's vision and identify with it. Furthermore, the statement must be congruent with the organization's core values. Managers should use it to assess whether new project proposals are within the scope of the company's mission.[4]

Consider Edge Learning Institute, an employee-training firm based in Tacoma, Washington. Edge executives were considering mass-marketing their training videos through television "infomercials." However, they realized that doing so would be contrary to the company's mission of using "the human touch when providing individuals and organizations with information." So they decided instead to expand Edge's reach by developing a network of franchises that follow the company's training methods.[5]

4 LEARNING OBJECTIVE

Discuss the benefits of conducting a SWOT analysis

Assess the Company's Strengths, Weaknesses, Opportunities, and Threats
Before establishing long-term goals, a firm must have a clear assessment of its strengths and weaknesses compared with the opportunities and threats it faces. Such analysis is commonly referred to as SWOT, which stands for strengths, weaknesses, opportunities, and threats.

Strengths are positive internal factors that contribute to a company's success, such as having a steady supply of knowledgeable employees or having a dynamic leader such as Michael Dell at the helm. *Weaknesses* are negative internal factors that inhibit the company's success,

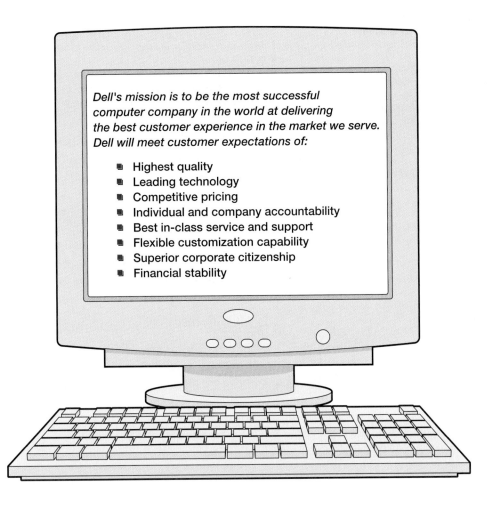

*Dell's mission is to be the most successful
computer company in the world at delivering
the best customer experience in the market we serve.
Dell will meet customer expectations of:*

- Highest quality
- Leading technology
- Competitive pricing
- Individual and company accountability
- Best in-class service and support
- Flexible customization capability
- Superior corporate citizenship
- Financial stability

EXHIBIT 7.3
Mission Statement
The mission statement for Dell
Computer embodies the firm's
high standards for quality and
customer service.

such as obsolete facilities, inadequate financial resources to fund the company's growth, or lack of managerial depth and talent. Identifying a firm's internal strengths and weaknesses helps management understand its current abilities so it can set proper goals. If a firm finds that its managers and employees do not possess the necessary abilities to meet desired goals, they must focus on learning such abilities, or they will have to modify their goals.

One particular strength worth noting is a firm's *core competence*. A **core competence** is a bundle of skills and technologies that enable a company to provide a particular benefit to customers. It sets the company apart from its competitors and is difficult for competitors to duplicate. Sony's core competence, for example, is miniaturization. Federal Express's core competence is its efficient delivery process. And Dell's core competence is not its direct-sales approach, but rather the company's execution of this approach. By identifying and improving a core competence, a firm has a greater chance for success.

What make's Dell's core competence so unique? As Dell puts it, the company is like a living organism. It is constantly adapting and changing and finding new ways to build flexibility and speed into its systems. The company moves quickly and keeps its costs low, which allows it to ruthlessly undercut prices and devour market shares at rates that make competitors gag. Moreover, its obsession with speed and thrift come straight from the boss, Michael Dell, whose rallying cry is: to be direct, cut out the bells and whistles, and be the fastest. As a result, managerial and operational brilliance is deeply embedded in the company's DNA: Over 80 percent of Dell's PCs are built, customized, and shipped within eight hours; production uses just-in-time inventory; and every component in every machine has a bar code that enables the company to know exactly what has been put on that machine if the customer has a problem.[6] As the Dell example shows, a core competence represents the sum of knowledge across the organization. Thus, it lasts even though individual employees may leave the firm.

core competence
Distinct skills and capabilities
that a firm has or does
especially well so that it sets
the firm apart from its
competitors

EXHIBIT 7.4   **Greatest Management Decisions Ever Made**
Visionary leaders spot opportunities early and make great decisions. Here are some of the greatest management decisions made in the 20th century.

Coca-Cola

During WWII, Robert Woodruff, president of Coca-Cola, committed to selling bottles of Coke to members of the armed services for a nickel a bottle. Customer loyalty never came cheaper.

Diners Club

In 1950, when Frank McNamara found himself in a restaurant with no money, he came up with the idea of the Diners Club Card. The first credit card changed the nature of buying and selling throughout the world.

Holiday Inn

When the Wilson family of Memphis went on a motoring vacation, they discovered it was not much fun staying in motels that were either too expensive or too slovenly. So Kemmons Wilson built his own. The first Holiday Inn opened in Memphis in 1952.

Honda

When Honda arrived in America in 1959 to launch its big motor bikes, customers weren't keen on their problematic performance. However, they did admire the little Supercub bikes Honda's managers used. So Honda bravely changed direction and transformed the motorbike business overnight.

Weight Watchers

When Jean Nidetch was put on a diet by the Obesity Clinic at the New York Department of Health, she invited six dieting friends to meet in her apartment every week. In 1961 she created Weight Watchers and launched the slimming industry.

CNN

Ignoring market research, Ted Turner launched the Cable News Network in 1980. No one thought a 24-hour news network would work.

Sony

Sony chief Akito Morita noticed that young people liked listening to music wherever they went. So in 1980 he and the company developed what became the Walkman. There was no need for market research, because according to Morita, "The public does not know what is possible. We do."

Tylenol

When Johnson & Johnson pulled Tylenol from store shelves in 1982 after capsules were found to be poisoned, the company put customer safety before corporate profit. And it provided a lesson in media openness.

Dell

In 1984 Michael Dell decided to sell PCs direct and built to order. Now everybody in the industry is trying to imitate Dell Computer's strategy.

Once managers have taken inventory of a company's internal strengths and weaknesses, they must next identify the external opportunities and threats that might significantly affect their ability to attain certain goals. *Opportunities* are positive external factors such as new markets or new customers. Dell, for example, sees the printer market as an opportunity for additional sales. Shrewd managers, of course, recognize an opportunity before others do and then promptly act on their ideas (see Exhibit 7.4). *Threats* are negative external forces that could inhibit the firm's ability to achieve its objectives. Threats include new competitors or entrants into the market, new government regulations, economic recession, increase in interest rates, technological advances that could make a company's product obsolete, and so on. Harvard Business School Professor Clayton Christensen notes that graveyards are full of big firms that ignored the competitive threats from start-ups.[7] Hewlett-Packard, for example, now sees Dell as an external threat to its printer business. (Threats and external analysis will be discussed in detail in Chapter 12 in the context of developing a strategic marketing plan.)

Develop Forecasts   To develop forecasts, managers must make a number of educated assumptions about future trends and events and modify those assumptions once new information becomes available. Some managers rely on expert forecasts such as those found in *Industry Week*'s "Trends and Forecasts," *Business Week*'s "Survey of Corporate Performance," and Standard & Poor's *Earnings Forecast* as a foundation for their projections. However, these sources may not always include key variables specific to an individual company or industry. Therefore, managers must also develop their own forecasts.

Managerial forecasts fall under two broad categories: *quantitative forecasts*, which are typically based on historical data or tests and which involve complex statistical computations; and *qualitative forecasts*, which are based on intuitive judgments or consumer research. Statistically analyzing the cycles of economic growth and recession over several decades to predict when the economy will take a downward turn is an example of quantitative forecasting. Making predictions about sales of a new product on the basis of experience and consumer responses to a survey is an example of qualitative forecasting. Neither method is foolproof, but both are valuable tools, enabling managers to fill in the unknown variables that inevitably crop up in the planning process.

Analyze the Competition   "Business is like any battlefield. If you want to win the war, you have to know who you're up against," says one management consultant.[8] Thus, sizing up the competition is another important task in planning for a company's future. It gives management a realistic view of the market, the company's position in it, and its ability to attain certain goals and a competitive edge.

A company can gain a competitive edge through one or more of three strategies:

- *Differentiation.* A company using differentiation develops a level of service, a product image, unique product features (including quality), or new technologies that distinguish its product from competitors' products. Volvo, for instance, stresses the safety of its cars. Caterpillar Tractor emphasizes product durability.

- *Cost leadership.* Businesses that pursue this strategy aim to become the low-cost leader in an industry by producing or selling products more efficiently and economically than competitors. Cost leaders have a competitive advantage by reaching buyers whose primary purchase criterion is price. Wal-Mart is a typical industry cost leader. So are Dell and Southwest Airlines.

- *Focus.* When using a focus strategy, companies concentrate on a specific regional market or consumer group, such as the Southwest United States or drivers of economy cars. This type of strategy enables organizations to develop a better understanding of their customers and to tailor their products specifically to customer needs. Examples of focused strategies include Abercrombie and Fitch (high-end apparel for young adults) and Williams-Sonoma (quality cookware and appliances for serious cooks).

Managers begin the competitive analysis process by identifying existing and potential competitors. Next they determine the competencies, strengths, and weaknesses of the major competitors they've identified. Armed with competitive information, they look for ways to capitalize on a competitor's weaknesses or match or surpass their strengths to gain a competitive edge, as Dell did when it entered into an agreement with printer manufacturer Lexmark International to produce Dell-branded inkjet and laser printers and cartridges. Although the decision ended Dell's eight-year agreement with Hewlett Packard (HP) to sell HP-branded computers to Dell customers, Dell recognized that it was missing out on a highly profitable opportunity by not selling its own brand of printers.

Dell's research showed that companies sell most printers at a loss but earn hefty profits—as high as 60 percent—on the sale of printer ink cartridges. Moreover, retailers such as

You won't find cheap frying pans at Williams-Sonoma. This retailer competes by focusing on a narrow market—top-of-the-line cookware for gourmet or serious cooks.

5 LEARNING OBJECTIVE

List the benefits of setting long-term goals and objectives

goal
Broad, long-range target or aim

objective
Specific, short-range target or aim

tactical plans
Plans that define the actions and the resource allocation necessary to achieve tactical objectives and to support strategic plans; usually defined for a period of one to three years and developed by middle managers

Immediately following the September 11 attacks, American Express CEO Ken Chenault, who was in Salt Lake City at the time, made the necessary calls to address the crisis. Foremost was the safe evacuation of employees from its headquarters building. Next was to help thousands of stranded card members get home. American Express responded to the crisis by waiving delinquency fees, providing cash advances, and increasing credit limits—putting customers' needs and safety above all else.

Staples and Office Depot mark up the price of ink cartridges another 30 percent, earning substantial profits from their sales. In other words, Dell was missing out on the highly profitable and recurring sales of ink refills.[9] Moreover, by eliminating the middleman, Dell could price its cartridges and printers below competition.

Such a move could seriously wound HP—a major Dell competitor for computer sales—by attacking HP's highly-profitable printer unit. That's because HP relies on its printing and imaging profits to subsidize its money-losing PC business.[10] To match Dell's ink cartridge prices, HP would have to sell cartridges directly to customers at wholesale prices. Such a move would discourage retailers from selling HP printers and would have a negative effect on sales of HP printers, on company profits, and ultimately on its ability to compete in the PC and PC server markets.[11]

Establish Company Goals and Objectives   As mentioned earlier, establishing goals and objectives is the key task in the planning process. Although these terms are often used interchangeably, a **goal** is a broad, long-range accomplishment that the organization wishes to attain in typically five years or more, whereas an **objective** is a specific, short-range target designed to help reach that goal. In 2002 Dell set a goal of doubling annual sales to $60 billion within four or five years.[12] To be effective, organizational goals and objectives should be specific, measurable, relevant, challenging, attainable, and time-limited. For example, it is better to state "increase our sales by 25 percent over the next five years" than "substantially increase our sales."

Setting appropriate goals has many benefits: It provides direction and guidance for managers at all levels; it helps firms allocate resources to projects with the greatest financial potential; it guides employee activity and increases motivation; it clarifies management's expectations; and it establishes standards for measuring individual and group performance. By establishing organizational goals, managers set the stage for the actions needed to achieve those goals. If actions aren't planned, the chances of reaching company goals are slim.

Develop Action Plans   Once managers have established a firm's long-term strategic goals and objectives, it must then develop a plan of execution. **Tactical plans** lay out the actions and the allocation of resources necessary to achieve specific, short-term objectives that support the company's broader strategic plan. Tactical plans typically focus on departmental goals and cover a period of one to three years. Their limited scope permits them to be changed more easily than strategic plans. **Operational plans** designate the actions and resources required to achieve the objectives of tactical plans. Operational plans usually define actions for less than one year and focus on accomplishing a firm's specific objectives, such as developing a strategic partnership with another company.

Planning for a Crisis

No matter how well a company plans for its future, any number of problems can arise to threaten its existence. An ugly fight for control of a company, a product failure, a breakdown in routine operations (as a result of fire, for example), or an environmental accident could develop into a serious and crippling crisis. Managers can help a company survive these setbacks through **crisis management**, a plan for handling such unusual and serious problems.

The goal of crisis management is to keep the company functioning smoothly both during and after a crisis. Successful crisis management requires comprehensive contingency plans in addition to speedy, open communication with all who are affected by the crisis. Experts suggest setting up a crisis communications team, with a knowledgeable spokesperson, to handle the many requests for information that

Managing in the 21st Century

JetBlue: Making Tough Management Decisions in Tough Times

When David Neeleman launched JetBlue Airways in February 2000, he was determined to succeed in an industry where a number of other ambitious entrants had failed: Kiwi International, People Express, and Tower Air, to name a few. With $130 million from private investors, Neeleman hoped to fill a niche left empty by the big air carriers—all-coach leather seats, seatback satellite TV, excellent service, candor about delays, and more. Still, nothing could have prepared Neeleman for the events of September 11 or for their impact on the airline industry. Overnight, Neeleman had to operate the most ambitious start-up in U.S. aviation on pure instinct.

JetBlue's management developed a crisis strategy that bucked the industry trend. From company headquarters, 9 miles from ground zero, Neeleman vowed not to lay off any of the airline's 2,000 employees, even though its planes were flying mostly empty. Then, while rivals scaled back flights and postponed deliveries of new planes, JetBlue expanded services to new markets and ordered additional planes. It was a daring move, indeed. Not only did the newcomer have an all-important instinct for survival, but its innovative strategies were paying off as well. JetBlue posted profits while others posted losses.

How did JetBlue beat the odds? To begin with, Neeleman based the airline at New York's JFK airport, an international gateway that is crowded only a few hours per day. This location allows JetBlue to bypass congested and delay-plagued La Guardia Airport. Then to keep costs down, it adopted Southwest Airlines' point-to-point service—flying busy routes between some 20 secondary airports. Moreover, JetBlue pays its workforce—which is nonunion—far less than major carriers do and keeps pilots happy by granting them stock options and promoting first officers to captains relatively quickly. The company also reduces training and maintenance costs by flying only one type of aircraft—factory-fresh, state-of-the art Airbus A320s, each with ample amounts of legroom. And it saves fuel by configuring all planes with emergency over-water equipment so its flights can swing out over the ocean to avoid congestion on popular East Coast routes.

JetBlue's innovative strategic flight plan has gained altitude even during turbulent times. Still, critics note that it's one thing to execute a smooth takeoff; it's another to expand cross country. JetBlue plans to add 60 jetliners in five years to an existing fleet of 23. Of course, only time will tell whether JetBlue can outfox the major carriers, which have historically grounded newcomers. Neeleman knows the risks are high. But as he sees it, where there's chaos, there's opportunity.

Questions for Critical Thinking

1. What is JetBlue's strategic flight plan for success?
2. How did JetBlue handle the September 11 crisis differently from its rivals?

---

arise during a crisis. The individuals selected should be able to remain honest and calm when a crisis hits. Moreover, top managers should be visible in the hours immediately following the crisis to demonstrate that the company will do whatever is necessary to control the situation as best it can, find the cause, and prevent a future occurrence.[13]

Ford and Bridgestone/Firestone were criticized for not taking these actions when reports started surfacing about the faulty tires manufactured by Bridgestone/Firestone and fitted on Ford Explorer sport utility vehicles. When the vehicles were driven at high speed, the treads separated from the tires, causing the cars to roll over, injuring—and even killing—passengers. Although both Ford and Firestone eventually recalled 6.5 million tires, both companies paid the price for making serious mistakes in handling the crisis.[14] (See "Firestone and Ford: Failure to Yield . . . or Asleep at the Wheel?" on page 51).

operational plans
Plans that lay out the actions and the resource allocation needed to achieve operational objectives and to support tactical plans; usually defined for less than 1 year and developed by first-line managers

crisis management
System for minimizing the harm that might result from some unusually threatening situations

The Organizing Function

organizing
Process of arranging resources to carry out the organization's plans

Organizing, the process of arranging resources to carry out the organization's plans, is the second major function of managers. During the organizing stage, managers think through all the activities that employees carry out (from programming the organization's computers to mailing its letters), as well as all the facilities and equipment employees need in order to complete those activities. They also give people the ability to work toward organizational goals by determining who will have the authority to make decisions, to perform or supervise activities, and to distribute resources.

The organizing function is particularly challenging because most organizations undergo constant change. Long-time employees leave, and new employees arrive. Equipment breaks down or becomes obsolete, and replacements are needed. The public's tastes and interests change, and the organization has to reevaluate its plans and activities. Shifting political and economic trends can lead to employee cutbacks—or perhaps expansion. Long-time competitors take unexpected actions, and new competitors enter the market. Every week the organization faces new situations, so management's organizing tasks are never finished. Consider Microsoft. The company continually challenges itself by asking: "Are we making what customers want and working on products and technologies they'll want in the future? Are we staying ahead of all our competitors? What don't our customers like about what we do, and what are we doing about it? Are we organized most effectively to achieve our goals?"[15]

management pyramid
Organizational structure comprising top, middle, and lower management

The organizing function will be discussed in detail in Chapter 8. In this chapter, however, we will discuss the three levels of a corporate hierarchy—top, middle, and bottom—commonly known as the **management pyramid** (see Exhibit 7.5). In general, **top managers** are the upper-level managers who have the most power and who take overall responsibility for the organization. An example is the chief executive officer (CEO). Top managers establish the structure for the organization as a whole, and they select the people who fill the upper-level positions. Top managers also make long-range plans, set a direction for their organization, establish major policies, inspire employees and others to achieve the company's vision, and represent the company to the outside world at official functions and fundraisers.

top managers
Those at the highest level of the organization's management hierarchy; they are responsible for setting strategic goals, and they have the most power and responsibility in the organization

middle managers
Those in the middle of the management hierarchy; they develop plans to implement the goals of top managers and coordinate the work of first-line managers

Middle managers have similar responsibilities, but usually for just one division or unit. They develop plans for implementing the broad goals set by top managers, and they coordinate the work of first-line managers. In traditional organizations, managers at the

EXHIBIT 7.5
The Management Pyramid
Separate job titles are used to designate the three basic levels in the management pyramid.

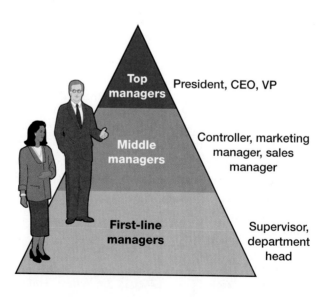

middle level are plant managers, division managers, branch managers, and other similar positions, all reporting to top-level managers. But in more innovative management structures, middle managers often function as team leaders, who are expected to supervise and lead small groups of employees in a variety of job functions. Similar to consultants, they must understand every department's function, not just their own area of expertise. Furthermore, they are granted decision-making authority previously reserved for only high-ranking executives.[16]

At the bottom of the management pyramid are **first-line managers** (or *supervisory managers*). They oversee the work of operating employees, and they put into action the plans developed at higher levels. Positions at this level include supervisor, department head, and office manager. Even though more managers are at the bottom level than at the top, today's leaner companies such as Dell tend to have fewer levels, flattening the organizational structure, as Chapter 8 points out.

first-line managers
Those at the lowest level of the management hierarchy; they supervise the operating employees and implement the plans set at the higher management levels; also called supervisory managers

The Leading Function

Leading—the process of influencing and motivating people to work effectively and willingly toward company goals—is the third basic function of management. As Michael Dell knows, leading is even more challenging in today's business environment because individuals with different backgrounds and unique interests, ambitions, and personal goals must work together productively in teams. Managers with good leadership skills have greater success in influencing the attitudes and actions of others, both through the demonstration of specific tasks and through the manager's own behavior and spirit. Furthermore, effective leaders are good at *motivating*, or giving employees a reason to do the job and to put forth their best performance (see Chapter 10).

leading
Process of guiding and motivating people to work toward organizational goals

What makes a good leader? When early researchers studied leadership, they looked for specific characteristics, or *traits*, common to all good leaders. At the time, they were unable to prove any link between particular traits and leadership ability. However, researchers found that leaders who have specific traits, such as decisiveness and self-confidence, are likely to be more effective.[17] Additional studies have shown that managers with strong interpersonal skills and high emotional quotients (EQs) tend to be more effective leaders. The characteristics of a high EQ include[18]:

- *Self-awareness.* Self-aware managers have the ability to recognize their own feelings and how they, their job performance, and other people are affected by those feelings. Moreover, managers who are highly self-aware know where they are headed and why.

- *Self-regulation.* Self-regulated managers have the ability to control or reduce disruptive impulses and moods. They can suspend judgment and think before acting. Moreover, they know how to use the best emotion for a given situation.

- *Motivation.* Motivated managers are driven to achieve beyond expectations—their own and everyone else's.

- *Empathy.* Empathetic managers thoughtfully consider employees' feelings, along with other factors, in the process of making intelligent decisions.

- *Social skill.* Socially skilled managers tend to have a wide circle of acquaintances, and they have a knack for finding common ground with people of all kinds. They assume that nothing important gets done by one person alone and have a network in place when the time for action comes.

Keep in mind that these traits alone do not define a leader. Different leadership traits are appropriate under different leadership situations.

Adopting an Effective Leadership Style

Leadership style is the way a manager uses authority to lead others. Every manager, from the baseball coach to the university chancellor, has a definite style. The three broad categories of leadership style are *autocratic*, *democratic*, and *laissez-faire*.

Autocratic leaders make decisions without consulting others. "My way or the highway" summarizes this style, which tends to go with traditional, hierarchical organizational structures. Although autocratic leadership can be highly effective when quick decisions are necessary, it does little to empower employees or encourage innovation. Al Dunlap, past CEO of Sunbeam, used an autocratic leadership style to try to turn the failing household appliance maker around, as this chapter's Case for Critical Thinking shows.

In contrast, **democratic leaders** such as Michael Dell delegate authority and involve employees in decision making. Even though their approach can lead to slower decisions, soliciting input from people familiar with particular situations or issues may result in better decisions. No one knows this better than Meg Whitman, CEO of eBay. Whitman is known for delegating responsibility to other managers and focusing on strategic issues. She will dive into details when things go awry, as she did in 1999 after a series of computer crashes threatened to derail eBay's business. But at management meetings, Whitman insists that all executives voice their opinions on troublesome issues. And she listens carefully before she expresses her own opinion.[19] Whitman's approach, known as **participative management** or *open-book management*, focuses on sharing information at all levels of the organization. Involving employees in decision making increases employees' power in an organization and improves the flow of information between employees and managers.

As more companies adopt the principles of teamwork, democratic leadership continues to gain in popularity. For example, managers at Rhone-Poulenc, the U.S. subsidiary of France's leading chemical and pharmaceutical manufacturer, gradually made the transition from autocratic to democratic leadership as the organization moved from a hierarchical structure to a team-based environment. CEO Peter Neff says, "I don't look over people's shoulders anymore. . . . My role now is to enable people to do the best they know how to do." For Neff, this means acting as an opportunity seeker, coach, facilitator, motivator, and mentor rather than as a controller or problem solver.[20]

The third leadership style, laissez-faire, is sometimes referred to as free-rein leadership. The French term *laissez faire* can be translated as "leave it alone," or more roughly as "hands off." **Laissez-faire leaders** take the role of consultant, encouraging employees' ideas and offering insights or opinions when asked. The laissez-faire style may fail if workers pursue goals that do not match the organization's. However, the style has proven effective in some situations. Managers at Hewlett-Packard's North American distribution organization adopted a laissez-faire style when they were given nine months to reorganize their order-fulfillment process. The managers eliminated all titles, supervision, job descriptions, and plans, and they made employees entirely responsible for the project. At first there was chaos. However, employees soon began to try new things, make mistakes, and learn as they went. In the end, the team finished the reorganization ahead of schedule, reduced product delivery times from 26 days to 8 days, and cut inventory by 20 percent. Moreover, the employees experienced a renewed sense of challenge, commitment, and enjoyment in their work.[21]

Meg Whitman, CEO of eBay, is a perfect example of a democratic leader. She attributes much of eBay's success to the involvement of employees and managers in decision making. "I'm really proud of what we've created at eBay, but I haven't done it alone," says Whitman. "It really has been our management team and the people that come to eBay that has built our community. It's a partnership."

EXHIBIT 7.6   Continuum of Leadership Behavior
Leadership style occurs along a continuum, ranging from boss-centered to employee-centered. Situations that require managers to exercise greater authority fall toward the boss-centered end of the continuum. Other situations call for a manager to give workers the leeway to function more independently.

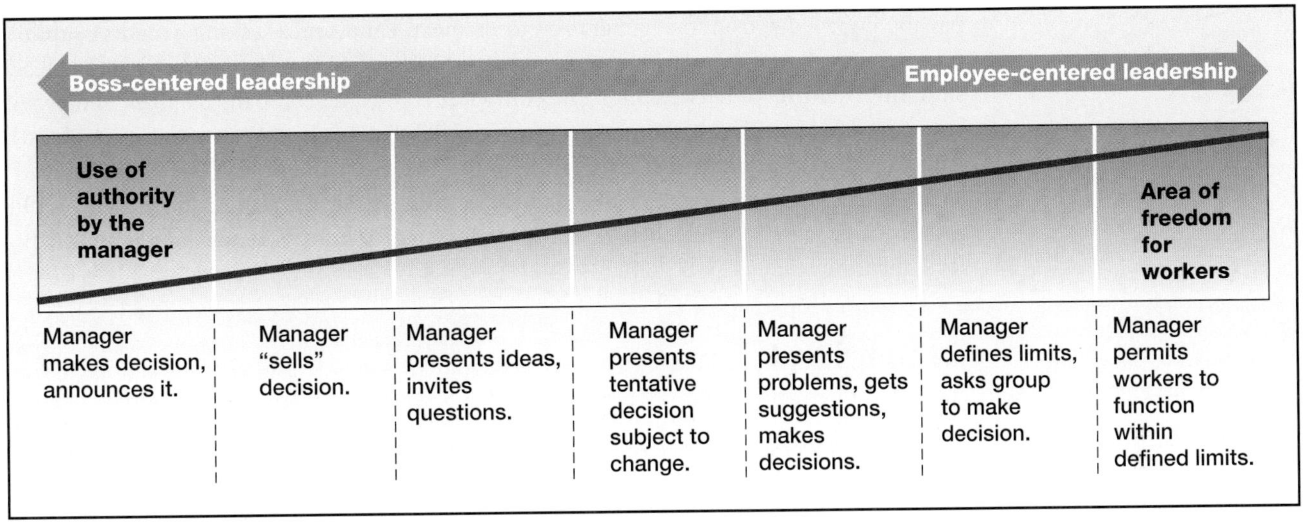

More and more businesses are adopting democratic and laissez-faire leadership as they reduce the number of management layers in their corporate hierarchies and increase the use of teamwork. However, experienced managers know that no one leadership style works every time. In fact, new research shows that leaders with the best results do not rely solely on one leadership style; instead they adapt their approach to match the requirements of the particular situation.[22] Adapting leadership style to current business circumstances is called **contingency leadership**. You can think of leadership styles as existing along a continuum of possible leadership behaviors, as suggested by Exhibit 7.6.

contingency leadership
Adapting the leadership style to what is most appropriate, given current business conditions

Coaching and Mentoring

Managers can provide effective leadership by coaching and mentoring their employees. On a winning sports team, the coach focuses on helping all team members perform at their highest potential. In a similar way, *coaching* managers strive to bring out the best in their employees.

Coaching involves taking the time to meet with employees, discussing any problems that may hinder their ability to work effectively, and offering suggestions and encouragement to help them find their own solutions to work-related challenges. This process requires keen powers of observation, sensible judgment, and both a willingness and an ability to take appropriate action. However, just as a sports coach cannot play the game for team members, a coaching manager must step back and let employees perform when it's "game time." Coaching managers develop a solid game plan and empower their team to carry it out. If the team gets behind, the manager offers encouragement to boost morale. And when team members are victorious, the manager recognizes and praises their outstanding achievement.[23] Tom Gegax, co-founder of Tires Plus stores, has been using internal coaches in his organization for years. "People are more willing to take feedback from a coach than from a boss because so many of us have been coached before," says Gegax.[24]

Acting as a mentor is similar to coaching, but mentoring also emphasizes helping employees understand how the organization works. A **mentor** is usually an experienced manager or employee who can help guide other employees through the corporate maze. Mentors have a deep knowledge of the business and a useful network of industry colleagues. In addition, they can explain office politics, serve as a role model for appropriate business behavior, and provide valuable advice about how to succeed within the organization.

coaching
Helping employees reach their highest potential by meeting with them, discussing problems that hinder their ability to work effectively, and offering suggestions and encouragement to overcome these problems

mentor
Experienced manager or employee with a wide network of industry colleagues who can explain office politics, serve as a role model for appropriate business behavior, and help other employees negotiate the corporate structure

Your mentor won't necessarily be your boss. Relationships with mentors often develop informally between the individuals involved. Some companies have formal programs that link up-and-comers to an old hand for years of personal development and career advice. Others take a more innovative approach. Intel's mentor program, for instance, focuses on passing knowledge from one generation to the next. Employees seeking a mentor submit an intranet-based questionnaire, listing topics and skills they want to master, such as leadership, Intel culture, or networking. The computer combs the company database and provides recommended matches based on the specific skills that are in demand. For example, when Ann Otero needed help with leadership and time-management skills, she was teamed up with a senior manager who was strong in those skills. After working with her mentor, Otero says she now has enough leadership know-how to feel comfortable speaking up in the high-level meetings that she sits in on.[25]

Managing Change

Another important function of leaders is to manage the process of change. As competitive pressures get worse, the pace of change accelerates while companies search for even higher levels of quality, service, and overall speed. But managing change is a formidable task. According to one recent study, about 70 percent of all change initiatives fail.[26] Resistance to change often arises because people don't understand how it will affect them. Mention change and most people automatically feel victimized. Some worry that they may have to master new skills—ones that might be difficult. Others fear that their jobs will be in jeopardy. Experts advise that if managers want less resistance to change, they should build trust with employees long before the change arrives and, when it does, explain to them how it will affect their jobs. Moreover, cultivating constant change on a small scale can prepare employees for even larger changes; it's the difference between asking someone to run a race who has never even practiced versus asking someone to run a race who jogs every day.[27]

Sometimes change is imposed from outside the company, as was the case with the airline industry (see Chapter 1 Case for Critical Thinking "Turmoil in the Airline Industry" on page 31). At other times managers initiate change, as Dell continually does. Dell stays one step ahead of its competitors by constantly pushing the envelope of change. Michael Dell has the ability to visualize and capitalize on changes in the business world before they occur. "If you sat in on our management meetings, you would find that we are a remarkable self-critical bunch with a disdain for complacency that motivates us," says Dell. "We are always looking to do things more efficiently. We are 99 percent focused on what is going to happen and what could change the business in the future. We ask ourselves, what are the risks to the business, what could go wrong."[28] As Dell knows, to successfully initiate and implement change, you must build it into your corporate culture.

Building a Strong Corporate Culture

Strong leadership is a key element in establishing a productive *corporate culture*—the set of underlying values, norms, and practices shared by members of an organization. When you visit an organization, observe how the employees work, dress, communicate, address each other, and conduct business. Each organization has a special way of doing things. In corporations, this force is often referred to as **corporate culture**.

A company's culture influences the way people treat and react to each other. It shapes the way employees feel about the company and the work they do; the way they interpret and perceive the actions taken by others; the expectations they have regarding changes in their work or in the business; and their ability to lead, be productive, and choose the best course of action. But as Dell's president Kevin Rollins knows "you can't buy cultural change off the shelf." Successful companies don't mimic programs at GE, IBM, or Wal-Mart; they devise a

corporate culture
A set of shared values and norms that support the management system and that guide management and employee behavior

Managing in the 21st Century

How Much Do You Know About the Company's Culture?

Before you accept a job at a new company, it's a good idea to learn as much as possible about the company's culture. Use this list of questions to guide you in your investigation.

Company Values

- Is there a compelling vision for the company?
- Is there a mission statement supporting the vision that employees understand and can implement?
- Do employees know how their work relates to this vision?
- Is there a common set of values that bind the organization together?
- Do officers/owners follow these values, or is there a gap between what they say and what they do?

People

- How are people treated?
- Is there an atmosphere of civility and respect?
- Is teamwork valued and encouraged, with all ideas welcomed?
- Are employee ideas acknowledged, encouraged, and acted upon?
- Are employees given credit for their ideas?
- Is there a positive commitment to a balance between work and life?
- Is there a commitment from top management to support working parents?

Community Involvement

- Is the company involved in the community?
- Is there a corporate culture of service?

- Is there a stated policy of community involvement by the company and its employees?

Communication

- Is there open communication?
- Do officers/owners regularly communicate with all levels?
- Are the customer service and financial results widely distributed?
- Is there meaningful two-way communication throughout the organization?
- Are employee surveys on workplace issues conducted and published? Are employees asked for input on solutions?
- Is there an open-door policy for access to management?

Employee Performance

- How are personnel issues handled?
- Is employee feedback given regularly?
- Are employee valuations based on agreed upon objectives that have been clearly communicated?
- Are employees asked to provide a summary of their accomplishments for placement into their evaluations?

Questions for Critical Thinking

1. How might a job candidate find the answers to these questions?
2. Why is it important to learn about the company's culture before accepting a job?

---

culture that fits their own organization. And they work on improving the firm's culture as things change.

As this chapter's vignette explains, Dell's recent initiative, "Soul of Dell," was developed to examine its company's culture and to find new ways for Dell to be more than just the world's most efficient and competitive machine. Dell launched the program after quarterly employee surveys, called "Tell Dell," showed that employees were concerned about their future with Dell. Moreover, Dell wanted employees to cite respect, integrity, honesty, and forthrightness as some of the reasons they choose Dell as an employer.

By contrast, one of the reasons Enron (once the world's leading broker in electricity and natural gas) failed was its culture, which emphasized earnings growth and rewarded aggressive behavior to such an extent that it fostered unethical behavior. Top performers were rewarded with huge cash bonuses and stock option grants—a system that encouraged "every man for himself" instead of teamwork. Moreover, monetary and stock rewards were granted by a performance review committee. This system bred a culture in which people were afraid to go against anyone who could influence their review. Thus, the whole environment at the vice-president level and above turned into a "yes-man" culture. Things weren't much better in the lower ranks. Young people—many just out of undergraduate or MBA programs with little experience and perspective—were handed extraordinary authority and decision-making power. Some were even swiftly advanced to senior-level positions. It was like a bunch of kids running loose without adult supervision. So if senior managers were fudging earnings, the inexperienced managers assumed that this was the way it was done at most businesses.[29]

The Controlling Function

controlling
Process of measuring progress against goals and objectives and correcting deviations if results are not as expected

quality
A measure of how closely a product conforms to predetermined standards and customer expectations

standards
Criteria against which performance is measured

Controlling is the fourth basic managerial function. In management, **controlling** means monitoring a firm's progress toward meeting its organizational goals and objectives, resetting the course if goals or objectives change in response to shifting conditions, and correcting deviations if goals or objectives are not being attained.

Managers strive to maintain a high level of **quality**—a measure of how closely goods or services conform to predetermined standards and customer expectations. Many firms control for quality through a four-step cycle that involves all levels of management and all employees (see Exhibit 7.7). In the first step, top managers set **standards**, or criteria for measuring the performance of the organization as a whole. At the same time, middle and first-line managers set departmental quality standards so they can meet or exceed company standards. Establishing control standards is closely tied to the planning function and depends on information supplied by employees, customers, and other external sources. Examples of specific standards might be "Produce 1,500 circuit boards monthly with less than 1 percent failures."

EXHIBIT 7.7 The Control Cycle
The control cycle has four basic steps: (1) On the basis of strategic goals, top managers set the standards by which the organization's overall performance will be measured. (2) Managers at all levels measure performance. (3) Actual performance is compared with the standards. (4) Appropriate corrective action is taken (if performance meets standards, nothing other than encouragement is needed; if performance falls below standards, corrective action may include improving performance, establishing new standards, changing plans, reorganizing, or redirecting efforts).

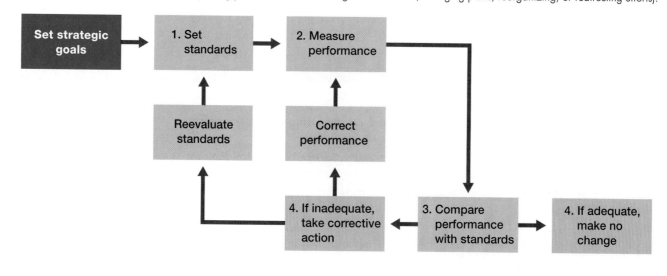

In the second step of the control cycle, managers assess performance, using both quantitative (specific, numerical) and qualitative (subjective) performance measures. In the third step, managers compare performance with the established standards and search for the cause of any discrepancies. If the performance falls short of standards, the fourth step is to take corrective action, which may be done by either adjusting performance or reevaluating the standards. If performance meets or exceeds standards, no corrective action is taken. As Exhibit 7.7 shows, if everything is operating smoothly, controls permit managers to repeat acceptable performance. If results are below expectations, controls help managers take any necessary action.

Take Dell. Suppose the company does not reach its goal of doubling annual sales in four or five years. With proper control systems in place, managers will evaluate why this goal was not reached. Perhaps they will find that a shortage of parts created manufacturing delays. Or perhaps the market where sales were targeted became saturated with PCs and printers made by competitors. Regardless, management will search for the cause of the discrepancies before modifying the company's objectives or trying a different approach to achieve the company's long-term goals. Control methods are examined in greater detail in Chapter 9.

7 LEARNING OBJECTIVE

Identify and explain important types of managerial skills

interpersonal skills
Skills required to understand other people and to interact effectively with them

technical skills
Ability and knowledge to perform the mechanics of a particular job

Management Skills

Managers rely on a number of skills to perform their functions and maintain a high level of quality in their organizations. These skills can be classified into five basic categories: *interpersonal, technical, administrative, conceptual, and decision making*. As managers rise through the organization's hierarchy, they may need to strengthen their abilities in one or more of these skills; fortunately, managerial skills can usually be learned.

Interpersonal Skills

The various skills required to communicate with other people, work effectively with them, motivate them, and lead them are **interpersonal skills**. Because managers mainly get things done through people at all levels of the organization, they use good interpersonal skills in countless situations. Encouraging employees to work together toward common goals, interacting with employees and other managers, negotiating with partners and suppliers, developing employee trust and loyalty, and fostering innovation—all these activities require interpersonal skills.

Communication, or exchanging information, is the most important and pervasive interpersonal skill that managers use. Effective communication not only increases the manager's and the organization's productivity but also shapes the impressions made on colleagues, employees, supervisors, investors, and customers. Communication allows you to perceive the needs of these stakeholders (your first step toward satisfying them), and it helps you respond to those needs.[30] Moreover, as the workforce becomes more and more diverse, managers will need to adjust their interactions with others, communicating in a way that considers the different needs, backgrounds, and experiences of people.

Jenny J. Ming, president of Old Navy, oversees everything from store operations to marketing and advertising. Her passion for fashion has helped drive the company's record growth. So has her ability to communicate effectively with others. Ming recognizes that people's needs change as quickly as the latest fashion trend. So when communicating with others, she takes extra care to focus on her audience's special needs and differing backgrounds.

Technical, Administrative, and Conceptual Skills

A person who knows how to operate a machine, prepare a financial statement, program a computer, or pass a football has **technical skills**; that is, the individual has the knowledge and ability to perform the mechanics of a particular job.

Technical skills are most important at lower organizational levels because managers at these levels work directly with employees who are using the tools and techniques of a particular specialty, such as automotive assembly or computer programming. Still, 21st-century managers must have a strong technology background. They must find new computer applications that can complete daily work routines faster or provide more accurate information sooner.

administrative skills
Technical skills in information gathering, data analysis, planning, organizing, and other aspects of managerial work

Managers at all levels use **administrative skills**, which are the technical skills necessary to manage an organization. Administrative skills include the abilities to make schedules, gather information, analyze data, plan, and organize. Managers often develop such skills through education and then improve them by working in one or more functional areas of an organization, such as accounting or marketing. Project management skills are becoming an increasingly important administrative skill. Managers must know how to start a project or work assignment from scratch, map out each step in the process to its successful completion, develop project costs and timelines, and establish checkpoints at key project intervals. They must have time-management skills (the ability to manage their time efficiently) so that communicating via phone or e-mail, handling volumes of information, and attending meetings does not interfere with their business productivity.

conceptual skills
Ability to understand the relationship of parts to the whole

Managers need **conceptual skills** to see the organization as a whole, in the context of its environment, and to understand how the various parts interrelate. Conceptual skills are especially important to top managers, who must acquire and analyze information, identify both problems and opportunities, understand the competitive environment in which their companies operate, develop strategies, and make decisions.

Decision-Making Skills

decision-making skills
Ability to identify and analyze a problem, weigh the alternatives, choose an alternative, implement it, and evaluate the results

Decision-making skills involve the ability to define problems and select the best course of action. Most managers make decisions by following a process such as the one highlighted in Exhibit 7.8. Using a formal process helps ensure that the best decision is made—a critical success factor for most companies. To show the steps in this process, we'll use the example of Boeing. Developing a new airplane takes years and billions of dollars. Moreover, carriers purchase planes years before they need them and fly them for decades. "You make a decision and then you don't find out whether they make sense until 10 years later," notes one Boeing executive.[31] Needless to say, the decision of what kinds of planes to build is crucial for this company.

8 LEARNING OBJECTIVE

Summarize the six steps involved in the decision-making process

Recognizing and Defining the Problem or Opportunity   The first step in the decision-making process is to recognize that an opportunity or a problem exists. Most companies look for problems or opportunities by gathering customer feedback, conducting studies, or monitoring such warning signals as declining sales or profits, excess inventory buildup, or high customer turnover. Such was the case with Boeing.

For years, Boeing built some 85 percent of the world's jetliners. But in the 1990s Boeing began to steadily lose ground to rival Airbus, as the popularity of the European jet maker's

EXHIBIT 7.8
Steps in the Decision-Making Process
Following these six steps will help you make better decisions.

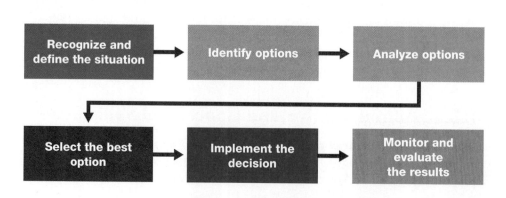

single-aisle airplanes took off. By 1994 Airbus had increased its total market share for new jets from 30 percent to nearly 50 percent, while Boeing's market share dropped from 85 percent to 50 percent. Then in 1999 rival Airbus sold twice as many planes as Boeing. It was a huge wake-up call for Boeing. One year later, Airbus announced its plans to go after Boeing's lucrative 747 market by building the A380, a state-of-the-art, 555-passenger, double-decker flying behemoth. The A380 will use the latest technology such as lightweight materials, making it cheaper to operate per seat-mile than Boeing's 747-400 (which seats 416 passengers). But the superjumbo will fly no faster than today's jets and cost more than $12 billion to develop.[32]

Identifying and Developing Options   Once a problem or opportunity has been defined, the next step is to develop a list of alternative courses of action. Boeing knew that to regain its decisive market lead, it would have to develop a new airplane. Management identified several options: It could build a similar superjumbo plane to compete with the A380; it could build a larger version of its 747-400 to accommodate more than 416 passengers (the plane's current capacity); it could build the Sonic Cruiser, a technologically advanced version of a midsize plane that travels at a speed just below the sound barrier and could cut travel time by 20 percent; or it could build a cheaper, fuel-efficient jet that is more economical to operate.[33]

Analyzing Options   Once the ideas have been generated, most companies develop criteria such as cost, feasibility, availability of existing resources, market acceptance, potential for revenue generation, and compatibility with the company's mission and vision, to evaluate the options. Some companies rank their criteria by importance, assigning a numerical value to criteria so that important criteria receive more weight in the decision-making process. This weighting is especially important in cases in which certain criteria, such as cost, labor, or implementation time, are scarce. As you can imagine, this step involves a great deal of discussion and debate among managers.

After analyzing the relevant information, challenges, opportunities, and competitive environment, and applying specific criteria, Boeing concluded that the superjumbo was too risky and too expensive. Boeing saw demand for new jets in the 400-plus passenger category increasing slightly but felt it could service this demand with its current 747 model. Moreover, Boeing thought the challenges posed by the superjumbo were too risky. One such challenge is the need for airports to spend hundreds of millions of dollars to upgrade terminals and taxiways to service the A380 and its two levels of jetways.

Selecting the Best Option   After all options have been analyzed and debated, management selects the best one. Some companies turn to customers and employees for feedback before finalizing their decision. This process can be cumbersome but rewarding. For instance, Boeing initially concluded that the company's best option was to build a new version of the 747 that could match or beat the A380's economics and cost only $4 billion to develop versus the $12 billion to develop a superjumbo. But after presenting this option to potential customers, Boeing discovered that the market acceptance for a modified 747 did not exist. So the company investigated an alternative option—developing a Sonic Cruiser. But that option was thrown off course after the September 11 terrorist attacks and the resulting drop in passenger traffic. With travelers becoming more price-sensitive and with airlines altering and cutting back schedules—and some even fighting for their lives—potential customers were reluctant to endorse a plane that could cost more to run and hence require them to raise ticket prices.[34] Thus, Boeing began exploring a different option: developing a futuristic, triangle-shaped aircraft that would be cheaper to build and fly than anything rival Airbus had on its drawing boards.[35]

Implementing the Decision and Monitoring the Results   Once a final option has been selected, it's time to implement the decision. This step generally requires the development of action plans that may be similar in scope to those developed for a strategic plan. Next, managers monitor the results of decisions over time to see whether the chosen alternative works, whether any new problems or opportunities arise because of the decision, and whether the decision should be modified to meet changing circumstances. Boeing and Dell, for example, must always keep a close eye on the changing nature of their respective industries.

In the next chapter, we show how a company's managerial structure defines the way decisions are made. Today's flatter organizations, for example, allow information to flow more freely among all levels of the organization, and they push decision making down to lower organizational levels. Moreover, as more and more organizations empower their employees, they delegate the task of decision making to teams.

Summary of Learning Objectives

1. **Define the four basic management functions.**

   The four management functions are (1) planning—establishing objectives and goals for the organization and translating them into action plans; (2) organizing—arranging resources to carry out the organization's plans; (3) leading—influencing and motivating people to work effectively and willingly toward company goals; and (4) controlling—monitoring progress toward organizational goals, resetting the course if goals or objectives change in response to shifting conditions, and correcting deviations if goals or objectives are not being attained.

2. **Outline the tasks involved in the strategic planning process.**

   The strategic planning process begins with a clear vision for the company's future. This vision is then translated into a mission statement so it can be shared with all members of the organization. Next, managers assess the company's strengths, weaknesses, opportunities, and threats; they develop forecasts about future trends that affect their industry and products; and they analyze the competition—paying close attention to their strengths and weaknesses so that they can use this information to gain a competitive edge. Managers use this information to establish company goals and objectives. Finally, they translate these goals and objectives into action plans.

3. **Explain the purpose of a mission statement.**

   A mission statement defines why the organization exists, what it does, what it hopes to achieve, and the principles it will abide by to meet its goals. It is used to bring clarity of focus to members of the organization and to provide guidelines for the adoption of future projects.

4. **Discuss the benefits of conducting a SWOT analysis.**

   An organization identifies its strengths, weaknesses, opportunities, and threats prior to establishing long-term goals. Iden-

   tifying internal strengths and weaknesses gives the firm insight into its current abilities. The organization must then decide whether new abilities must be learned to meet current or more ambitious goals. Internal strengths become a firm's core competence if they are a bundle of skills and technologies that set the company apart from competitors. Identifying a firm's external opportunities and threats helps prepare it for challenges that might interfere with its ability to reach its goals.

5. **List the benefits of setting long-term goals and objectives.**

   Goals and objectives establish long- and short-range targets that help managers fulfill the company's mission. Setting appropriate goals increases employee motivation, establishes standards by which individual and group performance can be measured, guides employee activity, and clarifies management's expectations.

6. **Cite three leadership styles and explain why no one style is best.**

   Three leadership styles are autocratic, democratic, and laissez-faire (also called free-rein). Each may work best in a different situation: autocratic when quick decisions are needed, democratic when employee participation in decision making is desirable, and laissez-faire when fostering creativity is a priority. Good leaders are flexible enough to respond with the best approach for the situation.

7. **Identify and explain important types of managerial skills.**

   Managers use interpersonal skills to communicate with other people, work effectively with them, and lead them; technical skills to perform the mechanics of a particular job; administrative skills to manage an organization efficiently; conceptual skills to see the organization as a whole, to see it in the context of its environment, and to understand how the various parts interrelate; and decision-making skills to ensure that the best decisions are made.

8. **Summarize the six steps involved in the decision-making process.**
   The decision-making process begins by recognizing that a problem or opportunity exists. Next, managers identify and develop options using a variety of brainstorming techniques. Once the options have been put forth, they analyze the options using appropriate criteria. Then they select the best option, implement the decision, and monitor the results, making changes as needed.

KEY TERMS

administrative skills **(182)**

autocratic leaders **(176)**

coaching **(177)**

conceptual skills **(182)**

contingency leadership **(177)**

controlling **(180)**

core competence **(169)**

corporate culture **(178)**

crisis management **(172)**

decision-making skills **(182)**

democratic leaders **(176)**

first-line managers **(175)**

goal **(172)**

interpersonal skills **(181)**

laissez-faire leaders **(176)**

leading **(175)**

management **(166)**

management pyramid **(174)**

mentor **(177)**

middle managers **(174)**

mission statement **(168)**

objective **(172)**

operational plans **(172)**

organizing **(174)**

participative management **(176)**

planning **(167)**

quality **(180)**

standards **(180)**

strategic plans **(167)**

tactical plans **(172)**

technical skills **(181)**

top managers **(174)**

vision **(167)**

TEST YOUR KNOWLEDGE

Questions for Review

1. What is management? Why is it so important?
2. What is forecasting, and how is it related to the planning function?
3. What is the goal of crisis management?
4. What are some common characteristics of effective leaders?
5. Why are interpersonal skills important to managers at all levels?

Questions for Analysis

6. Is the following statement an example of a strategic goal or an objective? "To become the number-one retailer of computers and computer accessories in terms of revenue, growth, and customer satisfaction." Explain your answer.
7. How do the three levels of management differ?
8. How do autocratic, democratic, and laissez-fair leaders differ?
9. Why are coaching and mentoring effective leadership techniques?

10. *Ethical Considerations:* When an organization learns about a threat that could place the safety of its workers or its customers at risk, is management obligated to immediately inform these parties of the threat? Explain your answer.

Questions for Application

11. What are your long-term goals? Develop a set of long-term career goals for yourself and several short-term objectives that will help you reach those goals. Make sure your goals are specific, measurable, and time-limited.
12. Do you have the skills it takes to be an effective manager? Find out by taking the Keirsey Temperament Sorter II personality test at www.keirsey.com.
13. *Integrated:* Using Dell Computer's mission statement in Exhibit 7.3 as a model and the material you learned in Chapter 2, develop a mission statement for a socially responsible company such as Patagonia or Ben & Jerry's.
14. *Integrated:* What is the principal difference between a business plan (as discussed in Chapter 5) and a strategic plan?

PRACTICE YOUR KNOWLEDGE

Handling Difficult Situations on the Job: Managing Fraud Risks

"Isn't there anything consumers can do to protect themselves?" you ask in disbelief. You're a midlevel manager at Capital One, where vice president Shauna Perkins has just concluded a presentation on "skimming," the latest twist in credit card fraud.

"What we don't want customers to do is become afraid to use their credit cards," Perkins replies. "They can monitor accounts through our online or toll-free services, reporting discrepancies immediately. They're not liable for charges they didn't make, but they'll have to prove the fraud. And if they wait for mailed statements, the crooks may have 30-60 days to ring up charges!"

The "crooks" she's referring to are using small devices, about the size of a pager, to "skim" vital information from a credit card's magnetic strip, including cardholder name, account number, expiration date, and the invisible verification codes introduced in the early 1990s to foil counterfeit cards. With the verification codes, an electronically indistinguishable duplicate card can be created.

The actual "skimming" is done by a dishonest waiter or store clerk who has been paid to conceal the device in a coat pocket, inside a jacket, or under a counter. The data they steal are downloaded into a computer and transmitted via the Internet, often to Europe, Asia, or Latin America. Phony cards are embedded with the stolen codes and within hours, the thieves can make purchases anywhere in the world.[36]

Your task: Since you manage the consumer fraud division, Perkins has assigned you the decision-making task: Should you warn customers about this new scam? New technologies may soon solve the problem: Visa is trying a tape with a stronger magnetic pull, and MasterCard is experimenting with embedding the last three digits of the account number in the plastic, not the magnetic stripe. Fingerprinting may also be used. If you do warn customers, what will you say? What might be the drawbacks for Capital One if you speak up? What will be the benefits?

Building Your Team Skills

A good mission statement should define the organization's purpose and ultimate goals and outline the principles that are to guide managers and employees in working toward those goals. Using library sources such as annual reports or Internet sources such as organizational websites, locate mission statements from one nonprofit organization, such as a school or a charity, and one company with which you are familiar.

Bring these statements to class and, with your team, select four mission statements to evaluate. How many of the mission statements contain all five of the typical components (product or service; primary market; concern for survival, growth, and profitability; managerial philosophy; commitment to quality and social responsibility)? Which components are most often absent from the mission statements you are evaluating? Which components are most often included? Of the mission statements your team is analyzing, which is the most inspiring? Why?

Now assume that you and your teammates are the top management team at each organization or company. How would you improve these mission statements? Rewrite the four mission statements so that they cover the five typical components, show all organization members how their roles are related to the vision, and inspire commitment among employees and managers.

Summarize your team's work in a written or oral report to the class. Compare the mission statement that your team found the most inspiring with the statements that other teams found the most inspiring. What do these mission statements have in common? How do they differ? Of all the inspiring mission statements reported to the class, which do you think is the best? Why? Does this mission statement inspire you to consider working for or doing business with this organization?

EXPAND YOUR KNOWLEDGE

Discovering Career Opportunities

If you become a manager, how much of your day will be spent performing each of the four basic functions of management? This is your opportunity to find out. Arrange to shadow a manager (such as a department head, a store manager, or a shift supervisor) for a few hours. As you observe, categorize the manager's activities in terms of the four management functions and note how much time each activity takes. If observation is not possible, interview a manager in order to complete this exercise.

1. How much of the manager's time is spent on each of the four management functions? Is this the allocation you expected?

2. Ask whether this is a typical work day for this manager. If it isn't, what does the manager usually do differently? During a typical day, does this manager tend to spend most of the time on one particular function?

3. Of the four management functions, which does the manager believe is most important for good organizational performance? Do you agree?

Developing Your Research Skills

Find two articles in business journals or newspapers (print or online editions) that profile two senior managers who lead a business or a nonprofit organization.

1. What experience, skills, and business background do the two leaders have? Do you see any striking similarities or differences in their backgrounds?

2. What kinds of business challenges have these two leaders faced? What actions did they take to deal with those challenges? Did they establish any long-term goals or objectives for their company? Did the articles mention a new change initiative?

3. Describe the leadership strengths of each person as they are presented in the articles you selected. Is either leader known as a team builder? Long-term strategist? Shrewd negotiator? What are each leader's greatest areas of strength?

Exploring the Best of the Web

URLs for all Internet exercises are provided at the website for this book, www.prenhall.com/bovee. *When you log on to this text's website, select Chapter 7, then select "Student Resources," click on the name of the featured website, and review the website to complete these exercises.*

Explore these chapter-related websites, review their content, and answer the following questions for each website you visit:

1. What is the purpose of this website?
2. What kinds of information does this website contain? Please be specific.
3. How is the information provided at this website useful for businesspeople? Consumers?
4. How did you expand your knowledge of management by reviewing the material at this website? What new things did you learn about this topic?

Become a Better Manager

ManagementFirst.com can help you become a better manager. Focused on management theory and practice, this website is a management portal that explores in-depth management issues including leadership, time management, training, strategy, knowledge management, personal development, customer relationship management, and more. Each channel provides lengthy articles, advice, and a collection of carefully annotated links. Log on today and join ManagementFirst.com to become information rich and well orga-nized. Learn why knowledge management is important. Discover what emotional intelligence is all about. And find out why companies form strategic alliances. www.managementfirst.com

Linking to Organizational Change

Looking for more information on every aspect of organizational change management? You'll find a comprehensive collection of links on the website of the Management Assistance Program for Nonprofits. This is the place to access articles, discussion groups, and other resources related to organizational change in businesses and in not-for-profit organizations. Start with the overview, which sets the stage for browsing the many links devoted to exploring management and employee perspectives on the challenges and goals of managing change. www.managementhelp.org/org_chng/org_chng.htm

Admire America's Most Admired

Find out who is in the most exclusive corporate club around—*Fortune's* Most Admired. Log on and learn why some companies seem to perform their best when the heat is on. These club members consistently deliver to shareholders, customers, and employees. Not only do they have the right stuff and the shiniest reputation, but they can predict changes in the marketplace, adapt to them, and capitalize on them when it counts. Check out the archives for a list of club members all the way back to 1983. What qualities will we admire most in years ahead? There's no mystery about it. Today, it's not enough to have a great brand or charming CEO. Now more than ever, companies must be credible and trustworthy. www.fortune.com/fortune/mostadmired/index.html

Learning Interactively

Companion Website

Visit the Companion Website at www.prenhall.com/bovee. For Chapter 7, take advantage of the interactive "Study Guide" to test your chapter knowledge. Get instant feedback on whether you need additional studying. Read the "Current Events" articles to get the latest on chapter topics, and complete the exercises as specified by your instructor. Expand your learning with a visit to the "Research Area." There you will find a wealth of information you can use to complete your course assignments.

A CASE FOR CRITICAL THINKING

The Ax Falls on Sunbeam's Chainsaw Al

It seemed like the perfect match: a self-confident CEO with a history of successfully saving troubled companies, and one of America's largest household appliance makers in desperate need of restructuring. That was the case when Al Dunlap arrived at Sunbeam in 1996, vowing to turn around the company within a year. True to his word, Dunlap turned Sunbeam inside out and upside down—and nearly destroyed the company with his autocratic, "chainsaw" management style.

Rambo in Pinstripes

Dunlap had garnered high praise from corporate America by restructuring and selling such companies as Scott Paper Company and Crown-Zellerbach. In every case, Dunlap engineered the turnarounds by axing thousands of jobs, slashing costs, and setting up the company for a quick sale. Confident and boastful, Dunlap called himself "Rambo in Pinstripes." Everyone else called him "Chainsaw Al."

Banking on Dunlap's successful track record, Sunbeam recruited the experienced CEO to jump-start its sagging sales and reverse its declining profits on such products as electric blankets and barbecue gear. Within days after arriving at Sunbeam, Dunlap developed an ambitious tactical plan for a company turnaround.

The first step of his strategy focused on cutting costs. He fired half of the company's 12,000 employees and outsourced as many functions as possible. Then he eliminated 87 percent of Sunbeam's products and closed or sold two-thirds of the company's 18 manufacturing facilities. Hoping to increase sales of new products, Dunlap expanded Sunbeam's product mix by acquiring Coleman, the camping gear maker; First Alert, the smoke alarm producer; and Signature Brands, the maker of Mr. Coffee.

Sliced and Diced

At first, Dunlap's strategy seemed to be on track. Sunbeam reduced overall annual expenses by $225 million and racked up big sales and profits gains during 1997. But Dunlap's chainsaw had sliced deep into the company, leaving shortages of experienced employees and wreaking havoc on day-to-day operations. Factories suffered from a lack of parts for production and a shortage of workers to produce goods and fulfill orders. Furthermore, his downsizing efforts often backfired, creating additional costs. After firing the entire computer staff, for example, Dunlap hired contract workers who demanded higher pay rates—including some workers who had just been fired. Moreover, Dunlap's changes occurred just as Sunbeam was upgrading its computer system. No backups existed, and Sunbeam couldn't track shipments or orders. Computers were down for months, forcing employees to manually invoice such major customers as Wal-Mart and Sears Roebuck.

Crushing Pressure

To make matters worse, Sunbeam executives recognized that Dunlap had set unrealistic goals for the company. Chances were slim that Sunbeam could meet Dunlap's goal of boosting profit margins to 20 percent, considering the current 2.5 percent margin on household appliances. Moreover, to meet Dunlap's goal of doubling revenues to $2 billion within the next year, Sunbeam needed to increase sales five times faster than the competition. And the chief executive's aim of generating $600 million in new product sales would require extraordinary sales of every new product.

Still, Chainsaw Al refused to acknowledge any weakness in his tactical plans. Instead of motivating employees to meet his goals, he threatened to place their jobs on the chopping block if they failed to perform. Managers, in turn, passed that intimidation down the line. Though his actions crushed morale and created unbearable stress on employees, Dunlap continued to exert excruciating pressure on his staff. "I don't get heart attacks; I give them," he boasted.

Al Gets the Chainsaw

But Dunlap's boastful ways halted when Sunbeam reported a first-quarter loss for 1998. Then Sunbeam's board of directors made an alarming discovery: Dunlap hadn't executed a turnaround at all. Sunbeam had persuaded retailers to buy seasonal goods such as gas grills before the normal selling season by offering hefty discounts, easy payment terms, and the promise to hold the goods in Sunbeam's warehouses for later delivery. Although the "bill-and-hold" strategy allowed Dunlap to show an impressive sales jump for 1997, the sales and accounting gimmicks backfired in the subsequent year. Stocked to the max, retailers had no need for additional sales.

So Sunbeam's board of directors turned the chainsaw on Dunlap, immediately firing the CEO. Although Dunlap's strategy of cutting jobs and selling assets had worked at other companies, his autocratic management style and fraudulent tactics nearly destroyed Sunbeam. The company was forced to restate financial results for the six quarters of Dunlap's tenure at Sunbeam, and the company filed for Chapter 11 bankruptcy in 2001. Meanwhile, Dunlap has been accused of massive financial fraud, has agreed to be banned from ever serving as a public-company official, and has agreed to pay the SEC a $500,000 penalty and shareholders $15 million to settle a lawsuit.

Critical Thinking Questions

1. Why were Dunlap's goals unrealistic for Sunbeam?
2. Was Dunlap's slice-and-dice plan a long-term or short-term strategy? Please explain.
3. Why did Dunlap's turnaround strategy backfire?
4. Expand your knowledge about leadership. Using a metasearch engine, enter the word "leadership" and follow the links. What kinds of leadership information can you find on the web? How might this information be helpful to a beginning business student?

VIDEO CASE

Creative Management: Creative Age Publications

Learning Objectives

The purpose of this video is to help you:

1. Understand how and why managers set organizational goals.
2. Identify the basic skills that managers need to be effective.
3. Discuss how corporate culture can affect an organization.

Synopsis

Creative Age Publications uses creativity in managing its beauty-industry publications. With offices or franchised operations in Europe, Japan, Russia, and other areas of the world, the company has expanded rapidly—thanks to sound management practices. In fact, one of the company's goals is to avoid overtaxing its management team by growing more slowly in the near future. The CEO is working toward delegating most or all of the decisions to her management team rather than making these decisions herself. As Creative Age's managers moved up through the ranks, they honed their technical skills as well as their skill in working with others. "Having heart" is a major part of the company's culture—an important element that, in the CEO's opinion, many companies lack.

Discussion Questions

1. *For analysis:* How does global growth affect Creative Age's emphasis on the management skill of interacting well with other people?
2. *For analysis:* How does moving Creative Age's managers up through the ranks help them develop their conceptual skills?
3. *For application:* How would you suggest that the CEO spread Creative Age's culture throughout its global offices?
4. *For application:* How might the CEO manage Creative Age's growth through the process of controlling?
5. *For debate:* Do you agree with the CEO's policy of allowing managers and employees to work on any company magazine they choose? Support your position.

Online Exploration

Visit Creative Age's website at www.creativeage.com and follow the link to *Day Spa* magazine. Scan the magazine's homepage and then click on the About Us link to read more about the magazine and its parent company. Why would Creative Age call attention to each magazine's goals and market rather than focusing on the parent company? How might Creative Age use a corporate website to communicate with other people and organizations that affect its ability to achieve its goals?

Organization and Teamwork

American Express has continuously transformed itself to become a leading global travel, financial, and network services provider.

INSIDE BUSINESS TODAY

Don't Leave Home to Go to Work: American Express's Virtual Environment

"Don't leave home without it!" sends a powerful message about the dangers of traveling without an American Express card tucked into your pocket. Millions of customers heed that advice each day, making American Express Company the world's largest travel agency and a leading provider of financial services. But offering a seamless network of services for customers around the globe requires effective teamwork by all employees, no matter whether they're working from the New York headquarters or telecommuting from home in Los Angeles. And David House makes sure that his employees have everything they need to work together and contribute to the company's success—even if they don't leave home to go to work.

As president of American Express Global Establishment Services and Travelers Cheque Group, the division that recruits new American Express merchants, House encourages his staff members to work together to achieve their goals. But uniting employees in sales offices across the country demands more than a few rousing pep talks. To build a successful team, House turns to technology for promoting communication within his division. He provides every employee with access to the company's highly efficient computer network. Employees are given the opportunity to work from home, eliminating the time, expense, and stress of daily commutes to the office. Furthermore, House contracts with outside sources to set up the home offices, arranging for everything from the installation of phone lines to home safety checks for such things as carbon monoxide levels and availability of fire extinguishers. And he even provides employees with computer training, software and

hardware setup, and selection and delivery of office furniture to complete their virtual office environment.

Still, House knows that effective teams need more than equipment to produce quality work. They need to communicate. House's telecommuters conduct virtual meetings with colleagues around the world, taking advantage of e-mail and videoconferencing to brainstorm and collaborate on projects. Several units in House's division use a buddy system that requires remote workers to chat with on-site colleagues by phone every morning, covering topics ranging from new customers to office politics. Other telecommuters report to a local or regional office several times each week, meeting with co-workers for specific purposes. Office meetings have predetermined agendas and follow regular schedules to reduce wasted meeting time and to allow team members to communicate face to face.

To encourage team members to work together, House commends outstanding team efforts. Each year, he awards lavish prizes to the top 75 sales reps for their contributions, and he makes a special point of recognizing team members who share information with their peers. For example, House acknowledged one outstanding rep who focused on her team's regional sales objectives instead of her own quotas. She not only accompanied other reps on sales calls in her region but made an effort to share her sales strategies by distributing copies of her winning presentations to every rep in the country.

House's knack for developing and using virtual teams at American Express has indeed paid off. Not only have virtual teams saved the company time and travel costs, but they have increased employee productivity and improved customer satisfaction rates.[1]

1 LEARNING OBJECTIVE

Discuss the function of a company's organizational structure

organizational structure
Framework enabling managers to divide responsibilities, ensure employee accountability, and distribute decision-making authority

organization chart
Diagram showing how employees and tasks are grouped and where the lines of communication and authority flow

formal organization
A framework officially established by managers for accomplishing tasks that lead to achieving the organization's goals

Designing an Effective Organizational Structure

Whether employees work from home as part of a virtual team or in a traditional office setting, the decision-making authority of employees and managers is supported by the company's **organizational structure**. This structure helps the company achieve its goals by providing a framework for managers to divide responsibilities, effectively distribute the authority to make decisions, coordinate and control the organization's work, and hold employees accountable for their work. In some organizations, this structure is a relatively rigid, vertical hierarchy like the management pyramid described in Chapter 7. In other organizations, teams of employees and managers from across levels and functions work together to make decisions and achieve the organization's goals.

When managers design the organization's structure, they use an **organization chart** to provide a visual representation of how employees and tasks are grouped and how the lines of communication and authority flow. Exhibit 8.1 shows the organization chart for a grocery store chain. An organization chart depicts the official design for accomplishing tasks that lead to achieving the organization's goals, a framework known as the **formal organization**. Every company also has an **informal organization**—the network of interactions that develop on a personal level among workers. Sometimes the interactions among people in the informal organization parallel their relationships in the formal organization, but often interactions transcend formal boundaries. Crossing formal boundaries can help establish a more pleasant work environment, but it can also undermine formal work processes and hinder a company's ability to get things done.

How do companies design an organizational structure, and which organizational structure is the most effective? In the past, organizations were designed around management's

EXHIBIT 8.1   Organization Chart for Food Lion Grocery Store Chain
Many organization charts look like this one for Food Lion. The traditional model of an organization is a pyramid in which numerous boxes form the base and lead up to fewer and fewer boxes on higher levels, ultimately arriving at one box at the top. A glance at Food Lion's organization chart reveals who has authority over whom, who is responsible for whose work, and who is accountable to whom.

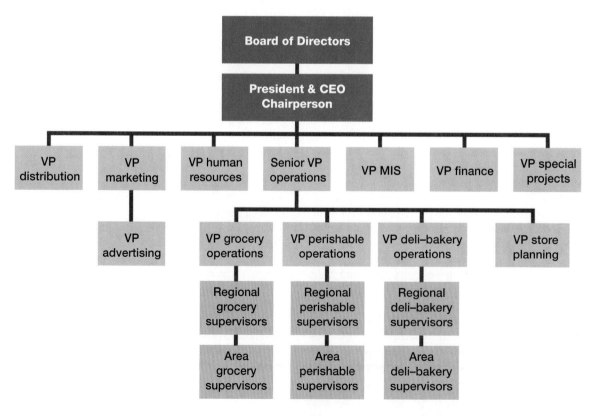

desire to control workers, with everything set up in a hierarchy. Today, however, more and more companies are designing organizational structures around the need to make fast decisions. Dell Computer, for example, is deliberately anti-hierarchical so that employees and managers can make timely decisions. Some Dell managers are in charge of segments; some are in charge of products. When an area grows too big, it's broken up to make everyone nimbler. Newcomers at Dell are told they must be comfortable with a high level of ambiguity. Even old-timers are hard pressed to draw a company organization chart.[2]

As this chapter will discuss later, more and more companies like Dell are eliminating layers of management, or flattening their organizational structures, to give more decision-making authority to employees who deal directly with customers. In fact, as management guru Peter Drucker sees it, "There is no such thing as one right organization. Each has distinct strengths, distinct limitations, and specific applications." In other words, today's managers require a toolbox full of organizational structures so they can select the right tool for each specific task.[3] Regardless of which organizational structure a company selects, four factors must be taken into consideration during the design phase: work specialization, chain of command, vertical organization, and horizontal organization and coordination.

Work Specialization

When designing an organizational structure, management must first decide on the optimal level of **work specialization**—the degree to which organizational tasks are broken down into separate jobs. Few employees have the skills to perform every task a company needs. Therefore, work specialization can improve organizational efficiency by enabling each worker to perform tasks that are well defined and that require specific skills. For example, in 1776 Scottish economist Adam Smith found that if each of 10 workers went through every step needed to make a pin, the entire group could make 200 pins a day. However, if each worker performed only a few steps and no one made a pin from start to finish, the same 10 workers could make 48,000 pins a day. When employees concentrate on the same specialized tasks, they can perfect their skills and perform their tasks more quickly. A classic example of work specialization is the automobile assembly line.

However, organizations can overdo specialization. If a task is defined too narrowly, employees may become bored with performing the same tiny, repetitive job over and over. They may also feel unchallenged and alienated. Managers must think carefully about how specialized or how broad each task should be. In fact, a growing number of companies are balancing specialization and employee motivation through teamwork. This approach enables group members to decide how to break down a complex task, and it allows employees to rotate among the jobs for which the team is collectively responsible. The team then shares credit for the results, and workers feel that they have created something of value. The team approach to organization is discussed in more depth later in this chapter.

Chain of Command

Besides incorporating work specialization into an organizational structure, companies must also establish a **chain of command**, the unbroken line of authority that connects each level of management with the next level. The chain of command helps organizations function smoothly by making two things clear: who is responsible for each task, and who has the authority to make official decisions.

All employees have a certain amount of **responsibility**—the obligation to perform the duties and achieve the goals and objectives associated with their jobs. As they work toward the organization's goals, employees must also maintain their **accountability**, their obligation to report the results of their work to supervisors or team members and to justify any outcomes that fall below expectations. Managers ensure that tasks are accomplished by

informal organization
Network of informal employee interactions that are not defined by the formal structure

work specialization
Specialization in or responsibility for some portion of an organization's overall work tasks; also called division of labor

2 LEARNING OBJECTIVE

Explain the concepts of accountability, authority, and delegation

chain of command
Pathway for the flow of authority from one management level to the next

responsibility
Obligation to perform the duties and achieve the goals and objectives associated with a particular position

accountability
Obligation to report results to supervisors or team members and to justify outcomes that fall below expectations

authority
Power granted by the organization to make decisions, take actions, and allocate resources to accomplish goals

delegation
Assignment of work and the authority and responsibility required to complete it

line organization
Chain-of-command system that establishes a clear line of authority flowing from the top down

line-and-staff organization
Organization system that has a clear chain of command but that also includes functional groups of people who provide advice and specialized services

span of management
Number of people under one manager's control; also known as span of control

flat organizations
Organizations with a wide span of management and few hierarchical levels

tall organizations
Organizations with a narrow span of management and many hierarchical levels

exercising **authority**, the power to make decisions, issue orders, carry out actions, and allocate resources to achieve the organization's goals. Authority is vested in the positions that managers hold, and it flows down through the management pyramid. **Delegation** is the assignment of work and the transfer of authority and responsibility to complete that work.

Look again at Exhibit 8.1. The senior vice president of operations delegates responsibilities to the vice presidents of grocery operations, perishable operations, deli-bakery operations, and store planning. These department heads have the authority to make certain decisions necessary to fulfill their roles, and they are accountable to the senior VP for the performance of their respective divisions. In turn, the senior VP is accountable to the company CEO.

The simplest and most common chain-of-command system is known as **line organization** because it establishes a clear line of authority flowing from the top down, as Exhibit 8.1 depicts. Everyone knows who is accountable to whom, as well as which tasks and decisions each is responsible for. However, line organization sometimes falls short because the technical complexity of a firm's activities may require specialized knowledge that individual managers don't have and can't easily acquire. A more elaborate system, called **line-and-staff organization**, was developed out of the need to combine specialization with management control. In such an organization, managers in the chain of command are supplemented by functional groupings of people, known as *staff*, who provide advice and specialized services but who are not in the line organization's chain of command (see Exhibit 8.2).

Span of Management The number of people a manager directly supervises is called the **span of management** or *span of control*. When a large number of people report directly to one person, that person has a wide span of management. This situation is common in **flat organizations** that have relatively few levels in the management hierarchy. Sun Microsystems, Visa, and Oticon (a hearing-aid manufacturer in Denmark) are all companies that have flat organizations. British Petroleum (BP) is also amazingly flat and lean for an organization with $148 billion in revenues and 107,000 employees. At BP there is no level between the general managers of the business units and the group of nine operating executives who oversee the businesses.[4]

In contrast, **tall organizations** have many hierarchical levels, usually with only a few people reporting to each manager. In such cases, the span of management is narrow (see Exhibit 8.3). General Motors traditionally had a tall organizational structure, with as many as 22 layers of management. Under tall organizational structures, employees who want to

EXHIBIT 8.2

Simplified Line-and-Staff Structure
A line-and-staff organization divides employees into those who are in the direct line of command (from the top level of the hierarchy to the bottom) and those who provide staff (or support) services to line managers at various levels. Staff report directly to top management.

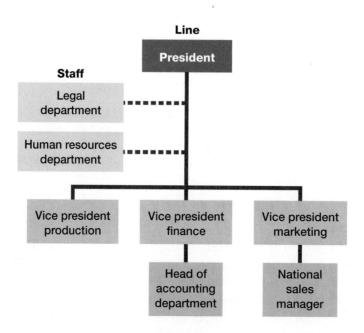

EXHIBIT 8.3
Tall Versus Flat Organizations
A tall organization, such as the U.S. Army, has many levels with a narrow span of management at each level so that relatively few people report to each manager on the level above them. In contrast, a flat organization, such as the Catholic Church, has relatively few levels with a wide span of management, so that more people report to each manager.

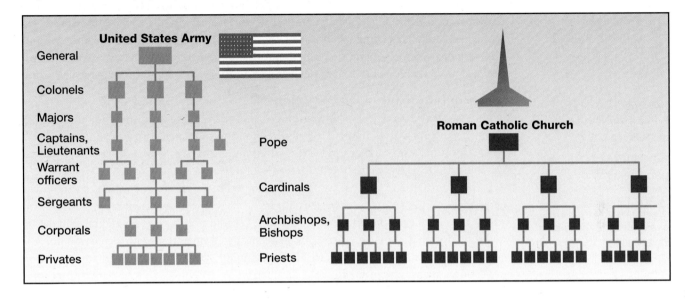

institute a change must ask a supervisor, who in turn must ask a manager, who in turn must ask another manager at the next level up, and so on. To reduce the time it takes to make decisions, many companies are now flattening their organizational structures by removing layers of management and by delegating increased responsibilities and authority to middle managers, work teams, and individual employees.[5]

No formula exists for determining the ideal span of management. How well people work together is more important than the number of people reporting to one person. Still, several factors affect the number of people a manager can effectively supervise, including the manager's personal skill and leadership ability, the skill of the workers, the motivation of the workers, and the nature or complexity of the job. In general, employees who are highly skilled or who are trained in many work tasks don't require as much supervision as employees who are less skilled.

Centralization Versus Decentralization   Organizations that focus decision-making authority near the top of the chain of command are said to be centralized. **Centralization** benefits a company by using top management's rich experience and broad view of organizational goals. Both line organizations and line-and-staff organizations tend to be centralized.

However, the trend in business today is to decentralize. **Decentralization** pushes decision-making authority down to lower organizational levels—such as department heads—while control over essential companywide matters remains with top management. Implemented properly, decentralization can stimulate responsiveness because decisions don't have to be referred up the hierarchy. But decentralization does not work in every situation or in every company. At times, strong authority from the top of the chain of command may be needed to keep the organization focused on immediate goals. Managers should select the level of decision making that will most effectively serve the organization's needs given the individual circumstances.

centralization
Concentration of decision-making authority at the top of the organization

decentralization
Delegation of decision-making authority to employees in lower-level positions

Vertical Organization

Choosing between a vertical and a horizontal model is one of the most critical decisions a company can make. Many organizations use a traditional vertical structure to define formal

vertical organization
Structure linking activities at the top of the organization with those at the middle and lower levels

departmentalization
Grouping people within an organization according to function, division, matrix, or network

3 LEARNING OBJECTIVE

Define four types of departmentalization

departmentalization by function
Grouping workers according to their similar skills, resource use, and expertise

departmentalization by division
Grouping departments according to similarities in product, process, customer, or geography

product divisions
Divisional structure based on products

process divisions
Divisional structure based on the major steps of a production process

customer divisions
Divisional structure that focuses on customers or clients

geographic divisions
Divisional structure based on location of operations

relationships and the division of tasks among employees and managers. **Vertical organization** links the activities at the top of the organization with those at the middle and lower levels. This structure also helps managers delegate authority to positions throughout the organization's hierarchy. Besides authority, the structure defines specific jobs and activities across vertical levels. In a vertical organization, companies define jobs and activities by using **departmentalization**—the arrangement of activities into logical groups that are then clustered into larger departments and units that form the total organization. Four common ways of departmentalizing are by function, division, matrix, and network. An organization may use more than one method of departmentalization, depending on its particular needs.

Departmentalization by Function **Departmentalization by function** groups employees according to their skills, resource use, and expertise. Common functional departments include marketing, human resources, operations, finance, research and development, and accounting, with each department working independently of the others. As depicted in Exhibit 8.1, functional departmentalization is highly centralized.

Splitting the organization into separate functional departments offers several advantages: (1) Grouping employees by specialization allows for the efficient use of resources and encourages the development of in-depth skills; (2) centralized decision making enables unified direction by top management; and (3) centralized operations enhance communication and the coordination of activities within departments. Despite these advantages, functional departmentalization can create communication barriers between departments, thereby slowing response to change, hindering effective planning for products and markets, and overemphasizing work specialization (which alienates employees).[6] Moreover, employees may become too narrowly focused on departmental goals and lose sight of larger company goals. For these reasons, most large companies have abandoned the functional structure in the past decade or so.

Departmentalization by Division **Departmentalization by division** establishes self-contained departments that encompass all the major functional resources required to achieve their goals—such as research and design, manufacturing, finance, and marketing. These departments are typically formed according to similarities in product, process, customer, or geography.

- *Product divisions.* Many organizations use a structure based on **product divisions**—grouped around each of the company's products or family of products. The logic behind this organizational structure is that each department can manage all the activities needed to develop, manufacture, and sell a particular product or product line.

- *Process divisions.* **Process divisions**, also called *process-complete* departments, are based on the major steps of a production process. For example, a table-manufacturing company might have three divisions, one for each phase of manufacturing a table.

- *Customer divisions.* The third approach, **customer divisions**, concentrates activities on satisfying specific groups of customers. For example, Acer America, a manufacturer of computer equipment, restructured into six customer-centric divisions to facilitate the fulfillment of the company's mission—to provide customers with the highest level of quality, reliability, and support (see Exhibit 8.4).[7]

- *Geographic divisions.* **Geographic divisions** enable companies spread over a national or an international area to respond more easily to local customs, styles, and product preferences. For example, Quaker Oats has two main geographic divisions: U.S. and Canadian Grocery Products and International Grocery Products. Each division is further subdivided to allow the company to focus on the needs of customers in specific regions.

Divisional departmentalization offers both advantages and disadvantages. First, because divisions are self-contained, they can react quickly to change, thus making the organization more flexible. In addition, because each division focuses on a limited number of products,

EXHIBIT 8.4 *Departmentalization by Customer Divisions*
Acer America's organizational structure supports the company's mission to be more customer-focused.

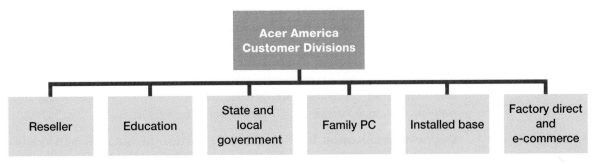

processes, customers, or locations, divisions can offer better service to customers. Moreover, top managers can focus on problem areas more easily, and managers can gain valuable experience by dealing with the various functions in their divisions. However, divisional departmentalization can also increase costs by duplicating the use of resources such as facilities and personnel. Furthermore, poor coordination between divisions may cause them to focus too narrowly on divisional goals and neglect the organization's overall goals. Finally, divisions may compete with one another for employees, money, and other resources, causing rivalries that hurt the organization as a whole.

Departmentalization by Matrix   **Departmentalization by matrix** is a structural design in which employees from functional departments form teams to combine their specialized skills (see Exhibit 8.5). This structure allows the company to pool and share resources across divisions and functional groups. The matrix may be a permanent feature of the organization's design, or it may be established to complete a specific project. Consider Black & Decker, which formed a matrix organization in the early 1990s. Departments such as mechanical design, electrical engineering, and model shop assigned employees with specific technical skills to work on product-development projects in such categories as saws, cordless appliances, and woodworking.[8]

Matrix departmentalization can help big companies function like smaller ones by allowing teams to devote their attention to specific projects or customers without permanently reorganizing the company's structure. But matrix structures are not without drawbacks. One problem of a matrix structure is that team members usually continue to report to their functional department heads as well as to a project team leader. Another drawback is that authority tends to be more ambiguous and up for grabs, creating power struggles and other interpersonal conflicts. Black & Decker realized this problem soon after implementing its

departmentalization by matrix
Assigning employees to both a functional group and a project team (thus using functional and divisional patterns simultaneously)

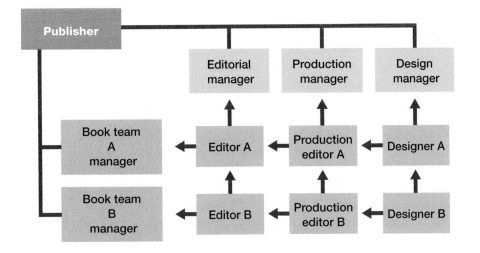

EXHIBIT 8.5
Departmentalization by Matrix
In a matrix structure, each employee is assigned to both a functional group (with a defined set of basic functions, such as production manager) and a project team (which consists of members of various functional groups working together on a project, such as bringing out a new consumer product).

matrix organization. The manager with the most authority was always the functional department head, and the project team did not really hold any control. The company has since redesigned its organizational structure, which is now based on product divisions that include teams of people from many functional areas.[9]

In a matrix organization, excellent communication and coordination are necessary to avoid conflicts. In addition, companies may find it difficult to coordinate the tasks of diverse functional specialists so that projects are completed efficiently. However, because it facilitates the pooling of resources across departments, a matrix organization can also enable a company to respond better to changes in the business environment.

departmentalization by network
Electronically connecting separate companies that perform selected tasks for a small headquarters organization

Departmentalization by Network   **Departmentalization by network** is a method of electronically connecting separate companies that perform selected tasks for a headquarters organization. Also called a *virtual organization*, the network organization *outsources* engineering, marketing, research, accounting, production, distribution, or other functions. That is, the organization hires other organizations under contracts to handle one or more of those functions. In fact, companies such as Nike, Liz Claiborne, and Dell Computer sell hundreds of millions of dollars' worth of products even though they outsource most of their manufacturing. As these companies have learned, the network approach is especially appropriate for international operations, allowing every part of the business to draw on resources no matter where in the world they may be.

The biggest advantage of the network structure is its flexibility. Companies hire whatever services are needed and then change them once they are no longer needed. The limited hierarchy required to manage a network organization also permits the company to make decisions and react to change quickly. Additional advantages are that the organization can continually redefine itself, and employees tend to have greater job variety and satisfaction. However, the network approach lacks hands-on control, because the functions are not in one location or company. Also, if one company in the network fails to deliver, the headquarters organization could suffer or even go out of business. Finally, strong employee loyalty and team spirit are less likely to develop, because the emotional connection between the employee and the organization is weak.

Horizontal Organization

More and more businesses are transforming their traditional bureaucratic and hierarchical vertical structure into a horizontal organization.[10] The horizontal approach uses the team concept to flatten hierarchies and integrate the many tasks of a business into a few smooth-flowing operations. The biggest benefit of horizontal organization is that everyone works together. Employees from various departments or functions are grouped around a few organization-wide, cross-functional core processes, and they are responsible for an entire core process from beginning to end. Employees who create new product designs, for instance, work with engineers and marketing personnel to make sure the designs can be manufactured and marketed.

A typical core process group might include staff from finance, research and development, manufacturing, and customer service. All core processes lead to one objective: creating and delivering something of value to the customer.

While some companies completely dismantle their vertical structure to create horizontal organizations, others prefer a hybrid organization—one that combines vertical and horizontal functions. In these firms, core processes are supported by organization-wide functional departments such as human resources and finance. The Xerox corporation, for example, organized its business operations around five core processes based on five types of products. The core processes are supported by two company-wide vertical operations: technology management and customer service. This way researchers are not constrained by specific markets, and customers face only one customer service representative even if they buy different product types.[11]

By now you can see that whether it uses a traditional vertical or an innovative horizontal organizational structure, every organization must coordinate activities and communication among its employees. Without such coordination, functional departments would be isolated from one another, and they would be unable to align their objectives. As David House knows, designing an organizational structure that facilitates teamwork and communication is an important first step.

A modular office layout such as this one at Continental Packaging Products encourages open communication climate and the sharing of information among employees.

Working in Teams

While the vertical chain of command is a tried-and-true method of organizing for business, it is limited by the fact that decision-making authority is often located high up the management hierarchy. Companies that organize vertically may become slow to react to change, and high-level managers may overlook many great ideas for improvement that originate in the lower levels of the organization. As this section will show, the value of involving employees from all levels and functions of the organization in the decision-making process cannot be overstated. As a result, most companies now use a variety of team formats in day-to-day operations.

A **team** is a unit of two or more people who work together to achieve a goal. Teams differ from work groups in that work groups interact primarily to share information and to make decisions to help one another perform within each member's area of responsibility. In other words, the performance of a work group is merely the summation of all group members' individual contributions.[12] By contrast, the members of a team have a shared mission and are collectively responsible for their work. By coordinating their efforts, team members generate a positive synergy and achieve a level of performance that exceeds what would have been accomplished if members had worked individually.

team
A unit of two or more people who share a mission and collective responsibility as they work together to achieve a goal

Of course, shifting to a team structure can be a challenging task, as Wainwright Industries discovered. In the early 1990s, this family-run manufacturer of components for automotive and aerospace companies was growing, but its employees and middle managers were frustrated because top managers controlled all the decisions. So management implemented a team approach. Instead of following managers' orders, employees would participate in making and implementing decisions through a new team structure, with leaders serving as trainers and coaches to six members. This shift was initially unsettling to both managers and employees. Employees had to develop confidence in their abilities. And managers had to learn how to show strong support for team concepts and empower teams to make important decisions about the work they do. But the hard work paid off. Wainwright employees now aspire to be great leaders and accomplish things as a team. "I can't imagine going back to the old way of doing things now," commented one employee.[13]

Studies show that successful teams have clear goals that are tied to the company's strategic goals, outcomes that are

Embracing a people-first strategy has paid off for Wainwright Industries. Winner of the coveted Malcolm Baldrige National Quality Award, Wainwright impressed examiners by the extent to which employees assumed responsibility for making improvements.

measured and compared with benchmarks, and employees who are motivated to work together in teams. Such motivation requires extensive training and a compensation system that is based, at least in part, on team performance. This last objective is sometimes accomplished by using stock options, profit sharing, performance bonuses, and other employee incentives, as Chapter 10 discusses. At Wainwright Industries, for instance, 25 percent of profits are set aside and split equally. This means the chairman, plant manager, punch-press operator, custodian, and everyone else in the organization gets the same amount.[14]

4 LEARNING OBJECTIVE

Describe the five most common forms of teams

Types of Teams

The type, structure, and composition of individual teams within an organization all depend on the organization's strategic goals and the objective for forming the team. The five most common forms of teams are *problem-solving teams*, *self-managed teams*, *functional teams*, *cross-functional teams*, and *virtual teams*. Such classifications are not exclusive. For example, a problem-solving team may also be self-managed and cross-functional. Similarly, some teams are established on an informal basis. That is, they are designed to encourage employee participation but do not become part of the formal organizational structure.

Competing in the Global Marketplace

Mervyn's Calls SWAT Team to the Rescue

The situation is tense. The stakes are high. Time is short. So who do you call for help if you're an executive at Mervyn's California facing the Christmas rush or the loss of a key manager? You call the company's SWAT team, of course.

Mervyn's is a department store chain with 28,000 employees and 264 locations in 14 states. Its SWAT team consists of 19 managers who race from division to division, usually at a moment's notice, to help with the kinds of crises that inevitably erupt in a high-pressure retail environment. SWAT team members must have experience in at least one specific discipline: buying, merchandising, or advertising. Assignments are as short as a week or as long as six months. Even though SWAT team members don't travel around in armored vehicles, life on the team can be pretty hectic.

This group of highly trained people can be deployed anywhere in the company's buying divisions, at any time, wherever they are needed. They can perform jobs quickly and efficiently, without a long learning curve. They help the company manage its unpredictable staffing needs, meet the requirements of its erratic markets, and seize unanticipated opportunities.

Originally created as an experiment to fill in for vacancies created by managers working flextime or on family leave, Mervyn's SWAT team has become something bigger. It has become an effective vehicle for moving talent around the company. SWAT team members aren't just good at learning fast; they're good at sharing what they've learned in other departments. And because team members have had a lot of exposure to various areas in the company, they're the most valued and highly sought-after employees in the organization.

It's no surprise that the team's biggest problem is turnover: Members are frequently hired away for full-time positions by managers whom they've impressed. In fact, joining the SWAT team has become a high-priority career tactic for young people who want to move up or for veterans who want a change of pace.

Questions for Critical Thinking

1. How could Mervyn's parent company, Target, use the SWAT team concept to benefit all its stores—Target, Dayton's, Hudson's, and Marshall Fields? (*Hint:* Think about the benefits of cross-functional teams.)
2. How does Mervyn's benefit from using the SWAT team concept on both a short-term and a long-term basis?

Problem-Solving Teams The most common type of informal team is the **problem-solving team**. Also referred to as *quality circles*, problem-solving teams usually consist of 5 to 12 employees from the same department who meet voluntarily to find ways of improving quality, efficiency, and the work environment. Any recommendations they come up with are then submitted to management for approval. Land Rover, a manufacturer of luxury sport-utility vehicles, was able to save millions of dollars, improve productivity, and sell more vehicles by using problem-solving teams.[15] If such teams are able to successfully contribute to the organization, as Land Rover's were, they may evolve into formal teams, a change that represents a fundamental shift in the way the organization is structured.

Self-Managed Teams Self-managed teams take problem-solving teams to the next level. As the name implies, **self-managed teams** manage their own activities and require minimum supervision. Typically they control the pace of work and determination of work assignments. Fully self-managed teams select their own members. As you might imagine, many managers are reluctant to embrace self-managed teams because doing so requires them to give up significant control.

At SEI Investments, administrator for over $100 billion in investor assets, the defining unit of operation is the self-managed team. Finding itself indistinguishable from other competitors, SEI took a wrecking ball to the traditional corporate pyramid and organized its 1,500 employees into 140 self-managed teams to speed up reaction time, innovate more quickly, and get closer to the customer. Most SEI employees belong to one "base" team and to three or four additional teams. The teams range from 2 members to as many as 30, and they are structured according to project. Some SEI teams are permanent, designed to serve big customers or important markets. Other teams are temporary, bringing employees together to solve a problem and disbanding after the solution is achieved.

SEI's flexible team structure is supported by having all office furniture and workstations on wheels so that teams can easily create their own work areas. No one, including the CEO, has an office. Cables dangle like vines from the vaulted ceilings, providing instant connections to electricity, phone lines, and the Internet from any location. Employees can easily move their desks to collaborate with other team members and serve as effective members of several different teams. In fact, employees move their desks so often that the company created special computer software to map every employee's location.[16]

Functional Teams Functional teams, or *command teams*, are organized along the lines of the organization's vertical structure and thus may be referred to as vertical teams. They are composed of managers and employees within a single functional department. For example, look again at Exhibit 8.1. Functional teams could be formed in Food Lion's marketing, human resources, and finance departments. The structure of a vertical team typically follows the formal chain of command. In some cases, the team may include several levels of the organizational hierarchy within the same functional department.

Cross-Functional Teams In contrast to functional teams, **cross-functional teams**, or horizontal teams, draw together employees from various functional areas and expertise. In many cross-functional teams, employees are cross-trained to perform a variety of tasks. At Pillsbury the most experienced workers can handle 23 different jobs.[17] Cross-functional teams have many benefits: (1) They facilitate the exchange of information between employees, (2) they generate ideas for how best to coordinate the

problem-solving team
Informal team of 5 to 12 employees from the same department who meet voluntarily to find ways of improving quality, efficiency, and the work environment

self-managed teams
Teams in which members are responsible for an entire process or operation

functional teams
Teams whose members come from a single functional department and that are based on the organization's vertical structure

cross-functional teams
Teams that draw together employees from different functional areas

Working in teams is a way of life at companies such as SEI Investments.

organizational units that are represented, (3) they encourage new solutions for organizational problems, and (4) they aid the development of new organizational policies and procedures.

Boeing used hundreds of "design—build" teams that integrated design engineers and production workers to develop its 777 airplane.[18] Cross-functional teams have also become a way of life at Harley-Davidson, as this chapter's Case for Critical Thinking shows.[19] Cross-functional teams can take on a number of formats:

task force
Team of people from several departments who are temporarily brought together to address a specific issue

- *Task forces.* A **task force** is a type of cross-functional team formed to work on a specific activity with a completion point. Several departments are usually involved so that all parties who have a stake in the outcome of the task are able to provide input. However, once the goal has been accomplished, the task force is disbanded. Saint Francis Hospital in Tulsa, Oklahoma, established a task force to find ways to reduce the cost of supplies. The team members came from many departments, including surgery, laboratory, nursing, financial planning, administration, and food service. The team not only helped the hospital save money by curbing supply waste but also generated excitement among hospital employees about working together for common goals.[20]

special-purpose teams
Temporary teams that exist outside the formal organization hierarchy and are created to achieve a specific goal

- *Special-purpose teams.* Like task forces, **special-purpose teams** are created as temporary entities to achieve specific goals. However, special-purpose teams are different because they exist outside the formal organization hierarchy. Such teams remain a part of the organization but have their own reporting structures, and members view themselves as separate from the normal functions of the organization. A special-purpose team might be used to develop a new product when complete creative freedom is needed. By operating outside the formal organization, the team would be able to test new ideas and new ways of accomplishing tasks.

committee
Team that may become a permanent part of the organization and is designed to deal with regularly recurring tasks

- *Committees.* In contrast to a task force, a **committee** usually has a long life span and may become a permanent part of the organizational structure. Committees typically deal with regularly recurring tasks. For example, a grievance committee may be formed as a permanent resource for handling employee complaints and concerns. Because many committees require official representation in order to achieve their goals, committee members are usually selected on the basis of their titles or positions rather than their personal expertise.

virtual teams
Team that uses communication technology to bring geographically distant employees together to achieve goals

Virtual Teams Virtual teams, such as those used by David House's division, are groups of physically dispersed members who work together to achieve a common goal. Virtual team members communicate using a variety of technological formats and devices such as company intranets, e-mail, electronic meeting software, and telephones. Occasionally, they may meet face-to-face. The biggest advantage of virtual teams is that members are able to work together even if they are thousands of miles and several time zones apart. At Texas Instruments, for instance, microchip engineers in India, Texas, and Japan are able to pool ideas, design new chips, and collaboratively debug the chips—even though they're separated by 8,000 miles and 12 time zones.[21]

The three primary factors that differentiate virtual teams from face-to-face teams are the absence of nonverbal cues, a limited social context, and the ability to overcome time and space constraints. Because virtual teams must function with less direct interaction among members, team members require certain competencies. Among these are project-management skills, time management skills, the ability to use electronic communication and collaboration technologies, the ability to work across cultures, and heightened interpersonal awareness.[22]

Managing a virtual team involves training team members to communicate effectively using different types of technology.

In many cases, virtual teams are as effective as teams that function under a single roof. At British Petroleum, for example, virtual teams link workers in the Gulf of Mexico with teams working in the eastern Atlantic and around the globe. By using a virtual team network, the company has decreased the number of helicopter trips to offshore oil platforms, has avoided refinery shutdowns because technical experts at other locations were able to handle problems remotely, and has experienced a significant reduction in construction rework, among other benefits.[23]

Advantages and Disadvantages of Teams

5 **LEARNING OBJECTIVE**

Highlight the advantages and disadvantages of working in teams

Teams can play a vital role in helping an organization reach its goals. However, teams are not appropriate for every situation. Managers must weigh both the advantages and disadvantages of teams when deciding whether to use them.

At their best, teams can be an extremely useful forum for making key decisions. The interaction of the participants and the combined intelligence of the group produce better decisions than what would have been achieved had the members worked independently. In short, team decision making can benefit an organization by delivering:

- *Increased information and knowledge.* By pooling the resources of several individuals, teams bring more information to the decision-making process.

- *Increased diversity of views.* Team members bring a variety of perspectives to the decision-making process.

- *Increased acceptance of a solution.* Those who participate in making a decision are more likely to support the decision enthusiastically and encourage others to accept it. Because they share in the final product, they are committed to seeing it succeed.

- *Higher performance levels.* Working in teams can unleash vast amounts of creativity and energy in workers who share a sense of purpose and mutual accountability. Teams fill the individual worker's need to belong to a group, reduce employee boredom, increase feelings of dignity and self-worth, reduce stress and tension between workers, and encourage employees to handle more authority and responsibility.

- *Increased organizational flexibility.* Employees who work in teams become familiar with the work performed by other employees. Thus, they are more willing to be assigned to other company jobs. Such flexibility helps companies meet changing customer needs more effectively and respond more quickly to the challenges of the competitive global workplace.

- *Increased operational efficiencies.* Companies that use teamwork to organize, plan, and control activities enjoy greater productivity, increased profits, fewer defects, lower employee turnover, less waste, and even increased market value.[24] Consider the results the following companies achieved by using employee teams: Kodak has halved the amount of time it takes to move a new product from the drawing board to store shelves; Tennessee Eastman, a division of Eastman Chemical, increased labor productivity by 70 percent; Texas Instruments increased revenues per employee by over 50 percent; and Ritz-Carlton Hotels jumped to the top of the J.D. Power and Associates consumer survey of luxury hotels.[25]

Doug Jaeger, interactive creative director of TBWA/Chiat/Day ad agency, stimulates this team of advertising people to think creatively by walking on the conference room table.

Although teamwork has many advantages, it also has a number of potential disadvantages. At their worst, teams are unproductive and frustrating, and they waste everyone's time. Some may actually be counterproductive, because they may arrive at bad decisions. For instance, when individuals are pressured to conform, they may abandon their sense of personal responsibility and agree to ill-founded plans. Similarly, a team may develop *groupthink*, the willingness of individual members to set aside their personal opinions and go along with everyone else simply because belonging to the team is more important to them than making the right decision. Groupthink can hinder effective decision making because some possibilities will be overlooked. It can even induce people to act unethically.

Some team members may have a *hidden agenda*—private motives that affect the group's interaction. Sam might want to prove that he's more powerful than Laura, Laura might be trying to share the risk of making a decision, and Don might be looking for a chance to postpone doing "real" work. Each person's hidden agenda can detract from the team's effectiveness. Other team members may be **free riders**—team members who don't contribute their fair share to the group's activities because they aren't being held individually accountable for their work. The free-ride attitude can lead to certain tasks going unfulfilled.

Still another drawback to teamwork is the high cost of coordinating group activities. Aligning schedules, arranging meetings, and coordinating individual parts of a project can eat up a lot of time and money. The fact is that teams simply aren't effective for all situations. As management guru Peter Drucker puts it, "When the ship goes down, you don't call a meeting. The captain gives an order or everybody drowns."[26]

free riders
Team members who do not contribute sufficiently to the group's activities because members are not being held individually accountable for their work

Developing Effective Teams

6 LEARNING OBJECTIVE

Review the five stages of team development

Developing an effective team is an ongoing process. Like the members who form them, teams grow and change as time goes by. You may think that each team evolves in its own way. However, research shows that teams typically pass through five definitive stages of development, nicknamed forming, storming, norming, performing, and adjourning.

- *Forming.* The forming stage is a period of orientation and breaking the ice. Members get to know each other, determine what types of behaviors are appropriate within the group, identify what is expected of them, and become acquainted with each other's task orientation.

- *Storming.* In the storming stage, members show more of their personalities and become more assertive in establishing their roles. Conflict and disagreement often arise during the storming stage as members jockey for position or form coalitions to promote their own perceptions of the group's mission.

- *Norming.* During the norming stage, these conflicts are resolved, and team harmony develops. Members come to understand and accept one another, reach a consensus on who the leader is, and reach agreement on what each member's roles are.

- *Performing.* In the performing stage, members are really committed to the team's goals. Problems are solved, and disagreements are handled with maturity in the interest of task accomplishment.

- *Adjourning.* Finally, if the team has a limited task to perform, it goes through the adjourning stage after the task has been completed. In this stage, issues are wrapped up and the team is dissolved.

As the team moves through the various stages of development, three things happen. First, the team develops a certain level of **cohesiveness**, a measure of how committed the members are to the team's goals. The team's cohesiveness is reflected in meeting attendance, team interaction, work quality, and goal achievement. Cohesiveness is influenced by many factors. Two primary factors are competition and evaluation. If a team is in competi-

cohesiveness
A measure of how committed the team members are to their team's goals

tion with other teams, cohesiveness increases as the team strives to win. In addition, if a team's efforts and accomplishments are recognized by the organization, members tend to be more committed to the team's goals. Strong team cohesiveness generally results in high morale. Moreover, when cohesiveness is coupled with strong management support for team objectives, teams tend to be more productive.

The second thing that happens as teams develop is the emergence of **norms**—informal standards of conduct that members share and that guide their behavior. Norms define what is acceptable behavior. They also set limits, identify values, clarify what is expected of members, and facilitate team survival. Norms can be established in various ways: from early behaviors that set precedents for future actions, from significant events in the team's history, from behaviors that come to the team through outside influences, and from a leader's or member's explicit statements that have an impact on other members.

Finally, team members assume one of four roles: task specialist, socioemotional role, dual role, or nonparticipator. People who assume the *task-specialist role* focus on helping the team reach its goals. In contrast, members who take on the *socioemotional role* focus on supporting the team's emotional needs and strengthening the team's social unity. Some team members

norms
Informal standards of conduct that guide team behavior

Thinking About Ethics

Ben & Jerry's Organizes Old Ideals Under a New Boss

After an acquisition, how much control should the parent company give management and staff to retain the mission, values, and culture of the acquired company? This was a key concern for employees, shareholders, and customers before, during, and after Dutch-owned Unilever's $326 million purchase of Ben & Jerry's Homemade, the offbeat company that wraps its diet-busting ice cream in messages of social responsibility.

After the deal, co-founders Ben Cohen and Jerry Greenfield remained involved with the company, though their relationships with Unilever—and each other—became strained. Things were especially difficult when Unilever replaced their hand-picked CEO, Perry Odak, with Yves Couette, a 25-year Unilever veteran. Born in France, Couette made his mark by turning around Unilever's once-troubled ice cream business in Mexico.

When he took over as Ben & Jerry's CEO, Couette understood the value customers place on the company's funky, irreverent brand and its long-held ethical standards. He also recognized the need to satisfy Unilever's desire for growth and profits. While some think these goals are incompatible, Couette stated his intent to run a socially responsible business that also meets Unilever's financial targets.

As he adjusted to the casual atmosphere of Ben & Jerry's Vermont headquarters, Couette also accepted the "us and them" mentality of the staff, acknowledging the importance of maintaining independence from the company's Dutch headquarters. He knew morale would suffer if people thought Rotterdam was calling the shots.

Couette also knew the competition might take aggressive action while the company dealt with internal issues—Haagen-Dazs, for one, is always trying to scoop up market share at Ben & Jerry's expense. To brace the company for tough times, Couette introduced aggressive sales targets but also delegated decision making to as many people as possible to encourage them to be more entrepreneurial. This is the strategy he used in Mexico, returning that unit to profitability in just two years.

Increasing Ben & Jerry's profits will keep Unilever happy and at the same time increase the amount given to charity, which will please customers and employees. However, to retain free rein for Ben & Jerry's, Couette will have to keep proving that socially responsible business can also be good business.

Questions for Critical Thinking

1. What kinds of organizational issues does a company face after a merger or acquisition?
2. How might Unilever use teams to help grow its global ice cream revenues while still retaining Ben & Jerry's culture and social mission?

EXHIBIT 8.6 Team Member Roles
Team members assume one of these four roles. Members who assume a dual role often make effective team leaders.

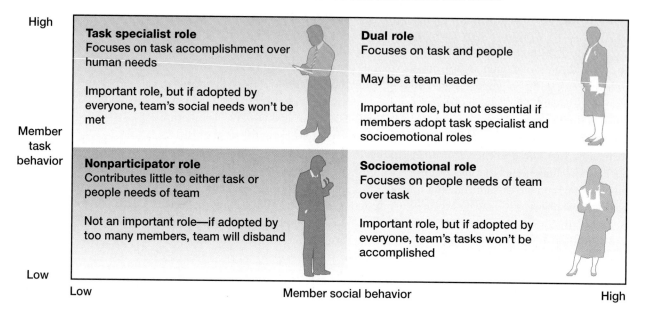

are able to assume *dual roles*, contributing to the task and still meeting members' emotional needs. Other members may be *nonparticipators*, contributing little to reaching the team's goals or to meeting members' emotional needs. Exhibit 8.6 outlines the behavior patterns associated with each of these roles.

Characteristics of Effective Teams

7 LEARNING OBJECTIVE

List the characteristics of effective teams

At Microsoft, almost all work is completed in teams. Two factors that have made Microsoft teams so successful are clear goals and strong leadership. Although the team's goals may be set by either the team or upper management, the team leader makes sure the team stays on track to achieve its goals. Team leaders are often appointed by senior managers, but sometimes they emerge naturally as the team develops.

Team size is another important factor that contributes to a team's overall effectiveness. The optimal size for teams is generally thought to be between 5 and 12 members. Teams smaller than 5 may be lacking in skill diversity and may, therefore, be less effective at solving problems. Teams of more than 12 may be too large for group members to bond properly and may discourage some members from sharing their ideas. Larger groups are also prone to disagreements and factionalism because so many opinions must be considered, thus making the team leader's job more difficult. Moreover, studies have shown that turnover and absenteeism are higher in larger teams because members tend to feel that their presence makes less of a difference.

Other characteristics of effective teams include the following:[27]

- *Clear sense of purpose.* Team members clearly understand the task at hand, what is expected of them, and their role on the team.

- *Open and honest communication.* The team culture encourages discussion and debate. Team members speak openly and honestly, without the threat of anger, resentment, or retribution. They listen to and value feedback from others. As a result, all team members participate.

- *Creative thinking.* Effective teams encourage original thinking, considering options beyond the usual.

- *Focused.* Team members get to the core issues of the problem and stay focused on key issues.

- *Diverse membership.* Effective teams are comprised of stakeholders, creative thinkers, and members who have a wide range of views.
- *Decision by consensus.* All decisions are arrived at by consensus. No easy, quick votes are taken. Instead, all members express their opinions and engage in debate. The decision that emerges is generally supported by all team members.

In addition to these characteristics, effective teams recognize that each individual brings valuable assets, knowledge, and skills to the team. They are willing to exchange information, examine issues, and work through conflicts that arise. They trust each other, looking toward the greater good of the team and organization rather than focusing on personal agendas, making unilateral decisions, or pulling power plays.

Of course, learning effective team skills takes time and practice, so many companies now offer employees training in building their team skills. At Saturn, for example, every team member goes through a minimum of 92 hours of training in problem solving and people skills. Saturn teaches team members how to reach a consensus point they call "70 percent comfortable but 100 percent supportive." At that level of consensus, everybody supports the solution.[28] For a brief review of characteristics of effective teams, see Exhibit 8.7.

Conflict in Teams

By now you can see that being an effective team member requires many skills. One of the most important skills is the ability to handle *conflict*—the antagonistic interactions resulting

8 **LEARNING OBJECTIVE**

Highlight six causes of team conflict and three styles of conflict resolution

EXHIBIT 8.7 Characteristics of Effective Teams
Effective teams practice these good habits.

Build a sense of fairness in decision making
✓ Encourage debate and disagreement without fear of reprisal
✓ Allow members to communicate openly and honestly
✓ Consider all proposals
✓ Build consensus by allowing team members to examine, compare, and reconcile differences
✓ Avoid quick votes
✓ Keep everyone informed
✓ Present all the facts

Select team members wisely
✓ Involve stakeholders
✓ Limit size to no more than 12 to 15 members
✓ Select members with a diversity of views
✓ Select creative thinkers

Make working in teams a top management priority
✓ Recognize and reward individual and group performance
✓ Provide ample training opportunities for employees to develop interpersonal, decision-making, and problem-solving skills
✓ Allow enough time for the team to develop and learn how to work together

Manage conflict constructively
✓ Share leadership
✓ Encourage equal participation
✓ Discuss disagreements
✓ Focus on the issues, not the people
✓ Keep things under control

Stay on track
✓ Make sure everyone understands the team's purpose
✓ Communicate what is expected of team members
✓ Stay focused on the core assignment
✓ Develop and adhere to a schedule
✓ Develop rules and obey norms

from differences in ideas, opinions, goals, or ways of doing things. Conflict can be both constructive and destructive to a team's effectiveness. Conflict is constructive if it increases the involvement of team members and results in the solution to a problem. Conflict is destructive if it diverts energy away from more important issues, destroys the morale of teams or individual team members, or polarizes or divides the team.[29]

Causes of Team Conflict   Team conflicts can arise for a number of reasons. First, teams and individuals may feel they are in competition for scarce or declining resources, such as money, information, and supplies. Second, team members may disagree about who is responsible for a specific task; this type of disagreement is usually the result of poorly defined responsibilities and job boundaries. Third, poor communication can lead to misunderstandings and misperceptions about other team members or other teams. In addition, intentionally withholding information can undermine trust among members. Fourth, basic differences in values, attitudes, and personalities may lead to clashes. Fifth, power struggles may result when one party questions the authority of another or when people or teams with limited authority attempt to increase their power or exert more influence. Sixth, conflicts can arise because individuals or teams are pursuing different goals. For example, a British cardboard-manufacturing company switched from a hierarchical, functionally oriented organization to a team-based structure with the hope of empowering employees and reducing scrap. However, once they got started, the teams realized that the company had many problems to solve. Conflicts resulted when team members couldn't agree on which problems to tackle first.[30]

Ways to Resolve Team Conflict   Each team member has a unique style of dealing with conflict, but the members' styles are primarily based on how competitive or cooperative team members are when a conflict arises. Depending on the particular situation, the same individual may use one of several styles, which include avoidance, defusion, and confrontation. *Avoidance* may involve ignoring the conflict in the hope that it will subside on its own, or it may even involve physically separating the conflicting parties. *Defusion* may involve several actions, including downplaying differences and focusing on similarities between team members or teams, compromising on the disputed issue, taking a vote, appealing to a neutral party or higher authority, or redesigning the team. *Confrontation* is an attempt to work through the conflict by getting it out in the open, which may be accomplished by organizing a meeting between the conflicting parties.

These three styles of conflict resolution come into play after a conflict has developed, but team members and team leaders can take several steps to prevent conflicts. First, by establishing clear goals that require the efforts of every member, the team reduces the chance that members will battle over their objectives or roles. Second, by developing well-defined tasks for each member, the team leader ensures that all parties are aware of their responsibilities and the limits of their authority. And finally, by facilitating open communication, the team leader can ensure that all members understand their own tasks and objectives as well as those of their teammates. Communication builds respect and tolerance, and it provides a forum for bringing misunderstandings into the open before they turn into full-blown conflicts.

The important thing to remember about resolving conflict is that people can usually get what they want if they are willing to work together. In many cases, the resolution process is an exchange of opinions and information that gradually leads to a mutually acceptable solution.

Summary of Learning Objectives

1. **Discuss the function of a company's organizational structure.**

   An organizational structure provides a framework through which a company can coordinate and control the work, divide responsibilities, distribute authority, and hold employees accountable. An organization chart provides a visual representation of this framework.

2. **Explain the concepts of accountability, authority, and delegation.**

   Accountability is the obligation to report work results to supervisors or team members and to justify any outcomes that fall below expectations. Authority is the power to make decisions, issue orders, carry out actions, and allocate resources to achieve the organization's goals. Delegation is the assignment of work and the transfer of authority and responsibility to complete that work.

3. **Define four types of departmentalization.**

   Companies may departmentalize in any combination of four ways: (1) by function, which groups employees according to their skills, resource use, and expertise; (2) by division, which establishes self-contained departments formed according to similarities in product, process, customer, or geography; (3) by matrix, which assigns employees from functional departments to interdisciplinary project teams and requires them to report to both a department head and a team leader; and (4) by network, which connects separate companies that perform selected tasks for a headquarters organization.

4. **Describe the five most common forms of teams.**

   The five most common forms of teams are (1) problem-solving teams, which seek ways to improve a situation and then submit their recommendation to management; (2) self-managed teams, which manage their own activities and seldom require supervision; (3) functional teams, which are composed of employees within a single functional department; (4) cross-functional teams, which draw together employees from various departments and expertise in a number of formats such as task forces, special-purpose teams, and committees; and (5) virtual teams, which bring together employees from distant locations.

5. **Highlight the advantages and disadvantages of working in teams.**

   Teams have the potential to produce more effective decisions by pooling the resources, knowledge, and diverse views of individual members. They can lead to increased acceptance of a solution, higher performance levels, increased organizational flexibility, and increased operational efficiencies. The potential disadvantages of working in teams include the possibilities of groupthink, distractions from members' hidden agendas, the failure of free riders to contribute to the group, and the costs and time needed to coordinate members' schedules and project parts.

6. **Review the five stages of team development.**

   Teams typically go through five stages of development. In the forming stage, team members become acquainted with each other and with the group's purpose. In the storming stage, conflict often arises as coalitions and power struggles develop. In the norming stage, conflicts are resolved and harmony develops. In the performing stage, members focus on achieving the team's goals. In the adjourning stage, the team dissolves upon completion of its task.

7. **List the characteristics of effective teams.**

   Effective teams have clear goals, a clear sense of purpose, strong leadership, and an optimal size of between 5 and 12 members. They communicate openly and honestly, think creatively, stay focused on key issues, and select team members wisely by involving stakeholders, creative thinkers, and members with different views. Moreover, effective teams arrive at decisions by consensus, manage conflict constructively, and place the good of the team ahead of their personal needs.

8. **Highlight six causes of team conflict and three styles of conflict resolution.**

   Conflict can arise from competition for scarce resources; confusion over task responsibility; poor communication and misinformation; differences in values, attitudes, and personalities; power struggles; and goal incongruity. Conflict can be resolved by avoiding it and hoping that it will go away; by defusing it—downplaying team member differences or focusing on member similarities; or by confronting it and working hard to resolve the issues at hand.

KEY TERMS

accountability **(193)**

authority **(194)**

centralization **(195)**

chain of command **(193)**

cohesiveness **(204)**

committee **(202)**

cross-functional teams **(201)**

customer divisions **(196)**

decentralization **(195)**

delegation **(194)**

departmentalization **(196)**

departmentalization by division **(196)**

departmentalization by function **(196)**

departmentalization by matrix **(197)**

departmentalization by network **(198)**

flat organizations **(194)**

formal organization **(192)**

free riders **(204)**

functional teams **(201)**

geographic divisions **(196)**

informal organization **(192)**

line organization **(194)**

line-and-staff organization **(194)**

norms **(205)**

organization chart **(192)**

organizational structure **(192)**

problem-solving team **(201)**

process divisions **(196)**

product divisions **(196)**

responsibility **(193)**

self-managed teams **(201)**

span of management **(194)**

special-purpose teams **(202)**

tall organizations **(194)**

task force **(202)**

team **(199)**

vertical organization **(196)**

virtual teams **(202)**

work specialization **(193)**

TEST YOUR KNOWLEDGE

Questions for Review

1. Why is organizational structure important?

2. What are the characteristics of tall organizations and flat organizations?

3. What are the advantages and disadvantages of work specialization?

4. What are the advantages and disadvantages of functional departmentalization?

5. What are the advantages and disadvantages of working in teams?

Questions for Analysis

6. Why would you expect a manager of a group of nuclear physicists to have a wide span of management?

7. How does horizontal organization promote innovation?

8. What can managers do to help teams work more effectively?

9. How can companies benefit from using virtual teams?

10. **Ethical Considerations:** You were honored that you were selected to serve on the salary committee of the employee negotiations task force. As a member of that committee, you reviewed confidential company documents listing the salaries of all department managers. You discovered that managers at your level are earning $5,000 more than you, even though you've been at the company the same amount of time. You feel that a raise is justified on the basis of this confidential information. How will you handle this situation?

Questions for Application

11. You are the leader of a cross-functional work team whose goal is to find ways of lowering production costs. Your team of eight employees has become mired in the storming stage. They disagree on how to approach the task, and they are starting to splinter into factions. What can you do to help the team move forward?

12. Your warehouse operation is currently functioning at capacity. To accommodate anticipated new business, your company must either build a major addition to your current warehouse operation or build a new warehouse that would be located at a distant site. As director of warehouse operations, you would like several people to participate in this decision. Should you form a task force, a committee, or a special-purpose team? Explain your choice.

13. **Integrated:** One of your competitors has approached you with an intriguing proposition. The company would like to merge with your company. The economies of scale are terrific. So are the growth possibilities. There's just one issue to be resolved. Your competitor is organized under a horizontal structure and uses lots of cross-functional teams. Your company is organized under a traditional vertical structure that is departmentalized by function. Using your knowledge about culture clash, what are the likely issues you will encounter if these two organizations are merged?

14. **Integrated:** In Chapter 7 we discussed three styles of leadership: autocratic, democratic, and laissez-faire. Using your knowledge about the differences in these leadership styles, which style would you expect to find under the following organizational structures? (a) vertical organization—departmentalization by function; (b) vertical organization—departmentalization by matrix; (c) horizontal organization; (d) self-directed teams.

PRACTICE YOUR KNOWLEDGE

Handling Difficult Situations on the Job: Dehiring Campus Recruits

The economy is steadily slipping. As a human resources manager at Intel, you've stopped hiring to fill vacancies (as the company closes plants); you've deferred payment of management raises for six months; and you've split the rank-and-file raises into "half now, half in six months." You're trying to hit the numbers management has targeted for immediate cuts in staff and salary expenses. But you know that others' sacrifices will be small consolation to the talented college graduates Intel recruited last winter. They're about to feel the pinch of a soft economy.

You've seen the days in which the quest for college talent was so hot that you fought with competitors to hire the best recruits—

and then figured out later what jobs to put them in. Times have changed. Today you've learned a new buzz phrase: "reverse hiring."

Should Intel do as others are now doing and "dehire" the grads you recruited last winter? Or should you let them come on board as planned, get placed in lesser jobs than expected, and risk finding themselves "reorganized" out of work? Being last hired, they could easily wind up in the growing pool of laid-off Intel employees awaiting new positions.

Some of your competitors are offering "reverse hiring bonuses," say two months' worth of the promised salary, if recruits will dismiss all legal claims and agree not to come to work. Some also let recruits keep their signing bonuses. Like Intel, these companies are trying to meet job-reduction goals, but they want their reputations on campus to remain strong. As soon as the economy picks up, you'll all be battling over the same individuals getting dehired today.[31]

Your task: Determine the best course of action. Should Intel dehire recruits? How might dehiring recruits have an impact on the firm's organizational structure? What alternatives can you offer? If you choose reverse hiring, what will you say to recruits and how will you reach them (letters, phone calls, e-mail)? What offers will you make, if any? How can you prevent hard feelings against Intel?

Building Your Team Skills

What's the most effective organizational structure for your college or university? With your team, obtain a copy of your school's organization chart. If this chart is not readily available, gather information by talking with people in administration, and then draw your own chart of the organizational structure.

Analyze the chart in terms of span of management. Is your school a flat or a tall organization? Is this organizational structure appropriate for your school? Does decision making tend to be centralized or decentralized in your school? Do you agree with this approach to decision making?

Finally, investigate the use of formal and informal teams in your school. Are there any problem-solving teams, task forces, or committees at work in your school? Are any teams self-directed or virtual? How much authority do these teams have to make decisions? What is the purpose of teamwork in your school? What kinds of goals do these teams have?

Share your team's findings during a brief classroom presentation, and then compare the findings of all teams. Is there agreement on the appropriate organizational structure for your school?

EXPAND YOUR KNOWLEDGE

Discovering Career Opportunities

Whether you're a top manager, first-line manager (supervisor), or middle manager, your efforts will have an impact on the success of your organization. To get a closer look at what the responsibilities of a manager are, log on to the Prentice Hall Student Success SuperSite at www.prenhall.com/success. Click on Majors Exploration, and select "management" in the drop down box. Then scroll down and read about careers in management.

1. What can you do with a degree in management?

2. What is the future outlook for careers in management?

3. Follow the link to the American Management Association website and click on Research. Then scroll down and click on Administrative Professionals Current Concerns Survey. According to the survey, what has affected administrative professionals most recently? On which five tasks do managers spend most of their time?

Developing Your Research Skills

Although teamwork can benefit many organizations, introducing and managing team structures can be a real challenge. Search past issues of business journals or newspapers (print or online editions) to locate articles about how an organization has overcome problems with teams.

1. Why did the organization originally introduce teams? What types of teams are being used?

2. What problems did each organization encounter in trying to implement teams? How did the organization deal with these problems?

3. Have the teams been successful from management's perspective? From the employees' perspective? What effect has teamwork had on the company, its customers, and its products?

Exploring the Best of the Web

URLs for all Internet exercises are provided at the website for this book, www.prenhall.com/bovee. *When you log on to the text website, select Chapter 8, then select "Student Resources," click on the name of the featured website, and review the website to complete these exercises.*

Explore these chapter-related websites, review their content, and answer the following questions for each website you visit:

1. What is the purpose of this website?

2. What kinds of information does this website contain? Please be specific.

3. How is the information provided at this website useful for businesspeople? Consumers?

4. How did you expand you knowledge of organizational structures and teams by reviewing the material at this website? What new things did you learn about these topics?

Build Teams in the Cyber Age

Let Teamworks, the Virtual Team Assistant, help you build a more effective team, resolve team conflict, manage projects, solve team problems, be a team leader, encourage team feedback, and teach with teams. Each of the site's nine information modules contains background information, self-assessment vehicles, skill development exercises, and links to helpful resources. Log on now and increase your effectiveness as a team member by learning more about why teams work, the stages of team development, tips for communicating with team members during a project, and some creative problem-solving techniques. www.vta.spcomm.uiuc.edu

Team Up with Industry Week

If you want to learn more about building effective teams and how companies are using teams in the workplace, you can read many excellent books on the subject. But you might be surprised by just how much information on teams you can find on the Internet. One good starting point is *Industry Week*. This publication (available in print or online) contains excellent articles about how companies are using teams in their manufacturing and day-to-day operations. Log on to the *Industry Week* website and enter the search term "teams." Review the list of articles produced by your search, read several of the articles, and get a jump start on improving your team-building skills. You'll be glad you did. www.industryweek.com

Resolve Conflict Like a Pro

The field of conflict resolution has been growing very quickly and includes practices such as negotiation, mediation, arbitration, international peacebuilding, and more. Learn more about each of these topics along with basic information about conflict resolution by visiting CRInfo. Be sure to check out the web resources, where you'll find links to communication and facilitation skills, consensus building, and more. Find out why BATNA is important. Discover what a mediator does. Learn how to conduct effective meetings. And don't leave without testing your knowledge of common negotiation terms. www.crinfo.org

Learning Interactively

Companion Website

Visit the Companion Website at www.prenhall.com/bovee. For Chapter 8, take advantage of the interactive "Study Guide" to test your chapter knowledge. Get instant feedback on whether you need additional studying. Read the "Current Events" articles to get the latest on chapter topics, and complete the exercises as specified by your instructor. Expand your learning with a visit to the "Research Area." There you will find a wealth of information you can use to complete your course assignments.

A CASE FOR CRITICAL THINKING

Harley-Davidson—From Dysfunctional to Cross-Functional

Richard Teerlink knows what it's like being at the bottom looking up. When he joined Harley-Davidson in 1981 as chief financial officer, the motorcycle manufacturer was as low as it could go. The company had acquired a poor reputation for quality and reliability. It was behind the curve on product design and development. And its big-iron cruisers and long-distance touring bikes were heavy, chrome-laden, and expensive. Moreover, they leaked oil and they vibrated excessively. Some customers even joked that they should buy two Harleys—one to ride and one for parts. Tired of tolerating frequent breakdowns, motorcycle buyers turned to smooth-riding imports.

Harley Goes Full Throttle

Facing some of the toughest competition in the world from such companies as Honda, Suzuki, and Yamaha, Harley-Davidson had to improve quality, introduce new products, and cut costs. So Teerlink and the management team set out to rebuild the company's production processes from the ground up.

Harley had survived several arduous years of crisis and had overcome its obstacles under the direction of a very strong hierarchical, centralized leadership group. By 1986 Harley's future looked bright. New products were coming to market, quality had improved, and products were snapped up as quickly as they could be cranked out. In fact, product demand rebounded so strongly that dealers reported long waiting lists of riders eager to climb on a Harley. Some fiercely loyal fans even tattooed the company's logo on their chests.

Harley-Davidson's inspiring comeback was a cheering symbol of American industrial renaissance. So when Teerlink climbed into the CEO saddle in 1989, he thought the hard work of saving the company was behind him. But competition from Japanese companies soon heated up.

More Potholes Ahead

The Japanese began introducing new bikes in the American market. Their first attempts at sport bikes and cruisers with sleek, modern designs fumbled. But eventually they caught on. Then in 1995 they introduced Harley clones. The bikes were spitting images of Harleys with one exception—they had many technical improvements. Once again, Harley faced a daunting challenge. In spite of its many improvements, Harley's quality standards were not on a par with those of its foreign competitors. Moreover, Harley's cost structure was among the highest in the industry. Teerlink had his work cut out for him—again.

Harley Revs Up Its Engines

Teerlink knew that the best way to improve quality and reliability and lower production costs was to create an environment in which everyone took responsibility for the company's present and future. Of course, such an approach would not come naturally to Harley. The previous crisis had been managed with an unmistakable top-down approach, as is so often the case with turnarounds. But times had changed. Employees could no longer be privates, taking orders and operating within strict limits.

So Teerlink flattened the corporate hierarchy and established teams of cross-functional leaders to work collaboratively and provide senior leadership with direction. This is the structure under which Harley currently operates. At the heart of the organizational structure are three cross-functional teams called Circles—the Create Demand Circle, the Produce Product Circle, and the Provide Support Circle. Each Circle includes design engineers, purchasing professionals, manufacturing personnel, marketing personnel, and others. The cross-functional teams are responsible for every motorcycle produced by Harley—from product conception to final design. Within each team, the leadership role moves from person to person, depending on the issue being addressed.

Recognizing that suppliers' input is crucial to Harley's new-product development, all cross-functional teams include key suppliers who work elbow-to-elbow with Harley personnel. "Suppliers are the experts. They have expertise in not only what they're developing today but also what's going on in their industry," says one Harley purchasing director. "The more input we have up front, the better our products will be."

Making a U-Turn

Cross-functional teamwork has indeed paid off for Harley. Output and productivity soon soared, as did sales around the world. By 2001 Harley was selling 243,000 bikes a year and the company's 6,000-plus employees had much to celebrate. At a time when automakers were whacking at their profit margins, Harley had plenty of gas. It sold every bike it made, and dealers often charged $2,000 to $4,000 *above* the sticker price.

Teerlink attributes much of Harley's success to its move from a top-down hierarchy to one based on cross-functional teams. Everyone must now add value to the organization. Still, "the work is not done," says Teerlink (who retired as CEO in 1999 and is now a member of the board of directors). "Transforming a culture takes time. . . . It's a journey that will never end unless we let it." In fact, Harley is headed for a nasty spill if it doesn't navigate its generational speed bump. The median age of a Harley buyer is 46, and Harley must make inroads with today's 20-something bikers—who prefer sleeker, sportier, and more technically advanced machines. In 2002 Harley unveiled the V-Rod—its first small, cheap bike in more than 20 years. Still, the road ahead is full of rough patches. And if Harley takes a wrong turn, it may be facing some serious time in the dirt.

Critical Thinking Questions

1. During Teerlink's tenure as Harley's CFO was the organizational structure flat or tall? Centralized or decentralized? Explain your answers

2. As CEO, how did Teerlink change the organizational structure?

3. Why does Harley-Davidson include outside suppliers on its cross-functional teams?

4. Go to Chapter 8 of this text's website at www.prenhall.com/bovee and click on the hot link to get to the Harley-Davidson website. Navigate the site to answer the following questions: How many motorcycles did Harley produce in the most recent quarter? What is the output trend? What is the trend in Harley's worldwide sales?

VIDEO CASE

Juicing Up the Organization: Nantucket Nectars

Learning Objectives

The purpose of this video is to help you:

1. Recognize how growth affects an organization's structure.
2. Discuss why businesses organize by departmentalization.
3. Understand how flat organizations operate.

Synopsis

Tom Scott and Tom First founded Nantucket Nectars in 1989 with an idea for a peach drink. At first, the two ran the entire operation from their boat. Today, Nantucket Nectars has more than 130 employees split between headquarters in Cambridge, Massachusetts, and several field offices. As a result, management has developed a more formalized organizational structure to keep the business running smoothly. The company relies on cross-functional teams to handle special projects, such as the implementation of new accounting software. These strategies have helped Nantucket Nectars successfully manage its rapid growth.

Discussion Questions

1. *For analysis:* What type of organization is in place at Nantucket Nectars?

2. *For analysis:* How would you describe the top-level span of management at Nantucket Nectars?

3. *For application:* Nantucket Nectars may need to change its organizational structure as it expands into new products and new markets. Under what circumstances would some form of divisional departmentalization be appropriate for the firm?

4. *For application:* Assume that Nantucket Nectars is purchasing a well-established beverage company with a tall structure stressing top-down control. What are some of the problems that management might face in integrating the acquired firm into the existing organizational structure of Nantucket Nectars?

5. *For debate:* Assume that someone who is newly promoted into a management position at Nantucket Nectars cannot adjust to delegating work to lower-level employees. Should this new manager be demoted? Support your chosen position.

Online Exploration

Visit the Nantucket Nectars site at www.juiceguys.com and follow the links to read about the company and its products. Then use Hoover's Online at www.hoovers.com to search for the latest news about the company, which is formally known as Nantucket Allserve. Has it been acquired by a larger company or has it acquired one or more smaller firms? What are the implications for the chain of command, decision making, and organizational structure of Nantucket Nectars?

CHAPTER 9

Production of Quality Goods and Services

LEARNING OBJECTIVES

After studying this chapter, you will be able to

1. Explain what production and operations managers do

2. Identify the key tasks involved in designing a production process

3. Discuss the role of computers and automation technology in production

4. Explain the strategic importance of managing inventory

5. Distinguish among JIT, MRP, and MRP II inventory management systems

6. Highlight five approaches for monitoring, controlling, and improving quality in the production of goods and services

7. Describe the supply chain and explain how companies today are managing their supply chains

It takes more than a quality mix to produce perfect Krispy Kreme doughnuts all the time. To ensure consistent quality, Krispy Kreme supplies its stores with everything they need to produce premium doughnuts—including the production machinery and equipment.

INSIDE BUSINESS TODAY

Sweet Success: Producing Perfect Krispy Kreme Doughnuts

Take one bite of a Krispy Kreme doughnut, and you'll understand why people have been buying them by the dozen for more than 60 years. They're doughnuts to die for—sinfully sweet with a delicate sugar glaze and a light, airy melt-in-your-mouth taste that keeps customers coming back for more. In fact, Americans treat themselves to more than 5 million Krispy Kreme doughnuts each day. And the Krispy Kreme Company makes sure that every doughnut meets the high standards of taste and quality that customers have come to expect from the legendary product.

Every day, Krispy Kreme stores across the country produce and sell about 20 types of doughnuts, ranging from dunking sticks to the popular glazed variety. Stores are specially designed with glass walls to showcase the doughnut-making process so customers can view the glazed delicacies making their way through the automated production line. Between mixing the dough with water and sugar-glazing the finished product, the procedure for making Krispy Kreme doughnuts takes about an hour. But the manufacturing process begins long before stores in Arizona or Nebraska crank up their doughnut production lines. Every Krispy Kreme doughnut starts from a special mix created at the company's headquarters in Winston-Salem, North Carolina.

Whether you're indulging in a doughnut in New York or California, Krispy Kreme wants you to enjoy the same, delicious taste from every bite. So the company maintains consistent product quality by carefully controlling each step of the production process. First, Krispy Kreme tests all raw ingredients—such as shortening, sugars, and flours—against established quality standards. Every delivery of wheat flour, for instance, is sampled and measured for such things as moisture content and protein levels. If a sample from a 25-ton delivery fails to meet Krispy Kreme's quality standards, the entire delivery is rejected.

After blending the approved ingredients, the company seasons the mix in its warehouse for at least a week. Then Krispy Kreme tests the doughnut mix for quality. Technicians in the company's test kitchen make doughnuts from every 2,500-pound batch of mix to make sure that all ingredients have been blended correctly. Because the characteristics of the flour produced from different crops of wheat may require adjustments in the mixing time or the amount of water added to the dough mix, the technicians note such differences and pass the information along to the stores.

But it takes more than a quality mix to produce perfect Krispy Kreme doughnuts all the time. To ensure consistent quality, Krispy Kreme supplies stores with everything they need to produce premium doughnuts, from ingredients to equipment. The company produces all of its own icings and fillings, then ships the goods by truck from its North Carolina warehouse to stores across the country. Krispy Kreme even makes the production machinery and equipment for its retail sites, following the tradition established by founder Vernon Rudolph, who invented and built the world's first doughnut-making equipment.

Such high standards of product quality have created sweet success for Krispy Kreme. The company now sells more than $400 million of doughnuts annually and has a loyal customer base that extends far beyond the company's Southern roots.[1]

Understanding Production and Operations Management

As managers at Krispy Kreme know, the extremely competitive nature of the global business environment requires companies to produce high-quality goods and services in the most efficient way possible. Few defects, fast production, low costs, excellent customer service, broad market reach, innovative products and processes, less waste, and high flexibility are all objectives that improve quality by adding value to the good or service being produced. Companies pursue these objectives to maintain a competitive advantage.[2] Moreover, managers understand that the level of quality that a company aspires to in the production of goods and services affects its long-term ability to address the needs of its customers.

What Is Production?

production
Transformation of resources into goods or services that people need or want

production and operations management (POM)
Coordination of an organization's resources for the manufacture of goods or the delivery of services

What exactly is production, and what does it involve? To many people, the term *production* suggests images of factories, machines, and assembly lines staffed with employees making automobiles, computers, furniture, Krispy Kreme doughnuts, or other tangible goods. That's because in the past people used the terms *production* and *manufacturing* interchangeably. With the growth in the number of service-based businesses and their increasing importance to the economy, however, the term **production** is now used to describe the transformation of resources into goods and services that people need or want. The broader term **production and operations management (POM)**, or simply *operations management*, refers to all the activities involved in producing a firm's goods and services.

Like other types of management, POM involves the basic functions of planning, organizing, leading, and controlling. It also requires careful consideration of a company's goals, the strategies for attaining those goals, and the standards against which results will be measured. In both manufacturing and service organizations, the production and operations manager is the person responsible for performing these functions. One of the principal responsibilities of the production and operations manager is to design and oversee an efficient conversion process—one that lowers costs by optimizing output from each resource used in the process. These resources include money, materials, inventories, people, buildings, and time.

What Is the Conversion Process?

analytic system
Production process that breaks incoming materials into various component products and divisional patterns simultaneously

synthetic system
Production process that combines two or more materials or components to create finished products; the reverse of an analytic system

At the core of production is the *conversion process*, the sequence of events that convert resources (or inputs) into products and services. This process applies to both intangible services and tangible goods. An airline, for example, uses such processes as booking flights, flying airplanes, maintaining equipment, and training crews to transform tangible and intangible inputs such as the plane, pilot's skill, fuel, time, and passengers into the delivery of customers to their destinations. For a clothing manufacturer to produce a jacket, inputs such as cloth, thread, and buttons are transformed by the seamstress into the finished product (see Exhibit 9.1).

Conversion is of two basic types. An **analytic system** breaks raw materials into one or more distinct products, which may or may not resemble the original material in form and function. In meatpacking, for example, a steer is divided into hide, bone, steaks, and so on. A **synthetic system** combines two or more materials to form a single product. For example, in steel manufacturing, iron is combined with small quantities of other minerals at high temperatures to make steel.

Another thing to keep in mind is that the conversion process for a service operation and goods-production operation is similar in terms of *what* is done—that is, inputs are transformed into outputs. However, the two differ in how the processes are performed (see

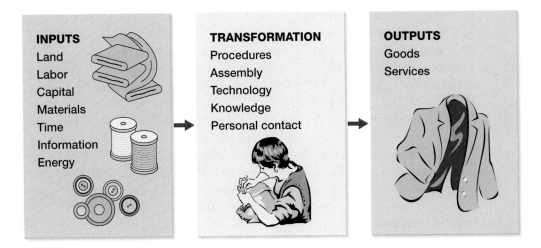

EXHIBIT 9.1
The Conversion Process
Production of goods or services is basically a process of conversion. Inputs (the basic ingredients) are transformed (by the application of labor, equipment, and capital) into outputs (the desired product or service).

Exhibit 9.2). That's because the production of goods results in a tangible output—something you can see or touch, such as a jacket, motorcycle, desk, or bicycle—while the production of a service results in an intangible act. As such, the production of services involves a much higher degree of customer contact, is subject to greater variability, is more labor intensive, and results in a lower uniformity of output than the production of goods.

Designing the Production Process

Designing an effective production process is one of the key responsibilities of production and operations managers. It involves five tasks: forecasting demand, planning for capacity, choosing a facility location, designing a facility layout, and scheduling work. Executing these tasks effectively can make the difference between an operation that is efficient and one that is inefficient and costly.

Consider Boeing, the world's largest aerospace company. For years, Boeing's assembly lines were morasses of inefficiency. The company used a manual numbering system to keep

2 LEARNING OBJECTIVE

Identify the key tasks involved in designing a production process

EXHIBIT 9.2

Input-Transformation-Output Relationships for Typical Systems
Both goods and services undergo a conversion process, but the components of the process vary to accommodate the differences between tangible and intangible outputs.

SYSTEM	INPUTS	TRANSFORMATION COMPONENTS	TRANSFORMATION FUNCTION	TYPICAL DESIRED OUTPUT
Hospital	Patients, medical supplies	Physicians, nurses, equipment	Health care	Healthy individuals
Restaurant	Hungry customers, food	Chef, waitress, environment	Well-prepared and well served food	Satisfied customers
Automobile factory	Sheet steel, engine parts	Tools, equipment, workers	Fabrication and assembly of cars	High-quality cars
College or university	High school graduates, books	Teachers, classrooms	Impart knowledge and skills	Educated individuals
Department store	Shoppers, stock of goods	Displays, salesclerks	Attract shoppers, promote products, fill orders	Sales to satisfied customers

Many of the newer, larger cruise ships have elegant restaurants, boutiques, luxury spas, high-tech fitness rooms, conference and meeting rooms, theatres, playrooms, ice-skating rinks, and even rock-climbing walls. With passenger counts of 2,600 and upward, forecasting customer demand for food, supplies, and entertainment is no easy task.

production forecasts
Estimates of how much of a company's goods and services must be produced in order to meet future demand

track of an airplane's 4 million parts and 170 miles of wiring. Changing a part on a 737's landing gear meant renumbering 464 pages of drawings. Worse yet, Boeing built airplanes like customized houses: Airlines could select from 109 shades of white paint and some 20,000 galley and lavatory arrangements. Previous attempts to automate Boeing's systems had metastasized into 450 separate computer systems, few of which could talk to one another.[3]

Trouble began to brew for Boeing in the early 1990s, as the global economy emerged from recession. Aerospace companies were enjoying an unprecedented surge in orders. And Airbus, Boeing's sole competitor, was gaining ground on Boeing's market share lead. So Boeing began to offer deep discounts on sales prices of new planes, banking on its ability to overhaul its inefficient operations and cut production costs by 25 percent by the time production on the planes began. But the plan backfired.

Boeing was besieged with more orders than it could deliver on time. Boeing's antiquated parts-tracking system couldn't keep up with the increased production volume. And supply problems prevented it from getting enough seats and electronic gear on time. By 1997 Boeing's factories were boiling over. Workers were toiling around the clock, pushing the assembly line to the breaking point. At the same time the company was struggling to overhaul outdated production methods. These pressures were building up to what was, in essence, a manufacturing nervous breakdown. Overtime, parts shortages, rework, defective parts, and out-of-sequence work resulted in late deliveries—a catastrophe that aircraft makers avoid at all costs, since it triggers enormous late fees and wreaks havoc on customers' business plans.

It took Boeing years to recover from the manufacturing mess. In the late 1990s the company underwent a massive reengineering of its production process. Now Boeing is a much leaner production operation, and the company works closely with suppliers. Doing so helps eliminate problems that arise when forecasts for demand change, as they did following the September 11 terrorist attacks.

Forecasting Demand

The first step in designing an effective production process for a manufacturing operation is to determine how much the company will need to produce in a certain time span. Whether a company is building airplanes or producing Krispy Kreme doughnuts, operations managers use customer feedback, market research, past sales figures, industry analyses, and educated guesses about the future behavior of the economy and competitors to prepare **production forecasts**, estimates of future demand for the company's products. These estimates are then used to plan, budget, and schedule the use of resources. Of course, many factors in the business environment cannot be predicted or controlled with certainty. For this reason, managers must regularly review and adjust their forecasts to account for these uncertainties.

Service companies must also forecast demand. For example, dentists must be able to project approximately how many patients they will treat in a given time period so they can staff their offices properly and have enough dental supplies on hand. Without such forecasts, dentists can't run their production process (treating patients) efficiently. Similarly, cruise ship operators must forecast exactly how much food and supplies to stock for one week's journey, because once the ship sets sail, there are no last-minute deliveries.

Planning for Capacity

Once product demand has been estimated, management must determine the company's capacity to produce the goods or services. The term *capacity* refers to the volume of manufacturing or service capability that an organization can handle. For example, having only one examining room limits the number of patients a doctor can see each day, having 750 staterooms limits the number of passengers that a cruise ship can accommodate in any given week, and having only one conveyor belt and one local warehouse limits the number of beverage products a bottling plant can produce.

Capacity planning is a long-term strategic decision that establishes the overall level of resources needed to meet customer demand. The neighborhood convenience store needs to consider traffic volume throughout the day and night in order to plan staffing levels appropriately. At the other extreme of complexity, when managers at Boeing plan for the production of an airliner, they have to consider not only the staffing of thousands of people but also factory floor space, material flows from hundreds of suppliers, internal deliveries, cash flow, tools and equipment, and dozens of other factors. Because of the potential impact on finances, customers, and employees, capacity planning involves some of the most difficult decisions that managers have to make.

Top management uses long-term capacity planning to make significant decisions about an organization's ability to produce goods and services, such as expanding existing facilities, constructing new facilities, or phasing out unneeded ones. Such decisions entail a great deal of risk, for two reasons: (1) Large shifts in demand are difficult to predict accurately, and (2) long-term capacity decisions can be difficult to undo. For example, if a new facility is built to produce a new product that then fails, or if demand for a popular product suddenly declines, the company will find itself with expensive excess capacity. Managers must decide what they should do with this excess capacity. If they keep it, they might try to find an alternative use for the space. If they eliminate it and demand picks up again, the company will have to forgo profits because it is unable to meet customer demand.

capacity planning
A long-term strategic decision that determines the level of resources available to an organization to meet customer demand

Choosing a Facility Location

One long-term issue that management must resolve early when designing the production process is where to locate production facilities. The goal is to choose a location that minimizes costs while increasing operational efficiencies and product quality. To accomplish this goal, management must consider such regional costs as land, construction, labor, local taxes, energy, and local living standards. In addition, management must consider whether the local labor pool has the skills that the firm needs. For example, firms that need highly trained accountants, engineers, or computer scientists often locate in areas near university communities, such as Boston. On the other hand, if most of the jobs can be filled by unskilled or semiskilled employees, firms can choose locations where such labor is available at a relatively low cost. The search for low-cost labor has led many U.S. companies to locate their manufacturing operations in countries such as China, Mexico, Taiwan, and Indonesia, where wages are relatively low.

Also affecting location decisions are transportation costs, which cover the shipping of supplies and finished goods. Almost every company needs easy, low-cost access to ground transportation such as highways and rail lines. Moreover, companies that sell a lot of products overseas must be able to arrange for efficient air or water transportation. Finally, companies must consider the costs for raw materials. For example, the location of a coal-based power

U.S. companies aren't the only ones manufacturing overseas. Japan's Sony has six factories in mainland China. Its two Shanghai factories make camcorders and televisions. Its two Suzhou factories make circuit boards and assemble Vaio multimedia computers. Its Huizhou factory makes parts for DVDs, Handycams, and Play Stations. And its Beijing factory makes cell phones.

plant must be chosen to minimize the cost of distributing electrical power to customers and to minimize the cost and *lead time* of shipping coal to the plant.

Location considerations may be different for some service organizations. Although they may also take regional costs into consideration, the main objective for many service firms is to locate where the profit potential is the greatest. Unlike manufacturing operations, in which low production costs are an important consideration, services tend to focus on more customer-driven factors.[4] Because they often require one-on-one contact with customers, service organizations such as gas stations, restaurants, department stores, and charities must locate where their target market is large and sustainable. Therefore, market research often plays a central role in site selection. However, for service companies that reach customers primarily by telephone, mail, or the Internet, proximity to customers is less of a consideration.

Designing a Facility Layout

After a site has been selected, managers must turn their attention to *facility layout*, the arrangement of production work centers and other elements (such as materials, equipment, and support departments) needed to process goods and services. Layout includes the efforts involved in selecting specific locations for each department, process, machine, support function, and other activity required for the operation or service. The need for a new layout design can occur for a number of reasons besides new construction; for instance, a new process or method might become available, the volume of business might change, a new product or service may be offered, an outdated facility may be remodeled, the mix of goods or services offered may change, or an existing product or service may be redesigned.

Facility layout affects the amount of on-hand inventory, the efficiency of materials handling, the utilization of equipment, and the productivity and morale of employees. In goods manufacturing, the primary concern is the efficient movement of resources and inventory. In the production of services, facility layout controls the flow of customers through the system and influences the customer's satisfaction with the service. In both services and goods operations, the major goals of a good layout design are to minimize materials-handling costs, reduce bottlenecks in moving material or people, provide flexibility, provide ease of supervision, use available space effectively and efficiently, reduce hazards, and facilitate coordination and communications wherever appropriate. Four typical facility layouts are the *process layout*, *product layout*, *cellular layout*, and *fixed-position layout* (see Exhibit 9.3).

A **process layout** is also called a *functional layout* because it concentrates everything needed to complete one phase of the production process in one place. Specific functions, such as drilling or welding, are performed in one location for different products or customers (see Exhibit 9.3A). The process layout is often used in machine shops as well as in service industries. For example, a medical clinic might dedicate one room to X-rays, another room to routine examinations, and still another to outpatient surgery.

An alternative to the process layout is the **product layout**, also called the assembly-line layout, in which the main production process occurs along a line, and products in progress move from one workstation to the next. Materials and subassemblies of component parts may feed into the main line at several points, but the flow of production is continuous. Electronics and personal-computer manufacturers are just two of many industries that typically use this layout (see Exhibit 9.3B).

Some production of services is also organized by product. For example, when you go to your local department of motor vehicles to renew a driver's license, you usually go through a series of steps administered by several people: registering, taking a written or computerized test, having an eye exam, paying a cashier, and getting your picture taken. You emerge from this system a licensed driver (unless, of course, you fail one of the tests).

A **cellular layout** groups dissimilar machines into work centers (or cells) to process parts that have similar shapes and processing requirements (see Exhibit 9.3C). Arranging

process layout
Method of arranging a facility so that production tasks are carried out in separate departments containing specialized equipment and personnel

product layout
Method of arranging a facility so that production proceeds along a line of workstations

cellular layout
Method of arranging a facility so that parts with similar shapes or processing requirements are processed together in work centers

EXHIBIT 9.3
Types of Facility Layouts

Facility layout is often determined by the type of product an organization is producing. (A) Process layout: Typically, a process layout is used for an organization producing made-to-order products. A process layout is arranged according to the specialized employees and materials involved in various phases of the production process. (B) Product layout: A product layout is used when an organization is producing large quantities of just a few products. In a product or assembly-line layout, the developing product moves in a continuous sequence from one workstation to the next. (C) Cellular layout: A cellular layout works well in organizations that practice mass customization. In a cellular layout, parts with similar shapes or processing requirements are processed together in work centers, an arrangement that facilitates teamwork and flexibility. (D) Fixed-position layout: A fixed-position layout requires employees and materials to be brought to the product and is used when the product is too large to move.

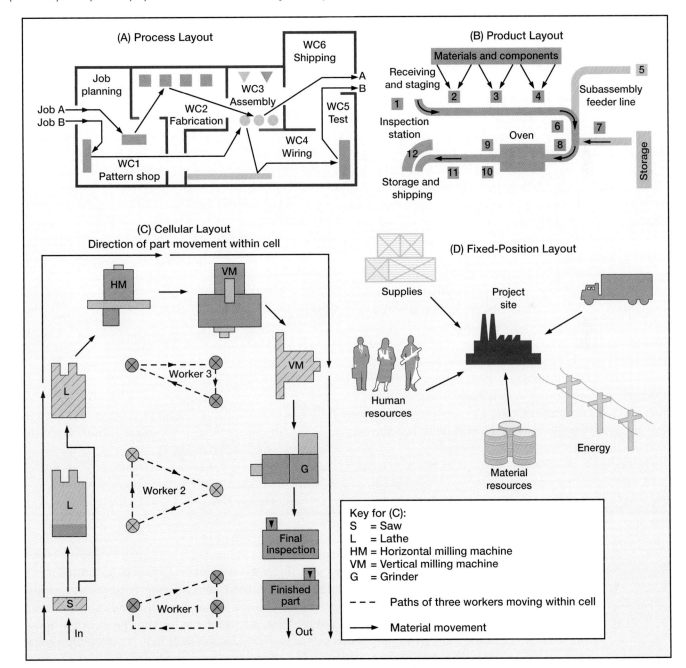

work flow by cells can improve the efficiency of a process layout while maintaining its flexibility. At the same time, grouping smaller numbers of workers in cells facilitates teamwork and joint problem solving. Employees are also able to work on a product from start to finish, and they can move between machines within their cells, thus increasing the flexibility of the team. Cellular layouts are commonly used in computer chip manufacturing and metal fabricating.

Competing in the Global Marketplace

A Bike That Really Travels

When bike industry veteran Hanz Scholz decided to pedal across Europe in 1987, his vision of packing a folding bike in a suitcase when it was time to board a plane or train soon began to fade. Scholz was disappointed by the poor quality of the available folding bikes. So he set out to build his own: one compact enough to fit into a large suitcase but sturdy enough to tackle steep hills and long, rugged stretches.

Five years later, the first commercial orders for Scholz's Bike Friday were rolling in. Unlike its fold-up predecessors—often one-size-fits-all models available in retail stores—all Bike Fridays are custom made by manufacturer Green Gear Cycling to meet the rider's size and component/color preference. The bike fits into a car trunk, a tight storage space, or an optional suitcase to travel on a plane like regular baggage.

Green Gear's operations are as distinctive as its product. The relatively small company ($3 million in sales, 30 employees, 17,000 square feet of production space) uses advanced manufacturing principles adopted from Toyota Motor and other large manufacturers. Built individually, each Bike Friday begins its life as a bundle of tubes, components, and other structures. These elements are processed through a build-to-order, flow-manufacturing configuration organized in a series of cells. The cells are designed so that any one cell can do some of the work of the previous or next cell if production runs behind or ahead.

Once work on a bike has begun, it flows though the process without hesitation at any point. "It works like a track relay with a transition area," says Scholz. "We've set up everything with single-process-specific tools so there is no process changeover time." The flow motto is "touch it once, do it now." When a quality problem is discovered, the operator switches on a red light and all procedures stop until the production cell is adjusted to eliminate the problem.

Operating in a one-at-a-time flow system rather than in batches maximizes the chances for continuous improvement. "For us, every bike is a batch, so we have 150 to 200 chances per month to make process improvements," says Scholz. "A small manufacturer operating in a large-batch mode can be put out of business if he ruins just one. If you can make improvements as you find them, you can survive as a small manufacturer."

Today Green Gear Cycling builds about 2,000 bikes annually. At an average selling price of $1,700, Bike Friday commands a premium price. "We give people what they want, when they want it," says Scholz. "If you do that, people are willing to pay you for it."

Questions for Critical Thinking

1. What are the advantages of using a cellular layout to manufacture Bike Friday?
2. Does Green Gear Cycling mass-produce or mass-customize folding bikes? Explain your answer.

Dell, which builds each computer made to order, recently adapted a cellular layout for its manufacturing process. Visit Dell's Topfer Manufacturing Center in Austin and it's hard to conceive of a more efficient operation. Gathered in six-person cells, workers assemble computers from batches of parts that arrive via a computer-directed conveyor system overhead. If a worker encounters a problem, that batch can instantly be shifted to another cell, avoiding the stoppages that plague conventional assembly lines. By adopting a cellular layout, Dell workers can now assemble 18 units an hour, double the pace of a few years ago.[5]

fixed-position layout
Method of arranging a facility so that the product is stationary and equipment and personnel come to it

Finally, the **fixed-position layout** is a facility layout in which labor, materials, and equipment are brought to the location where the good is being produced or the customer is being served. Buildings, roads, bridges, airplanes, and ships are examples of the types of large products that are typically constructed using a fixed-position layout (see Exhibit 9.3D). Service companies also use fixed-position layouts; for example, a plumber goes to a job site bringing the tools, material, and expertise needed to repair a broken pipe.

Routing is the task of specifying the sequence of operations and the path through the facility that the work will take. The way production is routed depends on the type of product and the layout of the plant. A table-manufacturing company, for instance, uses a process layout because it has three departments, each handling a different phase of the table's manufacture and each equipped with specialized tools, machines, and employees. Department 1 cuts wood into tabletops and legs. These pieces are then sent to department 2, where holes are drilled and rough finishing is done. Finally, the individual pieces are routed to department 3, where the tables are assembled and painted.

routing
Specifying the sequence of operations and the path the work will take through the production facility

Scheduling Work

An important aspect of any production process is **scheduling**—determining how long each operation takes and setting a starting and ending time for each. A master schedule, often called a *master production schedule (MPS)*, is a schedule of planned completion of items. In services such as a doctor's office, the appointment book serves as the master schedule.

When a job has relatively few activities and relationships, many production managers keep the process on schedule with a **Gantt chart**. Developed by Henry L. Gantt in the early 1900s, the Gantt chart is a bar chart showing the amount of time required to accomplish each part of a process. It allows managers to see at a glance whether the process is in line with the schedule they had planned (see Exhibit 9.4).

For more complex jobs, the **program evaluation and review technique (PERT)** is helpful. It is a planning tool that helps managers identify the optimal sequencing of activities, the expected time for project completion, and the best use of resources within a complex project. To use PERT, the manager must (1) identify the activities to be performed, (2) determine the sequence of activities, (3) establish the time needed to complete each activity, (4) diagram the network of activities, (5) calculate the longest path through the network that leads to project completion, and (6) refine the network's timing or use of resources as activities are completed. The longest path through the network is known as the **critical path** because it represents the minimum amount of time needed to complete the project.

In place of a single time projection for each task, PERT uses four figures: an *optimistic* estimate (if things go well), a *pessimistic* estimate (if they don't go well), a *most likely* estimate (how long the task usually takes), and an *expected* time estimate—an average of the other

scheduling
Process of determining how long each production operation takes and then setting a starting and ending time for each

Gantt chart
Bar chart used to control schedules by showing how long each part of a production process should take and when it should take place

program evaluation and review technique (PERT)
A planning tool that managers of complex projects use to determine the optimal order of activities, the expected time for project completion, and the best use of resources

critical path
In a PERT network diagram, the sequence of operations that requires the longest time to complete

EXHIBIT 9.4
A Gantt Chart
A chart like this one enables a production manager to immediately see the dates on which production steps must be started and completed if goods are to be delivered on schedule. Some steps may overlap to save time. For instance, after 3 weeks of cutting table legs, cutting tabletops begins. This overlap ensures that the necessary legs and tops are completed at the same time and can move on together to the next stage in the manufacturing process.

ID	Task Name	Start Date	End Date	Duration	2004
1	Make legs	8/1/04	8/28/04	20d	
2	Cut tops	8/22/04	8/28/04	5d	
3	Drill	8/29/04	9/4/04	5d	
4	Sand	9/5/04	9/11/04	5d	
5	Assemble	9/12/04	9/25/04	10d	
6	Paint	9/19/04	9/25/04	5d	

EXHIBIT 9.5
PERT Diagram for Manufacturing Shoes
In the manufacture of shoes, the critical path involves receiving, cutting the pattern, dyeing the leather, sewing the tops, sewing the tops to soles and heels, finishing, packaging, and shipping—a total of 61 days.

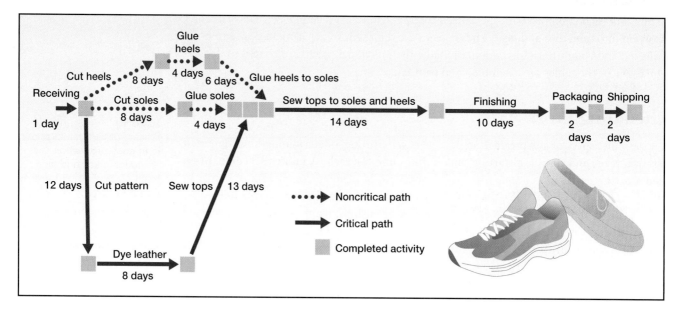

three estimates. The expected time is used to diagram the network of activities and determine the length of the critical path.

Consider the manufacture of shoes in Exhibit 9.5. At the beginning of the process, three paths deal with heels, soles, and tops. All three processes must be finished before the next phase (sewing tops to soles and heels) can be started. However, one of the three paths—the tops—takes 33 days, whereas the other two take only 18 and 12 days. The shoe tops, then, are on the critical path because they will delay the entire operation if they fall behind schedule. In contrast, soles can be started up to 21 days after starting the tops without slowing down production. This free time in the soles schedule is called *slack time* because managers can choose to produce the soles anytime during the 33-day period required by the tops.

Included in the scheduling process is the **dispatching** function, or the issuing of work orders to department supervisors. These orders specify the work to be done and the schedule for its completion. Work orders also inform department supervisors of their operational priorities and the schedule they must maintain.

Of course, once the schedule has been set and the orders have been dispatched, a production manager cannot just sit back and assume that the work will get done correctly and on time. Even the best scheduler may misjudge the time needed to complete an operation, and production may be delayed by accidents, mechanical breakdowns, or supplier problems. Therefore, the production manager needs a system for handling delays and preventing a minor disruption from growing into a major one. A successful system is based on good communication between the employees and the production manager.

Suppose a machine breakdown causes department 2 of a manufacturing company to lose half a day of drilling time. If the schedule is not altered to direct other work to department 3 (the next department), the employees and equipment in department 3 will sit idle for some time. However, if department 2 informs the production manager of its machine problem right away, the production manager can immediately reschedule some fill-in work for department 3.

dispatching
Issuing work orders and schedules to department heads and supervisors

Improving Production Through Technology

Today more and more companies are taking advantage of new production technologies to improve their efficiency and productivity. Two of the most visible advances in production technology are computers and **robots**—programmable machines that work with tools and materials to perform various tasks. Although industrial robots may seem exotic, like some science fiction creation, they are quite common and are really nothing more than smart tools. Industrial robots can easily perform precision functions as well as repetitive, strenuous, or hazardous tasks. When equipped with machine vision (electronic eyes), robots can place doors on cars in precise locations, cull blemished vegetables from frozen-food processing lines, check the wings of aircraft for dangerous ice buildup, make sure that drug capsules of the right color go into the correct packages before they are shipped to pharmacies, and even assist with surgery.[6]

Today's industrial robots do much more than repetitive manufacturing tasks such as inserting screws and assembling components. They can perform a variety of highly technical and hazardous tasks.

Computer-Aided Design and Computer-Aided Engineering

In addition to robots, companies are using **computer-aided design (CAD)**, the application of computer graphics and mathematical modeling to the design of products. A related process is **computer-aided engineering (CAE)**, in which engineers use computer-generated three-dimensional images and computerized calculations to test products. With CAE, engineers can subject proposed products to changing temperatures, various stresses, and even simulated accidents without ever building preliminary models. Moreover, the *virtual reality* capability of today's computers allows designers to see how finished products will look and operate before physical prototypes are built.

Using computers to aid design and engineering saves time and money because revising computer designs is much faster than revising hand-drafted designs and building physical models. In fact, computer technology allows companies to perfect a product or abandon a bad idea before production even begins. The result is better overall product quality. For example, when Boeing engineers designed the 777 airplane, they corrected problems and tried out new ideas entirely on their computer screens. Digitally preassembling the 3 million parts of the 777 allowed Boeing to exceed its goals for reducing errors, changes, and rework.[7]

Computer-Aided Manufacturing and Computer-Integrated Manufacturing

The use of computers to control production equipment is called **computer-aided manufacturing (CAM)**. In a CAD/CAM system, computer-aided design data are converted automatically into processing instructions for production equipment to manufacture the part or product. This integration of design and production can increase the output, speed, and precision of assembly lines, as well as make customized production much easier. In addition, the latest CAD/CAM software allows company departments to share designs and data over intranets and the Internet, enabling geographically dispersed departments to work

---

3 **LEARNING OBJECTIVE**

Discuss the role of computers and automation technology in production

robots
Programmable machines that can complete a variety of tasks by working with tools and materials

computer-aided design (CAD)
Use of computer graphics and mathematical modeling in the development of products

computer-aided engineering (CAE)
Use of computers to test products without building an actual model

computer-aided manufacturing (CAM)
Use of computers to control production equipment

together on complex projects. For example, Ford uses a CAD/CAM/CAE system it calls C3P to develop new vehicle prototypes. Whereas it once took two to three months to build, assemble, and test a car chassis prototype, with C3P the entire process can now be completed in less than two weeks.[8]

The highest level of computerization in operations management is **computer-integrated manufacturing (CIM)**, in which all the elements of production—design, engineering, testing, production, inspection, and materials handling—are integrated into one automated system. Computer-integrated manufacturing is not a specific technology but rather a strategy that uses technology for organizing and controlling a factory. Its role is to link the people, machines, databases, and decisions involved in each step of producing a good.

computer-integrated manufacturing (CIM)
Computer-based systems, including CAD and CAM, that coordinate and control all the elements of design and production

Mass Production Versus Mass Customization

Mass production—manufacturing goods in large quantities—means little or no customization. Because of the high volume of similar goods produced, this process reduces production costs per unit and makes products available to more people. Even though mass production has economic advantages, the competitive pressures of the global economy often require production techniques that are flexible, customer focused, and quality oriented.

mass production
Manufacture of uniform products in great quantities

Many companies today are adopting mass production techniques to tailor goods to individuals on a large scale. Called **mass customization**, this production system recognizes that consumers have individual needs and are best served by products that can be easily customized for them. The key to customizing on a mass scale is digital technology—a combination of hardware, software, and new machines that fine-tune the production process.

mass customization
Producing customized goods and services through mass production techniques

From colored bits of candy to hockey sticks and complex plastics, lots of items are now being tailored to individual needs. Procter & Gamble, for instance, lets shoppers design everything from eye moisturizer to liquid foundation makeup at its reflect.com website. Engineers at Rockwell Collins use virtual online labs to tailor materials for fighter-pilot visors.[9] Levi Strauss & Company and Brooks Brothers are among those using an assembly-line process to produce machine-customized clothing that are matched to a customer's body measurements. Nike has Nike ID, which allows customers to alter the color, design, and even the construction of their shoes. And Meridian Golf mass-customizes golf clubs in 1,100 different combinations. Customers are fitted by swinging a club on a special in-store platform, where computers measure 14 dimensions of their golf swing. Such mass customization has helped Meridian Golf reach a 99.5 percent customer satisfaction rate.[10]

Companies say that letting customers design products from the start cuts waste, design time, and inventory costs.[11] But retooling a factory to spit out thousands of faultless variations of a product is no easy task. Such mass customization requires manufacturing flexibility.

Flexible Manufacturing Systems

To facilitate mass customization, many companies have changed the way their production process is organized. Traditional automated manufacturing equipment is *fixed* or *hard-wired*, meaning it is capable of handling only one specific task. Although fixed automation is efficient when one type or model of good is mass produced, a change in product design requires extensive equipment changes. Such adjustments may involve high **setup costs**, the expenses incurred each time a manufacturer begins a production run of a different type of item. In addition, the initial investment for fixed automation equipment is high because specialized equipment is required for each of the operations involved in making a single item. Only after much production on a massive scale can a company recoup the cost of that specialized equipment. Harley-Davidson, for example, invested $4.8 million in fixed manufacturing equipment to make a particular motorcycle—only to dismantle the operation when the product faded.[12]

setup costs
Expenses incurred each time a producer organizes resources to begin producing goods or services

An alternative to a fixed layout is a flexible layout or a **flexible manufacturing system (FMS)**. Such systems are easily modifiable so that one machine may manufacture a variety of products. Moreover, changing from one product design to another requires only a few signals from a central computer. Each machine changes tools automatically, making appropriate selections from built-in storage carousels that can hold more than 100 tools. In addition, the sequence of events involved in building an item can be completely rearranged. This flexibility saves both time and setup costs. Moreover, producers can outmaneuver less agile competitors by moving swiftly into profitable new fields. Flexible manufacturing also allows producers to adapt their products quickly to changing customer needs. For instance, a flexible manufacturing system at Porsche allows 11 different versions of the Porsche 911 to be assembled on the same line.[13]

Flexible manufacturing systems are particularly well suited for large companies that mass customize or for smaller *job shops*, such as small machine shops, that make dissimilar items or produce at so irregular a rate that repetitive operations won't help. As a $10 million manufacturer of precision metal parts, Cook Specialty is one such operation that competes with larger manufacturers through flexible manufacturing. Cook used to make only certain products, such as basketball hoops and display racks. Now the company has transformed its production facilities so that it is capable of manufacturing custom-engineered medical instruments and precision parts for high-tech equipment. Technical innovations for these devices advance rapidly, but Cook is able to adapt its production facilities to keep up with the changes. In fact, almost one-third of the products Cook manufactures each year are new.[14]

Managing and Controlling the Production Process

During the production design phase, operations managers forecast demand, plan for capacity, choose facility locations, design facility layouts and configurations, and develop production schedules and sequences. Once the design of the production process has been completed, operations managers are responsible for managing and controlling the production process. Included in their responsibilities are programs to control and monitor inventory and quality.

Inventory Management

Forward-thinking companies know that maintaining a competitive advantage requires continuously seeking ways to reduce costs, increase manufacturing efficiency, and improve customer value. They recognize that tying up large sums of money in **inventory**—the goods and materials kept in stock for production or sale—is wasteful. But, not having an adequate supply of inventory can delay production and result in unhappy customers. So they use great care when purchasing and handling the materials they need to produce goods and services.

Purchasing Inventory   **Purchasing** is the acquisition of the raw materials, parts, components, supplies, and finished products required to produce goods and services. The goal of purchasing is to make sure that the company has all of the materials and supplies it needs, when it needs them, at the lowest possible cost. To accomplish this goal, a company must always have enough supplies on hand to cover a product's **lead time**—the period that elapses between placing the supply order and receiving materials.

E-procurement is the Internet-based purchase of products and services needed for business operations. Using web-based purchasing systems helps companies eliminate multiple purchase orders, automate requisition-approval processes, reduce errors, compare competitors' prices, save money, eliminate the need to call and fax suppliers for updates, and shorten waits for approvals, quotes, or delivery information. Owens Corning, the $5 billion

Johnathan W. Ayers, president of Carrier Corp, the world's largest manufacturer of air conditioners, runs an extremely web-savvy operation. By purchasing more than 50 percent of its components and services through a web-based procurement system, Carrier saved an estimated $100 million in one year.

5 LEARNING OBJECTIVE

Distinguish among JIT, MRP, and MRP II inventory management systems

just-in-time (JIT) system
Continuous system that pulls materials through the production process, making sure that all materials arrive just when they are needed with minimal inventory and waste

material requirements planning (MRP)
Method of getting the correct materials where they are needed, on time, and without carrying unnecessary inventory

global manufacturer of advanced glass and building materials systems, has saved over 10 percent of its annual corporate purchasing costs by using an e-procurement process.[15]

In the past, companies would buy supply inventories large enough to make sure they would not run out of parts during peak production times. As soon as inventory levels dropped to a predetermined level, the purchasing department would order new parts. Many companies continue to operate this way, which does offer certain benefits. For example, companies typically get a better price when they buy inventory in bulk, and having a large supply on hand enables them to meet customer demand quickly. Unfortunately, carrying a large inventory also ties up the company's money and increases the risk that products will become obsolete.

To minimize this risk and cost, and to increase manufacturing efficiency, many companies establish a system of **inventory control**—some way of (1) determining the right quantities of supplies and products to have on hand and (2) tracking where those items are. Three methods that companies use to control inventory and manage the production process are *just-in-time systems*, *material requirements planning*, and *manufacturing resource planning*.

Just-in-Time Systems An increasingly popular method of managing operations, including inventory control and production planning, is the **just-in-time (JIT) system**. The goal of just-in-time systems is to have only the right amounts of materials arrive at precisely the times they are needed. Because supplies arrive just as they are needed, and no sooner, inventories are eliminated and waste is reduced. When JIT systems work, the manufacturer achieves *lean production*; that is, it can do more with less.

The maintenance of a "zero inventory" under JIT also has some indirect benefits. For instance, reducing stocks of parts to practically nothing encourages factories to keep production flowing smoothly, from beginning to end, without any holdups. And a constant production flow requires good teamwork. On the other hand, JIT exposes a company to greater risks, because a disruption in the flow of raw materials from suppliers can slow or stop the production process. Shortly after the September 11 terrorist attacks, for instance, Toyota Motor Corp. came within 15 hours of halting production of its Sequoia sport-utility vehicle at its Princeton, Indiana, plant. One of its suppliers was waiting for steering sensors normally imported by plane from Germany, but the planes weren't flying.[16] Post–September 11 transportation snarls such as thorough cargo inspections and slower border crossings into the United States are now forcing many industrial operators to stockpile more parts, components, and materials.

A JIT system also places a heavy burden on suppliers, because poor quality simply cannot be tolerated in a stockless manufacturing environment. One defective part can bring production to a grinding halt. Moreover, suppliers must be able to meet the production schedules of their customers. For instance, an increasingly strong demand for electronic and computer components at the beginning of the 21st century left many electronic equipment manufacturers battling one another for computer chips and other components. "Just-in-time has become just-in-trouble," says the chief financial officer of one electronics company.[17]

Material Requirements Planning (MRP) Material requirements planning (MRP) is another inventory-control technique that helps a manufacturer get the correct materials where they are needed, when they are needed, and without unnecessary stockpiling. Managers use computer programs to calculate when certain materials will be required, when they should be ordered, and when they should be delivered so that storage costs will be minimal. These systems are so effective at reducing inventory levels that they are used almost universally in both large and small manufacturing firms.

Keeping Pace with Technology and Electronic Commerce

Your Inventory Wants to Talk to You

In the warehouse of the not-so-distant future, the wares may talk. Truckloads of consumer products will announce their arrival to workers on the loading dock. Boxes will record each time they are moved, and missing items will reveal their location by emitting a distinctive electronic shout. Empty store shelves will signal when it's time to haul out a few more cases from the stockroom, and when inventories run low vendors will receive an automated heads up that it's time to ship more product.

All of this will be made possible by an emerging technology called *radio frequency identification*, or RFID. The technology relies on memory chips the size of a grain of sand that are equipped with tiny radio antennas. Embedded in a product, the chip or tag is designed to identify and track billions of individual objects all over the world, all in real time. For instance, the chip identifies where and when the product was manufactured, how long it has sat on store shelves, whether it is beyond its expiration date, and when it is time to reorder. These chips can also track shipments from a warehouse to the store, protect against theft, and manage returns and exchanges.

Wal-Mart is investing heavily in RFID tags with an eye toward dramatically reducing supply-chain management expenses, trimming inventories, cutting theft, and eliminating misdirected shipments. In the first large-scale test of its kind, Wal-Mart is tracking cases of Coca-Cola, Bounty paper towels, and Mach3 razors and is experimenting with individually tagged products to track their movement from manufacturer to warehouse to store aisle to checkout counter. Wal-Mart hopes to give suppliers a real-time view of what's happening on store shelves by pumping information from RFID tags into Wal-Mart's 101-terabyte sales-transaction database.

The potential for RFID tags is enormous. But the technology faces several hurdles. One such hurdle is that radio waves can't pass through metal, or through water at certain frequencies. And they are easily confused in "noisy" environments like warehouses and factory floors, where communication systems and heavy machinery emit plenty of potentially distracting radio signals. Researchers think that these technical issues can be resolved. But the cost of both RFID chips and readers is another big obstacle. Currently RFID tags cost anywhere from 50 cents to a few dollars each, which makes them too expensive to replace the magnetic antitheft tags used by stores to control shoplifting or to be introduced on high-volume, low-priced goods like bars of soap. But work is in progress to get costs down to a few cents each—not much more than manufacturers now pay for barcodes. Plus RFID tags will give users much more for their money.

Nonetheless, it may be several years before RFID tags are widely used. But you'll know when that happens. You may enter a store only to discover that the objects around you are having conversations of their very own.

Questions for Critical Thinking

1. How can RFID tags help companies manage their inventory?
2. How can companies use RFID tags to improve the quality of their operation?

A more automated form of material requirements planning is the **perpetual inventory** system, in which computers monitor inventory levels and automatically generate purchase orders when supplies fall below a certain level. The price scanners found at the checkout counters of many stores are part of perpetual inventory systems. Every time a product is purchased, the scanner deletes that particular item from the computer system's inventory data. When inventory of the product reaches a predetermined level, the system generates an order for more. Often the store's system is linked to the supplier's own computer system, which enables the order to be placed with virtually no human involvement.

perpetual inventory
System that uses computers to monitor inventory levels and automatically generate purchase orders when supplies are needed

EXHIBIT 9.6
MRP II

An MRP II computer system gives managers and workers in every department easy access to data from all other departments, which in turn makes it easier to generate—and adhere to—the organization's overall plans, forecasts, and schedules.

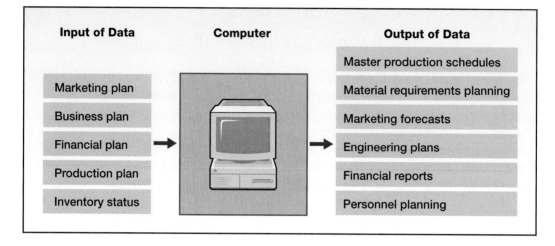

Input of Data	Computer	Output of Data
Marketing plan		Master production schedules
Business plan		Material requirements planning
Financial plan		Marketing forecasts
Production plan		Engineering plans
Inventory status		Financial reports
		Personnel planning

manufacturing resource planning (MRP II)
Computer-based system that integrates data from all departments to manage inventory and production planning and control

Manufacturing Resource Planning (MRP II) The MRP systems on the market today are made up of various modules, including inventory control, purchasing, customer order entry, production planning, shop-floor control, and accounting. With the addition of more and more modules that focus on capacity planning, marketing, and finance, an MRP system evolves into a **manufacturing resource planning (MRP II)** system.

Because it draws together all departments, an MRP II system produces a companywide game plan that allows everyone to work with the same numbers (see Exhibit 9.6). Employees can now draw on data, such as inventory levels, back orders, and unpaid bills, once reserved for only top executives. Moreover, the system can track each step of production, allowing managers throughout the company to consult other managers' inventories, schedules, and plans. In addition, MRP II systems are capable of running simulations (models of possible operations systems) that enable managers to plan and test alternative strategies. An extension of MRP II is **enterprise resource planning (ERP)**, which expands the scope of the production planning process to include customer and supplier information. ERP is based on software developed by SAP AG, a German software company. Using this software and ERP, manufacturers can tap into huge databases of company information to improve production processes.

enterprise resource planning (ERP)
A comprehensive database system that includes information about the firm's suppliers and customers as well as data generated internally

Quality Initiatives

Besides maintaining optimal inventory levels, companies today must produce high-quality goods as efficiently as possible. In almost every industry you can name, this global challenge has caused companies to reexamine their definition of quality and reengineer their production processes. Still, adopting high quality standards is not an easy task, because the manufacture of complex goods is not simply a matter of adding part A to part B to part C and so forth until a product emerges ready to ship. For example, the Mercedes M-Class sport-utility vehicle is assembled from subunits built by 65 major suppliers and many other smaller ones.[18] Making sure that all the pieces are put together in the proper sequence and at the proper time requires large-scale planning and scheduling. The same process is true for the production of complex services, as the following example from China illustrates.

Opening day at Chek Lap Kok, Hong Kong's new airport, was a monumental disaster. The state-of-the-art facility, designed to handle 80 million passengers annually, was promoted as a symbol of Swiss-watch efficiency. But on the airport's first day of operations, every single thing broke down—or so it seemed.

The airport lurched from crisis to crisis. Planes were stranded on the tarmac with no directions to parking gates. Passengers missed flights because of malfunctions in the Flight Information Display system. Some planes left without food for their passengers; others went without passengers altogether. Arriving passengers were imprisoned in the aircraft while mechanics repaired broken jetway doors. And baggage systems (designed to handle 13,700 pieces of luggage an hour) crashed, leaving passengers without luggage while luggage was loaded onto planes without passengers—a serious security breach.

Then, just as the chaos in the passenger terminal seemed under control, computer glitches all but paralyzed air-cargo operations. A software bug disabled the computer system running the new $1.2 billion on-site automated cargo handling facilities—one of the largest in the world. Thousands of air freight containers were strewn across the tarmac. And perishable goods rotted in state-of-the-art warehouses while new shipments were rerouted.[19]

Computer failures at Hong Kong's huge new airport, Chek Lap Kok, left cargo, including perishables, sitting on the tarmac for days.

Poor communications, overconfidence, and lack of system testing and contingency planning—even incompetence—are just a few of the reasons that the debut of Hong Kong's international airport at Chek Lap Kok turned into a nightmare. For example, communications systems and software on which the modern airport depended had not been thoroughly tested. Sample tests of 10,000 transactions had produced some minor problems, but when 70,000 actual transactions hit the systems on opening day, the systems were pushed to the breaking point.

Chek Lap Kok is a good example of what can happen without sufficient quality control. Besides inflicting serious damage on Hong Kong's image, the airport's poor opening cost all parties involved over $5 billion—one-fifth of the airport's $25 billion construction cost. The government wanted Chek Lap Kok to be world famous, and it was—but for all the wrong reasons.

Quality Assurance   The traditional means of maintaining quality is called **quality control**—the process of measuring quality against established standards after the good or service has been produced and weeding out any defects. A more comprehensive approach to quality improvement is **quality assurance**, a system of companywide policies, practices, and procedures to ensure that every product meets preset quality standards. Quality assurance includes quality control as well as doing the job right the first time by designing tools and machinery properly, demanding quality parts from suppliers, encouraging customer feedback, training employees, empowering them, and encouraging them to take pride in their work.

Companies approach quality assurance in various ways. As a builder of sheet-metal components and electromechanical assemblies, Trident Precision Manufacturing empowers workers to make decisions on the shop floor, and it spends 4.7 percent of payroll on employee training.[20] High-end computer maker Sequent Computer Systems has a "customer process engineering manager," whose primary responsibility is to continually communicate with customers and identify any recurring problems. These companies know that eliminating only one inefficiency, such as a defect or an excessively complex process, can reduce total product costs because less money is spent on inspection, complaints, and product service.[21]

6 LEARNING OBJECTIVE

Highlight five approaches for monitoring, controlling, and improving quality in the production of goods and services

quality control
Routine checking and testing of a finished product for quality against an established standard

quality assurance
System of policies, practices, and procedures implemented throughout the company to create and produce quality goods and services

statistical quality control (SQC)
Monitoring all aspects of the production process to see whether the process is operating as it should

statistical process control (SPC)
Use of random sampling and control charts to monitor the production process

Statistical Quality Control and Continuous Improvement Quality assurance also includes a widely used concept of **statistical quality control (SQC)**, in which all aspects of the production process are monitored so that managers can see whether the process is operating as it should. The primary tool of SQC is **statistical process control (SPC)**, which involves taking samples from the process periodically and plotting observations of the samples on a *control chart*. A large enough sample provides a reasonable estimate of the entire process. By observing the random fluctuations graphed on the chart, managers and workers can identify whether such changes are normal or whether they indicate that some corrective action is required in the process. In this way SPC can prevent poor quality.

Statistical quality control is not limited to goods-producing industries. For example, financial services provider GE Capital uses statistical control methods to make sure the bills it sends to customers are correct. The company's use of SQC lowers the cost of making adjustments while improving customer satisfaction.[22]

In addition to using SQC, companies can empower each employee to continuously improve the quality of goods production or service delivery. The Japanese word for continuous improvement is *kaizen*. Japanese manufacturers learned long before many U.S. manufacturers that continuous improvement is not something that can be delegated to one or a few people. Instead it requires the full participation of every employee, which means encouraging all workers to spot quality problems, halt production when necessary, generate ideas for improvement, and adjust work routines as needed.

total quality management (TQM)
Comprehensive, strategic management approach that builds quality into every organizational process as a way of improving customer satisfaction

Total Quality Management Total quality management (TQM) is both a management philosophy and a strategic management process that focuses on delivering the optimal level of quality to customers by building quality into every organizational activity (see Exhibit 9.7). Companies that adopt TQM create a value for all stakeholders—customers, employees, owners, suppliers, and the community.[23] The four key elements of TQM are employee involvement, customer focus, benchmarking, and continuous improvement:

- *Employee involvement.* Total quality management involves every employee in quality assurance. Workers are trained in quality methods and are empowered to stop a work process if they feel that products or services are not meeting quality standards. Managers also encourage employees to speak up when they think of better ways of doing things.

- *Customer focus.* Focusing on the customer simply means finding out what customers really want and then providing it. This approach requires casting aside assumptions about customers and relying instead on accurate research. It also requires developing long-term relationships with customers, as Chapter 12 discusses in detail.

- *Benchmarking.* This element of TQM involves comparing your company's processes and products against the standards of the world's best companies and then working to match or exceed those standards. Among the world-class organizations frequently cited as benchmarks for production are Toyota, IBM, and Hewlett-Packard; for distribution, L.L. Bean and FedEx; and for customer service, American Express and Nordstrom.

- *Continuous improvement.* This key feature of TQM requires an ongoing effort to reduce defects, cut costs, slash production and delivery times, and offer customers innovative products. Improvements are often small, incremental changes that add up to greater competitiveness over the long run.

Although many U.S. companies are enjoying greater success as a result of quality control, quality assurance, and total quality management, a recent study of the largest U.S. companies indicates that such initiatives have fallen short of expectations in a large number of companies. As a result, many companies are now turning to a quality program called Six Sigma.

EXHIBIT 9.7   Total Quality Management
These 14 points, based on the work of W. Edwards Deming, can help managers improve their goods and services through total quality management.

1. **Create constancy of purpose for the improvement of goods and services.**
   The organization should constantly strive to improve quality, productivity, and consumer satisfaction to improve performance today and tomorrow.

2. **Adopt a new philosophy to reject mistakes and negativism.**
   Customers, managers, and employees all need to change their attitudes toward unacceptable work quality and sullen service.

3. **Cease dependence on mass inspection.**
   Instead of inspecting products after production to weed out bad quality, improve the process to build in good quality.

4. **End the practice of awarding business on price alone.**
   Create long-term relationships with suppliers who can deliver the best quality.

5. **Improve constantly and forever the system of production and service.**
   Improvement is not a one-time effort; managers must lead the way to continuous improvement of quality, productivity, and customer satisfaction.

6. **Institute training.**
   Train all organization members to do their jobs consistently well.

7. **Institute leadership.**
   Managers must provide the leadership to help employees do a better job.

8. **Drive out fear.**
   Create an atmosphere in which employees are not afraid to ask questions or to point out problems.

9. **Break down barriers between units.**
   Ensure that people in organizational departments or units do not have conflicting goals and are able to work as a team to achieve overall goals.

10. **Eliminate slogans, exhortations, and targets for the workforce.**
    These alone cannot help anyone do a better job, and they imply that employees could do better if they tried harder; instead, management should provide methods for improvement.

11. **Eliminate numerical quotas.**
    Quotas count only finished units, not quality or methods, and they generally lead to defective goods, wasted resources, and demoralized employees.

12. **Remove barriers to pride in work.**
    Most people want to do a good job but are prevented from doing so by misguided management, poor communication, faulty equipment, defective materials, and other barriers that managers must remove to improve quality.

13. **Institute a vigorous program of education and retraining.**
    Both managers and employees have to be educated in the new quality methods.

14. **Take action to accomplish the transformation.**
    With top-management commitment, have the courage to make the changes throughout the organization that will improve quality.

Six Sigma   Motorola created the concept of Six Sigma in the 1980s when engineers concluded that new products, which often failed to meet customer expectations, could be produced error-free from the start. This represented a fairly radical idea in manufacturing: measuring customer requirements and performance against these targets during production, rather than after a product's completion. The basic idea behind **Six Sigma** is to achieve product perfection by eliminating defects in the business processes that create the product. Sigma is a Greek term for variation. To reach Six Sigma, a process must yield no more than 3.4 errors or defects per million chances at generating them.[24] The process is applicable to services as well as manufacturing.

Like other quality initiatives, Six Sigma can cut costs, improve processes, and reduce business cycle times. But it differs substantially from quality control and quality assurance, whose focus is on defect elimination for the sake of defect elimination. Such programs teach employees to become more quality-focused in their jobs, with the hope that incremental improvements will bubble up. In other words, quality is for perfection's sake.

Six Sigma
Management approach that uses customer feedback and collaboratively set goals to improve the quality of products, services, and operations so that they yield no more than 3.4 errors or defects per million chances of generating them

In contrast, Six Sigma aligns a company's people and processes behind commonly agreed-upon goals. Often, quality is defined by the needs and preferences of a firm's customers. For instance, if customers say that speed in receiving products or services is most relevant to them, the company determines which activities most affect its ability to act on a request quickly and measures those activities to create the defect-per-million opportunity.[25]

Starwood Hotels & Resorts Worldwide, owner of the Sheraton and Westin brands, is a good example of this customer-driven approach. Starwood found that 85 percent of guests were checked in within a three-minute goal. But in interviews, guests said they became annoyed after standing in line more than 20 seconds, suggesting that lines should be eliminated altogether. So Starwood adopted the Six Sigma quality-improvement model to cut down on everything from front desk check-in waits to collecting on bills more quickly. They are using it to overhaul their corporate culture, drastically improve customer service experiences, and radically alter the nature of their hospitality services. One possibility Starwood is considering is for guests to go straight to preassigned rooms and swipe their credit card to gain entry.[26]

ISO Standards   Companies that choose to do business in Europe may have to leap an extra quality hurdle. Many manufacturers and service providers in Europe require that suppliers comply with standards set by the International Organization for Standardization (ISO), a nongovernment entity based in Geneva, Switzerland. Recently revised into a family of quality-management-system standards and guidelines known as **ISO 9000**, ISO 9001, and ISO 9004, such standards are voluntary by definition. Companies may choose to comply with these standards and, if met, to promote their certification to gain recognition for their quality achievements.

In the past, ISO 9000 standards applied mostly to products that have health and safety-related features. However, the newer 9001 and 9004 standards place a greater focus on customer satisfaction, user needs, and continuous improvement.[27] The standards are recognized in over 100 countries, and about one-fourth of the world's corporations insist that all their suppliers be ISO certified.[28]

ISO standards help companies become *world-class manufacturers*, a term used to describe the level of quality and operational effectiveness that puts a company among the top performers in the world. Some companies view ISO standards as a starting point to achieving other national quality awards such as Japan's Deming Prize, a highly regarded industrial quality award, or the U.S. Malcolm Baldrige National Quality Award, which honors the quality achievements of U.S. companies (see Exhibit 9.8). Of course, even if an organization doesn't want to actually apply for an award, it can improve quality by measuring its performance against an award's standards and working to overcome any problems uncovered by this process.

> **ISO 9000**
> Global standards set by the International Organization for Standardization establishing a minimum level of acceptable quality

Supply-Chain Management

As Krispy Kreme knows, a company's ability to deliver quality products and services is often tied to the dynamics of its suppliers. Whether you're making doughnuts or airplanes, one faulty part, one late shipment, can send rippling effects through the production system and can even bring operations to a grinding halt. For instance, when a surge of orders for new Boeing 747s stepped up demand for parts, Boeing's suppliers were caught flat-footed. "We had $25,000 engine mounts that couldn't be finished because we were waiting for $40 nuts and bolts," noted one Boeing supplier. As a result, promised aircraft delivery dates were delayed and Boeing suffered huge losses. To avoid such problems in the future, Boeing now works hand in hand with its suppliers to refine products and delivery schedules.[29]

The group of firms that provides all the various processes required to make a finished product is called the *supply chain*. The chain begins with the provider of raw materials and

> **7 LEARNING OBJECTIVE**
>
> Describe the supply chain and explain how companies today are managing their supply chains

EXHIBIT 9.8 Criteria for the Malcolm Baldrige National Quality Award
The Malcolm Baldrige National Quality Award is given annually to companies that demonstrate an outstanding commitment to quality. Named after former Secretary of Commerce Malcolm Baldrige, the awards are given to companies in each of four categories: manufacturing, services, small businesses, and universities and hospitals. This chart lists the criteria on which companies are judged for the award.

✓ **Leadership.** Have senior leaders clearly defined the company's values, goals, and ways to achieve the goals? Is the company a model "corporate citizen"?

✓ **Information and analysis.** Does the company effectively use data and information to support customer-driven performance excellence and marketplace success?

✓ **Strategic planning.** How does the company develop strategies and business plans to strengthen its performance and competitive position?

✓ **Human resources development and management.** How does the company develop the full potential of its workforce? How are its human resource capabilities and work systems aligned with its strategic and business plans?

✓ **Process management.** How does the company design, manage, and improve key processes, such as customer-focused design and product and service delivery?

✓ **Business results.** How does the company address performance and improvement in key business areas—product and service quality, productivity and operational effectiveness, supply quality, and financial performance indicators linked to these areas?

✓ **Customer focus and satisfaction.** How does the company determine requirements, expectations, and preferences of customers? What are its customer satisfaction results?

ends with the company that produces the finished product that is delivered to the final customer. The members of the supply chain vary according to the nature of the operation and type of product, but typically include suppliers, manufacturers, distributors, and retailers. For example, if the finished product is a wood table, the supply chain going backward would include the retail store where it was sold, the shipping company that delivered it to the retail store, the furniture manufacturer, the hardware manufacturer, and the lumber company that acquired the wood from the forest.

Through a process known as **supply-chain management**, many companies now integrate all of the facilities, functions, and activities involved in the production of goods and services going from suppliers to customers. The process is based on the belief that because one company's output is another company's (or consumer's) input, all companies involved will benefit from working together more closely. Building high-trust relationships was once thought possible only with internal suppliers. But today, more and more companies are reducing the number of outside suppliers they use, working collaboratively with them, sharing information with them, and even involving them in the production and design processes.

Consider Seagate. In the mid-1990s, this leading disk-drive manufacturer discovered that overspecialization was jacking up its manufacturing costs—making it difficult to achieve economies of scale. Every new-product rollout was a one-of-a-kind adventure that was prone to delays and manufacturing bottlenecks. So company president Bill Watkins concluded that if Seagate wanted to be really fast, it would have to fix its supply chain.

Watkins began his quest by mandating that Seagate develop basic manufacturing platforms that would allow the company to make a variety of disk drives within a single plant without having to retool the entire production line. Then he focused on the supply chain. Instead of squeezing suppliers for the deepest discounts, he created incentive contracts that let suppliers earn more if they could help Seagate get to market faster with drives that surpassed those made by competitors.

Seagate's supply-chain overhaul was put to the test when Seagate raced to bring the Barracuda IV drive to market. In late-stage developmental work, Seagate realized that a crucial part of the disk was overheating and causing errors when the disk drive tried to write data. The best solution was to use a new heat-diffusing material—one that Seagate had

supply-chain management
Integrating all of the facilities, functions, and processes associated with the production of goods and services, from suppliers to customers

never used before. So Seagate worked collaboratively with the material's supplier. "We spent more than $1 million to help our supplier fabricate the material in high enough volume," recalls Seagate's project leader Emil Yappert. "But we cut the amount of time needed to get that part by one-third. In the old days, it would have taken us eight weeks. We got it done in five weeks. On a project like this one, each day that we save—or lose—means about $500,000 to the bottom line. So it's worth it."[30]

Like Seagate, Honda's engineers, designers, and technologists work side by side with suppliers in the very early stages of a new project. Honda believes in maintaining a frank, open, and collaborative relationship with its suppliers and even extends this philosophy to sharing cost data. "We show our suppliers our logic in coming up with the cost, and they show us theirs," notes Honda's senior purchasing manager.[31] This sharing of information with members of the supply chain has many benefits. Among them are increased sales, cost savings, inventory reductions, improved quality, accelerated delivery time, and improved customer service.[32]

Outsourcing the Manufacturing Function

As companies strive to find better ways to produce goods, many are turning to outsourcing the manufacturing function. Outsourcing this function has several advantages. For one thing, it allows companies to redirect the capital and resources spent on manufacturing to new product research and development, marketing, and customer service. For another, many contract manufacturers are industry specialists with state-of-the art facilities and production efficiencies that would be costly to duplicate on an individual scale.

Such highly regarded companies as Hewlett-Packard, IBM, Boeing, Airbus, and Porsche outsource their production processes. Porsche suppliers, for example, manufacture at least 75 percent of every Porsche sports car.[33] Computer manufacturers typically outsource production to contract electronic manufacturers (CEMs). Solectron is a California CEM that assembles everything from pagers to printers to computers to television decoding boxes for some of the biggest brand names in electronics. It is the only company that has twice won the Malcolm Baldrige Award for manufacturing excellence.[34] Outsourced electronic products manufactured by Solectron still bear the original equipment manufacturer's (OEMs) brand name—such as Hewlett-Packard, Cisco, IBM, and Lucent. In some cases the CEM provides additional services beyond the manufacturing function, including inventory management, delivery, and after-sales service.[35]

In some companies, in-house manufacturing operations consist of nothing more than bolting together fabricated chunks that have been manufactured by suppliers. DaimlerChrysler's Smart car is a good example of this process. Just about everything in Smartville, the production center where the Smart is assembled, is relegated to suppliers—from inventorying nuts and bolts on the assembly line to delivering cars to dealers in Europe and Japan. Over half of the 1,900 people working in Smartville aren't even on the manufacturer's payroll. The biggest suppliers are right on-site, building most of the car in the form of large modules—body, doors, rear section with engine, and so on. Conveyors link major suppliers' plants directly to the assembly building

In automotive manufacturing circles, the way the Smart car is built has attracted as much attention as the vehicle. Outsourcing the manufacturing function integrates the Smart car supply chain to the maximum.

where the cars are bolted together. Suppliers carry much of the cost of work-in-progress inventory, since they don't get paid until the car comes off the line and is accepted for sale by inspectors—about every 90 seconds, which is quick time for the auto industry. Meanwhile, DaimlerChrysler hopes to incorporate what it has learned about suppliers, modules, pay-on-build, and new technologies into its global operation. "We are getting more and more into learning from others," says one Smart plant manager. "We take good things in other places and install them at our plant."[36]

Summary of Learning Objectives

1. **Explain what production and operations managers do.**

   Production and operations managers design and oversee an efficient conversion process—the sequence of events that converts resources into goods and services. To do this, they must coordinate a firm's resources and optimize output from each resource. In addition, production and operations managers perform the four basic functions of planning, organizing, leading, and controlling, but the focus of these activities is the production of a company's goods and services.

2. **Identify the key tasks involved in designing a production process.**

   Managers must first prepare production forecasts, or estimates of future demand for the company's products. Next they must consider capacity, which is a business's volume of manufacturing or service delivery. The next step is to find a facility location that minimizes regional costs (land, construction, labor, local taxes, leasing, energy), transportation costs, and raw materials costs. Once a location has been selected, managers need to consider facility layout—the arrangement of production work centers and other facilities (such as material, equipment, and support departments) needed for the processing of goods and services. Finally, managers must develop a master production schedule.

3. **Discuss the role of computers and automation technology in production.**

   Computers and automation technology improve the production process in several ways: (1) Robots perform repetitive or mundane tasks quickly and with great precision; (2) CAD and CAE systems allow engineers to design and test virtual models of products; (3) CAM systems easily translate CAD data into production instructions; (4) CIM systems link the people, machines, databases, and decisions involved in each step of producing a good; and (5) flexible manufacturing systems (FMSs) reduce setup costs and time by linking programmable, multifunctional machine tools through a computer network and an automated materials-handling system.

4. **Explain the strategic importance of managing inventory.**

   The goods and materials kept in stock for production or sale make up inventory, which must be managed to minimize costs and ensure that the right supplies are in the right place at the right time. Having too much inventory is costly and increases the risk that products will become obsolete. Having too little inventory can result in production delays and unfilled orders.

5. **Distinguish among JIT, MRP, and MRP II inventory management systems.**

   Just-in-time (JIT) systems reduce waste and improve quality by producing only enough to fill orders when they are due, thus eliminating finished-goods inventory. Furthermore, under the JIT system, parts or materials are ordered only when they are needed, thus eliminating supplies inventories. Material requirements planning (MRP) and perpetual inventory systems are used to determine when materials are needed, when they should be ordered, and when they should be delivered. A more advanced system is manufacturing resource planning (MRP II), which brings together data from all parts of a company (including financial, design, and engineering departments) to better manage inventory and production planning and control.

6. **Highlight five approaches for monitoring, controlling, and improving quality in the production of goods and services.**

   Quality control focuses on measuring finished products against a preset standard and weeding out any defects. Quality assurance is a system of companywide policies, practices, and procedures that builds quality into a product and ensures that each product meets quality standards. Statistical quality control monitors all aspects of the production process to determine whether the process is operating properly. Total quality management focuses on building quality in every organizational activity by involving employees in quality assurance, focusing on customers, benchmarking, and making improvements on a continual basis. Six

Sigma begins with an agreed-upon set of customer-focused goals that are jointly established by employees and managers. Companies reach Six Sigma if a process yields no more than 3.4 errors or defects per million chances of generating them.

7. **Describe the supply chain and explain how companies today are managing their supply chains.**
The supply chain consists of all companies involved in making a finished product. The members of the chain vary according to the nature of the operation and the type of product, but typically include suppliers, manufacturers, distributors, and retail outlets. Today, more and more companies are working closely with their supply chains to be more responsive to the changing needs of their customers. To do this, companies are reducing the number of firms in their supply chain, developing long-term relationships with remaining members, and sharing information with them. Some companies are even involving members of their supply chain in the design and production processes.

KEY TERMS

analytic system **(216)**

capacity planning **(219)**

cellular layout **(220)**

computer-aided design (CAD) **(225)**

computer-aided engineering (CAE) **(225)**

computer-aided manufacturing (CAM) **(225)**

computer-integrated manufacturing (CIM) **(226)**

critical path **(223)**

dispatching **(224)**

enterprise resource planning (ERP) **(230)**

fixed-position layout **(222)**

flexible manufacturing system (FMS) **(227)**

Gantt chart **(223)**

inventory **(227)**

inventory control **(228)**

ISO 9000 **(234)**

just-in-time (JIT) system **(228)**

lead time **(227)**

manufacturing resource planning (MRP II) **(230)**

mass customization **(226)**

mass production **(226)**

material requirements planning (MRP) **(228)**

perpetual inventory **(229)**

process layout **(220)**

product layout **(220)**

production **(216)**

production and operations management (POM) **(216)**

production forecasts **(218)**

program evaluation and review technique (PERT) **(223)**

purchasing **(229)**

quality assurance **(231)**

quality control **(231)**

robots **(225)**

routing **(223)**

scheduling **(223)**

setup costs **(226)**

Six Sigma **(233)**

statistical process control (SPC) **(232)**

statistical quality control (SQC) **(232)**

supply-chain management **(235)**

synthetic system **(216)**

total quality management (TQM) **(232)**

TEST YOUR KNOWLEDGE

Questions for Review

1. What is the conversion process?

2. What factors need to be considered when selecting a site for a production facility?

3. What is mass customization?

4. Why is an effective system of inventory control important to every manufacturer?

5. Why might a company want to outsource its manufacturing function?

Questions for Analysis

6. Why is capacity planning an important part of designing operations?

7. How do JIT systems go beyond simply controlling inventory?

8. Why have companies moved beyond total quality management to Six Sigma?

9. How can supply-chain management help a company establish a competitive advantage?

10. *Ethical Considerations:* How does society's concern for the environment affect a company's decisions about facility location and layout?

Questions for Application

11. Assume you are the production manager for a small machine shop that manufactures precision parts for industrial equipment. How can you use CAD, CAE, CAM, CIM, and FMS to manufacture better parts more easily?

12. If your final product requires several unique subunits that are all produced with different machinery and in differing lengths of time, what facility layout will you choose and why?

13. *Integrated:* Review the discussion of franchises in Chapter 5. From an operational perspective, why is purchasing a franchise such as Wendy's or Jiffy Lube an attractive alternative for starting a business?

14. *Integrated:* Review the discussion of corporate cultures in Chapter 7. What things could you learn about a company's culture by observing the layout and design of its production facility? Discuss both goods and service operations.

PRACTICE YOUR KNOWLEDGE

Handling Difficult Situations on the Job: Giving Suppliers a Report Card

Just when you thought there was nothing left to measure and evaluate, your boss at Microsoft, Roxanna Frost, suggested something new. Frost, who is the program manager for Microsoft's Executive Management and Development Group, thinks that, like employees who get performance reviews, suppliers also need improved clarity in terms of goals and expectations, accomplishments, and improvements. "There's a gap between what we want our suppliers to do and the feedback they're getting," says Frost.

Thinking about this observation, you realize that 60 percent of the employee services your group monitors (travel assistance, retirement plans, the library at Microsoft's Redmond, Washington, campus) are outsourced to independent suppliers. This is nothing unusual at Microsoft, where many departments outsource both goods and services. What is new is Frost's idea of providing suppliers with performance feedback.

Frost suggested at a recent meeting that it would be a good idea to periodically evaluate *all* the outside suppliers that serve the company. When she asks for a volunteer to coordinate this new project, you raise your hand. This is just the kind of challenge you relish.[37]

Your task: To get the project underway, you'll first need to resolve several issues. For instance, what criteria should Microsoft departments use for evaluating suppliers? List four to six of these criteria (such as on-time delivery). How often should suppliers be evaluated?

Why? What response should Microsoft expect from suppliers after their evaluation? What will you do to encourage positive responses?

Building Your Team Skills

Facility layout is one of the most critical decisions production managers must make. In this exercise, you and your team are playing the role of production managers for the following companies, some producing a specific good and some producing a specific service:

- Mountain Dew—soft drinks
- H & R Block—tax consultation
- Bob Mackie—custom-made clothing
- Burger King—fast food
- Boeing—commercial jets
- Massachusetts General Hospital—medical services
- Hewlett-Packard—printers
- Toyota—sport-utility vehicles

For each company on the list, discuss and recommend a specific facility layout, referring to Exhibit 9.3 for an overview of the four layouts. Why does your team believe the recommended layout is best suited to the product or service each company produces? How would the recommended layouts affect the movement of resources and inventory for the manufacturers on the list? How would the layouts affect customer interaction for the service providers on the list?

EXPAND YOUR KNOWLEDGE

Discovering Career Opportunities

Whether you prefer to work with products or services, many possible careers await you in production and operations. From input to transformation to output, companies are looking for resourceful, results-oriented employees able to meet the demands of ever-changing schedules and specifications. Start your research by scanning the help-wanted classified and display ads in your local newspaper and in *The Wall Street Journal;* also check help-wanted ads in business magazines such as *Industry Week.* If you have Internet access, search the production and manufacturing jobs listed in America's Job Bank at www.ajb.dni.us.

1. As you read through these want ads, note all the production-related job titles you find. How many of these jobs include quality or technology (or both) among the duties and responsibilities?

2. Select two job openings that interest you. Reread the ads for those jobs to find out what kind of work experience and educational background are required. What further preparation will you need to qualify for these jobs?

3. Assume you have the qualifications for the two jobs you have selected. What key words should you include on your electronic résumé to show the employers that you are a good job candidate?

Developing Your Research Skills

Seeking increased efficiency and productivity, a growing number of producers of goods and services are applying technology to improve the production process. Find an article in business journals or newspapers (print or online edition) that discusses how one company used CAD, CAE, robots, or other technological innovations to refit or reorganize its production operations.

1. What problems led the company to rethink its production process? What kind of technology did it choose to address these problems? What goals did the company set for applying technology in this way?

2. Before adding the new technology, what did the company do to analyze its existing production process? What changes, if any, were made as a result of this analysis?

3. How did technology-enhanced production help the company achieve its goals for financial performance? For customer service? For growth or expansion?

Exploring the Best of the Web

URLs for all Internet exercises are provided at the website for this book, www.prenhall.com/bovee. *When you log on to the text website, select Chapter 9, then select "Student Resources," click on the name of the featured website, and review the website to complete these exercises.*

Explore these chapter-related websites, review their content, and answer the following questions for each website you visit:

1. What is the purpose of this website?

2. What kinds of information does this website contain? Please be specific.

3. How is this information provided at this website useful for businesspeople? Consumers?

4. How did you expand your knowledge of operations management by reviewing the material at this website? What new things did you learn about this topic?

Step Inside ISO Online

The International Organization for Standardization (ISO) is a worldwide federation of national standards bodies from some 130 countries, one from each country. Established in 1947, ISO is a nongovernmental organization with the following mission: to promote the development of standardization and related activities in the world with a view to facilitating the international exchange of goods and services, and to developing cooperation in the spheres of intellectual, scientific, technological, and economic activity. Step inside ISO Online and take a closer look at how ISO standards are developed, why international standardization is needed, and what fields are covered by ISO standards. www.iso.ch

Make Quality Count

In today's competitive business environment, companies have to be concerned about the quality of their goods and services. For information and advice, many turn to the American Society for Quality (ASQ). There you can find out about ISO 9000 and the Malcolm Baldrige Award. Find out who Malcolm Baldrige was and why the award was established. Discover how winning companies are selected, which companies have won the award, and how the award differs from ISO 9000. Follow the links to other quality-related websites. At the ASQ, quality is only a click away. www.asq.org

Follow This Path to Continuous Improvement

The business of manufacturing is more complex than ever before. Today's operations managers must address the conflicting needs of customers, suppliers, employees, and shareholders. Discover why many operations managers turn to *Industry Week* magazine to stay on top of trends, technologies, and strategies to help drive continuous improvement throughout their organization. Log on to this magazine's website and read about the world's best-managed companies. Find out which manufacturing plants have won awards. Check out the surveys and special industry reports. Take a peek at the factories of the future. Don't leave without browsing the current articles or reviewing the glossary of manufacturing terms. www.industryweek.com

Learning Interactively

Companion Website

Visit the Companion Website at www.prenhall.com/bovee. For Chapter 9, take advantage of the interactive "Study Guide" to test your chapter knowledge. Get instant feedback on whether you need additional studying. Read the "Current Events" articles to get the latest on chapter topics, and complete the exercises as specified by your instructor. Expand your learning with a visit to the "Research Area." There you will find a wealth of information you can use to complete your course assignments.

A CASE FOR CRITICAL THINKING

Porsche—Back in the Fast Lane

The German automaker Porsche enjoyed a long ride of success with its sleek, high-performance sports cars, cruising straight into the hearts of both consumers and racing fans with the introduction of its first model back in 1948. Producing such classics as the 356, the 550 Spyder, and the legendary 911, Porsche garnered a winning reputation for engineering excellence and for its victories in the racing world. Owning a Porsche became the ultimate fantasy of car lovers around the world, and the company's annual sales grew to more than 50,000 cars by the mid-1980s. Then everything changed, driving Porsche toward a collision course with disaster.

Faced with a global recession during the early 1990s, consumers postponed buying cars—especially expensive sports cars. Demand dropped sharply for Porsche's 911 model, and sales plummeted by nearly 75 percent. By the time Wendelin Wiedeking took over the company's production and materials management, Porsche was racing toward record losses of $150 million.

Few people believed Wiedeking could get Porsche back on track. After all, the German engineer was the fourth person in five years to manage the company. But Wiedeking was determined to save Porsche from bankruptcy. "It was a question of 'to be or not to be'—as simple as that," Wiedeking recalls.

Steering away from Disaster

To start the process of implementing changes, Wiedeking obtained benchmarks on every aspect of production by measuring the amount of time, money, and effort that was being spent on making a Porsche. Then he compared Porsche's production methods to those of Japanese automakers. After touring the production facilities of Honda, Toyota, and Nissan, Wiedeking and his managers were convinced they could apply the Japanese's lean, efficient production system at Porsche and turn the company around by slashing production costs and increasing productivity. Back at home, Wiedeking launched an improvement program to eliminate waste and to establish standards for quality and efficiency. Moreover, he paved the way for change by simplifying the management structure and assigning new responsibilities to every employee.

Meeting Challenges Head-On

Despite Wiedeking's efforts, Porsche's losses continued to mount. Drastic measures were needed to save the company, and Wiedeking had to act fast. He needed to overhaul the entire production system, and he needed the full cooperation of every worker to implement the changes. So he consulted a team of former Toyota managers who were experts in the concept of *kaizen*, a system developed by Toyota that emphasized continuous improvement in the quality of production.

The consultants quickly pointed out ways to save time and effort in Porsche's production assembly process. Under the existing system, for example, workers searched through shelves crammed with 30 days of inventory to find the components for assembling an engine. To save time and distance, the consultants replaced the shelves with robotic carts that carried the necessary parts for one engine straight to workers on the assembly line.

A New Sense of Direction

Wiedeking worked swiftly to implement the new production methods throughout the entire assembly process. He slashed the company's spiraling costs and introduced leaner, more flexible production processes. Then to keep things even leaner, Porsche began outsourcing everything it could get away with—working hand in hand with suppliers to improve products and delivery schedules. Within a week of implementing the changes, productivity increased dramatically.

As the company began to recover, Wiedeking instructed Porsche's engineers to apply the concepts of lean production to the development process. Instead of building expensive prototypes, the engineers used computer simulation to revamp the 911 model and to design a new two-seat roadster, the Boxster. They also incorporated the 911's basic engine and parts into the new Boxster and created a common assembly line to produce the two cars, eliminating waste and saving time and money. As a result, Porsche's profits leaped into high gear, totaling $50 million on sales of $2.2 billion in 1996.

Driving the Future

Thanks to Wiedeking's dramatic turnaround of the company, Porsche was back in the fast lane at the close of the century. After implementing the production changes, the company slashed production time for each 911 from 120 to 30 hours, built more engines with half the space, decreased the number of manufacturing defects, and cut its stockpiles of inventory from seven days to one. The company even established a new division, Porsche Consulting, to advise other businesses on how to improve productivity. Porsche is now the world's most profitable auto company. The company manufactures some 50,000 cars a year (compared to GM's 8.6 million) and boasts the highest profit margins of any manufacturer in the automobile industry.

Critical Thinking Questions

1. Why did Porsche run into problems during the early 1990s?

2. What steps did Wiedeking take to overhaul Porsche's production methods?

3. Why does Porsche outsource manufacturing functions to suppliers?

4. Go to Chapter 9 of this text's website at www.prenhall. com/bovee and click on the hot link to get the Porsche website. Review the website so you can answer these questions: What has Porsche learned from its past mistakes? Is Porsche prepared to meet the competitive and business challenges of the future? Does Porsche consider its relatively small company size an advantage or disadvantage? Why?

VIDEO CASE

Managing Production Around the World: Body Glove

Learning Objectives

The purpose of this video is to help you:

1. Recognize the production challenges faced by a growing company.

2. Understand the importance of quality in the production process.

3. Discuss how and why a company may shift production operations to other countries and other companies.

Synopsis

Riding the wave of public interest in water sports, Body Glove began manufacturing wetsuits in the 1950s. The founders, dedicated surfers and divers, came up with the idea of making the wetsuits from neoprene, offering more comfortable insulation than the rubber wetsuits of the time. The high costs of neoprene and labor were major considerations in Body Glove's eventual decision to have its wetsuits made in Thailand. The company's constant drive for higher quality was also a factor. Now company management can focus on building Body Glove's image as a California lifestyle brand without worrying about inventory and other production issues. In licensing its brand for a wide range of goods and services—from cell phone cases to flotation devices, footwear, resorts, and more—Body Glove has created a network of partners around the world.

Discussion Questions

1. *For analysis:* Even though Body Glove makes its wetsuits in Thailand, why must its managers continually research how U.S. customers use its products?

2. *For analysis:* Which aspects of product quality would wetsuit buyers be most concerned about?

3. *For application:* When deciding whether to license its name for a new product, what production issues might Body Glove's managers research in advance?

4. *For application:* How might Body Glove's Thailand facility use forecasts of seasonal demand to plan production?

5. *For debate:* Should the products that Body Glove does not manufacture be labeled to alert buyers that they are produced under license? Support your chosen position.

Online Exploration

Visit the Body Glove website at www.bodyglove.com and follow the links to read the Body Glove story and see the variety of products sold under the Body Glove brand. Also look at the electronics products, including the cell phone cases. Then browse the contacts listing to find out which U.S. and international companies have licensed the Body Glove brand for different products. How do these licensed products fit with the Body Glove brand image? What challenges might Body Glove face in coordinating its work with so many different companies and licensed products?

PART 3

Mastering Global and Geographical Skills—Why Is the Silicon Valley in California Rather than Colorado or Kentucky?

Comparing geographic information about companies and industries can lead to some interesting questions. For some industries, patterns of location and development seem fairly obvious. Florida has an ideal climate for citrus trees. Various cities along the East, West, and Gulf coasts have excellent natural harbors, which aided the development of a healthy shipping industry in those areas. Sometimes studying physical geography leads you to answers fairly quickly. And why are so many high-tech companies located in California's Silicon Valley (an area encompassing San Jose, Santa Clara, Palo Alto, and surrounding cities south of San Francisco)?

In other industries, however, the geographic connection seems weaker. For instance, why is so much of the insurance industry centered in Hartford, Connecticut? Why is Washington's manufacturing output (measured in dollar value) so much higher than Maryland's, even though the two states have similar populations?[38] Why are the three largest U.S. steel producers headquartered in Ohio and Pennsylvania when most iron ore (source of the primary ingredient in steel) is mined in Minnesota, Michigan, Utah, and Missouri?

Exploring these geographic patterns helps you understand how industries develop and how they affect local and regional economies and societies. Choose one of the following five industries:

- Computer software
- Automobiles
- Carpeting
- Commercial passenger aircraft
- Poultry processing

Using the research tools in your library and on the Internet, answer these questions:

1. Where did the industry start in the United States?
2. Who are the biggest competitors today?
3. Where are they located?
4. What influence has geography had on the industry's growth?
5. How strong is the influence of physical geography compared with the influence of other factors (such as where an industry pioneer happened to be living or where the cost for labor happened to be less expensive)?
6. Search the World Wide Web for specific companies in the industry you are researching. Visit the companies' websites, and find out in how many different geographic locations each company now operates. Based on your research and on what you have learned from the text, what are some of the factors that have influenced the geographic expansion of these particular companies?

CHAPTER

10

Employee Motivation, Today's Workforce, and Labor Relations

LEARNING OBJECTIVES

After studying this chapter, you will be able to

1. Identify and explain four important theories of employee motivation

2. Highlight three demographic challenges employers are facing in today's workplace

3. Discuss three staffing challenges employers are facing in today's workplace

4. Discuss three popular alternative work arrangements companies are offering their employees

5. Explain the two steps unions take to become the bargaining agent for a group of employees

6. Cite three options unions can exercise when negotiations with management break down

7. Cite three options management can exercise when negotiations with a union break down

EXHIBIT 10.1
Management by Objectives
The MBO process has four steps. This cycle is refined and repeated as managers and employees at all levels work toward establishing goals and objectives, thereby accomplishing the organization's strategic goals.

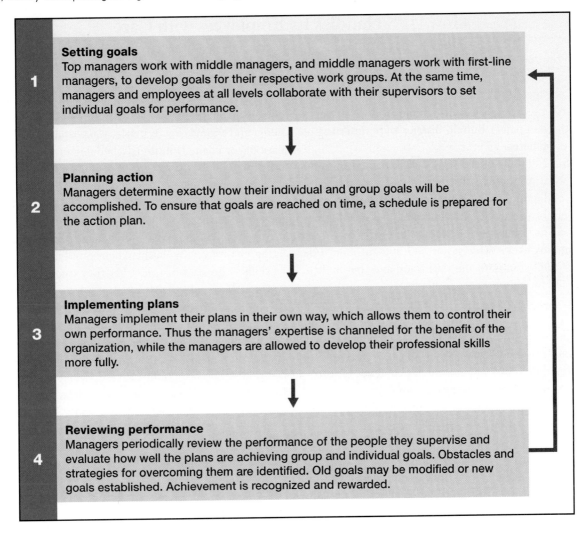

1 **Setting goals**
Top managers work with middle managers, and middle managers work with first-line managers, to develop goals for their respective work groups. At the same time, managers and employees at all levels collaborate with their supervisors to set individual goals for performance.

2 **Planning action**
Managers determine exactly how their individual and group goals will be accomplished. To ensure that goals are reached on time, a schedule is prepared for the action plan.

3 **Implementing plans**
Managers implement their plans in their own way, which allows them to control their own performance. Thus the managers' expertise is channeled for the benefit of the organization, while the managers are allowed to develop their professional skills more fully.

4 **Reviewing performance**
Managers periodically review the performance of the people they supervise and evaluate how well the plans are achieving group and individual goals. Obstacles and strategies for overcoming them are identified. Old goals may be modified or new goals established. Achievement is recognized and rewarded.

consequences by behaving in the desired way. For example, fear of losing a job (unpleasant consequences) may move an employee to finish a project on time (desired behavior). Such negative motivation, however, is much less effective than encouraging an individual's own sense of direction, creativity, and pride in doing a good job.

Another proven motivation technique used by many organizations is **management by objectives (MBO)**, a companywide process that empowers employees and involves them in goal setting and decision making. This process consists of four steps: setting goals, planning actions, implementing plans, and reviewing performance (see Exhibit 10.1). Because employees at all levels are involved in all four steps, they learn more about company objectives and feel that they are an important part of the companywide team. Furthermore, they understand how even their small job function contributes to the organization's long-term success.

One of the key elements of MBO is a collaborative goal-setting process. Together, a manager and employee define the employee's goals, the responsibilities for achieving those goals, and the means of evaluating individual and group performance so that the employee's activities are directly linked to achieving the organization's long-term goals. Jointly setting clear and challenging—but achievable—goals can encourage employees to reach higher levels of performance. MBO and behavior modification are two ways companies motivate

management by objectives (MBO)
A motivational tool whereby managers and employees work together to structure personal goals and objectives for every individual, department, and project to mesh with the organization's goals

Managing in the 21st Century

How UPS Handles Its Employees with Care

How does a company keep its employees engaged when the work isn't exactly engaging? UPS struggled with that question in the late 1990s, when part-time workers who load, unload, and sort packages in the company's Buffalo district were deserting at the rate of 50 percent a year.

UPS's 270,000-square-foot distribution center in Buffalo, New York, is an austere, three-story-high maze of belts and ramps. Every hour or so throughout the night, a big brown truck backs into a bay, where employees unload its packages and place them on a conveyor belt—one box every three seconds; 1,200 an hour. The packages don't stop until the shift does, and there's little opportunity for chitchat.

To produce a dramatic change in this work environment, UPS had to come up with a winning solution. After talking to employees, UPS management learned that many employees who were hired as part-timers wanted full-time jobs, which rarely opened up. So management started emphasizing the benefits of part-time jobs: short, flexible shifts that could complement the schedules of students.

Next, UPS strived to create a positive work environment: The company improved lighting throughout the building and upgraded break rooms to make them feel more inviting. It installed more personal computers on the floor, giving workers easier access to training materials and human-resources information on the company's intranet. And the company tried to make work more fun. Management added after-hours outings such as baseball games, a basketball tournament, and floorwide "super loader" contests. "We know that these are monotonous jobs," says one UPS manager. "We want to make them less mechanical and more social. People don't want to feel like robots."

UPS also recognized that "what motivates people changes over the course of their careers." College students and moms, for example, tend to need occasional days off or changes in their schedules—the sort of flexibility that supervisors in UPS's demanding production system weren't eager to grant. But it turned out to be something that was relatively easy to do. "Instead of just saying, 'We can't do this,' we started looking at ways we could do it," recalls one UPS manager. Moreover, college kids aren't especially loyal to their jobs, but they are loyal to skills—the kind of skills that they can apply to other work as they build their careers. So UPS began offering its employees Saturday classes for computer-skill development and career-planning discussions.

Finally, UPS realized that not everyone wants to spend the rest of his or her life loading and unloading boxes. "People are going to leave," acknowledges UPS. But now they will leave after years instead of weeks. And instead of worrying about them leaving, UPS now takes an interest in their future. "We had to learn that part of making people successful means letting go." That was the crucial insight that now helps UPS attract and keep young workers in Buffalo.

Questions for Critical Thinking

1. Why were UPS part-time package loaders leaving the company?
2. What changes did UPS make to encourage part-timers to stay?

---

employees to perform. As you can imagine, humans are motivated by many factors. Thus, the challenge for managers is to select motivators that will inspire employees to achieve organizational goals. But which ones are the most effective? Several theories of motivation have attempted to answer that question.

1 LEARNING OBJECTIVE

Identify and explain four important theories of employee motivation

Theories of Motivation

Motivation has been a topic of interest to managers for more than a hundred years. Frederick W. Taylor was a machinist and engineer from Philadelphia who became interested in employee efficiency and motivation late in the 19th century. Taylor developed

EXHIBIT 10.2
Maslow's Hierarchy of Needs
According to Maslow, lower-level work-related needs such as salary and insurance must be satisfied before employees will focus on higher-level needs such as job recognition and leadership.

scientific management, an approach that sought to improve employee efficiency through the scientific study of work. In Taylor's view, people were motivated almost exclusively by money, so he set up pay systems that rewarded employees when they were productive. Under Taylor's piecework system, for example, employees who just met or fell short of the quota were paid a certain amount for each unit produced. Those who produced more were paid a higher rate for *all* units produced, not just for those that exceeded the quota; this pay system gave employees a strong incentive to boost productivity.

scientific management
Management approach designed to improve employees' efficiency by scientifically studying their work

Although money has always been a powerful motivator, scientific management fails to take into account other motivational elements, such as opportunities for personal satisfaction or individual initiative. Thus, scientific management can't explain why someone still wants to work even though his or her spouse already makes a good living or why a Wall Street lawyer will take a hefty pay cut to serve in government. Therefore, other researchers have looked beyond money to discover what else motivates people.

Maslow's Hierarchy of Needs   In 1943 psychologist Abraham Maslow proposed the theory that behavior is determined by different types of needs, which can be organized into five categories and then arranged in a hierarchy. As Exhibit 10.2 shows, the most basic needs are at the bottom of this hierarchy, and the more advanced needs are toward the top. In Maslow's hierarchy, all of the requirements for basic survival—food, clothing, shelter, and the like—fall into the category of *physiological needs*. These basic needs must be satisfied before the person can consider higher-level needs such as *safety needs*, *social needs* (the need to give and receive love and to feel a sense of belonging), and *esteem needs* (the need for a sense of self-worth and integrity).

At the top of Maslow's hierarchy is *self-actualization*—the need to become everything one can become. This need is also the most difficult to fulfill. Employees who reach this point work not only to make money or to impress others but also because they feel their work is worthwhile and satisfying in itself. Self-actualization needs partially explain why some people make radical career changes or strike out on their own as entrepreneurs.

Although Maslow's hierarchy is a convenient way to classify human needs, it would be a mistake to view it as a rigid sequence. A person need not completely satisfy each level of needs before being motivated by a higher need. Indeed, at any one time, most people are motivated by a combination of needs.

Herzberg's Two-Factor Theory   In the 1960s Frederick Herzberg and his associates undertook their own study of human needs. They asked accountants and engineers to

EXHIBIT 10.3
Two-Factor Theory
Hygiene factors such as working conditions and company policies can influence employee dissatisfaction. On the other hand, motivators such as opportunities for achievement and recognition can influence employee satisfaction.

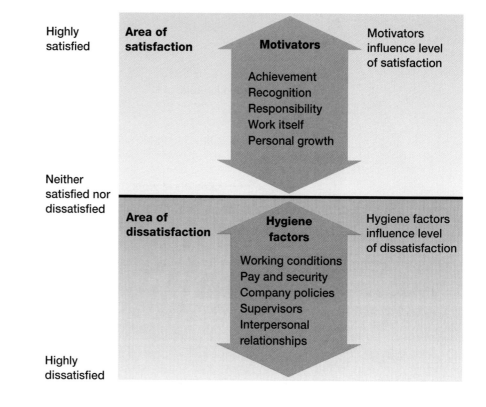

hygiene factors
Aspects of the work environment that are associated with dissatisfaction

motivators
Factors of human relations in business that may increase motivation

Theory X
Managerial assumption that employees are irresponsible, unambitious, and distasteful of work and that managers must use force, control, or threats to motivate them

Theory Y
Managerial assumption that employees like work, are naturally committed to certain goals, are capable of creativity, and seek out responsibility under the right conditions

describe specific aspects of their jobs that made them feel satisfied or dissatisfied. Upon analyzing the results, they found that two entirely different sets of factors were associated with satisfying and dissatisfying work experiences: *hygiene factors* and *motivators* (see Exhibit 10.3).

What Herzberg called **hygiene factors** are associated with *dissatisfying* experiences. The potential sources of dissatisfaction include working conditions, company policies, and job security. Management can lessen worker dissatisfaction by improving hygiene factors that concern employees, but such improvements seldom influence satisfaction. On the other hand, managers can help employees feel more motivated and, ultimately, more satisfied by paying attention to **motivators** such as achievement, recognition, responsibility, and other personally rewarding factors. Herzberg's theory is related to Maslow's hierarchy of needs: The motivators closely resemble the higher-level needs, and the hygiene factors resemble the lower-level needs.

Should managers concentrate on motivators or on hygiene factors? It depends. A skilled, well-paid, middle-class, middle-aged employee may be motivated to perform better if motivators are supplied. However, a young, unskilled worker who earns low wages, or an employee who is insecure, will probably still need the support of strong hygiene factors to reduce dissatisfaction before the motivators can be effective.

McGregor's Theory X and Theory Y In the 1960s psychologist Douglas McGregor identified two radically different sets of assumptions that underlie most management thinking. He classified these sets of assumptions into two categories: *Theory X* and *Theory Y* (see Exhibit 10.4).

According to McGregor, managers with a **Theory X** approach believe that employees dislike work and can be motivated only by the fear of losing their jobs or by *extrinsic rewards* such as money, promotions, and tenure. This management style emphasizes physiological and safety needs and tends to ignore the higher-level needs in Maslow's hierarchy. In contrast, managers with a **Theory Y** orientation believe that employees like work and can be motivated by working for goals that promote creativity or for causes they believe in. Thus, Theory Y–oriented managers seek to motivate employees through *intrinsic rewards*.

THEORY X	THEORY Y
1. Employees inherently dislike work and will avoid it whenever possible.	1. Employees like work and consider it as natural as play and rest.
2. Because employees dislike work, they must be threatened with punishment to achieve goals.	2. People naturally work toward goals they are committed to.
3. Employees will avoid responsibilities whenever possible.	3. The average person can learn to accept and even seek responsibility.
4. Employees value security above all other job factors.	4. The average person's intellectual potential is only partially realized.

EXHIBIT 10.4
Theory X and Theory Y
McGregor proposed two distinct views of human nature: The assumptions of Theory X are basically negative, whereas those of Theory Y are basically positive.

The assumptions behind Theory X emphasize authority; the assumptions behind Theory Y emphasize growth and self-direction. It was McGregor's belief that, although some employees need the strong direction demanded by Theory X, those who are ready to realize their social, esteem, and self-actualization needs will not work well under Theory X assumptions.[5]

Ouchi's Theory Z Another perspective on motivation was developed by William Ouchi, who studied Japanese and U.S. management practices. Ouchi's **Theory Z** assumes that employees are more motivated if you involve them in all aspects of company decision making and treat them like family. Managers who adopt these practices believe that employees with a sense of identity and belonging are more likely to perform their jobs conscientiously and will try more enthusiastically to achieve company goals. Embraced in one form or another by most Fortune 500 companies, Theory Z is the core of such practices as self-directed work teams, quality circles, and other forms of participative management that make employees more responsible for the outcome of their efforts.

Theory Z
Human relations approach that emphasizes involving employees at all levels and treating them like family

Keeping Pace with Today's Workforce

When trying to apply motivational techniques, managers must keep in mind that today's workforce comprises people with a wide variety of needs. They must recognize that employees come from a diversity of backgrounds and have interests and obligations outside of work, such as family, volunteer activities, and hobbies. Addressing employees' many needs becomes even more critical in a work environment plagued with a number of demographic and staffing challenges.

Demographic Challenges

The U.S. workforce is undergoing significant changes that require major alterations in how managers keep employees happy and productive. One of the most significant demographic trends facing companies today is increasing workforce diversity.

Workforce Diversity The U.S. workforce is diverse in race, gender, age, culture, family structures, religion, and educational backgrounds—and will become even more diverse in the years ahead. Although nearly three-fourths of the U.S. population is still classified as white, that's changing fast. By 2050 whites will represent only 53 percent of the U.S. population. Hispanics will make up about 24 percent, African Americans 14 percent, Asian Americans 8 percent, and Native Americans 1 percent.[6]

2 LEARNING OBJECTIVE

Highlight three demographic challenges employers are facing in today's workplace

Managing this changing mixture of ages, races, values, and views is, of course, increasingly difficult. A diverse workforce brings with it a wide range of skills, traditions, backgrounds, experiences, outlooks, and attitudes toward work that can affect individuals' job performance. Moreover, a diverse workforce brings language and communication challenges. One trend contributing to the diversity of the U.S. workforce is the influx of immigrants.

Influx of Immigrants Immigrants—legal and illegal—now make up about 13 percent of the nation's workers, the highest percentage since the 1930s. They dominate job categories at both ends of the economic spectrum. Many fill the U.S. demand for nurses, doctors, scientists, and teachers. Others work in jobs that native-born Americans prefer not to do—such as meatpackers, hotel maids, hamburger flippers, waiters, gardeners, seamstresses, and construction workers. "There are places in this country where we wouldn't survive without immigrants," says a lobbyist for the American Hotel and Lodging Association.[7] The influx of immigrants to the United States is expected to continue and will help hold down wages in unskilled jobs in addition to providing companies with the numbers of employees they need in order to expand.

Diversity Initiatives To cope with increasing workforce diversity, many companies offer employees sensitivity or awareness training to help them understand the various attitudes and beliefs that minorities and immigrants bring to their jobs. At Allstate Insurance, for example, all nonagent employees with service of more than one year are expected to complete diversity training—a company investment in excess of 540,000 hours of classroom time.[8] And at the Marriott Marquis Hotel in New York, mandatory diversity-training classes teach managers how to avoid defining problems in terms of gender, culture, or race. These classes also help managers become more sensitive to the behavior and communication patterns of employees with diverse backgrounds.

The number of U.S. workers over 65 has edged up during the past decade from 3 million to 3.8 million and is expected to rise to 4.3 million by 2005. In the meantime, the number of workers aged 25–44 is falling.

Minority employees say they gain a sense of belonging in the workplace when their employers create opportunities for workers with diverse backgrounds to interact with others and become involved as part of a group. Moreover, a company's diversity efforts enable it to uncover new opportunities by rethinking primary tasks and redefining markets, products, strategies, missions, business practices, and even cultures. Consider the small public-interest law firm of Dewey & Levin. In the mid-1980s the firm had an all-white legal staff. Concerned about its ability to serve ethnically diverse populations, the firm hired a Hispanic female attorney. She introduced Dewey & Levin to new ideas about what kinds of cases to take on, and many of her ideas were pursued with great success. Hiring more women of color brought even more fresh perspectives. The firm now pursues cases that the original staff members would never have considered because they would not have understood the link between the issues involved in the cases and the firm's mission.[9] In short, diversity is an asset, and one of the challenges of corporate human relations is to make the most of this asset.

The Aging Population The population in the United States is aging, a situation that creates new challenges and concerns for employers and employees alike. About 84 percent of baby boomers participate in today's labor market.[10] Experts predict that because of inadequate pensions, high medical costs, large debts, and a general desire to stay active, many baby boomers will put off retirement until they are in their 70s. A study by the American Association for Retired People (AARP) reports that about 70 percent of workers age 45 and older plan to work in some capacity during their retirement years.[11]

Widespread delayed retirement presents challenges for all parties involved. For one thing, even though the 1967 Age Discrimination in Employment Act (ADEA) makes workers over 40 a protected class, charges of age discrimination filed with the Equal Employment Opportunity Commission (EEOC) are on the rise.[12] Also, older, more experienced employees command higher salaries. "For my salary, the company could hire two twenty-somethings," says a 41-year-old. "I'm good at what I do. But am I better than two people? Even I know that's not true." Not only do older employees earn more, but the costs of employee benefits such as medical insurance and pensions rise with age as well.[13] Furthermore, as the speed of change gets faster, it can be difficult for older employees to keep up unless they have the stamina of a 25-year-old.

Age has its advantages, of course. According to one recent study, older employees have more experience, better judgment, and a greater commitment to quality. They are also more likely to show up on time and less likely to quit. But these traits pale by comparison with the highly desired traits characteristic of younger workers, who appear to be more flexible, more adaptable, more accepting of new technology, and better at learning new skills.[14]

Gender-Related Issues Another demographic challenge companies have been grappling with for years is the gender gap in compensation. Women today earn about 76 percent of men's median pay.[15] Moreover, even though women now hold 46 percent of executive, administrative, and managerial positions (up from 34 percent in 1983), only 12 percent of the senior executives at Fortune 500 companies are women.[16] Some attribute this inequality to the *glass ceiling.*

The Glass Ceiling The **glass ceiling** is an invisible barrier that keeps women and minorities from reaching the highest-level positions. One theory about the glass ceiling suggests that top management has long been dominated by white males, who tend to hire and promote employees who look, act, and think as they do. Another theory holds that stereotyping by male middle managers leads them to believe that family life will interfere with a woman's work. As a result, women are relegated to less visible assignments in the company, so their work goes unnoticed by top executives and their careers stagnate.

glass ceiling
Invisible barrier attributable to subtle discrimination that keeps women out of the top positions in business

sexism
Discrimination on the basis of gender

In recent years, women have made significant strides toward overcoming the glass ceiling and **sexism**—job discrimination on the basis of gender—thanks to a combination of changing societal attitudes and company commitments to workplace diversity. A recent study by Catalyst, an organization that focuses on the advancement of female executives, reports that the percentage of women holding titles such as executive vice president and higher increased from 1.9 percent in 1995 to 7.9 percent in 2002. Moreover, nearly 16 percent of Fortune 500 corporate officers are now women, up from 12.5 percent in 2000 and 8.7 percent in 1995.[17]

Recent initiatives by corporations to advance women in the corporate hierarchy include long-term commitments to hiring more women, company-sponsored networking and career planning for women, diversity training and workshops, and mentoring programs designed to help female employees move more quickly through the ranks. Pitney Bowes's long-term commitment to diversity, for instance, has resulted in women holding 5 of the top 11 jobs at the company. Patagonia boasts that women now hold more than half of the company's top-paying jobs and almost 60 percent of managerial jobs. And the appointment of Carly Fiorina to CEO of Hewlett-Packard (HP) was hailed by many as a

Women hold only 12 percent of corporate-office positions and 12 percent of board seats at 500 of the largest companies.

milestone for women. With women accounting for more than a quarter of HP's managers, it seems that the glass ceiling at this company has been shattered. Still, the battle for equal opportunities for women persists at most companies.[18] Some say it will take an additional thirty-some years before women occupy half of all corporate officer jobs.[19]

sexual harassment
Unwelcome sexual advance, request for sexual favors, or other verbal or physical conduct of a sexual nature within the workplace

Sexual Harassment   Another sensitive issue that women often face in the workplace is sexual harassment. As defined by the EEOC, **sexual harassment** takes two forms: the obvious request for sexual favors with an implicit reward or punishment related to work, and the more subtle creation of a sexist environment in which employees are made to feel uncomfortable by off-color jokes, lewd remarks, and posturing. Even though male employees may also be targets of sexual harassment and both male and female employees may experience same-sex harassment, sexual harassment of female employees by male colleagues continues to make up the majority of reported cases.

In a recent survey, 21 percent of women and 7 percent of men reported being sexually harassed at work.[20] To put an end to sexual harassment, many companies are now enforcing strict harassment policies. Moreover, recent Supreme Court rulings explain (for the first time) how all employers—large and small—can insulate themselves from potential sexual harassment lawsuits. In short, a company can defend itself successfully if it can prove that it had an effective policy against sexual harassment in place and that the employee alleging harassment failed to take advantage of this policy. To be effective, the policy must be in writing, must be communicated to all employees, and must be enforced.[21] This means that the company must train all employees on the policy, and the company must have clear procedures for reporting such behavior—including allowing employees access to management other than their supervisors. Without such policies, companies can be held indirectly responsible for a harasser's actions even when top managers had no idea that such practices were going on.[22]

Staffing Challenges

3 LEARNING OBJECTIVE

Discuss three staffing challenges employers are facing in today's workplace

If you ask business leaders what their biggest challenges are today, you will most likely get these answers: finding, attracting, and keeping talented people; rightsizing their workforces; and satisfying employees' desire for a work–life balance.[23] Finding and keeping good workers is especially difficult for small-company owners, who often trail bigger companies in salary, benefits, job security, and other criteria that lead workers to choose one company over another.

Shortage of Skilled Labor   Even though many baby boomers are delaying retirement, fewer new workers exist to fill the vacancies that are created when baby boomers leave the workforce. This gap is creating a skilled-labor shortage for many businesses. Most affected are blue-collar jobs that require specialized skills or training. According to a recent survey by the National Association of Manufacturers, more than two-thirds of manufacturers are facing skilled-labor shortages. Companies like Hommer Tool and Manufacturing in Illinois claim that it is so hard to find skilled employees, they are reluctant to let people go even though business is down.[24]

To meet their skilled-labor needs, some companies are being creative. For instance, when UPS could not find the 6,000 additional employees the company needed for its growing air-freight business in Louisville, Kentucky, the company partnered with the city of Louisville to attract new employees to the area. Together they built "UPS University" and special dormitories so student-workers could sleep during the day, attend classes taught by professors from the University of Louisville at night, and then work the UPS graveyard shift (from 11:30 P.M. to 3:30 A.M.) and still have time to study.[25]

Rightsizing   In spite of this skilled-labor shortage, many companies are laying off employees or downsizing for a number of reasons. Weak revenues and profits are the primary force behind the massive employee layoffs. Other factors include company reorganizations, elimination of unprofitable product lines, outsourcing, mergers and acquisitions, and a general mismatch between employee job skills and job demands. In short, companies are trying to *rightsize*, or realign their workforces to match their current needs. For example, employees from Department A may be let go while new hires are sought to keep up with the growth demands of Department B. Such was the case at Hewlett-Packard when the company shed marketing jobs but added new positions in consulting and sales.[26]

Employee Loyalty   As you can imagine, layoffs and rightsizing take their toll on employee loyalty. The experience of losing a job is devastating and demoralizing. This is especially true for loyal employees who worked for the same company for years as well as new hires who were promised a bright future. For instance, during the 1990s the best and brightest talent earned fat signing bonuses, big salaries, and fancy perks. With their futures seemingly secure, many young and mid-career workers took on big debts and splurged on expensive houses, cars, and vacations. Now, they feel like a lost generation—worried that their peak earning years are behind them even as their expenses jump. Many laid-off workers now realize that the jobs they lost may never return, so they are striking out in new directions.

Devastated by the lack of job security, employees quickly learn to "do what's best for me," as Exhibit 10.5 shows. For some, that means putting job security and a long-term financial future ahead of finding challenging work. Public affairs specialist Yara Lizarraga didn't even consider looking for another job when her employer Agilent Technologies asked her to take a 10 percent pay cut. "If I said it didn't hurt, I'd be lying," says Lizarraga. "But I'm just so grateful to have a job."[27]

Like Lizarraga, today's employees have more realistic expectations. They recognize that the old idea of a paternal company taking care of employees has, for the most part, died. Hardworking, loyal employees no longer expect to move up the organizational hierarchy. Moreover, they know that companies are going to do whatever they have to do to succeed—including moving manufacturing to South America, eliminating layers of management, closing down plants, or cutting salaries and perks.

Employee Burnout   Employee layoffs and tough times can put pressure on remaining employees to work longer hours. "I'm tired, cranky, and frustrated," says one vice-president of a Chicago bank. "We don't have any support, so you have to do everything yourself."[28] Working long hours can lead to employee *burnout* or stress, which is characterized by emotional exhaustion, depersonalization, and lower levels of achievement. "When you feel under stress, you find your mental wheels spinning and you work mechanically rather than creatively," says one human resources expert. "The tasks that normally would take a few minutes sit unfinished for days because you lose the capacity to prioritize and you put off larger, important projects that take more energy and concentration." Severe burnout or stress may even lead to clinical depression.[29]

Employee burnout is notorious at high-end consulting companies such as McKinsey, Accenture, and Boston Consulting Group. Lured by promises of corporate luxury and high

CHARACTERISTIC	THEN	NOW
Attachment to employer	Long-term	Near-term
Readiness to change jobs	Not interested	Not looking (but will listen)
Priorities on the job	The firm and its goals	Personal life and career
Devotion to employer goals	Follows orders	Buys in (usually)
Effort on the job	100 percent	110 percent
Motto	Always faithful	Seize the day

EXHIBIT 10.5
The Committed Employee—Then and Now
Employee loyalty isn't what it used to be. A recent survey confirms that even today's most valuable committed workers often put career development and life and family issues ahead of company goals. This chart illustrates this shift in workforce commitment.

salaries, bright Ivy League graduates learned the hard way that in exchange for the perks, they were expected to work 70 to 100 hours a week through the best years of their lives. Now that many have been laid off, they wonder whether the tradeoff was worth it.[30]

Besides increasing employer demands, other workplace conditions that are fueling the pressure to work longer and harder hours are job insecurity, technological advancements, and information overload:

- *Job insecurity.* Workers anxious about job security feel they have to give 150 percent (or more) or risk being seen as expendable. What once were considered crisis-mode workloads have now become business as usual. In some cases, keeping your job means working extra hours, which don't always bring extra pay. Such conditions can leave employees feeling burned out and resentful.[31]

- *Technological advancements.* New technology allows employees to work from home. But being wired to the office 24 hours a day can add extra pressure. Commonplace tools such as laptop computers, mobile phones, personal digital assistants, and wireless and high-speed Internet access are blurring the boundaries between work and home.[32] "We have all these great tools to save our time," notes one career expert. "Instead, it just extends our week. We're never out of touch anymore."[33]

- *Information overload.* Managers claim they're unable to handle the vast amounts of information they now receive. In fact, more information has been produced in the past 30 years than the previous 5,000, and the total quantity of printed material is doubling every 5 years, and accelerating.[34]

Quality of Work Life   A recent survey by True Careers revealed that 70 percent of more than 1,500 respondents don't think there is a healthy balance between their work and personal lives.[35] For some employees the primary work–life issue is caring for an elder parent; for others it's child care, rising college tuition costs, or a desire to return to school part-time.[36] Regardless, achieving a work–life balance is especially difficult when both parents work or in situations in which downsizing and restructuring have left remaining employees with heavier workloads than in the past.

Europeans are known for a more balanced work–life style than Americans. Many Europeans enjoy six weeks of vacation annually and most European countries maintain a standard 35-hour workweek. The average German worker puts in about 1,400 hours a year, a 17 percent decrease from 1980, and far below the standard 2,000-plus hours for American workers. Nonetheless, shortened work hours do not necessarily mean less work. Many Europeans are complaining that they now squeeze the same amount of work into fewer hours, which means they must work harder on the job.[37]

To help U.S. employees balance the demands of work and family, businesses, such as SAS Institute, are offering child-care assistance, family leave, flexible work schedules, telecommuting, and other solutions that are explored later in this chapter and in Chapter 11. They are also focusing on improving the **quality of work life (QWL)**, the environment created by work and job conditions. Hewlett-Packard, for instance, is addressing the fundamental problems of how much time a job really demands and how to build a life beyond work by encouraging employees to set leisure goals and focus on developing their personal lives. As Hewlett-Packard knows, an improved QWL benefits both the individual and the organization. Employees gain the chance to use their specialized abilities, improve their skills, and balance their lives. The organization gains a more motivated and loyal employee.[38]

Two common ways of improving QWL are through **job enrichment**, which reduces specialization and makes work more meaningful by expanding each job's responsibilities, and **job redesign**, which restructures work to provide a better fit between employees' skills and their jobs. Quality of work life can be improved in other ways, too. Like SAS and Hewlett-Packard, many organizations are providing their employees with a number of ben-

quality of work life (QWL)
Overall environment that results from job and work conditions

job enrichment
Reducing work specialization and making work more meaningful by adding to the responsibilities of each job

job redesign
Designing a better fit between employees' skills and their work to increase job satisfaction

Thinking About Ethics

Hershey's Bittersweet Surrender

It's hard to find towns like Hershey, Pennsylvania anymore—where street lamps are shaped like Hershey kisses and streets bear names like Chocolate Avenue and Cocoa Avenue. Here generations of families all work for the same company, and here company, community, and charity intertwine. But the town, which has long proclaimed itself as the sweetest place on earth, is now bittersweet.

Milton Hershey opened his first chocolate factory in 1905, in what was then rich dairy farmland. The candy magnate was considered as much a philanthropist as an entrepreneur. So while building the chocolate empire, he also raised a town—erecting a bank, department store, churches, golf courses, zoo, trolley system, museum, hotel, free amusement park, and arena with more seats than town residents. But a school soon became his focus.

In 1909, Milton Hershey founded the Milton Hershey School, an academy for orphaned children. And in 1918, he put his entire share of Hershey stock, then valued at $60 million, into a charitable trust—directing the trust to funnel nearly all of its profits to the school and ensuring that the school—not chocolate—would be his legacy. Today the academy is set on 2,700 acres just southeast of downtown Hershey and has an endowment of some $5 billion. The school serves some 1,500 disadvantaged students, who get a free education, health care, and room and board. You eat a chocolate kiss and you're putting money in a trust for orphans.

To protect the assets of the Milton Hershey School, the 17 trustees (who govern the trust and ultimately the company) gradually reduced the trust's stake in Hershey stock from 80 percent to 50 percent of the trust's total assets. But in 2002, with corporate disasters such as Enron in the wind, the trustees considered a possible sale of Hershey Foods. By selling the trust's controlling interest in Hershey at a premium and reinvesting the money in diversified assets, they hoped to make the $5.9 billion Hershey trust even stronger.

But the town's reaction was so heated over the proposal it could have melted the 33 million chocolate Kisses the company produces daily. Huge protests from workers, retirees, and the officials of the township where the plant and school are located forced the trustees to turn down both a $12.5 billion offer from William Wrigley Jr. Co. and a joint offer of $11.2 billion from Nestlé and Cadbury Schweppes. The townspeople feared that a new owner would eliminate jobs and ruin the town's image as a paternalistic yet profitable sanctuary in the tooth-and-claw world of American commerce.

Meanwhile, the trustees learned that the right thing to do is not always the popular thing. But they also know that businesses such as Hershey don't come on the sales block very often. And they worry that the townspeople's victory may leave the perception that Hershey can never be sold. Moreover, they fear that they merely postponed changes that will eventually unravel the cocoon that Milton Hershey built. After all, you don't have to look far to see what can happen when the winds of change start to blow in a one-industry town. A few miles to the southeast of Hershey is the small city of Steelton. This town is still trying to recover from the collapse of Bethlehem Steel, the once-mighty company whose furnaces made girders for the Empire State Building but couldn't survive the global competition in the 1990s.

Questions for Critical Thinking

1. What ethical dilemma did the Hershey trustees face?
2. What impact did the quality of work life have on the trustees' decision?

---

efits designed to help them balance their work with personal responsibilities. Pepsi has an on-site dry cleaning drop-off at its New York headquarters, SAS Institute's on-site day-care center caters to over 700 children, and American Banker's Insurance Group and Hewlett-Packard have sponsored schools at company sites that allow employees to visit their children during lunchtime and after school. Such measures can improve employees' lives by freeing up their time and by making work a more enjoyable place to be.[39]

Alternative Work Arrangements

flextime
Scheduling system in which employees are allowed certain options regarding time of arrival and departure

To meet today's staffing challenges, many companies are also adopting alternative work arrangements. Three of the most popular arrangements are flextime, telecommuting, and job sharing. Many organizations find that a mix of these arrangements and other employee benefits works better than a one-size-fits-all approach.[40]

Flextime One increasingly important alternative work arrangement is **flextime**, a scheduling system that allows employees to choose their own hours within certain limits. For instance, a company may require everyone to be at work between 10:00 A.M. and 2:00 P.M., but employees may arrive or depart whenever they want as long as they work a total of 8 hours every day. Another popular flextime schedule is to work four 10-hour days each week, taking one prearranged day off (see Exhibit 10.6).

Whether it's a four-day week or staggered work hours, flexible work programs and the ability to control one's own work schedule are motivating factors for some. At accounting firm Ernst & Young (E&Y), all employees can be considered for the company's flextime program as long as they build a business case for it. Today, 1,600 of E&Y's employees formally take advantage of flextime options. Moreover, a recent E&Y survey showed that 84 percent of flextimers cite the program as the primary reason why they stay with the firm.[41]

Like E&Y, companies have found that flextime reduces turnover, enables the company to adapt to business cycles, allows operation of a round-the-clock business, and helps maintain morale and performance after reengineering or downsizing. Still, flextime is not without drawbacks. They include supervisors who feel uncomfortable and less in control when employees are coming and going, and co-workers who resent flextimers because they assume that people who work flexible hours don't take their jobs seriously enough.[42]

telecommuting
Working from home and communicating with the company's main office via computer and communication devices

Telecommuting Related to flexible schedules is **telecommuting**—working from home or another location using computers and telecommunications equipment to stay in touch with the employer's offices. An estimated 28.8 million Americans—one-fifth of the adult working population—worked from home, on the road, at a telework center, or at a satellite office at least one day a week in 2001.[43]

The trend toward "telework"—an umbrella term for all kinds of remote work from home, satellite offices, and the road—is stretching forecasters' definitions. While the exodus from traditional offices was once confined mostly to working from home, millions of people are now working in places forecasters never anticipated. Take Bob Long. As a global

EXHIBIT 10.6
9-to-5 Not for Everyone
For many full-time employees and independent contractors, their degree of job satisfaction is closely linked to the availability of these job conditions or attributes.

Full-time, permanent employees and independent contractors who say these are "extremely important" in job satisfaction:

	Full-time	Independent
Ability to work from home	15%	44%
Flexible work schedule	40%	62%
Freedom from office politics	44%	60%
Believing in what they do	72%	83%
Making right amount of money	50%	46%
Work they find challenging	55%	59%

field-sales manager from Dow Chemical, Long is about as easy to pin down as a tiger roaming Africa's Serengeti. He spends 10 percent of his time at Dow headquarters and divides the rest of his time about evenly among hotels, airports, cars, and his New Jersey home office, with brief stints elsewhere. One recent day, he even toyed with the idea of working out of gas stations. The sight of a fax machine and picturephone, installed near the station's ATM, sparked the idea.[44]

Today's organizations are investing more in technology, which makes telecommuting more feasible. Companies such as AT&T, IBM, and Lucent Technologies provide employees with laptops, dedicated phone lines, software support, fax-printer units, help lines, and full technical backup at the nearest corporate facility. Some even provide employees who work at home with a generous allowance for furnishings and equipment to be used at their discretion.[45] Still, some company operations clearly are not designed for telecommuting. For example, a printer who runs giant color presses can't run the presses from home. But for the kinds of jobs that can be performed from remote sites, telecommuting helps meet employees' needs for flexibility while boosting their productivity as much as 20 percent.[46]

Thanks to virtual-office technology, the definition of telecommuting has expanded.

Telecommuting offers other advantages too. It can save the company money by eliminating offices people don't need, consolidating others, and reducing related overhead costs.[47] It enables a company to hire talented people in distant areas without requiring them to relocate. This benefit expands the company's pool of potential job candidates because employees who have an employed spouse, children in school, or elderly parents are reluctant to move. Moreover, it allows employees to set their own hours, save on job-related expenses such as commuting costs, and spend more time with their families.

Still, telecommuting does have its limitations. The challenges of managing the cultural changes required by telecommuting are substantial. In telecommuting situations, midlevel managers relinquish direct, visual employee supervision. Some find it scary to be in the position of managing people they can't see. Others are concerned that people working at home will slack off or that telecommuting could cause resentment among office-bound colleagues or weaken company loyalty.[48] Regardless, companies are learning that you can't just give people computers, send them home, and call them telecommuters. You have to teach an employee how to think like a telecommuter.

Prospective telecommuters at Merrill Lynch, for example, must submit a detailed proposal that covers when and how they're going to work at home, and even what their home office will look like. Next they participate in a series of meetings. Finally, they spend two weeks in a simulation lab that lets employees and their managers experience the change. Once at home, telecommuters are required to document their at-home working hours and submit weekly progress reports.[49] But even for companies that provide support, some telecommuters are finding that this "ideal setup" is not for everyone.

Job Sharing Job sharing, which lets two employees share a single full-time job and split the salary and benefits, has been slowly gaining acceptance as a way to work part-time in a full-time position. According to a recent survey by Hewitt Associates (a firm specializing in employee benefits), 37 percent of employers offer job-sharing arrangements to their employees.[50] But such arrangements are usually offered to people who already work for the company and who need to cut back their hours. Rather than lose a good employee or have to find and train someone new, the company finds a way to split responsibilities.

job sharing
Splitting a single full-time job between two employees for their convenience

Consider UnumProvident, a leading provider of insurance products. When two of its employees approached the company about sharing a job, the company decided to let them do it. Now one employee works all day Monday and Tuesday, the other works all day Thursday and Friday, and the two overlap on Wednesday. The personal benefits are exactly what the employees had hoped for—more time at home. Meanwhile, the company benefits from the job sharing because the position is rarely left uncovered during times of vacation or illness and because two people, instead of just one person, bring their ideas and creativity to the job.[51]

Most companies have no hard and fast rules for splitting the work load in a job share arrangement. Some people split the day, others split the work week. Still others have overlapping days or work alternate weeks.

Working with Labor Unions

At the most basic level, employees want safe and comfortable working conditions and sufficient pay. At the same time, however, business owners must focus on using company resources to increase productivity and profits. In the best of times and in the most enlightened companies, these two sets of needs can often be met simultaneously. However, when the economy slows down and competition speeds up, balancing the needs of employees with those of management can be a challenge.

labor unions
Organizations of employees formed to protect and advance their members' interests

Because of this potential for conflict, many employees join **labor unions**, organizations that seek to protect employee interests by negotiating with employers for better wages and benefits, improved working conditions, and increased job security. Historically, labor unions have played an important role in U.S. employee-management relations and are largely responsible for the establishment of worker's compensation, child-labor laws, overtime rules, minimum-wage laws, severance pay, and more. (See Exhibit 10.7 for a summary of the most significant laws relating to labor unions.)

EXHIBIT 10.7
Key Legislation Relating to Unions
Most major labor legislation was enacted in the 1930s and 1940s. Subsequent legislation amends and clarifies earlier laws.

LEGISLATION	PROVISION
Norris-La Guardia Act of 1932	Limits companies' ability to obtain injunctions against union strikes, picketing, membership drives, and other activities.
National Labor Relations Act of 1935 (Wagner Act)	Gives employees the right to form, join, or assist labor organizations; the right to bargain collectively with employers through elected union representatives; and the right to engage in strikes, pickets, and boycotts. Prohibits certain unfair labor practices by the employer and union. Established the National Labor Relations Board to supervise union elections and to investigate charges of unfair labor practices by management.
Labor–Management Relations Act of 1947 (Taft–Hartley Act)	Amends Wagner Act to reaffirm employees' rights to organize and bargain collectively over working conditions. Establishes specific unfair labor practices both for management and for unions, and prohibits strikes in the public sector.
Landrum–Griffin Act of 1959	Amends Taft–Hartley Act and Wagner Act to control union corruption and to add the secondary boycott as an unfair labor practice. A secondary boycott occurs when a union appeals to firms or other unions to stop doing business with an employer who sells or handles goods of a company whose employees are on strike. The act requires all unions to file annual financial reports with the U.S. Department of Labor, making union officials more personally responsible for the union's financial affairs. The act guarantees individual member rights such as the right to vote in union elections, the right to sue unions, and the right to attend and participate in union meetings.
Plant-Closing Notification Act of 1988	Requires employers to give employees and local elected officials 60 days advance notice of plant shutdowns or massive layoffs.

Employees are most likely to turn to unions if they are deeply dissatisfied with their current job conditions, if they believe that unionization can be helpful in improving those conditions, and if they are willing to overlook negative stereotypes that have surrounded unions in recent years. Joining a union can give employees stronger bargaining power. By combining forces, union employees can put more pressure on management than they could as individuals. Still, not all employees support labor unions. Many believe that unions stifle individual initiative and are not necessary to ensure fair treatment from employers. Moreover, companies that have most successfully resisted unionization seem to have adopted participative management styles and an enhanced sense of responsibility toward employees.

Still, even the best working conditions are no guarantee that employees won't seek union representation. For instance, although Starbucks is renowned for its generous employee benefit programs and supportive work environment, employees at the company's stores in Vancouver, British Columbia, organized and successfully bargained for higher wages.[52]

How Unions Are Structured

Many unions are organized at local, national, and international levels. **Locals**, or local unions, represent employees in a specific geographic area or facility; an example is Local 1853, which represents GM's Saturn employees. Each local union is a hierarchy with a broad base of *rank-and-file* members, the employees the union represents. These members pay an initiation fee, pay regular dues, and vote to elect union officials. Each department or facility also has or elects a **shop steward**, who works in the facility as a regular employee and serves as a go-between with supervisors when a problem arises. In large locals and in locals that represent employees at several locations, an elected full-time **business agent** visits the various work sites to negotiate with management and enforce the union's agreements with those companies.

By comparison, a **national union** is a nationwide organization composed of many local unions that represent employees in specific locations; examples are the United Auto Workers (UAW) of America and the United Steelworkers of America. *International unions* have members in more than one country, such as the Union of Needletrades, Industrial, and Textile Employees (UNITE). A national union is responsible for such activities as organizing new areas or industries, negotiating industrywide contracts, assisting locals with negotiations, administering benefits, lobbying Congress, and lending assistance in the event of a strike. Local unions send representatives to the national delegate convention, submit negotiated contracts to the national union for approval, and provide financial support in the form of dues. They have the power to negotiate with individual companies or plants and to undertake their own membership activities.

The AFL-CIO is a **labor federation** consisting of a variety of national unions and of local unions that are not associated with any other national union. The AFL-CIO's two primary roles are to promote the political objectives of the labor movement and to provide assistance to member unions in their collective-bargaining efforts.[53] In recent years, the AFL-CIO has also become much more active in recruiting new members, organizing new locals, and publicizing unions in general.

How Unions Organize

Union organizers, whether professional or rank-and-file, generally start by visiting with employees, although dissatisfied employees may also approach the union (see Exhibit 10.8). The organizers survey employees by asking questions such as "Have you ever been treated unfairly by your supervisor?" Employees who express interest are sent information about the union, along with **authorization cards**—sign-up cards used to designate the union as their bargaining agent. If 30 percent or more of the employees in the group sign the union's

locals
Relatively small union groups, usually part of a national union or a labor federation, that represent members who work in a single facility or in a certain geographic area

shop steward
Union member and employee who is elected to represent other union members and who attempts to resolve employee grievances with management

business agent
Full-time union staffer who negotiates with management and enforces the union's agreements with companies

national union
Nationwide organization made up of local unions that represent employees in locations around the country

labor federation
Umbrella organization of national unions and unaffiliated local unions that undertakes large-scale activities on behalf of their members and that resolves conflicts between unions

5 **LEARNING OBJECTIVE**

Explain the two steps unions take to become the bargaining agent for a group of employees

authorization cards
Sign-up cards designating a union as the signer's preferred bargaining agent

EXHIBIT 10.8
The Union-Organizing Process
This diagram summarizes the steps a labor union takes when organizing a group of employees and becoming certified to represent them in negotiations with management. The certification election is necessary only if management is unwilling to recognize the union.

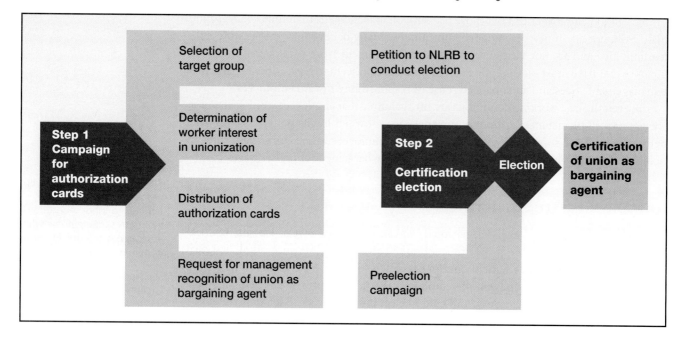

authorization cards, the union may ask management to recognize it. Usually, however, unions do not seek to become the group's bargaining agent unless a majority of the employees sign.

Often the company's management is unwilling to recognize the union at this stage. The union can then ask the National Labor Relations Board (NLRB), an independent federal agency created in 1935, to administer and enforce the National Labor Relations Act, to supervise a **certification** election, the process by which a union becomes the official bargaining agent for a company's employees. If a majority of the affected employees choose to make the union their bargaining agent, the union becomes certified. If not, that union and all other unions have to wait a year before trying again.

Once a company becomes aware that a union is seeking a certification election, management may mount an active campaign to point out the disadvantages of unionization. A company is not allowed, however, to make specific threats or promises about how it will respond to the outcome of the election, and it is not allowed to change general wages or working conditions until the election has been concluded.

Even when a union wins a certification election, there's no guarantee that it will represent a particular group of employees forever. Sometimes employees become dissatisfied with their union and no longer wish to be represented by it. When this happens, the union members can take a **decertification** vote to take away the union's right to represent them. If the majority votes for decertification, the union is removed as the bargaining agent.

certification
Process by which a union is officially recognized by the National Labor Relations Board as the bargaining agent for a group of employees

decertification
Process employees use to take away a union's official right to represent them

collective bargaining
Process used by unions and management to negotiate work contracts

The Collective Bargaining Process

As long as a union has been recognized as the exclusive bargaining agent for a group of employees, its main job is to negotiate employment contracts with management. In a process known as **collective bargaining**, union and management negotiators work together to forge the human resources policies that will apply to the unionized employees—and other employees covered by the contract—for a certain period, usually three years.

EXHIBIT 10.9
The Collective Bargaining Process
Contract negotiations go through the four basic steps shown here.

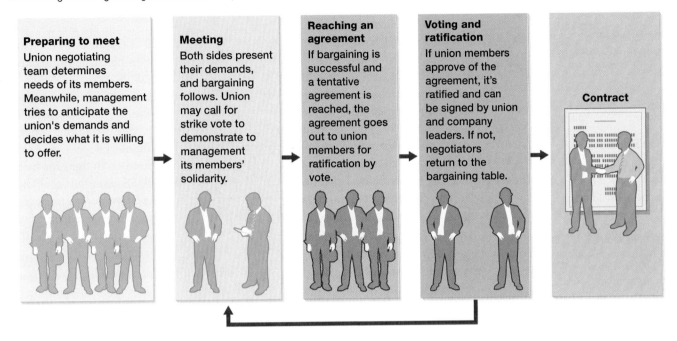

Preparing to meet
Union negotiating team determines needs of its members. Meanwhile, management tries to anticipate the union's demands and decides what it is willing to offer.

Meeting
Both sides present their demands, and bargaining follows. Union may call for strike vote to demonstrate to management its members' solidarity.

Reaching an agreement
If bargaining is successful and a tentative agreement is reached, the agreement goes out to union members for ratification by vote.

Voting and ratification
If union members approve of the agreement, it's ratified and can be signed by union and company leaders. If not, negotiators return to the bargaining table.

Contract

Most labor contracts are a compromise between the desires of union members and those of management. The union pushes for the best possible deal for its members, and management tries to negotiate agreements that are best for the company (and the shareholders, if a corporation is publicly held). Exhibit 10.9 illustrates the collective bargaining process.

Meeting and Reaching an Agreement   When the negotiating teams made up of representatives of the union and management actually sit down together, they state their opening positions and each side discusses its position point by point. Labor usually wants additions to the current contract. In a cooperative atmosphere, the real issues behind the demands gradually come to light. For example, management may begin by demanding the right to determine the sizes of work crews when all it really wants is smaller work crews; the union, however, wants to protect the jobs of its members and keep crew sizes as large as possible but may agree to certain reductions in exchange for, say, higher pay. After many stages of bargaining, each party presents its package of terms, and any gaps between labor and management demands are then dealt with.

If negotiations reach an impasse, outside help may be needed. The most common alternative is **mediation**—bringing in an impartial third party to study the situation and make recommendations for resolving the differences. Mediators are generally well-respected community leaders whom both sides will listen to. However, mediators can only offer suggestions, and their solutions are not binding. When a legally binding settlement is needed, the negotiators may submit to **arbitration**—a process in which an impartial referee listens to both sides and then makes a judgment by accepting one side's view. In *compulsory arbitration*, the parties are required by a government agency to submit to arbitration; in *voluntary arbitration*, the parties agree on their own to use arbitration to settle their differences.

mediation
Process for resolving a labor-contract dispute in which a neutral third party meets with both sides and attempts to steer them toward a solution

arbitration
Process for resolving a labor-contract dispute in which an impartial third party studies the issues and makes a binding decision

Exercising Options When Negotiations Break Down   The vast majority of management-union negotiations are settled quickly, easily, and in a businesslike manner. Nevertheless, sometimes negotiations reach an impasse, and neither side is willing to compromise. Both labor and management are able to draw on many powerful options when negotiations or mediation procedures break down.

6 **LEARNING OBJECTIVE**

Cite three options unions can exercise when negotiations with management break down

strike
Temporary work stoppage by employees who want management to accept their union's demands

picketing
Strike activity in which union members march before company entrances to persuade nonstriking employees to walk off the job and to persuade customers and others to cease doing business with the company

boycott
Union activity in which members and sympathizers refuse to buy or handle the product of a target company

Labor's Options   Strikes and picket lines are perhaps labor's best-known tactics, but other options are also used.

- *Strike.* The most powerful weapon that organized labor can use is the **strike**, a temporary work stoppage aimed at forcing management to accept union demands. An essential part of any strike is **picketing**, in which union members positioned at entrances to company premises march back and forth with signs and leaflets, trying to persuade nonstriking employees to join them and to persuade customers and others to stop doing business with the company. The basic idea behind the strike is that, in the long run, it costs management more in lost earnings to resist union demands than to give in. A 15-day strike by UPS drivers in 1997 cost the company $750 million in lost revenue. Teamsters officials were concerned about the company's growing reliance on part-time employees, who were paid half the hourly rate of full-time workers. So the union geared up to fight for better pay for part-timers, more full-time jobs, and better benefits. As UPS customers took their business to competitors, management worried that the defectors might never return. The loss of business and pressure from customers eventually forced UPS management to settle the strike—agreeing to nearly every union demand, including the creation of 2,000 full-time positions annually for the duration of the five-year contract.[54]

- *Boycott.* A less direct union weapon is the **boycott**, in which union members and sympathizers refuse to buy or handle the product of a target company. Millions of union members form an enormous bloc of purchasing power, which may be able to pressure management into making concessions. One of the best-known boycotts was the grape boycott organized by Cesar Chavez in the early 1970s. To pressure California growers into accepting the United Farm Workers (UFW) as the bargaining agent for previously unorganized farm laborers, he and his colleagues persuaded an estimated 17 million people in the United States to stop buying grapes. Eventually, the California legislature passed the country's first law guaranteeing farmworkers the right to hold union elections.[55]

- *Publicity.* Increasingly, labor is pressing its case by launching publicity campaigns, often called *corporate campaigns*, against the target company and companies affiliated with it. These campaigns might include sending investors alerts that question the firm's solvency, staging rallies during peak business hours, sending letters to charitable groups questioning executives' motives, handing out leaflets that allege safety and health-code violations, and stimulating negative stories in the press.

Labor's other options include *slowdowns*, in which employees continue to do their jobs but at a snail's pace, and *sickouts*, in which employees feign illness and stay home. Both can cripple a company. For instance, in 2000 United Airlines was forced to cancel more than 20,000 flights during the peak summer travel months because company pilots refused to fly overtime hours and called in sick to protest the slow pace of contract negotiations.[56] Similarly, American Airlines was forced to cancel more than 6,600 flights when its pilots staged a sickout in 1999 to protest a lower wage scale for pilots of newly acquired Reno Air. A federal judge later ordered the pilots' union at American Airlines to pay the carrier $45.5 million to compensate the company for the costs it incurred and the business it lost as a result of the sickout.[57]

7 **LEARNING OBJECTIVE**

Cite three options management can exercise when negotiations with a union break down

strikebreakers
Nonunion workers hired to replace striking workers

Management's Options   As powerful as the union's tactics are, companies are not helpless when it comes to fighting back. Management can use a number of legal methods to pressure unions when negotiations stall:

- *Strikebreakers.* When union members walk off their jobs, management can legally replace them with **strikebreakers**, nonunion workers hired to do the jobs of striking workers. (Union members brand them as "scabs.") For example, when over 2,000 union workers struck at the *Detroit News* and *Detroit Free Press* newspapers, management kept the presses rolling by hiring 1,400 replacement workers. Although the strike caused both papers to lose customers, advertisers, and profits, the papers persevered for 19 months until the union gave in. By that time, many temporary replacements had been hired permanently, an action that management is legally permitted to take if it's necessary to keep a business going.[58]

Idle cranes tower behind union longshoremen protesting at the Port of Oakland over being locked out by shipping companies.

- *Lockouts.* The U.S. Supreme Court has upheld the use of **lockouts**, in which management prevents union employees from entering the workplace, in order to pressure the union to accept a contract proposal. A lockout is management's counterpart to a strike. It is a preemptive measure designed to force a union to accede to management's demands. Lockouts are legal only if the union and management have come to an impasse in negotiations and the employer is defending a legitimate bargaining position. For instance, in September 2002 the Pacific Maritime Association (which represents international shipping lines and terminal operators) ordered a lockout, accusing the West Coast union dockworkers of staging illegal work slowdowns as negotiations between the Association and the union dockworkers came to a standstill. Members of the Pacific Maritime Association wanted to update technology at the ports but the union dockworkers feared that the introduction of scanners and remote cameras could eliminate hundreds of union jobs. Because the lockout was costing the U.S. economy billions (up to $2 billion a day) and jeopardizing the nation's security, President George W. Bush invoked the Taft–Hartley Act for the first time in nearly 25 years, forcing the 29 West Coast ports to reopen after a 10-day worker lockout. Both sides reached a deal shortly thereafter.[59]

- *Injunctions.* An **injunction** is a court order prohibiting union workers from taking certain actions. Management used this weapon without restriction in the early days of unionism, when companies typically sought injunctions to order striking employees back to work on the grounds that the strikers were interfering with business. Today, injunctions are legal only in certain cases. For example, the president of the United States has the right, under the Taft–Hartley Act, to obtain a temporary injunction to halt a strike deemed harmful to the national interest. In 1997 Bill Clinton used that power to intervene in American Airlines' labor dispute with its pilots' union. The president designated a 60-day period during which an arbitration panel was specially appointed to help the two sides reach an agreement. Although the workers were free to strike after 60 days, an agreement was reached and the strike was avoided.[60]

lockouts
Management tactics in which union members are prevented from entering a business during a strike in order to force union acceptance of management's last contract proposal

injunction
Court order prohibiting certain actions by striking workers

The Labor Movement Today

Unions remain a significant force in employee-management relations in the United States, but their membership continues to decline. Unions now represent only 13.5 percent (16.3 million) of workers in the United States (down from 20 percent in 1983 and 35 percent in the 1950s).[61] One key reason for the decrease in union membership is the shift from a manufacturing-based economy to one dominated by service industries, which tend to appeal less to unions. Another factor contributing to the decline is the changing nature of the labor force. Women, young workers, and highly skilled workers have been harder to organize with traditional methods, as have workers in less hierarchical organizations.[62]

Dynamic labor leaders have recognized that their own inertia is partly to blame for the unions' decline, and they are taking corrective measures. Even though unions are sticking to their traditional causes—good wages, safe conditions, and benefits—progressive labor leaders are pursuing new workplace issues such as job security, increasing health

Maurice Miller, a meat cutter at Wal-Mart in Jacksonville, Texas, got the unionizing ball rolling when he was promised management training that didn't materialize. To throw off the butchers' unionization attempts, Wal-Mart announced it would stop cutting meat at all its stores and buy "case-ready" prepackaged beef products. Wal-Mart insisted the change was made for quality and cost purposes.

care costs, labor involvement in management decisions, child care, and more job training.[63] In the United States, AFL-CIO president John Sweeney has beefed up recruiting efforts—especially among low-wage service workers, minorities, and women—and has targeted new industries, including technology and health care, along with smaller businesses and self-employed workers. But despite Sweeney's efforts, union membership continues to decline.

What does the future hold for employee-management relations? It is difficult to make predictions. Interest in unionization has surged in the United States, in part because of corporate scandals and a troubled economy. Yet unions lose about half of the elections they call. That's because most run poor sign-up campaigns and don't spend anywhere near the 30 percent of their budgets on recruiting, as Sweeney has requested they do. Still, another big reason for their defeat is that companies facing labor drives routinely use countertactics to get workers to change their minds. Many of these actions are perfectly legal, such as holding anti-union meetings or inundating workers with anti-union literature and videos.[64] And they can make winning a union election today a formidable task, as the example of Wal-Mart shows.

Wal-Mart—America's largest private employer and the world's largest retailer—has long resisted the unionization of its employees. With its generous employee benefits program and "open door" policy about hearing employee complaints, the company insists that Wal-Mart workers have no need for a union. So when employees at the Sam's Club store on Spring Mountain Road in Las Vegas tried to bring in the United Food & Commercial Workers (UFCW), Wal-Mart promptly responded by challenging the unionization attempt. The union successfully garnered enough support in 2001 to petition the National Labor Relations Board for a union vote, by using a website and a weekly radio call-in show, among other tactics. But on the other side, retailing behemoth Wal-Mart brought in a dozen labor-relations experts from its Bentonville, Arkansas, headquarters and instructed local managers on how to fight a fierce anti-union campaign— including surveillance of employees and the handling of union demands. Wal-Mart managers held mandatory employee meetings every week to express their anti-union sentiments and sent in labor experts to "educate associates about how the union election process works." The union claims store managers harassed union supporters and fired several union sympathizers, but Wal-Mart denies doing anything illegal. In the end, the union lost the election. Union leaders claim that the Sam's Club workers were too intimidated to proceed with a vote.[65]

Summary of Learning Objectives

1. **Identify and explain four important theories of employee motivation.**
Maslow organized individual needs into five hierarchical categories and proposed that the individual must satisfy the most basic needs before being able to address higher-level needs. Herzberg's two-factor theory suggests that hygiene factors—

such as working conditions, company policies, and job security—can influence employee dissatisfaction, but an improvement in these factors will not motivate employees. Only motivational factors such as recognition and responsibility can improve employee performance. McGregor's theory proposes two distinct views of individuals: Theory X–oriented managers believe that people dislike work and can be motivated only by fear, whereas Theory Y–oriented managers believe that people like work and are motivated by exposure to opportunities and challenges. Ouchi's Theory Z assumes that employees will be more motivated if you involve them in company decision making. It is the core thinking of companies that use teams in the workplace and adopt a more participative management style.

2. **Highlight three demographic challenges employers are facing in today's workplace.**

The influx of immigrants to the United States and their entry into the workforce is one to challenge employers are facing. Employers must learn how to manage a multicultural workforce and train all employees to become more culturally sensitive. The increasing number of women and minorities in the workforce poses another challenge. Companies must remove the invisible barriers that exist for women and minorities so that they can advance to senior-level positions much as their male counterparts do. An aging workforce resulting from the decline in the number of young people entering the workforce and the decision of baby boomers to delay retirement poses the third challenge. Older employees require higher salaries and more benefits than younger employees do. Furthermore, older employees may not be willing to change their work habits or learn new skills to meet today's workplace demands. Nor may they have the stamina to work longer hours.

3. **Discuss three staffing challenges employers are facing in today's workplace.**

A shortage of skilled labor, rightsizing the workforce, and an increasing employee desire to balance work and life responsibilities are making it difficult for employers to find and keep talented people. Other factors contributing to these staffing challenges are the increasing use of technology in the workplace, a stagnant U.S. economy, the conversion of a manufacturing-based economy to a service-based economy, a general mismatch between employee job skills and job demands, declining employee loyalty, and increasing employee burnout.

4. **Discuss three popular alternative work arrangements companies are offering their employees.**

To meet today's staffing and demographic challenges, companies are offering their employees flextime (the ability to vary their work hours and days), telecommuting (the ability to work from home or another location), and job sharing (the ability to share a single full-time job with a co-worker).

5. **Explain the two steps unions take to become the bargaining agent for a group of employees.**

First, unions distribute authorization cards to employees, which designate the union as the bargaining agent, and if at least 30 percent (but usually a majority) of the target group sign the cards, the union asks management to recognize it. Second, if management is unwilling to do so, the union asks the National Labor Relations Board to sponsor a certification election. If a majority of the employees vote in favor of being represented by the union, the union becomes the official bargaining agent for the employees.

6. **Cite three options unions can exercise when negotiations with management break down.**

Unions can conduct strikes, organize boycotts, and use publicity to pressure management into complying with union proposals. A strike is a temporary work stoppage, which the union hopes will cost management enough in lost earnings so that management will be forced to accept union demands. A boycott is a union tactic designed to pressure management into making concessions by convincing sympathizers to refuse to buy or handle the product of the target company. A negative publicity campaign against the target company is a pressure tactic designed to smear the reputation of the company in hopes of gaining management's attention.

7. **Cite three options management can exercise when negotiations with a union break down.**

To pressure a union into accepting its proposals, management may continue running the business with strikebreakers (nonunion workers hired to do the jobs of striking workers), institute a lockout of union members by preventing union employees from entering the workplace, or seek an injunction against a strike or other union activity.

KEY TERMS

arbitration (**263**)	glass ceiling (**253**)	locals (**261**)
authorization cards (**261**)	human relations (**246**)	lockouts (**265**)
behavior modification (**246**)	hygiene factors (**250**)	management by objectives (MBO) (**247**)
boycott (**264**)	injunction (**265**)	mediation (**263**)
business agent (**261**)	job enrichment (**256**)	morale (**246**)
certification (**262**)	job redesign (**256**)	motivation (**246**)
collective bargaining (**262**)	job sharing (**259**)	motivators (**250**)
decertification (**262**)	labor federation (**261**)	national union (**261**)
flextime (**258**)	labor unions (**260**)	picketing (**264**)

quality of work life (QWL) **(256)**

scientific management **(249)**

sexism **(253)**

sexual harassment **(254)**

shop steward **(261)**

strike **(264)**

strikebreakers **(264)**

telecommuting **(258)**

Theory X **(250)**

Theory Y **(250)**

Theory Z **(251)**

TEST YOUR KNOWLEDGE

Questions for Review

1. What is the goal of human relations?
2. What is the glass ceiling?
3. What is rightsizing?
4. What are the principal causes of employee burnout?
5. What is quality of work life, and how does it influence employee motivation?

Questions for Analysis

6. Why do managers often find it difficult to motivate employees who remain after downsizing?
7. How can diversity initiatives benefit a company?
8. What are some of the advantages and disadvantages of alternative work arrangements?
9. Why do employees choose to join labor unions? Why do they not join labor unions?
10. *Ethical Considerations:* You've got a golf game scheduled for Sunday afternoon, and you've worked all weekend to write a proposal to be presented Monday morning. The proposal is more or less finished, but a few more hours of work would make it polished and persuasive. Do you cancel the game?

Questions for Application

11. Some of your talented and hardworking employees come to you one day and say they do not feel challenged. They expected to be able to diversify their skills more and take on greater responsibility than they now have. How do you respond?
12. Assume you are the plant manager for a company that manufactures tires for cars and light trucks. To compete more economically in the global market, the company is seriously considering closing the plant within the next year and moving manufacturing operations to Southeast Asia. Upon hearing about the possible plant closing, the union votes to launch a strike in one week if its demands for job security aren't met. Because of a recent surge in orders, the company is not in a position to close the plant yet. What are your options as you continue to negotiate with union representatives? Which option would you choose and why?
13. *Integrated:* How do economic concepts such as profit motive and competitive advantage (see Chapter 1) affect today's workforce?
14. *Integrated:* Why is it difficult for small businesses to allow employees to telecommute, share jobs, and work flexible hours?

PRACTICE YOUR KNOWLEDGE

Handling Difficult Situations on the Job: Luring Dot-com Deserters

After a recent human resources department meeting your boss, director Tom Templeton, cornered you in the hallway. "Have you seen New Direction Consulting's full-page ad in *The Wall Street Journal* this morning? They invited Internet consulting firm employees to leave their current positions and come to work for an 'innovative firm with a rock-solid foundation.' I love that phrase. I'm tempted to steal it."

"What are you suggesting?" you counter. As his assistant director, you know Tom well; he's about to propose something radical.

"We've lost more than 500 good employees to e-commerce start-ups in recent years. Now that the technology bubble has burst, I keep hearing stories about 'dot-com deserters.' Companies like EDS are luring back their best talent by offering steady work

hours, regular pay, stability—all the things these same individuals rejected when they went off to pursue their stock-options!"

You know what he's thinking: No training required. Rapid orientation periods. They already know the business.

"It's not that these people were traitors or hated us," he adds. "They were merely seeking good opportunities like any intelligent person would do. Which is why they're valuable to us. And guess whose pasture is greener now?"[66]

Your task: Templeton is mulling over the idea of contacting employees who left for dot-coms and making them an offer. He wants to know your thoughts on the subject. Do you agree that encouraging their return is a good move? Why or why not? What could they offer EDS? If you were to contact them, what would you say? How could you motivate them to come back to a company they once considered a dead-end? Which types of motivators do you think would appeal most to these individuals?

Building Your Team Skills

Debate the pros and cons of telecommuting for an accounting, computer programming, or graphics design firm. Break into groups of four students with two students taking the employees' pro side, and the other two taking management's con side. As you prepare for this debate, consider the following factors: employee motivation, staffing challenges, quality of work life, costs, control, and feasibility.

During your team's debate, let one side present its arguments while the other side takes notes on the major points. After both sides have completed their presentations, discuss all the supporting points and try to reach a consensus as to whether or not your firm will support telecommuting. Draft a one-page statement outlining your team's conclusion and reasoning, and then share it during a class discussion.

Compare your team's conclusion and reasoning with those of other teams. Do most teams believe telecommuting is a good or a bad idea? What issues do most teams agree on? What issues do they disagree on?

EXPAND YOUR KNOWLEDGE

Discovering Career Opportunities

Is an alternative work arrangement such as flextime, job sharing, or telecommuting in your career future? This exercise will help you think about whether these work arrangements fit into your career plans.

1. Jot down a list of possible careers that interest you. Of the careers on your list, which ones seem best suited to flextime? To job sharing? To telecommuting?

2. Select one of the careers that seems suited to telecommuting. What job functions do you think could be performed at home or from another remote location?

3. Thinking about the same career, do you think it would be possible to split the job's responsibilities with a co-worker under a job-sharing arrangement? What issues, if any, might you need to resolve first?

Developing Your Research Skills

Select one or two articles from recent issues of business journals or newspapers (print or online editions) that relate to employee motivation or morale.

1. What is the problem or trend discussed in the article(s) and how is it influencing employee attitudes or motivation?

2. Is this problem unique to this company, or does it have broader implications? Who is affected by it now, and who do you think might be affected by it in the future?

3. What challenges and opportunities does this situation present to the company or industry? The employees? Management?

Exploring the Best of the Web

URLs for all Internet exercises are provided at the website for this book www.prenhall.com/bovee. *When you log on to the text website, select Chapter 10, then select "Student Resources," click on the name of the featured website, and review the website to complete these exercises.*

Explore these chapter-related websites, review their content, and answer the following questions for each website you visit:

1. What is the purpose of this website?

2. What kinds of information does this website contain? Please be specific.

3. How is the information provided at this website useful for businesspeople? Consumers?

4. How did you expand your knowledge of motivation and employee-management relations by reviewing the material at this website? What new things did you learn about these topics?

Staying on Top of Today's Workforce

Expand your human resources knowledge by visiting Workforce online. Visit the website's research center, where you'll find thousands of HR archived articles, tips, and tools that can be searched by topic or keyword. Log on to the Community Center to network with HR professionals and experts. Check out the channels to learn more about compensation, benefits, rewards, legal issues, recruiting, staffing, training, development, and other hot human resources topics. Finally, be sure to catch the Buzz where you can participate in a news poll, ask a question, or just share your views. www.workforce.com

Telecommuting Your Way to Success

Does telecommuting reality match the hype? Follow the links at this website and decide for yourself. Read the guidelines and articles. Learn some telecommuting basics to find out if you possess the skills and qualifications required to succeed in telecommuting. Get some facts and figures so you can use them effectively in a telecommuting proposal to your boss. Then read some success stories. Finally, explore your flexible options by learning about other alternative working arrangements. Which ones are suited for you? www.telecommuting.about.com

Spreading the Union Message

Of all the websites devoted to union causes, the AFL-CIO's site offers perhaps the most extensive collection of statistics, information, and commentaries on union issues and programs. The site is designed to educate members and prospective members about union activities and campaigns. Topics include union membership campaigns, safety and family issues, and much more. The AFL-CIO also maintains online directories with the e-mail addresses of members of Congress plus sample letters to encourage communication with legislators. Browse this site to get the latest on union initiatives as well as information about trends in the labor movement today. What worker issues and advantages of union membership are being highlighted? www.aflcio.org/home.htm

Learning Interactively

Companion Website

Visit the Companion Website at www.prenhall.com/bovee. For Chapter 10, take advantage of the interactive "Study Guide" to test your chapter knowledge. Get instant feedback on whether you need additional studying. Read the "Current Events" articles to get the latest on chapter topics, and complete the exercises as specified by your instructor. Expand your learning with a visit to the "Research Area." There you will find a wealth of information you can use to complete your course assignments.

A CASE FOR CRITICAL THINKING

Brewing Up People Policies at Starbucks

Hiring, training, and compensating a diverse workforce of 40,000 employees worldwide would be a difficult task for any company. But it was an especially daunting challenge in an industry whose annual employee turnover rate approached 300 percent. It was even more of a challenge for a company that was striving to open a new store every day.

This was the high-pressure situation facing Starbucks Coffee Company in the 1990s, when CEO Howard Schultz set a torrid pace for global expansion. The rich aroma of fresh-brewed espresso was already wafting through hundreds of neighborhoods all over North America, and new stores were planned for the United Kingdom, Japan, even China. But Schultz and his management team knew that good locations and top-quality coffee were just part of the company's formula for success.

To keep up with its ambitious schedule of new store openings, Starbucks had to find, recruit, and train 700 new employees every month, no easy feat "when there is a shortage of labor and few people want to work behind a retail counter," as Schultz noted. Moreover, Starbucks's employees had to deliver consistently superior customer service in every store and every market. In other words Starbucks' employees (known internally as *partners*) had to do more than simply pour coffee—they had to believe passionately in the product and pay attention to all the details that can make or break the retail experience for the chain's 10 million weekly customers. In short, Starbucks managers had to ensure that their stores provided the best service along with the best coffee.

Perking Up Benefits

Schultz, of course, knew that attracting and motivating employees would take more than good pay and company declarations to "provide a great work environment and treat each other with respect and dignity." So, guided by the company mission statement, the CEO and his managers designed a variety of human resources programs to motivate Starbucks partners.

First they raised employees' base pay. Next, management bucked the trend in the industry by offering full medical, dental, life, and disability insurance benefits to every partner who worked at least 20 hours per week. These partners were also eligible for paid vacation days and retirement savings plans, benefits not commonly available to part-time restaurant workers. Finally, to help partners better balance their work and family obligations—another priority for Starbucks—the human resources department designed a comprehensive work–life program. This program featured flexi-ble work schedules, access to employee assistance specialists, and referrals for child-care and elder-care support.

A Taste of the Good Life

The most innovative benefit brewed up by management, however, was its Bean Stock, a program offering stock options not just to upper-echelon managers but to all partners who worked 20 or more hours per week. "We established Bean Stock in 1991 as a way of investing in our partners and creating ownership across the company," explained Bradley Honeycutt, vice president of human resources. "It's been a key to retaining good people and building loyalty." For those who wanted to enlarge their financial stake in Starbucks, management devised a program that permitted partners to buy company stock at a discount. Owning a piece of the company motivated employees to take customer service to an even higher level of excellence.

The Perfect Blend

Of course, Starbucks recognizes that good pay and benefits, while attractive, are not enough to meet the company's future growth plans. So to stay on schedule and on top, Starbucks continually invests in its workforce. Each new hire is provided with 24 hours of training about the finer points of coffee brewing as well as the company's culture and values. To encourage more and better feedback and communication, management holds a series of open forums in which company performance, results, and plans are openly discussed. Finally, Starbucks honors employees whose achievements exemplify the company's values.

Grounds for Concern

In all, putting the focus on partners has helped Starbucks grow from 17 coffee shops in Seattle to some 5,600 outlets in 28 countries. Sales, which have climbed an average of 20 percent annually since the company want public in 1992, now top $3.2 billion. But with 1,200 new stores planned to open each year, Starbucks, faces a big human resources challenge. During its growth spurt of the mid- to late-1990s, Starbucks boasted the lowest employee turnover rate of any restaurant or fast-food company, attributable largely to its innovative employee benefits. Now the question remains whether such perks will be enough to keep employees from bolting. Some employees are already complaining that the benefits and pay don't match the workload Starbucks expects from them. Moreover, as

Starbucks expands, such as its recent acquisition of Seattle's Best Coffee, the company may find it increasingly difficult to keep new hires connected to the original mission of high service. And for a company modeled around enthusiastic service, waning employee morale could have dire consequences for both image and sales.

Critical Thinking Questions

1. Why do Starbucks's human resources managers need to be advised of company plans for new store openings?
2. What are the advantages and disadvantages of using a part-time workforce at Starbucks?

3. How does Starbucks use liberal employee-benefits to motivate its employees?
4. Go to Chapter 10 of this text's website at www.prenhall.com/bovee and click on the hot link to get to the Starbucks website. Then visit the site's job section to see how Starbucks presents its HR policies to potential employees. Browse the pages that discuss working at Starbucks. Read about company culture, diversity, benefits, and learning and career development. Why would Starbucks post information about company culture in this section of the website? Why would job candidates be interested in learning about the culture as well as the employee benefits and training at Starbucks?

VIDEO CASE

Feeling Like Part of the Family: Kingston Technology

Learning Objectives

The purpose of this video is to help you:

1. Understand the importance of motivating employees.
2. Consider how financial and nonfinancial rewards can motivate employees.
3. Explain how high morale can affect organizational performance.

Synopsis

Kingston Technology, based in California, is the world's largest independent manufacturer of computer memory products. Founded by John Tu and David Sun, Kingston employs more than 1,500 people—yet makes each employee feel like part of the family. The company returns 10 percent of its company profits to employees every year through a profit-sharing program. Just as important, it fosters mutual trust and respect between employees and management. Senior managers stay in touch with employees at all levels and conduct surveys to obtain employee feedback. For their part, employees report high job satisfaction and develop both personal and professional connections with their colleagues—boosting morale and motivation.

Discussion Questions

1. *For analysis:* After the sale to Softbank, employees learned from news reports that Kingston's $100 million profit-sharing

distribution was one of the largest in U.S. history. What was the likely effect of this publicity on employee morale?
2. *For analysis:* Are Kingston's managers applying Theory X or Theory Y to their employees? How do you know?
3. *For application:* What kinds of questions should Kingston ask through employee surveys to gauge satisfaction and morale?
4. *For application:* What else might Kingston's management do to motivate employees by offering opportunities to satisfy higher-level needs such as self-actualization?
5. *For debate:* Do you agree with Kingston's policy of giving new employees profit-sharing bonuses even when they join the company just one week before profits are distributed? Support your position.

Online Exploration

Visit Kingston Technology's website at www.kingston.com and follow the link to browse company information and read about its awards. From the company information page, follow the link to learn about the organization's values. How do these values support the founders' intention to create a family feeling within the company? How do they support employees' achievement of higher-level needs? Why would Kingston post this listing of milestones on its website, starting with the company's founding and continuing with honors bestowed by *Fortune* and others?

Managing Human Resources

LEARNING OBJECTIVES

After studying this chapter, you will be able to

1. List six main functions of human resources departments

2. Cite eight methods recruiters use to find job candidates

3. Identify the six stages in the hiring process

4. Discuss how companies incorporate objectivity into employee performance appraisals

5. List seven popular types of employee incentive programs

6. Highlight five popular employee benefits

7. Describe four ways an employee's status may change and discuss why many employers prefer to fill job vacancies from within

Thanks to Jamba Juice's management incentives, such as bonuses and paid sabbaticals, employee turnover at the company is substantially below industry average.

INSIDE BUSINESS TODAY

Blending a Successful Workforce: Jamba Juice Whips Up Creative Recruiting Strategies

Finding and keeping employees is no easy feat—especially for a high-growth company in the fast-food industry. But as a leading retailer of smoothies, freshly squeezed juices, healthy soups, and breads, San Francisco–based Jamba Juice meets the challenge of building a successful workforce with an appealing blend of savvy recruiting strategies and creative incentive tools.

Since founder Kirk Perron opened his first smoothie store in 1990, Jamba Juice has grown to 325 nationwide outlets and plans to open 60 to 70 new stores annually for the next several years. The majority of Jamba's 4,000 employees are part-time workers, primarily high school and college students who whip up healthy concoctions between classes and during school breaks. To attract part-time "team members," Perron promotes the key ingredients of the company's success: nutrition, fitness, and fun. And he quickly points out that the company's name reflects the enjoyable working environment—*jamba* is a West African word meaning "to celebrate."

As Jamba Juice expands its operations, Perron and his human resources staff work closely with the company's real estate committee to forecast demand for the number of workers needed in specific locations. Human resources begins the search at least four months before an official store opening, allowing time for finding, interviewing, and training new employees.

Searches are conducted using a variety of resources, and they are customized for each market. For instance, to attract young, cyber-savvy candidates who fit the profile of a typical Jamba employee, human resources uses the Internet.

Jamba Juice lists job openings on recruiting websites such as restaurantrecruit.com, a site popular with managers in the food industry. In turn, these sites provide a direct link to Jamba Juice's website so that job seekers can find out more about the company or send an e-mail requesting additional information.

Of course, Internet ads can generate responses from applicants who live as far away as Australia and France. So Perron and his staff must sift through the piles of applications and identify the strongest candidates to interview. Initial interviews are conducted by telephone. During 30-minute phone screenings, human resources staff look for personable candidates with a strong work ethic—the type of candidate who wants to stick with the company.

But recruiting new staff is only one of the challenges that Jamba Juice faces. Perron must also retain current store managers. To do that, Perron offers incentives to reward store performance. Managers receive a percentage of their store's sales every eight weeks. Furthermore, managers accrue retention bonuses for building the store's business. After accumulating three years of retention bonuses, managers receive a cash payment for their efforts. And managers who sign up for three more years of employment are rewarded with a three-week paid sabbatical.

Jamba's aggressive recruiting strategies and management incentives have paid off. In an industry that regularly sees a 50 percent turnover rate at the managerial level, Jamba reports a turnover rate in the 30 to 50 percent range.[1]

Understanding What Human Resources Managers Do

human resources management (HRM)
Specialized function of planning how to obtain employees, oversee their training, evaluate them, and compensate them

As Kirk Perron knows, hiring the right people to help a company reach its goals and then overseeing their training and development, motivation, evaluation, and compensation is critical to a company's success. These activities are known as **human resources management (HRM)**, which encompasses all the tasks involved in acquiring, maintaining, and developing an organization's human resources. Because of the accelerating rate at which today's workforce, economy, and corporate cultures are being transformed, the role of HRM is increasingly viewed as a strategic one.

Human resources (HR) managers must figure out how to attract qualified employees from a shrinking pool of entry-level candidates; how to train less-educated, poorly skilled employees; how to keep experienced employees when they have few opportunities for advancement; and how to lay off employees equitably when downsizing is necessary. They must also retrain employees to cope with increasing automation and computerization, manage increasingly complex (and expensive) employee benefits programs, shape workplace policies to address changing workforce demographics and employee needs (as discussed in Chapter 10), and cope with the challenge of meeting government regulations in hiring practices and equal opportunity employment.

One company that consistently gets human resources management right is Southwest Airlines, the only profitable U.S. airline among the top eight. Although starting pay for some positions at Southwest lags behind that of other carriers, the company makes up the difference with generous profit sharing and stock options. It also offers something even scarcer than a valuable stock: job security. While other major airlines are shrinking their service and laying off workers, Southwest Airlines is adding routes and flights, accelerating delivery of planes, hiring workers, and scooping up market share from its rivals.

But Southwest's advantage isn't that its employees are paid less for their work; rather, it's that they work more for their pay. They work more productively, more flexibly, and more creatively. Southwest pilots are paid for each trip, so they have a strong interest in keeping flights on schedule. And because a big chunk of their compensation comes in the form of stock options, they tend to watch costs like bean counters. Flight attendants at Southwest work as many as 150 hours a month, compared with 80 hours at many other airlines. And Southwest's mechanics operate like a Nascar pit crew—priding themselves on changing airplane tires faster then their counterparts at other airlines. Moreover, although Southwest has a higher proportion of union members among its employees than other major airlines, the 30-year-old carrier has never suffered a layoff or strike.

Management at Southwest works hard to maintain high employee morale and good customer service through careful recruitment and training. The airline received 200,000 résumés in 2001 but hired only 6,000 workers—making it more selective than Harvard. For many positions, candidates undergo a rigorous interview process that can take as long as six weeks before they are hired. Southwest wants to make sure that new employees will fit in with the company's culture. The payback: low turnover and high customer satisfaction.[2]

1 LEARNING OBJECTIVE

List six main functions of human resources departments

As the Southwest Airline example shows, human resources managers and staff are an important part of an organization's overall success. They keep the organization running smoothly at every level by planning for a company's staffing needs, recruiting and hiring employees, training and developing employees and managers, and appraising employee performance. The HR staff also administer compensation and employee benefits and oversee changes in employment status (promotion, reassignment, termination or resignation, and retirement). This chapter explores each of these human resources responsibilities, beginning with planning (see Exhibit 11.1 on page 276).

Managing in the 21st Century

Packing Up Great Service at The Container Store

The Container Store inspires its customers with the words "Contain Yourself." But the company encourages its employees to do just the opposite by asking them to continuously think outside the box. Store employees are expected to help customers solve every storage problem imaginable, from sweaters to DVDs to rubber stamps, with an array of boxes, baskets, hangers, hooks, and more. As frustrated retail consumers everywhere know all too well, delivering great customer service isn't easy.

When selecting new employees, The Container Store goes to great lengths to find the perfect person for each position, driven by the belief that one great person equals three good ones. Most employees are college educated, almost half come from employee referrals, and most have been customers of the store. They are also self-motivated, team-oriented, and passionate about customer service.

Those traits are enhanced by extensive employee development: New employees receive 235 hours of training in their first year, and after that full-timers get 160 hours per year. In comparison, most retailers give new workers less than 10 hours of training per year. The Container Store also pays three to four times minimum wage, which builds loyalty and helps keep annual turnover below 20 percent (versus the 100 percent that is common within the industry). What's more, salespeople are not paid commissions. Without the constant pressure to "make the numbers," it's easier for them to take their time, work in teams, and create complete storage solutions for their customers.

Teamwork is reinforced twice a day, before and after closing, through a gathering called "the huddle." Similar to a huddle in football, the goal is to give everyone a common purpose: set goals, share information, boost morale, and bond as a team. Morning sessions feature spirited discussions of sales goals and product applications, and may include a chorus of "Happy Birthday" for celebrating team members. Evening huddles include more team building and friendly competitions such as guessing the daily sales figures.

Maintaining solid company values and human resources practices helps The Container Store deliver great customer service. But the company seals the package of success by recognizing that employees are its greatest asset.

Questions for Critical Thinking

1. Why does The Container Store go to such great lengths to find the right employees?
2. How does the effort to treat employees well lead to better customer service?

Planning for a Company's Staffing Needs

One of the six functions of the human resources staff members is to plan for a company's staffing needs. Proper planning is critical because a miscalculation could leave a company without enough employees to keep up with demand, resulting in customer dissatisfaction and lost business. Yet if a company expands its staff too rapidly, profits may be eaten up by payroll, or the firm may have to lay off people who were just recruited and trained at considerable expense.

No one knows this situation better than Wal-Mart's executive vice president of human resources, Coleman Peterson, who is overseeing the hiring of more than 1 million employees within a five-year period—the equivalent of hiring the entire population of San Antonio, Texas. Wal-Mart's aggressive hiring program is founded on careful planning (see Exhibit 11.2). The company must forecast new store openings as well as employee turnover at existing stores. Once forecasts have been presented, Wal-Mart's managers must evaluate job requirements for each store.[3]

EXHIBIT 11.1
The Functions of the Human Resources Department
Human resources departments are responsible for these six important functions.

1. Planning for staffing needs
2. Recruiting and hiring
3. Training and development
4. Appraising performance
5. Administering compensation and benefits
6. Overseeing changes in employment status

Forecasting Supply and Demand

Effective human resources planning begins with forecasting *demand*, the numbers and kinds of employees that will be needed at various times. For example, suppose Jamba Juice plans to open another store in San Francisco within six months. The HR department would forecast that the store will need a store manager and an assistant manager as well as part-time salespeople. Although Jamba Juice might start looking immediately for someone as highly placed as the manager, it may postpone hiring part-time employees until just before the store opens.

The next task is to estimate the *supply* of available employees. In many cases, that supply is within the company already—perhaps just needing training to fill future requirements. Jamba Juice may well find that the assistant manager at an existing store can be promoted to manage the new store, and one of the current salespeople can be named assistant manager. If existing employees cannot be tapped for new positions, the human resources manager must determine how to find people outside the company who have the necessary skills. In

EXHIBIT 11.2
Steps in Human Resources Planning
Careful attention to each phase of this sequence helps ensure that a company will have the right human resources when it needs them.

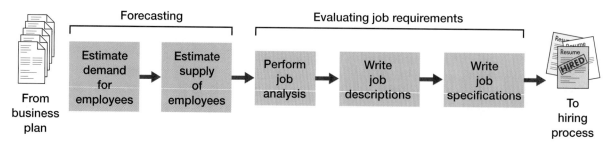

some cases, managers will want to consider strategic staffing alternatives such as hiring part-time and temporary employees to avoid drastic overstaffing or understaffing.

Part-Time and Temporary Employees More and more businesses try to save money and increase flexibility by building their workforces around part-time and temporary employees, or "temps," whose schedules can be rearranged to suit the company's needs. As a result, this segment of the labor force has increased by leaps and bounds in recent years. The Bureau of Labor Statistics projects that the temp-agency workforce will reach 4 million by 2006 (an increase of over 200 percent since 1997).[4] The temporary ranks include computer systems analysts, human resources directors, accountants, doctors, and even CEOs, with technical fields making up the fastest-growing segment of temporary employment.

Companies are incorporating temporary workers in long-term plans, whereas 15 years ago they used temps to fill occasional vacancies. The use of temps is an excellent recruiting technique because it allows companies to try out employees before hiring them permanently. Thus, what often begins as a temp assignment can turn into multiyear employment. Some 29 percent of workers employed by temp agencies remain on the job assignment for one year or more, says the Bureau of Labor Statistics. Many of these "permatemps" hold high-prestige, high-skilled technology jobs at leading firms. In fact, they often do the same work as the company's permanent employees, but because they are temps, they do not qualify for the benefits enjoyed by regular workers. However, some permatemps have sued companies, saying that they are, in fact, full-time employees and as such deserve employee benefits.[5]

Outsourcing Outsourcing is another way that companies fulfill their human resources needs without hiring permanent employees. Companies outsource some tasks or projects because the outside source can provide materials, parts, or services better, at a lower price, and more efficiently. Outsourcing is also used to take advantage of others' expertise and to increase flexibility. Outsourcing has many advantages: It gives companies access to new resources and world-class capabilities; it shares the risk of getting the work done; and it frees company resources for other purposes. Still, outsourcing has its share of risks, including loss of control, greater dependency on suppliers, and loss of in-house skills. Some companies have also experienced work delays, unhappy customers, and labor union battles as a result of outsourcing.

Evaluating Job Requirements

The second step of the planning function is to evaluate job requirements. If you were the owner of a small business, you might have a good grasp of the requirements of all the jobs in your company. However, in large organizations, where hundreds or thousands of employees are performing a wide variety of jobs, management needs a more formal and objective method of evaluating job requirements. That method is called **job analysis**.

To obtain the information needed for a job analysis, the human resources staff asks employees or supervisors several questions: What is the purpose of the job? What tasks are involved in the job? What qualifications and skills are needed to do it effectively? In what kind of setting does the job take place? Is there much public contact involved? Does the job entail much time pressure? Sometimes they obtain job information by observing employees directly. At other times they ask employees to keep daily diaries describing exactly what they do during the workday.

Once job analysis has been completed, the human resources staff develops a **job description**, a formal statement summarizing the tasks involved in the job and the conditions under which the employee will work. In most cases, the staff will also develop a **job specification**, a statement describing the skills, education, and previous experience that the job requires.

job analysis
Process by which jobs are studied to determine the tasks and dynamics involved in performing them

job description
Statement of the tasks involved in a given job and the conditions under which the holder of the job will work

job specification
Statement describing the kind of person who would be best for a given job—including the skills, education, and previous experience that the job requires

Recruiting, Hiring, and Training New Employees

2 LEARNING OBJECTIVE

Cite eight methods recruiters use to find job candidates

recruiting
Process of attracting appropriate applicants for an organization's jobs

Having forecast a company's supply and demand for employees and evaluated job requirements, the human resource manager's next step is to match the job specification with an actual person or selection of people. This task is accomplished through **recruiting**, the process of attracting suitable candidates for an organization's jobs. One recent study shows that companies with excellent recruiting and retention policies provide a nearly 8 percent higher return to shareholders than those that don't.[6]

Recruiters are specialists on the human resources staff who are responsible for locating job candidates. They use a variety of methods and resources, including internal searches, newspaper and Internet advertising, public and private employment agencies, union hiring halls, college campuses and career offices, trade shows, corporate "headhunters" (people who try to attract people from other companies), and referrals from employees or colleagues in the industry (see Exhibit 11.3). One of the fastest-growing recruitment resources for both large and small businesses is the Internet. As Chapter 4 points out, many companies now recruit online through their websites and a variety of popular online recruiting services (see "Job Recruiting Moves to the Net," page 98).

The Hiring Process

3 LEARNING OBJECTIVE

Identify the six stages in the hiring process

After exploring at least one—but usually more—of the available recruitment channels to assemble a pool of applicants, the human resources department may spend weeks and sometimes months on the hiring process. Most companies go through the same basic stages in the hiring process as they sift through applications to come up with the person (or persons) they want.

The first stage is to select a small number of qualified candidates from all of the applications received. Finalists may be chosen on the basis of a standard application form that all candidates fill out or on the basis of a résumé—a summary of education, experience, and personal data compiled by each applicant (see "Preparing Your Résumé" in Component Chapter C for further details). Sometimes both sources of information are used. Many organizations now use computer scanners to help them quickly sort through résumés and weed out those that don't match the requirements of the job.

The second stage in the hiring process is to interview each candidate to clarify qualifications and to fill in any missing information (see "Interviewing with Potential Employers" in Component Chapter C for further details). Another goal of the interview is to get an idea of the applicant's personality and ability to work well with others.

EXHIBIT 11.3

How Employers and Job Seekers Approach the Recruiting Process

Studies show that employers prefer to fill job openings with people from within their organization or from an employee's recommendation. Placing want ads is often viewed as a last resort. In contrast, typical job seekers begin their job-search process from the opposite direction (starting with reading a newspaper or Internet ads).

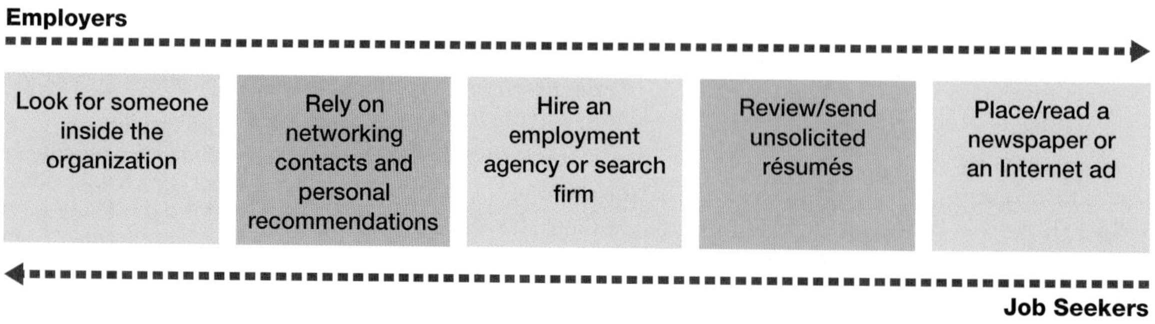
Employers
Look for someone inside the organization
Rely on networking contacts and personal recommendations
Hire an employment agency or search firm
Review/send unsolicited résumés
Place/read a newspaper or an Internet ad
Job Seekers

Depending on the type of job at stake, candidates may also be asked to take a test or a series of tests.

After the initial prescreening interviews comes the third stage, when the best candidates may be asked to meet with someone in the human resources department who will conduct a more probing interview. For higher-level positions, candidates may go through a series of interviews with managers, potential co-workers, and the employees who will make up the successful candidate's staff. Sometimes this process can take weeks.

When all the interviews have been completed, the process moves to the final stages. In the fourth stage, the department supervisor evaluates the candidates, sometimes in consultation with a higher-level manager, the human resources department, and staff. During the fifth stage, the employer checks the references and backgrounds of the top few candidates. In the sixth stage, the supervisor selects the most suitable person for the job. Now the search is over—if the candidate accepts the offer.

Background Checks Employers are carrying out more rigorous background checks on current employees as well as new hires since the September 11 terrorist attacks. In some cases, employers may look at credit reports, civil court records, motor vehicle records, workers' compensation claims, and criminal records going back 10 years or more (see Exhibit 11.4). Critics of this practice say that employers are trampling workers' privacy rights by going beyond traditional checks. But employers say they have good reason. A review of 2.6 million background checks by Automatic Data Processing reported that about 5 percent of job applicants had a criminal record in the past seven years, and more than 30 percent had credit records with black marks such as collection agency activity.[7]

Using background checks can add hundreds of dollars to the cost of hiring, but can save millions by avoiding the wrong hiring choice.[8] Violence in the workplace is an increasing threat that can harm employees and customers, hurt productivity, and lead to expensive lawsuits and higher health care costs. More than 1 million physical assaults and thousands of homicides occur at work each year. If an employer fails to address "preventable violences," that employer will likely be found liable. Thus, companies need to be especially careful about negligent hiring.[9] Background checks are particularly important for jobs in which employees are in a position to possibly harm others. For example, a trucking company must check applicants' driving records to avoid hiring a trucker with numerous violations.

Meanwhile, as more companies carry out background checks on employees, workers who have stretched the truth to get hired are finding themselves and their jobs in jeopardy.

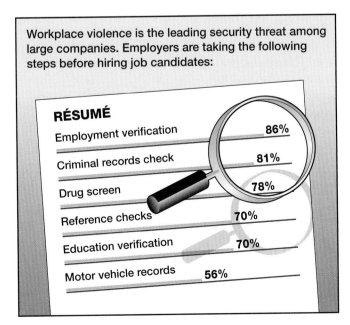

Workplace violence is the leading security threat among large companies. Employers are taking the following steps before hiring job candidates:

RÉSUMÉ
Employment verification — 86%
Criminal records check — 81%
Drug screen — 78%
Reference checks — 70%
Education verification — 70%
Motor vehicle records — 56%

EXHIBIT 11.4
Checking Out New Hires
Today's employers are scrutinizing new employees more closely.

It's a concern for thousands of workers who have exaggerated accomplishments on their résumés or lied about job history or pay. A study by Automatic Data Processing shows that more than 40 percent of applicants misrepresented their education or employment history. Some attribute the increase in résumé falsification to the economic downturn, because job seekers are more desperate in tough economic times.[10]

Hiring and the Law Federal and state laws and regulations govern many aspects of the hiring process. In particular, employers must be careful to avoid discrimination in the wording of their application forms, in interviewing, and in testing. Employers must also respect the privacy of applicants. Consider the dilemma this situation presents for employers.

On the one hand, asking questions about unrelated factors such as citizenship, marital status, age, and religion violates the Equal Employment Opportunity Commission's regulations because such questions may lead to discrimination. In addition, employers are not allowed to ask questions about whether a person has children, whether a person owns or rents a home, what caused a physical disability, whether a person belongs to a union, whether a person has ever been arrested, or when a person attended school. The exception is when such information is related to a bona fide occupational qualification for the specific job.

On the other hand, employers must also obtain sufficient information about employees to avoid becoming the target of a negligent-hiring lawsuit. Moreover, the Immigration Reform and Control Act (passed in 1986) forbids almost all U.S. companies from hiring illegal aliens. The act also prohibits discrimination in hiring on the basis of national origin or citizenship status. This creates a difficult situation for employers who must try to determine their applicants' citizenship so they can verify that the newly hired are legally eligible to work, without asking questions that violate the law. As you can imagine, striking the balance can be quite a challenge.

Testing One much-debated aspect of the hiring process is testing—using not only the tests that prospective employers give job applicants but any devices that can evaluate employees when making job decisions. Tests are used to gauge abilities, intelligence, interests, and sometimes even physical condition and personality. Many companies rely on pre-employment testing to determine whether applicants are suited to the job and whether they'll be worth the expense of hiring and training. Research shows that bad hiring decisions can cost a company as much as 150 percent of the person's annual salary, if you factor in the costs of recruiting, training, and lost productivity.[11]

Companies use three main testing procedures: job-skills testing, psychological testing, and drug testing. Job-skills tests are the most common type, designed to assess competency or specific abilities needed to perform a job. Nearly 65 percent of employers use a job-skills test of some kind.[12] Psychological tests usually take the form of questionnaires. These tests can be used to assess overall intellectual ability, attitudes toward work, interests, managerial potential, or personality characteristics—including dependability, commitment, and motivation. People who favor psychological testing say that it can predict how well employees will actually perform on the job. However, critics say that such tests are ineffective and potentially discriminatory.

Over the past 15 years, drug testing has become a standard business practice in the U.S. workplace.[13] The percentage of major U.S. firms that perform drug tests on employees and/or job applicants has risen from 22 percent in 1987 to 67 percent in 2001.[14] "We use drug testing as a condition of hire and continued employment," says one manager of Azteca Construction Company. "We believe that it's our company's responsibility to provide a safe working environment. Having an employee who is using drugs running a 60,000 pound excavator is not safe."[15]

Companies with mandatory testing have found real advantages, including lower accident rates, fewer disability claims, and decreased violence and absenteeism. Nevertheless, some employers prefer not to incur the extra expense to administer drug tests; others consider such tests an invasion of privacy.[16] And critics of drug testing say that it can be inaccurate and produce false-positive results.

Training and Development

To make sure that all new employees understand the company's goals, policies, and procedures, most large organizations and many small ones have well-defined **orientation** programs. Although they vary, such programs usually include information about company history and structure, equal opportunity practices, safety regulations, standards of employee conduct, company culture, employee compensation and benefit plans, work times, and other topics that newly hired employees might have questions about. Orientation programs help new employees understand and feel more comfortable in their role in the organization.

At Intel, for instance, all new hires participate in a six-month "integration" curriculum. Day One begins when new hires receive a packet at their home. The packet contains material about the company's culture and values, along with some forms to fill out. During the first month, all new hires attend a class called "Working at Intel," a formal eight-hour introduction to the company's corporate culture. At the end of the six-month period, each new hire participates in a two-hour structured question-and-answer session, in which an executive reviews the employee's transition into Intel and then asks a final question: "What do you think it will take to succeed at Intel?"[17]

Yasuko Ishikawa, a Delta Air Lines flight attendant, was fired after a random urine test showed her sample had been tampered with. So Ishikawa took her case to court. The jury found that the lab conducting the drug test was negligent and awarded Iskikawa $400,000. Delta also offered to reinstate her.

orientation
Session or procedure for acclimating a new employee to the organization

In addition to orientation programs, most companies offer training (and retraining), because employee competence has a direct effect on productivity and profits. Wal-Mart's Coleman Peterson believes that training is the most important part of human resources management. As Peterson puts it, "Wal-Mart is in the business of keeping and growing talent."[18] Although some employers worry that employees who develop new or improved skills might leave them for higher-paying jobs, studies show that the contrary is true. The more training given to employees, the more likely they will want to stay, because training gives them a sense that they are going somewhere in their careers, even if they're not getting a promotion.[19]

Tires Plus is one of a growing number of companies that invests heavily in employee training to become more competitive. Some 1,700 employees spend a total of 60,000 hours annually attending formal training programs at Tires Plus University. In addition, Tires Plus offers special training programs to develop inexperienced but promising workers into mechanics and managers. While training programs cost Tires Plus more than $3 million a year, they help the company retain talented workers and fill leadership positions—a small price to pay in today's tight labor market.[20] Southwest Airlines is another company that offers its employees training through its "University for People." Employees can choose courses that will help them to do their jobs more effectively and be more flexible in the tasks they can perform.[21]

Job training often focuses on teaching employees the required skills and procedures to operate company equipment in a safe and efficient manner. Such training is critical in industries that employ heavy machinery, dangerous substances, and highly technical equipment. Studies show that proper training can help reduce workplace injuries, illnesses, and fatalities—a growing concern among employers and employees. Approximately 6,500 job-related deaths, 13.2 million nonfatal injuries, and 862,200 occupational illnesses occur in the workplace annually—costing businesses some $170 billion.[22]

Circuit City trains most of its employees using self-paced e-learning modules. Here Andrew Harris (left) and Demetrius Toler try out what they've learned from the company's online tutorial for selling digital cameras.

performance appraisal
Evaluation of an employee's work according to specific criteria

4 LEARNING OBJECTIVE

Discuss how companies incorporate objectivity into employee performance appraisals

In many companies, training takes place at the work site, where an experienced employee oversees the trainee's on-the-job efforts, or in a classroom, where an expert lectures groups of employees. Employee training may also involve a self-study component using training manuals, computers, tests, and interactive modules. For example, employees at Days Inn of America participate in interactive self-paced web-based training to learn reservation operations, housekeeping duties, supervision, and even ways to deal with surly guests.[23]

Appraising Employee Performance

How do employees know whether they are doing a good job? How can they improve their performance? What new skills should they learn? Most human resources managers attempt to answer these questions by developing **performance appraisal** systems to objectively evaluate employees according to set criteria. Such systems promote fairness because their standards are usually job-related.

The ultimate goal of performance appraisals is not to judge employees but rather to improve their performance. Thus, experts recommend that performance reviews be an ongoing discipline—not just a once-a-year event linked to employee raises. Periodic performance evaluations are especially important in today's project-driven, results-oriented workplace. Employees need fast feedback so they can correct their deficiencies in a timely manner.

Most companies require regular written evaluations of each employee's work. Written evaluations also provide a record of the employee's performance, which may protect the company in cases of disputed terminations. To ensure objectivity and consistency, firms generally use a standard company performance appraisal form to evaluate employees (see Exhibit 11.5). The evaluation criteria are in writing so that both employee and supervisor understand what is expected and are therefore able to determine whether the work is being done adequately. Some companies require employees to prepare written self-evaluations, highlighting their job accomplishments and strengths as well as specific areas of improvement they plan on addressing in the near future.

In some organizations, performance appraisals are completed by several people (including more than one supervisor and perhaps several co-workers). This practice further promotes fairness by correcting for possible biases. One appraisal format that moves the review process from a one-dimensional perspective to a multidimensional format is the 360-degree review. Designed to provide employees with a broader range of perspectives, the *360-degree review* solicits feedback from colleagues above, below, and around the employee to provide observations of the person's performance in several skill and behavioral categories. This means that employees rate the performance of their superiors as well as that of their peers.[24]

One of the biggest problems with any employee appraisal system is finding a way to measure productivity. In a production job, the person who assembles the most defect-free microprocessors in a given amount of time is clearly the most productive. But how does an employer evaluate the productivity of the registration clerk at a hotel or the middle manager at a large television station? Although the organization's overall productivity can be mea-

Keeping Pace with Technology and Electronic Commerce

Click and Learn: E-Training Today's Employees

Employers from automakers and software firms to hospitals and pharmaceutical companies are turning to computers to train today's employees. Electronic training, or e-learning, uses computers and live or taped webcasts, web-based self-paced tutorials, and other forms of electronic media such as CD-ROMs to instruct employees on new products, customer service, sales techniques, and more. What makes e-learning possible are the technological advances in today's workplace—more desktop computers, increased Internet access, more bandwidth.

Dell Computer expects 90 percent of its learning solutions to be totally or partially technology enabled. General Motors University uses interactive satellite broadcasts to teach salespeople the best way to highlight features on new cars. Pharmaceutical companies such as Merck use live interactive Internet classes to instruct sales reps on the latest product information rather than fly them to a conference center. And IBM has moved online virtually all the content of the first three phases of management training for its first-line managers—eliminating the need to send them to offsite locations over the course of a training period that stretched out over six months.

As these companies have learned, e-training has many benefits:

- *Reduced costs.* Much of the cost savings comes from reduced travel expenses and time savings. Intel has saved over $1 million annually by using e-training programs. "If we save our 70,000 employees just 20 minutes a year, that alone is $1 million in savings," says one Intel training manager.

- *Increased productivity.* "Our salesforce can't come in for three-day conferences anymore," says one Black & Decker vice president. "But they still need to understand the company's new products and features." So the company has instituted online training courses—which means the company's 700 person sales force can spend a combined 12,000 more days a year with customers.

- *Individualized pace.* E-learning allows you to learn at your own pace—skipping over material you already know and spending more time learning material that meets your specific needs.

- *Increased consistency.* Companies can create one set of instructional materials that are used consistently by everyone in the organization. Thus, everyone is learning the same thing—regardless of their location.

While still in its infancy, e-learning is effectively changing the way companies transfer knowledge and information to employees and customers. Some experts predict that 80 percent of corporate training will soon be delivered electronically.

Questions for Critical Thinking

1. Why is e-learning an increasingly popular training approach for companies?
2. How might an economic slowdown or global terrorism impact e-learning?

sured (number of rooms booked per night, number of viewers per hour), often the employer can't directly relate the results to any one employee's efforts.

Evaluating productivity becomes an even greater challenge in organizations where employees work in teams. Some companies, such as Con-Way Transportation Services, meet this challenge by having teams evaluate themselves. About every three months a neutral facilitator leads a discussion in which team members rate team performance on a 1 to 5 scale for 31 criteria, which can include customer satisfaction, the ability to meet goals, employee behavior toward co-workers and customers, job knowledge, motivation, and skills. During the meetings, members discuss the team's performance. Individual performance is also discussed, but only in the context of the team. Each person creates two columns on a

EXHIBIT 11.5
Sample Performance Appraisal Form
Many companies use forms like this one to ensure that performance appraisals are as objective as possible.

Name _____ Title _____ Service Date _____ Date _____

Location _____ Division _____ Department _____

Length of Time in Present Position   Period of Review   Appraised by _____

_____ From: _____ To: _____   Title of Appraisor _____

Area of Performance	Comment	Rating
Job Knowledge and Skill Understands responsibilities and uses background for job. Adapts to new methods/techniques. Plans and organizes work. Recognizes errors and problems.		5 4 3 2 1
Volume of Work Amount of work output. Adherence to standards and schedules. Effective use of time.		5 4 3 2 1
Quality of Work Degree of accuracy–lack of errors. Thoroughness of work. Ability to exercise good judgment.		5 4 3 2 1
Initiative and Creativity Self-motivation in seeking responsibility and work that needs to be done. Ability to apply original ideas and concepts.		5 4 3 2 1
Communication Ability to exchange thoughts or information in a clear, concise manner. Dealing with different organizational levels of clientele.		5 4 3 2 1
Dependability Ability to follow instructions and directions correctly. Performs under pressure. Reliable work habits.		5 4 3 2 1
Leadership Ability/Potential Ability to guide others to the successful accomplishment of a given task. Potential for developing subordinate employees.		5 4 3 2 1

5. Outstanding   Employee who consistently exceeds established standards and expectations of the job.

4. Above Average   Employee who consistently meets established standards and expectations of the job. Often exceeds and rarely falls short of desired results.

3. Satisfactory   Generally qualified employee who meets job standards and expectations. Sometimes exceeds and may occasionally fall short of desired expectations. Performs duties in a normally expected manner.

2. Improvement Needed   Not quite meeting standards and expectations. An employee at this level of performance is not quite meeting all the standard job requirements.

1. Unsatisfactory   Employee who fails to meet the minimum standards and expectations of the job.

I have had the opportunity to read this performance appraisal.   How long has this employee been under your supervision?

Signature   Date   Signature of Supervisor   Date

_____   _____

sheet of paper, one labeled "strengths" and the other, "something to work on." Team members self-assess and then pass the list around the room so other team members can add their comments.[25]

Administering Compensation and Employee Benefits

On what basis should employees be paid? How much should they be paid? When should they be paid? What benefits should they receive? Every day, company leaders confront these types of decisions. Administering **compensation**, a combination of payments in the form of wages or salaries, incentive payments, employee benefits, and employer services, is another major responsibility of a company's human resources department.

compensation
Money, benefits, and services paid to employees for their work

Wages and Salaries

Many blue-collar (production) and some white-collar (management and clerical) employees receive compensation in the form of **wages**, which are based on calculating the number of hours worked, the number of units produced, or a combination of both time and productivity. Wages provide a direct incentive to an employee: The more hours worked or the more pieces completed, the higher the employee's paycheck. Moreover, employers in the United States must comply with the Fair Labor Standards Act of 1938, which sets a minimum hourly wage for most employees and mandates overtime pay for employees who work longer than 40 hours a week. Most states also have minimum wage laws intended to protect employees not covered by federal laws or to set higher wage floors.

wages
Cash payment based on the number of hours the employee has worked or the number of units the employee has produced

Employees whose output is not always directly related to the number of hours worked or the number of pieces produced are paid **salaries**. As with wages, salaries base compensation on time, but the unit of time is a week, two weeks, a month, or a year. Salaried employees such as managers normally receive no pay for the extra hours they sometimes put in; overtime is simply part of their obligation. However, they do get a certain amount of leeway in their schedules.

salaries
Fixed weekly, monthly, or yearly cash compensation for work

Both wages and salaries are, in principle, based on the contribution of a particular job to the company. Thus, a sales manager, who is responsible for bringing in sales revenue, is paid more than a secretary, who handles administrative tasks but doesn't sell or supervise. However, pay often varies widely by position, industry, and location. Among the best-paid employees in the world are chief executive officers of large U.S. corporations.

5 LEARNING OBJECTIVE

List seven popular types of employee incentive programs

Incentive Programs

To encourage employees to be more productive, innovative, and committed to their work, many companies like Jamba Juice provide managers and employees with **incentives**, cash payments that are linked to specific individual, group, and companywide goals; overall productivity; and company success. In other words, achievements, not just activities, are made the basis for payment. For example, employees of Jamba Juice receive healthy bonuses provided the company meets its goals for net income and annual sales growth.[26] Still, the success of these incentive programs often depends on how closely incentives are linked to actions within the employee's control:

incentives
Cash payments to employees who produce at a desired level or whose unit (often the company as a whole) produces at a desired level

- *Bonuses.* For both salaried and wage-earning employees, one type of incentive compensation is the **bonus**, a payment in addition to the regular wage or salary. As an incentive to reduce turnover during the year, some firms pay an annual year-end bonus, amounting to

bonus
Cash payment, in addition to the regular wage or salary, that serves as a reward for achievement

a certain percentage of each employee's wages. Other cash bonuses are tied to company performance. Nucor, a North Carolina steel producer with 8,000 employees, pays much lower base wages—sometimes half of what the competition pays hourly workers. The company uses the savings to pay employees handsome bonuses—some 100 to 200 percent or more of their regular hourly wage. The bonuses are based on the amount of quality steel produced by, or passed through, a work team or shift. Thanks to the bonus system, Nucor has the highest productivity of any steel mill in the United States and the highest-paid steelworkers on earth, but the lowest labor costs per ton produced. "If you give a bonus to somebody of 15 percent, of course they like it, or 20 percent, even 25 percent, of course they love it. But if you give them a bonus of 100 percent you get their attention big-time and when they start seeing a 150 percent bonus, they are focused on that bonus," says one Nucor manager.[27]

commissions
Payments to employees equal to a certain percentage of sales made

profit sharing
System for distributing a portion of a company's profits to employees

gain sharing
Plan for rewarding employees not on the basis of overall profits but in relation to achievement of goals such as cost savings from higher productivity

pay for performance
Accepting a lower base pay in exchange for bonuses based on meeting production or other goals

- *Commissions.* In contrast to bonuses, **commissions** are a form of compensation that pays employees a percentage of sales made. Used mainly for sales staff, they may be either the sole compensation or an incentive payment in addition to a regular salary.

- *Profit sharing.* Employees may be rewarded for staying with a company and encouraged to work harder through **profit sharing**, a system in which employees receive a portion of the company's profits. Depending on the company, profits may be distributed quarterly, semiannually, or annually.

- *Gain sharing.* Similar to profit sharing, **gain sharing** ties rewards to profits (or cost savings) achieved by meeting specific goals such as quality and productivity improvement. For example, gain sharing is one tool that the city of College Station, Texas, uses to encourage savings and innovative ideas. In 1997, 520 full-time city employees each received $460 as a reward for helping to save the city $884,000.[28]

- *Pay for performance.* A variation of gain sharing, **pay for performance** requires employees to accept a lower base pay but rewards them with bonuses, commissions, or stock options if they reach production targets or other goals. Pay for performance must be re-earned each year and doesn't permanently increase base salary. Individuals can be evaluated on a number of variables, including whether they show partnership, demonstrate teamwork, or improve their skills. At a time of economic slowdown, pay for performance is becoming increasingly popular. A recent survey by Hewitt Associates found that nearly 80 percent of all companies have some kind of variable pay system, up from fewer than 50 percent in 1990. Proponents of the incentive say that rigorous, long-term pay-for-performance systems offer effective methods of helping companies continually improve the workforce while getting and keeping the best employees. Opponents argue that such pay plans tend to pit employees against one another, erode trust and teamwork, and create white-collar sweatshops.[29]

knowledge-based pay
Pay tied to an employee's acquisition of skills; also called skill-based pay

- *Knowledge-based pay.* Another approach to compensation being explored by companies is **knowledge-based pay**, or skill-based pay, which is tied to employees' knowledge and abilities rather than to their job per se. Typically, the pay level at which a person is hired matches that person's current level of skills; as the employee acquires new skills, the pay level goes up. Because employees do not compete with each other to increase their pay through promotions, knowledge-based pay enhances teamwork, flexibility, and motivation.[30]

broadbanding
Payment system that uses wide pay grades, enabling the company to give pay raises without promotions

- *Broadbanding.* Like knowledge-based pay, **broadbanding** gives pay raises without promoting employees. Instead of having many narrow pay grades, the company has fewer, broader pay grades. For example, instead of a range of $30,000 to $40,000 for a particular job, a broadband range may be $20,000 to $50,000. This approach allows today's flatter organizations to reward employees without having to move them up a hierarchy. It also allows companies to move employees to different positions without being restricted by the pay grades normally associated with specific jobs.

These incentive programs are so popular in today's workplace that many employees consider their dollar value as part of their overall salary package.

Employee Benefits and Services

Companies also regularly provide **employee benefits**—financial benefits other than wages, salaries, and incentives. For example, Starbucks offers medical and dental insurance, vacation and holiday pay, stock options, discounts on Starbucks products, and a free pound of coffee every week. The benefits package is available to part-time as well as full-time employees, so Starbucks attracts and retains good people at every level.

Companies may offer employee benefits either as a preset package—that is, the employee gets whatever insurance, paid holidays, pension plan, and other benefits the company sets up—or as flexible benefits, recognizing that people have different priorities and needs at different stages of their lives. Flexible plans allow employees to pick their benefits—up to a certain dollar amount—to create a benefits package tailored to their individual needs. Moreover, they smooth out imbalances in benefits received by single employees and workers with families.[31] An employee with a young family might want extra life or health insurance, for example, and might feel no need for a pension plan, while a single employee might choose to "buy" an extra week or two of vacation time by giving up some other benefit.

The benefits most commonly provided by employers are insurance, retirement benefits, employee stock-ownership plans, stock options, and family benefits. In the following sections, we will explore how these benefits and services are undergoing considerable change to meet the needs of today's workforce.

Insurance Although it is entirely optional, insurance is the most popular employee benefit. Many businesses offer substantial compensation in the form of life and health insurance, but dental and vision plans, disability insurance, and long-term-care insurance are also gaining in popularity, as Component Chapter B points out. Today only about 62 percent of employees are covered by a company health plan.[32]

In the past, a company would negotiate a group insurance plan for employees and pay most of the premium costs. However, faced with exploding health care costs, many companies now require employees to pay part of their insurance premiums or more of the actual doctor bills.[33] In addition, more companies are hiring part-time and temporary workers, who typically receive few company benefits. Nonetheless, some companies, like Jamba Juice, provide benefits because doing so discourages employee turnover.

Retirement Benefits Social Security was created by the federal government following the Great Depression of the 1930s to provide basic support to those who could not accumulate the retirement money they would need later in life. Today, nearly everyone who works regularly is eligible for Social Security payments during retirement. This income is paid for by the Social Security tax, part of which is withheld by the employer from employees' wages and part of which is paid by the employer. If you are self-employed, you pay the full tax amount.

In addition to Social Security, many employees receive company-sponsored retirement benefits. Studies show that 72 percent of workers at large firms (those with more than 500 employees) have some form of company-sponsored retirement coverage.[34] The most popular type of retirement coverage is the **pension plan**, which is funded by company contributions. Each year, enough money is set aside in a separate pension account to cover employees' future retirement benefits. These plans are

6 LEARNING OBJECITIVE

Highlight five popular employee benefits

employee benefits
Compensation other than wages, salaries, and incentive programs

pension plan
Company-sponsored program for providing retirees with income

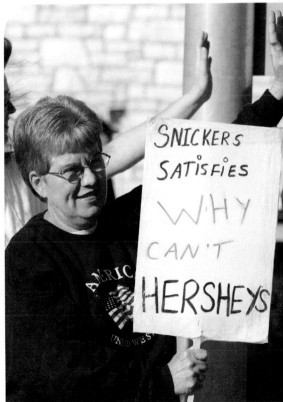

In Hershey, PA, workers like Bonnie Witmer are striking over Hershey Foods' insistence that employees pay more for their health care.

regulated by the Employees' Retirement Income Security Act of 1974 (ERISA), which established a federal agency to insure the assets of pension plans.

Three of the most popular types of company-sponsored pension plans are *defined contribution plans, defined benefit plans,* and *401(k) plans.* Defined contribution plans provide a future benefit based on annual employer contributions, voluntary employee matching contributions, and accumulated investment earnings. Less popular are defined benefit plans, which are formula-based plans in which employers typically promise to pay their employees a benefit on retirement based on the employee's retirement age, final average salary, and years of service.[35]

The employer-sponsored 401(k) plan allows eligible participants to contribute pre-tax dollars to a tax-qualified retirement plan. One special feature of a 401(k) plan is the deferral of federal and state income taxes and Social Security taxes on contributions up to a maximum of $10,500 per year until the time of withdrawal.[36] But these plans have drawbacks. For one thing, they put the burden on workers to set aside money for retirement and invest it wisely. For another, many employees invest their plans almost entirely in the employer's stock—subjecting their entire retirement savings to the vagaries of one company.

No company illustrates the promise—and the pitfall—of the 401(k) more than Enron, the Houston energy firm that filed for bankruptcy in December 2001. Some 11,000 Enron workers participated in the company's 401(k), receiving 50 cents worth of Enron shares for each dollar they contributed, up to 6 percent of their salaries. But when Enron's stock plummeted from $85 a share to less than 60 cents, employees lost about $1 billion in retirement savings. Some were like Roger Boyce, a 30-year employee who had accumulated more than $900,000 in his Enron 401(k) account; he watched the value of his account collapse to less than $10,000. Now Boyce is rethinking retirement—besides suing his former employer.[37]

employee stock-ownership plan (ESOP)
Program enabling employees to become partial owners of a company

stock options
Contract allowing the holder to purchase or sell a certain number of shares of a particular stock at a given price by a certain date

Employee Stock-Ownership Plans   Another employee benefit being offered by a number of companies is the **employee stock-ownership plan (ESOP)**, under which a company places a certain amount of its stock in trust for some or all of its employees, with each employee entitled to a certain share. These plans allow employees to later purchase the shares at a fixed price. If the company does well, the ESOP may provide a substantial employee benefit. Of course, linking the financial success of employees to the success of the company is a worthy goal, but some say that in the long run ESOPs are not effective performance motivators, as this chapter's United Airlines case study shows.

Stock Options   A related method for tying employee compensation to company performance is the stock option plan. **Stock options** grant employees the right to purchase a set number of shares of the employer's stock at a specific price, called the *grant* or *exercise* price, during a certain time period. Options typically "vest" over five years, at a rate of 20 percent annually. This means that at the end of one year employees can purchase up to 20 percent of the shares in the original grant, at the end of two years 40 percent, and so on. If the stock's market price exceeds the exercise price, the option holder can exercise the option and sell the stock at a profit. If the stock's price falls below the exercise price, the options become worthless.

Stock options can be a win–win situation for employers and employees. From the employer's perspective, stock options cost little, provide long-term incentives for good people to stay with the company, and encourage employees to work harder because they have a vested interest in the com-

After United Airlines employees bought a majority stake in their company, managers began referring to employees as "owners" and the airline changed its motto to "fly *our* friendly skies." The company's ESOP was even trumpeted on the cover of *Business Week* as a beacon for corporate America. But the era of harmony flickered briefly because the plan had several flaws.

pany's doing well. Options inspire creativity, hard work, and enough loyalty to stick around for the payoff because quitting would require an employee to forfeit stock option gains that could not yet be exercised. From the employee's perspective, stock options can be better than cash, offering the chance for riches far and beyond any salary.

But stock options lose their appeal when the stock does not perform as expected. When stocks retreat, as many did at the turn of the century, the value of the options decline considerably. And, as the Enron debacle illustrates, employees lose considerable profits when the stock's price falls below the option grant price.[38]

Family Benefits   The Family Medical and Leave Act (FMLA), signed into law in 1993, requires employers with 50 or more workers to provide up to 12 weeks of unpaid leave per year for childbirth, adoption, or the care of oneself, a child, a spouse, or a parent with serious illness. In spite of the law's good intentions, some claim that the FMLA is almost worthless to most American workers because few workers can afford to take up to 12 weeks off without pay. In fact, since Congress enacted the FMLA, employers report that only 6.5 percent of workers have used the law to take time off.[39]

Day care is another important family benefit, especially for two-career couples. Ford Motor Company, for instance, plans to open more than a dozen centers providing employees with 24-hour child care—part of a sweeping plan to provide family-related services in more than 30 locations around the United States. "Not only will [the centers] attract and retain the best, but the workforce, when they're at work, won't have to worry about their children and where they are," says one company spokesperson.[40] Today only 10 percent of companies provide day-care facilities on the premises, but 86 percent of companies surveyed by Hewitt & Associates offer some form of child-care assistance. Types of assistance include dependent-care spending accounts and resource and referral (R&R) services, which help employees find suitable child care. Firms estimate that they save anywhere from $2.00 to $6.75 in lost productivity and employee absenteeism for every $1.00 they spend on R&R programs.[41]

A related family issue is care for aging parents. An estimated 50 percent of employers offer some form of elder-care assistance, ranging from referral services that help find care providers to dependent-care allowances. Some companies will even agree to move elderly relatives when they transfer an employee to another location.[42]

Other Employee Benefits   Although sometimes overlooked, paid holidays, sick pay, premium pay for working overtime or unusual hours, and paid vacations are important benefits. Companies handle holiday pay in various ways. To provide incentives for employee loyalty, most companies grant employees longer paid vacations after they've been with the organization for a prescribed number of years. Some companies let employees buy additional vacation time or sell unused days back to the employer. Sick-day allowances also vary from company to company and from industry to industry. Some U.S. companies have begun offering paid-time-off banks that combine vacation, personal use, and sick days into one package. Employees can then take a certain number of days off each year for whatever reason necessary, with no questions asked.

Among the many other benefits that companies sometimes offer are sabbaticals, tuition loans and reimbursements, professional development opportunities, personal computers, financial counseling and legal services, assistance with buying a home, paid expenses for spouses who travel

Child care is a growing concern for all working mothers. These Harvard Business graduates balance their families and careers by working part time or by making alternate arrangements with their employers. Some have even put their careers on hold and have left the workplace to raise a family.

By offering benefits to all employees (including part-timers), Starbucks attracts and keeps quality employees.

with employees, employee assistance programs, nap time, and wellness programs. Typical wellness programs include health screenings, health and wellness education programs, and fitness programs. Children's clothier Osh Kosh B'Gosh, for example, provides wellness education classes in nutrition, heart disease, cancer, diabetes, prescription medication, and others.[43] Wellness programs have been reported to reduce absenteeism, health care costs, sickness, and work-related accidents.[44]

According to the U.S. Labor Department, 48 percent of all employers with more than 100 workers now offer **employee assistance programs (EAPs)**. EAPs offer private and confidential counseling to employees who need help with issues related to drugs, alcohol, finances, stress, family, and other personal problems. Studies by the National Council on Alcoholism and Drug Dependence (NCADD) show that the average annual cost for EAP services run from $12 to $20 per employee. However, these services save between $5 and $16 for each dollar spent as a result of improved safety and productivity, as well as reduced employee turnover.[45]

Benefits such as company cars, paid country club memberships, free parking, and expanded casual dress days are often referred to as perks. In a tight job market companies offer perks to attract the best managers.[46] "But recruitment perks only go so far," says one compensation expert. "Organizations must offer the total work experience to attract talent." And to keep talent from leaving, they must offer workers challenging jobs and training, more family-related benefits, and better management supervision.[47]

employee assistance programs (EAPs)
Company-sponsored counseling or referral plans for employees with personal problems

7 LEARNING OBJECTIVE

Describe four ways an employee's status may change and discuss why many employers prefer to fill job vacancies from within

Overseeing Changes in Employment Status

Of course, providing competitive compensation and good employee benefits is no guarantee that employees will stay with the company. Employees leave companies for a variety of reasons. Some may decide to retire. Others may resign voluntarily to pursue a better opportunity. Still others may make a change because they are promoted, reassigned, or terminated. Whatever the reason, when a vacancy occurs, companies must go to the trouble and expense of finding a replacement, whether from inside or outside the company. Overseeing changes in employment status is another responsibility of the human resources department.

Promoting and Reassigning Employees

As Exhibit 11.3 shows, many companies prefer to look within the organization to fill job vacancies. In part, this "promote from within" policy allows a company to benefit from the training and experience of its own workforce. This policy also rewards employees who have worked hard and demonstrated the ability to handle more challenging tasks. In addition, morale is usually better when a company promotes from within because employees see that they can advance.

However, a potential pitfall of internal promotion is that a person may be given a job beyond his or her competence. A common practice is for someone who is good at one kind of job to be made a manager. Yet managing often requires a completely different set of skills.

Someone who consistently racks up the most sales in the company, for example, is not necessarily a good candidate for sales manager. If the promotion is a mistake, the company not only loses its sales leader but also risks losing the employee altogether. People who can't perform well in a new job generally become demoralized and lose confidence in the abilities they do have. At the very least, support and training are needed to help promoted employees perform well.

Terminating Employees

A company invests time, effort, and money in each new employee it recruits and trains. This investment is lost when an employee is removed by **termination**—permanently laying off the employee because of cutbacks or firing the employee for poor performance. Many companies facing a downturn in business have avoided large-scale layoffs by cutting administrative costs (curtailing travel, seminars, and so on), freezing wages, postponing new hiring, implementing job-sharing programs, or encouraging early retirement. However, sometimes a company has no alternative but to reduce the size of its workforce, leaving the human resources department to handle layoffs and their resulting effects on both the terminated and the remaining employees.

Union official John Drueke said his "heart just dropped" after learning about the closing of Life Savers's Holland, Michigan, plant. The plant employed 600 workers and was the city's third-largest taxpayer. The company shifted production to Quebec, citing high U.S. sugar prices as the major factor behind the relocation.

termination
Act of getting rid of an employee through layoffs or firing

layoffs
Termination of employees for economic or business reasons

Layoffs are the termination of employees for economic or business reasons unrelated to employee performance. Companies are free to make layoffs in any manner they choose, just as long as certain demographic groups are not disproportionately affected. But as Michael Dell puts it, making cuts "is one of the hardest, most gut-wrenching decisions you can make as a leader." Layoffs are "an admission that we screwed up" by overhiring, admits Dell. If there's a lesson, says Dell, it's that "when things heat up quite a bit, we should take some pause."[48]

To help ease the pain of layoffs, many companies provide laid-off employees with job-hunting assistance. *Outplacement* aids such as résumé-writing courses, career counseling, office space, and secretarial help are offered to laid-off executives and blue-collar employees alike. Moreover, outplacement centers offer courses and tests to help employees decide what types of jobs are best suited for them.

Some companies adopt no-layoff, or guaranteed-employment, policies. This means that in an economic downturn, employees may be shifted to other types of jobs, perhaps at reduced pay, or given the chance to participate in work-sharing programs. Such no-layoff policies help promote employee loyalty and motivation, which benefit the company over the long run. Rhino Foods realized the benefit of this policy when the company hit a downturn in the mid-1990s. Employees voluntarily took temporary jobs with other companies, which Rhino helped them find. If the new companies paid lower wages than the employees normally received, Rhino made up the difference. Employees also kept their Rhino seniority, benefits, and accrued vacation time. When business picked up again, the employees returned. As a result of the exchange program, Rhino enjoys much higher employee morale, loyalty, and trust than it would had it laid off workers.[49]

Retiring Employees

As Chapter 10 discussed, the U.S. population is aging rapidly. For the business community, an aging population presents two challenges. The first is to give job opportunities to people

mandatory retirement
Required dismissal of an employee who reaches a certain age

worker buyout
Distribution of financial incentives to employees who voluntarily depart, usually undertaken in order to reduce the payroll

who are willing and able to work but who happen to be past the traditional retirement age. Many older citizens are concerned about their ability to live comfortably on fixed retirement incomes. Others simply prefer to work. For several decades, many companies and industries had **mandatory retirement** policies that made it necessary for people to quit working as soon as they turned a certain age. Then in 1967 the Age Discrimination in Employment Act outlawed discrimination against anyone between the ages of 40 and 65. In 1986 Congress amended the act to prohibit mandatory retirement for most employees. As a corollary, employers are also forbidden to stop benefit contributions or accruals because of age.

The second challenge posed by an aging workforce is to find ways to encourage older employees to retire early. One method a company may use is to offer older employees financial incentives to resign, such as enhanced retirement benefits or one-time cash payments. Inducing employees to depart by offering them financial incentives is known as a **worker buyout**. This method can be a lot more expensive than firing or laying off employees. However, the method has several advantages: The morale of the remaining employees is preserved because they feel less threatened about their own security, younger employees see increased chances for promotion, and the risk of age-discrimination lawsuits is minimized.

Summary of Learning Objectives

1. **List six main functions of human resources departments.**

   Human resources departments plan for a company's staffing needs, recruit and hire new employees, train and develop employees, appraise employee performance, administer compensation and employee benefits, and oversee changes in employment status.

2. **Cite eight methods recruiters use to find job candidates.**

   Recruiters find job candidates by (1) promoting internal candidates, (2) advertising in newspapers and on the Internet, (3) using public and private employment agencies, (4) contacting union hiring halls, (5) recruiting at college campuses and career placement offices, (6) attending trade shows, (7) hiring corporate "headhunters," and (8) soliciting referrals from employees or colleagues in the industry.

3. **Identify the six stages in the hiring process.**

   The stages in the hiring process are (1) narrowing down the number of qualified candidates, (2) performing initial screening interviews, (3) administering a series of follow-up interviews, (4) evaluating candidates, (5) conducting reference checks, and (6) selecting the right candidate.

4. **Discuss how companies incorporate objectivity into employee performance appraisals.**

   Employee performance appraisals are an effective way to inform employees if they are doing a good job and how they can improve their performance. To ensure objectivity and fairness, most firms use a standard, companywide format, provide a written record of appraisals for future reference, and solicit several perspectives by engaging superiors, peers, and colleagues at different levels in the organization in the review process.

5. **List seven popular types of employee incentive programs.**

   The most popular employee incentive programs are bonuses, commissions, profit sharing, gain sharing, pay for performance, knowledge-based pay, and broadbanding. In addition to these seven popular employee benefits, many companies offer paid holidays and vacations, sick pay, overtime pay, sabbaticals, tuition loans and reimbursements, professional development opportunities, wellness programs, and employee assistance programs.

6. **Highlight five popular employee benefits.**

   The two most popular employee benefits are insurance (health, life, disability, and long-term care) and retirement benefits, such as pension plans that help employees save for later years. Employee stock-ownership plans and stock options, two additional benefits, allow employees to receive or purchase shares of the company's stock, and thus obtain a stake in the company. Family benefits programs, also popular, include maternity and paternity leave, child-care assistance, and elder-care assistance.

7. **Describe four ways an employee's status may change and discuss why many employers prefer to fill job vacancies from within.**

An employee's status may change through promotion or through reassignment to a different position; through termination (removal from the company's payroll); through voluntary resignation; or through retirement. Employers like to fill vacancies created from such changes by promoting from within for these reasons: The employee has been trained by the company and knows the ropes; it boosts employee morale; and it sends a message to other employees that good performance will be rewarded.

KEY TERMS

bonus **(285)**

broadbanding **(286)**

commissions **(286)**

compensation **(285)**

employee assistance programs (EAPs) **(290)**

employee benefits **(287)**

employee stock-ownership plan (ESOP) **(288)**

gain sharing **(286)**

human resources management (HRM) **(274)**

incentives **(285)**

job analysis **(277)**

job description **(277)**

job specification **(277)**

knowledge-based pay **(286)**

layoffs **(291)**

mandatory retirement **(292)**

orientation **(281)**

pay for performance **(286)**

pension plan **(287)**

performance appraisal **(282)**

profit sharing **(286)**

recruiting **(278)**

salaries **(285)**

stock options **(288)**

termination **(291)**

wages **(285)**

worker buyout **(292)**

TEST YOUR KNOWLEDGE

Questions for Review

1. What do human resources managers do?

2. What are some strategic staffing alternatives that organizations use to avoid overstaffing and understaffing? Explain the advantages and disadvantages of each alternative.

3. What is the purpose of conducting a job analysis? What are some of the techniques used for gathering information?

4. What are the three types of preemployment tests administered by companies, and how are each of these tests used to assist with the hiring decision?

5. What functions do orientation programs serve?

Questions for Analysis

6. How do incentive programs encourage employees to be more productive, innovative, and committed to their work?

7. Why do some employers offer comprehensive benefits even though the costs of doing so have risen significantly in recent years?

8. What are the advantages and disadvantages of 401(k) retirement plans?

9. The 1986 Immigration Reform and Control Act forbids companies to hire illegal aliens but at the same time prohibits discrimination in hiring on the basis of national origin or citizenship status. How can companies satisfy both requirements of this law?

10. *Ethical Considerations:* Corporate headhunters have been known to raid other companies of their top talent to fill vacant or new positions for their clients. Is it ethical to contact the CEO of one company and lure him or her to join the management team of another company?

Questions for Application

11. If you were on the human resources staff at a large health care organization that was looking for a new manager of information systems, what recruiting method(s) would you use and why?

12. Assume you are the manager of human resources at a manufacturing company that employs about 500 people. A recent cyclical downturn in your industry has led to financial losses, and top management is talking about laying off workers. Several supervisors have come to you with creative ways of keeping employees on the payroll, such as exchanging workers with other local companies. Why might you want to consider this option? What other options exist besides layoffs?

13. *Integrated:* Of the five levels in Maslow's hierarchy of needs (discussed in Chapter 10), which is satisfied by offering salary? By offering health care benefits? By offering training opportunities? By developing flexible job descriptions?

14. *Integrated:* What are some of the human resources issues managers are likely to encounter when two companies (in the same industry) merge?

PRACTICE YOUR KNOWLEDGE

Handling Difficult Situations on the Job: Juggling Diversity and Performance

As billing adjustments department manager at SBC Pacific Bell, you've been trained to handle a culturally diverse workforce. For example, the company does not condone behaviors that interfere with work performance, no matter who commits them or why.

When a supervisor working for you suggested hiring Jorge Gutierrez after an interview, you agreed. No company rules forbid you to hire your 22-year-old nephew, especially since he was so well qualified. In record time, he was entering and testing complex price changes, mastering the challenges of your monumental computerized billing software. He was a real find—except for one problem he hasn't been able to surmount.

Every morning your Mexican American nephew's mother calls to be sure he got to work safely. Then his father calls. Afternoon calls are from his baseball buddies (he plays in a Mexican league). Later it's his girlfriend, also Mexican American. In one month's time, he left work for three "family emergencies": to change his girlfriend's flat tire, to deliver an extra car key because she locked herself out, and to "defend" her from an aggressive and unsavory boss at a job she quit that afternoon.

Gutierrez says he's asked friends and family not to call his office number. Now they dial his cell phone instead. He still lives with his parents, which may be why they seem insensitive to his appeals. You're not Mexican American but you understand completely, being married to his mother's sibling. In their culture, family comes first.

Your task: How will you reprimand Gutierrez while understanding his need to balance the demands of work with his personal life? Should you wait for a formal performance appraisal or do it sooner? Why? Should you terminate Gutierrez? Would alternative work arrangements be a good idea for Gutierrez? Why or why not?

Building Your Team Skills

Team up with a classmate to practice your responses to interview questions. Use the list of common interview questions provided in Component Chapter C, Exhibit C.9 (see p. 524), and take turns posing and responding to those questions. Which questions did you find most difficult to answer? What insights did you gain about your strengths and weaknesses by answering those questions? Why is it a good idea to rehearse your answers before going to an interview?

EXPAND YOUR KNOWLEDGE

Discovering Career Opportunities

If you pursue a career in human resources, you'll be deeply involved in helping organizations find, select, train, evaluate, and retain employees. You have to like people and be a good communicator to succeed in HR. Is this field for you? Using your local Sunday newspaper, the *Wall Street Journal*, or online sources such as Monster Board (www.monster.com), find ads seeking applicants for jobs in the field of human resources.

1. What educational qualifications, technical knowledge, or specialized skills are applicants for these jobs expected to have? How do these requirements fit with your background and educational plans?

2. Next, look at the duties mentioned in the ad for each job. What do you think you would be doing on an average day in these jobs? Does the work in each job sound interesting and challenging?

3. Now think about how you might fit into one of these positions. Do you prefer to work alone, or do you enjoy teamwork? How much paperwork are you willing to do? Do you communicate better in person, on paper, or by phone? Considering your answers to these questions, which of the HR jobs seems to be the closest match for your personal style?

Developing Your Research Skills

Locate one or more articles in business journals or newspapers (print or online editions) that illustrate how a company or industry is adapting to changes in its workforce. (Examples include retraining, literacy or basic-skills training, flexible benefits, and benefits aimed at working parents or people who care for aging relatives.)

1. What changes in the workforce or employee needs caused the company to adapt? What did the company do to respond to these changes? Was the company's response voluntary or legally mandated?

2. Is the company alone in facing these changes, or is the entire industry trying to adapt? What are other companies in the industry doing to adapt to the changes?

3. What other changes in the workforce or in employee needs do you think this company is likely to face in the next few years? Why?

Exploring the Best of the Web

URLs for all Internet exercises are provided at the website for this book, www.prenhall.com/bovee. *When you log on to the text website, select Chapter 11, then select "Student Resources," click on the name of the featured website, and review the website to complete these exercises.*

Explore these chapter-related websites, review their content, and answer the following questions for each website you visit:

1. What is the purpose of this website?
2. What kinds of information does this website contain? Please be specific.
3. How is the information provided at this website useful for businesspeople? Consumers?
4. How did you expand your knowledge of human resources management by reviewing the material at this website? What new things did you learn about this topic?

Staying on Top of the HR World

Like all areas of business, the world of human resources changes quickly. To stay informed about trends in recruiting, compensation, benefits, and employee satisfaction, turn to HR Live. Browse through some of the top recruiting markets for occupations that interest you. Read one of the recent layoff reports. This comprehensive online resource provides HR professionals with information about employment markets and trends, labor statistics, recruiting methods, layoffs, and much more. The site also offers convenient links to job fairs and conventions in a variety of industries so recruiters (and job seekers) can plan ahead. www.hrlive.com

Digging Deeper at the Bureau of Labor Statistics

By now you're probably aware that the U.S. government has an agency for almost every purpose. Many of these agencies gather facts and statistics on trends in the United States, and the Bureau of Labor Statistics is no exception. When you need to research detailed information about national or regional employment conditions—such as wages, unemployment, productivity, and benefits—point your web browser to this site. www.bls.gov

Maximizing Your Earning Potential

You know you should be making more money. So now what? Log on to Salary.com to find out what you are worth. Then maximize your earning potential by exploring the basics of negotiation. Sharpen your skills so you can get the job, salary, and benefits you want. Contemplating a move? Use the cost-of-living wizard to find out if it makes economic sense. You may even want to prepare for your next performance review by taking one of the site's self tests. Finally, don't leave without learning how to manage your take-home pay or getting some facts about tuition assistance. Many companies will reimburse you for your career course work. But you may not get it if you don't ask. www.salary.com

Learning Interactively

Companion Website

Visit the Companion Website at www.prenhall.com/bovee. For Chapter 11, take advantage of the interactive "Study Guide" to test your chapter knowledge. Get instant feedback on whether you need additional studying. Read the "Current Events" articles to get the latest on chapter topics, and complete the exercises as specified by your instructor. Expand your learning with a visit to the "Research Area." There you will find a wealth of information you can use to complete your course assignments.

A CASE FOR CRITICAL THINKING

Hard Landing for United's Employee Stock-Ownership Program

In the terrorist attacks of September 11, 2001, United Airlines lost two aircraft, 18 employees, and 92 passengers. The disaster was a huge emotional blow to a company already weakened by high labor costs and low-fare competitors. Eight days later, morale sank again as United announced plans to cut service and lay off 20,000 workers. In the ensuing months, the soft U.S. economy continued to decline and companies slashed spending on business travel—a major source of airline revenues. It was all too much for United, leading the company to file for Chapter 11 bankruptcy protection on December 9, 2002. United was the largest airline to ever go bankrupt and, in terms of assets, the fifth-largest bankruptcy ever.

Exchanging Pay for Ownership

United's problems started in the early 1990s, when its lackluster customer service and high fares helped drive passengers to upbeat, low-fare competitors such as Southwest Airlines. To get back on course, United entered into discussions with the unions representing its pilots, machinists, and flight attendants. In 1994, pilots, machinists, and nonunion workers agreed to $4.8 billion in pay cuts and work-rule changes in exchange for a 55 percent stake in the airline. Flight attendants, however, refused to participate because they didn't want to trade pay for stock.

Through its uniquely generous employee stock-ownership plan (ESOP), United became one of the world's largest employee-controlled companies. The new employee-owners hoped to recover the value of their lost wages through increased market value of their ESOP shares, and the company hoped to gain enhanced morale and improved customer service. Ultimately, neither occurred.

An ESOP Fable

In the beginning, the deal did help United streamline operations and cut costs. The company posted record profits from 1995 to 1997, and the stock soared in value. The innovative deal looked like a win–win for employees and management.

Unfortunately, the glow of success flickered all too briefly. United's stock soon began to struggle under the weight of competitive pressures, rising fuel costs, and internal battling among union members—either because they were not part of the ESOP or because they had joined reluctantly. What's more, because federal ESOP rules barred employees from selling their stock until they retired or quit, the shares were useless for financing a home or a college education. Ultimately, ESOP participants felt they had been taken for a ride.

Most ESOPs succeed in part because employees typically own less than 10 percent of the company—enough to give them a sense of ownership but not enough to take control. At United, the ESOP used its controlling stake to put three employees on the company board of directors, two of them union members and one non-union. Having union members participate in management created a conflict of interest and made it practically impossible for the board to have open discussions about cost reductions, which are often part of contract negotiations with airline unions. In effect, the ESOP became an enemy of the company and complicated the already tough job of managing an airline.

A Bumpy Ride

In 2000, the United ESOP and the 1994 union contracts all expired. Rather than renewing the ESOP, the unions fought for wage increases that would bring pay up to industry averages. Negotiations with the pilots union were brutal, forcing United to cancel thousands of flights during peak summer months. The resulting growth in compensation costs eroded United's profitability and hammered its stock. As the stock price fell, so did employee morale and customer satisfaction.

Things only got worse as crisis after crisis piled up like outbound jets at O'Hare. The year 2001 brought a failed merger with U.S. Airways and the 9-11 terrorist attacks. In 2002, tense contract negotiations with the machinists union also resulted in substantial wage increases. After posting huge losses in the second and third quarters of 2002, bankruptcy was United's inevitable destination.

The day after the bankruptcy announcement, United ran full-page ads in major newspapers along its routes, promising to keep flying while it worked out its problems. The ads called the bankruptcy a new beginning and promised customers they would feel new energy and optimism when boarding a United flight. It was a risky promise because it had to be fulfilled by employees who had watched the market value of their company shares become worthless.

While experts debate the reasons that the United Airlines ESOP failed, most agree that the plan's main flaw was its short-term nature. Because it failed to create long-term harmony between employees and management, the United ESOP will be remembered as an experiment in employee ownership that ultimately made it more difficult for the company to pull out of its nosedive.

Critical Thinking Questions

1. Why did United's pilots and machinists fight so hard for wage increases in 2000 and 2002?

2. How might benefit programs such as an ESOP ultimately affect customer service?

3. What lessons can other companies learn from United's failed ESOP?

4. Visit the United Airlines website at www.ual.com and review the information posted in the Employment section. What kind of employee benefits are described in the Employment section?

VIDEO CASE

Managing the Human Side of the Business: Park Place Entertainment

Learning Objectives

The purpose of this video is to help you:

1. Recognize how human resources management contributes to organizational performance.

2. Understand how and why HR managers make plans and decisions about staffing.

3. Identify some of the ways in which HR managers handle staff evaluation and development.

Synopsis

Park Place Entertainment owns and operates many resorts and casinos around the world. Its human resources department is responsible for hiring, training, and managing a diverse group of more than 52,000 employees. HR managers have created specific job descriptions for each position, instituted training programs for employee and management development, and established incentive programs to reward good performance. Park Place's 360-degree evaluation method allows supervisors to get performance feedback from the employees they supervise. Because its customers come from many countries and speak many languages, the company seeks out employees from diverse backgrounds, varying the recruitment process for different properties in different areas.

Discussion Questions

1. *For analysis:* What are the advantages and disadvantages of centralizing the recruiting process at a company such as Park Place Entertainment?

2. *For analysis:* Why did Park Place begin the restructuring of its HR department by standardizing training for supervisors?

3. *For application:* What steps might Park Place's HR executives take to reduce turnover among the employees at particular resorts?

4. *For application:* How might Park Place encourage its employees to refer friends as candidates for open positions?

5. *For debate:* Rather than hiring employees when business booms and then laying some off when business falls off, should Park Place temporarily rehire some of its retired supervisors and employees during peak periods? Support your chosen position.

Online Exploration

Visit the Park Place Entertainment website at www.ballys.com and browse the homepage to see the locations and names of the com-pany's resorts and casinos. Then follow the company information link to look at career opportunities and company benefits. What kinds of jobs are being featured on the website? Why would Park Place arrange jobs by region? How does the firm make it convenient for applicants to submit résumés online? Why would Park Place put so much emphasis on Internet recruiting?

Managing Employees

PART 4

Mastering Global and Geographical Skills: People Are the Same Everywhere, Aren't They?

Companies that expand across national or cultural borders sometimes run into unexpected barriers in human resources management. For example, Japanese automakers were surprised when they tried to get workers in their new U.S. plants to join in for daily warm-up exercises. Even though the activity is commonplace in Japan, it simply didn't catch on in the United States. And DaimlerChrysler's U.S. managers were surprised by the German managers' extravagant travel and dining practices.

When companies operate across national and cultural borders, understanding cultural expectations and norms is crucial to effective management. Some of the concepts to consider involve personal space, conversational formalities (or lack thereof), friendliness, willingness to "job hop," respect for authority figures, and awareness of social class distinctions.

You can identify a number of potentially important workplace issues by exploring a country's general culture. Egyptians, for instance, address each other by first names only in informal, private settings. When in public, even good friends may add titles when addressing each other. Egyptians tend to be more conscious of social classes than are people in the United States. Moreover, they place great value on visiting friends and relatives.

Assume that you're the president of a financial-services firm based in Indianapolis and that you're ready to expand overseas. To ease your first attempt at international expansion, you're trying to find a country with workplace characteristics most similar to those in the United States. Gather as much relevant information as you can about the four countries that follow. Choose the one with work styles that feel most like those of the United States, and explain your choice. In addition to the resources in your library, explore the information available on the Internet. Possible Internet resources include the *Region and Country Information* of the International Trade Administration, *Background Notes* published by the U.S. Department of State, the Library of Congress' *Country Studies*, and the *CIA World Factbook*. Go to this text's website at www.prenhall.com/bovee for direct links to these resources. (Your instructor may want you to do this as a group exercise.)

- England
- France
- South Korea
- Mexico

CHAPTER

12

Fundamentals of Marketing, Customers, and Strategic Marketing Planning

LEARNING OBJECTIVES

After studying this chapter, you will be able to

1. Explain what marketing is

2. Describe the four utilities created by marketing

3. Explain how the Internet is affecting the marketing function

4. Explain why and how companies learn about their customers

5. Discuss how marketing research helps the marketing effort, and highlight its limitations

6. Outline the three steps in the strategic marketing planning process

7. Define market segmentation and cite six factors used to identify segments

8. Identify the four elements of a company's marketing mix

Capital One is winning big in the cutthroat world of credit cards by analyzing customer information.

INSIDE BUSINESS TODAY

Driven by Data: Banking on Information at Capital One

If you think credit cards are merely banking products, think again. According to the co-founder, chairman, and CEO of Capital One Financial Corp, "Credit cards aren't banking—they're *information*." In fact, information is the driving force behind Richard Fairbank's successful strategy for building Capital One into one of America's leading credit card companies.

Fairbank collects extensive records on millions of consumers, maintaining massive databases on everything from customer demographics to individual card transactions. Then he uses that information not only to identify customers who would make good credit risks but to develop customized marketing strategies for different customer segments.

First, Fairbank applies data-mining techniques to his records of potential customers to find individuals who match the profile of the ideal credit card holder: the person who maintains a credit card balance but always makes a minimum monthly payment on time. And to build his customer base, he creates customized mailing lists by studying such demographics as educational levels and club memberships. For instance, Fairbank used data mining to develop his own profile of college students after he discovered that the credit card industry's mailing lists covered only one-third of the college population. Students overlooked by other credit card companies responded eagerly to Capital One's offers, returning 70 percent more applications than the industry's standard lists.

Next, Fairbank analyzes information about current Capital One customers to figure out how customers use their cards and to find meaningful patterns in consumer buying behavior. Finally, he conducts 40,000 tests every year, experimenting with everything from annual credit card fees to the color of the envelopes used for mailings. One of Fairbank's early experiments featured the "teaser rate," offering low interest rates for an introductory period. When the experiment attracted millions of new customers, competitors launched similar programs.

With test results in hand, Fairbank uses that information to produce and sell 7,000 types of customized credit cards—each with slightly different terms and conditions—aimed at different customer segments. Some customers, for example, pay $20 per year for a card with $200 worth of credit. Others carry no-fee cards with credit lines of $10,000 or $20,000. And many of the cards cater to customer preferences or interests, featuring images that range from Mt. Fuji to a Mercedes-Benz or a Canadian moose.

Fairbank even uses data mining to predict what customers might buy and how Capital One can sell those products and services to them. For example, after tests revealed that customers preferred to buy things when they call Capital One—rather than when Capital One calls them—Fairbank decided to offer additional products and services to incoming callers. He partnered with other businesses to sell callers such products as MCI long distance, Hartford insurance, and Damark International catalog club memberships. And he used an analysis of each customer's buying habits and demographics to develop a computer software system that recommends which products to sell specific customer types when they call Capital One.

Such aggressive marketing tactics have indeed paid off. Started in 1995, Capital One has quickly risen to the top of the credit card industry in the United States. But Fairbank isn't sitting still. He continues to bank on Capital One's extensive databases to identify new marketing opportunities and to test, produce, and sell a constant stream of new products to Capital One's 48 million customers.[1]

Marketing in a Changing World

Even though you are just beginning a formal classroom study of business, you probably already know quite a bit about marketing. Companies like Capital One have been trying to sell you products for years, and you've learned something about their techniques—contests, advertisements, tantalizing displays of merchandise, price markdowns, and product giveaways, to name but a few. However, marketing involves much more than a fancy display of merchandise, a clever commercial, or a special contest. In fact, a lot of planning and execution are needed to develop a new product, set its price, get it into stores, and convince people to buy it.

Think about all the decisions you would have to make if you worked for Richard Fairbank, for example. How many credit card customers would you need in order to be profitable? Which types of customers would you serve? How would you attract new customers? What fees would you charge for your services? What would you do if another credit card operation offered more attractive services or lower fees? These are just a few of the many marketing decisions that all companies make in order to be successful. This chapter explores some of the marketing fundamentals that will help you answer these questions. We begin with a definition of marketing.

What Is Marketing?

marketing
Process of planning and executing the conception, pricing, promotion, and distribution of ideas, goods, and services to create and maintain relationships that satisfy individual and organizational objectives

customer service
Efforts a company makes to satisfy its customers to help them realize the greatest possible value from the products they are purchasing

place marketing
Marketing efforts to attract people and organizations to a particular geographical area

cause-related marketing
Identification and marketing of a social issue, cause, or idea to selected target markets

The American Marketing Association (AMA) defines **marketing** as planning and executing the conception, pricing, promotion, and distribution of ideas, goods, and services to create exchanges that satisfy individual and organizational objectives.[2] With respect to products, marketing involves all decisions related to determining a product's characteristics, price, production specifications, market-entry date, distribution, promotion, and sales. With respect to customers, marketing involves understanding customers' needs and their buying behavior, creating consumer awareness, providing **customer service**—which is everything a company does to satisfy its customers—and maintaining relationships with customers long after the sales transaction is complete (see Exhibit 12.1).

Most people, of course, think of marketing in connection with selling tangible goods for a profit (the term *product* refers to any "bundle of value" that can be exchanged in a marketing transaction). But marketing applies to services, nonprofit organizations, people, places, and causes too. Politicians always market themselves. So do places (such as Paris or Poland) that want to attract residents, tourists, and business investment. **Place marketing** describes efforts to market geographical areas ranging from neighborhoods to entire countries. **Cause-related marketing** promotes a cause or a social issue, such as physical fitness, cancer awareness, recycling, or highway safety.

Cause-related marketing has become one of the hottest forms of corporate giving. Linking purchases of the company's products and services with fundraising for worthwhile causes or charitable organizations helps companies do well by doing good. Avon, the world's largest direct seller of cosmetics and beauty items, has for years sponsored programs aimed at raising national and global awareness of breast cancer. Other companies have also jumped on the corporate-giving bandwagon. Drink Tang and earn money for Mothers Against Drunk Driving. Donate Delta Airlines frequent flyer miles to Share Our Strength (SOS), a hunger relief organization, and Delta will add 1,000 miles for every 5,000 miles

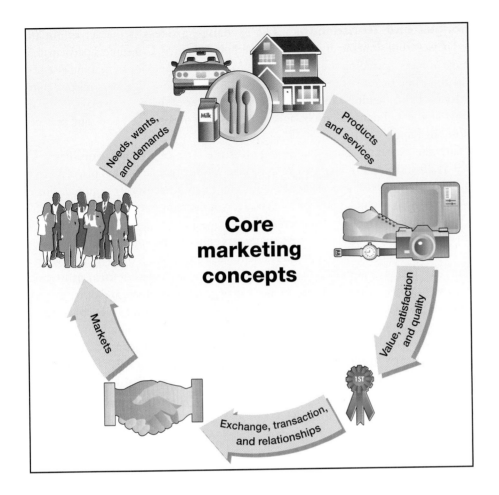

EXHIBIT 12.1
What Is Marketing?
Each of the core marketing concepts—needs, wants, demands, products, services, value, satisfaction, quality, exchanges, transactions, relationships, and markets—builds on the ones before it.

contributed by Sky Miles members. And purchase a pint of Ben & Jerry's One Sweet Whirled ice cream and support the company's grassroots promotion to encourage the reduction of greenhouse gases.[3]

Of course, marketing serves other functions besides promoting products, places, and causes. As the AMA definition suggests, marketing serves two important functions: It helps people satisfy their needs and wants, and it encourages consumer purchases.

need
Difference between a person's actual state and his or her ideal state; provides the basic motivation to make a purchase

wants
Things that are desirable in light of a person's experiences, culture, and personality

Needs and Wants A fundamental goal of marketing is to channel the customer's basic need for various products into the desire to purchase specific brands. To survive, people need food, water, air, shelter, and clothing. A **need** represents a difference between your actual state and your ideal state. If you're hungry; you need food in order to return to the non-hungry state. Needs create the motivation to buy products and are therefore at the core of any discussion of marketing.

Your **wants** are based on your needs but are more specific. Producers do not create needs, but they do shape your wants by exposing you to alternatives. For instance, when you need some food, you may want a Snickers bar or an orange. Al Ries and Jack Trout, co-authors of *The 22 Immutable Laws of Marketing*, note that customers' wants are directed by changing people's perception of products.[4] After all, what's the real difference between Viva and Bounty paper towels? Is one actually more absorbent than the other, or do you only perceive it that way?

The breast cancer awareness campaign is an example of cause-related marketing that attracts millions of marketing dollars from companies such as Kellogg's.

exchange process
Act of obtaining a desired object from another party by offering something of value in return

transaction
Exchange between parties

2 **LEARNING OBJECTIVE**

Describe the four utilities created by marketing

utility
Power of a good or service to satisfy a human need

form utility
Consumer value created by converting raw materials and other inputs into finished goods and services

time utility
Consumer value added by making a product available at a convenient time

place utility
Consumer value added by making a product available in a convenient location

possession utility
Consumer value created when someone takes ownership of a product

EXHIBIT 12.2
Examples of the Four Utilities
The utility of a good or service has four aspects, each of which enhances the product's value to the consumer.

Exchanges and Transactions The **exchange process** is the act of obtaining a desired object from someone by offering something in return. Consumers participate in the exchange process by trading something of value (usually money) for something else of value, such as an airline ticket, a car, or a college education. When consumers make a purchase, they cast a vote for that item and encourage the producer of that item to make more of it. In this way, supply and demand are balanced, and society obtains the goods and services that are most satisfying.

When the exchange actually occurs, it takes the form of a **transaction**. Party A gives Party B $1.29 and gets a medium Coke in return. A trade of values takes place. Most transactions in today's society involve money, but money is not necessarily required. For example, when you were a child, you may have traded your peanut butter sandwich for a friend's bologna and cheese in a barter transaction that involved no money.

To encourage the exchange process, marketers enhance the appeal of their products and services by adding **utility**, something of value to customers (see Exhibit 12.2). When organizations change raw materials into finished goods, they are creating **form utility** for consumers. For example, when Nokia combines plastic, computer chips, and other materials to make digital phones, the company is providing form utility. In other cases, marketers try to make their products available when and where customers want to buy them, creating **time utility** and **place utility**. Overnight couriers such as Airborne Express create time utility, whereas coffee carts in offices and ATM machines in shopping malls create place utility. The final form of utility is **possession utility**—the satisfaction that buyers get when they actually possess a product, both legally and physically. First Union Mortgage, for example, creates possession utility by offering loans that allow people to buy homes they could otherwise not afford.

Fundamental Marketing Concepts

A firm's marketing efforts are defined by its general marketing beliefs. Some companies believe that offering a good product or service is the key to marketing success. Others focus on selling the products they make, regardless of how consumer needs may be changing. Still others focus on doing whatever they can do to satisfy customers' changing needs and wants; they recognize the value of customer loyalty and they strive to maintain long-term relationships with their customers. Here's a closer look at these fundamental marketing concepts.

Product Concept Companies whose marketing is based on a product concept believe that consumers will favor products that offer the most in quality, performance, and innovative features. Thus, they devote their marketing resources to making continuous product

UTILITY	EXAMPLE
Form utility	Sunkist Fun Fruits are nutritious, bite-sized snacks that appeal to youngsters because of their shapes—numbers, letters, dinosaurs, spooks, and animals.
Time utility	LensCrafters has captured a big chunk of the market for eyeglasses by providing on-the-spot one-hour service.
Place utility	By offering convenient home delivery of the latest fashion apparel and accessories, the Delia*s catalog and website have become favorites of teenaged girls.
Possession utility	RealNetworks, producer of software for listening to music from the Internet, allows customers to download and install its programs directly from the company's website.

improvements. But building a better product does not guarantee sales, especially if consumers don't view the product as something they need. Moreover, even if a company develops a truly innovative product, it must package and price the product attractively, place it in a convenient distribution channel, bring it to the attention of consumers, and convince them to buy it. In short, focusing on a product's characteristics is seldom enough to compete successfully in today's global marketplace.

Selling Concept   Companies practicing the **selling concept** believe that consumers will buy whatever they sell. They rely on a good, solid product to sell itself, and they comfortably limit their marketing efforts to taking orders and shipping goods. The selling concept takes an *inside-out* perspective. It starts with the factory, focuses on the company's existing products, and calls for heavy selling and promotion to obtain profitable sales. Such a concept is generally successful only in a *sellers' market*, where demand for products exceeds supply. In a *buyers' market*, where supply exceeds demand, it becomes increasingly difficult to push whatever you produce on all consumers. Under these circumstances, companies must become more customer-centered. They must shift their focus from a sellers' perspective to a buyers' perspective.

selling concept
Approach to marketing in which firms emphasize selling what they make rather than making what consumers want

Marketing Concept   Companies that practice a **marketing concept** determine the needs and wants of target markets and deliver products and services that meet consumer needs and wants more conveniently and efficiently than competitors do. In contrast to the selling concept, the marketing concept takes an *outside-in* perspective (see Exhibit 12.3). Companies focus on customers' needs and wants first, then produce products that fill those needs. Land's End, Target, Costco, Nordstrom, Disney, Hyatt Hotels, and hundreds of well-known successful companies have adopted the marketing concept. These companies modify their marketing strategies and product offerings to satisfy customers' changing needs and wants while seeking long-term profitability and other long-term company goals.

marketing concept
Approach to marketing that stresses customer needs and wants, seeks long-term profitability, and integrates marketing with other functional units within the organization

Relationship Concept   Some organizations take the marketing concept to a higher level. They practice **relationship marketing** by building and maintaining long-term satisfying relationships with key parties—customers, suppliers, distributors—in order to retain their long-term business. In other words, they view the relationship between customer and company as an ongoing process instead of one that ends with the sales transaction. Frequently referred to as *customer relationship management* (CRM), relationship marketing gets smarter with each interaction—you learn something about your customer from each transaction, which helps you modify your product or service to meet the customer's changing needs.

relationship marketing
A focus on developing and maintaining long-term relationships with customers, suppliers, and distributors for mutual benefit

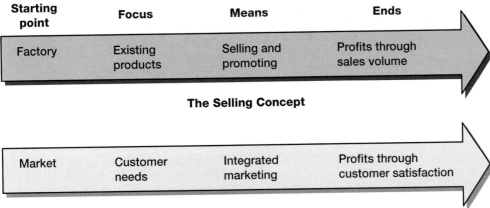

EXHIBIT 12.3
The Selling and Marketing Concepts Contrasted
Firms that practice the selling concept sell what they make rather than make what the market wants. Firms that practice the marketing concept determine the needs and wants of a market and deliver the desired product or service more effectively and efficiently than competitors do.

The Internet's Impact on the Marketing Function

Without a doubt, the most dramatic new technology affecting the marketing function today is the Internet. In a relatively short time, the Internet has opened new channels for distributing tangible goods and intangible services worldwide, and it is changing the way we buy, sell, advertise, and communicate with customers, as Chapter 4 points out. Moreover, the Internet offers a number of marketing benefits to buyers and sellers in the global marketplace.

Benefits to Buyers   The Internet provides buyers with options they never had before—countless brands to choose from, searchable databases, personal attention, shipping and delivery options, built-to-order merchandise, instant access to information, and more. In short, the Internet

- Enables customers to shop or conduct other transactions 24 hours a day, every day, from almost any location
- Allows customers to research a product online before purchasing it in a physical store
- Provides customers with more choices; they can select from any vendors and from more products and price levels
- Allows for quick delivery of digitized products and information
- Allows customers to interact with other customers and exchange ideas as well as compare experiences
- Facilitates competition—which can keep prices in line

Benefits to Sellers   The Internet yields many benefits to sellers as well. As Exhibit 12.4 shows, the Internet is a powerful tool for learning about and building relationships with customers. Companies are using the Internet to obtain information about customers, answer customers' questions, test their reaction to new products, sell products, obtain customer feedback, and better understand who their customers are and what they want. The Internet also brings the outside world closer and allows businesses to reach out and establish relationships with customers beyond their borders and market to the world. Finally, as Chapter 4 discusses, companies are using the Internet and e-commerce to generate new revenue, cut costs, enhance communication, and find information.

EXHIBIT 12.4   How the Internet Enhances Customer Relations
The Internet is a powerful tool for conducting marketing research, establishing new markets, testing customer interest in emerging products, and engaging in a dialogue with customers.

Internet capability →	Marketing and product research	Sales and distribution	Support and customer feedback
Benefits to company →	• Provides data for market research • Establishes consumer response to new products	• Reaches new customers • Provides a low-cost distribution method • Allows for electronic catalogs	• Improves customer access • Puts more staff in contact with customers • Allows immediate response to customer problems
Opportunities →	Increased market share	Lower costs	Enhanced customer satisfaction

Understanding Today's Customers

To compete in the global marketplace, companies must have good information about what customers want. They must "know and understand the customer so well that the product or service fits him and sells itself," says management consultant and author Peter Drucker.[5] Doing so is a challenge because customers today are not very easy to understand.

Priva, a Canadian manufacturer and distributor of a full range of reusable, waterproof, and absorbent protectors for beds, furniture, and clothing designed for people with incontinence, knows this situation all too well. Priva's target market are elderly who are often embarrassed by their physical condition. The fact that customers seldom talk openly about Priva's products makes it especially challenging for the company to understand what customers want. So to meet the challenge, Priva developed and inserted a postage-paid confidential questionnaire into every product package. It wasn't long before completed questionnaires started pouring in by the hundreds. "The information that the respondents included was more detailed than we ever imagined we'd get," recalls company CEO David Horowitz. For example, Priva discovered that product buying decisions often are made by home caregivers versus actual product users. To appeal to this target market, Priva established the Caregiver of the Year award. The award recognizes caregivers while boosting awareness of Priva's products to these important decision makers. Today, some 20 percent of the Priva's products are a result of customer input. Moreover, the company routinely receives thank-you cards from customers along with a steady stream of suggestions for product improvements and ideas for new items.[6]

Coach's experience also highlights the importance of understanding customers' needs and wants. In the early 1990s, Coach, a sleepy division of Sara Lee, was known for making briefcases and handbags as indestructible as tanks—and about as stylish. Priced about 50 percent lower than high-end designer bags, the items were sold in department stores such as Bloomingdale's and Saks Fifth Avenue, in Coach retail outlets, and in Coach catalogues. When "business casual" transformed women's fashion in the 1990s, consumers flocked to trend-conscious competitors such as Gucci, Prada, and new-comer Kate Spade. Coach was an American icon, but its offerings were out of date. Something was missing, so Coach turned to customers to find out. Spending about $2 million a year on consumer surveys, Coach began asking hundreds of customers about everything from comfort and strap length to style. Thanks to survey respondents, Coach has radically expanded its product line to include gloves, shoes, jewelry, watches, men's and women's apparel, outerwear, and luggage. Now Coach styles are dictated by what customers think is cool. New products are tested in a cross-section of stores six months before the collection is launched. And the company's growth is skyrocketing.[7]

As Priva, Coach, and others have learned, today's customers are sophisticated, price sensitive, and demanding. They live time-compressed lifestyles and have little patience for manufacturers, wholesalers, and retailers who do not understand them or will not adapt business practices to meet their needs. They expect products and services to be delivered faster and more conveniently. This is especially true of Internet shoppers, who have high expectations, such as service around the clock. They are less patient and more demanding than in-store shoppers because they've been sold on the idea that the Internet will improve their daily lives. They want to be treated as individuals, and they want immediate answers to their questions. For instance, they want to

4 **LEARNING OBJECTIVE**

Explain why and how companies learn about their customers

"Our surveys strongly suggest that the e-tailer [online retailer] who ignores customer service is doomed to fail," says Robert LoCascio, founder of LivePerson, a company that sells live chat systems to online retailers.

know whether goods are actually in stock and what the retailer's shipping and return policies are before they submit a credit card number.

Today's customers are also more informed. Armed with facts, prices, data, product reviews, advice, how-to guides, and databases, today's customers make buying decisions as if they had an army of intelligent helpers running to all the stores around the world to find the best products and prices. With a few clicks of the mouse, travelers can plan and price trips, purchase tickets, receive travel confirmations, review current reservations, and review the status of their mileage rewards accounts. Home buyers can use real estate websites to gain more control of the house-hunting process. Home descriptions, room dimensions, photographs, virtual tours, property tax information, and school and town information are all provided on home sales websites—enabling customers to do their research online before setting foot in the real estate office.[8] Similarly, car buyers can walk into dealerships with spec sheets (obtained from websites) that disclose the dealer's invoice cost, dealer rebates, and other purchasing incentives.[9] From travel agents to supermarkets to auto dealers to furniture stores to realtors, today's customers are indeed in an unprecedented position of control, which is why more and more businesses are finding it a challenge to satisfy them and service their changing needs.

Satisfying Customers

Companies strive to satisfy their customers and keep them coming back for several reasons:[10]

- Acquiring a new customer can cost up to five times as much as keeping an existing one
- Long-term customers buy more, take less of a company's time, bring in new customers, and are less price sensitive
- Satisfied customers are the best advertisement for a product
- Firms perceived to offer superior customer service find that they can charge as much as 10 percent more than their competitors
- Research shows that dissatisfied customers may tell as many as 20 other people about their bad experiences

One of the best ways to measure customer satisfaction, of course, is to analyze your customer base: Are you getting new customers? Are good ones leaving? What is your customer retention rate? What are you doing to keep your customers loyal?

Capital One takes great pains to retain its customers. When a current customer calls the company to close his or her account, the customer is immediately transferred to a customer retention specialist, whose job is to offer the customer a better deal (interest rate, line of credit, and so on) to keep the customer's business. Other companies promote customer loyalty by offering extra-long product guarantees. For example, Hewlett-Packard's 99.999 percent product reliability and availability guarantees keep customers loyal and willing to buy additional goods and services.[11] A.T. Cross pens carry a lifetime guarantee, and Le Creuset cookware is guaranteed for 101 years.[12] Software maker Intuit is so focused on retaining customers that every employee—including the president—spends a few hours each month working the customer-service phone lines. This intense focus helps Intuit make its Quicken program so user-friendly that customers are fiercely loyal. As one marketing consultant put it: "People would rather change their bank than switch from Quicken."[13]

But such customer loyalty is the exception, not the norm. On average, U.S. companies lose half their customers every five years. Why are customers less loyal today? First, they have more choices—more styles, options, services, and products are available than ever before. Second, customers have more information from brochures, consumer publications, the Internet, and other sources, which empowers buyers and raises expectations. Third, when more and more products start to look the same, nothing stands out to attract customer loyalty. And fourth, time is scarce. If it's easier to buy gas at a different service station each

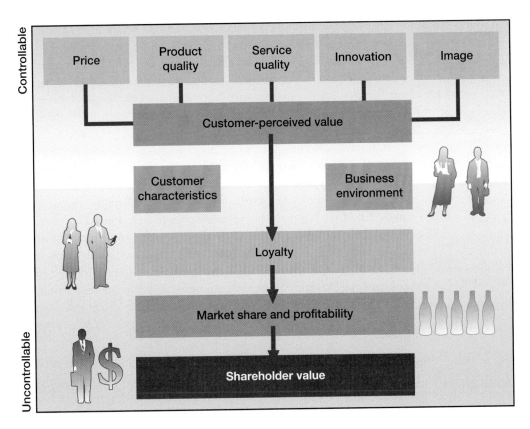

EXHIBIT 12.5   Beyond Customer Satisfaction
Satisfying the customer is no longer the ultimate business virtue. Companies today are looking for more and better ways of cementing customer loyalty to boost market share, profitability, and shareholder value.

week, customers will. Furthermore, customer loyalty must be earned every day, because customer needs and buying habits change constantly (see Exhibit 12.5).

Of course, not every customer is worth keeping. Some customers cost a great deal to service; others spend little but demand a lot. "We've gotten a lot smarter about separating the customers we do want from the customers we don't want," says C. Michael Armstrong, CEO of AT&T. Facing $500 million in yearly losses on the millions of customers who make few long-distance calls, AT&T routes customer service calls from low spenders to automated systems and lavishes human attention on higher-spending customers.[14]

Servicing Customers

Providing exceptional customer service is one way that companies try to retain their customers. Commerce Bank, for example, prides itself on being "America's most convenient bank." Based in Cherry Hill, New Jersey, with branches throughout the state, as well as in Delaware, New York, and Pennsylvania, Commerce doesn't observe traditional banking hours. Typically, the branch offices are open from 7:30 A.M. to 8:00 P.M. during the week and for most of the day on weekends. Moreover, while other banks try to steer customers away from their branch offices by offering incentives to use ATMs, Commerce does just the opposite. In fact, customer service is so critical to Commerce that the bank sends mystery shoppers to every branch twice a week to evaluate the overall condition of the branch as well as the level of service provided. Such attention to customers has helped Commerce grow its deposits in one year by 38 percent (compared to the industry average of 8 percent). As Commerce sees it, building strong customer relationships that start with checking accounts eventually leads to mortgages.

Galyan's, a retail sporting goods chain, is another good example of a company that provides exceptional customer service. Sales associates receive at least 45 hours of training at "Galyan's University" and are tested on details before they are allowed to sell company products and service customers. "We've chosen to make customer service what we stand for," says company president Joel Silverman.[15]

At the Lands' End website, customers can get more than answers to their questions. Personal shoppers can recommend additional products that match customers' preferences and even split the computer screen to display apparel combinations

Providing good customer service is important whether you are selling via a physical store or via a website. Many e-tailers have learned the hard way that selling via a website doesn't eliminate the need for human interaction. E-tailers who don't offer good customer support run the risk of losing customers to online competitors who do. Confused web shoppers are more likely to abandon their virtual electronic "shopping cart" in the middle of a transaction or before checking out.

Effective e-tailers, such as Amazon.com, Landsend.com, and Dell.com, offer a variety of online support services. These include self-help web pages, toll-free phone support, e-mail, online chat, and live support. Customers of Landsend.com, for example, simply click on the Lands' End Live button to immediately engage a customer service representative in an electronic chat. If customers would prefer to talk on the phone, they ask the representative to call them back. Called "personal shoppers," the online service reps can answer customer questions, solve problems, and even make suggestions about appropriate merchandise—all in real time. They can even split the computer screen and display apparel combinations (such as a shirt and tie) to help the customer make a decision.

Learning About Customers

To satisfy and service customers, companies must first learn about their needs, wants, and buying behavior. How do companies learn about customers? In the past, most businesses obtained information about changing customer preferences, changing market trends, and new competitor products by using a variety of marketing research techniques. But today, companies are using technology to engage in two-way, ongoing dialogues with customers through e-mail, web pages, fax machines, and toll-free telephone numbers. Some companies even go to extremes for a glimpse into the shopper's mind by hiring Minneapolis-based Once Famous, a home accessories and gift boutique and fully operational testing lab. Manufacturers and retail chains pay a lot of money to test their products in Once Famous, which uses mirrors, cameras, and microphones to capture customers' every move. Then Once Famous summarizes the data to provide clients with a detailed report on how best to sell their goods. Shoppers, of course, are made aware that they are being filmed and taped via a prominently placed blinking sign in the store. But the store still succeeds in catching customers off guard by cluttering displays with attractive merchandise to distract shoppers from the cameras.[16]

consumer buying behavior
Behavior exhibited by consumers as they consider and purchase various products

Consumer Buying Behavior   To learn what induces individuals to buy one product instead of another, companies study **consumer buying behavior**. For instance, when Israeli-based Sky Is the Ltd. needed to know where and how U.S. consumers buy crackers, its executives conducted marketing research studies and found that the firm's little-known brand would get lost among the sea of crackers on supermarket shelves but could attract some attention in gourmet food stores.[17]

When analyzing consumer buying behavior, companies must take into consideration the differences between organizational and consumer markets, the buyer's decision process, and factors that influence the buyer's decision process.

organizational market
Consumers who buy goods or services for resale or for use in conducting their own operations

Organizational Versus Consumer Buyers   The **organizational market** is made up of three main subgroups: the industrial/commercial market (companies that buy goods and services to produce their own goods and services, such as Toyota), the reseller market (wholesalers such as Ingram Micro, which wholesales computers, and retailers such as Ann Taylor, which sells women's clothing), and the government market (federal, state, and local agencies such as the state of Texas and the city of Dallas).

EXHIBIT 12.6 The Consumer Decision-Making Process
Consumers go through a decision-making process that can include up to five steps.

Organizations buy raw materials (grain, steel, fabric) and highly technical and complex products (printing presses, management consultation, buildings). They also buy many of the same products that consumers do—such as food, paper products, cleaning supplies, and landscaping services—but they generally purchase larger quantities and use a more complex buying process. By contrast, the **consumer market** consists of individuals or households that purchase goods and services for personal use. In most cases, consumers purchase smaller quantities of items and use a decision-making process that we will discuss next.

The Buyer's Decision-Making Process Suppose you want to buy a car. Do you rush to the dealer, plunk down money, and buy the first car you see? Of course not. Like most buyers, you go through a decision-making process, outlined in Exhibit 12.6, that begins with identifying a problem, which in this case is the need for a car. Your next step is to look for a solution to your problem. Possibilities occur to you on the basis of your experience (perhaps you recently drove a certain make or model) and on your exposure to marketing messages. If none of the obvious solutions seems satisfying, you gather additional information. The more complex the problem, the more information you are likely to seek from friends or relatives, magazines, salespeople, store displays, and sales literature.

Once you have all the information in hand, you are ready to make a choice. You may select one of the alternatives, such as a new Chevy Blazer or a used Ford Explorer. You might even postpone the decision or decide against making any purchase at all, depending on the magnitude of your desire, the outside pressure to buy, and your financial resources. If you decide to buy, you will evaluate the wisdom of your choice. If the item you bought is satisfying, you might buy the same product again under similar circumstances, thus developing a loyalty to the brand. If it is not satisfying, you will probably not repeat the purchase.

If the purchase was a major one, you will sometimes suffer from **cognitive dissonance**, commonly known as *buyer's remorse*. You will think about all the alternatives you rejected and wonder whether one of them might have been a better choice. At this stage, you're likely to seek reassurance that you have done the right thing. Realizing this tendency, many marketers try to reinforce their sales with guarantees, phone calls to check on the customer's satisfaction, user hot lines, follow-up letters, and so on. Such efforts help pave the way for repeat business.

Factors That Influence the Buyer's Decision-Making Process Throughout the buying process, various factors may influence a buyer's purchase decision. An awareness of the following factors and consumer preferences enables companies to appeal to the group most likely to respond to its products and services:

- *Culture.* The cultures and subcultures that people belong to shape their values, attitudes, and beliefs and influence the way they respond to the world around them. Understanding culture is therefore an increasingly important step in international business and in marketing to diverse populations within a country such as the United States.

consumer market
Individuals or households that buy goods or services for personal use

cognitive dissonance
Anxiety following a purchase that prompts buyers to seek reassurance about the purchase; commonly known as *buyer's remorse*

- *Social class.* In addition to being members of a particular culture, people also belong to a certain social class—be it upper, middle, lower, or somewhere in between. In general, members of various classes pursue different activities, buy different goods, shop in different places, and react to different media.

- *Reference groups.* A reference group consists of people who have a good deal in common: family members, friends, co-workers, sports enthusiasts, music lovers, computer buffs. Individuals are members of many such reference groups, and they use the opinions of the appropriate group as a benchmark when they buy certain types of goods or services.

- *Self-image.* The tendency to believe that "you are what you buy" is especially prevalent among young people. Marketers capitalize on people's need to express their identity through their purchases by emphasizing the image value of goods and services. That's why professional athletes and musicians frequently appear as product endorsers—so that consumers will identify with these celebrities and want to emulate their behavior and incorporate it into their own self-images.

- *Situational factors.* Events or circumstances in people's lives can influence buying patterns. Such factors might include having a coupon, being in a hurry, celebrating a holiday, being in a bad mood, and so on.

5 LEARNING OBJECTIVE

Discuss how marketing research helps the marketing effort, and highlight its limitations

marketing research
The collection and analysis of information for making marketing decisions

Marketing Research Many companies obtain information about customers' changing needs by engaging in **marketing research**—the process of gathering and analyzing information about customers, markets, and related marketing issues. Companies rely on research when they set product goals, develop new products, and plan future marketing programs. They also use research to monitor a program's effectiveness by analyzing the number of consumers using a product or purchasing it more than once. In addition, they use marketing research to keep an eye on the competition, track industry trends, and measure customer satisfaction. Popular marketing research tools include personal observations, customer surveys and questionnaires, experiments, telephone or personal interviews, studies of small samples of the consumer population, and focused interviews of six to 10 people (called focus groups). According to management expert Peter Drucker, the most important sources of information for strategic decision making come from customers.[18] Amazon.com, for example, uses the information it obtains from customers to make buying recommendations for them. But it also uses that information to, as Amazon CEO Jeff Bezos puts it, "invent things we suspect people will want."[19]

Each marketing research tool has its advantages and limitations, whether it is focus groups, consumer surveys, or other tools for probing customers' wants and needs. Take customer surveys, for example. In 1985 when Bell Labs first invented the cell phone, AT&T asked a big consulting firm to do a customer survey. The results convinced management that there was no market for the cell phone, and AT&T shelved the new product. Eight years later, AT&T ended up acquiring McCaw Cellular to catch up with the irreversible trend of cell-phone usage.[20]

Part of the problem with surveys is that they are administered in artificial settings that do not accurately represent the marketplace. Moreover, surveys generally measure the level of service that the company currently provides instead of identifying ways to propel a company beyond its current of service. Furthermore, if not carefully worded and administered, surveys can be misleading, as well as being poor predictors of future buying behavior. For example, more than 90 percent of car buyers are either "satisfied" or "very satisfied" when they drive away from the dealer's showroom, but less than half wind up buying the same car the next time around.[21]

In-person marketing surveys are a common way to gathering data directly from consumers. Many companies are now collecting consumer data over the Internet because it saves time and money in addition to expanding the survey's reach.

In addition, marketing research can suggest, in a narrow way, what people might prefer or dislike today, but it is seldom a good predictor of what will excite consumers in the future. The Walkman is one of the most successful consumer products ever introduced, yet it was greeted by skepticism during the prototype test.[22] FedEx and CNN were also met with public nay saying. So was the Chrysler minivan.[23]

Finally, marketing research is not a substitute for good judgment. When used inappropriately, research can be the source of expensive mistakes. Coca-Cola's experience with New Coke is a classic example of how marketing research can lead a company astray when data are not used correctly. In an effort to stem the growth of arch competitor Pepsi, Coca-Cola conducted extensive taste tests to find a cola taste consumers liked better than either Coke or Pepsi. On the basis of this research, the company launched New Coke, replacing the 100-year-old Coca-Cola formula. But New Coke simply did not sell, and Coca-Cola had to mount an expensive marketing effort to salvage the brand. At the same time, public outcry drove the company to bring back the original formula, renamed Coke Classic. What went wrong? First, researchers focused only on taste and failed to look at the emotional attachment consumers had to traditional Coke soft drink. Second, many of the people who participated in the test did not realize that old Coke would be taken off the shelf. If the company had asked the right questions, the rocky course of New Coke's introduction might have been smoother.[24]

Customer Databases   Another way to learn about customer preferences is to gather and analyze all kinds of customer-related data. **Database marketing** is the process of recording and analyzing customer interactions, preferences, and buying behavior for the purpose of contacting and transacting with customers. The underlying principle of database marketing is simple: All customers share the same common needs and characteristics, but each customer has his or her own twist. By analyzing data collected on each customer's key attributes, companies can determine which customers to target, which to avoid, and how to customize marketing offers for the best response (see Exhibit 12.7).

The growth in database marketing has been facilitated by computer technology, which is able to combine information from many sources and assemble it in usable form. For example, by merging information about an individual with census data for that person's ZIP-code-plus-four area, it is possible to make reliable inferences about income, lifestyle, and other personal characteristics. Companies that specialize in data collection can provide direct marketers with customized mailing lists that target groups with the desired characteristics.[25]

Capital One, for example, has become a leading credit card company by collecting extensive records on millions of consumers and using that information to plan its marketing strategies. As Capital One's CEO Richard Fairbank knows, every credit card transaction,

database marketing
Process of building, maintaining, and using customer databases for the purpose of contacting customers and transacting business

EXHIBIT 12.7

Typical Database for Customers' Orders
Designing a user-friendly database to record customer information is the key to building an effective database marketing program. The information from this simple order-entry screen will eventually be transferred to a customer history file so that the company can rank its customers by total dollars spent and other criteria.

Internet sale, and frequent-buyer purchase leaves behind a trail of information that retailers can use to their advantage. Frequent-shopper card programs, good for a wealth of discounts at supermarket checkouts, have convinced customers to share some of the most intimate details about their lives. For instance, grocery purchases reveal preferences for everything from hygiene products to junk food to magazines.

Once companies gather data about customers, they enter this information into customer databases to remember customer preferences and priorities and to make the customer's shopping experience more personal and compelling. Allstate, for example, uses database marketing to amass huge amounts of data about applicants (credit reports, driving records, claims histories) in order to swiftly price a customer's insurance policy.[26] Ritz Carlton records all customer requests, comments, and complaints in a worldwide database that now contains individual profiles of more than 500,000 guests. By accessing these pro-

Thinking About Ethics

Your Right to Privacy Versus the Marketing Databases

Are all the details of your personal life really private? Consider this: Your bank knows your account balance, your credit history, and your Social Security number. Government agencies know how much money you made last year, the kind of car you own, and how many parking tickets you've gotten. Credit agencies know to whom you owe money, and how much. This list of organizations keeping track of you goes on and on, from video stores to insurance companies. Plus every time you register online, or even click on a website, all sorts of data are being collected about you. By depositing "cookies" on your hard drive, web marketers can follow your path and track the sites you visit.

Of course, there's nothing unethical about collecting data or maintaining a database. The ethical problems arise when marketers buy, borrow, rent, or exchange information, usually without your knowledge or permission. Who should have the right to see your records? The answer depends on where you live. In Europe, strict privacy regulations prevent companies from using data about individuals without asking permission and explaining how the data will be used. But in the United States and most other countries, marketers can easily buy information about who you are, where you live, how much you earn, and what you buy—for as little as a nickel.

Many web marketers post privacy policies showing how they use personal data. Moreover, a 1999 law requires U.S. companies to send privacy policies to customers once a year—offering customers the opportunity to "opt out," which, if elected, prohibits companies from selling customer information to unrelated firms. But as privacy advocates note, companies are still allowed to share data with subsidiaries and with companies they purchase, merge with, affiliate with, and so on.

As you can imagine, the consumer's right to privacy is an ongoing debate—one that has intensified and taken on new dimensions since the September 11 terrorist attacks. Privacy advocates argue that companies should not take personal information when consumers aren't looking and that consumers should have more control over what is collected about them and how it can be used. Marketers, on the other hand, claim that collecting customer data allows them to target ads to consumers who are most likely interested in the products, thus slashing wasteful marketing costs. The argue that companies should have the right to freedom of speech—the right to inform customers about their offers. Thus, the ultimate dilemma: Does a marketer's needs and freedom of speech outweigh the consumer's right to privacy? What's your opinion?

Questions for Critical Thinking

1. Should a marketer selling long-distance telephone service be allowed to see your telephone records without your knowledge or permission?
2. Should web marketers be required to conspicuously post their privacy policies and ask consent before collecting and using visitors' personal data?

files, employees at any Ritz Carlton hotel can accommodate the individual tastes of its customers from anywhere in the world.[27] And Capital One has enough customer information in its databases to fill the hard drives of more than 200,000 personal computers.[28]

Treating Customer Individually

Smart companies gain a competitive edge by using their customer databases to make customers' experiences more personal and compelling. *One-to-one marketing* involves individualizing a firm's marketing efforts for a single customer to accommodate the specific customer's needs. Capital One, for instance, attracts millions of customers by presenting itself a little differently to each customer. Besides offering more than 7,000 variations of its credit card, it has up to 20,000 variations of other products, from phone cards to insurance.[29] Similarly, American Airlines and Amazon.com display websites that look different to registered members. Visitors who log in are greeted by their name and sometimes by a direct marketing offer.

Such one-to-one marketing programs require a thorough understanding of each customer's preferences and a detailed history of each customer's interactions with the company. But the payoff can be increased customer loyalty. The more time and energy a customer spends teaching a firm about his or her own preferences, the more difficult it becomes for the customer to obtain the same level of individualized service from a competitor.

Planning Your Marketing Strategies

6 **LEARNING OBJECTIVE**

Outline the three steps in the strategic marketing planning process

strategic marketing planning
The process of determining an organization's primary marketing objectives and then adopting courses of action and allocating resources to achieve those objectives

By now you can see why successful marketing rarely happens without carefully analyzing and understanding your customers. Once you have learned about your customers, you're ready to begin planning your marketing strategies. **Strategic marketing planning** is a process that involves three steps: (1) examining your current marketing situation, (2) assessing your opportunities and setting your objectives, and (3) developing a marketing strategy to reach those objectives (see Exhibit 12.8). The purpose of strategic marketing planning is to help you identify and create a competitive advantage, something that sets you apart from your rivals and makes your product more appealing to customers. Most companies record the results of their planning efforts in a document called the *marketing plan*. Here's a closer look at the three steps in the process.

EXHIBIT 12.8 The Strategic Marketing Planning Process
Strategic marketing planning comprises three steps: (1) examining your current marketing situation, (2) assessing your opportunities and setting objectives, and (3) developing your marketing strategy.

Step 1: Examining Your Current Marketing Situation

Examining your current marketing situation includes reviewing your past performance (how well each product is doing in each market where you sell it), evaluating your competition, examining your internal strengths and weaknesses, and analyzing the external environment.

Reviewing Performance Unless you're starting a new business, your company has a history of marketing performance. Maybe sales have slowed in the past year; maybe you've had to cut prices so much that you're barely earning a profit; or maybe sales are going quite well and you have money to invest in new marketing activities. Reviewing where you are and how you got there is critical, because you will want to repeat your successes and learn from your mistakes.

Evaluating Competition In addition to reviewing past performance, you must also evaluate your competition. If you own a McDonald's franchise, for example, you need to watch what Burger King and Wendy's are doing. You also have to keep an eye on Taco Bell, KFC, Pizza Hut, and other restaurants in addition to paying attention to any number of ways your customers might satisfy their hunger—including fixing a sandwich at home. Furthermore, you need to watch the horizon for competition that does not yet exist, such as the next big food craze. Consider McDonald's, for example. America's immigrants have made once-exotic foods like sushi and burritos everyday options. Quick meals of all sorts can now be found in supermarkets, convenience stores, even vending machines—creating new competition for McDonald's and stunting the burger giant's sales growth.[30]

Examining Internal Strengths and Weaknesses Successful marketers try to identify both sources of competitive advantage and areas that need improvement. They look at such things as management, financial resources, production capabilities, distribution networks, managerial expertise, and promotional capabilities. This step is important because you can't develop a successful marketing strategy if you don't know your strengths as well as your limitations. On the basis of your internal analysis, you will be able to decide whether your business should (1) limit itself to the opportunities for which it has the required strengths or (2) challenge itself to reach higher goals by acquiring and developing new strengths.

Understanding your strengths and weaknesses is especially important when evaluating the merits of global expansion. Selling products overseas requires not only managerial expertise and financial resources but also the ability to adjust your operation to different cultures, customs, legal requirements, and product specifications. Even selling on the Internet requires technological expertise and commitment as well as a thorough understanding of customer buying behavior.

Analyzing the External Environment Marketers must also analyze a number of external environmental factors when planning their marketing strategies. These factors include:

- *Economic conditions.* Marketers are greatly affected by trends in interest rates, inflation, unemployment, personal income, and savings rates. In tough times, consumers may put off buying expensive items such as major appliances, cars, and homes. They cut back on travel, entertainment, and luxury goods. Conversely, when the economy is good, consumers open their wallets and satisfy their pent-up demand for higher-priced goods and services.

- *Natural environment.* Changes in the natural environment can affect marketers, both positively and negatively. Interruptions in the supply of raw materials can upset even the most carefully conceived marketing plans. Floods, droughts, and cold weather can affect the price and availability of many products as well as the behavior of target customers.

- *Social and cultural trends.* Planners also study the social and cultural environment to determine shifts in consumer values. If social trends are running against a product, the producer might need more advertising to educate consumers about the product's benefits or might need to alter the product to make it more appealing. For example, when beef consumption fell out of favor, marketers used ads to educate consumers on the benefits of including more beef in their diet.

- *Laws and regulations.* Like every other function in business today, marketing is controlled by laws at the local, state, national, and international levels. From product design to pricing to advertising, virtually every task you'll encounter in marketing is affected in some way by laws and regulations. For example, the Nutritional Education and Labeling Act of 1990 forced marketers to put standardized nutritional labels on food products. Although this regulation cost manufacturers millions of dollars, it was a bonanza for food-testing laboratories.

- *Technology.* When technology changes, so must your marketing approaches. Look at *Encyclopaedia Britannica.* It didn't take long for computer technology to almost wreck this 230-year-old publishing company. In 1990 the company reported record sales of $650 million, but then the bottom fell out. With a set of books costing over $1,500, weighing 118 pounds, and taking 4.5 feet of shelf space, consumers soon opted for affordable CD-ROM and Internet reference works offered by competitors. Scrambling to survive, Britannica tried a number of electronic options. Today *Encyclopaedia Britannica* delivers information via the Internet and CD-ROMs, but only time will tell whether the company can thrive in the digital age.[31]

Marketers must not only keep on top of today's external environment, they must also think about tomorrow's changes. Car manufacturers, for example, are responding to increasing consumer and governmental pressure to clean up the environment by announcing plans to produce hybrid gas-and-electric vehicles.

Step 2: Assessing Your Opportunities and Setting Your Objectives

Once you've examined your current marketing situation, you're ready to assess your marketing opportunities and set your objectives. Successful companies are always on the lookout for new marketing opportunities, which can be classified into four options: selling more of your existing products in current markets (market penetration), creating new products for your current markets (new product development), selling your existing products in new markets (geographic expansion), and creating new products for new markets (diversification). These four options are listed in order of increasing risk; trying new products in unfamiliar markets is usually the riskiest choice of all.

With opportunities in mind, you are ready to set your marketing objectives. A common marketing objective is to achieve a certain level of **market share**, which is a firm's portion of the total sales within a market. Objectives must be specific and measurable. Establishing a goal to "increase sales in the future" is not a good objective; it doesn't say by how much or by what date. On the other hand, a goal to "increase sales 25 percent by the end of next year" provides a clear target and a reference against which progress can be measured. Objectives should also be challenging enough to be motivating. As CEO Mitchell Leibovitz of the Pep Boys auto parts chain says: "If you want to have ho-hum performance, have ho-hum goals."[32] Whatever objectives you set, be sure all employees know and understand what the organization wants to accomplish. Every Ritz Carlton employee, for example, attends a daily 15-minute meeting in which managers reiterate the hotel chain's business goals and commitment to customer service.[33]

market share
A firm's portion of the total sales in a market

Step 3: Developing Your Marketing Strategy

Using your current marketing situation and your objectives as your guide, you're ready to move to the third step. During this stage, you develop your **marketing strategy**, which

marketing strategy
Overall plan for marketing a product

consists of dividing your market into *segments* and *niches*, choosing your *target markets* and the *position* you'd like to establish in those markets, and then developing a *marketing mix* to help you get there.

7 LEARNING OBJECTIVE

Define market segmentation and cite six factors used to identify segments

market
People or businesses who need or want a product and have the money to buy it

market segmentation
Division of total market into smaller, relatively homogeneous groups

demographics
Study of statistical characteristics of a population

geographic segmentation
Categorization of customers according to their geographical location

psychographics
Classification of customers on the basis of their psychological makeup

geodemographics
Method of combining geographical data with demographic data to develop profiles of neighborhood segments

behavioral segmentation
Categorization of customers according to their relationship with products or response to product characteristics

Dividing Markets into Segments   A **market** contains all the customers or businesses that might be interested in a particular product and can afford to pay for it. Most companies subdivide the market in an economical and feasible manner by identifying *market segments*, or homogeneous groups of customers within a market that are significantly different from each other. This process is called **market segmentation;** its objective is to group customers with similar characteristics, behavior, and needs. Each of these market segments can then be targeted by offering products that are priced, distributed, and promoted differently.

The goal of market segmentation is to understand why certain customers buy what they buy so that you can sell them your products and services by targeting their needs. Here are six factors marketers frequently use to identify market segments:

- *Demographics.* When you segment a market using **demographics**, the statistical analysis of a population, you subdivide your customers according to such characteristics as age, gender, income, race, occupation, and ethnic group. Be aware, however, that according to recent studies, demographic variables are poor predictors of behavior. For instance, not all American men aged 35 to 44 making $100,000 per year want to buy a Mercedes. In fact, some don't even buy a luxury car, and those that do may not purchase such cars for the same reasons.[34]

- *Geographics.* When differences in buying behavior are influenced by where people live, it makes sense to use **geographic segmentation**. Segmenting the market into different geographical units such as regions, cities, counties, or neighborhoods allows companies to customize and sell products that meet the needs of specific markets. For instance, car rental agencies stock more four-wheel-drive vehicles in mountainous and snowy regions than they do in the South.

- *Psychographics.* Whereas demographic segmentation is the study of people from the outside, **psychographics** is the analysis of people from the inside, focusing on their psychological makeup, including attitudes, interests, opinions, and lifestyles. Psychographic analysis focuses on why people behave the way they do by examining such issues as brand preferences, media preferences, reading habits, values, and self-concept.

- *Geodemographics.* The goal of **geodemographics** is to divide markets into distinct neighborhoods by combining geographical and demographic data. The geodemographic system developed by Claritas Corporation divides the United States into 40 neighborhood types, with labels such as "Blue Blood Estates" and "Old Yankee Rows." This system, known as PRIZM, uses postal ZIP codes for the geographic segmentation part, making it easy to use specialized marketing programs to reach people in targeted neighborhoods.[35]

- *Behavior.* Markets can also be segmented according to customers' knowledge of, attitude toward, use of, or response to products or product characteristics. This approach is known as **behavioral segmentation**. Many web-based companies ask first-time visitors to fill out a personal profile so they can gear product recommendations and even display customized web pages that appeal to certain behavioral segments.

- *Internet usage.* An increasingly popular way to segment e-commerce customers is by Internet usage patterns. Companies are finding that categorizing web users by their session length, time per page, category concentration, and so on helps define the types of marketing that are best suited for each user type.[36]

Segmenting a market produces several customer groups, each representing a potentially productive focal point for marketing efforts. However, marketers also segment customers using multiple variables in order to produce more narrowly defined target groups known as

Thinking About Ethics

Questionable Marketing Tactics on Campus

College students are bombarded with credit card offers from the moment they step on campus as freshmen. Marketers have shown up on campuses unannounced and without permission to hawk cards in dorms and other areas. They stuff applications into bags at college bookstores. They entice students to apply for cards and take on debt with free T-shirts, music CDs, and promises of an easy way to pay for spring break vacations. Some yell at students to get their attention and follow them through hallways to make a sale. And they even get student organizations to work for them so that friends pressure friends.

Alarmed by how quickly college students can bury themselves in debt, and fed up with aggressive sales tactics, about 15 percent of schools have banned credit card marketers from soliciting on campus. Still, such moves seldom deter solicitors. Vendors just set up shop across the street from campus or move to other locations frequented by students, such as spring break vacation hot spots.

College campuses are a prime target for credit card marketers for a number of reasons. Marketing to college students allows lenders to build relationships with people who are likely to need loans, home mortgages, and other financial services in the future. And with most students carrying just one or two cards, competition to be the first card in the students' wallets is keen. Moreover, credit card issuers seldom take big losses on student accounts, because the balances are relatively small and because parents often bail out their children if they get into financial trouble.

Only about half of those students pay their bills in full each month, and the number who usually make just the minimum payment is rising. It is estimated that in one year 150,000 people younger than 25 will declare personal bankruptcy. That means for 150,000 young people, their first significant financial event as an adult will be to declare themselves a failure. And for each one who goes

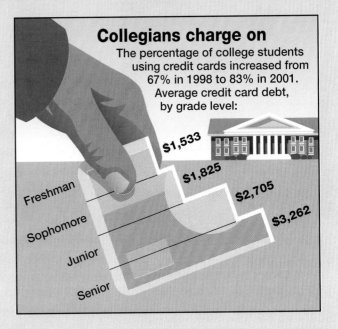

Collegians charge on
The percentage of college students using credit cards increased from 67% in 1998 to 83% in 2001. Average credit card debt, by grade level:

Freshman $1,533
Sophomore $1,825
Junior $2,705
Senior $3,262

into bankruptcy, there are dozens just behind them, struggling with credit card bills—like Katy Spivak, for instance. Within her first three years at college, Spivak ran up $9,000 in credit card debt—forcing her to work two part-time jobs just to pay off her credit card bills.

But the credit card industry says such cases are the exception. In fact, they claim that cards provide students with an opportunity to learn financial responsibility. What's your opinion? Do credit cards teach students how to be financially responsible?

Questions for Critical Thinking

1. Should credit card companies be prohibited from soliciting on college campuses? Why or why not?
2. Why do credit card companies target students even though they have little or no income?

microsegments or *niches*. A typical marketing niche might be young adult tennis players. Members of this niche would be interested in tennis products such as rackets, shoes, and tennis wear.

Choosing Your Target Markets Once you have segmented your market, the next step is to find appropriate target segments or **target markets** on which to focus your

target markets
Specific customer groups or segments to whom a company wants to sell a particular product

Health-conscious young adults are a highly sought-after target market for products such as bottled water.

efforts. Deciding exactly which segment to target—and when—is not an easy task. Sometimes the answer will be obvious, such as when you lack the necessary technological skills or financial power to enter a particular market segment. At other times, you'll have the resources to compete in several segments but not enough resources to compete in all of them. In general, marketers use a variety of criteria to narrow their focus to a few suitable market segments. These criteria can include the size of the segment, competition in the segment, sales and profit potential, compatibility with company resources and strengths, costs, growth potential, and risks.

Targeting is such a critical part of strategic marketing that missteps can be costly, as Motorola found out. The company stayed focused on the traditional cell phone market segment long after rivals Nokia and Ericsson had expanded into the digital phone segment. Furthermore, Motorola didn't respond when it was asked to develop digital phones for AT&T's digital network. By the time Motorola began to work on digital phones, its competitors had grabbed market share and brand loyalty in that fast-growing segment.[37]

Exhibit 12.9 diagrams three popular strategies for reaching target markets. Companies that practice *undifferentiated marketing* (or mass marketing) ignore differences among buyers and offer only one product or product line to satisfy the entire market. This strategy, which assumes that all buyers have similar needs that can be served with the same standardized product, was more popular in the past then it is today. Henry Ford, for instance, sold only one car type (the Model T Ford) and in one color (black) to the entire market.

By contrast, companies that manufacture or sell a variety of products to several target customer groups practice *differentiated marketing.* General Motors, for instance, manufactures a car for every personality, and Nike produces a shoe for every athlete. Differentiated marketing is a popular approach, but it requires substantial resources because you have to tailor products, prices, promotional efforts, and distribution arrangements for each customer group.

When company resources are limited, *concentrated marketing* may be the best marketing strategy. You acknowledge that different market segments exist and you choose to target just one. Southwest Airlines, for instance, began its operation by originally concentrating on servicing the submarket of intrastate, no-frills commuters.[38] The biggest advantage of concentrated marketing is that it allows you to focus all your time and resources on a single type of customer. The strategy can be risky, however, because you've staked your company's fortune on just one segment.

Positioning Your Product Once a company has decided which segments of the market it will enter, it must then decide what position it wants to occupy in those segments. **Positioning** your product is the act of designing your company's offerings and image so that it occupies a meaningful and distinct competitive position in your target customers' minds.

Even though consumers position products with or without the help of marketers, marketers do not want to leave their product's position to chance. Instead, they choose positions that will give their products the greatest advantage in selected target markets.[39] They can position their products on specific product features or attributes (such as size, ease of use, style, performance, quality, durability, or design), on the services that accompany the product (such as convenient delivery, lifetime customer support, or installation methods), on the product's image (such as reliability or sophistication), on price (such as low cost or premium), on category leadership (such as the leading online bookseller), and so forth. For example, BMW and Porsche associate their products with performance, Mercedes Benz with luxury, and Volvo with safety. Organizing products and services into categories based on the perceived position helps consumers simplify the buying process. Instead of test-driving all cars, for instance, they may focus on those they perceive to be high-performance vehicles.

positioning
Using promotion, product, distribution, and price to differentiate a good or service from those of competitors in the mind of the prospective buyer

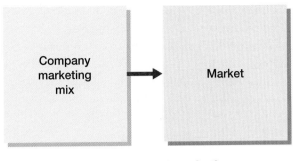

1. Undifferentiated marketing

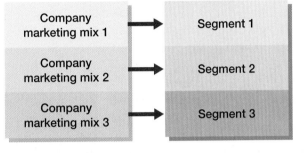

2. Differentiated marketing

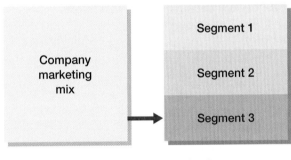

3. Concentrated marketing

Developing the Marketing Mix   After you've segmented your market, selected your target market, and positioned your product, your next task is to develop a marketing mix. A company's **marketing mix** (often called the *four Ps*) consists of product, price, place (or distribution), and promotion (see Exhibit 12.10).

Products   The most basic marketing-mix element is *product*, which covers the product itself plus brand name, design, packaging, services, quality, and warranty. From a marketing standpoint, a **product** is anything offered for the purpose of satisfying a want or a need in a marketing exchange. If you were asked to name three popular products off the top of your head, you might think of Doritos tortilla chips, the Volkswagen Beetle, and Gatorade drinks. You might not think of the Boston Celtics, Disney World, and the television show *60 Minutes*. That's because we tend to think of products as *tangible* objects, or things that we can actually touch and possess. Basketball teams, amusement parks, and television programs provide an *intangible* service for our use or enjoyment, not for our ownership; nevertheless, these and other services are products just the same. In fact, broadly defined, products can be persons, places, physical objects, ideas, services, and organizations.

Pricing   Price, the amount of money customers pay for the product (including any discounts) is the second major component of a marketing mix. Developing a product's price is one of the most critical decisions a company must make, because price is the only element

8 LEARNING OBJECTIVE

Identify the four elements of a company's marketing mix

marketing mix
The four key elements of marketing strategy: product, price, place (distribution), and promotion

product
Good or service used as the basis of commerce

price
The amount of money charged for a product or service

EXHIBIT 12.10
Positioning and the Marketing Environment
When positioning products for target markets, you need to consider the four marketing-mix elements plus the external environment.

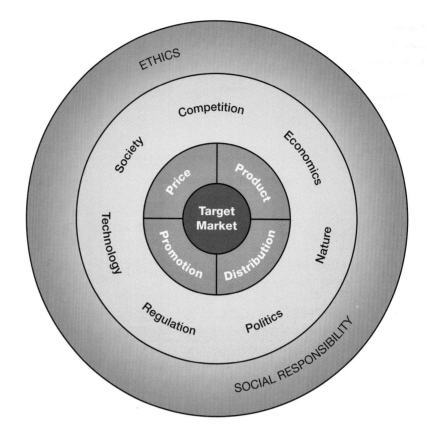

in a company's marketing mix that produces revenue—all other elements represent cost. Thus, setting a product's price not only determines the amount of income your company will generate from sales of that product but can also differentiate the product from competition. As you can imagine, determining the right price is not an easy task. If a company charges too much, it will generate fewer sales. If it charges too little, it will sacrifice potential profits.

Place or Distribution   *Place* (which is commonly referred to as *distribution*) is the third marketing-mix element. It covers the organized network of businesses that move goods and services from the producer to the consumer. This network is also known as *marketing channels* or **distribution channels**. A company's channel decisions directly affect all other marketing decisions. For instance, a company's pricing depends on whether it uses mass merchandisers or high-quality specialty stores. And a firm's salesforce and advertising decisions depend on how much training, motivation, and support the dealers need.

distribution channels
Systems for moving goods and services from producers to customers; also known as marketing channels

promotion
Wide variety of persuasive techniques used by companies to communicate with their target markets and the general public

Promotion   **Promotion**, the fourth marketing-mix element, includes all the activities the firm undertakes to communicate and promote its products to the target market. Among these activities are advertising, personal selling, public relations, and sales promotion. Promotion may take the form of direct, face-to-face communication, or indirect communication through such media as television, radio, magazines, newspapers, direct mail, billboards, bus ads, the Internet, and other channels. Of the four components in a firm's marketing mix, promotion is perhaps the one most often associated with marketing. Although it is no guarantee of success, promotion does have a profound impact on a product's performance in the marketplace.

We take a closer look at each of these four marketing-mix elements in the remaining chapters in this part of the book. Chapter 13 takes a closer look at what's involved in developing product and pricing strategies, Chapter 14 discusses the steps involved in developing a firm's distribution strategies, and Chapter 15 discusses promotional strategies.

Summary of Learning Objectives

1. **Explain what marketing is.**

   Marketing is the process of planning and executing the conception, pricing, promotion, and distribution of ideas, goods, and services to create exchanges that satisfy individual and organizational objectives. It involves all decisions related to a product's characteristics, price, production specifications, market-entry date, distribution, promotion, and sale. It involves understanding and satisfying customers' needs and buying behavior to encourage consumer purchases, in addition to maintaining long-term relationships with customers after the sale.

2. **Describe four utilities created by marketing.**

   Marketers enhance the appeal of their products and services by adding utility. Form utility is created when companies turn raw materials into finished goods desired by consumers. Time utility is created by making the product available when the consumer wants to buy it. Place utility is created when a product is made available at a location that is convenient for the consumer. Possession utility is created by facilitating the transfer of ownership from seller to buyer.

3. **Explain how the Internet is affecting the marketing function.**

   The Internet opens new channels of distribution for goods and services, in addition to new channels for marketing to and communicating with customers. It expands consumer product choices, extends shopping hours, provides extensive product research, and facilitates the building of relationships between sellers and customers. The Internet also serves as a vehicle for generating new revenues and cutting costs at the retail and wholesales levels.

4. **Explain why and how companies learn about their customers.**

   Today's customers generally are sophisticated, price sensitive, demanding, more impatient, more informed, and difficult to satisfy. Companies learn about their customers so they can stay in touch with their current needs and wants, deliver quality products, and provide effective customer service. Such attention tends to keep customers satisfied and helps retain their long-term loyalty. Moreover, studies show that sales to repeat customers are more profitable. Most companies learn about their customers by studying consumer buying behavior, conducting marketing research, and capturing and analyzing customer data.

5. **Discuss how marketing research helps the marketing effort, and highlight its limitations.**

   Marketing research can help companies set goals, develop new products, segment markets, plan future marketing programs, evaluate the effectiveness of a marketing program, keep an eye on competition, and measure customer satisfaction. On the other hand, marketing research is a poor predictor of what will excite consumers in the future. It is sometimes ineffective because it is conducted in an artificial setting. And, it is not a substitute for good judgment.

6. **Outline the three steps in the strategic marketing planning process.**

   The three steps in the strategic marketing planning process are (1) examining your current marketing situation, which includes reviewing your past performance, evaluating your competition, examining your internal strengths and weaknesses, and analyzing the external environment; (2) assessing your opportunities and setting your objectives; and (3) developing your marketing strategy, which covers segmenting your market, choosing your target markets, positioning your product, and creating a marketing mix to satisfy the target market.

7. **Define market segmentation and cite six factors used to identify segments.**

   Market segmentation is the process of subdividing a market into homogeneous groups to identify potential customers and to devise marketing approaches geared to their needs and interests. The six most common factors used to identify segments are demographics, geographics, psychographics, geodemographics, behavior, and Internet usage patterns.

8. **Identify the four elements of a company's marketing mix.**

   The four elements, known as the 4Ps, are products, price, place, and promotion. Products are persons, places, physical objects, ideas, services, organizations, or anything which is offered for the purpose of satisfying a want or need in a marketing exchange. Price is the amount of money customers pay for the product. Place (also known as distribution) is the organized network of firms that move the goods and services from the producer to consumer. Promotion involves the activities used to communicate and promote a product to the target market.

KEY TERMS

behavioral segmentation **(316)**	cognitive dissonance **(309)**	consumer market **(309)**
cause-related marketing **(300)**	consumer buying behavior **(308)**	customer service **(300)**

TEST YOUR KNOWLEDGE

Questions for Review

1. What are some of the characteristics of today's customers?

2. How does the organizational market differ from the consumer market?

3. What is strategic marketing planning, and what is its purpose?

4. What external environmental factors affect strategic marketing decisions?

5. What are the four basic components of the marketing mix?

Questions for Analysis

6. If relationship marketing is such a good idea, why don't more businesses do it?

7. How can marketing research and database marketing help companies improve their marketing efforts?

8. Why does a marketer need to consider its current marketing situation, including competitive trends, when setting objectives for market share?

9. Why do companies segment markets?

10. *Ethical Considerations:* Thanks to the Internet you can contact a company for product information with a click of a mouse. But while many companies promote a variety of online customer service features, few respond in a timely manner to customers' questions and some don't respond at all. Companies claim that they simply can't keep up with the number of customer e-mail queries they receive. And they can't afford to increase their customer service staff either. Website promises such as "Click here to talk to customer service," or "Got a question, let us help" look good, but the reality is too many companies promote a service they can't support. Review a few of your favorite retail websites and analyze the different online customer service options these companies offer. Do they provide a projected response time? Do they send an auto reply message for e-mail queries? Do they offer a self-service help page for frequently asked questions. In your opinion, how could companies better handle online customer support when they are short of resources?

Questions for Application

11. How might a retailer use relationship and database marketing to improve customer loyalty?

12. Think of a product you recently purchased and review your decision process. Why did you need or want that product? How did the product's marketing influence your purchase decision? How did you investigate the product before making your purchase decision? Did you experience cognitive dissonance after your decision?

13. *Integrated:* Why is it important to analyze a firm's marketing plan before designing the production process for a service or a good? What kinds of information are generally included in a marketing plan that might affect the design of the production process as discussed in Chapter 9?

14. *Integrated:* How might these economic indicators, discussed in Chapter 1, affect a company's marketing decisions: consumer price index, inflation, unemployment?

PRACTICE YOUR KNOWLEDGE

Handling Difficult Situations on the Job: Making Marketing Gimmicks Safer for Kids

Fast-food giveaways account for one-third of all toys distributed in the United States. So when two babies died in 1999 after suffocating on plastic Pokemon balls their parents got from Burger King, the fast-food industry took notice. Some restaurants implemented safety tests on the billions of free toys being distributed with kids' meals. But few took the strict steps now followed by Burger King and McDonald's. Burger King has hired independent testers, strengthened safety standards, and conducted tests before, during, and after manufacturing. McDonald's has developed a testing doll, "McBaby," with artificial lungs to check suffocation risks.

Ann W. Brown, the chairman of the Consumer Product Safety Commission (and your boss) wants other fast-food vendors to follow in their footsteps. "Just because a toy is inexpensive and is given away doesn't mean it shouldn't be as safe as the safest toys," Brown believes. Brown wants restaurants that profit from such promotions to be responsible for safety tests. After all, a popular giveaway can increase a restaurant's sales by about 4 percent; a really big hit, by 15 percent, so it's to their advantage to protect child safety. In addition to legal liabilities and reputation damage if children are injured or die from giveaway toys, restaurants can lose the millions they've spent to promote a toy that has to be recalled.[40]

Your task: Brown wants you to write to fast-food vendors in the United States, urging them to follow McDonalds' and Burger King's lead in pretesting giveaway toys. She also wants you to think of other ways to encourage vendors to adopt stricter safety standards. Knowing that a variety of situational factors also influence a buyer's decision-making process, how might you put further pressure on fast-food vendors to test the toys?

Building Your Team Skills

In the course of planning a marketing strategy, marketers need to analyze the external environment to consider how forces outside the firm may create new opportunities and challenges. One important environmental factor for merchandise buyers at Sears is weather conditions. For example when merchandise buyers for lawn and garden products think about the assortment and number of products to purchase for the chain's stores, they don't place any orders without first poring over long-range weather forecasts for each market.

In particular, temperature and precipitation predictions for the coming 12 months are critical to the company's marketing plan, because they offer clues to consumer demand for barbecues, lawn furniture, gardening tools, and other merchandise. What other products would benefit from examining weather forecasts? With your team, brainstorm to identify at least three types of products (in addition to lawn and garden items) for which Sears should examine the weather as part of its analysis of the external environment. Share your recommendations with the entire class. How many teams identified the same products your team did?

EXPAND YOUR KNOWLEDGE

Discovering Career Opportunities

Jobs in the four Ps of marketing cover a wide range of activities, including a variety of jobs such as personal selling, advertising, marketing research, product management, and public relations. You can get more information about various marketing positions by consulting the *Career Information Center* guide to jobs and careers, the U.S. Employment Service's *Dictionary of Occupational Titles*, and online job-search websites such as Career Builder, www.careerbuilder.com.

1. Select a specific marketing job that interests you. Using one or more of the preceding resources, find out more about this chosen job. What specific duties and responsibilities do people in this position typically handle?

2. Search through help-wanted ads in newspapers, specialized magazines, or websites to find two openings in the field you are researching. What educational background and work experience are employers seeking in candidates for this position? What kind of work assignments are mentioned in these ads?

3. Now think about your talents, interests, and goals. How do your strengths fit with the requirements, duties, and responsibilities of this job? Do you think you would find this field enjoyable and rewarding? Why?

Developing Your Research Skills

From recent issues of business journals and newspapers (print or online editions), select an article that describes in some detail a particular company's attempt to build relationships with its customers (either in general or for a particular product or product line).

1. Describe the company's market. What geographic, demographic, behavioral, or psychographic segments of the market is the company targeting?

2. How does the company hold a dialogue with its customers? Does the company maintain a customer database? If so, what kinds of information does it gather?

3. According to the article, how successful has the company been in understanding its customers?

Exploring the Best of the Web

URLs for all Internet exercises are provided at the website for this book, www.prenhall.com/bovee. *When you log on to the text website, select Chapter 12, then select "Student Resources," click on the name of the featured website, and review the website to complete these exercises.*

Explore these chapter-related websites, review their content, and answer the following questions for each website you visit:

1. What is the purpose of this website?

2. What kinds of information does this website contain? Please be specific.

3. How is the information provided at this website useful for businesspeople? Consumers?

4. How did you expand your knowledge of marketing and customers by reviewing the material at this website? What new things did you learn about these topics?

Sign Up for Electronic Commerce 101

Think you may be interested in moving your business onto the Net but you don't know where to start? Study the basics at Electronic Commerce 101 before you plan your marketing strategies. Find out how to succeed in electronic commerce. Read the beginners guide and the step-by-step process of becoming e-commerce enabled. Learn how to process payments, credit cards, and e-cash. Find out the top 10 ways websites lose customers. Still have a question? This site has free advice from over 7,000 experts. www.ecommerce. about.com/smallbusiness/ecommerce/library/bl101

Gather Some Demographical Data for Your Marketing Toolbox

How much does the typical family spend on food away from home? On entertainment? Are these consumer expenditures increasing each year? Find out by visiting the American Demographics Marketing Tools website and explore its toolbox of useful information. Read some of the current marketing articles. Follow the link to the Bureau of Labor Statistics (BLS) website. With all these sources, no wonder marketers today have more and better data about today's customers. www.marketingtools.com

See Why It's "As Easy As Dell"

Everybody talks about Dell's exceptional customer service and sales approach but few have been able to duplicate Dell's success. Dell's website demonstrates its commitment to customer service. The webpages include product benefits, product information, online help, and a variety of customer-care services. Log on and explore the website. See why the company has adopted the slogan "Easy as Dell." How does Dell use its website to build relationships with customers? How does the Dell website employ the marketing concept? What kinds of online customer service features does the Dell website offer? www.dell.com

Learning Interactively
Companion Website

Visit the Companion Website at www.prenhall.com/bovee. For Chapter 12, take advantage of the interactive "Study Guide" to test your chapter knowledge. Get instant feedback on whether you need additional studying. Read the "Current Events" articles to get the latest on chapter topics, and complete the exercises as specified by your instructor. Expand your learning with a visit to the "Research Area." There you will find a wealth of information you can use to complete your course assignments.

A CASE FOR CRITICAL THINKING

Is Levi Strauss Coming Apart at the Seams?

Throughout most of the 20th century, Levi Strauss had the jeans world sewn up. Its riveted, five-pocket denim bottoms were a must-have for the teenage set, as well as a wardrobe icon for middle-aged baby boomers who grew up with the brand. Aging boomers loved their Levi's, and the company's Dockers apparel line had been a solid hit with those core customers.

But young consumers formed a different perception of the famous brand during the 1990s. Teens and young adults found little appeal in the straight-leg Levi's that their parents loved, preferring more trendy, fashionable styles. Sticking with its "one brand fits all" marketing strategies that had worked successfully for years, Levi's ignored the fashion statements of the younger generation. And losing touch with youthful customers—the company's future market—created denim disaster at Levi Strauss.

Faded Jeans

Throughout the 1990s, Levi's looked the other way as competitors such as the Gap, Lee, Faded Glory, and specialty retailers gained market share among consumers aged 14 to 19. And failing to pay close attention to the youth market spelled trouble for Levi's. As the youth segment turned to competitors for jeans with baggier fits, wide pant legs, and bigger pockets, Levi's share of the denim jeans market plummeted and annual revenues dropped from nearly $7 billion to just over $4 billion.

To curb the losses, Levi's top management closed more than two dozen factories, laid off thousands of employees worldwide, and moved production to cheaper offshore factories owned by others. But instead of immediately focusing on ways to regain market share, Levi's launched an ambitious project for improving delivery to retailers. Distracted by the project, the company lost its focus on reaching out to younger customers. Moreover, the company executives, descendents of founder Levi Strauss, failed to encourage immediate innovation of the company's core brand.

Expanding Levi's Pockets

Still losing market share, Levi's finally scrambled to learn more about the perceptions and needs of two targeted consumer segments: youth, ages 13 to 25, and young adults, ages 25 to 35. After learning that younger buyers were interested in unique, uncommon styles, Levi's launched several programs to attract younger consumers. First, Levi's developed the Limited Edition product line, inspired by the movie *Mod Squad*, and restricted the availability of the product to 60 days. In return for featuring Levi's in the film, the company promoted the movie in TV commercials and print ads. "We hear from kids that they want something different and exclusive, and this limited, short product offering is a new strategy for Levi's," explained Levi's communications manager.

Next, the company moved away from its traditional "one brand fits all" marketing strategy by creating a series of individual brands. For instance, Red Line jeans were positioned as more fashionable and upscale. Nothing on the jeans indicated that they were related to Levi's, and distribution was limited to 25 trendy stores—including Barney's New York, an upscale retailer that had never carried Levi's before. To reach the youth segment, Levi's introduced such new products as the Silver Tab brand with a baggier fit, Mobile Zip-Off pants with legs that unzipped to create shorts, and Engineered Jeans, a "reinvention" of the traditional five-pocket style with big pockets to hold such items as pagers and cell phones. Furthermore, Levi's designed new brands specifically for its core customers, the baby boomer segment—customers that the company couldn't afford to lose. These new brands included Dockers

Equipment for Legs and K-1 Khakis, a hipper version of the popular Dockers product line.

Going further, the company created Original Spin, a high-tech program that allowed consumers to design their own jeans by accessing computerized kiosks at selected stores. And Levi's introduced Type 1 and Pure Blue mid-line brands and focused on more colorful packaging to give its products an exciting, youthful look.

Will Levi's Jean Therapy Work?

Despite Levi's efforts, few experts are convinced that Levi's has gotten its groove back. In 2002 Moody's Investor Service downgraded Levi's $2.1 billion debt to junk-bond status, and only time will tell whether Levi's can stitch together a strategy to keep the brand from fading further. But, as CEO Philip Marineau sees it, it took a while to get the brand in trouble and it will take a while to get it out of trouble.

Critical Thinking Questions

1. Why did Levi's lose serious market share during the 1990s?
2. Why was Levi's unresponsive to the demands of younger consumers?
3. What steps did Levi's take to regain its market share?
4. Go to Chapter 12 of this text's website at www.prenhall. com/bovee. Click on the Levi's link to answer these questions: How is Levi's using its website to attract younger consumers? How do the graphics and content reflect the needs and interests of the targeted segment? What points of differentiation are emphasized?

VIDEO CASE

In Consumers' Shoes: Skechers USA

Learning Objectives

The purpose of this video is to help you:

1. Describe the role of the four Ps in a company's marketing mix
2. Explain how a company shapes its market research to fit its marketing goals
3. Discuss the effectiveness of target marketing and segmentation in analyzing consumers

Synopsis

Skechers USA enjoys a reputation for producing footwear that combines comfort with innovative design, and the company has built its product line into a globally recognized brand distributed in more than 110 countries and territories throughout the world. From its corporate headquarters in Manhattan Beach, California, Skechers has engineered steady growth in market share while competing against some powerful players in the high-ticket, branded athletic shoe industry.

Since its start in 1992, Skechers has solidified its image as a maker of hip footwear through a savvy marketing strategy that calls for catering to a closely targeted consumer base. Maintaining brand integrity and its reputation for innovation is a crucial goal in all of Skechers' product development and marketing activities.

Director of public relations Kelly O'Connor discusses her work and the marketing activities that are critical to maintaining Skechers' edge in the highly competitive footwear marketplace. She describes the company's goal of creating a megabrand with an image, personality, and "feel" that can be translated and marketed globally. Skechers has been successful in brand building by means of an "Ask, Don't Tell" approach to product development and marketing—that is, it aims to find out what the market wants and then appeal to customers' wants rather than trying to influence the market with the products that it makes available.

Discussion Questions

1. *For analysis:* Which of the four Ps of the marketing mix seems to govern Skechers' marketing strategy? Why?
2. *For analysis:* How do you suppose Skechers alters elements of its American marketing mix to attract consumers in international markets?
3. *For application:* Skechers collects a lot of *primary* data in its market research. What kinds of primary data does the company prefer to gather? Why do these kinds of data suit the company's marketing goals? How do the data suit its consumer base? Given Skechers' fairly limited consumer base, are there other types of research data that you would recommend to company marketers?
4. *For application:* Describe Skechers' target market and explain how company marketers segment it. How effective is this strategy in analyzing customers? How successful are Skechers' marketing efforts among 12- to 24-year-olds (and consumers wishing they were in that demographic segment)?
5. *For debate:* Building brand loyalty is a major effort that presents both opportunities and challenges to marketers and product developers. How might Skechers increase loyalty for its brand? Do you think Skechers should expand its current product lines to include other new products such as clothing or accessories? How could the company go about investigating the market potential for such products?

Online Exploration

Go online to find out about the product lines and target markets of such companies as Nike (www.nike.com), Reebok (www.reebok.com), Lady Foot Locker (www.ladyfootlocker.com), and FUBU (www1.fubu.com). How does the approach to segmentation at these companies compare with that of Skechers?

13

Product and Pricing Strategies

After studying this chapter, you will be able to

1. Describe the four stages in the life cycle of a product

2. Describe six stages of product development

3. Cite three levels of brand loyalty

4. Discuss the functions of packaging and labeling

5. Identify four ways of expanding a product line, and discuss two risks that product-line extensions pose

6. Highlight several factors that should be considered when developing product strategies for international markets

7. List seven factors that influence pricing decisions, and cite several common pricing strategies

Laugh lines, frown lines, crow's feet: who needs them? Botox has become the most popular anti-aging treatment in the U.S. with more than two million people expected to have treatments this year.

INSIDE BUSINESS TODAY

Marketing a Facelift in a Bottle

It started in the late 1990s as a rumor, then it became a whisper, then a buzz. By 2001 every cosmetically correct woman on both U.S. coasts knew the secret: When you inject Botox—an obscure drug normally used to paralyze overactive muscles—into facial wrinkles, they disappear almost overnight.

Botox was developed in the 1970s by a San Francisco doctor looking for ways to correct crossed eyes, or strabismus. He found that injections of small amounts of purified botulinum toxin (the same bacterium that causes botulism) paralyzed the overactive muscles that causes strabismus, allowing other eye muscles to operate normally. The injections also improved uncontrollable eye blinking and uncontrollable neck spasms. Allergan, an Irvine, California, company, purchased the rights to the doctor's discovery in 1987 and started marketing Botox after receiving FDA approval in 1989.

Prior to Botox, Allergan was content to maintain a low profile. The company had paddled the backwaters of the pharmaceuticals industry, selling little-known eye and skin drugs, some surgical devices, and a line of over-the-counter lens cleaners. Because it was too small to attract much attention from pharmaceutical giants 20 times it size, Allergan adopted a narrowcast marketing approach, focusing on two attractive submarkets: ophthalmology and dermatology. This narrow focus meant that Allergan didn't have to spend a fortune on marketing or hire a large salesforce to call on hundreds of thousands of internists and family practitioners.

Then in the mid-1990s, doctors noticed something intriguing: Botox's paralyzing properties seemed to greatly reduce frown lines and wrinkles in patients using it for eye problems. As word of the Botox effect spread, more and more doctors began using it to relax the facial muscles that create eyebrow furrows, crow's feet, and horizontal forehead lines. Allergan conducted clinical trials and in 2002 received FDA regulatory approval to use Botox for cosmetic procedures.

Nothing in Allergan's history could have prepared it for the transformation of one of its oddest drugs into a glamorous sensation—and fame. The injections, which can be given in five to 15 minutes, make a perfect lunch-hour treatment. Soon the early buzz and media splash boosted Botox sales in high-glamour cities such as New York and Los Angeles. But Allergan recognized that selling the general public on the elective joys of injecting poison to paralyze their foreheads would require more than word-of-mouth promotion. Moreover, the effects of each treatment, which costs about $500, last for only four months. And the treatments are not covered by health insurance.

To meet these challenges, Allergan decided to promote the entire Botox experience. It began training doctors on how to inject Botox. And the company showed doctors how to design and decorate their offices to appeal to patients who want to be pampered.

How far will a people go for beauty? Using too much Botox can freeze the face into an inexpressive mask. Eyelid droop, slurred speech, and dropped mouth are just some of Botox's other side effects. In spite of these risks, Allergan's management believes that the product's convenience and quick-fix aspect will make the treatment increasingly popular among people who are beginning to despair as they see the wrinkles in the mirror. Already reaping some $175 million in worldwide revenues from sales of Botox, Allergan is developing new product and pricing strategies to help the product grow by several hundred million dollars a year. If successful, Botox could eventually fuel Allergan's transformation into a specialty-pharmaceuticals-only business.[1]

Characteristics of Products

As Allergan's management knows, companies face a number of wrinkles when it comes to developing marketing and pricing strategies for products. This chapter discusses some of the important product decisions marketers must make to compete effectively in the global marketplace. We begin the chapter by explaining product fundamentals, such as product types, product life cycles, and the new product development process. Next, we explore a variety of decisions companies must make with respect to product identities, brand sponsorship, product lines and mixes, positioning, and international markets. We conclude the chapter by explaining popular pricing strategies.

Types of Products

Think about Botox, Doritos tortilla chips, Disney World, and your favorite rock group. You wouldn't market all these products in the same way, because buyer behavior, product characteristics, market expectations, competition, and other elements of the equation are entirely different.

Marketers frequently classify products on the basis of tangibility and use. Some products are predominantly tangible; others are mostly intangible. Most products, however, fall somewhere between those two extremes. When you buy software such as Norton's AntiVirus, for example, you get service features along with the product—such as product updates, customer assistance, and so on. The *product continuum* indicates the relative amounts of tangible and intangible components in a product (see Exhibit 13.1). Education is a product at the intangible extreme, whereas salt and shoes are at the tangible extreme. TGI Friday's restaurants fall in the middle because they involve both tangible (food) and intangible (service) components.

Service Products   Service products have some special characteristics that affect the way they are marketed. *Intangibility* is one fundamental characteristic. You can't usually show a

EXHIBIT 13.1   The Product Continuum
Products contain both tangible and intangible components; predominantly tangible products are categorized as goods, whereas predominantly intangible products are categorized as services.

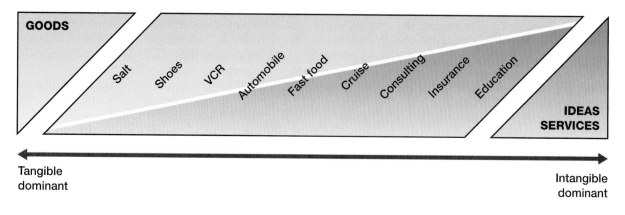

service in an ad, demonstrate it before customers buy, mass produce it, or give customers anything tangible to show for their purchase. Services marketers often compensate for intangibility by using tangible symbols or by adding tangible components to their products. Prudential Insurance, for example, uses the Rock of Gibraltar as a symbol of stability, and its ads invite you to get "your piece of the rock."

Another unique aspect of service products is *perishability*. Because services cannot usually be created in advance or held in storage until people are ready to buy, services are time sensitive. For instance, if airlines don't sell seats on a particular flight, once the flight takes off an unsold seat can never produce revenue. Hotel rooms, movie theatre seats, and restaurants are similar. For this reason, many services try to shift customer demand by offering discounts or promotions during slow periods.

Marketers also classify products by use. Both organizations and consumers use many of the same products, but they use them for different reasons and in different ways. Individual consumers or households generally purchase smaller quantities of goods and services for personal use. Products that are primarily sold to consumers for personal consumption are known as *consumer products*.

Consumer Products Consumer products can be classified into four subgroups, depending on how people shop for them:

- *Convenience products* are the goods and services that people buy frequently, without much conscious thought, such as toothpaste, dry cleaning, film developing, and photocopying.
- *Shopping products* are fairly important goods and services that people buy less frequently: a stereo, a computer, a refrigerator, or a college education. Such purchases require more thought and comparison shopping to check on price, features, quality, and reputation.
- *Specialty products* are particular brands that the buyer especially wants and will seek out, regardless of location or price, such as CK perfume, Armani suits, and Suzuki violin lessons. Specialty products are not necessarily expensive, but they are products that customers go out of their way to buy and for which they rarely accept substitutes.
- *Unsought goods* are products that people do not normally think of buying, such as life insurance, cemetery plots, and new products they must be made aware of through promotion.

Industrial Products In contrast to consumer products, *industrial products* are generally purchased by firms in large quantities and are used for further processing or in conducting a business. Two categories of industrial products are expense items and capital items. *Expense items* are relatively inexpensive goods and services that organizations generally use within a year of purchase. Examples are pencils and printer cartridges. *Capital items* are more expensive organizational products and have a longer useful life. Examples include desks, photocopiers, and computers.

Aside from dividing products into expense and capital items, industrial buyers and sellers often classify products according to their intended use:

- *Raw materials* such as iron ore, crude petroleum, lumber, and chemicals are used in the production of final products.
- *Components* such as spark plugs and printer cartridges are similar to raw materials; they also become part of the manufacturers' final products.
- *Supplies* such as pencils, nails, and light bulbs that are used in a firm's daily operations are considered expense items.
- *Installations* such as factories, power plants, airports, production lines, and semiconductor fabrication machinery are major capital projects.
- *Equipment* includes less-expensive capital items such as desks, telephones, and fax machines that are shorter lived than installations.

• *Business services* range from simple and fairly risk-free services such as landscaping and cleaning to complex services such as management consulting and auditing.

The Product Life Cycle

1 LEARNING OBJECTIVE

Describe the four stages in the life cycle of a product

product life cycle
Four basic stages through which a product progresses: introduction, growth, maturity, and decline

Regardless of a product's classification, few products last forever. Most products go through a **product life cycle**, passing through four distinct stages in sales and profits: introduction, growth, maturity, and decline (see Exhibit 13.2). As the product passes from stage to stage, various marketing approaches become appropriate.

The product life cycle can describe a product class (gasoline-powered automobiles), a product form (sports-utility vehicles), or a brand (Ford Explorer). Product classes and forms tend to have the longest life cycles, whereas specific brands tend to have shorter life cycles. The amount of time that a product remains in any one stage depends on customer needs and preferences, economic conditions, the nature of the product, and the marketer's strategy. Still, the proliferation of new products, changing technology, globalization, and the ability to quickly imitate competitors is hurtling product forms and brands through their life cycles much faster today than in the past.

Consider electronics, where product life is now a matter of months: Panasonic replaces its consumer electronic products with new models every 90 days.[2] Why? Smart companies know that if they don't keep innovating, competitors who do will capture the business. Polaroid learned this lesson the hard way. The company failed to properly respond to digital technology, and Polaroid customers soon defected to digital cameras or other technologies. In 2001 Polaroid filed for Chapter 11 bankruptcy protection. The company was partially salvaged by Bank One Corp's venture-capital group, One Equity Partners, which purchased almost all of Polaroid's assets in 2002 and hopes to revive the brand.[3]

Not only are existing products advancing through product life cycles at a rapid pace, but many companies are finding it increasingly hard to maintain a unique advantage long enough to make good profits on product innovations. Years ago, companies could milk an innovative product for years before cut-rate clones arrived. Now new TVs, packaged foods, telecom routers, e-commerce concepts, and wireless services are barely out the door before rivals are on their tails, bludgeoning prices. Procter & Gamble, for example, had high profit hopes for its innovative $50 Swiffer WetJet mop, which sprays water on floors. But soon after the product's launch, Clorox Co. developed ReadyMop and priced it competitively.

EXHIBIT 13.2
The Product Life Cycle
Most products and product categories move through a life cycle similar to the one represented by the curve in this diagram. However, the duration of each stage varies widely from product to product.

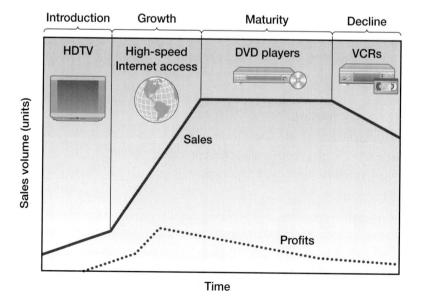

P&G was then forced to cut the price of its Swiffer WetJet mop price by half—only seven months after it was introduced into the marketplace.[4]

Introduction The first stage in the product life cycle is the *introductory stage*, during which producers launch a new product and stimulate demand. In this stage, companies typically spend heavily on conducting research-and-development efforts to create the new product, on developing promotions to build awareness of the product, and on establishing the distribution system to get the product into the marketplace. Every product—from personal computers to digital cameras—gets its start in this stage. The producer makes little profit during the introduction; however, these start-up costs are a necessary investment if the new product is to succeed. Procter & Gamble, for example, spent millions of dollars to develop and promote Dryel, a home dry-cleaning product.[5]

Growth After the introductory stage comes the *growth stage*, marked by a rapid jump in sales and, usually, an increase in the number of competitors and distribution outlets. As competition increases, so does the struggle for market share. This situation creates pressure to introduce new product features and to maintain large promotional budgets and competitive prices. In fact, marketing in this stage is so expensive that it can drive out smaller, weaker firms. With enough growth, however, a firm can often produce and deliver its products more economically than in the introduction phase. Thus, the growth stage can reap handsome profits for those who survive.

Procter & Gamble thinks Dryel has the potential to become a leading company product if it can convince consumers of the product's benefits.

Maturity During the *maturity stage*, the longest in the product life cycle, sales begin to level off or show a slight decline. Most products are in the maturity stage of the life cycle where competition increases and market share is maximized—making further expansion difficult. Because the costs of introduction and growth have diminished in this stage, most companies try to keep mature products alive so they can use the resulting profits to fund the development of new products. Some companies extend the life of a mature product by modifying the product's characteristics to improve the product's quality and performance. Keebler, for instance, has extended the life of its popular cookies by selling them in convenient mini-versions. Packaged in resealable cans, the mini-cookies are sold at convenience stores to appeal to consumers on the run.[6]

Decline Although maturity can be extended for many years, most products eventually enter the *decline stage*, when sales and profits slip and then fade away. Declines occur for several reasons: changing demographics, shifts in popular taste, product competition, and advances in technology. When a product reaches this point in the life cycle, the company must decide whether to keep it and reduce the product's costs to compensate for declining sales or discontinue it and focus on developing newer products. General Motors, for instance, decided to kill off the 103-year-old Oldsmobile brand. "The decision was long overdue," notes one marketing expert. Sales of Olds had been declining for over a decade, and the brand had lost its identity.[7]

Product Makeovers Most new products are not really new at all; only about 5 percent are true innovations.[8] The rest are variations of familiar products, created by changing the packaging, improving the formula, or modifying the form or flavor—in hopes of injecting new life into the brand. For example, when Kraft took its decade-old Crystal Light powdered fruit drink, added water, and packaged it in fancy plastic bottles, sales of the reinvented brand swiftly surpassed those of Coke's lavishly launched Fruitopia.[9]

Like Crystal Light, many declining products sometimes just need a makeover. Banana Republic, for example, started out as a clothing retailer with a gimmick: safari clothing sold in stores decorated with fake palm trees and shipping crates. That version of Banana Republic soon became an endangered species until the brand was rescued and reinvented as an upscale business-casual retailer when the Gap acquired it in 1983.[10] Similarly, the Old Spice brand, once mainly know for the aftershave used by dads or granddads, has recently gotten a makeover. The brand is now targeted to males in the 12 to 34 age group. Moreover, its hip new packaging and products, such as body spray for men, has made Old Spice a favorite fragrance among teenage boys.[11]

Jeffrey Himmel, chairman and CEO of New York's Himmel group, has made a business of seeking out and resuscitating deceased brands. As Himmel sees it, any brand that had lasted a long time must have had something going for it. "A company may have spent $10 million building up a brand, and then they let it slip," says Himmel. "But the value is still there, lodged in the backs of people's memory." Take Breck shampoo, for example. The 72-year-old brand peaked in the 1970s and then declined as the Breck Girl ads lost their power. The brand was taken off the shelf in 2000. But Himmel, who is licensing the marketing rights from Dial, has brought the brand back to life by focusing on the shampoo's light floral fragrance (which he thinks consumers will remember fondly) instead of introducing a new generation of Breck Girls.[12]

2 LEARNING OBJECTIVE

Describe six stages of product development

The New-Product Development Process

Suppose your company decides to develop a new product. Where do you begin? As Exhibit 13.3 shows, companies launch new products for a number of reasons: They may have a terrific new concept like P&G's Swiffer WetJet mop. They may be following in the footsteps of

EXHIBIT 13.3 Six Great Product Innovations
Some of the greatest product breakthroughs of the 20th century happened by chance, on a hunch, or because of impatience. Here are six product innovations that have changed our lives in a profound way.

YEAR	INNOVATION
1924	Frozen food: Until Clarence Birdseye came around, cooking and cryogenics had little in common. Birdseye noticed how natives in Labrador froze fresh fish to preserve its taste. Experimenting with other foods, he perfected the freezing process in the United States, and by 1934 Birdseye's frozen meats and vegetables filled grocers' coolers around the country.
1929	Synthetic rubber: In 1929 Julius Nieuwland discovered that acetylene could be polymerized into an elastic substance. Two years later, DuPont, which funded his research, marketed the material as a synthetic rubber, which today is still favored for cable insulation, wet suits, and beverage coolers.
1930	Jet engine: As a cadet in the Royal Air Force, Sir Frank Whittle predicted that a system of turbines and compressed air that burned vaporized fuel would make propellered craft obsolete. He patented the turbine engine in 1930 but spent another decade getting it off the ground. In a 1941 test flight, the world's first jet reached 370 miles per hour, far faster than propped planes.
1933	Wallboard: One of the cleverest ideas in home building since the invention of bricks was unveiled in 1933—preformed plaster walls. This mixture of recycled paper and the cheap mineral gypsum ended the huge cost of lath-and-plaster crews that used to finish the insides of buildings. Inventor U.S. Gypsum has lots of imitators now but still owns the popular moniker for the product, Sheetrock.
1938	Xerography: Tedium, not toner, was the mother of this invention. Working as a patent lawyer in New York, Chester Floyd Carlson grew tired of making copies of patent applications and law textbooks. In 1934 he began working on a machine that could transfer an image produced on a photoconductive plate with exposed light to a plain sheet of paper. He succeeded four years later. In 1946 he struck a deal with Haloid Co., which introduced the first commercial copying machine. They called it xerography: "xeros" for dry, "graphos" for picture. Haloid became Haloid Xerox before dropping the first part of its name.
1947	Microwave oven: Raytheon engineer Percy Spencer brought kitchens into the space age. In 1945, when he was standing in front of an active magnetron tube, the heart of shortwave radar systems, a chocolate bar in his pocket began to melt. He struck gold after placing kernels of corn on the tube and watching them pop. Two years later the world's first microwave oven was produced.

EXHIBIT 13.4 The Product Development Process
For every hundred ideas generated, only one or two salable products may emerge from the lengthy and expensive process of product development.

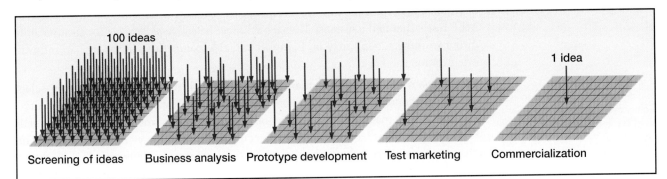

100 ideas

1 idea

Screening of ideas   Business analysis   Prototype development   Test marketing   Commercialization

their competitors, as Clorox did with its ReadyMop. Or they may discover a new product by chance, as Allergan did with Botox.

Companies that do develop new products generally use a *product-development process*—a series of stages through which a product idea passes. Still, not all ideas become new products. As Exhibit 13.4 shows, some ideas are killed midstream because they do not meet the criteria that specify what needs to be accomplished before a product moves from one stage into the next. Here are the six stages of the product-development process:

- **Idea generation.** The first step in the product-development process is to come up with ideas that will satisfy unmet needs. Customers, competitors, and employees are often the best source of new-product ideas. For instance, when Rubbermaid sent 15 two-person teams to willing consumers' homes to observe home-storage practices, the group returned with 300 new-product ideas in just three days.[13]

- **Idea screening.** From the mass of ideas suggested, the company culls a few that appear to be worthy of further development, applying broad criteria such as whether the product can use existing production facilities and how much technical and marketing risk is involved. In the case of industrial or technical products, this phase is often referred to as a "feasibility study," in which the product's features are defined and its workability is tested. In the case of consumer products, marketing consultants and advertising agencies are often called in to help evaluate new ideas. In some cases, potential customers are asked what they think of a new product idea—a process known as concept testing.

- **Business analysis.** A product idea that survives the screening stage is subjected to a business analysis. During this stage the company reviews the sales, costs, and profit projections to see if they meet the company's objectives. For instance, one question the company must answer is whether the company can make enough money on the product to justify the investment. To answer this question, the company forecasts the probable sales of the product, assuming various pricing strategies. In addition, it estimates the costs associated with various levels of production. Given these projections, the company calculates the potential profit that will be achieved if the product is introduced. If the product meets the company's objectives, it can then move to the product-development stage.

- **Prototype development.** At this stage the firm actually develops the product concept into a physical product. The firm creates and tests a few samples, or *prototypes*, of the

Product testing is a critical step in the new product development process for jet engines. Pairs of this GE90-115B giant engine will power all new Boeing 777 models, including one able to fly 18 hours nonstop—enough for Los Angeles to Paris if you care to sit that long.

product, including its packaging. During this stage, the various elements of the marketing mix are put together. In addition, the company evaluates the feasibility of large-scale production and specifies the resources required to bring the product to market. As noted by MIT researcher and journalist Michael Schrage: Effective *prototyping* (or turning an idea into a working model) may be the most valuable competitive advantage an innovative organization can have.[14]

test marketing
Product-development stage in which a product is sold on a limited basis—a trial introduction

- *Test marketing.* During **test marketing**, the firm introduces the product in selected areas of the country and monitors consumer reactions. Test marketing gives the marketer experience with marketing the product before going to the expense of a full introduction. Fisher-Price's Play Lab is the centerpiece of the company's success. There, marketers observe as children and infants play with dozens of new toy concepts. "Kids are pretty humbling," notes one product designer. "You can have what you think is a great idea, and they shoot it down in minutes." Infants are even harsher critics. Show babies something that they don't like, and they'll cry, push it away, or throw it on the floor. Drool, however, is the highest praise.[15]

commercialization
Large-scale production and distribution of a product

- *Commercialization.* The final stage of development is **commercialization**, the large-scale production and distribution of products that have survived the testing process. This phase (also referred to as a *product launch*) requires the coordination of many activities—manufacturing, packaging, distribution, pricing, and promotion. A classic mistake is letting marketing get out of phase with production by promoting the product before the company can supply it in adequate quantity. Many companies roll out their new products gradually, going from one geographic area to the next. This plan enables them to spread the costs of launching the product over a longer period and to refine their strategy as the rollout proceeds.

Product Identities

Creating an identity for your products is one of the first decisions marketers make. A **brand** is a unique name, symbol, or design that sets the product apart from those offered by competitors. Branding helps a product in many ways. It provides customers with a way of recognizing and specifying a particular product so that they can choose it again or recommend it to others. It provides consumers with information about the product. It facilitates the marketing of the product. And it creates value for the product. This notion of the value of a brand is also called *brand equity*.

brand
A name, term, sign, symbol, design, or combination of those used to identify the products of a firm and to differentiate them from competing products

3 LEARNING OBJECTIVE

Cite three levels of brand loyalty

Brand Equity

A brand name is often an organization's most valuable asset. Strong brands often command a premium price in the marketplace, as Nike shoes, North Face ski wear, Bobbie Brown cosmetics, and Evian water do. Customers who buy the same brand again and again are evidence of the strength of **brand loyalty**, or commitment to a particular brand. Brand loyalty can be measured in degrees. The first level is **brand awareness**, which means that people are likely to buy a product because they are familiar with it. The next level is **brand preference**, which means people will purchase the product if it is available, although they may still be willing to experiment with alternatives if they cannot find the preferred brand. The third and ultimate level of brand loyalty is **brand insistence**, the stage at which buyers will accept no substitute.

Companies can take various approaches to building brand equity. One approach is to create separate brands for products targeted to different customer segments. For example, Second Cup Limited, a Canadian company, uses three distinct coffeehouse brands—Coffee

brand loyalty
Commitment to a particular brand

brand awareness
Level of brand loyalty at which people are familiar with a product; they recognize it

brand preference
Level of brand loyalty at which people habitually buy a product if it is available

brand insistence
Level of brand loyalty at which people will accept no substitute for a particular product

Plantation, Gloria Jean's, and Coffee People—to target three geographical segments. The opposite approach is illustrated by Starbucks, which operates under one brand everywhere in the world.[16] Yet another approach is illustrated by the Gap. The $8 billion company has put its main brand on BabyGap and GapBody stores as well as its GapScents fragrances. Yet it has maintained separate brand identities for Banana Republic and Old Navy, two chains aimed at distinctly different customer segments.[17]

Brand Name Selection

Botox, Jeep, Levi's 501, Apple, and Martha Stewart are **brand names**, the portion of a brand that can be spoken, including letters, words, or numbers. McDonald's golden arches symbol is an example of a **brand mark**, the portion of a brand that cannot be expressed verbally. The choice of a brand name and any associated brand marks can be a critical success factor. A well-known brand name, for instance, can generate more sales than an unknown name. As a result, manufacturers zealously protect their names.

Brand names and brand symbols may be registered with the Patent and Trademark Office as trademarks. As Component Chapter A explains, a **trademark** is a brand that has been given legal protection so that its owner has exclusive rights to its use. The Lanham Trademark Act, a federal law, prohibits the unauthorized use of a trademark on goods or services when the use would likely confuse consumers as to the origin of those goods and services. For trademark infringement, the evidence must show that an appreciable number of ordinary prudent purchasers are likely to be confused as to the source, sponsorship, affiliation, or connection of the goods or services.[18] Nonetheless, when a name becomes too widely used it no longer qualifies for protection under trademark laws. Cellophane, kerosene, linoleum, escalator, zipper, shredded wheat, and raisin bran are just a few of the many brand names that have passed into public domain, much to their creators' dismay.

One of the most recognized trademarks in the world is the Nike Swoosh.

brand names
Portion of a brand that can be expressed orally, including letters, words, or numbers

brand mark
Portion of a brand that cannot be expressed verbally

trademark
Brand that has been given legal protection so that its owner has exclusive rights to its use

national brands
Brands owned by the manufacturers and distributed nationally

private brands
Brands that carry the label of a retailer or a wholesaler rather than a manufacturer

generic products
Products characterized by a plain label, with no advertising and no brand name

co-branding
Partnership between two or more companies to closely link their brand names together for a single product

Brand Sponsorship

Brand names may be associated with a manufacturer, retailer, wholesaler, or a combination of business types. Brands offered and promoted by a national manufacturer, such as Procter & Gamble's Tide detergent and Pampers disposable diapers, are called **national brands**. **Private brands** are not linked to a manufacturer but instead carry a wholesaler's or a retailer's brand. DieHard batteries and Kenmore appliances are private brands sold by Sears. As an alternative to branded products, some retailers also offer **generic products**, which are packaged in plain containers that bear only the name of the product. Generic products can cost up to 40 percent less than brand-name products because of uneven quality, plain packaging, and lack of promotion. Yet generic goods have found a definite market niche, as a look at your local supermarket shelves will confirm.

Co-branding occurs when two or more companies team up to closely link their names in a single product. Two examples of successful co-branding include Kellogg's Pop Tarts made with Smucker's jam and Nabisco Cranberry Newtons filled with Ocean Spray cranberries. Co-branding can help companies reach new audiences and tap the equity of particularly strong brands.[19] Moreover, it can help change a product's image. In an attempt to associate the Kodak brand with the output side of digital photography, the company has been co-branding its name with all things digital. The Kodak name sits above Lexmark's

Heinz's StarKist Tuna in a Pouch is the biggest innovation in tuna packaging since canned tuna was introduced over 80 years ago. The company hopes the innovative package will make a big splash with consumers.

license
Agreement to produce and market another company's product in exchange for a royalty or fee

Discuss the functions of packaging and labeling

Universal Product Codes (UPCs)
A bar code on a product's package that provides information read by optical scanners

logo on an inkjet printer (one of the first to print photographic inkjet paper), and it's all over the websites of companies that trumpet their use of Kodak processing and papers.[20]

Sometimes companies, such as Warner Brothers, **license** or sell the rights to specific well-known names and symbols—such as Looney Tunes cartoon characters—and then manufacturers use these licensed labels to help sell products. Licensing is an especially hot growth area for automotive marketers, where sales of licensed goods amount to over $6 billion annually. For instance, thousands of children now ride in Jeep and Land Rover strollers.[21]

Packaging

Another way that marketers create an identity for their products is through packaging. Most products need some form of packaging to protect the product from damage or tampering. Packaging can also make it convenient for customers to purchase or use a product. Examples of innovative packaging are Frito-Lay's Go Snacks—plastic canisters filled with 3-D Doritos, Cheetos, or Fritos Hoops—and 7-Eleven's Candy Gulp, a plastic cup filled with gummy animals. Both conveniently fit in a car's cup holder.[22] Other examples of innovative packaging with strong consumer appeal are Gatorade's ergonomically designed bottle, Quaker Oats cereal in bags, Hidden Valley Ranch Dressing's "Easy-Squeeze" inverted bottle, Coca-Cola's 12-pak can refrigerator dispenser, and Mentadent toothpaste's two-chamber package with pump.

In some cases, packaging is an essential part of the product itself, such as microwave popcorn or toothpaste in pump dispensers. Besides function, however, packaging plays an important role in a product's marketing strategy. Packaging makes products easier to display, facilitates the sale of smaller products, serves as a means of product differentiation, and enhances the product's overall appeal and convenience.

Companies spend a lot of money on packaging to attract consumer attention and to promote a product's benefits through the package's shape, composition, and design. Once a packaging design has been set, making a change can cost hundreds of thousands of dollars because most packaging changes require changes in the manufacturing lines. Coca-Cola's decision to convert its boxy 12-pack cans to a slimmer dispenser style that conveniently fits in a refrigerator (called the new fridge pack) was a costly endeavor indeed. Converting the 80 production lines around the country cost the company about $40 million.[23]

Labeling

Labeling is an integral part of packaging. Whether the label is a separate element attached to the package or a printed part of the container, it serves to identify a brand. Labels also provide grading information about the product and information about ingredients, operating procedures, shelf life, and risks. The labeling of foods, drugs, cosmetics, and many health products is regulated under various federal laws, which often require disclosures about potential dangers, benefits, and other issues consumers need to consider when making a buying decision.

Labels do more than communicate with consumers. They are also used by manufacturers and retailers as a tool for monitoring product performance and inventory. **Universal Product Codes (UPCs)**, those black stripes on packages, give companies a cost-effective method of tracking the movement of goods. Store checkout scanners read UPC codes and relay the identity, sales, and prices of all products to the retailer's computer system. Such data can help retailers and manufacturers measure the effectiveness of promotions such as coupons and in-store displays, as well as control inventory.

Product-Line and Product-Mix Strategies

In addition to developing product identities, a company must decide how many products it will offer. To stay competitive, most companies continually add and drop products to ensure that declining items will be replaced by growth products. Large companies may assign the responsibilities of managing a company's brand to a **brand manager**, who must develop and implement a strategic marketing plan for a specific brand and create a marketing mix for that brand's products as they move through the product life cycle.

brand manager
The person who develops and implements a complete strategy and marketing program for a specific product or brand

Product Lines

A **product line** is group of products that are similar in terms of use or characteristics. The General Mills snack-food product line, for example, includes Bugles, Fruit Roll-Ups, Nature Valley Granola Bars, and Pop Secret Popcorn. Within each product line, a company confronts decisions about the number of goods and services to offer. Hewlett Packard, for example, must decide on how many different types of products to manufacture in its printer and personal computer product lines. Similarly, Home Depot must decide how many types of garden hoses it should sell in its retail stores.

product line
A series of related products offered by a firm

Product Mix

An organization with several product lines has a **product mix**—a collection of goods or services offered for sale. The General Mills product mix consists of cereals, baking products, desserts, snack foods, main meals, and so on (see Exhibit 13.5). Three important dimensions of a company's product mix are *width*, *length*, and *depth*. A company's product mix is *wide* if it

product mix
Complete list of all products that a company offers for sale

EXHIBIT 13.5   The Product Mix at General Mills
Selected products from General Mills show a product mix that is fairly wide but that varies in length and depth within each product line.

	READY-TO-EAT CEREALS	SNACK FOODS AND BEVERAGES	BAKING PRODUCTS AND DESSERTS	MAIN MEALS AND SIDE DISHES	DAIRY PRODUCTS
PRODUCT LINES	Cheerios	Bugles Corn Snacks	Bisquick	Bacon Bits	Columbo Yogurt
	Cinnamon Toast Crunch	Chex Snack Mix	Gold Medal Flour	Chicken Helper	Yoplait Yogurt
	Cocoa Puffs	Fruit by the Foot	Hungry Jack Biscuits	Green Giant Vegetables	
	Kix	Fruit Roll-Ups	Pet Ritz Pie Crusts	Hamburger Helper	
	Oatmeal Crisp	Nature Valley Granola Bars	Softasilk Cake Flour	Potato Buds	
	Raisin Nut Bran	Pop Secret Popcorn	Supermoist Cake Mix	Suddenly Salad	

has several different product lines. General Mills's product mix, for instance, is fairly wide, with five or more product lines. A company's product mix is long if it carries several items in its product lines, as General Mills does. A product mix is deep if it has a number of versions of *each* product in a product line. General Mills, for example, produces several different versions of Cheerios—frosted, multi-grain, and honey nut. The same is true for many other products in the company's other product lines.

When deciding on the dimensions of a product mix, a company must weigh the risks and rewards associated with various approaches. Some companies limit the number of product offerings and focus on selling a few selected items to be economical: Doing so keeps the production costs per unit down and limits selling expenses to a single salesforce. Other companies adopt a full-line strategy as a protection against shifts in technology, taste, and economic conditions.

Product Expansion Strategies

family branding
Using a brand name on a variety of related products

As Exhibit 13.6 shows, you can expand your product line and mix in a number of ways. You can introduce additional items in a given product category under the same brand name—such as new flavors, forms, colors, ingredients, or package sizes. Old Spice, for example, put a new spin on its product line by entering the body-wash category with its Old Spice High Endurance.[24] And Heinz squeezed more sales out of ketchup by adding green ketchup to its product line after young consumers identified color change as a desirable selling feature.[25]

You can also expand your product line by adding new but similar products bearing the same product name—a strategy known as **family branding**. Kraft, for example, has extended its Jell-O product line with new products such as gelatin in a cup, pudding in a cup, and cheesecake snacks in a cup. These products build on the convenience-with-quality image of the Jell-O family brand.

Building on the name recognition of an existing brand cuts the costs and risks of introducing new products. However, there are limits to how far a brand name can be stretched to accommodate new products and still fit the buyer's perception of what the brand stands for. Snickers ice cream bars and Dr. Scholl's socks and shoes worked as brand extensions, but Bic perfume and Rubbermaid computer accessories did not. An overextended brand name might lose its specific meaning, and sales of an extension may come at the expense of other items in the line. A line extension works best when it takes sales away from competing brands, not when it cannibalizes the company's other items.

Richard Branson, founder of Virgin, has been accused of overextending the Virgin brand. Branson has slapped the Virgin name and logo on a chaotic jumble of hundreds of products—from airplanes to cola to financial services—putting it in danger of losing its identity. "Virgin makes no sense; it's completely unfocused," says the head of one New York communications firm.[26]

EXHIBIT 13.6   Expanding the Product Line
Knowing that no product or category has an unlimited life cycle, companies use one or more of these product-line expansion methods to keep sales strong.

METHOD OF EXPANSION	HOW IT WORKS	EXAMPLE
Line filling	Developing items to fill gaps in the market that have been overlooked by competitors or have emerged as consumers' tastes and needs shift	Alka-Seltzer Plus cold medicine
Line extension	Creating a new variation of a basic product	Tartar Control Crest toothpaste
Brand extension	Putting the brand for an existing product category into a new category	Virgin Cola
Line stretching	Adding higher- or lower-priced items at either end of the product line to extend its appeal to new economic groups	Marriott Marquis hotel

Product Positioning Strategies

In Chapter 12 we defined a product's position as the place it occupies in the consumer's mind relative to competing products. For example, BMW and Porsche are associated with performance, Mercedes Benz with luxury, and Volvo with safety. By organizing products and services into categories based on the perceived position, consumers simplify the buying process. Instead of test-driving all cars, for instance, they may focus on those they perceive to be high-performance vehicles.

Even though consumers position products with or without the help of marketers, marketers do not want to leave their product's position to chance. Companies such as Allergan define the position they want to occupy in the consumer's mind before developing their marketing strategies. Then they choose positions that will give their products the greatest advantage in selected target markets. For example, at a cost of $400 to $1,000 per Botox treatment, Allergan has decided to position Botox as a premium product. The company increases the product's appeal by assisting doctors with redesigning their waiting rooms to appear more upscale and comforting.

Marketers can follow several positioning strategies. They can position their products on specific product features or attributes (such as size, ease of use, style), on the services that accompany the product (such as convenient delivery or lifetime customer support), on the product's image (such as reliability or sophistication, as Allergan does), on price (such as low cost or premium), on category leadership (such as the leading online bookseller), and so on.

When choosing the number of distinguishing variables to promote, companies try to avoid three major positioning errors: underpositioning (failing to ever really position the product at all); overpositioning (promoting too many benefits so that no one actually stands out); and confused positioning (mixing benefits that confuse the buyer such as sophisticated image and low-cost). Consider McDonald's, for instance. To convince U.S. consumers that McDonald's McCafe coffee shops stand for premium, McDonald's decided to locate the cafes in a separate area of its fast-food franchises. The cafes have their own counter, sign, and coffeehouse-like furniture. Employees wear upscale outfits, beans are gourmet quality, and drinks are served in ceramic mugs—but prices are below those of competitors such as Starbucks.[27]

Product Strategies for International Markets

In the course of developing strategies for marketing products internationally, companies must consider a variety of factors. First, they must decide on which products and services to introduce in which countries. When selecting a country, they must take into consideration the type of government, market-entry requirements, tariffs and other trade barriers, cultural and language differences, consumer preferences, foreign-exchange rates, and differing business customs. Then they must decide whether to *standardize* the product, selling the same product everywhere, or to *customize* the product to accommodate the lifestyles and habits of local target markets. Keep in mind that the degree of customization can vary. A company may change only the product's name or packaging, or it can modify the product's components, size, and functions.

Of course, understanding the country's culture and regulations will help a company make important choices regarding international product strategies, but even the most successful U.S. companies sometimes blunder. After being slammed for its alleged ignorance of European ways and losing $1 billion in Euro-Disney's first year of operation, Disney realized that Paris was not Anaheim or Orlando. Disney had insulted its French employees with a required dress code and angered its European customers, who were not accustomed to standing in line for rides or eating fast food standing up. "When we first launched Euro-Disney there was the belief that it was enough to be Disney," says Euro-Disney CEO Jay

6 **LEARNING OBJECTIVE**

Highlight several factors that should be considered when developing product strategies for international markets

When Mars Incorporated designs and promotes its M&M candy products for the Russian market, it takes cultural context into account.

Rasulo. "Now we realize that our guests need to be welcomed on the basis of their own culture and travel habits."[28] To cease alienating the Europeans, Disney switched from a standardized to a customized product strategy by modifying its theme park for the European culture. The company ditched its controversial dress code, authorized wine with meals, lowered admission prices, hired a French investor relations firm, and changed the name of the complex from Euro-Disney to Disneyland Paris to lure the French tourists. Today Disneyland Paris is Europe's leading tourist attraction.[29]

Like Disney, many U.S. manufacturers have customized their products after learning that international customers are not all alike. For instance, KFC's parent company, Tricon, believes that business, like politics, is local. So it doesn't just open restaurants based on the U.S. model and expect success. It adapts KFC's products offerings to local tastes. In Japan, for example, KFC sells tempura crispy strips. In northern England, KFC stresses gravy and potatoes, while in Thailand it offers fresh rice with soy or sweet chili sauce. In Holland the company makes a potato-and-onion croquette. In France it sells pastries alongside chicken. And in China the chicken gets spicier the farther inland you travel.[30]

McDonald's has also customized its products overseas. The French have been consuming *les Big Macs* from the moment McDonald's first arrived in 1972, and France is now the company's third largest market in Europe, but the burger giant has a unique look in that country. To accommodate a culture known for its cuisine and dining experience, many McDonald's outlets in France have upgraded their decor to a level that would make them almost unrecognizable to an American. Gone are the Golden Arches, utilitarian chairs and tables, and other plastic fixtures. Instead the restaurants have hardwood floors, exposed brick, armchairs, and extras such as music videos that entice customers to linger over their meals. And while the basic burger offerings remain the same, menus at the upscale restaurants include a premiere line of sandwiches, espresso, and brioche.[31]

Pricing Strategies

7 **LEARNING OBJECTIVE**

List seven factors that influence pricing decisions, and cite several common pricing strategies

The second key factor in the marketing mix is pricing. The pricing decisions for a product are determined by manufacturing and selling costs, competition, and the needs of wholesalers and retailers who distribute the product to the final customer. In addition, pricing is influenced by a firm's marketing objectives, government regulations, consumer perceptions, and consumer demand.

- **Marketing objectives.** The first step in setting a price is to match it to the objectives you set in your strategic marketing plan. Is your goal to increase market share, increase sales, improve profits, project a particular image, or combat competition? Consider Intel. This Silicon Valley chipmaker slashed prices on its Pentium brand microprocessors to boost sales and fend off lower-priced rival brands.[32] Rolex and Botox take a different approach, using premium pricing along with other marketing-mix elements to give its products a luxury position.

Thinking About Ethics

The Price of Life-Saving Drugs: How Much Is Too Much?

Although it's easy to characterize the debate over drug prices as social responsibility versus corporate greed, the question is not that simple. It's a murky brew of complex financial, scientific, legal, and ethical issues.

At the heart of the problem is the extraordinary cost of developing new drugs, from the years of research to the cost of laboratories, factories, and clinical tests. And many promising compounds don't make it through this long gauntlet, putting even more profit pressure on the few drugs that do. Drug makers can patent their successful creations to protect profits, but after these patents run out, other companies can produce competing "generic" versions that often sell for far less because these producers don't have to recoup the development costs. Consequently, the search for blockbuster drugs is a risky venture that can make or break the companies that discover them.

Patents are a hot button in the medical cost debate, partly because the collaborative and unpredictable nature of research can make it hard to identify who really discovered what. The patent on the pioneering AIDS medication AZT in particular has been mired in controversy since day one. AZT was discovered by the nonprofit Michigan Cancer Foundation in the 1960s as a possible cancer treatment. Two decades later, British firm GlaxoSmithKline claims it discovered AZT's effective-

ness in suppressing the AIDS virus; the AIDS Healthcare Foundation (AHF), the world's largest specialized provider of AIDS treatment services, and others argue that government scientists at the National Institutes of Health (NIH) made the discovery. Glaxo was awarded the U.S. patent nevertheless.

But AHF sued Glaxo, asking the government to invalidate Glaxo's patent on AZT and hoping to force the company to reduce the price of its AIDS drugs. Three months after the 2002 lawsuit was filed, Glaxo reduced its prices, but AHF called this a "hollow gesture" because Glaxo's prices were still significantly higher than those for comparable generics. Glaxo says it is only trying to cover its production costs and that continued lawsuits will only delay work on other life-saving drugs. What's your opinion? Are pharmaceutical companies under any greater social burden to lower prices than companies in other industries?

Questions for Critical Thinking

1. Why does the AIDS Healthcare Foundation dispute Glaxo's U.S. patent on AZT?
2. What role does patent protection play in the pricing of pharmaceuticals? Why are patents critical to the pharmaceutical industry?

- *Government regulations.* Government plays a big role in pricing in many countries. To protect consumers and encourage fair competition, the U.S. government has enacted various price-related laws over the years. Three important classes of pricing are regulated: (1) *price fixing*—an agreement among two or more companies supplying the same type of products as to the prices they will charge, (2) *price discrimination*—the practice of unfairly offering attractive discounts to some customers but not to others, and (3) *deceptive pricing*—pricing schemes that are considered misleading.

- *Consumer perceptions.* Another consideration is the perception of quality that your price will elicit from your customers. When people shop, they usually have a rough price range in mind. An unexpectedly low price triggers fear that the item is of low quality. South Korean carmaker Hyundai, for example, decided not to cut prices when the dollar gained strength against the Korean won, because the company did not want to reinforce an image of shoddy goods.[33] On the other hand, an unexpectedly high price makes buyers question whether the product is worth the money.

- *Consumer demand.* Whereas a company's costs establish a floor for prices, demand for a product establishes a ceiling. Theoretically, if the price for an item is too high, demand falls and the producers reduce their prices to stimulate demand. Conversely, if the price for an item is too low, demand increases and the producers are motivated to raise prices. As prices climb and profits improve, producers boost their output until supply and demand are in balance and prices stabilize. Nonetheless, the relationship between price and demand isn't always this perfect. Some goods and services are relatively insensitive to changes in price; others are highly responsive. Marketers refer to this sensitivity as **price elasticity**—how responsive demand will be to a change in price.

price elasticity
A measure of the sensitivity of demand to changes in price

When companies set their prices, they take these factors—among others—into account before choosing a general pricing approach. Common pricing approaches include cost-based, price-based, optimal, skimming, and penetration pricing, and a variety of price adjustment methods.

Cost-Based Pricing

Many companies simplify the pricing task by using *cost-based pricing* (also known as cost plus pricing). They price by starting with the cost of producing a good or a service and then add a markup to the cost of the product to produce a profit. How does a company determine the amount of profit it will earn by selling a certain product? **Break-even analysis** is a tool companies use to determine the number of units of a product they must sell at a given price to cover all manufacturing and selling costs, or to break even.

break-even analysis
Method of calculating the minimum volume of sales needed at a given price to cover all costs

In break-even analysis, you consider two types of costs. **Variable costs** change with the level of production. These include raw materials, shipping costs, and supplies consumed during production. **Fixed costs**, by contrast, remain stable regardless of the number of products produced. These costs include rent payments, insurance premiums, and real estate taxes. The total cost of operating the business is the sum of a firm's variable and fixed costs. The **break-even point** is the minimum sales volume the company must achieve to avoid losing money. Sales volume beyond the break-even point will generate profits; sales volume below the break-even amount will result in losses.

variable costs
Business costs that increase with the number of units produced

fixed costs
Business costs that remain constant regardless of the number of units produced

break-even point
Sales volume at a given price that will cover all of a company's costs

You can determine the break-even point in number of units with this simple calculation:

$$\text{Break-even point} = \frac{\text{Fixed costs}}{\text{Selling price} - \text{Variable costs per unit}}$$

For example, if you wanted to price haircuts at $20 and you had fixed costs of $60,000 and variable costs per haircut of $5, you would need to sell 4,000 haircuts to break even:

$$\text{Break-even point (in units)} = \frac{\$60,000}{\$20 - \$5} = 4{,}000 \text{ units}$$

Of course, $20 isn't your only pricing option. Why not charge $30 instead? When you charge the higher price, you need to give only 2,400 haircuts to break even (see Exhibit 13.7). However, before you raise your haircut prices to $30, bear in mind that a lower price may attract more customers and enable you to make more money in the long run.

Break-even analysis doesn't dictate what price you should charge; rather, it provides some insight into the number of units you have to sell at a given price to make a profit. This analysis is especially useful when you are trying to calculate the amount to mark up a price to earn a profit.

Cost-based pricing, while simple, makes little sense. First, any pricing that ignores demand and competitor prices is not likely to lead to the best price. Second, although cost-based pricing may ensure a certain profit, companies using this strategy tend to sacrifice profit opportunity.

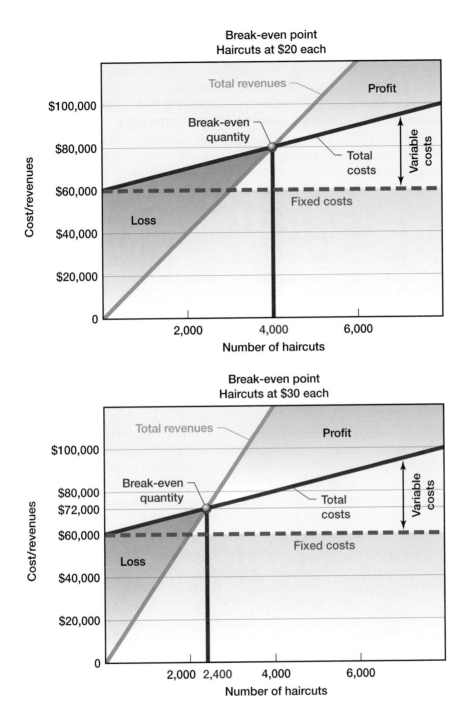

Break-even point
Haircuts at $20 each

Break-even point
Haircuts at $30 each

EXHIBIT 13.7
Break-Even Analysis
The break-even point is the point at which revenues just cover costs. After fixed costs and variable costs have been met, any additional income represents profit. The graphs show that at $20 per haircut, the break-even point is 4,000 haircuts; charging $30 yields a break-even point at only 2,400 haircuts.

Price-Based Pricing

Most manufacturers design a product, then try to figure out how to make it for a price. But recent thinking holds that cost should be the last item analyzed in the pricing formula, not the first. Companies that use *priced-based pricing* can maximize their profit by first establishing an optimal price for a product or service. The product's price is based on an analysis of a product's competitive advantages, the users' perception of the item, and the market being targeted. Once the desired price has been established, the firm focuses its energies on keeping costs at a level that will allow a healthy profit.

At Ikea, the price literally comes first. Ikea's corporate mantra is "Low price with meaning." The goal is to make products less expensive without making customers feel that the products are cheap. Striking that balance demands a special kind of design, manufacturing, and distribution expertise. New products are born at Ikea by first establishing a price point. The company surveys competition to figure out how much the new product should cost and then targets a price 30 to 50 percent below that of rivals. After settling on a target price for a product, Ikea determines what materials will be used and what manufacturer will do the assembly work—even before the new item is actually designed. The company chooses among its 1,800 suppliers in 55 countries by posting a description of the product's target cost and basic specifications to suppliers. Once a manufacturer is selected, Ikea uses the same competitive process to find a designer and select a design for production. To reduce costs, Ikea designers focus on using materials as efficiently as possible, analyzing the function of every furniture surface to determine which materials, finishes, and construction techniques will work best for the least amount of money.

Ikea's price-driven manufacturing process is a key factor in its success. While the price of other companies' products tends to rise over time, Ikea has reduced its retail prices by about 20 percent during the past four decades. The price of a basic Pöang chair, for example, has fallen from $149 in 2000 to $99 in 2001 to $79 today.[34]

Optimal Pricing

Optimal pricing uses computer software to generate the ideal price for every item, at each individual store, at any given time. Research shows that many retailers routinely underprice or overprice the merchandise on their shelves. They generally set a price by marking up from cost, by benchmarking against the competition's prices, or simply by hunch.

A price-optimization program plugs reams of data from checkout scanners, seasonal sales figures, and so on into probability algorithms to come up with an individual demand curve for each product in each store. From that, retailers can identify which products are the most price sensitive. Then they can adjust prices up or down according to each store's priorities—profit, revenue, or market share—to achieve a theoretically maximum profit margin for their goals. This means that an item priced at $2.07 in one store's location might be going for $1.86 at a different location.

Longs Drug Stores in California have reported increased sales and margins after adopting a price-optimization program. But considerable obstacles stand in the way of broader adoption. First, the software can cost $1 million to $10 million depending on the number of stores and the complexity of the inventory. That limits price optimization to large retailers. Another problem is psychological: The software requires users to accept, on faith, pricing recommendations that are sometimes counterintuitive. "You have to trust it," says the chief operating officer of Longs Drug Stores.[35]

Price Skimming

skimming
Charging a high price for a new product during the introductory stage and lowering the price later

A product's price seldom remains constant and will vary depending on the product's stage in its life cycle. During the introductory phase, for example, the objective might be to recover product development costs as quickly as possible. To achieve this goal, the manufacturer might charge a high initial price—a practice known as **skimming**—and then drop the price later, when the product is no longer a novelty and competition heats up. Products such as HDTV and flat-screen monitors are perfect examples of this practice. Price skimming makes sense under two conditions: if the product's quality and image support a higher price; and if competitors cannot easily enter the market with competing products and undercut the price.

Penetration Pricing

Rather than setting a high initial price to skim off a small but profitable market segment, a company might try to build sales volume by charging a low initial price, a practice known as

penetration pricing. This approach has the added advantage of discouraging competition, because the low price (which competitors would be pressured to match) limits the profit potential for everyone. Southwest Airlines uses this strategy when it enters new markets.

Penetration pricing can also help expand the entire product category by attracting customers who wouldn't have purchased at higher, skim-pricing levels. Furthermore, if a company is new to a category pioneered by another company, this strategy can help take customers away from the pioneer. Still, the strategy makes most sense when the market is highly price sensitive so that a low price generates additional sales and the company can maintain its low-price position long enough to keep out competition.

penetration pricing
Introducing a new product at a low price in hopes of building sales volume quickly

Competing in the Global Marketplace

Sun Microsystems Tries to Grab a Slice of the Microsoft Pie

Not too many years ago, PC users could choose from several leading word processors and spreadsheets, along with a variety of other software applications for presentations, graphics, and database management. When these "office productivity" products started to appear together in discounted bundles, however, the competition narrowed quickly, first to Lotus, Corel, and Microsoft, then pretty much to Microsoft and, well, Microsoft. Before long, Microsoft Office dominated the market, commanding retail prices that can top $500.

More than a few software companies have no doubt looked at this juicy market and speculated they could offer a competitive product for much less. The latest and boldest competitor to make a run at the king of the software hill is Sun Microsystems, with its StarOffice bundle. Sun is a major player in the computer industry, best known for servers that help power the Internet and technical computers for animation, engineering, and other high-end tasks. And even though it offers many "behind-the-scenes" software products, the company isn't nearly as well known as a software supplier.

Nonetheless, Sun is challenging Microsoft Office. And the component of the marketing mix Sun is relying on more than any other is price. StarOffice 6.0, released in 2002, retailed for around $75 for a single copy—about 85 percent less than Microsoft Office. And prior to the release of 6.0, StarOffice was free. Sun only began charging so it could afford to provide better customer support.

Practically giving software away is not automatically successful, however. First, there's the question of perceived quality: Many buyers will wonder how good a product can be if it's free or really cheap. Even more important are a host of support costs and compatibility issues. In fact, the installation, downtime, and relearning costs of switching office software can far exceed the cost of buying it in the first place. Then there's the file-compatibility issue. Even though StarOffice users can share files with Microsoft Office users, the transition is not always seamless or trouble free.

In spite of the challenges, Sun does claim some early success. Within a week of its launch on Amazon.com, StarOffice was the most popular business software product offered at the site. And Sun is aggressively staking a claim in the education market, too, having donated more than $6 billion worth of StarOffice with the hope of making it the de facto standard among students around the world—brand loyalty it hopes will carry over into the post-graduation workplace, too.

Questions for Critical Thinking

1. What pricing strategy is Sun using to gain a foothold in the competitive marketplace?
2. Why is the purchase price not always the most important cost consideration for software buyers?

Wal-Mart's price rollbacks are just one way the company passes on cost savings to customers.

discount pricing
Offering a reduction in price

bundling
Combining several products and offering the bundle at a reduced price

dynamic pricing
Charging different prices depending on individual customers and situations

Price Adjustment Strategies

Once a company has set a product's price, it may choose to adjust that price from time to time to account for changing market situations or changing customer preferences. Three common price adjustment strategies are price discounts, bundling, and dynamic pricing.

Price Discounts When you use **discount pricing**, you offer various types of temporary price reductions, depending on the type of customer being targeted and the type of item being offered. You may decide to offer a trade discount to wholesalers or retailers as a way of encouraging orders, or you may offer cash discounts to reward customers who pay cash or pay promptly. You may offer a quantity discount to buyers who buy large volumes, or you may offer a seasonal discount to buyers who buy merchandise or services out of season.

Another way to discount products is by *value pricing* them, charging a fairly affordable price for a high-quality offering. Many restaurants, including Friendly's, offer value menus for certain times of the day or certain customer segments, such as seniors. This strategy builds loyalty among price-conscious customers without damaging a product's quality image.

Although discounts are a popular way to boost sales of a product, the down side is that they can touch off price wars between competitors. Price wars encourage customers to focus only on a product's pricing and not on its value or benefits. Thus, they can hurt a business—even an entire industry—for years. A whopper of a price war among burger chains has thrown the $105 billion fast-food world into a tizzy.[36] Dollar value menus condition consumers to expect full-sized burgers for a buck. Such promotions boost business in the short term, but over the long term they become money-losers and ultimately hurt a company's bottom line.

Bundling Sometimes sellers combine several of their products and sell them at one reduced price. This practice, called **bundling**, can promote sales of products consumers might not otherwise buy—especially when the combined price is low enough to entice them to purchase the bundle. Examples of bundled products are season tickets, vacation packages, sales of computer software with hardware, and wrapped packages of shampoo and conditioner. Bundling products and services can make it harder for consumers to make price comparisons.

Dynamic Pricing **Dynamic pricing** is the opposite of fixed pricing. Using Internet technology, companies continually reprice their products and services to meet supply and demand. Dynamic pricing not only enables companies to move slow-selling merchandise instantly but also allows companies to experiment with different pricing levels. Because price changes are immediately posted to electronic catalogs or websites, customers always have the most current price information. Airlines and hotels are notorious for this type of continually adjusted pricing. In addition to posting current prices on their homepages and many travel websites, many major airlines and hotels send customers weekly e-mail notifications listing special discount fares.[37]

Three popular dynamic pricing tactics are

- *auction pricing,* in which buyers bid against each other and the highest bid buys the product;
- *group buying,* in which buyers obtain volume discount prices by joining buying groups;
- *name-your-price,* in which buyers specify how much they are willing to pay for a product and sellers can choose whether to sell at that price.

Nonetheless, putting these pricing tactics into practice has been a formidable challenge for many e-merchants, who are still struggling to find ways to use dynamic pricing to sell products at attractive prices and earn a healthy profit.

Summary of Learning Objectives

1. **Describe the four stages in the life cycle of a product.**
   Products start in the introductory stage, during which marketers focus on stimulating demand for the new product. As the product progresses through the growth stage, marketers focus on increasing the product's market share. During the maturity stage, marketers try to extend the life of the product by highlighting improvements or by repackaging the product in different sizes. Eventually, all products move to a decline stage, where the marketer must decide whether to keep the product and reduce its costs to compensate for declining sales or to discontinue it.

2. **Describe six stages of product development.**
   The first two stages of product development involve generating and screening ideas to isolate those with the most potential. In the third stage, promising ideas are analyzed to determine their likely profitability. Those that appear worthwhile enter the fourth, or prototype development stage, in which a limited number of the products are created. In the fifth stage, the product is test marketed to determine buyer response. Products that survive the testing process are then commercialized, the final stage.

3. **Cite three levels of brand loyalty.**
   The first level of brand loyalty is brand awareness, in which the buyer is familiar with the product. The next level is brand preference, in which the buyer will select the product if it is available. The final level is brand insistence, in which the buyer will accept no substitute.

4. **Discuss the functions of packaging and labeling.**
   Packaging provides protection for the product, makes products easier to display, and attracts attention. In addition, packaging enhances the convenience of the product and communicates its attributes to the buyer. Labels help identify and distinguish the brand and product. They provide information

about the product—including ingredients, risks, shelf life, and operating procedures. And they contain UPC codes, which are used for scanning sales information and monitoring inventory and pricing.

5. **Identify four ways of expanding a product line, and discuss two risks that product-line extensions pose.**
   A product line can be expanded by filling gaps in the market, extending the line to include new varieties of existing products, extending the brand to new product categories, and stretching the line to include lower- or higher-priced items. Two of the biggest risks with product-line extensions include a loss of brand identity (weakening of the brand's meaning), and cannibalization of sales of other products in the product line.

6. **Highlight several factors that should be considered when developing product strategies for international markets.**
   Before entering international markets, a company must consider the type of government, market entry requirements, tariffs and other trade barriers, cultural and language differences, consumer preferences, foreign-exchange rates, and business customs. Then the company must decide whether to standardize the product or customize it to meet the needs of individual markets.

7. **List seven factors that influence pricing decisions and cite several common pricing strategies.**
   Pricing decisions are influenced by manufacturing and selling costs, competition, the needs of wholesalers and retailers who distribute the product to the final customer, a firm's marketing objectives, government regulations, consumer perceptions, and consumer demand. Common pricing methods include cost-based, price-based, optimal pricing, price skimming, penetration pricing, and a number of price adjustment strategies such as discounting, bundling, and dynamic pricing.

KEY TERMS

brand **(334)**

brand awareness **(334)**

brand insistence **(334)**

brand loyalty **(334)**

brand manager **(337)**

brand mark **(335)**

brand names **(335)**

brand preference **(334)**

break-even analysis **(342)**

break-even point **(342)**

bundling **(346)**

co-branding **(335)**

commercialization **(334)**

discount pricing **(346)**

dynamic pricing **(346)**

family branding **(338)**

fixed costs **(342)**

generic products **(335)**

license **(336)**

national brands **(335)**

penetration pricing **(345)**

price elasticity **(342)**

private brands **(335)**

product life cycle **(330)**

TEST YOUR KNOWLEDGE

Questions for Review

1. What are the four main subgroups of consumer products?
2. Why are most services perishable?
3. What are the functions of packaging?
4. How many books will a publisher have to sell to break even if fixed costs are $100,000, the selling price per book is $60, and the variable costs per book are $40?
5. How does cost-based pricing differ from price-based pricing?

Questions for Analysis

6. Why do businesses continually introduce new products, given the high costs of the introduction stage of the product life cycle?
7. How could a marketer confuse a consumer when developing a product's positioning strategies?
8. Why are brand names important?
9. Why is it important to review the objectives of a strategic marketing plan before setting a product's price?
10. **Ethical Considerations:** Why might an employee with high personal ethical standards act less ethically when developing packaging, labeling, or pricing strategies?

Questions for Application

11. In what ways might Mattel modify its pricing strategies during the life cycle of a toy product?
12. As the international marketing manager for Coca-Cola's Dasani bottled water, you are responsible for investigating the possibility of selling bottled water in other countries. What are some of the product-related issues you should consider during your study?
13. **Integrated:** Review the theory of supply and demand in Chapter 1 (see pages 9–14). How do skimming and penetration pricing strategies influence a product's supply and demand?
14. **Integrated:** Review the discussion of cultural differences in international business in Chapter 3 (see pages 62–63). Which cultural differences do you think Disney had to consider when planning its product strategies for Disneyland Paris? Originally the company offered a standardized product but was later forced to customize many of the park's operations. What might have been some of the cultural challenges Disney experienced under a standardized product strategy?

PRACTICE YOUR KNOWLEDGE

Handling Difficult Situations on the Job: Defending Freddy Pumpkin

Allen White had a bit of a shock when he opened his March phone bill a while back—and April's bill was no better. The statements for both months listed $40 worth of phone calls that White was sure he had not made. Finally, in May, when the mystery calls totaled $100, White figured out that his four-year-old son was placing calls to "Freddy Pumpkin"—a 900 telephone line advertised on children's television shows. The irate Mr. White paid the telephone bill but fired off a letter of protest to Robert H. Lorsch, president of Teleline, a company that operates children's phone-line services.

You are Mr. Lorsch's assistant, and you were in the office when White's letter arrived. Lorsch has asked you to draft a letter responding to this complaint. He believes that Teleline offers a legitimate service. Children who call the firm's 900 numbers hear a taped message featuring cartoon or fantasy characters. At $2.45 for the first minute and 45 cents for each additional minute, the calls aren't cheap; but they aren't a big problem unless a child develops a serious habit. Teleline receives fewer than 12 complaints a month.

The company is careful to state its prices in its television ads for the phone lines, and it clearly warns children to ask their parents for permission before calling.[38]

Your task: Before you draft the response, consider whether pricing is really the problem in this situation. What should you say about pricing in your letter? Can you defend Teleline's promotional ethics? How? Now that you've given it some thought, what suggestions might you make to Mr. Lorsch about changing Teleline's promotional or pricing strategies to minimize the number of parental complaints?

Building Your Team Skills

Select a high-profile product with which you and your teammates are familiar. Do some online research to learn more about that brand. Then answer these questions and prepare a short group presentation to your classmates summarizing your findings.

- Is the product a consumer product, industrial product, or both?
- At what stage in its life cycle is this product?
- Is the product a national brand or a private brand?

- How do the product's packaging and labeling help boost consumer appeal?
- How is this product promoted?
- Is the product mix to which this product belongs wide? Long? Deep?

- Is the product sold in international markets? If so, does the company use a standardized or a customized strategy?
- How is the product priced in relation to competing products?

EXPAND YOUR KNOWLEDGE

Discovering Career Opportunities

Being a marketing manager is a big responsibility, but it can be a lot of fun at the same time. Don't take our word for it, however. Read what the U.S. Department of Labor has to say about the nature of the work, working conditions, qualifications, and job outlook for marketing managers by accessing the Bureau of Labor Statistics Occupational Outlook Handbook at www.bls.gov/oco/home.htm.

1. What does a marketing manager do?
2. What are some key questions you might want to ask when interviewing for a job in marketing?
3. What training and qualifications should a marketing manager have?

Developing Your Research Skills

Scan recent business journals and newspapers (print or online editions) for an article related to one of the following:

- New-product development
- The product life cycle
- Pricing strategies
- Packaging

1. Does this article report on a development in a particular company, several companies, or an entire industry? Which companies or industries are specifically mentioned?
2. If you were a marketing manager in this industry, what concerns would you have as a result of reading the article? What questions do you think companies in this industry (or related ones) should be asking? What would you want to know?
3. In what ways do you think this industry, other industries, or the public might be affected by this trend or development in the next five years? Why?

Exploring the Best of the Web

URLs for all Internet exercises are provided at the website for this book, www.prenhall.com/bovee. When you log on to the text website, select Chapter 13, then select "Student Resources," click on the name of the featured website, and review the website to complete these exercises.

Explore these chapter-related websites, review their content, and answer the following questions for each website you visit:

1. What is the purpose of this website?
2. What kinds of information does this website contain? Please be specific.

3. How is the information provided at this website useful for businesspeople? Consumers?
4. How did you expand your knowledge of products and pricing by reviewing the material at this website? What new things did you learn about these topics?

Be a Sharp Shopper

Put your marketing knowledge to practice. Visit the Sharper Image website and think like a marketer. Evaluate the company's product mix. Is the product mix wide? Deep? What types of consumer products does this company sell? Who is its target market? Do the products have recognizable brand names? Which other stores carry this type of product? Be sure to read about the company's mission. And don't leave without checking out the new products. www.sharperimage.com

Protect Your Trademark

Got a winning idea for a new product? Don't forget to protect your trademark by registering it with the U.S. Patent and Trademark Office. Visit this government agency's website and learn the basic facts about registering a trademark, such as who is allowed to use the TM symbol and how a trademark differs from a service mark. Find out how the process works and how much it costs. In fact, why not search its database now to see whether anyone has already registered your trademark? www.uspto.gov

Uncover Hidden Costs

When you buy something online, the selling price is usually only part of your *total* cost. Factor in hidden costs such as shipping and sales tax, and the total cost can vary dramatically from one website to another. Using comparison-shopping sites can help you ferret out hidden costs. Take a look at Best Book Buys, which compares the total cost of buying a book from a variety of Internet sources. Check out one of the best-selling books or search for your favorite book. Click to see a table comparing the item price, shipping cost, and total cost at different retail websites. Then simply click to buy. www.bestbookbuys.com

Learning Interactively

Companion Website

Visit the Companion Website at www.prenhall.com/bovee. For Chapter 13, take advantage of the interactive "Study Guide" to test your chapter knowledge. Get instant feedback on whether you need additional studying. Read the "Current Events" articles to get the latest on chapter topics, and complete the exercises as specified by your instructor. Expand your learning with a visit to the "Research Area." There you will find a wealth of information you can use to complete your course assignments.

A CASE FOR CRITICAL THINKING

Coke Unpacks a Winner

In 2002 Coca-Cola was a company in need of some good news. Although the company was still profitable and the Coca-Cola brand was one of the world's most valuable, as measured by future profit potential, bad news seemed to be bubbling over everywhere. A $300 million ad campaign failed to make much of an impression on consumers. An attempt to buy Quaker Oats, which would've brought Gatorade into the Coke beverage portfolio, got nixed at the last minute by Coke's board of directors; Quaker was then snatched up by Coke's arch rival PepsiCo. A deal to partner Coke's Minute Maid orange juice brand with Procter & Gamble's Pringles potato chips—to better compete against PepsiCo's Frito-Lay and Tropicana brands—also fell apart.

Perhaps most troubling, sales were growing at only 2.4 percent a year, a far cry from the growth rates of 10 percent or more Coke enjoyed during its glory days. Among carbonated drinks, upstarts such as the repositioned Mountain Dew were growing at the expense of Coke's primary brands. PepsiCo (with its Aquafina brand) also moved into the surging bottled water market two years before Coke got there with Dasani. Coca-Cola's legendary marketing magic seemed to have fizzled out.

Thinking Like a Customer

Sometimes in marketing, good news can come from the smallest details. Researchers at Alcoa, which supplies aluminum cans to Coca-Cola, learned that the typical refrigerator is too full of food for the blocky 12-pack box consumers bring home from the store. Most beverage drinkers pull a few cans out of a box, throw them in the fridge, and shove the rest of the box in a pantry or other room-temperature storage. When the chilled cans are consumed, though, many people are slow to grab a few more from storage to restock the fridge. Consequently, the warm cans sit in storage longer, and people find something else in the fridge to drink.

Coke's product strategists picked up on this behavioral detail and reasoned that a package more compatible with today's refrigerators would let people keep the entire 12-pack chilled and ready to drink. The more chilled cans, the faster they get consumed and the faster those thirsty consumers need to head back to the grocery store for more Coke.

A New Fit for the Fridge

Conventional 12-pack stacked cans in a three-by-four configuration are too tall for many overloaded fridge shelves. Front to back, though, fridges tend to have more empty space. The solution was something shorter but deeper: two cans high by six cans deep. It was one of those simple ideas that everyone thinks is obvious once somebody else comes up with it.

While a product's package may seem far less important than the product itself, packaging can be a major influence if it affects consumer behavior. Coke's own research suggested that consumers could respond more to changes in packaging than to changes in branding.

The idea of the Fridge Pack is about as simple as ideas get, but execution is another matter entirely. To keep prices low, the beverage business is both highly automated and complex, involving multiple local and regional bottlers who produce the beverage and deliver it to thousands of retail outlets. Just studying the system to figure out what needs to be modified can take months. For instance, everything from production lines to store shelves is set up for certain packaging sizes . Changes can ripple all the way through the system, from production facilities to in-store stacking procedures. Changing a single production line to accommodate the Fridge Pack costs a half million dollars, and Coca-Cola has some 80 production lines around the country. Executives needed to be reasonably sure such a large gamble would pay off.

Passing the Test

Coke chose its hometown of Atlanta and the city of Chicago—a Pepsi stronghold—as sites to test the new package. It was a hit; sales of Coke in cans rose 10 percent. The next step was rolling out regionally in the Southeastern United States. The success continued: Sales of 12-packs climbed 25 percent. The packaging was also adapted for Dasani bottled water, Coke's fastest-growing brand, and that beverage is "flying off the shelves," in the words of the regional bottler. Something as simple as a reconfigured box seems to really be shaking up the fiercely competitive and generally stagnant soft drink market. Then Coke took the new 12-pack packaging nationwide.

Coca-Cola needs more success stories to get its marketing magic back, but the dramatic success of the Fridge Pack shows it can be done.

Critical Thinking Questions

1. Why was Alcoa interested in the behavior of Coca-Cola's customers?

2. Why were the market tests in Atlanta and Chicago so important?

3. Why would beverage consumers be more sensitive to packaging than branding?

4. Browse the websites of several beverage products and examine how they package their products. As a consumer, what other ways could beverage companies use packaging to make their products easier for you to purchase and consume?

VIDEO CASE

Sending Products into Space: MCCI

Learning Objectives

The purpose of this video is to help you:

1. Recognize how and why a company develops specialized products for organizational customers.
2. Describe some of the decisions a company faces in pricing specialized products under long-term contracts for organizational customers.
3. Understand how a company can use quality to differentiate its products.

Synopsis

MCCI, a 55-person company based in California, designs and produces highly specialized products that are customized to the detailed specifications of its organizational customers. When a telecommunications company or government agency needs a radio frequency filter for a new satellite, it calls on MCCI to design one especially for that situation. Custom-made from tiny components and precious materials, this filter must be top quality to withstand powerful vibration and temperature extremes in space—and continue to perform exactly as promised for 20 years. Because some contracts cover products purchased over a decade or more, MCCI must carefully assess the risks of designing a product and pricing it for long-term profit. Yet speed is also a factor: MCCI once created a new product during a single weekend to win a contract from an important customer.

Discussion Questions

1. *For analysis:* Are MCCI's products capital or expense items? How do you know?

2. *For analysis:* Given its in-depth knowledge of the market, why does MCCI develop new products for individual customers rather than creating new products to meet general industry needs?
3. *For application:* The price of gold can fluctuate widely, depending on market conditions. How might this affect MCCI's pricing decisions for products that incorporate components made from gold?
4. *For application:* What factors must MCCI analyze as it prices a custom-designed product?
5. *For debate:* At the start of a long-term contract, should MCCI price a product to return little or no profit in the hope that it will be able to generate more profit from other products sold to this customer later in the contract period? Support your chosen position.

Online Exploration

One of MCCI's products went to Mars on the *Sojourner Rover* sent by NASA. What other kinds of goods and services does NASA buy? Visit its procurement website, acquisition.jpl.nasa.gov, and follow the link to see some of the requests for proposals on this site. Do any contain a document with questions and answers? Why would MCCI need to read such a document before preparing a proposal to develop a product for NASA? Now examine the listing of other links. How could MCCI use information from the sites on this listing in planning a product for NASA?

Distribution Strategies

Unlike other discounters, Costco has figured out how to successfully affix a low price to high-quality, high-end merchandise.

INSIDE BUSINESS TODAY

Costco Makes the Good Life More Affordable

With low prices that magically promote thrift, Costco Wholesale has become the country's largest and most profitable warehouse club chain. The company knows that a low price on high-quality, high-end merchandise can transcend the common notion of "discount." And, in what amounts to a treasure hunt played out along Costco's cement-floor aisles, the high/low shopping experience is a powerful elixir for middle-class shoppers.

Once new members get the hang of the treasure hunt mentality, they get hooked on Costco because even though they don't know what will be on display, they're sure it will be something at a price that will make the good life more affordable. It's not unusual, for instance, for a 1,000-piece lot of Ralph Lauren golf jackets, selling 75 percent below retail at $19.99 each, to vanish in an afternoon. Like other warehouse clubs, Costco Wholesale sells seemingly everything from giant boxes of cereal to patio furniture to diamond rings. In fact, Costco often asks vendors to change their factory runs to produce specially built packages that are bigger and cheaper. So you can only buy toilet paper if you want a 24-roll pack, and laundry detergent and Italian olive oil come in drums.

The merchandise sold at Costco may be similar to that of its two main competitors—Sam's Club and BJ's—but Costco aims to be a cut above. Its stores look slightly more upscale than other club stores, the brands it carries have more cachet, and the products are often a bit more expensive, but they still offer extremely good value. Moreover, Costco does not offer everything under the sun. The stores actually carry only about 4,000 products, which is a small fraction of the more than 100,000 items stocked by conventional discounters such as Target or Wal-Mart. About 3,000 of Costco's carefully chosen products are a consistent array of everyday basics, from canned tuna to laundry detergent to printer cartridges. The other 1,000 items are a fast-moving assortment of luxury goods such as designer-label clothing, big-name watches, and premium wines. These items change week to week, reinforcing the idea of buying something when you see it because it'll probably be gone next week.

Costco would prefer to offer only name-brand products, but since many high-end suppliers such as Cartier and Cannondale flinch at the idea of their goods being sold in a warehouse setting, this isn't always possible. Some suppliers, hoping to protect their higher-end retail customers, have been known to spurn Costco's offers "officially," only to call back later to quietly cut a deal. In other cases, Costco goes on its own treasure hunts, using third-party distributors to track down hot products, even though these "gray market" channels can be unpredictable. And if that doesn't work, Costco can commission another manufacturer to create a look-alike product—leather handbags are one example—with its own Kirkland Signatures label. Roughly 12 percent of the Costco's products bear the Kirkland Signatures label.

To give its 40 million members the best prices on everything, Costco negotiates directly—and fiercely—with suppliers. Aiming to be known as the toughest negotiators in the business, Costco's buyers won't let up until they get their target price on the merchandise. Often, the "right" price is determined by how much cheaper Costco can make a product itself.

The company has managed to bully down price points in several categories, including photo film and over-the-counter drugs. Costco, of course, passes on the savings to customers, who never pay more than 14 percent above Costco's cost.

Costco has also added ancillary departments to several of its stores, including food courts, pharmacies, optical shops, one-hour photo labs, and even hearing aid centers. These additions are just one more way Costco entices members to visit more often and spend more money on every visit.

All in all, the company is relentless in its mission. With annual sales topping $34 billion, over 40 million members, and a cult-like 86 percent membership renewal rate, Costco is the shining star of wholesale clubs. The company has ambitious expansion plans for the United States and is even exporting its business model—and buying power—to the United Kingdom, Taiwan, South Korea, and Japan.[1]

Understanding the Role of Marketing Intermediaries

1 **LEARNING OBJECTIVE**

Explain what marketing intermediaries do, and list their seven primary functions

distribution strategy
Firm's overall plan for moving products to intermediaries and final customers

marketing intermediaries
Businesspeople and organizations that channel goods and services from producers to consumers

wholesalers
Firms that sell products to other firms for resale or for organizational use

retailers
Firms that sell goods and services to individuals for their own use rather than for resale

Costco is just one example of how marketing intermediaries work. Getting products to consumers is the role of distribution, the third element of a firm's marketing mix—also known as *place*. As Chapter 12 points out, a distribution channel, or *marketing channel*, is an organized network of firms that work together to get goods and services from producer to consumer. A company's **distribution strategy**, which is its overall plan for moving products to buyers, plays a major role in the firm's success.

Think of all the products you buy: food, toiletries, clothing, sports equipment, train tickets, haircuts, gasoline, stationery, appliances, CDs, videotapes, books, and all the rest. How many of these products do you buy directly from the producer? For most people, the answer is not many. Most companies do not sell their goods directly to the final users, even though the Internet is making that easier to do these days. Instead, producers in many industries work with **marketing intermediaries** (also called *middlemen*) to bring their products to market.

Two main types of marketing intermediaries are wholesalers and retailers. **Wholesalers** sell primarily to retailers, to other wholesalers, and to organizational users such as government agencies, institutions, and commercial operations. In turn, the customers of wholesalers either resell the products or use them to make products of their own. Ingram Book Group, for example, is the leading wholesale book distributor in the United States. The company ships more than 175 million books and audiotapes produced by a variety of publishers to some 32,000 retail outlets annually.

Unlike wholesalers, **retailers** sell products to the final consumer for personal use. Retailers can operate out of a physical facility (department store, gas station, kiosk), through vending equipment (soft drink machine, newspaper box, or automated teller), or from a virtual store (via telephone, catalog, or website). Most retailers today reach shoppers through a carefully balanced blend of store and nonstore retail outlets. The major types of retailers are described in Exhibit 14.1.

Wholesalers and retailers are instrumental in creating three of the four forms of utility mentioned in Chapter 12: place utility, time utility, and possession utility. If you need a ream of paper or a printer cartridge for your printer, you don't call up Hewlett Packard to order these products. Instead, you go to the nearest retailer, such as Costco, where you can purchase not only office supplies, but groceries, small kitchen appliances, and a number of other products. Stores such as Costco create utility for consumers in several ways. They provide the items you need in a convenient location (place utility), they save you the time of having to contact each manufacturer to purchase a good (time utility), and they provide an efficient process for transferring products from the producer to the customer (possession

EXHIBIT 14.1   Types of Retail Stores
The term *retailer* covers many types of outlets. This table shows some of the most common types.

TYPE OF RETAILER	DESCRIPTION	EXAMPLES
Category killer	Type of specialty store focusing on specific products on giant scale and dominating retail sales in respective product categories	Office Depot Toys "R" Us
Convenience store	Offers staple convenience goods, long service hours, quick checkouts	7-Eleven
Department store	Offers a wide variety of merchandise under one roof in departmentalized sections and many customer services	Sears J.C. Penney Nordstrom
Discount store	Offers a wide variety of merchandise at low prices and few services	Wal-Mart
Factory/retail outlet	Large outlet store selling discontinued items, overruns, and factory seconds	Nordstrom Rack Nike outlet store
Hypermarket/ superstore	Giant store offering food and general merchandise at discount prices	Wal-Mart Super Center Super Target
Off-price store	Offers designer and brand-name merchandise at low prices and few services	T.J. Maxx Marshall's
Specialty store	Offers a complete selection in a narrow range of merchandise	Athlete's Foot The Body Shop
Supermarket	Large, self-service store offering a wide selection of food and nonfood merchandise	Kroger Safeway
Warehouse club	Large, warehouse style store that sells food and general merchandise at discount prices; some require club membership	Sam's Club Costco

utility). In addition to creating utility, wholesalers and retailers perform the following distribution functions (see Exhibit 14.2):

- *Match buyers and sellers.* By making sellers' products available to multiple buyers, intermediaries such as Costco reduce the number of transactions between producers and customers.

- *Provide market information.* Retail intermediaries, such as Macy's, collect valuable data about customer purchases: who buys, how often, and how much. Many stores now use frequent shopper cards to help them spot buying patterns and share marketplace information with producers.

- *Provide promotional and sales support.* Many intermediaries, such as Pepsi distributors, create advertising, produce eye-catching displays, and use other promotional devices for some or all of the products they sell. Some employ a salesforce, which can perform a number of selling functions.

- *Gather an assortment of goods.* Nordstrom, Sportmart, Office Max, and other intermediaries receive bulk shipments from producers and break them into more convenient units by sorting, standardizing, and dividing bulk quantities into smaller packages.

- *Transport and store the product.* Intermediaries such as Borders, Best Buy, and Pier 1 maintain an inventory of merchandise that they acquire from producers so they can quickly fill customers' orders. In many cases retailers purchase this merchandise from wholesalers who, in addition to breaking bulk, may also transport the goods from the producer to the retail outlets.

- *Assume risks.* When intermediaries accept goods from manufacturers, they take on the risks associated with damage, theft, product perishability, and obsolescence. For example, if products stocked or displayed at Costco are stolen or become obsolete, Costco assumes responsibility for the loss.

- *Provide financing.* Large intermediaries sometimes provide loans to smaller producers.

EXHIBIT 14.2
Seven Roles of Marketing Intermediaries
These important functions performed by marketing intermediaries make life easier for both producers and consumers.

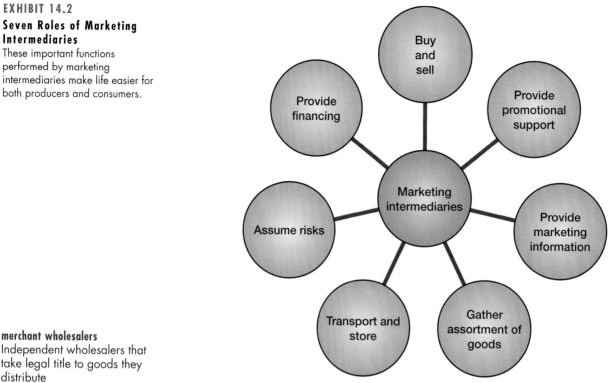

merchant wholesalers
Independent wholesalers that take legal title to goods they distribute

full-service merchant wholesalers
Merchant wholesalers that provide a wide variety of services to their customers, such as storage, delivery, and marketing support

rack jobbers
Merchant wholesalers that are responsible for setting up and maintaining displays in a particular section of a retail store

limited-service merchant wholesalers
Merchant wholesalers that offer fewer services than full-service merchant wholesalers; they often specialize in particular markets, such as agriculture

drop shippers
Limited-service merchant wholesalers that assume ownership of goods but don't take physical possession; commonly used to market agricultural and mineral products

agents and brokers
Independent wholesalers that do not take title to the goods they distribute but may or may not take possession of those goods

As Exhibit 14.3 shows, without marketing intermediaries, the buying and selling process would be expensive and time-consuming.

Wholesalers

Because wholesalers seldom deal directly with consumers, you may not be familiar with the various players in the wholesale distribution arena. Most U.S. wholesalers are independent, and they can be classified as *merchant wholesalers*, *agents*, or *brokers*.

Types of Wholesalers The majority of wholesalers are **merchant wholesalers**, independently owned businesses that buy from producers, take legal title to the goods, then resell them to retailers or to organizational buyers. **Full-service merchant wholesalers** provide a wide variety of services, such as storage, selling, order processing, delivery, and promotional support. **Rack jobbers**, for example, are full-service merchant wholesalers that set up displays in retail outlets, stock inventory, and mark prices on merchandise displayed in a particular section of a store. **Limited-service merchant wholesalers**, on the other hand, provide fewer services. Natural resources such as lumber, grain, and coal are usually marketed through a class of limited-service wholesalers called **drop shippers**, which take ownership but not physical possession of the goods they handle.

In contrast to merchant wholesalers, **agents and brokers** never take title to the products they handle, and they perform fewer services. Their primary role is to bring buyers and sellers together; they are generally paid a commission (a percentage of the money received) for arranging sales. Real estate agents, insurance brokers, and securities brokers, for example, match up buyers and sellers for a fee or a commission, but they don't own the items that are sold. Producers of commercial parts often sell to business customers through brokers. Manufacturers' representatives, another type of agent, sell various noncompeting products to customers in a specific region and arrange for product delivery. By representing several manufacturers' products, these reps achieve enough volume to justify the cost of a direct sales call.

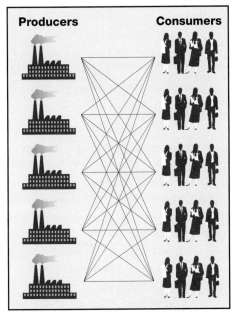

Number of transactions required when consumers buy directly from manufacturers

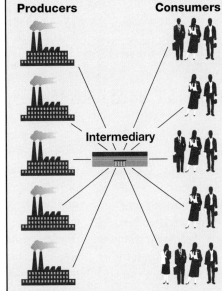

Number of transactions required when buying is conducted via intermediary

EXHIBIT 14.3
How Intermediaries Simplify Commerce
Intermediaries actually reduce the price customers pay for many goods and services, because they reduce the number of contacts between producers and consumers that would otherwise be necessary. They also create place, time, and possession utility.

The Changing Role of Wholesalers The Internet's efficient and effective global reach is revolutionizing the way goods and services are sold and distributed. As Chapter 4 points out, an increasing number of businesses are using the Internet to improve the efficiency of their distribution systems and to expand their market reach. But for some wholesalers the Internet is as much a threat as it is a promise for others.

After 110 years of offering medical insurance through 20,000 insurance agents, Provident American Life & Health Insurance Company dropped its agent network, changed its name to HealthAxis.com, and launched a website to sell a full line of insurance products directly to consumers. CEO Michael Ashker says that eliminating "costly middlemen in an industry where distribution is inefficient" allowed the company to cut its prices by 15 percent.[2]

Other industries are following suit. The livelihoods of travel agents, retailers, real-estate agents, and independent sales representatives are also being threatened as the Internet increasingly allows sellers and buyers to find each other and do business directly or differently. About 15 percent of all airline tickets are now sold on the web, and that number is growing.[3]

While some companies are using the Internet to bypass the middleman, others are using the Internet as a springboard for new businesses that function as a middleman where a void existed before. For years the hotel industry enjoyed the enviable success of selling many of its rooms directly to customers via toll-free numbers and websites. But many hotels now unload their vacant rooms to discount intermediaries such as Hotels.com and Expedia.com, which buy blocks of unsold rooms at discount prices and sell them over the Internet to the public at a small markup.

This situation creates a vexing challenge for the hotel chains. On the one hand, using a middleman helps chain members fill their vacancies. On the other hand, using a middleman removes the control parent companies have over hotel room pricing. To combat the pricing problem, several major hotel chains are requiring franchisees to offer their lowest rates on the parent company's own website. Moreover, five of the largest hotel chains are joining forces and launching a website similar to the airlines' Orbitz. Hopes are high that

Keeping Pace with Technology and Electronic Commerce

Carvin Strikes a Chord with Factory-Direct Guitars

Budding young guitarists dream of trading up from $300, Asian-made guitars to brand-name models from companies such as Fender and Gibson, whose American-made instruments retail for $800 to $3,000. Experienced players dream of moving up from these respected but still mass-produced guitars to custom-built instruments that reflect their style and personality. For $4,000 to $8,000—and a months-long wait—a skilled instrument maker called a luthier can create a truly custom guitar.

Carvin Guitars of San Diego, California, has built a successful business in the gap between mass-produced and fully custom guitars. In two to six weeks, and for $700 to $1,500, Carvin can customize one of 24 electric guitar models and 16 electric bass models. All are available in a dizzying array of woods, paints, stains, finishes and electronics—so many choices that the discussion boards on carvin.com buzz with debates about which combinations are "best" for specific styles of music.

Carvin's slogan tells part of the story: "World's #1 factory-direct music store." By eliminating distributors and retailers, Carvin says, it can create higher-quality products with lower prices. The rest of the story is a flexible, highly automated factory staffed by skilled technicians and instrument makers. In business since 1946, Carvin builds a broad line of instruments, amplifiers, professional sound systems, and more, and sells the products through its catalog, toll-free number, and website.

Although the catalog is revised and mailed six times a year, the website goes much farther in helping people visualize their dream instrument. It presents each guitar or bass on a page that lists standard features, provides an interactive list of customization options, and computes and displays the total price for the desired configuration. A pop-up browser window called the "virtual custom shop" lets online shoppers select and preview most of the possible wood, paint, and stain variations.

With one click and a credit card, they can order their sonic dream machine. Of course, buying a guitar without playing it makes most potential buyers nervous. To alleviate that fear, Carvin offers a 10-day trial period that doesn't start until the instrument is delivered. If buyers aren't satisfied—for any reason—they can return purchases for a refund. The guarantee is low risk for Carvin, because it resells returned instruments via the "Guitars in Stock" section of carvin.com. In-stock instruments can't be modified, but they ship within three days and the 10-day trial still applies. That's just one more reason why Carvin earns rave reviews from serious players who want truly unique guitars.

Questions for Critical Thinking

1. How has its website enhanced Carvin's formerly catalog-only business?
2. Why is the 10-day trial period important to Carvin's success?

---

this cooperative hotel-booking website called Travelweb.com will take business away from independent third-party online travel brokers and allow chains to gain back control of how hotel rooms are sold and priced online.[4]

2 LEARNING OBJECTIVE

Identify at least six types of store retailers and four types of nonstore retailers

scrambled merchandising
Policy of carrying merchandise that is ordinarily sold in a different type of outlet

Retailers

In contrast to wholesalers, retailers are a highly visible element in the distribution chain. Retail stores provide many benefits to consumers. Some, such as Target, save people time and money by providing an assortment of merchandise under one roof. Others, such as Trader Joe's, give shoppers access to goods and delicacies that they would have difficulty finding on their own. Still other retailers build traffic and add convenience by diversifying their product lines, a practice known as **scrambled merchandising**. For example, you can rent videos, eat pizza, and buy T-shirts at Grand Union supermarkets, and you can buy cosmetics, stationery, and toys at Walgreen drugstores. Such mixed product assortments cut across retail classifications and blur store identities in the consumers' minds.

Many stores begin as discount operations and then upgrade their product offerings to become more like department stores in appearance, merchandise, and price. This process of store evolution, known as the **wheel of retailing**, follows a predictable pattern: An innovative retailer with low operating costs attracts a following by offering low prices and limited service. As this store adds more services to broaden its appeal, its prices creep upward, opening the door for lower-priced competitors. Eventually, these competitors also upgrade their operations and are replaced by still other lower-priced stores that later follow the same upward pattern.

Specialty Stores, Category Killers, and Discount Stores   When you shop in a pet store, a shoe store, or a stationery store, you are in a **specialty store**—a store that carries only particular types of goods. The basic merchandising strategy of a specialty shop is to offer a limited number of product lines but an extensive selection of brands, styles, sizes, models, colors, materials, and prices within each line. Specialty shops are particularly strong in certain product categories: books, children's clothing, and sporting goods, for example.

At the other end of the retail spectrum are the **category killers**—superstores that dominate a particular product category by stocking every conceivable variety of merchandise in that category. Home Depot, Toys "R" Us, Office Depot, and Barnes and Noble are category killers.

In contrast to category killers, **discount stores** offer a wider variety of merchandise, lower prices, and fewer services. One of the newest categories of discounters is supercenters, large discount stores that offer a broad selection of groceries, toys, household items, and other products at discount prices. Since the early 1990s, Wal-Mart has opened over 1,140 U.S. supercenters with an average size of 190,000 square feet and is now one of the nation's largest food retailers.[5]

Since the 1980s, Americans have migrated to such giant discount stores as Wal-Mart, but now some consumers are getting tired of trudging through stores the size of airplane hangars. To expand their customer base, some of the nation's leading large discount stores and category killers—Wal-Mart, Home Depot, and Best Buy among them—are opening smaller versions of their big-box stores. At 41,000 square feet, Home Depot's new "urban format" design is less than one-third the size of the chain's typical orange warehouse.[6] Smaller stores help boost profits because they are less costly to run and carry only top-selling items.[7]

Nonstore Retailers

Nonstore retailing has its roots in the mail-order catalogs sent out by Sears and Montgomery Ward during the late 1800s, selling everything from household goods to ready-to-assemble housing materials. Today you can order clothing, electronics, flowers, and almost every other type of tangible and intangible product from anywhere in the world at any time of day without actually visiting a store. Nonstore retailing includes everything from mail-order catalog companies to online-only stores:

- *Mail-order firms.* Among the most popular types of nonstore retailers are **mail-order firms**. These companies provide customers and businesses with a wide variety of goods ordered from catalogs and shipped by mail or private carrier. Catalog

wheel of retailing
Evolutionary process by which stores that feature low prices gradually upgrade until they no longer appeal to price-sensitive shoppers and are replaced by new low-price competitors

specialty store
Store that carries only a particular type of goods

category killers
Discount chains that sell only one category of products

discount stores
Retailers that sell a variety of goods below the market price by keeping their overhead low

mail-order firms
Companies that sell products through catalogs and ship them directly to customers

Wal-Mart stores has been aggressively opening scaled-down versions of its supercenters.

shopping is big business, but mailing thick catalogs is expensive. Thus, this venue is facing stiff competition from the Internet. To increase sales, many firms now include electronic versions of their catalogs on company websites, and some, such as Harry and David, have even opened physical stores.

- *Automatic vending.* For certain types of products, vending machines are an important nonstore retail outlet. In Japan, soft drinks, coffee, candy, sandwiches, and cigarettes are all commonly sold this way. From the consumer's point of view, the chief attraction of vending machines is their convenience: They are open 24 hours a day and may be found in a variety of handy locations, from college dormitories to laundromats. On the other hand, vending-machine prices are usually no bargain. The cost of servicing the machines is relatively high, and vandalism is a factor. So high prices are required in order to provide the vending-machine company and the product manufacturer with a reasonable profit.

- *Telemarketing.* You have probably experienced telephone retailing, or *telemarketing*, in the form of calls from insurance agents, long-distance telephone companies, and assorted nonprofit organizations, all trying to interest you in their products and causes.

- *Door-to-door sales.* Gone are the days when a large salesforce called directly on customers in their homes or offices to demonstrate merchandise, take orders, and make deliveries, simply because in many households both parents work outside the home. However, two famous names in door-to-door selling (and its variant, the party plan)—Avon and Tupperware—are trying to stay in business by changing their approach. Both have recently launched initiatives to sell directly to the customers over the Internet and in retail stores. So far, Avon's debut in J.C. Penney stores has produced disappointing retail sales.[8]

- *Electronic catalogs.* Catalogs on computer disk or published over the Internet have many advantages: They offer an easy way for customers to search for products; they allow businesses to reach an enormous number of potential customers at a relatively low cost; and they present timely information about a product's price and availability. Consider AMP, an electronics manufacturer in Harrisburg, Pennsylvania. The company was spending about $8 million to $10 million a year on its paper-based catalog, and some of the information was already out of date by the time the catalog was mailed. So, like many companies, AMP switched to electronic catalogs. W. W. Grainger, a 73-year-old industrial-parts supplier is another company that has moved its catalog, with over 80,000 items, to the web.[9]

Mall shoppers try out computers, printers, and other equipment at a Dell kiosk in Austin, Texas.

- *Cybermalls.* These web-based retail complexes house dozens of *virtual storefronts*, or Internet-based stores. Consumers can buy everything from computer software to gourmet chocolates in cybermalls maintained by Yahoo, America Online, and Microsoft. Like their physical counterparts, these Internet storefronts rely on a lot of "walk-in" traffic. For instance, cybermall shoppers looking to buy a CD might also click on the cyber shoe store. A key advantage of the cybermall is that tenants do not have to create their own web page or find a server to house it. Typically, the cybermall operator does all that for a sizable fee.[10]

- *Interactive kiosks.* These small free-standing electronic structures vend products and services in convenient locations and introduce new products in dynamic ways. Located in showrooms or shopping areas, kiosks can inform customers about inventory, products, and store

EXHIBIT 14.4
What Lures Online Shoppers
Shoppers prefer to do online business with retailers that have a physical store.

promotions; take and process orders; help people fill out applications; sell small items such as entertainment and transportation tickets; and even let customers demonstrate products. Toyota customers, for example, can sample audio options, order fog lights, and customize their Scion car orders using special Internet kiosks at Toyota dealerships.[11] Dell recently launched mall-based kiosks that allow customers to sample and select PCs, printers, and other peripheral devices. "We see [kiosks] as another marketing vehicle to extend the direct sales model," says a Dell senior vice president.[12]

- *E-commerce websites.* Amazon.com's Jeff Bezos was a pioneer in recognizing the Internet's potential for making goods and services available to buyers. He reasoned that given a choice, many people would prefer the ease and convenience of online shopping to visiting a store every time they wanted to buy a book. He also believed that publishers would welcome Amazon.com as yet another way to get their books into the hands of readers. Today, a growing number of businesses sell a huge selection of goods and services online. For some, such as Amazon, the Internet is their only marketing channel. But for others, such as Costco and REI, the Internet offers an additional way to sell to customers. Regardless, as Exhibit 14.4 shows, it takes more than a spectacular website to entice shoppers.

Retail Industry Challenges Like wholesalers, retailers are facing a number of pressing challenges in today's competitive marketplace. Chief among them is an oversupply of physical retail store space. The United States now has about 1,800 malls, which industry watchers say is about one-third too many.[13] This oversupply is a result of rapid growth during the past decade or so, when the retail industry added three square feet of new store space for every man, woman, and child in the United States. That 20 percent growth rate was double the rate of population growth during the decade.[14] To make matters worse, many retail locations are looking their age: Nearly half of the malls in the United States were built in the 1970s or earlier.[15]

To entice shoppers, some malls are being reinvented through extensive remodeling and the addition of newer stores, restaurants, and short-term shows and exhibits. This trend toward "retail-tainment" is adding a touch of friendly theatrics to local outlets of giant chains. Customers who attend a cooking class at Williams Sonoma or get tips from golf pros at the Sports Authority are likely to come back for the next in-store event—and buy something when they do.[16]

3 LEARNING OBJECTIVE

Discuss the challenges wholesalers and retailers are facing today

Once the ultimate destination for bargain hunters, Kmart filed for Chapter 11 bankruptcy protection in 2002. The retailer's troubles began when management decided to shine the blue light on the entire store and slashed prices on 38,000 items.

4 **LEARNING OBJECTIVE**

Discuss how customers and retailers benefit from a clicks-and-bricks distribution strategy

In addition to an oversupply of stores, retailers are grappling with a weakened economy and changing consumer demographics, lifestyles, and shopping patterns. Discount- and moderate-priced chains such as Wal-Mart and Target are pulling business away from department stores and apparel retailers as more and more shoppers become less enamored with famous design names and big brands. Citing a bleak retail environment, clothing maker Tommy Hilfiger closed most of its U.S. retail stores in 2002.[17]

These challenges are not only intensifying competition among players but have forced some retailers to merge; others, such as K-Mart, filed for Chapter 11 bankruptcy, then reemerged, although with significantly fewer stores; still others are closing up shop, as Montgomery Ward did in 2001. Finally, the growth of nonstore retailing and e-commerce is forcing many retailers to revise their sales and marketing strategies to accommodate new technologies.

Internet Strategies for Retailers In the midst of the Internet boom, conventional wisdom held that shoppers, lured by the convenience of online buying, would disappear from physical retail stores. So traditional retailers rushed to establish websites and engage in *e-tail* (conducting retail business over the Internet). Industry experts advised retailers to keep their fledgling e-tail operations separate by spinning off the web enterprise and operating it independently. Their thinking was that an independent web operation could make faster decisions, be more flexible, and be more entrepreneurial and thus could compete more effectively with *pure-play* e-businesses (operations that exist only on the Internet, such as Amazon and eBay).

Some retailers, such as REI, ignored this advice and adopted a *clicks-and-bricks* strategy from inception. (See this chapter's Case for Critical Thinking: "REI's Perfect Blend of Retail and E-Tail" on page 374). A clicks-and-bricks strategy integrates a company's website (clicks) with its existing physical stores (bricks) and other retail channels so that all logistics and marketing programs are shared. In a perfect mesh, all retail channels operate seamlessly so that consumers see the company as one operation.

Disadvantages of a Pure-Play Strategy The disadvantages of running a company's retail and Internet operation independently became apparent during the dot-com meltdown at the end of the 20th century. Difficulty in acquiring brand recognition, high customer-acquisition costs, logistical snags, and competition among siblings were just a few of the problems encountered by retailers who chose to run their e-tail operations independently. As high-profile e-businesses such as eToys.com, Pets.com, and Webvan.com went under, retailers began to reel in their independent spin-offs. The benefits of the clicks-and-bricks approach soon became clear: an enhanced shopping experience for consumers and increased business for retailers.

Advantages of a Clicks-and-Bricks Strategy Using multiple channels—Internet, telemarketing, mail order, and physical stores—has many advantages. A clicks-and-bricks strategy allows customers to purchase what they want, where they want, and when they want. It also facilitates the product exchange and return process. Customers can gather production information from a company's website before heading to the store, where they can use salespeople to answer specific product questions and to demonstrate products. Customers can also order merchandise online and pick up or return their purchases at a nearby physical outlet. "This synchronization of multiple sales channels is absolutely the future of retail," says one industry consultant.[18]

In addition to enhancing the customer shopping experience, a clicks-and-bricks strategy can help boost sales at physical retail stores. Studies show that "multichannel" customers, or those who shop both online and in physical stores, tend to be more loyal and to spend more.[19] Sears reports that 1 of every 10 in-store purchases comes directly from customers who logged on to Sears.com first.[20] Clicks-and-bricks retailers can boost sales by using their different venues to cross-sell products. For instance they may use their websites to promote or advertise in-store merchandise. Similarly they may use their retail store to promote products that are available only on their website. Prada's flagship store in Manhattan encourages sales with a unique clicks-and-brick approach. Shoppers can create a webpage showing the outfits they've tried on and then e-mail that page to friends for wardrobe advice.[21]

REI has grown into a renowned supplier of specialty outdoor gear and clothing by using a clicks-and-bricks strategy: retail stores, the Internet, telephone, and direct mail.

Setting Distribution Strategies

Should you sell directly to end users or rely on intermediaries? Which intermediaries should you choose? Should you try to sell your product in every available outlet or limit its distribution to a few exclusive outlets? Should you use more than one channel? These are some of the critical decisions that managers face when designing and selecting marketing channels for any product.

Building an effective channel system takes years and, as with all marketing relationships, requires commitment. Thus, companies take extra care when establishing their initial marketing channels because changing distribution arrangements at a later date may prove difficult. As Chris DeNove, a channel expert puts it, "It's much more difficult to modify an existing system than to start with a clean slate." Citing the automobile industry, for example, DeNove points out that "if automakers could start over now, none of them would create a franchise distribution system that looks like the existing one."[22]

A company's decision about the number and type of intermediaries to use—its **distribution mix**—depends on the kind of product being sold and the marketing practices of the industry. An arrangement that works well for a power-tool and appliance manufacturer like Black & Decker or a book publisher like Prentice Hall would not necessarily work for an insurance company, a restaurant, a steel manufacturer, or a movie studio. In general, consumer products and business products tend to move through different channels. When choosing marketing channels, companies must also consider channel length, market coverage, cost, control, and channel conflict.

Channel Length

Distribution channels come in all shapes and sizes. Some channels are short and simple; others are complex and involve many people and organizations. Most businesses purchase goods they use in their operations directly from producers, so the distribution channel is short. Boeing, for example, purchases the parts and supplies it needs to build airplanes directly from over 15,800 companies, such as C&D Aerospace (builders of stowage bins, lavatories, and baggage compartment liners), and Crissair (manufacturer of fuel system

5 LEARNING OBJECTIVE

Discuss six key factors that marketers should consider when choosing distribution channels

distribution mix
Combination of intermediaries and channels a producer uses to get a product to end users

EXHIBIT 14.5 Alternative Channels of Distribution
Producers of consumer and business goods and services must analyze the alternative channels of distribution available for their products so they can select the channels that best meet their marketing objectives and their customers' needs.

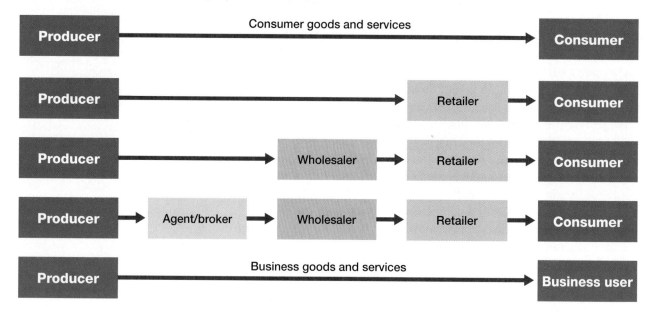

components). In contrast, the channels for consumer goods are usually longer and more complex (see Exhibit 14.5). The four primary channels for consumer goods are

- *Producer to consumer.* Producers who sell directly to consumers through catalogs, tele-marketing, infomercials, and the Internet are using the shortest, simplest distribution channel. Dell Computer is an example of a company using a producer-to-consumer channel. By selling directly to consumers, Dell gains more control over pricing, promotion, service, and delivery. Although this approach eliminates payments to channel members, it also forces producers to handle distribution functions such as storing inventory and delivering products.

- *Producer to retailer to consumer.* Many producers create longer channels by selling their products to retailers, who then resell them to consumers. Weber grills, Benjamin Moore paint, and GE light bulbs are typical of the many products distributed in this way.

- *Producer to wholesaler to retailer to consumer.* Most manufacturers of supermarket and pharmaceutical items rely on longer channels when selling to such retailers as Albertsons, Safeway, and Walgreens. They sell their products to wholesalers, who in turn sell to the retailers. This approach works particularly well for small producers who lack the resources to sell or deliver merchandise to individual retail sites. It is also beneficial to retailers who lack the space to store container-size shipments of each product they sell.

- *Producer to agent/broker to wholesaler to retailer to consumer.* Additional channel levels are common in certain industries, such as agriculture, where specialists are required to negotiate transactions or to perform interim functions such as sorting, grading, or subdividing the goods.

6 LEARNING OBJECTIVE

Differentiate between intensive, selective, and exclusive distribution strategies

intensive distribution
Market coverage strategy that tries to place a product in as many outlets as possible

Market Coverage

The appropriate *market coverage*—the number of wholesalers or retailers that will carry a product—varies by type of product. Inexpensive convenience goods or organizational supplies such as computer paper and pens sell best if they are available in as many outlets as possible. Such **intensive distribution** requires wholesalers and retailers of many types. In contrast, shopping goods (goods that require some thought before being purchased) such as

Sub Zero refrigerators require different market coverage, because customers shop for such products by comparing features and prices. For these items, the best strategy is usually **selective distribution**, selling through a limited number of outlets that can give the product adequate sales and service support.

If producers of expensive specialty or technical products do not sell directly to customers, they may choose **exclusive distribution**, offering products in only one outlet in each market area. Vehicle manufacturers have traditionally relied on exclusive distribution agreements to sell through one dealership in each local area. In contrast, other firms use multiple channels to increase their market coverage and reach several target markets. Apparel manufacturers such as Champion frequently sell through a combination of channels, including department stores, specialty stores, the Internet, and catalogs.

selective distribution
Market coverage strategy that uses a limited number of outlets to distribute products

exclusive distribution
Market coverage strategy that gives intermediaries exclusive rights to sell a product in a specific geographical area

Cost

Costs play a major role in determining a firm's channel selection. It takes money to perform all the functions that are handled by intermediaries. Small or new companies often cannot afford to hire a salesforce large enough to sell directly to end users or to call on a host of retail outlets. Neither can they afford to build large warehouses and distribution centers to store large shipments of goods. These firms need the help of intermediaries, who can spread the cost of such activities across a number of noncompeting products. With time and a larger sales base, a producer may build enough strength to take over some of these functions and reduce the length of the distribution channel.

Control

A third issue to consider when selecting distribution channels is control of how, where, when, and for how much your product is sold. Longer distribution channels mean less control for producers, who become increasingly distant from sellers and buyers as the number of intermediaries multiplies. Shorter distribution channels, on the other hand, give producers more control over how the goods are sold in the market, but there is a tradeoff. Concentrating too many distribution functions in the hands of too few intermediaries can increase the negotiating power of distributors.

Control becomes critical when a firm's reputation is at stake. For instance, a designer of high-priced purses, such as Kate Spade or Louis Vitton, generally limits distribution to exclusive boutiques or high-end retail stores such as Neiman Marcus. Otherwise, the brand could lose some of its appeal if the purses were sold by mid-priced retailers such as J.C. Penney. Similarly, producers of complex technical products such as X-ray machines don't want their products handled by unqualified intermediaries that can't provide adequate customer service.

Channel Conflict

Because the success of individual channel members depends on the overall channel success, ideally all channel members should work together smoothly. However, individual channel members must also run their own businesses profitably, which means that they often disagree on the roles each member should play. Such disagreements create *channel conflict*.[23]

Channel conflict may arise when suppliers provide inadequate product support, when markets are oversaturated with intermediaries, or when companies sell products via multiple channels, each of which is competing for the same customers. For instance, Hallmark's decision to sell cards to mass-market outlets such as discount stores, supermarkets, and drugstores angered its 8,200 independent dealers and forced them to compete with large chains.[24] Similarly, when producers choose to sell directly to consumers via the Internet, they run the risk of damaging their existing relationships with other channel members. Such

Managing in the 21st Century

The Nautilus Group Flexes Its Muscles in Multiple Channels

Adults in over half of all American households own at least one piece of exercise equipment, and studies say the equipment is being used regularly. For busy people, a home gym is often more convenient than going to a health club or taking an exercise break while at work.

Many home gyms contain equipment from The Nautilus Group, which markets, develops, and manufactures health and fitness products under four well-known brands: Bowflex, Nautilus, Schwinn, and StairMaster.

Founded in 1986 as Bowflex of America, the company began marketing its strength-training products directly to consumers in 1993, using cable TV spots and infomercials. The success of the Bowflex products helped the company bulk up through acquisition, buying Nautilus International in 1999, Schwinn Fitness in 2001, and StairMaster in 2002. Those acquisitions and several successful new products helped revenues grow 10-fold in only four years: from $57 million in 1998 to over $580 million in 2002. That same year, the company changed its name to The Nautilus Group, since Nautilus is the most highly respected brand in its portfolio.

Along the way, the company kept the distribution channels it inherited with these acquired brands but worked to make the various channels more productive by giving them broader product offerings. For example, Nautilus, Schwinn, and StairMaster commercial fitness equipment is sold to health clubs, universities, and other institutions through the company's own salesforce and via selected dealers. It also sells a diverse line of consumer fitness equipment under the same three brands through a network of specialty dealers, distributors, and retailers worldwide.

The flagship Bowflex products remain the star of the direct channel, which uses a brawny combination of television commercials, infomercials, response mailings, the Internet, toll-free call centers, and outbound telemarketing. Its well-developed direct marketing process begins with thorough market research, centered on the company's extensive database of existing and potential customers. Next, it uses accumulated business intelligence and calculated estimates of consumer response rates to place carefully designed and targeted TV commercials and infomercials. Consumers who respond by calling a toll-free number or accessing a product-specific website will receive multiple informational mailings and follow-up phone calls. This integrated program produces a very high purchase rate and provides additional consumer data that pumps up the company's business intelligence for future campaigns.

By combining effective management of its various commercial, retail, and direct channels with in-depth knowledge of buyers in every target segment, The Nautilus Group plans to continue flexing its muscles in the health and fitness industry.

Questions for Critical Thinking

1. How did The Nautilus Group more fully utilize the distribution channels for the brands it acquired?
2. For the Bowflex line, what supporting activities make the direct channel so successful?

was the case when Levi Strauss decided to sell its jeans on the company website. Worried that they might lose jeans sales, retail channel members protested. Some even fought back by giving Levi's jeans less prominent display space in their stores. Eventually Levi Strauss caved in to retailer pressure and ceased selling merchandise directly to consumers via its website.[25]

Other Factors

In addition to channel length, market coverage, cost, control, and possible channel conflict, managers should consider several other factors when selecting distribution channels. These factors include the nature and price of the product, the market's growth rate, the geographical concentration of the customer base, customers' need for service, the impor-

EXHIBIT 14.6   Factors Involved in Selecting Distribution Channels
The choice of distribution channels depends on the product, the customer, and the company's capabilities.

FACTOR	EXPLANATION
Number of transactions	When many transactions are likely, the channel should provide for many outlets and several levels of intermediaries. If only a few transactions are likely, the number of outlets can be limited, and the channel can be relatively short.
Value of transactions	If the value of each transaction is high, the channel can be relatively short and direct, because the producer can better absorb the cost of making firsthand contact with each customer. If each transaction has a low value, a long channel is used to spread the cost of distribution over many products and outlets.
Market growth rate	In a rapidly growing market, many outlets and a long channel of distribution may be required to meet demand. In a shrinking market, fewer outlets are required.
Geographic concentration of market	If customers are clustered in a limited geographic area, the channel can be short, because the cost of reaching each account is relatively low. If customers are widely scattered, a multilevel channel with many outlets is preferable.
Need for service and sales support	Complex, innovative, or specialized products require sophisticated outlets where customers can receive information and service support; short, relatively direct channels are generally used. If the product is familiar and uncomplicated, the consumer requires little assistance; long channels with many self-service outlets can be used.

tance of rapid delivery, the strengths and weaknesses of the various types of intermediaries within the channel, and international laws and customs when selling in other countries (see Exhibit 14.6).

Managing Physical Distribution

Developing a distribution strategy involves more than selecting the most effective channels for selling a product. Companies must also decide on the best way to move their products and services through the channels so that they are available to the customers at the right place, at the right time, and in the right amount. **Physical distribution** encompasses all the activities required to move finished products from the producer to the consumer, including forecasting, order processing, inventory control, warehousing, materials handling, and outbound transportation (see Exhibit 14.7).

The physical movement of goods may not appear glamorous or exciting, but it is vital to a company's success. To illustrate the importance of physical distribution, consider this: A typical box of breakfast cereal can spend as long as 104 days getting from factory to

7 LEARNING OBJECTIVE

Highlight the major components of a physical distribution process and the key factors to consider when choosing a mode of outbound transportation

physical distribution
All the activities required to move finished products from the producer to the consumer

EXHIBIT 14.7
Steps in the Physical Distribution Process
The phases of a distribution system should mesh as smoothly as the cogs in a machine. Because the steps are interrelated, a change in one phase can affect the other phases. The objective of the process is to provide a target level of customer service at the lowest overall cost.

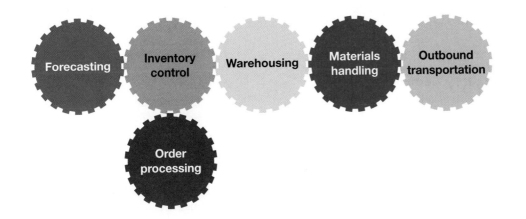

Forecasting · Inventory control · Warehousing · Materials handling · Outbound transportation · Order processing

supermarket, moving haltingly through a series of wholesalers and distributors, each of which has a warehouse. In fact, so many physical distribution systems are burdened with duplication and inefficiency that in industry after industry executives have been placing one item near the top of the corporate agenda: **logistics**—the planning and movement of goods and information throughout the supply chain.

Hard pressed to knock out competitors on quality or price, companies are trying to gain an edge by streamlining processes that traverse companies and continents—no easy task, although the payback can be enormous. The key to success in managing physical distribution is to coordinate the activities of everyone involved, from the sales staff who are trying to satisfy demanding customers to the production staff who are trying to manage factory workloads. The overriding objective should be to achieve a competitive level of *customer-service standards* (the quality of service that a firm provides for its customers) at the lowest total cost. In general, as the level of service improves, the cost of distribution increases. A producer must analyze whether it is worthwhile to deliver the product in, say, three days as opposed to five, if doing so increases the price of the item.

This type of trade-off can be difficult because the components of a physical distribution process are all interrelated. A change in one affects the others. For example, if you use slower forms of transportation, you reduce your shipping costs, but you probably increase your storage costs. Similarly, if you reduce the level of inventory to cut your storage costs, you run the risk of being unable to fill orders in a timely fashion. The trick is to optimize the *total* cost of achieving the desired level of service. This optimization requires a careful analysis of each component in the distribution process in relation to every other component. Let's take a closer look at each of these components.

In-House Operations

The components of the distribution process can be divided into in-house operations and outbound transportation. The in-house steps include forecasting, order processing, inventory control, warehousing, and materials handling.

Forecasting   To control the flow of products through the distribution system, a firm must have an accurate estimate of demand. To some degree, historical data can be used to project future sales; however, the firm must also consider the impact of unusual events (such as special promotions) that might temporarily boost demand. For example, if Costco decided to offer a special discount price on television sets during September, management would need to project how many additional sets will be sold because of the sale and order enough sets so that they arrive in time for the promotion.

Order Processing   Order processing involves preparing orders for shipment and receiving orders when shipments arrive. It includes a number of activities, such as checking the customer's credit, recording the sale, making the appropriate accounting entries, arranging for the item to be shipped, adjusting the inventory records, and billing the customer. Because order processing involves direct interaction with the customer, it affects a company's reputation for customer service. Most companies establish standards for filling orders within a specified time period.

Inventory Control   As Chapter 9 discusses, in an ideal world a company would always have just the right amount of goods on hand to fill the orders it receives. In reality, however, inventory and sales are seldom in perfect balance. Most firms like to build a supply of finished goods so that they can fill orders in a timely fashion. But how much inventory is enough? If your inventory is too large, you incur extra expenses for storage space, handling, insurance, and taxes; you also run the risk of product obsolescence. On the other hand, if your inventory is too low, you may lose sales when the product is not in stock. The objective of *inventory control* is to resolve these issues. Inventory managers decide how much product

---

logistics
The planning, movement, and flow of goods and related information throughout the supply chain

order processing
Functions involved in preparing and receiving an order

to keep on hand and when to replenish the supply of goods in inventory. They also decide how to allocate products to customers if orders exceed supply.

Warehousing Products held in inventory are physically stored in a **warehouse**, which may be owned by the manufacturer, by an intermediary, or by a private company that leases space to others. Some warehouses are almost purely holding facilities, in which goods are stored for relatively long periods. Other warehouses, known as **distribution centers**, serve as command posts for moving products to customers. In a typical distribution center, goods produced at a company's various locations are collected, sorted, coded, and redistributed to fill customer orders.

Some of today's most advanced physical distribution centers use satellite navigation and communication, voice-input computers, machine vision, robots, onboard computer logbooks, and planning software that relies on artificial intelligence. FedEx, for instance, runs a fully automated distribution center. The Memphis hub has 2.4 million square feet of floor space and processes an average of 1.5 million shipments per night—at a rate of 1,000 bar code scans per minute. As packages arrive at the Memphis headquarters, they're placed on a conveyor belt that is part of a 200-mile labyrinth of belts traversing the hub. Packages pass through scanners that capture data such as destination ZIP codes. Metal diverters strategically placed along a belt automatically snap forward to move each package to one of the 22 FedEx geographic locations.

This $25 million sorting machine at Amazon.com's warehouse in Fernley, Nevada, reads bar codes on items, routes them into one of 2,100 chutes, and signals when an order is ready to be packed in a box.

Each parcel is scanned multiple times, weighed, and measured, and its digital image is recorded on a computer. In addition, the company's world shipping software streamlines customer billing, reduces shipping paperwork, and allows customers to track their shipments over the Internet.[26]

Materials Handling An important part of warehousing activities is **materials handling**, the movement of goods within and between physical distribution facilities. One main area of concern is storage method—whether to keep supplies and finished goods in individual packages, in large boxes, or in sealed shipping containers. The choice of storage method depends on how the product is shipped, in what quantities, and to which locations. For example, a company that typically sends small quantities of goods to widely scattered customers wouldn't want to use large containers. Materials handling also involves keeping track of inventory so that the company knows where in the distribution process its goods are located and when they need to be moved.

warehouse
Facility for storing inventory

distribution centers
Warehouse facilities that specialize in collecting and shipping merchandise

materials handling
Movement of goods within a firm's warehouse terminal, factory, or store

Outbound Transportation

For any business, the cost of transportation is normally the largest single item in the overall cost of physical distribution. When choosing a mode of transportation, managers must also evaluate other marketing issues: storage, financing, sales, inventory size, speed, product perishability, dependability, flexibility, and convenience—to name a few. The goal is to maximize the efficiency of the entire distribution process while minimizing overall cost. Each of the five major modes of transportation has distinct advantages and disadvantages:

- *Rail.* Railroads can carry heavier and more diverse cargo and a larger volume of goods than any other mode of transportation. However, trains are constrained to tracks, so they can rarely deliver goods directly to customers.

FedEx Ground is North America's second-largest small-package ground delivery service. With some 13,000 trucks, FedEx Ground delivers more than 2.1 million packages every business day.

- *Truck.* Trucks are a preferred form of transportation for two reasons: (1) the convenience of door-to-door delivery, and (2) the ease and efficiency of travel on public highways, which do not require the use of expensive terminals or the execution of right-of-way agreements (customary for air and rail transportation). Trucks cannot, however, carry all types of cargo cost effectively; for example, commodities such as steel and coal are too large and heavy.

- *Water.* The cheapest method of transportation is via water, and is the preferred method for such low-cost bulk items as oil, coal, ore, cotton, and lumber. However, ships are slow, and service to any given location is infrequent. Furthermore, another form of transportation is usually needed to complete delivery to the final destination, as it is for rail.

- *Air.* Air transportation offers the advantage of speed—but at a price. Airports are not always convenient to the customers. Moreover, air transport imposes limitations on the size, shape, and weight of shipments and is the least dependable and most expensive form of transportation. Weather may cause flight cancellations, and even minor repairs may lead to serious delays. But when speed is a priority, air is usually the only way to go.

- *Pipeline.* For products such as gasoline, natural gas, and coal or wood chips (suspended in liquid), pipelines are an effective mode of transportation. Although they are expensive to build, they are extremely economical to operate and maintain. The downside is transportation via pipeline is slow (three to four miles per hour), and routes are inflexible.

Shippers can combine the benefits of each mode by using *intermodal transportation* (a combination of multiple modes). For instance, a company may ship goods in over-the-road trailers that ride part of the way on flat bed railroad freight cars and part of the way on highways.

Summary of Learning Objectives

1. **Explain what marketing intermediaries do, and list their seven primary functions.**
   Wholesalers buy from producers and sell to retailers, to other wholesalers, and to organizational customers such as businesses, government agencies, and institutions. Retailers buy from producers or wholesalers and sell the products to the final consumers. These marketing intermediaries, or middlemen, bring products to market and help ensure that the goods and services are available in the right time, place, and amount. More specifically, intermediaries match buyers and sellers; provide market information; provide promotional and sales support; sort, standardize, and divide merchandise; transport and store the product; assume risks; and provide financing.

2. **Identify at least six types of store retailers and four types of nonstore retailers.**
   Some of the most common types of store retailers are department stores, discount stores, specialty stores, supermarkets, convenience stores, category killers, and superstores. Common nonstore retailers are mail-order firms, vending machines, telemarketers, door-to-door sales, and electronic approaches (which include electronic catalogs, cybermalls, interactive kiosks, and websites).

3. **Discuss the challenges wholesalers and retailers are facing today.**
   The biggest challenge facing today's wholesalers is the attempt by retailers to bypass the middleman and deal directly with pro-

ducers. The Internet and other technologies facilitate this producer-to-consumer direct sales channel. Retailers are also being affected by the Internet. The growth of nonstore retail options such as e-commerce websites and kiosks is forcing retailers to revise their distribution strategies. Most are adopting a clicks-and-bricks strategy or using multiple retail channels to conduct business with customers. An oversupply of physical stores and shopping malls is an additional challenge forcing change within the retail industry. Many retailers are finding they must either reinvent their concepts to stay alive or close up shop.

4. **Discuss how customers and retailers benefit from a clicks-and-bricks distribution strategy.**

Clicks and bricks, or the integration of e-commerce with physical retail in a multiple-channel strategy, provides customers with more shopping options. Essentially, customers can get what they want, where they want it, and when they want it. A clicks-and-bricks approach also facilitates the product return process. Customers who buy on the web can return unwanted merchandise to physical stores. Traditional retailers benefit from a clicks-and-bricks strategy by using their existing name recognition and goodwill to attract e-commerce customers. Moreover, studies show that customers who shop at both a company's website and physical stores tend to be more loyal. Finally, retailers can use their multiple venues to cross-sell products. That is, they use their physical stores to promote their website sales and use their websites to promote their physical stores.

5. **Discuss six key factors that marketers should consider when choosing distribution channels.**

When choosing distribution channels, companies should consider the type of product and industry practices, channel length, a firm's desired market coverage (intense, selective, or exclusive), costs, desire for control, and potential for channel conflict.

6. **Differentiate between intensive, selective, and exclusive distribution strategies.**

With an intensive distribution strategy, a company attempts to saturate the market with its products by offering them in every available outlet. Companies that use a more selective approach to distribution choose a limited number of retailers that can adequately support the product. Firms that use exclusive distribution grant a single wholesaler or retailer the exclusive right to sell the product within a given geographic area.

7. **Highlight the major components of a physical distribution process and the key factors to consider when choosing a mode of outbound transportation.**

The major components of a firm's distribution process are order processing, inventory control, warehousing, materials handling, and outbound transportation. When choosing the best method of outbound transportation, such as truck, rail, ship, airplane, and pipeline, you should consider cost, storage, sales, inventory size, speed, product perishability, dependability, flexibility, and convenience.

KEY TERMS

agents and brokers **(356)**

category killers **(359)**

discount stores **(359)**

distribution centers **(369)**

distribution mix **(363)**

distribution strategy **(354)**

drop shippers **(356)**

exclusive distribution **(365)**

full-service merchant wholesalers **(356)**

intensive distribution **(364)**

limited-service merchant wholesalers **(356)**

logistics **(368)**

mail-order firms **(359)**

marketing intermediaries **(354)**

materials handling **(369)**

merchant wholesalers **(356)**

order processing **(368)**

physical distribution **(367)**

rack jobbers **(356)**

retailers **(354)**

scrambled merchandising **(358)**

selective distribution **(365)**

specialty store **(359)**

warehouse **(369)**

wheel of retailing **(359)**

wholesalers **(354)**

TEST YOUR KNOWLEDGE

Questions for Review

1. What is a distribution channel?
2. What are the two main types of intermediaries, and how do they differ?
3. What forms of utility do intermediaries create?
4. What are some of the main causes of channel conflict?
5. How does a specialty store differ from a category killer and a discount store?

Questions for Analysis

6. How does the presence of intermediaries in the distribution channel affect the price of products?
7. What are some of the challenges facing retailers and wholesalers today?
8. What trade-offs must you consider when adopting a physical distribution system?

9. If a manufacturer starts to sell its goods on its company website, why might this arouse channel conflict?

10. *Ethical Considerations:* Direct-mail marketers often publish different prices in different catalogs targeted at different market segments. When you call to order, the sales representative asks for your customer number or catalog number first so that he or she knows what to charge you.[27] Is this practice ethical?

Questions for Application

11. Imagine that you own a small specialty store selling hand-crafted clothing and jewelry. What are some of the nonstore retail options you might explore to increase sales? What are the advantages and disadvantages of each option?

12. Compare the prices of three products offered at a retail outlet with the prices charged if you purchase those products by mail order (catalog or phone) or over the Internet. Be sure to include hidden costs such as handling and delivery charges. Which purchasing format produced the lowest price for each of your products?

13. *Integrated:* In Chapter 9 we discussed the fact that supply chain management integrates all the activities involved in the production of goods and services from suppliers to customers. What are the benefits of involving wholesalers and retailers in the design, manufacturing, or sale of a company's product or service?

14. *Integrated:* Which of the four basic functions of management discussed in Chapter 7 would be involved in decisions that establish or change a company's channels of distribution? Explain your answer.

PRACTICE YOUR KNOWLEDGE

Handling Difficult Situations on the Job: Lining Up the Right Channels

Nearly every automobile company offers branded clothing and accessories for proud vehicle owners or wanna-be's: ties, T-shirts, watches, shoes, hats, jackets, sweaters. Most are sold right in the showrooms, and they're extremely popular, whether they be Saturn sneakers or Land Rover tweeds.

Steve Beaty, vice president of accessories marketing for Mercedes-Benz, is reaching out to car owners with a 55-page, glossy, full-color Mercedes-Benz Personal & Automotive Accessories catalog loaded with expensive logoed items. Mercedes-Benz has recruited world-class, top-of-the-line manufacturers and designers to produce merchandise worthy of the company's highly refined clientele. The new catalog presents Wittnauer watches, Caran D'Ache ballpoints, Bally bomber jackets, and silk boxers designed by artist Nicole Miller—all emblazoned with the triangle logo or images of Mercedes-Benz models, past and present. The catalog even features a $3,300 collapsible aluminum mountain bike for slipping into the trunk of your 500SL. As Beaty's assistant, you wonder whether mail-order retailing is the best—or the only—way to sell these items.[28]

Your task: Beaty has asked for your feedback on the mail-order strategy; now that the first catalog is completed, he's weighing other channels. What are the advantages and disadvantages of the catalog approach? Should the classy accessories be sold in Mercedes-Benz showrooms? What would be the challenges and opportunities? What about other nonstore retail options? List a few, noting advantages and disadvantages for each. How might the Mercedes-Benz website play a role?

Building Your Team Skills

In managing the transportation side of physical distribution, companies have to look at more than cost. Paying less to ship products is certainly an important consideration, but dependability—knowing that carriers can be counted on to deliver products—is equally vital. Smaller businesses such as Noah's Ark Original Deli in Teaneck, New Jersey, can't afford to maintain their own fleet of delivery vans; they rely on FedEx and other common carriers to whisk their products to customers around the United States.

Noah's Ark is one of thousands of businesses that contract with FedEx to fulfill customer orders that come in via the Internet. But what can the deli do if FedEx employees go on strike? David Sokolow, the deli's manager, is especially concerned about disrupting deliveries during the crucial year-end holiday gift-giving season, when orders for knishes and other specialty foods come from as far away as Puerto Rico and Hawaii.[29]

With your team, identify at least four transportation options that Noah's Ark might consider if FedEx is not able to make deliveries during the holidays. Next to each option, list both advantages and disadvantages. Then assess FedEx in the same way.

Now think about the way transportation will affect the deli's products during the delivery period. What product characteristics must Sokolow consider when he makes plans to deal with a possible FedEx strike? What additional information should he obtain about each transportation option before making a decision? What criteria should he use to choose among the many options? And what can he do in advance to be better prepared before any delivery disruptions occur?

Summarize and share your team's listing of options, advantages, and disadvantages with the class. Also share your team's thinking about additional information needed and criteria for deciding among the various options. Did other teams identify the same options and criteria as your team? Which option do most teams recommend for Noah's Ark? Why?

EXPAND YOUR KNOWLEDGE

Discovering Career Opportunities

Retailing is a dynamic, fast-paced field with many career opportunities in both store and nonstore settings. In addition to hiring full-time employees when needed, retailers of all types often hire extra employees on a temporary basis for peak selling periods, such as the year-end holidays. You can find out about seasonal and year-round job openings by checking newspaper classified ads, looking for signs in store windows, and browsing the websites of online retailers.

1. Select a major retailer, such as a chain store in your area or a retailer on the Internet. Is this a specialty store, discount store, department store, or another type of retailer?

2. Visit the website of the retailer you selected. Does the site discuss the company's hiring procedures? If so, what are they? What qualifications are required for a position with the company?

3. Research your chosen retailer using library sources or online resources. Is this retailer expanding? Is it profitable? Has it recently acquired or been acquired by another firm? What are the implications of this acquisition for job opportunities?

Developing Your Research Skills

Find an article in a business journal or newspaper (online or print editions) discussing changes a company is making to its distribution strategy or channels. For example, is a manufacturer selling products directly to consumers? Is a physical retailer offering goods via a company website? Is a company eliminating the middleman? Has a nonstore retailer decided to open a physical store? Is a category killer opening smaller stores? Has a major retail tenant closed its stores in a mall?

1. What changes in the company's distribution structure or strategy have taken place? What additional changes, if any, are planned?

2. What were the reasons for the changes? What role, if any, did electronic commerce play in the changes?

3. If you were a stockholder in this company, would you view these changes as positive or negative? What, if anything, might you do differently?

Exploring the Best of the Web

URLs for all Internet exercises are provided at the website for this book, www.prenhall.com/bovee. *When you log on to the text website, select Chapter 14, then select "Student Resources," click on the name of the featured website, and review the website to complete these exercises.*

Explore these chapter-related websites, review their content, and answer the following questions for each website you visit:

1. What is the purpose of this website?

2. What kinds of information does this website contain? Please be specific.

3. How is the information provided at this website useful for businesspeople? Consumers?

4. How did you expand your knowledge of distribution by reviewing the material at this website? What new things did you learn about this topic?

Explore the World of Wholesaling

Thinking about a career as a wholesale sales representative? The Occupational Outlook Handbook is a terrific source for learning about careers in business. Read the online material discussing the functions wholesale sales reps perform, the skills and experience manufacturers look for in candidates, and how to acquire any necessary training. Find out what a typical day on the job involves. How will you be compensated? Will travel be required? Will you be required to work long hours? What types of reports will you be expected to submit? Log on and learn now. A career in wholesale sales may be just the thing for you. http://stats.bls.gov/oco/ocos119.htm

Explore the World of Retailing

Thinking about opening up a small store or building a career in retailing? Need some statistics? Find out what's hot in the retail industry by visiting the National Retail Federation website. Browse the FAQs and read the Washington Update. Learn which government proposals might affect your retail business and how to do something about them. Opening a retail store can be an exciting venture—especially if you're prepared. www.nrf.com

Get a Move On

How much freight are companies moving around the United States? To find the answer, visit the website of the U.S. Department of Transportation's Commodity Flow Survey Program. Read the results of the latest survey to find out how many *billion* tons of raw materials and finished goods—worth *trillions* of dollars—are being shipped within the country. Surprisingly, more than half the shipments (as measured by tonnage) are headed to a destination less than 50 miles from their point of origin. So physical distribution is critical even when you are buying and selling locally. www.bts.gov/ntda/cfs

Learning Interactively

Companion Website

Visit the Companion Website at www.prenhall.com/bovee. For Chapter 14, take advantage of the interactive "Study Guide" to test your chapter knowledge. Get instant feedback on whether you need additional studying. Read the "Current Events" articles to get the latest on chapter topics, and complete the exercises as specified by your instructor. Expand your learning with a visit to the "Research Area." There you will find a wealth of information you can use to complete your course assignments.

A CASE FOR CRITICAL THINKING

REI's Perfect Blend of Retail and E-Tail Channels

During the mid-1990s, many retailers were reluctant to establish an online presence for fear of competing against existing distribution channels. But Recreational Equipment, Inc. (REI) viewed the web as an exciting new channel that could reach markets far beyond the limits of its physical stores and paper catalogs. And the outdoor gear retailer quickly developed a winning multichannel approach that successfully blended its online store with its offline businesses.

On Solid Ground

Established in 1938 by two Seattle mountain climbers as a consumer cooperative, REI developed a reputation for providing enthusiasts with high-quality sports equipment at reasonable prices. By the mid-1990s, REI had grown into the nation's largest supplier of specialty outdoor gear, serving customers in the Pacific Northwest and California through some 50 retail stores and a thriving catalog business.

Offering everything from canoes to hiking gear, each REI store was a true interactive experience. Spanning from 10,000 to 95,000 square feet, the stores gave shoppers an avalanche of opportunities to test, touch, and play with products most stores kept in boxes or behind glass. Footwear test trails, water filter testing stations, binocular demo stations, and rock climbing walls were just a few of the reasons that shoppers flocked to REI stores.

Gearing Up

Despite its success, REI was unknown outside the western United States. Moreover, the company needed to find a way to keep customers and employees informed of the increasingly changing array of products in the outdoor gear industry. The Internet seemed like a perfect channel for accomplishing both objectives, but in the mid-1990s it was still a wild frontier—largely populated by net surfers and techno-enthusiasts. Furthermore, experts warned retailers that opening an online store would likely steal business from a company's existing retail channels.

But the advantages of venturing into the world of e-tailing outweighed the risks for REI. Start-up costs for REI's website—$500,000 for all computers and programming—paled in comparison to building and equipping the typical $6 million REI store. And six decades of experience, powerful name recognition, and a loyal customer base placed REI in a strong position to move into cyberspace.

The First Step

So REI pressed ahead with its web store in 1996. Launching www.rei.com in five languages to attract customers around the world, the company made every effort to integrate the online store with its established channels. Unlike pure-play retailers that must start from scratch, REI called on its existing retail and catalog distribution systems for processing e-tail orders. The co-op also extended its web strategy into its retail channels by placing Internet kiosks in stores. With in-store access to REI's website, retail shoppers can place online orders, interact with experts, or download customized items such as topographic hiking maps. Furthermore, store cash registers are web-linked, so clerks can look up product information or sell items that are out of stock at one store but available at another. And because REI's online and offline channels offer the same merchandise and use the same computer system, customers can return web purchases to REI's physical stores without any hassles.

With the success of its online store, the company launched a second site in 1998 to attract bargain hunters. The website, www.REI-outlet.com, carries limited quantities of manufacturers' overstocks, seconds, and product closeouts at rock-bottom prices. It features items that are not available at REI's physical stores, in its catalog, or on the main website, and it is linked to the company's main website. This strategy allows REI to tailor messages to each consumer segment.

Flying High

With some 78,000 items—more than any physical REI store—and more than 45,000 pages of detailed product information, the web stores operate around the clock, seven days per week. REI's top-rate service appeals to e-tail shoppers, who place nearly one-third of online orders after regular retail hours. "Our value proposition for rei.com is to deliver any product, at any time, to any place, and to answer any question," says an REI executive.

And the strategy works. Today REI's annual sales top $116 million. Online sales account for 13 percent of the company's total retail sales and are growing twice as fast as the sales of its busiest store. REI credits its multichannel approach to serving customers as one of the key reasons for the company's success. "We've recognized that we can't choose how our customers want to shop, but we can make it easier for them to access us and provide the same high-quality shopping experience however they interact with REI," says a company spokesperson.

Critical Thinking Questions

1. Why did REI venture into e-commerce?
2. How has REI's success as a traditional retailer benefited its online business?
3. How does REI blend its online and offline channels?
4. Go to the REI website at www.rei.com. Review the website and then answer these questions: How does REI promote its physical stores? What are REI's return policies for online customers? What outdoor information does this site offer?

VIDEO CASE

Through the Grapevine: Clos du Bois Winery

Learning Objectives

The purpose of this video is to help you:

1. Understand how a company works with wholesalers and retailers to make its products available to consumers.
2. Discuss the factors that affect a company's distribution strategy.
3. Consider the goals and challenges of physical distribution.

Synopsis

Riding a tidal wave of U.S. consumer interest in California wines, Clos du Bois Winery sells its wines from coast to coast. The company now produces and ships more than 1 million cases of wine every year, although less than 20 percent is sold in California. The winery works through a network of statewide and regional distributors that sell to retailers and restaurants, which in turn sell the wine to consumers. For efficient order fulfillment and inventory management, Clos du Bois ships its wines from a central warehouse to more than 300 wholesalers' warehouses around the United States. The company also pays close attention to the details of physical distribution so wine quality is not compromised by temperature extremes. Now the company is tapping the infrastructure of parent company Allied Domecq to arrange for wider distribution in Europe.

Discussion Questions

1. *For analysis:* Why does Clos du Bois sell through wholesalers rather than selling directly to retailers and restaurants?

2. *For analysis:* How does the U.S. pattern of table wine consumption affect the winery's domestic distribution strategy?

3. *For application:* What might Clos du Bois do when its supply of a certain vintage is very limited?

4. *For application:* What effect does the cost of storing and shipping Clos du Bois wine have on the prices paid by retailers and, ultimately, consumers?

5. *For debate:* Given its long-term relationships with established wholesalers, should Clos du Bois lobby against direct sales of wine to U.S. consumers through Internet channels? Support your position.

Online Exploration

Visit the website of the Clos du Bois Winery at www.closdubois. com/home.html and (if you are of legal drinking age in your state) check out what the company says about its wines, winery, and wine club. Also follow the link to explore the trade site and find out where Clos du Bois wines are sold. Considering the winery's dependence on distributors, why would it invest so heavily in a consumer-oriented website? What channel conflict might be caused by this site? If you cannot legally enter the winery's website, use your favorite search engine (such as www.google.com) to see whether other online retailers are selling this wine. If so, why would Clos du Bois make its wine available through these intermediaries?

Promotional Strategies

LEARNING OBJECTIVES

After studying this chapter, you will be able to

1. Identify the five basic categories of promotion

2. Highlight factors you should consider when developing a promotional mix

3. List the seven steps in the personal-selling process

4. Identify five common types of advertising

5. Explain the difference between logical and emotional advertising appeals

6. Name four popular direct marketing vehicles

7. Distinguish between the two main types of sales promotion, and give at least two examples of each

8. Explain the role of public relations in marketing

9. Discuss the use of integrated marketing communications

Richard Rebh, founder of Floorgraphics, wants customers to walk all over his products.

INSIDE BUSINESS TODAY

Flooring It: Mini-Billboards at Your Feet from Floorgraphics

In-store advertisers try to influence your final purchasing decisions by planting messages on everything from shopping carts to end-of-aisle displays. But the CEO of Floorgraphics uses a different approach to catch the attention of store customers: Richard Rebh places colorful ads directly at the feet of shoppers, delivering messages that literally stop consumers in their tracks at the final point of sale.

Rebh's company produces, distributes, and installs mini-billboards on the floors of major retailers across the country, carefully positioning each advertiser's message directly below the shelf location of the featured product. Since studies show that 70 percent of brand decisions are made in the store, Rebh insists that floor ads make a powerful impact on final buying decisions. "We believe we have the most crucial piece of real estate in the media world—right where every manufacturer wants to be, right in front of their product, right at the moment of decision," Rebh contends.

Rebh paves the way for Floorgraphics ads by leasing advertising floor space from stores for periods of three to five years. Then he sells the space to advertisers for 4-, 8-, or 12-week cycles and oversees every detail necessary for properly producing and installing each ad. After transforming an advertiser's digital photographs into six square feet of colorful, laminated decals, Floorgraphics' technicians affix the mini-billboards to the floors of participating stores. Advertisers can promote their products with a single floor ad or divide their allotted space into smaller, separate components. Campbell Soup, for instance, uses a trail of small floor ads in the shape of

O's to lead customers directly to the shelf location for SpaghettiOs.

Rebh of course avoids cluttering up every square inch of floor tile with splashy ads. To maintain the effectiveness of each message, he limits the number of floor ads to two per store aisle. Furthermore, he grants advertisers exclusive coverage in their brand categories. Floor ads for such competing brands as Pepsi and Coca-Cola, for example, do not appear in the same store.

To entice merchants to sign on with Floorgraphics, Rebh offers participating retailers a cut of ad revenue, usually about 25 percent of sales. And he provides advertisers a showcase for their advertising dollars that is economical, especially when compared to the costs of advertising on outdoor billboards, in TV commercials, and in other traditional media. For each mini-billboard, the cost-per-thousand impressions averages about $1 a day for advertisers, including production and installation charges.

Since the launch of Floorgraphics in 1998, Rebh has installed floor ads for more than 100 national advertisers in over 13,000 grocery, mass-merchandise, drug, and auto retail stores. The unique promotional medium not only stimulates immediate sales but also reminds consumers of brand names and increases impulse purchases. Surveys commissioned by Floorgraphics reveal that floor ads increase brand sales by 15 to 30 percent, more than doubling the effect of advertising venues such as shopping cart ads.

Rebh's future plans call for creating animated and electronic floor ads—complete with voice, sound, music, and full-motion images—that can be changed by remote control. He envisions floor ads with scrolling text and interactive floor displays that will allow customers to alter messages or register preferences by stepping on the ads. In fact, as far as Rebh is concerned, the floor's the limit for in-store consumer promotions.[1]

What Is Promotion?

1 LEARNING OBJECTIVE

Identify the five basic categories of promotion

Richard Rebh knows that promotions such as floor ads can increase brand awareness and stimulate customers to buy. Of the four ingredients in the marketing mix (product, price, place/distribution, and promotion), promotion is perhaps the one element you associate most with the marketing function. That's because promotion is highly visible to consumers. In Chapter 12 we defined promotion as a form of persuasive communication that motivates people to buy whatever an organization is selling—goods, services, or ideas. Promotion may take the form of direct, face-to-face interaction or indirect communication through such media as floor ads, television, radio, magazines, newspapers, direct mail, billboards, the Internet, and other channels. How does a firm decide on which forms of promotion to use? Many companies develop a **promotional strategy**; that is, they define the direction and scope of the promotional activities they will take to meet their marketing objectives by setting promotional goals and developing a promotional mix.

promotional strategy
Statement or document that defines the direction and scope of the promotional activities that a company will use to meet its marketing objectives

Setting Your Promotional Goals

You can use promotion to achieve three basic goals: to inform, to persuade, and to remind. *Informing* is the first promotional priority, because people cannot buy something until they are aware of it and know what it can do for them. Potential customers need to know where the item can be purchased, how much it costs, and how to use it. *Persuading* is also an important priority, because most people need to be encouraged to purchase something new or to switch brands. Advertising that meets this goal is classified as **persuasive advertising**. *Reminding* the customer of the product's availability and benefits is also important, because such reminders stimulate additional purchases. The term for such promotional efforts is **reminder advertising.**

persuasive advertising
Advertising designed to encourage product sampling and brand switching

reminder advertising
Advertising intended to remind existing customers of a product's availability and benefits

Beyond these general goals, your promotional goals should accomplish specific objectives: They should attract new customers, increase usage among existing customers, aid distributors, stabilize sales, boost brand-name recognition, create sales leads, differentiate the product, and influence decision makers.

2 LEARNING OBJECTIVE

Highlight factors you should consider when developing a promotional mix

Developing the Promotional Mix

A company's **promotional mix** consists of a specific blend of personal selling, sales promotion, advertising, direct-marketing tools, and public relations that work best for the firm's product variables, market, and desired objectives (see Exhibit 15.1).

promotional mix
Particular blend of personal selling, advertising, direct marketing, sales promotion, and public relations that a company uses to reach potential customers

• *Personal selling.* **Personal selling** is the interpersonal arm of the promotional mix. It involves person-to-person presentation—face-to-face, by phone, or by interactive media such as Web TV's videoconferencing or customized websites—for the purpose of making sales and building customer relationships. Personal selling allows for immediate interaction between the buyer and seller. It also enables the seller to adjust the message to the specific needs, interests, and reactions of the individual customer. The chief disadvantage of face-to-face personal selling is its relatively high cost—about $170 per sales call according to one recent study.[2]

personal selling
In-person communication between a seller and one or more potential buyers

EXHIBIT 15.1 The Five Elements of Promotion
The promotional mix typically includes a blend of elements. The most effective mix depends on the nature of the market and the characteristics of the good or service being marketed. Over time the mix for a particular product may change.

ACTIVITY	REACH	TIMING	COST FLEXIBILITY	EXPOSURE
Personal selling	Direct personal interaction with limited reach	Regular, recurrent contact	Message tailored to customer and adjusted to reflect feedback	Relatively high
Advertising	Indirect interaction with large reach	Regular, recurrent contact	Standard, unvarying message	Low to moderate
Direct marketing	Direct personal interaction with large reach	Intermittent, based on short-term sales objectives	Customized, varying message	Relatively high
Sales promotion	Indirect interaction with large reach	Intermittent, based on short-term sales objectives	Standard, unvarying message	Varies
Public relations	Indirect interaction with large reach	Intermittent, as newsworthy events occur	Standard, unvarying message	No direct cost

- *Advertising.* **Advertising** consists of messages paid for by an identified sponsor and transmitted through a mass communication medium such as television, radio, or newspapers. The primary role of advertising is to create product awareness and stimulate demand by bringing a consistent message to a large targeted consumer group economically. As we shall see later in the chapter, advertising can take many forms—each with its own advantages and disadvantages.

- *Direct marketing.* **Direct marketing** is defined by the Direct Marketing Association as distributing one or more promotional materials directly to a consumer or business recipient for the purpose of generating (1) a response in the form of an order, (2) a request for further information, or (3) a visit to a store or other place of business for purchase of a specific product or service.[3]

- *Sales promotion.* **Sales promotion** includes a wide range of events and activities designed to stimulate immediate interest in and encourage the purchase of a product or service. The impact of sales promotion activities is often short term; thus, sales promotions are not as effective as advertising or personal selling in building long-term brand preference.[4]

- *Public relations.* **Public relations** encompasses all the nonsales communications that businesses have with their many audiences—communities, investors, industry analysts, government agencies and officials, and the news media. Companies rely on public relations to build a favorable corporate image and foster positive relations with these groups.

When developing a promotional mix, companies weigh the advantages and disadvantages of the five elements of promotion (which are discussed more fully later in this chapter). They also consider a number of product and market variables.

Product Variables Various types of products lend themselves to differing forms of promotion. Simple, familiar items such as laundry detergent can be explained adequately through advertising, but personal selling is generally required to communicate the features of unfamiliar and sophisticated goods and services such as office-automation equipment or municipal waste-treatment facilities. Direct, personal contact is particularly important in promoting customized services such as interior design, financial advice, or legal counsel. As this chapter will later explain, the complexity of a product and its familiarity in the marketplace will dictate the best forms of promotion to use.

advertising
Paid, nonpersonal communication to a target market from an identified sponsor using mass communications channels

direct marketing
Direct communication other than personal sales contacts designed to effect a measurable response

sales promotion
Wide range of events and activities (including coupons, rebates, contests, in-store demonstrations, free samples, trade shows, and point-of-purchase displays) designed to stimulate interest in a product

public relations
Nonsales communication that businesses have with their various audiences (includes both communication with the general public and press relations)

The product's price is another factor to consider in selecting an appropriate promotional mix. Inexpensive items such as shaving cream or breakfast cereal sold to a mass market are well suited to advertising and sales promotion, which have a relatively low per-unit cost. At the other extreme, products with a high unit price such as in-ground swimming pools lend themselves to personal selling because the high cost of a sales call is justified by the price of the product. Furthermore, the nature of the selling process often demands face-to-face interaction between the buyer and seller.

The product's position in its life cycle also influences promotional choices. Early on, when the seller is trying to inform the customer about the product and build the distribution network, promotional efforts are in high gear. Selective advertising, sales promotion, and public relations are good tools for building awareness and for encouraging early adopters to try the product, while personal selling is an effective tool for gaining the cooperation of intermediaries. Gillette, for example, spent $300 million to promote the launch of the Mach3 razor during its first year—on top of $750 million-plus in development costs—to accelerate the Mach3's transition from the costly introduction stage to the profitable growth stage faster than any previous Gillette razors. Just 18 months after the Mach3 was launched, sales for the product hit $1 billion, making it the company's most successful new product ever.[5]

As the market expands during the growth phase, the seller broadens its advertising and sales-promotion activities to reach a wider audience and continues to use personal selling to expand the distribution network. When the product reaches maturity and competition is at its peak, the seller's primary goal is to differentiate the product from rival brands. Advertising generally dominates the promotional mix during this phase, but sales promotion is an important supplemental tool, particularly for low-priced consumer products. As the product begins to decline, the level of promotion generally tapers off. Advertising and selling efforts are carefully targeted toward loyal, steady customers.

Market Variables Selection of an appropriate promotional mix is also influenced by the size and concentration of the target market. In markets with many widely dispersed buyers, advertising is generally the most economical way of communicating the product's features. In markets with relatively few customers, particularly when they are clustered in a limited area, personal selling is a practical promotional alternative. Many marketers use a combination of methods, often relying on advertising and public relations to build awareness and interest, following up with personal selling to complete the sale.

When selecting a promotional mix, a firm must also decide whether it will focus its marketing effort on intermediaries or on final customers. If the focus is on intermediaries, the producer uses a **push strategy** to persuade wholesalers and retailers to carry the item. Producers may, for instance, offer wholesalers or retailers special discounts or incentives for purchasing larger quantities of the item. Thus, you would expect to see personal selling and trade promotions dominate the promotional mix aimed at intermediaries. These marketing intermediaries then use a number of promotional tools to push the products into the market channels.

If the marketing focus is on end users, the producer uses a **pull strategy** to appeal directly to the ultimate customer, using advertising, direct mail, contests, discount coupons, and so on. With this approach, consumers learn of the product through sales promotions. They pull it through the market channels by requesting the product from retailers, who in turn request it from wholesalers, who request it from producers (see Exhibit 15.2).

Viking Range Corporation, manufacturer of commercial-type stoves and kitchen appliances, used a pull strategy to gain brand recognition and market share when it first entered the marketplace in 1984. Instead of pushing products on wholesalers and retailers, Viking marketed the products to a select group of end-users—kitchen designers and gourmet cooks—by advertising in elite home-decorating magazines and by hosting in-store cooking demonstrations. Consumers reading the magazines and attending the cook-

push strategy
Promotional strategy that uses the salesforce and a number of trade promotions to motivate wholesalers and retailers to push products to end users

pull strategy
Promotional strategy that stimulates consumer demand via advertising and a number of consumer promotions, thereby exerting pressure on wholesalers and retailers to carry a product

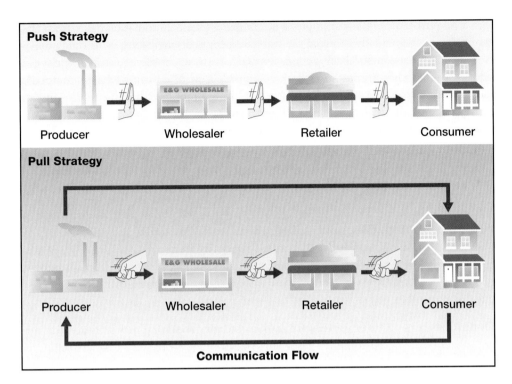

EXHIBIT 15.2
Push and Pull Strategies
Push strategies "push" products through distribution channels to final consumers by persuading wholesalers and retailers to carry the product. Pull strategies use consumer promotions and advertising to induce consumers to buy the product and "pull" it through the distribution channels.

ing demos soon began asking stores and home-building contractors for Viking stoves. High consumer demand eventually encouraged retailers and contractors to carry the Viking brand.[6]

Most companies use a combination of push and pull tactics to increase the impact of their promotional efforts. For example, when Schering-Plough introduced Claritin antihistamine, it used push tactics to educate physicians about the prescription drug's use and effectiveness, while it used pull tactics such as television and print advertising to increase market awareness and encourage consumers to ask for the new medication. This diverse, high-powered promotional mix helped Claritin capture a whopping 54 percent of the antihistamine drug market within a short time.[7] By 2001, U.S. sales of Claritin totaled $2.7 billion. The allergy drug is now sold in the over-the-counter market.[8]

Personal Selling

By almost any measure, personal selling is the dominant form of promotional activity. Most companies spend twice as much on personal selling as they do on all other marketing activities combined, even as technology is drastically changing the entire selling process.

Today's sales reps are plugged in—to headquarters and to their customers. Many are walking electronic wonders, virtual offices with laptop computer, cell phone, and pager. These new technologies provide online proposal-generation and order-management systems to relieve salespeople of nonproductive tasks, freeing them to spend more time attending to customers' specific needs. Consider the sales

The Owens-Corning FAST salesforce automation system makes working directly with customers easier than ever.

reps at Owens-Corning, for example. The company's Field Automation Sales Team (FAST) system has fundamentally changed the way salespeople do their jobs. Now they use laptops to learn about customers' backgrounds and sales histories, resolve customer service issues on the spot, modify pricing information as needed, print customized sales material, and more. By using the latest technology, Owens-Corning reps have become more empowered. "They become the real managers of their own business and their own territories," says Owens-Corning's regional general manager.[9]

Types of Sales Personnel

order getters
Salespeople who are responsible for generating new sales and for increasing sales to existing customers

creative selling
Selling process used by order getters, which involves determining customer needs, devising strategies to explain product benefits, and persuading customers to buy

order takers
Salespeople who generally process incoming orders without engaging in creative selling

sales support personnel
Salespeople who facilitate the selling effort by providing such services as prospecting, customer education, and customer service

missionary salespeople
Salespeople who support existing customers, usually wholesalers and retailers

The people who do personal selling go by many names: salespeople, account executives, marketing representatives, sales representatives, and sales consultants, to cite only a few. Regardless of their title, salespeople can be categorized according to three broad areas of responsibility: order getting, order taking, and sales support services. Although some salespeople focus primarily on one area of responsibility, others may have broader responsibilities that span all three.

Order Getters **Order getters** are responsible for generating new sales and for increasing sales to existing customers. Order getters can range from telemarketers selling home security systems and stockbrokers selling securities to engineers selling computers and nuclear physicists selling consulting services. Order getting is sometimes referred to as **creative selling**, particularly if the salesperson must invest a significant amount of time in determining what the customer needs, devising a strategy to explain how the product can meet those needs, and persuading the customer to buy. This type of creative selling requires a high degree of empathy, and the salesperson focuses on building a long-term relationship with the customer.

Order Takers **Order takers** do little creative selling; they primarily process orders. Unfortunately, the term *order taker* has assumed negative overtones in recent years because salespeople often use it to refer to someone too lazy to work for new customers or actively close orders, or they use it to refer to someone whose territory is so attractive that the individual can just sit by the phone and wait for orders to roll in. Regardless of how salespeople use the term, order takers in the true sense play an important role in the sales function.

With the aim of generating additional sales, many companies are beginning to train their order takers to think more like order getters. You've probably noticed that nearly every time you order a meal at McDonald's and don't ask for French fries, the person at the counter will ask, "Would you like an order of fries to go with that?" Such suggestions can prompt customers to buy something they may not otherwise order.

Sales Support Personnel **Sales support personnel** generally don't sell products, but they facilitate the overall selling effort by providing a variety of services. Their responsibilities can include looking for new customers, educating potential and current customers, building goodwill, and providing service to customers after the sale. The three most common types of sales support personnel are missionary, technical, and trade salespeople.

Missionary salespeople are employed by manufacturers to disseminate information about new products to exist-

In-store sales reps can help companies generate sales for products. Here a Tupperware representative sells products to Target customers.

ing customers (usually wholesalers and retailers) and to motivate them to sell the product to their customers. Manufacturers of pharmaceuticals and medical supplies use missionary salespeople to call on doctors and pharmacists. They leave samples and information, answer questions, and persuade doctors to prescribe their products.

Technical salespeople contribute technical expertise and assistance to the selling function. They are usually engineers and scientists or have received specialized technical training. In addition to providing support services to existing customers, they may also participate in sales calls to prospective customers. Companies that manufacture computers, industrial equipment, and sophisticated medical equipment use technical salespeople to sell their products as well as to provide support services to existing customers.

technical salespeople
Specialists who contribute technical expertise and other sales assistance

Trade salespeople sell to and support marketing intermediaries. Producers such as Hormel, Nabisco, and Sara Lee use trade salespeople to give in-store demonstrations, offer samples to customers, set up displays, restock shelves, and work with retailers to obtain more shelf space. Increasingly, producers work to establish lasting, mutually beneficial relationships with their channel partners, and trade salespeople are responsible for building those relationships.

trade salespeople
Salespeople who sell to and support marketing intermediaries by giving in-store demonstrations, offering samples, and so on

The Personal-Selling Process

3 LEARNING OBJECTIVE

List the seven steps in the personal-selling process

Although it may look easy, personal selling is not a simple task. Some sales, of course, are made in a matter of minutes. However, other sales, particularly for large organizational purchases, can take months to complete. Many salespeople follow a carefully planned process from start to finish, as Exhibit 15.3 suggests. But personal selling involves much more than performing a series of steps. Successful salespeople help customers understand their problems and show them new and better solutions to those problems. Moreover, they're willing to invest the time and effort to build a long-term relationship with customers both before and after the sale.[10]

Step 1: Prospecting   Prospecting is the process of finding and qualifying potential customers. This step involves three activities: (1) *generating sales leads*—names of individuals and organizations that *might* be likely prospects for the company's product; (2) *identifying prospects*—potential customers who indicate a need or a desire for the seller's product; and (3) *qualifying prospects*—the process of figuring out which prospects have both the authority and the available money to buy. Those who pass the test are called **qualified prospects**.

prospecting
Process of finding and qualifying potential customers

Step 2: Preparing   With a list of hot prospects in hand, the salesperson's next step is to prepare for the sales call. Without this preparation, the chances of success are greatly reduced. Preparation starts with creating a prospect profile, which includes the names of key people, their role in the decision-making process, and other relevant information, such as the prospect's buying needs, motive for buying, current suppliers, income/revenue level, and so on.

qualified prospects
Potential buyers who have both the money needed to make the purchase and the authority to make the purchase decision

Next, the salesperson decides how to approach the prospect. Possible options for a first contact include sending a letter or making a cold call in person or by telephone. For an existing customer, the salesperson can either drop by unannounced or call ahead for an appointment, which is generally preferred.

EXHIBIT 15.3   The Personal Selling Process
The personal-selling process can involve up to seven steps, starting with prospecting for sales leads and ending with following up after the sale has been closed.

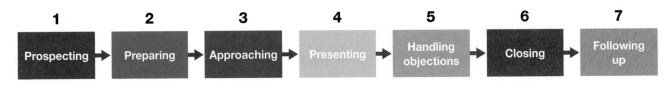

Before meeting with the prospect, the salesperson establishes specific objectives to achieve during the sales call. Depending on the situation, objectives can range anywhere from "getting the order today" to simply "persuading prospects to accept the company as a potential supplier." After establishing the objectives, the salesperson prepares the actual presentation, which can be as basic as a list of points to discuss or as elaborate as a product demonstration or multimedia presentation.

Step 3: Approaching the Prospect Whether the approach is by telephone, by letter, or in person, a positive first impression results from three elements. The first is an appropriate *appearance*—you wouldn't wear blue jeans to call on a banker, and you probably wouldn't wear a business suit to call on a farmer. Appearance also covers the things that represent you, including business cards, letters, and automobiles. Second, a salesperson's *attitude and behavior* can make or break a sale. A salesperson should come across as professional, courteous, and considerate. Third, a salesperson's *opening lines* should include a brief greeting and introduction, followed by a few carefully chosen words that get the prospect's attention and generate interest. The best way to get a prospect's attention is to focus on a benefit to the customer rather than on the product itself.

Step 4: Making the Presentation The most crucial step in the selling process is the presentation. It can take many forms, but its purpose never varies: to personally communicate a product message that will persuade a prospect to buy. Most sellers use one of two methods. The **canned approach** is a memorized presentation (easier for inexperienced sellers, but inefficient for complex products or for sellers who don't know the customer's needs). The **need-satisfaction approach** (now used by most professionals) identifies the customer's needs and creates a presentation to specifically address them.

Step 5: Handling Objections No matter how well a presentation is delivered, it doesn't always conclude with an immediate offer that might move the prospect to buy. Often the prospect will express various types of objections and concerns throughout the presentation. In fact, the absence of objections is often an indication that the prospect is not all that interested. Many successful salespeople look at objections as a sign of the prospect's interest and as an opportunity to develop new ideas that will strengthen future presentations. Smart salespeople know that objections to price are often a mask for some other issue. They also know *not* to argue with the customer. If you do, you may prove how smart you are by winning the argument, but you will probably lose the sale.

Step 6: Closing Closing is the stage of the selling process when you persuade the customer to place an order. Companies don't make any money unless the prospect decides to buy. Closing techniques are numerous; among the more popular are the alternative proposal close, the assumptive close, the silent close, and the direct close. The *alternative proposal close* asks the prospect to choose between some minor details, such as method of shipment. Example: "Should we ship this standard freight or overnight?" With the *assumptive close*, the salesperson simply proceeds with processing the order, assuming that the prospect has already decided to buy. Another alternative is the *silent close*, in which the salesperson finishes the presentation and sits quietly, waiting for the customer to respond with a buying decision. Finally, many salespeople prefer the *direct close*, where they just come right out and ask for the order.

These closing techniques might strike you as tricks, and in the hands of unethical salespeople, some closing approaches certainly can be. However, the professional salesperson uses these techniques to make the selling process effective, and efficient, and as painless for the customer as possible—not to trick people into buying when they aren't ready.

Step 7: Following Up Most salespeople depend on repeat sales and referrals from satisfied customers, so it's important that they follow up on all sales and not ignore the customer once the first sale is made. During this stage of the selling process, the salesperson

canned approach
Selling method based on a fixed, memorized presentation

need-satisfaction approach
Selling method that starts with identifying the customer's needs and then creating a presentation that addresses those needs; this is the approach used by most professional salespeople

closing
Point at which a sale is completed

Competing in the Global Marketplace

Three Steps to an Effective Sales Presentation

The sales presentation is a chance to show and tell, but it's not *all* show and tell. Successful sales reps know their audience's needs and concerns, goals and objectives, and hot buttons. They know what motivates them and how they make decisions. If you want to make a sale, you should follow this tried and true set of steps:

1. *Establish a Bond.* Prospects are much more inclined to buy from people who make them feel good and with whom they have developed a personal bond. Don't plunge into the presentation immediately. First build rapport—a sense of psychological connection— with the prospect. Build a feeling of agreement by discussing items of mutual interest or concern with the audience. These topics can range from industry issues to current events, sports, or even the weather— anything you and your audience will agree on.

2. *Focus on Buyer's Benefit.* After you've established a bond, use a "probing" period to find out the prospect's real needs and problems. Then describe and demonstrate the product in a way that the prospect can easily see and comprehend. Most important, focus on the buyer's benefits—showing how the product or service will meet the buyer's needs or solve a problem.

3. *Make an Artful Close.* The most striking characteristic of a great sales rep is the ability to close the sale and walk away with the prospect's signature on an order blank. Here are some proven closing techniques:

- *Summarize the presentation.*   Use a simple anecdotal statement that clearly positions the need for the product in the buyer's mind.
- *Make the offer available for a limited time only.* This approach often gets immediate action.
- *Ask for a small "trial" order.*   This trial can reduce the customer's risk.
- *Turn the buyer's last objection into a close.*   By saying, "Then you'd order if I could guarantee a one-year warranty in writing?," you leave the buyer in the position of having run out of valid objections.

Remember, some sales reps botch the sale because they can't stop talking—they effectively sell the product and then buy it back. So be sure that when you go for the final close you are able to keep quiet while the customer orders.

Questions for Critical Thinking

1. Why is it important to understand your audience before giving a sales presentation?
2. Why are closing techniques necessary?

---

needs to make sure that the product has been delivered properly and that the customer is satisfied. Inexperienced salespeople may avoid the follow-up stage because they fear facing an unhappy customer. However, an important part of a salesperson's job is to ensure customer satisfaction and to build goodwill.

Advertising and Direct Marketing

All forms of advertising and direct marketing have three objectives: to create product awareness, to create and maintain the image of a product, and to stimulate consumer demand. Advertising and direct marketing are also the promotional approaches that best reach mass audiences quickly at a relatively low per-person cost. But, to be effective, messages must be persuasive, stand out from competition, and motivate the target audience—a lofty goal, considering that the average U.S. resident is exposed to roughly 250 ads every day.[11]

Basically, marketers can say whatever they want in an advertisement, just as long as they stay within the boundaries of the law and conform to the moral and ethical standards of the advertising medium and trade associations. To limit promotional abuses, the Federal Trade Commission (FTC) and other government agencies have passed strict rules and regulations. One such rule is that *all statements of fact must be supported by evidence.* For example, the Food and Drug Administration ordered Glaxo Wellcome PLC, makers of flu drug Relenza, to stop showing a widely aired commercial because it suggested that Relenza was more effective than had actually been demonstrated.[12] Another rule is that *sellers must not create an overall impression that is incorrect.* So they cannot claim that doctors recommend a product if doctors do not; nor can they dress an actor in a doctor's white jacket to deliver the message. Neither can they use whipped cream in a shaving-cream commercial to create an impression of a firm, heavy lather. Most states also regulate promotional practices by certain businesses, such as liquor stores, stock brokerages, employment agencies, and loan companies.

Many individual companies and industries also practice self-regulation to restrain false and misleading promotion. The National Advertising Review Board, whose members include advertisers, agencies, and the general public, has a full-time professional staff who investigate complaints of deceptive advertising. If the complaint appears justified, the board tries to get the offending company to stop—even if it means referring the offender to proper government enforcement agencies.

Types of Advertising

4 **LEARNING OBJECTIVE**

Identify five common types of advertising

product advertising
Advertising that tries to sell specific goods or services, generally by describing features, benefits, and, occasionally, price

competitive advertising
Ads that specifically highlight how a product is better than its competitors

comparative advertising
Advertising technique in which two or more products are explicitly compared

institutional advertising
Advertising that seeks to create goodwill and to build a desired image for a company rather than to sell specific products

advocacy advertising
Ads that present a company's opinions on public issues such as education and health

Business professionals generally refer to advertising by its type. Common types of advertising include product advertising, institutional advertising, national and local advertising, word-of-mouth advertising, and stealth advertising. Here's a closer look at each.

Product Advertising   **Product advertising** is the most common type, designed to sell specific goods or services, such as Kellogg's cereals, Sega video games, or Esteé Lauder cosmetics. Product advertising generally describes the product's features and may mention its price.

You can argue that all product advertising is competitive, but the term **competitive advertising** is applied to ads that specifically highlight how a product is better than its competitors. When two or more products are directly contrasted in an ad, the technique being used is **comparative advertising**. In some countries, comparative ads are tightly regulated and sometimes banned; that is clearly not the case in the United States. Indeed, the Federal Trade Commission encourages advertisers to use direct product comparisons with the intent of better informing customers. Comparative advertising is frequently used by competitors vying with the market leader, but it is useful whenever a company believes it has some specific product strengths that are important to customers. Burger King uses it on McDonald's, Pepsi uses it on Coke, Apple Computer uses it on IBM and other PC makers, and car manufacturers from Ford to Toyota use it on each other. This approach is bare-knuckle marketing and, when done well, is effective.

Institutional Advertising   **Institutional advertising** is designed to create goodwill and build a desired image for a company rather than to sell specific products. As discussed in Chapter 2, many companies are now spending large sums for institutional advertising that focuses on *green marketing*, creating an image of companies as corporate conservationists. Institutional advertisers tout their actions, contributions, and philosophies not only as supporting the environmental movement but as leading the way. When used as *corporate advertising*, institutional advertising often promotes an entire line of a company's products. Institutional ads can also be used to remind investors that the company is doing well.

Institutional ads that address public issues are called **advocacy advertising**. Mobil and W. R. Grace are well known for running ads that deal with taxation, environmental regula-

Competing in the Global Marketplace

Will "Real People" Create Real Sales for Apple Computer?

Apple Computer can be forgiven for occasionally adopting an "us versus the world" attitude: The company more or less competes with the entire world in its struggle to take market share from Windows-based personal computers. Buyers who opt to stay on the PC side of the fence can choose from a number of well-known brands, including Dell, IBM, Toshiba, Gateway, HP and others, all running Microsoft Windows. In a sense, Apple's Macintosh has to compete with the entire field of PC companies at once.

Over the years, computer users have migrated into two camps, PCs and Macs, with PCs holding around 95 percent of the market. Getting people to switch from a PC to a Mac is more difficult than getting PC users to switch from, say, a Dell to an HP. It's almost a lifestyle change for some. Beyond technical issues such as compatibility and networking, this decision has a strong emotional aspect, particularly on the Mac side of the fence. Consequently, Mac advertising has often featured a strong emotional element, whether it focuses on the joys of using a Mac or on the supposed frustrations of using a PC.

Apple has sometimes been known as much for its marketing efforts as for its computers. The company's Orwellian "1984" ad that aired once during the 1984 Super Bowl is still discussed in advertising circles today. The "Think Different" campaign of more recent years featured images of icons such as Albert Einstein who dared to think differently, with the implication that switching to a Mac is a creative and wise choice.

In 2002 Apple introduced a campaign called "Real People" that featured interviews with people who had switched from PCs to Macs. Most of the people in the campaign were unknown, regular folk, but one ad featured renowned cellist Yo-Yo Ma saying that "Macs are friendly to technically challenged people like me." The message woven through all these comparative ads was that PCs were frustrating and unfriendly compared to Macs.

Even in the rough computer market in 2002 and into 2003, the campaign did have a modest impact on sales while generating plenty of heated discussion. Some thought the ads were clever and that it was about time Apple tackled Microsoft head on. Others thought the ads were desperate, attacking not only PCs but the people who chose to use them. It wouldn't be the first time an Apple marketing effort generated both sales and spirited discussions on both sides of the computer fence.

Questions for Critical Thinking

1. What product strengths did Apple promote in its comparative ads?
2. What are the risks of positioning Macintosh as the computer for people intimidated by technology?

---

tion, and other issues. Advocacy advertising has recently expanded beyond issues in which the organization has a stake. Some companies now run advocacy ads that don't directly benefit their business, such as ads that project opinions and attitudes supporting those of their target audiences.

National Versus Local Advertising   Advertising can also be classified according to the sponsor. **National advertising** is sponsored by companies that sell products on a nationwide basis. The term *national* refers to the level of the advertiser, not the geographic coverage of the ad. If a national manufacturer places an ad in only one city, the ad is still classified as a national ad. As Exhibit 15.4 shows, national advertisers spend over $231 billion annually.[13]

In contrast, **local advertising** is sponsored by a local merchant. Grocery store ads in the local newspaper are a good example. **Cooperative advertising** is a financial arrangement in which companies with products sold nationally share the costs of local advertising with local merchants and wholesalers. As a result, it is a cross between local and national advertising.

national advertising
Advertising sponsored by companies that sell products on a nationwide basis; refers to the geographic reach of the advertiser, not the geographic coverage of the ad

local advertising
Advertising sponsored by a local merchant

cooperative advertising
Joint efforts between local and national advertisers, in which producers of nationally sold products share the costs of local advertising with local merchants and wholesalers

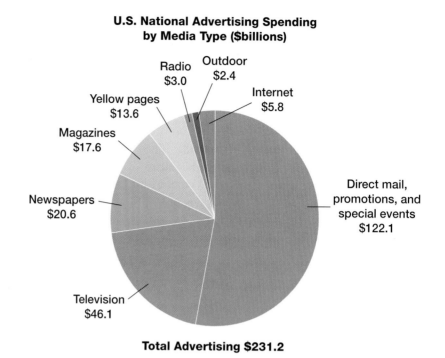

U.S. National Advertising Spending by Media Type ($billions)

Radio $3.0
Outdoor $2.4
Internet $5.8
Yellow pages $13.6
Magazines $17.6
Newspapers $20.6
Direct mail, promotions, and special events $122.1
Television $46.1

Total Advertising $231.2

Word-of-Mouth Advertising

Many companies with tight advertising budgets rely on word-of-mouth advertising to build their market share. Jiffy muffin and biscuit mixes, produced by Chelsea Milling, have never used TV commercials, print ads, or coupons. The brand's success is based entirely on repeat customers and word-of-mouth. "Our approach is to give people the best value," says the product's founder. Jiffy gives consumers the highest-quality ingredients with the best price by eliminating advertising, marketing, merchandising, and similar costs that are customarily passed on to consumers. This pricing advantage has given Jiffy a huge boost over the years.[14]

TiVo, a personal video recorder that allows viewers to record their favorite TV shows, pause live TV, rewind for instant replays, and fast forward through ads, has also amassed a base of devoted users by relying on word-of-mouth advertising. TiVo does not have the financial resources to advertise its product features to the masses, so it encourages customers to host TiVo-ware parties. Similar to Tupperware parties, the hosted events bring together friends for an event like the Grammy Awards or Superbowl to give nonusers the chance to experience TiVo's special features. Presenting TiVo in action is one of the company's strongest marketing strategies.[15]

Buzz marketing is similar to word-of-mouth advertising. Companies seek out trendsetters in communities and subtly push them into talking up a brand or product to friends and admirers. For example, they may give expensive sneakers, colognes, and even cars to young trendsetters on college campuses so that they will use and talk up the product. Vespa promoted U.S. sales of its scooters by paying influential people to ride the scooters around such cities as Los Angeles and Houston.[16]

Stealth Advertising

Stealth advertising is a commercial message that sneaks up on consumers where they least expect it. These messages blur programming and advertising by hyping products and services in TV news and talk shows and interviews with celebrities who are actually paid endorsers. Movies are notorious for stealth ads. Characters driving BMWs, drinking Coca-Cola, and flying on American Airlines are just a few examples of how marketers sneak their products into our lives without calling them commercials.[17]

Hershey's store in New York City's Times Square is decorated with 4,000 chasing lights, 380 feet of neon lighting, and a moving message board—making the store's exterior the ultimate outdoor advertisement.

Digital photography facilitates the use of stealth advertising. Fans watching Major League Baseball on ESPN, for example, can see what appears to be product billboards on the walls behind home plate. But fans at the game will not see the billboards because the ads do not physically exist. Instead, they are digitally inserted into network broadcasts.[18]

Advertising Appeals

All well-designed ads make a carefully planned appeal to whatever motivates the audience. The specific motivator depends largely on the target audience. By segmenting along age, ethnic group, lifestyles, and other variables, advertisers try to identify which groups of people can be reached with logical or emotional appeals to get their points across.

Logical Appeal Some ads use a logical appeal to persuade the audience with data. When selling technical products, some industrial and high-tech marketers assume that logic is the only reasonable approach. Discussing price or product value is one way to appeal to consumers' logic. Promising to give buyers more for their money or highlighting product benefits is an effective way to stimulate interest. A value appeal can be accomplished in other ways too: lowering the price and making people aware of the new bargain price, keeping the price the same but adding value, or keeping the price and the product the same and trying to convince people that the product is worth whatever price you are charging.

Emotional Appeal Even with the most unemotional sort of product, emotions can be a significant factor in the decision process because all people have hopes, fears, desires, and dreams, regardless of the products they buy. Emotional appeals range from the most syrupy and sentimental to the downright terrifying. On the lighter side, some companies try to convince you of how good it will feel to use their products. Flowers, greeting cards, and gifts are among the products usually sold with a positive emotional appeal. Other companies appeal to a broad range of fears: personal and family safety, financial security, social acceptance, and business success or failure. Insurance companies are notorious for using fear in advertising campaigns when they air commercials that show extensive losses from burglary, fire, hurricanes, or other catastrophic events. To be effective, appeals to fear must be managed carefully. Laying it on too thick can anger the audience or even cause them to block out the message entirely.

Celebrity Appeal Using celebrities in ads is a common emotional appeal tactic. Celebrities can bring new value, excitement, humor, and energy to a product that may not be possible with other types of advertising. The idea is that people will be more inclined to use products endorsed by a celebrity because they will identify with and want to be like the celebrity. American Express, for example, ran several ads featuring golf champion Tiger Woods because he characterizes traits such as discipline, hard work, and preparation—the pillars of American Express. "It's hard to visualize anyone he wouldn't appeal to," says the company president.[19] Nike agrees. Since Nike signed Tiger Woods in 1996, sales of Nike golf balls have seen a $50 million revenue growth. "He's definitely influenced sales," says Nike's director of sports marketing. "We were able to grow at a time when the rest of the industry was flat."[20]

Sales of Salton's countertop grill soared when it signed on former heavyweight champ George Forman as the product's spokesman. The promotion was such a success that the company eventually bought the rights to use George Forman's name in perpetuity in association with its food preparation appliances.

Car dealers frequently use celebrity endorsements to increase a product's appeal. For instance, Best Actor nominee Russell Crowe arrived at the 2002 Academy Awards in a General Motors black Cadillac Escalade instead of a block-long limousine. The $50,000 SUV was lent to him courtesy of GM. Ben Affleck, Adam Sandler, Calista Flockhart, and pop stars Pink and Justin Timberlake have also been seen driving Escalades—thanks to GM.[21]

Nonetheless, celebrity ads are not always successful. Consumers don't always find them convincing (or at least don't claim to find them convincing). In one survey on the power of various advertising appeals, 70 percent of the respondents ranked celebrity endorsements as the least convincing. Another danger is that linking the celebrity to the product also links the celebrity's behavior (both good and bad) to the product. Madonna, Mike Tyson, O.J. Simpson, and Michael Jackson are among celebrities who have lost endorsement contracts when negative aspects of their private lives became public news.

Sex Appeal A tenet of advertising is that "sex sells." The classic technique is to have an attractive, scantily attired model share the page or TV screen with the product. The model may bring nothing to the ad beyond a visual focus point. The goal is to have the audience associate the product with pleasure. Guess Jeans and Calvin Klein's Obsession perfume are well-known examples of this approach. The sex appeal has to be used with some caution, however. At the extreme, using sex as the appeal can keep an ad from running, when media refuse to accept it for publication or broadcast. In addition, attempts to present a sexy image may cross the line, offending some readers and viewers as simply sexist, not sexy.

Direct Marketing

6 LEARNING OBJECTIVE

Name four popular direct marketing vehicles

In addition to personal selling and advertising, direct marketing is an effective promotional tool used by many companies. Direct marketing enables companies to more precisely target and personalize messages to specific consumer and business segments and build long-term customer relationships.[22] Direct marketers use print, TV, and radio advertising like mass advertisers do but with one critical difference: Their offer includes a response method such as an 800 number. The most popular direct marketing vehicles are direct mail, targeted e-mail, web advertising, telemarketing, infomercials, and interactive television.

direct mail
Advertising sent directly to potential customers, usually through the U.S. Postal Service

Direct Mail and Targeted E-Mail The principal method of direct marketing is **direct mail**, which includes catalogs, brochures, videotapes, computer disks, and other materials delivered through the U.S. Postal Service and private carriers. Direct mail can be an effective way to increase sales, although companies must take into account the cost of printing and postage. The goal of direct mail is to encourage action—to get a recipient to pick up the phone, mail in a reply card, or place an order.

Increasingly, companies are replacing their direct mail campaigns with targeted e-mail. Companies poured $927 million into e-mail marketing in 2001, up 87 percent from 2000.[23] Sending e-mails to highly targeted lists of prospects is a cost-efficient way to reach potential and existing customers. E-mailing a company's own customer list, for example, costs only $1 per sale, according to Forester Research. By contrast, sending a direct mail solicitation costs $20 per sale.[24]

E-mail marketing works much the same way as mailing a letter. Companies build databases of e-mail addresses by enticing customers to register on a website in exchange for information or access to a special offer.[25] For example, when Jive Records wanted to push 'N Sync's album *No Strings Attached*, it sent e-mails to thousands of the band's fans. The e-mail featured a click-and-play video message from band members, encouraging fans to spread the word about the album. As you can imagine, this form of direct marketing has more impressive response rates than U.S. mail. Moreover, targeted e-mail campaigns allow marketers to gauge how many people open and forward the e-mail, as well as track how long the user views the message and whether or not they click through to the website.[26]

Still, e-mail marketing does have a drawback. Targeted consumers could resent companies that mass-distribute e-mail ads and view such abuse as a form of spam.

Web Advertising   Like targeted e-mail, web ads can be sent to specific interest groups or individuals. Advertisers can tailor a unique pitch to the individual and use interactive options to gather information about the viewer. For example, companies can (1) track the exact information accessed by any particular visitor to their website, (2) develop a profile for each of their regular visitors, (3) present information that may be of special interest to a particular visitor by customizing the webpage based on the user's profile, and (4) alert customers to special savings or remind them of past purchases.

Banner ads are one of the most popular forms of web advertising. Called banners because of their long, thin shape, the ads generally appear at the top and bottom of websites and contain a short text or graphical message that can be customized for target audiences. In addition to clicking on the ad to go to the advertiser's website, *rich media*, a combination of high-grade graphics with audio and interactive capabilities, allows users to interact with the banner ad by opening dropdown lists, selecting buttons, or performing other actions with a mouse inside the ad. Banner ads are sold on what is known as a cost per mil, or CPM basis. This means that an advertiser pays a website a fixed amount for every one thousand "impressions," or webviews. (For a list of popular cybermarketing terms, consult Exhibit 15.5.)

banner ads
Rectangular graphic displays on a webpage that are used for advertising and linked to an advertiser's webpage

Web advertising is expected to reach $9 billion annually in the near future.[27] The principal advantages of this form of advertising include[28]

- *Timeliness.* Web ads can be updated any time at a minimal cost.
- *Reach.* Web ads can reach very large numbers of potential buyers globally.
- *Cost.* Web ads can be less expensive than television, newspaper, or radio ads. The cost for banner ads is considerably less than the cost for direct mail campaigns.[29]
- *Interactive options.* Chat, e-mail, and instant messaging can be incorporated in a web ad at a reasonable cost.

In spite of these benefits, web advertising is not without challenges. Many web surfers ignore banner ads or click away to another website. Moreover, a TV commercial has 30 to

EXHIBIT 15.5   Popular Cybermarketing Terms
Using the Internet as a marketing vehicle has given birth to these popular cybermarketing terms.

TERM	EXPLANATION
Banner	Small, usually rectangular graphic display that appears on a website like a roadside billboard. Clicking on the banner will transfer you to the advertiser's website.
Click through	How often a viewer will respond to an ad by clicking on it.
Cost per click (CPC)	The ad rate charged only if the web surfer responds to a displayed ad.
CPM (cost per thousand impressions)	The cost of delivering an impression to 1,000 people.
Impressions	The total number of times users call up a page with a banner during a specific period.
Interactive advertisement	Any advertisement that requires or allows the viewer/consumer to take some action.
Interstitials	Brief ad message that appears as a new webpage download. Intrusive style can create an impact but can also be annoying.
Pointcasting	Mass delivery of Internet information using push technology. Also known as webcasting.
Pop-up windows	Linked ad messages that appear within a new browser window.
Splash screen	An initial webpage used as a promotion or lead-in to the site homepage and designed to capture the user's attention for a short time by using multimedia effects.

60 seconds to influence a potential customer, but web surfers may spend only 5 to 10 seconds before clicking to another webpage.[30]

telemarketing
Selling or supporting the sales process over the telephone

Telemarketing Telemarketing, or selling over the telephone, is another popular form of direct marketing. Telemarketing is a low-cost way to efficiently reach many people. But it can be intrusive. Each day telemarketers place some 100 million commercial calls hawking credit cards, house painting, and a number of other products and services.[31]

To respond to a flood of consumer complaints, the federal government passed a law in 2003 that creates a national "do not call" list, similar to the lists established by individual states. Customers can add their phone numbers to the list by registering with the U.S. government over the Internet or by dialing a toll-free number. Companies are banned from calling numbers on the federal list for five years, and violators could be fined up to $11,000 per call. Furthermore, companies are required to reveal their phone numbers on Caller ID systems.[32]

The Direct Marketing Association, of course, opposed the legislation. The organization filed a lawsuit against the FTC in 2003 claiming that a national "do-not-call" list will devastate the business of telemarketers and that it infringes on the right of free speech. Meanwhile, some companies are circumventing the law by training customer-service agents to double as telemarketers. For instance, if you call AT&T's customer service with a question about billing, the representative might spend part of the call trying to persuade you to sign up for local service.[33]

media
Communications channels, such as newspapers, radio, and television

media plan
Written plan that outlines how a company will spend its media budget, including how the money will be divided among the various media and when the advertisements will appear

media mix
The combination of print, broadcast, and other media used for the advertising campaign

Infomercials and Interactive Advertising Television *infomercials* are longer forms of commercials—30 to 60 minutes—that have the appearance of regular TV programs but provide viewers with a toll-free number to place an order. Infomercials are useful selling tools for products that need some form of demonstration or technical explanation. Tae-Bo infomercials, for example, sold more than $75 million worth of videos in one year by demonstrating the grueling combination of punches and kicks that can help you lose weight, and free your spirit.[34] Still, only 10 percent of infomercials are successful. Most fail because promoters don't understand how to generate sales by making the ads entertaining and informative.[35]

The Media Mix

Once you select which forms of advertising you will use, you must get your message to your target audience by choosing suitable **media**, or channels of communication. Your **media plan** is a document that shows your advertising budget, how you will divide your money among various media, and when your ads will appear. The goal of your media plan is to make the most effective use of your advertising dollar.

The critical task in media planning is to select a **media mix**, the combination of print, broadcast, and other media used for the advertising campaign. When selecting the media mix, the first step is to determine the characteristics of the target audience and the types of media that will reach the largest audience at the lowest cost per exposure. The choice is also based on what the medium can do (show the product in use, list numerous sale items and prices, and so on). The second step in choosing the media mix is to pick specific vehicles in each of the chosen media categories, such as individual magazines (*Time, Rolling Stone, Sports Illustrated*) or individual radio stations (a rock station, a classical station).

Advertising media fall into seven major categories, each with its own strengths and weaknesses, as highlighted in

At an average cost of $2 million for 30 seconds of air time, national Super Bowl ads are the most expensive real estate on TV. Advertisers such as MTV capture viewers' attention by lining up pop stars such as 'N Sync (pictured here) to appear in national sponsored halftime bashes.

EXHIBIT 15.6   Advantages and Disadvantages of Major Advertising Media
When selecting the media mix, companies attempt to match the characteristics of the media audiences with the characteristics of the customer segments being targeted. A typical advertising campaign involves the use of several media.

MEDIUM	ADVANTAGES	DISADVANTAGES
Newspapers	Extensive market coverage; low cost; short lead time for placing ads; good local market coverage; geographic selectivity	Poor graphic quality; short life span; cluttered pages; visual competition from other ads
Television	Great impact; broad reach; appealing to senses of sight, sound, and motion; creative opportunities for demonstration; high attention; entertainment carryover	High cost for production and air time; less audience selectivity; long preparation time; commercial clutter; short life for message; vulnerability to remote controls
Direct mail	Can deliver large amounts of information to narrowly selected audiences; excellent control over quality of message; personalization	High cost per contact; delivery delays; difficulty of obtaining desired mailing list; consumer resistance; generally poor image (junk mail)
Radio	Low cost; high frequency; immediacy; highly portable; high geographic and demographic selectivity	No visual possibilities; short life for message; commercial clutter; lower attention than television; easy to switch stations
Magazines	Good reproduction; long life; local and regional market selectivity; authority and credibility; multiple readers	Limited demonstration possibilities; long lead time between placing and publishing ads; high cost; less compelling than other major media
Outdoor	Broad coverage; impression frequency; geographic flexibility; low cost per message; large image, high impact	Image is passed by quickly; long message can't be used; high preparation cost
Internet	Fast-growing reach; low cost; ability to personalize; can appeal to senses of sight, sound, and motion	Difficulty in measuring audiences; consumer resistance; increasing clutter

Exhibit 15.6. However, imaginative marketers go beyond these categories, taking advantage of such venues as free movie magazines distributed in theater lobbies, in-flight advertising, and supermarket shopping bags, shopping carts, and even floors, thanks to Floorgraphics.

Sales Promotion

The fourth element of promotion, sales promotion, consists of short-term incentives to encourage the purchase of a product or service. Because the impact of sales promotion activities is often short term, sales promotions are not as effective as advertising or personal selling in building long-term brand preference.[36] Sales promotion consists of two basic categories: consumer promotion and trade promotion.

Consumer Promotions

Consumer promotion is aimed directly at the final users of the product. Companies use a variety of consumer promotional tools and incentives to stimulate repeat purchases and to entice new users:

- *Coupons.* The biggest category of consumer promotion—and the most popular with consumers—is **coupons**, certificates that spur sales by giving buyers a discount when they purchase specified products. Customers redeem their coupons at the time of purchase. Companies offer coupons on packages, in print ads, in direct mail, at the checkout, and on the Internet to encourage trial of new products, reach out to nonusers of mature products, encourage repeat buying, and temporarily lower a product's price. Couponing is a fairly inefficient technique, however: A lot of money is wasted on advertising and delivering

7 LEARNING OBJECTIVE

Distinguish between the two main types of sales promotion, and give at least two examples of each

consumer promotion
Sales promotion aimed at final consumers

coupons
Certificates that offer discounts on particular items and are redeemed at the time of purchase

Once a mundane afterthought to costlier, more glamorous forms of advertising, product sampling is now seen by many marketers as a more cost-effective way to promote some products. Here a representative of Odwalla juice is giving away samples.

coupons that are never redeemed. Of the 328 billion manufacturers' coupons distributed in 2001, shoppers redeemed only 1.1 percent, according to coupon clearinghouse Carolina Manufacturer's Services.[37] Moreover, critics say couponing instills a bargain-hunting mentality, leading some people to avoid buying unless they have a coupon.

- *Rebates.* With rebates, buyers generally get reimbursement checks from the manufacturer by submitting proofs of purchase along with a prepared manufacturer's rebate form. Because many buyers neglect to redeem the rebates, the costs of running such programs remains relatively low. Moreover, rebates allow the manufacturer to promote the reduced price even though customers pay the full price at checkout.[38]

- *Point-of-purchase.* The **point-of-purchase (POP) display** is a device for showing a product in a way that stimulates immediate sales. It may be simple, such as an end-of-aisle stack of soda six-packs in a supermarket, or it may be more elaborate, such as specially designed product "dumps" with signs and coupons. Simple or elaborate, point-of-purchase displays really work: Studies show that 70 percent of all consumer purchase decisions are made in the store.[39]

point-of-purchase (POP) display
Advertising or other display materials set up at retail locations to promote products to potential customers as they are making their purchase decisions

- *Samples.* Samples are an effective way to introduce a new product, encourage nonusers to try an existing product, encourage current buyers to use the product in a new way, or expand distribution into new areas. Neutrogena places sample sizes of its glycerin soap in hotel bathrooms. Butler and Procter & Gamble give dentists toothbrushes to pass on to their patients. Hall's puts bins heaped with cough drops in theatre lobbies. And Kellogg hands out single-serving packs of Smart Start cereal on street corners.[40]

- *Special-event sponsorship.* Sponsoring special events has become one of the most popular sales promotion tactics. Thousands of companies spend billions of dollars to sponsor events ranging from golf to opera. The 2002 Winter Olympic Games in Salt Lake City, Utah, drew over 64 corporate sponsors, which contributed over $800 million in cash, goods, and services. Eastman Kodak, Visa, John Hancock, Coca-Cola, and McDonald's were some of the games' largest sponsors.[41]

cross-promotion
Jointly advertising two or more noncompeting brands

- *Cross-promotion.* With **cross-promotion**, one brand is used to advertise another, noncompeting brand. For example, in 2002 Air New Zealand (ANZ) signed a two-year agreement with New Line Cinema, producer of the Lord of the Rings trilogy, to cross-promote each other's products. ANZ will paint imagery from the movies on a jumbo jet, turning the Boeing 747 into a flying billboard for the movies. It will also place similar land billboards in ANZ's major route cities. The airline will benefit from the agreement because the movies show spectacular scenery from New Zealand. Thus, the airline hopes the movies will increase travel to the country. Similarly, New Line Cinema hopes the billboards will increase demand for the movies.[42]

premiums
Free or bargain-priced items offered to encourage consumers to buy a product

specialty advertising
Advertising that appears on various items such as coffee mugs, pens, and calendars, designed to help keep a company's name in front of customers

Other popular consumer sales promotion techniques include in-store demonstrations, loyalty and frequency programs such as frequent-flyer miles, and **premiums**, which are free or bargain-priced items offered to encourage the consumer to buy a product. Contests, sweepstakes, and games are also quite popular in some industries and can generate a great deal of public attention, particularly when valuable or unusual prizes are offered. **Specialty advertising** (on pens, calendars, T-shirts, and so on) helps keep a company's name in front of customers for a long period of time.

CHAPTER 15   Promotional Strategies   **395**

Trade Promotions

Although shoppers are more aware of consumer promotion, trade promotion actually accounts for the larger share of promotional spending. **Trade promotions** are aimed at inducing distributors or retailers to sell a company's products. The most popular trade promotion is a **trade allowance**, which involves a discount on the product's price or free merchandise that brings down the cost of the product. The wholesaler can either pocket the savings and increase company profits or pass the savings on to the consumer to generate additional sales. Trade allowances are commonly used when adopting a push marketing strategy. Their chief downside is that they can create the controversial practice of **forward buying**, in which the distributor stocks up on merchandise while the price is low. For example, say that the producer of Bumble Bee tuna offers retailers a 20 percent discount for a period of 6 weeks. A retailer might choose, however, to buy enough tuna to last 8 or 10 weeks. Purchasing this excessive amount at the lower price increases the retailer's profit, but at the expense of the producer's profit.

Besides trade allowances, other popular trade promotions are display premiums, dealer contests or sweepstakes, and travel bonus programs. All are designed to motivate distributors or retailers to push particular merchandise. As this chapter's case study shows, one increasingly controversial form of trade promotions is prescription drug giveaways. Pharmaceutical companies try to influence which drugs doctors prescribe by giving them free samples of medications—nearly $11 billion worth in 2001—as well as gifts and entertainment perks. To curb the potential for bias when prescribing drugs, leaders of the drug industry enacted voluntary guidelines in 2001. The guidelines ban drug companies from such lavish freebies as sports gear, tickets to Broadway shows, ski trips, and expensive meals.[43]

trade promotions
Sales-promotion efforts aimed at inducing distributors or retailers to push a producer's products

trade allowance
Discount offered by producers to wholesalers and retailers

forward buying
Retailers taking advantage of trade allowances by buying more products at discounted prices than they hope to sell

Public Relations

Public relations, the fifth element of promotion, plays a vital role in the success of most companies, and that role applies to more than just the marketing of goods and services. Smart businesspeople know that a good reputation is one of a business's most important assets. A recent study shows that companies with a good public image have a big edge over less-respected companies. Consumers are more than twice as likely to buy new products from companies they admire, which is why smart companies work hard to build and protect their reputations. When United Airlines filed for Chapter 11 bankruptcy protection in 2002, it immediately launched a public relations campaign, notifying customers and travel agents via letters, newspapers, and e-mail that the company would continue to operate as usual while the bankruptcy proceedings were under way.[44]

Sometimes companies hire public relations firms to help them maintain or restore their public image. Tire maker Bridgestone/Firestone hired a public relations firm to help restore its tattered image following the 2000 recall of 6.5 million Firestone tires that had been implicated in over 170 U.S. traffic deaths. A spokesperson for Bridgestone/Firestone acknowledged that the company had been slow to respond to public concerns. "We underestimated the intensity of the situation, and we have been too focused on internal details," he said. "We are determined to change all that."[45]

Another way that companies build good reputations is by maintaining good relations with both the general news media and specialized trade media. **Press relations** is the process of communicating with newspapers, magazines, and broadcast media. In the personal computer industry, for example, manufacturers know that many people look to *ComputerWorld*, *PC*, *Byte*, and other computer publications as influential sources of information about new products. Editors and reporters often review new products and then make recommendations to their readers, pointing out both strengths and weaknesses. Companies

8 LEARNING OBJECTIVE

Explain the role of public relations in marketing

press relations
Process of communicating with reporters and editors from newspapers, magazines, and radio and television networks and stations

news release
Brief statement or video program released to the press announcing new products, management changes, sales performance, and other potential news items; also called a *press release*

news conference
Gathering of media representatives at which companies announce new information; also called a *press briefing* or *press conference*

9 **LEARNING OBJECTIVE**

Discuss the use of integrated marketing communications

integrated marketing communications (IMC)
Strategy of coordinating and integrating communications and promotions efforts with customers to ensure greater efficiency and effectiveness

EXHIBIT 15.7
Integrated Marketing Communications
Coordinating the five elements of promotion delivers a consistent message to the marketplace.

roll out the proverbial red carpet for these media figures, treating them to hospitality suites at conventions, factory tours, and interviews with company leaders. When introducing products, manufacturers often send samples to reporters and editors for review, or they visit the media offices themselves.

Two standard public relations tools are the news release and the news conference. A **news release** is a short memo sent to the media covering topics that are of potential news interest; a *video news release* is a brief video clip sent to television stations. Companies use news releases to get favorable news coverage about themselves and their products. When a business has significant news to announce, it will often arrange a **news conference**. Both tools are used when the company's news is of widespread interest, when products need to be demonstrated, or when company officials want to be available to answer questions from the media.

Integrated Marketing Communications

With five major promotional methods available—personal selling, advertising, direct marketing, sales promotion, and public relations—how do you decide on the right mix for your product? There are no easy answers, because you must take many factors into account. In fact, when you consider all the ways that audiences can receive marketing messages today, the potential for confusion is not all that surprising. Besides the traditional media—radio, television, billboards, print ads, and direct-mail promotions—marketers are using websites, e-mail, faxes, kiosks, sponsorships, and a number of clever vehicles to deliver messages to targeted audiences. Coordinating promotional and communication efforts is becoming vital if a company is to send a consistent message and boost that message's effectiveness.

All too often, companies fail to integrate their various marketing communications. The result is confusing to consumers: Mass media advertisements say one thing, a price promotion sends a different message, a product label creates yet another message, and company sales literature says something altogether different. **Integrated marketing communications (IMC)** is a strategy of coordinating and integrating all of a company's communications and promotion efforts to provide customers with clarity, consistency, and maximum communications impact. "It's everything from running ads to developing new media, to creating custom media, licensing, promotion, sweepstakes—every aspect of communicating to consumers," says one media expert.[46] The basics of IMC are quite simple: communicating with one voice and one message to the marketplace, as Exhibit 15.7 suggests.

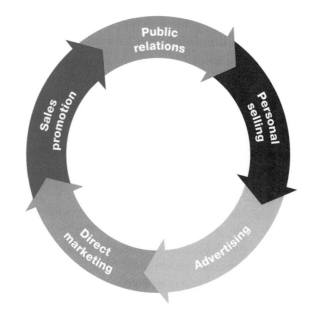

Properly implemented, IMC increases marketing and promotional effectiveness. Look at Southwest Airlines. The company coordinates all marketing to establish and maintain a consistent image of low-fare, high-frequency service in new and existing markets. For example, when the Texas-based airline beefed up service on the East Coast, it used public relations, special events, and advertising to whip up excitement by promoting a special Thanksgiving Day cross-country flight from Baltimore, Maryland, to Oakland, California, at the bargain rate of $99. The resulting media coverage effectively communicated the airline's low-price, flyer-friendly position. "We always start out with the public relations side in announcing inaugural services. Then we integrate government relations, community affairs, service announcements, special events, advertising, and promotion," says the head of Southwest's ad agency. "We try to fire all guns at once so that by the time Southwest comes into the market, the airline already is part of the community."[47]

Summary of Learning Objectives

1. **Identify the five basic categories of promotion.**

   The five basic categories of promotion are: (1) personal selling, which involves contacting customers by phone, interactive media, or in person to make a sale; (2) advertising, which consists of paid sponsored messages transmitted by mass communication media; (3) direct marketing, which is the distribution of promotional material to consumers via direct mail, e-mail, the Internet, telemarketing, or infomercials to generate an order or other consumer response; (4) sales promotion, which includes a number of consumer and promotional tools designed to stimulate consumer interest in a product and encourage a purchase; and (5) public relations, which includes nonsales communications between businesses and their stakeholders to foster positive relationships.

2. **Highlight factors you should consider when developing a promotional mix.**

   When establishing a promotional mix you should consider a product's characteristics, price, and position in its life cycle. You should also consider the target market size and concentrations and whether you will focus your marketing efforts on intermediaries (using a push strategy) or on end users (adopting a pull strategy).

3. **List the seven steps in the personal-selling process.**

   The seven steps are prospecting (finding prospects and qualifying them), preparing (creating a prospect profile and deciding on the appropriate approach), approaching the prospects (using appropriate behavior and language for your prospect), making the sales presentation (using either a canned or personalized approach), handling objections (using audience comments as an opportunity to strengthen the presentation), closing (focusing on making a sale), and following up after the sale has been made.

4. **Identify five common types of advertising.**

   Product advertising, which is the most common type, may be competitive or comparative. Institutional advertising creates goodwill and focuses on building a company's image. National advertising is sponsored by companies that sell on a nationwide basis. Local advertising is sponsored by companies that sell locally. Cooperative advertising is an agreement to share the advertising costs with merchants and wholesalers. Word-of-mouth advertising focuses on providing customers with good experiences so that they will promote the product to other potential customers. Stealth advertising is the act of disguising an ad as normal programming material and may involve the everyday discussion of a product's benefits or the use of a branded product on TV programs or movie sets.

5. **Explain the difference between logical and emotional advertising appeals.**

   You can view the difference between logical and emotional appeals as the difference between appealing to the head and appealing to the heart. Logical appeals try to convince the audience with facts, reasons, and rational conclusions; they tend to focus on important product features and the product's price or value. Emotional appeals, as the name implies, persuade through emotion—which can range from heart-warming tenderness to stark fear. Use of celebrities and sex appeal are two ways marketers appeal to emotions. It's important to remember, however, that nearly all ads contain a mixture of both logic and emotion; most just lean heavily in one direction or the other.

6. **Name four popular direct marketing vehicles.**

   The most popular direct marketing vehicles are direct mailings of catalogs and other materials; targeted e-mail messages; web advertising, such as banners or company websites that may be customized according to individual user profiles; telemarketing, or selling over the telephone; and infomercials or longer informative ads.

7. **Distinguish between the two main types of sales promotion, and give at least two examples of each.**
The two main types of sales promotion are consumer promotion and trade promotion. Consumer promotions are intended to motivate the final consumer to try new products or to experiment with the company's brands. Examples include coupons, rebates, cross-promotion, specialty advertising, point-of-purchase displays, samples, special event sponsorship, and cross-promotion. Trade promotions are designed to induce wholesalers and retailers to stimulate sales of a producer's products. Examples include trade allowances, trade shows, display premiums, dealer contests, and travel bonus programs.

8. **Explain the role of public relations in marketing.**
Because consumers and investors support companies with good reputations, smart companies use public relations to build and protect their reputations. They communicate with consumers, investors, industry analysts, and government officials through the media. They pursue and maintain press relations with representatives of newspapers, television, and other broadcast media so that they can give effective news releases and hold effective news conferences.

9. **Discuss the use of integrated marketing communications.**
When companies use a greater variety of marketing communications, the likelihood of sending conflicting marketing messages to consumers increases. Integrated marketing communications (IMC) is a process of coordinating all of a company's communications and promotions efforts so that they present only one consistent message to the marketplace. Properly implemented, IMC increases marketing and promotional effectiveness.

KEY TERMS

advertising **(379)**
advocacy advertising **(387)**
banner ads **(391)**
canned approach **(384)**
closing **(384)**
comparative advertising **(386)**
competitive advertising **(386)**
consumer promotion **(393)**
cooperative advertising **(387)**
coupons **(393)**
creative selling **(382)**
cross-promotion **(394)**
direct mail **(380)**
direct marketing **(379)**
forward buying **(395)**
institutional advertising **(386)**
integrated marketing communications (IMC) **(396)**

local advertising **(387)**
media **(392)**
media mix **(392)**
media plan **(392)**
missionary salespeople **(382)**
national advertising **(387)**
need-satisfaction approach **(384)**
news conference **(396)**
news release **(396)**
order getters **(382)**
order takers **(382)**
personal selling **(378)**
persuasive advertising **(378)**
point-of-purchase (POP) display **(394)**
premiums **(394)**
press relations **(395)**
product advertising **(386)**
promotional mix **(378)**

promotional strategy **(378)**
prospecting **(383)**
public relations **(379)**
pull strategy **(380)**
push strategy **(380)**
qualified prospects **(383)**
reminder advertising **(378)**
sales promotion **(379)**
sales support personnel **(382)**
specialty advertising **(394)**
technical salespeople **(383)**
telemarketing **(392)**
trade allowance **(395)**
trade promotions **(395)**
trade salespeople **(383)**

TEST YOUR KNOWLEDGE

Questions for Review

1. What are the three basic goals of promotion?
2. What is the difference between using a push strategy and using a pull strategy to promote products?
3. What is the biggest advantage of personal selling over other forms of promotion?
4. What techniques do skilled salespeople use when closing a sale?
5. What are some common types of consumer promotion?

Questions for Analysis

6. Why is it important to prepare for a sales call?

7. How do advertisers determine the type of appeal to use in designing an ad, and why must they use caution with celebrity appeals?

8. Why is e-mail becoming an increasingly popular form of direct marketing?

9. What are the principal advantages and disadvantages of web advertising?

10. *Ethical Considerations:* Scan your local papers and highlight or clip ads that could possibly mislead the public. What do you find misleading about the ad? How would you improve the ad?

Questions for Application

11. If you were a realtor, how would you determine whether it's worth investing a significant amount of time in a particular prospect?

12. Find three newspaper or magazine ads that you think are particularly effective and three more that you think are ineffective. What do you like about the effective ads? How might you improve the ineffective ads?

13. *Integrated:* Should companies involve their marketing channels in the design of their promotional programs? What are the advantages and disadvantages of doing so?

14. *Integrated:* Review the five forms of promotion discussed in this chapter. How can companies use each of these forms to build relationships with their customers?

PRACTICE YOUR KNOWLEDGE

Handling Difficult Situations on the Job: Extolling a Better Way to Buy Insurance

The great thing about Quotesmith.com is that no one is obligated to buy a thing, which makes your job in the company's marketing department easier. Free of charge, consumers can log on to your website, ask for dozens of insurance quotes, then go off and buy elsewhere. They can look at instant price-comparison quotes from more than 300 insurers, covering every kind of insurance from term life and medical, to private passenger auto insurance.

Quotesmith.com is now the largest single source for comprehensive insurance price comparisons in the United States. All rates are guaranteed up-to-the-day accurate, against a $500 reward. And so far the online service has received positive press from *Nation's Business, Kiplinger's Personal Finance, Good Housekeeping, The Los Angeles Times, Money, U.S. News & World Report,* and *Forbes.*

Quotesmith.com generates revenues primarily from the receipt of commissions and fees paid by insurers based on the volume of business produced. Customers can purchase insurance from the company of their choice via the Quotesmith.com website or they can call Quotesmith's toll-free number to speak to one of the

company's insurance-experienced reps. The reps are paid salaries versus commissions, and do not directly benefit by promoting one insurance company's product over another.[48]

Your task: It's your job to lure more insurance customers to Quotesmith.com. How will you promote the site and the service it offers? Describe how you might use both logical and emotional appeals. Rate the potential effectiveness of each of the five promotional categories for Quotesmith; explain your reasoning. For direct marketing, what strategies might be most efficient? Why?

Building Your Team Skills

In small groups discuss three or four recent ads or consumer promotions that you think were particularly effective. Using the knowledge you've gained from this chapter, try to come to agreement on which attributes contributed to the success of each ad or promotion. For instance was it persuasive? Informative? Competitive? Creative? Did it have logical or emotional appeal? Did it stimulate you to buy the product? Why? Compare your results with those of other teams. Did you mention the same ads? Did you list the same attributes?

EXPAND YOUR KNOWLEDGE

Discovering Career Opportunities

Jobs in promotion—personal selling, advertising, direct marketing, sales promotion, and public relations—are among the most exciting and challenging in all of marketing. Choose a particular job in one of these five areas, such as public relations or media planning. Using personal contacts, local phone or Chamber of Commerce directories, or Internet resources such as company websites or search engines, arrange a brief phone, e-mail, or per-

sonal interview with a professional working in your chosen marketing field.

1. What are the daily activities of this professional? What tools and resources does this person use most often on the job? What does this professional like most and least about the job?

2. What talents and educational background does this professional bring to the job? How are the person's skills and knowledge applied to handle the job's daily activities?

3. What advice does the person you are interviewing have for newcomers entering this field? What can you do now to get yourself started on a career path toward this position?

Developing Your Research Skills

Choose an article from recent issues of business journals or newspapers (print or online editions) that describe the advertising or promotion efforts of a particular company or trade association.

1. Who is the company or trade association targeting?
2. What specific marketing objectives is the organization trying to accomplish?
3. What role does advertising play in the promotion strategy? What other promotion techniques does the article mention? Are any of them unusual or noteworthy? Why?

Exploring the Best of the Web

URLs for all Internet exercises are provided at the website for this book, www.prenhall.com/bovee. *When you log on to the text website, select Chapter 15, then select "Student Resources," click on the name of the featured website, and review the website to complete these exercises.*

Explore these chapter-related websites, review their content, and answer the following questions for each website you visit:

1. What is the purpose of this website?
2. What kinds of information does this website contain? Please be specific.
3. How is the information provided at this website useful for businesspeople? Consumers?
4. How did you expand your knowledge of promotion by reviewing the material at this website? What new things did you learn about this topic?

Learn the Consumer Marketing Laws

Visit the Federal Trade Commission (FTC) website and click on Consumer Protection to learn how this agency protects consumers against unfair and deceptive marketing practices. Do you know what the FTC's policies are on deceptive pricing, use of the word *free*, or use of endorsements and testimonials? Find out what it means to substantiate product claims such as "tests prove," or "studies show." Learn what the rules are for unsolicited telephone calls and telephone slamming before you telemarket your product. www.ftc.gov

Take an Idea Journey

Looking for a way to market your product or service? Perhaps what you really need is a new marketing idea. How about hundreds of them—many of which are quite unusual? Start your idea journey now by visiting the Sales and Marketing Management website. Learn some creative strategies for increasing your sales. Check out the tip of the week. Help solve a sticky management situation. Explore the list of resources for the sales and marketing professional. Follow the hot links. This journey never ends. www.salesandmarketing.com

Sample Success on the Sales Marketing Network

Want to know the fastest way to get the sales and marketing how-to and reference information you need? Tune in to the Sales Marketing Network (SMN), where you'll find over 100 how-to and reference articles, along with a wealth of sales and marketing trends, statistics, and legal issues. Check out the information on marketing strategies, promotions, trade shows, event marketing, direct marketing, and more. Learn how to incorporate the Internet into your promotional strategies. Discover the most effective sampling strategies. Find out how to attract and keep long-term customers using frequency marketing. And learn some tips for building customer profiles. www.info-now.com/SMN

Learning Interactively

Companion Website

Visit the Companion Website at www.prenhall.com/bovee. For Chapter 15, take advantage of the interactive "Study Guide" to test your chapter knowledge. Get instant feedback on whether you need additional studying. Read the "Current Events" articles to get the latest on chapter topics, and complete the exercise as specified by your instructor. Expand your learning with a visit to the "Research Area." There you will find a wealth of information you can use to complete your course assignments.

A CASE FOR CRITICAL THINKING

Polyclinic Closes the Door on Sales Reps

When you walk out of the doctor's office and head to the pharmacy to get that prescription filled, do you ever wonder if the doctor recommended the best medication possible? What if the person who visited the doctor right before you was not another patient but a sales rep pushing the very medication the doctor just prescribed for you?

Many organizations are concerned about the role of personal selling in medicine. They wonder how much personal selling—including the $7 billion worth of free samples the industry gives to doctors every year—influences both the choices doctors make and the overall cost of health care. The management team at Polyclinic, an 80-doctor clinic in Seattle, got so worried about personal selling that they took the drastic step of locking drug company sales reps out of the clinic.

Information Versus Persuasion

A look inside the pharmaceutical sales process helps to shed some light on Polyclinic's bold decision. Doctors have two primary sources of information about drugs: professional medical journals and the marketing materials and sales presentations from drug companies. Information from a drug company, understandably, seeks to present that specific company's products in the most positive light possible. To the worry of many, though, studies show that doctors who rely heavily on drug company information tend to exhibit prescription patterns that are both more expensive than their peers and sometimes less effective.

The Cost of Sales

For the past decade, Polyclinic and other health providers have watched as the cost of prescription drugs and supplies has increased an average of 13 percent per year, a rate significantly above the general rate of inflation. A number of factors contribute to rising costs, but two relate directly to personal selling. The first issue is the cost of all that marketing and selling, costs that must be covered by the prices patients pay. Drug companies spend $5 billion a year to send nearly 90,000 salespeople out on 60 million sales calls. And like many sales personnel, drug company reps employ a variety of promotional gifts as part of their effort to build customer relationships. These gifts can be as insignificant as pens and coffee cups or as expensive as trips to resorts for informational seminars.

The second issue involves the specific drug recommendations that doctors make. Because patients, not doctors, have to pay for the drugs, there is no systematic pressure on doctors to prescribe less-expensive drugs. Moreover, free samples make the problem even worse, according to Howard Springer, an associate administrator at Polyclinic. He suggests it's simply too easy for a doctor to hand a patient a few doses from the samples left by a sales rep, then prescribe a full course of treatment with that drug if the samples prove to be effective—even if it's not the least-expensive choice.

Wearing Out Their Welcome

As if an expensive selling process and expensive prescription choices weren't enough, drug reps were wearing out their welcome with their demands on doctors' time. On a slow day, more than a dozen sales reps visited Polyclinic's offices, and on busy days it could get a lot worse. This time crunch is a common complaint among doctors today, according to the American Medical Association.

Polyclinic decided it had had enough. Dr. Ralph Rossi, who chairs the clinic's pharmacy and therapeutics panel, said the onsite sales calls weren't benefiting patients, the clinic, or the community. Following the lead of some other clinics around the United States, the clinic first started charging reps $30 an hour just to enter the building, then announced a ban on sales calls entirely in January 2003.

The Right Prescription?

Is Polyclinic's response the right answer to this complicated dilemma? Even the clinic's own doctors didn't all agree with it; many liked to give the free samples away to low-income patients. To counter that loss, the clinic will help low-income patients apply for free medication directly from drug companies. And to make sure doctors continue to get needed information, the clinic is planning quarterly seminars hosted by an outside consultant and an internal team of doctors.

Not surprisingly, pharmaceutical companies don't applaud the decision, saying that Polyclinic's doctors will lose access to vital information.

With enormous pressure on one side to sell medications that cost millions to develop and enormous pressure on the other to contain health care costs, the battle over personal selling in the pharmaceutical industry has only just begun.

Critical Thinking Questions

1. Why did Polyclinic decide to ban drug company sales representatives?

2. How might drug companies continue to reach Polyclinic's doctors with persuasive messages about their products?

3. A new law in Vermont requires sales reps to report any gift to doctors worth more than $25 (not including samples); will this law reduce the inappropriate influence of promotional gifts?

4. Visit the Pharmaceutical Research and Manufacturers of America website at www.phrma.org. What effect will the new code of marketing ethics adopted by this organization have on the drug industry?

VIDEO CASE

Revving Up Promotion: BMW Motorcycles

Learning Objectives

The purpose of this video is to help you:

1. Describe the purpose of product promotion.
2. Understand how and why a company must coordinate all the elements in its promotional mix.
3. Discuss how the message and the media work together in an effective advertising campaign.

Synopsis

Although U.S. car buyers are extremely familiar with the BMW brand, the brand has much lower awareness among motorcycle buyers. Increasing customer awareness is a major challenge for BMW Motorcycles, which has been producing high-end motorcycles for more than 80 years. The company's main promotional goal is to attract serious buyers who are looking for an exceptional riding experience. To do so, its marketers carefully coordinate every promotional detail to convey a unified brand message positioning the BMW motorcycle as "the ultimate riding machine," as its advertising slogan states. Using print and television advertising, personal selling in dealerships, sales promotion, and a virtual showroom on the web, BMW is driving its brand message home to motorcycle enthusiasts across the United States.

Discussion Questions

1. *For analysis:* What are the advantages of using more personal advertising copy and encouraging customers to become missionaries for BMW motorcycles?

2. *For analysis:* Why would BMW use its website as a virtual showroom rather than also selling online directly to consumers?

3. *For application:* What are some ways that BMW might use public relations to build brand awareness?

4. *For application:* How might BMW use direct mail to bring potential buyers into its motorcycle dealerships?

5. *For debate:* Should BMW develop and promote a new brand to differentiate its motorcycles from competing motorcycle brands as well as from BMW cars? Support your chosen position.

Online Exploration

Visit the BMW Motorcycle site, www.bmwmotorcycle.com, and notice the links on the home page. Then look at the pages promoting new models and preowned motorcycles. Finally, follow the link to look at the contact page. Which elements of the promotional mix are in evidence on this site? How does this site support the company's "ultimate riding machine" brand message? How does the site make it easy for customers to obtain more information and ask questions about BMW motorcycles and dealer services?

Developing Marketing Strategies to Satisfy Customers

PART 5

Mastering Global and Geographical Skills: What's the Best Location for Your New Store?

You've probably heard the remark that the three most important things to look for when buying real estate are location, location, and location. The same basic concern applies to businesses such as restaurants (although other factors certainly affect your chances of success).

Assume you're going to open a restaurant. Where would you put a restaurant in your city or town? Begin your decision process by outlining the type of restaurant you will open and the type of menu you will offer. Then determine who your target customers are. Next, using a street map, the Yellow Pages, and the Internet, work through the following questions (if you're in a large city, you may want to restrict yourself to one particular section of the city):

1. Where do your target customers work, live, or travel regularly? For instance, if you've defined your business as an expensive restaurant, most of your customers are likely to come from business districts and affluent neighborhoods.

2. How will these people reach you? Can they walk? Will they have to drive? Will they use public transportation? Depending on the business you choose to start, you'll encounter different transportation needs. Think about how far people are willing to drive to eat at a special restaurant.

3. Where do your competitors seem to be? You can get a good idea from the yellow pages. Identify the restaurants you'll compete with and mark their locations on your map. (Again, you may want to restrict the geographic scope of this project; you don't want to track down a thousand restaurants!)

4. Using the Internet, find out more about your desired location.
   a. How is the area changing? Are any new buildings, offices, or residential properties scheduled for construction in the near future? (*Hint:* Local Chamber of Commerce websites frequently include this information.)
   b. Does the area offer forms of entertainment such as movies, plays, or sporting events that would help drive business to your restaurant? (*Hint:* Websites such as Digital City at http://home.digitalcity.com/ or City Search at www.citysearch.com/ provide this information.)
   c. How easy will it be for customers to get to your restaurant? Log on to MapBlast at www.mapblast.com and check it out. Enter the location for your desired restaurant (as much information as you have) and generate the map. Now get *Driving Directions* from some main location points by entering their respective street locations and then clicking on *Drive*. Is your selected location near a major highway or thoroughfare?

CHAPTER 16

Accounting

LEARNING OBJECTIVES

After studying this chapter, you will be able to

1. Discuss how managers and outsiders use a company's financial information

2. Describe what accountants do

3. State the basic accounting equation, and explain the purpose of double-entry bookkeeping and the matching principle

4. Differentiate between cash basis and accrual basis accounting

5. Explain the purpose of the balance sheet and identify its three main sections

6. Explain the purpose of the income statement

7. Explain the purpose of the statement of cash flows

8. Explain the purpose of ratio analysis, and list the four main categories of financial ratios

When Craig Conway took the helm at PeopleSoft in 1999, he accelerated bill collection time, brought discipline to the ranks, and introduced a revolutionary suite of products.

INSIDE BUSINESS TODAY

PeopleSoft Takes a Hard Look at the Bottom Line

When Craig Conway took the reins at PeopleSoft in 1999, he took over a company with accounting problems on the inside and a collapsing market on the outside. PeopleSoft had been successful during the technology boom market of the 1990s with its enterprise resource planning (ERP) software. But the company had developed some decidedly unhealthy financial habits.

Employees enjoyed such perks as $1 million worth of free breakfasts every year, and customers routinely got away with paying their bills late. Conway's predecessor, David Duffield, had taken pride in doing what was best for customers, but he sometimes went too far, allowing customers who hadn't paid their outstanding bills to purchase additional software on credit. As a result, PeopleSoft's accounts receivables averaged 103 days old—meaning customers were taking nearly three and a half months to pay their bills.

External market forces quickly magnified the internal accounting problems. First, the approaching year 2000 brought widespread fear of a global computer meltdown, leading many customers to stop buying new technology so they could fix old systems instead. Then a recession hammered the entire industry. And as if all that weren't enough, the company's software needed to be reengineered to make it more Internet compatible.

To restore profitability, Conway wasted little time in applying much-needed discipline. The company immediately sent out collection notices, and Conway leaned on his accounts receivable staff to follow up on unpaid bills, reducing their average number of days for outstanding receivables to a more acceptable 63 days. Then he tackled expenses. Out went the free breakfasts and freewheeling spending, and in came formal budgets and a requirement that he personally approve any purchase over $100,000.

Next Conway focused on making the company's suite of business software compatible with the Internet. He pumped up research and development to 25 percent of revenues—more than double the industry average. He eliminated dozens of ongoing projects and assigned most of the company's 2,000 programmers to a single, massive program: rewriting the PeopleSoft product suite into HTML, the language of the Internet. This new version, the Internet-based PeopleSoft 8, saved customers huge software maintenance costs because it didn't require every company computer to be programmed with special software. PeopleSoft 8 was an instant hit.

By the turn of the century, PeopleSoft appeared to be on the road to recovery. Then some past accounting trickery came back to bite the company. Six months before Conway's predecessor, David Duffield, stepped aside, Duffield had transferred $250 million to a newly created subsidiary with just one employee. PeopleSoft hired that subsidiary, Momentum Business Applications, to write new software. Momentum, in turn, contracted the project out to PeopleSoft programmers at a markup. This creative accounting arrangement transformed the high cost of creating software programs into a source of revenue for PeopleSoft and boosted profits, too. Although the move was legal and within the boundaries of accepted accounting practices, it misled investors, according to accounting experts. PeopleSoft defended the maneuver as a good idea, but as the scrutiny of corporate bookkeeping intensified in the

405

1 **LEARNING OBJECTIVE**

Discuss how managers and outsiders use a company's financial information

accounting
Measuring, interpreting, and communicating financial information to support internal and external decision making

financial accounting
Area of accounting concerned with preparing financial information for users outside the organization

management accounting
Area of accounting concerned with preparing data for use by managers within the organization

2 **LEARNING OBJECTIVE**

Describe what accountants do

bookkeeping
Record keeping, clerical aspect of accounting

cost accounting
Area of accounting focusing on the calculation of manufacturing and storage costs of products for use or sale in a business

wake of Enron's collapse, Conway decided to reverse the accounting maneuver. In 2002, PeopleSoft paid $90 million to buy back Momentum, ending a convenience that had turned into controversy.

Conway's discipline and resulting changes helped PeopleSoft weather the prolonged tech market downturn better than many other technology companies. Its stock dropped only 50 percent when others dropped 80 or 90 percent, and the company made it through 2002 without laying off a single employee. With a renewed product offering and a stable accounting foundation, Conway and PeopleSoft were ready to face the future again.[1]

The Nature of Accounting

As Craig Conway knows, it's difficult to manage a business today without accurate, up-to-date financial information. **Accounting** is the system a business uses to identify, measure, and communicate financial information to others, inside and outside the organization. Financial information is important to businesses such as PeopleSoft for two reasons: First, it helps managers and owners plan and control a company's operation and make informed business decisions. Second, it helps outsiders evaluate a business. Suppliers, banks, and other lenders want to know whether a business is creditworthy; investors and shareholders are concerned with a company's profit potential; government agencies are interested in a business's tax accounting.

Because outsiders and insiders use accounting information for different purposes, accounting has two distinct facets. **Financial accounting** is concerned with preparing financial statements and other information for outsiders such as stockholders and *creditors* (people or organizations that have lent a company money or have extended them credit); **management accounting** is concerned with preparing cost analyses, profitability reports, budgets, and other information for insiders such as management and other company decision makers. Regardless of who is using the information or why, all accounting information must be accurate, objective, consistent over time, and comparable to information supplied by other companies.

What Accountants Do

Some people confuse the work accountants do with **bookkeeping**, which is the clerical function of recording the economic activities of a business. Although some accountants do perform bookkeeping functions, their work generally goes well beyond the scope of this activity. Accountants design accounting systems, prepare financial statements, analyze and interpret financial information, prepare financial forecasts and budgets, and prepare tax returns. In addition to traditional accounting work, many accountants analyze and interpret company information, help improve business processes, plan for the future, evaluate product performance, analyze profitability by customer and product groups, design and install new computer systems, assist companies with decision making, and provide a variety of other management consulting services. Performing these functions requires a strong business background and a variety of business skills beyond accounting (see Exhibit 16.1).

Some accountants specialize in certain areas of accounting, such as **cost accounting** (computing and analyzing pro-

Accountants perform a variety of services for their clients beyond tax preparation and auditing. Many serve on strategic planning teams and help companies plan for the future.

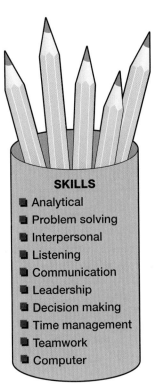

SKILLS
- ■ Analytical
- ■ Problem solving
- ■ Interpersonal
- ■ Listening
- ■ Communication
- ■ Leadership
- ■ Decision making
- ■ Time management
- ■ Teamwork
- ■ Computer

EXHIBIT 16.1
Ten Most Important Skills for Accountants
Besides having a thorough knowledge of accounting, today's accountants need the right mix of personal and business skills to increase their chances for a successful career.

duction costs), **tax accounting** (preparing tax returns and interpreting tax law), or **financial analysis** (evaluating a company's performance and the financial implications of strategic decisions such as product pricing, employee benefits, and business acquisitions). Regardless of the specific functions performed, accountants are classified into two broad groups: private accountants and public accountants.

Private and Public Accountants   **Private accountants** (sometimes called corporate accountants) work for a business, a government agency (such as the Internal Revenue Service, a school, or a local police department), or a nonprofit corporation (such as a church, charity, or hospital).[2] Private accountants generally work together as a team under the supervision of the organization's **controller**, who reports to the vice president of finance. Exhibit 16.2 shows the typical finance department of a large company. In smaller organizations, the controller may be in charge of the company's entire finance operation and report directly to the president.

Public accountants, by contrast, are independent of the businesses, organizations, and individuals they serve. Most public accountants are employed by public accounting firms that provide a variety of accounting and auditing services to their clients. Members of the firm generally are CPAs and must obtain CPA and state licensing certifications to be eligible to conduct an audit.

To become a **certified public accountant (CPA)**, an accountant must pass a rigorous state-certified licensing exam. Eligibility requirements to sit for the exam are strict. Candidates must first complete the equivalent of 150 semester hours of education at an accredited college or university, specific courses, and a number of other requirements specified by the licensing state.[3] Many private accountants are CPAs, but a growing number are becoming **certified management accountants (CMAs)**. To become a CMA, you must pass a four-part exam (given by the Institute of Management Accountants) that is comparable in scope and difficulty to the CPA exam.[4] However, eligibility requirements to take the CMA exam are not as strict as those for the CPA exam.

A study by the American Institute of Certified Public Accountants (AICPA) reported that from 1990 to 2000, the percentage of college students majoring in accounting dropped

tax accounting
Area of accounting focusing on tax preparation and tax planning

financial analysis
Process of evaluating a company's performance and analyzing the costs and benefits of a strategic action

private accountants
In-house accountants employed by organizations and businesses other than a public accounting firm; also called corporate accountants

controller
Highest-ranking accountant in a company, responsible for overseeing all accounting functions

public accountants
Professionals who provide accounting services to other businesses and individuals for a fee

certified public accountant (CPA)
Professionally licensed accountant who meets certain requirements for education and experience and who passes a comprehensive examination

certified management accountants (CMAs)
Accountants who have fulfilled the requirements for certification as specialists in management accounting

EXHIBIT 16.2 Typical Finance Department
Here is a typical finance department of a large company. In smaller companies, the controller may be the highest-ranking accountant and report directly to the president.

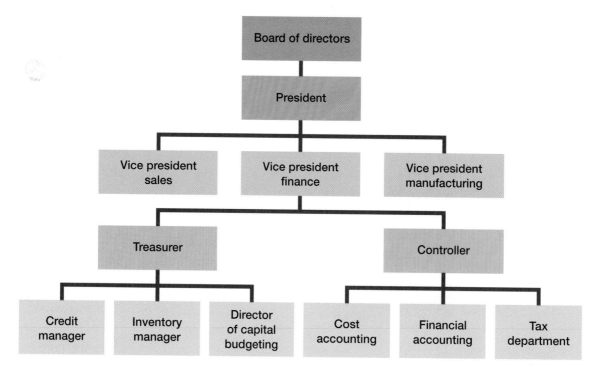

from 4 percent to 2 percent.[5] Some attribute this decline to new stricter eligibility requirements imposed by state licensing agencies on CPA candidates, such as the increased course requirement from 120 to 150 semester-hours and the requirement to take specific courses within those hours. To meet these stricter requirements, accounting students must stay in school one additional year—something that many students can't afford or are not willing to do. Nonetheless, the downward trend of students electing to major in accounting is especially troublesome for public accounting firms, which rely on a steady stream of newly licensed CPAs to assist with audits.

Auditors Companies whose stock (ownership shares) is publicly traded in the United States are required to file quarterly financial statements and audited annual reports with the SEC. An **audit** is a formal evaluation of a company's accounting records and processes to ensure the integrity and reliability of a company's financial statements. An independent audit serves to give stockholders confidence in the company's operations and its management. Many people, such as creditors, shareholders, investors, and government agencies, rely on the integrity of a company's financial statements and place great trust and confidence in the independence of auditors whose detached position allows them to be objective and, when necessary, critical.

During an audit, CPAs who work for an independent accounting firm (also known as *external* auditors) review a client's financial records to determine whether the statements that summarize these records have been prepared in accordance with **generally accepted accounting principles (GAAP)**, basic accounting standards and procedures that have been agreed on by regulators, auditors, and companies over decades. GAAP aims to give a fair and true picture of a company's financial position.

Once the auditors have completed an audit, they report their findings to the company's management, board of directors, and stockholders via an audit report included in the company's published annual report. Audit reports must be signed by an independent auditor who is a CPA. Sometimes the audit report discloses information that might materially affect

audit
Formal evaluation of the fairness and reliability of a client's financial statements

generally accepted accounting principles (GAAP)
Professionally approved U.S. standards and practices used by accountants in the preparation of financial statements

the client's financial position, such as the bankruptcy of a major supplier, a large obsolete inventory, costly environmental problems, or questionable accounting practices. Most companies, however, receive a clean audit report, which means that to the best of the auditors' knowledge the company's financial statements are accurate.

To assist with the auditing process, many large organizations employ **internal auditors**—company employees who investigate and evaluate the organization's internal operations and data to determine whether they are accurate and whether they comply with GAAP, federal laws, and industry regulations. This self-checking process is vital to an organization's financial health, but an internal audit is not a substitute for having an independent auditor look things over and render an unbiased opinion.

internal auditors
Employees who analyze and evaluate a company's operations and data to determine their accuracy

The Rules of Accounting

All U.S. public companies such as PeopleSoft must publish their financial statements in accordance with GAAP. This requirement makes it possible for external users to compare the financial results of one company with those of another and to gain a general idea of a firm's relative effectiveness and its standing within a particular industry. In the United States, the Financial Accounting Standards Board (FASB) is responsible for establishing GAAP. Other countries, of course, have similar governing boards, which means that foreign companies such as Nissan or Toyota may report accounting data using rules that are different from those used by U.S. companies such as Ford or General Motors.

Foreign companies that list their securities on a U.S. stock exchange must, however, convert financial statements prepared under foreign accounting rules to GAAP. This requirement ensures that all companies listed on U.S. stock exchanges are on even ground. But it can also create problems for foreign companies. For instance, when Daimler-Benz listed its stock on the New York Stock Exchange in 1993, the company's $102 million profit changed to a $579 million loss for the same period because of a difference between German accounting rules and U.S. GAAP.[6]

Recent proposals to develop a uniform set of global accounting rules known as International Accounting Standards (IAS) could help eliminate such differences and simplify the bookkeeping process for multinational companies. Most European Union companies have adopted the International Accounting Standards, but such global rules are meeting strong resistance from the U.S. Securities and Exchange Commission (SEC) and other regulators.[7]

How Strict Is GAAP?   GAAP sets forth the principles and guidelines that companies and accountants must follow when preparing financial reports or recording accounting transactions (which we will discuss later in this chapter). But, as with any rules, GAAP can be interpreted aggressively or conservatively. In other words, the rules give executives the freedom to use their judgment in areas that can dramatically affect the company's bottom line without breaking any rules. Unfortunately, some companies take advantage of this flexibility by resorting to a number of accounting tricks that overstate expenses, puff up income, and hide problems from the public.

Recently, some of the nation's brightest executives have been caught lying about the financial status of their company after they tried to cover their lies by restating the company's profit and loss in subsequent years. Over 900 accounting restatements were reported during the five-year period ending 2002—that's more than the total number of restatements reported in previous accounting history.[8]

WorldCom is one such company that used accounting trickery. In June 2002 the SEC accused WorldCom of fraud after the telecommunications giant revealed that it had concealed $3.8 billion in expenses, allowing the company to report a $1.5 billion profit for a five-quarter period when, in fact, the company actually suffered a loss. Coming fast on the heels of the Enron scandal, WorldCom's disclosure further jolted the public's already

Thinking About Ethics

Where Were the Auditors?

Where were the auditors when nearly $2 billion in revenue disappeared at Xerox Corp., more than $3.8 billion in expenses were wiped out at WorldCom, and over $1.2 billion in shareholders' equity vaporized at Enron? Why did auditors give a clean bill of health to 42 percent of the 228 publicly traded companies that filed for Chapter 11 bankruptcy-court protection during the first 18 months of the new millennium? These are questions that lawmakers, stakeholders, and accountants hope to soon resolve.

Auditors maintain that in many cases it's impossible to detect deliberately misleading bookkeeping, and it's unfair to hold them accountable when they don't spot the trickery. An auditor "cannot provide 100 percent guarantee against fraud," says Chuck Landes, director of auditing for the AICPA, although statistics show that auditors do a good job. Of more than 15,000 public companies examined by auditors every year, only 0.1 percent of the audits fail. But the price of those few failures is high. The Sunbeam, Waste Management, Enron, Global Crossing, Qwest, and WorldCom scandals have cost investors more than $300 billion and have put tens of thousands of people out of work.

Some experts link the rise in bad corporate bookkeeping to a change in review methods used by auditing firms. They claim that auditors aren't looking in the right places. In the past, auditors used a labor-intensive process of sifting through thousands of transactions to determine whether bookkeeping entries were correct. Now, auditors focus on analyzing the computerized bookkeeping programs and internal controls that are supposed to prevent errors. The flaw in this approach is that while it prevents low-level employees from swiping petty cash, it doesn't catch the executives who shift millions or billions using creative and manipulative accounting schemes.

Others blame the recent parade of scandals on the conflict of interest that exists when an accounting firm earns millions performing consulting work for an audit client. "If you are auditing your own creations, it is very difficult to criticize them," says one accounting expert. The potential conflict indeed played a role in Enron's demise. The energy giant paid Andersen accountants $27 million in consulting fees and $25 million in audit fees in 2000, while the two maintained an unusually close relationship (see "A Case for Critical Thinking: Consulting Pushes Arthur Andersen Out of Balance").

To curb the potential conflicts of interest, the SEC now requires companies to disclose consulting fees paid to auditors. The SEC has also proposed that accounting firms be banned from directly basing audit partners' compensation on the volume of consulting services they bring into the firm. Meanwhile, several accounting firms have split their consulting operations into separate companies and have sold their technology consulting operations. But some have retained other consulting functions such as tax management, human resources, and merger and acquisition advice. They argue that providing these consulting services helps them learn more about their clients' operations, which makes it more likely they will spot fraud. Others disagree. The debate continues, but this much is certain: Auditing is a vital function upon which free enterprise and the health of the global economy depend. So expect to see some major changes ahead as lawmakers, regulators, and other stakeholders hammer out new ways to restore investor confidence in corporate financial reporting.

Questions for Critical Thinking

1. Should accounting firms be allowed to perform management consulting functions for their audit clients? Why or why not?
2. Why is the auditing function of such vital importance to the global economy? (*Hint:* Think of the outcome of the Enron scandal.)

shaken confidence in the reliability of corporate financial reporting and put pressure on regulators to clamp down on financial wrongdoings. In July 2002 WorldCom filed for bankruptcy court protection.[9]

Of course, no one can calculate how many other companies are resorting to accounting trickery, because such offenses get counted only when companies get caught. What is clear, however, is that in most cases "accounting irregularities don't start with dishonesty; rather they start with pressure for financial performance," says one financial expert.[10] Such pressure comes from employee-shareholders whose life savings are invested in company stock, executives whose bonuses are tied to a company's bottom line, and financial managers who must meet Wall Street estimates or pump up a company's stock price.

The Changes Ahead "Accounting is the lifeblood of our capital market systems, and we have great need for improvement," notes former SEC chairman Arthur Leavitt.[11] From outdated rules to lax procedures to multiple loopholes to corporate boards and overseers, "the whole process has failed," he adds.[12]

Hoping to put an end to financial wrongdoings, President George W. Bush signed the Sarbanes-Oxley Act into law in 2002. This act, triggered by the glut of corporate scandals, makes both executives and audit firms liable for claims from shareholders and subject to criminal penalties if the financial condition of a company is misrepresented.

The Sarbanes-Oxley Act is being implemented by the SEC, whose first move was to establish the Public Company Accounting Oversight Board. The board will oversee the audits of the financial statements of public companies and will make decisions about implementing provisions of the act. These decisions include establishing standards for auditing, lawyer conduct, auditor independence, stock analysts, and audit committees. [13]

Companies bend and stretch accounting rules to make their numbers prettier. It's not fraud—it's even legal—but it's deceptive.

Fundamental Accounting Concepts

As pressure mounts for companies to produce cleaner financial statements and to disclose material information promptly, the need increases for all businesspeople—not just accountants—to understand basic accounting concepts. In the following sections we discuss the fundamental accounting concepts, explore the key elements of financial statements, and explain how managers and investors analyze a company's financial statements to make decisions.

In their work with financial data, accountants are guided by three basis concepts: the *fundamental accounting equation*, *double-entry bookkeeping*, and the *matching principle*. Let's take a closer look at each of these concepts.

The Accounting Equation

For thousands of years, businesses and governments have kept records of their **assets**—valuable items they own or lease, such as equipment, cash, land, buildings, inventory, and investments. Claims against those assets are **liabilities**, or what the business owes to its creditors—such as banks and suppliers. For example, when a company borrows money to purchase a building, the lender or creditor has a claim against the company's assets. What remains after liabilities have been deducted from assets is **owners' equity**:

$$Assets - Liabilities = Owners' \ equity$$

Using the principles of algebra, this equation can be restated in a variety of formats. The most common is the simple **accounting equation**, which serves as the framework for the entire accounting process:

$$Assets = Liabilities + Owners' \ equity$$

3 LEARNING OBJECTIVE

State the basic accounting equation, and explain the purpose of double-entry bookkeeping and the matching principle

assets
Any things of value owned or leased by a business

liabilities
Claims against a firm's assets by creditors

owners' equity
Portion of a company's assets that belongs to the owners after obligations to all creditors have been met

accounting equation
Basic accounting equation stating that assets equals liabilities plus owners' equity

Since 1993, Arthur Andersen has been embroiled in a number of accounting scandals. But it was the firm's unusually close ties with Enron that sealed the accounting firm's fate.

This equation suggests that either creditors or owners provide all the assets in a corporation. Think of it this way: If you were starting a new business, you could contribute cash to the company to buy the assets you needed to run your business, you could borrow money from a bank (the creditor), or you could do both. The company's liabilities are placed before owners' equity in the accounting equation because creditors get paid first. After liabilities have been paid, anything left over belongs to the owners or, in the case of a corporation, to the shareholders. As a business engages in economic activity, the dollar amounts and composition of its assets, liabilities, and owners' equity change. However, the equation must always be in balance; in other words, one side of the equation must always equal the other side.

Double-Entry Bookkeeping and the Matching Principle

double-entry bookkeeping
Way of recording financial transactions that requires two entries for every transaction so that the accounting equation is always kept in balance

matching principle
Fundamental principle requiring that expenses incurred in producing revenue be deducted from the revenues they generate during an accounting period

To keep the accounting equation in balance, companies use a **double-entry bookkeeping** system that records every transaction affecting assets, liabilities, or owners' equity. For example, if PeopleSoft purchased a $6,000 computer system on credit, assets would increase by $6,000 (the cost of the system) and liabilities would also increase by $6,000 (the amount the company owes the vendor), keeping the accounting equation in balance. But if PeopleSoft paid cash outright for the equipment (instead of arranging for credit), the company's total assets and total liabilities would not change, because the $6,000 increase in equipment would be offset by an equal $6,000 reduction in cash. In fact, the company would just be switching assets—cash for equipment.

The **matching principle** requires that expenses incurred in producing revenues be deducted from the revenue they generated during the same accounting period. This matching of expenses and revenue is necessary for the company's financial statements to present an accurate picture of the profitability of a business. Accountants match revenue to expenses by adopting the **accrual basis** of accounting, which states that revenue is recognized when you make a sale or provide a service, not when you get paid. Similarly, your expenses are recorded when you receive the benefit of a service or when you use an asset to produce revenue—not when you pay for it. Accrual accounting focuses on the economic substance of the event instead of on the movement of cash. It's a way of recognizing that revenue can be earned either before or after cash is received and that expenses can be incurred when you receive a benefit (such as a shipment of supplies) whether before or after you pay for it.

Differentiate between cash basis and accrual basis accounting

accrual basis
Accounting method in which revenue is recorded when a sale is made and expense is recorded when it is incurred

cash basis
Accounting method in which revenue is recorded when payment is received and expense is recorded when cash is paid

depreciation
Accounting procedure for systematically spreading the cost of a tangible asset over its estimated useful life

If a business runs on a **cash basis**, the company records revenue only when money from the sale is actually received. Your checkbook is an easy-to-understand cash-based accounting system: You record checks at the time of purchase and deposits at the time of receipt. Revenue thus equals cash received, and expenses equal cash paid. The trouble with cash-based accounting, however, is that it can be misleading. You can misrepresent expenses and income by the way you time payments. It's easy to inflate income, for example, by delaying the payment of bills. For that reason, public companies are required to keep their books on an accrual basis.

Depreciation, or the allocation of the cost of a tangible long-term asset over a period of time, is another way that companies match expenses with revenue. During the normal course of business, a company enters into many transactions that benefit more than one accounting period—such as the purchase of buildings, inventory, and equipment. When you buy a piece of real estate or equipment, instead of deducting the entire cost of the item at the time of purchase, you depreciate it, or spread its cost over the asset's useful life (because the asset will likely generate income for years to come). If the company were to expense long-term assets at the time of purchase, the financial performance of the company would be distorted in the year of purchase as well as in all future years when these assets generate revenue.

Financial Statements

An accounting system is made up of thousands of individual transactions—debits and credits to be exact. During the accounting process, sales, purchases, and other transactions are recorded and classified into individual accounts. Once these individual transactions are recorded and then summarized, accountants must review the resulting transaction summaries and adjust or correct all errors or discrepancies before they can **close the books**, or transfer net revenue and expense items to retained earnings. Exhibit 16.3 presents the process for putting all of a company's financial data into standardized formats that can be used for decision making, analysis, and planning. To make sense of these individual transactions, accountants summarize them by preparing financial statements.

Financial statements consist of three separate yet interrelated reports: the *balance sheet*, the *income statement*, and the *statement of cash flows*. Together these statements provide information about an organization's financial strength and ability to meet current obligations, the effectiveness of its sales and collection efforts, and its effectiveness in managing its assets. Organizations and individuals use financial statements to spot opportunities and problems, to make business decisions, and to evaluate a company's past performance, present condition, and future prospects. In sum, they're indispensable.

In the following sections we will examine the financial statements of Computer Central, a company engaged in direct sales and distribution of brand-name personal computers (such as Compaq, Toshiba, and Macintosh) and related computer products (such as software, printer cartridges, and scanners). The company conducts its primary business

close the books
The act of transferring net revenue and expense account balances to retained earnings for the period

EXHIBIT 16.3   The Accounting Process
The traditional printed accounting forms are shown here. Today, nearly all companies use the computer equivalents of these forms.

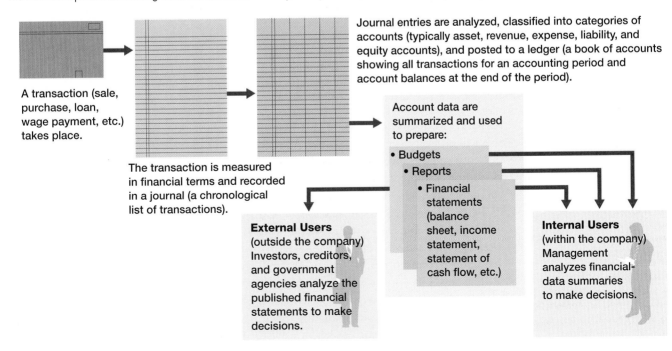

A transaction (sale, purchase, loan, wage payment, etc.) takes place.

The transaction is measured in financial terms and recorded in a journal (a chronological list of transactions).

Journal entries are analyzed, classified into categories of accounts (typically asset, revenue, expense, liability, and equity accounts), and posted to a ledger (a book of accounts showing all transactions for an accounting period and account balances at the end of the period).

Account data are summarized and used to prepare:
• Budgets
  • Reports
    • Financial statements (balance sheet, income statement, statement of cash flow, etc.)

External Users (outside the company) Investors, creditors, and government agencies analyze the published financial statements to make decisions.

Internal Users (within the company) Management analyzes financial-data summaries to make decisions.

from a combined telemarketing, corporate office, warehouse, and showroom facility in Denver, Colorado. There, Computer Central's 600-plus account executives service over 634,000 customers annually. In 2003 the company shipped over 2.3 million orders, amounting to more than $1.7 billion in sales—a 35 percent increase in sales from the previous year. The company's daily sales volume has grown exponentially over the past decade—from $232,000 to $6.8 million. Because of this tremendous growth and the increasing demand for new computer products, the company recently purchased a 276,000-square-foot building. Keep these points in mind as we discuss Computer Central's financial statements in the next sections.

5 LEARNING OBJECTIVE

Explain the purpose of the balance sheet and identify its three main sections

balance sheet
Statement of a firm's financial position on a particular date; also known as a statement of financial position

calendar year
Twelve-month accounting period that begins on January 1 and ends on December 31

fiscal year
Any 12 consecutive months used as an accounting period

current assets
Cash and items that can be turned into cash within one year

fixed assets
Assets retained for long-term use, such as land, buildings, machinery, and equipment; also referred to as property, plant, and equipment

Balance Sheet

The **balance sheet**, also known as the *statement of financial position*, is a snapshot of a company's financial position on a particular date, such as December 31, 2003. In effect, it freezes all business actions and provides a baseline from which a company can measure change. This statement is called a balance sheet because it includes all elements in the accounting equation and shows the balance between assets on one side of the equation and liabilities and owners' equity on the other side. In other words, as in the accounting equation, a change on one side of the balance sheet means changes elsewhere. Exhibit 16.4 is the balance sheet for Computer Central as of December 31, 2003.

In reality, however, no business can stand still while its financial condition is being examined. A business may make hundreds of transactions of various kinds every working day. Even during a holiday, office fixtures grow older and decrease in value, and interest on savings accounts accumulates. Yet the accountant must set up a balance sheet so that managers and other interested parties can evaluate the business's financial position as if it were static, rather than ever-changing.

Every company prepares a balance sheet at least once a year, most often at the end of the **calendar year**, covering from January 1 to December 31. However, many business and government bodies use a **fiscal year**, which may be any 12 consecutive months. For example, a company may use a fiscal year of June 1 to May 31 because its peak selling season ends in May. Its fiscal year would then correspond to its full annual cycle of manufacturing and selling. Some companies prepare a balance sheet more often than once a year, perhaps at the end of each month or quarter. Thus, every balance sheet is dated to show the exact date when the financial snapshot was taken.

By reading a company's balance sheet you should be able to determine the size of the company, the major assets owned, any asset changes that occurred in recent periods, how the company's assets are financed, and any major changes that have occurred in the company's debt and equity in recent periods. Most companies classify assets, liabilities, and owners' equity into categories like those shown in the Computer Central balance sheet.

Assets As discussed earlier in this chapter, an asset is something owned by a company that will be used to generate income. Assets can consist of cash, items that can be converted into cash (such as investments), and equipment needed to make products or to provide services. For example, Computer Central needs a warehouse and a sizable inventory to sell computer products to its customers. Most often, the asset section of the balance sheet is divided into current assets and *fixed assets*. **Current assets** include cash and other items that will or can become cash within the following year. **Fixed assets** (sometimes referred to as *property, plant, and equipment*) are long-term investments in buildings, equipment, furniture and fixtures, transportation equipment, land, and other tangible property used in running the business. Fixed assets have a useful life of more than one year. Computer Central's principal fixed asset is the company's warehouse facility.

Assets are listed in descending order by *liquidity*, or the ease with which they can be converted into cash. Thus, current assets are listed before fixed assets. The balance sheet gives

EXHIBIT 16.4 **Balance Sheet for Computer Central**
The categories used on Computer Central's year-end balance sheet are typical.

Computer Central

Balance Sheet
As of December 31, 2003
(in thousands)

ASSETS

Current Assets
Cash and other items that will or can be converted to cash within one year.

Current Assets		
Cash	$ 4,230	
Marketable Securities	36,458	
Accounts Receivable	158,204	
Inventory	64,392	
Miscellaneous Prepaid and Deferred Items	6,504	
Total Current Assets		**$ 269,788**

Fixed Assets
Long-term investments in buildings, equipment, furniture, and any other tangible property expected to be used in running the business for a period longer than one year.

Fixed Assets		
Property and Equipment	$ 53,188	
Less: Accumulated Depreciation	–16,132	
Total Fixed Assets		**$ 37,056**
Other Assets		4,977
Total Assets		**$311,821**

LIABILITIES AND SHAREHOLDERS' EQUITY

Current Liabilities
Amounts owed by the company that are to be repaid within one year.

Current Liabilities		
Accounts Payable	$ 41,358	
Accrued Expenses	29,700	
Total Current Liabilities		**$ 71,058**

Long-Term Liabilities
Debts that are due a year or more after the date of the balance sheet.

Long-Term Liabilities		
Loans Payable	15,000	
Total Long-Term Liabilities		15,000
Total Liabilities		**$ 86,058**

Shareholders' Equity
Money contributed to the company for ownership interests, as well as the accumulation of profits that have not been paid out as dividends (retained earnings).

Shareholders' Equity		
Common Stock		
(21,571 shares @ $.01 par value)	216	
Less: Treasury Stock (50,000 shares)	–2,089	
Paid-in Capital	81,352	
Retained Earnings	146,284	
Total Shareholders' Equity		**$ 225,763**
Total Liabilities and Shareholders' Equity		**$311,821**

a subtotal for each type of asset and then a grand total for all assets. Computer Central's current assets consist primarily of cash, investments in short-term marketable securities such as money-market funds, accounts receivable (or amounts due from customers), and inventory (such as computers, software, and other items the company sells to customers).

Some companies list an asset called *goodwill* on their balance sheets. This asset refers to the premium one company pays to buy another—specifically, the amount spent for intangible assets such as brand recognition, a loyal customer base, or the assumed value of synergies arising from a merger. The accounting for goodwill has always inspired debate. Under old accounting rules, firms had up to 40 years to write off or amortize goodwill on the theory that its long-term value inevitably deteriorated (amortization is similar to depreciation of a fixed asset under the matching principle). But recent accounting rules state that a company should compute what it thinks goodwill is actually worth annually and expense or write down on the company books the amount of goodwill that exceeds the market valuation. As a result, it's quite common today to find companies announcing large write-offs. One such example is Qwest, a telecommunications company, that took a $30 billion goodwill write-down in 2002 to reflect the evaporated value of its merger with regional telecom company US West.[14]

Liabilities Liabilities come after assets because they represent claims against the company's assets, as shown in the basic accounting equation: *Assets = Liabilities + Owners' equity*. Liabilities may be current or long-term, and they are listed in the order in which they will come due. The balance sheet gives subtotals for **current liabilities** (obligations that will have to be met within one year of the date of the balance sheet) and **long-term liabilities** (obligations that are due one year or more after the date of the balance sheet), and then it gives a grand total for all liabilities.

Current liabilities include accounts payable, short-term financing, and accrued expenses. *Accounts payable* includes the money the company owes its suppliers (such as Compaq and Toshiba) as well as money it owes vendors for miscellaneous services (such as electricity and telephone charges). *Short-term financing* consists of trade credit—the amount owed to suppliers for products purchased but not yet paid for—and commercial paper—short-term promissory notes of major corporations sold in denominations of $100,000 or more, with maturities of up to 270 days (the maximum allowed by the SEC without registration). *Accrued expenses* are expenses that have been incurred but for which bills have not yet been received. For example, because Computer Central's account executives earn commissions on computer sales to customers, the company has a liability to its account executives once the sale is made—regardless of when a check is issued to the employee. Thus, the company must record this liability because it represents a claim against company assets. If such expenses and their associated liabilities were not recorded, the company's financial statements would be misleading and would violate the matching principle (because the commission expenses that were earned at the time of sale would not be matched to the revenue generated from the sale).

Long-term liabilities include loans, leases, and bonds. As Chapter 17 will point out, bank loans may be secured or unsecured. The borrowing company makes principal and interest payments to the bank over the term of the loan, and its obligation is limited to these payments. Leases are an alternative to loans. Rather than borrowing money to buy a piece of equipment, a firm may enter into a long-term **lease**, under which the owner of an item allows another party to use it in exchange for regular payments. Bonds are certificates that obligate the company to repay a certain sum, plus

current liabilities
Obligations that must be met within a year

long-term liabilities
Obligations that fall due more than a year from the date of the balance sheet

lease
Legal agreement that obligates the user of an asset to make payments to the owner of the asset in exchange for using it

Businesses rely on bank loans as a chief source of long-term financing. Here, bankers review a company's financial statements to determine if the firm is creditworthy.

interest, to the bondholder on a specific date. Bonds are traded on organized securities exchanges and are discussed in detail in Chapter 18.

Computer Central's long-term liabilities are relatively small for a company its size. In 2003 the company purchased a new $30 million warehouse facility with $15 million in cash it had saved over many years and a five-year, $15 million bank loan. The company invests its excess cash in short-term marketable securities so it can earn interest on these funds until they are needed for future projects.

Owners' Equity   The owners' investment in a business is listed on the balance sheet under owners' equity (or shareholders' equity for a corporation such as Computer Central). Sole proprietorships list owner's equity under the owner's name with the amount (assets minus liabilities). Small partnerships list each partner's share of the business separately, and large partnerships list the total of all partners' shares. Shareholders' equity for a corporation is presented in terms of the amount of common stock that is outstanding, meaning the amount that is in the hands of the shareholders. The combined amount of the assigned or par value of the common stock plus the amount paid over the par value (paid-in capital) represents the shareholders' total investment. Roughly $81 million was paid into the corporation by Computer Central shareholders at the time the company's shares were issued. In 2003 the company repurchased 50,000 shares of the company's own stock in the open market for $948,000. The company will use this *treasury stock* for its employee stock option plan and other general corporate purposes.

Shareholders' equity also includes a corporation's **retained earnings**—the portion of shareholders' equity that is not distributed to its owners in the form of dividends. Computer Central's retained earnings amount to $146 million. The company did not pay dividends. Instead it is building its cash reserves for future asset purchases and to finance future growth.

Income Statement

If the balance sheet is a snapshot, the income statement is a movie. The **income statement** shows an organization's profit performance over a specific period of time, typically one year. It summarizes all **revenues** (or sales), the amounts that have been or are to be received from customers for goods or services delivered to them, and all **expenses**, the costs that have arisen in generating revenues. Expenses and income taxes are then subtracted from revenues to show the actual profit or loss of a company, a figure known as **net income**—profit, or the *bottom line*. By briefly reviewing a company's income statements you should have a general sense of the company's size, its trend in sales, its major expenses, and the resulting net income or loss. Owners, creditors, and investors can evaluate the company's past performance and future prospects by comparing net income for one year with net income for previous years. Exhibit 16.5 is the 2003 income statement for Computer Central, showing net income of almost $66 million. This is a 32 percent increase over the company's net income of $50 million for the previous year.

Expenses, the costs of doing business, include both the direct costs associated with creating or purchasing products for sale and the indirect costs associated with operating the business. Whether a company manufactures or purchases its inventory, the cost of storing the product for sale (such as heating the warehouse, paying the rent, and buying insurance on the storage facility) is added to the difference between the cost of the beginning inventory and the cost of the ending inventory in order to compute the actual cost of items that were sold during a period—or the **cost of goods sold.** The computation can be summarized as follows:

Cost of goods sold = Beginning inventory + Net purchases − Ending inventory

As shown in Exhibit 16.5, the cost of goods sold is deducted from sales to obtain a company's **gross profit**—a key figure used in financial statement analysis. In addition to the costs directly associated with producing goods, companies deduct **operating expenses**, which

EXHIBIT 16.5   Income Statement for Computer Central
An income statement summarizes the company's financial operations over a particular accounting period, usually a year.

Revenues
Funds received from sales of goods and services to customers as well as other items such as rent, interest, and dividends. Net sales are gross sales less returns and allowances.

Cost of Goods Sold
Cost of merchandise or services that generate a company's income by adding purchases to beginning inventory and then subtracting ending inventory.

Operating Expenses
Generally classified as selling and general expenses. Selling expenses are those incurred through the marketing and distributing of the company's products. General expenses are operating expenses incurred in the overall administration of a business.

Net Income After Taxes
Profit or loss over a specific period determined by subtracting all expenses and taxes from revenues.

Computer Central

Income Statement
Year ended December 31, 2003
(in thousands)

Revenues		
Gross Sales	$1,991,489	
Less Sales Returns and Allowances	−258,000	
Net Sales		$1,733,489
Cost of Goods Sold		
Beginning Inventory	$ 61,941	
Add: Purchases During the Year	1,515,765	
Cost of Goods Available for Sale	−1,577,706	
Less: Ending Inventory	64,392	
Total Cost of Goods Sold		−1,513,314
Gross Profit		$ 220,175
Operating Expenses		
Selling Expenses	$ 75,523	
General Expenses	40,014	
Total Operating Expenses		115,537
Net Operating Income (Gross Profit Less Operating Expenses)		104,638
Other Income		4,373
Net Income Before Income Taxes		109,011
Less: Income Taxes		−43,170
Net Income After Taxes		**$ 65,841**

---

selling expenses
All the operating expenses associated with marketing goods or services

general expenses
Operating expenses, such as office and administrative expenses, not directly associated with creating or marketing a good or a service

7 LEARNING OBJECTIVE

Explain the purpose of the statement of cash flows

statement of cash flows
Statement of a firm's cash receipts and cash payments that presents information on its sources and uses of cash

include both *selling expenses* and *general expenses*, to compute a firm's *net operating income*, or the income that is generated from business operations. **Selling expenses** are operating expenses incurred through marketing and distributing the product (such as wages or salaries of salespeople, advertising, supplies, insurance for the sales operation, depreciation for the store and sales equipment, and other sales department expenses such as telephone charges). **General expenses** are operating expenses incurred in the overall administration of a business. They include professional services (accounting and legal fees), office salaries, depreciation of office equipment, insurance for office operations, supplies, and so on.

A firm's net operating income is then adjusted by the amount of any nonoperating income or expense items such as the gain or loss on the sale of a building. The result is the firm's net income or loss before income taxes (losses are shown in parentheses), a key figure used in budgeting, cash flow analysis, and a variety of other financial computations. Finally, income taxes are deducted to compute the company's net income or loss for the period.

Statement of Cash Flows

In addition to preparing a balance sheet and an income statement, all public companies and many privately owned companies prepare a **statement of cash flows** to show how much cash the company generated over time and where it went (see Exhibit 16.6). The statement of cash flows tracks the cash coming into and flowing out of a company's bank accounts. It

EXHIBIT 16.6 Statement of Cash Flows for Computer Central
A statement of cash flows shows a firm's cash receipts and cash payments as a result of three main activities—operating, investing, and financing—for a period of time.

Cash flows from operations
How much cash a company's business generates or uses contains clues to how healthy earnings are. Most companies start with net income from the income statement and detail items that cause income to differ from cash.

Cash flows from investments
Cash used to buy or received from selling stock, assets, and businesses, plus capital expenditures.

Cash flows from financing
Cash from or paid to outsiders—such as banks or stockholders. If positive, the company relied on outsiders for funds. If negative, the company may have paid down debt or bought back stock.

Computer Central
Statement of Cash Flows
Year ended December 31, 2003
(in thousands)

Cash Flows from Operating Activities*:		
Net Income	$ 65,841	
Adjustments to Reconcile Net Income to Net Cash Provided by Operating Activities	−61,317	
Net Cash Provided by or Used in Operating Activities		$ 4,524
Cash Flows from Investing Activities:		
Purchase of Property and Equipment	−30,110	
Purchase of Securities	−114,932	
Redemptions of Securities	112,463	
Net Cash Provided by or Used in Operating Activities		−32,579
Cash Flows from Financing Activities		
Loan Proceeds	15,000	
Purchase of Treasury Stock	−2,089	
Proceeds from Exercise of Stock Options	1,141	
Net Cash Provided by or Used in Financing Activities		14,052
Net (Decrease) Increase in Cash		−14,003
Cash and Cash Equivalents at Beginning of Year		$18,233
Cash and Cash Equivalents at End of Year		$ 4,230

* Note: Numbers preceded by minus sign indicate cash outflows

reveals the increase or decrease in the company's cash for the period and summarizes (by category) the sources of that change. From a brief review of this statement you should have a general sense of the amount of cash created or consumed by daily operations, the amount of cash invested in fixed or other assets, the amount of debt borrowed or repaid, and the proceeds from the sale of stock or payments for dividends. In addition, an analysis of cash flows provides a good idea of a company's ability to pay its short-term obligations when they become due.

As Exhibit 16.6 shows, the cash flow statement is organized into three parts. Computer Central's statement of cash flows shows that the company used $15 million of its cash reserves and the proceeds of a $15 million bank loan in 2003 to pay for its new facility.

Financial Analysis

Once financial statements have been prepared, managers and outsiders use these statements to evaluate the financial health of the organization, make business decisions, and spot opportunities for improvements by looking at the company's performance in relation to its past performance, the economy as a whole, and the performance of its competitors.

Trend Analysis

The process of comparing financial data from year to year in order to see how they have changed is known as *trend analysis*. You can use trend analysis to uncover shifts in the nature of the business over time. Most large companies provide data for trend analysis in their annual reports. Their balance sheets and income statements typically show three to five years or more of data (making comparative statement analysis possible). Changes in other key items—such as revenues, income, earnings per share, and dividends per share—are usually presented in tables and graphs.

Of course, when you are comparing one period with another, it's important to take into account the effects of extraordinary or unusual items such as the sale of major assets, the purchase of a new line of products from another company, weather, or economic conditions that may have affected the company in one period but not the next. These extraordinary items are usually disclosed in the text portion of a company's annual report or in the notes to the financial statements.

Ratio Analysis

8 **LEARNING OBJECTIVE**

Explain the purpose of ratio analysis, and list the four main categories of financial ratios

ratio analysis
Use of quantitative measures to evaluate a firm's financial performance

Managers and others compute financial ratios to facilitate the comparison of one company's financial results with those of competing firms and with industry averages. **Ratio analysis** compares two elements from the same year's financial figures. These statistics are called *ratios* because they are computed by dividing one element of a financial statement by another. The advantage of using ratios is that it puts companies on the same footing; that is, it makes it possible to compare different-size companies and changing dollar amounts. For example, by using ratios, you can easily compare a large supermarket's ability to generate profit out of sales with a similar statistic for a small grocery store.

The benefit of converting numbers into ratios can be explained by the following example: Suppose you wanted to know how well your favorite baseball player is performing this year. To find out, you would check the player's statistics—batting average, runs batted in (RBIs), hits, and home runs. In other words, you would look at data that have been arranged into meaningful statistics that allow you to compare present performance with past performance and with the performance of other players in the league. Financial ratios do the same thing. They convert the raw numbers from the current and previous years' financial statements into ratios that highlight important relationships or measures of performance.[15]

Just as baseball statistics focus on various aspects of performance (such as hitting or pitching), financial ratios help companies understand their current operations and answer key questions: Is inventory too large? Are credit customers paying too slowly? Can the company pay its bills? Ratios also set standards and benchmarks for gauging future business by comparing a company's scores with industry averages that show the performance of competition. Every industry tends to have its own "normal" ratios, which act as yardsticks for individual companies. Dun and Bradstreet, a credit rating firm, and Robert Morris Associates publish both average financial figures and ratios for a variety of industries and company sizes.

Before reviewing specific ratios, consider two rules of thumb: First, avoid drawing too strong a conclusion from any one ratio. For instance, even with a low batting average, a baseball player's RBIs may prove valuable in the team's lineup. Second, once ratios have presented a general indication, refer back to the specific data involved to see whether the numbers confirm what the ratios suggest. In other words, do a little investigating, because statistics can be misleading. For example, a baseball player who has been at bat only two times and has one hit has a batting average of .500.

Financial ratios can be organized into the following groups, as Exhibit 16.7 shows: profitability, liquidity, activity, and leverage (or debt).

EXHIBIT 16.7 How Well Does This Company Stack Up?
Nearly all companies use ratios to evaluate how well the company is performing in relation to previous performance, the economy as a whole, and the company's competitors.

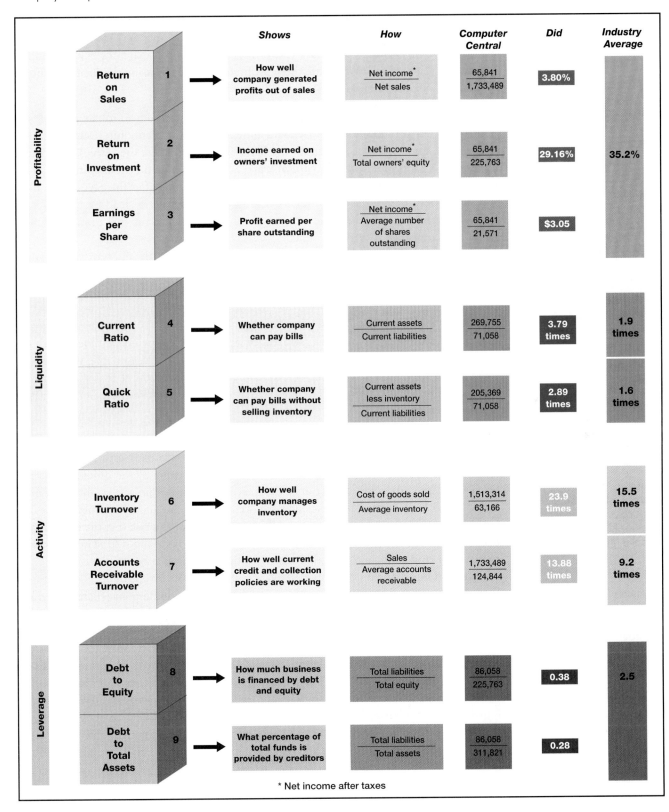

		Shows	How	Computer Central	Did	Industry Average
Profitability	Return on Sales 1	How well company generated profits out of sales	Net income* / Net sales	65,841 / 1,733,489	3.80%	35.2%
	Return on Investment 2	Income earned on owners' investment	Net income* / Total owners' equity	65,841 / 225,763	29.16%	
	Earnings per Share 3	Profit earned per share outstanding	Net income* / Average number of shares outstanding	65,841 / 21,571	$3.05	
Liquidity	Current Ratio 4	Whether company can pay bills	Current assets / Current liabilities	269,755 / 71,058	3.79 times	1.9 times
	Quick Ratio 5	Whether company can pay bills without selling inventory	Current assets less inventory / Current liabilities	205,369 / 71,058	2.89 times	1.6 times
Activity	Inventory Turnover 6	How well company manages inventory	Cost of goods sold / Average inventory	1,513,314 / 63,166	23.9 times	15.5 times
	Accounts Receivable Turnover 7	How well current credit and collection policies are working	Sales / Average accounts receivable	1,733,489 / 124,844	13.88 times	9.2 times
Leverage	Debt to Equity 8	How much business is financed by debt and equity	Total liabilities / Total equity	86,058 / 225,763	0.38	2.5
	Debt to Total Assets 9	What percentage of total funds is provided by creditors	Total liabilities / Total assets	86,058 / 311,821	0.28	

* Net income after taxes

profitability ratios
Ratios that measure the overall financial performance of a firm

return on sales
Ratio between net income after taxes and net sales; also known as profit margin

return on investment (ROI)
Ratio between net income after taxes and total owners' equity; also known as return on equity

earnings per share
Measure of a firm's profitability for each share of outstanding stock, calculated by dividing net income after taxes by the average number of shares of common stock outstanding

liquidity ratios
Ratios that measure a firm's ability to meet its short-term obligations when they are due

working capital
Current assets minus current liabilities

current ratio
Measure of a firm's short-term liquidity, calculated by dividing current assets by current liabilities

quick ratio
Measure of a firm's short-term liquidity, calculated by adding cash, marketable securities, and receivables, then dividing that sum by current liabilities; also known as the acid-test ratio

activity ratios
Ratios that measure the effectiveness of the firm's use of its resources

inventory turnover ratio
Measure of the time a company takes to turn its inventory into sales, calculated by dividing cost of goods sold by the average value of inventory for a period

accounts receivable turnover ratio
Measure of time a company takes to turn its accounts receivable into cash, calculated by dividing sales by the average value of accounts receivable for a period

Profitability Ratios   You can analyze how well a company is conducting its ongoing operations by computing **profitability ratios**, which show the state of the company's financial performance or how well it's generating profits. Three of the most common profitability ratios are **return on sales**, or profit margin (the net income a business makes per unit of sales); **return on investment (ROI)**, or return on equity (the income earned on the owner's investment); and **earnings per share** (the profit earned for each share of stock outstanding). Exhibit 16.7 shows how to compute these profitability ratios by using the financial information from Computer Central.

Liquidity Ratios   **Liquidity ratios** measure the ability of the firm to pay its short-term obligations. As you might expect, lenders and creditors are keenly interested in liquidity measures. Liquidity can be judged on the basis of *working capital*, the *current ratio*, and the *quick ratio*. A company's **working capital** (current assets minus current liabilities) is an indicator of liquidity because it represents current assets remaining after the payment of all current liabilities. The dollar amount of working capital can be misleading, however. For example, it may include the value of slow-moving inventory items that cannot be used to help pay a company's short-term debts.

A different picture of the company's liquidity is provided by the **current ratio**—current assets divided by current liabilities. This figure compares the current debt owed with the current assets available to pay that debt. The **quick ratio**, also called the *acid-test ratio*, is computed by subtracting inventory from current assets and then dividing the result by current liabilities. This ratio is often a better indicator of a firm's ability to pay creditors than the current ratio because the quick ratio leaves out inventories—which at times can be difficult to sell. Analysts generally consider a quick ratio of 1.0 to be reasonable, whereas a current ratio of 2.0 is considered a safe risk for short-term credit. Exhibit 16.7 shows that both the current and quick ratios of Computer Central are well above these benchmarks and industry averages.

Activity Ratios   A number of **activity ratios** may be used to analyze how well a company is managing its assets. The most common is the **inventory turnover ratio**, which measures how fast a company's inventory is turned into sales; in general, the quicker the better, because holding excess inventory can be expensive. When inventory sits on the shelf, money is tied up without earning interest; furthermore, the company incurs expenses for its storage, handling, insurance, and taxes. In addition, there is always a risk that the inventory will become obsolete before it can be converted into finished goods and sold. The firm's goal is to maintain enough inventory to fill orders in a timely fashion at the lowest cost.

Keep in mind that it's difficult to judge a company by its inventory level. For example, lower inventories might mean one of many things: You're running an efficient operation, the right inventory is not being stocked, or sales are booming and you need to increase your orders. Likewise, higher inventories could signal a decline in sales, careless ordering, or stocking up because of favorable pricing. The "ideal" turnover ratio varies with the type of operation. In 2003 Computer Central turned over its inventory 23.9 times (see Exhibit 16.7). This rate is unusually high when compared with industry averages, and it suggests that the company stocks only enough inventory to fill current orders and cover a product's reorder time, as discussed in Chapter 8.

Another popular activity ratio is the **accounts receivable turnover ratio**, which measures how well a company's credit and collection policies are working by indicating how frequently accounts receivable are converted to cash. The volume of receivables outstanding depends on the financial manager's decisions regarding several issues, such as who qualifies for credit and who does not, how long customers are given to pay their bills, and how aggressive the firm is in collecting its debts. Be careful here as well. If the ratio is going up, you need to determine whether the company is doing a better job of collecting or whether sales are rising. If the ratio is going down, it may be because sales are decreasing or because

Managing in the 21st Century

How to Read an Annual Report

Whether you're thinking of investing in companies, becoming a supplier for them, or applying for a job with them, you'll need to know how to read annual reports in your career. Thus, it's worth your while to consider the advice of *Newsweek* columnist Jane Bryant Quinn, who provides these pointers.

Read the Letters

First, turn to the report of the certified public accountant. This third-party auditor will tell you right off the bat if the report conforms with generally accepted accounting principles. Now turn to the letter from the chairman. This letter should tell you how the company fared this year, but more important, the letter should tell you why. Keep an eye out for sentences that start with "Except for . . . " and "Despite the . . . " They're clues to problems. The chairman's letter should also give you insights into the company's future. For example, look for what's new in each line of business. Is management getting the company in good shape to weather the tough and competitive years ahead?

Dig into the Numbers

Check out the trend in the company's working capital (the difference between current assets and current liabilities). If working capital is shrinking, it could mean trouble. One possibility: The company may not be able to keep dividends growing rapidly.

Another important number to analyze is earnings per share. Management can boost earnings by selling off a plant or by cutting the budget for research and advertising. See the footnotes; they often tell the whole story. If earnings are down only because of a change in account-

ing, maybe that's good! The company owes less tax and has more money in its pocket. If earnings are up, maybe that's bad. They may be up because of a special windfall that won't happen again next year. One good indicator is the trend in net sales. If sales increases are starting to slow, the company may be in trouble.

Get Out Your Calculator and Compare

High and rising debt, relative to equity, may be no problem for a growing business. But it shows weakness in a company that's leveling out. So get out your calculator and divide long-term liabilities by shareholders' equity. That's the debt-to-equity ratio. A high ratio means the company borrows a lot of money to fund its growth. That's okay, if sales grow too, and if there's enough cash on hand to meet the payments. But if sales fall, watch out. The whole enterprise may slowly sink.

Remember, one ratio, one annual report, one chairman's letter won't tell you much. You have to compare. Is the company's debt-to-equity ratio better or worse than it used to be? Better or worse than the industry norms? In company-watching, comparisons are all. They tell you if management is staying on top of things.

Questions for Critical Thinking

1. Why might a job seeker want to read a company's annual report before applying for a job with that company?
2. What types of valuable nonfinancial information might an annual report disclose to a potential supplier?

---

collection efforts are sagging, as they were at PeopleSoft. In 2003 Computer Central turned over its accounts receivable 13.88 times—considerably higher than the industry average (see Exhibit 16.7).

Leverage, or Debt, Ratios You can measure a company's ability to pay its long-term debts by calculating its **debt ratios**, or leverage ratios. Lenders look at these ratios to determine whether the potential borrower has put enough money into the business to serve as a protective cushion for the loan. The **debt-to-equity ratio** (total liabilities divided by total equity) indicates the extent to which a business is financed by debt, as opposed to invested capital (equity). From the lender's standpoint, the lower this ratio, the safer the company, because the company has less existing debt and may be able to repay additional money it

debt ratios
Ratios that measure a firm's reliance on debt financing of its operations (sometimes called leverage ratios)

debt-to-equity ratio
Measure of the extent to which a business is financed by debt as opposed to invested capital, calculated by dividing the company's total liabilities by owners' equity

wants to borrow. However, a company that is conservative in its long-term borrowing is not necessarily well managed; often a low level of debt is associated with a low growth rate. Computer Central's low debt-to-equity ratio of 38 percent (as shown in Exhibit 16.7) reflects the company's practice of financing its growth by using excess cash flow from operations and by selling shares of common stock to the public.

debt-to-total-assets ratio
Measure of a firm's ability to carry long-term debt, calculated by dividing total liabilities by total assets

The **debt-to-total-assets ratio** (total liabilities divided by total assets) also serves as a simple measure of a company's ability to carry long-term debt. As a rule of thumb, the amount of debt should not exceed 50 percent of the value of total assets. For Computer Central, this ratio is a very low 28 percent and again reflects the company's policy of using retained earnings to finance its growth (see Exhibit 16.7). However, this ratio, too, is not a magic formula. Like grades on a report card, ratios are clues to performance. Managers, creditors, lenders, and investors can use a selection of ratios to get a fairly accurate idea of how a company is doing.

Summary of Learning Objectives

1. **Discuss how managers and outsiders use a company's financial information.**
Managers use financial information to control a company's operations and to make informed business decisions. Outsiders use financial information to evaluate whether a business is creditworthy or a good investment. Specifically, banks want to know if a business is able to pay back a loan; investors want to know if the company is earning a profit; and governments want to be assured the company is paying the proper amount of taxes.

2. **Describe what accountants do.**
Accountants design and install accounting systems, prepare financial statements, analyze and interpret financial information, prepare financial forecasts and budgets, prepare tax returns, interpret tax law, compute and analyze production costs, evaluate a company's performance, and analyze the financial implications of business decisions. In addition to these functions, accountants help managers improve business procedures, plan for the future, evaluate product performance, analyze the firm's profitability, and design and install computer systems. Accountants may be employed by a business or organization or by a public accounting firm. They may pass exams to become certified management accountants (CMAs) or certified public accountants (CPAs). But auditors must be licensed CPAs. Auditors review accounting records and processes to assess whether they conform to GAAP and whether the company's financial statements fairly present the company's financial position and operating results.

3. **State the basic accounting equation, and explain the purpose of double-entry bookkeeping and the matching principle.**
Assets = Liabilities + Owners' equity is the basic accounting equation. Double-entry bookkeeping is a system of recording financial transactions to keep the accounting equation in balance. The matching principle makes sure that expenses incurred in producing revenues are deducted from the revenue they generated during the same accounting period.

4. **Differentiate between cash basis and accrual basis accounting.**
Cash basis accounting recognizes revenue at the time payment is received, whereas accrual basis accounting recognizes revenue at the time of sale, even if payment is not made.

5. **Explain the purpose of the balance sheet and identify its three main sections.**
The balance sheet provides a snapshot of the business at a particular point in time. It shows the size of the company, the major assets owned, how the assets are financed, and the amount of owners' investment in the business. Its three main sections are assets, liabilities, and owners' equity.

6. **Explain the purpose of the income statement.**
The income statement reflects the results of operations over a period of time. It gives a general sense of a company's size and performance.

7. **Explain the purpose of the statement of cash flows.**
The statement of cash flows shows how a company's cash was received and spent in three areas: operations, investments, and financing. It gives a general sense of the amount of cash created or consumed by daily operations, fixed assets, investments, and debt over a period of time.

8. **Explain the purpose of ratio analysis, and list the four main categories of financial ratios.**
Financial ratios provide information for analyzing the health and future prospects of a business. Ratios facilitate financial

comparisons between different-size companies and between a company and industry averages. Most of the important ratios fall into one of four categories: profitability ratios, which show how well the company generates profits; liquidity ratios, which measure the company's ability to pay its short-term obligations; activity ratios, which analyze how well a company is managing its assets; and debt ratios, which measure a company's ability to pay its long-term debt.

KEY TERMS

accounting **(406)**

accounting equation **(411)**

accounts receivable turnover ratio **(422)**

accrual basis **(412)**

activity ratios **(422)**

assets **(411)**

audit **(408)**

balance sheet **(414)**

bookkeeping **(406)**

calendar year **(414)**

cash basis **(412)**

certified management accountants (CMAs) **(407)**

certified public accountant (CPA) **(407)**

close the books **(413)**

controller **(407)**

cost accounting **(406)**

cost of goods sold **(417)**

current assets **(414)**

current liabilities **(416)**

current ratio **(422)**

debt ratios **(423)**

debt-to-equity ratio **(423)**

debt-to-total-assets ratio **(424)**

depreciation **(412)**

double-entry bookkeeping **(412)**

earnings per share **(422)**

expenses **(417)**

financial accounting **(406)**

financial analysis **(407)**

fiscal year **(414)**

fixed assets **(414)**

general expenses **(418)**

generally accepted accounting principles (GAAP) **(408)**

gross profit **(417)**

income statement **(417)**

internal auditors **(409)**

inventory turnover ratio **(422)**

lease **(416)**

liabilities **(411)**

liquidity ratios **(422)**

long-term liabilities **(416)**

management accounting **(406)**

matching principle **(412)**

net income **(417)**

operating expenses **(417)**

owners' equity **(411)**

private accountants **(407)**

profitability ratios **(422)**

public accountants **(407)**

quick ratio **(422)**

ratio analysis **(420)**

retained earnings **(417)**

return on investment (ROI) **(422)**

return on sales **(422)**

revenues **(417)**

selling expenses **(418)**

statement of cash flows **(418)**

tax accounting **(407)**

working capital **(422)**

TEST YOUR KNOWLEDGE

Questions for Review

1. What is the primary difference between a public accountant and a private accountant?

2. What is GAAP?

3. What is an audit, and why is it performed?

4. What is the matching principle?

5. What are the three main profitability ratios, and how is each calculated?

Questions for Analysis

6. Why is accounting important to business?

7. Why do some companies resort to accounting tricks, and what steps are being taken to clamp down on such wrongdoings?

8. Why are the costs of fixed assets depreciated?

9. Why do companies use ratios to analyze financial information?

10. *Ethical Considerations:* In the process of closing the company books, you encounter a problematic transaction. One of the company's customers was charged twice for the same project materials, resulting in a $1,000 overcharge. You immediately notify the controller, whose response is, "Let it go, it happens often." What should you do now?

Questions for Application

11. The senior partner of an accounting firm is looking for ways to increase the firm's business. What other services besides traditional accounting can the firm offer to its clients? What new challenges might this additional work create?

12. Log on to Hoovers website at www.hoovers.com, and click on Companies and Industries. Find and print the annual financials for Ford Motor Company and General Motors Corporation.

Using these financials, compute the working capital, current ratio, and quick ratio for each company. Does one company appear to be more liquid than the other? Why?

13. *Integrated:* Review the Chapter 2 Case for Critical Thinking, "Enron: A Case Study in Unethical Behavior" (see pages 58–59). Then review this chapter's Case for Critical Thinking: "Consulting Pushes Arthur Andersen out of Business." Answer the following question based on your analysis of these two case studies: Why did the Arthur Andersen auditors look the other way—even as warning lights began to flash?

14. *Integrated:* Your appliance manufacturing company recently implemented a just-in-time inventory system (see Chapter 9) for all parts used in the manufacturing process. How might you expect this move to affect the company's inventory turnover rate, current ratio, and quick ratio?

PRACTICE YOUR KNOWLEDGE

Handling Difficult Situations on the Job: Raising Funds for a Nonprofit

For nearly 50 years, New Jersey's nonprofit Morris County Senior Center has relied on financial support from government, businesses, and individuals. Unfortunately, recent state and federal cutbacks have dug into the organization's budget despite the center's growing needs. For many of the county's roughly 1,000 seniors who live alone, it's the only place where they can meet their peers, use a special library, avoid extreme weather, or get a well-balanced meal. Most individuals get to the facility on one of the three shuttle-type buses belonging to the center. The buses are also used for day trips to museums, plays, and similar functions, or to help the temporarily disabled get to doctors' offices or pharmacies.

Unfortunately, each bus is more than eight years old and constant repairs are costing the center an average of $300 per month. When buses aren't working, seniors can't get to the center, trips are canceled, and drivers are sometimes paid for coming to work even though they aren't able to drive. Conservatively, it would cost about $28,000 to replace each van with a new one: $84,000 total, includ-

ing trade-in value on the old buses. Your board of directors believes that buying new vans is a better choice than continuously repairing the old ones or risking the purchase of used ones.

Your task: As director of the center, you'll be drafting a fundraising letter to send to county businesses, seeking donations to pay for the new buses. You'll stress the good work the center does and the fact that this is a special fundraising effort. But what specific financial information should you include in your letter?

Building Your Team Skills

Divide into small groups and compute the following financial ratios for Alpine Manufacturing using the company's Balance Sheet and Income Statement on the facing page. Compare your answers to those of your classmates:

- Profitability ratios: return on sales; return on equity; earning per share
- Liquidity ratios: current ratio; quick ratio
- Activity ratios: inventory turnover; accounts receivable turnover
- Leverage ratios: debt to equity; debt to total assets

EXPAND YOUR KNOWLEDGE

Discovering Career Opportunities

People interested in entering the field of accounting can choose among a wide variety of careers with diverse responsibilities and challenges. Using library sources or the Internet, dig deeper to learn more about what accountants do.

1. What are the day-to-day duties of most accountants? How would these duties contribute to the financial success of a company?

2. What skills and educational qualifications would you need to become an accountant? How do these qualifications fit with your current plans, skills, and interests?

3. What kinds of employers hire people for accounting positions? According to your research, does the number of employers seem to be increasing or decreasing? How do you think this trend will affect your employment possibilities if you choose this career?

Developing Your Research Skills

Select an article from a business journal or newspaper (print or online editions) that discusses the quarterly or year-end performance of a company that industry analysts consider notable for either positive or negative reasons.

1. Did the company report a profit or a loss for this accounting period? What other performance indicators were reported? Did the company's performance improve or decline over previous accounting periods?

2. Did the company's performance match industry analysts' expectations, or was it a surprise? How did analysts or other experts respond to the firm's actual quarterly or year-end results?

3. What reasons were given for the company's improvement or decline in performance?

Alpine Manufacturing
Balance Sheet
As of December 31, 2003

ASSETS

Cash	$ 100
Accounts Receivable (beginning balance $350)	300
Inventory (beginning balance $250)	300
Current Assets	700
Fixed Assets	2,300
Total Assets	**$ 3,000**

LIABILITIES AND SHAREHOLDERS' EQUITY

Current Liabilities (beginning balance $300)	$ 400
Long-Term Debts	1,600
Shareholders' Equity (100 common shares outstanding valued at $12 each)	1,000
Total Liabilities and Shareholders' Equity	**$ 3,000**

Alpine Manufacturing
Income Statement
Year ended December 31, 2003

Sales	$ 1,800
Less: Cost of Goods Sold	1,000
Gross Profit	800
Less: Total Operating Expenses	450
Net Operating Income Before Income Taxes	350
Less: Income Taxes	50
Net Income After Income Taxes	**$ 300**

Exploring the Best of the Web

URLs for all Internet exercises are provided at the website for this book, www.prenhall.com/bovee. *When you log on to the text website, select Chapter 16, then select "Student Resources," click on the name of the featured website, and review the website to complete these exercises.*

Explore these chapter-related websites, review their content, and answer the following questions for each website you visit:

1. What is the purpose of this website?

2. What kinds of information does this website contain? Please be specific.

3. How is the information provided at this website useful for businesspeople? Consumers?

4. How did you expand your knowledge of accounting by reviewing the material at this website? What new things did you learn about this topic?

Link Your Way to the World of Accounting

Looking for one accounting supersite packed with information and links to financial resources? Check out the Electronic Accountant, an online launching point for accountants. This is the place to find answers to all kinds of questions about accounting, financial analysis, taxes, and more. Participate in one of the many focused discussion groups. Visit the niche sites for information on financial planning, practice management, technology consulting, or CPE requirements. Read the latest issues of *Accounting Technology* or the *Practical Accountant.* Don't leave without checking out the Career Center, where you'll find information on the latest accounting hot jobs and opportunities. www.electronicaccountant.com

Sharpen Your Pencil

You never know what you'll find at a gallery these days. How about annual reports—lots of them! Sharpen your pencil and start thinking like an accountant. Take a virtual field trip to the Report

Gallery, where you can click to view the annual reports of Allstate, Boeing, and many other U.S. and international firms. Select an annual report for any company and examine the financial statements, chairman's letter, and auditor's report. Was it a good or bad year for the company? Who are the company's auditors? Did they issue a clean audit report? www.reportgallery.com

Think Like an Accountant

Find out how the world of accounting is changing by exploring the valuable links at CPAnet. Learn about the many facets of accounting such as taxes, finance, auditing, and more. Follow the link to your state CPA society, and discover what it takes to become a CPA or how to prepare for the CPA exam. Learn how to read a financial report, and discover what financial statements say about your business. Check out the financial calculators. Increase your knowledge

of accounting terms and accounting basics before participating in one of the site's discussion forums. CPAnet claims to be a complete resource for the accounting profession. Log on and find out why. www.cpanet.com

Learning Interactively

Companion Website

Visit the Companion Website at www.prenhall.com/bovee. For Chapter 16, take advantage of the interactive "Study Guide" to test your chapter knowledge. Get instant feedback on whether you need additional studying. Read the "Current Events" articles to get the latest on chapter topics, and complete the exercises as specified by your instructor. Expand your learning with a visit to the "Research Area." There you will find a wealth of information you can use to complete your course assignments.

A CASE FOR CRITICAL THINKING

Consulting Pushes Arthur Andersen out of Balance

The descent of accounting firm Arthur Andersen from role model to convicted felon didn't happen overnight. It stemmed from external forces and internal decisions that gradually eroded the company's core values. Founded in 1913 by Arthur Andersen, the firm built its reputation by putting integrity ahead of profits. Its new hires recited the founder's motto, "Think straight, talk straight." And they learned Andersen's four cornerstones: provide good service, produce quality audits, manage staff well, and generate profits.

Assets and Liabilities

As the firm grew from a close-knit partnership to a globe-spanning giant, its auditing services practically sold themselves. Andersen also offered business consulting, but this service was considered secondary to the accounting practice.

In the early 1970s businesses started clamoring for computers, and Andersen was ready: its small consulting practice had been helping clients set up computer systems since 1954. As more clients began using computers to automate bookkeeping, Andersen's consulting practice exploded. It was soon bringing in as much money as the firm's accounting business; meanwhile, however, the rise of computers was driving down the demand for auditing.

As the consulting business grew larger and more profitable, the accountants struggled to retain control of the company. This conflict put a tremendous strain on the partnership, and in 1989 the consultants made their break. The firm separated into two units: Arthur Andersen and Andersen Consulting. Both reported to a new parent company called Andersen Worldwide SC, but under a complex formula, the less profitable unit would receive a share of the other's profits.

Sibling Rivalry

The annual race for profits turned into a brutal internal battle. When efforts to expand the accounting business faltered, the

accountants began offering consulting to audit clients—sometimes competing head-to-head with Andersen Consulting. The accountants couldn't keep pace with their sibling, though, which by 1994 was contributing twice as much revenue to the parent. Worse yet, the separation agreement required Andersen Consulting to subsidize the Arthur Andersen partners by $200 million annually. This understandably upset Andersen Consulting, which in 1997 voted unanimously to sever all ties with the accounting side. The siblings battled for three years over the terms of separation until an arbitrator finally settled the dispute. Andersen Consulting won its freedom but lost the prize it wanted most: the Andersen name. Reborn reluctantly as Accenture, the consultants would soon be glad they had a new name.

Unsettling Settlements

During the separation fight, pressure mounted at Arthur Andersen to make up for the $200 million it was about to lose every year. Auditors were pushed to sell more audit work or to recommend that clients outsource their internal bookkeeping operations to Andersen. Critics of this practice believed such services would damage the firm's integrity because Andersen would in effect be checking its own work.

Ultimately, partners who faced accounting dilemmas with clients had much more at stake when deciding whether to reject questionable practices uncovered by audits. Some fell short of the founder's high standards. In 1997 audit and consulting client Waste Management reported an unprecedented earnings restatement, wiping out $1.7 billion in profits. Securities regulators alleged that Andersen had bent rules so badly that it had committed fraud; Andersen paid $75 million to settle the shareholder suits that followed. In 2001 Andersen paid investors $110 million for its botched 1997 audit of home-appliance maker Sunbeam, and in 2002 the firm paid $10.3 million to settle a shareholders' lawsuit related to audit client Boston Market. But it was Andersen's role in the Enron scandal that sealed the firm's fate.

Paying the Piper

During the 1990s Arthur Andersen formed unusually close ties with energy-trading company Enron, serving as its external auditors, internal auditors, and consultants. Not only did Andersen's staff maintain permanent offices at Enron's headquarters, but Andersen's Houston office became a recruiting pool for Enron. In fact, the hiring became so relentless, Andersen had to cap the number of people Enron could hire away.

In 2001 the scandal surrounding Enron exploded (see Chapter 2, pages 58–59). The U.S. Justice Department rejected Andersen's settlement overtures—citing its repeated offenses—and took the company to court. After a six-week trial, a jury convicted Andersen of federal obstruction of justice for interfering with the Enron investigation. The court imposed the maximum punishment—a $500,000 fine and five years of court monitoring—for obstructing the government's investigation into Enron's collapse. But the fine was just the tip of the iceberg for Andersen.

In the midst of the scandal and trial, audit clients and employees bolted from the firm, to protect their own integrity and seek new relationships before Andersen went under. In the aftermath, the firm surrendered its licenses to practice accounting in every U.S. state, ending its 89-year history. The demise of Arthur Andersen made an indelible mark on the public image of accounting and prompted a tidal wave of reform within the industry.

Critical Thinking Questions

1. How did the growth of consulting services seal Arthur Andersen's fate?
2. How did Arthur Andersen's troubles affect the accounting industry?
3. Why was Andersen Consulting ultimately relieved to have a new name?
4. Visit the AICPA website at www.aicpa.org and review the AICPA Code of Professional Conduct. Which sections of the Code did Arthur Andersen accountants violate in their dealings with clients?

VIDEO CASE

Accounting for Billions of Burgers: McDonald's

Learning Objectives

The purpose of this video is to help you:

1. Understand the challenges a company may face in managing financial information from operations in multiple countries.
2. Consider how management and investors use the financial information reported by a public company.
3. Recognize how differing laws and monetary systems can affect the accounting activities of a global corporation.

Synopsis

Collecting, analyzing, and reporting financial data from 27,000 restaurants in 119 countries is no easy task, as the accounting experts at McDonald's are well aware. Every month, the individual restaurants send their sales figures to be consolidated with data from other restaurants at the local or country level. From there, the figures are sent to country-group offices and then to one of three major regional offices before going to their final destination at the McDonald's headquarters in Oak Brook, Illinois. In the past, financial information arrived in Illinois in bits and pieces, sent by courier, mail, or fax. Today, local and regional offices log onto a special secure website and enter their month-end figures, enabling the corporate controller to quickly produce financial statements and projections for internal and external use.

Discussion Questions

1. *For analysis:* Why does McDonald's use "constant currency" comparisons when reporting its financial results?
2. *For analysis:* What types of assets might McDonald's list for depreciation in its financial statements?
3. *For application:* What effect do the corporate income tax rates in the countries where McDonald's operates have on the income statements prepared in local offices?
4. *For application:* What problems might arise if individual McDonald's restaurants were required to enter sales data directly on the company's centralized accounting website, instead of following the current procedure of sending it through country and regional channels?
5. *For debate:* To help investors and analysts better assess the company's worldwide financial health, should McDonald's be required to disclose detailed financial results for every country and region? Support your chosen position.

Online Exploration

Visit the McDonald's corporate website at www.mcdonalds.com/corporate. Look for the most recent financial report (quarterly or annual), and examine both overall and regional results. What aspects of its results does McDonald's highlight in this report? What does McDonald's say about its use of constant currency reporting? Which regions are doing particularly well? Which are lagging? How does management explain any differences in performance? What does McDonald's say about its use of constant currency reporting?

Financial Management and Banking

1. Identify the responsibilities of a financial manager

2. Discuss how financial managers improve a company's cash flow

3. Differentiate between a master budget and a capital budget

4. Cite three factors financial managers must consider when selecting an appropriate funding vehicle

5. Identify five common types of debt financing

6. Identify three common financial services that banks provide customers, and list electronic banking vehicles that facilitate these services

7. Explain how the U.S. banking industry has evolved

8. Identify four ways the Federal Reserve System influences the U.S. money supply

After years of mismanagement at Bank One, its board of directors looked for a savior. They seem to find it in Jamie Dimon, a back-to-basics manager, who is a brutally tough businessman and unforgiving of failure.

INSIDE BUSINESS TODAY

Bank One's Dimon in the Rough

When Jamie Dimon took over the helm at Bank One in 2000, the Midwestern financial giant was in a heap of trouble. Years of mismanagement and a raft of problems stemming from multiple mergers—including the 1998 merger of Bank One and First Chicago NBD—had turned the nation's sixth-largest bank into a mess. The highly decentralized group of regional banks had no strong central control. Dimon immediately recognized an opportunity. "This was my one big shot," said Dimon, who put his money where his mouth was and purchased $58 million in his new employer's stock. "I just thought I should eat my own home cooking," recalls the former president of Citigroup.

Dimon wasted no time. He immediately whacked 12,000 jobs—on top of the 10,000 already lopped off. Then, he replaced 12 of his top 13 managers, and shaved the board of directors from 20 to 12 members. With a new management team in place, Dimon set out to attack Bank One's problems one at a time.

First he went after problem loans. Dimon discovered that different regions had set their own guidelines for making loans, sewing a crazy quilt of credit standards. Car loans, brokered home-equity loans, and huge corporate credits looked profitable, but no one had really bothered to check to see whether they were making money or to analyze what would happen when a recession inevitably rolled in. So Dimon systematically examined the profitability of each relationship, company by company. He dropped less-profitable customers—those that borrowed money but had no other profitable business with the bank, such as cash-management services. And he established rigorous nationwide credit guidelines for loans. The big loans—$30 million and up—would require approval from a credit committee or top officers. All in all, Dimon shrank Bank One's loan portfolio by 33 percent. By limiting the amount of credit extended to risky businesses, Bank One managed to avoid about $1 billion in losses when the economy started to weaken.

Auto leases were another disaster area. Bank One had amassed an $11 billion car loan portfolio. Managers had predicted that once the leases expired, the bank would resell the cars at an average of $25,000 per vehicle. But Dimon was suspicious. "There were smelly, stinky, old used cars," he fumed, after discovering that used-car prices had dropped 10 percent and the bank had overestimated their value in the first place. To reflect their lower resale value, Dimon booked $757 million in losses and write-downs, and he cut the number of future auto leases by 90 percent.

Finally, Dimon demanded that Bank One accomplish what his troops regarded as impossible: knitting together the hodge-podge of computer systems inherited from a series of poorly integrated mergers. Bank One was running seven deposit systems, three clearing networks, and five wire-transfer platforms. This situation required Bank One to have separate maintenance contracts for each system and to pay a king's ransom in software programming. So Dimon hired a systems-integration wizard to merge the systems, and in doing so saved the company an estimated $200 million annually.

In two short years, Dimon set in motion a dramatic turnaround at Bank One. He pared expenses by some 16 percent and cushioned Bank One from big loan losses that could have pushed it into bankruptcy. Still, Dimon is nowhere close to his goal. Moving to a low-cost, integrated money center could take a decade. "I want to build one of the best financial services companies in America," says Dimon. "Something everybody who works here can be proud of. I've seen a lot of great companies with strategies," he adds. "But if you don't execute, you fail."[1]

The Role of Financial Management

financial management
Effective acquisition and use of money

As Bank One's Jamie Dimon knows, all companies need to pay their bills and still have some money left over to improve the business. Furthermore, a key goal of any business is to increase the value to its owners (and other stakeholders) by making it grow. Maximizing the owner's wealth sounds simple enough: Just sell a good product for more than it costs to make. Before you can earn any revenue, however, you need money to get started. Once the business is off the ground, your need for money continues—whether it's to buy new road repair equipment or to build a new warehouse.

Planning for a firm's current and future money needs is the foundation of **financial management**, or finance. In most smaller companies, the owner is responsible for the firm's financial decisions, whereas in larger operations financial management is the responsibility of the finance department, which reports to a vice president of finance or a chief financial officer (CFO). This department also includes the accounting function. In fact, most financial managers are accountants.

Financial management involves making decisions about alternative sources and uses of funds, with the goal of maximizing a company's value (see Exhibit 17.1). To achieve this goal, financial managers develop and implement a firm's financial plan; monitor a firm's cash flow and decide how to create or use excess funds; budget for current and future expenditures and for capital investments; raise capital to finance the enterprise for future growth; and interact with banks and capital markets. Here's a closer look at these important tasks.

financial plan
A forecast of financial requirements and the financing sources to be used

Developing and Implementing a Financial Plan

One way companies make sure they have enough money is by developing a *financial plan*. Normally in the form of a budget, a **financial plan** is a document that shows the funds a

EXHIBIT 17.1

Sources and Uses of a Company's Funds
Financial management involves finding suitable sources of funds and deciding on the most appropriate uses for those funds.

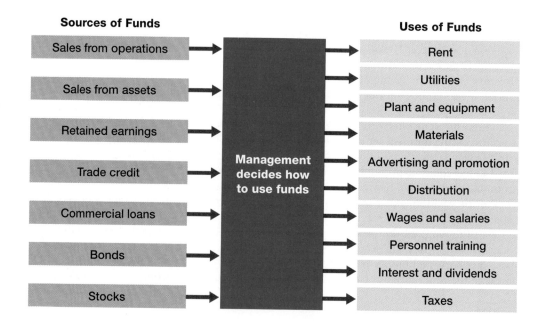

firm will need for a period of time as well as the sources and uses of those funds. An underlying concept of any financial plan is that all money should be used productively. When you prepare a financial plan for a company, you have two objectives: achieving a positive cash flow and efficiently investing excess cash flow to make your company grow. Financial planning requires looking beyond the four walls of the company to answer such questions as: Is the company introducing a new product in the near future or expanding its market? Is the industry growing? Is the national economy declining? Is inflation heating up? Would an investment in new technology improve productivity?

Monitoring Cash Flow   In accounting, income statements are prepared to determine the net income of a firm. In finance, however, the focus is on cash flows. Although the firm's income is important, cash flows are even more important, because cash is necessary to purchase the assets and supplies a company needs to operate and to pay dividends to shareholders. Cash flows are generally related to net income; that is, companies with relatively high accounting profits generally have relatively high cash flows, but the relationship is not precise.

One way financial managers improve a company's cash flow is by monitoring its *working capital accounts:* cash, inventory, accounts receivable, and accounts payable. They use common-sense procedures, such as shrinking collection periods for accounts receivable, dispatching bills on a timely basis without paying bills earlier than necessary, controlling the level of inventory, and investing excess cash.

Managing Accounts Receivable and Accounts Payable   Keeping an eye on *accounts receivable*—the money owed to the firm by its customers—is one way to manage cash flow effectively. The volume of receivables depends on the financial manager's decisions regarding several issues: who qualifies for credit and who does not, how long customers are given to pay their bills, and how aggressive the firm is in collecting its debts. In addition to setting guidelines and policies for handling these issues, the financial manager analyzes the firm's outstanding receivables to identify patterns that might indicate problems and establishes procedures for collecting overdue accounts.

The flip side of managing receivables is managing *payables*—the bills that the company owes to its creditors. Here the objective is generally to postpone paying bills until the last moment, since accounts payable represent interest-free loans from suppliers. However, the financial manager also needs to weigh the advantages of paying promptly if doing so entitles the firm to cash discounts. In addition, paying on time is a good way to maintain the company's credit standing, which in turn influences a lender's decision to approve a loan. Of course, paying bills online is one way to manage cash aggressively and efficiently, as this chapter points out later.

Managing Inventory   Inventory is another area in which financial managers can fine-tune the firm's cash flow. In Chapter 9 we discussed that inventory sitting on the shelf represents capital that is tied up without earning interest. Furthermore, the firm incurs expenses for storage and handling, insurance, and taxes. In addition, there is always the risk that inventory will become obsolete before it can be converted into finished goods and sold. Thus, the firm's goal is to maintain enough inventory to fill orders in a timely fashion at the lowest cost. To achieve this goal, financial managers work with operations managers and marketing managers to determine the *economic order quantity* (EOQ), or quantity of materials that, when ordered regularly, results in

2 LEARNING OBJECTIVE

Discuss how financial managers improve a company's cash flow

Managing cash reserves is especially challenging for a seasonal business such as a major league ballpark. Revenues generated during the months of March through September must be invested to cover year-round expenses, which include stadium maintenance and pre-season start-up costs.

Financial managers help their companies determine how much money they need for operations and for expansion. They're also responsible for identifying the right combination of funding sources at the lowest cost.

the lowest ordering and storage costs. (Inventory control techniques and efficient ordering systems are discussed in Chapter 9.)

Managing Cash Reserves   Sometimes companies find themselves with more cash on hand than they need. A seasonal business may experience a quiet period between the time when revenues are collected from the last busy season and the time when suppliers' bills are due. Department stores, for example, may have excess cash during a few weeks in February and March. A firm may also accumulate cash to meet a large financial commitment in the future or to finance future growth. Using a company's own money instead of borrowing from an outside source such as a bank has one chief attraction: No interest payments are required. Finally, every firm keeps some surplus cash on hand as a cushion in case its needs are greater than expected.

Part of the financial manager's job is to make sure that excess cash is invested so that it earns as much interest as possible. Aggressive financial managers use electronic cash management (the ability to access bank account information online) to move cash between accounts and pay bills on a daily basis; they also invest excess cash on hand in short-term

marketable securities
Stocks, bonds, and other investments that can be turned into cash quickly

investments called **marketable securities**. These interest-bearing or dividend-paying investments include money-market funds or publicly traded stocks such as IBM or Sears. They are said to be "marketable" because they can be easily converted back to cash. Because marketable securities are generally used as contingency funds, however, most financial managers invest these funds in securities of solid companies or the government—ones with the least amount of risk. (Securities are discussed in detail in Chapter 18.)

Budgeting

3 LEARNING OBJECTIVE

Differentiate between a master budget and a capital budget

budget
Planning and control tool that reflects expected revenues, operating expenses, and cash receipts and outlays

In addition to developing a financial plan and monitoring cash flow, financial managers are responsible for developing a **budget**, a financial blueprint for a given period (often one year). Master (or operating) budgets help financial managers estimate the flow of money into and out of the business by structuring financial plans within a framework of a firm's total estimated revenues, expenses, and cash flows. Accountants provide much of the data required for budgets and are important members of the budget development team because they have a complete understanding of the company's operating costs.

The master budget sets a standard for expenditures, provides guidelines for controlling costs, and offers an integrated and detailed plan for the future. For example, by reviewing the budget of any airline, you can determine whether the company plans on increasing its fleet of aircraft, adding more routes, hiring more employees, increasing employees' pay, or continuing or abandoning any discounts for travelers. No wonder companies like to keep their budgets confidential.

financial control
The process of analyzing and adjusting the basic financial plan to correct for forecasted events that do not materialize

Once a budget has been developed, the finance manager compares actual results with projections to discover variances and recommends corrective action—a process known as **financial control**. Companies also periodically adjust their budgets to meet their changing financial needs and goals. Bank One's Jamie Dimon, for example, cut the company's budget for office decorating when he discovered that workers were spending too much money wallpapering the posh corporate offices. "I had just finished telling people I didn't want anyone spending any more money on real estate," recalls Dimon, who then told workers to leave the walls half-beige, half-brown as a reminder of a bygone era.[2]

Capital Budgeting In contrast to operating budgets, capital budgets forecast and plan for a firm's **capital investments** such as major expenditures in buildings or equipment. Capital investments generally cover a period of several years and help the company grow. Before investments can be made, however, a firm must decide on which of the many possible capital investments to make, how to finance those that are undertaken, and even whether to make any capital investments at all. This process is called **capital budgeting**.

The process generally begins by having all divisions within a company submit their capital requests—essentially, "wish lists" of investments that would make the company more profitable and thus more valuable to its owners over time. Next, the financial manager decides which investments need evaluating and which don't. For example, the routine replacement of old equipment probably wouldn't need evaluating; however, the construction of a new manufacturing facility would. Finally, a financial evaluation is performed to determine whether the amount of money required for a particular investment will be greater than, equal to, or less than the amount of revenue it will generate. On the basis of this analysis, the financial manager can determine which projects to recommend to senior management for purchase approval.

Forecasting Capital Requirements As with any poorly made decision, an erroneous forecast of capital requirements can have serious consequences. If the firm invests too much in assets, it will incur unnecessarily heavy expenses. If it does not replace or upgrade existing assets on a regular basis, the assets will likely become obsolete. For example, old manufacturing equipment may be incapable of handling increasing capacities. This situation could even result in a loss of market share to competitors. For these important reasons, firms try to match capital investments with the company's goals. In other words, if the firm is growing, projects that would produce the greatest growth rates would receive the highest priority. However, if the company is trying to reduce costs, projects that enhance the company's efficiency and productivity would be ranked toward the top. Because asset expansion frequently involves large sums of money and affects the company's productivity for an extended period of time, finance managers must carefully evaluate the best way to finance or pay for these investments, another major responsibility of financial managers.

capital investments
Money paid to acquire something of permanent value in a business

capital budgeting
Process for evaluating proposed investments in select projects that provide the best long-term financial return

Financing Operations and Growth

Most companies can't operate and grow without a periodic infusion of money. Firms need money to cover the day-to-day expenses of running a business, such as paying employees and purchasing inventory. They also need money to acquire new assets such as land, production facilities, and equipment. Furthermore, as Chapter 5 pointed out, start-up companies need money to fund the costs involved in launching a new business.

Where can existing firms obtain the money they need to operate and grow? The most obvious source would be revenues: cash received from sales, rentals of property, interest on short-term investments, and so on. Another likely source would be suppliers who may be willing to do business on credit, thus enabling the company to postpone payment. Most firms also obtain money in the form of loans from banks, finance companies, or other commercial lenders. In addition, public companies can raise funds by selling shares of stock, and large corporations can sell bonds.

Companies plan for construction projects such as this one years in advance and reflect the costs of such long-term projects in their capital budgets.

LEARNING OBJECTIVE

Cite three factors financial managers must consider when selecting an appropriate funding vehicle

short-term financing
Financing used to cover current expenses (generally repaid within a year)

long-term financing
Financing used to cover long-term expenses such as assets (generally repaid over a period of more than one year)

cost of capital
Average rate of interest a firm pays on its combination of debt and equity

prime interest rate (prime)
Lowest rate of interest charged by banks for short-term loans to their most creditworthy customers

discount rate
Interest rate charged by the Federal Reserve on loans to commercial banks and other financial institutions

As you can imagine, financing an enterprise is a complex undertaking. The process begins by assessing the firm's financing needs and determining whether funds are needed for the short or the long term. Next, the firm must assess the cost of obtaining those funds. Finally, it must weigh the advantages and disadvantages of financing through debt or equity, taking into consideration the firm's special needs and circumstances. The financing process is further complicated by the fact that many sources of long-term and short-term financing exist—each with their own special attributes, risks, and costs.

Length of Term Financing can be either short-term or long-term. **Short-term financing** is any financing that will be repaid within one year, whereas **long-term financing** is any financing that will be repaid in a period longer than one year. The primary purpose of short-term financing is to ensure that a company maintains its liquidity, or its ability to meet financial obligations (such as inventory payments) as they become due. By contrast, long-term financing is used to acquire long-term assets such as buildings and equipment or to fund expansion via any number of growth options. Long-term financing can come from both internal and external sources, as Exhibit 17.2 highlights.

Cost of Capital In general, a company wants to obtain money at the lowest cost and least amount of risk. However, lenders and investors want to receive the highest possible return on their investment, also at the lowest risk. A company's **cost of capital**, the average rate of interest it must pay on its debt and equity financing, depends on three main factors: the risk associated with the company, the prevailing level of interest rates, and management's selection of funding vehicles.

Risk Lenders, such as Bank One, who provide money to businesses expect their returns to be in proportion to the two types of risk they face: the quality and length of time of the venture. Obviously, the more financially solid a company is, the less risk investors face. However, time also plays a vital role. Because a dollar will be worth less tomorrow than it is today, lenders need to be compensated for waiting to be repaid. As a result, long-term financing generally costs a company more than short-term financing.

Interest Rates Regardless of how financially solid a company is, the cost of money will vary over time because interest rates fluctuate. The **prime interest rate (prime)** is the lowest interest rate offered on short-term bank loans to preferred borrowers. The prime changes irregularly and, at times, quite frequently. Sometimes it changes because of supply and demand; at other times it changes because the prime rate is closely tied to the **discount rate**, the interest rate Federal Reserve Banks charge on loans to commercial banks and other depository institutions. We will discuss the importance of the discount rate later in the chapter when we discuss the money supply.

EXHIBIT 17.2

Sources of Long-Term Financing
To finance long-term projects, financial managers rely on both internal and external sources of capital.

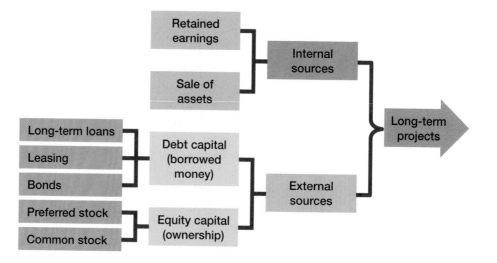

Companies must take such interest rate fluctuations into account when making financing decisions. For instance, a company planning to finance a short-term project when the prime rate is 3 percent would want to reevaluate the project if the prime rose to 6 percent a few months later. Even though companies try to time their borrowing to take advantage of drops in interest rates, this option is not always possible. A firm's need for money doesn't always coincide with a period of favorable rates. At times, a company may be forced to borrow when rates are high and then renegotiate the loan when rates drop. Sometimes projects must be put on hold until interest rates become more affordable.

Opportunity Cost   Using a company's own cash to finance its growth has one chief attraction: No interest payments are required. Nevertheless, such internal financing is not free; using this money has an *opportunity cost.* That is, a company might be better off investing its excess cash in external opportunities, such as another company's projects or stocks of growing companies, and borrowing money to finance its own growth. Doing so makes sense as long as the company can earn a greater *rate of return* (the percentage increase in the value of an investment) on external investments than the rate of interest paid on borrowed money. This concept is called **leverage**, because the loan acts like a lever: It magnifies the power of the borrower to generate profits (see Exhibit 17.3). However, leverage works both ways: Borrowing may magnify your losses as well as your gains. Because most companies require some degree of external financing from time to time, the issue is not so much whether to use outside money; rather, it's a question of how much should be raised, by what means, and when. The answers to such questions determine the firm's **capital structure**, the mix of debt and equity.

Debt Versus Equity Financing   *Debt financing* refers to what we normally think of as a loan. A creditor agrees to lend money to a debtor in exchange for repayment, with accumulated interest, at some future date. *Equity financing* is achieved by selling shares of a company's stock. (The advantages and disadvantages of selling stock to the public are discussed in Chapter 6.) When choosing between debt and equity financing, companies consider a variety of issues, including the prevailing interest rates, maturity, the claim on income, the claim on assets, and the desire for ownership control. Exhibit 17.4 summarizes these issues.

Of course, some companies get into trouble by taking on too much debt. For example, when Quaker Oats unloaded Snapple for $300 million (after plunking down a whopping $1.7 billion to purchase the brand from its creators less than three years earlier), the company

leverage
Technique of increasing the rate of return on an investment by financing it with borrowed funds

capital structure
Financing mix of a firm

5 **LEARNING OBJECTIVE**

Identify five common types of debt financing

EXHIBIT 17.3
How Leverage Works
If you invest $10,000 of your own money in a business venture and it yields 15 percent (or $1,500), your return on equity is 15 percent. However, if you borrow an additional $30,000 at 10 percent interest and invest a total of $40,000 with the same 15 percent yield, the ultimate return on your $10,000 equity is 30 percent (or $3,000). The key to using leverage successfully is to try to make sure that your profit on the total funds is greater than the interest you must pay on the portion of it that is borrowed.

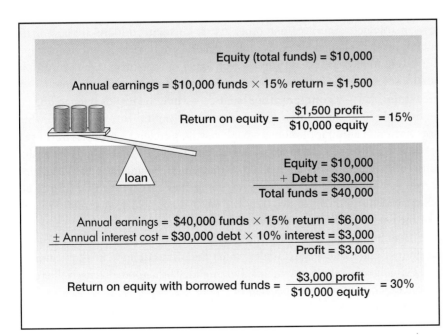

EXHIBIT 17.4 Debt Versus Equity
When choosing between debt and equity financing, companies evaluate the characteristics of both types of funding.

CHARACTERISTIC	DEBT	EQUITY
Maturity	**Specific:** Specifies a date by which it must be repaid.	**Nonspecific:** Specifies no maturity date.
Claim on income	**Fixed cost:** Company must pay interest on debt held by bondholders and lenders before paying any dividends to shareholders. Interest payments must be met regardless of operating results.	**Discretionary cost:** Shareholders may receive dividends after creditors have received interest payments; however, company is not required to pay dividends.
Claim on assets	**Priority:** Lenders have prior claims on assets.	**Residual:** Shareholders have claims only after the firm satisfies claims of lenders.
Influence over management	**Little:** Lenders are creditors, not owners. They can impose limits on management only if interest payments are not received.	**Varies:** As owners of the company, shareholders can vote on some aspects of corporate operations. Shareholder influence varies, depending on whether stock is widely distributed or closely held.

trade credit
Credit obtained by the purchaser directly from the supplier

commercial paper
An IOU, backed by the corporation's reputation, issued to raise short-term capital

secured loans
Loans backed up with something of value that the lender can claim in case of default, such as a piece of property

collateral
Tangible asset a lender can claim if a borrower defaults on a loan

unsecured loans
Loan requiring no collateral but a good credit rating

compensating balance
Portion of an unsecured loan that is kept on deposit at the lending institution to protect the lender and increase the lender's return

line of credit
Arrangement in which the financial institution makes money available for use at any time after the loan has been approved

recorded a $1.4 billion loss on the sale. Analysts estimate that Quaker lost $1.6 million for every day it owned Snapple because the net revenue generated from sales of the brand did not cover the costs of financing the acquisition.[3]

Common Types of Debt Financing   Two common types of short-term debt financing are **trade credit** (or open-account purchases) from suppliers—allowing purchasers to obtain products before paying for them; and **commercial paper**—short-term promissory notes of major corporations usually sold in denominations of $100,000 or more, with maturities of up to 270 days (the maximum allowed by the SEC without registration).

Loans, another common source of debt financing, can be long term or short term and secured or unsecured. **Secured loans** are those backed by something of value, known as **collateral**, which may be seized by the lender in the event that the borrower fails to repay the loan. The most common type of secured loan is a *mortgage*, in which a piece of property such as a building is used as collateral. Other types of loan collateral are accounts receivable, inventories, marketable securities, and other assets. **Unsecured loans** are ones that require no collateral. Instead, the lender relies on the general credit record and the earning power of the borrower. To increase the returns on such loans and to obtain some protection in case of default, most lenders insist that the borrower maintain some minimum amount of money on deposit at the bank—a **compensating balance**—while the loan is outstanding.

One example of an unsecured loan is a working capital **line of credit**, which is an agreed-on maximum amount of money a bank is willing to lend a business during a specific period of time, usually one year. Once a line of credit has been established, the business may obtain unsecured loans for any amount up to that limit, provided the bank has funds. The line of credit can be canceled at any time, so companies that want to be sure of obtaining credit when needed should arrange a *revolving line of credit*, which guarantees that the bank will honor the line of credit up to the stated amount.

Rather than borrowing from a commercial lender to buy a piece of property or equipment, a firm may enter into a lease, under which the owner of an item allows another party to use it in exchange for regular payments. Leasing may be a good alternative for a company that has difficulty obtaining loans because of a poor credit rating. Creditors are more willing to provide a lease than a loan because, should the company fail, the lessor need not worry about a default on loan payments; it can simply repossess equipment it legally owns. Some firms use leases to finance up to 35 percent of their total assets, particularly in industries such as airlines, where assets are mostly large, expensive pieces of equipment.

When a company needs to borrow a large sum of money, it may not be able to get the entire amount from a single source. Under such circumstances, it may borrow from many individual investors by issuing *bonds*—certificates that obligate the company to repay a certain sum, plus interest, to the bondholder on a specific date. (Both bonds and stocks are traded on organized securities exchanges and are discussed in detail in Chapter 18.)

The U.S. Financial System

Whether a company finances with debt, equity, or cash reserves, financial managers must interact with financial institutions to satisfy their financial needs. The variety of financial institutions that operate within the U.S. banking environment can be classified into two broad categories: *deposit institutions* and *nondeposit institutions*. Deposit institutions accept deposits from customers or members and offer checking and savings accounts, loans, and other banking services. Among the many deposit institutions are

- *Commercial banks.* These include institutions such as Bank One, which operate under state or national charters.
- *Thrifts.* These include savings and loan associations (which use most of their deposits to make home mortgage loans) and mutual savings banks (which are owned by their depositors).
- *Credit unions.* These include institutions that take deposits only from members, such as one company's employees or one union's members or another designated group.

Nondeposit institutions offer specific financial services but do not accept deposits. Among the many nondeposit institutions are

- *Insurance companies.* These institutions provide insurance coverage for life, property, and other potential losses; they invest the payments they receive in real estate, in construction projects, and in other ways.
- *Pension funds.* These institutions are set up by companies to provide retirement benefits for employees; money contributed by the company and its employees is put into securities and other investments.
- *Finance companies.* These institutions lend money to consumers and businesses for home improvements, expansion, purchases, and other purposes.
- *Brokerage firms.* These institutions buy and sell stocks, bonds, and other investments for investors; many also offer checking accounts, high-paying savings accounts, and loans to buy securities. (Brokerage firms are discussed more fully in Chapter 18.)

In the past, services such as checking accounts, savings accounts, and loans were not offered at all financial institutions; instead, each institution focused on offering a particular set of financial services for specific customer groups. However, the competitive situation changed dramatically after the passage of the Depository Institutions Deregulation and Monetary Control Act of 1980. This law deregulated banking and made it possible for all financial institutions to offer a wider range of services—blurring the line between banks and other financial institutions and encouraging more competition between various types of institutions. Before we take a look at the changing U.S. banking environment, let's examine the types of traditional services offered by financial institutions.

Once restricted to taking deposits and making loans, banks now offer customers a wide range of services, including selling securities.

6 LEARNING OBJECTIVE

Identify three common financial services that banks provide customers, and list electronic banking vehicles that facilitate these services

checks
Written orders that tell the customer's bank to pay a specific amount to a particular individual or business

credit cards
Plastic cards that allow the customer to buy now and pay back the loaned amount at a future date

Financial Services

No matter where in the world you live, work, or travel, today's businesses and individuals require a wide range of financial services. Banks of all sizes—from the largest multinational bank to the tiniest community bank—provide customers with a variety of financial services that include checking and savings accounts, loans, and credit, debit, and smart cards. Moreover, thanks to technological advances and the Internet, customers can now access their money and account information at any hour and from almost anywhere. Of course, the human touch is still a big part of banking. But in today's time-pressured world, more people want to handle banking transactions from different locations and at different times, not during traditional bankers' hours.

Checking and Savings Accounts Money you put into your checking account is a *demand deposit*, available immediately (on demand) through the use of **checks**, written orders that direct your bank to pay the stated amount of money to you or to someone else. Banks traditionally paid no interest on money in checking accounts. Since the laws changed in 1980, however, financial institutions have been allowed to offer interest-bearing NOW (Negotiable Order of Withdrawal) checking accounts. Most NOW accounts limit the number of checks customers can write and impose a fee if the account balance falls below a minimum level.

You earn interest on the money you put away in savings accounts; credit unions typically pay slightly higher savings rates than commercial banks. Originally, these accounts were known as *passbook savings accounts* because customers received a small passbook in which the bank recorded all deposits, withdrawals, and interest. Today, banks send out statements instead of passbooks, so these accounts have become known as *statement savings accounts*. In general, money in savings accounts can be withdrawn at any time. Money in a *money-market deposit account* earns more interest, but you are allowed only a limited number of monthly withdrawals. Money held in a *certificate of deposit (CD)* earns an even higher interest rate, but you cannot withdraw the funds for a stated period, such as six months or more. If you want to make an early withdrawal from a CD, you will lose some or all of the interest you've earned.

Loans Businesses of all sizes rely on banks to provide loans for expansion, purchases of new equipment, construction or renovation of plants and facilities, or other large-scale projects. Banks are a major source of loans for customers who need money for a particular purpose. Bank One's primary loan market is geared toward small and mid-tier companies with sales of $10 million to $500 million. But, like most banks, Bank One also lends money to individuals to buy or make improvements to a home, to purchase a car, to finance an education, and for many other reasons. Customers, of course, shop around to compare interest rates, fees, and repayment schedules before they take out a loan.

Credit, Debit, and Smart Cards For everyday access to short-term credit, banks issue **credit cards**, plastic cards that entitle customers to make purchases now and repay the loaned amount later. Nondeposit institutions such as Merrill Lynch also issue credit cards.

Credit cards have become immensely popular with consumers because they are convenient and allow people to make purchases without cash. Nearly every store accepts credit cards, and mail-order merchants and Internet retailers are especially dependent on credit cards to facilitate purchases. Credit cards also help people manage their finances by either choosing to repay the full amount when they are billed or making small payments month by month until the debt has been repaid.

Credit card companies make money by charging customers interest on their unpaid account balances and by charging businesses a processing fee, which can range from 2 to 5 percent of the value of each sales transaction paid by credit card. Many banks also charge credit card holders an annual fee in addition to late-payment, cash advance, over-the-limit, and currency exchange fees. In fact, fees paid by consumers jumped 10 percent in 2001 to $13.6 billion and are becoming a growing source of revenue for credit card issuers.

Credit card companies generally advertise the lowest interest rate they charge, but actual rates are often higher: There's an attractive introductory rate, a standard rate that kicks in after a set period, and a penalty rate that may exceed

Credit card issuers are getting craftier about applying fees and penalties, and they are shortening grace periods.

20 percent. Some card issuers slap a penalty rate on cardholders for being late on as few as one or two payments.[4] For example, in a desperate attempt to woo customers, First USA, the credit card business that Bank One bought in 1997, offered a teaser introductory interest rate of 3.9 percent. But anyone missing a payment twice in a six-month period—even by a day—paid a much higher penalty rate. Once customers discovered this "hidden" rate, many bolted to other credit card companies—a situation that Jamie Dimon tried to rectify once he took over the helm.[5]

In addition to credit cards, many banks offer **debit cards**, plastic cards that function like checks in that the amount of a purchase is electronically deducted from the user's checking account and is transferred to the retailer's account at the time of the sale. Debit cards are ideal for customers who must control their spending or stick to a budget.

Smart cards are plastic cards with tiny computer chips that can store amounts of money (from the user's bank account) and selected data (such as shipping address, credit card information, frequent-flyer account numbers, health and insurance details, or other personal information). When a purchase is made, the store's equipment electronically deducts the amount from the value stored on the smart card and reads and verifies requisite customer information. Users reload money from their bank accounts to their smart cards as needed.

Although popular in Europe, smart cards have been slow to catch on in the United States for two reasons: Low U.S. telephone rates (compared to those of European countries) make it affordable to verify credit card transactions over the phone, and the costs to replace current credit card infrastructures with smart card readers and computer chip technology are not cost effective for most U.S. businesses. Nevertheless, American Express has made some inroads with its combination smart card and credit card, Blue. The card boasts a transparent, blue hologram in the center and an embedded microchip that holds customer information. Customers who purchase online can insert Blue into a small smart card reader that plugs into the user's serial port. Once the card is inserted, customers type in a password to transfer the digital information stored on the smart card (such as the credit card number, expiration date, and shipping address) to the vendor. A similar process is used for purchases at physical stores, provided the store has a smart card reader. If not, the card also has a standard magnetic strip to accommodate those merchants.[6]

debit cards
Plastic cards that allow the bank to take money from the user's demand-deposit account and transfer it to a retailer's account

smart cards
Plastic cards that include an embedded chip to store money drawn from the user's demand-deposit account and information that can be used for purchases

Thinking About Ethics

Surprise! You've Been Swiped

Skimming. It's the fastest-growing area of credit card fraud. A skimmer is someone who steals customer account information by swiping a credit card through a handheld magnetic card reader—about the size of a pager. The reader copies the cardholder's name, account number, and even the card validation code—stored on the magnetic stripe—giving the counterfeiter all the data needed to create a perfect clone of the credit card. These readers can be purchased for as little as $100 over the Internet and are intended for legitimate use by banks, restaurants, retailers, and hotels. Unfortunately, some end up in the wrong hands.

Thieves, and increasingly organized crime groups, pay waiters and store clerks to steal information from credit cards using the concealed devices. By skimming 14 to 20 accounts, crooks can generate $50,000 to $60,000 worth of fraud that will probably go undiscovered until the victims get their bills—30 to 60 days after the crime. Moreover, skimmed data from say a customer in New York City or Dallas can be e-mailed to Taiwan, Japan, or Europe and used for mail-order, telephone-order, or e-commerce overseas transactions within 24 to 48 hours of the theft. Professionals can even encode the stolen codes into a stripe and use equipment to produce an electronically indistinguishable counterfeit card.

Although credit card issuers decline to say how much they are losing to skimmers—in part because they don't want to scare consumers out of using their plastic—industry analysts estimate skimmers reap over $125 mil-

lion annually. To curb the fraud, major credit card issuers are cooperating with the U.S. Secret Service to pool information about fraudulent transactions. For example, issuers can generate computer analyses that flag locations where numerous cards may have been skimmed. Or if someone in Hong Kong tries to buy something with a credit card that was used two hours earlier in Chicago, the computer will reject the transaction.

What can you do to prevent your credit cards from getting skimmed? Not much, say experts, besides reading your bills closely, checking your accounts on the web or by phone during the month to make sure there are no surprises, and reporting improper charges promptly. Although you're not liable for fraudulent charges made to your accounts by skimmers or other scam artists, you do have to face the hassle of getting the unauthorized transactions removed from your bills. Of course, you can ditch the credit cards and pay with old-fashioned cash. But if you carry lots of that around, you may have to worry about the old-fashioned robber.

Questions for Critical Thinking

1. To curb the abuse, why don't credit card issuers require customers to present additional personal validation data at the time of sale?
2. Why don't thieves skim debit cards too?

Electronic Banking Electronic banking includes various banking activities conducted from sites other than a physical bank location. For instance, all over the world, customers rely on **automated teller machines (ATMs)** to withdraw money from their demand-deposit accounts at any hour. The number of ATMs nationwide now tops 324,000.[7] By linking with regional, national, and international ATM networks, banks let customers withdraw cash far from home, make deposits, and handle other transactions such as check cashing, purchasing prepaid wireless phone cards or gift cards, and transferring funds between bank and brokerage accounts.[8]

Electronic funds transfer systems (EFTS) are another form of electronic banking. These computerized systems allow users to conduct financial transactions efficiently from remote locations. More than half of all U.S. workers take advantage of EFTS when their employers use *direct deposit* to transfer wages directly into employees' bank accounts. Workers with direct deposit won't find a check inside their pay envelopes on payday.

automated teller machines (ATMs)
Electronic terminals that permit people with plastic cards to perform simple banking transactions 24 hours a day without the aid of a human teller

electronic funds transfer systems (EFTS)
Computerized systems for performing financial transactions

Instead, they get a stub showing the amounts earned, withheld, deducted, and directly deposited into their bank account. Some companies are even eliminating the pay stub and instead giving employees a password so they can access their personal payroll records online.[9]

The benefits of direct deposit are many. Companies save about $1.20 a person for each pay period they use direct deposits. They can save even more if they omit paper stubs and provide payroll information in an electronic format. American Greetings Corp., one of the world's largest greeting-card companies, saved about $20 per employee a year by switching to direct deposits, and expects to save $500,000 a year after converting to online paperless pay. Employees also benefit from paperless pay systems. They can get their pay-stub information at least two days before payday, and the information is available 24 hours a day, seven days a week.[10]

In addition to automated teller machines and electronic funds transfer systems, most major banks and many thrifts and community banks now offer Internet or online banking to accommodate the growing number of individuals and businesses that want to transfer money between accounts, check account balances, pay bills, apply for loans, and handle other transactions at any hour. About 25 million U.S. households in 2002 paid or viewed their bills online, according to one study. That number is expected to double to 50 million households by 2006.[11]

Online banking has many advantages. It's fast and easy for customers, and it's extremely cost-efficient for banks. Billers can also save money by switching from paper bills to online ones—about $1.50 to $2 for each customer every month. The savings include postage, printing, and return envelopes as well as the cost of handling checks and bill stubs. But the biggest advantage of online banking is increased customer loyalty. Online banking customers have an 80 percent lower attrition rate than customers who aren't online. Moreover, their loan and deposit balances are 35 percent higher than those of customers who aren't online.[12]

Automated teller machines (ATMs) allow customers to perform certain bank transactions 24 hours a day in places other than a branch office.

7 LEARNING OBJECTIVE

Explain how the U.S. banking industry has evolved

The Evolving U.S. Banking Environment

The U.S. banking environment has changed radically over the past few decades. Seeking strength, efficiency, and access to more customers and markets, U.S. banks underwent a series of mergers, acquisitions, and takeovers during the 1980s and 1990s. In 1934 there were 14,146 main bank offices in the United States; by 1999 the number had plummeted to only 8,581.[13]

The deregulation of the banking industry in 1980 paved the way for such industry consolidation. The Riegle–Neal Interstate Banking and Branching Efficiency Act of 1994, a landmark law, reversed legislation dating back to 1927 that allowed banks to enter new markets by opening branch operations or merging with banks across state lines.[14] As a result, customers can now make deposits, cash checks, or handle any banking transaction in any branch of their bank, regardless of location. In 1999 Congress opened the floodgates for consolidation among banks, brokerage firms, and insurance companies by repealing the Glass–Steagall Act.

Ever since Scott Cook developed the first edition of Quicken in 1984, Intuit has dominated the market for personal finance software with its Quicken, QuickBooks, and Turbo Tax. Millions of customers and small-business owners now use the software to track their finances and pay their bills electronically.

Repeal of Glass–Steagall Act The 1999 Financial Services Modernization Act repealed the Glass–Steagall Act (also known as the Banking Act of 1933) and portions of the 1956 Bank Holding Act, which for decades had kept banks out of the securities and insurance businesses. Originally enacted after the stock market crash of 1929 and the Great Depression, the Glass–Steagall Act was designed to restore confidence in U.S. financial houses by restricting investment banks and commercial banks from crossing into each others' businesses and potentially abusing their fiduciary duties at the expense of customers. Regulators hoped to protect corporations, borrowers, and investors from banks' potential conflicts of interest. The act also ensured that a catastrophic failure in one part of the finance industry did not invade every other part, as it did in 1929.[15]

Emergence of Financial Supermarkets The repeal of the Glass–Steagall Act accelerated the existing merger trend and facilitated the growth of financial supermarkets. Commercial and investment banks soon began invading one another's turf.

Financial institutions, once restricted to taking deposits and making loans, broke into the business of selling securities. Citigroup (formed by a 1998 merger of Travelers Group with Citicorp) was a pioneer in bringing together a large corporate lender, Citibank, with a major investment house, Salomon Smith Barney. The combined entity soon began to offer a number of financial and security services under one roof. These included loans, sales of securities, merger advice, and the underwriting of IPOs. Rivals soon followed Citigroup's lead, combining banks and insurance companies to create financial supermarkets that offer customers a full range of services—from traditional loans to investment banking services to public stock offerings to insurance.

At the same time, securities firms, such as Merrill Lynch, expanded their financial services to include loans, mortgages, credit cards, online bill payment, and checking accounts to entice customers to leave their banks and run all of their finances through their brokerage accounts.[16] Online broker E*Trade bought Telebanc Financial, the nation's largest online bank, and mortgage lender Loans Direct. The company also began selling life insurance and offering credit cards. E*Trade even got physical, setting up investor centers in large cities, a network of ATMs, and nationwide "financial zones" inside Target superstores.[17]

Bank and brokerage executives believed that size was the answer to everything. Larger institutions, they figured, could take advantage of economies of scale and make a mint on fees by cross-selling an extensive arsenal of products. But these benefits did not evolve as projected. So much energy and resources were devoted to making the mergers work that cross-selling services was often put on the back burner.[18] And in their race to become jacks-of-all-trades (one-stop financial shops selling everything from merger advice to credit cards), many financial supermarkets ended up mastering none.[19]

Look at Bank One. With 1,800 branches, 7.3 million households, 500,000 small-business customers, and 5,000 ATMs, the newly merged Bank One operation hoped to become a huge delivery system for a range of services—mutual funds, credit cards, investment management, and lines of credit. In fact, when Bank One bought First USA in 1997, it projected that combined earnings would rise 16 to 20 percent through 2000, much higher than its traditional growth rate.[20] But the deal posed the classic problem of mergers of equals: Neither side was in charge. "The two camps would argue for months over whether retail or corporate should get the big resources, which people from which former bank should run the businesses, and everything else," says Dave Donovan, head of human resources at Bank One and a veteran of First Chicago. It seemed top management could agree on just one thing: Everyone wanted to grow revenues as rapidly as possible. And the quickest route was piling on risky loans.[21]

Breaches in the Chinese Wall Regulators refer to the separation of securities research functions and bank lending functions within the same company as a "Chinese wall." This *invisible wall*, in theory, prevents bankers from influencing opinions written by securities personnel and securities personnel from influencing bank loans. Such influence could give rise to biased securities research reports and encourage the investing public to purchase the securities of companies with whom the company's bankers also have a debt relationship. Moreover, by influencing analysts' ratings of stocks, bankers could strengthen relationships with corporate clients in order to win lucrative investment-banking business.[22]

The potential conflict resulting from a breach of the "Chinese wall" is illustrated in Citigroup's dealings with WorldCom.[23] In May 2001 Citigroup won an assignment to sell an $11.8 billion WorldCom bond offering—one of the biggest such bond offerings ever. Citigroup was also one of the main arrangers of loans and credit lines to WorldCom. So when WorldCom filed for bankruptcy-court protection in 2002, the bonds Citigroup helped sell became worthless. Bond investors sued Citigroup on the grounds that the firm should have known about WorldCom's dire financial condition and should have warned bond buyers of the risk. Moreover, they claim that Citigroup went ahead and sold investors WorldCom bonds anyway and by doing so prevented WorldCom from drawing on its Citigroup credit line.[24]

Meanwhile, disclosures of similar breaches of the "Chinese wall" separation at the beginning of the 21st century has since prompted reform in this area. Pressure from securities regulators and the government has forced many financial supermarkets to separate their investment banking from stock brokering and research units.[25]

Resurgence of Community Banks   *Community banks* are smaller banks that concentrate on serving the needs of local consumers and businesses. Following a wave of consolidation in the banking industry, many industry analysts predicted that community banks would not be able to compete with the growing depth of services offered by financial supermarkets. But according to a recent Federal Reserve study, small banks are now earning more on assets than their huge competitors. A number of factors are contributing to their increasing popularity and competitiveness.

Community banks cater to markets that large banks have traditionally neglected or ignored, such as minorities, small businesses, rural communities, and inner cities; they provide faster decisions on loans and more flexible terms; and they give exceptional personalized customer service. Most community bankers, if they believe in a small business owner, will go out of their way to make a loan. They typically try to help their local customers by thinking creatively—offering customized services that a large branching operation may not have the flexibility to do. Acknowledging that smaller players have an edge in personal service, some large financial institutions are shortening their loan approval times, beefing up small-business and minority programs, and adding new services to compete with smaller rivals.[26]

Struggling Internet Banks   Amid predictions of exponential growth in the number of Internet users, Bank One started a stand-alone Internet bank called Wingspanbank.com in 1999. It was an early attempt by a big bank to operate solely on the Internet—without tellers or branches. Others soon followed in Bank One's footsteps. But Internet banks or cyberbanks did not catch on for a number of reasons. Customers of cyberbanks found it difficult to deposit and withdraw funds online. And they had to pay higher fees to use ATMs. Moreover, Internet banks weren't making money, especially after advertising heavily to convince customers their PC was better than a teller. In 2001 Bank One shuttered Wingspan.com after spending more than $150 million. Today, most stand-alone Internet banks have closed.[27]

Community bankers excel at personal service. They will meet with small-business owners and work with them on their business plan, and they will lend them money to help them grow their business to the next level.

Bank Safety and Regulation

Regardless of where or how you conduct your financial transactions, everyone (including Congress, regulators, and the financial community) worries about bank failure. As many as 9,000 U.S. banks failed during the Depression years from 1929 to 1934. In response to concerns about bank safety during that period, the government established the Federal Deposit Insurance Corporation (FDIC) to protect money in customer accounts. Today, money on deposit in U.S. banks is insured by the FDIC up to a maximum of $100,000 through the Savings Association Insurance Fund (for thrifts) and the Bank Insurance Fund (for commercial banks). Similarly, the National Credit Union Association protects deposits in credit unions.

In addition, a number of government agencies supervise and regulate banks. State-chartered banks come under the watchful eyes of each state's banking commission, nationally chartered banks are under the federal Office of the Comptroller of the Currency, and thrifts are under the federal Office of Thrift Supervision. The overall health of the country's banking system is, ultimately, the responsibility of the Federal Reserve System.

The Functions of the Federal Reserve System

The Federal Reserve System was created in 1913. Commonly known as the Fed, it is the most powerful financial institution in the United States, serving as the central bank. The Fed's primary role is to manage the money supply so that the country avoids both recession and inflation. It also supervises and regulates banks and serves as a clearinghouse for checks.

The Fed is a network of 12 district banks that controls the nation's banking system. The overall policy of the Fed is established by a seven-member board of governors who meet in Washington, D.C. To preserve the board's political independence, the members are appointed by the president to 14-year terms, staggered at two-year intervals. Although all national banks are required to be members of the Federal Reserve System, membership for state-chartered banks is optional. Still, the Fed exercises regulatory power over all deposit institutions, members and nonmembers alike. The Federal Reserve System has three major functions: influencing the U.S. money supply, supplying currency, and clearing checks.

Influencing the U.S. Money Supply

8 LEARNING OBJECTIVE

Identify four ways the Federal Reserve System influences the U.S. money supply

money
Anything generally accepted as a means of paying for goods and services

Money is anything generally accepted as a means of paying for goods and services. Before it was invented, people got what they needed by trading their services or possessions; in some societies, such as Russia, this system of trading, or bartering, still exists. However, barter is inconvenient and impractical in a global economy, where many of the things we want are intangible, come from places all over the world, and require the combined work of many people.

To be an effective medium for exchange, money must have these important characteristics: It must be divisible, portable (easy to carry), durable, and difficult to counterfeit, and it should have a stable value. In addition, money must perform three basic functions: First, it must serve as a medium of exchange—a tool for simplifying transactions between buyers and sellers. Second, it must serve as a measure of value so that you don't have to negotiate the relative worth of dissimilar items every time you buy something. Finally, money must serve as a temporary store of value—a way of accumulating your wealth until you need it.

Keeping Pace with Technology and Electronic Commerce

How Will You Be Paying for That?

For years, companies and customers have been trying to figure out new and better ways to pay for items purchased online. Despite all the effort, credit cards seem to be working pretty well. An estimated 95 percent of Internet purchases are completed with a credit card. Yet there are problems with using a credit card online. One is security—although most credit card transactions are safe. Another is privacy. So, as electronic commerce grows, people are trying to find new ways to make money off of it.

E-money is one idea. Also know as *digital cash*, e-money is a way to store money for use on the web that is the virtual equivalent of a phone card or a gift certificate. Here's how it works: A company creates a virtual currency that will be accepted only on the Internet. Retailers download the software that accepts the currency, and customers download the software that offers the currency. Customers buy the Internet currency using real money or a credit card and then use the e-money to make purchases online. Then retailers exchange the e-money for real currency. E-money, of course, limits fraud because even if the currency is stolen, it can only be used for e-purchases at online stores equipped with the software. Nonetheless, e-money faces one big hurdle. Retailers don't want to install new software unless they see a lot of customers using it. And customers don't want to download software unless they see a lot of retailers accepting it.

Digital wallets are another idea. Similar in concept to smart cards, digital or electronic wallets speed up online checkout by reading pertinent purchaser information from a customer's digital wallet. Customers download software that stores their credit card numbers, shipping and billing addresses, and other personal information. Participating sites download software that enables them to receive payment from the wallet. Like e-money, digital wallets can make transactions speedier and solve the problem of having to remember a different password and user name for each web store. But this approach has the same flaw—the difficulty of signing up retailers.

Despite these challenges, e-money, digital wallets, and new online payment options are expected to gain ground as Internet shopping grows even more. A slew of competitors, including PayPal, BillPoint, eCash, eCHEQs, c2it, eCoin, the Internet Dollar, Modex, Pay Hound, and Yahoo! PayDirect, already exist. So next time an online clerk asks you "And how you will be paying for your purchase?" you may be surprised at the number of options you will have.

Questions for Critical Thinking

1. What events might stimulate wider acceptance of e-money and digital wallets?
2. Why do some consumers not like to pay for online purchases with credit cards?

The Fed's main job is to establish and implement *monetary policy*, guidelines for handling the nation's economy and the money supply. The U.S. money supply has three major components:

- **Currency**: Money in the form of coins, bills, traveler's checks, cashier's checks, and money orders
- **Demand deposits**: Money available immediately on demand, such as checking accounts
- **Time deposits**: Accounts that pay interest and restrict the owner's right to withdraw funds on short notice, such as savings accounts, certificates of deposit, and money-market deposit accounts

The Fed influences the money supply to make certain that enough money and credit are available to fuel a healthy economy. However, it must act carefully, because altering the

currency
Bills and coins that make up the cash money of a society

demand deposits
Money in a checking account that can be used by the customer at any time

time deposits
Bank accounts that pay interest and require advance notice before money can be withdrawn

money supply affects interest rates, inflation, and the economy. When the money supply is increased, more money is available for loans, so banks can charge lower interest rates to borrowers. On the other hand, an increased money supply can lead to more consumer spending and can result in the demand for goods exceeding supply. When demand exceeds supply, sellers may raise their prices, leading to inflation. In turn, inflation can slow economic growth—a situation the Fed wants to avoid. And, because so many companies now buy and sell across national borders, Fed changes may affect the interlinked economies of many countries, not just the United States. That's why the Fed moves cautiously and keeps a close eye on the size of the money supply.

How the Money Supply Is Measured

To get a rough idea of the size of the money supply, the Fed looks at various combinations of currency, demand deposits, and time deposits (see Exhibit 17.5). The narrowest measure, known as **M1**, consists of currency, demand deposits, and NOW accounts that are common forms of payment. **M2**, a broader measure of the money supply, includes M1 plus savings deposits, money-market funds, and time deposits under $100,000. **M3**, the broadest measure of the money supply, includes M2 plus time deposits of $100,000 and higher and other restricted deposits.

Tools for Influencing the Money Supply

The Fed can use four basic tools to influence the money supply:

- *Changing the reserve requirement.* All financial institutions must set aside *reserves*, sums of money equal to a certain percentage of their deposits. The Fed can change the **reserve requirement**, the percentage of deposits that banks must set aside, to influence the money supply. However, the Fed rarely uses this technique because a small change can have a drastic effect. Increasing the reserve requirement slows down the economy: Banks have less money to lend, so businesses can't borrow to expand and consumers can't borrow to buy goods and services. Conversely, reducing this requirement boosts the economy, because banks have more money to lend to businesses and consumers (see Exhibit 17.6).

- *Changing the discount rate.* The Fed can also change the discount rate, the interest rate it charges on loans to commercial banks and other depository institutions. When the Fed

---

M1
That portion of the money supply consisting of currency and demand deposits

M2
That portion of the money supply consisting of currency, demand deposits, and small time deposits

M3
That portion of the money supply consisting of M1 and M2 plus large time deposits and other restrictive deposits

reserve requirement
Percentage of a bank's deposit that must be set aside

EXHIBIT 17.5
The Total Money Supply
The U.S. money supply is measured at three levels: M1, M2, and M3. Here's a closer look at the size and composition of these three components.

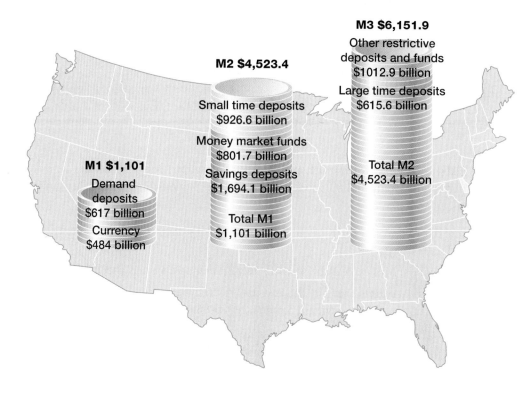

M1 $1,101
Demand deposits $617 billion
Currency $484 billion

M2 $4,523.4
Small time deposits $926.6 billion
Money market funds $801.7 billion
Savings deposits $1,694.1 billion
Total M1 $1,101 billion

M3 $6,151.9
Other restrictive deposits and funds $1012.9 billion
Large time deposits $615.6 billion
Total M2 $4,523.4 billion

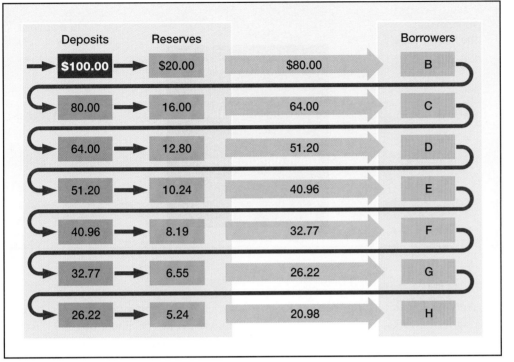

Deposits	Reserves		Borrowers
$100.00	$20.00	$80.00	B
80.00	16.00	64.00	C
64.00	12.80	51.20	D
51.20	10.24	40.96	E
40.96	8.19	32.77	F
32.77	6.55	26.22	G
26.22	5.24	20.98	H

EXHIBIT 17.6
How Banks Create Money
Banks stay in business by earning more on interest from loans than they pay out in the form of interest on deposits; they can increase their earnings by "creating" money. When customer A deposits $100, the bank must keep some in reserve but can lend, say, $80 to customer B (and earn interest on that loan). If customer B deposits the borrowed $80 in the same bank, the bank can lend 80 percent of *that* amount to borrower C. The initial $100 deposit, therefore, creates a much larger pool of funds from which customer loans may be made.

raises the discount rate, member banks generally raise the prime interest rate. This situation discourages loans, and in so doing tightens the money supply, which can slow down economic growth. By contrast, lowering the discount rate results in lower lending rates, which can encourage more borrowing and stimulate economic growth. As Chapter 1 points out, the Fed lowered interest rates 11 times in 2001 to stimulate the economy into recovery.[28]

- *Conducting open-market operations.* The tool the Fed uses most often to influence the money supply is the power to buy and sell U.S. government bonds. Because anyone can buy these bonds on the open market, this tool is known as **open-market operations**. If the Fed is concerned about inflation, it can reduce the money supply by selling U.S. government bonds, which takes cash out of circulation. And when the Fed wants to boost the economy, it can buy back government bonds, putting cash into circulation and increasing the money supply.

open-market operations
Activity of the Federal Reserve in buying and selling government bonds on the open market

- *Establishing selective credit controls.* The Fed can also use **selective credit controls** to set the terms of credit for various kinds of loans. This tool includes the power to set *margin requirements*, the percentage of the purchase price that an investor must pay in cash when purchasing a stock or a bond on credit. By altering the margin requirements, the Fed is able to influence how much cash is tied up in stock market transactions.

selective credit controls
Federal Reserve's power to set credit terms on various types of loans

Exhibit 17.7 summarizes the effects of using these four tools.

Supplying Currency and Clearing Checks

The second function of the Fed is to supply currency to keep the U.S. financial system running smoothly. Regional Federal Reserve Banks are responsible for providing member banks with adequate amounts of currency throughout the year. For example, in preparation for potential disruptions due to year-2000 computer problems, the Fed was ready to provide U.S. banks with another $50 billion in cash.[29]

EXHIBIT 17.7

Influencing the Money Supply
The Federal Reserve uses four tools to influence the money supply as it attempts to stimulate economic growth while keeping inflation and interest rates at acceptable levels.

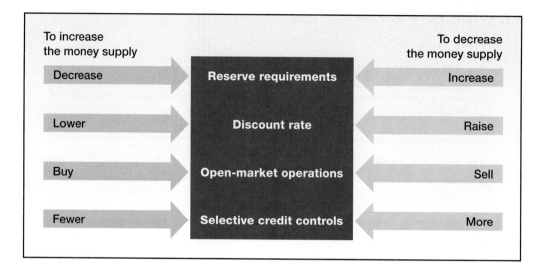

Another function of the Federal Reserve is to act as a clearinghouse for checks. After peaking in the 1990s, the number of checks being written has declined. In 2000 the total number of checks written was 42.5 billion, down from 49.5 billion in 1995. The chief factors contributing to the decline in check use are the increased use of electronic payments, direct payroll deposits, direct drafts from consumer bank accounts, credit and debit cards, and online banking.[30] Regardless, Exhibit 17.8 shows the operation of this automated clearinghouse function, which is invisible yet indispensable to consumers and businesses.

EXHIBIT 17.8   How the Fed Clears Checks
The Federal Reserve acts as a clearinghouse for checks in the United States. This example shows how the Fed clears a check that has been drawn on a bank in one city but deposited by a store in a bank in another city.

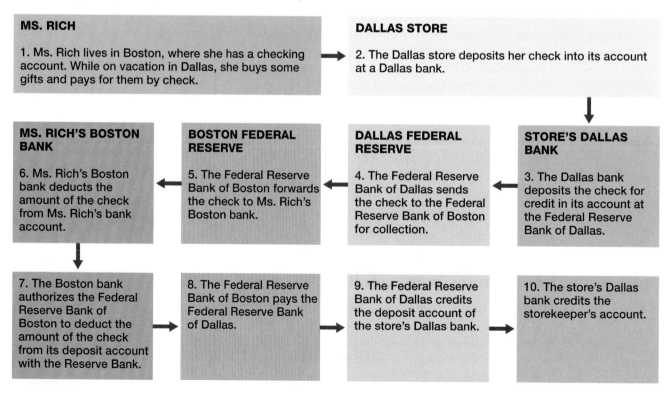

Summary of Learning Objectives

1. **Identify the responsibilities of a financial manager.**
The responsibilities of a financial manager include developing and implementing a firm's financial plan; monitoring a firm's cash flow and deciding how to create or use excess funds; budgeting for current and future expenditures and capital investments; raising capital to finance the enterprise for future growth; and interacting with banks and capital markets.

2. **Discuss how financial managers improve a company's cash flow.**
Monitoring working capital accounts is one way financial managers improve a company's cash flow. Such monitoring includes establishing effective accounts receivable credit and collection policies; paying bills strategically to obtain discounts and to conserve cash; establishing inventory procedures to maintain enough inventory to fill orders on time at the lowest purchase cost; and investing excess cash so it earns as much interest as possible.

3. **Differentiate between a master budget and a capital budget.**
Master or operating budgets handle all revenues, expenses, and cash flows of the firm. Moreover, they provide guidelines for a firm's total expenditures. By contrast, capital budgets forecast and plan for a firm's capital investments such as buildings and equipment while matching a firm's capital investments with the company's overall long-term goals.

4. **Cite three factors financial managers must consider when selecting an appropriate funding vehicle.**
Finance managers must determine whether the financing is for the short term or the long term. They must minimize the cost of capital by weighing the risk, interest costs, and opportunity costs of different financing alternatives. Finally, they must evaluate the merits of debt versus equity financing in light of their own needs.

5. **Identify five common types of debt financing.**
Five common types of debt financing are trade credit (paying for products after they are purchased); commercial paper (short-term promissory notes of major corporations); loans (money borrowed from the bank which is secured or unsecured, long term or short term); leases (paying for the use of someone else's property over a fixed term); and bonds (issuing corporate certificates to individual investors that obligate the company to repay a certain sum plus interest on a specific date).

6. **Identify three common financial services that banks provide customers, and list electronic banking vehicles that facilitate these services.**
Banks provide customers with checking and savings accounts so they can pay bills and earn interest on money they save. They provide loans so customers can purchase homes, cars, and finance educational expenses, among other things. They issue credit cards so customers can purchase now and repay the loaned amount later, as well as debit and smart cards, which facilitate retail transactions without the physical use of money. Banks facilitate these services by providing a number of electronic banking options. These include ATMs, electronic funds transfers, and online banking.

7. **Explain how the U.S. banking industry has evolved.**
Passage of the 1999 Financial Services Modernization Act, which repealed the Glass–Steagall Act, has fueled a raft of megamergers among banks, insurance companies, and brokerage firms and has increased the competition among these institution types. Such industry consolidation has blurred the line between the types of financial services offered by banks, securities brokers, and insurance companies and has transformed banks into multistate financial powerhouses. These large financial supermarkets can cross-sell products and reap economies of scale. But first they must overcome the challenges posed by merging operations. Moreover, a number of reported breaches in the "Chinese" wall has fueled pressure from security regulators to separate investment banking from stock-brokering functions. Meanwhile, the popularity of community banks has increased, as smaller banks fill the customer-service void created by large banking institutions. Electronic banking is also changing the competitive landscape. More and more customers are seeking banks with a good network of ATMs and services such as direct deposit and online banking.

8. **Identify four ways the Federal Reserve System influences the U.S. money supply.**
The Fed influences the U.S. money supply by changing reserve requirements (the percentage of deposits that banks must set aside), by changing the discount rate (the interest rate it charges on loans to commercial banks and other depository institutions), by carrying out open-market operations (selling and buying government bonds), and by setting selective credit controls (setting the amount of cash investors must pay when purchasing a stock or bond on credit).

KEY TERMS

automated teller machines (ATMs) **(442)**	demand deposits **(447)**	marketable securities **(434)**
budget **(434)**	discount rate **(436)**	money **(446)**
capital budgeting **(435)**	electronic funds transfer system (EFTS) **(442)**	open-market operations **(449)**
capital investments **(435)**	financial control **(434)**	prime interest rate (prime) **(436)**
capital structure **(437)**	financial management **(432)**	reserve requirement **(448)**
checks **(440)**	financial plan **(432)**	secured loans **(438)**
collateral **(438)**	leverage **(437)**	selective credit controls **(449)**
commercial paper **(438)**	line of credit **(438)**	short-term financing **(436)**
compensating balance **(438)**	long-term financing **(436)**	smart cards **(441)**
cost of capital **(436)**	M1 **(448)**	time deposits **(447)**
credit cards **(440)**	M2 **(448)**	trade credit **(438)**
currency **(447)**	M3 **(448)**	unsecured loan **(438)**
debit cards **(441)**		

TEST YOUR KNOWLEDGE

Questions for Review

1. What is the primary goal of financial management?
2. What types of projects are typically considered in the capital budgeting process?
3. What is the difference between a secured and an unsecured loan?
4. How do credit cards, debit cards, and smart cards work?
5. What is the main function of the Federal Reserve System?

Questions for Analysis

6. Why do companies prepare budgets?
7. Why does internal financing have an opportunity cost?
8. How can smaller community banks compete with large commercial banks?
9. Besides shipping information and credit card information, what types of customer information might smart cards store in their chip that would be useful to e-businesses?

10. *Ethical Considerations:* What issues regarding privacy of personal information must Bank One and other financial supermarkets address to protect consumers?

Questions for Application

11. The financial manager for a small manufacturing firm wants to improve the company's cash flow position. What steps can he or she take?
12. Why might a company's board of directors decide to lease a piece of property even though it would be more economical to purchase the property and finance it with a long-term loan?
13. *Integrated:* Which of the four forms of utility discussed in Chapter 12 do ATMs and online banking create?
14. *Integrated:* How does the money supply affect the economy and inflation? (*Hint:* Think about the theory of supply and demand discussed in Chapter 1.)

PRACTICE YOUR KNOWLEDGE

Handling Difficult Situations on the Job: Dealing with Electronic Banking Errors

The ATM Error Resolution Department at Union Bank of California (where you work as an operations officer) often adjusts customer accounts for multiple electronic debit errors. Such errors are usually the result of an honest mistake: A merchant will run a customer's debit card two or three times through the card machine,

thinking the first few times didn't "take," when in fact the machine *was* working. For genuine errors, your routine is to authorize a correcting credit.

This time, you're questioning a claim from customer Margaret Caldwell. According to her letter and bank statement, her account was debited three times on the same day, using her debit card and crediting the same market, Wilson's Gourmet. The amounts differed: $23.02, $110.95, and $47.50. That doesn't strike you as a multiple-card-swipe situation. She hasn't enclosed any store receipt, and she claims that Wilson's Gourmet was trying to steal from her.

The store manager, Ronson Tibbits, tells you on the phone that his equipment is working fine, so it's unlikely that any card could be run repeatedly. He also mentions that food shoppers often return on the same day to make additional purchases, particularly for highly consumable products, or to pick up merchandise they forgot. Some buy a deli lunch at noon, then return later to shop for dinner.[31]

Your task: Margaret Caldwell and her husband are wealthy customers who keep large sums on deposit; they also use your investment and lending services. You're convinced that Mrs. Caldwell is merely mistaken or confused. But bank roles are clear: Deny the request politely. How will you convey your decision to the Caldwells without losing their valued business?

Building Your Team Skills

You and your team are going to build an operating expense budget worksheet for a neighborhood Domino's pizza franchise. Begin by brainstorming a list of expenses that are typical of a franchise/delivery restaurant. One way to do so is to think about the company's process—from making the pizza to delivering it. List the types of expenses and then group your list into categories such as delivery, marketing, manufacturing, financing, and so on. Leave the budget dollar amounts blank. Finally, develop a list of capital investments your company will make over the next three to five years. Compare your budget worksheets to those of the other teams in your class. Which operating and capital expenses did other teams have that your team did not? Which expenses did your team have that other teams omitted? Did all the teams categorize the expenses in a similar manner?

EXPAND YOUR KNOWLEDGE

Discovering Career Opportunities

Is a career in community banking for you? Bankers in smaller banks deal with a wide variety of customers, products, transactions, and inquiries every working day. To get a better idea of what community bankers do, visit a local bank where you do business.

1. Talk with a customer service representative or an officer about the kinds of customers this bank serves. Does it handle a high volume of business banking transactions, or is it more geared to consumer banking needs? How does the mix of consumer and business customers affect the branch's staffing and working hours?

2. What banking services are offered by this bank? Does the bank have specialized experts on staff to service these customers? What kind of skills, experience, education, and licenses must these experts have?

3. What kinds of entry-level jobs in this bank are appropriate for your background? What are the advancement opportunities within the bank and within the bank organization? Now that you have a better idea of what branch banking is, how does this career fit with your interests and goals?

Developing Your Research Skills

Choose a recent article from a business journal or newspaper (print or online editions) that discusses the financing arrangements or strategies of a particular company.

1. What form of financing did the company choose? Did the article indicate why the company selected this form of financing?

2. Who provided the financing for the company? Was this arrangement considered unusual, or was it routine?

3. What does the company intend to do with the arranged financing—purchase equipment or other assets, finance a construction project, finance growth and expansion, or do something else?

Exploring the Best of the Web

URLs for all Internet exercises are provided at the website for this book, www.prenhall.com/bovee. *When you log on to the text website, select Chapter 17, then select "Student Resources," click on the name of the featured website, and review the website to complete these exercises.*

Explore these chapter-related websites, review their content, and answer the following questions for each website you visit:

1. What is the purpose of this website?

2. What kinds of information does this website contain? Please be specific.

3. How is the information provided at this website useful for businesspeople? Consumers?

4. How did you expand your knowledge of banking and financial management by reviewing the material at this website? What new things did you learn about these topics?

Plan Ahead

Start your personal financial planning now by using the tools at the Financenter. This website has loads of information on the best way to buy, finance, or refinance major assets such as cars and houses. Use the calculators to compute what it will take to pay off your credit card balance. Find out whether you should consolidate your debts. Compute your available line of credit. Calculate how much money you can save by cutting your spending and investing the savings for 10 years. Better hurry. You may be losing interest. www.financenter.com

Take a Field Trip to the Fed

Visit the Fed. Find out what the Board of Governors of the Federal Reserve System does. Read summaries of their regulations. Learn what "Truth in Lending" means or how to file a consumer complaint against a bank. Brush up on your credit card knowledge. Do you know what a grace period is or how finance charges are calculated? Take a side trip to the Federal Reserve Banks. Don't leave without meeting Carmen Cents. She's at the FDIC and she has a wonderful tour planned for you. www.federalreserve.gov

Tour the U.S. Treasury

Take a virtual tour of the U.S. Treasury and discover what this department does. Visit the Learning Vault and find out how much paper currency is printed in one day or one year. Click on the Site Map and explore this department from the inside out. Learn about the benefits of electronic funds transfer. Take the link to the Bureau of Engraving and Printing, where you can play money trivia and get some money production figures. Discover how money gets into circulation. Find out whose picture is on the $500 bill. Bet you wish you had one! www.ustreas.gov

Learning Interactively

Companion Website

Visit the Companion website at www.prenhall.com/bovee. For Chapter 17, take advantage of the interactive "Study Guide" to test your chapter knowledge. Get instant feedback on whether you need additional studying. Read the "Current Events" articles to get the latest on chapter topics, and complete the exercises as specified by your instructor. Expand your learning with a visit to the "Research Area." There you will find a wealth of information you can use to complete your course assignments.

A CASE FOR CRITICAL THINKING

Cablevision Slims Down to Beef Up Profits

It's a dilemma most college students can certainly relate to: running a few dollars short when expenses pile up faster than income. If you can't earn more, the only choices are to spend less or to borrow enough to bridge the gap. James L. Dolan and the management team at Cablevision Systems ran into the same problem in 2002. Their only difference—the gap was $600 million wide.

Financing High-Speed Growth

In recent years, the name of the game in the media business has been size—bigger is better and biggest is best of all. From local cable companies to international giants such as Time Warner and Viacom, media firms acquired smaller companies and grew on the theory that market share was the key to success. One by one, though, many of these behemoths began to struggle under the challenge of financing their complex, far-flung operations.

New York–based Cablevision Systems started as a tiny local cable service with 1,500 subscribers and grew into a multibillion-dollar conglomerate with three million cable customers, a chain of electronics stores (The Wiz), a local telephone company, Rainbow Media Holdings (whose cable channels include American Movie Classics and the Independent Film Channel), a chain of movie theaters (Clearview Cinemas), stakes in a fledging wireless phone service, entertainment properties (Madison Square Garden and Radio City Music Hall), and—if all that weren't enough—the New York Knicks and several other professional sports teams.

Repairing a Weak Signal

Like most public companies, Cablevision relies heavily on sales of its own stock as a potential source of cash and as collateral for loans (if it needs to borrow). Unfortunately, like too many media and technology-related stocks, in the summer of 2002 Cablevision's market value took a nasty tumble, from a typical range of $60 to $70 a share to as low as $5 a share. It was also losing cable subscribers, thanks in large part to its refusal to carry New York Yankees games (Cablevision certainly wanted to carry the games, but not at the price the Yankees channel was demanding). Moreover, advertising business was down as a result of a general recession stretching back to 2001. The company was losing money, and the trend was not encouraging.

At the same time, Cablevision needed to keep investing in new cable and Internet technologies in order to retain existing customers and attract new subscribers. By midsummer, the cash-flow crunch reached a critical point, with cable revenues in danger and the company's ability to generate funds by selling stocks or securing attractive loans on the decline. Financial projections showed the company would need a cash infusion of $600 million in 2003. Borrowing enough to close the gap would be tough, given the company's sinking stock-collateral value and the fact that it was already $7 billion in debt after acquiring all those business units over the years.

Banking on New Business

The company had to act, both to shore up its finances and to give investors some reason to buy Cablevision stock and thereby help push the price back up. Dolan knew how much money he needed to find; the question was how to get it. Cutting capital investments in the cable operation would delay attractive new features and run the risk of losing more subscribers to the competition. Reducing staff could affect customer service, at a time when Cablevision was already in hot water with many New Yorkers for not carrying the Yankees games.

With no single place to make enough cuts to solve the problem, Dolan developed a multipart plan for increasing revenues and cutting costs. To both protect and grow the core cable business, which offered multiple opportunities for selling new digital services such as high-speed Internet access and video on demand, Cablevision announced plans to accelerate completion of its advanced broadband network. Meanwhile, the company maintained existing staff in the customer service call centers and field service operations to handle increased customer inquiries. Then Dolan sold the wireless phone licenses, sold the Bravo cable channel, put Clearview Cinemas up for sale, closed more than two dozen unprofitable stores in The Wiz chain, refocused the Lightpath business, and laid off 3,000 employees.

The moves were drastic, but so far they've seemed to pay off. In February 2003 the company announced a profitable fourth quarter, ending 2002 on a positive note. Cablevision lost 5,300 more basic cable subscribers that quarter but gained 136,000 higher-revenue digital customers. Net income for the quarter was over $500 million, compared to a loss of nearly $300 million for the same quarter the previous year. Dolan is confident the company is back on track, predicting plenty of money in the bank by the end of 2003 and continued growth into the future.

Critical Thinking Questions

1. Why did Nolan decide not to reduce customer service staff in the cable operation?

2. How did the company's sinking stock price affect its financial management?

3. Why couldn't Cablevision simply borrow $600 million to close the cash flow gap?

4. Visit the investor information section of Cablevision's website, www.cablevision.com, and check out the financial news. How has the company performed financially in recent quarters?

VIDEO CASE

Funding the Business World: Coast Business Credit

Learning Objectives

The purpose of this video is to help you:

1. Recognize how and why banks use customer deposits as the basis of loans.

2. Understand the role of banks and financial services firms in providing funding for business expansion, operations, and acquisitions.

3. Identify the risks that financial services firms take when loaning money to companies.

Synopsis

Coast Business Credit, a division of Southern Pacific Bank, provides the money that fuels businesses. As a lender, Coast carefully considers a business's collateral, cash flow, and management when evaluating the risk that a loan will not be repaid as promised. Business customers may apply for a short-term line of credit, a long-term loan, or another type of financing for a variety of purposes. One company may need operating capital; another may need money to make a major acquisition or expand more aggressively. Coast analyzes each lending opportunity in terms of the potential risk, the potential profit, and—in some cases—the ability to create or save jobs, which benefits the community at large.

Discussion Questions

1. *For analysis:* How might the amount of time deposits gathered by parent company, Southern Pacific Bank, affect the loans made by Coast Business Services?

2. *For analysis:* If the Federal Reserve lowers the discount rate by a significant amount, what would be the likely effect on business loan rates?

3. *For application:* What type of collateral might Coast Business Services prefer when considering a business's loan application?

4. *For application:* In addition to collateral, Coast Business Services looks at cash flow and management when considering a loan application. Why is management such an important element?

5. *For debate:* Should Coast Business Services establish a separate lending department specifically for financing Internet start-ups? Support your chosen position.

Online Exploration

Visit Coast Business Credit's website at www.coastbusinesscredit.com, and after browsing the homepage, follow the link to learn more about Coast Business Credit. Then follow the link to find out what types of loans Coast will make and to what types of businesses. Why does Coast explain its financial offerings in such detail? Why would it mention the names of the parent company, its affiliates, and the bank's FDIC coverage on its website? How does Coast make it easy for businesses to make contact?

Securities

First Charles Schwab grabbed huge chunks of market share from traditional brokers. Then it cleaned up in the discount online trading markets. Now it's going after the full-service brokers— again.

INSIDE BUSINESS TODAY

Charles Schwab Takes On Wall Street—Again and Again and Again

Since its founding in 1974, Charles Schwab has been at the leading edge of a series of industry-transforming changes. When the SEC ended fixed-stock commissions in the 1970s, the company forged new ground by opening the discount brokerage house that now bears the founder's name. When mutual funds became popular in the 1980s, the trendsetter revolutionized the mutual-fund industry by creating a mutual-fund supermarket where investors could buy and sell hundreds of mutual funds in one account without incurring heavy fees. And, when e-commerce took off in the mid-1990s, Schwab took a giant leap of faith by leveraging the power of the Internet and the company's nationwide network of customer centers to provide a convenient and economical way for investors to trade stocks online. Merrill Lynch, one of the last Wall Street firms to offer online trading, eventually had to give in or continue losing customers to Schwab.

Through it all, Schwab developed a reputation as a bold innovator that responds to market changes and isn't afraid to take on anybody in the business. That attitude was put to the test time and again after the dot-com collapse in 2000 and 2001, the persistent recession that followed soon after, corporate financial scandals that scared investors away, and the market-depressing effects of terrorist attacks and global political uncertainty. Schwab responded in true character, redefining the company to meet changing conditions and taking on old-school Wall Street at every step. The internal changes were painful: The company laid off nearly a quarter of its staff in 2001, and the cuts continued into 2002, when company executives became convinced that the investment market would not turn around anytime soon.

But the company didn't simply retreat. With the online discount business in trouble, Schwab expanded from its discounter roots in order to recapture wealthier customers who had been migrating to Merrill Lynch and other full-service firms. Schwab purchased U.S. Trust Co, an old-line money-management firm, in order to pursue the wealthiest and most profitable investment customers. The acquisition set the stage for Schwab to move one step closer to becoming a full-service firm. Soon thereafter, Schwab began offering personalized investment advice, wireless trading, account management, financial planning, and portfolio evaluations.

Next came an aggressive marketing campaign with hard-hitting print and TV ads that tried to turn Wall Street's woes into a competitive advantage for Schwab. The ads explained that unlike its competitors, Schwab did not pay brokers based on how much they encouraged customers to trade. Nor was Schwab tied to big corporate clients via investment banking relationships. The ads also promoted Schwab's new stock-rating system, which used an unbiased computer model. Schwab hoped the new rating system would attract investors who had lost faith in the advice of brokers possibly influenced by commissions or investment banking relationships.

All in all, Schwab has blazed a trail that competitors inevitably followed, and in doing so the company has built a durable business. Schwab now has over 8 million active accounts, or 25 percent of the discount brokerage market. It also has some pretty lofty goals: "Our goal is to show 20 percent year-over-year growth in revenues and maintain profit margins of 12 percent and above," says CEO David Pottruck.

But only time—and a better investment climate—will tell if the new Schwab model will succeed. "The changes we're making are profound," admits Pottruck. We are "retesting what the company stands for." No one is sure when the investment business will recover, but whatever actions Schwab needs to take to survive and succeed in the future, one thing is clear: Charles Schwab won't be afraid to take on anybody or to redefine the company to meet new market realities.[1]

Types of Securities Investments

securities
Instruments such as stocks, bonds, options, futures, and commodities

As David Pottruck knows, **securities**—stocks, bonds, and other investments—are much in the news these days. Look at the business section of any newspaper or magazine, and you'll read about a corporation selling stocks or bonds to finance operations or expansion. Similarly, governments and municipalities issue bonds to raise money for building or public expenses, from national defense to road improvements. These securities are traded in organized markets where investors (individuals and institutions) can buy and sell them to meet their investment goals.

This chapter discusses the types of securities investments issued by corporations and governments, the marketplaces where securities are sold, and the recommended approach and standard procedures for buying and selling securities.

Stocks

1 LEARNING OBJECTIVE

Differentiate among a stock's par value, its market value, and its book value

stock certificate
Document that proves stock ownership

authorized stock
Shares that a corporation's board of directors has decided to sell eventually

issued stock
Authorized shares that have been released to the market

unissued stock
Authorized shares that are to be released in the future

par value
Arbitrary value assigned to a stock that is shown on the stock certificate

stock split
Increase in the number of shares of ownership that each stock certificate represents

As discussed in Chapter 6, a share of stock represents ownership in a corporation and is evidenced by a **stock certificate**. The number of stock shares a company sells depends on the amount of equity capital the company will require and on the price of each share it sells. A corporation's board of directors sets a maximum number of shares into which the business can be divided. In theory, all these shares—called **authorized stock**—may be sold at once. In practice, however, the company sells only a part of its authorized stock. The part sold and held by shareholders is called **issued stock**; the unsold portion is called **unissued stock**.

When stock is first issued, the company assigns a **par value**, or dollar value, to the stock primarily for bookkeeping purposes. Par value is also used to calculate dividends (for certain kinds of stock). Par value should not be confused with a stock's *market value*, the price at which a share currently sells, or its *book value*, the amount of net assets of a corporation represented by one share of common stock.

From time to time a company may announce a **stock split**, in which it increases the number of shares that each stock certificate represents while proportionately lowering the value of each share. Companies generally use a stock split to make the share price more affordable. For instance, if a company with 1 million shares outstanding and a stock price of $50 per share announces a two-for-one split, it is doubling the number of shares outstanding without altering the total market value of the shares. After the split, the company will have 2 million shares outstanding, and each original share will become two shares worth $25 each. The total market value of the company's stock will remain at $50 million.

Companies may also announce a *reverse split*. This strategy reduces the number of shares outstanding and boosts the price per share, but the total market value of the company shares also remains the same. For example, in a 10-for-1 reverse split, 10 million shares trading at 90 cents become 1 million shares trading at $9. The total market value of the company's stock remains at $9 million. Some companies use a reverse split to make the stock price appear more attractive to investors or to keep the stock from being delisted by stock exchanges. NASDAQ, for example, requires that a company maintain a minimum stock price of $1. Regardless of the reason, reverse splits are rarely effective, because smart investors recognize the ploy. Of 37 tech firms listed on NASDAQ that used reverse splits in 2002, only five were trading above their reverse split price at the end of that year.[2]

Common Stock   Most investors buy common stock, which represents an ownership interest in a publicly traded corporation. As Chapter 6 points out, shareholders of this class of stock vote to elect the company's board of directors, vote on other important corporate issues, and receive dividends—payments from the company's profits. But they have no say in the day-to-day business activities. Still, common shareholders have the advantage of limited liability if the corporation gets into trouble, and as part owners, they share in the fortunes of the business and are eligible to receive dividends as long as they hold the stock. In addition, common shareholders stand to make a profit if the stock price goes up and they sell their shares for more than the purchase price. The reverse is also true: Shareholders of common stock can lose money if the market price drops and they sell the stock for less than they paid for it.

Stock certificates represent a share of ownership of a company.

Preferred Stock   Investors who own preferred stock, the second major class of stock, enjoy higher dividends and a better claim (after creditors) on assets if the corporation fails. The amount of the dividend on preferred stock is printed on the stock certificate and set when the stock is first issued. If interest rates fluctuate, the market price of preferred stock will go up or down to adjust for the difference between the market interest rate and the stock's dividend.

Preferred stock often comes with special privileges. *Convertible preferred stock* can be exchanged, if the shareholder chooses, for a certain number of shares of common stock issued by the company. *Cumulative preferred stock* has an additional advantage: If the issuing company stops paying dividends for any reason, the dividends on these shares will be held (accumulate) until preferred shareholders have been paid in full—before common stockholders are paid.

2 LEARNING OBJECTIVE

Highlight the distinguishing features of common stock, preferred stock, bonds, and mutual funds

bond
Method of funding in which the issuer borrows from an investor and provides a written promise to make regular interest payments and repay the borrowed amount in the future

Bonds

Unlike stock, which gives the investor an ownership stake in the corporation, bonds are a form of debt financing. A **bond** is a method of raising money in which the issuing organization borrows from an investor and issues a written pledge to make regular interest payments and then repay the borrowed amount later. When you invest in this type of security, you are lending money to the company, municipality, or government agency that issued the bond. Bonds are usually issued in multiples of $1,000, such as $5,000, $10,000 and $50,000. Also like stocks, bonds are evidenced by a certificate, which shows the issuer's name, the

Bell South Telecommunications Bond Certificate
(1) Name of corporation issuing bond; (2) type of bond (debenture); (3) face value of the bond; (4) annual interest rate (8.25%); (5) maturity date (due 2032).

principal
Amount of a debt, excluding any interest

amount borrowed (the **principal**), the date this principal amount will be repaid, and the annual interest rate investors receive.

The interest is stated in terms of an annual percentage rate but is usually paid at six-month intervals. For example, the holder of a $1,000 bond that pays 8 percent interest due January 15 and July 15 could expect to receive $40 on each of those dates. A look at the financial section of any newspaper will show that some corporations sell new bonds at an interest rate two or three percentage points higher than that offered by other companies. Yet the terms of the bonds seem similar. Why? Because bonds are not guaranteed investments. The variations in interest rates reflect the degree of risk associated with the bond, which is closely tied to the financial stability of the issuing company.

Agencies such as Standard & Poor's (S&P) and Moody's rate bonds on the basis of the issuers' financial strength. Exhibit 18.1 shows that the safest corporate bonds are rated AAA (S&P) and Aaa (Moody's). Low-rated bonds, known as *junk bonds*, pay higher interest rates to compensate investors for the higher risk. Companies with AAA (S&P) ratings don't necessarily get material advantages over those rated one notch down at AA. The AAA rating merely indicates that the company borrows less than it can—a sacrifice few companies are willing to make. In fact, only one company, General Electric, has kept its S&P's AAA rating since 1960.[3]

secured bonds
Bonds backed by specific assets

debentures
Corporate bonds backed only by the reputation of the issuer

convertible bonds
Corporate bonds that can be exchanged at the owner's discretion into common stock of the issuing company

Corporate Bonds Companies issue a variety of corporate bonds. **Secured bonds** are backed by company-owned property (such as airplanes or plant equipment) that will pass to the bondholders if the issuer does not repay the amount borrowed. *Mortgage bonds*, one type of secured bond, are backed by real property owned by the issuing corporation. **Debentures** are unsecured bonds, backed only by the corporation's promise to pay. Because debentures are riskier than other types of bonds, investors who buy these bonds receive higher interest rates. **Convertible bonds** can be exchanged at the investor's option for a certain number of shares of the corporation's common stock. Because of this feature, convertible bonds generally pay lower interest rates.

U.S. Government Securities and Municipal Bonds Just as corporations raise money by issuing bonds, so do federal, state, city, and local governments and agencies. As an investor, you can buy a variety of U.S. government securities, including three types of

3 LEARNING OBJECTIVE

List five types of bonds issued by governments

EXHIBIT 18.1
Corporate Bond Ratings
Standard & Poor's (S&P) and Moody's Investors Service are two companies that rate the safety of corporate bonds. When its bonds receive a low rating, a company must pay a higher interest rate to compensate investors for the higher risk.

S&P	INTERPRETATION	MOODY'S	INTERPRETATION
AAA	Highest rating	Aaa	Prime quality
AA	Very strong capacity to pay	Aa	High grade
A	Strong capacity to pay; somewhat susceptible to changing business conditions	A	Upper-medium grade
BBB	More susceptible than A rated bonds	Baa	Medium grade
BB	Somewhat speculative	Ba	Somewhat speculative
B	Speculative	B	Speculative
CC	Vulnerable to nonpayment	Caa	Poor standing; may be in default
CCC	Highly vulnerable to nonpayment	C	Highly speculative; often in default
C	Bankruptcy petition filed or similar action taken	C	Lowest rated; extremely poor chance of ever attaining real investment standing
D	In default		

bonds issued by the U.S. Treasury, U.S. savings bonds, and bonds issued by various U.S. municipalities.

Treasury bills (also referred to as T-bills) are short-term U.S. government bonds that are repaid in less than one year. Treasury bills are sold at a discount and redeemed at face value. The difference between the purchase price and the redemption price is, in effect, the interest earned for the time periods. **Treasury notes** are intermediate-term U.S. government bonds that are repaid one to 10 years after they were initially issued. **Treasury bonds** are long-term U.S. government bonds that are repaid more than 10 years after they were initially issued. Both treasury notes and treasury bonds pay a fixed amount of interest twice a year. But in general, U.S. government securities pay lower interest than corporate bonds because they are considered safer: There is very little risk that the government will fail to repay bondholders as promised. Another benefit is that investors pay no state or local income tax on interest earned on these bonds. Also, these bonds can easily be bought or sold through the Treasury or in organized securities markets.

A traditional choice for many individual investors, **U.S. savings bonds** are issued by the U.S. government in amounts ranging from $50 to $10,000. Investors who buy Series EE savings bonds pay just 50 percent of the stated value and receive the full face amount in as little as 17 years (the difference being earned interest). Once the bond's face value equals its redemption value, the bond continues to earn interest, but only until 30 years after the bonds were issued (the bond's final maturity date). Other savings bonds are Series HH, which can be bought only by exchanging Series EE bonds, and Series I, which pay interest indexed to the inflation rate.

Municipal bonds (often called *munis*) are issued by states, cities, and special government agencies to raise money for public services such as building schools, highways, and airports. Investors can buy two types of municipal bonds: general obligation bonds and revenue bonds. A **general obligation bond** is a municipal bond backed by the taxing power of the issuing government. When interest payments come due, the issuer makes payments out of its tax receipts. In contrast, a **revenue bond** is a municipal bond backed by the money to be generated by the project being financed. As an example, revenue bonds issued by a city airport are paid from revenues raised by the airport's operation. To encourage investment, the federal government doesn't tax the interest that investors receive from municipal bonds. Also exempt from state income tax is the interest earned on municipal bonds that are issued by the governments within the taxpayer's home state. However, **capital gains**—the return investors get from selling a security for more than its purchase price—are taxed at both the federal and state levels.

Retirement of Debt Issuers of bonds must eventually repay the borrowed amount to the bondholders. Normally, this repayment is done when the bonds mature—say, 10, 15, or 20 years after the bond is issued. The cost of retiring the debt can be staggering, because bonds are generally issued in quantity—perhaps thousands of individual bonds in a single issue. To ease the cash flow burden of redeeming its bonds all at once, a company sometimes issues *serial bonds*, which mature at various times, as opposed to *term bonds*, which all mature at the same time.

Another way of relieving the financial strain of retiring many bonds all at once is to set up a **sinking fund**. When a corporation issues a bond payable by a sinking fund, it must set aside a certain sum of money each year to pay the debt. This money may be used to retire a few bonds each year, or it may be set aside to accumulate until the issue matures.

With most bond issues, a corporation retains the right to pay off the bonds before maturity. Bonds containing this provision are known as *callable bonds*, or *redeemable bonds*. If a company issues bonds when interest rates are high and then rates fall later on, it may want to pay off its high-interest bonds and sell a new issue at a lower rate. However, this feature carries a price tag: Investors must be offered a higher interest rate to encourage them to buy callable bonds. The portion of the percentage rate that is above market rates is actually a "call premium."

Treasury bills
Short-term debt issued by the federal government; also referred to as *T-bills*

Treasury notes
Debt securities issued by the federal government that mature within one to 10 years

Treasury bonds
Debt securities issued by the federal government that mature in 10 to 30 years

U.S. savings bonds
Debt instruments sold by the federal government in small denominations

municipal bonds
Debt issued by a state or a local agency; interest earned on municipal bonds is exempt from federal income tax and from taxes in the issuing jurisdiction

general obligation bond
Municipal bonds backed by the issuing agency's general taxing authority

revenue bond
Municipal bonds backed by revenue generated from the projects financed with the bonds

capital gains
Difference between the price at which a financial asset is sold and its original cost (assuming the price has gone up)

sinking fund
Account into which a company makes annual payments for use in redeeming its bonds in the future

Other Investments

Stocks and bonds are the most common marketable securities available for investors. However, other securities have been developed. For the most part, mutual funds, options, financial futures, commodities, and their variations are used by money managers and savvy traders. In recent years, some of these securities, particularly options, have been used more by individual investors.

mutual funds
Pools of money raised by investment companies and invested in stocks, bonds, or other marketable securities

Mutual Funds **Mutual funds** are financial organizations that pool money from many investors to buy a diversified mix of stocks, bonds, or other securities. Charles Schwab made this type of investment popular when the company launched its OneSource no-fee mutual-fund supermarket in 1992. Mutual funds are particularly well suited for investors who wish to spread a fixed amount of money over a variety of investments and do not have the time or experience to search out and manage investment opportunities. *No-load* funds charge no fee to buy or sell shares, whereas *load funds* charge investors a commission to buy or sell shares. The most common types of loads are front end (assessed when you purchase the fund) and back end (assessed when you sell the fund).

Investment companies offer two types of mutual funds. An *open-end fund* issues additional shares as new investors ask to buy them. In essence, the fund's books never close. The number of shares outstanding changes daily as investors buy new shares or redeem old ones. These shares aren't traded in a separate market. *Closed-end funds*, on the other hand, raise all their money at once by distributing a fixed number of shares that trade much like stocks on major security exchanges. As soon as a certain number of shares are sold, the fund closes its books.

money-market funds
Mutual funds that invest in short-term securities

Various mutual funds have different investment priorities. Among the most popular mutual funds are **money-market funds**, which invest in short-term securities and other liquid investments. *Growth funds* invest in stocks of rapidly growing companies. *Income funds* invest in securities that pay high dividends and interest. *Balanced funds* invest in a carefully chosen mix of stocks and bonds. *Sector funds* (also known as specialty or industry funds) invest in companies within a particular industry. *Global funds* invest in foreign and U.S. securities, whereas *international funds* invest strictly in foreign securities. And *index funds* buy stocks in companies included in specific market averages, such as the Standard & Poor's 500. You can buy shares in mutual funds through your broker or directly from the mutual fund company.

Options and Financial Futures As Chapter 11 points out, a stock option is the purchased right—but not the obligation—to buy or sell a specified number of shares of a stock at a predetermined price during a specified period. Options can be used for wild speculation, or they can be used to **hedge** your positions—that is, partially protect against the risk of a sudden loss. By trading options, the investor doesn't have to own shares of stock in a company—only an option to buy or sell those shares. Investors who trade stock options are betting that the price of the stock will either rise or fall. The cost of buying an option on shares of stock is only the premium paid to the seller, or the price of the option.

hedge
To make an investment that protects the investor from suffering loss on another investment

All options fall into two broad categories: *puts* and *calls*. Exhibit 18.2 explains the rights acquired with each type of option. **Financial futures** are similar to options, but they are legally binding contracts to buy or sell a financial instrument (stocks, Treasury bonds, foreign currencies) for a set price at a future date.

financial futures
Legally binding agreements to buy or sell financial instruments at a future date

Commodities For the investor who is comfortable with risky investments, nothing compares with speculating in **commodities**—raw materials and agricultural products, such as petroleum, gold, coffee beans, pork bellies, beef, and coconut oil. Commodities markets originally sprang up as a convenience for buyers and sellers interested in trading the actual commodities. A manufacturer of breakfast cereals, for example, must buy wheat, rye, oats, and sugar from hundreds of farmers. The easiest way to arrange these transactions is to meet in a forum where many buyers and sellers come to trade. Because the commodities are

commodities
Raw materials used in producing other goods

primary market
Market where firms sell new securities issued publicly for the first time

EXHIBIT 18.2   Options
All stock options fall into two broad categories: puts and calls.

RIGHT	BUYER'S BELIEF	SELLER'S BELIEF
CALL OPTION		
The right to buy the stock at a fixed price until the expiration date.	Buyer believes price of underlying stock will increase. Buyer can buy stock at a set price and sell it at a higher price for a capital gain.	Seller believes price of underlying stock will decline and that the option will not be exercised. Seller earns a premium.
PUT OPTION		
The right to sell the stock at a fixed price until the expiration date.	Buyer believes price of underlying stock will decline and wants to lock in a fixed profit. Buyer usually already owns shares of underlying stock.	Seller believes price of underlying stock will rise and that the option will not be exercised. Seller earns a premium.

too bulky to bring to the marketplace, the traders buy and sell contracts for delivery of a given amount of these raw materials at a given time.

Trading contracts for immediate delivery of a commodity is called *spot trading*, or *cash trading*. Most commodity trading is for future delivery, usually months in advance, sometimes a year or more; this is called trading commodities futures. The original purpose of futures trading was to allow producers and consumers of commodities to hedge their position, or protect themselves against violent price swings. For example, say you're a cattle rancher in Montana and each month you purchase 20,000 bushels of feed corn. A big rise in corn prices resulting from a flood in the Midwest could ruin you. To hedge against such risk, you purchase futures contracts guaranteeing you 20,000 bushels of corn at a given price when you need them at a later date. Now you know what you'll have to pay. But for every hedger, there must be a speculator—a person willing to take on the risk the hedger wants to shed. The person on the other end of your corn trade probably has no business interest in corn or cattle; he simply wants to gamble that he can buy an offsetting corn contract at a lower price and thus make a profit on the deal.[4] But such speculation is risky—even seasoned veterans have been known to lose literally millions of dollars within a few days.

Securities Exchanges and Marketplaces

Where can you purchase bonds, stocks, and other securities? Stocks and bonds are bought and sold in two kinds of marketplaces: primary markets and secondary markets. Newly issued shares or initial public offerings (IPOs) are sold in the **primary market**. Once these shares have been issued, subsequent investors can buy and sell them in the organized **secondary market** known as **stock exchanges** (or securities exchanges). The process for buying and selling securities varies according to the type of exchange.

Auction Exchanges Versus Dealer Exchanges

In an **auction exchange** all buy and sell orders (and all information concerning companies traded on that exchange) are funneled onto an auction floor. There, buyers and sellers are matched by a **stock specialist**, a broker who occupies a post on the trading floor and conducts all the trades in specific stocks via a central clearinghouse. If buying or selling imbalances occur in that stock, a specialist can

secondary market
Market where subsequent owners trade previously issued shares of stocks and bonds

stock exchanges
Location where traders buy and sell stocks and bonds

4 **LEARNING OBJECTIVE**

Differentiate among an auction exchange, a dealer exchange, and an electronic communication network (ECN)

auction exchange
Centralized marketplace where securities are traded by specialists on behalf of investors

stock specialist
Intermediary who trades in a particular security on the floor of an auction exchange; "buyer of last resort"

At the Chicago Mercantile Exchange (CME) orders stream in from customers trading futures and options from all over the world. Each CME trader acts as buyer and seller, communicating with hand signals and by shouting bids to buy and offers to sell.

The New York Stock Exchange began under a buttonwood tree on Wall Street in 1792 as an agreement among a group of brokers to trade with one another. In 1817 the institution was established, with members taking seats in a room to trade stocks at designated times. For a long time, the floor was an important center of power in brokerage firms. Then came the Internet and ECNs. Today, the NYSE is under competitive pressure to automate its trading systems.

halt trading to prevent the price from plunging without adequate cause. Specialists can also sell stock to customers out of their own inventory.[5]

The New York Stock Exchange (NYSE), also known as the "Big Board," is the world's largest auction exchange. The stocks and bonds of about 3,000 companies, with a combined market value topping $11 trillion, are traded on the exchange's floor.[6] After the NYSE, some of the largest stock exchanges are located in Tokyo, London, Frankfurt, Paris, Toronto, and Montreal. Many companies list their securities on more than one securities exchange. Thus, NYSE-listed stocks can also be bought and sold at one or more of the U.S. regional exchanges, such as the Pacific or Philadelphia exchanges.

In contrast, a **dealer exchange** has no central marketplace for making transactions. Instead, all buy and sell orders are executed through computers by **market makers**, registered stock and bond representatives who sell securities out of their own inventories. Most use a nationwide computer network owned by the National Association of Securities Dealers (NASD). This network, called **NASDAQ (National Association of Securities Dealers Automated Quotations)**, is the second-largest stock market in the United States. In 1998 NASD (owners of NASDAQ) acquired the American Stock Exchange (the world's third-largest auction exchange), making NASDAQ an even stronger competitor against the New York Stock Exchange.[7]

dealer exchange
Decentralized marketplace where securities are bought and sold by dealers out of their own inventories

market makers
Dealers in dealer exchanges who sell securities out of their own inventories so that a market is always available for buyers and sellers

NASDAQ (National Association of Securities Dealers Automated Quotations)
National over-the-counter securities trading network

Electronic communication networks (ECNs)
Internet-based networks that match up buy and sell orders without using a middleman

Electronic Communication Networks

Electronic communication networks (ECNs) use the Internet to link buyers and sellers. Frequently referred to as virtual stock markets or cybermarkets, ECNs have no exchange floors, specialists, or market makers. In fact, they are nothing more than computer networks with software programs that match buy and sell orders directly, cutting out the once dominant market makers and specialists. Like other securities marketplaces, ECNs make money by providing a place where stocks can be traded and by collecting commissions on each trade. Most ECNs operate globally and economically—which is why they are becoming increasingly popular. In 2002 the two biggest ECNs, Instinet and Island, joined forces when Instinet acquired Island in a stock transaction valued at about $508 million.[8]

ECNs give customers an additional way to buy and sell stocks (see Exhibit 18.3). For example, if a company's stock is listed on an auction or dealer exchange, its shares may also be traded on an ECN. In fact, many brokerage firms use a combination of auction exchanges, dealer exchanges, and ECNs to execute their trades. Over 40 percent of NASDAQ shares are now traded on ECNs.[9]

As this chapter's Case for Critical Thinking shows, the increasing popularity of ECNs is putting older trading systems to the test. Until recently, big Wall Street firms have lived with costly stock exchange floors, specialists, and market makers because the system worked well enough. But even the Chairman of the NASD now admits that "the old methods of exchanging stocks no longer meet the needs of the investing consumer."[10] Discount brokers, ECNs, large securities institutions such as Merrill Lynch and Goldman Sachs (which are investing in ECNs), and consumers are pushing traditional securities exchanges to offer electronic trading options within their exchanges.[11]

EXHIBIT 18.3   Old and New Ways to Buy Stocks
Some think that floor trading will become a thing of the past as electronic communication networks become increasingly popular.

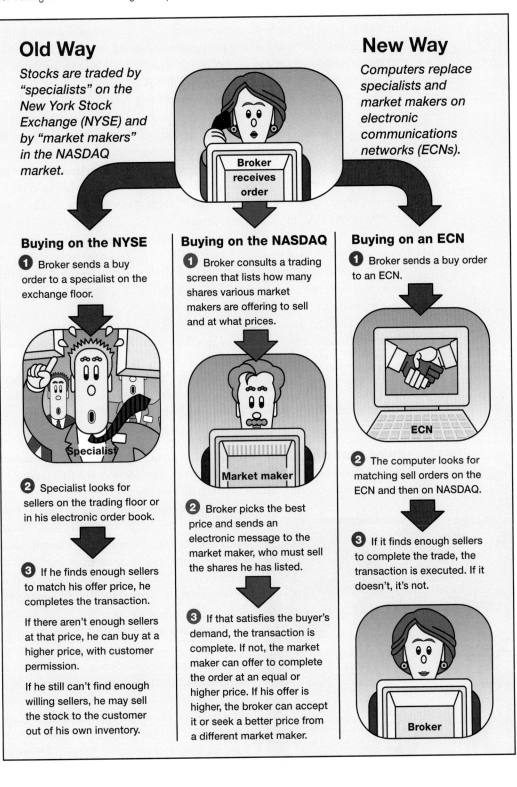

5 **LEARNING OBJECTIVE**

Discuss how securities
marketplaces are changing

The Changing Nature of Securities Marketplaces

The securities marketplaces we know today are really a creation of the past quarter-century. The deregulation of trading commissions in 1975, the rise of discount brokers like Charles Schwab, and the 20-year bull market have transformed once-small Manhattan partnerships that specialized in advice and the occasional deal into publicly traded financial supermarkets with tens of thousands of employees and millions of customers.

Most of the business that defines what the big New York–based investment banks and brokerage firms do today—stock and bond trading, IPO underwriting, merger and acquisition advice, securities analysis, asset management for institutions and individuals—exploded in the 1990s. At the same time, the lines between commercial banking and investment banking blurred, giving rise to new players such as Citigroup and J.P. Morgan Chase. The prospects of growth in new deals and services also sparked a hiring frenzy among the big security firms. Between 1990 and 2000, securities-industry employment soared from 417,000 to 783,000, an 88 percent increase.[12]

But at the beginning of the 21st century the floor fell out. Wall Street became mired in its deepest bear market since the Crash of 1929. By 2002 the stock market turned in its third consecutive year of losses—something it hadn't done in 60 years—and investors in U.S. stocks had suffered annual paper losses of over $2.8 trillion. The services that drove the great profit boom of the 1990s slowed to a crawl.[13]

Some industry experts believe that the era of dramatic industry growth is now over. Many don't expect these services to come roaring back even when the stock markets rebound. To compensate for the loss of business, securities firms are entering new markets, reorganizing, and thinning their staffs. The brokerage sector laid off some 78,000 people from mid-2001 through 2002. Many seasoned investment bankers and brokers who once raked in more than $1 million a year are either jobless or have seen their paychecks shrivel by two-thirds.[14]

Online Trading Online trading is also changing how securities marketplaces operate. When online trading first became popular in the 1990s, many full-service brokerage firms, such as Merrill Lynch, resisted offering this service because they did not want to lose their lucrative sales commissions. But to remain competitive in the marketplace, they were eventually forced to offer some form of online trading. Some of the most notable discount online trading firms today are Ameritrade, E*Trade, Charles Schwab, and TD Waterhouse. Some, such as E*Trade, are expanding their market share by adding banking, loan, insurance, and advisory services.[15]

Investors who choose online trading execute their trades via a brokerage firm's website instead of phoning a firm's brokers. Convenience, control, and lower commissions are the main customer advantages of online trading. Still, online trading is not for everyone. When you trade online, you trade alone, with no one to check for mistakes or to offer advice. Moreover, online trading websites have had their share of problems. The top five consumer complaints filed with the SEC against online brokers include (1) failure to process orders or delays in executing orders, (2) difficulty in accessing one's account or contacting a broker, (3) errors in processing orders, (4) execution of orders at higher prices than posted on the website, and (5) errors and omissions in account records and documents.[16]

Many investors now use online discount brokers to trade securities.

Extended Hours   To respond to changing times, many securities exchanges have extended their traditional trading hours of 9:30 A.M. to 4 P.M. (Eastern U.S. time zone) to include early-morning and late-night trading sessions. *After-hours trading* or *extended-hours trading* refers to the purchase and sale of publicly traded stocks mostly in the 90 minutes before the NYSE and NASDAQ open and the 90 minutes after they close, although some after-hours trading takes place 24 hours a day. After-hours trading was once limited to sophisticated institutional investors. But with online trading, ECNs, and favorable regulatory changes, individual investors can now get in the game as well.

The biggest advantages to extended-hours trading are that it accommodates traders who live in regions outside the Eastern U.S. time zone, and it allows shrewd investors to beat others to the punch. The biggest disadvantage, however, is the lack of volume. Most institutional investors close up shop after the NYSE closing bell.[17] An average of 70 million shares change hands after hours, but that's only a fraction of the 1.2 billion shares traded each day on the NYSE.[18]

Regulation of Securities Markets

Whether you buy and sell securities online or use a traditional full-service house, your trades are governed by a network of state and federal laws (see Exhibit 18.4). Combined with industry self-regulation, these laws are designed to ensure that you and all investors receive accurate information and that no one artificially manipulates the market price of a given security.

6 **LEARNING OBJECTIVE**

Explain how government regulation of securities trading tries to protect investors

EXHIBIT 18.4   Major Federal Legislation Governing the Securities Industry
Although you have no guarantee that you'll make money on your investments, you are protected by laws against unfair securities trading practices.

LEGISLATION	PROVISION
Securities Act (1933)	Requires full disclosure of relevant financial information from companies that want to sell new stock or bond issues to the general public; also known as the Truth in Securities Act
Securities Exchange Act (1934)	Creates the Securities and Exchange Commission (SEC) to regulate the national stock exchanges and to establish trading rules
Maloney Act (1938)	Creates the National Association of Securities Dealers to regulate over-the-counter securities trading
Investment Company Act (1940)	Extends the SEC's authority to cover the regulation of mutual funds
Amendment to the Securities Exchange Act (1964)	Extends the SEC's authority to cover the over-the-counter market
Securities Investor Protection Act (1970)	Creates the Securities Investor Protection Corporation (SIPC) to insure individual investors against losses in the event of dealer fraud or insolvency
Commodity Futures Trading Commission Act (1974)	Creates the Commodity Futures Trading Commission (CFTC) to establish and enforce regulations governing futures trading
Insider Trading and Securities Fraud Act (1988)	Toughens penalties, authorizes bounties for information, requires brokerages to establish written policies to prevent employee violations, and makes it easier for investors to bring legal action against violators
Securities Market Reform Act (1990)	Increases SEC market control by granting additional authority to suspend trading in any security for 10 days, to restore order in the event of a major disturbance, to establish a national system for settlement and clearance of securities transactions, to adapt rules for actions affecting market volatility, and to require more detailed record keeping and reporting of brokers and dealers
Private Securities Litigation Reform Act (1995)	Protects companies from frivolous lawsuits by investors: limits how many class-action suits can be filed by the same person in a three-year period, and encourages judges to penalize plaintiffs who bring meritless cases

One such regulation recently adopted by the SEC is Regulation Fair Disclosure (FD). The 2000 law was designed to create a level playing field for all investors. Specifically, the regulation mandates that any news with the potential to affect the price of a stock must be released to everyone simultaneously. In other words, the regulation prohibits companies from "selectively disclosing" important information (such as earnings estimates) to big institutional shareholders and Wall Street analysts ahead of regular investors. Otherwise, early news recipients would be able to "make a profit or avoid a loss at the expense of those kept in the dark."[19]

In spite of its good intentions, critics argue that the regulation could have unintended negative consequences. They worry that instead of giving small and large investors equal access to market-sensitive information, the regulation could cut down on the amount of information received by everyone. Part of the problem stems from the fact that the SEC has not clearly defined what it means by *market-sensitive* information, so companies are opting to err on the side of silence. Moreover, some companies claim it's too difficult to give small investors the same level of information that they have selectively provided to investment analysts.[20]

Trading Oversight   The SEC is the principal overseer of the U.S. securities markets. The SEC works closely with the stock exchanges and NASD to police securities transactions and maintain the system's integrity. NASD is in charge of policing Wall Street and settling disputes between brokerages and investors. All Wall Street firms and brokers must belong to the NASD and fund its $400 million annual budget. The association has the power to suspend or expel members as well as levy fines and seize ill-gotten profits. NASD can also order a broker or firm to repay an investor, but it rarely does.[21] In addition to obeying SEC and NASD policies, all brokers must operate according to the rules of the exchanges, rules that are largely designed to protect investors.

SEC Filing Requirements   Public companies must file a number of periodic documents with the SEC, as listed in Exhibit 18.5. Investors can view, download, and print many of the documents filed by public companies by visiting the SEC's Edgar website. One such document required by the SEC is a *prospectus*, which must be filed before offering securities for sale. A prospectus gives a detailed description of the company issuing the securities as well as the securities being issued. In addition, a prospectus provides information regarding the company's products, financial status, future projects, and pending litigation.

As you can imagine, overseeing the filing and content of these documents keeps the SEC very busy indeed. The SEC's goal is to review 33 percent of all documents filed and to review 100 percent of annual reports filed by Fortune 500 companies. Nevertheless, in 2001 the SEC reviewed only 16 percent of the 14,000 annual reports filed by public companies for that year.[22] Part of the problem is that the agency is chronically understaffed and beset with high turnover and increasing workloads. Still, some say that's no excuse. "The SEC's reticence at the turn of the century will go down in history as one of the great failures of an organization that is supposed to protect investors," says a former SEC attorney. "There have been red flags for years . . . and the SEC simply sat on its hands."[23]

Securities Fraud   As Chapters 2 and 17 point out, insider trading, corporate bookkeeping trickery, and other forms of securities fraud are also on the rise. In fact, securities fraud has become so pervasive today that the SEC, the Department of Justice, the FTC, the U.S. Attorney's offices, and even the FBI have stepped up efforts to police such fraud.

Experts attribute the recent rise in the number of securities fraud cases to a combination of a "get rich" mindset, large numbers of people now investing in securities markets, and the ease of online trading. Recent breaches in the "Chinese wall" are also to blame. For example, Merrill Lynch, the nation's largest brokerage firm, tarred its image when several of Merrill's analysts were caught defrauding investors. The analysts were touting stocks of corporate clients while ridiculing them privately. In 2002 Merrill Lynch agreed to pay a $100 million fine and apologized publicly for misleading investors.[24]

EXHIBIT 18.5
An Edgar Scorecard
To successfully navigate the
Securities and Exchange
Commission's Edgar database of
corporate filings, it helps to know
the most common filings required
of publicly traded companies and
their content.

An Edgar Scorecard

10K ➡ The official version of a company's annual report, with a comprehensive overview of the business.

10Q ➡ An abridged version of the 10K, filed quarterly for the first three quarters of a company's fiscal year.

8K ➡ An interim report disclosing significant company events that occur before the company files its next 10Q or 10K.

12B-25 ➡ Request for a deadline extension to file a required report, like a 10K or 10Q. When the late report is ultimately filed, NT is appended to the report's name.

S1 ➡ Basic registration form for new securities, most often initial or secondary public offerings.

Proxy Statement ➡ Information and ballot materials for shareholder votes, including election of directors and approval of mergers and acquisitions when required.

Forms 3, 4, and 5 ➡ Directors, officers, and owners of more than 10 percent of a company's stock report their initial purchases on Form 3 and subsequent purchases or sales on Form 4; they file an annual statement of their holdings on Form 5.

One of the largest securities fraud settlements ever recorded involved seven former traders and executives of Datek Online, an online stock brokerage firm. In 2003 the seven defendants agreed to pay $70 million in fines for what regulators called illegal trading and fraudulent bookkeeping during the market boom of the 1990s. Regulators accused the defendants of making tens of millions of dollars by manipulating NASDAQ's small-order executing system. The defendants pretended to be using the system to make trades for smaller investors with accounts at Datek. But they were, in fact, trading on their own behalf. To hide their involvement, the seven executives and traders recruited family members, friends, and others to create so-called nominee accounts. Datek also created fictitious books and records and filed false reports with securities regulators.[25]

In March 2003, federal and state regulators reached a landmark settlement in a fraud suit in which ten of Wall Street's biggest investment firms agreed to $1.4 billion. As part of the settlement, firms will have to physically separate their research and investment banking departments, analysts will be barred from having meetings with clients to win certain types

The Betrayed Investor

High-profile companies go bust. Business leaders fall into disrepute. The stock market tumbles. Is America's long infatuation with the stock market coming to an end?

In the 1990s owning stocks was simply a part of life. Expecting to see steady stockmarket gains, investors were given a fresh dose of reality when a stunning 113-month bull run ended in March 2000 and the turmoil began. "We were just riding the market, and we all felt like we were brilliant because our stocks were going up," says one accountant. But the dot-com crash, the September 11 terrorist attacks, and a wave of corporate scandals sent America's financial markets into a tailspin, a chilling situation reminiscent of the 1930s. Some 100 million investors—about half of all adult Americans—collectively lost more than $5 trillion over a 24-month period starting in the spring of 2000. That's equal to the gross domestic product of Japan and France combined. It was money earmarked for retirement, college tuition, and medical bills.

Déjà vu

The stock market tumble of the new millennium and the crash of the 1930s had some common elements. In both eras, self-dealing, or the act of profiting at the expense of other investors, led to the misallocation of trillions of invested dollars and the ensuing collapse of investor confidence. Before the Great Crash of the 1930s, insiders used holding companies and other stock-watering schemes to bilk both investors and consumers. Banking houses combined brokerage, underwriting, and commercial banking to sell securities to the gullible. And more and more people invested "on margin."

The policy innovations of the 1930s were designed to block a repetition of such investor abuses by regulating securities markets, separating commercial banking from investment via the Glass–Steagall Act, limiting margin investing, and so on. But back then no one could imagine the investor abuses that brought today's stock market to its knees: auditors who had become servants of managers rather than of shareholders; brokers serving their own accounts rather than offering dispassionate advice to investors; bankers who put aside their fiduciary duties to cut deals with dubious investment partners; directors who were subservient to CEOs rather than vice versa; and executives who put their own short-term enrichment through stock options ahead of creating wealth for shareholders.

Fed Up

Can Wall Street regain its golden image as the place for Americans to invest money? "Not in this generation," say John Challenger, chief executive of outplacement firm Challenger, Gray & Christmas. Investors assumed during the gold rush that they were going to become millionaires. But the rug has been pulled out, and it's been a very hard fall. Investors don't trust the word of their brokers and corporations. Consumers feel like dupes, and they are laying the blame on Wall Street.

"There is a loss of confidence in corporate America," says one leading securities lawyer. Today's investors are angry and disillusioned. They are fed up with disappointing earnings, accounting scandals, the threat of terrorism, and global instability. The Investor Class has lost its appetite for risk and is parking its cash in unglamorous, low-yielding, money-market brokerage accounts. They simply don't want to make long-term commitments until they believe that the worst is over.

Change Is Inevitable

The 2002 market meltdown could indeed be a historic turning point in American business—similar to the wave of reforms enacted during the 1930s. Proposals under current debate include making audits more strict, preventing executive and director abuses, restricting the use of stock options, reducing the potential for conflict of interest among security analysts, and punishing offenders more severely. Hopes are that such reform will restore investor confidence in the stock market so that companies can get the funding they need to grow. Still, with or without such reform, earnings aren't likely to boom and rekindle the force of the last bull market. "It's not that we can't get back to where we were," notes one corporate chief economist. "It's just that we were never really there to begin with."

Questions for Critical Thinking

1. Why is investor confidence important to the health of the U.S. economy?
2. Why did securities rules and regulations enacted in the 1930s fail to block investor abuses? What can we learn from this?

of business, and interaction between analysts and investment bankers will have to be chaperoned by compliance officers. The firms also agreed to adopt reforms to resolve allegations that they issued biased ratings on stocks to gain investment bank business that resulted in deceiving investors.

Approximately $400 million of the settlement is being set aside for investors to recoup their losses, although this figure amounts to only pennies on the dollar because the collective damages ran into billions of dollars. This fund will be held by the Securities and Exchange Commission and will be administered by a federal court appointee.

The settlement does provide investors with volumes of documents, including memos and e-mails, that contain highly damaging evidence about security firms. These documents could be used by investors to bring their own lawsuits or by institutions or other individuals on behalf of all those harmed. Customers of brokerage firms usually sign an agreement stating that disputes would be handled by binding arbitration rather than by the courts; such cases can be brought before the New York Stock Exchange or the National Association of Securities Dealers. [26]

Investors and Investing

As an investor, how do you guard against securities fraud? Experts claim that your best defense against fraud is to carefully research securities before you buy and to steer clear of any investment that seems too good to be true (see Exhibit 18.6). Your goal is to put your money to work to earn more money. Done wisely, investing in stocks and bonds can help you meet your financial goals. But you must first make decisions about how much you want to invest and where to invest it. To choose wisely, you need to know what options you have and what risks they entail. Before you start to trade, take time to think about your objectives, both long term and short term. Next, look at how various securities match your objectives and your attitude toward risk, because investing in stocks and bonds can involve potential losses.

7 **LEARNING OBJECTIVE**

Name five criteria to be considered when making investment decisions

EXHIBIT 18.6   Ten Questions to Ask Before You Invest
You can avoid getting taken in an online stock scam by asking yourself these 10 questions before you invest.

1. Is the investment registered with the SEC and your state's securities agency?
2. Have you read the company's audited financial statements?
3. Is the person recommending this investment a registered broker?
4. What does the person promoting the investment have to gain?
5. If the tip came from an online bulletin board or e-mail, is the author identifiable or using an alias? Is there any reason to trust that person?
6. Are you being pressured to act before you can evaluate the investment?
7. Does the investment promise you'll get rich quick, using words like "guaranteed," "high return," or "risk free"?
8. Does the investment match your objectives? Could you afford to lose all of the money you invest?
9. How easy would it be to sell the investment later? Remember, stocks with fewer shares are easy for promoters to manipulate and hard for investors to sell if the price starts falling.
10. Does the investment originate overseas? If yes, beware: It is tougher to track money sent abroad and harder for burned investors to have recourse to justice.

Investment Objectives

yield
Income received from securities, calculated by dividing dividend or interest income by market price

Many investors seek the highest **yield** or return to supplement their income. Yield on a stock is calculated by dividing the stock's dividends by its annualized market price. Some investors want to make a large profit in a short period of time. Others may be looking for a long-term steady return to fund retirement activities or provide money to send their children to college. In general, people make investment decisions on the basis of five criteria: *income, growth, safety, liquidity,* and *tax consequences.*

If an investor wants a steady, reasonably predictable flow of cash, he or she will seek an investment that provides fixed or dividend income. Fixed income investments include certificates of deposit, government securities, corporate bonds, and preferred stocks. A retired person wanting to supplement Social Security or pension benefits would be a customer for this type of investment.

growth stocks
Equities issued by small companies with unproven products or services

Many investors are concerned with wealth accumulation, or growth. Their objective is to maximize capital gains. **Growth stocks** are issued by younger companies, such as Amazon.com, that have strong growth potential. These companies normally pay no dividends because they reinvest earnings in the company to expand operations. High-growth stocks attract a breed of investors who buy stocks with rapidly accelerating earnings and sell them on the tiniest of disappointments over a company's prospects. For this reason, they are considered the most *volatile* in the market—that is, their stock prices tend to rise more quickly, but they can fall just as quickly.

speculators
Investors who purchase securities in anticipation of making large profits quickly

Safety is another concern. Generally, the higher the potential for income or growth, the greater the risk of the investment. **Speculators** are investors who accept high risks in order to realize large capital gains. Of course, every investor must make some kind of trade-off. Government bonds are safer than corporate bonds, which are safer than common stocks, which are safer than futures contracts, which are safer than commodities.

Moreover, before you get too caught up in focusing on your own assessment of a specific security, you need to understand what other investors are thinking. You may see an abundance of value, or substantial growth potential, but if other investors don't share your view, your insights won't do you much good. The market is a voting machine, wherein countless individuals register choices—sometimes based on reason and sometimes based on emotion.[27]

Two additional investment objectives you should consider when selecting investments are liquidity and tax consequences. Liquidity is the measure of how quickly an investor can change an investment into cash. For example, common stock is more liquid than real estate; most financial assets can be changed into cash within a day. Some, like certificates of deposit, can be cashed in before maturity, but only after paying a penalty. All investors must consider the tax consequences of their decisions. Historically, dividend and interest income have been taxed heavily, and capital gains have been taxed relatively lightly. In addition, the income from most state and local municipal bonds is exempt from federal income tax.

Investment Portfolio

investment portfolios
Assortment of investment instruments

rate of return
Percentage increase in the value of an investment

asset allocation
Method of shifting investments within a portfolio to adapt them to the current investment environment

No single investment instrument will provide income, growth, and a high degree of safety. For this reason, all investors—whether institutions or individuals—build **investment portfolios**, or collections of various types of investments. Money managers and financial advisers are often asked to determine which investments should be in an investor's portfolio and to buy and sell securities and maintain the client's portfolio. Sometimes they must structure a portfolio to provide a desired **rate of return**, the percentage of gain or interest yield on investments.

Managing a portfolio to gain the highest rates of return while reducing risk as much as possible is known as **asset allocation**. A portion of the portfolio might be devoted to cash instruments such as money-market mutual funds, a portion to income instruments such as government and corporate bonds, and a portion to equities (mainly common stock). The money manager then determines how much each portion should be, on the basis of economic and market conditions—not an easy task. If the economy is booming and the stock market is performing well, the money manager might take advantage of the good environment by shifting 75 percent of the total portfolio into stocks, 20 percent into bonds, and 5 percent into cash. If the economy turns bad, the stock market heads downward, and inflation heats up, the money manager might readjust the portfolio and invest 30 percent in stocks, 40 percent in short-term government securities, and 30 percent in cash. This adjustment helps protect the value of the portfolio during poor investment conditions.[28]

Another major concern for these managers is **diversification**—reducing the risk of loss in a client's total portfolio by investing funds in several different securities so that a loss experienced by any one will not hurt the entire portfolio. One way to diversify is by investing in securities from unrelated industries and a variety of countries. Another way is by allocating your assets among different investment types.

How to Buy and Sell Securities

Regardless of when, where, or how you trade securities, you must execute all trades by using a securities broker. Currently, individuals cannot interact with securities marketplaces or ECNs directly; purchases must be made through traditional stock brokers—although some hope this will change soon.[29]

A **broker** is an expert who has passed a series of formal examinations and is legally registered to buy and sell securities on behalf of individual and institutional investors. As an investor, you pay *transaction costs* for every buy or sell order, to cover the broker's commission, which varies with the type of broker and the size of your trade: A *full-service broker* provides financial management services such as investment counseling and planning; a *discount broker* provides fewer or limited services and generally charges lower commissions than a full-service broker. Still, some discount brokers offer a range of services and resources that include free or low-cost research, customized tracking of securities, e-mails confirming trades, and electronic newsletters packed with investment advice.

Your broker can buy or sell securities in a number of ways. A **market order** tells the broker to buy or sell at the best price that can be negotiated at the moment. A **limit order** specifies the highest price you are willing to pay when buying or the lowest price at which you are willing to sell. A **stop order** tells the broker to sell if the price of your security drops to or below the price you set, protecting you from losing more money if prices are dropping. You can also place a time limit on your orders. An **open order** instructs the broker to leave the order open until you cancel it. A **day order** is valid only on the day you place it and should not be confused with a *day trader*, a stock trader who holds positions for a very short time (minutes to hours) and closes out these positions within the same day.

If you have special confidence in your broker's ability, you may place a **discretionary order**, which gives the broker the right to buy or sell your securities at the broker's discretion. In some cases, discretionary orders can save you from taking a loss, because the broker may have a better sense of when to sell a stock. If the broker's judgment proves wrong, however, you cannot hold the broker legally responsible for the consequences; so investigate your broker's background and think carefully before you give anyone the right to trade your securities.

Investors sometimes borrow cash to buy stocks, a practice known as **margin trading**. Instead of paying for the stock in full, you borrow some of the money from your stockbroker, paying interest on the borrowed money and leaving the stock with the broker as collateral. As we mentioned in Chapter 17, the Federal Reserve Board establishes margin requirements. Be aware, however, that margin trading increases risk. If the price of a stock you bought on margin goes down, you will have to give your broker more money or the broker will sell your stock. Such forced sales can cause prices to fall even further, triggering a vicious cycle of sales and margin calls.[30]

diversification
Assembling investment portfolios in such a way that a loss in one investment won't cripple the value of the entire portfolio

broker
Individual registered to sell securities

market order
Authorization for a broker to buy or sell securities at the best price that can be negotiated at the moment

limit order
Market order that stipulates the highest or lowest price at which the customer is willing to trade securities

stop order
An order to sell a stock when its price falls to a particular point to limit an investor's losses

open order
Limit order that does not expire at the end of a trading day

day order
Any order to buy or sell a security that automatically expires if not executed on the day the order is placed

discretionary order
Market order that allows the broker to decide when to trade a security

margin trading
Borrowing money from brokers to buy stock, paying interest on the borrowed money, and leaving the stock with the broker as collateral

short selling
Selling stock borrowed from a broker with the intention of buying it back later at a lower price, repaying the broker, and pocketing the profit

If you believe that a stock's price is about to drop, you may choose a trading procedure known as **short selling**. With this procedure, you sell stock you borrow from a broker in the hope of buying it back later at a lower price. After you return the borrowed stock to the broker, you keep the price difference. For example, you might decide to borrow 25 shares that are selling for $30 per share and sell short because you think the share price is going to plummet. When the stock's price declines to $15, you buy 25 shares on the open market and make $15 profit on every share (minus transaction costs). Selling short is risky. If the stock had climbed to $32, you would have had to buy shares at that higher price, even though you would be losing money.

8 **LEARNING OBJECTIVE**

Name several sources of investment information

How to Analyze Financial News

Whether you are purchasing, holding, or selling securities, as an investor you will want to keep current on the market, the world, and the performance of specific companies and industries. Good sources of financial information include daily newspaper reports on securities markets, newspapers aimed specifically at investors (such as *Investor's Business Daily* and *Barron's*), and general-interest business publications that follow the corporate world and give hints about investing (such as the *Wall Street Journal*, *Forbes*, *Fortune*, and *Business Week*). Standard & Poor's, Moody's Investor Service, and Value Line also publish newsletters and special reports on securities. Online sources include your brokerage firm's website plus a growing number of excellent financial websites listed in "Put Your Money Where Your Mouse Is!"

What types of financial information should you be looking for? First, you want to determine the general direction of stock prices. If stock prices have been rising over a long period, the industry and the media will often describe this situation as a **bull market**. The reverse is a **bear market**, one characterized by a long-term trend of falling prices. You can see these broad market movements in Exhibit 18.7 on page 476. Once you have the general picture, look at the timing. Has a bull market lasted for too long, suggesting that stocks are overvalued and a correction (tumbling prices) might be imminent? Also watch the volume of shares traded each day.

bull market
Rising stock market

bear market
Falling stock market

institutional investors
Companies that invest money entrusted to them by others

Institutional investors—such as pension funds, insurance companies, investment companies, banks, and colleges and universities—buy and sell securities in large quantities, often in blocks of at least 10,000 shares per transaction. Because these institutions have such large pools of money to work with, their investment decisions have a major impact on the marketability of a company's shares as well as the overall behavior of the securities market. If the stock market is down on heavy volume (that is, if prices are moving downward and a lot of trading is going on), institutional investors may be trying to sell before prices go down further—a bearish sign.

market indexes
Measures of security markets calculated from the prices of a selection of securities

Watching Market Indexes and Averages   One way to determine whether the market is bullish or bearish is to watch **market indexes** and averages, which use the performance of a representative sampling of stocks, bonds, or commodities as a gauge of broader market activity. The most famous U.S. stock index is the Dow Jones Industrial Average (DJIA), which tracks the prices of 30 *blue-chip* or well-established stocks, each representing a particular sector of the U.S. economy. Critics say the Dow is too narrow and too susceptible to short-term swings, lacks the right stocks, and gives too much weight to higher-priced shares. But advocates say the Dow's 30 stocks serve as a general barometer of market conditions. To make the DJIA more representative of the new economy, in 1999 the *Wall Street Journal* editors (guardians of the Dow) replaced time-honored blue chips Chevron, Goodyear, Sears Roebuck, and Union Carbide with Microsoft, Intel, Home Depot, and SBC Communications.[31]

Keeping Pace with Technology and Electronic Commerce

Put Your Money Where Your Mouse Is!—Investment Information on the Net

The Internet has been hailed as the great equalizer between individual investors and Wall Street. Today's investors have access to a staggering amount of valuable information and investment tools—many of which are used by Wall Street professionals. But having access to information is one thing; using it wisely is another. So before you put a dollar (or a euro) into any investment, learn as much as possible about the market, the security, its issuer, and its potential. Here are some tips to point you in the right direction.

For "how to" advice, try the Motley Fool (www. fool.com), Quicken's financial site (www.quicken. com/investments), or *CNN/Money*'s website (http:// money.cnn.com). For the latest online news and commentary about stocks, check out The Street (www. thestreet.com), CBS Market Watch (www.marketwatch. com), Jag Notes (www.jagnotes.com), and Wall Street Research Net (www.wsrn.com). Then research individual securities using Yahoo! (www.yahoo.com) or another Internet search tool. Plug in the company name and click to see the latest news. Go to Hoover's Online (www.hoovers.com) to read a little about the company's history and recent results. Be sure to stop by the company's website to read its press releases and financial statements. You can burrow even further into potential investments using these websites:

- Corporate financial data filed with the SEC (www. edgar-online.com)

- Morningstar mutual fund reports (www.morningstar. com)

- Stock analysis (www.premierinvestor.com)

Construct a hypothetical portfolio on Quicken, Yahoo!, or another financial website and watch how your investments fare. Track your favorite market index on MSN MoneyCentral (http://moneycentral.msn.com), and compare it with your personal investment portfolio. Are your proposed investments meeting, missing, or beating the market index?

Now you're in a better position to buy securities, but your research shouldn't end here. Even after you start trading, you need to stay on top of the latest news and industry developments that can affect the securities in which you have invested. And if a potential investment seems too good to be true, point your web browser to the North American Securities Administrators Association (www.nasaa.org) and get some tips on investment fraud. Remember, when it comes to investments, your web surfing can really pay off.

Questions for Critical Thinking

1. Why is it important to learn about a company's financial results and background before buying its stock or bonds?
2. What are the disadvantages of searching for investment information on the Internet?

Another widely watched index is the Standard & Poor's 500 Stock Average (S&P 500), which tracks the performances of 500 corporate stocks, many more than the DJIA. This index is weighted by market value, not by stock price, so large companies carry far more weight than small companies.[32] The Wilshire 5000 Index, which actually covers some 7,000 stocks, is the broadest index measuring U.S. market performance. To get a sense of how technology stocks are doing, check the NASDAQ Composite Index, covering more than 3,000 over-the-counter stocks, including many high-tech firms. You can also look at indexes to learn about the performance of foreign markets, such as Japan's Nikkei 225 Index and the United Kingdom's FT-SE 100 Index.

Interpreting the Financial News   In addition to watching market trends, you will want to follow the securities you own and others that look like promising investments. For stocks, you can turn to the stock exchange report in major daily newspapers. Exhibit 18.8 on page 477

EXHIBIT 18.7 **The Stock Market's Ups And Downs**
The peaks and valleys on this chart represent swings in the Dow Jones Industrial Average, the most widely used indicator of U.S. stock prices.

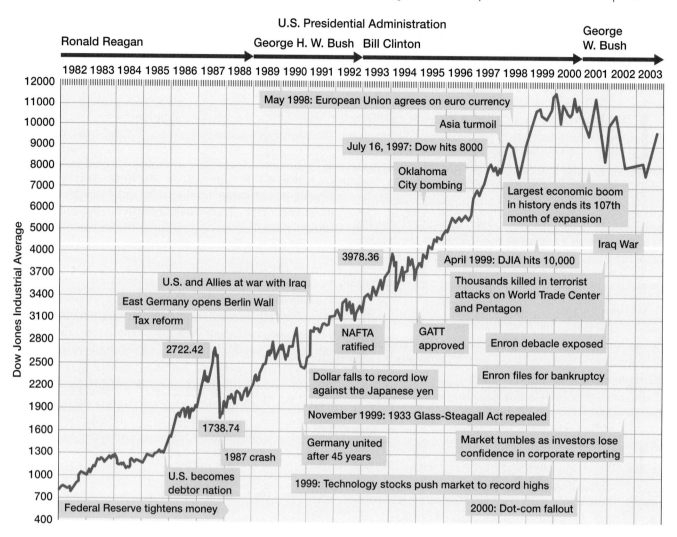

shows how to read this report, which includes high and low prices for the past 52 weeks, the number of shares traded (volume), and the change from the previous day's closing price. U.S. securities markets began quoting security prices in decimals (dollars and cents) in 2000. Prior to that year, prices were quoted in fractions as small as 1/16. Using decimals in trading makes stock prices easier for many investors to understand. Moreover, quoting shares down to the penny permits stocks to be priced in smaller increments.[33]

price-earnings ratio (p/e ratio)
Stock's current market price divided by issuer's annual earnings per share; also known as the price-earnings multiple

Included in the stock exchange report is the **price-earnings ratio**, or *p/e ratio* (also known as the price-earnings multiple), which is computed by dividing a stock's market price by its *previous* year's earnings per share. Some investors also calculate a forward p/e ratio using *expected* year earnings in the ratio's denominator. Bear in mind that if a stock's p/e ratio is well below the industry norm, either the company is in trouble or it's an undiscovered gem with a relatively low stock price. For more detailed data on a stock, consult the company's annual reports or documents filed with the Securities and Exchange Commission (SEC).

To follow specific bonds, check the bond quotation tables in major newspapers (see Exhibit 18.9). When reading these tables, remember that the price is quoted as a percentage of the bond's value. For example, a $1,000 bond shown closing at 65 actually sold at $650.

EXHIBIT 18.8   How to Read a Newspaper Stock Quotation
Even before you invest, you will want to follow the latest quotations for your stock. This table shows you how to read the newspaper stock quotation tables.

(1) 52-WEEK HIGH	52-WEEK LOW	(2) STOCK	(3) SYM	(4) DIV	(5) YLD%	(6) PE	(7) VOL 100S	(8) HI	LOW	(9) CLOSE	(10) NET CHG
42.88	27.00	BankOne		.84	2.5	14	107778	34.64	31.60	34.00	−1.20
47.94	22.25	Maytag		.72	2.3	33	9027	31.48	29.40	31.36	+1.16
39.50	23.53	Neiman Marc	NMG	...	...	18	4217	27.03	23.75	27.03	+2.15
21.96	10.06	Office Depot		...	...	15	33898	12.80	11.05	12.77	+0.98

1. **52-week high/low:** Indicates the highest and lowest trading price of the stock in the past 52 weeks plus the most recent week but not the most recent trading day (adjusted for splits). Stocks are quoted in dollars and cents. In most newspapers, boldfaced entries indicate stocks whose price changed by at least 4%, but only if the change was at least 75 cents a share.

2. **Stock:** The company's name may be abbreviated. A capital letter usually means a new word. In this example, Neiman Marc is Neiman Marcus.

3. **Symbol:** Symbol under which this stock is traded on stock exchanges.

4. **Dividend:** Dividends are usually annual payments based on the last quarterly or semiannual declaration, although not all stocks pay dividends. Special or extra dividends or payments are identified in footnotes.

5. **Yield:** The percentage yield shows dividends as a percentage of the share price.

6. **PE:** Price-to-earnings ratio, calculated by dividing the stock's closing price by the earnings per share for the latest four quarters.

7. **Volume:** Daily total of shares traded, in hundreds. A listing of 888 indicates 88,800 shares were traded during that day.

8. **High/Low:** The stock's highest and lowest price for that day.

9. **Close:** Closing price of the stock that day.

10. **Net change:** Change in share price from the close of the previous trading day.

Common Stock Footnotes: d—new 52-week low; n—new; pf—preferred; s—stock split or stock dividend of 25 percent or more in previous 52 weeks; u—52-week high; v—trading halted on primary market; vi—in bankruptcy; x—ex dividend (the buyer won't receive a recently declared dividend, but the seller will)

(1) COMPANY	(2) CUR YLD	(3) VOL	(4) CLOSE	(5) NET CHG
NYTel 6 1/8 10	6.6	11	93.40	−.25
PacBell 6 1/4 05	6.4	10	98.40	+.25
Safwy 9 7.8 07	8.4	20	117.50	+3.60
StoneC 11 1/4	11.1	24	103.50	−1.10
TimeWar 9 1/8 13	8.3	30	109.75	−.50

EXHIBIT 18.9
How to Read a Newspaper Bond Quotation
When newspapers carry bond quotations, they show prices as a percentage of the bond's value, which is typically $1,000.

1. **Company:** Name of company issuing the bond, such as New York Telephone, and bond description, such as 6 1/8 percent bond maturing in 2010.

2. **Current Yield:** Annual interest of $1,000 bond divided by the closing price shown. The yield for New York Telephone is $61.24 ÷ $933.75 = 0.06559, or approximately 6.6 percent.

3. **Volume:** Number of bonds traded (in thousands) that day.

4. **Close:** Price of the bond at the close of the last day's business.

5. **Net change:** Change in bond price from the close of the previous trading day.

Newspapers and business publications also include tables of price quotations for investments such as mutual funds, commodities, options, and government securities (see Exhibit 18.10). These same publications also carry news about current challenges the securities industry is facing, securities regulations, reported frauds, and proposals to improve investor protection.

EXHIBIT 18.10   How to Read a Newspaper Mutual Fund Quotation
A mutual fund listing shows the new asset value of one share (the price at which one share is trading) and the change in trading price from one day to the next.

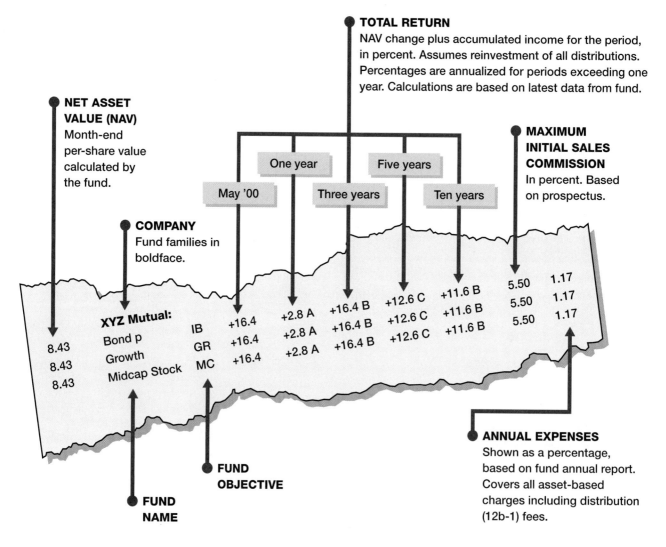

Summary of Learning Objectives

1. **Differentiate among a stock's par value, its market value, and its book value.**

   Par value is the dollar value assigned to a stock for bookkeeping and for dividend calculations. Market value is the price at which a share of stock is currently selling. Book value is the portion of a corporation's net assets represented by a single share of common stock.

2. **Highlight the distinguishing features of common stock, preferred stock, bonds, and mutual funds.**

   Common stock gives shareholders an ownership interest in a company, the right to elect directors and vote on important issues, and the chance to earn dividends and share in the fortunes of the company, while limiting the shareholder's liability to the price paid for the shares. Preferred stock gives shareholders a higher dividend than common stock and a preferred claim on creditors if the corporation fails. Special types of preferred stock have certain privileges. Bonds are long-term loans investors make to the issuing entity in return for a stated interest amount. The loan or principal is paid back to the bondholder over the life of the bond. Bonds may be secured, unsecured, or convertible. They may be issued by corporations or federal, state, city, and local agencies. Mutual funds are pools of money drawn from many investors to buy a variety of stocks, bonds, and other marketable securities. The primary benefit of this investment is diversification.

3. **List five types of bonds issued by governments.**

   The U.S. government issues treasury bills (short-term bonds), treasury notes (intermediate-term bonds), and treasury bonds (long-term bonds). In addition, the U.S. government issues U.S. savings bonds. These bonds are issued at a discount and grow to their full redemption value at maturity (generally 17 years or more). Cities, states, and special government agencies issue municipal bonds to fund public services such as building schools, highways, and airports. Municipal bonds backed by the taxing power of the issuing government are general obligation bonds. Municipal bonds backed by money to be generated from the financial project are revenue bonds.

4. **Differentiate among an auction exchange, a dealer exchange, and an electronic communication network (ECN).**

   Auction exchanges such as the New York Stock Exchange funnel all buy and sell orders into one centralized location. Dealer exchanges such as NASDAQ are decentralized marketplaces in which dealers, known as market makers, are connected electronically to handle buy and sell orders without a single, centralized trading floor. Electronic computerized networks (ECNs) match buy and sell orders directly (cutting out the market makers and specialists); ECNs operate globally, and they operate economically.

5. **Discuss how securities marketplaces are changing.**

   Overstaffing of securities firms, stemming from a hiring frenzy during the 1990s, are forcing many investment banks and brokerage firms to lay off employees. Declines in services such as IPO underwriting, mergers and acquisitions, and in overall individual investment activity is forcing securities firms to enter new markets and reorganize to compensate for the lost business. The rapid growth and public acceptance of online trading is forcing most full-service firms to offer and expand online trading options to remain competitive. Increased competition and public pressure is forcing securities exchanges to extend traditional trading hours. Securities exchanges are responding by using ECNs to offer limited after-hours trading.

6. **Explain how government regulation of securities trading tries to protect investors.**

   The government tries to prevent fraud in the securities markets by issuing securities laws and regulations, and by requiring companies to file registration papers, fulfill certain requirements, and file periodic information reports so that investors receive accurate information. Regulations also try to monitor the use of insider information and police fraudulent manipulation of securities. The SEC is the chief agency responsible for the oversight of the securities industry. The SEC works closely with NASD and stock exchanges to police the industry and maintain the integrity of trading in the security marketplaces.

7. **Name five criteria to be considered when making investment decisions.**

   Investors should consider the income, growth, safety, liquidity, and tax consequences of alternative investments.

8. **Name several sources of investment information.**

   Daily newspaper reports on securities markets, general-interest business publications, investor newsletters, and special reports are good sources of investment information. So are online resources such as brokerage firm websites, company websites, and a number of financial websites. Market indexes are another source of financial information and are good indicators of market performance and market trends. Reports filed with the SEC such as prospectuses and annual reports are other good information sources.

KEY TERMS

asset allocation **(472)**	hedge **(462)**	rate of return **(472)**
auction exchange **(463)**	institutional investors **(474)**	revenue bond **(461)**
authorized stock **(458)**	investment portfolios **(472)**	secondary market **(463)**
bear market **(474)**	issued stock **(458)**	securities **(458)**
bond **(459)**	limit order **(473)**	secured bonds **(460)**
broker **(473)**	margin trading **(473)**	short selling **(474)**
bull market **(474)**	market indexes **(474)**	sinking fund **(461)**
capital gains **(461)**	market makers **(464)**	speculators **(472)**
commodities **(462)**	market order **(473)**	stock certificate **(458)**
convertible bonds **(460)**	money-market funds **(462)**	stock exchanges **(463)**
day order **(473)**	municipal bonds **(461)**	stock specialist **(463)**
dealer exchange **(464)**	mutual funds **(462)**	stock split **(458)**
debentures **(460)**	NASDAQ (National Association of Securities Dealers Automated Quotations) **(464)**	stop order **(473)**
discretionary order **(473)**		Treasury bills **(461)**
diversification **(473)**	open order **(473)**	Treasury bonds **(461)**
electronic communication networks (ECNs) **(464)**	par value **(458)**	Treasury notes **(461)**
	price-earnings ratio (p/e ratio) **(476)**	unissued stock **(458)**
financial futures **(462)**	primary market **(463)**	U.S. savings bonds **(461)**
general obligation bond **(461)**	principal **(460)**	yield **(472)**
growth stocks **(472)**		

TEST YOUR KNOWLEDGE

Questions for Review

1. What are the differences between a Treasury bill, a Treasury note, and a U.S. savings bond?

2. What is the difference between a general obligation bond and a revenue bond?

3. What happens during a 2-for-1 stock split?

4. What is a p/e ratio, and what does it signify to an investor?

5. What is the function of the Securities and Exchange Commission?

Questions for Analysis

6. What are some of the advantages of mutual funds?

7. What are some of the ways an investor can diversify investments to reduce the risk of loss?

8. Why are debentures considered riskier than other types of bonds?

9. When might an investor sell a stock short? What risks are involved in selling short?

10. **Ethical Considerations:** You work in the research and development department of a large corporation and have been involved in a discovery that could lead to a new, profitable product. News of the discovery has not been made public. Is it legal for you to buy stock in the company? Now assume the same scenario but you talk to your friend about your discovery while dining at a restaurant. The person at the next table overhears the conversation. Is it legal for the eavesdropper to buy the company's stock before the public announcement of the news?

Questions for Application

11. If an investor wants a steady, predictable flow of cash, what types of investments should she seek and why?

12. If you were thinking about buying shares of AT&T, under what circumstances would you place a market order, a limit order, an open order, and a discretionary order?

13. **Integrated:** Look back at Chapter 7 and review the discussion of mission statements. Suppose you were thinking about purchasing 100 shares of common stock in General Electric. Why might you want to first review the company's mission statement? What would you be looking for in the company's mission statement that could help you decide whether or not to invest?

14. **Integrated:** In Chapter 6 we mentioned that one disadvantage of going public was the burdensome SEC filing requirements. Why do you think the SEC requires companies to file the documents listed in Exhibit 18.5, page 469?

PRACTICE YOUR KNOWLEDGE

Handling Difficult Situations on the Job: Calming an Angry Online Trader

You are a customer service representative for a popular online broker. One of the company's investors, Ian Stevens, placed an online market order for a hot new Internet stock, Theglobe.com, thinking it would cost between $15 and $25 a share. His order was filled for 2,300 shares, but at a price of $90 a share and a bill of $207,000—nearly $150,000 more than he expected. Irate, Stevens called E*Trade—and you're the lucky rep to get his call.

Your company boldly posts statements on its website warning customers about possible delays and other potential problems with online trades. For example, it warns customers that high trading volume can delay the execution of an order, which may mean that a stock's price is significantly different from when the order was placed. It also informs customers of the difference between a market order and a limit order. Doesn't matter. Stevens is making all kinds of threats and he wants to speak to the president of the company NOW! You have been told to turn over situations such as these to your department manager, but only after you input all the facts in an electronic customer file.[34]

Your task: To complete the file, you need to ask Stevens a series of questions, but first you have to calm him down—without making any promises, of course. What kinds of information should you try to obtain from Stevens?

Building Your Team Skills

You and your team are going to pool your money and invest $5,000. Before you plunge into any investments, how can you prepare yourselves to be good investors? First, consider your group's goals. What will you and your teammates do with any profits generated by your investments? Once you have agreed on a goal for your team's profits, think about how much money you will need to achieve this goal and how soon you want to achieve it.

Next, think about how much risk you personally are willing to take to achieve the goal. Bear in mind that safer investments generally offer lower returns than riskier investments—and certain investments, such as stocks, can lose money. Now hold a group discussion to find a level of risk that feels comfortable for everyone on your team.

Once your team has decided how much risk to take, consider which investments are best suited to your group's goals and chosen risk level. Will you choose stocks, bonds, a combination of both, or other securities? What are the advantages and disadvantages of each type of investment for your team's situation? Then come to a decision about specific investment opportunities—particular stocks, for example—that your group would like to investigate further.

Compare your group's goal, risk level, and investment possibilities with those of the other teams in your class and discuss the differences and similarities you see.

EXPAND YOUR KNOWLEDGE

Discovering Career Opportunities

Think you might be interested in a job in the securities and commodities industry? This industry has one of the most highly educated and skilled workforces of any industry. And the requirements for entry are high—most brokerage clerks have a college degree. Log on to the Bureau of Labor Statistics, Career Guide to Industries at www.bls.gov/oco/cg/home.htm, and click on Financial and Insurance, then click on Securities and Commodities. Read the article, then answer these questions:

1. What are the licensing and continuing education requirements for securities brokers?
2. What is the typical starting position for many people in the securities industry?
3. What factors are expected to contribute to the projected long-term growth of this industry?

Developing Your Research Skills

Since the turn of the century, the stocks of several high-profile companies, such as Tyco, Enron, and WorldCom, tumbled following their disclosures of negative company information. Use computer resources or business journals to find a company whose disclosure of negative information had a dramatic impact on its securities. Then perform some research on that company so you can answer the following questions:

1. On what exchanges do the company's shares trade and under what ticker symbol?
2. What negative information did the company disclose? When? Did the company commit a fraudulent act? How did the information have an impact on the company as a whole?
3. How did the negative information have an impact on the company's securities? What was the company's stock price prior to the release of the negative information? Following the release of the information? What was the stock's 52-week high and low during the year the disclosure was made?
4. How did the DJIA and NASDAQ perform on the day the negative information was made public?

Exploring the Best of the Web

URLs for all Internet exercises are provided at the website for this book, www.prenhall.com/bovee. *When you log on to the text website, select*

Chapter 18, select "Student Resources," then click on the name of the featured website, and review the website to complete these exercises.

Explore these chapter-related websites, review their content, and answer the following questions for each website you visit:

1. What is the purpose of this website?
2. What kinds of information does this website contain? Please be specific.
3. How is the information provided at this website useful for businesspeople? Consumers?
4. How did you expand your knowledge of securities by reviewing the material at this website? What new things did you learn about this topic?

Stock Up at the NYSE

Tour the New York Stock Exchange. Visit the trading floor and learn about the hectic pace of trading. Find out why having a seat doesn't necessarily mean you'll have a chance to sit down. Listen in on a stock transaction and discover how a stock is bought and sold. Learn how investors are protected and how unusual stock transactions are spotted. Get the latest market information as well as a historical perspective of the Exchange. Don't leave without checking out your favorite stock price. Maybe it's time to sell. www.nyse.com

Invest Wisely, Don't Be a Fool

Here's a fun securities website you can fool around at for a while. Visit the Motley Fool and don't be afraid to ask a foolish investment question or two. Roll up your sleeves and do a little work on your own. Discover the strategies, ideas, and information needed to make investment decisions at Fool's School. Learn the steps to investing foolishly. Read the investing basics and learn how to value stocks, analyze stocks, or pick a stockbroker. Expand your knowledge of stocks, bonds, and mutual funds. Finally, discover the keys to successful investing. www.fool.com

Make a Pile of Money

Looking to learn about the stock market and investing but don't know where to turn? Try the Financial Info Centers at Investorama and get a head start on your investment education without wading through dense textbooks full of Wall Street jargon. Get the lowdown on the Dow. Learn some fundamental analysis techniques. Read some tips on choosing a broker. And find out which questions you should ask your broker before you invest. Aren't sure whether you should invest globally? Ask Investorama. You may discover a world of opportunity. www.investorama.com

Learning Interactively

Companion Website

Visit the Companion Website at www.prenhall.com/bovee. For Chapter 18, take advantage of the interactive "Study Guide" to test your chapter knowledge. Get instant feedback on whether you need additional studying. Read the "Current Events" articles to get the latest on chapter topics, and complete the exercises as specified by your instructor. Expand your learning with a visit to the "Research Area." There you will find a wealth of information you can use to complete your course assignments.

A CASE FOR CRITICAL THINKING

Floored by Technology at the NYSE

Ever since a group of brokers gathered on Wall Street to trade stocks in 1792, the New York Stock Exchange has provided a central marketplace for buying and selling securities. Its floor-based auction system met the needs of large and small investors for years. But at the close of the 20th century new technologies threatened its established trading system, and the world's largest and most prestigious securities exchange seemed doomed.

At the height of Internet mania, its chief competitor, NASDAQ, had touted itself as the "stock market for the next 100 years." Its volume was bigger than the NYSE's, and its top companies—Microsoft, Intel, Dell, Sun, Oracle, and Cisco—seemed more important. Moreover, the NASDAQ seemed to be more efficient. Trades were either completed by market makers sitting at banks of computer screens, or increasingly, by computerized systems. The NYSE, by contrast, looked like something Norman Rockwell would have painted. Jackets and ties were still required on the trading floor. Uniformed porters in cloakrooms took members' coats and shined their shoes. And while many parts of the exchange were computer-

ized, stocks still traded more or less the same way they had since the specialist system was invented in 1871—at a trading post in a sea of paper on the floor. "The exchange simply looked like it wasn't going to be able to compete," said the former SEC commissioner.

Moves on the Big Board

As more and more customers bypassed the Big Board in favor of trading through electronic markets, Richard Grasso, the NYSE's former chairman and CEO, acknowledged that the NYSE could no longer cling to its old ways. "These are no longer the days of old, when we were the only game in town . . . Reinvention is absolutely essential," Grasso said in early 2000. Still, he had no desire to switch to an all-electronic market that could turn the NYSE into "a museum."

To meet demands for change without abolishing the existing auction system, the NYSE developed a strategy that offers a combination of human and electronic services. First, the exchange invested millions in new technology to maintain a competitive edge in the electronic market. Then the NYSE introduced Network NYSE, a portfolio of products and services that adopt ECN techniques. The network offers investors the benefits of trading instantly and electronically while continuing to retain the floor-based auction system. Direct Plus, for example, automatically executes orders for up to 2,099 shares on the NYSE without human intervention, enabling floor traders to preserve their roles for larger orders. Another service, Institutional Xpress, allows big investors to bypass brokers and send orders to a specialist on the trading floor for automatic execution. Yet another new feature is MarkeTrac, which allows investors to navigate the trading floor in real time on the web.

Nevertheless, the NYSE has no plans to eliminate the auction floor. It is, however, doing something critics thought it would never do: offering investors ways of trading stocks without a specialist, and letting investors see chunks of the specialist's once closely guarded order book. Specialists, who used to record trades on paper tickets, now use special software to fill orders electronically. A trading platform with a bandwidth of 50 gigabits per second, enough to handle 30 million simultaneous phone calls, allows them to process 6.5 trades a second, up from 1.6 trades a second at the turn of the century. Paper use on the exchange floor has fallen dramatically.

Weathering the Storm

Since the NYSE began fighting for its survival, a lot has changed in the United States. But it was the dot-com crash and a parade of corporate scandals that turned the exchange's biggest gripers into its biggest supporters. They now see the NYSE as a place where companies of quality list. Moreover, if the September 11 attacks, which shut down Wall Street for six days, were symbols of America's vulnerability, the NYSE's reopening on September 17, 2001, was a symbol of its resolve. For many, the idea of the Big Board's disappearing seems almost laughable now.

Some experts question how long the exchange can continue to process higher and higher volume with a 131-year-old specialist system. "As computers make trading more and more commoditized, the NYSE will find that its costs are simply too high to be competitive," notes one critic. The NYSE's answer: Continue automating until specialists handle only the biggest and most complicated trades and the rest don't get touched by human hands at all. Specialists are still needed, as Grasso has argued, because computerized trading fueled by the 24-hour news cycle allows investors to react instantaneously. "That makes the markets more sensitive and more volatile," he adds. And investors don't like it when stocks jump around, because they have a harder time getting the price they want. Electronic exchanges, by their very nature, can't dampen this volatility. So, in Grasso's view, now more than ever specialists are needed to step in and calm things down.

Critical Thinking Questions

1. How does electronic trading threaten the NYSE's auction system?

2. Why does the NYSE want to maintain the existing auction system?

3. How did the NYSE respond to the demand for change?

4. Go to New York Stock Exchange's website at www.nyse.com. Review the site to answer these questions: What is the mission of the NYSE? How does Network NYSE add a new dimension to the exchange? What makes the NYSE unique?

VIDEO CASE

Information Pays Off: Understanding Investments

Learning Objectives

The purpose of this video is to help you:

1. Identify the wide variety of investments available to individuals.

2. Describe the process by which securities are bought and sold.

3. Recognize the risks involved in commodities and other investments.

Synopsis

Despite news reports about lottery winners and others who have become millionaires overnight, individuals have a better chance of getting rich if they learn to select investments that are appropriate for their long-term financial goals. Experts advise looking for investments that will beat inflation and keep up with or—ideally—beat general market returns. Individuals can invest in preferred or common stock, newly issued stock from initial public offerings (IPOs), managed or index mutual funds, bonds, or commodities. These investments are far from risk-free, however; commodities and IPOs can be particularly risky. Therefore, individuals should become educated about securities and investment strategies by surfing websites such as the Motley Fool (www.fool.com).

Discussion Questions

1. *For analysis:* Why is the Securities and Exchange Commission concerned about stock rumors that circulate on the Internet?

2. *For analysis:* Why do Motley Fool's experts advise individuals to invest in index funds rather than in actively managed mutual funds?

3. ***For application:*** What should you consider when deciding whether to buy and sell stock through a broker, through a web-based brokerage, or directly through the company issuing the stock?

4. ***For application:*** If you were about to retire, why might you invest in preferred stock rather than common stock?

5. ***For debate:*** Should stock rumors that circulate on the Internet be covered by the individual's constitutional right to freedom of speech rather than being regulated by the SEC? Support your chosen position.

Online Exploration

Mutual funds that seek out environmentally and socially conscious firms in which to invest are becoming more popular because they offer investors a way to earn returns that don't offend their principles. Investigate the following websites: www.socialfunds.com, www.ethicalfunds.com, and www.domini.com. What types of firms does each fund avoid? What type does each prefer to invest in? Would you choose one of these funds if you wanted to invest in a mutual fund? Explain your answer.

PART 6

Mastering Global and Geographical Skills—Monitoring the World Markets

The Dow Jones Industrial Average (DJIA), the Standard & Poor's 500, the Wilshire Index—these and other such stock market indexes provide good indications of where U.S. markets are headed. Unfortunately, they aren't much help for markets in other countries. You can find similar indexes in all the other major industrialized countries of the world; perhaps the best known is Japan's Nikkei index.

Understanding the composition of a market index is vital (1) to interpret the index's movement up or down and (2) to compare it with the DJIA or other U.S. indexes. Select one of the following stock market indexes and use the Internet or financial newspapers to answer the questions that follow:

- Nikkei (Japan)
- XETRA-DAX (Germany)
- FSE (Britain)
- CAC (France)
- Hang Seng (Hong Kong)

1. Does the index have more or fewer companies than the DJIA? Than the S&P 500?

2. Over the past 5 or 10 years, how has your chosen index performed, compared with the DJIA?

3. Does the index appear to represent the stock market as a whole or just one sector?

4. Go to the CNNfn Financial Network website (www.cnnfn. com) to answer these questions:

   a. Do you spot any trends or patterns between the performance of the international stock market indexes and the U.S. market indexes?

   b. What explanation was provided in the CNNfn news capsules for Europe, Asia, and the U.S. that might have contributed to the performance of these world market indexes?

   c. Was the performance of either Europe's or Asia's markets linked in any way to U.S. news events?

CHAPTER COMPONENT

A

The U.S. Legal System and Business Law

The U.S. Legal System

Throughout this textbook, we have discussed a number of regulatory agencies such as the FDA, FTC, EPA, and SEC, whose function is to protect society from the potential abuses of business. In this chapter we explore how the U.S. government protects its citizens from corporate wrong-doings through its legal system. The law protects both businesses and individuals against those who threaten society. It also spells out accepted ways of performing many essential business functions—along with the penalties for failing to comply. In other words, like the average person, companies must obey the law or face the consequences.

As you read this chapter, keep in mind that many companies conduct business overseas. Thus, in addition to knowing U.S. laws, these companies must also be familiar with **international law**, the principles, customs, and rules that govern the relationships between sovereign states and international organizations and persons. Successful global business requires an understanding of the domestic laws of trading partners as well as of established international trading standards and legal guidelines.

A *law* is a rule developed by a society to govern the conduct of, and relationships among, its members. The U.S. Constitution, including the Bill of Rights, is the foundation for U.S. laws. Because the Constitution is a general document, laws offering specific answers to specific problems are constantly embellishing its basic principles. However, law is not static; it develops in response to changing conditions and social standards. Individual laws originate in various ways: through legislative action (*statutory law*), through administrative rulings (*administrative law*), and through customs and judicial precedents (*common law*). To one degree or another, all three forms of law affect businesses. Moreover, at times the three forms of law may overlap so that the differences between them become indistinguishable. Nonetheless, in cases in which the three forms of law appear to conflict, statutory law generally prevails.

Statutory Law

Statutory law is law written by the U.S. Congress, state legislatures, and local governments. One very important part of statutory law affecting businesses is the **Uniform Commercial Code (UCC)**. Designed to mitigate differences between state statutory laws and to simplify interstate commerce, this code is a comprehensive, systematic collection of statutes in a particular legal area. For example, the UCC provides a nationwide standard in many issues of commercial law, such as sales contracts, bank deposits, and warranties. The UCC has been adopted in its entirety in 49 states and the District of Columbia, and about half of it has been adopted in Louisiana.

Administrative Law

Once laws have been passed by a state legislature or Congress, an administrative agency or commission typically takes responsibility for enforcing them. That agency may be

Global companies, such as Coca-Cola, must have a firm grasp of international law.

called on to clarify a regulation's intent, often by consulting representatives of the affected industry. The administrative agency may then write more specific regulations, which are considered **administrative law**.

Administrative agencies also have the power to investigate corporations suspected of breaking administrative laws. A corporation found to be misbehaving may agree to a **consent order**, which allows the company to promise to stop doing something without actually admitting to any illegal behavior. As an alternative to entering into a consent order, the administrative agency may start legal proceedings against the company in a hearing presided over by an administrative law judge. During such a hearing, witnesses are called and evidence is presented to determine the facts of the situation. The judge then issues a decision, which may impose corrective actions on the company. If either party objects to the decision, the party may file an appeal with the appropriate federal court.

Regulations created by administrative agencies must be linked to specific statutes to be legal. For example, the FTC (Federal Trade Commission) issues regulations and enforces statutory laws concerning such deceptive trade practices as unfair debt collection and false or deceptive advertising. Diet ads that literally promise that you can eat all the cake, fried chicken, and hot fudge you want and still lose weight by using dietary supplements are a good example of deceptive advertising. A recent report showed that 55 percent of 300 weight-loss ads studied made claims that lack proof or probably were false.[1] Some diet ads even bolster the false claims with user testimonials such as "Seven weeks ago, I weighed 268 pounds. Now I am down to just 148! During this time, I didn't change my eating habits at all."[2]

To curb such advertising abuse, the FTC is pursuing enforcement action on a number of producers of diet-related products. For example, the federal government and two states sued Mark Nutritionals for deceiving the public via advertising claims that its product, Body Solutions Evening Weight Loss Formula, burned away fat while dieters slept. The FTC said there was no scientific proof that any of the product's ingredients promoted weight loss.[3]

Inadequate disclosure of risks is another form of deceptive advertising. The FTC, for example, accused Pfizer of misrepresenting the effectiveness of its drug Zithromax and failing to disclose the risks of overusing antibiotics. For years, Pfizer promoted Zithromax to treat ear infections in children by creating a fictional mascot, Max, a zebra. Pediatricians would find medical journals wrapped in paper covered with Max's stripes in their mailboxes. Zithromax sales representatives would hand out small plastic zebras that doctors could hang from their stethoscopes. Pfizer even donated a zebra to the San Francisco Zoo. Sales of the drug brought in more than $1 billion in 2002. But in 2003 Pfizer

In 2002 Enron executives testified before an administrative agency to defend the company's actions. Among other things, lawmakers had accused Enron of illegally manipulating California's energy market.

agreed to pay $6 million to settle an investigation brought by 19 states into how the company advertised the effectiveness of Zithromax. Admitting no wrongdoing, Pfizer agreed to settle to avoid unnecessary legal costs and to finance a three-year, $2 million public service campaign to inform parents that antibiotics can't be used to treat an ear infection that is caused by a virus.[4]

Common Law

Common law, the type of law that comes out of courtrooms and judges' decisions, began in England many centuries ago and was transported to the United States by the colonists. It is applied in all states except Louisiana (which follows a French model). Common law is sometimes called the "unwritten law" to distinguish it from legislative acts and administrative-agency regulations, which are written documents. Instead, common law is established through custom and the precedents set in courtroom proceedings.

Despite its unwritten nature, common law has great continuity, which derives from the doctrine of *stare decisis* (Latin for "to stand by decisions"). What the *stare decisis* doctrine means is that judges' decisions establish a precedent for

EXHIBIT A.1 The U.S. Court System
A legal proceeding may begin in a trial court or an administrative agency (examples of each are given here). An unfavorable decision may be appealed to a higher court at the federal or state level. (The court of appeals is the highest court in states that have no state supreme court; other states have no intermediate appellate court.) The U.S. Supreme Court, the country's highest court, is the court of final appeal.

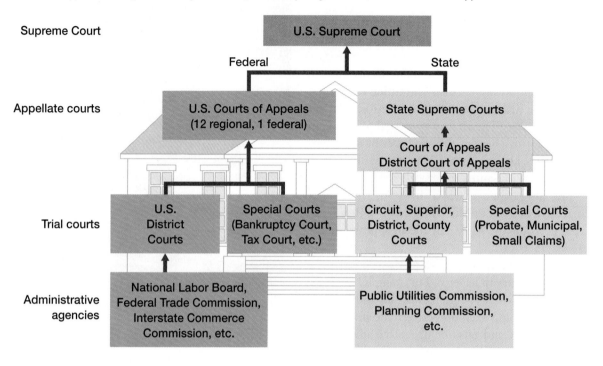

deciding future cases of a similar nature. Because common law is based on what has gone before, the legal framework develops gradually.

In the United States, common law is applied and interpreted in the system of courts (see Exhibit A.1). Common law thus develops through the decisions in trial courts, special courts, and appellate courts. The U.S. Supreme Court (or the highest court of a state when state laws are involved) sets precedents for entire legal systems. Lower courts must then abide by those precedents as they pertain to similar cases.

In all but six states, business cases are heard in standard trial courts. However, many corporations and states are pushing for the establishment of a network of special business courts. Advocates say that the special nature of business legal disputes requires experienced judges who understand business issues. They also feel that a system of business courts would go a long way toward reducing the expense and unpredictability of business litigation. However, opponents say that business courts are likely to favor local companies in disputes involving out-of-state litigants. Moreover, they say that the courts are likely to come under the influence of powerful business special-interest groups. Regardless, the national trend appears to be moving in the direction of special business courts. The states of New York and Connecticut now have business-only court sessions. And a two-year business court experiment by Suffolk County, Massachusetts, which assigned one Superior Court to hear only business cases, was a reported success.[5]

Business Law

Although businesses must comply with the full body of laws that apply to individuals, a subset of laws can be defined more precisely as **business law**. This includes the elements of law that directly affect business activities. For example, laws pertaining to business licensing, employee safety, and corporate income taxes can all be considered business law. For the remainder of this chapter, we will examine some of the specific categories of laws affecting business, including torts; contracts; agency; property transactions; patents, trademarks, and copyrights; negotiable instruments; and bankruptcy.

Torts

A **tort** is a noncriminal act (other than breach of contract) that results in injury to a person or to property. A tort can be either intentional or the result of negligence. The victim of a tort is legally entitled to some form of financial compensation, or **damages**, for his or her loss and suffering. This compensation is also known as a *compensatory damage award*. In some cases, the victim may also receive a *punitive damage award* to punish the wrongdoer if the misdeed was glaringly bad. For example, in 2002 jurors slapped Philip Morris with $28 billion in punitive damages—the largest punitive award in U.S. history—after jurors saw documentary evidence that

Philip Morris knew for decades that cigarettes cause cancer and that nicotine is highly addictive, but the company failed to disclose such information to the public.[6]

Intentional Torts   An **intentional tort** is a willful act that results in injury. For example, accidentally hitting a softball through someone's window is a tort, but purposely cutting down someone's tree because it obstructs your view is an intentional tort. Note that *intent* in this case does not mean the intent to cause harm; it is the intent to commit a specific physical act. Some intentional torts involve communication of false statements that harm another's reputation. If the communication is in writing or on television, it is called *libel*; if it is spoken, it is *slander*. For example, a group of Texas cattlemen sued television talk show host Oprah Winfrey for more than $12 million in damages because they said her disparaging remarks about beef in a 1996 television program caused beef prices to plummet. The jury found Winfrey not guilty of food-libel laws designed to protect perishable food products from disparagement or misinformation that could diminish their market value.[7]

Negligence and Product Liability   In contrast to intentional torts, torts of **negligence** involve a failure to use a reasonable amount of care necessary to protect others from unreasonable risk of injury. Cases of alleged negligence often involve **product liability**, which is a product's capacity to cause damages or injury for which the producer or seller is held responsible. Product-liability lawsuits can cost business owners billions of dollars.

Consider American Home Products (AHP), for instance. In 2002 AHP agreed to set aside $13.2 billion to resolve lawsuits brought by thousands of individuals who contended they were injured by taking the company's popular diet pill combination fen-phen. The product, which had been hailed as a miracle weight-loss pill for the obese, was removed from the market in 1997 at the request of the FDA after studies linked the drugs to heart valve damage and fatal lung diseases. Over six million people took fen-phen.[8]

A company may also be held liable for injury caused by a defective product even if the company used all reasonable care in the manufacture, distribution, or sale of its product. Such **strict product liability** makes it possible to assign liability without assigning fault. It must only be established that (1) the company is in the business of selling the product; (2) the product reached the customer or user without substantial change in its condition; (3) the product was defective; (4) the defective condition rendered the product unreasonably dangerous; and (5) the defective product caused the injury.[9]

Although few people would argue that individual victims of harmful products shouldn't be entitled to some sort of compensation, many question whether such strict

Facing the potential for product liability lawsuits, makers of cold and cough remedies removed products containing phenylpropanolamine (PPA) from drugstore shelves in 2000. The FDA banned the ingredient after reports showed that PPA could increase the risk of stroke in young women. Reformulated products using a safer ingredient soon appeared in their place.

interpretation of product-liability laws is good for society. Many individuals try to take advantage of the system by filing "frivolous" lawsuits. The large compensatory, and sometimes punitive, damages that plaintiffs are awarded make it difficult for many companies to obtain product-liability insurance at a reasonable price. As a result, manufacturers have withheld products from the market that might otherwise benefit society. Although Congress passed a bill in 1996 that restricted the amounts of compensatory and punitive damages awarded in product-liability suits, the bill was vetoed by President Clinton, who felt that it was too restrictive and would have a negative impact on consumers. Nonetheless, the issue continues to be a priority with lawmakers.[10] In 2000 the U.S. House of Representatives passed a bill capping product-liability punitive damages faced by businesses with fewer then 25 employees at the lesser of $250,000 or three times the amount of actual damages.[11]

Contracts

Broadly defined, a **contract** is an exchange of promises between two or more parties that is enforceable by law. Many business transactions—including buying and selling products, hiring employees, purchasing group insurance, and licensing technology—involve contracts. Contracts may be either express or implied. An **express contract** is derived from the words (either oral or written) of the parties; an **implied contract** stems from the actions or conduct of the parties.[12] Iris Kapustein learned the hard way how important written contracts can be in the business world. When she first started her trade show management and consulting firm, she operated on the principle of "my word is my bond." But after losing $15,000 to clients who didn't pay, she adopted a new principle: All clients must sign contracts, and all contracts supplied by clients must be reviewed by her attorney.[13]

Elements of a Contract The law of contracts deals largely with identifying the exchanges that can be classified as contracts. The following factors must usually be present for a contract to be valid and enforceable:

- *An offer must be made.* One party must propose that an agreement be entered into. The offer may be oral or written, but it must be firm, definite, and specific enough to make it clear that someone intends to be legally bound by the offer. Finally, the offer must be communicated to the intended party or parties.

- *An offer must be accepted.* For an offer to be accepted, there must be clear intent (spoken, written, or by action) to enter into the contract. An implied contract arises when a person requests or accepts something and the other party has indicated that payment is expected. If, for example, your car breaks down on the road and you call a mobile mechanic and ask him or her to repair it, you are obligated to pay the reasonable value for the services, even if you didn't agree to specific charges beforehand. However, when a specific offer is made, the acceptance must satisfy the terms of the offer. For example, if someone offers you a car for $18,000, and you say you would take it for $15,000, you have not accepted the offer. Your response is a *counteroffer*, which may or may not be accepted by the salesperson.

- *Both parties must give consideration.* A contract is legally binding only when the parties have bargained with each other and have exchanged something of value, which is called the **consideration**. The relative value of each party's consideration does not generally matter to the courts. In other words, if you make a deal with someone and later decide you didn't get enough in the deal, that result is not the court's concern. You entered into the deal with the original consideration in mind, and that fact is legally sufficient.[14]

- *Both parties must give genuine assent.* To have a legally enforceable contract, both parties must agree to it voluntarily. The contract must be free of fraud, duress, undue influence, and mutual mistake.[15] If only one party makes a mistake, it ordinarily does not affect the contract. On the other hand, if both parties made a mistake, the agreement would be void. For example, if both the buyer and the seller of a business believed the business was profitable, when in reality it was operating at a loss, their agreement would be void.

- *Both parties must be competent.* The law gives certain classes of people only a limited capacity to enter into contracts. Minors, people who are senile or insane, and in some cases those who are intoxicated cannot usually be bound by a contract for anything but the bare necessities: food, clothing, shelter, and medical care.

- *The contract must not involve an illegal act.* Courts will not enforce a promise that involves an illegal act. For example, a drug dealer cannot get help from the courts to enforce a contract to deliver illegal drugs at a prearranged price.

- *The contract must be in proper form.* Most contracts can be made orally, by an act, or by a casually written document; however, certain contracts are required by law to be in writing. For example, the transfer of goods worth $500 or more must be accompanied by a written document. The written form is also required for all real estate contracts.

A contract need not be long; all these elements of a contract may be contained in a simple document (see Exhibit A.2). In fact, a personal check is one type of simple contract.

Contract Performance Contracts normally expire when the agreed-to conditions have been met, called *performance* in legal terms. However, not all contracts run their expected course. Both parties involved can agree to back out of the contract, for instance. In other cases, one

EXHIBIT A.2 Elements of a Contract
This simple document contains all the essential elements of a valid contract.

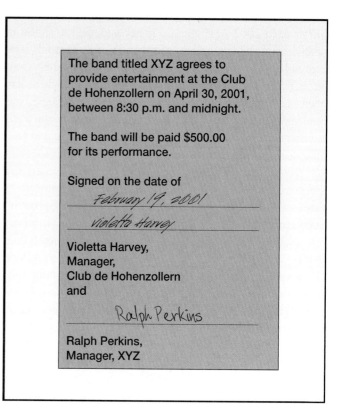

The band titled XYZ agrees to provide entertainment at the Club de Hohenzollern on April 30, 2001, between 8:30 p.m. and midnight.

The band will be paid $500.00 for its performance.

Signed on the date of
February 19, 2001
Violetta Harvey

Violetta Harvey,
Manager,
Club de Hohenzollern
and

Ralph Perkins

Ralph Perkins,
Manager, XYZ

party fails to live up to the terms of the contract, a situation called **breach of contract**. The other party has several options at that point:

- *Discharge.* When one party violates the terms of the agreement, generally the other party is under no obligation to continue with his or her end of the contract. In other words, the second party is discharged from the contract.

- *Damages.* A party has the right to sue in court for damages that were foreseeable at the time the contract was entered into and that result from the other party's failure to fulfill the contract. The amount of damages awarded usually reflects the amount of profit lost and often includes court costs as well.

- *Specific performance.* A party can be compelled to live up to the terms of the contract if money damages would not be adequate.

Jeffrey Katzenberg, former Walt Disney studio chief, settled a bitter breach-of-contract lawsuit in 1999. Katzenberg, who left the company upon learning he would not be promoted to president, contended that he was owed as much as $581 million. The amount was based on a unique contractual bonus arrangement whereby Katzenberg was to receive 2 percent of the projected future profits of films and television shows created during the 10 years he oversaw Disney's movie and television operations. The settlement figure was private, but analysts speculate that Katzenberg received about $250 million.[16]

To control the increasing costs of litigation, more and more companies are now experimenting with alternatives to the courtroom. These include independent mediators, who sit down with the two parties and try to hammer out a satisfactory solution to contract problems, and *mandatory arbitration*, in which an impartial arbitrator or arbitration panel hears evidence from both sides and makes a legally binding decision.

Throughout the United States, businesses slip mandatory arbitration agreements into legal contracts every day, forcing people to give up their right to access the nation's counts. For example, AT&T sends customers a short notice in their bills stating that the company requires mandatory arbitration. Customers agree to such arbitration provisions simply by using AT&T's services. Credit card companies use similar tactics. Customers automatically agree to mandatory arbitration terms if they use a credit card after receiving notice of the mandatory arbitration provision by the card's issuing company.[17]

Despite its widespread use, mandatory arbitration has come under fire by consumer groups because it can wipe out a customer's right to sue. Although some consumers prefer to use this form of alternative dispute resolution, those who do not wish to waive their right to sue are advised to read the fine print of all contracts and purchase agreements. The same advice applies to employment and service contracts.[18]

Warranties The Uniform Commercial Code specifies that everyday sales transactions are a special kind of contract (although this provision applies only to tangible goods, not to services), even though they may not meet all the exact requirements of regular contracts. Related to the sales contract is the notion of a **warranty**, which is a statement specifying what the producer of a product will do to compensate the buyer if the product is defective or if it malfunctions. Several types of warranties exist. *Express warranties* are specific, written statements, whereas *implied warranties* are unwritten but involve certain protections under the law. Warranties may also be *full* or *limited*. The former obligates the seller to repair or replace the product, without charge, in the event of any defect or malfunction, whereas the latter imposes restrictions on the defects or malfunctions that will be covered. Warranty laws also address a number of other details, including giving consumers instructions on how to exercise their rights under the warranty.[19]

Agency

These days it seems that nearly every celebrity has an agent. Basketball players hire agents to get them athletic shoe commercials and handle their contract negotiations; authors' agents sell manuscripts to the publishers that offer the largest advances; actors' agents try to find choice movie and television roles for their clients. These relationships illustrate a common legal association known as **agency**, which exists when one party, known as the *principal*, authorizes another party, known as the *agent*, to act on his or her behalf in contractual matters.[20]

All contractual obligations come into play in agency relationships. The principal usually creates this relationship by explicit authorization. In some cases—when a transfer of property is involved, for example—the authorization must be written in the form of a document called **power of attorney**, which states that one person may legally act for another (to the extent authorized).

Usually, an agency relationship is terminated when the objective of the relationship has been met or at the end of a period specified in the contract between agent and principal. It may also be ended by a change of circumstances, by the agent's breach of duty or loyalty, or by the death of either party.

Property Transactions

Anyone interested in business must know the basics of property law. Most people think of property as some object they own (a book, a car, a house). However, **property** is actually the relationship between the person having the rights to any tangible or intangible object and all other persons. The law recognizes two primary types of property: real and personal.

Real property is land and everything permanently attached to it, such as trees, fences, or mineral deposits. **Personal property** is all property that is not real property; it may be tangible (cars, jewelry, or anything having a physical existence) or intangible (bank accounts, stocks, insurance policies, customer lists). A piece of marble in the earth is real property until it is cut and sold as a block, when it becomes personal property. Property rights are subject to various limitations and restrictions. For example, the government monitors the use of real property for the welfare of the public, to the point of explicitly prohibiting some property uses and abuses.[21]

Two types of documents are important in obtaining real property for factory, office, or store space: a deed and a lease. A **deed** is a legal document by which an owner transfers the *title*, or right of ownership, to real property to a new owner. A lease is used for a temporary transfer of interest in real property. The party that owns the property is commonly called the landlord; the party that occupies or gains the right to occupy the property is the tenant. The tenant pays the landlord, usually in periodic installments, for the use of the property. Generally, a lease may be granted for any length of time that the two parties agree on.

Patents, Trademarks, and Copyrights

If you invent a product, write a book, develop some new software, or simply come up with a unique name for your business, you probably want to prevent other people from using or prospering from your **intellectual property** without fairly compensating you. Several forms of legal protection are available for your creations. They include patents, trademarks, and copyrights. Which one you should use depends on what you have created. Having a patent, copyright, or trademark still doesn't guarantee that your idea or product will not be copied. However, they do provide you with legal recourse if your creations are infringed upon.

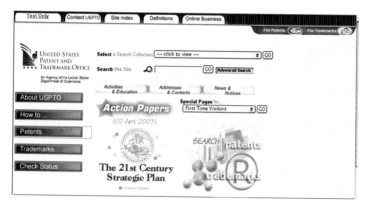

The U.S. Patent and Trademark office website has a wealth of information on how to apply for patents and register a trademark.

Patents A **patent** protects the invention or discovery of a new and useful process, an article of manufacture, a machine, a chemical substance, or an improvement on any of these. Issued by the U.S. Patent and Trademark Office (USPTO), a patent grants the owner the right to exclude others from making, using, or selling such an invention or discovery for 20 years from the date the patent application is filed.[22] Because patent law guarantees the originator the right to use the discovery exclusively for a relatively long period of time, it encourages people to devise new machines, gadgets, and processes. The inventor can stop anyone who tries to steal his or her invention by suing them. Once the 20 years expires, however, the patented item becomes available for common use.

The economic rewards from patenting are enormous. If a patent is granted, you may collect fees from those who want to use your patented product. IBM, for instance, was awarded 3,411 patents and collected $1.5 billion in licensing royalties in 2001 alone. Nationwide, an estimated $120 billion is generated each year from patent licenses, up from $15 billion in 1990.[23]

Nonetheless, winning a patent isn't easy. There's market research to do, legal hurdles to jump, and a relatively long waiting period because the number of patent applications in the system grows annually and receiving a patent is a comprehensive process.

Before granting a patent, examiners must assiduously search for any evidence that proves the invention is not new or is based on an existing design. That evidence, called prior art, includes everything from earlier patents to published material from anywhere in the world that describes the same invention. The enormity of the search is mind-boggling. In a perfect world, an examiner would scour everything worldwide—from graduate dissertations to marketing brochures for small businesses. But obstacles exist, which some say allow too many questionable patents to slip through the system.[24]

One such obstacle is jargon. Once patents have been awarded, they're filed electronically, giving examiners the ability to search the archives by a word or phrase. But when applicants use different adjectives to describe their invention, the examiner can easily miss previous inventions that might prevent a patent from being awarded. Another obstacle is dwindling agency resources. Congress has diverted funds earmarked for the USPTO to other national concerns, putting the agency's efforts to modernize its research methods and data systems off track. As a result, the USPTO is drowning under its workload. The agency's Virginia offices house row after row of floor-to-ceiling shelves jammed with file applications that collect dust as they await their turn to be sent to an examiner. And to make matters worse, the agency is shorthanded. During the economic boom of the late 1990s, the USPTO lost hundreds of examiners to the more lucrative private sector. At the same time, patent applications grew over 50 percent. Approximately

350,000 cases were on backlog in 2002.[25] This backlog puts pressure on examiners to accelerate their pace and has resulted in poorly researched applications and conflicts with existing patents. Such conflicts generally wind up in court.

Defending a patent can be costly and time consuming. The average cost to litigate a patent-infringement case is $1.5 million.[26] Big companies have been known to flagrantly copy products they see on shelves and risk patent infringement because they know that many smaller firms cannot afford the high cost of a drawn-out legal battle. Still, persistence can pay off, as the case of Tom and Tracy Hazzard will demonstrate.

The Hazzards launched their company, ttools, in 1998, selling a combination stylus-ink pen that can be used for writing on paper and electronic PDA organizers. Tom Hazzard received patents on the stylus tip and the ink pen in 1998 and 1999, respectively. In March 1998, before the formal launch of the product, the husband and wife team went to 3Com (owners of Palm, which makes the Palm PDA) for the first time, revealing their design plans in order to gauge the company's interest in their invention. 3Com didn't have anything like the combination pen and was very excited about it, though no deal between the two was struck. Encouraged, the Hazzards officially launched ttools in May 1998. They sold their invention online to individuals, and soon began to do customized bulk orders for companies such as AT&T, Casio, Motorola, and ESPN. After a few months on the market, ttools thought it was ready for the Palm catalog and approached 3Com for a second time. Only this time the company wasn't interested because Palm was developing its *own* two-in-one stylus-ink pen. Shortly thereafter, Palm advertised its new dual stylus-ink pen in a magazine. The product looked so similar to ttools' pen, that ttools got e-mail from customers wondering whether the new Palm stylus was ttools' creation. "We were devastated," recalls Tom Hazzard, who decided to file a patent-infringement lawsuit.

3Com tried to win the legal battle by stalling, asking for court extensions, and dragging out proceedings for more than a year. The stall tactics worked: ttools' business ground to a halt because retailers and investors did not want to deal with a small business involved in a pending lawsuit.

Still, the Hazzards persisted in their claim against 3Com. Tom had retained his sketchpad and a bound book that had extensive records documenting his innovative idea for the two-in-one pen. Each design sketch, every minor change, was dated, creating a complete picture of the product's development. Whenever Tom showed the sketches to anyone, including Palm executives, he had them initial and date the page. Phone conversations, patent applications, brainstorming sessions, were all documented. The bound book told a compelling story.

Forty-eight hours before a mandatory court appearance in November 2000, 3Com settled. Ttools halted the unfair competition suit after 3Com agreed not to produce any new versions of the dual-stylus pen. 3Com also agreed to pay ttools royalties and licensing fees for the Palm two-in-one pen already on the market. Today, ttools stylus pens are available in Wal-Mart, Target, Circuit City, and Office Depot, and the company generates millions in product sales.[27]

Trademarks   As Chapter 13 points out, a trademark is any word, name, symbol, or device used to distinguish the product of one manufacturer from those made by others. Trademark laws also protect logos, shapes, and fonts associated with specific companies, even in digital form. A service mark is the same thing for services. McDonald's golden arches are one of the most visible of modern trademarks. Brand names can also be registered as trademarks. Examples are Exxon, Polaroid, and Chevrolet.

If properly registered and renewed every 20 years, a trademark generally belongs to its owner forever. Among the exceptions are popular brand names that have become generic terms, meaning that they describe a whole class of products. A brand-name trademark can become a generic term if the trademark has been allowed to expire, if it has been incorrectly used by its owner (as in the case of Borden's ReaLemon lemon juice, which the Federal Trade Commission ruled was being used by Borden to maintain a monopoly in bottled lemon juice), or if the public comes to equate the name with the class of products, as was the case with zipper, linoleum, aspirin, Xerox, and many other brand names.

Trade dress, defined as the general appearance or image of a product, has been easier to legally protect since 1992, when the U.S. Supreme Court extended trademark protection to products with "inherently distinctive" appearances.

A well-recognized trademark is an effective advertising tool. Many companies use their trademarks to promote their sponsorship of an athletic event. In this example, Mercedes uses the trademark in sponsored athletic events, such as tennis, by hanging the trademark on the tennis net, a sign, or other display items.

For instance, in 1999 Apple Computer filed suit against Future Power for allegedly infringing on the iMac trade dress with its look-alike E-Power PC. Apple Computer asked the court to prohibit the sale of E-Power in addition to an award of actual and punitive damages. A U.S. District Court granted a preliminary injunction against Future Power from making, distributing, and selling a 15-inch all-in-one computer with a colored plastic cover while the case was being heard. The two parties settled the lawsuit in 2001 when Future Power agreed to refrain from producing the look-alike until 2004.[28]

One particularly problematic area of trademark law involves webpages. When it comes to the design of a webpage, the interpretation of trademark law gets murky. That's because the basic elements of smart web design—such as navigation bars, shopping carts, and fill-in forms—are fair game. They're considered ideas, and you can't protect an idea. But if you create an original expression for the idea, you can protect that trademark. An example would be the blue navigational monorail that scrolls across the Disney webpage at www.Disney.com. Protected by trademark law, that monorail design prevents the public from using a similar navigational device and from copying the code to create a similar device from scratch.[29]

Napster became an Internet phenomenon by allowing its 32 million users to download virtually any popular music for free. In 2000, major music labels went to court to try to force Napster to curb its music-transfer service, which the record industry regards as a violation of copyright laws. Napster's inventor Shawn Fanning (pictured here) argued in court that noncommercial music downloading is indeed legal. In 2001, a U.S. Federal District judge ruled against Napster, shutting down the operation.

Copyrights A **copyright** protects the creators of literary, dramatic, musical, artistic, scientific, and other intellectual works. Any printed, filmed, or recorded material can be copyrighted. The copyright gives its owner the exclusive right to reproduce (copy), sell, or adapt the work he or she has created. Copyright law covers reproduction by photocopying, videotape, and magnetic storage.

The Library of Congress Copyright Office will issue a copyright to the creator or to whomever the creator has granted the right to reproduce the work. (A book, for example, may be copyrighted by the author or the publisher.) Copyrights issued through 1998 are good for 75 years from the date of publication. Copyrights issued after 1998 are valid for the lifetime of the creator plus 70 years.[30]

Copyright protection on the Internet has become an especially important topic as more businesses and individuals include original material on their websites. Technically, copyright protection exists from the moment material is created. Therefore, anything you post on a website is protected by copyright law. However, loose Internet standards and a history of sharing information via the Net has made it difficult for some users to accept this situation. But the No Electronic Theft Act (enacted in 1998) makes it clear that the sanctity of the copyright extends into the area of cyberspace. This law makes it a crime to possess or distribute multiple copies of online copyrighted material for profit or not. Specifically, it closes the loophole that had allowed the distribution of copyrighted material as long as the offender didn't seek profit. Penalties include fines up to $250,000 and five years in prison.[31]

To avoid potential trademark and copyright infringements, experts suggest that authors include copyright and trademark notices on webpages that contain protected material, include a link on each page to a detailed copyright notice that explains what users can and cannot do, and place disclaimers on all pages that contain links to other sites.[32]

Still, the ease of electronic file sharing and the growing supply of new recording devices makes it increasingly difficult for creators to protect their rights. A recent CNN/USA Today/Gallup Poll reported that 18 percent of Internet users have downloaded music from an Internet site that was not authorized by a record company.[33] Entertainment companies claim that such piracy cuts into their profit margins, and many are waging war to gain more control over digital copies of movies, music, and TV shows. One such war was with Napster, who argued for years that the noncommercial music downloading was legal. But in 2001, a U.S. Federal District judge ruled against Napster, effectively shutting down the operation. The ruling ultimately forced Napster to file for Chapter 11 bankruptcy protection. Now Hollywood and the recording companies are going after Napster look-alikes. They are also waging war with technology companies that produce products that make digital copying easier and cheaper.

Sonicblue is one such company. Sonicblue builds gadgets that let people download, copy, and share digital music and video. The company's ReplayTV, for example, lets viewers skip commercials and send TV shows to friends over the Internet. In 2002, 28 entertainment companies sued Sonicblue to get its ReplayTV off the shelves. Hollywood is also trying to push legislation that would force tech companies such as Sonicblue to build piracy protection into products, from PCs to MP players. A processor chip inside a PC, for example, would check each file for a digital watermark. Files without watermarks wouldn't play. But experts say such a law is unlikely to pass because it's too controversial.[34]

Negotiable Instruments

Negotiable instruments are another important area of business law. Whenever you write a personal check, you are creating a **negotiable instrument**, a transferable document that represents a promise to pay a specified amount. (*Negotiable* in this sense means that it can be sold or used as payment of a debt; an *instrument* is simply a written document that expresses a legal agreement.) In addition to checks, negotiable instruments include certificates of deposit, promissory notes, and commercial paper. To be negotiable, an instrument must meet several criteria:[35]

- It must be in writing and signed by the person who created it.

- It must have an unconditional promise to pay a specified sum of money.

- It must be payable either on demand or at a specified date in the future.

- It must be payable either to some specified person or organization or to the person holding it (the bearer).

You can see how a personal check meets those criteria; when you write one, you are agreeing to pay the amount of the check to the person or organization to whom you're writing it.

Bankruptcy

Even though the U.S. legal system establishes the rules of fair play and offers protection from the unscrupulous, it can't prevent most businesses from taking on too much debt. The legal system does, however, provide help for businesses that find themselves in deep financial trouble. **Bankruptcy** is the legal means of relief for debtors (either individuals or businesses) who are unable to meet their financial obligations.

Voluntary bankruptcy is initiated by the debtor; *involuntary bankruptcy* is initiated by creditors. The law provides for several types of bankruptcy, which are commonly referred to by chapter number of the Bankruptcy Reform Act. In a Chapter 7 bankruptcy, the debtor company is liquidated and its assets are sold. The proceeds are then divided equitably among the creditors. Under Chapter 11 (which is usually aimed at businesses but does not exclude individuals other than stockbrokers), a business is allowed to get back on its feet and continue functioning while it arranges to pay its debts. For the steps involved in a Chapter 11 bankruptcy, see Exhibit A.3.

EXHIBIT A.3   Steps in Chapter 11 Bankruptcy Proceedings
Chapter 11 bankruptcy may buy a debtor time to reorganize finances and continue operating. However, using this device to evade financial obligations is extremely risky from a legal standpoint, and declaring bankruptcy may severely damage the reputation and credit rating of a firm or an individual.

Step 1: All current legal proceedings against the firm are halted. A decision is made to either liquidate or reorganize the firm, based on the value of the firm's assets. If liquidation is chosen, the firm's assets are transferred to a trustee, who sells them to pay the firm's debts. If reorganization is chosen, go to step 2.

Step 2: The courts may appoint a trustee to operate the firm, or current management may continue to operate it. A reorganization plan is developed either by current management, by the trustee, or by a committee of creditors. When plan is developed, go to step 3.

Step 3: Creditors and shareholders vote on the reorganization plan. Plan is ratified if (1) at least one-half of creditors vote in favor and if their claims against the company represent at least two-thirds of total claims; (2) at least two-thirds of shareholders approve the plan; and (3) the plan is confirmed by the court. When plan is ratified, go to step 4.

Step 4: The plan guarantees creditors new securities, and sometimes cash, in exchange for dismissal of their claims. With the firm discharged from its debts, it is free to start anew without the weight of past failures.

EXHIBIT A.4
20 Largest U.S. Company Bankruptcies 1987–2002
Twelve of the 20 largest U.S. bankruptcies occurred in the first two years of the new millennium.

COMPANY	BANKRUPTCY DATE	TOTAL ASSETS (BILLIONS) PREBANKRUPTCY
Worldcom	7/21/02	$103.9
Enron	12/2/01	63.4
Conseco	12/18/02	61.4
Texaco	4/12/87	35.8
Financial Corp. of America	9/9/88	33.9
Global Crossing	1/28/02	30.1
UAL Corp (United Airlines parent)	12/9/02	25.2
Adelphia Communications	6/25/02	21.5
Pacific Gas and Electric	4/6/02	21.5
MCorp	3/31/89	20.2
First Executive	5/13/91	15.2
Gibraltar Financial	2/8/90	15.0
Kmart	1/22/02	14.7
NTL	5/8/02	13.0
FINOVA Group	3/7/01	14.0
HomeFed	10/22/92	13.9
Southeast Banking	9/20/91	13.4
Reliance Group Holdings	6/12/01	12.6
Imperial Corp. of America	2/28/90	12.3
Federal-Mogul	10/1/01	10.2
Total		**$551.20**

As Exhibit A.4 shows, a number of Chapter 11 bankruptcies of epic proportions were filed during the first two years of the new millennium. If a company emerges from Chapter 11 as a leaner, healthier organization, creditors generally benefit. That's because once a company is back on its financial feet it can resume payments to creditors. Polaroid, for example, emerged from Chapter 11 bankruptcy in 2002, less than nine months after it filed for such protection. The outcome resulted in a court-approved sale of substantially all of Polaroid's business to One Equity Partners. Both the secured and unsecured creditors supported the sale in anticipation of receiving payments on their outstanding debt balances.[36]

TEST YOUR KNOWLEDGE

Questions for Review

1. What are the three types of U.S. laws, and how do they differ? What additional laws must global companies consider?
2. What is the difference between negligence and intentional torts?
3. What are the seven elements of a valid contract?
4. How can companies protect their intellectual property?
5. What criteria must an instrument meet to be negotiable?

Questions for Analysis

6. What is precedent, and how does it affect common law?

7. What does the concept of strict product liability mean to businesses?
8. Why is agency important to business?
9. What is the advantage of declaring Chapter 11 bankruptcy? What is the disadvantage?
10. *Ethical Considerations:* For a small investment, anyone can purchase a CD copier, called a CD burner, and record a free CD by downloading music off the Internet. If the 1998 Electronic Theft Act makes it a crime to possess or distribute multiple copies of online copyrighted material, for profit or not, why doesn't the government simply ban such copying devices?

CHAPTER GLOSSARY

administrative law   Rules, regulations, and interpretations of statutory law set forth by administrative agencies and commissions

agency   Business relationship that exists when one party (the principal) authorizes another party (the agent) to enter into contracts on the principal's behalf

bankruptcy   Legal procedure by which a person or a business that is unable to meet financial obligations is relieved of debt

breach of contract   Failure to live up to the terms of a contract, with no legal excuse

business law   The elements of law that directly influence or control business activities

common law   Law based on the precedents established by judges' decisions

consent order   Settlement in which an individual or organization promises to discontinue some illegal activity without admitting guilt

consideration   Negotiated exchange necessary to make a contract legally binding

contract   Legally enforceable exchange of promises between two or more parties

copyright   Exclusive ownership right belonging to the creator of an article, book, photo, film, design, or musical work

damages   Financial compensation to an injured party for loss and suffering

deed   Legal document by which an owner transfers the title, or ownership rights, to real property to a new owner

express contract   Contract derived from words, either oral or written

implied contract   Contract derived from actions or conduct

intellectual property   Intangible personal property, such as ideas, songs, trade secrets, and computer programs, that are protected by patents, trademarks, and copyrights

intentional tort   Willful act that results in injury

international law   Principles, customs, and rules that govern the international relationships between states, organizations, and persons

negligence   Tort in which a reasonable amount of care to protect others from risk of injury is not used

negotiable instrument   Transferable document that represents a promise to pay a specified amount

patent   The exclusive right to make, use, or sell (or license others to make or sell) a newly invented product or process

personal property   All property that is not real property

power of attorney   Written authorization for one party to legally act for another

product liability   The capacity of a product to cause harm or damage for which the producer or seller is held accountable.

property   Rights held regarding any tangible or intangible object

real property   Land and everything permanently attached to it

stare decisis   Concept of using previous judicial decisions as the basis for deciding similar court cases

statutory law   Statute, or law, created by a legislature

strict product liability   Liability for injury caused by a defective product when all reasonable care is used in its manufacture, distribution, or sale; no fault is assigned

tort   Noncriminal act (other than breach of contract) that results in injury to a person or to property

Uniform Commercial Code (UCC)   Set of standardized laws, adopted by most states, that govern business transactions

warranty   Statement specifying what the producer of a product will do to compensate the buyer if the product is defective or if it malfunctions

Risk Management and Insurance

Protection Against Risk

All businesses face the risk of loss. Fire, lawsuits, accidents, natural disasters, theft, illness, disability, and death are common occurrences that can devastate any business—large or small—if they are not prepared for. Of course, managers cannot guard against every conceivable threat of loss. Still, they know that in any given situation, the greater the number of outcomes that may occur, the greater their company is at *risk*.

Understanding Risk

Risk is a daily fact of life for both businesses and individuals. Most businesses accept the possibility of losing money in order to make money. In fact, risk prompts people to go into business in the first place. Although the formal definition of **risk** is the variation, based on chance, in possible outcomes of an event, it's not unusual to sometimes hear the term used to mean exposure to loss. This second definition is helpful, because it explains why people purchase **insurance**, a contractual arrangement whereby one party agrees to compensate another party for losses.

Speculative risk refers to those exposures that offer the prospect of making a profit or loss—such as investments in stock. Because in most cases speculative risks are not insurable, the idea is to identify the risks, take steps to minimize them, and provide for the funding of potential losses. **Pure risk**, on the other hand, is the threat of loss without the possibility of gain. Disasters such as an earthquake or a fire at a manufacturing plant are examples of pure risk. Nothing good can come from an exposure to pure risk.

An **insurable risk** is one that meets certain requirements in order for the insurer to provide protection, whereas an **uninsurable risk** is one that an insurance company will not cover (see Exhibit B.1). For example, most insurance

companies are unwilling to cover potential losses that can occur from general economic conditions such as a recession. Such uncertainties are beyond the realm of insurance. In general, a risk is insurable if it meets these requirements:

- *The loss must be accidental and beyond the insured's control.* For example, a fire insurance policy excludes losses caused by the insured's own arson, but losses caused by an employee's arson would be covered.

- *The loss must be financially measurable.* Although the loss of an apartment building is financially measurable, the loss suffered by having an undesirable tenant is not.

- *A large number of similar cases must be subject to the same peril.* In order for the likelihood of a loss to be predictable, insurance companies must have data on the frequency and severity of losses caused by a given peril. If this information covers a long period of time and is based on a large number of cases or observations, the **law of large numbers** will usually allow insurance companies to predict accurately how many losses will occur in the future. For example, insurers keep track of the number of automobile accidents by age group in the United States so they can estimate the likelihood of a customer's becoming involved in a collision.

- *The risk should be spread over a wide geographical area.* Unless an insurance company spreads its coverage over a large geographical area or a broad population base, a single disaster might force it to pay out on all its policies at once. Consider Hurricane Andrew. This 1992 catastrophe caused over $20 billion in insured losses, and the temporary insolvency of State Farm Fire & Casualty, along with the demise of a dozen smaller insurers. Andrew's staggering losses prompted the insurance industry to rethink how it spreads risk. These days insurers employ sophisticated computer models to predict payouts and avoid covering more than they can handle for a single event. For instance, U.S. insurance claims from the September 11 terrorist attacks on the

INSURABLE	UNINSURABLE
Property risks: Uncertainty surrounding the occurrence of loss from perils that cause 1. Direct loss of property 2. Indirect loss of property Personal risks: Uncertainty surrounding the occurrence of loss due to 1. Premature death 2. Physical disability 3. Old age Legal liability risks: Uncertainty surrounding the occurrence of loss arising out of 1. Use of automobiles 2. Occupancy of buildings 3. Employment 4. Manufacture of products 5. Professional misconduct	Market risks: Factors that may result in loss of property or income, such as 1. Price changes, seasonal or cyclical 2. Consumer indifference 3. Style changes 4. Competition offered by a better product Political risks: Uncertainty surrounding the occurrence of 1. Overthrow of the government 2. Restrictions imposed on free trade 3. Unreasonable or punitive taxation 4. Restrictions on free exchange of currencies Production risks: Uncertainties surrounding the occurrence of 1. Failure of machinery to function economically 2. Failure to solve technical problems 3. Exhaustion of raw-material resources 4. Strikes, absenteeism, labor unrest Personal risks: Uncertainty surrounding the occurrence of 1. Unemployment 2. Poverty from factors such as divorce, lack of education or opportunity, loss of health from military service

EXHIBIT B.1   Insurable and Uninsurable Risk
Insurance companies consider some pure risks insurable. They usually view speculative risks as uninsurable. (Some pure risks, such as flood and strike, are considered uninsurable.)

World Trade Center and the Pentagon could run between $30 to $58 billion, but no major insurance insolvencies are expected to occur as a result of the record-setting payouts. Moreover, to prepare for the possibility of future terrorist attacks, most insurance companies have raised their rates for coverage pertaining to acts of terrorism.[1]

- **The possible loss must be financially serious to the insured.** An insurance company could not afford the paperwork involved in handling numerous small **claims** (demands by the insured that the insurance company pay for a loss) of a few dollars each, nor would a business be likely to insure such a small loss. For this reason, many policies have a clause specifying that the insurance company will pay only that part of a loss greater than an amount stated in the policy. This amount, the **deductible**, represents small losses (such as the first $250 of covered repairs) that the insured has agreed to absorb.

Managing risk is indeed an important part of running a business. The process of reducing the threat of loss from uncontrollable events and funding potential losses is called **risk management**, which includes assessing risk, controlling risk, and financing risk by shifting it to an insurance company or by self-insuring to cover possible losses.

Assessing Risk

One of the first steps in managing risk is to identify where it exists. Those areas of risk in which a potential for loss exists, called **loss exposures**, fall under four headings: (1) loss of property (due to destruction or theft of tangible or intangible assets), (2) loss of income (either through decreased revenues or through increased expenses resulting from an accidental event), (3) legal liability to others, including employees, and (4) loss of the services of key personnel (through accidental injury or death).

Consider just one of the many loss exposures that a manufacturer of stuffed toys must face: First, the manufacturer must identify the ways a consumer (most likely a child) can be injured by a stuffed toy. The child might choke on button eyes, get sick from eating the stuffing, or have an allergic reaction to any material in the toy. Second, the company must identify any possible flaws in the production or marketing of the toy that might lead to one of these injuries. For example, a child may have an allergic reaction to the toy if its materials are not carefully tested for allergenic substances, if impurities enter the toy during manufacture, or if the toy is not properly packaged (allowing foreign substances to reach it). Third, the manufacturer must analyze these possibilities in order to predict product-liability losses accurately.

Theft and destruction of company information are two loss exposures that more and more companies are taking seriously. "High-tech crime is the wave of the future," says the head of the FBI's computer crime department.

Once you have identified your potential for risk, you have three reasonable choices: you can accept risk, eliminate or control it, or shift the responsibility for it.

Controlling Risk

Whereas some companies choose to fully accept the financial consequences of a loss themselves—especially when the potential loss costs are small or can be financed by the company itself—others choose to control risk by using a number of *risk-control techniques* to minimize the organization's losses:

- **Risk avoidance.** A risk manager might try to eliminate the chance of a particular type of loss. With rare exceptions, such risk avoidance is not practical. The stuffed-toy manufacturer could avoid being sued for a child's allergic reaction by not making stuffed toys, but, of course, the company would also be out of business.

- **Loss prevention.** A risk manager may try to reduce (but not totally eliminate) the *chance* of a given loss by removing hazards or taking preventive measures. Security guards at banks, warnings on medicines and dangerous chemicals, and safety locks are examples of loss prevention measures.

- **Loss reduction.** A risk manager may try to reduce the *severity* of the losses that do occur. Examples include installing overhead sprinklers to reduce damage during a fire and paying the medical expenses of an injured consumer to reduce the likelihood of litigation and punitive damages.

- **Risk-control transfer.** A risk manager may try to eliminate risk by transferring to some other person or group either (1) the actual property or activity responsible for the risk

or (2) the responsibility for the risk. For example, a firm can sell a building to eliminate the risks of ownership.

Of course, not all risk is controllable. Thus, many companies will shift risk to an outside insurance company or self-insure against risk.

Shifting Risk to an Insurance Company

Insurance is an intangible good—a contingent promise to be delivered in the future. When companies purchase insurance, they transfer a group's (but not an individual's) predicted losses to an insurance pool. The pool combines the cost of the potential losses to be financed and then redistributes them back to the individuals exposed (in advance) by charging them a fee known as an **insurance premium**.

Actuaries determine how much income insurance companies need to generate from premiums by compiling statistics of losses, predicting the amount needed to pay claims over a given period, and calculating the amount needed to cover these expenses plus any anticipated operating costs. Insurance companies don't count on making a profit on any particular policy, nor do they count on paying for a single policyholder's losses out of the premium paid by that particular policyholder. Rather, the insurance company pays for a loss by drawing the money out of the pool of funds it has received from all its policyholders in the form of premiums (see Exhibit B.2). In this way, the insurance company redistributes the cost of predicted losses from a single individual or company to a large number of policies.

Avoiding accidents and injuries through such measures as protective clothing is an important step in managing corporate risk.

EXHIBIT B.2 How Insurance Works

An insurance company covers the cost of a policyholder's loss out of the premiums paid by a large pool of policyholders. Thus, if 100 policyholders pay $400 each to insure against fire damage, the insurance company can afford to compensate one policyholder who actually suffers fire damage with $40,000.

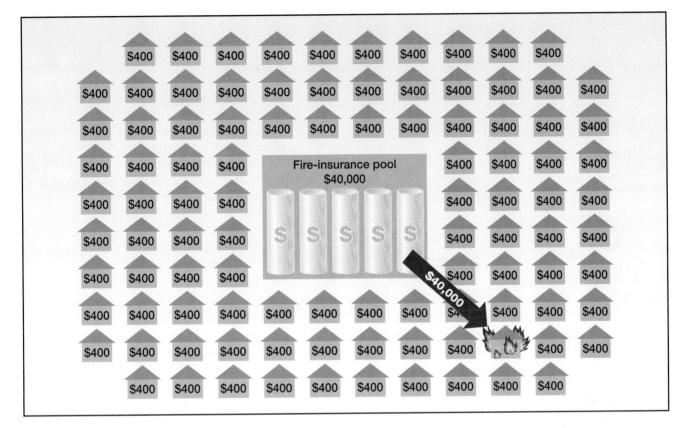

If you were starting a business, what types of insurance would you need? To some extent, the answer to that question would depend on the nature of your business and your potential for loss. In general, however, you would probably want to protect yourself against the loss of property, loss of income, liability, and loss of services of key personnel (see Exhibit B.3).

Property Insurance Property loss can have a variety of causes, including accidental damage, natural disaster, and theft. Property can also be lost through employee dishonesty and nonperformance. When a cannery in California ships jars of pizza sauce by a truck to New York, for example, the goods face unavoidable risks in transit. One wrong turn could cover a whole hillside with broken glass and gallons of sauce, which would represent a sizable loss to the manufacturer. The factory itself is vulnerable to fire, flood, and (especially in California) earthquakes.

Property insurance covers the insured for physical damage to or destruction of property and also for its loss by theft. When purchasing property insurance, the buyer has three coverage options: replacement cost, actual cash value, or functional replacement cost. **Replacement-cost coverage** means that the insurer promises to pay an amount equal to the full cost of repairing or replacing the property even if the property was old or run-down before the loss occurred. Because the insured is often better off after the loss, the premium for this type of coverage is generally quite expensive.

Actual cash value coverage assumes that the property that was lost or damaged was worth less than new property because of normal aging or use. Thus, the insurance company will pay the amount that allows the insured to return the property to its same state before the incident. Sometimes, however, it does not pay to restore a property to its same state because the replacement cost of a building is greater than its market value (as is often the case with older, inner-city structures). **Functional-replacement-cost coverage** allows for the substitution of modern construction materials such as wall board instead of plaster to restore a property to a similar, functioning state.

Consequential Loss Insurance When a disaster strikes, such as a fire or a flood or terrorism, property loss is only one part of the story. Disasters not only disrupt the business operation; they often result in a temporary shutdown, costing the company far more than the equipment repairs or replacement of damaged stock. That's because expenses continue—salaries, interest payments, rent—even

EXHIBIT B.3

Business Risks and Protection

Here are some of the more common types of business insurance purchased.

RISK	PROTECTION
Loss of property	
Due to destruction or theft	Fire insurance
	Disaster insurance
	Marine insurance
	Automobile insurance
Due to dishonesty or nonperformance	Fidelity bonding
	Surety bonding
	Credit life insurance
	Crime insurance
Loss of income	Business interruption insurance
	Extra-expense insurance
	Contingent business-interruption insurance
Liability	Comprehensive general liability insurance
	Automobile liability insurance
	Workers' compensation insurance
	Umbrella liability insurance
	Professional liability insurance
Loss of services of key personnel	Key-person insurance

though the company is not earning revenues. Disruption also results in extra expenses: leasing of temporary space, paying overtime to meet work schedules with a reduced capacity, buying additional advertising to assure the public that the business is still a going concern. In fact, a prolonged interruption of business could even cause bankruptcy.

For this reason, many companies carry *consequential loss insurance*. Available coverage includes **business-interruption insurance**, which protects the insured against lost profits and pays continuing expenses when a fire or other disaster causes a

Businesses with business interruption insurance that had losses from a temporary shutdown resulting from the September 11 terrorist attacks received reimbursement for lost net profits and for reasonable continuing expenses.

company to shut down temporarily; **extra-expense insurance**, which pays the additional costs of maintaining the operation in temporary quarters; and **contingent business-interruption insurance**, which protects against a company's loss of profit due to the misfortune of another business, such as a fire or other disaster that interrupts the operation of an important supplier or the closing of an anchor store in the mall where the business is located.

Many small companies such as Scott Printing Corporation, a specialist in securities-offering prospectuses and other regulatory documents, discovered the value of business-interruption insurance following the September 11 terrorist attacks. Located four blocks south of the World Trade towers, Scott Printing had a business-interruption liability policy and received $100,000 from Hartford Financial Services Group because its business was shut-down for weeks following the catastrophe. Payouts for business-interruption claims can cover everything from renting temporary office space to setting up temporary phone systems to estimating lost revenue. But most business-interruption insurance policies apply only if a business has been shut down for at least 72 hours.[2] Moreover, the claimants need not be located in the disaster area, just affected by the disaster. For example, the post–September 11, 2001, four-day closure of the biggest U.S. stock exchanges also stopped business at brokerage houses across the country.[3]

Liability Insurance Liability insurance provides protection against a number of perils. **Liability losses** are financial losses suffered by firms or individuals held responsible for property damage or for injuries suffered by others. In general, liability losses arise from three sources: (1) the costs of legal damages awarded by a court to the injured party if the company is found negligent; (2) the costs of a legal defense, which can be quite expensive; and (3) the costs of loss prevention or identifying potential liability problems so they may be handled in an appropriate way. To accommodate these sources of liability, the insurance industry has created these types of liability policies:

- *Commercial general liability.* This basic coverage automatically provides protection against all forms of liability not specifically excluded under the terms of the policy. Examples would be liability for operations on business premises, product liability, completed operations, and operations of independent contractors.

- *Product liability.* Manufacturers of a product have a legal duty to design and produce a product that will not injure people in normal use. In addition, products must be packaged carefully and accompanied by adequate instructions and warnings, so consumers may use them properly and avoid injury. If these duties are not fulfilled and result in an injured user, a potential for a product-liability lawsuit exists. **Product-liability coverage** protects insured companies from being threatened financially when someone claims that one of their products caused damage, injury, or death.

- *Automobile liability.* Many companies also carry insurance that specifically covers liability connected with any vehicles owned or operated by the company. Some states have **no-fault insurance laws**, which means that all parties involved in an automobile accident receive compensation for their injuries from their own insurer, regardless of who causes the accident. According to current no-fault plans, after some threshold of damage has been reached, the injured party may revert to the liability system to seek compensation for loss.

- *Professional liability.* Also known as *malpractice insurance* or *errors and omissions insurance*, **professional liability insurance** covers people who are found liable for professional negligence. Because this type of coverage protects professionals from financial ruin if sued by dissatisfied clients, it is very expensive.

- *Employment practices liability.* Recent increases in employee lawsuits and hefty judgments against employers have generated increased interest in employment practices liability insurance. Such insurance reimburses employers for defense costs, settlements, and judgments arising from employment claims related to discrimination, sexual harassment, wrongful termination, breach of employment contract, negligent evaluation, failure to employ or promote, wrongful discipline, deprivation of career opportunity, wrongful infliction of emotional stress, and mismanagement of employee benefits.

- *Umbrella liability.* Because many liability policies have limits, or maximum amounts that may be paid out, businesses sometimes purchase **umbrella policies** to provide

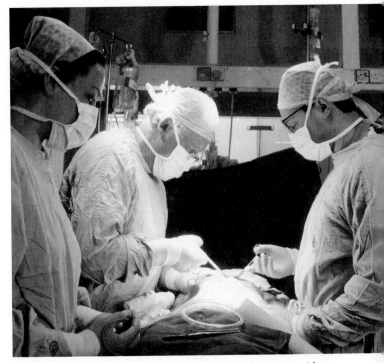

Professional liability insurance is a must for health-care providers, in order to avoid the financially devastating effects of malpractice lawsuits. The high cost of this type of insurance is a major reason that health-care costs have risen so rapidly.

coverage after underlying liability policies have been exhausted. Sometimes an umbrella policy is called *excess liability insurance.*

Key-Person Insurance   Sometimes one executive or employee has expertise or experience that is crucial to the company's operation. If a business loses this key person by illness, disability, death, or unplanned retirement, the effect may be felt in lost income. **Key-person insurance** can be purchased to protect a company against the financial impact of losing such a key employee under the circumstances described. Part of identifying the key-employee exposure is developing an estimate of where, at what cost, and how quickly a replacement may be hired and trained. For example, when fashion designer Gianni Versace was murdered, his key-man policy paid $21 million to his company.[4]

Self-Insuring Against Risk

Self-insurance is becoming an increasingly popular method of insuring against risk. Because self-insurance plans are not subject to state regulation, mandates, and premium taxes (typically 2 percent), companies that use **self-insurance** often save quite a bit of money. Deciding to self-insure with a liability reserve fund means putting aside a certain sum each year to cover predicted liability losses. Unless payments to the self-insurance fund are calculated scientifically and paid regularly, a true self-insurance system does not exist.

Keep in mind that self-insurance differs greatly from "going bare," or having no reserve funds. Self-insurance implies an attempt by business to combine a sufficient number of its own similar exposures to predict the losses accurately. It also implies that adequate financial arrangements have been made in advance to provide funds to pay for losses should they occur. For instance, companies that self-insure often set aside a revenue or self-insurance contingency fund to cover any unexpected or large losses. That way, if disaster strikes, companies won't have to borrow funds to cover their losses, or be forced out of business. In addition, they generally protect themselves from unexpected losses or disasters by purchasing excess insurance from commercial insurers, called *stop-loss insurance*. This additional insurance is designed to cover losses that would exceed a company's own financial capabilities.

Experts advise companies to consider self-insurance plans only if they are prepared to handle the worst-case scenario (usually the point at which stop-loss insurance kicks in) and to use self-insurance only as a long-term strategy. That's because in some years the cost to self-insure will be lower than the cost of commercial insurance, whereas in other years it will be higher. In the long run, however, statistics show that the good and bad years should average out in the company's favor.[5]

Most self-insurers protect themselves from disasters by purchasing stop-loss insurance.

Monitoring the Risk-Management Program

Risk management is an ongoing activity. Managers must periodically reevaluate the company's loss exposures by asking these questions: What does the company have? What can go wrong? What's the minimum we need to stay in business? What's the best way to protect the company's assets? By answering these questions, managers can then revise a company's risk-management program to address changing needs and circumstances. Of course, smart managers recognize that risk management is really everybody's job. Practically every employee can take steps to reduce his or her company's exposure to risk by preventing it or controlling it.

Employee Insurance

Besides protecting company property and assets, many businesses look out for the well-being of employees by providing them with health, disability, workers' compensation, and life insurance coverage. Disease and disability may cost employees huge sums of money unless they are insured. In addition, death carries the threat of financial hardship for an employee's family.

Health Insurance

Approximately 41.2 million Americans are without health insurance today.[6] Most Americans who have health insurance get it from their employers. The type of insurance varies, but typically covers the employee and eligible dependents. Exhibit B.4 lists the most common types of health expense coverage offered by employers.

The Rising Cost of Medical Care Employers typically pay a large portion of the premium costs of health insurance for their employees; however, as costs rise, many employers are shifting more of the cost burden to employees by requiring them to pay a larger portion of their own premiums and larger deductibles through a payroll deduction plan. Small companies and the self-employed often get hit the hardest. Because their insurance groups are smaller, premiums tend to be more costly, forcing some small companies to drop health insurance altogether.

Several factors have led to the escalating costs of health care and health insurance. Insurers blame rising drug costs. Drug companies blame increased hospital operating costs. Doctors blame lawyers for the high costs of professional-liability insurance. And nearly all of the health care industry's players blame consumers for rising health costs. Patients, they

Basic medical	Designed to pay for most inpatient and some outpatient hospital costs
Major medical	Protects the insured against catastrophic financial losses by covering medical expenses that exceed the coverage limits of the basic policies
Disability income	Designed to protect against the loss of short-term or long-term income while the insured is disabled as a result of an illness or accident
Medicare supplemental	Designed specifically to supplement benefits provided under the Medicare program
Long-term care	Designed to cover stays in long-term care facilities

EXHIBIT B.4
Common Types of Health Insurance
Here are five of the most common types of health insurance policies sold by insurers.

say, naturally want the best and latest treatments—but they also want others to pay for it.[7] Other factors causing the escalation of health insurance premiums include costly state mandates. Over the past four decades state legislatures have passed more than 1,500 mandates that require insurers to cover everything from infertility treatments to wigs for cancer patients. Large employers that "self-insure," are exempt from state mandates so the burden falls on small businesses and the self-employed. According to one PriceWaterhouseCoopers study, mandates were responsible for 15 percent of the $67 billion increase in health spending in 2001.[8]

Cost Containment Measures   To help keep the cost of employee health insurance in line, companies have adopted a variety of cost-containment practices. These include preadmission testing (to qualify health insurance applicants), second opinions, home health care, hospice care (long-term home care for the terminally ill), and generic drugs. Many companies have also established worksite disease-prevention programs, referred to as "wellness programs" or "well care," because studies show that keeping employees healthy reduces absenteeism and lowers health costs.

Another way companies choose to contain their health insurance costs is by joining **health maintenance organizations (HMOs)**, which are comprehensive, prepaid, group-practice medical plans in which consumers pay a set fee (called a capitation payment) and in return receive most of their health care at little or no additional costs. Because the capitation payment does not change with usage, HMOs shift the risk from the employer to the health-care provider. Unlike hospitals and doctors in private practice, which charge on a fee-for-service basis, HMOs charge a fixed fee with which they must cover all their expenses. Certain HMOs (called "open HMOs") allow members the option of using hospitals and doctors outside the network. These variations are actually a form of **managed care** programs where employers (usually through an insurance carrier) set up their own network of doctors and hospitals that agree to discount the fees they charge in return for the flow of patients.

As an alternative to HMOs, some employers opt for **preferred-provider organizations (PPOs)**, health-care providers that contract with employers, insurance companies,

or other third-party payers to deliver health-care services to an employee group at a reduced fee. In most companies, employees are not required to use preferred providers, but they are offered incentives to do so—such as reduced deductibles, lower copayments, and well care. Preferred-provider organizations not only save employers money but also allow them to control the quality and appropriateness of services provided. However, employees are restricted in their choice of hospitals and doctors, and preventive services are generally not covered.

National Health Insurance   The rising cost of health care has employers and employees alike clamoring for reform. The problem is getting more attention from Congress, which has been struggling with the issue for over a decade. Much of the debate on health-care reform focuses on the idea of *national health care*, which is generally interpreted as some form of centralized government support or control. One of the strongest motivations for national health care is the goal of providing coverage for people who either aren't covered by employer programs or can't afford to cover themselves. England, Canada, and many other countries

Cutting health-care costs by improving employees' health is the goal of the Hewlett Packard Fitness Center.

have national health care programs; however, many of these programs are struggling to stay afloat because of the need to increase taxes to pay for escalating health care costs.

National health care proposals have generally met with strong opposition in the United States, for a variety of reasons. Some people want to let free-market forces drive the system; others believe the only way to get everyone covered is through government intervention. Some argue that a centralized, so-called single-payer system is the best way to make health care more efficient and more widely available, but opponents are skeptical that any government program—particularly one as massive as national health care—could ever be efficient. In fact, because of the huge amounts of money involved, any changes to the current system are likely to meet opposition from somebody, whether it's health-care professionals, insurance companies, taxpayers, employers, or employees.

Disability Income Insurance

Disability income insurance, which replaces income not earned because of illness or accident, is often included as part of the health insurance package provided by employers. Such policies are designated as either short-term or long-term, depending on the period for which coverage is provided. Short-term policies are more common and provide a specific number of weeks of coverage (often 30), after a brief waiting or elimination period—a period that must elapse before an employee is eligible to receive insurance payments. The purpose of the elimination period is to exclude payments for minor illness. Long-term disability income, on the other hand, provides a number of years of protection after a substantial elimination period has elapsed (generally six months of continuous disability).

The amount of disability payment depends on whether the disability is partial or total, temporary or permanent, short-term or long-term. In general, the amount received is decreased by the amount of disability payments received from Social Security. To encourage employees to return to work as soon as possible, some policies will continue partial payments if an employee is able to perform some type of work, even if he or she is unable to maintain the same pace of career advancement or hours of labor per week as before the disability.

Workers' Compensation Insurance

As Chapter 2 points out, each year thousands of workers die or are injured permanently because of job-related injuries. **Workers' compensation insurance** pays the medical bills of employees who are hurt or become ill as a result of their work. It covers loss of income by occupationally injured or diseased workers, full payment of medical expenses, and rehabilitation expenses for these workers. Plus, it provides death benefits to the survivors of any employee killed on the job. In most cases, it covers both full- and part-time employees.

Workers' compensation insurance is required by U.S. law, and the benefits are enumerated in the workers' compensation statute. Premiums for workers' compensation insurance are based on the employer's payroll and past experience. Thus, employers with relatively good safety records will pay lower workers' compensation insurance rates than employers with poor safety records. This approach rewards loss prevention and loss reduction efforts. Insurers also classify employers by industry, giving recognition to the fact that some industries involve more danger to workers than others. For instance, an employer in a mining industry would pay higher rates than an employer in the food services industry.

Life Insurance

One of the most unfortunate circumstances that could strike a family would be the loss of its main source of income. Life insurance policies provide some protection against the financial problems associated with premature death by paying predetermined amounts to **beneficiaries** when the covered individual dies.

There are many types of life insurance, and each is used for a variety of purposes. For example, *credit life insurance* is required by many lending institutions to guarantee that a mortgage or other large loan will be paid off in the case of the borrower's death. Some life insurance policies provide a type of savings fund for retirement or other purposes by building a *cash value* from excess premiums. In some policies, owners

Each day thousands of workers are injured on the job and file workers' compensation claims. The increasing number of claims has more than doubled the cost of workers' compensation insurance for companies.

can borrow against the cash value by paying interest to the insurer (sometimes at a lower rate than banks charge), and they can withdraw the accumulated cash value in one lump sum or in annual payments if they want to end the policy.

Term insurance, as the name implies, covers a person for a specific period of time—the term of the policy. If the insured outlives the period, no payment is made by the insurer, and the policy has no cash value. Group life insurance is term insurance that is commonly purchased by employers for their employees. It may generally be renewed without the proof of insurability (also known as guaranteed renewable), but not past the age of 65. **Whole life insurance** provides a combination of insurance and savings. The policy stays in force until the insured dies, provided that the premiums are paid. In addition to paying death benefits, whole life insurance accumulates cash value. Because this type of insurance tends to be more expensive than term insurance, it is not typically provided by employers.

Variable life insurance was developed in response to the soaring inflation of the late 1970s and early 1980s. The difference between variable life insurance and whole life insurance is that variable is most often associated with an investment portfolio because the underlying investments are securities, and the policy owner has some investment choice. If the insured's investment decisions are good, the policy's cash value and death benefit (the amount paid at death) will increase. On the other hand, if the investments do poorly, the cash value may drop to $0 and the death benefit may decrease—although not below the original amount purchased (the face value) as long as the policy remains in force and accumulates cash value.

Universal life insurance is also a flexible policy. It allows the insured to buy term insurance and invest an additional amount with the insurance company. Premiums on a universal life insurance policy are used to fund, in essence, term insurance and a savings account. The accumulated premium payments produce a cash value, which then earns two types of interest: A guaranteed interest rate specified in the contract, and an excess interest rate if policy conditions are met. The interest that accumulates on the savings portion of the policy is pegged to current money-market rates (but generally guaranteed to stay above a certain level). Premium payments may vary too, depending on the insured's preferences and as long as cash value is large enough to fund the term-insurance portion of the policy. Because of low market interest rates, this type of policy has lost popularity during the past few years.

Social Insurance Programs

When most people think of insurance, they think of the kind of insurance purchased from a private insurance company.

Actually, the largest single source of insurance in the United States is the government, which accounts for nearly half of the total insurance premiums collected for all types of coverage combined. Most social insurance programs are designed to protect people from loss of income, either because they have reached retirement age or because they have lost their jobs or become disabled. Unlike private insurance, which is voluntarily chosen by the insured, government-sponsored programs are compulsory.

Social Security

Social Security was created by the federal government following the Great Depression of the 1930s. Officially known as Old-Age, Survivors, Disability, and Health Insurance, this program covers just about every wage earner in the United States.

The basic purpose of the Social Security program is to provide a minimum level of income for retirees, their survivors, and their dependents, as well as for the permanently disabled. The program also provides hospital and supplemental medical insurance—known as Medicare—for people age 65 and over. Social Security benefits vary, depending on a worker's average indexed monthly earnings and number of dependents. The program is funded by a payroll tax paid half by workers and half by their employers. In most cases, these taxes are automatically deducted from each paycheck. Self-employed people pay the full amount of the tax as part of their federal income tax liability. It's important to note that Social Security is not a needs-based program; every eligible person is entitled to the benefits of the system, regardless of his or her financial status.

The future of Social Security is questionable. Recent studies show that unless federal law or current financial assumptions change, the retirement and disability program's trust fund will be exhausted by 2042. After that, the government will be able to pay only 73 percent of benefits from current income. The hospital insurance fund, also financed by payroll taxes, will be depleted in 2026.[9] Increased longevity and a low birth rate are the chief blame for this financial dilemma. In the past, the system worked because a far greater number of workers supported every retiree, and many potential beneficiaries died before collecting their first check. This is no longer the case.

Several alternative solutions have been proposed to restore the system's financial stability. These include increasing the tax rate paid by employees and employers, subjecting more earnings of higher-paid workers to the tax, subjecting all social security benefits to the federal income tax, and privatizing or replacing some or all of the current system with privately funded individual retirement accounts.

Unemployment Insurance

Under the terms of the Social Security Act of 1935, employers in all 50 states finance special **unemployment insurance** to benefit employees who are unemployed. The cost is borne by employers. Currently, the unemployment insurance program is a joint federal–state program, with about 90 percent of the funding coming from the states.

The unemployment insurance program is designed to meet the peril of short-term unemployment caused by the business cycle and other factors over which workers have little control. Thus, an employee who becomes unemployed for reasons not related to performance is entitled to collect benefits—typically for 26 weeks, which may be extended during periods of very high unemployment.

TEST YOUR KNOWLEDGE

Questions for Review

1. What is the difference between pure risk and speculative risk?
2. What are the five characteristics of insurable risks?
3. What are the four types of loss exposure?
4. How can you control risk?
5. What is the difference between workers' compensation insurance and disability income insurance?

Questions for Analysis

6. How do insurance companies calculate their premiums?

7. What is self-insurance, and why is it becoming an increasingly popular risk-shifting technique?
8. Why is it a good idea to purchase consequential loss insurance?
9. If you were starting a new accounting practice with 15 employees, what types of insurance might you need?
10. *Ethical Consideration:* A survey by the Society of Chartered Property Casualty Underwriters rated ethical behavior as the number-one attribute insurance industry employers look for in job candidates when making hiring decisions.[10] Why is ethics of such critical concern in the insurance industry? (*Hint:* Think about the nature and length-of-term of the product.)

CHAPTER GLOSSARY

actual cash value coverage Property insurance in which the insurer pays for the replacement cost of property at the time of loss, less an allowance for depreciation

actuaries People employed by an insurance company to compute expected losses and to calculate the cost of premiums

beneficiaries People named in a life insurance policy who receive the proceeds of an insurance contract when the insured dies

business-interruption insurance Insurance that covers losses resulting from temporary business closings

claims Demands for payments from an insurance company because of some loss by the insured

contingent business-interruption insurance Insurance that protects a business from losses due to losses sustained by other businesses such as suppliers or transportation companies

deductible Amount of loss that must be paid by the insured before the insurer will pay for the rest

disability income insurance Short-term or long-term insurance that protects an individual against loss of income while that individual is disabled as the result of an illness or accident

extra-expense insurance Insurance that covers the added expense of operating the business in temporary facilities after an event such as a fire or a flood

functional-replacement-cost coverage Property insurance that allows for the substitution of construction materials to restore a property to a similar, functioning state

health maintenance organizations (HMOs) Prepaid medical plans in which consumers pay a set fee in order to receive a full range of medical care from a group of medical practitioners

insurable risk Risk for which an acceptable probability of loss may be calculated and that an insurance company might, therefore, be willing to cover

insurance Written contract that transfers to an insurer the financial responsibility for losses up to specified limits

insurance premium Fee that the insured pays the insurer for coverage against loss

key-person insurance Insurance that provides a business with funds to compensate for the loss of a key employee by unplanned retirement, resignation, death, or disability

law of large numbers   Principle that the larger the group on which probabilities are calculated, the more accurate the predictive value

liability losses   Financial losses suffered by a business firm or individual held responsible for property damage or injuries suffered by others

loss exposures   Areas of risk in which a potential for loss exists

managed care   Health care set up by employers (usually through an insurance carrier) who provide networks of doctors and hospitals that agree to discount the fees they charge in return for the flow of patients

no-fault insurance laws   Laws limiting lawsuits connected with auto accidents

preferred-provider organizations (PPOs)   Health-care providers offering reduced-rate contracts to groups that agree to obtain medical care through the providers' organization

product-liability coverage   Insurance that protects companies from claims for injuries or damages that result from use of a product the company manufactures or distributes

professional liability insurance   Insurance that covers losses arising from damages or injuries caused by the insured in the course of performing professional services for clients

property insurance   Insurance that provides coverage for physical damage to or destruction of property and for its loss by theft

pure risk   Risk that involves the chance of loss only

replacement-cost coverage   Property insurance in which the insurer pays for the full cost of repairing or replacing the property rather than the actual cash value

risk   Uncertainty of an event or exposure to loss

risk management   Process used by business firms and individuals to deal with their exposures to loss

self-insurance   Accumulating funds each year to pay for predicted liability losses, rather than buying insurance from another company

speculative risk   Risk that involves the chance of both loss and profits

term insurance   Life insurance that provides death benefits for a specified period

unemployment insurance   Government-sponsored program for assisting employees who are laid off for reasons not related to performance

uninsurable risk   Risk that few, if any, insurance companies will assume because of the difficulty of calculating the probability of loss

universal life insurance   Combination of term life insurance policy and a savings plan with flexible interest rates and flexible premiums

umbrella policies   Insurance that provides businesses with coverage beyond what is provided by a basic liability policy

variable life insurance   Whole life insurance policy that allows the policyholder to decide how to invest the cash value

whole life insurance   Insurance that provides both death benefits and savings for the insured's lifetime, provided premiums are paid

workers' compensation insurance   Insurance that partially replaces lost income and that pays for employees' medical costs and rehabilitation expenses for work-related injuries

Careers in Business and the Employment Search

Thinking About Your Career

Getting the job that's right for you takes more than sending out a few letters and signing up with the college placement office. Planning and research are important if you want to find a company and a position that suit you. Before you limit your job search to a particular industry or functional specialty, analyze what you have to offer and what you hope to get from your work. Then you can identify employers who are likely to want you and vice versa.

What Do You Have to Offer?

Get started by jotting down 10 achievements you're proud of, such as learning to ski, taking a prize-winning photo, tutoring a child, or editing your school paper. Think carefully about what specific skills these achievements demanded. For example, leadership skills, speaking ability, and artistic talent may have helped you coordinate a winning presentation to your school's administration. As you analyze your achievements, you'll begin to recognize a pattern of skills. Which of them might be valuable to potential employers?

Next, look at your educational preparation, work experience, and extracurricular activities. What do your knowledge and experience qualify you to do? What have you learned from volunteer work or class projects that could benefit you on the job? Have you held any offices, won any awards or scholarships, mastered a second language?

Take stock of your personal characteristics. Are you aggressive, a born leader? Or would you rather follow? Are you outgoing, articulate, great with people? Or do you prefer working alone? Make a list of what you believe are your four or five most important qualities. Ask a relative or friend to rate your traits as well.

If you're having trouble figuring out your interests, characteristics, or capabilities, consult your college placement office. Many campuses administer a variety of tests to help you identify interests, aptitudes, and personality traits. These tests won't reveal your "perfect" job, but they'll help you focus on the types of work best suited to your personality.

What Do You Want to Do? Knowing what you *can* do is one thing. Knowing what you *want* to do is another. Don't lose sight of your own values. Discover the things that will bring you satisfaction and happiness on the job.

- *What would you like to do every day?* Talk to people in various occupations about their typical workday. You might consult relatives, local businesses, or former graduates (through your school's alumni relations office). Read about various occupations. Start with your college library or placement office.

- *How would you like to work?* Consider how much independence you want on the job, how much variety you like, and whether you prefer to work with products, machines, people, ideas, figures, or some combination thereof. Do you like physical work, mental work, or a mix? Constant change or a predictable role?

- *What specific compensation do you expect?* What do you hope to earn in your first year? What kind of pay increase do you expect each year? What's your ultimate earnings goal? Would you be comfortable getting paid on commission, or do you prefer a steady paycheck? Are you willing to settle for less money in order to do something you really love?

- *Can you establish some general career goals?* Consider where you'd like to start, where you'd like to go from there, and the ultimate position you'd like to attain. How soon after joining the company would you like to receive your first promotion? Your next one? What additional training or preparation will you need to achieve them?

- *What size company would you prefer?* Do you like the idea of working for a small, entrepreneurial operation? Or would you prefer a large corporation?

- *What type of operation is appealing to you?* Do you prefer to work for a profit-making company or a nonprofit organization? Are you attracted to service businesses or manufacturing operations? Do you want regular, predictable hours, or do you thrive on flexible, varied hours? Would you enjoy a seasonally varied job such as education (which may give you summers off) or retailing (with its selling cycles)?

- *What location would you like?* Would you like to work in a city, a suburb, a small town, an industrial area, or an uptown setting? Do you favor a particular part of the country? A country abroad? Do you like working indoors or outdoors?

- *What facilities do you envision?* Is it important to you to work in an attractive place, or will simple, functional quarters suffice? Do you need a quiet office to work effectively, or can you concentrate in a noisy, open setting? Is access to public transportation or freeways important?

- *What sort of corporate culture are you most comfortable with?* Would you be happy in a formal hierarchy with clear reporting relationships? Or do you prefer less structure? Are you looking for a paternalistic firm or one that fosters individualism? Do you like a competitive environment? One that rewards teamwork? What qualities do you want in a boss?

Seeking Employment Opportunities and Information

Whether your major is business, biology, or political science, once you know what you have to offer and what you want, you can start finding an employer to match. If you haven't already committed yourself to any particular career field, review the career tables in the *Occupational Outlook Handbook*, a nationally recognized source of career information published by the U.S. Bureau of Labor Statistics. Revised every two years, the handbook (available in print and online at www.bls.gov/oco) describes what workers do on the job, working conditions, the training and education needed, earnings, and expected job prospects in a wide range of occupations.[1]

Here is a brief overview of the future outlook for a number of careers in business:

- *Careers in Management.* Today's business environment requires the skills of effective managers to reduce costs, streamline operations, develop marketing strategies, and supervise workers. As discussed in Chapter 7, managers perform four basic functions: planning, organizing, leading, and controlling. Facing increased competition, many businesses are becoming more dependent on the expertise of outside management consultants—one of the fastest-growing occupations of all jobs. Outside management consultants perform many important tasks, but chief among them is evaluating operating conditions and making recommendations to improve effectiveness. To find out more about what you can do with a degree in management and the typical courses management majors take, log on to the Prentice Hall Student Success SuperSite at www.prenhall.com/success/MajorExp/management.html.

- *Careers in Human Resources.* As discussed in Chapters 10 and 11, human resources managers plan and direct human resource activities that include recruiting, training and development, compensation and benefits, employee and labor relations, health and safety. In addition, human resources managers develop and implement human resources systems and practices to accommodate a firm's strategy and to motivate and manage diverse workforces. Large numbers of job openings are expected in the human resources field in the near future. Efforts to recruit quality employees and to provide more employee training programs should create new human resources positions. With a vast supply of qualified workers and new college graduates, however, the job market for human resources is likely to remain competitive.

- *Careers in Computers and Information Systems.* Job opportunities abound for trained information technology workers. As competition and advanced technologies force companies to upgrade and improve their computer systems, the number of computer-related positions continues to escalate. Within the computer field, only two categories of jobs are expected to decrease: computer operators and data entry clerks. More user-friendly computer software has greatly reduced the need for operators and data entry processors, but displaced workers who keep up with changing technology should have few problems moving into other areas of computer support. To find out more about careers in computer science and information systems, log on to the Prentice Hall Student Success SuperSite at www.prenhall.com/success/MajorExp/index.html, and select Computer Science or Information Technology.

- *Careers in Sales and Marketing.* Increasing competition in products and services should create greater needs for effective sales and marketing personnel in the future. Employment opportunities for retail salespersons look good because of the need to replace the large number of workers who transfer to other occupations or leave the workforce each year. Opportunities for part-time work should be abundant. Employment for insurance and real estate agents, however, is expected to grow more slowly than average. Computer technology will allow established agents to increase their sales volume and eliminate the need for additional marketing personnel in these fields. For additional information on the types of courses marketing majors take and what you can do with a degree in marketing see

Chapters 12 through 15 and log on to the Prentice Hall Student Success SuperSite at www.prenhall.com/success/MajorExp/marketing.html.

- *Careers in Finance and Accounting.* As Chapter 16 points out, accountants and financial managers are needed in almost every industry. Most positions in finance and accounting are expected to grow as fast as the average for all occupations in the near future, as continued growth in the economy and population is expected to create more demand for trained financial personnel. To find out more about careers in finance and accounting, log on to the Prentice Hall Student Success SuperSite at www.prenhall.com/success/MajorExp/index.html, and select finance or accounting.

EXHIBIT C.1

The 20 Fastest-Growing Occupations

The 20 occupations shown here will account for over one-third of all new jobs during the first 10 years of the 21st century.

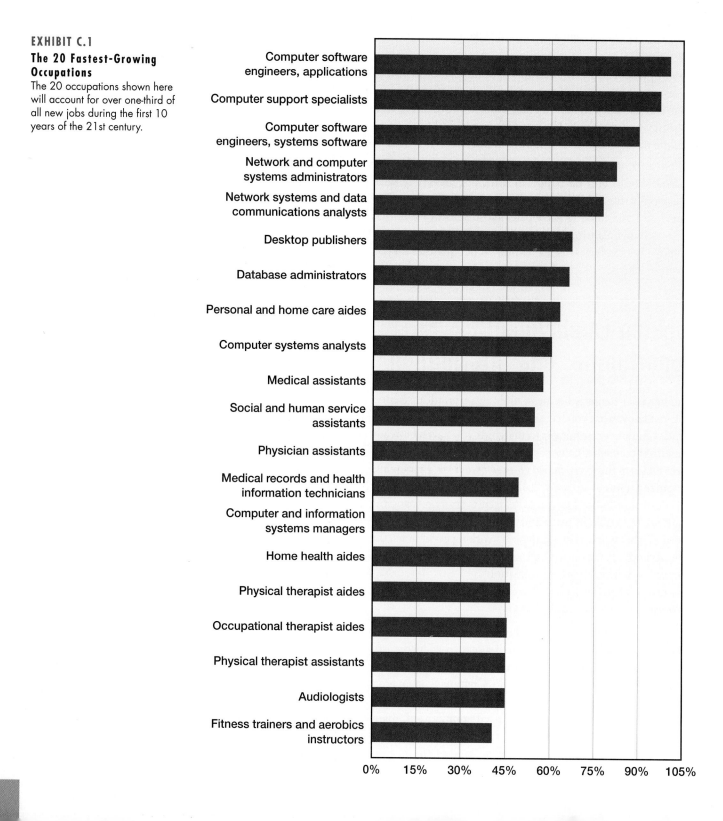

• **_Careers in Economics._** As Chapter 1 discusses, economists study how society distributes scarce resources such as land, labor, raw materials, and machinery to produce goods and services. They conduct research, collect and analyze data, monitor economic trends, and develop forecasts. Economists are needed in many industries and spend time applying economic theory to analyze issues that are important to their firms. For example, they might analyze the effects of global economic activity on the demand for the company's product, conduct a cost–benefit analysis of the projects the company is considering, or determine the effects of government regulations or taxes on the company. Employment of economists is expected to grow about as fast as the average for all occupations, with the best opportunities in private industry—especially research, testing, and consulting firms—as more companies contract out for economic research services. To find out more about what you can do with a degree in economics and the typical courses economic majors take, log on to the Prentice Hall Student Success SuperSite at www. prenhall.com/success/MajorExp/economic.html.

• **_Careers in Communications._** As businesses recognize the need for effective communications with their customers and the public, employment of communications personnel is expected to grow as fast or faster than the average for all occupations in the near future. Recent college graduates may face keen competition for entry positions in communications as the number of applicants is expected to exceed the number of job openings. Newly created jobs in the ever-expanding computer world—such as graphic designers for websites or technical writers for instruction manuals—are expected to improve the career outlook for new communications graduates.

Professional and related occupations are expected to grow by 26 percent from 2000 to 2010. As Exhibit C.1 shows, nearly three-quarters of the job growth will come from computer and mathematical occupations, and education, training, and library occupations. By contrast, employment in management occupations is expected to increase by 13.6 percent over the same 10-year period. General and operations managers will add the most new jobs.[2]

Exhibit C.2 shows that job growth will also vary by education and training requirements. Occupations that require a bachelor's degree, for example, are expected to grow 21.6 percent by 2010. Categories that do not require a college degree are projected to grow slower than average in the future. Moreover, the hottest jobs in today's business world demand technological and computer skills. Even if you're interested in finance, human resources, or marketing positions, you'll need basic computer skills to snare the best jobs in your desired field of work.

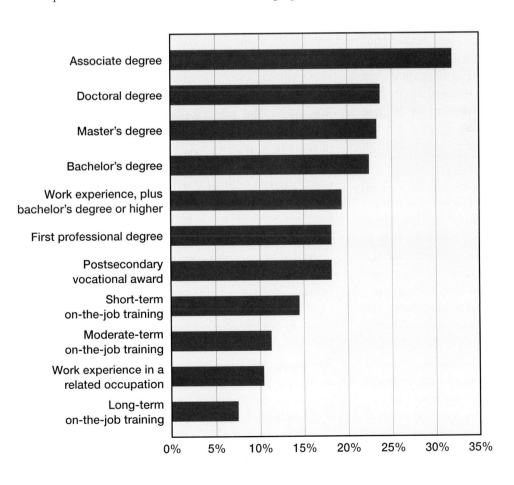

EXHIBIT C.2

Projected Job Growth by Source of Education or Training 2000–2010
Having a college degree can make a big difference when looking for a job in today's competitive marketplace.

Cisco Systems participates in college job fairs as one way to recruit new employees.

Sources of Employment Information

One effective approach to the employment process is to gather as much information as you can, narrowing it as you go until you know precisely the companies you want to contact. Begin by finding out where the job opportunities are, which industries are strong, which parts of the country are booming, and which specific job categories offer the best prospects for the future. From there you can investigate individual organizations, doing your best to learn as much about them as possible. Here are some good information sources:

- **Business and Financial News.** If you don't already do so, subscribe to a major newspaper (print or online editions) and scan the business pages every day. Watch some of the television programs that focus on business, such as *Wall Street Week.* You can find information about the future of specific jobs in the *Dictionary of Occupational Titles* (U.S. Employment Service), the employment publications of Science Research Associates, and the *Occupational Outlook Handbook* (U.S. Bureau of Labor Statistics).

- **Networking.** You have any number of options for networking with people who work at the organizations you're interested in or who work in a field you would like to investigate. You may be able to network with executives in your field by joining or participating in student business organizations, especially those with ties to real-world

organizations such as the American Marketing Association or the American Management Association. You might try visiting some organizations, contacting their personnel departments, and talking with key employees.

- **College Placement Offices.** Also known as career centers, college placement offices offer individual counseling, credential services, job fairs, on-campus interviews, and job listings. Advisors can give you advice on résumé writing and provide workshops in job-search techniques, interview techniques, and more.

Employment Information on the Web

The web offers an amazing amount of company and employment information, both general and specific:

- **Discussion groups.** Using the web, you can locate and communicate with potential employers through numerous types of discussion groups dedicated to your field. Usenet newsgroups provide an electronic bulletin board so that members can leave and retrieve messages whenever they visit. Listservs (Internet mailing lists) send each message to every member's e-mail address. Commercial systems (Prodigy, America Online, etc.) have their own discussion groups (and make a profit from the time users spend accessing their services). Once you locate a potential contact, you can use e-mail to request information about the company or inquire about job openings.

- **Career counseling websites.** You can also find job counseling online. You might begin your self-assessment, for example, with the Keirsey Temperament Sorter, an online personality test at www.keirsey.com. For excellent job-seeking pointers and counseling, visit college- and university-run online career centers. Commercial career centers range from award winning to depressing, so seek out those whose advice is both useful and sensible.

- **Company websites.** Find out whether a company you're interested in maintains a website. Those that do generally include a company profile, press releases, financial information, descriptive brochures, and information on employment opportunities. You'll also find information about an organization's mission, products, and employee benefits.

- **Job boards.** An increasing number of large and small companies are posting job openings on Internet job boards such as the ones listed in Exhibit C.3. You can locate job board websites by knowing the URL (web address), using links from other sites, or using your favorite search engine. Job boards are an excellent place to post your résumé.

WEBSITE	DESCRIPTION AND FEATURES
America's Career InfoNet www.acinet.org	Good place to begin. Offers information on typical wages and employment trends. Gives education, knowledge, and skills requirements for most occupations. Includes links to multiple career resources on the Internet.
America's Job Bank www.ajb.dni.us	State agencies post an average of 5,000 new openings each day on this government site. Companies contribute another 3,000.
CareerBuilder www.careerbuilder.com	Offers a network of career services, job-search information, and tips on how to succeed once you're hired. Includes a database of 20,000 openings.
Careers in Business www.careers-in-business.com	Provides free information on a wide variety of business careers. Posts job openings by company name and by industry. Focuses on careers in accounting, finance, and marketing.
HotJobs.com http://hotjobs.yahoo.com	A member-based website that charges companies a hefty fee to post openings or search through résumés. Job seekers can create a personal page to manage their search and collect statistics on how many companies have retrieved their résumé.
Monster Trak www.monstertrak.com	Has formed partnerships with 750 campuses nationwide and serves as a virtual career center for students and alumni. Many entry-level postings.
Net-Temps www.net-temps.com	Maintained by career consultants; offers several thousand updated listings and real-time seminars. Network forums help you develop new contacts and job leads. Includes chat room for online interviews.
The Monster Board www.monster.com	Posts more than 25,000 openings and 300,000 résumés. Heavily marketed, it brings a flood of employers (many with under 500 employees).
Yahoo! Classifieds Classifieds.yahoo.com	Offers extensive listing of companies by city, in addition to a wealth of job-related information at the parent website, www.yahoo.com. Click on Business & Economy/Jobs/Company Job Listings.
4Work www.4work.com	One of the few sites that includes listings of internships and volunteer opportunities.

EXHIBIT C.3

10 Places to Start Your Online Job Search
Begin your job search with these helpful online career resources.

Preparing Your Résumé

A **résumé** is a structured, written summary of a person's education, employment background, and job qualifications. Although many people have misconceptions about résumés (see Exhibit C.4), the fact is that a résumé is a form of advertising. It is intended to stimulate an employer's interest in you—in meeting you and learning more about you. A successful résumé inspires a prospective employer to invite you to interview with the company. Thus, your purpose in writing your résumé is to create interest—*not* to tell readers everything about you. In fact, it may be best to only hint at some things and leave the reader wanting more. The potential employer will then have even more reason to contact you.

To write a successful résumé, you need to convey seven qualities that employers seek. You want to show that you (1) think in terms of results, (2) know how to get things done, (3) are well rounded, (4) show signs of progress, (5) have personal standards of excellence, (6) are flexible and willing to

EXHIBIT C.4

Fallacies and Facts About Résumés

Many people incorrectly believe that a good résumé will get them the job they want.

FALLACY	FACT
The purpose of a résumé is to list all your skills and abilities.	The purpose of a résumé is to kindle employer interest and generate an interview.
A good résumé will get you the job you want.	All a résumé can do is get you in the door.
Your résumé will be read carefully and thoroughly by an interested employer.	Your résumé probably has less than 45 seconds to make an impression.
The more good information you present about yourself in your résumé, the better.	Too much information on a résumé may actually kill the reader's appetite to know more.
If you want a really good résumé, have it prepared by a résumé service.	Prepare your own résumé—unless the position is especially high-level or specialized. Even then, you should check carefully before using a service.

try new things, and (7) possess strong communication skills. As you organize and compose your résumé, think about how you can convey those seven qualities.

Controlling the Format and Style

With less than a minute to make a good impression, your résumé needs to look sharp and grab a recruiter's interest in the first few lines. A typical recruiter devotes 45 seconds to each résumé before tossing it into either the "maybe" or the "reject" pile. Most recruiters skim a résumé rather than read it from top to bottom. If yours doesn't stand out, chances are the recruiter won't look at it long enough to judge your qualifications.

To give your printed résumé the best appearance possible, use a clean typeface on high-grade, letter-size bond paper (in white or some light earth tone). Your stationery and envelope should match. Leave ample margins all around, and make sure that any corrections are unnoticeable. Avoid italic typefaces, which are difficult to read, and use a quality printer.

Try to keep your résumé to one page. If you have a great deal of experience and are applying for a higher-level position, you may need to prepare a somewhat longer résumé. The important thing is to have enough space to present a persuasive, but accurate, portrait of your skills and accomplishments.

Lay out your résumé so that the information is easy to grasp. Break up the text with headings that call attention to various aspects of your background, such as work experience and education. Underline or boldface key points, or set them off in the left margin. Use indented lists to itemize your most important qualifications. Leave plenty of white space, even if you're forced to use two pages. Pay attention to mechanics and details. Make sure that headings and itemized lists are grammatically parallel and that grammar, spelling, and punctuation are correct.

Write in a simple and direct style to save your reader time. Use short, crisp phrases instead of whole sentences, and focus on what your reader needs to know. Absolutely avoid using the word *I*. You might say, "Coached a Little League team to the regional playoffs" or "Managed a fast-food restaurant and four employees."

Think about your résumé from the employer's perspective. Ask yourself: What key qualifications will an employer be looking for? Which of these are my greatest strengths? What will set me apart from other candidates? What are my greatest accomplishments, and what was produced as a result? Then tailor your résumé to appeal to the employer's needs.

Organizing Your Résumé Around Your Strengths

As you compose your résumé, try to emphasize the information that has a bearing on your career objective, and minimize or exclude any that is irrelevant or counterproductive. To interest potential employers in your résumé, call attention to your best features and downplay your weaknesses—but be sure you do so without distorting or misrepresenting the facts. Do you have something in your history that might trigger an employer's red flag? The following are some common problems and some quick suggestions for overcoming them:[3]

- *Frequent job changes.* Group all contract and temporary jobs under one heading if they're similar.

- *Gaps in work history.* Mention relevant experience and education gained during time gaps, such as volunteer or community work. If gaps are due to personal problems such as drug or alcohol abuse or mental illness, offer honest but general explanations about your absences ("I had serious health concerns and had to take time off to fully recover.").

- *Inexperience.* List related volunteer work. List relevant course work and internships. Offer hiring incentives such as "willing to work nights and weekends."

- *Overqualification.* Tone down your résumé, focusing exclusively on pertinent experience and skills.

- *Long-term employment with one company.* Itemize each position held at the firm to show "interior mobility" and increased responsibilities. Don't include obsolete skills and job titles.

- *Job termination for cause.* Be honest with interviewers. Show you're a hard-working employee and counter their concerns with proof such as recommendations and examples of completed projects.

- *Criminal record.* Consider sending out a "broadcast letter" about your skills and experience, rather than a résumé and cover letter. Prepare answers to questions that interviewers will probably pose ("You may wonder whether I will be a trustworthy employee. I'd like to offer you a list of references from previous bosses and co-workers who will attest to my integrity. I learned some hard lessons during that difficult time in my life, and now I'm fully rehabilitated.").

To focus attention on your strongest points, adopt the appropriate organizational approach—make your résumé chronological, functional, or a combination of the two. The "right" choice depends on your background and your goals.

The Chronological Résumé In a **chronological résumé,** the "Work Experience" section dominates and is placed in the most prominent slot, immediately after the name and address and the objective. You develop this section by listing your jobs sequentially in reverse order, beginning with the most recent position and working backward toward earlier jobs. Under each listing, describe your responsibilities and accomplishments, giving the most space to the most recent positions. If you're just graduating from college, you can vary this chronological approach by putting your educational qualifications before your experience, thereby focusing attention on your academic credentials.

The chronological approach is the most common way to organize a résumé, and many employers prefer it (see Exhibit C.5). This approach has three key advantages: (1) employers are familiar with it and can easily find information, (2) it highlights growth and career progression, and (3) it highlights employment continuity and stability. As vice president with Korn/Ferry International, Robert Nesbit speaks for many recruiters: "Unless you have a really compelling reason, don't use any but the standard chronological format. Your résumé should not read like a treasure map, full of minute clues to the whereabouts of your jobs and experience. I want to be able to grasp quickly where a candidate has worked, how long, and in what capacities."

The Functional Résumé A **functional résumé** emphasizes a list of skills and accomplishments, identifying employers and academic experience in subordinate sections. This pattern stresses individual areas of competence, so it's useful for people who are just entering the job market, want to redirect their careers, or have little continuous career-related experience. The functional approach also has three advantages: (1) without having to read through job descriptions, employers can see what you can do for them, (2) you can emphasize earlier job experience, and (3) you can de-emphasize any lack of career progress or lengthy unemployment. Bear in mind, however, that many seasoned employment professionals are suspect of this résumé style. They assume that candidates who use it are trying to hide something.

The Combination Résumé A **combination résumé** includes the best features of the chronological and functional approaches. Nevertheless, it is not commonly used because it has two major disadvantages: (1) it tends to be longer and (2) it can be repetitious if you have to list your accomplishments and skills in both the functional section and the chronological job descriptions.

Converting Your Traditional Résumé to a Scannable Format

You need to format your résumé in at least two and maybe three ways: (1) as a traditional printed document such as the one just discussed, (2) as a plain-text (or ASCII) document that can be scanned from a hard copy or submitted electronically, and (3) as an HTML-coded document that would be uploaded to the Internet to post on a webpage (should you choose to).

Most Fortune 1000 companies today encourage applicants to submit electronic or scannable résumés. By scanning these résumés into their electronic databases, companies can narrow down a pile of job applicants quickly.

Scannable résumés should convey the same information as traditional résumés, but the format and style must be changed to one that is computer-friendly because scannable résumés are not intended to be read by humans. To make your traditional résumé a scannable one, format it as plain text (ASCII) document, improve its look, and modify its content slightly by providing a list of key words and by balancing common language with current jargon (see Exhibit C.6).

Prepare Your Résumé in ASCII Format ASCII is a common plain-text language that allows your résumé to be read by any scanner and accessed by any computer, regardless

EXHIBIT C.5 Chronological Résumé

Roberto Cortez calls attention to his most recent achievements by setting them off in list form with bullets. The section titled "Intercultural and Technical Skills" emphasizes his international background, fluency in Spanish, and extensive computer skills—all of which are important qualifications for his target position.

Combines accounting expertise with international experience in the minds of employers by stating it in an overall objective

Organizes information chronologically and emphasizes that organization with format

Makes each description concise, easy to read, and informative:

- Avoids the word "I" throughout

- Uses no unnecessary words

Highlights important skills by breaking them out into a list in a separate section

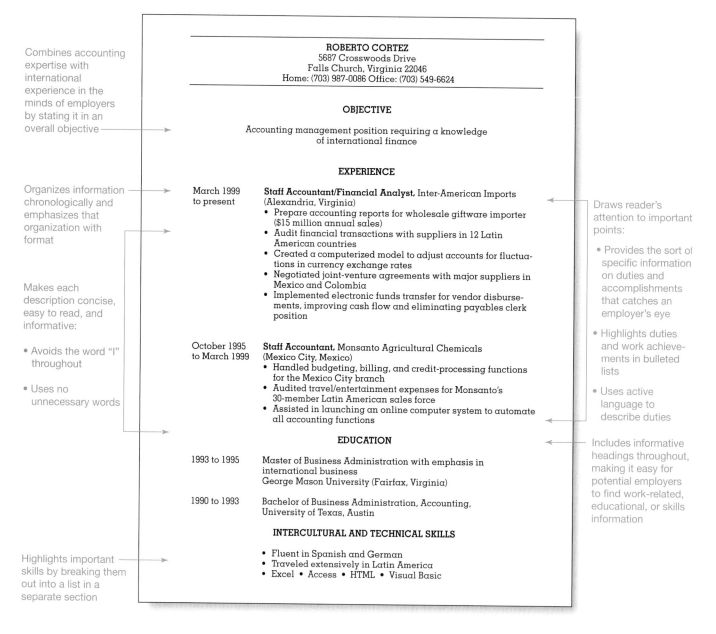

ROBERTO CORTEZ
5687 Crosswoods Drive
Falls Church, Virginia 22046
Home: (703) 987-0086 Office: (703) 549-6624

OBJECTIVE

Accounting management position requiring a knowledge
of international finance

EXPERIENCE

March 1999 to present — **Staff Accountant/Financial Analyst,** Inter-American Imports (Alexandria, Virginia)
- Prepare accounting reports for wholesale giftware importer ($15 million annual sales)
- Audit financial transactions with suppliers in 12 Latin American countries
- Created a computerized model to adjust accounts for fluctuations in currency exchange rates
- Negotiated joint-venture agreements with major suppliers in Mexico and Colombia
- Implemented electronic funds transfer for vendor disbursements, improving cash flow and eliminating payables clerk position

October 1995 to March 1999 — **Staff Accountant,** Monsanto Agricultural Chemicals (Mexico City, Mexico)
- Handled budgeting, billing, and credit-processing functions for the Mexico City branch
- Audited travel/entertainment expenses for Monsanto's 30-member Latin American sales force
- Assisted in launching an online computer system to automate all accounting functions

EDUCATION

1993 to 1995 — Master of Business Administration with emphasis in international business
George Mason University (Fairfax, Virginia)

1990 to 1993 — Bachelor of Business Administration, Accounting, University of Texas, Austin

INTERCULTURAL AND TECHNICAL SKILLS

- Fluent in Spanish and German
- Traveled extensively in Latin America
- Excel • Access • HTML • Visual Basic

Draws reader's attention to important points:

- Provides the sort of specific information on duties and accomplishments that catches an employer's eye

- Highlights duties and work achievements in bulleted lists

- Uses active language to describe duties

Includes informative headings throughout, making it easy for potential employers to find work-related, educational, or skills information

of the word-processing software you used to prepare the document. All word-processing programs allow you to save files as plain text. To convert your résumé to an ASCII plain-text file

- Remove all formatting (boldfacing, underlining, italics, centering, bullets, graphic lines, etc.) and all formatting codes such as tab settings or tables.

- Remove shadows and reverse print (white letters on black background).

- Remove graphics and boxes.

- Use scannable typefaces (such as Helvetica, Futura, Optima, Univers, Times New Roman, Palatino, New Century Schoolbook, and Courier).

- Use a font size of 10 to 14 points.

- Remove multicolumn formats that resemble newspapers or newsletters.

- Save your document under a different name by using your word processor's "save as" option and selecting "text only with line breaks."

EXHIBIT C.6   Electronic Résumé

Because some of his target employers will be scanning his résumé into a database, and because he wants to submit his résumé via e-mail or post it on the Internet, Roberto Cortez created an electronic résumé by changing his formatting and adding a list of key words. However, the information remains essentially the same.

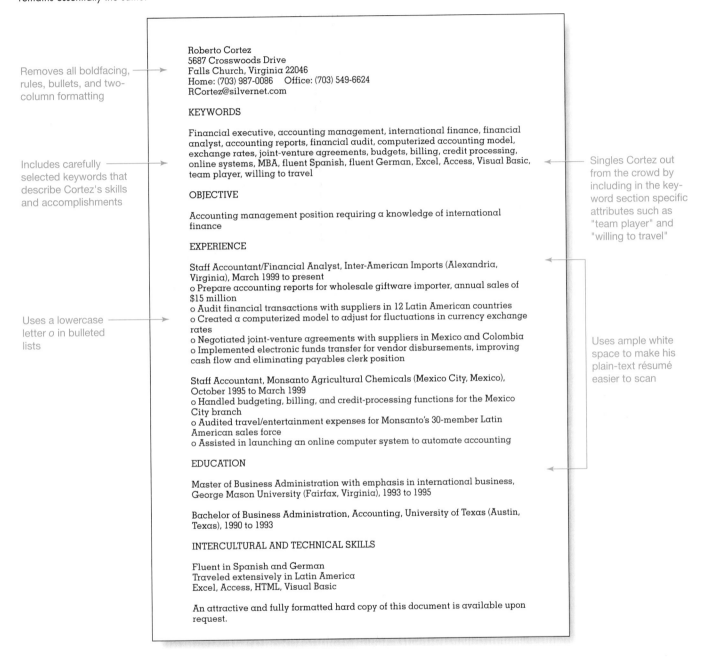

Removes all boldfacing, rules, bullets, and two-column formatting

Includes carefully selected keywords that describe Cortez's skills and accomplishments

Uses a lowercase letter *o* in bulleted lists

Singles Cortez out from the crowd by including in the key-word section specific attributes such as "team player" and "willing to travel"

Uses ample white space to make his plain-text résumé easier to scan

Roberto Cortez
5687 Crosswoods Drive
Falls Church, Virginia 22046
Home: (703) 987-0086   Office: (703) 549-6624
RCortez@silvernet.com

KEYWORDS

Financial executive, accounting management, international finance, financial analyst, accounting reports, financial audit, computerized accounting model, exchange rates, joint-venture agreements, budgets, billing, credit processing, online systems, MBA, fluent Spanish, fluent German, Excel, Access, Visual Basic, team player, willing to travel

OBJECTIVE

Accounting management position requiring a knowledge of international finance

EXPERIENCE

Staff Accountant/Financial Analyst, Inter-American Imports (Alexandria, Virginia), March 1999 to present
o Prepare accounting reports for wholesale giftware importer, annual sales of $15 million
o Audit financial transactions with suppliers in 12 Latin American countries
o Created a computerized model to adjust for fluctuations in currency exchange rates
o Negotiated joint-venture agreements with suppliers in Mexico and Colombia
o Implemented electronic funds transfer for vendor disbursements, improving cash flow and eliminating payables clerk position

Staff Accountant, Monsanto Agricultural Chemicals (Mexico City, Mexico), October 1995 to March 1999
o Handled budgeting, billing, and credit-processing functions for the Mexico City branch
o Audited travel/entertainment expenses for Monsanto's 30-member Latin American sales force
o Assisted in launching an online computer system to automate accounting

EDUCATION

Master of Business Administration with emphasis in international business, George Mason University (Fairfax, Virginia), 1993 to 1995

Bachelor of Business Administration, Accounting, University of Texas (Austin, Texas), 1990 to 1993

INTERCULTURAL AND TECHNICAL SKILLS

Fluent in Spanish and German
Traveled extensively in Latin America
Excel, Access, HTML, Visual Basic

An attractive and fully formatted hard copy of this document is available upon request.

Improve the Look of Your Scannable Résumé

Résumés in ASCII format (without special formatting) look ugly in comparison with traditional résumés. Use the following formatting techniques (which are acceptable for scannable résumés) to enhance the résumé's overall look and effectiveness:

• Align text by adding some blank spaces (rather than tabs).

• Create headings and separate paragraphs by adding a few blank lines.

• Indicate bullets with an asterisk or the lowercase letter *o*.

• Use white space so that scanners and computers can tell when one topic ends and another begins.

• Do not condense the spacing between letters.

• Use all capital letters for section headings as long as the letters do not touch each other.

• Put your name at the top of each page on its own line (with no text appearing above or beside your name).

• Use the standard address format below your name.

- List each phone number on its own line.
- Use white or light-colored 8- by 11-inch paper, printing on one side only.

Keep in mind that scannable résumés are designed to be read by computers, so it's fine to submit multiple pages; just don't get carried away. To increase your chances of a quality scan, do not fold or staple the résumé, and do not send a photocopy. Provide a printed original, if possible.

Provide a List of Key Words When converting your résumé to a scannable format, emphasize certain key words to help potential employers select your résumé from the thousands they scan. Employers generally search for nouns (since verbs tend to be generic rather than specific to a particular position or skill). To maximize the number of matches (or hits), include a key word summary of 20 to 30 words and phrases that define your skills, experience, education, professional affiliations, and so on. Place this list right after your name and address. A key word summary for an accountant, for example, might include these terms: Accountant, Corporate Controller, Fortune 1000, Receivables, Payables, Inventory, Cash Flow, Financial Analysis, Payroll Experience, Corporate Taxes, Activity Based Accounting, Problem Solving, Computer Skills, Excel, Access, Networks, HTML, Peachtree, Quick Books, BA Indiana University–Accounting, CPA, Dean's List, Articulate, Team Player, Flexible, Willing to Travel, Fluent Spanish.

Balance Common Language with Current Jargon
Another way to maximize hits on your résumé is to use words that potential employers will understand (for example, say *keyboard*, not *input device*). Also, use abbreviations sparingly (except for common ones such as BA or MBA). At the same time, learn and use the important buzzwords in your field. Look for current jargon in the want ads of major newspapers such as the *Wall Street Journal* and in other résumés in your field that are posted online. Be careful to check and recheck the spelling, capitalization, and punctuation of any jargon you include, and use only the words you see most often.

Submit Your Scannable Résumé If an employer gives you an option of submitting a scannable résumé by mail, by fax, or by e-mail, choose e-mail. E-mail puts your résumé directly into the employer's database, bypassing the scanning process. If you send your résumé in a paper format by regular mail or by fax, you run the risk that an OCR scanning program will create an error when reading it. In fact, increasing numbers of job applicants are submitting both a traditional and a scannable résumé, explaining in their cover letter that the scannable résumé is for downloading into a database if the company desires.

When submitting your résumé by e-mail, don't attach it as a separate document. Most human resources departments

Under Jeff Taylor's guidance, monster.com now lists more than 20 million résumés on its recruitment website.

won't accept attached files (they're concerned about computer viruses). Instead, paste your résumé into the body of your e-mail message. Whenever you know a reference number or a job ad number, include it in your e-mail subject line.

If you're posting your scannable résumé to a résumé builder at a recruitment or company website, copy and paste the appropriate sections from your electronic file directly into the employer's form. This method avoids rekeying and eliminates errors.

If you fax your scannable résumé, set your machine to "fine" mode (to ensure a high-quality printout on the receiving end). If you're mailing your résumé, you may want to send both a well-designed traditional résumé and a scannable one. Simply attach Post-It notes, labeling one "visual résumé" and the other "scannable résumé."

Building an Online Résumé

If you wish to post your résumé on your webpage, provide employers with your URL; most recruiters won't take the time to use search engines to find your site. As you design your website résumé, think of important key words to use as hyperlinks—words that will grab an employer's attention and make the recruiter want to click on that hyperlink to learn more about you. You can make links to papers you've written, recommendations, and sound or video clips. Don't distract potential employers from your credentials by using hyperlinks to organizations or other websites.

Do not use photos, and avoid providing information that reveals your age, gender, race, marital status, or religion. Because a website is a public access area, you should also leave out the names of references and previous employers. Either mention that references are available on request, or say nothing. Also, instead of naming companies, simply refer to "a large accounting firm" or "a wholesale giftware importer." Finally, include an ASCII version of your résumé on your webpage so that prospective employers can download it into their company's database.

Preparing Your Application Letter

Whenever you submit your résumé, accompany it with a cover, or application, letter to let readers know what you're sending, why you're sending it, and how they can benefit from reading it. Because your application letter is in your own style (rather than the choppy, shorthand style of your résumé), it gives you a chance to show your communication skills and some personality.

Always send your résumé(s) and application letter together, because each has a unique job to perform. The purpose of your résumé is to get employers interested enough to contact you for an interview. The purpose of your application letter is to get employers interested enough to read your résumé.

Before drafting a letter, learn something about the organization you're applying to; then focus on your audience so that you can show you've done your homework. Imagine yourself in the recruiter's situation, and show how your background and talents will solve a particular problem or fill a specific need the company has. The more you can learn about the organization, the better you'll be able to capture the reader's attention and convey your interest in the company. During your research, find out the name, title, and department of the person you're writing to. Reaching and addressing the right person is the most effective way to gain attention. Avoid phrases such as "To Whom It May Concern" and "Dear Sir."

When putting yourself in your reader's shoes, remember that this person's in-box is probably overflowing with résumés and cover letters. So respect your reader's time. Steer clear of gimmicks, which almost never work, and include nothing in your cover letter that already appears in your résumé. Keep your letter straightforward, fact-based, short, upbeat, and professional (see Exhibit C.7).

Following Up on Your Application

If your application letter and résumé fail to bring a response within a month or so, follow up with a second letter to keep your file active. This follow-up letter also gives you a chance to update your original application with any recent job-related information. Even if you've received a letter acknowledging your application and saying that it will be kept on file, don't hesitate to send a follow-up letter three months later to show that you are still interested. Such a letter can demonstrate that you're sincerely interested in working for the organization, that you're persistent in pursuing your goals, and that you're upgrading your skills to make yourself a better employee. And it might just get you an interview.

Interviewing with Potential Employers

Approach job interviews with a sound appreciation of their dual purpose: The organization's main objective is to find the best person available for the job; the applicant's main objective is to find the job best suited to his or her goals and capabilities.

In general, the easiest way to connect with a big company is through your campus placement office; the most efficient way to approach a smaller business is by contacting the company directly. In either case, you move to the next stage and prepare to meet with a recruiter during an **employment interview,** a formal meeting during which an employer and an applicant ask questions and exchange information to see whether the applicant and the organization are a good match.

Most employers conduct two or three interviews before deciding whether to offer a person a job. The first interview, generally held on campus, is the **preliminary screening interview,** which helps employers eliminate unqualified applicants from the hiring process. Candidates who best meet the organization's requirements are invited to visit company offices for further evaluation. Some organizations make a decision at that point, but many schedule a third interview to complete the evaluation process before extending a job offer.

Because the interview takes time, start seeking interviews well in advance of the date you want to start work. It takes an average of 10 interviews to get one job offer. If you hope to have several offers to choose from, you can expect to go through 20 or 30 interviews during your job search. Some students start their job search as early as nine months before graduation. Early planning is even more crucial during downturns in the economy because many employers become more selective when times are tough.

What Employers Look For

Today's employers want candidates who are experienced, intelligent, good communicators, enthusiastic, creative, and

EXHIBIT C.7 Application Letter
In her unsolicited application letter, Glenda Johns manages to give a snapshot of her qualifications and skills without repeating what is said in her résumé.

1254 Main Street
Council Bluffs, IA 51505
June 16, 2003

Ms. Patricia Downings, Store Manager
Wal-Mart
840 South Oak
Iowa Falls, IA 50126

Dear Ms. Downings:

You want retail clerks and managers who are accurate, enthusiastic, and experienced. You want someone who cares about customer service, who understands merchandising, and who can work with others to get the job done. When you're ready to hire a manager trainee or a clerk who is willing to work toward promotion, please consider me for the job.

Working as a clerk and then as an assistant department manager in a large department store has taught me how challenging a career in retailing can be. Moreover, my AA degree in retailing (including work in such courses as retailing, marketing, and business information systems) will provide your store with a well-rounded associate. Most important, I can offer Wal-Mart's Iowa Falls store more than my two years of study and field experience. You'll find that I'm interested in every facet of retailing, eager to take on responsibility, and willing to continue learning throughout my career. Please look over my résumé to see how my skills can benefit your store.

I understand that Wal-Mart prefers to promote its managers from within the company, and I would be pleased to start out with an entry-level position until I gain the necessary experience. Do you have any associate positions opening up soon? Could we discuss my qualifications? I will phone you early next Wednesday to arrange a meeting at your convenience.

Sincerely,

Glenda Johns

Glenda Johns

Enclosure

Annotations:
- Gains attention in the first paragraph
- Interests reader with knowledge of the company's policy toward promotion
- Points out personal qualities that aren't specifically stated in her résumé
- Focuses on the audience, even though the last paragraph uses the word *I*

---

motivated. In addition to these qualities, candidates must also fit in with the organization and meet the basic qualifications for the job.

To determine whether a candidate will be compatible with the other people in the organization, some interviewers may ask you questions about your interests, hobbies, awareness of world events, and so forth. Others may consider your personal style. You're likely to impress an employer by being open, enthusiastic, and interested. Still others may look for courtesy, sincerity, willingness to learn, and a style that is positive and self-confident. All of these qualities help a new employee adapt to a new workplace and new responsibilities.

When you're invited to interview for a position, the interviewer may already have some idea of whether you have the right qualifications, based on a review of your résumé.

But during the interview, you'll be asked to describe your education and previous jobs in more depth so that the interviewer can determine how well your skills match the requirements. When describing your skills, be honest. If you don't know how to do something, say so. In many cases, the interviewer will be seeking someone with the flexibility to apply diverse skills in several areas.

What Applicants Need to Find Out

What things should you find out about the prospective job and employer? By doing a little advance research and asking the right questions during the interview (see Exhibit C.8), you can probably find answers to these questions and more:

QUESTIONS ABOUT THE JOB	QUESTIONS ABOUT THE ORGANIZATION
What are the job's major responsibilities?	What are the organization's major strengths? Weaknesses?
What qualities do you want in the person who fills this position?	Who are your organization's major competitors, and what are their strengths and weaknesses?
Do you want to know more about my related training?	What makes your organization different from others in the industry?
What is the first problem that needs the attention of the person you hire?	What are your organization's major markets?
Would relocation be required now or in the future?	Does the organization have any plans for new products? Acquisitions?
Why is this job now vacant?	How would you define your organization's managerial philosophy?
What can you tell me about the person I would report to?	What additional training does your organization provide?
	Do employees have an opportunity to continue their education with help from the organization?

EXHIBIT C.8
Fifteen Questions to Ask the Interviewer
Learn as much as you can about potential employers by asking these questions.

- Are these my kind of people?
- Can I do this work?
- Will I enjoy the work?
- Is this job what I want?
- Does the job pay what I'm worth?
- What kind of person would I be working for?
- What sort of future can I look forward to with this organization?

How to Prepare for a Job Interview

It's perfectly normal to feel a little anxious before an interview. Don't worry too much, however; preparation will help you perform well. Learning about the organization and the job is important because it enables you to consider the employer's point of view. Here are some pointers to guide that preparation:

- *Think ahead about questions.* Most job interviews are essentially question-and-answer sessions: You answer the interviewer's questions about your background, and you ask questions of your own to determine whether the job and the organization are right for you. By planning for your interviews, you can handle these exchanges intelligently (see Exhibit C.9). Of course, you don't want to memorize responses or sound overrehearsed.

- *Bolster your confidence.* By overcoming your tendencies to feel self-conscious or nervous during an interview, you can build your confidence and make a better impression. If

some aspect of your background or appearance makes you uneasy, correct it or exercise positive traits to offset it, such as warmth, wit, intelligence, or charm. Instead of dwelling on your weaknesses, focus on your strengths so that you can emphasize them to an interviewer.

- *Polish your interview style.* Confidence helps you walk into an interview and give the interviewer an impression of poise, good manners, and good judgment. In the United States, you're more likely to be invited back for a second interview or offered a job if you maintain eye contact, smile frequently, sit in an attentive position, and use frequent hand gestures. These nonverbal signals convince the interviewer that you're alert, assertive, dependable, confident, responsible, and energetic. Work on eliminating speech mannerisms such as "you know," "like," and "um." Speak in your natural tone, and try to vary the pitch, rate, and volume of your voice to express enthusiasm and energy.

- *Plan to look good.* The best policy is to dress conservatively. Wear the best-quality businesslike clothing you can, preferably in a dark, solid color. Avoid flamboyant styles, colors, and prints. Clean, unwrinkled clothes, well-shined shoes, neatly styled and combed hair, clean fingernails, and fresh breath help make a good first impression. Don't spoil the effect by smoking cigarettes before or during the interview. Finally, remember that one of the best ways to look good is to smile at appropriate moments.

- *Be ready when you arrive.* Be sure you know when and where the interview will be held. Take a small notebook, a pen, a list of your questions, a folder with two copies of your résumé, an outline of your research findings about the

EXHIBIT C.9

Twenty-Five Common Interview Questions

Prepare for an interview in advance by thinking about your answers to these questions.

QUESTIONS ABOUT COLLEGE

1. What courses in college did you like most? Least? Why?
2. Do you think your extracurricular activities in college were worth the time spent on them? Why or why not?
3. When did you choose your college major? Did you ever change your major? If so, why?
4. Do you feel you did the best scholastic work you are capable of?
5. Which of your college years was the toughest? Why?

QUESTIONS ABOUT EMPLOYERS AND JOBS

6. What jobs have you held? Why did you leave?
7. What percentage of your college expenses did you earn? How?
8. Why did you choose your particular field of work?
9. What are the disadvantages of your chosen field?
10. Have you served in the military? What rank did you achieve? What jobs did you perform?
11. What do you think about how this industry operates today?
12. Why do you think you would like this particular type of job?

QUESTIONS ABOUT PERSONAL ATTITUDES AND PREFERENCES

13. Do you prefer to work in any specific geographic location? If so, why?
14. How much money do you hope to be earning in 5 years? In 10 years?
15. What do you think determines a person's progress in a good organization?
16. What personal characteristics do you feel are necessary for success in your chosen field?
17. Tell me a story.
18. Do you like to travel?
19. Do you think grades should be considered by employers? Why or why not?

QUESTIONS ABOUT WORK HABITS

20. Do you prefer working with others or by yourself?
21. What type of boss do you prefer?
22. Have you ever had any difficulty getting along with colleagues or supervisors? With instructors? With other students?
23. Would you prefer to work in a large or a small organization? Why?
24. How do you feel about overtime work?
25. What have you done that shows initiative and willingness to work?

organization, and any correspondence about the position. You may also want to take a small calendar, a transcript of your college grades, a list of references, and, if appropriate, samples of your work. After you arrive, relax. You may have to wait, so bring something to read or to occupy your time (the less frivolous or controversial, the better).

How to Follow Up After the Interview

Touching base with the prospective employer after the interview, either by phone or in writing, shows that you really want the job and are determined to get it. It also brings your name to the interviewer's attention again and reminds him or her that you're waiting to know the decision.

The two most common forms of follow-up, the thank-you message and the inquiry, are generally handled by letter or e-mail. But a phone call can be just as effective, particularly if the employer favors a casual, personal style. Express your thanks within two days after the interview, even if you feel you have little chance for the job. In a brief message, acknowledge the interviewer's time and courtesy, convey your continued interest, and ask politely for a decision. If you're not advised of the interviewer's decision by the promised date or within two weeks, you might make an inquiry, particularly if you don't want to accept a job offer from a second firm before you have an answer from the first. Assume that a simple oversight is the reason for the delay, not outright rejection.

Building Your Career

Having the right skills is one way to build toward a career. Employers seek people who are able and willing to adapt to diverse situations, who thrive in an ever-changing workplace, and who continue to learn throughout their careers. In addition, companies want team players with strong work records and leaders who are versatile. Many companies encourage managers to get varied job experience. In some cases, your chances of being hired are better if you've studied abroad or learned another language. Many employers expect college graduates to have a sound understanding of international affairs, and they're looking for employees with intercultural sensitivity and an ability to adapt in other cultures.

Compile an employment portfolio. Get a three-ring notebook and a package of plastic sleeves that open at the top. Collect anything that shows your ability to perform, such as classroom or work evaluations, certificates, awards, and papers you've written. An employment portfolio serves as an excellent resource when writing your résumé and provides employers with tangible evidence of your professionalism.

As you search for a permanent job that fulfills your career goals, take interim job assignments, participate in an internship program, and consider temporary work or freelance jobs. Not only will these temporary assignments help you gain valuable experience and relevant contacts, but they will also provide you with important references and with items for your portfolio. Employers will be more willing to find (or even to create) a position for someone they've learned to respect, and your temporary or freelance work gives them a chance to see what you can do.

If you're unable to find actual job experience, work on polishing and updating your skills. Network with professional colleagues and friends who can help you stay abreast of your occupation and industry. While you're waiting for responses to your résumé or your last interview, take a computer course or gain some other educational or life experience that would be difficult while working full time. Become familiar with the services offered by your campus career center (or placement office). These centers offer individual placement counseling, credential services, job fairs, on-campus interviews, job listings, advice on computerized résumé-writing software, workshops in job-search techniques, résumé preparation, interview techniques, and more.

Once an employer hires you and you're on the job, don't think you've reached the end of the process. The best thing you can do for your long-term career is to continue learning. Listen to and learn from those around you who have experience. Be ready and willing to take on new responsibilities, and actively pursue new or better skills. Employers appreciate applicants and employees with willingness and enthusiasm to learn, to listen, and to gain experience.

CHAPTER GLOSSARY

chronological résumé   Most traditional type of résumé, listing employment history sequentially in reverse order so that the most recent experience is listed first

combination résumé   A hybrid of a chronological and functional résumé that contains elements of both

employment interview   Formal meeting during which an employer and an applicant ask questions and exchange information to see whether the applicant and the organization are a good match

functional résumé   Résumé organized around a list of skills and accomplishments, subordinating employers and academic experience in order to stress individual areas of competence

preliminary screening interview   Meeting between an employer's representative and a candidate for the purpose of eliminating unqualified applicants from the hiring process

résumé   Form of advertising that lists a person's education, employment background, and job qualifications in order to obtain an interview

Your Business Plan

Getting Started with Business PlanPro Software

Business PlanPro (BPP) software is a template for crafting a winning business plan. The software is designed to stimulate your thinking about the many tasks and decisions that go into planning and running a business. The software does not do your thinking for you. Instead, it leads you through a thought process by asking you to respond to questions about your business and to provide data for the preformatted tables and charts. Accompanying instructions, examples, and sample business plans provide you with a full range of assistance you can use to draft your own comprehensive business plan. By working these exercises, you will gain a practical skill for your business career.

When installing BPP, be sure to install Adobe Acrobat Reader, so you can view the sample business plans included with the disk and download them from the web. You can get an overview of the BPP software by clicking on the Help menu from the main screen, then selecting About Business PlanPro. Under the Help menu, you can click on Contents and then Getting Help for operational instructions or to look up business terms in the software's Glossary. For quick answers to questions about using the software, look under the How Do I menu at the top right of the screen. An overview of the software's features is also on the web at www.paloalto.com/prenticehall.

Navigating the Software

One of the best ways to become familiar with the BPP software is by navigating one of the BPP sample business plans. Launch the BPP software, then click on Create a New Business Plan to reach the main screen. Now choose File from the menu and click Open Sample. This brings you to the Sample Plan Browser. An alternate way to get to this screen is by clicking on the Research It menu along the left of the screen, then selecting Sample Plan Browser.

The names of the sample plans are listed on the left, and the first page of plans bundled with the software can be seen on the right. To view a sample plan, double-click on the plan name. To page through a plan, simply click on the arrows on the bottom of the frame in which the plan pages appear. If you have an Internet connection, the software will download the latest version of the sample plan. You can also check the web at www.bplans.com/sp to search through more than 60 sample plans created using BPP software.

To see how a sample plan in the BPP software is organized or to move between sections in your order, click the Show/Hide Navigation icon to the right of the printer icon on the menu above the sample plan page. When you click on a section name, the plan displays that page.

As you will see when exploring the sample plans, the Executive Summary section provides a brief overview of the business plan. The Company Summary discusses company specifics such as the mission and ownership. The Products and Services section describes exactly what the company is selling. The Market Analysis examines the company's market, including competitors and customers. The Strategy and Implementation section indicates the company's broad course of action in the market, its sales goals, and how it will implement the plan. The Management Summary introduces the organizational structure and management personnel. Finally, the Financial Plan section presents profit-and-loss projections and other financial plans.

You may find it helpful to print out a full copy of the sample plan you have selected and review it as you navigate its contents on your screen. This way you can see how the software uses the information to construct a formal business plan. To print out the sample plan, click on the Printer icon and select Plan. You may also choose to print selected sections or the instructions or examples for a business plan. Once you've finished viewing or printing sample plans, click to close the frame and return to the main screen.

You have multiple options for accessing the same information, as shown under the View menu. The Plan Manager option guides you through the process of researching a plan, building it, distributing and delivering it, and making it happen. The Plan Outline option allows you to develop the plan section by section in outline form. To access the text mode option, where you write your business plan's text, select Text Mode from the View menu. You can move between sections by selecting from topics in the Topic drop-down menu above the text screen or using the forward and backward arrows at the right of the Topic menu. To view related tables and charts, click the Table mode or the Chart mode under the View menu.

Creating a Winning Business Plan

The exercises included in this appendix allow you to use the knowledge you've gained from reading a specific part in this textbook. Each exercise has two tasks: Think Like a Pro tasks require you to navigate the software, find and review information in the sample business plans, and evaluate and critique some of the thinking that went behind these plans. By reviewing these sample plans with a critical eye you will begin to sharpen your own business planning skills. Create Your Own Business Plan tasks are an opportunity for you to apply your business planning skills to create your own winning business plan. So begin thinking now about the type of business you'd like to own or manage some day. Then develop and refine your business strategies as you work through the exercises on the pages that follow.

Conducting Business in the Global Economy

PART 1

Think Like a Pro

Objective: By completing these exercises you will become acquainted with the sections of a business plan that address forms of competition, company and product/service descriptions, and the economic outlook for the related industry. You will use the sample business plan for Adventure Excursions Unlimited (listed as Travel Agency-Adventure Sports in the Sample Plan Browser) in this exercise. Use the table of contents to move from section to section as you explore the plan and answer these questions.

1. What products and services does Adventure Excursions provide? Will the company compete on the basis of price, speed, quality, service, or innovation to gain a competitive advantage?

2. What is the economic outlook for the travel industry? What competition does Adventure Excursions face?

3. How does Adventure Excursions plan to use the Internet?

Create Your Own Business Plan

Now start a new plan for your own business. Answering the following questions will help you think about different aspects of your business plan. Enter your answers in the appropriate sections of the new business plan.

What information should you include about your product or service when creating a business plan? Describe in detail the product or service your company will provide. Indicate whether you will compete on price, speed, quality, service, or innovation. What are some of the things you should discuss about your competition in a business plan? In what industry will you compete? What is the economic outlook for that industry? What kinds of competition do you expect to face?

Starting and Organizing a Small Business

PART 2

Think Like a Pro

Objective: By completing these exercises you will become acquainted with the sections of a business plan that address forms of ownership, financing the enterprise, and the franchising alternative. You will use the sample business plan for Pegasus Sports (listed as Inline Skating Products in the Sample Plan Browser) in this exercise.

1. What form of ownership does Pegasus currently use? What are the advantages of selecting that form of ownership? What change in ownership form is Pegasus planning to make?

2. How is Pegasus financing its start-up operations? Has the company gone public (or does the plan indicate it wants to go public)?

3. Would you recommend that Pegasus use franchising to grow its business? Explain your answer.

Create Your Own Business Plan

Think about your own business. What form of ownership will you choose? Why? How much start-up money will you need? How will you finance your start-up costs? Where will you obtain the money you will need to grow your business? Enter your answers in the appropriate sections of your business plan.

Managing a Business

PART 3

Think Like a Pro

Objective: By completing these exercises you will become acquainted with the sections of a business plan that address a company's mission, goals and objectives, and management team. You will use the sample business plan for JavaNet (listed as Internet Cafe in the Sample Plan Browser) in this exercise.

1. Evaluate JavaNet's mission statement. Does it summarize why the organization exists, what it seeks to accomplish, and the principles that the company will adhere to as it tries to reach its goals? How might you improve this mission statement?

2. Evaluate JavaNet's objectives. Are they clearly stated? Are they measurable? Do they seem realistic? Which objectives might need some refining?

3. Assess the risks facing JavaNet. How do you expect these threats to affect the company's ability to compete?

4. Read about the company's management structure and personnel plan. What challenges might JavaNet face as a result of its chosen structure and personnel plan?

Create Your Own Business Plan

Return to the plan you are creating for your own business. List your company's goals and objectives, and be sure they are clearly stated and measurable. How will you reach these goals and objectives? What might prevent you from achieving them? What information should you include about your management team? Should you mention the team's weaknesses in addition to its strengths? Why?

PART 4

Think Like a Pro

Objective: By completing these exercises you will become acquainted with the sections of a business plan that address staffing the enterprise and managing employees. You will use the sample business plan for Sagebrush Sam's (listed as Restaurant-Steak Buffet in the Sample Plan Browser) in this exercise.

1. What do the mission statement and keys to success sections say about Sagebrush Sam's approach to employee relations? Why are good relations with employees so important to the success of this type of business?
2. What workforce challenges is Sagebrush Sam's likely to encounter as it grows?
3. What are the company's estimates for manager and employee compensation, and how do these estimates change over the years covered by the plan?
4. According to the business plan, Sagebrush Sam's will need a director of store operations when it has more than five units.

How might the company recruit a manager with the appropriate experience and background for this position?

Create Your Own Business Plan

The success of your business depends on hiring, training, and motivating the right employees. Answer these questions as you continue developing your own business plan. How many employees will your business require? Of these, how many will be managers? How will you motivate your staff? Will you pay them a salary or a commission? Will you offer alternative work arrangements? If so, which ones? Will you use part-time and temporary employees? Will you provide your employees with benefits? Which ones?

PART 5

Think Like a Pro

Objective: By completing these exercises you will become acquainted with the sections of a business plan that address a firm's product, pricing, promotion, and distribution strategies. You will use the sample business plan for Boulder Stop (listed as Sports Equipment-Cafe in the Sample Plan Browser) in this exercise.

1. Define the target market for Boulder Stop. How will the company differentiate its products and services from those of its competitors?
2. Describe the company's pricing, promotion, sales, and distribution strategies. Which distribution channels will the company use to deliver its products?
3. Rank the company's three market segmentation categories according to their importance.

4. According to the Keys to Success section, what must Boulder Stop do to be successful?

Create Your Own Business Plan

Consider your own target market and customers as you continue working on the business plan you are creating. How will you segment your target market? Which customers are likely to buy your product or service? Describe your product, pricing, promotion, and distribution strategies. Now make some preliminary sales forecasts. Under which section headings will you present this information?

Managing Financial Information and Resources

PART 6

Think Like a Pro

Objective: By completing these exercises you will become acquainted with the sections of a business plan that address a company's financial and operational projections. You will use the sample business plan for Fantastic Florals (listed as Import-Artificial Flowers in the Sample Plan Browser) in this exercise.

1. Identify the source(s) Fantastic Florals will use to fund its start-up costs. Why is it important to indicate how much start-up money will be used to fund assets versus expenses?

2. Review the financial assumptions, sales tables and graphs, and other financial information included in the Fantastic Florals plan. Assuming the financial projections are on target, would an investment of $75,000 for a 20 percent ownership stake in the company be prudent? Explain your answer. Which financial statement(s) did you use to make your decision?

3. Examine the company's projected gross margin for the years covered by the plan. How does Fantastic Florals' gross margin compare with the industry profile? How might a potential investor view this comparison?

Create Your Own Business Plan

Return to the plan you are developing for your own business. How will you categorize your revenue and expense items? Will you break down your sales by product type, by service, or by location? What general operating and product-related expenses will you incur? Set up your basic revenue and expense categories, and build the framework for your profit and loss statement. How do the categories in your plan compare with those used by Fantastic Florals?

Notes

Chapter 1

1. Adapted from Jerry Useem, "One Nation Under Wal-Mart," *Fortune*, 3 March 2003, 65–78; Stephanie Armour, "While Hiring at Most Firms Chills, Wal-Mart's Heats Up," *USA Today*, 26 August 2002, 3B; John Dicker, "Union Blues at Wal-Mart," *The Nation*, 8 July 2002, 14–19; Lorrie Grant, " Wal-Mart Bagging Success as Grocer," *USA Today*, 6 June 2002, B3; Cait Murphy, "Fortune 5 Hundred: Intro," *Fortune*, 15 April 2002, 94–98; Mark Gimein, "Sam Walton Made Us a Promise," *Fortune*, 18 March 2002, 120–130; Virginia Postrel, "Lessons in Keeping Business Humming, Courtesy of Wal-Mart U." *New York Times*, 28 February 2002, C2; Wal-Mart website [accessed 13 August 2002] www.walmart.com.

2. Michael J. Mandel, "The Painful Truth About Profits," *Business Week*, 4 November 2002, 107–109.

3. Wal-Mart corporate website, U.S. Operations [accessed 6 September 2002] www.walmartstores.com.

4. American Red Cross website [accessed 10 March 2002] www.redcross.org.

5. Ken Stammen, "Where Big Planes Are Born," *Cincinnati Post*, 12 September 2000, 7C.

6. IBM 2000 Annual Report, *IBM website* [accessed 9 September 2002] www.ibm.com.

7. Everette James, "Services—U.S. Firms Are Leaders in the Global Economy," *Business America*, April 1998, 5–7.

8. Peronet Despeignes, "Services Sector Figures Paint Picture of Economy at a Standstill," *Financial Times*, 6 September 2002, 8.

9. Robert L. Heilbroner and Lester C. Thurow, *Economics Explained* (New York: Simon & Schuster, 1994), 29–30.

10. Heilbroner and Thurow, *Economics Explained*, 250.

11. Heilbroner and Thurow, *Economics Explained*, 250.

12. Carol Matlack, "Vive L'Air France," *Business Week*, 9 September 2002, 114; Greg Steinmetz, "Her Majesty May Sell Part of London's Tube, Angering Some in U.K.," *Wall Street Journal*, 14 October 1999, A1, A12; Erik Eckholm, "Chinese Restate Goals to Reorganize State Companies," *New York Times*, 23 September 1999, A10; Dexter Roberts, "China's New Revolution," *Business Week*, 27 September 1999, 72–78.

13. Daniel Michaels, "In the Secret World of Airplane Deals, One Battle up Close," *Wall Street Journal*, 10 March 2003, A1, A9.

14. Jeff Wise, "How Skiboarding Became the New Snowboarding," *New York Times Magazine*, 21 March 1999, 58–61.

15. Adam Cohen, "No Split but Microsoft's a Monopolist," *Time*, 9 July 2001, 36–38; Ted Bridis and John R. Wilke, "Judge Orders Microsoft Broken in Two, Imposes Tough Restriction on Practices," *Wall Street Journal*, 8 June 2000, A3, A12; "Judge Suspends Restrictions on Microsoft," *Wall Street Journal*, 21 June 2000, A3; John R. Wilke and Rebecca Buckman, "Justices Decline Early Look at Microsoft," *Wall Street Journal*, 27 September 2000, A3, A17.

16. Steve Lohr, "For Microsoft Ruling Will Sting but Not Really Hurt," *New York Times*, 2 November 2002, B1, B5.

17. Kenneth N. Gilpin, "Antitrust Challenge Stops United Merger with U.S. Airways," *New York Times*, 26 July 2001, B1, B2.

18. Patrick M. Reilly, "Barnes & Noble Closes Book on Attempt to Buy Ingram Amid FTC Objections," *Wall Street Journal*, 3 June 1999, B16.

19. Richard J. Newman, "The Revenge of the Baby Bells," *U.S. News & World Report*, 13 August 2001, 34–36.

20. Louis Uchitelle, "Wild Card of the Recovery: Inflation," *New York Times*, 17 March 2002, 3–4.

21. Jeffrey E. Garten, "The Fed Should Look Farther Than Its Own Backyard," *Business Week*, 31 August 1998, 18.

22. Jeannine Aversa, "Fed Ends String of Rate Cuts," *Journal-Gazette*, 31 January 2001, 7B.

23. "National Debt Keeps Building," *USA Today Snapshot*, 25 November 2002, B1.

24. Martin Kasindorf and Ken Fireman, "The Clinton Budget/2002 Solution," *Newsday*, 7 February 1997, A4; Gilbert C. Alston, "Balancing the Federal Budget," *Los Angeles Times*, 14 February 1997, B8.

25. Make Allen, "Bush Pledges Effort to Balance Budget by 2004," *Washington Post*, 17 April 2002, A6; Richard W. Stevenson, "2 Parties Predict a Sharp Increase in Spending by U.S.," *New York Times*, 12 May 2002, sec. 1, 1.

26. Kathleen Madigan, "Keep Your Nest Egg Safe—Watch Housing Data," *Business Week*, 17 April 2000, 208–210.

27. Greg Ip, "Labor Department to Publish New Consumer Price Index," *Wall Street Journal*, 21 February 2002, A2.

28. Michael Moynihan, *The Coming American Renaissance* (New York: Simon & Schuster, 1987), 25.

29. William A. Sahlman, "The New Economy Is Stronger Than You Think," *Harvard Business Review*, November–December 1999, 99–106.

30. Sahlman, "The New Economy Is Stronger Than You Think," 99–106.

31. Michael van Biema and Bruce Greenwald, "Managing Our Way to Higher Service-Sector Productivity," *Harvard Business Review*, July–August 1997, 87–95.

32. Moynihan, *The Coming American Renaissance*, 42–43; "Through Seven Decades, Tracking Business and the World," *Business Week*, 4 October 1999, 118A–118P.

33. Rona Gindin, "Dealing with a Multicultural Workforce," *Nation's Restaurant News*, September–October 1998, 31, 83; Howard Gleckman, "A Rich Stew in the Melting Pot," *Business Week*, 31 August 1998, 76+.

34. Adapted from Bernard Weinraub, "New Harry Potter Book Becoming a Publishing Phenomenon," *New York Times*, 3 July 2000 [accessed 12 July 2000] www.nytimes.com/library/books/070300potter-parties.html; Laura Miller, "Pottermania at Midnight," *Salon.com*, 8 July 2000 [accessed 12 July 2000] www.salon.com/books/features/2000/07/08/potter/; David D. Kirkpatrick, "Harry Potter Magic Halts Bedtime for Youngsters," *New York Times*, 9 July 2000 [accessed 12 July 2000] www.nytimes.com/library/books/070900potter-goblet. html; David D. Kirkpatrick, "Vanishing off the Shelves," *New York Times*, 10 July 2000 [accessed 10 July 2000] www.nytimes.com/library/books/071000rowling-goblet.html.

Chapter 2

1. Marilyn Berlin Snell, "Where to Work," *Sierra*, May–June 2002, 21; Monte Burke, "The World According to Yvon," *Forbes*, 26 November 2001, 236; Dianna Edwards, "A Mountain of Trust," *Step-By-Step Graphics*, September–October 2001, 30–39; Jennifer Laabs, "Mixing Business With Passion," *Workforce*, March 2000, 80–87; Roger Rosenblatt, "The Root of All Good: Reaching the Top by Doing the Right Thing," *Time*, 18 October 1999, 88–91; Michael Lear-Olimpi, "Management Mountaineer," *Warehousing Management*, January–February 1999, 23–30; Larry Armstrong, "Patagonia Sticks to Its Knitting," *Business Week*, 7 December 1998, 68; Nancy Rivera Brooks, "Companies Give Green Power the Green Light," *Los Angeles Times*, 27 September 1998, D8; Charlene Marmer Solomon, "A Day in the Life of Terri Wolfe: Maintaining Corporate Culture," *Workforce*, June 1998, 94–95; Jacqueline Ottman, "Proven Environmental Commitment Helps Create Committed Customers," *Marketing News*, 2 February 1998, 5–6; Dawn Hobbs, "Patagonia Ranked 24th by Magazine," *Los Angeles Times*, 23 December 1997, B1; Jim Collins, "The Foundation for Doing Good," *Inc.*, December 1997, 41–42; "It's Not Easy Being Green," *Business Week*, 24 November 1997, 180; Paul C. Judge and Melissa Downing, "A Lean, Green Fulfillment Machine," *Catalog Age*, June 1997, 63; "Patagonia, A Green Endeavor," *Apparel Industry Magazine*, February 1997, 46–48; Polly LaBarre, "Patagonia Comes of Age," *Industry Week*, 3 April 1995, 42; John Steinbreder, "Yvon Chouinard, Founder and Owner of the Patagonia Outdoor," *Sports Illustrated*, 2 November 1991, 200.

2. Alicia Zappier, "P & G, Unilever Talk Settlement in Hair Care Spy Case," *Drug Store News*, 24 September 2001, 45.

3. Michael McCarthy, "Recent Crop of Sneaky Ads Backfires," *USA Today*, 17 July 2001, 3B; "Publishers Clearing House Strikes Deceptive-Practices Accord," *New York Times*, 23 August 2000, A16.

4. Aaron Bernstein, Brian Grow, Darnell Little, Stanley Holmes, and Diane Brady, "Bracing for a Backlash," *Business Week*, 4 February 2002, 32–36.

5. David Lieberman and Gregg Farrell, "Adelphia Founder, 2 Sons, 2 Others Arrested in Fraud," *USA Today*, 25 July 2002, B1; David Lieberman, "Feds Set to Indict Adelphia Family," *USA Today*, 15 July 2002, 1A; Devin Leonard, "The Adelphia Story," *Fortune*, 12 August 2002, 137–146.

6. Constance L. Hays, "Ex-ImClone Chief Admits Dome U.S. Charges," *New York Times*, 16 October 2002, 1; Thor Valdmanis and Jayne O'Donnell, "Martha Stewart's Stock Soars 14%," *USA Today*, 20 June 2002, 3B; Constance L. Hays, "House Panel Defers to Justice Dept. on Stewart," *New York Times*, 11 September 2002, C1, C11; Tracie Rozhon, "Stewart Quits as a Director of Big Board," *New York Times*, 4 October 2002, C1.

7. Deborah Solomon, "Leading the News: Ex Finance Chief May Strike Deal over WorldCom," *Wall Street Journal*, 12 November 2002, A3; Kevin Maney, "Latest Charges Leave WorldCom in Limbo," *USA Today*, 2 August 2002, 1B; Andrew Backover, Thor Valdmanis, and Matt Krantz, "WorldCom Finds Accounting Fraud," *USA Today*, 26 June 2002, 2A; Kevin Maney and Andrew Backover, "WorldCom's Bomb," *USA Today*, 22 July 2002, 2A.

8. Mark Maremont and Jerry Markon, "Former Tyco Executives Are Charged," *Wall Street Journal*, 13 September 2002, A3, A6; Mark Maremont and Laurie Cohen, "Tyco Probe Expands to Include Auditor PricewaterhouseCoopers," *Wall Street Journal*, 30 September 2002, A1, A8; William Symonds, "Tyco: The Vise Grows Ever-Tighter," *Business Week*, 7 October 2002, 48–49; Andrew Ross Sorkin, "Tyco Details Lavish Lives of Executives," *New York Times*, 18 September 2002, C1, C16.

9. Amy Zipkin, "Getting Religion on Corporate Ethics," *New York Times*, 18 October 2000, C1, C10.

10. John S. McClenahen, "Your Employees Know Better," *Industry Week*, 1 March 1999, 12–14.

11. Betsy Stevens, "Communicating Ethical Values: A Study of Employee Perceptions," *Journal of Business Ethics*, June 1999, 113–120.

12. Milton Bordwin, "The Three R's of Ethics," *Management Review*, June 1998, 59–61.

13. Mark Seivar, personal communication, 2 April 1998; "1-800-Jus-tice or 1-800-Rat-fink," *Reputation Management*, March–April 1995, 31–34; Margaret Kaeter, "The 5th Annual Business Ethics Awards for Excellence in Ethics," *Business Ethics*, December 1993, 26–29.

14. Elisabeth Bumiller, "Bush Signs Bill Aimed at Fraud in Corporations," *New York Times*, 31 July 2002, A1, C5; Jonathan Weisman, "Some See Cracks in Reform Law," *Washington Post*, 7 August 2002, E1.

15. See letters in *New York Times*, 25 August 1918, and *New York Herald*, 1 October 1918.

16. "Business of Social Responsibility," *Businessline*, 3 August 1999, 1.

17. Edward O. Welles, "Ben's Big Flop," *Inc.*, September 1998, 40+; Constance L. Hays, "Getting Serious at Ben & Jerry's," *New York Times*, 22 May 1998, C1, C3.

18. Welles, "Ben's Big Flop," 40+; Hays, "Getting Serious at Ben & Jerry's," C1, C3.

19. Constance L. Hays, "Ben & Jerry's to Unilever, with Attitude," *New York Times*, 13 April 2000, C1, C20; Fred Bayles, "Reviews in on Ben & Jerry's Sweet Deal," *USA Today*, 20 April 2000, 3A.

20. Thomas A. Fogarty, "Corporations Use Causes for Effect," *USA Today*, 10 November 1997, 7B; Peaceworks website [accessed 22 June 1999] www.peaceworks.net; Florence Fabricant, "A Young Entrepreneur Makes Food, Not War," *New York Times*, 30 November 1996, sec. International Business, 21.

21. Jim Hopkins, "Ben & Jerry's Co-Founder to Try 'Venture Philanthropy,'" *USA Today*, 7 August 2001, B1.

22. William H. Miller, "Cracks in the Green Wall," *Industry Week*, 19 January, 1998, 58–65.

23. Keith Naughton, "Growing a Green Plant," *Newsweek*, 13 November 2000, 58–59.

24. Joseph Weber, "3M's Big Cleanup," *Business Week*, 5 June 2000, 96–98.

25. "The IW Survey: Encouraging Findings," *Industry Week*, 19 January 1998, 62.

26. John Markoff, "Technology's Toxic Trash is Sent to Poor Nations," *New York Times*, 25 February 2002, C1, C4.
27. Anita Hamilton, "Mean Clean Machines," *Time*, 26 August 2002, A46–A47.
28. Julie Appleby, "No One Has to Tell You If Your Pacemaker's Recalled," *USA Today*, 22 October 2002, 1B.
29. Daniel Eisenberg and Adam Zagorin, "Firestone's Rough Road," *Time*, 18 September 2000, 38–40; Joann Muller and Nicole St. Pierre, "How Will Firestone and Ford Steer Through This Blowout?," *Business Week*, 28 August 2000, 54+.
30. Chris Burritt, "Fallout from the Tobacco Settlement," *Atlanta Journal and Constitution*, 22 June 1997, A14; Jolie Solomon, "Smoke Signals," *Newsweek*, 28 April 1997, 50–51; Marilyn Elias, "Mortality Rate Rose Through '80s," *USA Today*, 17 April 1997, B3; Mike France, Monica Larner, and Dave Lindorff, "The World War on Tobacco," *Business Week*, 11 November 1996; Richard Lacayo, "Put Out the Butt, Junior," *Time*, 2 September 1996, 51; Elizabeth Gleick, "Smoking Guns," *Time*, 1 April 1996, 50.
31. "Injuries, Illnesses, and Fatalities," Bureau of Labor Statistics [accessed 26 February 2002] www.bls.gov/iif.
32. Yochi J. Dreazen, "New OSHA Proposal Enrages Businesses," *Wall Street Journal*, 8 November 2000, A2, A6; Robert Manor, "OSHA's Ergonomic Rules Rile Business," *Chicago Tribune*, 14 November 2000, sec. 1, 1.
33. Wendy Bounds and Hilary Stout, "Sweatshop Pact: Good Fit or Threadbare?" *Wall Street Journal*, 10 April 1997, A2; Ellen Neuborne, "Nike to Take a Hit In Labor Report," *USA Today*, 27 March 1997, B1; William J. Holstein, et al., "Santa's Sweatshop," *U.S. News & World Report*, 16 December 1996, 50–60.
34. Adapted from Associated Press, "Children's Painkiller Recalled," CNN.com/Health, 16 August 2001 [accessed on 22 August 2001] www.cnn.com/2001/HEALTH/parenting/08/16/kids.drug.recalled.ap/index.html; Perrigo Company website, www.perrigo.com [accessed on 29 August 2001].
35. Geanne Rosenberg, "Truth and Consequences," *Working Woman*, June/August 1998, 79–80.

Chapter 3

1. Adapted from Bonnie Miller Rubin, "Quite a Ride for Trek," *Chicago Tribune*, 23 July 2002, sec. 3, 1, 4; Trek's website [accessed 26 May 2000] www.trekbikes.com; Michele Wucker, "Keep on Trekking," *Working Woman*, December/January 1998, 32–36; Christopher Elliott, "Zero Defects through Design," *Chief Executive*, 1998, 36–38; Randy Weston, "Trek Design System Cranks Out Changes," *Computerworld*, 15 December 1997, 37.
2. John Alden, "What in the World Drives UPS?" *International Business*," March/April 1998, 6–7; UPS website [accessed 4 March 2002] www.ups.com.
3. "Getting It Right in Japan," *International Business*, May–June 1997, 19.
4. Gary M. Wederspahn, "Exporting Corporate Ethics," *Global Workforce*, January 1997, 29–30; Dana Milbank and Marcus W. Brauchli, "Greasing Wheels," *Wall Street Journal*, 29 September 1995, A1, A7.
5. James Wilfong and Toni Seger, *Taking Your Business Global* (Franklin Lakes, N.J.: Career Press, 1997), 289.
6. Jules Abend, "Jockey Colors Its World," *Bobbin*, February 1999, 50–54.
7. Ricky W. Griffin and Michael W. Pustay, *International Business*, 3 ed. (Upper Saddle River, N.J.: Prentice Hall, 2003), 317.
8. "Padgett Surveys Franchise/Small Business Sectors," *Franchising World*, March–April 1995, 46; John Stansworth, "Penetrating the Myths Surrounding Franchise Failure Rates—Some Old Lessons for New Business," *International Small Business Journal*,

January–March 1995, 59–63; Laura Koss-Feder, "Building Better Franchise Relations," *Hotel & Motel Management*, 6 March 1995, 18; Carol Steinberg, "Franchise Fever," *World Trade*, July 1992, 86, 88, 90–91; John O'Dell, "Franchising America," *Los Angeles Times*, 25 June 1989, sec. IV, 1.
9. One World website [accessed 16 May 2000] www.oneworld alliance.com.
10. Stanley Holmes, Drake Bennett, Kate Carlisle, and Chester Dawson, "Planet Starbucks," *Business Week*, 9 September 2002, 100–110.
11. Lewis M. Simons, "High-Tech Jobs for Sale," *Time*, 22 July 1996, 59.
12. Alden, "What in the World Drives UPS?" 6–7.
13. Ernest Beck and Emily Nelson, "As Wal-Mart Invades Europe, Rivals Rush to Match Its Formula," *Wall Street Journal*, 6 October 1999, A1, A6.
14. Thomas W. Anderson, "Foreign Direct Investment in the United States," *Study of Current Business*, June 2002, 28–35.
15. *Big Emerging Markets: 1996 Outlook* (Washington D.C.: GPO, 1996); Nicholas D. Kristof and Sheryl WuDunn, "The World's Ills May Be Obvious, but Their Cure Is Not," *New York Times*, 18 February 1999 [accessed 19 February 1999] www.nytimes.com/library/world/global/021699global-econ. html.
16. Holley H. Ulbrich and Mellie L. Warner, *Managerial Economics* (New York: Barron's Educational Series, 1990), 190.
17. Patrick Lane, "World Trade Survey: Why Trade Is Good for You," *The Economist*, 3 October 1998, S4–S6.
18. Bureau of Economic Analysis website [accessed 17 September 2002] www.bea.doc.gov.
19. Robert J. Samuelson, "Trading with the Enemy," *Newsweek*, 1 April 1996, 41; Amy Borrus, Pete Engardio, and Dexter Roberts, "The New Trade Superpower," *Business Week*, 16 October 1995, 56–57; David A. Andelman, "Marco Polo Revisited," *American Management Association*, August 1995, 10–12; John Greenwald, "Get Asia Now, Pay Later," *Time*, 10 October 1994, 61; Simons, "High-Tech Jobs for Sale," 59.
20. Warren Vieth, "Free Trade? Only up to a Point," *Seattle Times*, 2 May 2002, A13.
21. James Cox, "Tariffs Shield Some U.S. Products," *USA Today*, 6 May 1999, 1B.
22. Eric Schmitt, "U.S. Backs off Sanctions, Seeing Poor Effect Abroad," *New York Times*, 31 July 1998, A1, A6; Robert T. Gray, "Book Review," *Nation's Business*, January 1999, 47.
23. Ken Stammen, "Chiquita Brand Files for Chapter 11," *Cincinnati Post*, 28 November 2001, 1A.
24. J. Lynn Lunsford and Daniel Michaels, "Jet Makers Differ on Strategy to Deal with Aviation Slump," *Wall Street Journal*, 29 July 2002, A2.
25. "Japanese Steelmakers Face U.S. Penalties in Antidumping Case," *Wall Street Journal*, 3 August 2000, C19.
26. Cox, "Tariffs Shield Some U.S. Products," 1B, 2B.
27. "APEC Ministers Commit to Sustainable Development," *Xinhau News Agency*, 11 June 1997; Fred C. Bergsten, "An Asian Push for World-Wide Free Trade: The Case For APEC," *The Economist*, 6 January 1996, 62; "U.S. Must Press to Reduce Trade Barriers in Asia, Pacific, Congress Told," *Gannett News Service*, 1995.
28. Michael M. Phillips, "One by One," *Wall Street Journal*, 26 April 1999, R4, R7.
29. Mary E. Thyfault, "Global Opportunities," *Information Week*, 26 March 2001, 65–66.
30. "Grand Illusions," *The Economist*, 4 March 1995, 87; Bob Davis, "Global Paradox: Growth of Trade Binds Nations, but It Also Can Spur Separatism," *Wall Street Journal*, 20 June 1994, A1, A6; Barbara Rudolph, "Megamarket," *Time*, 10 August 1992,

43–44; Peter Truell, "Free Trade May Suffer from Regional Blocs," *Wall Street Journal*, 1 July 1991, A1.

31. David I. Oyama, "World Watch," *Wall Street Journal*, 5 September 2001, A18.

32. Rafael A. Lecuona, "Economic Integration: NAFTA and MERCOSUR, A Comparative Analysis," *International Journal on World Peace*, December 1999, 27–49.

33. Thomas Catan, "Mercosur Seeks to Build Ties with Mexico," *Financial Times*, 6 July 2002, 2.

34. Anthony DePalma, "With the U.S. Economy Slumping, Canada and Mexico Are Reeling," *New York Times*, 17 December 2001, C13.

35. Charles J. Walen, "NAFTA's Scorecard: So Far, So Good," *Business Week*, 9 July 2001, 54–56.

36. Geri Smith, "Betting on Free Trade," *Business Week*, 23 April 2001, 60–62.

37. "Central and Eastern Europeans Already Sampling Life in EU," *Financial Times*, 24 July 2002, 9.

38. Brandon Mitchener, "Increasingly Rules of Global Economy Are Set in Brussels," *Wall Street Journal*, 23 April 2002, A1, A10.

39. Mitchener, "Increasingly Rules of Global Economy Are Set in Brussels," A1, A10.

40. Thomas Kamm, "EU Certifies Participants for Euro," *Wall Street Journal*, 26 March 1998, A14; Mitchener, "Increasingly Rules of Global Economy Are Set in Brussels," A1, A10.

41. Michael J. Mandel, "Rethinking the Economy," *Business Week*, 1 October 2001, 28–33.

42. James Cox, "U.S. Slowdown Would Ripple Around Globe," *USA Today*, 22 January 2001, 1B–2B.

43. Cox, "U.S. Slowdown Would Ripple Around Globe," 1B–2B.

44. Jeffrey E. Garten, "The Wrong Time for Companies to Beat a Global Retreat," *Business Week*, 17 December 2001, 22.

45. "Is It at Risk?—Globalization," *The Economist*, 2 February 2002, 65–68.

46. Brian O'Keefe, "Global Brands," *Fortune*, 26 November 2001, 102–110.

47. Ben Van Houten, "Where Are They Now?" *Restaurant Business*, 15 November 2001, 22–30.

48. Peter Engardio and Rich Miller, "What's at Stake?" *Business Week*, 22 October 2001, 34–37; Chris Woodyard, "Stepped-up Security Siphons Companies' Cash," *USA Today*, 22 October 2001, 1B, 2B.

49. Mandel, "Rethinking the Economy," 28–33.

50. Adapted from Courtland L. Bovée and John V. Thill, "Should Companies Stress English Only on the Job?" *Business Communication Today*, 6th ed. (Upper Saddle River, N.J.: Prentice Hall, 2000), 74.

51. Adam Zagorin, "The Great Banana War," *Time*, 8 February 1999 [accessed 11 May 1999] www.pathfinder.com.

52. "USAJobs: International Trade Specialist," USA Jobs website [accessed 17 June 1999] www.usajobs.opm.gov/wfjic/jobs/BL2896.htm.

Chapter 4

1. Michael Liedtke, "UPS Moves Beyond Delivering Packages," *USA Today*, 7 November 2002, 19A; Erick Schonfeld, "The Total Package," www.ecompany.com, June 2001, 91–97; Samuel Greengard, "UPS Delivers on Wireless Connectivity," *IQ Magazine*, May–June 2001, 63; *UPS Fact Sheet, UPS Technology Fact Sheet, Quick Facts—UPS Worldport^sm* (all published by UPS); Kelly Barron, "UPS Company of the Year," *Forbes*, 10 January 2000, 79–83.

2. Bill Gates, *Business @ the Speed of Thought* (New York: Warner Books, 1999), 3.

3. Larry Long and Nancy Long, *Computers*, 6th ed. (Upper Saddle River, NJ: Prentice Hall, 1999), MIS 5.

4. Jim Coates, "Going Mobile," *Los Angeles Times*, 18 April 2002, S1.

5. Jay Krall, "The Cordless Consumer: Coming Soon to Stores," *Wall Street Journal*, 15 July 2002, R7; Salina Khan, "Gadgets Help You Get Out of Line," *USA Today*, 20 December 1999, 3B.

6. Jesse Drucker, "New Ways to Surf the Web Is Giving Cell Carriers Static," *Wall Street Journal*, 29 November 2002, A1, A6.

7. Rebecca Buckman, "Lofty Goals," *Wall Street Journal*, 9 December 2002, R8.

8. Stanley Homes, "Planet Starbucks," *Business Week*, 9 September 2002, 100–110.

9. Bill Breen, "Lilly's R&D Prescription," *Fast Company*, April 2002, 44–48.

10. Karen Kaplan, "M is for Mobile," *Chicago Tribune*, 18 April 2002, sec. 7, 1, 4; Brian Nadel, "Waiting for the Wireless Revolution," *PC Magazine*, 21 May 2002, 84–86; Walter S. Mossberg, "A Guide to Lingo You'll Want to Learn for Wireless Technology," *Wall Street Journal*, 28 March 2002, B1.

11. Gary Armstrong and Philip Kotler, *Marketing: An Introduction*, 6th ed. (Upper Saddle River, N.J.: Prentice Hall, 2003) 89.

12. Melanie Wells, "D-Day for eBay," *Forbes*, 22 July 2002, 68.

13. Andy Reinhardt, "The Paperless Manual," *Business Week e.Biz*, 18 September 2000, EB92.

14. Fred Sandsmark, "Culture Shift," *IQ Magazine*, March–April 2001, 52–59.

15. Stephanie Armour, "Workers Just Click to Enroll for Benefits," *USA Today*, 8 November 2000, B1; Charlene Marmer Solomon, "Sharing Information Across Borders and Time Zones," *Global Workforce*, March 1998, 13–18; Eryn Brown, "9 Ways to Win on the Web," *Fortune*, 24 May 1999, 112.

16. Material for this section was taken from Courtland L. Bovée, John V. Thill, and Barbara E. Schatzman, *Business Communication Today*, 7th ed. (Upper Saddle River, N.J.: Prentice Hall, 2003), 365–366.

17. Eric Young, "Web Marketplaces That Really Work," *Fortune*, Winter 2002, 78–86.

18. Jason Zien, "Measuring the Internet," *About.com*, 13 July 1999 [accessed 17 July 1999] http://internet.about.com/library/weekly/1999/ aa071399a.htm; "FAST Aims for Largest Index," *Search Engine Watch*, 4 May 1999, [accessed 17 July 1999] http://searchenginewatch.internet.com/sereport/99/05-fast.htm.

19. John R. Boatright, *Ethics and the Conduct of Business*, 4th ed. (Upper Saddle River, New Jersey: Prentice Hall, 2003), 158.

20. Jeff Howe, "Big Boss Is Watching," *Yahoo! Internet Life*, October 2000, 105–107.

21. Elisa Deardorff, "With Voice Mail, You Never Know Who's Listening," *Chicago Tribune*, 1 June 1998, B1, B8; "40 Fired for Sex-Site Abuse," *CNN America*, 6 October 1999, http://cnnfn.com/1999/10/06/companies/xerox.

22. Nick Wingfield, "The Rise and Fall of Web Shopping at Work," *Wall Street Journal*, 27 September 2002, B1.

23. Scott Thurm, "New and Improved," *Wall Street Journal*, 11 February 2002, R13.

24. Jim Hopkins and Michelle Kessler, "Companies Squander Billions on Tech," *USA Today*, 20 May 2002, 1A.

25. Bob Tedeschi, "E-Commerce Report," *New York Times*, 27 January 2003, C4.

26. Tedeschi, "E-Commerce Report."

27. Del Jones, "Businesses Battle over Intellectual Property," *USA Today*, 2 August 2000, 1B, 2B; Greengard, "How Secure Is Your Data?"

28. Tedeschi, "E-Commerce Report."

29. "Corporate Security Gets Urgent: 10 Tips for Creating a Network Security Policy," *Interactive Week*, 23 October 2001, http://techupdate.zdnet.com/techupdate/stories/main/0,14179, 2819412-9,00.html.

30. Richard Behar, "Fear Along the Firewall," *Fortune*, 15 October 2001, 145–148; Brian Fonseca, "Study: Viruses Cost $12B in '99," *InfoWorld.com*, 17 January 2000 [cited 5 November 2001] www.computerworld.com.

31. David S. Bernstein, "We've Been Hacked," *Inc. Tech 2000*, no. 3, 106+.

32. Julian Borger, "US Fears al-Qaida Hackers Will Hit Vital Computer Networks," *The Guardian*, 28 June 2002, 2; Richard Behar, "Fear Along the Firewall," *Fortune*, 15 October 2001, 145–148.

33. Steve Patterson, "Congress to Weigh Privacy Right vs. Security Need; Legislation May Mean Intrusiveness," *Florida Times Union*, 24 September 2001, A-1.

34. Adapted from Stephanie Armour, "Technology's Burps Give Workers Heartburn," *USA Today*, 16 August 1999, 1B, 2B; "COM-PAQ: Employees Get 'IT' out of Their Systems," *M2 Presswire*, 27 May 1999; Jack Gordon, Kim Kiser, Michele Picard, and David Stamps, "Take That, You @!%#!* Machine!" *Training*, May 1999, 20.

35. Adapted from Rafael Behr, "Nation's Hopes Resting on the Next Generation," *Financial Times*, 5 July 2001, 5+; Marco R. Della Cava, "Wireless Nation," *USA Today*, 25 August 1999, 1A–2A.

Chapter 5

1. Abigail Leichman, "Oh, Baby—Novel Gifts for the Newborn," *The Record* (Bergen County, NJ), 7 September 2002, F01; Isabel M. Isidro, "GeniusBabies.com: Turning Passion into a Successful Business," *PowerHomeBiz.com*, [accessed online 10 November 2002] www.powerhomebiz.com/OnlineSuccess/ geniusbabies.htm; Isabel M. Isidro, "What Works on the Web? 12 Lessons From Successful Home-Based Online Entrepreneurs," *PowerHomeBiz.com* (www.powerhomebiz.com/ vol63/whatworks.htm); Karen Dash, "Dotcom Moms: Many Parents Have Discovered the Perfect Place to Balance Work and Family—The Web," *Raleigh News & Observer*, 14 May 2000 [accessed online 10 November 2002] www.baby university.com/about_us/raleigh_n_o.shtml; Barbara Whitaker, "For the Small Retailer, Life on the Internet Is One Big Bazaar," *New York Times*, 29 March 2000 [accessed online 10 November 2002] www.nytimes.com/library/tech/00/03/biztech/technology/ 29whit.html.

2. "Market Share," *Inc. State of Small Business 2001*, 25.

3. Jim Hopkins, "Entrepreneur 101: Supervising Employees," *USA Today*, 12 September 2001, 9B; Claudia H. Deutsch, "When a Big Company Hatches a Lot of Little Ideas," *New York Times*, 23 September 1998, D4.

4. Small Business Administration Office of Advocacy website [accessed 15 October 2002] www.sba.gov/advo/stats.

5. Small Business Administration Office of Advocacy website [accessed 15 October 2002] www.sba.gov/advo/stats.

6. National Science Foundation website, 2001 Data Briefs, NSF 01-326, 17 May 2001 [accessed 13 October 2002] www.nsf.gov/sbe/databrf/db.htm.

7. Paul C. Peralte, "SBA's Helping Hand Leads to Big Award for Nuclear Industry Firm," *Atlanta Journal-Constitution*, 9 September 2000, C1. Lloyd Gite and Dawn M. Baskerville, "Black Women Entrepreneurs on the Rise," *Black Enterprise*, August 1996, 73–74.

8. LeapFrog website [accessed 20 March 2002] www.leapfrogtoys. com.

9. Bill Meyers, "It's a Small-Business World," *USA Today*, 30 July 1999, B1, B2.

10. Donna Fenn, "The Buyers," *Inc.*, June 1996, 46–52.

11. Barbara Hagenbaugh, "Economics Majors Build Brand Name with Unmentionables," *USA Atlanta Journal-Constitution*, 20 May 2002, C1.

12. Donna Fenn and John Case, "Ordinary People, Extraordinary Creativity," *Inc Magazine*, October 2002, 83–86.

13. Fenn and Case, "Ordinary People, Extraordinary Creativity."

14. Michelle Conlin, "It's in the Bag," *Forbes*, 28 December 1998, 86, 90; Edie Cohen, "Ace of Spades," *Interior Design*, April 2001, 198–205.

15. Adam Cohen, "Her Own Bubble Economy," *Time Bonus Section—Your Business*, April 2001, Y14.

16. *NFIB Small Business Policy Guide* (Washington, DC: NFIB Education Foundation, 2000), 20; Joanne H. Pratt, "Small Business Research Summary, Homebased Business: The Hidden Economy," U.S. Small Business Administration Office of Advocacy, No. 194, March 2000, 1–2.

17. Small Business Association website [accessed 17 March 2002] www.sba.gov.

18. Hilary E. MacGregor, "The Sweet Life," *Los Angeles Times*, 9 July 2002, E1.

19. Small Business Administration Office of Advocacy website [accessed 17 March 2002] www.sba.gov/advo.

20. Stephanie Armour, "Many Turn to Start-Ups for Freedom," *USA Today*, 8 June 1998, 1B, 2B; "The Top 500 Women-Owned Businesses," *Working Woman*, May 1998, 50.

21. Jim Hopkins, "Bad Times Spawn Great Start-Ups," *USA Today*, 18 December 2001, 1B; Alan Cohen, "Your Next Business," *FSB*, February 2002, 33–40.

22. Susan Greco and Elaine Appleton Grant, "Creation Nation," *Inc Magazine*, October 2002, 72–79.

23. Hopkins, "Entrepreneur 101: Supervising Employees," 9B.

24. Norman M. Scarborough and Thomas W. Zimmerer, *Effective Small Business Management*, 7th ed. (Upper Saddle River, N.J.: Prentice Hall, 2003), 100.

25. "How Widespread Is Franchising?" International Franchise Association website [accessed 12 October 2002] www.franchise. org/resourcectr/faq/faq.asp.

26. Scarborough and Zimmerer, *Effective Small Business Management*, 93.

27. Michael Hopkins, "Zen and the Art of the Self-Managed Company," *Inc.*, November 2000, 54–63.

28. Constance L. Hays, "Franchisees on the Edge," *New York Times*, 22 August 2001, C1, C2.

29. "McBusiness," *Inc. State of Small Business 2001*, 58.

30. Juan Hovey, "Risky Business," *Industry Week*, 15 May 2000, 75–76.

31. Sharon Nelton, "Coming to Grips with Growth," *Nation's Business*, February 1998, 26–32.

32. Lee Smith, "Five Secrets of Growth," *FSB*, July–August 2001, 54–57.

33. Michael Selz, "Here's the Problem," *Wall Street Journal— Breakaway Special Report Winter 1999*, 22 February 1999, 12.

34. Jerry Useem, "The Secret of My Success," *Inc.*, May 1998, 67–80.

35. Marita Bon, "Mature Outlook: Keep SCORE," *Morning Star*, 5 February 2002, 3D; J. Tol Broome Jr., "SCORE's Impact on Small Firms," *Nation's Business*, January 1999, 41–43.

36. "With SCORE's Help, Virtual Skateboard Business in San Diego, Calif. Becomes an Internet Hit," SCORE website [accessed 13 December 2002] www.score.org/success/virtual skate/index. htm.

37. Broome, "SCORE's Impact on Small Firms"; Robert McGarvey, "Peak Performance," *American Way*, July 1996, 56–60.

38. Loren Fox, "Hatching New Companies," *Upside*, February 2000, 144–152.

39. Dale Buss, "Bringing New Firms out of Their Shell," *Nations Business*, March 1997, 48–50; Fox, "Hatching New Companies."

40. Jonathan Katz, "Hatching Ideas," *Industry Week*, 18 September 2000, 63–65.

41. Buss, "Bringing New Firms out of Their Shell."

42. Robert McGarvey, "Peak Performance," *American Way*, July 1996, 56–60.

43. Henry Wichmann Jr., Charles Harter, and H. Charles Sparks, "Big Cash for Small Business," *Journal of Accountancy*, July 1999, 64–72.

44. Susan Hodges, "Microloans Fuel Big Ideas," *Nation's Business*, February 1997, 34–35.

45. Ronaleen R. Roha, "Big Loans for Small Businesses," *Changing Times*, April 1989, 105–109; "Small Loans, Big Problems," *Economist*, 28 January 1995, 73; Elizabeth Kadetsky, "Small Loans, Big Dreams," *Working Woman*, February 1995, 46–49; Reid Rutherford, "Securitizing Small Business Loans: A Banker's Action Plan," *Commercial Lending Review*, Winter 1994–1995, 62–74.

46. Pete Lewis and Robert Schwab, SBA Delivers, *ColoradoBiz*, July 2002, 26–34.

47. Small Business Administration website [accessed 12 October 2002] www.sba.gov; Karen Gutloff, "Five Alternative Ways to Finance Your Business," *Black Enterprise*, March 1998, 81–85.

48. Jim Hopkins, "Corporate Giants Bankroll Start-Ups," *USA Today*, 29 March 2001, B1.

49. "Retail Entrepreneurs of the Year: Kirk Perron," *Chain Store Age*, December 2001, 66.

50. Bob Zider, "How Venture Capital Works," *Harvard Business Review*, November/December 1998, 131–139.

51. Cash Flow," *Inc. State of Small Business*, 2001, 76.

52. Dori Jones Yang, "Venture Capitalists Seek Less Adventure," *U.S. News & World Report*, 4 June 2001, 39.

53. Barbara Darrow, "Touched by an Angel," *Computer Reseller News*, 17 April 2000, 152, 156.

54. Jane Easter Bahls, "Cyber Cash; Startup Financing: Finding an Angel to Get Going," CCH Business Owners Toolkit website [accessed 20 May 1999] aol.toolkit.cch.com/columns/Starting/225-99AngelR.asp.

55. Darrow, "Touched by an Angel," 152, 156.

56. Jim Hopkins, "Entrepreneurial Spirit Suffering," *USA Today*, 18 September 2002, A1.

57. Joel Russell, "Credit Card Capitalism," *Hispanic Business*, March 1998, 40.

58. Adapted from Subway website [accessed 12 October 2002] www.subway.com; Maynard, Robert, "Choosing a Franchise," *Nation's Business*, October 1996, 54–55.

Chapter 6

1. Adapted from Rishawn Biddly, "Family Feud," *Forbes*, 10 June 2002, 54–56; Kinko's website [accessed 4 April 2002] www.kinkos.com; Shawn Tully, "A Better Taskmaster Than the Market," *Fortune*, 26 October 1998, 277–286; Laurie J. Flynn, "For the Officeless, A Place to Call Home," *New York Times*, 6 July 1998, 1, 4; Michele Marchetti, "Getting the Kinks Out," *Sales and Marketing Management*, March 1997, 56–64; "Man of Few Words," *Sales and Marketing Management*, March 1997, 63; "Kinko's Improves Image of Businesses with Top-Notch Proposals and Presentation Capabilities; Presentations a Growing Percentage of Customer Work at Kinko's," *Business Wire*, 28 September 1997; "Kinko's Strengthens Office Product Assortment," *Discount Store News*, 17 November 1997, 6, 70; Ann Marsh, "Kinko's Grows Up—Almost," *Forbes*, 1 December 1997, 270–272; "Kinko's Strikes Deal for Mideast Growth," *Graphic Arts Monthly*, January 1998, 22;

Lori Ioannou and Paul Orfalea, "Interview: The Brains Behind Kinko's," *Your Company*, 1 May 1999, 621.

2. Mitchell Pacelle and Ianthe Jeanne Dugan, "Partners Forever? Within Andersen, Personal Liability May Bring Ruin," *Wall Street Journal*, 2 April 2002, C1, C16.

3. Norman M. Scarborough and Thomas W. Zimmerer, *Effective Small Business Management* (Upper Saddle River, N.J.: Prentice Hall, 2000), 84.

4. James W. Cortada, "Do You Take This Partner?," *Total Quality Review*, November–December 1995, 11.

5. Vivien Kellerman, "A Growing Business Takes the Corporate Plunge," *New York Times*, 23 July 1994, sec. Your Money, 31.

6. "Fortune 5 Hundred Largest U.S. Corporations," *Fortune*, 15 April 2002, F1–F20.

7. Wal-Mart website [accessed 5 April 2002] www.walmart.com; U.S. Census Bureau website [accessed 5 April 2002], www.census.gov.

8. Scarborough and Zimmerer, *Effective Small Business Management*, 90.

9. Robert G. Goldstein, Russell Shapiro, and Edward A. Hauder, "So Many Choices of Business Entities—Which One Is Best for Your Needs?," *Insight (CPA Society)*, February/March 1999, 10–16.

10. Rana Dogar, "Crony Baloney," *Working Woman*, January 1997; Richard H. Koppes, "Institutional Investors, Now in Control of More Than Half the Shares of U.S. Corporations, Demand More Accountability," *National Law Journal*, 14 April 1997, B5; John A. Byrne, "The Best & Worst Boards," *Business Week*, 25 November 1996, 82–84; Anthony Bianco, John Byrne, Richard Melcher, and Mark Maremont, "The Rush to Quality on Corporate Boards," *Business Week*, 3 March 1997, 34–35.

11. Laurence Zuckerman, "UPS Hears Market's Song, and Plans to Sell Some Stock," *New York Times*, 22 July 1999, A1, C23.

12. Phyllis Berman, "Fashion Game," *Forbes*, 4 March 2002, 55–60.

13. John A. Byrne, "No Excuses for Enron's Board," *Business Week*, 29 July 2002, 50–51.

14. Gary Strauss, "From Public Service to Private Payday," *USA Today*, 17 April 2000, 1B, 2B.

15. Matt Krantz, "Web of Board Members Ties Together Corporate America," *USA Today*, 25 November 2002, 1B, 3B.

16. Carol Hymowitz, "How to Fix a Broken System," *Wall Street Journal*, 24 February 2003, R1, R3.

17. Louis Lavelle, "The Best & Worst Boards," *Business Week*, 7 October 2002, 104–114.

18. Hymowitz, "How to Fix a Broken System."

19. Lavelle, "The Best & Worst Boards," 104–114.

20. Emily Thorton and Louis Lavelle, "It's Getting Tough to Fill a Boardroom," *Business Week*, 29 July 2002, 80–81.

21. David A. Nadler, "10 Steps to a Happy Merger," *New York Times*, 15 March 1998, BU14.

22. Henry, "Mergers—Why Most Big Deals Don't Pay Off," 60–70.

23. Stephen Labaton, "800-Pound Gorillas," *New York Times*, 11 June 2000, sec. 4, 1.

24. Martin Peers, Nick Wingfield, and Laura Landro, "AOL, Time Warner Set Plan to Link in Mammoth Merger," *Wall Street Journal*, 11 January 2000, A1, A6; Thomas E. Weber, Martin Peers, and Nick Wingfield, "Two Titans in a Strategic Bind Bet on a Futuristic Megadeal," *Wall Street Journal*, 11 January 2000, B1, B12; "AOL and Time Warner Will Merge to Create World's First Internet-Age Media and Communications Company," America Online website [accessed 11 January 2000] http://media.web.aol.com/media/ press.cfm.

25. Eleena De Lisser, "Banking on Mergers," *Wall Street Journal*, 24 May 1999, R25.

26. Merrill Goozner and John Schmeltzer, "Mass Exodus Hits Corporate Names," *Chicago Tribune*, 12 May 1998, sec. 3, 1, 3; Bill Vlasic, "The First Global Car Colossus," *Business Week*, 18 May 1998, 40–43; Abid Aslam, "Exxon-Mobil Merger Could Poison the Well," *Inter Press Service English News Wire*, 2 December 1998, Electric Library [accessed 2 June 1999] www.elibrary.com; Agis Salpukas, "Do Oil and Bigger Oil Mix?," *New York Times*, 2 December 1998, C1, C4.

27. Christopher C. Williams, "Conglomerates Face Challenge," *Wall Street Journal*, 17 April 2002, B5A.

28. Steve Lipen, "Concentration: Corporations' Dreams Converge in One Idea: It's Time to Do a Deal," *Wall Street Journal*, 26 February 1997, A1, A8.

29. "Business: Pfizer's Prize," *Economist*, 12 February 2000, 69; Nikheil Deogun and Robert Langreth, "P&G Walks away from Merger Talks; Stock Decline Prompts End to Warner-AHP Link; Bidder Pfizer Bolstered," *Wall Street Journal*, 25 January 2000, A3.

30. Pui-Wing Tam, "Judge Dismisses Suit Over H-P Deal," *Wall Street Journal*, 1 May 2002, A3; Pui-Wing Tam, "H-P's Board Says It Won't Nominate Dissident Walter Hewlett for Re-Election," *Wall Street Journal*, 2 April 2002, A3, A6.

31. Joann S. Lublin, "Poison Pills Are Giving Shareholders a Big Headache, Union Proposals Assert," *Wall Street Journal*, 23 May 1997, C1.

32. Thomas Mulligan, "ITT Takes Starwood Offer," *Los Angeles Times*, 13 November 1997, D2; Kathleen Morris, "Behind the New Deal Mania," *Business Week*, 3 November 1997, 36.

33. Martha Groves and Stuart Silverstein, "Levi Strauss Offers Year's Pay as Incentive Bonus," *Los Angeles Times*, 13 June 1996, A1.

34. "RadioShack Recognized for Contributions to Wireless Industry," *PR Newswire*, 21 March 2002, 1; "Verizon Wireless and RadioShack to Unveil Nationwide Store-Within-A-Store," *PR Newswire*, 7 May 2001.

35. Ranjay Gulati, Sarah Huffman, and Gary Neilson, "The Barista Principle—Starbucks and the Rise of Relational Capital," *Strategy & Business*, Third Quarter 2002 [accessed 16 October 2002] www.strategy-business.com.

36. Michael Hickins, "Searching for Allies," *Management Review*, January 2000, 54–58.

37. Gary Dessler, *Management*, 2d ed. (Upper Saddle River, N.J.: Prentice Hall, 2001), 45.

38. Adapted from advertisement, *The Atlantic Monthly*, January 2000, 119; Endless Pools, Inc. website [accessed 31 August 2000] www.endlesspools.com/.

Chapter 7

1. Kathryn Jones, "The Dell Way," *Business 2.0*, February 2003, 61–66; Linda Tischler, "Can Kevin Rollins Find the Soul of Dell?," *Fast Company*, November 2002, 110–114; Pui-Wing Tam, Gary McWilliams, Scott Thurm, "Out of the Box: As Alliances Fade, Computer Firms Toss Out Playbook," *Wall Street Journal*, 15 October 2002, A1; John G. Spooner, "Dell Dives into Printer Market," News.com, 24 September 2002, http://news.com.com/2100-1001-959132.html; Andrew Park, Faith Keenan, Cliff Edwards, "Whose Lunch Will Dell Eat Next?," *Business Week*, 12 August 2002, 66–67; executive biography, Michael S. Dell, www.dell.com/us/en/gen/corporate/michael_bio.htm; executive biography, Kevin Rollins, www.dell.com/us/en/gen/corporate/kevin_bio.htm; Dell history, www.dell.com/us/en/gen/corporate/access_mdell_history_fact_pak.htm; Soul of Dell, www.dell.com/us/en/gen/corporate/vision_soulofdell.htm

2. Dell website [accessed 1 November 2002] www.dell.com; Daniel Roth, "Dell's Big New Act," *Fortune*, 6 December 1999, 152–156.

3. Michael A. Verespej, "Michael Dell's Magic," *IW*, 16 November 1998, 57–64; Richard Murphy, "Michael Dell," *Success*, January 1999, 50–53.

4. Leonard Goodstein, Timothy Nolan, and J. William Pfeiffer, *Applied Strategic Planning* (New York: McGraw-Hill, 1993), 169–192.

5. Aimee L. Stern, "Management: You Can Keep Your Staff on the Competitive Track If You . . . Inspire Your Team with a Mission Statement," *Your Company*, 1 August 1997, 36.

6. Betsy Morris, "Can Michael Dell Escape the Box?," *Fortune*, 16 October 2000, 92–110.

7. Toni Mack and Mary Summers, "Danger: Stealth Attack," *Forbes*, 25 January 1999, 88–92.

8. Norman M. Scarborough and Thomas W. Zimmerer, *Effective Small Business Management* (Upper Saddle River, N.J.: Prentice Hall, 2000), 50.

9. Mark Veverka, "Plugged In: Michael Dell's Plan to Hobble Hewlett-Packard," *Barron's*, 15 July 2002, T3.

10. Veverka, "Plugged In: Michael Dell's Plan to Hobble Hewlett-Packard."

11. Veverka, "Plugged In: Michael Dell's Plan to Hobble Hewlett-Packard."

12. Steve Lohr, "On a Roll, Dell Enters Uncharted Territory," *New York Times*, 25 August 2002, 1.

13. Judy A. Smith, "Crisis Communications: The War on Two Fronts," *Industry Week*, 20 May 1996, 136; John F. Reukus, "Hazard Communication," *Occupational Hazards*, February 1998, 39; Kim M. Gibson and Steven H. Smith, "Do We Understand Each Other?," *Journal of Accountancy*, January 1998, 53.

14. Timothy Aeppel, Clare Ansberry, Milo Geyelin, and Robert L. Simison, "Road Signs: How Ford, Firestone Let the Warnings Slide by as Debacle Developed," *Wall Street Journal*, 6 September 2000, A1; Joann Muller, David Welch, Jeff Green, Lorraine Woellert, and Nicole St. Pierre, "A Crisis of Confidence," *Business Week*, 18 September 2000, 40–42.

15. Michael Moeller, Steve Hamm, and Timothy J. Mullaney, "Remaking Microsoft," *Business Week*, 17 May 1999, 106–116.

16. Stephanie Armour, "Once Plagued by Pink Slips, Now They're in Driver's Seat," *USA Today*, 14 May 1998, 1B–2B.

17. Gary A. Yukl, *Leadership in Organizations*, 2d ed. (Upper Saddle River, N.J.: Prentice Hall, 1989), 9, 175–176.

18. Daniel Goleman, "What Makes a Leader?," *Harvard Business Review*, November–December 1998, 92–102; Shari Caudron, "The Hard Case for Soft Skills," *Workforce*, July 1999, 60–66.

19. Saul Hansell, "Meg Whitman and eBay, Net Survivors," *New York Times*, 5 May 2002, sec 3, 1.

20. Michael A. Verespej, "Lead, Don't Manage," *Industry Week*, 4 March 1996, 58.

21. Stratford Sherman, "Secrets of HP's 'Muddled' Team," *Fortune*, 18 March 1996, 116–120.

22. Daniel Goleman, "Leadership That Gets Results," *Harvard Business Review*, March–April 2000, 78–90.

23. Stephen P. Robbins and David A. De Cenzo, *Fundamentals of Management*, 2d ed. (Upper Saddle River, N.J.: Prentice Hall, 1998), 55–56; James Waldroop and Timothy Butler, "The Executive as Coach," *Harvard Business Review*, November–December 1996, 113.

24. Kathryn Tyler, "Scoring Big in the Workplace," *HR Magazine*, June 2000, 96–106.

25. Fara Warner, "Inside Intel's Mentoring Movement," *Fast Company*, April 2002, 116–119.

26. Michael Been and Nitin Nohria, "Cracking the Code of Change," *Harvard Business Review*, May–June 2000, 133–141.

27. Michael Barrier, "Managing Workers in Times of Change," *Nation's Business*, May 1998, 31–32.

28. Verespej, "Michael Dell's Magic," 57–64; Murphy, "Michael Dell," 50–53.

29. John A. Byrne, Mike France, and Wendy Zellner, "Enron and Beyond," *Business Week*, 25 February 2002, 118–120.

30. Courtland L. Bovée and John V. Thill, *Business Communication Today*, 6th ed. (Upper Saddle River, N.J.: Prentice Hall, 2000), 4.

31. Jeff Cole, "Wing Commander," *Wall Street Journal*, 10 January 2001, A1, A12.

32. "Boeing Puts a Price on Speedier Flights: $25," *Chicago Sun Times*, 4 August 2002, 42.

33. Stanley Holmes and Wendy Zellner, "Boeing: A Flight to Safety," *Business Week*, 29 July 2002, 70.

34. Holmes and Zellner, "Boeing: A Flight to Safety," 70; J. Lynn Lunsford, "Boeing Explores Plan B," *Wall Street Journal*, 11 June 2002, D5.

35. Stanley Holmes, "The Battle over a Radical New Plane," *Business Week*, 25 November 2002, 106–108.

36. Adapted from Tom Lowry, "Thieves Swipe Credit with Card Readers," *USA Today*, 28 June 1999, 1B; Elaine Shannon, "A New Credit-Card Scam," *Time*, 5 June 2000, 54–55; Linda Punch, "Card Fraud: Down but Not Out," *Credit Card Management*, June 1999, 30–42.

Chapter 8

1. American Express Company's website [accessed 15 November 2002] www.americanexpress.com; Sally Richards, "Make the Most of Your First Job," *Informationweek*, 21 June 1999, 183–186; Tim Greene, "American Express: Don't Leave Home to Go to Work," *Network World*, 8 March 1999, 25; Mahlon Apgar IV, "The Alternative Workplace: Changing Where and How People Work," *Harvard Business Review*, May/June 1998, 121–130; "How Senior Executives at American Express View the Alternative Workplace," *Harvard Business Review*, May/June 1998, 132–133; Michelle Marchetti, "Master Motivators," *Sales and Marketing Management*, April 1998, 38–44; Carrie Shook, "Leader, Not Boss," *Forbes*, 1 December 1997, 52–54.

2. Betsy Morris, "Can Michael Dell Escape the Box?," *Fortune*, 16 October 2000, 92–110.

3. Peter F. Drucker, "Management's New Paradigms," *Forbes*, 5 October 1998, 152–176.

4. "Sharing Knowledge Through BP's Virtual Team Network," *Harvard Business Review*, September–October 1997, 152–153; British Petroleum website [accessed 20 April 2002] www.bp.com.

5. Alan Webber, "The Best Organization Is No Organization," *USA Today*, 13A; Eve Tahmincioglu, "How GM's Team Approach Works," *Gannett News Service*, 24 April 1996, S11.

6. Gary Izumo, "Teamwork Holds Key to Organization Success," *Los Angeles Times*, 20 August 1996, D9; Daft, *Management*, 328–329; David, *Strategic Management*, 223.

7. Steven Burke, "Acer Restructures into Six Divisions," *Computer Reseller News*, 13 July 1998, 10; Acer America website [accessed 20 July 2000] www.acer.com/aac/about/profile.htm.

8. Dan Dimancescu and Kemp Dwenger, "Smoothing the Product Development Path," *Management Review*, 1 January 1996, 36.

9. Dimancescu and Dwenger, "Smoothing the Product Development Path."

10. "The Horizontal Organization," *Soundview Executive Book Summaries*, 21, no. 3 (March 1999): 1–8.

11. "The Horizontal Organization."

12. Stephen P. Robbins, *Essentials of Organizational Behavior*, 6th ed. (Upper Saddle River, N.J.: Prentice Hall, 2000), 105.

13. Arthur D. Wainwright, "People-First Strategies Get Implemented," *Strategy and Leadership*, January–February 1997, 12–17; "Profile: The Team's the Theme," *St. Louis Commerce Magazine*, 1 April 2000, 84.

14. Wainwright, "People-First Strategies Get Implemented," 12–17.

15. Jeffrey Pfeffer, "When It Comes to 'Best Practices'—Why Do Smart Organizations Occasionally Do Dumb Things?," *Organizational Dynamics*, Summer 96, Vol. 25, Issue 1, 33.

16. Andy Gotlieb, "Secret Is Out on SEI," *Philadelphia Business Journal*, 19 January 2001, 15; Anna Muoio, "Updating the Agenda: A Second Look at the 1998 Agenda Role Models," *Fast Company*, 1 April 1999, 184; "Doing the Work that Needs Doing: Conversations with the Leaders," *Training & Development*, January 1999, 56–60; Scott Kirsner, "Every Day, It's a New Place," *Fast Company*, April–May 1998, 132–134.

17. Jenny C. McCune, "On the Train Gang: In the New Flat Organizations, Employees Who Want to Be Competitive Must Be Versatile Enough to Perform a Variety of Tasks," *Management Review*, 1 October 1994, 57.

18. Seth Lubove, "Destroying the Old Hierarchies," *Forbes*, 3 June 1996, 62–64.

19. Clyde Fessler, "Rotating Leadership at Harley-Davidson: From Hierarchy to Interdependence," *Strategy & Leadership*, July–August 1997, 42–43; Mark A. Brunelli, "How Harley-Davidson Uses Cross-Functional Teams," *Purchasing*, 4 November 1999, 148.

20. Richard Moderow, "Teamwork Is the Key to Cutting Costs," *Modern Healthcare*, 29 April 1996, 138.

21. Robbins, *Essentials of Organizational Behavior*, 109.

22. Deborah L. Duarte and Nancy Tennant Snyder, *Mastering Virtual Teams* (San Francisco: Jossey-Bass, 1999), 23.

23. "Sharing Knowledge Through BP's Virtual Team Network," *Harvard Business Review*, September–October 1997, 152–153.

24. Ross Sherwood, "The Boss's Open Door Means More Time for Employees," *Reuters Business Report*, 30 September 1996.

25. Neuborne, "Companies Save, but Workers Pay," B2; Charles L. Parnell, "Teamwork: Not a New Idea, But It's Transforming the Workplace," *Vital Speeches of the Day*, 1 November 1996, 46.

26. Mike Verespej, "Drucker Sours on Teams," *Industry Week*, 6 April 1998, 16+.

27. Larry Cole and Michael Cole, "Why Is the Teamwork Buzz Word Not Working?," *Communication World*, February/March 1999, 29; Patricia Buhler, "Managing in the 90s: Creating Flexibility in Today's Workplace," *Supervision*, January 1997, 24+; Allison W. Amason, Allen C. Hochwarter, Wayne A. Thompson, and Kenneth R. Harrison, "Conflict: An Important Dimension in Successful Management Teams," *Organizational Dynamics*, Autumn 1995, 20+.

28. "Team Players," *Executive Excellence*, May 1999, 18.

29. Thomas K. Capozzoli, "Conflict Resolution—A Key Ingredient in Successful Teams," *Supervision*, November 1999, 14–16.

30. Steven Crom and Herbert France, "Teamwork Brings Breakthrough Improvements in Quality and Climate," *Quality Progress*, March 1996, 39–41.

31. Adapted from Dan Goodin, "Graduating Students Weigh New Job Incentive: Money to Stay Away," *Wall Street Journal*, 4 May 2001, B1; Mark Larson, "Intel Offering Buy-outs to Workers, College Recruits," *Sacramento Business Journal*, 4 May 2001, 1; Barbara Clements, "The Workplace: This Year's College Grads Will Face a More Challenging Job Hunt," *The News Tribune*, Tacoma, Wash., 7 May 2001, D1.

Chapter 9

1. Krispy Kreme website [accessed 15 November 2002] www.krispykreme.com; Olivia Barker, "Krispy Kreme Doughnuts Take the (Wedding) Cake," *USA Today*, 11 October 2002, D1; Brian O'Keefe, "Kreme of the Crop," *Fortune*, 23 July 2001, 247;

Lidia Kelly, "For Krispy Kreme, Doughnuts a Delicacy," *The Arizona Republic*, 20 June 2000, D1; Avital Louria Hahn, "Krispy Kreme IPO Brings Jelly-Filled to a Dot-Com World," *The Investment Dealers' Digest: IDD*, 17 January 2000, 9, 14; Karyn Strauss, "Looking to Raise Dough . . . The Public Way: Krispy Kreme Goes for IPO," *Nation's Restaurant News*, 3 January 2000, 26; Charles Fishman, "The King of Kreme," *Fast Company*, October 1999, 268–278; Scott McCormack, "Sweet Success," *Forbes*, 7 September 1998; Chuck Martin, "For the Love of a Good Doughnut: Krispy Kremes Gain Status Across the Nation," *Gannett News Service*, 10 September 1997; Fred Faust, "Doughnuts Holing on in Munch Crunch," *St. Louis Post-Dispatch*, 21 July 1997, 12; Paul Brown and Robert Siegel, "Krispy Kreme History," *All Things Considered*, National Public Radio, 17 July 1997.

2. Roberta A. Russell and Bernard W. Taylor III, *Operations Management: Focusing on Quality and Competitiveness*, 2d ed. (Upper Saddle River, N.J.: Prentice Hall, 1998), 21.

3. Stanley Holmes and Mike France, "Boeing's Secret," *Business Week*, 20 May 2002, 110–120; Jerry Useem, "Boeing vs. Boeing," *Fortune*, 2 October 2002, 148–160; Daniel Michaels, "Europe's Airbus Ready to Spread Wings as a Company," *Wall Street Journal*, 23 June 2000, A15; Alex Taylor III, "Blue Skies for Airbus," *Fortune*, 2 August 1999, 102–108.

4. Mark M. Davis, Nicholas J. Aquilano, and Richard B. Chase, *Fundamentals of Operations Management* (Boston: Irwin McGraw-Hill, 1999), 241–242.

5. Daniel Fisher, "The Best Little Factory in Texas," *Forbes*, 10 June 2002, 110.

6. Stuart F. Brown, "Giving More Jobs to Electronic Eyes," *Fortune*, 16 February 1998, 104B–104D.

7. "IBM and Dassault Awarded Boeing CATIA Contract," *CAD/CAM Update*, 1 January 1997, 1–8.

8. Drew Winter, "C3P: New Acronym Signals Big Change at Ford," *Ward's Auto World* 32 (1 August 1996): 34; Thomas Hoffman, "Ford to Cut Its Prototype Costs," *Computerworld*, 30 September 1996, 65; Drew Winter, "Massive Changes Coming in Computer Engineering," *Ward's Auto World* 32 (1 April 1996): 34.

9. Faith Keenan, "A Mass Market of One," *Business Week*, 2 December 2002, 68–72.

10. T. J. Becker, "Have It Your Way," *The Edward Lowe Report*, February 2002, 1–3, 12.

11. Jon Swartz, "Have It Your Way," *USA Today*, 30 October 2002, 3B.

12. Brian S. Moskal, "Born to Be Real," *Industry Week*, 2 August 1993, 14–18.

13. Robyn Meredith, "Porsche Goes Soccer Mom," *Forbes*, 4 February 2000, 54.

14. Brian McWilliams, "Re-engineering the Small Factory," *Inc. Technology*, 1 (1996): 44–45.

15. "E-Procurement Explosion," *Industry Week*, March 2002, 24–28.

16. Greg Ip, "Risky Business," *Wall Street Journal*," 24 October 2001, A1, A4.

17. Jon E. Hilsenrath, "Parts Shortages Hamper Electronics Makers; Surging Demand Shows Flaw in Just-in-Time Chains," *Wall Street Journal*, 7 July 2000, B5.

18. Karl Ritzler, "A Mercedes Made from Scratch," *Atlanta Journal and Constitution*, 30 May 1997, S1.

19. Adapted from Bruce Dorminey, "Overconfidence, Poor Planning Led to Hong Kong Airport Woes," *Aviation Week and Space Technology*, 15 February 1999, 53+; Sherrie E. Zhan, "No Kudos for Chek Lap Kok Airport," *World Trade*, October 1998, 32+; Martyn Warwick, "Not Tried, Not Tested," *Communications International*, August 1998, 24+; "Hong Kong Opens New Airport," *Material Handling Engineering*, August 1998, 12+; "Trouble-Shooting at Chek Lap Kok," *Transportation and Distribution*, August 1998, 12; Bruce Dorminey and Carole A. Shifrin, "Hong Kong Investigates What Went Wrong," *Aviation Week and Space Technology*, 20 July 1998, 45+; Megan Scott, "Vendors Take Blame for System Woes," *Computerworld*, 20 July 1998, 29–32; Kristin S. Krause, "Order out of Chaos," *Traffic World*, 20 July 1998, 23–24; Murray Hiebert, "Opening-Day Blues," *Far-Eastern Economic Review*, 16 July 1998, 62–63; Mark Landler, "Problems Continue to Mount at New Hong Kong Airport," *New York Times*, 9 July 1998, C6; Michael Mecham, "In Hong Kong, There's Still Room to Expand," *Aviation Week & Space Technology*, 27 March 2000, 44–46.

20. Del Jones, "Training and Service at Top of Winners' List," *USA Today*, 17 October 1996, 5B.

21. John A. Byrne, "Never Mind the Buzzwords. Roll up Your Sleeves," *Business Week*, 22 January 1996, 84.

22. William M. Carley, "Charging Ahead: To Keep GE's Profits Rising, Welch Pushes Quality-Control Plan," *Wall Street Journal*, 13 January 1997, A1, A6.

23. Kostas N. Dervitsiotis, "The Challenge of Managing Organizational Change," *Total Quality Management*, February 1998, 109–122.

24. John Berry, "Six Sigma Savvy," *Computerworld*, 5 August 2002, 37.

25. Dawne Shand, "Six Sigma," *Computerworld*, 5 March 2001, 38.

26. Christina Binkley, "Starwood Sets Effort to Enhance Quality and Improve Cash Flow," *Wall Street Journal*, 5 February 2001, B4.

27. Gillian Babicz, "ISO 9004: The Other Half of the Consistent Pair," *Quality*, June 2001, 50–53; David Drickhemer, "Standards Shake-Up," *Industry Week*, 5 March 2001, 37–40.

28. Hugh D. Menzies, "Global Guide: Quality Counts When Wooing Overseas Clients," *Your Company*, 1 June 1997, 64; Michael E. Raynor, "Worldwide Winners," *Total Quality Management*, July–August 1993, 43–48; Greg Bounds, Lyle Yorks, Mel Adams, and Gipsie Ranney, *Beyond Total Quality Management: Toward the Emerging Paradigm* (New York: McGraw-Hill, 1994), 212; Russell and Taylor, *Operations Management*, 115–116.

29. Ronald Henkoff, "Boeing's Big Problem," *Fortune*, 12 January 1998, 96–103; James Wallace, "How Boeing Blew It," *Sales and Marketing Management*, February 1998, 52–57; John Greenwald, "Is Boeing out of Its Spin?," *Time*, 13 July 1998, 67–69; John T. Landry, "Supply Chain Management: The Case for Alliances," *Harvard Business Review*, November–December 1998, 24–25.

30. George Anders, "The Innovator's Solution," *Fast Company*, June 2002, 132–138.

31. Timothy M. Laseter, "Balanced Sourcing the Honda Way," *Strategy and Business*, Fourth Quarter 1998, 24–31.

32. George Taninecz, "Forging the Chain," *Industry Week*, 15 May 2000, 40–46.

33. Meredith, "Porsche Goes Soccer Mom."

34. Gene Bylinsky, "For Sale: Japanese Plants in the U.S." *Fortune*, 21 February 2000, 240B–240D.

35. Saul Hansell, "Is This the Factory of the Future?," *New York Times*, 26 July 1998, sec. 3, 1, 12–13; Pete Engardio, "Souping Up the Supply Chain," *Business Week*, 31 August 1998, 110–112.

36. Philip Siekman, "The Smart Car Is Looking More So," *Fortune*, 15 April 2002, 310(I)–310(P).

37. "How Microsoft Reviews Suppliers," *Fast Company*, 17 [accessed 3 September 1998] fastcompany.com/online/17/msoftreviews.html

38. Gary Hoover, Alta Campbell, and Patrick J. Spain, eds., *Hoover's Handbook of American Business 1994* (Austin, Tex.: Reference Press, 1994), 268–269, 712–713, 1092–1093; State and Country Demographic and Economic Profiles, U.S. Census Bureau, [accessed 14 August 2000], www.census.gov/datamap/www/index.html.

Chapter 10

1. Thomas Watson, "Goodnight, Sweet Prince," *Canadian Business*, 27 May 2002, 77–78; Jennifer Schu, "Even in Hard Times, SAS Keeps Its Culture Intact," *Workforce*, October 2001, 21; Charles Fishman, "Moving Toward a Balanced Work Life," *Workforce*, March 2000, 38–42; Joanne Cole, "Case Study: SAS Institute Inc. Uses Sanity as Strategy," *HR Focus*, May 1999, 6; Charles Fishman, "Sanity Inc.," *Fast Company*, January 1999, 85–96.

2. Michael A. Verespej, "Balancing Act," *Industry Week*, 15 May 2000, 81–85.

3. John McMorrow, "Future Trends in Human Resources," *HR Focus*, September 1999, 8–9.

4. Robert B. Reich, "The Company of the Future," *Fast Company*, November 1998, 124–150.

5. Douglas McGregor, *The Human Side of Enterprise* (New York: McGraw-Hill, 1960).

6. Toby B. Gooley, "A World of Difference," *Logistics Management and Distribution Report*, June 2000, 51–55; William H. Miller, "Beneath the Surface," *Industry Week*, 20 September 1999, 13–16.

7. Laura Parker, "USA Just Wouldn't Work Without Immigrant Labor," *USA Today*, 23 July 2001, 1A, 2A.

8. Joan Crockett, "Winning Competitive Advantage Through a Diverse Workforce," *HR Focus*, May 1999, 9–10.

9. Crockett, "Winning Competitive Advantage Through a Diverse Workforce."

10. "Work Force Facts," *Chicago Tribune*, 10 September 2000, sec. 6, 1.

11. Stephanie Armour, "Younger Workers Feel Stuck As Older Ones Don't Retire," *USA Today*, 13 October 2002, 1A.

12. Stephanie Armour, "Maturing Boomers Smack 'Silver Ceiling,'" *USA Today*, 16 August 2001, 1A, 2A.

13. Nina Munk, "Finished at Forty," *Fortune*, 1 February 1999, 50–66.

14. Munk, "Finished at Forty."

15. "Is There Really Still a Gender Pay Gap?," *HR Focus*, June 2000, 3–4.

16. Genaro C. Armas, "Study Finds Women Still Trailing Men at Highest Salary Level," *Desert Sun*, 25 March 2003, E1; Gary Strauss and Del Jones, "Too Bright Spotlight Burns Female CEOs," *USA Today*, 18 December 2000, 3B.

17. Del Jones, "Women Gain Corporate Slots," *USA Today*, 19 November 2002, 3B.

18. Toddi Gutner, "The Rose-Colored Glass Ceiling," *Business Week*, 2 September 2000, 101.

19. Jones, "Women Gain Corporate Slots."

20. "One Fifth of Women Are Harassed Sexually," *HR Focus*, April 2002, 2.

21. Michael Barrier, "Sexual Harassment," *Nation's Business*, December 1998, 15–19.

22. Marianne Lavelle, "The New Rules of Sexual Harassment," *U.S. News & World Report*, 6 July 1998, 30–31.

23. Reich, "The Company of the Future."

24. Tammy Uyetake, "Skilled Labor Hard to Find," *Daily Herald*, 22 February 2002, 1.

25. Greg Jaffe and Douglas A. Blackmon, "Just in Time. When UPS Demanded Workers, Louisville Did the Delivering," *Wall Street Journal*, 24 April 1998, A1, A10.

26. Stephanie Armour, "Companies Hire Even As They Lay Off," *USA Today*, 15 May 2001, A1.

27. Michelle Kessler, "Days of BMW Signing Bonuses Long Gone," *USA Today*, 14 April 2002, 3B.

28. Lisa Tekevchi Cullen, "Where Did Everyone Go?," *Time*, 18 November 2002, 62–66.

29. Michael A. Verespej, "Stressed Out," *Industry Week*, 21 February 2000, 30–34.

30. Laura Vanderkamp, "White Collar Sweatshops Batter Young Workers," *USA Today*, 26 November 2002, A13.

31. Stephanie Armour, "Workplace Demands Taking Up More Weekends," *USA Today*, 24 April 1998, B1; Laabs, "Workforce Overload."

32. Dave Patel, "Vacation? What Vacation?," *HR Magazine*, August 2002, 144.

33. Armour, "Workplace Demands Taking Up More Weekends."

34. Laabs, "Workforce Overload."

35. Andy Cohen, "Survey Says: Workers Want Balance," *Sales and Marketing Management*, September 2002, 13.

36. Verespej, "Balancing Act."

37. Christopher Rhoads, "Clocking Out," *Wall Street Journal*, 8 August 2002, A1, A6.

38. Joanne Cole, "De-Stressing the Workplace," *HR Focus*, October 1999, 1, 10.

39. Diane Brady, "Rethinking the Rat Race," *Business Week*, 26 August 2002, 142; Jennifer Bresnehan, "The Elusive Muse," *CIO Enterprise*, 15 October 1997, 52; Kerry A. Dolan, "When Money Isn't Enough," *Forbes*, 18 November 1996, 164–170.

40. Mahlon Apgar IV, "The Alternative Workplace: Changing Where and How People Work," *Harvard Business Review*, May–June 1998, 121–136.

41. Sarah Fister Gale, "Formalizing Flextime: The Perk That Brings Productivity," *Workforce*, February 2001, 38–42.

42. Charlene Marmer Solomon, "Flexibility Comes Out of Flux," *Personnel Journal*, June 1996, 3840.

43. John Fetto, "You Can Take It with You," *American Demographics*, February 2002, 10–11.

44. Sue Shellenbarger, "Telework Is on the Rise, But It Isn't Just Done from Home Anymore," *Wall Street Journal*, 23 January 2002, B1.

45. Apgar, "The Alternative Workplace."

46. Carol Leonetti Dannhauser, "Who's in the Home Office?," *American Demographics*, June 1999, 50–56.

47. "Time to Take Another Look at Telecommuting," *HR Focus*, May 2002, 6–8.

48. Kemba J. Dunham, "Telecommuters' Lament," *Wall Street Journal*, 31 October 2000, B1, B8.

49. Lisa Chadderdon, "Merrill Lynch Works—At Home," *Fast Company*, April–May 1998, 70–72.

50. Shari Caudron, "Workers' Ideas for Improving Alternative Work Situations," *Work Force*, December 1998, 42–46.

51. Caudron, "Workers' Ideas for Improving Alternative Work Situations."

52. Martha Irvine, "Organizing Twentysomethings," *Los Angeles Times*, 7 September 1997, D5.

53. Thomas A. Kochan and Harry C. Katz, *Collective Bargaining and Industrial Relations* (Homewood, Ill.: Irwin, 1988), 173.

54. Linda Grant, "How UPS Blew It," *Fortune*, 29 September 1997, 29–30; Rick Brooks, "UPS and Teamsters Ready Themselves for Contract Brawl," *Wall Street Journal*, 28 January 2002, A2, A8; Rick Brooks, "UPS Customer Fearing Strike Contribute to Declining Volume," *Wall Street Journal*, 11 July 2002, B2.

55. *World Almanac and Book of Facts* (New York: Scripps Howard, 1989), 161.

56. Susan Carey, "United Grapples with Summer of Widespread Discontent," *Wall Street Journal*, 8 August 2000, A2; Laurence Zuckerman and Matthew L. Wald, "Crisis for Air Traffic System: More Passengers, More Delays," *New York Times*, 5 September 2000, A1, C12.

57. Stephanie Overman, "Unions: New Activism or Old Adversarial Approach?," *HR Focus*, May 1999, 7–8; Laurence

Zuckerman, "Pilots Lose a Battle, Not the War," *New York Times*, 17 April 1999, B1, B14.

58. Eugene H. Methvin, "The Union Label: With the Level of Union Violence on the Rise, Congress Must, Again, Deal with the Courts," *National Review*, 29 September 1997, 47; Anya Sacharow, "Walking the Line in Detroit," *Newspapers*, 22 July 1996, 8–13.

59. Nancy Cleeland, Joseph Menn, and Ronald D. White, "Lockout at West Coast Ports Racking Up Billions in Losses," *Chicago Tribune*, 1 October 2002, sec. 1, pp. 1, 8; Karen Brandon, "Bush Invokes Taft Hartley Act, Saying Crisis Is Harming the U.S.," *Chicago Tribune*, 9 October 2002, sec 1, 1, 18; Steven Greenhouse, "Ports, Workers Make a Deal," *Milwaukee Journal Sentinel*, 25 November 2002, 1D; Steven Greenhouse, "Longshoremen Accused of Slowdown in West," *New York Times*, 24 October 2002, A24.

60. David Field, "Airline Chief Has Become Key Figure in Labor Dispute," *USA Today*, 6 March 1997, B1, B2; Donna Rosato, "American Airlines Pilots Ask to Extend Deadline for Talks," *USA Today*, 18 March 1997, 2B; David Field, "Clinton Unlikely to Act Unless Both Sides Ask," *USA Today*, 10 February 1997, 2A.

61. Nancy Cleeland, "Union Membership Steady in 2001 at 13.5% of Nation's Workforce," *Los Angeles Times*, 18 January 2002, C3; Steven Greenhouse, "Unions Hit Lowest Point in 6 Decades," *New York Times*, 21 January 2001, 1, 20.

62. International Labour Organization, *World Labour Report*, 4 November 1997 [accessed 7 November 1997] www.ilo.org.

63. Lloyd G. Reynolds, Stanley H. Masters, and Colletta H. Moser, *Labor Economics and Labor Relations*, 11th ed. (Upper Saddle River, N.J.: Prentice Hall, 1998), 497; Indiana University News Bureau, "Trends in U.S. Labor Movement," *Futurist*, January–February 1996, 44.

64. Wendy Zellner, "How Wal-Mart Keeps Unions at Bay," *Business Week*, 28 October 2002, 94–96.

65. Zellner, "How Wal-Mart Keeps Unions at Bay."

66. Adapted from Carol Vinzant, "They Want You Back," *Fortune*, 2 October 2000, 271–272; Stephanie Armour, "Companies Recruiting Former Employees," *USA Today*, 2 February 2000, B1.

Chapter 11

1. Megan Rowe, "Jamba Juice," *Restaurant Business*, 1 July 2001, 42; Janet Moore, "Juicy Prospects," *Star Tribune*, 17 August 2001, 1D; "Here's How Jamba Juice Unsnagged a New Incentive Plan," *IOMA's Report on Managing Customer Service*, April 2001, 6–7; Brenda Paik Sunoo, "Blending a Successful Workforce," *Workforce*, March 2000, 44–48; Karyn Strauss, "Perron: Jamba's Juiced for Growth, Plans IPO," *Nation's Restaurant News*, 24 January 2000, 1, 76; Karyn Strauss, "Report: Smoothie Indies Face Rocky Road as Chains Slurp Up Market Share," *Nation's Restaurant News*, 14 June 1999, 8, 138; "Best Healthy Choice Menu Selection: Jamba Juice: Jambola Bread Is on the Rise," *Nation's Restaurant News*, 24 March 1999, 168; Michael Adams, "Kirk Perron: Jamba Juice," *Restaurant Business*, 15 March 1999, 38; Victor Wishna, "Leaving for Good," *Restaurant Business*, 1 May 2000, 64–74.

2. Sally B. Donnelly, "One Airline's Magic," *Time*, 28 October 2002, 45–47; George Donnelly, "Recruiting, Retention, and Returns," *CFO Magazine*, March 2000 [accessed 10 April 2000] www.cfonet.com/html/Articles/CFO/2000/00MArecr.html.

3. Stephanie Armour, "While Hiring at Most Firms Chills, Wal-Mart's Heats Up," *USA Today*, 26 August 2002, 3B.

4. Joanne Cole, "Permatemps Pose New Challenges for HR," *HR Focus*, December 1999, 7–8; Sharon R. Cohany, "Workers in Alternative Employment Arrangements: A Second Look," *Monthly Labor Review*, November 1998, 3–21.

5. Steven Greenhouse, "Equal Work, Less-Equal Perks," *New York Times*, 30 March 1998, C1, C6; Aaron Bernstein, "When Is a Temp Not a Temp?," *Business Week*, 7 December 1998, 90–92.

6. Stephanie Armour, "Some Companies Choose No-Layoff Policy," *USA Today*, 17 December 2001, 1B.

7. Stephanie Armour, "Worker Background Checks Raise Privacy Concerns," *USA Today*, 21 May 2002.

8. Jennifer Merritt, "Improv at the Interview," *Business Week*, 3 February 2003, 63.

9. Jonathan Segal, "When Norman Bates and Baby Jane Act Out at Work," *HR Magazine* 41, 1 February 1996, 31; Jenny C. McCune, "Companies Grapple with Workplace Violence," *Management Review*, March 1994, 52–57.

10. Stephanie Armour, "Security Checks Worry Workers," *USA Today*, 19 June 2002, 1B.

11. Lisa Frederiksen Bohannon, "Employment Testing—Be Prepared," *Career World*, January 2001, 12–14.

12. Bohannon, "Employment Testing—Be Prepared."

13. William F. Current, "Screening for Safety," *Occupational Health & Safety*, August 2001, 24–26.

14. Stephanie Armour, "Accused Workers Challenge Drug-Test Results in Court," *USA Today*, 16 July 2001, B1.

15. Bohannon, "Employment Testing—Be Prepared."

16. Armour, "Accused Workers Challenge Drug-Test Results in Court."

17. Katharine Mieszkowski, "Report from the Future," *Fast Company*, February–March 1998, 28–30.

18. Tonia L. Shakespeare, "High-Tech Training, Wal-Mart Style," *Black Enterprise*, July 1996, 54.

19. Michael Barrier, "Develop Workers and Your Business," *Nation's Business*, December 1998, 25–27.

20. Kevin Dobbs, "Tires Plus Takes the Training High Road," *Training*, April 2000, 56–63.

21. Adolph Haasen and Gordon F. Shea, *A Better Place to Work* (New York: American Management Association, 1997), 19–20.

22. Randall G. Kesselring and Jeffrey R. Pittman, "Drug Testing Laws and Employment Injuries," *Journal of Labor Research*, Spring 2002, 293–301.

23. Bill Roberts, "://Training Via the Desktop://" *HR Magazine*, August 1998, 98–104.

24. Kate Ludeman, "How to Conduct Self-Directed 360," *Training and Development*, July 2000, 44–47; Cassandra Hayes, "To Tell the Truth," *Black Enterprise*, December 1998, 55.

25. Gina Imperato, "How to Give Good Feedback," *Fast Company*, September 1998, 144–156.

26. Christopher Caggiano, "The Right Way to Pay," *Inc.*, November 2002, 84–92.

27. Susan J. Marks, "Incentives That Really Reward and Motivate," *Workforce*, June 2001, 108–114.

28. Jeff Kersten, "Gain Sharing in College Station," *PM: Public Management*, May 1998, 19.

29. Janet Wiscombe, "Can Pay for Performance Really Work?," *Workforce*, August 2001, 28–34.

30. Bobette M. Gustafson, "Skill-Based Pay Improves PFS Staff Recruitment, Retention, and Performance," *Healthcare Financial Management*, January 2000, 62–63; Rosalie Webster, "Both Sides of the Coin," *New Zealand Management*, November 1998, 122; Genevieve Capowski, "HR View Online," *HR Focus*, June 1998, 2.

31. Fiona Jebb, "Flex Appeal," *Management Today* (London), July 1998, 66–69; Milton Zall, "Implementing a Flexible Benefits Plan," *Fleet Equipment*, May 1999, B4–B8.

32. "Employees Prefer Finding Their Own Health Care Coverage," *Employee Benefit Plan Review*, March 2000, 49.

33. Michelle Conlin, "Going Sideways on the Corporate Ladder," *Business Week*, 30 September 2002, 39; Julie Appleby, "Workers

Pay More for Insurance Costs, Doctor Visits," *USA Today*, 6 September 2002, 1B.

34. Richard D. Pearce, "The Small Employer Retirement Plan Void," *Compensation and Benefits Management*, Winter 1999, 51–55.

35. James H. Dulebohn, Brian Murray, and Minghe Sun, "Selection Among Employer-Sponsored Pension Plans: The Role of Individual Differences," *Personnel Psychology*, Summer 2000, 405–432.

36. George Van Dyke, "Examining Your 401(k)," *Business Credit*, January 2000, 59.

37. Paul J. Lim and Matthew Benjamin, "The 401(k) Stumbles," *U.S. News & World Report*, 24 December 2001, 30–32.

38. Rebecca Buckman and David Bank, "For Silicon Valley, Stocks' Fall Upsets Culture of Options," *Wall Street Journal*, 18 July 2002, A1, A6.

39. Fay Hansen, "Few Workers Invoke U.S. Family-Leave Law," *Christian Science Monitor*, 26 August 2002, 16.

40. Stephanie Armour, "Ford Plans Ambitious Child-Care Program for Workers," *USA Today*, 22 November 2000, B1.

41. "Workplace Briefs," *Gannett News Service*, 24 April 1997; Julia Lawlor, "The Bottom Line," *Working Woman*, July–August 1996, 54–58, 74–76.

42. Stephanie Armour, "Employers Stepping Up in Elder Care," *USA Today*, 3 August 2000, 3B.

43. William Atkinson, "Wellness, Employee Assistance Programs: Investments, Not Costs," *Bobbin*, May 2000, 42–48.

44. Atkinson, "Wellness, Employee Assistance Programs."

45. Atkinson, "Wellness, Employee Assistance Programs."

46. "50 Benefits and Perks That Make Employees Want to Stay Forever," *HR Focus*, July 2000, S2–S3.

47. Edward Iwata, "Staff-Hungry Tech Firms Cast Exotic Lures," *USA Today*, 1 February 2000, B1.

48. Adam Cohen and Cathy Booth Thomas, "Inside a Layoff," *Time*, 16 April 2001, 38–40.

49. Gillian Flynn, "Why Rhino Won't Wait Until Tomorrow," *Personnel Journal*, July 1996, 36–39.

Chapter 12

1. Jane Eisinger, "Capitalizing on Corporate Success," *Association Management*, February 2000, 47–49; Mike McNamee, "Isn't There More to Life Than Plastic?," *Business Week*, 22 November 1999, 173–176; Charles Fishman, "This Is a Marketing Revolution," *Fast Company*, May 1999, 204–218; Leslie Goff, "Surviving the Data Minefield," *Computerworld*, 24 August 1998, 49–50.

2. "AMA Board Approves New Marketing Definition," *Marketing News*, 1 March 1985, 1.

3. "Delta Air Lines: Delta's Sky Wish Program Partners with Share Our Strength Sky Miles," *M2-Presswire*, 9 October 2002, 1; Matthew Grimm, "Earthy Crunch," *American Demographics*, June 2002, 46.

4. Al Ries and Jack Trout, *The 22 Immutable Laws of Marketing* (New York: HarperCollins, 1994), 19–25.

5. Terry G. Vavra, "The Database Marketing Imperative," *Marketing Management*, 2, no. 1 (1993): 47–57.

6. Mark Gottlieb, "Just Tell Me What You Want," *Industry Week*, 19 March 2001, 43–45.

7. Julia Boorstin, "How Coach Got Hot," *Fortune*, 28 October 2002, 131–134.

8. Barbara Whitaker, "House Hunting with Cursor and Click," *New York Times*, 24 September 1998, D1, D5.

9. Pierre M. Loewe and Mark S. Bonchek, "The Retail Revolution," *Management Review*, April 1999, 38–44.

10. Janet Willen, "The Customer Is Wrong," *Business 97*, October–November 1997, 40–42; William H. Davidow and Bro

Uttal, *Total Customer Service: The Ultimate Weapon* (New York: Harper & Row, 1989), 8; Valarie A. Zeithaml, A. Parasuraman, and Leonard L. Berry, *Delivering Quality Service* (New York: Free Press, 1990), 9; George J. Castellese, "Customer Service . . . Building a Winning Team," *Supervision*, January 1995, 9–13; Erica G. Sorohan and Catherine M. Petrini, "Dumpsters, Ducks, and Customer Service," *Training and Development*, January 1995, 9.

11. Peter Burrows, "HP: No Longer Lost in Cyberspace?," *Business Week*, 31 May 1999, 124, 126.

12. Avery Comarow, "Broken? No Problem," *U.S. News & World Report*, 11 January 1999, 68–69.

13. Ronald B. Lieber, "Storytelling: A New Way to Get Close to Your Customer," *Fortune*, 3 February 1997, 102–110.

14. Scott Woolley, "Get Lost, Buster," *Forbes*, 23 February 1998, 90; Jon Van, "$5 Question: When Does Not Calling Not Add Up?," *Chicago Tribune*, 8 April 1999, sec. 1, 1, 14.

15. Martin Kaufmann, "A Service Culture Permeates Galyan's," *Sporting Goods Business*, February 2002, 31.

16. Bruce Horwowitz, "Shop, You're On Candid Camera," *USA Today*, 6 November 2002, B1.

17. Joshua Macht, "The New Market Research," *Inc.*, July 1998, 87–94.

18. Mary J. Cronin, *Doing More Business on the Internet* (New York: Van Nostrand Reinhold, 1995), 13.

19. Eryn Brown, Mary J. Cronin, Ann Harrington, and Jane Hodges, "9 Ways to Win on the Web," Fortune, 24 May 1999, 112–125.

20. Louisa Wah, "The Almighty Customer," *Management Review*, February 1999, 16–22.

21. Thomas A. Stewart, "A Satisfied Customer Isn't Enough," *Fortune*, 21 July 1997, 112–113.

22. Oren Harari, "Six Myths of Market Research," *Management Review*, April 1994, 48–51.

23. Robert Passikoff, "Loyal Opposition—The Limits of Customer Satisfaction," *Brandweek*, 3 March 1997, 17.

24. Pamela G. Hollies, "What's New in Market Research," *New York Times*, 15 June 1986, sec. 3, 19; Phyllis M. Thornton, "Linking Market Research to Strategic Planning," *Nursing Homes*, January–February 1995, 34–37; Harari, "Six Myths of Market Research."

25. John R. Boatright, *Ethics and the Conduct of Business*, 4th ed. (Upper Saddle River, N.J.: Prentice Hall, 2003), 160–161.

26. Janet Novack, "The Data Miners," *Forbes*, 12 February 1996, 96–97; Don Peppers and Martha Rogers, *Enterprise One to One* (New York: Doubleday, 1997), 120–121.

27. Louisa Wah, "The Almighty Customer," *Management Review*, February 1999, 16–22; James Lardner, "Your Every Command," *U.S. News & World Report*, 5 July 1999, 44–46.

28. Charles Fishman, "This Is a Marketing Revolution," *Fast Company*, May 1999, 206–218.

29. Diane Brady, "Why Service Stinks," *Business Week*, 23 October 2000, 118–128.

30. Pallavi Gogoi and Michael Arndt, "Hamburger Hell," *Business Week*, 3 March 2003, 104–108.

31. Leslie Kaufman, "Playing Catch-Up at the On-Line Mall," *New York Times*, 21 February 1999, sec. 3, 1, 6; Gary Samuels, "CD-ROMs First Big Victim," *Forbes*, 28 February 1994, 42–44; Richard A. Melcher, "Dusting Off the Britannica," *Business Week*, 20 October 1997, 143–146.

32. Alex Taylor III, "How to Murder the Competition," *Fortune*, 22 February 1993, 87, 90.

33. Scott Hays, "Exceptional Customer Service Takes the 'Ritz' Touch," *Workforce*, January 1999, 99–102.

34. Jennifer Barron and Jill Hollingshead, "Making Segmentation Work," *MM*, January–February 2002, 24–28.

35. Michael J. Weiss, *The Clustering of America* (New York: Harper & Row, 1988), 41.

36. Horacio D. Rozanski, Gerry Bollman, and Martin Lipman, "Seize the Occasion," *Strategy and Business*, Third Quarter 2001, 42–51.

37. Daniel Roth, "First: From Poster Boy to Whipping Boy," *Fortune*, 6 July 1998, 28–29.

38. Gary Armstrong and Philip Kotler, *Marketing: An Introduction*, 5th ed. (Upper Saddle River, N.J.: Prentice Hall, 2000), 201–204.

39. Armstrong and Kotler, *Marketing: An Introduction*, 206.

40. Adapted from Julian E. Barnes, "Fast-Food Giveaway Toys Face Rising Recalls," *New York Times*, 16 August 2001, A1; Shirley Leung, "Burger King Recalls 2.6 Million Kids Meal Toys," *Wall Street Journal*, 1 August 2001, B2.

Chapter 13

1. David Lipschultz, "When Facial Wrinkles Are Ironed Away For Good," *New York Times*, 11 February 2003, D6; Brian O'Reilly, "Facelift in a Bottle," *Fortune*, 24 June 2002, 101–104; Ronald D. White, "Allergan Bets on Botox Lift," *Los Angeles Times*, 23 May 2002, C1; Michael McCarthy, "Botox Maker Plans $50 Million Ad Campaign," *USA Today*, 29 April 2002, B1; Reed Abelson, "FDA Approves Allergan Drug for Fighting Wrinkles," *New York Times*, 16 April 2002, C4.

2. "Preparing for a Point-to-Point World," *Marketing Management* 3, no. 4 (Spring 1995): 30–40.

3. Jeffrey Krasner, "Bank One Completes Polaroid Deal," *Boston Globe*, 1 August 2002, C1.

4. Pete Engardio and Faith Keenan, "The Copycat Economy," *Business Week*, 26 August 2002, 94–96.

5. Al Ries and Jack Trout, "Focused in a Fuzzy World," *Rethinking the Future* (London: Nicholas Brealey, 1997), 183.

6. Bruce Horovitz, "Cookie Makers Bake Up New Twists," *USA Today*, 27 March 2001, 3B.

7. Michael McCarthy, "Brands That Lose Their Punch Get Yanked," *USA Today*, 13 December 2000, 3B.

8. "New Product Winners—And Losers," *In Business*, April 1985, 64.

9. Yumiko Ono, "Kraft Searches Its Cupboard for Old Brands to Remake," *Wall Street Journal*, 12 March 1996, B1, B4.

10. Scott Bedbury, "Nine Ways to Fix a Broken Brand," *Fast Company*, February 2002, 72–77; Gap Website [accessed 17 January 2003] www.gap.com.

11. Don Baker Post, "Reviving a Classic: Today's Old Spice Isn't Just for the Old Guys," *Cincinnati Post*, 21 August 2002, 7C.

12. Rogier Van Bakel, "The Art of Brand Revival," *Business 2.0*, September 2002, 45–48.

13. Tim Stevens, "Lights, Camera, Innovation," *Industry Week*, 19 July 1999, 32–38.

14. Tom Peters, "We Hold These Truths to Be Self-Evident," *Organizational Dynamics*, 1 June 1996, 27–32.

15. Douglas McGray, "Babes in R&D Toyland," *Fast Company*, December 2002, 46.

16. Constance L. Hays, "No More Brand X," *New York Times*, 12 June 1998, C1, C4.

17. Kelly Barron, "The Cappuccino Conundrum," *Forbes*, 22 February 1999, 54–55.

18. Janell M. Kurtz and Cynthia Mehoves, "Whose Name Is It Anyway," *Marketing Management*, January–February 2002, 31–33.

19. Jagdish N. Sheth and Rajendra S. Sisodia, "Feeling the Heat," *Marketing Management* 4, no. 2 (Fall 1995): 9–23.

20. Claudia H. Deutsch, "Will That Be Paper or Pixel?," *New York Times*, 4 August 2000, C1, C4.

21. Laura Clark Geist, "Licensing Links Brands, People with Goods," *Automotive News*, 16 September 2002, 2M.

22. Roy Evans, "The Year in Ideas: Cup-Holder Cuisine," *New York Times Magazine*, 15 December 2002, 6, 80.

23. Scott Leith, "CCE Puts 'Fridge Pack' on Store Shelves Today," *Atlanta Journal*, 1 May 2002, D1.

24. Jack Neff, "P & G Shores Up Old Spice with Body-Wash Extension," *Advertising Age*, 30 December 2002, 8.

25. Gary Strauss, "Squeezing New from Old," *USA Today*, 4 January 2001, 1B–2B.

26. Melanie Wells, "Red Baron," *Forbes*, 3 July 2000, 151–160.

27. Bruck Horovitz, "Would You Like Fries with That Cappuccino?," *USA Today*, 22 September 2000, 1A.

28. Paulo Prado and Bruce Orwall, "A Certain 'Je Ne Sais Quoi' at Disney's New Park," *Wall Street Journal*, 12 March 2002, B1, B4.

29. Tim O'Brien, "Disneyland Paris Caters to European Tastes, Lowers Costs and Refines Service," *Amusement Business*, 5 May 1997, 18; "Disneyland Paris: How Beauty Became a Beast," *Reputation Management*, March–April 1995, 35–37.

30. Brian O'Keefe, "Global Brands," *Fortune*, 26 November 2001, 102–110.

31. Carol Matlack, "What's This? The French Love McDonald's?," *Business Week*, 13 January 2003, 50; Shirley Leung, "Armchairs, TVs and Espresso—Is It McDonald's?," *Wall Street Journal*, 30 August 2002, A1, A6.

32. Dean Takahashi, "Intel Steps Up Use of Price Cuts to Protect Its Turf and to Expand," *Wall Street Journal*, 9 June 1998, B6.

33. Terril Yue Jones, "Fearing the Old Shoddy Image," *Forbes*, 12 January 1998 [accessed 16 June 1999], www.forbes.com/forbes/98/0112/6101064a.htm.

34. Lisa Margonelli, "How Ikea Designs Its Sexy Price Tags," *Business 2.0*, October 2002, 106–112.

35. Amy Cortese, "The Power of Optimal Pricing," *Business 2.0*, September 2002, 68–70.

36. Bruce Horovitz, "Burger Wars Heat Up As Consumers Devour Value," *USA Today*, 11 November 2002, 4B.

37. Edwin McDowell, "Winging It with Internet Fares," *New York Times*, 7 March 1999, sec. 3, 1, 10.

38. Joanne Lipman, "Do Toll Phone Services Play Fair by Advertising Directly to Kids?," *Wall Street Journal*, 7 July 1989, B1.

Chapter 14

1. Suzanne Wooley, "Costco? More Like Costgrow," *Money*, August 2002, 44–46; J. Martin McOmber, *Seattle Times*, 17 July 2002, E1; "Costco: A Cut Above," *Retail Merchandiser*, July 2002, 44; Pete Hisey, "Costco.com Means Business," *Retail Merchandiser*, October 2001, 36; Shelly Branch, "Inside the Cult of Costco," *Fortune*, 6 September 1999, 184–188.

2. Marcia Stepanek, "Closed, Gone to the Net," *Business Week*, 7 June 1999, 113–114.

3. David Wessel, "Airlines' Orbitz: Consumers' Friend or Foe?," *Wall Street Journal*, 29 August 2002, A2.

4. Julia Angwin and Motoko Rich, "Inn Fighting," *Wall Street Journal*, 14 March 2003, A1, A7; Rob Lieber, "How to Get a Four-Star Hotel at Two-Star Prices," *Wall Street Journal*, 30 January 2003, D1, D5.

5. Wal-Mart home page [accessed 26 January 2003], www.walmart.com; Mike Troy, "Wal-Mart Supercenters: The Combo with the Midas Touch," *DSN Retailing Today*, 8 May 2000, 113–114; Wendy Zellner, "Look Out, Supermarkets—Wal-Mart Is Hungry," *Business Week*, 14 September 1998, 98, 100.

6. Daniel McGinn, "Honey, I Shrunk the Store," *Newsweek*, 3 June 2002, 36–37.

7. Bruce Horovitz, "Trend Shrinks Store Sizes to Save Money, Satisfy Customers," *USA Today*, 9 August 1999, B1.

8. Sherri Day, "Tupperware to Sell Products in SuperTarget Store," *New York Times*, 18 July 2001, C1; Katarzyna Moreno,

"UnbeComing," *Forbes*, 10 June 2002, 151–152; Nanette Byrnes, "Avon, The New Calling," *Business Week*, 18 September 2000, 136–140.

9. Jason Anders, "Yesterday's Darling," *Wall Street Journal*, 23 October 2000, R8.

10. Daniel S. Janal, "Net Profit Now," *Success*, July–August 1997, 57–63.

11. "Toyota Takes Aim at Young Buyers," *Grand Rapids Press*, 3 June 2002, A7.

12. Gary McWilliams and Ann Zimmerman, "Dell Plans to Peddle PCs Inside Sears, Other Large Chains," *Wall Street Journal*, 30 January 2003, B1, B3.

13. Dean Starkman, "As Malls Multiply, Developers Fight Fiercely for Turf," *Wall Street Journal*, 19 April 2002, A1, A6.

14. Robert Berner and Gerry Khermouch, "Retail Reckoning," *Business Week*, 10 December 2001, 72–77.

15. Michelle Pacelle, "The Aging Shopping Mall Must Either Adapt or Die," *Wall Street Journal*, 16 April 1996, B1, B14.

16. Ginia Bellafante, "That's Retail-tainment!" *Time*, 7 December 1998, 64–65.

17. "Tommy Hilfiger to Shut Most U.S. Stores," *Los Angeles Times*, 31 October 2002, C12.

18. Maryanne Murray Buechner, "Recharging Sears," *Time*, 27 May 2002, 46.

19. Kaplan, "Retailers Taking New Approach to Internet," *Knight Ridder Tribune News Service*, 11 June 2002, 1.

20. Maryanne Murray Buechner, "Attention Online Shoppers," *Time*, 28 January 2002, B12+.

21. Ann Grimes, "E-Commerce (A Special Report): Cover Story—What's in Store: Retailers Are Bringing the Clicks to the Bricks," *Wall Street Journal*, 15 July 2002, R6.

22. Gregory L. White, "GM Is Forming Unit to Buy Dealerships," *Wall Street Journal*, 24 September 1999, A3; Joann Muller, "Meet Your Local GM Dealer: GM," *Business Week*, 11 October 1999, 48.

23. Philip Kotler and Gary Armstrong, *Principles of Marketing*, 9th ed. (Upper Saddle River, N.J.: Prentice Hall, 2001), 435.

24. "Hallmark, a New Name in Mass Retailing," *Supermarket Business*, March 1997, 84; Daniel Roth, "Card Sharks," *Forbes*, 7 October 1996, 14; Julie Rygh, "Hallmark Cards Find Success with New Expressions Brand," *Knight-Ridder/Tribune Business News*, 31 August 1997, 831B0958.

25. Michael S. Katz and Jeffrey Rothfeder, "Crossing the Digital Divide," *Strategy & Business*, First Quarter 2000, 26–41; Anne Stuart, "Clicks & Bricks," *CIO*, 15 March 2000, 76–84.

26. Bob Brewin and Linda Rosencrance, "Follow That Package," *Computerworld*, 19 March 2001, 58–60; Colleen Gourley, "Retail Logistics in Cyberspace," *Distribution*, December 1996, 29; Dave Hirschman, "FedEx Starts Up Package Sorting System at Memphis Tenn. Airport," *Knight-Ridder/Tribune Business News*, 28 September 1997, 928B0953; "FedEx and Technology—Maintaining a Competitive Edge," *PressWIRE*, 2 December 1996.

27. Bill Gates, *Business @ the Speed of Thought* (New York: Warner Books, 1999), 76; Elizabeth Weise, "Sizing Up Web Shoppers for the Perfect Fit," *USA Today*, 21 April 1999, 4D.

28. Paul Dean, "Auto Makers Shift into New Gear," *Los Angeles Times*, 15 January 1997, E1, E6.

29. Bill Dedman, "Holiday Vigil for FedEx Customers," *New York Times*, 8 November 1998, sec. 3, 4.

Chapter 15

1. Floorgraphics website [accessed 2 February 2003] www. floorgraphics.com; Jack Neff, "Floors in Stores Start Moving," *Advertising Age*, 20 August 2001, 15; John Grossman, "Upstarts: Nontraditional Ads," *Inc.*, March 2000, 23–26; David Wellman,

"Floor 'Toons," *Supermarket Business*, 15 November 1999, 47; Skip Wollenberg, "Advertising Finds New Canvasses," *Boulder News*, 1 June 1999 [accessed 8 April 2000] http://community.bouldernews. com/business/01bads. html; "Floor Show," *Dallas Morning News*, 4 September 1998, 11D.

2. Michele Marchetti, "What a Sales Call Costs," *Sales and Marketing Management*, September 2000, 80–82.

3. Direct Marketing Association website [accessed 12 February 2003] www.the-dma.org/index.shtml.

4. Gary Armstrong and Philip Kotler, *Marketing: An Introduction* (Upper Saddle River, N.J.: Prentice Hall, 2000), 409.

5. Mark Maremont, "How Gillette Brought Its Mach3 to Market," *Wall Street Journal*, 15 April 1998, B1, B4; Jeremy Kahn, "Gillette Loses Face," *Fortune*, 8 November 1999, 147–148.

6. Ann Harrington, "A Brand Built to Last," *FSB*, July–August 2001, 88–91.

7. David J. Morrow, "From Lab to Patient, by Way of Your Den," *New York Times*, 7 June 1998, sec. 3, 1, 10.

8. Vicki Kemper, "Over-the-Counter Sale of Allergy Drug Approved," *Los Angeles Times*, 28 November 2002, A1; David Goetzl and Jack Neff, "OTC Claritin Given $40 Million Backing," *Advertising Age*, 18 November 2002, 3, 52.

9. David Prater, "The Third Time's the Charm," *Sales and Marketing Management*, September 2000, 100–104; Armstrong and Kotler, *Marketing: An Introduction*, 454.

10. "Rethinking the Sales Force," *Soundview Executive Book Summaries*, pt. 3, vol. 21, no. 7 (July 1999): 1–8.

11. Dennis K. Berman, "From Cell Phones to Sell Phones," *Business Week*, 11 September 2000, 88–90.

12. Chris Adams, "FDA Tells Glaxo to Halt Airing Flu Commercial," *Wall Street Journal*, 14 January 2000, B3.

13. Berman, "From Cell Phones to Sell Phones," 88–90.

14. Paul Lukas, "Jiffy's Secret Recipe," *FSB*, December 2001–January 2002, 56–60.

15. Scott Kirsner, "Can TiVo Go Prime Time?," *Fast Company*, August 2002, 82–88.

16. Daniel Eisenberg, "It's An Ad, Ad, Ad, Ad World," *Time*, 2 September 2002, 36–41.

17. Michael McCarthy, "Ads Show up in Unexpected Places," *USA Today*, 23 March 2001, 1B.

18. Pamela Paul, "Coming Soon: More Ads Tailored to Your Tastes," *American Demographics*, August 2001, 28–31.

19. Richard Sandomir, "Tiger Woods Signs Pact with American Express," *New York Times*, 20 May 1997, C1.

20. Sonia Alleyne, "The Celebrity Sell," *Black Enterprise*, September 2002, 74–81.

21. Richard J. Newman, "SUV to the Stars," *U.S. News & World Report*, 14 October 2002, 44.

22. "Direct Hit," *The Economist*, 9 January 1999, 55–57.

23. Chana R. Schoenberger, "Web? What Web?," *Forbes*, 10 June 2002, 132.

24. Schoenberger, "Web? What Web?"

25. Sarah Lorge, "Banner Ads vs. E-Mail Marketing," *Sales and Marketing Management*, August 1999, 15.

26. Christine Blank, "Beating the Banner Ad," *American Demographics*, June 2000, 42–44.

27. Tim Mack, "The Growth of Electronic Marketing," *USA Today*, March 2002, 22–24.

28. Efraim Turban, Jae Lee, David King, and H. Michael Chung, *Electric Commerce: A Managerial Perspective* (Upper Saddle River, N.J.: Prentice Hall, 2000), 120.

29. Mack, "The Growth of Electronic Marketing;" Rebecca Quick, "E-Tailers Say, 'Bah, Humbug!' to Lavish Ads," *Wall Street Journal*, 22 September 2000, B1, B4.

30. Mack, "The Growth of Electronic Marketing."

31. Yochi J. Dreazen and Jane Spencer, "Curbing Telemarketers: FTC Moves to Defend Your Dinner Hour," *Wall Street Journal*, 19 December 2002, D1.

32. "Do-Not-Call List Becomes Law," *Wall Street Journal*, 12 March 2003; Dreazen and Spencer, "Curbing Telemarketers: FTC Moves to Defend Your Dinner Hour."

33. Dreazen and Spencer, "Curbing Telemarketers: FTC Moves to Defend Your Dinner Hour."

34. Nadya Labi, "Tae-Bo or Not Tae-Bo?," *Time*, 15 March 1999, 77.

35. Walter Nichols, "Infomercials! What Makes People Order an Inside-the-Shell Electric Egg Scrambler at 3 in the Morning," *Washington Post*, 21 February 2001, F1.

36. Armstrong and Kotler, *Marketing: An Introduction*, 409.

37. Geoffrey A. Fowler, "Marketing: Click and Clip—Online Coupon Campaigns Can Be Cost-Efficient and Effective," *Wall Street Journal*, 21 October 2002.

38. William M. Bulkeley, "Rebates' Secret Appeal to Manufacturers: Few Customers Actually Redeem Them," *Wall Street Journal*, 10 February 1998, B1, B8.

39. David Botsford, "Getting the Retail Support You Want," *Brandweek*, 3 June 2002, 19.

40. "Effective Sampling Strategies," *Sales Marketing Network* [accessed 7 November 2000] www.info-now.com/html/1022dir1.asp.

41. Grace Shim, "Sponsorship of the Rings," *Omaha World-Herald*, 7 February 2002, 1D.

42. "Air New Zealand Links Up with the Lord of the Rings," *Marketing*, 9 January 2003, 5.

43. Pamela Sherrid, "Fewer Doc Freebies," *U.S. News & World Report*, 17 June 2002, 46.

44. "United Airlines to Send Out Mailing As Reassurance," *Marketing* (London), 12 December 2002, 3.

45. Kathryn Kranhold and Stephen Power, "Bridgestone Turns to Ketchum to Redo Image After Tire Recall," *Wall Street Journal*, 12 September 2000, A4.

46. Verne Gay, "Milk, the Magazine," *American Demographics*, February 2000, 32–33.

47. Wendy Zellner, "Southwest's New Direction," *Business Week*, 8 February 1999, 58–59; Jennifer Lawrence, "Integrated Mix Makes Expansion Fly," *Advertising Age—Special Integrated Marketing Report*, 4 November 1993, S10–S12.

48. Adapted from Quotesmith.com website, Investor Overview and FAQ [accessed 31 August 2000] http://investor.quotesmith.com/ireye/ir_site.zhtml?ticker=QUOT&script=2100.

Chapter 16

1. Adapted from Bill Snyder, "PeopleSoft Keeping the Hard Times at Bay," *TheStreet.com* [accessed 3 February 2003]; Jim Kerstetter and Jay Greene, "Software: Getting Its Groove Back," *Business Week*, 13 January 2003, 116; "The Top 25 Managers of the Year," *Business Week*, 14 January 2002, 69; Carleen Hawn, "Now, for My Next Trick," *Forbes*, 21 January, 2002, 90–92; Ian Mount, "Attention Underlings: That's Mister Conway to You. And I Am Not a PeoplePerson," *Business 2.0*, February 2002, 53–58; Elise Ackerman, "PeopleSoft to Buy Back Controversial Spinoff," *Knight Ridder Tribune Business News*, 25 January 2002, 1; Elise Ackerman, "Accounting Gimmick Puts Pleasanton, Calif.–Based PeopleSoft on the Spot," *Knight Ridder Tribune Business News*, 22 January 2002, 1; Jim Kerstetter, "PeopleSoft's Hard Guy," *Business Week*, 15 January 2001, 76–77.

2. Robert Stuart, "Accountants in Management—A Globally Changing Role," *CMA Magazine*, 1 February 1997, 5.

3. American Institute of Certified Public Accountants website [accessed 12 February 2003] www.aicpa.org.

4. Institute of Management Accountants website [accessed 12 February 2003] www.imanet.org.

5. Lynn J. Cook, "Next Time, Hire an Accountant," *Forbes*, 11 November 2002, 52; "National CPA Student Recruitment Campaign," *Journal of Accountancy*, September 2002, 72–73.

6. Steve Zwick, "The Price of Transparency," *Time*, 19 February 2001, B8–B11.

7. Francesco Guerrera and Andrew Parker, "Concern over New Rules and U.S. Companies," *Financial Times*, 9 October 2002, 9; Thomas Fuller, "EU to Press for Access to Wall Street," *International Herald Tribune*, 18 May 2002, 11; Jeffrey E. Garten, "Global Accounting Rules? Not So Fast," *Business Week*, 5 April 1999, 26.

8. Kelly Patricia O'Meara, "Feds Chasing Down Corporate Fraud," *Insight on the News*, 11 November 2002, 22–23.

9. James P. Miller, "Scandal Stuns Investors; Bush Promises Full Probe," *Chicago Tribune*, 27 June 2002, sec. 1, 1, 16; "WorldCom Files for Bankruptcy," *Wall Street Journal*, 22 July 2002, A3.

10. Matt Krantz and Gregg Farrell, "Fuzzy Accounting Raises Flags," *USA Today*, 22 June 2001, 1B.

11. Andy Serwer, "Dirty Rotten Numbers," *Fortune*, 18 February 2002, 74–84.

12. Mitchell Pacelle, "Former SEC Chairman Levitt Decries Business Ethics in U.S.," *Wall Street Journal*, 17 June 2002, C7.

13. "The Wrangling over Reform Is Far from Over," *Business Week*, October 21, 2002, 44; "Grapping with Sarbanes-Oxley," *Reactions*, March 2003, 58.

14. Joellen Perry, "The New Math of Mergers," *U.S. News & World Report*, 11 November 2002, 40.

15. Frank Evans, "A Road Map to Your Financial Report," *Management Review*, October 1993, 39–47.

Chapter 17

1. Shawn Tully, "The Jamie Dimon Show," *Fortune*, 22 July 2002, 88–96; Mark Tatge, "Rough-Cut Dimon," *Forbes*, 13 May 2002, 64–68; Joseph Weber and Margaret Popper, "Can Jamie Dimon Win at Cards?," *Business Week*, 23 April 2001, 94–95; Angela Key, "Dimon in the Rough," *Fortune*, 26 June 2000, 292; "Finance and Economics: Bank Not One," *Economist*, 1 April 2000, 69; Amy Kover, "Big Banks Debunked," *Fortune*, 21 February 2000, 187–194.

2. Tatge, "Rough-Cut Dimon."

3. Bruce Horovitz and Chris Woodyard, "Quaker Oats' $1.4 Billion Washout," *USA Today*, 28 March 1997.

4. Paul J. Lim, "Credit Squeeze," *U.S. News & World Report*, 17 June 2002, 38–39.

5. Kover, "Big Banks Debunked."

6. Charles Fishman, "What the Hell Do Smart Cards Do?," *Fast Company*, March 2002, 58.

7. Michelle Higgins, "ATMs to Go Far Beyond Cash," *Wall Street Journal*, 6 June 2002, D1.

8. Higgins, "ATMs to Go Far Beyond Cash."

9. Jerri Stroud, "Paperless Paydays Put Money in the Bank for Large Employers," *St. Louis Post*, 15 December 2002, G1.

10. Stroud, "Paperless Paydays Put Money in the Bank for Large Employers."

11. Jerri Stroud, "Customers Put Stamp of Approval on Paying Bills Online," *St. Louis Post-Dispatch*, 30 June 2002, E1.

12. Stroud, "Customers Put Stamp of Approval on Paying Bills Online."

13. "FDIC Statistics on Banking: Number of FDIC-Insured Commercial Banks, 1934 Through 1999," FDIC Databank [accessed 12 December 2000], www2.fdic.gov/hsob/ SelectRpt.asp?EntryTyp=10.

14. "Important Banking Legislation," FDIC [accessed 28 July 1999], www.fdic.gov/publish/banklaws.html; "Interstate Branching," The Federal Reserve Board [accessed 23 July 1999], www.bog.frb.fed.us/generalinfo/isb.

15. Stephan Labaton, "Accord Reached on Lifting Depression-Era Barriers Among Financial Industries," *New York Times*, 23 October 1999, A1, B4.

16. Stuart Elliott, "Merrill Campaign on Banking to Open," *New York Times*, 8 January 2003, 8.

17. Paul J. Lim, "Headed for Reality," *U.S. News & World Report*, 6 May 2002, 39.

18. Tatge, "Rough-Cut Dimon."

19. Emily Thornton, Peter Coy, and Heather Timmons, "The Breakdown in Banking," *Business Week*, 7 October 2002, 40–42. Thornton, Coy, and Timmons, "The Breakdown in Banking."

20. Kover, "Big Banks Debunked."

21. Tully, "The Jamie Dimon Show."

22. Walter Hamilton, "Wall Street in Separation Mode," *Los Angeles Times*, 27 September 2002, C3.

23. Thornton, Coy, and Timmons, "The Breakdown in Banking."

24. Paul Beckett and Jathon Sapsford, "Citigroup's Vast Reach Brings It Trouble from Many Quarters," *Wall Street Journal*, 26 July 2002, A1, A6.

25. Thor Valdmanis, "Citigroup Banks on Reform Plan," *USA Today*, 31 October 2002, 3B.

26. Derek Reveron, "Banks: Big vs. Small," *Hispanic Business*, October 2002, 36–38.

27. Bradley Meacham, "Online Banking Starts to Click," *Seattle Times*, 22 December 2002, F1.

28. "National Debt Keeps Building," *USA Today Snapshot*, 25 November 2002, B1.

29. Laura Cohn, "Are T-Bills Y2K Insurance?," *Business Week*, 26 July 1999, 34.

30. John M. Berry, "As Paper Checks Disappear, So May Some Fed Jobs," *Washington Post*, 31 December 2002, E1.

31. Adapted from Union Bank of California teleservices, personal communication, 16 August 2001.

Chapter 18

1. Adapted from Patrick McGeehan, "Charles Schwab to Give Up Title at Brokerage Firm," *New York Times*, 1 February 2003, C1; "Company News; Charles Schwab Reports a $79 Million Loss in Quarter," *New York Times*, 22 January 2003, C1; Walter Updegrave, "Is There a Better Way to Rate Stocks?," *Money*, September 2002, 93; Patrick McGeehan, "Seeing Long Trading Slump, Schwab Sets More Cutbacks," *New York Times*, 13 August 2002, C2; Erin E. Arvedlund, "Schwab Trades Up," *Barron's*, 27 May 2002, 19–20; Louise Lee and Emily Thornton, "Schwab vs. Wall Street," *Business Week*, 3 June 2002, 62–71; Louise Lee, "Will Investors Pay for Schwab's Advice?," *Business Week*, 21 January 2002, 36; Fred Vogelstein, "Can Schwab Get Its Mojo Back?," *Fortune*, 17 September 2001, 93–98; Susanne Craig, "Schwab Unveils a New Service, Chides Brokers," *Wall Street Journal*, 17 May 2002, C1, C13; Charles Gasparino and Ken Brown, "Discounted, Schwab's Own Stock Suffers from Move into Online Trading," *Wall Street Journal*, 19 June 2001, A1, A6; Rebecca Buckman, "Schwab, Once a Predator, Is Now Prey," *Wall Street Journal*, 8 December 1999, C1; Louise Lee, "When You're No. 1, You Try Harder," *Business Week E.Biz*, 18 September 2000, EB88.

2. Jon Swartz, "Tech Firms Try Reverse Splits to Lift Stocks," *USA Today*, 15 October 2002, 1A.

3. Matt Krantz, "Only 8 Companies Get AAA Debt Rating," *USA Today*, 30 May 2002, 1B.

4. David Rynecki, "CBOT Gazes into the Pit," *Fortune*, 15 May 2000, 279–294.

5. Julie Bort, "Trading Places," *Computerworld*, 27 May 1996, 1051.

6. New York Stock Exchange website [accessed 3 March 2003] www.nyse.com.

7. James K. Glassman, "Manager's Journal: Who Needs Stock Exchanges? Not Investors," *Wall Street Journal*, 8 May 2000, A42.

8. Gaston F. Ceron, "Instinet to Acquire Island ECN in a $508 Million Stock Deal," *Wall Street Journal*, 11 June 2002, C5.

9. Patrick Thibadeau, "Congress Examines Impact of ECNs on Stock Markets," *Computerworld*, 21 October 2002, 8.

10. Diana B. Henriques, "Stock Markets, Facing Threats, Pursue Changes," *New York Times on the Web*, 6 March 1999 [accessed 7 March 1999] www.nytimes.com/library/financial/030799 market-changes.htm.

11. Mike McNamee and Paula Dwyer, "A Revolt at NASD?," *Business Week*, 2 August 1999, 70–71.

12. Nelson D. Schwartz and Jeremy Kahn, "Can This Bull Run Again?," *Fortune*, 30 December 2002, 68–78.

13. Schwartz and Kahn, "Can This Bull Run Again?"

14. Schwartz and Kahn, "Can This Bull Run Again?"

15. Eileen Colkin Cuneo, "E-Trading Hangs On," *Information Week*, 9 December 2002, 43–49.

16. SEC website [accessed 21 December 2000] www.sec.gov/ consumer/jdatacom.htm.

17. Lee Copeland, "After-Hours Trading," *Computerworld*, 27 March 2000, 57.

18. Mara Der Hovanesian, "The Market's Closed—Wake Up," *Business Week*, 3 March 2003, 132–133.

19. Thor Valdmanis and Tom Lowry, "Wall Street's New Breed Revives Inside Trading," *USA Today*, 4 November 1999, 1B.

20. Joseph Nocera, "No Whispering Allowed," *Money*, December 2000, 71–74; Heather Timmons, "The Full Disclosure Rule Could Mean More Secrets," *Business Week*, 9 October 2000, 198; Lee Clifford, "The SEC Wants to Open the Info Vault," *Fortune*, 13 November 2000, 434.

21. Noelle Knox and Barbara Hansen, "Brokerage Watchdog Fights for Credibility," *USA Today*, 24 May 2002, 1B–2B.

22. Noelle Knox and Gary Strauss, "Mounting Workload Puts SEC Under the Gun," *USA Today*, 9 May 2002, 1B–2B.

23. Thor Valdmanis, "SEC Turns Up Heat on Analysts," *USA Today*, 26 April 2002, B1.

24. Thor Valdmanis, "Mighty Merrill Lynch Bogs Down in Legal Troubles," *USA Today*, 10 October, 2002, 1A–2A; Noelle Knox, "Merrill Lynch to Pay $100M Fine," *USA Today*, 22 May 2002, 1B.

25. David Barboza, "Online Brokers Fined Millions in Fraud Case," *New York Times*, 15 January 2003, A1.

26. Sharon Epperson, "Now Wall Street Pays," *Time* (March 12, 2003), 83.

27. Harvey Shapiro, "You Gotta Have A Style," *Hemispheres*, July 1997, 53–55.

28. Martin L. Leibowitz and Stanley Kogelman, "Asset Allocation Under Shortfall Constraints," *Journal of Portfolio Management*, Winter 1991, 18–23.

29. Copeland, "After-Hours Trading."

30. John R. Dorfman, "Crash Courses," *Wall Street Journal*, 28 May 1996, R12–R13.

31. Katrina Brooker, "Could the Dow Become Extinct?," *Fortune*, 15 February 1999, 194–195; Anita Raghavan and Nancy Ann Jeffrey, "What, How, Why—So What Is the Dow Jones Industrial Average, Anyway?," *Wall Street Journal*, 28 May 1996, R30; E.S. Browning, "New Economy Stocks Join Industrials," *Wall Street Journal*, 27 October 1999, C1, C15.

32. Jeffrey M. Laderman, "Why It's So Tough to Beat the S&P," *Business Week*, 24 March 1997, 82–83.

33. E.S. Browning, "Journal Goes 'Decimal' with NASDAQ Tables," *Wall Street Journal*, 2 August 2000, C1; "SEC Orders Decimal Stock Prices," *Chicago Tribune*, 29 January 2000, sec. 2, 2.
34. Adapted from Stephen Labaton, "On-line Trades Rise and So Do the Complaints," *New York Times*, 28 January 1999, A1, C21.

Component Chapter A

1. Ronald D. White, "FTC: Weight-Loss Ads Often Deceive," *Los Angeles Times*, 18 September 2002, C1.
2. "U.S. and 2 States File Suit over Claims in Diet Ads," *New York Times*, 6 December 2002, A26.
3. "U.S. and 2 States File Suit over Claims in Diet Ads."
4. Melody Petersen, "Pfizer Settles an Inquiry into Ads for an Antibiotic," *New York Times*, 7 January 2003, C7.
5. Louise Story, "Suffolk Business Court Wins Praises," *Boston Globe*, 5 July 2002, E1; Mike France, "Order in the Business Court," *Business Week*, 9 December 1996, 138–140.
6. Pamela Sherrid, "Smokers' Revenge," *U.S. News & World Report*, 4 November 2002, 44–47.
7. "For the Record, What's the Beef, Oprah," *London Free Press*, 14 February 1998, F5; Deborah Frazier, "Cattlemen Have Beef with Oprah—Stock Raisers Angry That TV Host Maligned Food They're Proud Of," *Denver Rocky Mountain News*, 21 January 1998, 30A; "United States: No Beef with Oprah," *The Economist*, 7 March 1998, 29; Scott Baldauf, "In Oprah Trial, Food Libel Charges Prove Hard to Swallow," *Christian Science Monitor*, 27 February 1998, 3.
8. "Fen-Phen Settlement Approved," *New York Times*, 11 January 2002, C12; Rick Schmitt and Scott Hensley, "Woman Wins $56.6 Million in AHP Case," *Wall Street Journal*, 9 April 2001, B7; David J. Morrow, "Maker of Diet Pill Agrees to Pay $3.75 Billion to Settle Liability Case," *New York Times* website [accessed 8 October 1999] www.nytimes.com.
9. Thomas W. Dunfee, Frank F. Gibson, John D. Blackburn, Douglas Whitman, F. William McCarty, and Bartley A. Brennan, *Modern Business Law* (New York: Random House, 1989), 569.
10. "Reasonable Product-Liability Reform"; Stephen Blakely, "Getting a Handle on Liability Coverage," *Nation's Business*, 1 September 1997, 87; John M. Broder, "Clinton Vetoes Bill to Limit Product-Liability Lawsuits," *Los Angeles Times*, 3 May 1996, A1.
11. "For the Record," *Washington Post*, 23 February 2000, M09.
12. Dunfee et al., *Modern Business Law*, 236.
13. Ethan A. Blumen, "Legal Land Mines," *Business 96*, June/July 1996, 53.
14. Dunfee et al., *Modern Business Law*, 284–297; Douglas Whitman and John William Gergacz, *The Legal Environment of Business*, 2d ed. (New York: Random House, 1988), 196–197; *The Lawyer's Almanac* (Englewood Cliffs, N.J.: Prentice Hall Law & Business, 1991), 888.
15. Brennan and Kubasek, *The Legal Environment of Business*, 128.
16. James Bates, "Disney Settles Up with Its Former Studio Boss," *Los Angeles Times*, 8 July 1999, 1; Bruce Orwall, "Katzenberg Wins Round in Lawsuit with Walt Disney," *Wall Street Journal*, 20 May 1999, B161.
17. Kristin Loiacono, "Congress Tackles Mandatory Arbitration," *Trial*, July 2002, 11.
18. Roy Furchgott, "Opposition Builds to Mandatory Arbitration at Work," *New York Times*, 20 July 1997, F11; Barry Meier, "In Fine Print, Customers Lose Ability to Sue," *New York Times*, 10 March 1997, A1, C7.
19. Richard M. Steuer, *A Guide to Marketing Law: What Every Seller Should Know* (New York: Harcourt Brace Jovanovich, 1986), 151–152.
20. Dunfee et al., *Modern Business Law*, 745, 749.
21. Whitman and Gergacz, *The Legal Environment of Business*, 260.

22. Jim Hopkins, "Entrepreneur 101: Patents," *USA Today*, 11 April 2001, 9B; Henry R. Cheeseman, *Business Law* (Upper Saddle River, N.J.: Prentice Hall, 2001), 324.
23. Megan Barnett, "Patents Pending," *U.S. News & World Report*," 10 June 2002, 33–34.
24. Barnett, "Patents Pending."
25. Barnett, "Patents Pending."
26. Cora Daniels, "Small Business Rip-Off," *FSB*, November 2001, 49–52.
27. Daniels, "Small Business Rip-Off."
28. James Connell, "Tech Brief: Apple Look-Alike Suit Settled," *International Herald Tribune*, 7 June 2001, 17; David P. Hamilton, "Apple Sues Future Power and Daewood, Alleging They Copied Design of iMac," *Wall Street Journal*, 2 July 1999, B4; "Injunction Is Issued Against Makers of iMac Look Alikes," *Wall Street Journal*, 9 November 1999, B25.
29. Jill Hecht Maxwell, "Copying Web Design: How Much Is Too Much?," *Inc. Tech*, 2001, 1, 20.
30. Cheeseman, *Business Law*, 330.
31. Mike Snider, "Law Targets Copyright Theft Online," *USA Today*, 18 December 1998, A1.
32. Tariq K. Muhammad, "Real Law in a Virtual World," *Black Enterprise*, December 1996, 44.
33. Michelle Kessler, "Hollywood, High-Tech Cross Swords over Digital Content," *USA Today*, 25 June 2002, 1E–2E.
34. Kessler, "Hollywood, High-Tech Cross Swords over Digital Content;" Lou Carlozo and Kathy Bergen, "Song-Sharing Napster Files for Bankruptcy," *Chicago Tribune*, 4 June 2002, sec. 3, 1, 6.
35. Jerry M. Rosenberg, *Dictionary of Business and Management* (New York: Wiley, 1983), 340.
36. "Polaroid Finalizes Sale, Emerges from Chapter 11," *TWICE*, 8 July 2002, 37; Polaroid website [accessed 29 July 2002], www.polaroid.com.

Component Chapter B

1. Jeremy Kahn and David Stipp, "The $30 Billion Explosion," *Fortune*, 1 October 2001, 100.
2. Cassell Bryan-Low, "Insurance Learns to Adjust to Ground Zero," *Wall Street Journal*, 9 October 2001, B9.
3. Christopher Oster and Cassell Bryan-Low, "Economic Recovery: Insurers Brace for Claims of Business Interruptions," *Wall Street Journal*, 5 October 2001, A6.
4. Judy Feldman, "What Daredevil CEO's Can Cost," *Money*, April 1999, 321.
5. Laura M. Litvan, "Switching to Self-Insurance," *Nation's Business*, March 1996, 16–21; Joseph B. Treaster, "Protecting Against the Little Risks," *New York Times*, 31 December 1996, C1, C15.
6. "Why You Can't Buy Insurance," *Wall Street Journal*, 1 October 2002, A20.
7. Julie Appleby, "Finger Pointers Can't Settle on Who's to Blame for Health Costs," *USA Today*, 21 August 2002, 1A.
8. "Why You Can't Buy Insurance."
9. Larry Lipman, "Social Security Outlook Improves," *Milwaukee Journal Sentinel*, 18 March 2003, 3A.
10. Amada Levin, "Ethics Rates Highest When Hiring Insurance Staff," *National Underwriter*, 12 April 1999, 4, 65.

Component Chapter C

1. Bureau of Labor Statistics, *2002–2003 Occupational Outlook Handbook* [accessed 8 April 2003], www.bls.gov/oco.
2. Bureau of Labor Statistics, *2002–2003 Occupational Outlook Handbook* [accessed 8 April 2003], www.bls.gov/oco.
3. Susan Vaughn, "Answer the Hard Questions Before Asked," *Los Angeles Times*, 29 July 2001, W1–W2.

Illustration and Text Credits

Chapter 1

Exhibit 1.1: Adapted from Christopher Caggiano, "Will the Real Bootstrappers Please Stand Up?," *Inc.*, August 1995, 34; Mike Hofman, "Capitalism—A Bootstrappers' Hall of Fame," *Inc.*, August 1997, 54–57; 1999 Amazon.com Annual Report, Amazon website-Investor Relations, accessed [10 June 2000] http://www.amazon.com.

Exhibit 1.2: U.S. Department of Commerce, Bureau of Economic Analysis [accessed 14 February 2002] http://beadata.bea.doc.gov/bea/dn2/gpoc.htm.

Acknowledgements—Sources for Boxes and Case for Critical Thinking

Is Big Government Back in Style?

Adapted from Jeffrey H. Birnbaum, "The Return of Big Government," *Fortune*, 16 September 2002, 112; David Boaz, "Is Big Government Back? No," *Milwaukee Journal Sentinel*, 27 May 2002, 17A; Bruce Nussbaum, "9.11.02," *Business Week*, 16 September 2002, 22–25; Jeanne Cummings, Jacob M. Schlesinger, and Michael Schroeder, "Securities Threat: Bush Crackdown on Business Fraud Signals New Era," *Wall Street Journal*, 10 July 2002, A1; Lorraine Woellert, "Just When the Right Thought Big Government Was History," *Business Week*, 5 November 2001, 53.

What's New About the New Economy?

Alan Murray, "Accounting Rules Should Still Adapt to New Economy," *Wall Street Journal*, 23 July 2002, A4; "Q&A: What Is the State of the New Economy?," *Fast Company*, September 2001, 101–104; "Fast Talk: The Old Economy Meets the New Economy," *Fast Company*, October 2001, 70–80; Jerry Useem, "Our 10 Principles of the New Economy, Slightly Revised," *Business 2.0*, August–September 2001, 85; Peter Coy, Rich Miller, Linda Himelstein et al, "Feeling the Heat," *Business Week*, 2 April 2001, 34–39.

A Case for Critical Thinking: Turmoil in the Airline Industry

Adapted from Scott McCartney and Susan Carey, "Shifts at Big Airlines Promise to Change the Industry's Course," *Wall Street Journal*, 17 April 2003, A1, A6; Wendy Zellner and Michael Arndt, "Holding Steady," *Business Week*, 3 February 2003, 66–68; Shawn Tully, "Friendly Skies Aren't out of the Picture," *Fortune*, 30 December 2002, 42–43; Edward Wong, "Winter's Frustrations Linger On Stubbornly for U.S. Airline Industry," *New York Times*, 15 June 2002, C1; George F. Will, "Always a Bumpy Ride," *Washington Post*, 9 May 2002, A31; Susan Carey, "Costly Race in the Sky," *Wall Street Journal*, 9 September 2002, B1, B3; Laurence Zuckerman, "A New Sense of Urgency in Debating the Future of Airlines," *New York Times*, 17 December 2001, C10; Adam Bryant, "The Cruel New Math," *Newsweek*, 26 November 2001, 22; "Business: Too Many Here, Too Few There," *Economist*, 13 January 2001, 58–59; Wendy Zellner, "It's Showtime for the Airlines," *Business Week*, 2 September 2002, 36–37; Peter Coy, "The Airlines: Caught Between a Hub and a Hard Place," *Business Week*, 5 August 2002, 83; Michael E. Levine, "Another Airline Nose-dives. Who's Next?," *Wall Street Journal*, 13 August 2002, A20; Scott McCartney, "Clipped Wings: American Airlines to Retrench in Bid to Beat Discount Carriers," *Wall Street Journal*, 13 August 2002, A1, A8; Melanie Trottman and Scott McCartney, "Executive Flight: The Age of 'Wal-Mart' Airlines Crunches the Biggest Carriers," *Wall Street Journal*, 18 June 2002, A1, A8. Shawn Tully, "From Bad to Worse," *Fortune*, 15 October 2001, 119–126; Alex Berenson, "Cry for Help: This Industry Doesn't Fly," *New York Times*, 18 November 2001, A5; . Perry Flint, "Hard Times," *Air Transport World*, November 2001, 22–28; Cynthia Wilson, "U.S. Airline Industry Faced Big Losses Even Before Terrorists Hijacked Jets," *St. Louis Post-Dispatch*, 23 September 2001, A13.

Chapter 2

Exhibit 2.1: Adapted from *The Institute of Electrical and Electronics Engineers* [accessed 21 July 1999] http://ieeeusa.org/documents/career/career_library/ethics.html.

Exhibit 2.2: "American Workers Do the Right Thing," *HR Focus*, March 1999, 4. Reprinted by permission of IOMA (the Institute of Management & Administration) © 2003 HRF. 212/244-0360. http://www.ioma.com

Exhibit 2.3: Adapted from Manuel G. Velasquez, *Business Ethics: Concepts and Cases* (Upper Saddle River, N.J.: Prentice Hall, 1998), 87; Joseph L. Badaracco, Jr., "Business Ethics: Four Spheres of Executive Responsibility," *California Management Review*, spring 1992, 64–79; Kenneth Blanchard and Norman Vincent Peale, *The Power of Ethical Management* (Reprint, 1989; New York: Fawcett Crest, 1991), 7–17; John R. Boatright, *Ethics and the Conduct of Business* (Upper Saddle River, N.J.: Prentice Hall, 1996), 35–39, 59–64, 79–86.

Acknowledgements—Sources for Boxes and Case for Critical Thinking

Actions Speak Louder Than Codes

Adapted from Dr. Craig Dreilinger, "Get Real (and Ethics Will Follow)," *Workforce*, August 1998, 101–102; Louisa Wah, "Workplace Conscience Needs a Boost," *American Management Association International*, July–August 1998, 6; "Ethics Are Questionable in the Workplace," *HR Focus*, June 1998, 7.

Firestone and Ford: Failure to Yield . . . or Asleep at the Wheel?

Adapted from Joann Muller, David Welch, and Jeff Green, "Would You Buy One?," *Business Week*, 25 September 2000, 46–47; Timothy Aeppel, Stephen Power, and Milo Geyelin, "Firestone Breaks with Ford over Tire Pressure," *Wall Street Journal*, 22 September 2000, A3; Keith Naughton and Mark Hosenball, "Ford vs. Firestone," *Newsweek*, 18 September 2000, 26–33; Keith Naughton, "Spinning out of Control," *Newsweek*, 11 September 2000, 58; Stephen Power and Bob Simison, "Firestone Knew of Tire Safety Problems," *Wall Street Journal*, 7 September 2000, A3; Timothy Aeppel, Clare Ansberry, Milo Geyelin, and Robert L. Simison, "Road Signs: How Ford, Firestone Let the Warnings Slide by as Debacle Developed," *Wall Street Journal*, 6 September 2000, A1; Robert L. Simison, Norihiko Shirouzu, and Timothy Aeppel, "Ford Says It Knew of Venezuelan Tire Failures in 1998," *Wall Street Journal*, 30 August 2000, A3; Robert L. Simison, Norihiko Shirouzu, Timothy Aeppel, and Todd Zaun, "Pressure Points: Tension Between Ford and Firestone Mounts Amid Recall Efforts," *Wall Street Journal*, 28 August 2000, A1.

A Case for Critical Thinking: Enron: A Case Study in Unethical Behavior

Adapted from Bethany Mclean, "Why Enron Went Bust," *Fortune*, 24 December 2001, 59–68; Michael Tackett, "Enron's Fall Piques

Congress' Interest in 401(k) Rules," *Chicago Tribune*, 25 January 2002, sec. 1, p. 1,12; Fred Tam, "Proper Controls Needed After Enron Debacle," *Business Times*, 14 February 2002, 18; Leslie Wayne, "Before Debacle, Enron Insiders Cashed in $1.1 Billion in Shares," *New York Times*, 13 January 2002, A1; Jacob M. Schlesinger, "O'Neill Weighs Stricter Corporate Penalties," *Wall Street Journal*, 25 February 2002, A1; Bethany McLean, "Monster Mess," *Fortune*, 4 February 2002, 93–96; Grag Hitt and Tom Hamburger, "Skilling Denies He Misled Enron Officials," *Wall Street Journal*, 27 February 2002, A3, A8. Daniel Kadlec, "Who's Accountable?" *Time*, 21 January 2002, 28–34; Jonathan Weil, "Enron's Auditors Debated Partnership Losses," *Wall Street Journal*, 3 April 2002, C1, C12; Kurt Eichenwald, "Andersen Guilty in Effort to Block Inquiry on Enron," *New York Times on the Web*, 16 June 2002 [accessed 19 June 2002] www.nytimes.com; E.A. Torriero and Robert Manor, "Jury Finds Andersen Guilty," *Chicago Tribune*, 16 June 2002, sec. 1, 1, 12.

Chapter 3

Exhibit 3.1: USA Today Snapshot: "Going Global Has Its Barriers," *USA Today*, 3 May 2000, B1.
Exhibit 3.2: John V. Thill and Courtland L. Bovée, *Excellence in Business Communication* (Upper Saddle River, N.J.: Prentice Hall, 2002), 33.
Exhibit 3.4: Adapted from U.S. Census Bureau website, foreign-trade statistics [accessed 17 September 2002] www.census.gov/foreign-trade.

Acknowledgements—Sources for Boxes and Case for Critical Thinking

When Will China Get Real?

Adapted from Karby Leggett and Todd Zaun, "In Yamaha Ruling, Sign of China's Piracy Stance," *Wall Street Journal*, 15 August 2002, A11; "China Vows to Continue Fight Against Fake Products," *Xinhau*, 28 December 2001; Todd Zaun and Karen Leggert, "Road Warriors," *Wall Street Journal*, 25 July 2001, A1, A4; Steve Friess, "Product Piracy Poses Biggest Threat to China's Economic Status," *USA Today*, 28 June 2001, 6B; Richard Behar, "Beijing's Phony War on Fakes," *Fortune*, 30 October 2000, 188+; Susan V. Lawrence, "For Better or Worse," *Far Eastern Economic Review*, 5 October 2000, 60; Lorien Holland, "A Brave New World," *Far Eastern Economic Review*, 5 October 2000, 46–48; Trish Saywell, "Fakes Cost Real Cash," *Far Eastern Economic Review*, 5 October 2000, 57–58; Dexter Roberts, Frederik Balfour, Paul Magnusson, Pete Engardio, and Jennifer Lee, "China's Piracy Plague," *Business Week*, 5 June 2000, 44–48.

How to Avoid Business Blunders Abroad

Adapted from David Ricks, "How to Avoid Business Blunders Abroad," *Business*, April–June 1984, 3–11.

A Case for Critical Thinking: Doing Everybody's Wash—Whirlpool's Global Lesson

Adapted from Regina Fazio Maruca, "The Right Way to Go Global," *Harvard Business Review*, March–April 1994, 135–145; Deborah Duarte and Nancy Snyder, "From Experience: Facilitating Global Organizational Learning in Product Development at Whirlpool Corporation," *Journal of Product Innovation Management* 14, no. 1 (January 1997): 48–55; Joe Jancsurak, "Whirlpool: U.S. Leader Pursues Global Blueprint," *Appliance Manufacturer* 45, no. 2 (February 1997): G21; Carl Quintanilla, "Despite Setbacks, Whirlpool Pursues Overseas

Markets," *Wall Street Journal*, 9 December 1997, B4; Ian Katz, "Whirlpool: In the Wringer," *Business Week*, 14 December 1998, 831; Gale Cutler, "Asia Challenges Whirlpool Technology," *Research Technology Management*," September–October 1998, 4–6; "Whirlpool Europe and Tupperware Europe Announce Strategic Alliance," Whirlpool Investor Relations, 28 April 1999, Whirlpool website, [accessed 15 September 2002] www.whirlpoolcorp.com; Sallie L. Gaines, "Washer War Spins on Investor Cycle," *Chicago Tribune*, 31 October 1999, sec. 5, 1, 7.

Chapter 4

Exhibit 4.6: Charles V. Callahan and Bruce A. Pasternack, "Corporate Strategy in the Digital Age," *Strategy and Business*, Issue 15, Second Quarter 1999, www.strategy-business.com/research/99202/page2.html [accessed 21 April 2000].
Exhibit 4.8: John Galvin, "Cheating, Lying, Stealing," *SmartBusinessMag.Com*, June 2000, 86–99.

Acknowledgements—Sources for Boxes and Case for Critical Thinking

Create a Winning Website

Adapted from Brian Hurley and Peter Birkwood, *A Small Business Guide to Doing Big Business on the Internet* (Bellingham, Wash.: International Self-Counsel Press), 1996, 124–134; "Design a Better Web Site," *Journal of Accountancy*, August 1998, 18; Anita Dennis, "A Home on the Web," *Journal of Accountancy*, August 1998, 29–31.

Job Recruiting Moves to the Net

Adapted from Stephanie Armour, "Online Résumés Create Quandary for Employers," *USA Today*, 6 November 2002, 3B; Efraim Turban, Jae Lee, David King, and H. Michael Chung, *Electronic Commerce, A Managerial Perspective* (Upper Saddle River, N.J.: Prentice Hall, 2000), 164–168; Marlene Piturro, "The Power of E-Cruiting," *Management Review*, January 2000, 33–38; "Online Recruiting: What Works, What Doesn't," *HR Focus*, March 2000, 11–15; "More Pros and Cons to Internet Recruiting," *HR Focus*, May 2000, 8; Christopher Caggiano, "The Truth About Internet Recruiting," *Inc.*, December 1999, 156; Peter Buxbaum, "Where's Dilbert?," *Chief Executive* [accessed 2 March 2000] www.chief executive.net/mag/150tech/part1c.htm; James R. Borck, "Recruiting Systems Control Résumé Chaos," *InfoWorld*, 24 July 2000, 47–48; Bill Leonard, "Online and Overwhelmed," *HR Magazine*, August 2000, 36–42; Milton Zall, "Internet Recruiting," *Strategic Finance*, June 2000, 66–72; "Why Your Web Site Is More Important Than Ever to New Hires," *HR Focus*, June 2000, 9; Rachel Emma Silverman, "Recruiters' Hunt for Résumés Is Nocturnal Game," *Wall Street Journal*, 20 September 2000, B1–B4.

A Case for Critical Thinking: Nokia Dials Up Wireless Innovations

Nokia Annual Report, 2001; Nokia website [accessed 12 December 2002] www.nokia.com; David Pringle and Matt Pottinger, "Nokia's China Connection May Grow Turbulent," *Wall Street Journal*, 29 August 2002, B4; David Pringle, "Nokia Widens Gap with Its Rivals," *Wall Street Journal*, 20 August 2002, B6; Alan Cowell, "Nokia Lowers Sales Target but Is Optimistic on Profits," *New York Times*, 11 September 2002, 1; Andy Reinhardt, "Nokia's Next Act," *Business Week*, 1 July 2002, 56–58; Stephen Baker with Inka Resch and Roger O. Crockett, "Nokia's Costly Stumble," *Business Week*, 14 August 2000, 42; "Business: Star Turn," *The Economist*, 5 August 2000, 60; Maryanne Murry

Buechner, "Making the Call," *Time*, 29 May 2000, 64–65; Justin Fox, "Nokia's Secret Code," *Fortune*, 1 May 2000; 160–174; Adrian Wooldridge, "Survey: Telecommunications: To the Finland Base Station," *The Economist*, 9 October 1999, S23–S27; Stephen Baker and Robert McNatt, "Now Nokia Is Net Crazy," *Business Week*, 5 April 1999, 6; "Jorma Ollila: Finn Fatale," *Business Week*, 11 January 1999, 78; Stephen Baker with Roger O. Crockett and Neil Gross, "Nokia," *Business Week*, 10 August 1998, 54.

Chapter 5

Exhibit 5.1: Adapted from Carrie Dolan, "Entrepreneurs Often Fail as Managers," *Wall Street Journal*, 15 May 1989, B1. Reprinted by permission of the Wall Street Journal, 1989 Dow Jones & Company, Inc. All Rights Reserved Worldwide.

Exhibit 5.2: Norman M. Scarborough and Thomas W. Zimmerer, *Effective Small Business Management*, 7th ed. (Upper Saddle River, N.J.: 2003), 4, and Dun and Bradstreet, *19th Annual Small Business Survey*, 2000.

Exhibit 5.3: Reprinted with permission of *USA Today*, Copyright March 1998.

Exhibit 5.4: Adapted from Norman M. Scarborough and Thomas W. Zimmerer, *Effective Small Business Management* (Upper Saddle River, N.J.: Prentice Hall, 2000), 8–13.

Exhibit 5.6: From *The Home Office and Small Business Answer Book*, 2nd Edition, by Janet Attard. © 1993 by Janet Attard. Revised Material © 2000 by Janet Attard. Reprinted by permission of Henry Hold and Company, LLC. *Business Know How* [accessed 19 September 1997] www.businessknowhow.com.

Exhibit 5.7: Adapted from Norman M. Scarborough and Thomas W. Zimmerer, *Effective Small Business Management* (Upper Saddle River, N.J.: Prentice Hall, 2000), 27–29.

Acknowledgements—Sources for Boxes and Case for Critical Thinking

Six Strategies for Working Effectively from Home

Adapted from "Two Dozen Do's and Don'ts for Home Business Success," *Small Business Administration* website [accessed 11 October 2002] www.sba.gov/gopher/Business-Development/ Success-Series/Vol9/twodozen.txt; Joyce M. Rosenberg, "Starting Home-Based Business Requires Lots of Thought," *Milwaukee Journal Sentinel*, 15 October 2001, 5D; Lori Gottlieb, "A Home Office Needs Its Boundaries," *New York Times*, 30 September 2001, 3, 11.

Why Did the Dot-Coms Fall to Earth?

Adapted from Paulette Thomas, "The Morning After," *Wall Street Journal*, 27 March 2002, R12; Michael Totty and Ann Grimes, "If at First You Don't Succeed," *Wall Street Journal*, 11 February 2002, R6–R7; J. William Gurley, "Startups, Beware: Obey the Law of Supply and Demand," *Fortune*, 29 May 2000, 278; William M. Bulkeley and Jim Carlton, "E-Tail Gets Derailed: How Web Upstarts Misjudged the Game," *Wall Street Journal*, 5 April 2000, A1, A6; Matt Krantz, "E-Retailers Run Low on Fuel," *USA Today*, 26 April 2000, 1B, 2B; "Survival of the Fastest," *Inc. Tech*, 16 November 1999, 44–58; Darnell Little, "Peapod Is in a Pickle," *Business Week*, 3 April 2000, 41; Heather Green, Nanette Byrnes, Norm Alster, and Arlene Weintraub, "The Dot.Coms Are Falling to Earth," *Business Week*, 17 April 2000, 48–49; John A. Byrne, "The Fall of a Dot-Com," *Business Week*, 1 May 2000, 150–160; Stephanie N. Mehta, "As Investors Play VC, It's Dot-Com Doomsday," *Fortune*, 1 May 2000, 40–41; David P. Hamilton and Mylene Mangalindan, "Angels of Death," *Wall Street Journal*, 25 May 2000, A1, A8; Luisa Kroll, "When the Music Stops," *Forbes*,

15 May 2000, 182; Chris Farrell, "Death of the Dot-Coms?," *Business Week*, 22 May 2000, 104E6; James Lardner and Paul Sloan, "The Anatomy of Sickly IPOs," *U.S. News & World Report*, 29 May 2000, 42; Hillary Stout, "Crunch Time," *Wall Street Journal*, 7 June 2000, B1; Jerry Useem, "Dot-Coms—What Have We Learned?," *Fortune*, 30 October 2000, 82–104; Heather Green and Norm Alster, "Guess What—Venture Capitalists Aren't Geniuses," *Business Week*, 10 July 2000, 98; Thomas E. Weber, "What Were We Thinking?," *Wall Street Journal*, 18 July 2000, B1, B4; Greg Ip, Susan Pulliam, Scott Thurm, and Ruth Simon, "The Color Green," *Wall Street Journal*, 14 July 2000, A1, A8.

A Case for Critical Thinking: Why Is Papa John's Rolling in Dough?

Adapted from Kate MacArthur, "Pizza Rut," *Advertising Age*, 21 January 2002, 4, 39; Susan Gosselin, "Pizza Wars," *The Lane Report*, 1 September 2001, 46; Kirsten Haukebo, "Papa John's Dad Finds His Calling," *USA Today*, 22 February 2000, 3B; Ron Ruggles, "John Schnatter: Mom Never Thought There'd Be Days Like This, but Papa John's CEO Is Rolling in Dough," *Nation's Restaurant News*, January 2000, 158–160; Amy Zuber, "Papa John's European Expansion to Mushroom via Perfect Pizza Buy," *Nation's Restaurant News*, 13 December 1999, 8; Alynda Wheat, "Striking It Rich The Low-Tech Way," *Fortune*, 27 September 1999, 86; Amy Zuber, "Papa John's Acquires Minnesota Pizza Co.," *Nation's Restaurant News*, 12 April 1999, 4, 91; Anne Field, "Piping-Hot Performance," *Success*, March 1999, 76–80; John Greenwald, "Slice, Dice, and Devour," *Time*, 26 October 1998, 64–66; Papa John's website [accessed 20 March 2002] www.papajohns.com.

Chapter 6

Exhibit 6.2: Adapted from "Business Enterprise," *Statistical Abstract of the United States, 1999*, 545.

Exhibit 6.3: Adapted from *Fortune* website [accessed 11 March 2003] www.fortune.com.

Acknowledgements—Sources for Boxes and Case for Critical Thinking

DaimlerChrysler: Merger of Equals or Global Fender Bender?

Adapted from Carol Hymowitz, "How to Fix a Broken System," *Wall Street Journal*, 24 February 2003, R1, R3; Bill Vlasic and Bradley A. Stertz, "How the DaimlerChrysler Marriage of Equals Got Taken for a Ride," *Business Week*, 5 June 2000, 86–92; Jeffrey Ball and Scott Miller, "Full Speed Ahead: Stuttgart's Control Grows with Shakeup at DaimlerChrysler," *Wall Street Journal*, 24 September 1999, A1, A8; Robert L. Simison and Scott Miller, "Making Digital Decisions," *Wall Street Journal*, 24 September 1999, B1, B4; Keith Bradsher, "A Struggle over Culture and Turf at Auto Giant," *New York Times*, 25 September 1999, B1, B14; "Message from DaimlerChrysler Chairmen to Company Employees," *Wall Street Journal*, 24 September 1999, A15; Joann Muller, Kathleen Kerwin, and Jack Ewing, "Man with a Plan," *Business Week*, 4 October 1999, 34–35; Frank Gibney Jr., "Worldwide Fender Bender," *Time*, 24 May 1999, 58–62; Daniel McGinn and Stefan Theil, "Hands on the Wheel," *Newsweek*, 12 April 1999, 49–52; Alex Taylor III, "The Germans Take Charge," *Fortune*, 11 January 1999, 92–96; Barrett Seaman and Ron Stodghill II, "The Daimler-Chrysler Deal: Here Comes the Road Test," *Time*, 18 May 1999, 66–69; Bill Vlasic, Kathleen Kerwin, David Woodruff, Thane Peterson, and Leah Nathans Spiro, "The First Global Car Colossus," *Business Week*, 18 May 1998, 40–43; Joann Muller, "Lessons from a Casualty of the Culture Wars,"

Business Week, 29 November 1999, 198; Rovert McNatt, "Chrysler: Not Quite So Equal," *Business Week*, 13 November 2000, 14.

Do Mergers Fulfill Management's Responsibility to Shareholders?

Adapted from David Henry, "Mergers—Why Most Big Deals Don't Pay Off," *Business Week*, 14 October 2002, 60–70; Amy Kover, "Big Banks Debunked," *Fortune*, 21 February 2000, 187–194; Erick Schonfeld, "Have the Urge to Merge? You'd Better Think Twice," *Fortune*, 31 March 1997, 114–116; Phillip L. Zweig et al., "The Case Against Mergers," *Business Week*, 30 October 1995, 122–130; Kevin Kelly et al., "Mergers Today, Trouble Tomorrow?," *Business Week*, 12 September 1994; "How to Merge," *The Economist*, 9 January 1999, 21–23; "Study Says Mergers Often Don't Aid Investors," *New York Times*, 1 December 1999, C9.

A Case for Critical Thinking: AOL and Time Warner: Fragile Promises

Adapted from Martin Peers and Julia Angwin, "AOL Reports Record Annual Loss and Says Ted Turner Will Resign," *Wall Street Journal*, 30 January 2003, A1, A2; Martin Peers and Julia Angwin, "Steve Case Quits as AOL Chairman Under Pressure," *Wall Street Journal*, 13 January 2003, A1, A8; Catherine Yang, "AOL: Anatomy of a Long Shot," *Business Week*, 16 December 2002, 58–60; Andy Kessler, "Here's the Sinking Case of AOL Time Warner," *Wall Street Journal Online*, 8 October 2002; Frank Ahrens, "At AOL and Disney, Uneasy Chairs," *Washington Post*, 18 September 2002, E01; Martin Peers, "Will Steve Case Leave AOL?," *Wall Street Journal*, 12 September 2002, B1, B7; Jeremy Kahn and Bill Powell, "Can These Guys Fix AOL?," *Fortune*, 2 September 2002, 95–100; Tom Lowry, "The Sinkhole of 'Synergy,'" *Business Week*, 26 August 2002, 22; Catherine Yang, "Can Miller Put the Oomph Back in AOL?," *Business Week*, 26 August 2002, 42; Frank Ahrens, Merissa Marr, "Old-School Media Reassert Control," *Toronto Star*, 30 July 2002; "Big Media Mergers Raise Big Doubts; Is Synergy Achievable–or Even Desirable?," *Washington Post*, 14 May 2002, A01.

Chapter 7

Exhibit 7.3: Adapted from Dell Computer website [accessed 5 November 2002] www.dell.com/corporate/vision/mission.htm.
Exhibit 7.4: Stuart Crainer, "The 75 Greatest Management Decisions Ever Made," *Management Review*, November 1998, 17–23.
Exhibit 7.6: Adapted from and reprinted by permission of *Harvard Business Review*, an exhibit from "How to Choose a Leadership Pattern" by Robert Tannenbaum and Warren H. Schmidt, May–June 1973. Copyright © 1973 by the President and Fellows of Harvard College, all rights reserved.

Acknowledgements—Sources for Boxes and Case for Critical Thinking

JetBlue: Making Tough Management Decisions in Tough Times

Adapted from Michael Arndt and Wendy Zellner, "American Draws a Bead on JetBlue," *Business Week*, 24 June 2002, 48; Sally B. Donnelly, "Blue Skies," *Time*, 30 July 2001, 23–27; Paul C. Judge, "How Will Your Company Adapt?," *Fast Company*, December 2001, 128–132; Robert Whalen, "JetBlue Turning Profit as Industry Struggles," *The Record*, 27 December 2001, B1; Tom Fredrickson, "Plane Sailing," *Crain's New York Business*, 12 November 2001, 1.

How Much Do You Know About the Company's Culture?

Adapted from Andrew Bird, "Do You Know What Your Corporate Culture Is?," *CPA Insight*, February/March 1999, 25–26; Gail H. Vergara, "Finding a Compatible Corporate Culture," *Healthcare Executive*, January/February 1999, 46–47; Hal Lancaster, "To Avoid a Job Failure, Learn the Culture of a Company First," *Wall Street Journal*, 14 July 1998, B1.

A Case for Critical Thinking: The Ax Falls on Sunbeam's Chainsaw Al

Adapted from Michael Barbaro, "Sunbeam Settlement Reached," *Washington Post*, 5 September 2002, E1; Kelly Greene, "Dunlap Agrees to Settle Suit over Sunbeam," *Wall Street Journal*, 15 January 2002, A3; James R. Fisher Jr., "Profits and People," *Executive Excellence*, January 2000, 18; Jenny Anderson, "Al Gets the Chainsaw," *Institutional Investor*, October 1999, 224; John A. Byrne, "Chainsawal: He Anointed Himself America's Best CEO," *Business Week*, 18 October 1999, 128; "Al Dunlap: Booted for Being a Shareholder Hero," *Fortune*, 26 April 1999, 413; Martha Brannigan, "Best and Worst Performing Companies: Worst 1-Year Performer: Sunbeam Corp," *Wall Street Journal*, 25 February 1999, R7; Geoffrey Colvin, "America's Most Hated," *Director*, September 1998, 35; Matthew Schifrin, "The Sunbeam Soap Opera: Act VI," *Forbes*, 6 July 1998, 44–45; John A. Byrne, "How Al Dunlap Self-Destructed," *Business Week*, 6 July 1998, 58; Daniel Kadlec, "Chainsaw Al Gets the Chop," *Time*, 29 June 1998, 46–47; David Morrison and Kevin Mundt, "Chainsaw Al Gets the Ax. What's Next for Sunbeam?," *Wall Street Journal*, 22 June 1998, A22; Jonathan R. Laing, ". . . And Take the Chainsaw with You!" *Barron's*, 22 June 1998, 13–14; "Business: Exit Bad Guy," *The Economist*, 20 June 1998, 70–75; Patricia Sellers, "Exit for Chainsaw?," *Fortune*, 8 June 1998, 30–31; James R. Hagerty and Martha Brannigan, "Inside Sunbeam: Raindrops Mar Dunlap's Parade," *Wall Street Journal*, 22 May 1998, B1.

Chapter 8

Exhibit 8.4: Adapted from Steven Burke, "Acer Restructures into Six Divisions," *Computer Reseller News*, 13 July 1998, 10.

Acknowledgements—Sources for Boxes and Case for Critical Thinking

Mervyn's Calls SWAT Team to the Rescue

Adapted from Mervyn's website [accessed 13 November 2002] www.mervyns.com; Peter Carvonara, "Mervyn's Calls in the SWAT Team," *Fast Company*, April–May 1998, 54–56; Richard Halverson, "Ulrich Delivers Ultimatum to Mervyn's: Improve Sales Performance, or Else," *Discount Store News*, 26 October 1998, 3, 126.

Ben & Jerry's Organizes Old Ideals Under a New Boss

Adapted from "Effect of Unilever Acquisition on Company Values," 24 September 2002, Ben & Jerry's website [accessed 23 December 2002] www.benjerry.com/ca/, reference #010402-000003; "Unilever Acquisition of Ben & Jerry's," 11 June 2002, Ben & Jerry's website [accessed 23 December 2002] www.benjerry.com/ca/, reference #000412-000001; Heather Tomlinson, "The Lowdown: Stop and Buy Me a Ben & Jerry's," *Independent on Sunday*, 9 December 2001, 7; Geoffrey Smith, "A Famous Brand on a Rocky Road," *Business Week*, 11 December 2000, 54; David Graham, "The Sad Saga of Ben & Jerry's Melting Ideals," *Toronto Star*, 12 May 2000; "Ben & Jerry's and Unilever to Join Forces," 12 April 2000, Ben & Jerry's website [accessed 23 December 2002] http://lib.benjerry.com/pressrel/join-forces.html

A Case for Critical Thinking: Harley-Davidson—From Dysfunctional to Cross-Functional

Adapted from John Teresko, "Fueled by Innovation," *Industry Week*, December 2002, 52–57; John Helyar, "Will Harley Davidson Hit the Wall?," *Fortune*, 12 August 2002, 120–124; Jonathan Fahey, "Love into Money," *Forbes*, 7 January 2002, 60–65; Rich Teerlink, "Harley's Leadership U-Turn," *Harvard Business Review*, July–August 2000, 43+; Kevin R. Fitzgerald, "Purchasing at Harley Links Supply with Design," *Purchasing*, 13 February 1997, 56–57; Machan Dyan, "Is the Hog Going Soft?," *Forbes*, 10 March 1997, 114–115; Ronald B. Lieber, "Selling the Sizzle," *Fortune*, 23 June 1997, 80; Clyde Fessler, "Rotating Leadership at Harley-Davidson: From Hierarchy to Interdependence," *Strategy & Leadership*, July–August 1997, 42–43; Tim Minahan, "Harley-Davidson Revs Up Development Process," *Purchasing*, 7 May 1998, 44S18–44S23; Michael A. Verespej, "Invest in People," *Industry Week*, 1 February 1999, 6–7; Leslie P. Norton, "Potholes Ahead?," *Barron's*, 1 February 1999, 16–17; Mark A. Brunelli, "How Harley-Davidson Uses Cross-Functional Teams," *Purchasing*, 4 November 1999, 148.

Chapter 9

Exhibit 9.2: Adapted from Mark M. Davis, Nicholas J. Aquilano, and Richard B. Chase, *Fundamentals of Operations Management* (Boston: Irwin McGraw-Hill, 1999), 7.
Exhibit 9.7: Adapted from Courtland Boveé, et al., *Management* (New York: McGraw Hill, 1993), 678.

Acknowledgements—Sources for Boxes and Case for Critical Thinking

A Bike That Really Travels

Adapted from Lisa Marshall, "A Bike That Really Travels," *Boulder Daily Camera*, June 1999; Bike Friday website [accessed 15 November 2002] www.bikefriday.com; Tim Stevens, "Pedal Pushers," *Industry Week*, 17 July 2000, 46–52.

Your Inventory Wants to Talk to You

Adapted from Mark Roberti, "Your Inventory Wants to Talk to You," *Business 2.0*, May 2002, 84–87; Craig Fuller, "Barcodes Get Smart," *Chain Store Age*, March 2002, 32; Daniel Thomas, "High Street Ships are Eager to Adopt RFID Electronic Tagging," *Computer Weekly*, 10 October 2002, 18.

A Case for Critical Thinking: Porsche—Back in the Fast Lane

Adapted from Alex Taylor III, "Porsche's Risky Recipe," *Fortune*, 17 February 2003, 91–94; Scott Miller, "Porsche Gambling that Cayenne Will Be Hot SUV," *Chicago Sun Times*, 26 August 2002, 4; "The Selling of an Anachronistic Dream; Porsche Is Now the World's Most Profitable Car Maker," *Irish Times*, 21 August 2002, 53; "The Stars of Europe: Turnaround Artists: Wendelin Wiedeking," *Business Week*, 19 June 2000, 186; Tom Mudd, "Back in High Gear," *Industry Week*, 21 February 2000, 38–46; Matthew Karnitschnig, "That Van You're Driving May Be Part Porsche," *Business Week*, 27 December 1999, 72; Peter Morgan, "Back to Winning Ways," *Professional Engineering*, 28 April 1999, 30–31; Karen Abramic Dilger, "Gear Up and Go," *Manufacturing Systems*, A24–A28; "Porsche Gears Up for Faster Parts Distribution," *Material Handling Engineering*, July 1998, 34–40; Richard Feast, "The Road Ahead for Porsche," *Independent*, 6 September 1996, 17.

Chapter 10

Exhibit 10.3: From Richard L. Daft, *Management, Fourth Edition* (South-Western, 1997.) Reproduced with permission of South-Western, a division of Thomson Learning: www.thomsonrights.com. Fax 800-730-2215.
Exhibit 10.4: Douglas McGregor, *The Human Side of Enterprise* (New York: McGraw-Hill, 1960). Twenty-fifth anniversary printing.
Exhibit 10.5: Jennifer Laabs, "The New Loyalty: Grasp It. Earn It. Keep It." *Workforce*, November 1998, 35–39.
Exhibit 10.6: *USA Today* Snapshot, "9-to-5 Not for Everyone," *USA Today*, 13 October 1999, B1. Reprinted with permission of *USA Today*. © October 2002.

Acknowledgements—Sources for Boxes and Case for Critical Thinking

How UPS Handles Its Employees with Care

Adapted from Keith H. Hammonds, "Handle with Care," *Fast Company*, August 2002, 102–107; Diane E. Lewis, "A Higher Value on Knowledge Companies Increase Education Spending to Retain, Improve Their Work Forces," *Boston Globe*, 31 March 2002, G1; United Parcel Services website [accessed 28 November 2002] www.ups.com.

Hershey's Bittersweet Surrender

Adapted from David B. Caruso, "Hershey Workers Aren't Resting Easy," *Milwaukee Journal Sentinel*, 22 September 2002, 8D; John Helyar, "Sweet Surrender," *Fortune*, 14 October 2002, 224–234; Francis S. Clines, "Whiff of Chocolate and the Sweet Smell of Success," *New York Times*, 19 September 2002, 6; Shelly Branch, Sarah Ellison, and Gordon Fairclough, "Sweet Deal: Hershey Foods Is Considering a Plan to Put Itself Up for Sale," *Wall Street Journal*, 25 July 2002, A1.

A Case for Critical Thinking: Brewing Up People Policies at Starbucks

Adapted from Stanley Homes, Drake Bennett, Kate Carlisle, and Chester Dawson, "Planet Starbucks," *Business Week*, 9 September 2002, 99–110; Ranjay Gulati, Sarah Huffman, and Gary Neilson, "The Barista Principle," *Strategy & Business*, Quarter 3 2002, 58–69; "Mr. Coffee," *Context*, August–September 2001, 20–25; Jennifer Ordonez, "Starbucks's Schulz to Leave Top Post, Lead Global Effort," *Wall Street Journal*, 7 April 2000, B3; Karyn Strauss, "Howard Schulz: Starbucks's CEO Serves a Blend of Community, Employee Commitment," *Nation's Restaurant News*, January 2000, 162–163; Carla Joinson, "The Cost of Doing Business?," *HR Magazine*, December 1999, 86–92; "Interview with Howard Schulz: Sharing Success," *Executive Excellence*, November 1999, 16–17; Kelly Barron, "The Cappuccino Conundrum," *Forbes*, 22 February 1999, 54–55; Naomi Weiss, "How Starbucks Impassions Workers to Drive Growth," *Workforce*, August 1998, 60–64; Scott S. Smith, "Grounds for Success," *Entrepreneur*, May 1998, 120–126; "Face Value: Perky People," *The Economist*, 30 May 1998, 66; Howard Schulz and Dori Jones Yang, "Starbucks: Making Values Pay," *Fortune*, 29 September 1997, 261–272.

Chapter 11

Exhibit 11.4: "Checking Out New Hires," *USA Today Snapshot*, 18 May 2000, B1. Reprinted with permission of *USA Today*. ©2000.

Acknowledgements—Sources for Boxes and Case for Critical Thinking

Packing Up Great Service at The Container Store

Adapted from Lorrie Grant, "Container Store's Workers Huddle Up to Help You Out," *USA Today*, 20 April 2002, 1B–2B; Bill Broadway, "Good for the Soul—and for the Bottom Line," *Washington Post*, 19 August, 2001, A01; Jennifer Koch Laabs, "Thinking Outside the Box at Container Store," *Workforce*, March 2001, Vol. 80, Issue 3, 34–37; "Learn About Us," www.container store.com/learn/index.jhtml

Click and Learn: E-Training Today's Employees

Adapted from Michael A. Verespej, "Click and Learn," *Industry Week*, 15 January 2001, 31–36; Elisabeth Goodridge, "Slowing Economy Sparks Boom in E-Learning," 12 November 2001, 100–104; Cynthia Pantazis, "Maximizing E-Learning to Train the 21st Century Workforce," Public Personnel Management, Spring 2002, 21–26; Mary Lord, "They're Online and on the Job," *U.S. News & World Report*, 15 October 2001, 72–78.

A Case for Critical Thinking: Hard Landing for United's Employee Stock-Ownership Program

Adapted from Melanie Trottman, "UAL's Move to Soothe Fliers Sets a Lofty Hurdle to Clear," *Wall Street Journal Online*, 11 December 2002, online.wsj.com/article0,, SB1039555126819405473.djm,00.html; Online news roundup, "UAL Files for Creditor Shield But Vows to Keep Flying," *Wall Street Journal Online*, 9 December 2002, online.wsj.com/ article0,, SB1039129716135801433.djm,00.html; Shirley Leung, "United's Staff Is Likely To Lose Its Equity Stake," *Wall Street Journal*, 6 December, 2002, online.wsj.com/article0, SB1039443152312445433.djm.00.html; Chris Woodyard, "Averting Strike Just First Stop on United's Trip Back," *USA Today*, 19 February 2002, 8B; John Helyar, "United We Fall," *Fortune*, 18 February 2002, 92–96; Suzanne I. Cohen, "United Airlines' ESOP Woes," Risk Management, June 2001, 9; Laurence Zuckerman, "Divided, an Airline Stumbles," *New York Times*, 14 March 2001, C1; Michael Arndt, "Will United's Woes Spread?," *Business Week*, 13 November 2000, 180–192; Michael Arndt, "The Industry Will Pay for United's Deal with Pilots," *Business Week*, 18 September 2000, 52; Floyd Norris, "Pilot Woes: Why Employee Ownership Didn't Help UAL," *New York Times*, 11 August 2000, C1; Michael Arndt, Aaron Bernstein, "From Milestone to Millstone?," *Business Week*, 30 March 2000, 120.

Chapter 12

Exhibit 12.1: Gary Armstrong and Philip Kotler, *Marketing: An Introduction*, 5th ed. (Upper Saddle River, N.J.: Prentice Hall, 2000), 5.
Exhibit 12.3: Gary Armstrong and Philip Kotler, *Marketing: An Introduction*, 5th ed. (Upper Saddle River, N.J.: Prentice Hall, 2000), 19.
Exhibit 12.4: Adapted from Mary J. Cronin, *Doing More Business on the Internet* (New York: Van Nostrand Reinhold, 1995), 61.
Exhibit 12.5: Joan O. Fredericks and James M. Salter, "Beyond Customer Satisfaction," *Management Review*, May 1995, 29. Artist: Elliot Bergman.
Exhibit 12.9: Gary Armstrong and Philip Kotler, *Marketing: An Introduction*, 5th ed. (Upper Saddle River, N.J.: Prentice Hall, 2000), 201. Reprinted by permission of Pearson Education, Inc., Upper Saddle River, N.J.

Acknowledgements—Sources for Boxes and Case for Critical Thinking

Your Right to Privacy Versus the Marketing Databases

Adapted from Linda Stern, "Is Orwell Your Banker?," *Newsweek*, 8 April 2002, 59; Mike France and Heather Green, "Privacy in an Age of Terror," *Business Week*, 5 November 2001, 83–87; Amy Harmon, "F.T.C. to Propose Laws to Protect Children on Line," *New York Times*, 4 June 1998, C1, C6; Andrew L. Shapiro, "Privacy for Sale," *The Nation*, 23 June 1997, 11–16; Bruce Horovitz, "Marketers Tap Data We Once Called Our Own," *USA Today*, 19 December 1995, 1A–2A; Stephen Baker, "Europe's Privacy Cops," *Business Week*, 2 November 1998, 49, 51.

Questionable Marketing Tactics on Campus

Adapted from Ruth Simon and Christine Whelan, "The New Credo on Campus: 'Just Charge It,'" *Wall Street Journal*, 3 September 2002, D1–D2; Charles Haddad, "Congratulations, Grads—You're Bankrupt," *Business Week*, 21 May 2001, 48; Christine Dugas, "Colleges Target Card Solicitors," *USA Today*, 12 March 1999, B1; Lisa Toloken, "Turning the Tables on Campus," *Credit Card Management*, May 1999, 76–79; "Credit Cards Given to College Students a Marketing Issue," *Marketing News*, 27 September 1999, 38.

A Case for Critical Thinking: Is Levi Strauss Coming Apart at the Seams?

Adapted from Fara Warner, "Levi's Fashions a New Strategy," *Fast Company*, November 2002, 48–49; Susan Chandler, "Low-Rise a Boon to Levi," *Seattle Times*, 21 September 2002, C1; Louise Lee, "Why Levi's Still Looks Faded," *Business Week*, 22 July 2002, 54; Brad Stone, "Jean Therapy For Levi's," *Newsweek*, 15 April 2002, 42–43; Louise Lee, "Can Levi's Be Cool Again?," *Business Week*, 13 March 2000, 144, 148; Shawn Meadows, "Levi Shifts Online Strategy," *Bobbin*, January 2000, 8; Luisa Kroll, "Denim Disaster," *Forbes*, 29 November 1999, 181; Stacey Collett, "Channel Conflicts Push Levi to Halt Web Sales," *Computerworld*, 8 November 1999, 8; Nina Munk, "How Levi's Trashed a Great American Brand," *Fortune*, 12 April 1999, 83–90; Betsy Spethmann, "Can We Talk?," *American Demographics*, March 1999, 42–44; Wayne D'Orio, "Clothes Make the Teen," *American Demographics*, March 1999, 34–37; Murray Forester, "Levi's Weaves a Tangled Web," *Chain Store Age*, January 1999, 10; Suzette Hill, "Levi Strauss & Co.: Icon in Revolution," *Apparel Industry Magazine*, January 1999, 66–69; Luisa Kroll, "Digit Denim," *Forbes*, December 28, 1998, 102–103; "Keep Reinventing the Brand or Risk Facing Extinction," *Marketing*, 25 February 1999, 5; Suzette Hill, "Levi Strauss Puts a New Spin on Brand Management," *Apparel Industry Magazine*, November 1998, 46–47; Linda Himlestein, "Levi's is Hiking Up Its Pants," *Business Week*, 1 December 1997, 70–75.

Chapter 13

Exhibit 13.3: Adapted from David Armstrong, Monte Burke, Emily Lambert, Nathan Vardi, and Rob Wherry, "85 Innovations," *Forbes*, 23 December 2002, 122–202.

Acknowledgements—Sources for Boxes and Case for Critical Thinking

The Price of Life-Saving Drugs: How Much Is Too Much?

Adapted from AIDS Healthcare Foundation press release, "AIDS Healthcare Foundation Calls Glaxo AIDS Drug Announcement A

'Hollow Gesture': New Price Remains Seven Times Higher Than Generics," 6 September 2002; AID Healthcare Foundation press release, "AZT Scientists Join GSK Patent Challenge," 5 December 2002; Harry Schwartz, "Patents—Whose Rights Do They Serve?," *Pharmaceutical Executive*, 1 September 1997; GlaxoSmithKline press release, "Statement in Response to Amended Litigation Filed by the AIDS Healthcare Foundation," 15 October 2002; Gautam Naik, "Glaxo to Face Suit over AIDS Drugs," *Wall Street Journal*, 1 July 2002.

Sun Microsystems Tries to Grab a Slice of the Microsoft Pie

Adapted from Richard Morochove, "Demand for StarOffice May Rise with Fee," *Toronto Star*, 25 March 2002; Sun Microsystems Press Release, "Sun Microsystems Donates More Than $6 Billion of StarOffice Productivity Software and Sun Technologies to Schools Worldwide, Reaching over 240 Million Students," 17 September 2002; Sun Microsystems Press Release, "StarOffice 6.0 Storms to the Top of Amazon.Com's Software Charts," 23 May 2002; Doug Bedell, "War on Word: Low-Cost and Free Office Suites May Delete Microsoft Dominance," *Dallas Morning News*, 1 August 2002.

A Case for Critical Thinking: Coke Unpacks a Winner

Adapted from Dean Foust and Gerry Khermouch, "Shaking up the Coke Bottle," *BusinessWeek*, 3 December 2001, 74–75; Patricia Sellers, "Who's in Charge Here?," *Fortune*, 24 December 2001, 77–86; Gerry Khermouch, "The Best Global Brands," *BusinessWeek*, 5 August 2002, 92+; Daniel Fisher, "Gone Flat," *Forbes*, 15 October 2001, 77–79; Betsy McKay, "Thinking Inside the Box—'Big Idea' Behind Fridge Pack Is That Consumers Will Drink More When Soft Drinks Are Kept Cold," *Wall Street Journal*, 2 August 2002, B1+; Scott Leith, "CCE Puts 'Fridge Pack' on Store Shelves Today," *Atlanta Journal Constitution*, 1 May 2002, D1+.

Chapter 14

Exhibit 14.3: Adapted from Philip Kotler, *Marketing Management*, 10th ed. (Upper Saddle River, N.J.: Prentice Hall, 2000), 491.
Exhibit 14.4: "Having Real-World Store a Plus for Online Buying," *USA Today*, 8 August 2000, B1. Reprinted with permission of *USA Today*, © August 2000.
Exhibit 14.5: Courtesy of REI
Exhibit 14.6: Adapted from Charles D. Schewe, *Marketing Principles and Strategies* (New York: McGraw-Hill), 1987, 294. Reprinted by permission of the publisher.

Acknowledgements—Sources for Boxes and Case for Critical Thinking

Carvin Strikes a Chord with Factory-Direct Guitars

Adapted from "The Carvin Factory Tour," Carvin website [accessed 2 January 2003] www.carvin.com/factorytour/; "10-day Trial," Carvin website [accessed 2 January 2003] www.carvin.com/mbg.html; "Custom Shop Guitar Models," Carvin website [accessed 2 January 2003] www.carvin.com/cgi-bin/Isearch.exe?P1=GTR; James Daw, "Dreamers Need More Than Loans, Advice," *Toronto Star*, 31 August 2002; Rich Krechel, "Some Custom-Made Guitars Can Cost $4,000 to $8,000," *St. Louis Post Dispatch*, 27 September 2001, 16.

The Nautilus Group Flexes Its Muscles in Multiple Channels

Adapted from "Nautilus Group Announces Preliminary Fourth Quarter 2002 Results," *Wall Street Journal* Online, 13 January 2003, http://online.wsj.com/article/0,,PR_CO_20030113_001783,00.html; "About the Nautilus Group," Nautilus Group website [accessed 20 December 2002], www.nautilusgroup.com/aboutus/index.asp; "Fitness Factoids," Nautilus Group website [accessed 20 December 2002], www.nautilusgroup.com/pressroom/fitfacts.asp; Elizabeth MacDonald, "Fiscal Fitness," *Forbes*, 11 November 2002, 80.

A Case for Critical Thinking: REI's Perfect Blend of Retail and E-tail Channels

Adapted from "REI Sure-Footed on Its Way to the Web," *Seattle Times*, 14 April 2002, D10; Ken Yamada, "Web Trails," *Forbes Best of the Web*, 3 December 2001, 15; Mike Troy, "REI.com Scales On-Line Heights," *DSN Retailing Today*, 8 May 2000, 6; Kellee Harris, "Online Travel Revs Up Revenues," *Sporting Goods Business*, 1 February 2000, 16; Lawrence M. Fisher, "REI Climbs Online: A Clicks-and-Mortar Chronicle," *strategy+business*, First Quarter 2000 [accessed 13 October 2000], www.strategy-business.com/casestudy/00111; "REI Scales New Heights with Second-Generation Websites and IBM," IBM E-Business Case Studies [accessed 10 March 2000], www.ibm.com/e-business/case_studies/rei.phtml; Kristin Carpenter, "REI.com," *Sporting Goods Business*, 6 July 1999, 57; David Orenstein, "Retailers Find Uses for Web Inside Stores," *Computerworld*, 11 January 1999, 41; Sharon Machlis, "Outdoor Goods Seller Creates Online Outlet," *Computerworld*, 14 December 1998, 51–53; Kerry A. Dolan, "Backpackers Meet Bottom Line," *Forbes*, 16 November 1998, 161; Kristin Carpenter, "REI Venturing Out with Off-Price Website," *Sporting Goods Business*, 10 August 1998, 22.

Chapter 15

Exhibit 15.4: "Leading National Advertisers," *Advertising Age*, 24 June 2002, S1–S6+. Reprinted with permission. © 2002, Crain Communications Inc.

Acknowledgements—Sources for Boxes and Case for Critical Thinking

Will "Real People" Create Real Sales for Apple Computer?

Adapted from Apple Computer press release, "Apple Launches 'Real People' Ad Campaign; PC to Mac 'Switchers' Tell Their Story," 10 June 2002; Apple Computer website [accessed 28 January 2003] www.apple.com/switch; Ian Fried, "Apple's 'Real People' Ad Seeks PC Crowd," News.com, 9 June 2002 [accessed 28 January 2003] www.news.com, Andrew Orlowski, "Monday Night at the Single's Club? Apple's Real People," *The Register*, 17 June 2002 [accessed 28 January 2003] www.theregister.co.uk; Jim Dalrymple, "Dvorak: Apple's 'Real People' Campaign Desperate," 25 June 2002 [accessed 28 January 2003] http://maccentral.macworld.com.

A Case for Critical Thinking: Polyclinic Closes the Door on Sales Reps

Adapted from Carol M. Ostrom, "Polyclinic Shuts Out Drug Reps, Samples," *Seattle Times*, 16 January 2003 [www.seattletimes.com]; Pharmaceutical Research and Manufacturers of America website [accessed 25 January 2003] www.phrma.org; Helen Jung, "Clinic Charges Drug Reps for Access," *AP Online*, 14 June 2002 [accessed 16 January 2003] www.elibrary.com; Jeffrey Kahn, "The Double-Edged Sword of Drug Marketing," *CNN Health, Ethics Matters*, 9 August 1999 [accessed 16 January 2003] www.cnn.com; Abigail Zuger, "Fever Pitch: Getting Doctors To Prescribe Is Big Business," *New York Times*, 11 January 1999 [accessed 16 January 2003] www.nyt.com; Michael A. Steinman, "Gifts to Physicians in the Consumer Marketing Era," *MSJAMA—Review*, 1 November 2000, 2243 [accessed 16 January 2003] www.ama-assn.org; Tony Pugh, "Drug Reps Get the Cold Shoulder," *Toronto Star*, 6 September 2002 [accessed 16 January] www.elibrary.com; "Sales Pitch: Drug Firms Use Perks to Push Pills; Companies Ply Doctors to Write Prescriptions," *USA Today*, 16 May 2001, 1B.

Chapter 16

Exhibit 16.1: Adapted from Gary Siegel and Bud Kulesza, "The Practice of Management Accounting," *Management Accounting*, April 1996, 20; "Up the Ladder of Success," *Journal of Accountancy*, November 2000, 24.

Acknowledgements—Sources for Boxes and Case for Critical Thinking

Where Were the Auditors?

Adapted from David S. Hilzenrath, "Auditors May Face Curbs on Incentives," *Washington Post*, 19 November 2002, E1; Johan A. Byrne, "Fall from Grace," *Business Week*, 12 August 2002, 50–56; Cassell Bryan-Low, "Auditors Fail to Foresee Bankruptcies," *Wall Street Journal*, 11 July 2002, C9; Ken Brown, "Auditors' Methods Make It Hard to Catch Fraud by Executives," *Wall Street Journal*, 8 July 2002, C1, C16; Thaddeus Herrick and Alexei Barrionuevo, "Were Auditor and Client Too Close-Knit?," *Wall Street Journal*, 21 January 2002, C1, C5; Jeremy Kahn, "One Plus One Makes What?," *Fortune*, 7 January 2002, 88–90; Nanette Byrnes, "Auditing Here, Consulting over There," *Business Week*, 8 April 2002, 34–36; Nanette Byrnes, "Accounting in Crisis," *Business Week*, 28 January 2002, 42–48.

How to Read an Annual Report

Adapted from Manual Schiffres, "All the Good News That Fits," *U.S. News & World Report*, 14 April 1998, 50–51; Janice Revell, "Annual Reports Decided," *Fortune*, 25 June 2001, 176; "The P&L: Your Score Card of Profitability," *The Edward Lowe Report*, August 2001, 1–3.

A Case for Critical Thinking: Consulting Pushes Arthur Andersen out of Balance

Adapted from Ameet Sachdev, "Judge Gives Andersen $500,000 Fine, Probation," *Chicago Tribune*, 17 October 2002, sec.1, 1; Flynn McRoberts, "Repeat Offender Gets Stiff Justice," *Chicago Tribune*, 4 September 2002, 1, 12, 13; Flynn McRoberts, "Ties to Enron Blinded Andersen," *Chicago Tribune*, 3 September 2002, 1; "Andersen Surrenders Accounting Licenses," *Wall Street Journal*, 3 September 2002, A6; Flynn McRoberts, "Civil War Splits Andersen," *Chicago Tribune*, 2 September 2002, 1; Flynn McRoberts, "The Fall of Andersen," *Chicago Tribune*, 1 September 2002, 1; Deepa Babington, "Curtain to Fall on Once-Proud Andersen," *Reuters Business*, 29 August 2002; Ken Brown and Ianthe Jeanne Dugan, "Andersen's Fall from Grace Is a Tale of Greed and Miscues," *Wall Street Journal*, 7 June 2002, A1, A6; Andrew Countryman and Delroy Alexander, "Bailing Out," *Chicago Tribune*, 2 June 2002, sec. 5, 1, 4; Ken Brown and Jonathan Weil, "How Andersen's Embrace of Consulting Altered the Culture of the Auditing Firm," *Wall Street Journal*, 12 March 2002, C1, C16;

Thaddeus Herrick and Alexei Barrionuevo, "Were Auditor and Client Too Close-Knit?," *Wall Street Journal*, 21 January 2002, C1, C5; Deepa Babington, "Accenture Now a Clear Winner Without Andersen Name," *Reuters Business*, 17 January 2002.

Chapter 17

Acknowledgements—Sources for Boxes and Case for Critical Thinking

Surprise! You've Been Swiped

Adapted from Sandra Block, "How to Protect Your Credit Card from Headaches of ID Theft," *USA Today*, 28 January 2003, B3; Lorien Holland, "How to Swipe a Million," *Far Eastern Economic Review*, October 2001, 68–69; Tom Lowry, "Thieves Swipe Credit with Card Readers," *USA Today*, 28 June 1999, 1B; Elaine Shannon, "A New Credit Card Scam," *Time*, 5 June 2000, 54–55; Linda Punch, "Card Fraud: Down but Not Out," *Credit Card Management*, June 1999, 30–42; Bill Orr, "Will E-Commerce Reverse Card Fraud Trend?," *American Bankers Association*, April 2000, 59–62.

How Will You Be Paying for That?

Adapted from Victor Smart, "Online: Show Me the Money," *The Guardian*, 11 April 2002; Julia Angwin, "E-Commerce: The Lessons We've Learned—E Money: And How Will You Be Paying for That?," *Wall Street Journal*, 23 October 2000, R37; Stacy Collett, "New Online Payment Options Emerging," *Computerworld*, 31 January 2000, 6; Kenneth Kiesnoski and Bob Curley, "Digital Wallets: Card Issuers Seek to Ease Web Shopping," *Bank Systems and Technology*, October 1999, 26–34; Thomas E. Weber, "On the Web, the Race for a Better Wallet," *New York Times*, 16 December 1998, B1, B4.

A Case for Critical Thinking: Cablevision Slims Down to Beef Up Profits

Adapted from NewsEdge, "Cablevision Clicks: Sales Strong, Earnings Up, Debt Down in 4Q," 12 February 2003 [accessed 13 February 2003] www.hoovers.com; Erin Joyce, "Digital Data Drives Cablevision's Outlook," Internetnews.com, 11 February 2003 [accessed 13 February 2003] www.internetnews.com; "Cablevision Puts 'For Sale' Sign on Wireless Unit," 9 August 2002 [accessed 13 February 2003] www.internetnews.com; Richard Sandomir, "Suit Dismissed Against Cablevision," *New York Times*, 15 June 2002, D7; Seth Schiesel, "Cablevision Will Retrench by Shedding Jobs and Stores," *New York Times*, 9 August 2002 [accessed 13 February 2003] www.nyt.com; Seth Schiesel, "Cablevision, Its Stock Price Battered, Will Retire Tracking Shares," *New York Times*, 6 August 2002, C3; Cablevision press release, "Cablevision Issues Statement Regarding Accounting," 10 June 2002; Ronald Grover, "Adelphia's Fall Will Bruise a Crowd," *Business Week*, 8 July 2002 [accessed 14 February 2003] www.businessweek.com; Cablevision press release, "Cablevision Systems Corporation Announces Fully-Funded Growth Plan," 8 August 2002.

Chapter 18

Exhibit 18.5: Richard Korman, "Mining for Nuggets of Financial Data," *New York Times*, 21 June 1998, BU5.
Exhibit 18.6: Amy Feldman, "The Seedy World of Online Stock Scams," *Money*, February 2000, 143–148. © 2002, Time Inc. All rights reserved.

Acknowledgements—Sources for Boxes and Case for Critical Thinking

The Betrayed Investor

Adapted from Gerald F. Seib and John Harwood, "What Could Bring 1930s-Style Reform of U.S Businesses?," *Wall Street Journal*, 24 July 2002, A1, A8; Marcia Vickers, Mike McNamee, and Peter Coy, "The Betrayed Investor," *Business Week*, 25 February 2002, 105–113; Michael McCarthy, "Wall Street's Woes Leave Its Glittery Image in Tatters," *USA Today*, 2 January 2002, 1A–1B; Floyd Norris, "A Hand over the Nose, A Hand Still in Stocks," *New York Times*, 27 June 2002, C1; James C. Cooper & Kathleen Madigan, "Don't Blame the Economy for the Bear Market," *Business Week*, 29 July 2002, 29–30; Robert Kuttner, "Today's Markets Need a Whole New Set of Rules," *Business Week*, 29 July 2002, 26.

A Case for Critical Thinking: Information Pays Off: Understanding Investments

Adapted from Fred Vogelstein, "The Man Who Saved the New York Stock Exchange," *Fortune*, 15 April 2002, 168–174; Peter Grant, "Big Board Signs Letter with State, City to Build $780 Million New York Home," *Wall Street Journal*, 21 December 2000, A8; Greg Ip and Peter Grant, "Deals & Deal Makers: NYSE's Deal for Staying in New York Draws Fire," *Wall Street Journal*, 6 December 2000, C22; Neil Weinburg, "The Big Board Comes back from the Brink," *Forbes*, 13 November 2000, 274–280; Pimm Fox, "Floored by Technology," *Computerworld*, 23 October 2000, 41; "Stock Exchanges: The Battle for Efficient Markets," *The Economist*, 17 June 2000, 69–71; Marcia Trombly, "Under Pressure, the NYSE Moves Online," *Computerworld*, 27 March 2000, 48; Marcia Vickers, "Getting off the NYSE Floor," *Business Week*, 7 February 2000, 80–81; Randall Smith, "Will NYSE Get Bowled over by Rivals?," *Wall Street Journal*, 19 January 2000, C1; Hal Lux, "Grasso Seeks a Floor Plan," *Institutional Investor*, January 2000, 42–43; Greg Ip and Randall Smith, "Tense Exchange: Big Board's Members Face Off on the Issue of Automated Trading," *Wall Street Journal*, 15 November 1999, A, 1:6; William P. Barrett, "End of an Era," *Forbes*, 11 October 1999, 121–126.

Component Chapter A

Exhibit A.1: Adapted from Bartley A. Brennan and Nancy Kubasek, *The Legal Environment of Business* (New York: Macmillan, 1988), 24; Douglas Whitman and John Gergacz, *The Legal Environment of Business*, 2d ed. (New York: Random House, 1988), 22, 25.

Exhibit A.3: Adapted from Richard A. Brealely and Stewart C. Myers, *Principles of Corporate Finance*, 4th ed. (New York: McGraw-Hill, 1991), 761–765.

Exhibit A.4: Adapted from BankruptcyData.Com [accessed 1 April 2003] www.bankruptcydata.com

Component Chapter C

Exhibit C.1: U.S. Department of Labor, *Occupational Outlook Handbook*, 2002–2003 Edition [accessed online 8 April 2003] www.bls.gov/oco.

Exhibit C.2: U.S. Department of Labor, *Occupational Outlook Handbook*, 2002–2003 Edition [accessed online 8 April 2003] www.bls.gov/oco.

Chapter 9

215 Jim West; **218** Jonathan Atkin; **219** Masterfile Corporation; **225** Charles O'Rear/CORBIS BETTMANN; **228** Dennis Kleiman Photography; **231** Larry Chan/Getty Images Inc.–Hulton Archive Photos; **236** Martyn Goddard/CORBIS BETTMANN

Chapter 10

245 SAS Institute Inc.; **252** AP/Wide World Photos; **253** CORBIS BETTMANN; **259** Ariel Skelley/Corbis/Stock Market; **265** DaSilva Photography; **266** AP/Wide World Photos

Chapter 11

273 Amy C. Etra/PhotoEdit; **281** John Klicker/John Klicker Photography; **282** Jeffrey Macmillan Photography; **287** Bradley C. Bower/Mercury Pictures; **288** Don Hogan Charles/New York Times Pictures; **289** Glaser Capital Partners, Inc.; **290** Michael Newman/PhotoEdit; **291** John Kringas/The Chicago Tribune/The Chicago Tribune

Chapter 12

299 Dann Tardif/Corbis/Stock Market; **301** The Susan G. Komen Breast Cancer Foundation; **305** Todd Plitt/Todd Plitt; **310** Rhoda Sidney/PhotoEdit; **318** David Young-Wolff/Getty Images-Stone Allstock

Chapter 13

327 AP/Wide World Photos; **331** Ted Rice; **333** Mate Airman Theron J. Godbold/via Bloomberg News/Ladov LLC; **335** Getty Images, Inc./Allsport Photography; **336** Kyoko Hamada; **340** David Kampfner/Getty Images, Inc.–Liaison; **346** PhotoCornett

Chapter 14

353 Landov LLC; **359** Tom Ewart/NWA Photography; **360** AP/Wide World Photos; **362** REUTERS/Joe Skipper/CORBIS BETTMANN; **369** Marilyn Newton/New York Times Pictures; **370** Kristine Larsen

Chapter 15

377 Rowhouse Pictures, Inc.; **381** Robin Nelson/Black Star; **382** Alan Klehr/Churchill & Klehr Photography; **388** Rudi Von Briel/PhotoEdit; **389** Karen Leitza/Karen Leitza; **392** AP/Wide World Photos; **394** Bill Aron/PhotoEdit

Chapter 16

405 AP/Wide World Photos; **406** Superstock, Inc.; **412** Ryan Reniorz/Canadian Press; **416** Terry Vine/Getty Images Inc.–Stone Allstock

Chapter 17

431 REUTERS/Jeff Christensen-Handout/Landov/LLC; **433** Olathe Daily News, Todd Feeback/AP/Wide World Photos; **434** Shotgun/Corbis/Stock Market; **435** Bob Firth Photography/ImageState/International Stock Photography Ltd.; **440** CORBIS BETTMANN; **441** CORBIS BETTMANN; **443** (Top), Ariel Skelley/CORBIS BETTMANN; **443** (Bottom), Robert Holmgren Photography; **445** Michael Krasowitz/Getty Images, Inc.–Taxi

Chapter 18

457 James Leynse/Corbis/SABA Press Photos, Inc.; **463** Mark Joseph/Getty Images Inc.–Stone Allstock; **464** Jeffrey Macmillan/PARS International Corporation; **466** Pat Sullivan/AP/Wide World Photos; **470** Superstock, Inc.

Component Chapter A

486 Panos Pictures; **487** Susana Raab; **489** AP/Wide World Photos; **493** The Image Works; **494** Chris Hondros, Newsmaker/Getty Images, Inc.–Liason

Component Chapter B

500 (Top) Stan Godlewski Photography; **500** (Bottom) Getty Images, Inc.–Stone Allstock; **502** Rudi Von Briel/PhotoEdit; **503** Tim Beddow/Photo Researchers, Inc.; **504** Susan Holtz; **505** Jason Grow/Corbis/SABA Press Photos, Inc.; **506** Mark Sherman/Photo Network

Component Chapter C

514 Mark Richards/PhotoEdit; **520** Mark Wilson Photographer

GLOSSARY

A

absolute advantage   A nation's ability to produce a particular product with fewer resources per unit of output than any other nation

accountability   Obligation to report results to supervisors or team members and to justify outcomes that fall below expectations

accounting equation   Basic accounting equation stating that assets equal liabilities plus owners' equity

accounting   Measuring, interpreting, and communicating financial information to support internal and external decision making

accounts receivable turnover ratio   Measure of time a company takes to turn its accounts receivable into cash, calculated by dividing sales by the average value of accounts receivable for a period

accrual basis   Accounting method in which revenue is recorded when a sale is made and expense is recorded when it is incurred

acquisition   Form of business combination in which one company buys another company's voting stock

activity ratios   Ratios that measure the effectiveness of the firm's use of its resources

administrative skills   Technical skills in information gathering, data analysis, planning, organizing, and other aspects of managerial work

advertising   Paid, nonpersonal communication to a target market from an identified sponsor using mass communications channels

advocacy advertising   Ads that present a company's opinions on public issues such as education and health

affirmative action   Activities undertaken by businesses to recruit and promote women and minorities, based on an analysis of the workforce and the available labor pool

agents and brokers   Independent wholesalers that do not take title to the goods they distribute but may or may not take possession of those goods

analytic system   Production process that breaks incoming materials into various component products and divisional patterns simultaneously

application software   Programs that perform specific functions for users, such as word processing or spreadsheet analysis

arbitration   Process for resolving a labor-contract dispute in which an impartial third party studies the issues and makes a binding decision

artificial intelligence   Ability of computers to reason, to learn, and to simulate human sensory perceptions

asset allocation   Method of shifting investments within a portfolio to adapt them to the current investment environment

assets   Anything of value owned or leased by a business

auction exchange   Centralized marketplace where securities are traded by specialists on behalf of investors

audit   Formal evaluation of the fairness and reliability of a client's financial statements

authority   Power granted by the organization to make decisions, take actions, and allocate resources to accomplish goals

authorization cards   Sign-up cards designating a union as the signer's preferred bargaining agent

authorized stock   Shares that a corporation's board of directors has decided to sell eventually

autocratic leaders   Leaders who do not involve others in decision making

automated teller machines (ATMs)   Electronic terminals that permit people with plastic cards to perform simple banking transactions 24 hours a day without the aid of a human teller

B

balance of payments   Sum of all payments one nation receives from other nations minus the sum of all payments it makes to other nations, over some specified period of time

balance of trade   Total value of the products a nation exports minus the total value of the products it imports, over some period of time

balance sheet   Statement of a firm's financial position on a particular date; also known as a statement of financial position

bandwidth   Maximum capacity of a data transmission medium

banner ads   Rectangular graphic displays on a webpage that are used for advertising and linked to an advertiser's webpage

barriers to entry   Factors that make it difficult to launch a business in a particular industry

bear market   Falling stock market

behavior modification   Systematic use of rewards and punishments to change human behavior

behavioral segmentation Categorization of customers according to their relationship with products or response to product characteristics

board of directors Group of people, elected by the shareholders, who have the ultimate authority in guiding the affairs of a corporation

bond Method of funding in which the issuer borrows from an investor and provides a written promise to make regular interest payments and repay the borrowed amount in the future

bonus Cash payment, in addition to the regular wage or salary, that serves as a reward for achievement

bookkeeping Record keeping, clerical aspect of accounting

Boolean operators The term boolean refers to a system of logical thought developed by the English mathematician George Boole; it uses the operators AND, OR, and NOT

boycott Union activity in which members and sympathizers refuse to buy or handle the product of a target company

brand awareness Level of brand loyalty at which people are familiar with a product; they recognize it

brand insistence Level of brand loyalty at which people will accept no substitute for a particular product

brand loyalty Commitment to a particular brand

brand manager The person who develops and implements a complete strategy and marketing program for a specific product or brand

brand mark Portion of a brand that cannot be expressed verbally

brand names Portion of a brand that can be expressed orally, including letters, words, or numbers

brand preference Level of brand loyalty at which people habitually buy a product if it is available

brand A name, term, sign, symbol, design, or combination of those used to identify the products of a firm and to differentiate them from competing products

break-even analysis Method of calculating the minimum volume of sales needed at a given price to cover all costs

break-even point Sales volume at a given price that will cover all of a company's costs

broadbanding Payment system that uses wide pay grades, enabling the company to give pay raises without promotions

broker Individual registered to sell securities

budget Planning and control tool that reflects expected revenues, operating expenses, and cash receipts and outlays

bull market Rising stock market

bundling Combining several products and offering the bundle at a reduced price

business agent Full-time union staffer who negotiates with management and enforces the union's agreements with companies

business cycle Fluctuations in the rate of growth that an economy experiences over a period of several years

business plan A written document that provides an orderly statement of a company's goals and how it intends to achieve those goals

business Activity and enterprise that provides goods and services that a society needs

business-to-business e-commerce Electronic commerce that involves transactions between companies and their suppliers, manufacturers, or other companies

business-to-consumer e-commerce Electronic commerce that involves transactions between businesses and the end user or consumer

C

calendar year Twelve-month accounting period that begins on January 1 and ends on December 31

canned approach Selling method based on a fixed, memorized presentation

capacity planning A long-term strategic decision that determines the level of resources available to an organization to meet customer demand

capital budgeting Process for evaluating proposed investments in select projects that provide the best long-term financial return

capital gains Difference between the price at which a financial asset is sold and its original cost (assuming the price has gone up)

capital investments Money paid to acquire something of permanent value in a business

capital structure Financing mix of a firm

capital The physical, human-made elements used to produce goods and services, such as factories and computers; can also refer to the funds that finance the operations of a business

capital-intensive businesses Businesses that require large investments in capital assets

capitalism Economic system based on economic freedom and competition

cash basis Accounting method in which revenue is recorded when payment is received and expense is recorded when cash is paid

category killers Discount chains that sell only one category of products

cause-related marketing Identification and marketing of a social issue, cause, or idea to selected target markets

cellular layout Method of arranging a facility so that parts with similar shapes or processing requirements are processed together in work centers

centralization Concentration of decision-making authority at the top of the organization

certification Process by which a union is officially recognized by the National Labor Relations Board as the bargaining agent for a group of employees

certified management accountants (CMAs) Accountants who have fulfilled the requirements for certification as specialists in management accounting

certified public accountant (CPA) Professionally licensed accountant who meets certain requirements for education and experience and who passes a comprehensive examination

chain of command Pathway for the flow of authority from one management level to the next

chat A form of interactive communication that enables computer users in separate locations to have real-time conversations. Usually takes place at websites called chat rooms.

checks Written orders that tell the customer's bank to pay a specific amount to a particular individual or business

chief executive officer (CEO) Person appointed by a corporation's board of directors to carry out the board's policies and supervise the activities of the corporation

chief information officer (CIO)   Top corporate executive with responsibility for managing information and information systems

close the books   The act of transferring net revenue and expense account balances to retained earnings for the period

closing   Point at which a sale is completed

coaching   Helping employees reach their highest potential by meeting with them, discussing problems that hinder their ability to work effectively, and offering suggestions and encouragement to overcome these problems

co-branding   Partnership between two or more companies to closely link their brand names together for a single product

code of ethics   Written statement setting forth the principles that guide an organization's decisions

cognitive dissonance   Anxiety following a purchase that prompts buyers to seek reassurance about the purchase; commonly known as buyer's remorse

cohesiveness   A measure of how committed the team members are to their team's goals

collateral   Tangible asset a lender can claim if a borrower defaults on a loan

collective bargaining   Process used by unions and management to negotiate work contracts

commercial paper   An IOU, backed by the corporation's reputation, issued to raise short-term capital

commercialization   Large-scale production and distribution of a product

commissions   Payments to employees equal to a certain percentage of sales made

committee   Team that may become a permanent part of the organization and is designed to deal with regularly recurring tasks

commodities   Raw materials used in producing other goods

common stock   Shares whose owners have voting rights and have the last claim on distributed profits and assets

communism   Economic system in which all productive resources are owned and operated by the government, to the elimination of private property

comparative advantage theory   Theory that states that a country should produce and sell to other countries those items it produces most efficiently

comparative advertising   Advertising technique in which two or more products are explicitly compared

compensating balance   Portion of an unsecured loan that is kept on deposit at the lending institution to protect the lender and increase the lender's return

compensation   Money, benefits, and services paid to employees for their work

competition   Rivalry among businesses for the same customer

competitive advantage   Ability to perform in one or more ways that competitors cannot match

competitive advertising   Ads that specifically highlight how a product is better than its competitors

computer-aided design (CAD)   Use of computer graphics and mathematical modeling in the development of products

computer-aided engineering (CAE)   Use of computers to test products without building an actual model

computer-aided manufacturing (CAM)   Use of computers to control production equipment

computer-integrated manufacturing (CIM)   Computer-based systems, including CAD and CAM, that coordinate and control all the elements of design and production

conceptual skills   Ability to understand the relationship of parts to the whole

conflict of interest   Situation in which a business decision may be influenced by the potential for personal gain

consolidation   Combination of two or more companies in which the old companies cease to exist and a new enterprise is created

consumer buying behavior   Behavior exhibited by consumers as they consider and purchase various products

consumer market   Individuals or households that buy goods or services for personal use

consumer price index (CPI)   Monthly statistic that measures changes in the prices of about 400 goods and services that consumers buy

consumer promotion   Sales promotion aimed at final consumers

consumerism   Movement that pressures businesses to consider consumer needs and interests

consumer-to-consumer e-commerce   Electronic commerce that involves transactions between consumers

contingency leadership   Adapting the leadership style to what is most appropriate, given current business conditions

controller   Highest-ranking accountant in a company, responsible for overseeing all accounting functions

controlling   Process of measuring progress against goals and objectives and correcting deviations if results are not as expected

convertible bonds   Corporate bonds that can be exchanged at the owner's discretion into common stock of the issuing company

cooperative advertising   Joint efforts between local and national advertisers, in which producers of nationally sold products share the costs of local advertising with local merchants and wholesalers

core competence   Distinct skills and capabilities that a firm has or does especially well so that it sets the firm apart from its competitors

corporate culture   A set of shared values and norms that support the management system and that guide management and employee behavior

corporation   Legally chartered enterprise having most of the legal rights of a person, including the right to conduct business, to own and sell property, to borrow money, and to sue or be sued; owners of the corporation enjoy limited liability

cost accounting   Area of accounting focusing on the calculation of manufacturing and storage costs of products for use or sale in a business

cost of capital   Average rate of interest a firm pays on its combination of debt and equity

cost of goods sold   Cost of producing or acquiring a company's products for sale during a given period

coupons   Certificates that offer discounts on particular items and are redeemed at the time of purchase

creative selling   Selling process used by order getters, which involves determining customer needs, devising strategies to explain product benefits, and persuading customers to buy

credit cards   Plastic cards that allow the customer to buy now and pay back the loaned amount at a future date

crisis management   System for minimizing the harm that might result from some unusually threatening situations

critical path   In a PERT network diagram, the sequence of operations that requires the longest time to complete

cross-functional teams   Teams that draw together employees from different functional areas

cross-promotion   Jointly advertising two or more noncompeting brands

currency   Bills and coins that make up the cash money of a society

current assets   Cash and items that can be turned into cash within one year

current liabilities   Obligations that must be met within a year

current ratio   Measure of a firm's short-term liquidity, calculated by dividing current assets by current liabilities

customer divisions   Divisional structure that focuses on customers or clients

customer service   Efforts a company makes to satisfy its customers to help them realize the greatest possible value from the products they are purchasing

cyberterrorism   Orchestrated attacks on a company's information systems for political or economic purposes

D

data mining   Sifting through huge amounts of data to identify what is valuable to a specific question or problem

data warehousing   Building an organized central database out of files and databases gathered from various functional areas, such as marketing, operations, and accounting

data   Recorded facts and statistics; data need to be converted to information before they can help people solve business problems

database marketing   Process of building, maintaining, and using customer databases for the purpose of contacting customers and transacting business

databases   Centralized, organized collections of data

day order   Any order to buy or sell a security that automatically expires if not executed on the day the order is placed

dealer exchange   Decentralized marketplace where securities are bought and sold by dealers out of their own inventories

debentures   Corporate bonds backed only by the reputation of the issuer

debit cards   Plastic cards that allow the bank to take money from the user's demand-deposit account and transfer it to a retailer's account

debt ratios   Ratios that measure a firm's reliance on debt financing of its operations (sometimes called leverage ratios)

debt-to-equity ratio   Measure of the extent to which a business is financed by debt as opposed to invested capital, calculated by dividing the company's total liabilities by owners' equity

debt-to-total-assets ratio   Measure of a firm's ability to carry long-term debt, calculated by dividing total liabilities by total assets

decentralization   Delegation of decision-making authority to employees in lower-level positions

decertification   Process employees use to take away a union's official right to represent them

decision support system (DSS)   Information system that uses decision models, specialized databases, and artificial intelligence to assist managers in solving highly unstructured and nonroutine problems

decision-making skills   Ability to identify and analyze a problem, weigh the alternatives, choose an alternative, implement it, and evaluate the results

deflation   Economic condition in which prices fall steadily throughout the economy

delegation   Assignment of work and the authority and responsibility required to complete it

demand curve   Graph of the quantities of product that buyers will purchase at various prices

demand deposits   Money in a checking account that can be used by the customer at any time

demand   Buyers' willingness and ability to purchase products

democratic leaders   Leaders who delegate authority and involve employees in decision making

demographics   Study of statistical characteristics of a population

departmentalization by division   Grouping departments according to similarities in product, process, customer, or geography

departmentalization by function   Grouping workers according to their similar skills, resource use, and expertise

departmentalization by matrix   Assigning employees to both a functional group and a project team (thus using functional and divisional patterns simultaneously)

departmentalization by network   Electronically connecting separate companies that perform selected tasks for a small headquarters organization

departmentalization   Grouping people within an organization according to function, division, matrix, or network

depreciation   Accounting procedure for systematically spreading the cost of a tangible asset over its estimated useful life

direct mail   Advertising sent directly to potential customers, usually through the U.S. Postal Service

direct marketing   Direct communication other than personal sales contacts designed to effect a measurable response

discount pricing   Offering a reduction in price

discount rate   Interest rate charged by the Federal Reserve on loans to commercial banks and other financial institutions

discount stores   Retailers that sell a variety of goods below the market price by keeping their overhead low

discretionary order   Market order that allows the broker to decide when to trade a security

discrimination   In a social and economic sense, denial of opportunities to individuals on the basis of some characteristic that has no bearing on their ability to perform in a job

discussion mailing lists   E-mail lists that allow people to discuss a common interest by posting messages, which are received by everyone in the group

dispatching   Issuing work orders and schedules to department heads and supervisors

distribution centers   Warehouse facilities that specialize in collecting and shipping merchandise

distribution channels   Systems for moving goods and services from producers to customers; also known as marketing channels

distribution mix   Combination of intermediaries and channels a producer uses to get a product to end users

distribution strategy   Firm's overall plan for moving products to intermediaries and final customers

diversification   Assembling investment portfolios in such a way that a loss in one investment won't cripple the value of the entire portfolio

diversity initiatives   Company policies designed to enhance opportunities for minorities and to promote understanding of diverse cultures, customs, and talents

dividends   Distributions of corporate assets to shareholders in the form of cash or other assets

double-entry bookkeeping   Way of recording financial transactions that requires two entries for every transaction so that the accounting equation is always kept in balance

drop shippers   Limited-service merchant wholesalers that assume ownership of goods but don't take physical possession; commonly used to market agricultural and mineral products

dumping   Charging less than the actual cost or less than the home-country price for goods sold in other countries

dynamic pricing   Charging different prices depending on individual customers and situations

E

earnings per share   Measure of a firm's profitability for each share of outstanding stock, calculated by dividing net income after taxes by the average number of shares of common stock outstanding

ecology   Study of the relationships between living things in the water, air, and soil, their environments, and the nutrients that support them

economic indicators   Statistics that measure variables in the economy

economic system   Means by which a society distributes its resources to satisfy its people's needs

economics   The study of how society uses scarce resources to produce and distribute goods and services

economies of scale   Savings from manufacturing, marketing, or buying in large quantities

electronic commerce (e-commerce)   The general term for the buying and selling of goods and services on the Internet

Electronic communication networks (ECNs)   Internet-based networks that match up buy and sell orders without using a middleman

electronic data interchange (EDI)   Information systems that transmit documents such as invoices and purchase orders between computers, thereby lowering ordering costs and paperwork

electronic funds transfer systems (EFTS)   Computerized systems for performing financial transactions

embargo   Total ban on trade with a particular nation (a sanction) or of a particular product

employee assistance programs (EAPs)   Company-sponsored counseling or referral plans for employees with personal problems

employee benefits   Compensation other than wages, salaries, and incentive programs

employee stock-ownership plan (ESOP)   Program enabling employees to become partial owners of a company

enterprise resource planning (ERP)   A comprehensive database system that includes information about the firm's suppliers and customers as well as data generated internally

entrepreneurs   People who accept the risk of failure in the private enterprise system

equilibrium price   Point at which quantity supplied equals quantity demanded

ethical dilemma   Situation in which both sides of an issue can be supported with valid arguments

ethical lapse   Situation in which an individual makes a decision that is morally wrong, illegal, or unethical

ethics   The rules or standards governing the conduct of a person or group

euro   A planned unified currency used by European nations that meet certain strict requirements

exchange process   Act of obtaining a desired object from another party by offering something of value in return

exchange rate   Rate at which the money of one country is traded for the money of another

exclusive distribution   Market coverage strategy that gives intermediaries exclusive rights to sell a product in a specific geographical area

executive information system (EIS)   Similar to decision support system but customized to strategic needs of executives

expenses   Costs created in the process of generating revenues

expert system   Computer system that simulates the thought processes of a human expert who is adept at solving particular problems

exporting   Selling and shipping goods or services to another country

extranet   Similar to an intranet, but extending the network to select people outside the organization

F

factors of production   Basic inputs that a society uses to produce goods and services, including natural resources, labor, capital, entrepreneurship, and knowledge

family branding   Using a brand name on a variety of related products

file transfer protocol (FTP)   A software protocol that lets you copy or move files from a remote computer-called an FTP site-to your computer over the Internet; it is the Internet facility for downloading and uploading files

financial accounting   Area of accounting concerned with preparing financial information for users outside the organization

financial analysis   Process of evaluating a company's performance and analyzing the costs and benefits of a strategic action

financial control   The process of analyzing and adjusting the basic financial plan to correct for forecasted events that do not materialize

financial futures   Legally binding agreements to buy or sell financial instruments at a future date

financial management   Effective acquisition and use of money

financial plan   A forecast of financial requirements and the financing sources to be used

firewall   Computer hardware and software that protects part or all of a private computer network attached to the Internet by preventing public Internet users from accessing it

first-line managers   Those at the lowest level of the management hierarchy; they supervise the operating employees and implement the plans set at the higher management levels; also called supervisory managers

fiscal policy   Use of government revenue collection and spending to influence the business cycle

fiscal year   Any 12 consecutive months used as an accounting period

fixed assets   Assets retained for long-term use, such as land, buildings, machinery, and equipment; also referred to as property, plant, and equipment

fixed costs   Business costs that remain constant regardless of the number of units produced

fixed-position layout   Method of arranging a facility so that the product is stationary and equipment and personnel come to it

flat organizations   Organizations with a wide span of management and few hierarchical levels

flexible manufacturing system (FMS)   Production system using computer-controlled machines that can adapt to various versions of the same operation

flextime   Scheduling system in which employees are allowed certain options regarding time of arrival and departure

foreign direct investment (FDI)   Investment of money by foreign companies in domestic business enterprises

form utility   Consumer value created by converting raw materials and other inputs into finished goods and services

formal organization   A framework officially established by managers for accomplishing tasks that lead to achieving the organization's goals

forward buying   Retailers taking advantage of trade allowances by buying more products at discounted prices than they hope to sell

franchise   Business arrangement in which a small business obtains rights to sell the goods or services of the supplier (franchisor)

franchisee   Small-business owner who contracts for the right to sell goods or services of the supplier (franchisor) in exchange for some payment

franchisor   Supplier that grants a franchise to an individual or group (franchisee) in exchange for payments

free riders   Team members who do not contribute sufficiently to the group's activities because members are not being held individually accountable for their work

free trade   International trade unencumbered by restrictive measures

free-market system   Economic system in which decisions about what to produce and in what quantities are decided by the market's buyers and sellers

full-service merchant wholesalers   Merchant wholesalers that provide a wide variety of services to their customers, such as storage, delivery, and marketing support

functional teams   Teams whose members come from a single functional department and that are based on the organization's vertical structure

G

gain sharing   Plan for rewarding employees not on the basis of overall profits but in relation to achievement of goals such as cost savings from higher productivity

Gantt chart   Bar chart used to control schedules by showing how long each part of a production process should take and when it should take place

general expenses   Operating expenses, such as office and administrative expenses, not directly associated with creating or marketing a good or a service

general obligation bond   Municipal bonds backed by the issuing agency's general taxing authority

general partnership   Partnership in which all partners have the right to participate as co-owners and are individually liable for the business's debts

generally accepted accounting principles (GAAP)   Professionally approved U.S. standards and practices used by accountants in the preparation of financial statements

generic products   Products characterized by a plain label, with no advertising and no brand name

geodemographics   Method of combining geographical data with demographic data to develop profiles of neighborhood segments

geographic divisions   Divisional structure based on location of operations

geographic segmentation   Categorization of customers according to their geographical location

glass ceiling   Invisible barrier attributable to subtle discrimination that keeps women out of the top positions in business

globalization   Tendency of the world's economies to act as a single interdependent market

goal   Broad, long-range target or aim

goods-producing businesses   Businesses that produce tangible products

gross domestic product (GDP)   Dollar value of all the final goods and services produced by businesses located within a nation's borders; excludes receipts from overseas operations of domestic companies

gross national product (GNP)   Dollar value of all the final goods and services produced by domestic businesses; includes receipts from overseas operations and excludes receipts from foreign-owned businesses within a nation's borders

gross profit   Amount remaining when the cost of goods sold is deducted from net sales; also known as gross margin

growth stocks   Equities issued by small companies with unproven products or services

H

hardware   Physical components of a computer system, including integrated circuits, keyboards, and disk drives

hedge   To make an investment that protects the investor from suffering loss on another investment

holding company   Company that owns most, if not all, of another company's stock but that does not actively participate in the management of that other company

hostile takeovers   Situations in which an outside party buys enough stock in a corporation to take control against the wishes of the board of directors and corporate officers

human relations   Interaction among people within an organization for the purpose of achieving organizational and personal goals

human resources management (HRM)   Specialized function of planning how to obtain employees, oversee their training, evaluate them, and compensate them

human resources   All the people who work for an organization

hygiene factors   Aspects of the work environment that are associated with dissatisfaction

I

importing   Purchasing goods or services from another country and bringing them into one's own country

incentives   Cash payments to employees who produce at a desired level or whose unit (often the company as a whole) produces at a desired level

income statement   Financial record of a company's revenues, expenses, and profits over a given period of time

incubators   Facilities that house small businesses during their early growth phase

inflation   Economic condition in which prices rise steadily throughout the economy

informal organization   Network of informal employee interactions that are not defined by the formal structure

initial public offering (IPO)   Corporation's first offering of stock to the public

injunction   Court order prohibiting certain actions by striking workers

insider trading   Use of material nonpublic information to further one's own fortune or those of one's family and friends

instant messaging (IM)   Technology that allows people to carry on real-time, one-on-one, and small-group text conversations. Unlike e-mail, instant messages are not automatically recorded or saved.

institutional advertising   Advertising that seeks to create goodwill and to build a desired image for a company rather than to sell specific products

institutional investors   Companies that invest money entrusted to them by others

integrated marketing communications (IMC)   Strategy of coordinating and integrating communications and promotions efforts with customers to ensure greater efficiency and effectiveness

intensive distribution   Market coverage strategy that tries to place a product in as many outlets as possible

internal auditors   Employees who analyze and evaluate a company's operations and data to determine their accuracy

Internet telephony   Using the Internet to converse vocally

Internet   A worldwide collection of interconnected networks that enables users to share information electronically and provides digital access to a wide variety of services

interpersonal skills   Skills required to understand other people and to interact effectively with them

intranet   A private network, set up within a corporation or organization, that operates over the Internet and may be used to link geographically remote sites

inventory control   System for determining the right quantity of various items to have on hand and keeping track of their location, use, and condition

inventory turnover ratio   Measure of the time a company takes to turn its inventory into sales, calculated by dividing cost of goods sold by the average value of inventory for a period

inventory   Goods kept in stock for the production process or for sales to final customers

investment portfolios   Assortment of investment instruments

ISO 9000   Global standards set by the International Organization for Standardization establishing a minimum level of acceptable quality

issued stock   Authorized shares that have been released to the market

J

job analysis   Process by which jobs are studied to determine the tasks and dynamics involved in performing them

job description   Statement of the tasks involved in a given job and the conditions under which the holder of the job will work

job enrichment   Reducing work specialization and making work more meaningful by adding to the responsibilities of each job

job redesign   Designing a better fit between employees' skills and their work to increase job satisfaction

job sharing   Splitting a single full-time job between two employees for their convenience

job specification   Statement describing the kind of person who would be best for a given job-including the skills, education, and previous experience that the job requires

joint venture   Cooperative partnership in which organizations share investment costs, risks, management, and profits in the development, production, or selling of products

just-in-time (JIT) system   Continuous system that pulls materials through the production process, making sure that all materials arrive just when they are needed with minimal inventory and waste

K

knowledge   Expertise gained through experience or association

knowledge-based pay   Pay tied to an employee's acquisition of skills; also called skill-based pay

L

labor federation   Umbrella organization of national unions and unaffiliated local unions that undertakes large-scale activities on behalf of their members and that resolves conflicts between unions

labor unions   Organizations of employees formed to protect and advance their members' interests

labor-intensive businesses   Businesses in which labor costs are more significant than capital costs

laissez-faire leaders   Leaders who leave the actual decision making up to employees

layoffs   Termination of employees for economic or business reasons

lead time   Period that elapses between the ordering of materials and their arrival from the supplier

leading   Process of guiding and motivating people to work toward organizational goals

lease   Legal agreement that obligates the user of an asset to make payments to the owner of the asset in exchange for using it

leverage   Technique of increasing the rate of return on an investment by financing it with borrowed funds

leveraged buyout (LBO)   Situation in which individuals or groups of investors purchase a company primarily with debt secured by the company's assets

liabilities   Claims against a firm's assets by creditors

license   Agreement to produce and market another company's product in exchange for a royalty or fee

licensing   Agreement to produce and market another company's product in exchange for a royalty or fee

limit order   Market order that stipulates the highest or lowest price at which the customer is willing to trade securities

limited liability companies (LLCs)   Organizations that combine the benefits of S corporations and limited partnerships without the drawbacks of either

limited partnership   Partnership composed of one or more general partners and one or more partners whose liability is usually limited to the amount of their capital investment

limited-service merchant wholesalers   Merchant wholesalers that offer fewer services than full-service merchant wholesalers; they often specialize in particular markets, such as agriculture

line of credit   Arrangement in which the financial institution makes money available for use at any time after the loan has been approved

line organization   Chain-of-command system that establishes a clear line of authority flowing from the top down

line-and-staff organization   Organization system that has a clear chain of command but that also includes functional groups of people who provide advice and specialized services

liquidity ratios   Ratios that measure a firm's ability to meet its short-term obligations when they are due

local advertising   Advertising sponsored by a local merchant

local area network (LAN)   Computer network that encompasses a small area, such as an office or a university campus

locals   Relatively small union groups, usually part of a national union or a labor federation, that represent members who work in a single facility or in a certain geographic area

lockouts   Management tactics in which union members are prevented from entering a business during a strike in order to force union acceptance of management's last contract proposal

logistics   The planning, movement, and flow of goods and related information throughout the supply chain

long-term financing   Financing used to cover long-term expenses such as assets (generally repaid over a period of more than one year)

long-term liabilities   Obligations that fall due more than a year from the date of the balance sheet

M

M1   That portion of the money supply consisting of currency and demand deposits

M2   That portion of the money supply consisting of currency, demand deposits, and small time deposits

M3   That portion of the money supply consisting of M1 and M2 plus large time deposits and other restrictive deposits

macroeconomics   The study of a country's overall economic issues, such as competition, the allocation of scarce resources, and government policies

mail-order firms   Companies that sell products through catalogs and ship them directly to customers

management accounting   Area of accounting concerned with preparing data for use by managers within the organization

management by objectives (MBO)   A motivational tool whereby managers and employees work together to structure personal goals and objectives for every individual, department, and project to mesh with the organization's goals

management information system (MIS)   Computer system that supplies information to assist in managerial decision making

management pyramid   Organizational structure comprising top, middle, and lower management

management   Process of coordinating resources to meet organizational goals

mandatory retirement   Required dismissal of an employee who reaches a certain age

manufacturing resource planning (MRP II)   Computer-based system that integrates data from all departments to manage inventory and production planning and control

margin trading   Borrowing money from brokers to buy stock, paying interest on the borrowed money, and leaving the stock with the broker as collateral

market indexes   Measures of security markets calculated from the prices of a selection of securities

market makers   Dealers in dealer exchanges who sell securities out of their own inventories so that a market is always available for buyers and sellers

market order   Authorization for a broker to buy or sell securities at the best price that can be negotiated at the moment

market segmentation   Division of total market into smaller, relatively homogeneous groups

market share   A firm's portion of the total sales in a market

market   People or businesses who need or want a product and have the money to buy it

marketable securities   Stocks, bonds, and other investments that can be turned into cash quickly

marketing concept   Approach to marketing that stresses customer needs and wants, seeks long-term profitability, and integrates marketing with other functional units within the organization

marketing intermediaries   Businesspeople and organizations that channel goods and services from producers to consumers

marketing mix   The four key elements of marketing strategy: product, price, place (distribution), and promotion

marketing research   The collection and analysis of information for making marketing decisions

marketing strategy   Overall plan for marketing a product

marketing   Process of planning and executing the conception, pricing, promotion, and distribution of ideas, goods, and services to create and maintain relationships that satisfy individual and organizational objectives

mass customization   Producing customized goods and services through mass production techniques

mass production   Manufacture of uniform products in great quantities

matching principle Fundamental principle requiring that expenses incurred in producing revenue be deducted from the revenues they generate during an accounting period

material requirements planning (MRP) Method of getting the correct materials where they are needed, on time, and without carrying unnecessary inventory

materials handling Movement of goods within a firm's warehouse terminal, factory, or store

media mix The combination of print, broadcast, and other media used for the advertising campaign

media plan Written plan that outlines how a company will spend its media budget, including how the money will be divided among the various media and when the advertisements will appear

media Communications channels, such as newspapers, radio, and television

mediation Process for resolving a labor-contract dispute in which a neutral third party meets with both sides and attempts to steer them toward a solution

mentor Experienced manager or employee with a wide network of industry colleagues who can explain office politics, serve as a role model for appropriate business behavior, and help other employees negotiate the corporate structure

merchant wholesalers Independent wholesalers that take legal title to goods they distribute

merger Combination of two companies in which one company purchases the other and assumes control of its property and liabilities

microeconomics The study of small economic units, such as individual consumers, businesses, and industries

middle managers Those in the middle of the management hierarchy; they develop plans to implement the goals of top managers and coordinate the work of first-line managers

mission statement A statement of the organization's purpose, basic goals, and philosophies

missionary salespeople Salespeople who support existing customers, usually wholesalers and retailers

mobile commerce (m-commerce) Transaction of electronic commerce using wireless devices and wireless Internet access instead of PC-based technology

modem Hardware device that allows a computer to communicate over a regular telephone line

monetary policy Government policy and actions taken by the Federal Reserve Board to regulate the nation's money supply

money Anything generally accepted as a means of paying for goods and services

money-market funds Mutual funds that invest in short-term securities

monopolistic competition Situation in which many sellers differentiate their products from those of competitors in at least some small way

monopoly Market in which there are no direct competitors, so that one company dominates

morale Attitude an individual has toward his or her job and employer

motivation Force that moves someone to take action

motivators Factors of human relations in business that may increase motivation

multinational corporations (MNCs) Companies with operations in more than one country

municipal bonds Debt issued by a state or a local agency; interest earned on municipal bonds is exempt from federal income tax and from taxes in the issuing jurisdiction

mutual funds Pools of money raised by investment companies and invested in stocks, bonds, or other marketable securities

N

NASDAQ (National Association of Securities Dealers Automated Quotations) National over-the-counter securities trading network

national advertising Advertising sponsored by companies that sell products on a nationwide basis; refers to the geographic reach of the advertiser, not the geographic coverage of the ad

national brands Brands owned by the manufacturers and distributed nationally

national union Nationwide organization made up of local unions that represent employees in locations around the country

natural resources Land, forests, minerals, water, and other tangible assets usable in their natural state

need Difference between a person's actual state and his or her ideal state; provides the basic motivation to make a purchase

need-satisfaction approach Selling method that starts with identifying the customer's needs and then creating a presentation that addresses those needs; this is the approach used by most professional salespeople

net income Profit earned or loss incurred by a firm, determined by subtracting expenses from revenues; also called the bottom line

network Collection of computers, communications software, and transmission media (such as telephone lines) that allows computers to communicate

news conference Gathering of media representatives at which companies announce new information; also called a press briefing or press conference

news release Brief statement or video program released to the press announcing new products, management changes, sales performance, and other potential news items; also called a press release

nonprofit organizations Firms whose primary objective is something other than returning a profit to their owners

norms Informal standards of conduct that guide team behavior

O

objective Specific, short-range target or aim

office automation systems (OAS) Computer systems that assist with the tasks that people in a typical business office face regularly, such as drawing graphs or processing documents

oligopoly Market dominated by a few producers

open order Limit order that does not expire at the end of a trading day

open-market operations Activity of the Federal Reserve in buying and selling government bonds on the open market

operating expenses All costs of operation that are not included under cost of goods sold

operating systems Class of software that controls the computer's hardware components

operational plans   Plans that lay out the actions and the resource allocation needed to achieve operational objectives and to support tactical plans; usually defined for less than 1 year and developed by first-line managers

order getters   Salespeople who are responsible for generating new sales and for increasing sales to existing customers

order processing   Functions involved in preparing and receiving an order

order takers   Salespeople who generally process incoming orders without engaging in creative selling

organization chart   Diagram showing how employees and tasks are grouped and where the lines of communication and authority flow

organizational market   Consumers who buy goods or services for resale or for use in conducting their own operations

organizational structure   Framework enabling managers to divide responsibilities, ensure employee accountability, and distribute decision-making authority

organizing   Process of arranging resources to carry out the organization's plans

orientation   Session or procedure for acclimating a new employee to the organization

owners' equity   Portion of a company's assets that belongs to the owners after obligations to all creditors have been met

P

par value   Arbitrary value assigned to a stock that is shown on the stock certificate

parent company   Company that owns most, if not all, of another company's stock and that takes an active part in managing that other company

participative management   Sharing information with employees and involving them in decision making

partnership   Unincorporated business owned and operated by two or more persons under a voluntary legal association

pay for performance   Accepting a lower base pay in exchange for bonuses based on meeting production or other goals

penetration pricing   Introducing a new product at a low price in hopes of building sales volume quickly

pension plan   Company-sponsored program for providing retirees with income

performance appraisal   Evaluation of an employee's work according to specific criteria

perpetual inventory   System that uses computers to monitor inventory levels and automatically generate purchase orders when supplies are needed

personal selling   In-person communication between a seller and one or more potential buyers

persuasive advertising   Advertising designed to encourage product sampling and brand switching

philanthropic   Descriptive term for altruistic actions such as donating money, time, goods, or services to charitable, humanitarian, or educational institutions

physical distribution   All the activities required to move finished products from the producer to the consumer

picketing   Strike activity in which union members march before company entrances to persuade nonstriking employees to walk off the job and to persuade customers and others to cease doing business with the company

place marketing   Marketing efforts to attract people and organizations to a particular geographical area

place utility   Consumer value added by making a product available in a convenient location

planned system   Economic system in which the government controls most of the factors of production and regulates their allocation

planning   Establishing objectives and goals for an organization and determining the best ways to accomplish them

point-of-purchase (POP) display   Advertising or other display materials set up at retail locations to promote products to potential customers as they are making their purchase decisions

pollution   Damage to or destruction of the natural environment caused by the discharge of harmful substances

positioning   Using promotion, product, distribution, and price to differentiate a good or service from those of competitors in the mind of the prospective buyer

possession utility   Consumer value created when someone takes ownership of a product

preferred stock   Shares that give their owners first claim on a company's dividends and assets after paying all debts

premiums   Free or bargain-priced items offered to encourage consumers to buy a product

press relations   Process of communicating with reporters and editors from newspapers, magazines, and radio and television networks and stations

price elasticity   A measure of the sensitivity of demand to changes in price

price   The amount of money charged for a product or service

price-earnings ratio (p/e ratio)   Stock's current market price divided by issuer's annual earnings per share; also known as the price-earnings multiple

primary market   Market where firms sell new securities issued publicly for the first time

prime interest rate (prime)   Lowest rate of interest charged by banks for short-term loans to their most creditworthy customers

principal   Amount of a debt, excluding any interest

private accountants   In-house accountants employed by organizations and businesses other than a public accounting firm; also called corporate accountants

private brands   Brands that carry the label of a retailer or a wholesaler rather than a manufacturer

private corporation   Company owned by private individuals or companies

privatizing   The conversion of public ownership to private ownership

problem-solving team   Informal team of 5 to 12 employees from the same department who meet voluntarily to find ways of improving quality, efficiency, and the work environment

process control systems   Computer system that uses special sensing devices to monitor conditions in a physical process and makes necessary adjustments to the process

process divisions   Divisional structure based on the major steps of a production process

process layout Method of arranging a facility so that production tasks are carried out in separate departments containing specialized equipment and personnel

producer price index (PPI) Monthly statistic that measures changes in the prices at the producer or wholesaler level

product advertising Advertising that tries to sell specific goods or services, generally by describing features, benefits, and, occasionally, price

product divisions Divisional structure based on products

product layout Method of arranging a facility so that production proceeds along a line of workstations

product life cycle Four basic stages through which a product progresses: introduction, growth, maturity, and decline

product line A series of related products offered by a firm

product mix Complete list of all products that a company offers for sale

product Good or service used as the basis of commerce

production and operations management (POM) Coordination of an organization's resources for the manufacture of goods or the delivery of services

production control systems Computer systems that manage production by controlling production lines, robots, and other machinery and equipment

production forecasts Estimates of how much of a company's goods and services must be produced in order to meet future demand

production Transformation of resources into goods or services that people need or want

profit sharing System for distributing a portion of a company's profits to employees

profit Money left over after expenses and taxes have been deducted from revenue generated by selling goods and services

profitability ratios Ratios that measure the overall financial performance of a firm

program evaluation and review technique (PERT) A planning tool that managers of complex projects use to determine the optimal order of activities, the expected time for project completion, and the best use of resources

promotion Wide variety of persuasive techniques used by companies to communicate with their target markets and the general public

promotional mix Particular blend of personal selling, advertising, direct marketing, sales promotion, and public relations that a company uses to reach potential customers

promotional strategy Statement or document that defines the direction and scope of the promotional activities that a company will use to meet its marketing objectives

prospecting Process of finding and qualifying potential customers

protectionism Government policies aimed at shielding a country's industries from foreign competition

proxy Document authorizing another person to vote on behalf of a shareholder in a corporation

psychographics Classification of customers on the basis of their psychological makeup

public accountants Professionals who provide accounting services to other businesses and individuals for a fee

public corporation Corporation that actively sells stock on the open market

public relations Nonsales communication that businesses have with their various audiences (includes both communication with the general public and press relations)

pull strategy Promotional strategy that stimulates consumer demand via advertising and a number of consumer promotions, thereby exerting pressure on wholesalers and retailers to carry a product

purchasing Acquiring the raw materials, parts, components, supplies, and finished products needed to produce goods and services

pure competition Situation in which so many buyers and sellers exist that no single buyer or seller can individually influence market prices

push strategy Promotional strategy that uses the salesforce and a number of trade promotions to motivate wholesalers and retailers to push products to end users

Q

qualified prospects Potential buyers who have both the money needed to make the purchase and the authority to make the purchase decision

quality assurance System of policies, practices, and procedures implemented throughout the company to create and produce quality goods and services

quality control Routine checking and testing of a finished product for quality against an established standard

quality of work life (QWL) Overall environment that results from job and work conditions

quality A measure of how closely a product conforms to predetermined standards and customer expectations

quick ratio Measure of a firm's short-term liquidity, calculated by adding cash, marketable securities, and receivables, then dividing that sum by current liabilities; also known as the acid-test ratio

quotas Fixed limits on the quantity of imports a nation will allow for a specific product

R

rack jobbers Merchant wholesalers that are responsible for setting up and maintaining displays in a particular section of a retail store

rate of return Percentage increase in the value of an investment

ratio analysis Use of quantitative measures to evaluate a firm's financial performance

recession Period during which national income, employment, and production all fall

recruiting Process of attracting appropriate applicants for an organization's jobs

relationship marketing A focus on developing and maintaining long-term relationships with customers, suppliers, and distributors for mutual benefit

reminder advertising Advertising intended to remind existing customers of a product's availability and benefits

reserve requirement Percentage of a bank's deposit that must be set aside

responsibility Obligation to perform the duties and achieve the goals and objectives associated with a particular position

retailers   Firms that sell goods and services to individuals for their own use rather than for resale

retained earnings   The portion of shareholders' equity earned by the company but not distributed to its owners in the form of dividends

return on investment (ROI)   Ratio between net income after taxes and total owners' equity; also known as return on equity

return on sales   Ratio between net income after taxes and net sales; also known as profit margin

revenue bond   Municipal bonds backed by revenue generated from the projects financed with the bonds

revenues   Amount earned from sales of goods or services and inflow from miscellaneous sources such as interest, rent, and royalties

robots   Programmable machines that can complete a variety of tasks by working with tools and materials

routing   Specifying the sequence of operations and the path the work will take through the production facility

S

S corporation   Corporations with no more than 75 shareholders that may be taxed as a partnership; also known as a subchapter S corporation

salaries   Fixed weekly, monthly, or yearly cash compensation for work

sales promotion   Wide range of events and activities (including coupons, rebates, contests, in-store demonstrations, free samples, trade shows, and point-of-purchase displays) designed to stimulate interest in a product

sales support personnel   Salespeople who facilitate the selling effort by providing such services as prospecting, customer education, and customer service

scheduling   Process of determining how long each production operation takes and then setting a starting and ending time for each

scientific management   Management approach designed to improve employees' efficiency by scientifically studying their work

scrambled merchandising   Policy of carrying merchandise that is ordinarily sold in a different type of outlet

search engines   Internet tools for finding websites on the topics of your choice

secondary market   Market where subsequent owners trade previously issued shares of stocks and bonds

secured bonds   Bonds backed by specific assets

secured loans   Loans backed up with something of value that the lender can claim in case of default, such as a piece of property

securities   Instruments such as stocks, bonds, options, futures, and commodities

selective credit controls   Federal Reserve's power to set credit terms on various types of loans

selective distribution   Market coverage strategy that uses a limited number of outlets to distribute products

self-managed teams   Teams in which members are responsible for an entire process or operation

selling concept   Approach to marketing in which firms emphasize selling what they make rather than making what consumers want

selling expenses   All the operating expenses associated with marketing goods or services

service businesses   Businesses that provide intangible products or perform useful labor on behalf of another

setup costs   Expenses incurred each time a producer organizes resources to begin producing goods or services

sexism   Discrimination on the basis of gender

sexual harassment   Unwelcome sexual advance, request for sexual favors, or other verbal or physical conduct of a sexual nature within the workplace

shareholders   Owners of a corporation

shop steward   Union member and employee who is elected to represent other union members and who attempts to resolve employee grievances with management

short selling   Selling stock borrowed from a broker with the intention of buying it back later at a lower price, repaying the broker, and pocketing the profit

short-term financing   Financing used to cover current expenses (generally repaid within a year)

sinking fund   Account into which a company makes annual payments for use in redeeming its bonds in the future

Six Sigma   Management approach that uses customer feedback and collaboratively set goals to improve the quality of products, services, and operations so that they yield no more than 3.4 errors or defects per million chances of generating them

skimming   Charging a high price for a new product during the introductory stage and lowering the price later

small business   Company that is independently owned and operated, is not dominant in its field, and meets certain criteria for the number of employees and annual sales revenue

smart cards   Plastic cards that include an embedded chip to store money drawn from the user's demand-deposit account and information that can be used for purchases

social audit   Assessment of a company's performance in the area of social responsibility

social responsibility   The concern of businesses for the welfare of society as a whole

socialism   Economic system characterized by public ownership and operation of key industries combined with private ownership and operation of less-vital industries

software   Programmed instructions that drive the activity of computer hardware

sole proprietorship   Business owned by a single individual

span of management   Number of people under one manager's control; also known as span of control

special-purpose teams   Temporary teams that exist outside the formal organization hierarchy and are created to achieve a specific goal

specialty advertising   Advertising that appears on various items such as coffee mugs, pens, and calendars, designed to help keep a company's name in front of customers

specialty store   Store that carries only a particular type of goods

speculators   Investors who purchase securities in anticipation of making large profits quickly

speech-recognition system   Computer system that recognizes human speech, enabling users to enter data and give commands vocally

stakeholders   Individuals or groups to whom a business has a responsibility

standards   Criteria against which performance is measured

start-up companies   New ventures

statement of cash flows   Statement of a firm's cash receipts and cash payments that presents information on its sources and uses of cash

statistical process control (SPC)   Use of random sampling and control charts to monitor the production process

statistical quality control (SQC)   Monitoring all aspects of the production process to see whether the process is operating as it should

stock certificate   Document that proves stock ownership

stock exchanges   Location where traders buy and sell stocks and bonds

stock options   Contract allowing the holder to purchase or sell a certain number of shares of a particular stock at a given price by a certain date

stock specialist   Intermediary who trades in a particular security on the floor of an auction exchange; "buyer of last resort"

stock split   Increase in the number of shares of ownership that each stock certificate represents

stock   Shares of ownership in a corporation

stop order   An order to sell a stock when its price falls to a particular point to limit an investor's losses

strategic alliance   Long-term relationship in which two or more companies share ideas, resources, and technologies in order to establish competitive advantages

strategic marketing planning   The process of determining an organization's primary marketing objectives and then adopting courses of action and allocating resources to achieve those objectives

strategic plans   Plans that establish the actions and the resource allocation required to accomplish strategic goals; usually defined for periods of two to five years and developed by top managers

strike   Temporary work stoppage by employees who want management to accept their union's demands

strikebreakers   Nonunion workers hired to replace striking workers

subsidiary corporations   Corporations whose stock is owned entirely or almost entirely by another corporation

supply curve   Graph of the quantities that sellers will offer for sale, regardless of demand, at various prices

supply   Specific quantity of a product that the seller is able and willing to provide

supply-chain management   Integrating all of the facilities, functions, and processes associated with the production of goods and services, from suppliers to customers

synthetic system   Production process that combines two or more materials or components to create finished products; the reverse of an analytic system

T

tactical plans   Plans that define the actions and the resource allocation necessary to achieve tactical objectives and to support strategic plans; usually defined for a period of one to three years and developed by middle managers

tall organizations   Organizations with a narrow span of management and many hierarchical levels

target markets   Specific customer groups or segments to whom a company wants to sell a particular product

tariffs   Taxes levied on imports

task force   Team of people from several departments who are temporarily brought together to address a specific issue

tax accounting   Area of accounting focusing on tax preparation and tax planning

team   A unit of two or more people who share a mission and collective responsibility as they work together to achieve a goal

technical salespeople   Specialists who contribute technical expertise and other sales assistance

technical skills   Ability and knowledge to perform the mechanics of a particular job

telecommuting   Working from home and communicating with the company's main office via computer and communication devices

telemarketing   Selling or supporting the sales process over the telephone

Telnet   A way to access someone else's computer (the host computer), and to use it as if it were right on your desk.

termination   Act of getting rid of an employee through layoffs or firing

test marketing   Product-development stage in which a product is sold on a limited basis-a trial introduction

Theory X   Managerial assumption that employees are irresponsible, unambitious, and distasteful of work and that managers must use force, control, or threats to motivate them

Theory Y   Managerial assumption that employees like work, are naturally committed to certain goals, are capable of creativity, and seek out responsibility under the right conditions

Theory Z   Human relations approach that emphasizes involving employees at all levels and treating them like family

time deposits   Bank accounts that pay interest and require advance notice before money can be withdrawn

time utility   Consumer value added by making a product available at a convenient time

top managers   Those at the highest level of the organization's management hierarchy; they are responsible for setting strategic goals, and they have the most power and responsibility in the organization

total quality management (TQM)   Comprehensive, strategic management approach that builds quality into every organizational process as a way of improving customer satisfaction

trade allowance   Discount offered by producers to wholesalers and retailers

trade credit   Credit obtained by the purchaser directly from the supplier

trade deficit   Unfavorable trade balance created when a country imports more than it exports

trade promotions   Sales-promotion efforts aimed at inducing distributors or retailers to push a producer's products

trade salespeople   Salespeople who sell to and support marketing intermediaries by giving in-store demonstrations, offering samples, and so on

trade surplus   Favorable trade balance created when a country exports more than it imports

trademark   Brand that has been given legal protection so that its owner has exclusive rights to its use

trading blocs   Organizations of nations that remove barriers to trade among their members and that establish uniform barriers to trade with nonmember nations

transaction processing system (TPS)   Computerized information system that processes the daily flow of customer, supplier, and employee transactions, including inventory, sales, and payroll records

transaction   Exchange between parties

Treasury bills   Short-term debt issued by the federal government; also referred to as T-bills

Treasury bonds   Debt securities issued by the federal government that mature in 10 to 30 years

Treasury notes   Debt securities issued by the federal government that mature within one to 10 years

U

U.S. savings bonds   Debt instruments sold by the federal government in small denominations

unissued stock   Authorized shares that are to be released in the future

Universal Product Codes (UPCs)   A bar code on a product's package that provides information read by optical scanners

unlimited liability   Legal condition under which any damages or debts attributable to the business can also be attached to the owner because the two have no separate legal existence

unsecured loans   Loan requiring no collateral but a good credit rating

Usenet newsgroups   One or more discussion groups on the Internet where people with similar interests can post articles and reply to messages

utility   Power of a good or service to satisfy a human need

V

variable costs   Business costs that increase with the number of units produced

venture capitalists   Investment specialists who provide money to finance new businesses or turnarounds in exchange for a portion of the ownership, with the objective of making a considerable profit on the investment; also called VCs

vertical organization   Structure linking activities at the top of the organization with those at the middle and lower levels

virtual teams   Team that uses communication technology to bring geographically distant employees together to achieve goals

viruses   Form of computer sabotage embedded in software or passed from one computer to the next that changes or deletes computer files or programs

vision   A viable view of the future that is rooted in but improves on the present

W

wages   Cash payment based on the number of hours the employee has worked or the number of units the employee has produced

wants   Things that are desirable in light of a person's experiences, culture, and personality

warehouse   Facility for storing inventory

wheel of retailing   Evolutionary process by which stores that feature low prices gradually upgrade until they no longer appeal to price-sensitive shoppers and are replaced by new low-price competitors

wholesalers   Firms that sell products to other firms for resale or for organizational use

wide area network (WAN)   Computer network that encompasses a large geographic area

work specialization   Specialization in or responsibility for some portion of an organization's overall work tasks; also called division of labor

worker buyout   Distribution of financial incentives to employees who voluntarily depart, usually undertaken in order to reduce the payroll

working capital   Current assets minus current liabilities

worms   Form of computer sabotage sent by e-mail that reproduces-taking up network space and snarling connections

Y

yield   Income received from securities, calculated by dividing dividend or interest income by market price

INDEXES

Name/Organization/Brand/Company Index

Subject Index